MANUAL
FOR
COURTS-MARTIAL
UNITED STATES
(2024 EDITION)

PREFACE

The Manual for Courts-Martial (MCM), United States (2024 edition) updates the MCM (2019 edition) and MCM (2023 edition). It is a complete republishing and incorporates the promulgation of and amendments to the Preamble, Rules for Courts-Martial, Military Rules of Evidence, Punitive Articles, Nonjudicial Punishment Procedure, and Appendices 12A-D made by the President in Executive Orders (E.O.) 12473 of April 13, 1984, to present and specifically including E.O. 14062 (January 26, 2022) and E.O. 14103 (July 28, 2023). This edition also contains amendments to the Uniform Code of Military Justice made by the National Defense Authorization Act for Fiscal Year 2020, Pub. L. No. 116-92, 133 Stat. 1198 (2019); the William M. (Mac) Thornberry National Defense Authorization Act for Fiscal Year 2021, Pub. L. No. 116-283, 134 Stat. 3388 (2020); the National Defense Authorization Act for Fiscal Year 2022, Pub. L. No. 117-81, 135 Stat. 1541 (2021); and the James M. Inhofe National Defense Authorization Act for Fiscal Year 2023, Pub. L. No. 117-263, 136 Stat. 2395 (2022). Finally, this edition incorporates amendments to the Appendices and the supplementary materials accompanying the MCM. These items are available at the Joint Service Committee on Military Justice's website at https://jsc.defense.gov.

JOINT SERVICE COMMITTEE ON MILITARY JUSTICE

CONTENTS

CHAPTER III. INITIATION OF CHARGES; APPREHENSION; PRETRIAL RESTRAINT; RELATED MATTERS

CHAPTER IV. FORWARDING AND DISPOSITION OF CHARGES

CHAPTER V. COURT-MARTIAL COMPOSITION AND PERSONNEL; CONVENING COURTS-MARTIAL

CHAPTER VI. REFERRAL, SERVICE, AMENDMENT, AND WITHDRAWAL OF CHARGES

CHAPTER VII. PRETRIAL MATTERS

CHAPTER VIII. TRIAL PROCEDURE GENERALLY

CHAPTER IX. TRIAL PROCEDURES THROUGH FINDINGS

CHAPTER X. SENTENCING

CHAPTER XII. APPEALS AND REVIEW

CHAPTER XIII. SUMMARY COURTS-MARTIAL

PART III MILITARY RULES OF EVIDENCE

SECTION I GENERAL PROVISIONS

SECTION VI WITNESSES

PART V NONJUDICIAL PUNISHMENT PROCEDURE

APPENDICES

PART I

PREAMBLE

1. Sources of military jurisdiction

The sources of military jurisdiction include the Constitution and international law. International law includes the law of war.

2. Exercise of military jurisdiction

(a) *Kinds*. Military jurisdiction is exercised by:

(1) A government in the exercise of that branch of the municipal law which regulates its military establishment. (Military law).

(2) A government temporarily governing the civil population within its territory or a portion of its territory through its military forces as necessity may require. (Martial law).

(3) A belligerent occupying enemy territory. (Military government).

(4) A government with respect to offenses against the law of war.

(b) *Agencies*. The agencies through which military jurisdiction is exercised include:

(1) Courts-martial for the trial of offenses against military law and, in the case of general courts-martial, of persons who by the law of war are subject to trial by military tribunals. *See* Parts II, III, and IV of this Manual for rules governing courts-martial.

(2) Military commissions and provost courts for the trial of cases within their respective jurisdictions. Subject to any applicable rule of international law or to any regulations prescribed by the President or by other competent authority, military commissions and provost courts shall be guided by the appropriate principles of law and rules of procedures and evidence prescribed for courts-martial.

(3) Courts of inquiry for the investigation of any matter referred to such court by competent authority. *See* Article 135. The Secretary concerned may prescribe regulations governing courts of inquiry.

(4) Nonjudicial punishment proceedings of a commander under Article 15. *See* Part V of this Manual.

3. Nature and purpose of military law

Military law consists of the statutes governing the military establishment and regulations issued thereunder, the constitutional powers of the President and Executive Orders and regulations issued thereunder, and the inherent authority of military commanders. Military law includes jurisdiction exercised by courts-martial and the jurisdiction exercised by commanders with respect to nonjudicial punishment. The purposes of military law are to promote justice, to deter misconduct, to facilitate appropriate accountability, to assist in maintaining good order and discipline in the armed forces, to promote efficiency and effectiveness in the military establishment, and thereby to strengthen the national security of the United States.

4. The Evolving Military Justice System

The military operates a modern criminal justice system that recognizes and protects the rights of both the victims of alleged offenses and those accused of offenses. The continuous evolution of the military justice system has progressed through statutes, Executive Orders, regulations, and judicial interpretations. The Uniform Code of Military Justice (UCMJ), enacted in 1950, significantly enhanced the fairness of military justice across the armed forces, including by establishing a civilian appellate court at the system's apex. The Military Justice Act of 1968, which created the position of military judge and enhanced the role of lawyers in the system, resulted in further improvements. The promulgation of the Military Rules of Evidence by a 1980 Executive Order brought court-martial practice into closer alignment with federal civilian criminal practice. In 2014, Congress added a victims' rights article to the UCMJ and also made counsel available to represent certain victims of alleged UCMJ offenses. The Military Justice Act of 2016 further modernized the military justice system by expanding pretrial judicial authorities, updating trial and post-trial procedures, and enacting new punitive articles. Most recently, the National Defense Authorization Act for Fiscal Year 2022 made historic reforms to the military justice system, including the unprecedented transfer of prosecutorial discretion from commanders to independent, specialized counsel to prosecute certain covered offenses, including sexual assault and domestic violence, as recommended by the Independent Review Commission on Sexual Assault in the Military to strengthen Service members' trust in the military justice system. These and many other improvements have been vital to maintaining a fair, just, and efficient military justice system. The system must continue to evolve to be worthy of those who protect our Nation and its freedoms.

5. Structure and application of the Manual for Courts-Martial

The Manual for Courts-Martial shall consist of this Preamble, the Rules for Courts-Martial, the Military Rules of Evidence, the Punitive Articles, the Nonjudicial Punishment Procedures (Parts I-V), and Appendixes 12A through 12D. This Manual shall be applied in a manner consistent with the purpose of military law.

The Department of Defense (DoD), in conjunction with the Department of Homeland Security, publishes supplementary materials to accompany the Manual for Courts-Martial. These materials consist of a Preface, a Table of Contents, Discussions, Appendices (other than Appendixes 12A through 12D, which were promulgated by the President), and an Index. These supplementary materials do not have the force of law.

The Manual shall be identified by the year in which it was printed; for example, "Manual for Courts-Martial, United States (20xx edition)." Any amendments to the Manual made by Executive Order shall be identified as "20xx" Amendments to the Manual for Courts-Martial, United States, "20xx" being the year the Executive Order was signed.

The DoD Joint Service Committee on Military Justice (JSC) reviews the Manual for Courts-Martial and proposes amendments to the DoD for consideration by the President on an annual basis. In conducting its annual review, the JSC is guided by DoD Instruction 5500.17, "Role and Responsibilities of the Joint Service Committee on Military Justice (JSC)." DoD Instruction 5500.17 includes provisions allowing public participation in the annual review process.

Discussion

The Department of Defense, in conjunction with the Department of Homeland Security, has published supplementary materials to accompany the Manual for Courts-Martial. These materials consist of a Discussion (accompanying the Preamble, the Rules for Courts-Martial, the Military Rules of Evidence, and the Punitive Articles), an Analysis, and various appendices. With the exception of Appendix 12A (lesser included offenses), which is issued by the President pursuant to Article 79, these supplementary materials do not constitute the official views of the Department of Defense, the Department of Homeland Security, the Department of Justice, the military departments, the United States Court of Appeals for the Armed Forces, or any other authority of the Government of the United States, and they do not constitute rules. *Cf., e.g.*, 5 U.S.C. § 551(4). The supplementary materials do not create rights or responsibilities that are binding on any person, party, or other entity (including any authority of the Government of the United States whether or not included in the definition of "agency" in 5 U.S.C. § 551(1)). Failure to comply with matter set forth in the supplementary materials does not, of itself, constitute error, although these materials may refer to requirements in the rules set forth in the Executive Order or established by other legal authorities (for example, binding judicial precedents applicable to courts-martial) that are based on sources of authority independent of the supplementary materials. *See* Appendix 15 in this Manual.

The 1995 amendment to paragraph 4 of the Preamble eliminated the practice of identifying the Manual for Courts-Martial, United States, by a particular year. Historically the Manual had been published in its entirety sporadically (*e.g.*, 1917, 1921, 1928, 1949, 1951, 1969, and 1984) with amendments to it published piecemeal. It was therefore logical to identify the Manual by the calendar year of publication, with periodic amendments identified as "Changes" to the Manual. Beginning in 1995, however, a new edition of the Manual was published in its entirety and a new naming convention was adopted. *See* Exec. Order No. 12960 of May 12, 1995. Beginning in 1995, the Manual was to be referred to as "Manual for Courts-Martial, United States (19xx edition)." In 2013, the Preamble was amended to identify new Manuals based on their publication date.

Amendments made to the Manual can be researched in the relevant Executive Order as referenced in Appendix 19. Although the Executive Orders were removed from Appendix 19 of the Manual in 2012 to reduce printing requirements, they can be accessed online. *See* Appendix 19.

PART II
RULES FOR COURTS–MARTIAL

CHAPTER I. GENERAL PROVISIONS

Rule 101. Scope, title

(a) *In general.* These rules govern the procedures and punishments in all courts-martial and, whenever expressly provided, preliminary, supplementary, and appellate procedures and activities.

(b) *Title.* These rules may be known and cited as the Rules for Courts-Martial (R.C.M.).

Rule 102. Purpose and construction

(a) *Purpose.* These rules are intended to provide for the just determination of every proceeding relating to trial by court-martial.

(b) *Construction.* These rules shall be construed to secure simplicity in procedure, fairness in administration, and the elimination of unjustifiable expense and delay.

Rule 103. Definitions and rules of construction

The following definitions and rules of construction apply throughout this Manual, unless otherwise expressly provided.

(1) "Appellate military judge" means a judge of a Court of Criminal Appeals.

(2) "Article" refers to articles of the Uniform Code of Military Justice unless the context indicates otherwise.

(3) "Capital case" means a general court-martial to which a capital offense has been referred with an instruction that the case be treated as a capital proceeding, and, in the case of a rehearing or new or other trial, for which offense death remains an authorized punishment under R.C.M. 810(d).

(4) "Capital offense" means an offense for which death is an authorized punishment under the UCMJ and Part IV of this Manual or under the law of war.

(5) "Commander" means a commissioned officer in command or an officer in charge except in Part V or unless the context indicates otherwise.

(6) "Convening authority" includes a commissioned officer in command for the time being and successors in command.

Discussion

See R.C.M. 504 concerning who may convene courts-martial.

---

(7) "Copy" means an accurate reproduction, however made. Whenever necessary and feasible, a copy may be made by handwriting.

(8) "Court-martial" includes, depending on the context:

(A) The military judge and members of a general or special court-martial;

(B) The military judge when a session of a general or special court-martial is conducted without members under Article 39(a);

(C) The military judge when a request for trial by military judge alone has been approved under R.C.M. 903;

(D) The military judge when the case is referred as a special court-martial consisting of a military judge alone under Article 16(c)(2)(A); or

(E) The summary court-martial officer.

(9) "Days." When a period of time is expressed in a number of days, the period shall be in calendar days, unless otherwise specified. Unless otherwise specified, the date on which the period begins shall not count, but the date on which the period ends shall count as one day.

(10) "Deferral" of an offense means a special trial counsel declines to prefer charges for an offense or declines to refer charges to court-martial. Once a special trial counsel declines to prefer or refer charges for an offense, a commander shall exercise authority within the scope of these rules.

(11) "Detail" means to order a person to perform a specific temporary duty, unless the context indicates otherwise.

(12) "Exercise authority over" means when a special trial counsel acts on a covered, related, or known offense in furtherance of a special trial counsel's statutory duties or authorities under Article 24a(c).

Discussion

See Article 24a(c)(2). If the special trial counsel determines that there is a known or related offense, the special trial counsel must affirmatively act in furtherance of special trial counsel's statutory duties under Article 24a(c) to exercise authority over that offense. When a special trial counsel exercises authority over any reported offense, the special trial counsel shall notify the suspect's special court-martial convening authority. *See* R.C.M. 303A(e).

---

(13) "Explosive" means gunpowders; powders used for blasting; all forms of high explosives; blasting materials; fuzes (other than electrical circuit breakers), detonators, and other detonating agents; smokeless powders; any explosive bomb, grenade, missile, or similar device; any incendiary bomb or grenade, fire bomb, or similar device; and any other compound, mixture, or device which is an explosive within the meaning of 18 U.S.C. § 232(5) or 844(j).

(14) "Firearm" means any weapon that is designed to or may be readily converted to expel any projectile by the action of an explosive.

(15) "Joint" in connection with military organization connotes activities, operations, organizations, and the like in which elements of more than one military service of the same nation participate.

(16) "Lead Special Trial Counsel" within the Department of Defense means a general or flag officer with significant experience in military justice who is responsible for a dedicated office within each Military Department from which office the Lead Special Trial Counsel will provide for the overall supervision and oversight of the activities of the special trial counsel of a Military Department or Military Service, and who reports directly to the Secretary concerned, without intervening authority.

(17) "Members." The members of a court-martial are the voting members detailed by the convening authority.

(18) "Military judge" means a judge advocate designated under Article 26(c) who is detailed under Article 26(a) or Article 30a to preside over a general or special court-martial or proceeding before referral. In the context of a summary court-martial, "military judge" means the summary court-martial officer. In the context of a pre-referral proceeding or a special court-martial consisting of a military judge alone, "military judge" includes a military magistrate designated under Article 19 or Article 30a.

(19) "Military magistrate" means a commissioned officer of the armed forces certified under Article 26a who is performing duties under Article 19 or 30a.

(20) "Party," in the context of parties to a court-martial or other proceeding under these rules, means:

(A) The accused and any defense or associate or assistant defense counsel and agents of the defense counsel when acting on behalf of the accused with respect to the court-martial or proceeding in question; and

(B) Any trial or assistant trial counsel representing the United States, and agents of the trial counsel or such counsel when acting on behalf of the United States with respect to the court-martial or proceeding in question.

(21) "Preferral" is the act by which a person subject to the UCMJ formally accuses another person subject to the UCMJ of an offense, in accordance with R.C.M. 307(b).

(22) "Referral" is the order of a convening authority or a special trial counsel that one or more charges and specifications against an accused will be tried by a specified court-martial.

(23) "Referral authority" means a convening authority or special trial counsel who may order that one or more charges and specifications against an accused be tried by a specified court-martial pursuant to R.C.M. 601.

(24) "Special trial counsel" means a judge advocate who is qualified, certified, and assigned as such by the Judge Advocate General of the armed force of which the officer is a member, or, in the case of the Marine Corps, by the Staff Judge Advocate to the Commandant of the Marine Corps, and who is independent of the military chains of command of both the victim and those accused of covered offenses over which a special trial counsel at any time exercises authority in accordance with Article 24a. Special trial counsel shall be well-trained, experienced, highly skilled and competent in handling cases involving covered offenses. Within the Department of Defense, special trial counsel work within dedicated offices under the overall supervision and oversight of a Lead Special Trial Counsel. Within the Coast Guard, special trial counsel work under the overall supervision and oversight of an officer designated under regulations prescribed by the Commandant of the Coast Guard.

(25) "Staff judge advocate" means a judge advocate so designated in the Army, Air Force, or Marine Corps, and means the principal legal advisor of a command in the Navy and Coast Guard who is a judge advocate.

(26) "*Sua sponte*" means that the person involved acts on that person's initiative, without the need for a request, motion, or application.

(27) "Trial counsel," unless otherwise specified in these rules, includes special trial counsel.

(28) "UCMJ" refers to the Uniform Code of Military Justice.

Discussion

The Uniform Code of Military Justice is set forth at Appendix 2.

---

(29) "War, time of." For purposes of R.C.M. 1004(c)(6) and of implementing the applicable paragraphs of Parts IV and V of this Manual only, "time of war" means a period of war declared by Congress, or the factual determination by the President that the existence of hostilities warrants a finding that a "time of war" exists for purposes of R.C.M. 1004(c)(6) and Parts IV and V of this Manual.

(30) The terms "writings" and "recordings" have the same meaning as in Mil. R. Evid. 1001.

Discussion

The definition of "writing" includes letters, words, or numbers set down by handwriting, typewriting, printing, photostating, photographing, magnetic impulse, mechanical or electronic recording, or any other form of data compilation. This section makes it clear that computers and other modern reproduction systems are included in this definition, and consistent with the definition of "writing" in Military Rule of Evidence 1001. The definition is comprehensive, covering all forms of writing or recording of words or word-substitutes.

---

(31) The definitions and rules of construction in 1 U.S.C. §§ 1 through 5 and in 10 U.S.C. §§ 101 and 801.

Discussion

The following provisions are set forth below:

(1) 1 U.S.C. §§ 1 through 5.

(2) 10 U.S.C. § 101.

(3) 10 U.S.C. § 801 (Article 1).

(1) 1 U.S.C. §1 through §5

§1. Words denoting number, gender, and so forth

In determining the meaning of any Act of Congress, unless the context indicates otherwise—

words importing the singular include and apply to several persons, parties, or things;

words importing the plural include the singular;

words importing the masculine gender include the feminine as well;

words used in the present tense include the future as well as the present;

the words "insane" and "insane person" shall include every idiot, insane person, and person non compos mentis;

the words "person" and "whoever" include corporations, companies, associations, firms, partnerships, societies, and joint stock companies, as well as individuals;

"officer" includes any person authorized by law to perform the duties of the office;

"signature" or "subscription" includes a mark when the person making the same intended it as such;

"oath" includes affirmation, and "sworn" includes affirmed;

"writing" includes printing and typewriting and reproductions of visual symbols by photographing, multigraphing, mimeographing, manifolding, or otherwise.

§2. "County" as including "parish", and so forth

The word "county" includes a parish, or any other equivalent subdivision of a State or Territory of the United States.

§3. "Vessel" as including all means of water transportation

The word "vessel" includes every description of watercraft or other artificial contrivance used, or capable of being used, as a means of transportation on water.

§4. "Vehicle" as including all means of land transportation

The word "vehicle" includes every description of carriage or other artificial contrivance used, or capable of being used, as a means of transportation on land.

§5. "Company" or "association" as including successors and assigns

The word "company" or "association", when used in reference to a corporation, shall be deemed to embrace the words "successors and assigns of such company or association", in like manner as if these last-named words, or words of similar import, were expressed.

(2) 10 U.S.C. § 101

§101. Definitions

(a) IN GENERAL.—The following definitions apply in this title:

(1) The term "United States", in a geographic sense, means the States and the District of Columbia.

[(2) Repealed. Pub. L. 109–163, div. A, title X, §1057(a)(1), Jan. 6, 2006, 119 Stat. 3440.]

(3) The term "possessions" includes the Virgin Islands, Guam, American Samoa, and the Guano Islands, so long as they remain possessions, but does not include any Commonwealth.

(4) The term "armed forces" means the Army, Navy, Air Force, Marine Corps, and Coast Guard.

(5) The term "uniformed services" means—

(A) the armed forces;

(B) the commissioned corps of the National Oceanic and Atmospheric Administration; and

(C) the commissioned corps of the Public Health Service.

(6) The term "department", when used with respect to a military department, means the executive part of the department and all field headquarters, forces, reserve components, installations,

activities, and functions under the control or supervision of the Secretary of the department. When used with respect to the Department of Defense, such term means the executive part of the department, including the executive parts of the military departments, and all field headquarters, forces, reserve components, installations, activities, and functions under the control or supervision of the Secretary of Defense, including those of the military departments.

(7) The term "executive part of the department" means the executive part of the Department of Defense, Department of the Army, Department of the Navy, or Department of the Air Force, as the case may be, at the seat of government.

(8) The term "military departments" means the Department of the Army, the Department of the Navy, and the Department of the Air Force.

(9) The term "Secretary concerned" means—

(A) the Secretary of the Army, with respect to matters concerning the Army;

(B) the Secretary of the Navy, with respect to matters concerning the Navy, the Marine Corps, and the Coast Guard when it is operating as a service in the Navy;

(C) the Secretary of the Air Force, with respect to matters concerning the Air Force; and

(D) the Secretary of Homeland Security, with respect to matters concerning the Coast Guard when it is not operating as a service in the Department of the Navy.

(10) The term "service acquisition executive" means the civilian official within a military department who is designated as the service acquisition executive for purposes of regulations and procedures providing for a service acquisition executive for that military department.

(11) The term "Defense Agency" means an organizational entity of the Department of Defense—

(A) that is established by the Secretary of Defense under section 191 of this title (or under the second sentence of section 125(d) of this title (as in effect before October 1, 1986)) to perform a supply or service activity common to more than one military department (other than such an entity that is designated by the Secretary as a Department of Defense Field Activity); or

(B) that is designated by the Secretary of Defense as a Defense Agency.

(12) The term "Department of Defense Field Activity" means an organizational entity of the Department of Defense—

(A) that is established by the Secretary of Defense under section 191 of this title (or under the second sentence of section 125(d) of this title (as in effect before October 1, 1986)) to perform a supply or service activity common to more than one military department; and

(B) that is designated by the Secretary of Defense as a Department of Defense Field Activity.

(13) The term "contingency operation" means a military operation that—

(A) is designated by the Secretary of Defense as an operation in which members of the armed forces are or may become involved in military actions, operations, or hostilities against an enemy of the United States or against an opposing military force; or

(B) results in the call or order to, or retention on, active duty of members of the uniformed services under section 688, 12301(a), 12302, 12304, 12304a, 12305, or 12406 of this title, chapter 15 of this title, section 712 of title 14, or any other provision of law during a war or during a national emergency declared by the President or Congress.

(14) The term "supplies" includes material, equipment, and stores of all kinds.

(15) The term "pay" includes basic pay, special pay, retainer pay, incentive pay, retired pay, and equivalent pay, but does not include allowances.

(16) The term "congressional defense committees" means—

(A) the Committee on Armed Services and the Committee on Appropriations of the Senate; and

(B) the Committee on Armed Services and the Committee on Appropriations of the House of Representatives.

(17) The term "base closure law" means the following:

(A) Section 2687 of this title.

(B) The Defense Base Closure and Realignment Act of 1990 (part A of title XXIX of Public Law 101–510; 10 U.S.C. 2687 note).

(C) Title II of the Defense Authorization Amendments and Base Closure and Realignment Act (Public Law 100–526; 10 U.S.C. 2687 note).

(18) The term "acquisition workforce" means the persons serving in acquisition positions within the Department of Defense, as designated pursuant to section 1721(a) of this title.

(b) PERSONNEL GENERALLY.—The following definitions relating to military personnel apply in this title:

(1) The term "officer" means a commissioned or warrant officer.

(2) The term "commissioned officer" includes a commissioned warrant officer.

(3) The term "warrant officer" means a person who holds a commission or warrant in a warrant officer grade.

(4) The term "general officer" means an officer of the Army, Air Force, or Marine Corps serving in or having the grade of general, lieutenant general, major general, or brigadier general.

(5) The term "flag officer" means an officer of the Navy or Coast Guard serving in or having the grade of admiral, vice admiral, rear admiral, or rear admiral (lower half).

(6) The term "enlisted member" means a person in an enlisted grade.

(7) The term "grade" means a step or degree, in a graduated scale of office or military rank, that is established and designated as a grade by law or regulation.

(8) The term "rank" means the order of precedence among members of the armed forces.

(9) The term "rating" means the name (such as "boatswain's mate") prescribed for members of an armed force in an occupational field. The term "rate" means the name (such as "chief boatswain's mate") prescribed for members in the same rating or other category who are in the same grade (such as chief petty officer or seaman apprentice).

(10) The term "original", with respect to the appointment of a member of the armed forces in a regular or reserve component, refers to that member's most recent appointment in that component that is neither a promotion nor a demotion.

(11) The term "authorized strength" means the largest number of members authorized to be in an armed force, a component, a branch, a grade, or any other category of the armed forces.

(12) The term "regular", with respect to an enlistment, appointment, grade, or office, means enlistment, appointment, grade, or office in a regular component of an armed force.

(13) The term "active-duty list" means a single list for the Army, Navy, Air Force, or Marine Corps (required to be maintained under section 620 of this title) which contains the names of all officers of that armed force, other than officers described in section 641 of this title, who are serving on active duty.

(14) The term "medical officer" means an officer of the Medical Corps of the Army, an officer of the Medical Corps of the Navy, or an officer in the Air Force designated as a medical officer.

(15) The term "dental officer" means an officer of the Dental Corps of the Army, an officer of the Dental Corps of the Navy, or an officer of the Air Force designated as a dental officer.

(16) The term "Active Guard and Reserve" means a member of a reserve component who is on active duty pursuant to section 12301(d) of this title or, if a member of the Army National Guard or Air National Guard, is on full-time National Guard duty pursuant to section 502(f) of title 32, and who is performing Active Guard and Reserve duty.

(c) RESERVE COMPONENTS.—The following definitions relating to the reserve components apply in this title:

(1) The term "National Guard" means the Army National Guard and the Air National Guard.

(2) The term "Army National Guard" means that part of the organized militia of the several States and Territories, Puerto Rico, and the District of Columbia, active and inactive, that—

(A) is a land force;

(B) is trained, and has its officers appointed, under the sixteenth clause of section 8, article I, of the Constitution;

(C) is organized, armed, and equipped wholly or partly at Federal expense; and

(D) is federally recognized.

(3) The term "Army National Guard of the United States" means the reserve component of the Army all of whose members are members of the Army National Guard.

(4) The term "Air National Guard" means that part of the organized militia of the several States and Territories, Puerto Rico, and the District of Columbia, active and inactive, that—

(A) is an air force;

(B) is trained, and has its officers appointed, under the sixteenth clause of section 8, article I, of the Constitution;

(C) is organized, armed, and equipped wholly or partly at Federal expense; and

(D) is federally recognized.

(5) The term "Air National Guard of the United States" means the reserve component of the Air Force all of whose members are members of the Air National Guard.

(6) The term "reserve", with respect to an enlistment, appointment, grade, or office, means enlistment, appointment, grade, or office held as a Reserve of one of the armed forces.

(7) The term "reserve active-status list" means a single list for the Army, Navy, Air Force, or Marine Corps (required to be maintained under section 14002 of this title) that contains the names of all officers of that armed force except warrant officers (including commissioned warrant officers) who are in an active status in a reserve component of the Army, Navy, Air Force, or Marine Corps and are not on an active-duty list.

(d) DUTY STATUS.—The following definitions relating to duty status apply in this title:

(1) The term "active duty" means full-time duty in the active military service of the United States. Such term includes full-time training duty, annual training duty, and attendance, while in the active military service, at a school designated as a service school by law or by the Secretary of the military department concerned. Such term does not include full-time National Guard duty.

(2) The term "active duty for a period of more than 30 days" means active duty under a call or order that does not specify a period of 30 days or less.

(3) The term "active service" means service on active duty or full-time National Guard duty.

(4) The term "active status" means the status of a member of a reserve component who is not in the inactive Army National Guard or inactive Air National Guard, on an inactive status list, or in the Retired Reserve.

(5) The term "full-time National Guard duty" means training or other duty, other than inactive duty, performed by a member of the Army National Guard of the United States or the Air National Guard of the United States in the member's status as a member of the National Guard of a State or territory, the Commonwealth of Puerto Rico, or the District of Columbia under section 316, 502, 503, 504, or 505 of title 32 for which the member is entitled to pay from the United States or for which the member has waived pay from the United States.

(6) The term "active Guard and Reserve duty" means—

(A) active duty performed by a member of a reserve component of the Army, Navy, Air Force, or Marine Corps, or full-time National Guard duty performed by a member of the National Guard pursuant to an order to full-time National Guard duty, for a period of 180 consecutive days or more for the purpose of organizing, administering, recruiting, instructing, or training the reserve components.

(B) Such term does not include the following:

(i) Duty performed as a member of the Reserve Forces Policy Board provided for under section 10301 of this title.

(ii) Duty performed as a property and fiscal officer under section 708 of title 32.

(iii) Duty performed for the purpose of interdiction and counter-drug activities for which funds have been provided under section 112 of title 32.

(iv) Duty performed as a general or flag officer.

(v) Service as a State director of the Selective Service System under section 10(b)(2) of the Military Selective Service Act (50 U.S.C. 3809(b)(2)).

(7) The term "inactive-duty training" means—

(A) duty prescribed for Reserves by the Secretary concerned under section 206 of title 37 or any other provision of law; and

(B) special additional duties authorized for Reserves by an authority designated by the Secretary concerned and performed by them on a voluntary basis in connection with the prescribed training or maintenance activities of the units to which they are assigned.

Such term includes those duties when performed by Reserves in their status as members of the National Guard.

(e) FACILITIES AND OPERATIONS.—The following definitions relating to facilities and operations apply in this title:

(1) RANGE.—The term "range", when used in a geographic sense, means a designated land or water area that is set aside, managed, and used for range activities of the Department of Defense. Such term includes the following:

(A) Firing lines and positions, maneuver areas, firing lanes, test pads, detonation pads, impact areas, electronic scoring sites, buffer zones with restricted access, and exclusionary areas.

(B) Airspace areas designated for military use in accordance with regulations and procedures prescribed by the Administrator of the Federal Aviation Administration.

(2) RANGE ACTIVITIES.—The term "range activities" means—

(A) research, development, testing, and evaluation of military munitions, other ordnance, and weapons systems; and

(B) the training of members of the armed forces in the use and handling of military munitions, other ordnance, and weapons systems.

(3) OPERATIONAL RANGE.—The term "operational range" means a range that is under the jurisdiction, custody, or control of the Secretary of a military department and—

(A) that is used for range activities, or

(B) although not currently being used for range activities, that is still considered by the Secretary to be a range and has not been put to a new use that is incompatible with range activities.

(4) MILITARY MUNITIONS.—

(A) The term "military munitions" means all ammunition products and components produced for or used by the armed forces for national defense and security, including ammunition products or components under the control of the Department of Defense, the Coast Guard, the Department of Energy, and the National Guard.

(B) Such term includes the following:

(i) Confined gaseous, liquid, and solid propellants.

(ii) Explosives, pyrotechnics, chemical and riot control agents, smokes, and incendiaries, including bulk explosives and chemical warfare agents.

(iii) Chemical munitions, rockets, guided and ballistic missiles, bombs, warheads, mortar rounds, artillery ammunition, small arms ammunition, grenades, mines, torpedoes, depth charges, cluster munitions and dispensers, and demolition charges.

(iv) Devices and components of any item specified in clauses (i) through (iii).

(C) Such term does not include the following:

(i) Wholly inert items.

(ii) Improvised explosive devices.

(iii) Nuclear weapons, nuclear devices, and nuclear components, other than nonnuclear components of nuclear devices that are managed under the nuclear weapons program of the Department of Energy after all required sanitization operations under the Atomic Energy Act of 1954 (42 U.S.C. 2011 et seq.) have been completed.

(5) UNEXPLODED ORDNANCE.—The term "unexploded ordnance" means military munitions that—

(A) have been primed, fused, armed, or otherwise prepared for action;

(B) have been fired, dropped, launched, projected, or placed in such a manner as to constitute a hazard to operations, installations, personnel, or material; and

(C) remain unexploded, whether by malfunction, design, or any other cause.

(f) RULES OF CONSTRUCTION.—In this title—

(1) "shall" is used in an imperative sense;

(2) "may" is used in a permissive sense;

(3) "no person may * * *" means that no person is required, authorized, or permitted to do the act prescribed;

(4) "includes" means "includes but is not limited to"; and

(5) "spouse" means husband or wife, as the case may be.

(g) REFERENCE TO TITLE 1 DEFINITIONS.—For other definitions applicable to this title, see sections 1 through 5 of title 1.

(3) 10 U.S.C. § 801 (Article 1)

§801. Article 1. Definitions

In this chapter (the Uniform Code of Military Justice):

(1) The term "Judge Advocate General" means, severally, the Judge Advocates General of the Army, Navy, and Air Force and, except when the Coast Guard is operating as a service in the Navy, an official designated to serve as Judge Advocate General of the Coast Guard by the Secretary of Homeland Security.

(2) The Navy, the Marine Corps, and the Coast Guard when it is operating as a service in the Navy, shall be considered as one armed force.

(3) The term "commanding officer" includes only commissioned officers.

(4) The term "officer in charge" means a member of the Navy, the Marine Corps, or the Coast Guard designated as such by appropriate authority.

(5) The term "superior commissioned officer" means a commissioned officer superior in rank or command.

(6) The term "cadet" means a cadet of the United States Military Academy, the United States Air Force Academy, or the United States Coast Guard Academy.

(7) The term "midshipman" means a midshipman of the United States Naval Academy and any other midshipman on active duty in the naval service.

(8) The term "military" refers to any or all of the armed forces.

(9) The term "accuser" means a person who signs and swears to charges, any person who directs that charges nominally be signed and sworn to by another, and any other person who has an interest other than an official interest in the prosecution of the accused.

(10) The term "military judge" means a judge advocate designated under section 826(c) of this title (article 26(c)) who is detailed under section 826(a) or section 830a of this title (article 26(a) or 30a)).

[(11) Repealed. Pub. L. 109–241, title II, §218(a)(1), July 11, 2006, 120 Stat. 526.]

(12) The term "legal officer" means any commissioned officer of the Navy, Marine Corps, or Coast Guard designated to perform legal duties for a command.

(13) The term "judge advocate" means—

(A) an officer of the Judge Advocate General's Corps of the Army, the Navy, or the Air Force;

(B) an officer of the Marine Corps who is designated as a judge advocate; or

(C) a commissioned officer of the Coast Guard designated

for special duty (law).

(14) The term "record", when used in connection with the proceedings of a court-martial, means—

(A) an official written transcript, written summary, or other writing relating to the proceedings; or

(B) an official audiotape, videotape, or similar material from which sound, or sound and visual images, depicting the proceedings may be reproduced.

(15) The term "classified information" means (A) any information or material that has been determined by an official of the United States pursuant to law, an Executive order, or regulation to require protection against unauthorized disclosure for reasons of national security, and (B) any restricted data, as defined in section 11(y) of the Atomic Energy Act of 1954 (42 U.S.C. 2014(y)).

(16) The term "national security" means the national defense and foreign relations of the United States.

Rule 104. Command influence

(a) *General prohibitions.*

(1) *Convening authorities and commanders.*

(A) No court-martial convening authority, nor any other commanding officer, may censure, reprimand, or admonish a court-martial or other military tribunal or any member, military judge, or counsel thereof, with respect to the findings or sentence adjudged by the court-martial or tribunal, or with respect to any other exercise of the functions of the court-martial or tribunal or such persons in the conduct of the proceedings.

(B) No court-martial convening authority, nor any other commanding officer, may deter or attempt to deter a potential witness from participating in the investigatory process or testifying at a court-martial. The denial of a request to travel at government expense or refusal to make a witness available shall not by itself constitute unlawful command influence.

(2) *All persons subject to the UCMJ.* No person subject to the UCMJ may attempt to coerce or, by any unauthorized means, attempt to influence the action of a court-martial or any other military tribunal or any member thereof, in reaching the findings or sentence in any case or the action of any preliminary hearing officer or convening, approving, or reviewing authority with respect to such preliminary hearing officer's or authority's acts concerning the following: any decision to place a Servicemember into pretrial confinement; disposition decisions; rulings on pre-referral matters; findings at a preliminary hearing; convening a court-martial; decisions concerning plea agreements; selecting members; decisions concerning witness requests; taking action on any clemency or deferment request; or any appellate or post-trial review of a case.

(3) *Scope.*

(A) *Instructions.* Paragraphs (a)(1) and (2) of this rule do not prohibit general instructional or informational courses in military justice if such courses are designed solely for the purpose of instructing personnel of a command in the substantive and procedural aspects of courts-martial.

(B) *Court-martial statements.* Paragraphs (a)(1) and (2) of this rule do not prohibit statements and instructions given in open session by the military judge or counsel.

(C) *Professional supervision.* Paragraphs (a)(1) and (2) of this rule do not prohibit action by the Judge Advocate General concerned under R.C.M. 109.

(D) *Offense.* Paragraphs (a)(1) and (2) of this rule do not prohibit appropriate action against a person for an offense committed while detailed as a military judge, counsel, or member of a court-martial, or while serving as individual counsel.

(E) *General statements regarding criminal activity or offenses.* Paragraphs (a)(1) and (2) of this rule do not prohibit statements regarding criminal activity or a particular criminal offense that do not advocate a particular disposition, do not advocate a particular court-martial finding or sentence, and do not relate to a particular accused.

(b) *Communication between superiors and subordinates.*

(1) A superior convening authority or officer may generally discuss matters to consider regarding the disposition of alleged violations of the UCMJ with a subordinate convening authority or officer, and a subordinate convening authority or officer may seek advice from a superior convening authority or officer regarding the disposition of an alleged offense under the UCMJ.

(2) *All persons subject to the UCMJ.* No person subject to the UCMJ may attempt to coerce or, by any unauthorized means, attempt to influence the action of:

(A) a court-martial or any other military tribunal or any member thereof, in reaching the findings or sentence in any case or the action of any case; or

(B) any preliminary hearing officer or convening, referral, approving, or reviewing authority with respect to such preliminary hearing officer's or authority's acts concerning the following:

(i) any decision to place a service member into pretrial confinement;

(ii) disposition decisions;

(iii) rulings on pre-referral matters;

(iv) findings at a preliminary hearing;

(v) convening a court-martial;

(vi) decisions concerning plea agreements;

(vii) selecting members;

(viii) decisions concerning witness requests;

(ix) taking action on the findings or sentence;

(x) taking action on any clemency or deferment request; or

(xi) any appellate or post-trial review of a case.

Discussion

See also Article 37(d)(2) ("Except as provided in paragraph (1) [Article 37(d)(1)] or as otherwise authorized by this chapter, a superior convening authority or commanding officer may not limit the discretion of a subordinate convening authority or officer to act with respect to a case for which the subordinate convening authority or officer has authority to dispose of the offenses.")

(c) *Prohibitions concerning evaluations.*

(1) *Evaluation of members, defense counsel, and special victims' counsel.* In the preparation of an effectiveness, fitness, or efficiency report or any other report or document used in whole or in part for the purpose of determining whether a member of the armed forces is qualified to be advanced in grade, or in determining the assignment or transfer of a member of the armed forces, or in determining whether a member of the armed forces should be retained on active duty, no person subject to the UCMJ may:

(A) Consider or evaluate the performance of duty of any such person as a member of a court-martial; or

(B) Give a less favorable rating or evaluation of any defense counsel or special victims' counsel because of the zeal with which such counsel represented any client. As used in this rule, "special victims' counsel" are judge advocates and civilian counsel, who, in accordance with 10 U.S.C. § 1044e, are designated as Special Victims' Counsel.

Discussion

For evaluations of military judges, see generally Article 26(c) and Article 37.

R.C.M. 104(c)(1)(B) applies when the counsel in question has been detailed, assigned, or authorized to represent the client as a defense or special victims' counsel. Nothing in this rule prohibits supervisors from taking appropriate action for violations of ethical, procedural, or other rules, or for conduct outside the scope of representation.

"Special victims' counsel," as used in R.C.M. 104(c)(1)(B), includes victims' legal counsel within the Navy and Marine Corps and victims' counsel within the Department of the Air Force.

See paragraph 87 of Part IV concerning prosecuting violations of Article 37 under Article 131f.

(d) *Command discretion.*

(1) A superior convening authority or commanding officer may withhold the authority of a subordinate convening authority or officer to dispose of offenses in individual cases, types of cases, or generally.

(2) Except as provided in paragraph (d)(1) of this rule or as otherwise authorized under the UCMJ, a superior convening authority or commanding officer may not limit the discretion of a subordinate convening authority or officer to act with respect to a case for which the subordinate convening authority or officer has the authority to dispose of the offenses.

Rule 105. Direct communications: convening authorities and staff judge advocates; among staff judge advocates; with special trial counsel

(a) *Convening authorities and staff judge advocates.* Convening authorities shall at all times communicate directly with their staff judge advocates in matters relating to the administration of military justice, and may communicate directly with special trial counsel, although any input by the convening authority regarding case dispositions shall be non-binding on the special trial counsel for cases involving covered, known, and related offenses.

Discussion

See R.C.M. 103(18) for a definition of staff judge advocate.

(b) *Among staff judge advocates and with the Judge Advocate General.* The staff judge advocate of any command is entitled to communicate directly with the staff judge advocate of a superior or subordinate command, the Judge Advocate General, or, in the case of the Marine Corps, the Staff Judge Advocate to the Commandant of the Marine Corps.

(c) *Communications among special trial counsel, staff judge advocates, and convening authorities.* Special trial counsel, staff judge advocates, and convening authorities may communicate directly while ensuring that all communications regarding case disposition for covered, related, and known offenses are non-binding on the special trial counsel.

(d) *Free from unlawful or unauthorized influence or coercion.* All communications referenced in this rule shall be free from unlawful or unauthorized influence or coercion.

Discussion

See Article 37, UCMJ and 10 U.S.C. §1044f.

Rule 106. Delivery of military offenders to civilian authorities

Under such regulations as the Secretary concerned may prescribe, a member of the armed forces accused of an offense against civilian authority may be delivered, upon request, to the civilian authority for trial. A member may be placed in restraint by military authorities for this purpose only upon receipt of a duly issued warrant for the apprehension of the member or upon receipt of information establishing probable cause that the member committed an offense, and upon reasonable belief that such restraint is necessary. Such restraint may continue only for such time as is reasonably necessary to effect the delivery.

Discussion

See R.C.M. 1102(b)(2)(C)(ii) for the effect of such delivery on the execution of a court-martial sentence.

Rule 107. Dismissed officer's right to request trial by court-martial

If a commissioned officer of any armed force is dismissed by order of the President under 10 U.S.C. § 1161(a)(3), that officer may apply for trial by general court-martial within a reasonable time.

Discussion

See Article 4 for the procedures to be followed. *See also* Article 75(c).

Rule 108. Rules of court

The Judge Advocate General concerned and persons designated by the Judge Advocate General may make rules of court not inconsistent with these rules for the conduct of court-martial proceedings. Such rules shall be disseminated in accordance with procedures prescribed by the Judge Advocate General concerned or a person to whom this authority has been delegated. Noncompliance with such procedures shall not affect the validity of any rule of court with respect to a party who has received actual and timely notice of the rule or who has not been prejudiced under Article 59 by the absence of such notice. Copies of all rules of court issued under this rule shall be forwarded to the Judge Advocate General concerned.

Rule 109. Professional supervision of military judges and counsel

(a) *In general.* Each Judge Advocate General is responsible for the professional supervision and discipline of appellate military judges, military judges, military magistrates, judge advocates, and other lawyers who practice in proceedings governed by the UCMJ and this Manual. To discharge this responsibility each Judge Advocate General may prescribe rules of professional conduct not inconsistent with this rule or this Manual. Rules of professional conduct promulgated pursuant to this rule may include sanctions for violations of such rules. Sanctions may include but are not limited to indefinite suspension from practice in courts-martial and in the Courts of Criminal Appeals. Such suspensions may only be imposed by the Judge Advocate General of the armed service of such courts. Prior to imposing any discipline under this rule, the subject of the proposed action must be provided notice and an opportunity to be heard. The Judge Advocate General concerned may upon good cause shown modify or revoke suspension. Procedures to investigate complaints against appellate military judges, military judges, and military magistrates are contained in subsection (c) of this rule.

(b) *Action after suspension or disbarment.* When a Judge Advocate General suspends a person from practice or the Court of Appeals for the Armed Forces disbars a person, any Judge Advocate General may suspend that person from practice upon written notice and opportunity to be heard in writing.

(c) *Investigation of judges.*

(1) *In general.* These rules and procedures promulgated pursuant to Article 6a are established to

investigate and dispose of charges, allegations, or information pertaining to the fitness of an appellate military judge, military judge, or military magistrate to perform the duties of the judge's or magistrate's office.

(2) *Policy*. Allegations of judicial misconduct or unfitness shall be investigated pursuant to the procedures of this rule and appropriate action shall be taken. Judicial misconduct includes any act or omission that may serve to demonstrate unfitness for further duty as a judge or magistrate, including, but not limited to violations of applicable ethical standards.

Discussion

The term "unfitness" should be construed broadly, including, for example, matters relating to the incompetence, impartiality, and misconduct of the appellate military judge, military judge, or military magistrate. Erroneous decisions of a judge are not subject to investigation under this rule. Challenges to these decisions are more appropriately left to the appellate process.

---

(3) *Complaints*. Complaints concerning an appellate military judge, military judge, or military magistrate will be forwarded to the Judge Advocate General of the Service concerned or to a person designated by the Judge Advocate General concerned to receive such complaints.

Discussion

Complaints need not be made in any specific form, but if possible complaints should be made under oath. Complaints may be made by judges, lawyers, a party, court personnel, members of the general public or members of the military community. Reports in the news media relating to the conduct of an appellate military judge, military judge, or military magistrate may also form the basis of a complaint.

An individual designated to receive complaints under this paragraph should have judicial experience. The chief trial judge of a Service may be designated to receive complaints against military judges and military magistrates. Military magistrates who perform other duties may be investigated in their capacity other than as a magistrate through the process established by the Judge Advocate General concerned in accordance with R.C.M. 109(a).

---

(4) *Initial action upon receipt of a complaint*. Upon receipt, a complaint will be screened by the Judge Advocate General concerned or by the individual designated in paragraph (c)(3) of this rule to receive complaints. An initial inquiry is necessary if the complaint, taken as true, would constitute judicial misconduct or unfitness for further service as an appellate military judge, a military judge, or military magistrate. Prior to the commencement of an initial inquiry, the Judge Advocate General concerned shall be notified that a complaint has been filed and that an initial inquiry will be conducted. The Judge Advocate General concerned may temporarily suspend the subject of a complaint from performing judicial duties pending the outcome of any inquiry or investigation conducted pursuant to this rule. Such inquiries or investigations shall be conducted with reasonable promptness.

Discussion

Complaints under this paragraph will be treated with confidentiality. Confidentiality protects the subject appellate military judge, military judge, or military magistrate and the judiciary when a complaint is not substantiated. Confidentiality also encourages the reporting of allegations of judicial misconduct or unfitness and permits complaints to be screened with the full cooperation of others.

Complaints containing allegations of criminality should be referred to the appropriate criminal investigative agency in accordance with Appendix 3 of this Manual.

---

(5) *Initial inquiry*.

(A) *In general*. An initial inquiry is necessary to determine if the complaint is substantiated. A complaint is substantiated upon finding that it is more likely than not that the subject appellate military judge, military judge, or military magistrate has engaged in judicial misconduct or is otherwise unfit for further service as a judge or magistrate.

(B) *Responsibility to conduct initial inquiry*. The Judge Advocate General concerned, or the person designated to receive complaints under paragraph (c)(3) of this rule will conduct or order an initial inquiry. The individual designated to conduct the inquiry should, if practicable, be senior to the subject of the complaint. If the subject of the complaint is a military judge or military magistrate, the individual designated to conduct the initial inquiry should, if practicable, be a military judge or an individual with experience as a military judge. If the subject of the complaint is an appellate military judge, the individual designated to conduct the inquiry should, if practicable, have experience as an appellate judge.

Discussion

To avoid the type of conflict prohibited in Article 66(i), the Judge Advocate General's designee should not ordinarily be a member of the same Court of Criminal Appeals as the subject of the complaint. If practicable, a former appellate military judge should be designated.

(C) *Due process.* During the initial inquiry, the subject of the complaint will, at a minimum, be given notice and an opportunity to be heard.

(D) *Action following the initial inquiry.* If the complaint is not substantiated pursuant to subsection (c)(5)(A) of this rule, the complaint shall be dismissed as unfounded. If the complaint is substantiated, minor professional disciplinary action may be taken or the complaint may be forwarded, with findings and recommendations, to the Judge Advocate General concerned. Minor professional disciplinary action is defined as counseling or the issuance of an oral or written admonition or reprimand. The Judge Advocate General concerned will be notified prior to taking minor professional disciplinary action or dismissing a complaint as unfounded.

(6) *Action by the Judge Advocate General.*

(A) *In general.* The Judge Advocates General are responsible for the professional supervision and discipline of appellate military judges, military judges, and military magistrates under their jurisdiction. Upon receipt of findings and recommendations required by paragraph (c)(5) of this rule the Judge Advocate General concerned will take appropriate action.

(B) *Appropriate actions.* The Judge Advocate General concerned may dismiss the complaint, order an additional inquiry, appoint an ethics commission to consider the complaint, refer the matter to another appropriate investigative agency or take appropriate professional disciplinary action pursuant to the rules of professional conduct prescribed by the Judge Advocate General under subsection (a) of this rule. Any decision of the Judge Advocate General, under this rule, is final and is not subject to appeal.

Discussion

Reassignment of appellate military judges, military judges, and military magistrates in accordance with Service regulations is not professional disciplinary action.

(C) *Standard of proof.* Prior to taking professional disciplinary action, other than minor professional disciplinary action as defined in subparagraph (c)(5)(D) of this rule, the Judge Advocate General concerned shall find, in writing, that the subject of the complaint engaged in judicial misconduct or is otherwise unfit for continued service as an appellate military judge, military judge, or military magistrate, and that such misconduct or unfitness is established by clear and convincing evidence.

(D) *Due process.* Prior to taking final action on the complaint, the Judge Advocate General concerned will ensure that the subject of the complaint is, at a minimum, given notice and an opportunity to be heard.

(7) *The Ethics Commission.*

(A) *Membership.* If appointed pursuant to subparagraph (c)(6)(B) of this rule, an ethics commission shall consist of at least three members. If the subject of the complaint is a military judge or military magistrate, the commission should include one or more military judges or individuals with experience as a military judge. If the subject of the complaint is an appellate military judge, the commission should include one or more individuals with experience as an appellate military judge. Members of the commission should, if practicable, be senior to the subject of the complaint.

(B) *Duties.* The commission will perform those duties assigned by the Judge Advocate General concerned. Normally, the commission will provide an opinion as to whether the subject's acts or omissions constitute judicial misconduct or unfitness. If the commission determines that the affected appellate military judge, military judge, or military magistrate engaged in judicial misconduct or is unfit for continued judicial service, the commission may be required to recommend an appropriate disposition to the Judge Advocate General concerned.

Discussion

The Judge Advocate General concerned may appoint an ad hoc or a standing commission.

(8) *Rules of procedure.* The Secretary of Defense or the Secretary of the service concerned may establish additional procedures consistent with this rule and Article 6a.

CHAPTER II. JURISDICTION

Rule 201. Jurisdiction in general

(a) *Nature of courts-martial jurisdiction.*

(1) The jurisdiction of courts-martial is entirely penal or disciplinary.

Discussion

"Jurisdiction" means the power to hear a case and to render a legally competent decision. A court-martial has no power to adjudge civil remedies. For example, a court-martial may not adjudge the payment of damages, collect private debts, order the return of property, or order a criminal forfeiture of seized property. A summary court-martial appointed under 10 U.S.C. §§ 4712 or 9712 to dispose of the effects of a deceased person is not affected by these Rules or this Manual.

---

(2) The UCMJ applies in all places.

Discussion

Except insofar as required by the Constitution, the UCMJ, or the Manual, such as jurisdiction over persons listed under Article 2(a)(10), jurisdiction of courts-martial does not depend on where the offense was committed.

---

(3) The jurisdiction of a court-martial with respect to offenses under the UCMJ is not affected by the place where the court-martial sits. The jurisdiction of a court-martial with respect to military government or the law of war is not affected by the place where the court-martial sits except as otherwise expressly required by this Manual or applicable rule of international law.

Discussion

In addition to the power to try persons for offenses under the UCMJ, general courts-martial have power to try certain persons for violations of the law of war and for crimes or offenses against the law of the territory occupied as an incident of war or belligerency whenever the local civil authority is superseded in whole or part by the military authority of the occupying power. *See* R.C.M. 201(f)(1)(B). In cases where a person is tried by general court-martial for offenses against the law of an occupied territory, the court-martial normally sits in the country where the offense is committed, and must do so under certain circumstances. *See* Articles 4, 64, and 66, Geneva Convention Relative to the Protection of Civilian Persons in Time of War, August 12, 1949, 6 U.S.T. 3516, 3559-60 T.I.A.S. No. 3365.

(b) *Requisites of court-martial jurisdiction.* A court-martial always has jurisdiction to determine whether it has jurisdiction. Otherwise for a court-martial to have jurisdiction:

(1) The court-martial must be convened by an official empowered to convene it;

Discussion

See R.C.M. 504; 1302.

---

(2) The court-martial must be composed in accordance with these rules with respect to number and qualifications of its personnel. As used here "personnel" includes only the military judge, the members, and the summary court-martial;

Discussion

See R.C.M. 501-504; 1301.

---

(3) Each charge before the court-martial must be referred to it by competent authority;

Discussion

See R.C.M. 601; *see also* R.C.M. 307. A commanding officer shall not be considered an accuser under Article 1(9) solely due to the role of the commanding officer in convening a general court-martial or a special court-martial to which charges and specifications were referred by a special trial counsel pursuant to Article 22(b) for general courts-martial or Article 23(b) for special courts-martial, as amended by Section 534 of the National Defense Authorization Act for Fiscal Year 2022, Pub. L. No. 117-81, 135 Stat. 1541, 1696 (2021).

---

(4) The accused must be a person subject to court-martial jurisdiction; and

Discussion

See R.C.M. 202.

---

(5) The offense must be subject to court-martial jurisdiction.

Discussion

See R.C.M. 203. The judgment of a court-martial without jurisdiction is void and is entitled to no legal effect. *See* R.C.M. 907(b)(2)(C)(iv). But see R.C.M. 810(d) concerning the effect of certain decisions by courts-martial without jurisdiction.

See R.C.M. 106 concerning delivery of offenders to civilian authorities.

See also R.C.M. 201(g) concerning the jurisdiction of other military tribunals.

(c) [Reserved].

(d) *Exclusive and nonexclusive jurisdiction.*

(1) Courts-martial have exclusive jurisdiction of purely military offenses.

(2) An act of omission that violates both the UCMJ and local criminal law, foreign or domestic, may be tried by a court-martial, or by a proper civilian tribunal, foreign or domestic, or, subject to R.C.M. 907(b)(2)(C) and regulations of the Secretary concerned, by both.

(3) Where an act or omission is subject to trial by court-martial and by one or more civil tribunals, foreign or domestic, the determination which nation, state, or agency will exercise jurisdiction is a matter for the nations, states, and agencies concerned, and is not a right of the suspect or accused.

Discussion

In the case of an act or omission that violates the UCMJ and a criminal law of a State, the United States, or both, the determination which agency shall exercise jurisdiction should normally be made through consultation or prior agreement between appropriate military officials and appropriate civilian authorities (United States Attorney, or equivalent). *See also* Memorandum of Understanding (MOU) Between the Departments of Justice (DOJ) and Defense Relating to the Investigation and Prosecution of Certain at Appendix 3; Memorandum of Understanding Between the Departments of Justice and Transportation (Coast Guard) Relating to the Investigations and Prosecution of Crimes Over Which the Two Departments Have Concurrent Jurisdiction at Appendix 4.

Under the Constitution, a person generally may not be tried for the same misconduct by both a court-martial and another federal court. *See* R.C.M. 907(b)(2)(C). Although it is constitutionally permissible to try a person by court-martial and by a state court for the same act, as a matter of policy, a person who is pending trial or has been tried by a state court should not ordinarily be tried by court-martial for the same act. International agreements might preclude trial by one state party to the treaty of a person acquitted or finally convicted of a given act by another state party.

Under international law, a friendly foreign nation has jurisdiction to punish offenses committed within its borders by members of a visiting force, unless it expressly or impliedly consents to relinquish its jurisdiction to the visiting sovereign. The procedures and standards for determining which nation will exercise jurisdiction are normally established by treaty. *See, e.g.*, NATO Status of Forces Agreement, June 19, 1951, 4 U.S.T. 1792, T.I.A.S. No. 2846. As a matter of policy, efforts should be made to maximize the exercise of court-martial jurisdiction over persons subject to the UCMJ to the extent possible under applicable agreements.

(e) *Reciprocal jurisdiction.*

(1) Each armed force has court-martial jurisdiction over all persons subject to the UCMJ.

(2)(A) A commander of a unified or specified combatant command may convene courts-martial over members of any of the armed forces.

(B) So much of the authority vested in the President under Article 22(a)(9), to empower any commanding officer of a joint command or joint task force to convene courts-martial is delegated to the Secretary of Defense, and such a commanding officer may convene general courts-martial for the trial of members of any of the armed forces assigned or attached to a combatant command or joint command.

(C) A commander who is empowered to convene a court-martial under subparagraphs (e)(2)(A) or (e)(2)(B) of this rule may expressly authorize a commanding officer of a subordinate joint command or subordinate joint task force who is authorized to convene special and summary courts-martial to convene such courts-martial for the trial of members of other armed forces assigned or attached to a joint command or joint task force, under regulations that the superior command may prescribe.

(3)(A) An accused should not ordinarily be tried by a court-martial convened by a member of a different armed force except when the circumstances described in subparagraphs (e)(2)(A) or (B) of this rule exist. However, failure to comply with this non-binding policy does not affect an otherwise valid referral.

(B) The non-binding policy stated by subparagraph (e)(3)(A) of this rule does not apply when one or more of the following circumstances exists:

(i) The court-martial is convened by a commander authorized to convene courts-martial under paragraph (e)(2) of this rule;

(ii) The accused cannot be delivered to the armed force of which the accused is a member without manifest injury to the armed forces;

(iii) The court-martial is convened by a member of the Space Force to try a member of the Air Force; or

(iv) The court-martial is convened by a member of the Air Force to try a member of the Space Force.

(4) Nothing in this rule prohibits detailing to a court-martial a military judge, member, or counsel who is a member of an armed force different from that of the accused, the convening authority, or both.

(5) When a member of one armed force is tried by a court-martial convened by a member of another armed force, the court-martial will use the implementing regulations and procedures prescribed by the Secretary concerned of the military service of the accused. In all cases, departmental review after that by the officer with authority to convene a general court-martial for the command that held the trial, where that review is required by the UCMJ, shall be carried out by the department that includes the armed force of which the accused is a member.

(6) Unless otherwise directed by the President or Secretary of Defense, whenever action under this Manual is required or authorized to be taken by a person superior to—

(A) a commander of a unified or specified combatant command; or

(B) a commander of any other joint command or joint task force that is not part of a unified or specified combatant command, the matter shall be referred to the Secretary of the armed force of which the accused is a member. The Secretary may convene a court-martial, take other appropriate action, or, subject to R.C.M. 504(c), refer the matter to any person authorized to convene a court-martial of the accused.

(7) When there is a disagreement between the Secretaries of two military departments or between the Secretary of a military department and the commander of a unified or specified combatant command or other joint command or joint task force as to which organization should exercise jurisdiction over a particular case or class of cases, the Secretary of Defense or an official acting under the authority of the Secretary of Defense shall designate which organization will exercise jurisdiction.

Discussion

As to the authority to convene courts-martial, see R.C.M. 504. "Manifest injury" does not mean minor inconvenience or expense. Examples of manifest injury include direct and substantial effect on morale, discipline, or military operations, substantial expense or delay, or loss of essential witnesses.

As to the composition of a court-martial for the trial of an accused who is a member of another armed force, see R.C.M. 503(a)(3) Discussion. Cases involving two or more accused who are members of different armed forces generally should not be referred to a court-martial for a common trial.

(f) *Types of courts-martial.*

[Note: R.C.M. 201(f)(1)(D) and (f)(2)(D) apply to offenses committed on or after 24 June 2014.]

(1) *General courts-martial.*

(A) *Cases under the UCMJ.*

(i) Except as otherwise expressly provided, general courts-martial may try any person subject to the UCMJ for any offense made punishable under the UCMJ. General courts-martial also may try any person for a violation of Article 103, 103b, or 104a.

(ii) Upon a finding of guilty of an offense made punishable by the UCMJ, general courts-martial may, within limits prescribed by this Manual, adjudge any punishment authorized under R.C.M. 1003.

(iii) Notwithstanding any other rule, the death penalty may not be adjudged if:

(a) Not specifically authorized for the offense by the UCMJ and Part IV of this Manual; or

(b) The case has not been referred with a special instruction that the case is to be tried as capital.

(B) *Cases under the law of war.*

(i) General courts-martial may try any person who by the law of war is subject to trial by military tribunal for any crime or offense against:

(a) The law of war; or

(b) The law of the territory occupied as an incident of war or belligerency whenever the local civil authority is superseded in whole or part by the military authority of the occupying power. The law of the occupied territory includes the local criminal law as adopted or modified by competent authority, and the proclamations, ordinances, regulations, or orders promulgated by competent authority of the occupying power.

Discussion

R.C.M. 201(f)(1)(B)(i)(b) is an exercise of the power of military government.

(ii) When a general court-martial exercises jurisdiction under the law of war, it may adjudge any punishment permitted by the law of war.

Discussion

Certain limitations on the discretion of military tribunals to adjudge punishment under the law of war are prescribed in international conventions. *See, e.g.*, Geneva Convention Relative to the Protection of Civilian Persons in Time of War, Aug. 12, 1949, art. 68, 6 U.S.T. 3516, T.I.A.S. No. 3365.

(C) *Limitations in judge alone cases.* A general court-martial composed only of a military judge does not have jurisdiction to try any person for any offense for which the death penalty may be adjudged unless the case has been referred to trial as noncapital.

Discussion

See R.C.M. 103(4) for the definition of the term "capital offense."

(D) *Jurisdiction for Certain Sexual Offenses.* Only a general court-martial has jurisdiction to try offenses under Articles 120(a), 120(b), 120b(a), and 120b(b), and attempts thereof under Article 80.

Discussion

Only a general court-martial has jurisdiction over penetrative sex offenses under subsections (a) and (b) of Article 120, subsections (a) and (b) of Article 120b, and attempts to commit such penetrative sex offenses under Article 80. *See* Article 18, as amended by Section 1705(b) of the National Defense Authorization Act for Fiscal Year 2014, Pub. L. No. 113-66, 127 Stat. 672 (2013), as further amended by Section 5162 of the Military Justice Act of 2016, Division E of the National Defense Authorization Act for Fiscal Year 2017, Pub. L. No. 114-328, 130 Stat. 2000 (2016).

---

(2) *Special courts-martial.*

(A) *In general.* Except as otherwise expressly provided, special courts-martial may try any person subject to the UCMJ for any noncapital offense made punishable by the UCMJ and, as provided in this rule, for capital offenses.

(B) *Punishments*

(i) Upon a finding of guilty, special courts-martial may adjudge, under limitations prescribed by this Manual, any punishment authorized under R.C.M. 1003 except death, dishonorable discharge, dismissal, confinement for more than 1 year, hard labor without confinement for more than 3 months, forfeiture of pay exceeding two-thirds pay per month, or any forfeiture of pay for more than 1 year.

(ii) A bad-conduct discharge, confinement for more than six months, or forfeiture of pay for more than six months, may not be adjudged by a special court-martial when the case is referred as a special court-martial consisting of a military judge alone under Article 16(c)(2)(A).

(C) *Capital offenses.*

(i) A capital offense for which there is prescribed a mandatory punishment beyond the punitive power of a special court-martial shall not be referred to such a court-martial.

(ii) Other than offenses described in (C)(i):

(I) a general court-martial convening authority over the command that includes the accused may permit any capital offense to be referred to a special court-martial for trial.

(II) a special trial counsel exercising authority over a capital offense may refer such an offense to a special court-martial for trial.

(III) The Secretary concerned may authorize, by regulation, special court-martial convening authorities to refer capital offenses to trial by a special court-martial without first obtaining the consent of the general court-martial convening authority.

(D) *Certain Offenses under Articles 120 and 120b.* Notwithstanding subparagraph (f)(2)(A), special courts-martial do not have jurisdiction over offenses under Articles 120(a), 120(b), 120b(a), and 120b(b), and attempts thereof under Article 80. Such offenses shall not be referred to a special court-martial.

Discussion

Only a general court-martial has jurisdiction over penetrative sex offenses under subsections (a) and (b) of Article 120, subsections (a) and (b) of Article 120b, and attempts to commit such penetrative sex offenses under Article 80. *See* UCMJ, Art. 18, as amended by Section 1705(b) of the National Defense Authorization Act for Fiscal Year 2014, Pub. L. No. 113-66, 127 Stat. 672 (2013), as further amended by Section 5162 of the Military Justice Act of 2016, Division E of the National Defense Authorization Act for Fiscal Year 2017, Pub. L. No. 114-328, 130 Stat. 2000 (2016).

(E) *Limitations on trial by special court-martial consisting of a military judge alone.*

(i) No specification may be tried by a special court-martial consisting of a military judge alone under Article 16(c)(2)(A) if, before arraignment, the accused objects on the grounds provided in subclause (I) or (II) of this subparagraph and the military judge determines that:

(I) the maximum authorized confinement for the offense it alleges would be greater than two years if the offense were tried by a general court-martial, with the exception of a specification alleging wrongful use or possession of a controlled substance in violation of Article 112a(b) or an attempt thereof under Article 80; or

(II) the specification alleges an offense for which sex offender notification would be required under regulations issued by the Secretary of Defense.

Discussion

See Department of Defense Instruction 1325.07, Administration of Military Correctional Facilities and Clemency and Parole Authority, for offenses requiring sex offender notification.

(ii) If the accused objects to trial by a special court-martial consisting of a military judge alone under Article 16(c)(2)(A), and the military judge makes a determination under clause (i), trial may be ordered by a special court-martial under Article 16(c)(1) or a general court-martial as may be appropriate.

(3) *Summary courts-martial. See* R.C.M. 1301(c) and (d)(1).

(g) *Concurrent jurisdiction of other military tribunals.* The provisions of the UCMJ and this Manual conferring jurisdiction upon courts-martial do not deprive military commissions, provost courts, or other military tribunals of concurrent jurisdiction with respect to offenders or offenses that by statute or by the law of war may be tried by military commissions, provost courts, or other military tribunals.

Discussion

See Articles 103 and 103b for some instances of concurrent jurisdiction.

Rule 202. Persons subject to the jurisdiction of courts-martial

(a) *In general.* Courts-martial may try any person when authorized to do so under the UCMJ.

Discussion

(1) *Authority under the UCMJ.* Article 2 lists classes of persons who are subject to the UCMJ. These include active duty personnel (Article 2(a)(1)); cadets, aviation cadets, and midshipmen (Article 2(a)(2)); certain retired personnel (Article 2(a)(4) and (5)); members of Reserve components not on active duty under some circumstances (Article 2(a)(3)); members of the Fleet Reserve and Fleet Marine Corps Reserve (Article 2(a)(6)); persons in the custody of the armed forces serving a sentence imposed by court-martial (Article 2(a)(7)); and, under some circumstances, specified categories of civilians (Article 2(a)(10), (11), and (12)); *see* paragraphs (3) and (4) of this discussion. In addition, certain persons whose status as members of the armed forces or as persons otherwise subject to the UCMJ apparently has ended may, nevertheless, be amendable to trial by court-martial. *See* Articles 3, 4, and 73. A person need not be subject to the UCMJ to be subject to trial by court-martial under Articles 103, 103b, and 104a. See also Article 48 and R.C.M. 809 concerning who may be subject to the contempt powers of a court-martial.

(2) *Active duty personnel.* Court-martial jurisdiction is most commonly exercised over active duty personnel. In general, a person becomes subject to court-martial jurisdiction upon enlistment in or induction into the armed forces, acceptance of a commission, or entry onto active duty pursuant to orders. Generally, three criteria are considered to determine when military jurisdiction over active duty personnel terminates: (1) the delivery of a discharge certificate; (2) a final accounting of pay; and (3) completion of any clearing process required under Military Service regulations. Orders transferring a person to the inactive reserve are the equivalent of a discharge certificate for purposes of jurisdiction over reserve personnel. There are several important qualifications and exceptions to these general guidelines."

(A) *Inception of court-martial jurisdiction over active duty personnel.*

(i) *Enlistment.*

"The voluntary enlistment of any person who has the capacity to understand the significance of enlisting in the armed forces shall be valid for purposes of jurisdiction under [Article 2(a)] and a change of status from civilian to member of the armed forces shall be effective upon taking the oath of enlistment." Article 2(b). A person who is, at the time of enlistment, insane, intoxicated, or under the age of 17 does not have the capacity to enlist by law. No court-martial jurisdiction over such a person may exist as long as the incapacity continues. If the incapacity ceases to exist, a "constructive enlistment" may result under Article 2(c). See discussion of "constructive enlistment" of this rule. Similarly, if the enlistment was involuntary, court-martial jurisdiction will exist only when the coercion is removed and a "constructive enlistment" under Article 2(c) is established.

Persons aged 17 (but not yet aged 18) may not enlist without parental consent. A parent or guardian may, within 90 days of the enlistment's inception, terminate the enlistment of a 17-year-old who enlisted without parental consent, if the person has not yet reached the age of 18. 10 U.S.C. § 1170. See also DOD Instruction 1332.14 and Service regulations for specific rules on separation of persons aged 17 based on a parental request. Absent effective action by a parent or guardian to terminate such an enlistment, court-martial jurisdiction exists over the person. An application by a parent for release does not deprive a court-martial of jurisdiction to try a person for offenses committed before action is completed on such an application.

Even if a person lacked capacity to understand the effect of enlistment or did not enlist voluntarily, a "constructive enlistment" may be established under Article 2(c).

Even if a person never underwent an enlistment or induction proceeding of any kind, court-martial jurisdiction could be established under this provision.

(ii) *Induction.* Court-martial jurisdiction does not extend to a draftee until: the draftee has completed an induction ceremony which was in substantial compliance with the requirements prescribed by statute and regulations; the draftee, by conduct after an apparent induction, has waived objection to substantive defects in it; or a "constructive enlistment" under Article 2(c) exists.

The fact that a person was improperly inducted (for example, because of incorrect classification or erroneous denial of exemption) does not of itself negate court-martial jurisdiction. When a person has made timely and persistent efforts to correct such an error, court-martial jurisdiction may be defeated if improper induction is found, depending on all the circumstances of the case.

(iii) *Call to active duty.* A member of a reserve component may be called or ordered to active duty for a variety of reasons, including training, service in time of war or national emergency, discipline, or as a result of failure to participate satisfactorily in unit activities.

When a person is ordered to active duty for failure to satisfactorily participate in unit activities, the order must substantially comply with procedures prescribed by regulations, to the extent due process requires, for court-martial jurisdiction to exist. Generally, the person must be given notice of the activation and the reasons therefor, and an opportunity to object to the activation. A person waives the right to contest involuntary activation by failure to exercise this right within a reasonable time after notice of the right to do so.

(B) *Termination of jurisdiction over active duty personnel.* As indicated in this rule, the delivery of a valid discharge certificate or its equivalent ordinarily serves to terminate court-martial jurisdiction.

(i) *Effect of completion of term of service.* Completion of an enlistment or term of service does not by itself terminate court-martial jurisdiction. An original term of enlistment may be adjusted for a variety of reasons, such as making up time lost for unauthorized absence. Even after such adjustments are considered, court-martial jurisdiction normally continues past the time of scheduled separation until a discharge certificate or its equivalent is delivered and certain other criteria are satisfied or until the Government fails to act within a reasonable time after the person objects to continued retention. As indicated in subsection (c) of this rule, service members may be retained past their scheduled time of separation, over protest, by action with a view to trial while they are still subject to the UCMJ. Thus, if action with a view to trial is initiated before discharge or the effective terminal date of self-executing orders, a person may be retained beyond the date that the period of service would otherwise have expired or the terminal date of such orders.

"(ii) *Effect of discharge and reenlistment.* For offenses occurring on or after October 23, 1992, under the 1992 National Defense Authorization Act's amendment to Article 3(a), a person who reenlists following a discharge may be tried for offenses committed during the earlier term of service. For offenses occurring prior to October 23, 1992, a person who reenlists following a discharge may be tried for offenses committed during the earlier term of service only if the offense was punishable by confinement for five years or more and could not be tried in the courts of the United States or of a State, a Territory, or the District of Columbia. *But see* (iii)(a) of this discussion."

(iii) *Exceptions.* There are several exceptions to the general principle that court-martial jurisdiction terminates on discharge or its equivalent.

(a) A person who was subject to the UCMJ at the time an offense was committed may be tried by court-martial for that offense despite a later discharge or other termination of that status if:

(1) For offenses occurring on or after October 23, 1992, the person is, at the time of the court-martial, subject to the UCMJ, by reentry into the armed forces or otherwise. *See* Article 3(a), as amended by the National Defense Authorization Act for Fiscal Year 1993, Pub. L. No. 102-484, 106 Stat. 2315, 2505 (1992);

(2) For offenses occurring before October 23, 1992,

(A) The offense is one for which a court-martial may adjudge confinement for 5 or more years;

(B) The person cannot be tried in the courts of the United States or of a State, Territory, or the District of Columbia; and

(C) The person is, at the time of the court-martial, subject to the UCMJ, by reentry into the armed forces or otherwise. *See* Article 3(a) prior to the 1992 National Defense Authorization Act Amendment.

(b) A person who was subject to the UCMJ at the time the offense was committed is subject to trial by court-martial despite a later discharge if—

(1) The discharge was issued before the end of the accused's term of enlistment for the purpose of reenlisting;

(2) The person remains, at the time of the court-martial, subject to the UCMJ; and

(3) The reenlistment occurred after 26 July 1982.

(c) Persons in the custody of the armed forces serving a sentence imposed by a court-martial remain subject to the UCMJ and court-martial jurisdiction. A prisoner who has received a discharge and who remains in the custody of an armed force may be tried for an offense committed while a member of the armed forces and before the execution of the discharge as well as for offenses committed after it.

(d) A person discharged from the armed forces who is later charged with having fraudulently obtained that discharge is, subject to the statute of limitations, subject to trial by court-martial on that charge, and is after apprehension subject to the UCMJ while in the custody of the armed forces for trial. Upon conviction of that charge such a person is subject to trial by court-martial for any offenses under the UCMJ committed before the fraudulent discharge.

(e) No person who has deserted from the armed forces is relieved from court-martial jurisdiction by a separation from any later period of service.

(f) When a person's discharge or other separation does not interrupt the status as a person belonging to the general category of persons subject to the UCMJ, court-martial jurisdiction over that person does not end. For example, when an officer holding a commission in a Reserve component of an armed force is discharged from that commission while on active duty because of acceptance of a commission in a Regular component of that armed force, without an interval between the periods of service under the two commissions, that officer's military status does not end. There is merely a change in personnel status from temporary to permanent officer, and court-martial jurisdiction over an offense committed before the discharge is not affected.

(3) *Public Health Service and National Oceanic and Atmospheric Administration.* Members of the Public Health Service and the National Oceanic and Atmospheric Administration become subject to the UCMJ when assigned to and serving with the armed forces.

(4) *Limitations on jurisdiction over civilians.* Court-martial

jurisdiction over civilians under the UCMJ is limited by the Constitution and other applicable laws, including as construed in judicial decisions. The exercise of jurisdiction under Article 2(a)(11) in peace time has been held unconstitutional by the Supreme Court of the United States. Before initiating court-martial proceedings against a civilian, relevant statutes, decisions, Service regulations, and policy memoranda should be carefully examined.

(5) *Members of a Reserve Component.* Members of a reserve component in federal service on active duty, as well as those in federal service on inactive-duty training or during any of the periods specified in Article 2(a)(3)(B), are subject to the UCMJ. Moreover, members of a reserve component are amenable to the jurisdiction of courts-martial notwithstanding the termination of a period of such duty. See R.C.M. 204.

(b) *Offenses under the law of war.* Nothing in this rule limits the power of general courts-martial to try persons under the law of war. *See* R.C.M. 201(f)(1)(B).

(c) *Attachment of jurisdiction over the person.*

(1) *In general.* Court-martial jurisdiction attaches over a person when action with a view to trial of that person is taken. Once court-martial jurisdiction over a person attaches, such jurisdiction shall continue for all purposes of trial, sentence, and punishment, notwithstanding the expiration of that person's term of service or other period in which that person was subject to the UCMJ or trial by court-martial. When jurisdiction attaches over a Servicemember on active duty, the Servicemember may be held on active duty over objection pending disposition of any offense for which held and shall remain subject to the UCMJ during the entire period.

Discussion

Court-martial jurisdiction exists to try a person as long as that person occupies a status as a person subject to the UCMJ. Thus, a service member is subject to court-martial jurisdiction until lawfully discharged or, when the service member's term of service has expired, the Government fails to act within a reasonable time on objection by the service member to continued retention. Articles 103, 103b, and 104a set forth offenses with expanded jurisdictional reach.

Court-martial jurisdiction attaches over a person upon action with a view to trial. Once court-martial jurisdiction attaches, it continues throughout the trial and appellate process, and for purposes of punishment.

If jurisdiction has attached before the effective terminal date of self-executing orders, the person may be held for trial by court-martial beyond the effective terminal date.

---

(2) *Procedure.* Actions by which court-martial jurisdiction attaches include: apprehension; imposition of restraint, such as restriction, arrest, or confinement; and preferral of charges.

Rule 203. Jurisdiction over the offense

To the extent permitted by the Constitution, courts-martial may try any offense under the UCMJ and, in the case of general courts-martial, the law of war.

Discussion

(a) *In general.* Courts-martial have power to try any offense under the UCMJ except when prohibited from so doing by the Constitution. The rule enunciated in *Solorio v. United States*, 483 U.S. 435 (1987), is that jurisdiction of courts-martial depends solely on the accused's status as a person subject to the Uniform Code of Military Justice, and not on the "service-connection" of the offense charged.

(b) *Pleading and proof.* Normally, the inclusion of the accused's rank or grade will be sufficient to plead the service status of the accused. Ordinarily, no allegation of the accused's armed force or unit is necessary for military members on active duty. See R.C.M. 307 regarding required specificity of pleadings. For jurisdictional punishment limitations applicable for specific types of courts-martial, see R.C.M. 201(f).

Rule 204. Jurisdiction over certain reserve component personnel

(a) *Service regulations.* The Secretary concerned shall prescribe regulations setting forth rules and procedures for the exercise of court-martial jurisdiction and nonjudicial punishment authority over reserve component personnel under Article 2(a)(3) and 2(d), subject to the limitations of this Manual and the UCMJ.

Discussion

See definitions in R.C.M. 103 (Discussion); paragraph 5.e and f., Part V, concerning limitations on nonjudicial punishments imposed on reservists while on inactive-duty training.

(b) *Courts-Martial*

(1) *General and special court-martial proceedings.* A member of a reserve component must be on active duty prior to arraignment at a general or special court-martial. A member ordered to active duty pursuant to Article 2(d) may be retained on active duty to serve any adjudged confinement or other restriction on liberty if the order to active duty was approved in accordance with Article 2(d)(5), but such member may not be retained on active duty pursuant to Article 2(d) after service of the confinement or other restriction on liberty. All punishments remaining unserved at the

time the member is released from active duty may be carried over to subsequent periods of inactive-duty training or active duty.

Discussion

An accused ordered to active duty pursuant to Article 2(d) may be retained on active duty after service of the punishment if permitted by other authority. For example, an accused who commits another offense while on active duty ordered pursuant to Article 2(d) may be retained on active duty pursuant to R.C.M. 202(c)(1).

(2) *Summary courts-martial.* A member of a reserve component may be tried by summary court-martial either while on active duty or inactive-duty training. A summary court-martial conducted during inactive-duty training may be in session only during normal periods of such training. The accused may not be held beyond such periods of training for trial or service or any punishment. All punishments remaining unserved at the end of a period of active duty or the end of any normal period of inactive duty training may be carried over to subsequent periods of inactive-duty training or active duty.

Discussion

A "normal period" of inactive-duty training does not include periods that are scheduled solely for the purpose of conducting court-martial proceeding.

(c) *Applicability.* This subsection is not applicable when a member is held on active duty pursuant to R.C.M. 202(c).

(d) *Changes in type of service.* A member of a reserve component at the time disciplinary action is initiated, who is alleged to have committed an offense while subject to the UCMJ, is subject to court-martial jurisdiction without regard to any change between active and reserve service or within different categories of reserve service subsequent to commission of the offense. This subsection does not apply to a person whose military status was completely terminated after commission of an offense.

Discussion

A member of a regular or reserve component remains subject to court-martial jurisdiction after leaving active duty for offenses committed prior to such termination of active duty if the member retains military status in a reserve component without having been discharged from all obligations of military service.

See R.C.M. 202(a), Discussion, paragraph (2)(B)(ii) and (iii), regarding the jurisdictional effect of a discharge from military service. A "complete termination" of military status refers to a discharge relieving the service member of any further military service. It does not include a discharge conditioned upon acceptance of further military service.

CHAPTER III. INITIATION OF CHARGES; APPREHENSION; PRETRIAL RESTRAINT; RELATED MATTERS

Rule 301. Report of offense

(a) *Who may report.* Any person may report an offense subject to trial by court-martial.

(b) *To whom reports are conveyed.* Ordinarily, any military authority who receives a report of an offense shall forward as soon as practicable the report and any accompanying information to the immediate commander of the suspect. Competent authority superior to that commander may direct otherwise.

(c) *Special trial counsel.* All reports of covered offenses shall be forwarded promptly to a special trial counsel. A special trial counsel shall have the authority to determine whether a reported offense is a covered, known, or related offense in accordance with R.C.M. 303A.

Discussion

Any military authority may receive a report of an offense. Typically such reports are made to law enforcement or investigative personnel, or to appropriate persons in the chain of command. A report may be made by any means, and no particular format is required. When a person who is not a law enforcement official receives a report of an offense, that person should forward the report to the immediate commander of the suspect unless that person believes it would be more appropriate to notify law enforcement or investigative authorities.

If the suspect is unidentified, the military authority who receives the report should refer it to a law enforcement or investigative agency.

Upon receipt of a report, the immediate commander of a suspect, or a special trial counsel, as appropriate, should refer to R.C.M. 306 (Initial disposition) or R.C.M. 306A (Initial determination by special trial counsel to exercise authority). *See also* R.C.M. 302 (Apprehension); R.C.M. 303 (Preliminary inquiry into reported offenses); R.C.M. 304, 305 (Pretrial restraint, confinement). Any doubt as to whether a report alleges a covered offense should be resolved in favor of forwarding the reported offense to a special trial counsel.

Rule 302. Apprehension

(a) *Definition and scope.*

(1) *Definition.* Apprehension is the taking of a person into custody.

Discussion

Apprehension is the equivalent of "arrest" in civilian terminology. (In military terminology, "arrest" is a form of restraint. *See* Article 9; R.C.M. 304.) See subsection (c) of this rule concerning the bases for apprehension. An apprehension is not required in every case; the fact that an accused was never apprehended does not affect the jurisdiction of a court-martial to try the accused. However, see R.C.M. 202(c) concerning attachment of jurisdiction.

An apprehension is different from detention of a person for investigative purposes, although each involves the exercise of government control over the freedom of movement of a person. An apprehension must be based on probable cause, and the custody initiated in an apprehension may continue until proper authority is notified and acts under R.C.M. 304 or 305. An investigative detention may be made on less than probable cause (see Mil. R. Evid. 314(f)), and normally involves a relatively short period of custody. Furthermore, an extensive search of the person is not authorized incident to an investigative detention, as it is with an apprehension. *See* Mil. R. Evid. 314(f) and (g). This rule does not affect any seizure of the person less severe than apprehension.

Evidence obtained as the result of an apprehension which is in violation of this rule may be challenged under Mil. R. Evid. 311(d). Evidence obtained as the result of an unlawful civilian arrest may be challenged under Mil. R. Evid. 311(d).

---

(2) *Scope.* This rule applies only to apprehensions made by persons authorized to do so under subsection (b) of this rule with respect to offenses subject to trial by court-martial. Nothing in this rule limits the authority of federal law enforcement officials to apprehend persons, whether or not subject to trial by court-martial, to the extent permitted by applicable enabling statutes and other law.

Discussion

R.C.M. 302 does not affect the authority of any official to detain, arrest, or apprehend persons not subject to trial under the UCMJ. The rule does not apply to actions taken by any person in a private capacity.

Several federal agencies have broad powers to apprehend persons for violations of federal laws, including the Uniform Code of Military Justice. For example, agents of the Federal Bureau of Investigation, United States Marshals, and Secret Service may apprehend persons for any offenses committed in their presence and for felonies. 18 U.S.C. §§ 3052, 3053, 3056. Other agencies with apprehension powers include the General Services Administration, 40 U.S.C. § 318 and the Veterans Administration, 38 U.S.C. § 902. The extent to which such agencies become involved in the apprehension of persons subject to trial by courts-martial may depend on the statutory authority of the agency and the agency's formal or informal relationships with the Department of Defense.

(b) *Who may apprehend.* The following officials may apprehend any person subject to trial by court-martial:

(1) *Military law enforcement officials.* Persons designated by proper authorities to perform military criminal investigative, guard, or police duties, whether subject to the UCMJ or not, when in each of the foregoing instances, the official making the apprehension is in the execution of law enforcement duties;

Discussion

Whenever enlisted persons, including police and guards, and civilian police and guards apprehend any commissioned or warrant officer, such persons should make an immediate report to the commissioned officer to whom the apprehending person is responsible.

The phrase "persons designated by proper authority to perform military criminal investigative, guard or police duties" includes special agents of the Defense Criminal Investigative Service, security forces, military police, master at arms personnel, and members of the shore patrol.

---

(2) *Commissioned, warrant, petty, and noncommissioned officers.* All commissioned, warrant, petty, and noncommissioned officers on active duty or inactive duty training;

Discussion

Noncommissioned and petty officers not otherwise performing law enforcement duties should not apprehend a commissioned officer unless directed to do so by a commissioned officer or in order to prevent disgrace to the Service or the escape of one who has committed a serious offense.

---

(3) *Civilians authorized to apprehend deserters.* Under Article 8, any civilian officer having authority to apprehend offenders under laws of the United States or of a State, Territory, Commonwealth, or possession, or the District of Columbia, when the apprehension is of a deserter from the armed forces.

Discussion

The UCMJ specifically provides that any civil officer with the authority to apprehend offenders under the laws of the United States or of a State, Commonwealth, possession, or the District of Columbia may summarily apprehend a deserter. *See* Article 8. However, this authority does not permit state and local law enforcement officers to apprehend persons for other violations of the UCMJ.

(c) *Grounds for apprehension.* A person subject to the UCMJ or trial thereunder may be apprehended for an offense triable by court-martial upon probable cause to apprehend. Probable cause to apprehend exists when there is a reasonable belief that an offense has been or is being committed and the person to be apprehended committed or is committing it. Persons authorized to apprehend under R.C.M. 302(b)(2) may also apprehend persons subject to the UCMJ who take part in quarrels, frays, or disorders, wherever they occur.

Discussion

A mere suspicion is not enough but proof which would support a conviction is not necessary. A person who determines probable cause may rely on the reports of others.

(d) *How an apprehension may be made.*

(1) *In general.* An apprehension is made by clearly notifying the person to be apprehended that person is in custody. This notice should be given orally or in writing, but it may be implied by the circumstances.

(2) *Warrants.* Neither warrants nor any other authorizations shall be required for an apprehension under these rules except as required in paragraph (e)(2) of this rule.

(3) *Use of force.* Any person authorized under these rules to make an apprehension may use such force and means as reasonably necessary under the circumstances to effect the apprehension.

Discussion

In addition to any other action required by law or regulation or proper military officials, any person making an apprehension under these rules should maintain custody of the person apprehended and inform as promptly as possible the immediate commander of the person apprehended, or any official higher in the chain of command of the person apprehended if it is impracticable to inform the immediate commander.

(e) *Where an apprehension may be made.*

(1) *In general.* An apprehension may be made at any place, except as provided in paragraph (e)(2) of this rule.

(2) *Private dwellings.* A private dwelling includes dwellings, on or off a military installation, such as single family houses, duplexes, and apartments. The quarters may be owned, leased, or rented by the residents, or assigned, and may be occupied on a

temporary or permanent basis. "Private dwelling" does not include the following, whether or not subdivided into individual units: living areas in military barracks, vessels, aircraft, vehicles, tents, bunkers, field encampments, and similar places. No person may enter a private dwelling for the purpose of making an apprehension under these rules unless:

(A) Pursuant to consent under Mil. R. Evid. 314(e) or 316(c)(3);

(B) There is a reasonable belief that the delay necessary to obtain a search warrant or search authorization would result in the person sought to be taken into custody evading apprehension;

(C) In the case of a private dwelling which is military property or under military control, or nonmilitary property in a foreign country

(i) if the person to be apprehended is a resident of the private dwelling, there exists, at the time of the entry, reason to believe that the person to be apprehended is present in the dwelling, and the apprehension has been authorized by an official listed in Mil. R. Evid. 315(d) upon a determination that probable cause to apprehend the person exists; or

(ii) if the person to be apprehended is not a resident of the private dwelling, the entry has been authorized by an official listed in Mil. R. Evid. 315(d) upon a determination that probable cause exists to apprehend the person and to believe that the person to be apprehended is or will be present at the time of the entry.

(D) In the case of a private dwelling not included in subparagraph (e)(2)(C) of this rule,

(i) if the person to be apprehended is a resident of the private dwelling, there exists at the time of the entry, reason to believe that the person to be apprehended is present and the apprehension is authorized by an arrest warrant issued by competent civilian authority; or

(ii) if the person to be apprehended is not a resident of the private dwelling, the apprehension is authorized by an arrest warrant and the entry is authorized by a search warrant, each issued by competent civilian authority. A person who is not a resident of the private dwelling entered may not challenge the legality of an apprehension of that person on the basis of failure to secure a warrant or authorization to enter that dwelling, or on the basis of the sufficiency of such a warrant or authorization. Nothing in paragraph (e)(2)) affects the legality of an apprehension which is incident to otherwise lawful presence in a private dwelling.

Discussion

For example, if law enforcement officials enter a private dwelling pursuant to a valid search warrant or search authorization, they may apprehend persons therein if grounds for an apprehension exist. This subsection is not intended to be an independent grant of authority to execute civilian arrest or search warrants. The authority must derive from an appropriate federal or state procedure. *See, e.g.*, Fed. R. Crim. P. 41 and 28 C.F.R. 60.1.

Rule 303. Preliminary inquiry into reported offenses

Except for covered offenses as defined by Article 1(17), upon receipt of information that a member of the command is accused or suspected of committing an offense or offenses triable by court-martial, the immediate commander shall make or cause to be made a preliminary inquiry into the charges or suspected offenses. A commander who receives a report of a covered offense shall promptly forward the report to a special trial counsel in accordance with R.C.M. 301(c) and regulations prescribed by the Secretary concerned.

Discussion

In serious or complex cases, including sexual offenses and sexual harassment, the commander should, and in some cases must, seek law enforcement or appropriate investigative assistance in conducting any inquiry or further investigation.

The Military Rules of Evidence should be consulted when conducting interrogations (*see* Mil. R. Evid. 301-306), searches (*see* Mil. R. Evid. 311-317), and eyewitness identifications (*see* Mil. R. Evid. 321).

If the offense is one for which the Department of Justice has investigative responsibilities, appropriate coordination should be made under the Memorandum of Understanding, *see* Appendix 3, and any implementing regulations.

If it appears that any witness may not be available for later proceedings in the case, this should be brought to the attention of appropriate authorities. *See also* R.C.M. 702 (depositions).

A person who is an accuser (*see* Article 1(9)) is disqualified from convening a general or special court-martial in that case. *See* R.C.M. 504(c)(1). Therefore, when the immediate commander is a general or special court-martial convening authority, the preliminary inquiry should be conducted by another officer of the command. That officer may be informed that charges may be preferred if the officer determines that preferral is warranted.

Rule 303A. Determination by special trial counsel to exercise authority

(a) *Initial determination.* A special trial counsel has the exclusive authority to determine if a reported offense is a covered offense.

(b) *Covered offense.* If a special trial counsel determines that a reported offense is a covered offense or receives a preferred charge alleging a covered offense, a special trial counsel shall exercise authority over that covered offense.

(c) *Related offenses.* If a special trial counsel exercises authority pursuant to R.C.M. 303A(b), the special trial counsel may also exercise authority over any reported offense or charge related to a covered offense, whether alleged to have been committed by the suspect of the covered offense or by anyone else subject to the UCMJ.

(d) *Known offenses.* If a special trial counsel exercises authority pursuant to R.C.M. 303A(b), the special trial counsel may also exercise authority over any offense or charge alleged to have been committed by the suspect of the covered offense.

(e) *Notification to command.* When a special trial counsel exercises authority over any reported offense, the special trial counsel shall notify the officer exercising special court-martial convening authority over the suspect.

Rule 304. Pretrial restraint

(a) *Types of pretrial restraint.* Pretrial restraint is moral or physical restraint on a person's liberty which is imposed before and during disposition of offenses. Pretrial restraint may consist of conditions on liberty, restriction in lieu of arrest, arrest, or confinement.

(1) *Conditions on liberty.* Conditions on liberty are imposed by orders directing a person to do or refrain from doing specified acts. Such conditions may be imposed in conjunction with other forms of restraint or separately.

(2) *Restriction in lieu of arrest.* Restriction in lieu of arrest is the restraint of a person by oral or written orders directing the person to remain within specified limits; a restricted person shall, unless otherwise directed, perform full military duties while restricted.

(3) *Arrest.* Arrest is the restraint of a person by oral or written order not imposed as punishment, directing the person to remain within specified limits; a person in the status of arrest may not be required to perform full military duties such as commanding or supervising personnel, serving as guard, or bearing arms. The status of arrest automatically ends when the person is placed, by the authority who ordered the arrest or a superior authority, on duty inconsistent with the status of arrest, but this shall not prevent requiring the person arrested to do ordinary cleaning or policing, or to take part in routine training and duties.

(4) *Confinement.* Pretrial confinement is physical restraint, imposed by order of competent authority, depriving a person of freedom pending disposition of offenses. *See* R.C.M. 305.

Discussion

Conditions on liberty include orders to report periodically to a specified official, orders not to go to a certain place (such as the scene of the alleged offense), and orders not to associate with specified persons (such as the alleged victim or potential witnesses). Conditions on liberty must not hinder pretrial preparation, however. Thus, when such conditions are imposed, they must by sufficiently flexible to permit pretrial preparation.

Restriction in lieu of arrest is a less severe restraint on liberty than is arrest. Arrest includes suspension from performing full military duties and the limits of arrest are normally narrower than those of restriction in lieu of arrest. The actual nature of the restraint imposed, and not the characterization of it by the officer imposing it, will determine whether it is technically an arrest or restriction in lieu of arrest.

Breach of arrest or restriction in lieu of arrest or violation of conditions on liberty are offenses under the UCMJ. See paragraphs 12, 13 and 18, Part IV. When such an offense occurs, it may warrant appropriate action such as nonjudicial punishment or court-martial. *See* R.C.M. 306. In addition, such a breach or violation may provide a basis for the imposition of a more severe form of restraint.

R.C.M. 707(a) requires that the accused be brought to trial within 120 days of preferral of charges or imposition of restraint under R.C.M. 304(a)(2)-(4).

(b) *Who may order pretrial restraint.*

(1) *Of civilians and officers.* Only a commanding officer to whose authority the civilian or officer is subject may order pretrial restraint of that civilian or officer.

Discussion

Civilians may be restrained under these rules only when they are subject to trial by court-martial. *See* R.C.M. 202.

---

(2) *Of enlisted persons.* Any commissioned officer may order pretrial restraint of any enlisted person.

(3) *Delegation of authority.* The authority to order

pretrial restraint of civilians and commissioned and warrant officers may not be delegated. A commanding officer may delegate to warrant, petty, and noncommissioned officers authority to order pretrial restraint of enlisted persons of the commanding officer's command or subject to the authority of that commanding officer.

(4) *Authority to withhold.* A superior competent authority may withhold from a subordinate the authority to order pretrial restraint.

(c) *When a person may be restrained.* No person may be ordered into restraint before trial except for probable cause. Probable cause to order pretrial restraint exists when there is a reasonable belief that:

(1) An offense triable by court-martial has been committed;

(2) The person to be restrained committed it; and

(3) The restraint ordered is required by the circumstances.

Discussion

The decision whether to impose pretrial restraint, and, if so, what type or types, should be made on a case-by-case basis. The factors listed in the Discussion of R.C.M. 305(h)(2)(B) should be considered. The restraint should not be more rigorous than the circumstances require to ensure the presence of the person restrained or to prevent foreseeable serious criminal misconduct.

Restraint is not required in every case. The absence of pretrial restraint does not affect the jurisdiction of a court-martial. However, see R.C.M. 202(c) concerning attachment of jurisdiction. See R.C.M. 305 concerning the standards and procedures governing pretrial confinement.

(d) *Procedures for ordering pretrial restraint.* Pretrial restraint other than confinement is imposed by notifying the person orally or in writing of the restraint, including its terms or limits. The order to an enlisted person shall be delivered personally by the authority who issues it or through other persons subject to the UCMJ. The order to an officer or a civilian shall be delivered personally by the authority who issues it or by another commissioned officer. Pretrial confinement is imposed pursuant to orders by a competent authority by the delivery of a person to a place of confinement.

(e) *Notice of basis for restraint.* When a person is placed under restraint, the person shall be informed of the nature of the offense which is the basis for such restraint.

Discussion

See R.C.M. 305(e) concerning additional information which must be given to a person who is confined. If the person ordering the restraint is not the commander of the person restrained, that officer should be notified.

(f) *Punishment prohibited.* Pretrial restraint is not punishment and shall not be used as such. No person who is restrained pending trial may be subjected to punishment or penalty for the offense which is the basis for that restraint. Prisoners being held for trial shall not be required to undergo punitive duty hours or training, perform punitive labor, or wear special uniforms prescribed only for post-trial prisoners. This rule does not prohibit minor punishment during pretrial confinement for infractions of the rules of the place of confinement. Prisoners shall be afforded facilities and treatment under regulations of the Secretary concerned.

Discussion

Offenses under the UCMJ by a person under restraint may be disposed of in the same manner as any other offenses.

(g) *Release.* Except as otherwise provided in R.C.M. 305, a person may be released from pretrial restraint by a person authorized to impose it. Pretrial restraint shall terminate when a sentence is adjudged, the accused is acquitted of all charges, or all charges are dismissed.

Discussion

Pretrial restraint may be imposed (or reimposed) if charges are to be reinstated or a rehearing or "other" trial is to be ordered.

(h) *Administrative restraint.* Nothing in this rule prohibits limitations on a Servicemember imposed for operational or other military purposes independent of military justice, including administrative hold or medical reasons.

Discussion

See R.C.M. 306.

Rule 305. Pretrial confinement

(a) *In general.* Pretrial confinement is physical restraint, imposed by order of competent authority, depriving a person of freedom pending disposition of charges.

Discussion

See Article 12 regarding the limitations on confinement of members of the armed forces of the United States in immediate association with enemy prisoners or other foreign nationals detained under the law of war.

(b) *Who may be confined.* Any person who is subject to trial by court-martial may be confined if the requirements of this rule are met.

Discussion

See R.C.M. 201 and 202 and the discussions therein concerning persons who are subject to trial by courts-martial.

(c) *Who may order confinement. See* R.C.M. 304(b)

Discussion

No provost marshal, commander of a guard, or master at arms may refuse to receive or keep any confinee committed to his charge by a commissioned officer of the armed forces, when the committing officer furnishes a statement, signed by him, of the offense charged against the confinee. *See* Article 11(a).

(d) *When a person may be confined.* No person may be ordered into pretrial confinement except for probable cause. Probable cause to order pretrial confinement exists when there is a reasonable belief that:

(1) An offense triable by court-martial has been committed;

(2) The person confined committed it; and

(3) Confinement is required by the circumstances.

Discussion

The person who directs confinement should consider the matters discussed under subparagraph (i)(2)(B) of this rule before ordering confinement. However, the person who initially orders confinement is not required to make a detailed analysis of the necessity for confinement. It is often not possible to review a person's background and character or even the details of an offense before physically detaining the person. For example, until additional information can be secured, it may be necessary to confine a person apprehended in the course of a violent crime.

"When a person subject to this chapter is charged only with an offense that is normally tried by summary court-martial, the person ordinarily shall not be ordered in confinement." Article 10(a)(2).

Confinement should be distinguished from custody. Custody is restraint which is imposed by apprehension and which may be, but is not necessarily, physical. Custody may be imposed by anyone authorized to apprehend (see R.C.M. 302(b)), and may continue until a proper authority under R.C.M. 304(b) is notified and takes action. Thus, a person who has been apprehended could be physically restrained, but this would not be pretrial confinement in the sense of this rule until a person authorized to do so under R.C.M. 304(b) directed confinement.

(e) *Advice to the accused upon confinement.* Each person confined shall be promptly informed of:

(1) The nature of the offenses for which held;

(2) The right to remain silent and that any statement made by the person may be used against the person;

(3) The right to retain civilian counsel at no expense to the United States, and the right to request assignment of military counsel; and

(4) The procedures by which pretrial confinement will be reviewed.

(f) *Notification to Special Trial Counsel.* If a person who is alleged to have committed a covered offense is ordered into or released from pretrial confinement, the individual ordering confinement or authorizing release shall immediately notify a special trial counsel in accordance with regulations prescribed by the Secretary concerned.

(g) *Military counsel.* If requested by the confinee and such request is made known to military authorities, military counsel shall be provided to the confinee before the initial review under R.C.M. 305(j) or within 72 hours of such a request being first communicated to military authorities, whichever occurs first. Counsel may be assigned for the limited purpose of representing the accused only during the pretrial confinement proceedings before charges are referred. If assignment is made for this limited purpose, the confinee shall be so informed. Unless otherwise provided by regulations of the Secretary concerned, a confinee does not have a right under this rule to have military counsel of the confinee's own selection.

(h) *Who may direct release from confinement.* Any commander of a confinee, an officer appointed under regulations of the Secretary concerned to conduct the review under R.C.M. 305(j) or (k), or, once charges have been referred, a military judge detailed to the court-martial to which the charges against the accused have been referred, may direct release from pretrial confinement. For purposes of this subsection (R.C.M. 305(h)), "any commander" includes the immediate or higher commander of the confinee and the commander of the installation on which the confinement facility is located.

(i) *Notification and action by commander.*

(1) *Report.* Unless the commander of the confinee ordered the pretrial confinement, the commissioned, warrant, noncommissioned, or petty officer into whose charge the confinee was committed shall, within 24 hours after that commitment, cause a report to be made to the commander that shall contain the name of the confinee, the offenses charged against the confinee, and the name of the person who ordered or authorized confinement.

Discussion

This report may be made by any means. Ordinarily, the immediate commander of the confinee should be notified. In unusual cases, any commander to whose authority the confinee is subject, such as the commander of the confinement facility, may be notified. In the latter case, the commander so notified must ensure compliance with R.C.M. 305(i)(2).

---

(2) *Action by commander.*

(A) *Decision.* Not later than 72 hours after the commander's ordering of a confinee into pretrial confinement or, after receipt of a report that a member of the commander's unit or organization has been confined, whichever situation is applicable, the commander shall decide whether pretrial confinement will continue. A commander's compliance with this paragraph (R.C.M. 305(i)(2)) may also satisfy the 48-hour probable cause determination of R.C.M. 305(j)(1), provided the commander is a neutral and detached officer and acts within 48 hours of the imposition of confinement under military control. Nothing in R.C.M. 305(d), this subparagraph (R.C.M. 305(i)(2)(A)), or R.C.M. (j)(1) prevents a neutral and detached commander from completing the 48-hour probable cause determination and the 72-hour commander's decision immediately after an accused is ordered into pretrial confinement.

(B) *Requirements for confinement.* The commander shall direct the confinee's release from pretrial confinement unless the commander believes upon probable cause, that is, upon reasonable grounds, that:

(i) An offense triable by a court-martial has been committed;

(ii) The confinee committed it;

(iii) Confinement is necessary because it is foreseeable that:

(a) The confinee will not appear at trial, pretrial hearing, or preliminary hearing, or

(b) The confinee will engage in serious criminal misconduct; and

(iv) Less severe forms of restraint are inadequate.

Serious criminal misconduct includes intimidation of witnesses or other obstruction of justice, serious injury of others, or other offenses which pose a serious threat to the safety of the community or to the effectiveness, morale, discipline, readiness, or safety of the command, or to the national security of the United States. As used in this rule, "national security" means the national defense and foreign relations of the United States and specifically includes: a military or defense advantage over any foreign nation or group of nations; a favorable foreign relations position; or a defense posture capable of successfully resisting hostile or destructive action from within or without, overt or covert.

Discussion

A person should not be confined as a mere matter of convenience or expedience.

Some of the factors which should be considered under this subsection are:

(1) The nature and circumstances of the offenses charged or suspected, including extenuating circumstances;

(2) The weight of the evidence against the confinee;

(3) The confinee's ties to the locale, including family, off-duty employment, financial resources, and length of residence;

(4) The confinee's character and mental condition;

(5) The confinee's service record, including any record of previous misconduct;

(6) The confinee's record of appearance at or flight from other pretrial investigations, trials, and similar proceedings; and

(7) The likelihood that the confinee can and will commit further serious criminal misconduct if allowed to remain at liberty.

Although the Military Rules of Evidence are not applicable, the commander should judge the reliability of the information available. Before relying on the reports of others, the commander must have a reasonable belief that the information is believable and has a factual basis. The information may be received orally or in writing. Information need not be received under oath, but an oath may add to its reliability. A commander may examine the confinee's personnel records and police records, and may consider the recommendations of others.

Less serious forms of restraint must always be considered before pretrial confinement may be approved. Thus the commander should consider whether the confine could be safely returned to the confinee's unit, placed on restriction, placed under arrest, or placed under conditions on liberty. *See* R.C.M. 304.

(C) *72-hour memorandum.* If continued pretrial confinement is approved, the commander shall prepare a written memorandum that states the reasons for the conclusion that the requirements for confinement in R.C.M. 305(i)(2)(B) have been met. This memorandum may include hearsay and may incorporate by reference other documents, such as witness statements, investigative reports, or official records. This memorandum shall be forwarded to the 7-day reviewing officer under R.C.M. 305(j)(2). If such a memorandum was prepared by the commander before ordering confinement, a second memorandum need not be prepared; however, additional information may be added to the memorandum at any time.

(j) *Procedures for review of pretrial confinement.*

(1) *48-hour probable cause determination.* Review of the adequacy of probable cause to continue pretrial confinement shall be made by a neutral and detached officer within 48 hours of imposition of confinement under military control. If the confinee is apprehended by civilian authorities and remains in civilian custody at the request of military authorities, reasonable efforts will be made to bring the confinee under military control in a timely fashion.

(2) *7-day review of pretrial confinement.* Within 7 days of the imposition of confinement, a neutral and detached officer appointed in accordance with regulations prescribed by the Secretary concerned shall review the probable cause determination and necessity for continued pretrial confinement. In calculating the number of days of confinement for purposes of this rule, the initial date of confinement under military control shall count as one day and the date of the review shall also count as one day.

(A) *Nature of the 7-day review.*

(i) *Matters considered.* The review under this clause (R.C.M. 305(j)(2)(A)(i)) shall include a review of the memorandum submitted by the confinee's commander under R.C.M. 305(i)(2)(C). Additional written matters may be considered, including any submitted by the confinee. The confinee and the confinee's counsel, if any, shall be allowed to appear before the 7-day reviewing officer and make a statement, if practicable. A representative of the command may also appear before the reviewing officer to make a statement.

(ii) *Rules of evidence.* Except for Mil. R. Evid., Section V (Privileges) and Mil. R. Evid. 302 and 305, the Military Rules of Evidence shall not apply to the matters considered.

(iii) *Standard of proof.* The requirements for confinement under R.C.M. 305(h)(2)(B) must be proved by a preponderance of the evidence.

(iv) *Victim's right to be reasonably heard.* A victim of an alleged offense committed by the confinee has the right to reasonable, accurate, and timely notice of the 7-day review; the right to confer with the representative of the command and counsel for the Government, if any; and the right to be reasonably heard during the review. However, the hearing may not be unduly delayed for this purpose. The right to be heard under this rule includes the right to be heard through counsel and the right to be reasonably protected from the confinee during the 7-day review. Notice of these rights shall be given to the victim, or victim's counsel, if any, in accordance with regulations of the Secretary concerned.

Discussion

Personal appearance by the victim is not required. A victim's right to be reasonably heard at a 7-day review may also be accomplished telephonically, by video conference, or by written statement. The right to be heard under this rule includes the right to be heard through counsel, in those instances in which a victim is represented by counsel.

(B) *Extension of time limit.* The 7-day reviewing officer may, for good cause, extend the time limit for completion of the review to 10 days after the imposition of pretrial confinement.

(C) *Action by 7-day reviewing officer.* Upon completion of review, the reviewing officer shall approve continued confinement or order immediate release. If the reviewing officer orders immediate release, a victim of an alleged offense committed by the confinee has the right to reasonable, accurate, and timely notice of the release, unless such notice may endanger the safety of any person.

(D) *Memorandum.* The 7-day reviewing officer's conclusions, including the factual findings on which they are based, shall be set forth in a written memorandum. The memorandum shall also state whether the victim was represented by counsel, whether the victim was notified of the review, was given the opportunity to confer with the representative of the command or counsel for the Government and was given a reasonable opportunity to be heard. A copy of the memorandum and all documents considered by the 7-day reviewing officer shall be maintained in accordance with regulations prescribed by the Secretary concerned and provided to the accused or the Government on request.

(E) *Reconsideration of approval of continued confinement.* The 7-day reviewing officer shall upon request, and after notice to the parties, reconsider the decision to confine the confinee based upon any significant information not previously considered.

(k) *Review by military judge.* Once the charges for which the accused has been confined are referred to trial, or in a pre-referral proceeding conducted in accordance with R.C.M. 309, the military judge shall review the propriety of pretrial confinement upon motion for appropriate relief.

(1) *Release.* The military judge shall order release from pretrial confinement only if:

(A) The 7-day reviewing officer's decision was an abuse of discretion, and there is not sufficient information presented to the military judge justifying continuation of pretrial confinement under R.C.M. 305(i)(2)(B);

(B) Information not presented to the 7-day reviewing officer establishes that the confinee should be released under R.C.M. 305(i)(2)(B); or

(C) The provisions of R.C.M. 305(j)(1) or (2) have not been complied with and information presented to the military judge does not establish sufficient grounds for continued confinement under R.C.M. 305(i)(2)(B).

Discussion

Upon a motion for release from pretrial confinement, a victim of an alleged offense committed by the confinee has the right to reasonable, accurate, and timely notice of the motion and any hearing, the right to confer with counsel representing the Government, and the right to be reasonably heard. Inability to reasonably afford the victim these rights shall not delay the proceedings. The right to be heard under this rule includes the right to be heard through counsel. *See* R.C.M. 906(b)(8).

(2) *Credit.* Upon sentencing, the military judge shall order administrative credit under R.C.M. 305(l) for any pretrial confinement served as a result of an abuse of discretion or failure to comply with the provisions of R.C.M. 305(g), (i), or (j).

(l) *Remedy.* The remedy for noncompliance with R.C.M. 305(g), (i), (j), or (k) shall be an administrative credit against the sentence adjudged for any confinement served as the result of such noncompliance. Such credit shall be computed at the rate of 1 day credit for each day of confinement served as a result of such noncompliance. The military judge may order additional credit for each day of pretrial confinement that involves an abuse of discretion or unusually harsh circumstances. This credit is to be applied in addition to any other credit to which the accused may be entitled as a result of pretrial confinement served. This credit shall be applied first against any confinement adjudged. If no confinement is adjudged, or if the confinement adjudged is insufficient to offset all the credit to which the accused is entitled, the credit shall be applied against hard labor without confinement using the conversion formula under R.C.M. 1003(b)(6), restriction, fine, and forfeiture of pay, in that order. For purposes of R.C.M. 305(l), 1 day of confinement shall be equal to 1 day of total forfeiture or a like amount of fine. The credit shall not be applied against any other form of punishment.

(m) *Confinement after release.* No person whose release from pretrial confinement has been directed by a person authorized in R.C.M. 305(h) may be confined again before completion of trial except upon discovery, after the order of release, of evidence or of misconduct which, either alone or in conjunction with all other available evidence, meets the criteria for confinement under R.C.M. 305(i)(2)(B).

Discussion

See R.C.M. 304(b) concerning who may order confinement.

(n) *Exceptions.*

(1) *Operational necessity.* The Secretary of Defense may suspend application of R.C.M. 305(e)(3), (e)(4), (g), (i)(2)(A) or (C), or (j) to specific units or in specified areas when operational requirements of such units or in such areas would make application of such provisions impracticable.

(2) *At sea.* R.C.M. 305(e)(3), (e)(4), (g), (i)(2)(C), and (j) shall not apply in the case of a person on board a vessel at sea. In such situations, confinement on board the vessel at sea may continue only until the person can be transferred to a confinement facility ashore. Such transfer shall be accomplished at the earliest opportunity permitted by the operational requirements and mission of the vessel. Upon such transfer, the memorandum required by R.C.M. 305(i)(2)(C) shall be transmitted to the reviewing officer under R.C.M. 305(j) and shall include an explanation of any delay in the transfer.

Discussion

Under this paragraph, the standards for confinement remain the same (although the circumstances giving rise to the exception could bear on the application of those standards). Also, pretrial confinement remains subject to judicial review. The confinee's commander still must determine whether confinement will continue under R.C.M. 305 (h)(2)(B). The suspension of R.C.M. 305(h)(2)(A) removes the 72-hour requirement because, in a combat environment, the commander may not be available to comply with it. The commander must make the pretrial confinement decision as soon as reasonably possible, however. (This provision is not suspended under paragraph (2) since the commander of a vessel is always available.)

Operational exceptions to the requirements under R.C.M. 305 (e)(3) and (4) do not constitute exceptions to the notice requirements under Article 31(b).

(o) *Notice to victim of escaped confinee.* Reasonable, accurate, and timely notice of the escape of the prisoner shall be provided to the victim of an alleged offense committed by the confinee for which the confinee has been placed in pretrial confinement or such victim's counsel, if any, unless such notice may endanger the safety of any person.

Discussion

For purposes of this rule, the term "victim of an alleged offense" has the same meaning as the term "victim of an offense under this chapter" in Article 6b.

Rule 306. Initial disposition of offenses over which special trial counsel does not exercise authority

(a) *Who may dispose of offenses.*

(1) Except for offenses over which a special trial counsel has exercised authority and has not deferred, each commander has discretion to dispose of offenses by members of that command in accordance with this rule.

(2) Ordinarily the immediate commander of a person accused or suspected of committing offenses over which a special trial counsel has not exercised authority or has deferred initially determines how to dispose of those offenses. A superior commander may withhold the authority to dispose of offenses in individual cases, types of cases, or generally. A superior commander may not limit the discretion of a subordinate commander to act on cases over which authority has not been withheld.

Discussion

Each commander in the chain of command has independent, yet overlapping, discretion to dispose of offenses within the limits of that officer's authority. Normally, in keeping with the policy in subsection (b) of this rule, the initial disposition decision is made by the official at the lowest echelon with the power to make it. A decision by a commander ordinarily does not bar a different disposition by a superior authority. *See* R.C.M. 401(c), 601(f). Once charges are referred to a court-martial by a convening authority competent to do so, they may be withdrawn from that court-martial only in accordance with R.C.M. 604 and R.C.M. 604A.

See Appendix 3 or 4 with respect to offenses for which coordination with the Department of Justice is required.

(b) *Policy.* Allegations of offenses should be disposed of in a timely manner at the lowest appropriate level of disposition listed in subsection (c) of this rule.

Discussion

In deciding how an offense should be disposed of, the commander should review and consider the disposition factors set forth in Appendix 2.1 (Non-binding disposition guidance).

(c) *Disposition of offenses.* Within the limits of the commander's authority and subject to R.C.M. 306A, a commander may take the actions set forth in this subsection (R.C.M. 306(c)) to initially dispose of a charge or suspected offense.

Discussion

Prompt disposition of charges is essential. *See* R.C.M. 707 (speedy trial requirements).

If charges have not already been preferred, the commander may, if appropriate, prefer them and dispose of them under this rule. But see R.C.M. 601(c) regarding disqualification of an accuser.

If charges have been preferred, the commander should ensure that the accused has been notified in accordance with R.C.M. 308, and that charges are in proper form. *See* R.C.M. 307. Each commander who forwards or disposes of charges may make minor changes therein. *See* R.C.M. 603(a) and (b). If major changes are necessary, the affected charge should be preferred anew. *See* R.C.M. 603(d).

When charges are brought against two or more accused with a view to a joint or common trial, see R.C.M. 307(c)(5), 601(e)(3). If it appears that the accused may lack mental capacity to stand trial or may not have been mentally responsible at the times of the offenses, see R.C.M. 706, 909, 916(k).

---

(1) *No action.* A commander may decide to take no action.

Discussion

A decision to take no action or dismissal of charges at this stage does not bar later disposition of the offenses under R.C.M. 306(c)(2) through (5).

See R.C.M. 401(a) concerning who may dismiss charges, and R.C.M. 401(c)(1) concerning dismissal of charges.

When a decision is made to take no action, the accused should be informed.

---

(2) *Administrative action.* A commander may take or initiate administrative action, in addition to or instead of other action taken under this rule, subject to regulations of the Secretary concerned.

Discussion

Other administrative measures, which are subject to regulations of the Secretary concerned, include matters related to efficiency reports, academic reports, and other ratings; rehabilitation and reassignment; career field reclassification; administrative reduction for inefficiency; bar to reenlistment; personnel reliability program reclassification; security classification changes; pecuniary liability for negligence or misconduct; and administrative separation.

---

(3) *Nonjudicial punishment.* A commander may consider the matter pursuant to Article 15, nonjudicial punishment. *See* Part V.

(4) *Disposition of charges.* Charges may be disposed of in accordance with R.C.M. 401.

Discussion

If charges have not been preferred, they may be preferred. See R.C.M. 307 concerning preferral of charges. But see R.C.M. 601(c) concerning disqualification of an accuser.

Charges may be disposed of by dismissing them, forwarding them to another commander for disposition, or referring them to a summary, special, or general court-martial. Before charges may be referred to a general court-martial, compliance with R.C.M. 405 and 406 is necessary. Therefore, if appropriate, a preliminary hearing under R.C.M. 405 may be directed. Additional guidance on these matters is found in R.C.M. 401-407.

Pursuant to Article 24a and R.C.M. 306A, a convening authority may not dispose of a covered offense at a general or special court-martial

---

(5) *Forwarding for disposition.* A commander may forward a report of suspected offenses or charges to a superior or subordinate authority for disposition.

Discussion

The immediate commander may lack authority to take action which that commander believes is an appropriate disposition. In such cases, the matter should be forwarded to a superior officer with a recommendation as to disposition. See also R.C.M. 401(c)(2) concerning forwarding charges. If allegations are forwarded to a higher authority for disposition, because of lack of authority or otherwise, the disposition decision becomes a matter within the discretion of the higher authority.

A matter may be forwarded for other reasons, such as for investigation of allegations and preferral of charges, if warranted (*see* R.C.M. 303, 307), or so that a subordinate can dispose of the matter.

(d) *National security matters.* If a commander not authorized to convene general courts-martial finds that an offense warrants trial by court-martial, but believes that trial would be detrimental to the prosecution of a war or harmful to national security, the matter shall be forwarded to the general court-martial convening authority for action under R.C.M. 407(b).

(e) *Sex-related offenses.*

(1) For purposes of this subsection (R.C.M. 306(e)), a "sex-related offense" means any allegation of a violation of Article 120, 120b, 120c, or 130, or any attempt thereof under Article 80, occurring on or before December 27, 2023.

(2) Under such regulations as the Secretary concerned may prescribe, for alleged sex-related offenses committed in the United States, the victim of the sex-related offense shall be provided an opportunity to express views as to whether the offense should be prosecuted by court-martial or in a civilian court with jurisdiction over the offense. The commander, and if charges are preferred, the convening authority, shall consider such views as to

the victim's preference for jurisdiction, if available, prior to making an initial disposition decision. For purposes of this rule, "victim" is defined as an individual who has suffered direct physical, emotional, or pecuniary harm as a result of the commission of an alleged sex-related offense as defined in paragraph (e)(1) of this rule.

(3) Under such regulations as the Secretary concerned may prescribe, if the victim of an alleged sex-related offense expresses a preference for prosecution of the offense in a civilian court, the commander, and if charges are preferred, the convening authority, shall ensure that the civilian authority with jurisdiction over the offense is notified of the victim's preference for civilian prosecution. If the commander and, if charges are preferred, the convening authority learns of any decision by the civilian authority to prosecute or not prosecute the offense in civilian court, the commander or convening authority shall ensure the victim is notified.

Rule 306A. Initial disposition of offenses over which a special trial counsel exercises authority

(a) *Disposition of offenses that are not the subject of preferred charges.* Once a special trial counsel has exercised authority over an offense, only a special trial counsel may dispose of that offense, unless a special trial counsel defers the offense. For each offense over which a special trial counsel has exercised authority that is not the subject of a preferred charge, a special trial counsel shall:

(1) Prefer, or cause to be preferred, a charge; or

(2) Defer the offense by electing not to prefer a charge. If a special trial counsel defers the offense, the special trial counsel shall promptly forward the offense to a commander or convening authority for disposition, and the commander or convening authority shall dispose of the offense pursuant to R.C.M. 306.

(b) *Disposition of a preferred specification.* A special trial counsel shall dispose of each preferred specification in accordance with R.C.M. 401A.

(c) *National security matters.* If a commander believes trial would be detrimental to the prosecution of a war or harmful to national security, the matter shall be forwarded to the Secretary concerned for action.

(d) *Sex-related offenses.*

(1) For purposes of this subsection (R.C.M. 306A(d)), "sex-related offense" means any allegation of a violation of Article 120, 120b, 120c, or 130, or any attempt thereof under Article 80.

(2) Under such regulations as the Secretary concerned may prescribe, for alleged sex-related offenses committed in the United States, the victim of the sex-related offense shall be provided an opportunity to express views as to whether the offense should be prosecuted by court-martial or in a civilian court with jurisdiction over the offense. A special trial counsel shall consider the victim's preference for jurisdiction, if available, prior to making an initial disposition decision. For purposes of this rule, "victim" is defined as an individual who has suffered direct physical, emotional, or pecuniary harm as a result of the commission of an alleged sex-related offense as defined in R.C.M. 306A(d)(1).

(3) Under such regulations as the Secretary concerned may prescribe, if the victim of an alleged sex-related offense expresses a preference for prosecution of the offense in a civilian court, a special trial counsel shall ensure that the civilian authority with jurisdiction over the offense is notified of the victim's preference for civilian prosecution. If a special trial counsel learns of any decision by the civilian authority to prosecute or not prosecute the offense in civilian court, the special trial counsel shall ensure the victim, or victim's counsel, if any, is notified.

Discussion

See Appendix 3 or 4 with respect to offenses for which coordination with the Department of Justice is required.

Rule 307. Preferral of charges

(a) *In general.* In accordance with R.C.M. 307(b), preferral is the act by which a person subject to the UCMJ formally accuses another person subject to the UCMJ of an offense. Any person subject to the UCMJ may prefer charges.

Discussion

No person may be ordered to prefer charges to which that person is unable to make truthfully the required oath. *See* Article 30(a) and R.C.M. 307(b). A person who has been the accuser or nominal accuser (*see* Article 1(9)) may not also serve as the convening authority of a general or special court-martial to which the charges are later referred. *See* Articles 22(b), 23(b), and 24a(c)(2)(A); R.C.M. 601; *but see* R.C.M. 1302(b) (summary court-martial convening authority is not disqualified by being the accuser). A person authorized to dispose of offenses (*see* R.C.M. 306-306A, 401-404, and 407) should not be ordered to prefer charges when this would disqualify that person from exercising that person's authority or would improperly restrict that person's discretion to act on the case. *See* R.C.M. 104 and 504(c).

Charges may be preferred against a person subject to trial by court-martial at any time but should be preferred without unnecessary delay. See the statute of limitations prescribed by Article 43. Preferral of charges should not be unnecessarily delayed. When a good reason exists—as when a person is permitted to continue a course of conduct so that a ringleader or other conspirators may also be discovered or when a suspected counterfeiter goes uncharged until guilty knowledge becomes apparent—a reasonable delay is permissible. However, see R.C.M. 707 concerning speedy trial requirements.

(b) *How charges are preferred; oath.* In preferring charges and specifications—

(1) The person preferring the charges and specifications must sign them under oath before a commissioned officer of the armed forces authorized to administer oaths; and

(2) The writing under paragraph (b)(1) must state that—

(A) the signer has personal knowledge of, or has investigated, the matters set forth in the charges and specifications; and

(B) the matters set forth in the charges and specifications are true to the best of the knowledge and belief of the signer.

(3) Any procedure, including those by remote means, which appeals to the conscience of the person to whom the oath is administered and which binds that person to properly perform that person's duties under this rule, is sufficient.

Discussion

See Article 136 for authority to administer oaths. The following form may be used to administer the oath:

"You (swear) (affirm) that you are a person subject to the Uniform Code of Military Justice, that you have personal knowledge of or have investigated the matters set forth in the foregoing charge(s) and specification(s), and that the same are true to the best of your knowledge and belief. (So help you God.)"

The accuser's belief may be based upon reports of others in whole or in part.

(c) *How to allege offenses.*

(1) *In general.* The format of charge and specification is used to allege violations of the UCMJ.

Discussion

See DD Form 458 for a template charge sheet.

---

(2) *Charge.* A charge states the article of the UCMJ, law of war, or local penal law of an occupied territory which the accused is alleged to have violated.

Discussion

The particular subdivision of an article of the UCMJ (for example, Article 118(1)) should not be included in the charge. When there are numerous infractions of the same article, there will be only one charge, but several specifications thereunder. There may also be several charges, but each must allege a violation of a different article of the UCMJ. For violations of the law of war, see (D) of this Discussion.

(A) *Numbering charges.* If there is only one charge, it is not numbered. When there is more than one charge, each charge is numbered by a Roman numeral.

(B) *Additional charges.* Charges preferred after others have been preferred are labeled "additional charges" and are also numbered with Roman numerals, beginning with "I" if there is more than one additional charge. These ordinarily relate to offenses not known at the time or committed after the original charges were preferred. Additional charges do not require a separate trial if incorporated in the trial of the original charges before arraignment. *See* R.C.M. 601(e)(2).

(C) *Preemption.* An offense specifically defined by Articles 81 through 132 may not be alleged as a violation of Article 134. *See* paragraph 91.c.(5)(a) of Part IV. *But see* R.C.M. 307(d).

(D) *Charges under the law of war.* In the case of a person subject to trial by general court-martial for violations of the law of war (*see* Article 18), the charge should be: "Violation of the Law of War"; or "Violation of __________, ______" referring to the local penal law of the occupied territory.

See R.C.M. 201(f)(1)(B). *But see* R.C.M. 307(d). Ordinarily persons subject to the UCMJ should be charged with a specific violation of the UCMJ rather than a violation of the law of war.

---

(3) *Specification.* A specification is a plain, concise, and definite statement of the essential facts constituting the offense charged. A specification is sufficient if it alleges every element of the charged offense expressly or by necessary implication; however, specifications under Article 134 must expressly allege the terminal element. Except for aggravating factors under R.C.M. 1003(d) and R.C.M. 1004, facts that increase the maximum authorized punishment must be alleged in order to permit the possible increased punishment. No particular format is required.

Discussion

How to draft specifications.

(A) *Sample specifications.* Before drafting a specification, the drafter should read the pertinent provisions of Part IV, where the elements of proof of various offenses and forms for specifications appear.

(B) *Numbering specifications.* If there is only one specification under a charge it is not numbered. When there is more than one specification under any charge, the specifications are numbered in Arabic numerals. The term "additional" is not used in connection with the specifications under an additional charge.

(C) *Name and description of the accused.*

(i) *Name.* The specification should state the accused's full name: first name, middle name or initial, last name. If the accused is known by more than one name, the name acknowledged by the accused should be used. If there is no such acknowledgment, the name believed to be the true name should be listed first, followed by all known aliases. For example: Seaman John P. Smith, U.S. Navy, alias Lt. Robert R. Brown, U.S. Navy.

(ii) *Military association.* The specification should state the accused's rank or grade. If the rank or grade of the accused has changed since the date of an alleged offense, and the change is pertinent to the offense charged, the accused should be identified by the present rank or grade followed by rank or grade on the date of the alleged offense. For example: In that Seaman ________ then Seaman Apprentice ________, etc.

(iii) *Social security number or service number.* The social security number or service number of an accused should not be stated in the specification.

(iv) *Basis of personal jurisdiction.*

(a) *Military members on active duty.* Ordinarily, no allegation of the accused's armed force or unit or organization is necessary for military members on active duty.

(b) *Persons subject to the UCMJ under Article 2(a), subsections (3) through (12), or subject to trial by court-martial under Articles 3 or 4.* The specification should describe the accused's armed force, unit or organization, position, or status which will indicate the basis of jurisdiction. For example: John Jones, (a person employed by and serving with the U.S. Army in the field in time of war) (a person convicted of having obtained a fraudulent discharge), etc.

(D) *Date and time of offense.*

(i) *In general.* The date of the commission of the offense charged should be stated in the specification with sufficient precision to identify the offense and enable the accused to understand what particular act or omission to defend against.

(ii) *Use of "on or about."* In alleging the date of the offense it is proper to allege it as "on or about" a specified day.

(iii) *Hour.* The exact hour of the offense is ordinarily not alleged except in certain absence offenses. When the exact time is alleged, the 24-hour clock should be used. The use of "at or about" is proper.

(iv) *Extended periods.* When the acts specified extend(s) over a considerable period of time it is proper to allege it (or them) as having occurred, for example, "from about 15 June 1983 to about 4 November 1983," or "did on divers occasions between 15 June 1983 and 4 November 1983."

(E) *Place of offense.* The place of the commission of the offense charged should be stated in the specification with sufficient precision to identify the offense and enable the accused to understand the particular act or omission to defend against. In alleging the place of the offense, it is proper to allege it as "at or near" a certain place if the exact place is uncertain.

(F) *Subject-matter jurisdiction allegations.* Pleading the accused's rank or grade along with the proper elements of the offense normally will be sufficient to establish subject-matter jurisdiction.

(G) *Description of offense.*

(i) *Elements.* The elements of the offense must be expressly alleged. If a specific intent, knowledge, or state of mind is an element of the offense, it must be alleged. To state an offense under Article 134, practitioners must expressly allege the terminal element. All offenses under Article 134 require proof of a single terminal element, but the terminal element is charged and proven differently for offenses charged under Clause (1) and (2) of Article 134, in contrast to those charged under Clause (3). For elements of offenses charged under Article 134, Clause (1), (2), or (3), see paragraph 91.b. in Part IV of this Manual.

(ii) *Words indicating criminality.* If the alleged act is not itself an offense but is made an offense either by applicable statute (including Articles 133 and 134), or regulation or custom having the effect of law, then words indicating criminality such as "wrongfully," "unlawfully," or "without authority" (depending upon the nature of the offense) should be used to describe the accused's acts.

(iii) *Specificity.* The specification should be sufficiently specific to inform the accused of the conduct charged, to enable the accused to prepare a defense, and to protect the accused against double jeopardy. Only those facts that make the accused's conduct criminal ordinarily should be alleged. Specific evidence supporting the allegations ordinarily should not be included in the specifications.

(iv) *Duplicitousness.* One specification should not allege more than one offense, either conjunctively (the accused "lost and destroyed") or alternatively (the accused "lost or destroyed"). However, if two acts or a series of acts constitute one offense, they may be alleged conjunctively. *See* R.C.M. 906(b)(5).

(v) *Lesser included offenses.* Article 79 contains two provisions concerning notice of lesser included offenses: (1) offenses that are "necessarily included" in the charged offense in accordance with Article 79(b)(1); and (2) offenses designated as lesser included offenses by the President under Article 79(b)(2). *See* Appendix 12A. Each provision sets forth an independent basis for providing notice of a lesser included offense. Where there is doubt as to whether an offense is a lesser included offense or whether a particular offense should be charged in the alternative, preferral of a separate charge or specification may be warranted. If the accused is convicted of two or more offenses, the trial counsel should consider asking the military judge to determine whether any convictions that were charged in the alternative or as potential lesser included offenses should be dismissed or conditionally dismissed subject to appellate review.

(H) *Other considerations in drafting specifications.*

(i) *Principals.* All principals are charged as if each was the perpetrator. See paragraph 1 of Part IV for a discussion of principals.

(ii) *Victim.* In the case of an offense against the person or property of a person, the first name, middle initial and last name of such person should be alleged, if known. If the name of the victim is unknown, a general physical description may be used. If this cannot be done, the victim may be described as "a person whose name is unknown." Military rank or grade should be alleged, and must be alleged if an element of the offense, as in an allegation of disobedience of the command of a superior officer. If the person has no military position, it may otherwise be necessary to allege the status as in an allegation of using provoking words toward a person subject to the UCMJ. *See* paragraph 55 of Part IV.

(iii) *Property*. In describing property generic terms should be used, such as "a watch" or "a knife," and descriptive details such as make, model, color, and serial number should ordinarily be omitted. In some instances, however, details may be essential to the offense, so they must be alleged. For example: the length of a knife blade may be important when alleging a violation of general regulation prohibiting carrying a knife with a blade that exceeds a certain length.

(iv) *Value*. When the value of property or other amount determines the maximum punishment which may be adjudged for an offense, the value or amount should be alleged, for in such a case increased punishments that are contingent upon value may not be adjudged unless there is an allegation, as well as proof, of a value which will support the punishment. If several articles of different kinds are the subject of the offense, the value of each article should be stated followed by a statement of the aggregate value. Exact value should be stated, if known. For ease of proof an allegation may be "of a value not less than_________." If only an approximate value is known, it may be alleged as "of a value of about ______." If the value of an item is unknown but obviously minimal, the term "of some value" may be used. These principles apply to allegations of amounts.

(v) *Documents*. When documents other than regulations or orders must be alleged (for example, bad checks in violation of Article 123a), the document may be set forth verbatim (including photocopies and similar reproductions) or may be described, in which case the description must be sufficient to inform the accused of the offense charged.

(vi) *Orders*.

(a) *General orders*. A specification alleging a violation of a general order or regulation (Article 92(1)) must clearly identify the specific order or regulation allegedly violated. The general order or regulation should be cited by its identifying title or number, section or paragraph, and date. It is not necessary to recite the text of the general order or regulation verbatim.

(b) *Other orders*. If the order allegedly violated is an "other lawful order" (Article 92(2)), it should be set forth verbatim or described in the specification. When the order is oral, see clause (H)(vii) of this discussion.

(c) *Negating exceptions*. If the order contains exceptions, it is not necessary that the specification contain a specific allegation negating the exceptions. However, words of criminality may be required if the alleged act is not necessarily criminal. *See* clause (G)(ii) of this discussion.

(vii) *Oral statements*. When alleging oral statements the phrase "or words to that effect" should be added.

(viii) *Joint offense*. In the case of a joint offense each accused may be charged separately as if each accused acted alone or all may be charged together in a single specification. For example:

(a) If Doe and Roe are joint perpetrators of an offense and it is intended to charge and try both at the same trial, they should be charged in a single specification as follows:

"In that Doe and Roe, acting jointly and pursuant to a common intent, did. . . ."

(b) If it is intended that Roe will be tried alone or that Roe will be tried with Doe at a common trial, Roe may be charged in the same manner as if Roe alone had committed the offense. However, to show in the specification that Doe was a joint actor with Roe, even though Doe is not to be tried with Roe, Roe may be charged as follows:

"In that Roe did, in conjunction with Doe, ..."

(ix) *Matters in aggravation*. Matters in aggravation that do not increase the maximum authorized punishment ordinarily should not be alleged in the specification. Prior convictions need not be alleged in the specification to permit increased punishment.

(x) *Abbreviations*. Commonly used and understood abbreviations may be used, particularly abbreviations for ranks, grades, units and organizations, components, and geographic or political entities, such as the names of states or countries.

---

(4) *Multiple offenses*. Charges and specifications alleging all known offenses by an accused may be preferred at the same time. Each specification shall state only one offense. What is substantially one transaction should not be made the basis for an unreasonable multiplication of charges against one person.

Discussion

Unreasonable multiplication of charges should not be confused with multiplicity, a double jeopardy concept. *See* R.C.M. 1003(c)(1)(C). Accordingly, the phrase "multiplicity in sentencing" is confusing and should be avoided. Unreasonable multiplication of charges is addressed in R.C.M. 906(b)(12); multiplicity is addressed in R.C.M. 907(b)(3)(B); and punishment limitations are addressed in R.C.M. 1003(c)(1)(C).

For example, a person should not be charged with both failure to report for a routine scheduled duty (*e.g.*, reveille) and absence without leave if the failure to report occurred during the period for which the accused is charged with absence without leave. There are times, however, when sufficient doubt as to the facts or the law exists to warrant making one transaction the basis for charging two or more offenses. In no case should both an offense and a lesser included offense thereof be separately charged.

See also R.C.M. 601(e)(2) concerning referral of several offenses.

---

(5) *Multiple offenders*. A specification may name more than one person as an accused if each person so named is believed by the accuser to be a principal in the offense which is the subject of the specification.

Discussion

See also R.C.M. 601(e)(3) concerning joinder of accused.

A joint offense is one committed by two or more persons acting together with a common intent. Principals may be charged jointly with the commission of the same offense, but an accessory after the fact cannot be charged jointly with the principal whom the accused is alleged to have received, comforted, or assisted. Offenders are properly joined only if there is a common unlawful design or purpose; the mere fact that several persons happen to have committed the same kinds of offenses at the time, although material as tending to show concert of purpose, does not necessarily establish this. The fact that several persons happen to have absented themselves without leave at about the same time will not, in the absence of evidence indicating a joint design, purpose, or plan, justify joining them in one specification, for they may merely have been availing themselves of the same opportunity. In joint offenses the participants may be separately or jointly charged. However, if the participants are members of different armed forces, they must be charged separately because their trials must be separately reviewed. The preparation of joint charges is discussed in R.C.M. 307 (c)(3), Discussion (H)(viii)(a). The advantage of a joint charge is that all accused will be tried at one trial, thereby saving time, labor, and expense. This must be weighed against the possible unfairness to the accused which may result if their defenses are inconsistent or antagonistic. An accused cannot be called as a witness except upon that accused's own request. If the testimony of an accomplice is necessary, the accomplice should not be tried jointly with those against whom the accomplice is expected to testify. *See also* Mil. R. Evid. 306.

See R.C.M. 603 concerning amending specifications.

See R.C.M. 906(b)(4) and (6) concerning motions to amend specifications and bills of particulars.

See R.C.M. 906(b)(5) pertaining to severance of duplicitous specifications.

(d) *Harmless error in citation.* Error in or omission of the designation of the article of the UCMJ or other statute, law of war, or regulation violated shall not be ground for dismissal of a charge or reversal of a conviction if the error or omission did not prejudicially mislead the accused.

Rule 308. Notification to accused of charges and required disclosures

(a) *Immediate commander.* The immediate commander of the accused shall cause the accused to be informed of the charges preferred against the accused, and the name of the person who preferred the charges and of any person who ordered the charges to be preferred, if known, as soon as practicable.

Discussion

When notice is given, a certificate to that effect on the charge sheet should be completed. *See* DD Form 458.

However, in cases where charges are immediately referred after preferral, service of referred charges under R.C.M. 602 fulfills the notice requirement of this rule. In those cases, the notice certificate on the charge sheet need not be completed and should be lined out.

Following notification of preferred charges, the Government shall comply with the requirements of R.C.M. 403(c).

(b) *Commanders at higher echelons.* When the accused has not been informed of the charges, commanders at higher echelons to whom the preferred charges are forwarded shall cause the accused to be informed of the matters required under R.C.M. 308(a) as soon as practicable.

(c) *Disclosures generally.* Except as otherwise provided in R.C.M. 308(d) and as soon as practicable after notification to the accused of preferred charges, counsel for the Government shall provide the defense with copies of the charges and any books, papers, documents, data, photographs, or tangible objects that accompanied the charge or charges when preferred. If extraordinary circumstances make it impracticable to provide copies, counsel for the Government shall permit the defense to inspect these items.

(d) *Information not subject to disclosure.*

(1) *Military Rules of Evidence.* Nothing in this rule shall be construed to require the disclosure of information protected from disclosure by the Military Rules of Evidence.

(2) *Work Product.* Nothing in this rule shall require the disclosure or production of notes, memoranda, or similar working papers prepared by counsel or counsel's assistants and representatives.

(3) *Contraband.* If items covered by R.C.M. 308(c) are contraband, the disclosure required under this rule is a reasonable opportunity to inspect said contraband prior to the preliminary hearing.

(4) *Privilege.* If items covered by R.C.M. 308(c) are privileged, classified, or otherwise protected under Section V of Part III, the Military Rules of Evidence, no disclosure of those items is required under this rule. However, counsel for the Government may disclose privileged, classified, or otherwise protected information covered by R.C.M. 308(a) if authorized by the holder of the privilege or, in the case of Mil. R. Evid. 505 or 506, if authorized by a competent

authority.

(5) *Protective order if privileged information is disclosed.* If the Government agrees to disclose to the accused information to which the protections afforded by Section V of the Military Rules of Evidence may apply, the convening authority, or other person designated by regulation of the Secretary concerned, may enter an appropriate protective order, in writing, to guard against the compromise of information disclosed to the accused. The terms of any such protective order may include prohibiting the disclosure of the information except as authorized by the authority issuing the protective order, as well as those terms specified by Mil. R. Evid. 505(g)(2)–(6) or 506(g)(2)–(5).

Discussion

This rule is not intended to limit or discourage counsel for the Government from providing additional materials to the defense. The purpose of this rule is to provide the accused with the documents used to make the determination to prefer charges.

(e) *Remedy.* The sole remedy for violation of this rule is a continuance or recess of sufficient length to permit the accused to adequately prepare a defense, and no relief shall be granted upon a failure to comply with this rule unless the accused demonstrates that the accused has been hindered in the preparation of a defense.

Rule 309. Pre-referral judicial proceedings

(a) *In general.*

(1) A military judge detailed under regulations of the Secretary concerned may conduct proceedings under Article 30a, before referral of charges and specifications to court-martial for trial, and may issue such rulings and orders as necessary to further the purpose of the proceedings. A military judge may issue such orders and rulings only when the matters would be subject to consideration by a military judge in a general or special court-martial.

Discussion

In determining whether to issue a ruling or order before referral, a military judge may consider chain of command recommendations as to disposition of a charged offense or offenses, representations of counsel or a federal law enforcement officer, the frequency or severity of a charged offense or offenses, and any other matter deemed relevant by the military judge.

(2) The matters that may be considered and ruled upon by a military judge under this rule are limited to those matters specified in R.C.M. 309(b).

(3) If any matter in a proceeding under this rule becomes a subject at issue with respect to charges that have been referred to a general or special court-martial, the matter, to include any motions, related papers, and the record of the hearing, if any, shall be provided to the military judge detailed to the court-martial.

(b) *Pre-referral matters.*

(1) *Pre-referral investigative subpoenas.* A military judge may, upon application by the Government, consider whether to issue a pre-referral investigative subpoena under R.C.M. 703(g)(3)(C). The proceeding may be conducted *ex parte* and may be conducted in camera.

(2) *Pre-referral warrants or orders for wire or electronic communications.* A military judge may, upon written application by a federal law enforcement officer or authorized counsel for the Government in connection with an ongoing investigation of an offense or offenses under the UCMJ, consider whether to issue a warrant or order for wire or electronic communications and related information as provided under R.C.M. 703A. The proceeding may be conducted *ex parte* and may be conducted in camera.

Discussion

The defense may request that the trial counsel or other counsel for the Government make an application under R.C.M. 309(b)(1) or (b)(2) of this rule. The military judge may, as a matter of discretion, afford the defense an opportunity to be heard.

(3) *Requests for relief from subpoena or other process.* A person in receipt of a pre-referral investigative subpoena under R.C.M. 703(g)(3)(C), a victim named in a specification whose personal and confidential information has been subpoenaed under R.C.M. 703(g)(3)(C)(ii), a service provider in receipt of a warrant or court order to disclose information about wire or electronic communications under R.C.M. 703A(a), or a person ordered to sit for a deposition under R.C.M. 702(b)(2) may request relief on grounds that compliance with the subpoena, warrant, or order is unreasonable, oppressive, or prohibited by law. The military judge shall review the request and shall either order the person or service provider to comply with the subpoena, warrant, or order, or modify or quash the

subpoena, warrant, or order, as appropriate. In a proceeding under this paragraph, the United States shall be represented by an authorized counsel for the Government.

Discussion

See Article 46; R.C.M. 703(g)(3)(G); R.C.M. 703A(c)(2).

---

(4) *Pre-referral matters referred by an appellate court.* When a Court of Criminal Appeals or the Court of Appeals for the Armed Forces, in the course of exercising the jurisdiction of such court, remands the case for a pre-referral judicial proceeding, a military judge may conduct such a proceeding under this rule. This includes matters referred by a Court of Criminal Appeals under subsection (e) of Article 6b.

(5) *Pre-referral matters under subsection (c) of Article 6b.* The military judge may designate a suitable person to assume the rights of a victim who is under 18 years of age (but who is not a member of the armed forces), or who is incompetent, incapacitated, or deceased. Upon appointment by the military judge, the legal guardian of the victim, the representative of the victim's estate, a family member, or any other person designated as suitable by the military judge, may assume the rights of the victim. Under no circumstances may the military judge designate the accused to assume the rights of the victim.

(6) *Pretrial confinement of an accused.* After action by the 7-day reviewing officer under R.C.M. 305(j)(2)(C), a military judge may, upon application of an accused for appropriate relief, review the propriety of pretrial confinement. A military judge may order release from pretrial confinement under the provisions of R.C.M. 305(k)(1).

(7) *The mental capacity or mental responsibility of an accused.*

(A) A military judge may, under the provisions of R.C.M. 706(b)(1), order an inquiry into the mental capacity or mental responsibility of an accused before referral of charges. The proceeding may be conducted *ex parte* and may be conducted in camera.

(B) A military judge may, under the provisions of R.C.M. 909, conduct a hearing to determine the mental capacity of the accused.

(8) *A request for individual military counsel.* When an accused requests individual military counsel prior to charges being referred to a general or special court-martial, a military judge may review the request subject to the provisions of R.C.M. 506(b).

(9) *Victim's petition for relief.*

(A) A victim of an offense under the UCMJ, as defined in Article 6b(b), may file a motion pre-referral requesting that a military judge require a preliminary hearing officer conducting a preliminary hearing under R.C.M. 405 to comply with:

(i) Articles 6b or 32;

(ii) R.C.M. 405; or

(iii) Mil. R. Evid. 412, 513, 514, or 615.

(B) The military judge may grant or deny such a motion. The ruling is subject to further review pursuant to Article 6b(e).

(10) *Pre-referral depositions.* A military judge may, upon application by a party, consider whether to order a pre-referral deposition under R.C.M. 702(c)(2).

(c) *Procedure for submissions.* The Secretary concerned shall prescribe the procedures for receiving requests for proceedings under this rule and for detailing military judges to such proceedings.

(d) *Hearings.* Any hearing conducted under this rule shall be conducted in accordance with the procedures generally applicable to sessions conducted under Article 39(a), and R.C.M. 803.

(e) *Record.* A separate record of any proceeding under this rule shall be prepared and forwarded to the convening authority, special trial counsel, or any combination thereof, with authority to dispose of the charges or offenses in the case. If charges are referred to trial in the case, such record shall be included in the record of trial.

(f) *Military magistrate.* If authorized under regulations of the Secretary concerned, a military judge detailed to a proceeding under this rule, other than a proceeding under paragraph (b)(2), (b)(7)(B), or (b)(8) of this rule, may designate a military magistrate to preside and exercise the authority of the military judge over the proceeding.

CHAPTER IV. FORWARDING AND DISPOSITION OF CHARGES

Rule 401. Forwarding and disposition of charges in general

(a) *Who may dispose of charges.* Only persons authorized to convene courts-martial or to administer nonjudicial punishment under Article 15 may dispose of charges, except for those charges over which a special trial counsel has exercised authority and which must be disposed of in accordance with R.C.M. 401A. A superior competent authority may withhold the authority of a subordinate to dispose of charges in individual cases, types of cases, or generally.

Discussion

R.C.M. 401 applies only to offenses over which a special trial counsel does not exercise authority. When a special trial counsel has exercised authority, a commander may not dispose of charges in accordance with this rule unless the special trial counsel defers. *See* R.C.M. 401A.

When a commander receives charges containing a covered offense that has not been reviewed by a special trial counsel, the commander shall forward the charges to a special trial counsel for an initial determination under R.C.M. 303A.

See R.C.M. 504 as to who may convene courts-martial and paragraph 2 of Part V as to who may administer nonjudicial punishment. If the power to convene courts-martial and to administer nonjudicial punishment has been withheld, a commander may not dispose of charges under this rule.

Ordinarily charges should be forwarded to the accused's immediate commander for initial consideration as to disposition. Each commander has independent discretion to determine how charges will be disposed of, except to the extent that the commander's authority has been withheld by superior competent authority. *See also* R.C.M. 104.

See R.C.M. 603 if major or minor changes to the charges are necessary after preferral. If a commander is an accuser (*see* Article 1(9); R.C.M. 307(a)) that commander is ineligible to refer such charges to a general or special court-martial. *See* R.C.M. 601(c). *But see* R.C.M. 1302(b) (accuser may refer charges to a summary court-martial).

(b) *Prompt determination.* When a commander with authority to dispose of charges receives charges, that commander shall promptly determine what disposition will be made in the interest of justice and discipline.

Discussion

In determining what level of disposition is appropriate, see R.C.M. 306(b) and (c) and Appendix 2.1 (Disposition Guidance). When charges are brought against two or more accused with a view to a joint or common trial, see R.C.M. 307(c)(5) and 601(e)(3). If it appears that the accused may lack mental capacity to stand trial or may not have been mentally responsible at the times of the offenses, see R.C.M. 706, 909, and 916(k).

As to the rules concerning speedy trial, see R.C.M. 707. *See also* Articles 10, 30, and 131f.

Before determining an appropriate disposition, a commander who receives charges should ensure that: (1) a preliminary inquiry under R.C.M. 303 has been conducted; (2) the accused has been notified in accordance with R.C.M. 308; and (3) the charges are in proper form.

(c) *How charges may be disposed of.* Unless the authority to do so has been limited or withheld by superior competent authority, a commander may dispose of charges by dismissing any or all of them, forwarding any or all of them to another commander for disposition, or referring any or all of them to a court-martial which the commander is empowered to convene. Charges should be disposed of in accordance with the policy in R.C.M. 306(b).

Discussion

A commander may dispose of charges individually or collectively.

See Appendix 3 or 4 when the charges may involve matters in which the Department of Justice has an interest.

See the Discussion to R.C.M. 306(b) and Appendix 2.1 (Disposition Guidance).

---

(1) *Dismissal.* When a commander dismisses charges further disposition under R.C.M. 306(c) of the offenses is not barred.

Discussion

Charges are ordinarily dismissed by lining out and initialing the deleted specifications or otherwise recording that a specification is dismissed. When all charges and specifications are dismissed, the accuser and the accused ordinarily should be informed.

A charge should be dismissed when it fails to state an offense, when it is unsupported by available evidence, or when there are other sound reasons why trial by court-martial is not appropriate. Before dismissing charges because trial would be detrimental to the prosecution of a war or harmful to national security, see R.C.M. 401(d) and 407(b).

If the accused has already refused nonjudicial punishment, charges should not be dismissed with a view to offering nonjudicial punishment unless the accused has indicated willingness to accept nonjudicial punishment if again offered. The decision whether to dismiss charges in such circumstances is within the sole discretion of the commander concerned.

Charges may be amended in accordance with R.C.M. 603. It is appropriate to dismiss a charge and prefer another charge anew when, for example, the original charge failed to state an offense, or was so defective that a major amendment was required (*see* R.C.M. 603(d)), or did not adequately reflect the nature or seriousness of the offense.

See R.C.M. 907(b)(2)(C) concerning the effect of dismissing charges after the court-martial has begun.

---

(2) *Forwarding charges.*

(A) *Forwarding to a superior commander.* When charges are forwarded to a superior commander for disposition, the forwarding commander shall make a personal recommendation as to disposition. If the forwarding commander is disqualified from acting as convening authority in the case, the basis for the disqualification shall be noted.

Discussion

A commander's recommendation is within that commander's sole discretion. No authority may direct a commander to make a specific recommendation as to disposition. However, in making a disposition recommendation, the forwarding commander should review Appendix 2.1 (Disposition Guidance).

When charges are forwarded to a superior commander with a view to trial by general or special court-martial, they should be forwarded by a letter of transmittal or indorsement. To the extent practicable without unduly delaying forwarding the charges, the letter should include or carry as enclosures: a summary of the available evidence relating to each offense; evidence of previous convictions and nonjudicial punishments of the accused; an indication that the accused has been offered and refused nonjudicial punishment, if applicable; and any other matters required by superior authority or deemed appropriate by the forwarding commander. Other matters which may be appropriate include information concerning the accused's background and military service, and a description of any unusual circumstances in the case. The summary of evidence should include available witness statements, documentary evidence, and exhibits. When practicable, copies of signed statements of the witnesses should be forwarded, as should copies of any investigative or laboratory reports. Forwarding charges should not be delayed, however, solely to obtain such statements or reports when it otherwise appears that sufficient evidence to warrant trial is or will be available in time for trial. If because of the bulk of documents or exhibits, it is impracticable to forward them with the letter of transmittal, they should be properly preserved and should be referred to in the letter of transmittal.

When it appears that any witness may not be available for later proceedings in the case or that a deposition may be appropriate, that matter should be brought to the attention of the convening authority promptly and should be noted in the letter of transmittal.

When charges are forwarded with a view to disposition other than trial by general or special court-martial, they should be accompanied by sufficient information to enable the authority receiving them to dispose of them without further investigation.

(B) *Other cases.* When charges are forwarded to a commander who is not a superior of the forwarding commander, no recommendation as to disposition may be made.

Discussion

Except when directed to forward charges, a subordinate commander may not be required to take any specific action to dispose of charges. *See* R.C.M. 104. *See also* paragraph 1.d.(2) of Part V. When appropriate, charges may be sent or returned to a subordinate commander for compliance with procedural requirements. *See, e.g.*, R.C.M. 303 (preliminary inquiry); R.C.M. 308 (notification to accused of charges).

---

(3) *Referral of charges. See* R.C.M. 403, 404, 407, 601.

(d) *National security matters.* If a commander who is not a general court-martial convening authority finds that the charges warrant trial by court-martial but believes that trial would probably be detrimental to the prosecution of a war or harmful to national security, the charges shall be forwarded to the officer exercising general court-martial convening authority.

Discussion

See R.C.M. 407(b).

Rule 401A. Disposition of charges over which a special trial counsel exercises authority and has not deferred

(a) *Who may dispose of preferred specifications.* Regardless of who preferred a specification, only a special trial counsel may dispose of a specification alleging a covered offense or another offense over which a special trial counsel has exercised authority and has not deferred. A superior competent authority may withhold the authority of a subordinate special trial counsel to dispose of offenses charged in individual cases, types of cases, or generally.

Discussion

The "superior competent authority" referenced in R.C.M. 401A(a) may include the Secretary concerned, the Lead Special Trial Counsel, or other supervisory special trial counsel.

(b) *Prompt determination.* Special trial counsel shall promptly determine what disposition will be made in the interest of justice and discipline.

Discussion

In determining what level of disposition is appropriate, see R.C.M. 306(b) and (c) and Appendix 2.1 (Disposition Guidance).

(c) *Disposition of preferred specifications.*

(1) *Referral.* For those offenses over which a special trial counsel has exercised authority and not deferred, a special trial counsel may refer a charge and any specification thereunder to a special or general court-martial. If a preliminary hearing in accordance with Article 32 and R.C.M. 405 is required, a special trial counsel shall request a hearing officer and a hearing officer shall be provided by the convening authority.

(2) *Dismissal.* For those offenses over which a special trial counsel has exercised authority and not deferred, a special trial counsel may dismiss any charge or specification thereunder. A dismissal may be accompanied by a deferral as defined in this rule. Further disposition by a special trial counsel in accordance with this rule or by a convening authority pursuant to RCM 306(c) is not barred.

(3) *Deferral.*

(A) *Pre-referral.* A special trial counsel may defer a charged offense by electing not to refer the charged offense to a special or general court-martial. Upon such a determination, the special trial counsel shall promptly forward the matter to the commander or convening authority for disposition. The commander or convening authority shall dispose of the offense pursuant to R.C.M. 306 or the charged offense pursuant to R.C.M. 401, as applicable. The commander or convening authority may dismiss a charge preferred by a special trial counsel. However, a convening authority may not refer a charge alleging a covered offense to a special or general court-martial.

(B) *Post-referral.* After referral, a charge referred to a general or special court-martial by a special trial counsel must be withdrawn before the offense alleged by that charge may be deferred.

Discussion

Following deferral by special trial counsel, a commander or convening authority may dispose of a charge pursuant to R.C.M. 401, including by dismissing charges preferred by special trial counsel. *See* R.C.M 401(c). However, after referral of charges by a special trial counsel, a special trial counsel must withdraw a charge before it can be deferred to a commander or convening authority. *See* R.C.M. 604(a)."

Rule 402. Action by commander not authorized to convene courts-martial

Except for covered offenses and other charges over which a special trial counsel has exercised authority and has not deferred, when in receipt of charges, a commander authorized to administer nonjudicial punishment but not authorized to convene courts-martial may:

(1) Dismiss any charge; or

Discussion

See R.C.M. 401(c)(1) concerning dismissal of charges, the effect of dismissal, and options for further action.

---

(2) Forward any charge to a superior commander for disposition.

Discussion

See R.C.M. 401(c)(2) for additional guidance concerning forwarding charges. See generally R.C.M. 303 (preliminary inquiry); 308 (notification to accused of charges) concerning other duties of the immediate commander when in receipt of charges.

When the immediate commander is authorized to convene courts-martial, see R.C.M. 403, 404, or 407, as appropriate.

Rule 403. Action by commander exercising summary court-martial jurisdiction

(a) *Recording receipt.* Immediately upon receipt of sworn charges, an officer exercising summary court-martial jurisdiction over the command shall cause the hour and date of receipt to be entered on the charge sheet. After recording receipt of charges over which a special trial counsel has exercised authority and has not deferred, the charge sheet shall be returned to the special trial counsel.

Discussion

See Article 24 and R.C.M. 1302(a) concerning who may exercise summary court-martial jurisdiction.

The entry indicating receipt is important because it stops the running of the statute of limitations. *See* Article 43; R.C.M. 907(b)(2)(B). Charges may be preferred and forwarded to an officer exercising summary court-martial jurisdiction over the command to stop the running of the statute of limitations even though the accused is absent without authority.

(b) *Disposition.* Except for covered offenses and other charges over which a special trial counsel has exercised authority and has not deferred, when in receipt of charges, a commander exercising summary court-martial jurisdiction may:

(1) Dismiss any charge;

Discussion

See R.C.M. 401(c) concerning dismissal of charges, the effect of dismissing charges, and options for further action.

(2) Forward any charge (or, after dismissing a charge, the matter) to a subordinate commander for disposition;

Discussion

See R.C.M. 401(c)(2)(B) concerning forwarding charges to a subordinate. When appropriate, charges may be forwarded to a subordinate even if the subordinate previously considered them.

(3) Forward any charge to a superior commander for disposition;

Discussion

See R.C.M. 401(c)(2)(A) for guidance concerning forwarding charges to a superior.

(4) Subject to R.C.M. 601(d) and 1301(c), refer any charge to a summary court-martial for trial; or

Discussion

See R.C.M. 1302(c) concerning referral of charges to a summary court-martial.

(5) Unless otherwise prescribed by the Secretary concerned, direct a preliminary hearing under R.C.M. 405, and, if appropriate, forward the report of preliminary hearing with the charges to a superior commander for disposition.

Discussion

A preliminary hearing should be directed when it appears that the charges are of such a serious nature that trial by general court-martial may be warranted. *See* R.C.M. 405. If a preliminary hearing of the subject matter already has been conducted,. see R.C.M. 405

Rule 404. Action by commander exercising special court-martial jurisdiction

Except for covered offenses and other charges over which a special trial counsel has exercised authority and has not deferred, when in receipt of charges, a commander exercising special court-martial jurisdiction may:

(1) Dismiss any charge;

Discussion

See R.C.M. 401(c) concerning dismissal of charges, the effect of dismissing charges, and options for further action.

(2) Forward any charge (or, after dismissing a charge, the matter) to a subordinate commander for disposition;

Discussion

See R.C.M. 401(c)(2)(B) concerning forwarding charges to a subordinate. When appropriate, charges may be forwarded to a subordinate even if the subordinate previously considered them.

(3) Forward any charge to a superior commander for disposition;

Discussion

See R.C.M. 401(c)(2)(A) for guidance concerning forwarding charges to a superior.

(4) Subject to R.C.M. 201(f)(2)(D) and (E), 601(d), and 1301(c), refer any charge to a summary court-martial or to a special court-martial for trial; or

Discussion

See Article 23 and R.C.M. 504(b)(2) concerning who may convene special courts-martial.

See R.C.M. 601 concerning referral of charges to a special court-martial. See R.C.M. 1302(c) concerning referral of charges to a summary court-martial.

See R.C.M. 201(f)(2)(D) and (E) and 1301(c) for limitations on the referral of certain offenses to special and summary courts-martial.

---

(5) Unless otherwise prescribed by the Secretary concerned, direct a preliminary hearing under R.C.M. 405, and, if appropriate, forward the report of preliminary hearing with the charges to a superior commander for disposition.

Discussion

A preliminary hearing should be directed when it appears that the charges are of such a serious nature that trial by general court-martial may be warranted. *See* R.C.M. 405. If a preliminary hearing of the subject matter already has been conducted, see R.C.M. 405(b) and 405(f)(2).

Rule 405. Preliminary hearing

(a) *In general.* Except as provided in R.C.M. 405(n), no charge or specification may be referred to a general court-martial for trial until completion of a preliminary hearing in substantial compliance with this rule. The issues for determination at a preliminary hearing are limited to the following: whether each specification alleges an offense; whether there is probable cause to believe that the accused committed the offense or offenses charged; whether the convening authority has court-martial jurisdiction over the accused and over the offense; and to recommend the disposition that should be made of the case. Failure to comply with this rule shall have no effect on the disposition of any charge if the charge is not referred to a general court-martial.

Discussion

The function of the preliminary hearing is to ascertain and impartially weigh the facts needed for the limited scope and purpose of the preliminary hearing. The preliminary hearing is not intended to perfect a case against the accused and is not intended to serve as a means of discovery or to provide a right of confrontation required at trial. Determinations and recommendations of the preliminary hearing officer are advisory.

Failure to substantially comply with the requirements of Article 32, which failure prejudices the accused, may result in delay in disposition of the case or disapproval of the proceedings. See R.C.M. 905(b)(1) and 906(b)(3) concerning motions for appropriate relief relating to the preliminary hearing.

The accused may waive the preliminary hearing. *See* R.C.M. 405(m). In such case, no preliminary hearing need be held. However, the convening authority authorized to direct the preliminary hearing may direct that it be conducted notwithstanding the waiver.

(b) *Earlier preliminary hearing.* If a preliminary hearing on the subject matter of an offense has been conducted before the accused is charged with an offense, and the accused was present at the preliminary hearing and afforded the rights to counsel, cross-examination, and presentation of evidence required by this rule, no further preliminary hearing is required.

(c) *Who may direct a preliminary hearing.*

(1) Subject to R.C.M. 405(c)(2), unless prohibited by regulations of the Secretary concerned, a preliminary hearing may be directed under this rule by any court-martial convening authority. That authority may also give procedural instructions not inconsistent with these rules.

(2) For charges and specifications over which a special trial counsel has exercised authority, the special trial counsel shall determine whether a preliminary hearing is required. If a special trial counsel determines that a hearing is required, the special trial counsel shall request that a convening authority provide a preliminary hearing officer. Upon such a request, the convening authority shall provide a preliminary hearing officer and direct a preliminary hearing in accordance with this rule. If a special trial counsel determines a previous preliminary hearing is required to be reopened, the convening authority shall direct the preliminary hearing to be reopened.

(d) *Disclosures after direction of a preliminary hearing.*

(1) As soon as practicable but no later than five days after direction of an Article 32 preliminary hearing, counsel for the Government shall provide the defense with copies of, or, if impracticable, permit the defense to inspect:

(A) the order directing the Article 32 preliminary hearing pursuant to this rule (R.C.M. 405);

(B) statements, within the control of military authorities, of witnesses that counsel for the Government intends to call at the preliminary hearing;

(C) evidence counsel for the Government intends to present at the preliminary hearing; and

(D) any matters provided to the convening authority when deciding to direct the preliminary hearing.

Discussion

This rule is not intended to limit or discourage counsel for the Government from providing additional materials to the defense.

(2) *Contraband.* If items covered by R.C.M. 405(d)(1) are contraband, the disclosure required under this rule is a reasonable opportunity to inspect said contraband prior to the preliminary hearing.

(3) *Privilege.* If items covered by R.C.M. 405(d)(1) are privileged, classified, or otherwise protected under Section V of Part III, the Military Rules of Evidence, no disclosure of those items is required under this rule. However, counsel for the Government may disclose privileged, classified, or otherwise protected information covered by R.C.M. 405(d)(1) if authorized by the holder of the privilege, or, in the case of Mil. R. Evid. 505 or 506, if authorized by a competent authority.

(4) *Protective order if privileged information is disclosed.* If the Government agrees to disclose to the accused information to which the protections afforded by Section V of Part III may apply, the convening authority, or other person designated by regulation of the Secretary concerned, may enter an appropriate protective order, in writing, to guard against the compromise of information disclosed to the accused. The terms of any such protective order may include prohibiting the disclosure of the information except as authorized by the authority issuing the protective order, as well as those terms specified by Mil. R. Evid. 505(g)(2)–(6) or 506(g)(2)–(5).

Discussion

The purpose of this rule is to provide the accused with the documents used to make the determination to direct a preliminary hearing and to allow the accused to prepare for the preliminary hearing. This rule is not intended to be a tool for discovery and does not impose the same discovery obligations found in R.C.M. 405 prior to amendments required by Section 1702 of the National Defense Authorization Act for Fiscal Year 2014, Pub. L. No. 113-66, 127 Stat. 980 (2013), as amended by Section 531 of the Carl Levin and Howard P. "Buck" McKeon National Defense Authorization Act for Fiscal Year 2015, Pub. L. No. 113-291, 128 Stat. 3371 (2014), or R.C.M. 701. Additional rules for disclosure of witnesses and other evidence in the preliminary hearing are provided in R.C.M. 405(j).

(e) *Personnel.*

(1) Preliminary hearing officer.

(A) The convening authority directing the preliminary hearing shall detail an impartial judge advocate, not the accuser, who is certified under Article 27(b)(2) to conduct the hearing. When it is impracticable to appoint a judge advocate certified under Article 27(b)(2) due to exceptional circumstances:

(i) The convening authority may detail an impartial commissioned officer as the preliminary hearing officer, and

(ii) An impartial judge advocate certified under Article 27(b)(2) shall be available to provide legal advice to the detailed preliminary hearing officer.

(B) Whenever practicable, the preliminary hearing officer shall be equal or senior in grade to the military counsel detailed to represent the accused and the Government at the preliminary hearing.

(C) The Secretary concerned may prescribe additional limitations on the detailing of preliminary hearing officers.

(D) The preliminary hearing officer shall not depart from an impartial role and become an advocate for either side. The preliminary hearing officer is disqualified to act later in the same case in any other capacity.

Discussion

The preliminary hearing officer, if not a judge advocate, should be an officer in the grade of O-4 or higher. The preliminary hearing officer may seek legal advice concerning the preliminary hearing officer's responsibilities from an impartial source, but may not obtain such advice from counsel for any party or counsel for a victim.

Because this is a preliminary hearing and not a trial, the requirement for the preliminary hearing officer to remain impartial does not preclude the preliminary hearing officer from identifying matters or sources of information that may warrant further inquiry. *See* R.C.M. 405(k)(1). The responsibility for requesting and producing such information, however, rests with the parties.

(2) *Counsel for the Government.*

(A) Subject to R.C.M. 405(e)(2)(B), a judge advocate, not the accuser, shall serve as counsel to represent the Government.

(B) For preliminary hearings requested by a special trial counsel, the special trial counsel shall detail counsel for the Government consistent with regulations prescribed by the Secretary concerned. Any determination by a special trial counsel to prefer or refer charges shall not act to disqualify that special trial counsel as an accuser.

(3) *Defense counsel.*

(A) *Detailed counsel.* Military counsel certified in accordance with Article 27(b) shall be detailed to represent the accused.

(B) *Individual military counsel.* The accused may request to be represented by individual military counsel. Such requests shall be acted on in accordance with R.C.M. 506(b).

(C) *Civilian counsel.* The accused may be represented by civilian counsel at no expense to the Government. Upon request, the accused is entitled to a reasonable time to obtain civilian counsel and to have such counsel present for the preliminary hearing. However, the preliminary hearing shall not be unduly delayed for this purpose. Representation by civilian counsel shall not limit the rights to military counsel under R.C.M. 405(e)(3)(A) or (B).

(4) *Others.* The convening authority who directed the preliminary hearing may also detail or request an appropriate authority to detail a reporter, an interpreter, or both.

(f) *Scope of preliminary hearing.*

(1) The preliminary hearing officer shall limit the inquiry to the examination of evidence, including witnesses, relevant to the issues for determination under R.C.M. 405(a).

(2) If evidence adduced during the preliminary hearing indicates that the accused committed any uncharged offense, the preliminary hearing officer may examine evidence and hear witnesses presented by the parties relating to the subject matter of such offense and make the determination specified in R.C.M. 405(a) regarding such offense without the accused first having been charged with the offense. The rights of the accused under R.C.M. 405(g), and, where it would not cause undue delay to the proceedings, the procedure applicable for production of witnesses and other evidence under R.C.M. 405(i), are the same with regard to both charged and uncharged offenses. When considering uncharged offenses identified during the preliminary hearing, the preliminary hearing officers shall inform the accused of the general nature of each offense considered and otherwise afford the accused the same opportunity for representation, cross-examination, and presentation afforded during the preliminary hearing of any charged offense.

(3) If evidence adduced during the preliminary hearing indicates that the accused committed any uncharged covered offense and the preliminary hearing was not requested by special trial counsel, the preliminary hearing officer shall provide prompt notice to the convening authority and a special trial counsel and shall submit a copy of the preliminary hearing report to a special trial counsel.

Discussion

Except as set forth in R.C.M. 405(j), the Military Rules of Evidence do not apply at a preliminary hearing. Except as prohibited elsewhere in this rule, a preliminary hearing officer may consider evidence, including hearsay, which would not be admissible at trial.

(g) *Rights of the accused.* At any preliminary hearing under this rule the accused shall have the right to:

(1) Be advised of the charges and uncharged misconduct under consideration;

(2) Be represented by counsel;

(3) Be informed of the purpose of the preliminary hearing;

(4) Be informed of the right against self-incrimination under Article 31;

(5) In accordance with the terms of R.C.M. 405(k)(4), be present throughout the taking of evidence;

(6) Cross-examine witnesses on matters relevant to the issues for determination under R.C.M. 405(a);

(7) Present matters relevant to the issues for determination under R.C.M. 405(a); and

(8) Make a sworn or unsworn statement relevant to the issues for determination under R.C.M. 405(a).

(h) *Notice to and presence of victim.*

(1) For the purposes of this rule, a "victim" is an individual who is alleged to have suffered a direct physical, emotional, or pecuniary harm as a result of the commission of an offense under the UCMJ.

(2) A victim of an offense under the UCMJ or the victim's counsel, if any, shall receive reasonable, accurate, and timely notice of a preliminary hearing relating to the alleged offense and a reasonable opportunity to confer with counsel for the Government.

(3) A victim has the right not to be excluded from any public proceeding of the preliminary hearing, except to the extent a similarly situated victim would be excluded at trial.

Discussion

See Article 6b, UCMJ.

(i) *Notice, Production of Witnesses, and Production of Other Evidence.*

(1) *Notice.* Prior to any preliminary hearing under this rule, the parties shall, in accordance with timelines set by the preliminary hearing officer, provide to the preliminary hearing officer and the opposing party the following notices:

(A) Notice of the name and contact information for each witness the party intends to call at the preliminary hearing;

(B) Notice of any other evidence that the party intends to offer at the preliminary hearing; and

(C) Notice of any additional information the party intends to submit under R.C.M. 405(l).

(2) *Production of Witnesses.*

(A) *Military Witnesses.*

(i) Prior to the preliminary hearing, defense counsel shall provide to counsel for the Government the names of proposed military witnesses whom the accused requests that the Government produce to testify at the preliminary hearing, and the requested form of the testimony, in accordance with the timeline established by the preliminary hearing officer. Counsel for the Government shall respond that either (1) the Government agrees that the witness' testimony is relevant, not cumulative, and necessary to a determination of the issues under R.C.M. 405(a) and will seek to secure the witness' testimony for the hearing; or (2) the Government objects to the proposed defense witness on the grounds that the testimony would be irrelevant, cumulative, or unnecessary to a determination of the issues under R.C.M. 405(a).

(ii) If the Government objects to the proposed defense witness, defense counsel may request that the preliminary hearing officer determine whether the witness is relevant, not cumulative, and necessary to a determination of the issues under R.C.M. 405(a).

(iii) If the Government does not object to the proposed defense military witness or the preliminary hearing officer determines that the military witness is relevant, not cumulative, and necessary, counsel for the Government shall request that the commanding officer of the proposed military witness make that person available to provide testimony. The commanding officer shall determine whether the individual is available, and if so, whether the witness will testify in person, by video teleconference, by telephone, or by similar means of remote testimony, based on operational necessity or mission requirements. If the commanding officer determines that the military witness is available, counsel for the Government shall make arrangements for that individual's testimony. The commanding officer's determination of unavailability due to operational necessity or mission requirements is final.

(iv) A victim who is alleged to have suffered a direct physical, emotional, or pecuniary harm as a result of the matters set forth in a charge or specification under consideration and is named in one of the specifications under consideration shall not be required to testify at a preliminary hearing.

Discussion

A commanding officer's determination of whether an individual is available, as well as the means by which the individual is available, is a balancing test. The more important the testimony of the witness, the greater the difficulty, expense, delay, or effect on military operations must be to deny production of the witness. Based on operational necessity and mission requirements, the witness' commanding officer may authorize the witness to testify by video teleconference, telephone, or similar means of remote testimony. Factors to be considered in making this determination include the costs of producing the witness; the timing of the request for production of the witness; the potential delay in the proceeding that may be caused by the production of the witness; and the likelihood of significant interference with operational deployment, mission accomplishment, or essential training. Before determining that a witness is unavailable, the witness' commanding officer should give due consideration to the alternative forms of testimony noted above, which generally can be facilitated with minimal impact on command operations.

(B) *Civilian Witnesses.*

(i) Defense counsel shall provide to counsel for the Government the names of proposed civilian witnesses whom the accused requests that the Government produce to testify at the preliminary hearing, and the requested form of the testimony, in accordance with the timeline established by the preliminary hearing officer. Counsel for the Government shall respond that either (1) the Government agrees that the witness' testimony is relevant, not cumulative, and necessary to a determination of the issues under R.C.M. 405(a) and will seek to secure the witness' testimony for the hearing; or (2) the Government objects to the proposed defense witness on the grounds that the testimony would be irrelevant, cumulative, or unnecessary to a determination of the issues under R.C.M. 405(a).

(ii) If the Government objects to the proposed defense witness, defense counsel may request that the preliminary hearing officer determine whether the witness is relevant, not cumulative, and necessary to a determination of the issues under R.C.M. 405(a).

(iii) If the Government does not object to the proposed civilian witness or the preliminary hearing officer determines that the civilian witness' testimony is relevant, not cumulative, and necessary, counsel for the Government shall invite the civilian witness to provide testimony and, if the individual agrees, shall make arrangements for the witness's testimony. If expense to the Government is to be incurred, the convening authority who directed the preliminary hearing, or the convening authority's delegate, shall determine whether the witness testifies in person, by video teleconference, by telephone, or by similar means of remote testimony.

Discussion

Factors to be considered in making this determination include the costs of producing the witness; the timing of the request for production of the witness; the potential delay in the proceeding that may be caused by the production of the witness; the willingness of the witness to testify in person; and, for child witnesses, the traumatic effect of providing in person testimony. Civilian witnesses may not be compelled to provide testimony at a preliminary hearing. Civilian witnesses may be paid for travel and associated expenses to testify at a preliminary hearing. *See generally* Department of Defense Joint Travel Regulations.

---

(3) *Production of other evidence.*

(A) *Evidence under the control of the Government.*

(i) Prior to the preliminary hearing, defense counsel shall provide to counsel for the Government a list of evidence under the control of the Government the accused requests the Government produce to the defense for introduction at the preliminary hearing. The preliminary hearing officer may set a deadline by which defense requests must be received. Counsel for the Government shall respond that either (1) the Government agrees that the evidence is relevant, not cumulative, and necessary to a determination of the issues under R.C.M. 405(a) and shall make reasonable efforts to obtain the evidence; or (2) the Government objects to production of the evidence on the grounds that the evidence would be irrelevant, cumulative, or unnecessary to a determination of the issues under R.C.M. 405(a).

(ii) If the Government objects to the production of the evidence, defense counsel may request that the preliminary hearing officer determine whether the evidence should be produced. The preliminary hearing officer shall determine whether the evidence is relevant, not cumulative, and necessary to a determination of the issues under R.C.M. 405(a). If the preliminary hearing officer determines that the evidence shall be produced, counsel for the Government shall make reasonable efforts to obtain the evidence.

(iii) The preliminary hearing officer may not order the production of any privileged matters; however, when a party offers evidence that an opposing party claims is privileged, the preliminary hearing officer may rule on whether a privilege applies.

(B) *Evidence not under the control of the Government.*

(i) Evidence not under the control of the Government may be obtained through noncompulsory means or by a pre-referral investigative subpoena issued by a military judge under R.C.M. 309 or counsel for the Government in accordance with the process established by R.C.M. 703(g)(3)(C).

(ii) Prior to the preliminary hearing, defense counsel shall provide to counsel for the Government a list of evidence not under the control of the Government that the accused requests the Government obtain. The preliminary hearing officer may set a deadline by which defense requests must be received. Counsel for the Government shall respond that either (1) the Government agrees that the evidence is relevant, not cumulative, and necessary to a determination of the issues under R.C.M. 405(a) and shall issue a pre-referral investigative subpoena for the evidence; or (2) the Government objects to the production of the evidence on the grounds that the evidence would be irrelevant, cumulative, or unnecessary to a determination of the issues under R.C.M. 405(a).

(iii) If the Government objects to production of the evidence, defense counsel may request that the preliminary hearing officer determine whether the evidence should be produced. If the preliminary hearing officer determines that the evidence is relevant, not cumulative, and necessary to a determination of the issues under R.C.M. 405(a) and that the issuance of a pre-referral investigative subpoena would not cause undue delay to the preliminary hearing, the preliminary hearing officer shall direct counsel for the Government to seek a pre-referral investigative subpoena for the defense-requested evidence from a military judge in accordance with R.C.M. 309 or authorization from the general court-martial convening authority to issue an investigative subpoena. If counsel for the Government refuses or is unable to obtain an investigative subpoena, the counsel shall set forth the reasons why the investigative subpoena was not obtained in a written statement that shall be included in the preliminary hearing report under R.C.M. 405(m).

Discussion

A pre-referral investigative subpoena to produce books, papers, documents, data, electronically stored information, or other objects for a preliminary hearing may be issued by counsel for the Government when authorized by the general court-martial convening authority or by a military judge under R.C.M. 309. The preliminary hearing officer has no authority to issue a pre-referral investigative subpoena.

(iv) The preliminary hearing officer may not order the production of any privileged matters; however, when a party offers evidence that an opposing party claims is privileged, the preliminary hearing officer may rule on whether a privilege applies.

(j) *Military Rules of Evidence.*

(1) *In general.*

(A) Only the following Military Rules of Evidence apply to preliminary hearings:

(i) Mil. R. Evid. 301-303 and 305.

(ii) Mil. R. Evid. 412(a), except as provided in R.C.M. 405(j)(2).

(iii) Mil. R. Evid., Section V, Privileges, except that Mil. R. Evid. 505(f)-(h) and (j); 506(f)-(h), (j), (k), and (m); and 514(d)(6) shall not apply.

(B) In applying the rules to a preliminary hearing in accordance with R.C.M. 405(j)(1)(A), the term "military judge," as used in such rules, means the preliminary hearing officer, who shall assume the military judge's authority to exclude evidence from the preliminary hearing, and who shall, in discharging this duty, follow the procedures set forth in such rules. Evidence offered in violation of the procedural requirements of the rules in R.C.M. 405(j)(1)(A) shall be excluded from the preliminary hearing, unless good cause is shown.

(2) *Sex-offense cases.*

(A) *Inadmissibility of certain evidence.* In a case of an alleged sexual offense, as defined under Mil. R. Evid. 412(d), evidence offered to prove that any alleged victim engaged in other sexual behavior or evidence offered to prove any alleged victim's sexual predisposition is not admissible at a preliminary hearing unless—

(i) the evidence would be admissible at trial under Mil. R. Evid. 412(b)(1) or (2); and

(ii) the evidence is relevant, not cumulative, and is necessary to a determination of the issues under R.C.M. 405(a).

(B) *Initial procedure to determine admissibility.* A party intending to offer evidence under R.C.M. 405(j)(2)(A) shall, no later than five days before the preliminary hearing begins, submit a written motion specifically describing the evidence and stating why the evidence is admissible. The preliminary hearing officer may permit a different filing time, but any motion shall be filed prior to the beginning of the preliminary hearing. The moving party shall serve the motion on the opposing party, who shall have the opportunity to respond in writing. Counsel for the Government shall cause the motion and any written responses to be served on the victim, or victim's counsel, if any, or, when appropriate, the victim's guardian or representative. After reviewing the motion and any written responses, the preliminary hearing officer shall either—

(i) deny the motion on the grounds that the evidence does not meet the criteria specified in R.C.M. 405(j)(2)(A)(i) or (ii); or

(ii) conduct a hearing to determine the admissibility of the evidence.

(C) *Admissibility hearing.* If the preliminary hearing officer conducts a hearing to determine the admissibility of the evidence, the admissibility hearing shall be closed and should ordinarily be conducted at the end of the preliminary hearing, after all other evidence offered by the parties has been admitted. At the admissibility hearing, the parties may call witnesses and offer relevant evidence. The victim shall be afforded a reasonable opportunity to attend and be heard, to include being heard through counsel. If the preliminary hearing officer determines that the evidence should be admitted, the victim may directly petition the Court of Criminal Appeals for a writ of mandamus pursuant to Article 6b.

Discussion

The preliminary hearing may be abated pending action by the Court of Criminal Appeals.

(D) *Sealing.* The motions, related papers, and the record of an admissibility hearing shall be sealed and remain under seal in accordance with R.C.M. 1113.

Discussion

When ordering an exhibit or proceeding sealed in accordance with R.C.M. 1113, the preliminary hearing officer should consider the purpose for which the exhibit or proceeding is to be sealed and determine if the person or entity whose interests are being protected should be permitted access to the sealed materials. The preliminary hearing officer should include language in the sealing order identifying the purpose for which the exhibit or proceeding is being sealed and, if applicable, provide parameters for examination by or disclosure to those persons or entities whose interests are being protected. See R.C.M. 1113(b)(4)-(5) for definitions of the terms "examination" and "disclosure."

(k) *Preliminary hearing procedure.*

(1) *Generally.* The preliminary hearing shall begin with the preliminary hearing officer informing the accused of the accused's rights under R.C.M. 405(g). Counsel for the Government will then present evidence. Upon the conclusion of counsel for the Government's presentation of evidence, defense counsel may present matters. Both counsel for the Government and defense counsel shall be afforded an opportunity to cross-examine adverse witnesses. The preliminary hearing officer may also question witnesses called by the parties. If the preliminary hearing officer determines that additional evidence is necessary for a determination of the issues under R.C.M. 405(a), the preliminary hearing officer may provide the parties an opportunity to present additional testimony or evidence. Except as provided in R.C.M. 405(m)(2)(J), the preliminary hearing officer shall not consider evidence not presented at the preliminary hearing in making the determination under R.C.M. 405(a). The preliminary hearing officer shall not call witnesses *sua sponte.*

Discussion

When the preliminary hearing officer finds that evidence offered by either party is not within the scope of the hearing, the preliminary hearing officer shall inform the parties and halt the presentation of that information.

---

(2) *Presentation of evidence.*

(A) *Testimony.* Witness testimony may be provided in person, by video teleconference, by telephone, or by similar means of remote testimony. All testimony shall be taken under oath, except that the accused may make an unsworn statement. The preliminary hearing officer shall only consider testimony that is relevant to the issues for determination under R.C.M. 405(a).

Discussion

The following oath may be given to witnesses:

"Do you (swear) (affirm) that the evidence you give shall be the truth, the whole truth, and nothing but the truth (so help you God)?"

All preliminary hearing officer notes of testimony and recordings of testimony should be preserved until the end of trial.

If during the preliminary hearing any witness subject to the UCMJ is suspected of an offense under the UCMJ, the preliminary hearing officer should comply with the warning requirements of Mil. R. Evid. 305(c), (d), and, if necessary, (e).

Bearing in mind that counsel are responsible for preparing and presenting their cases, the preliminary hearing officer may ask a witness questions relevant to the issues for determination under subsection (a). When questioning a witness, the preliminary hearing officer may not depart from an impartial role and become an advocate for either side.

(B) *Other evidence.* If relevant to the issues for determination under R.C.M. 405(a) and not cumulative, a preliminary hearing officer may consider other evidence offered by either counsel for the Government or defense counsel, in addition to or in lieu of witness testimony, including statements, tangible evidence, or reproductions thereof, that the preliminary hearing officer determines is reliable. This other evidence need not be sworn.

(3) *Access by spectators.* Preliminary hearings are public proceedings and should remain open to the public whenever possible, whether conducted in person or via remote means. If there is an overriding interest that outweighs the value of an open preliminary hearing, the convening authority or the preliminary hearing officer may restrict or foreclose access by spectators to all or part of the proceedings. Any restriction or closure must be narrowly tailored to protect the overriding interest involved. Before ordering any restriction or closure, a convening authority or preliminary hearing officer must determine whether any reasonable alternatives to such restriction or closure exist, or if some lesser means can

be used to protect the overriding interest in the case. The convening authority or preliminary hearing officer shall make specific findings of fact in writing that support the restriction or closure. The written findings of fact shall be included in the preliminary hearing report.

Discussion

Convening authorities or preliminary hearing officers must conduct a case-by-case, witness-by-witness, and circumstance-by-circumstance analysis of whether restriction or closure is necessary. Examples of overriding interests include: preventing psychological harm or trauma to a child witness or to an alleged victim of a sexual crime, protecting the safety or privacy of a witness or an alleged victim, protecting classified material, and receiving evidence where a witness is incapable of testifying in an open setting.

---

(4) *Presence of accused.* The accused shall be present for the preliminary hearing.

(A) *Remote presence of the accused.* The convening authority that directed the preliminary hearing may authorize the use of audio-visual technology between the parties and the preliminary hearing officer. In such circumstances, the "presence" requirement of the accused is met only when the accused has a defense counsel physically present at the accused's location or when the accused consents to presence by remote means with the opportunity for confidential consultation with defense counsel during the proceeding. Such technology may include two or more remote sites as long as all parties can see and hear each other.

(B) The accused shall be considered to have waived the right to be present at the preliminary hearing if the accused:

(i) After being notified of the time and place of the proceeding is voluntarily absent; or

(ii) After being warned by the preliminary hearing officer that disruptive conduct will cause removal from the proceeding, persists in conduct which is such as to justify exclusion from the proceeding.

(5) *Recording of the preliminary hearing.* Counsel for the Government shall ensure that the preliminary hearing is recorded by a suitable recording device. A victim named in a specification under consideration may request access to, or a copy of, the recording of the proceedings. Upon request, counsel for the Government shall provide the requested access to, or a copy of, the recording or, at the Government's discretion, a transcript, to the victim or victim's counsel, if any, not later than a reasonable time following dismissal of the charges, unless charges are dismissed for the purpose of rereferral, or court-martial adjournment. This rule does not entitle the victim to classified information or sealed materials consistent with an order issued in accordance with R.C.M. 1113(a).

Discussion

See Article 32(e)-(h), UCMJ.

---

(6) *Recording and broadcasting prohibited.* Video and audio recording, broadcasting, and the taking of photographs—except as required in R.C.M. 405(k)(5)—are prohibited. The convening authority may, as a matter of discretion, permit contemporaneous closed-caption video or audio transmission to permit viewing or hearing by an accused removed under R.C.M. 405(k)(4) or by spectators when the facilities are inadequate to accommodate a reasonable number of spectators.

(7) *Objections.* Any objection alleging a failure to comply with this rule, other than an objection under R.C.M. 405(m), shall be made to the preliminary hearing officer promptly upon discovery of the alleged error. The preliminary hearing officer is not required to rule on any objection. An objection shall be noted in the preliminary hearing report if the person objecting so requests. The preliminary hearing officer may require a party to file any objection in writing.

(8) *Sealed exhibits and proceedings.* The preliminary hearing officer has the authority to order exhibits, recordings of proceedings, or other matters sealed as described in R.C.M. 1113.

Discussion

When ordering an exhibit or proceeding sealed in accordance with R.C.M. 1113, the preliminary hearing officer should consider the purpose for which the exhibit or proceeding is to be sealed and determine if the person or entity whose interests are being protected should be permitted access to the sealed materials. The preliminary hearing officer should include language in the sealing order identifying the purpose for which the exhibit or proceeding is being sealed and, if applicable, provide parameters for examination by or disclosure to those persons or entities whose interests are being protected. See R.C.M. 1113(b)(4)-(5) for definitions of the terms "examination" and "disclosure."

(l) *Supplementary information.*

(1) No later than 24 hours from the closure of the preliminary hearing, counsel for the Government, defense counsel, and any victim named in a specification under consideration (or, if applicable, counsel for such a victim) may submit to the preliminary hearing officer, counsel for the Government, and defense counsel additional information that the submitter deems relevant to the disposition of the charges and specifications.

(2) Defense counsel may submit additional matters that rebut the submissions of counsel for the Government or any victim provided under R.C.M. 405(l)(1). Such matters must be provided to the preliminary hearing officer and to the counsel for the Government within 5 days of the closure of the preliminary hearing.

Discussion

The Military Rules of Evidence and other regulations may require the preliminary hearing officer to seal certain materials. Preliminary hearing officers have the discretion to seal other supplementary information that they determine should be protected from disclosure. Such information may include personally identifiable information, medical information, financial information, and any other information that may cause unnecessary harm to an individual or entity if released. When ordering an exhibit or proceeding sealed in accordance with R.C.M. 1113, the preliminary hearing officer should consider the purpose for which the exhibit or proceeding is to be sealed and determine if the person or entity whose interests are being protected should be permitted access to the sealed materials. The preliminary hearing officer should include language in the sealing order identifying the purpose for which the exhibit or proceeding is being sealed and, if applicable, provide parameters for examination by or disclosure to those persons or entities whose interests are being protected. See R.C.M. 1113(b)(4)-(5) for definitions of the terms "examination" and "disclosure."

---

(3) The preliminary hearing officer shall examine all supplementary information submitted under R.C.M. 405(l) and shall seal, in accordance with R.C.M. 1113, any matters the preliminary hearing officer deems privileged or otherwise not subject to disclosure.

(A) The preliminary hearing officer shall provide a written summary and an analysis of the supplementary information submitted under R.C.M. 405(l) that is not sealed and is relevant to disposition for inclusion in the report to the convening authority or special trial counsel, as applicable, under R.C.M. 405(m).

(B) If the preliminary hearing officer seals any supplementary information submitted under R.C.M. 405(l), the preliminary hearing officer shall provide an analysis of those materials. The analysis of the sealed materials shall be sealed. Additionally, the preliminary hearing officer shall generally describe those matters and detail the basis for sealing them in a separate cover sheet. This cover sheet shall accompany the sealed matters and shall not contain privileged information or be sealed.

(4) The supplementary information and any summary and analysis provided by the preliminary hearing officer, and any sealed matters and cover sheets, as applicable, shall be forwarded to the convening authority or special trial counsel, as applicable, for consideration in making a disposition determination.

(5) Submissions under R.C.M. 405(l) shall be maintained as an attachment to the preliminary hearing report provided under R.C.M. 405(m).

(m) *Preliminary hearing report.*

(1) *In general.* The preliminary hearing officer shall make a timely written report of the preliminary hearing to the convening authority or, for hearings requested by a special trial counsel, to the special trial counsel. This report is advisory and does not bind the staff judge advocate, convening authority, or special trial counsel, as applicable.

Discussion

As soon as practicable after receipt of supplementary information under R.C.M. 405(l), the charges and the report of preliminary hearing should be forwarded to the court-martial convening authority. *See* Article 10.

---

(2) *Contents.* The preliminary hearing report shall include:

(A) A statement of names and organizations or addresses of counsel for the Government and defense counsel and, if applicable, a statement of why either counsel was not present at any time during the proceedings;

(B) The recording of the preliminary hearing under R.C.M. 405(k)(5);

(C) For each specification, the preliminary hearing officer's reasoning and conclusions with respect to the issues for determination under R.C.M. 405(a), including a summary of relevant witness testimony and documentary evidence presented at the hearing and any observations concerning the testimony of witnesses and the availability and admissibility of evidence at trial;

(D) If applicable, a statement that an essential witness may not be available for trial;

(E) An explanation of any delays in the preliminary hearing;

(F) A notation if counsel for the Government refused to issue a pre-referral investigative subpoena that was directed by the preliminary hearing officer and the counsel's statement of the reasons for such refusal;

(G) Recommendations for any necessary modifications to the form of the charges and specifications;

(H) A statement of whether the preliminary hearing officer examined evidence or heard witnesses relating to any uncharged offenses in accordance with R.C.M. 405(f)(2), and, for each such offense, the preliminary hearing officer's reasoning and conclusions as to whether there is probable cause to believe that the accused committed the offense and whether the convening authority would have court-martial jurisdiction over the offense if it were charged;

(I) A notation of any objections if required under R.C.M. 405(k)(7);

(J) The recommendation of the preliminary hearing officer as to the disposition that should be made of the charges and specifications in the interest of justice and discipline. In making this disposition recommendation, the preliminary hearing officer may consider any evidence admitted during the preliminary hearing and matters submitted under R.C.M. 405(l);

(K) The written summary and analysis required by R.C.M. 405(l)(3)(A); and

(L) A notation as to whether the parties or the preliminary hearing officer considered any offense to be a covered offense.

Discussion

The preliminary hearing officer may include any additional matters useful to the convening authority or special trial counsel in determining disposition. For guidance concerning disposition of offenses, see Appendix 2.1 (Disposition Guidance). The preliminary hearing officer may recommend that the charges and specifications be amended or that additional charges be preferred. See R.C.M. 306 and 401 concerning other possible dispositions.

---

(3) *Sealed exhibits and proceedings*. If the preliminary hearing report contains exhibits, proceedings, or other matters ordered sealed by the preliminary hearing officer in accordance with R.C.M. 1113, counsel for the Government shall cause such materials to be sealed so as to prevent unauthorized viewing or disclosure.

(4) *Distribution of preliminary hearing report*. The preliminary hearing officer shall promptly cause the preliminary hearing report to be delivered to the convening authority or, for hearings requested by a special trial counsel, to the special trial counsel. Counsel for the Government shall promptly cause a copy of the report to be delivered to each accused. The convening authority or, for hearings requested by a special trial counsel, the special trial counsel shall promptly determine what disposition will be made in the interest of justice and discipline in accordance with R.C.M. 401 or R.C.M. 401A.

(5) *Objections to the preliminary hearing officer's report*. Upon receipt of the report, the parties shall have five days to submit objections to the preliminary hearing officer. Any objection to the preliminary hearing report shall be made to the convening authority who directed the preliminary hearing, via the preliminary hearing officer. The objection shall be served upon the opposing party, and government counsel must provide notice of the objection to any named victim or named victim's counsel, if any. The preliminary hearing officer will forward the objections to the convening authority as soon as practicable. The convening authority may direct that the preliminary hearing be reopened or take other action, as appropriate. For cases where a special trial counsel has exercised authority, the special trial counsel may request the convening authority reopen the preliminary hearing. Upon such request, the convening authority shall reopen the preliminary hearing. This paragraph does not prohibit a convening authority or special trial counsel from taking other action prior to the expiration of five days allotted for submitting objections. Failure to make a timely objection under this rule shall constitute waiver of the objection.

(n) *Waiver*. The accused may waive a preliminary hearing. However, the preliminary hearing may still be conducted notwithstanding the waiver. Relief from the waiver may be granted by the convening authority, a superior convening authority, or the military judge, as appropriate, for good cause shown. For offenses over which a special trial counsel has exercised authority, a special trial counsel may grant relief from the waiver. If a special trial counsel declines to grant relief from the waiver and the case is referred, the accused may request relief from the military judge.

Discussion

See also R.C.M. 905(b)(1); 906(b)(3).

Rule 406. Pretrial advice and special trial counsel determinations

(a) *Pretrial Advice by the Staff Judge Advocate.*

(1) *General court-martial.* Except as provided by R.C.M. 406(b), before any charge may be referred for trial by a general court-martial, it shall be submitted to the staff judge advocate of the convening authority for consideration and advice. The advice of the staff judge advocate shall include a written and signed statement which sets forth the staff judge advocate's:

(A) Conclusion with respect to whether each specification alleges an offense under the UCMJ;

(B) Conclusion with respect to whether there is probable cause to believe that the accused committed the offense charged in the specification;

(C) Conclusion with respect to whether a court-martial would have jurisdiction over the accused and the offense; and

(D) Recommendation as to the disposition that should be made of the charges and specifications by the convening authority in the interest of justice and discipline.

Discussion

A written pretrial advice need not be prepared in cases referred to special or summary courts-martial. A convening authority is required to consult with a judge advocate before referring charges to a special court-martial (*see* R.C.M. 406(a)(2)) and may seek the advice of a lawyer before referring charges to a summary court-martial. When charges have been withdrawn from a general court-martial (*see* R.C.M. 604) or when a mistrial has been declared in a general court-martial (*see* R.C.M. 915), supplementary advice is necessary before the charges may be referred to another general court-martial.

The staff judge advocate may make changes in the charges and specifications in accordance with R.C.M. 603.

For guidance concerning the disposition of charges and specifications, see Appendix 2.1 (Disposition Guidance).

The staff judge advocate is personally responsible for the pretrial advice and must make an independent and informed appraisal of the charges and evidence in order to render the advice. While the staff judge advocate may use a preliminary hearing officer's report in preparing pretrial advice, and another person may prepare the advice, the staff judge advocate is, unless disqualified, responsible for it and must sign it personally. Grounds for disqualification in a case include previous action in the case as preliminary hearing officer, military judge, trial counsel, defense counsel, or member.

The advice need not set forth the underlying analysis or rationale for its conclusions. Ordinarily, the charge sheet, forwarding letter, endorsements, and report of preliminary hearing are forwarded with the pretrial advice. In addition, the pretrial advice should include, when appropriate: a brief summary of the evidence; discussion of significant aggravating, extenuating, or mitigating factors; any recommendations for disposition of the case by commanders or others who have forwarded the charges; and any recommendations of the Article 32 preliminary hearing officer. However, there is no legal requirement to include such information, and failure to do so is not error.

Information which is incorrect or so incomplete as to be misleading may result in a determination that the advice is defective, necessitating appropriate relief. *See* R.C.M. 905(b)(1), 906(b)(3).

Defects in the pretrial advice are not jurisdictional and are raised by pretrial motion. *See* R.C.M. 905(b)(1) and its Discussion.

---

(2) *Special-court martial.* Subject to R.C.M. 406(b), before any charge may be referred for trial by a special court-martial, the convening authority shall consult a judge advocate on relevant legal issues. Such issues may include:

(A) Whether each specification alleges an offense under the UCMJ;

(B) Whether there is probable cause to believe the accused committed the offense(s) charged;

(C) Whether a court-martial would have jurisdiction over the accused and the offense;

(D) The form of the charges and specifications and any necessary modifications; and

(E) Any other factors relating to disposition of the charges and specifications in the interest of justice and discipline.

(b) *Special trial counsel determinations.* For all charges alleging covered offenses, and other charges over which special trial counsel has exercised authority and has not deferred, referral to a special or general court-martial may be made only by a special trial counsel and the referral must be accompanied by a special trial counsel's written determination that:

(1) each specification under a charge alleges an offense under the UCMJ;

(2) there is probable cause to believe that the accused committed the offense charged; and

(3) a court-martial would have jurisdiction over the accused and the offense.

(c) *Distribution.*

(1) Subject to R.C.M. 406(c)(2), a copy of the

written advice of the staff judge advocate shall be provided to the defense if charges are referred for trial by general court-martial.

(2) For those cases over which special trial counsel exercises exclusive authority, a copy of the written determination by special trial counsel shall be provided to the defense if charges are referred for trial by general or special court-martial.

Rule 407. Action by commander exercising general court-martial jurisdiction

(a) *Disposition.* Except for covered offenses and any other charges over which a special trial counsel has exercised authority and has not deferred, a commander exercising general court-martial jurisdiction, when in receipt of charges, may:

(1) Dismiss any charge;

Discussion

See R.C.M. 401(c)(1) concerning dismissal of charges and the effect of dismissing charges.

---

(2) Forward any charge (or, after dismissing charges, the matter) to a subordinate commander for disposition;

Discussion

See R.C.M. 401(c)(2)(B) concerning forwarding charges to a subordinate.

A subordinate commander may not be required to take any specific action or to dispose of charges. *See* R.C.M. 104. *See also* paragraph 1.d.(2) of Part V. When appropriate, charges may be sent or returned to a subordinate commander for compliance with procedural requirements. *See,* e.g., R.C.M. 303 (preliminary inquiry); R.C.M. 308 (notification to accused of charges).

---

(3) Forward any charge to a superior commander for disposition;

Discussion

See R.C.M. 401(c)(2)(A) for guidance concerning forwarding charges to a superior.

---

(4) Subject to R.C.M. 201(f)(2)(D) and (E), 601(d), and 1301(c), refer any charge to a summary court-martial or to a special court-martial for trial;

Discussion

See R.C.M. 201(f)(2)(D) and (E) and 1301(c) for limitations on the referral of certain offenses to special and summary courts-martial.

---

(5) Unless otherwise prescribed by the Secretary concerned, direct a preliminary hearing under R.C.M. 405, after which additional action under this rule may be taken;

Discussion

A preliminary hearing should be directed when it appears that the charges are of such a serious nature that trial by general court-martial may be warranted. *See* R.C.M. 405. If a preliminary hearing of the subject matter has already been conducted, *see* R.C.M. 405(b).

---

(6) Subject to R.C.M. 601(d), refer any charge to a general court-martial.

Discussion

See Article 22 and R.C.M. 504(b)(1) concerning who may exercise general court-martial jurisdiction.

See R.C.M. 601 concerning referral of charges. See R.C.M. 306 and 401 concerning other dispositions.

See Section 1744 (b)-(d) of the National Defense Authorization Act for Fiscal Year 2014, Pub. L. No. 113-66, 127 Stat. 980 (2013), as amended by Section 541 of the Carl Levin and Howard P. "Buck" McKeon National Defense Authorization Act for Fiscal Year 2015, Pub. L. 113-291, 128 Stat. 3371 (2014) and Service regulations for possible higher-level review requirements for decisions not to refer charges of certain sex-related offenses for trial by court-martial.

(b) *National security matters.*

(1) Subject to R.C.M. 407(b)(2), when in receipt of charges the trial of which the commander exercising general court-martial jurisdiction finds would probably be detrimental to the prosecution of a war or harmful to national security, that commander, unless otherwise prescribed by regulations of the Secretary concerned, shall determine whether trial is warranted and, if so, whether the security considerations involved are paramount to trial. As the commander finds appropriate, the commander may dismiss the charges, authorize trial of them, or forward them to a superior authority.

(2) For charges and specifications over which a

special trial counsel has exercised authority and has not deferred and a commander believes trial would be detrimental to the prosecution of a war or harmful to national security, the matter shall be forwarded to the Secretary concerned.

Discussion

In time of war, charges may be forwarded to the Secretary concerned for disposition under Article 43(e). Under Article 43(e), the Secretary may take action suspending the statute of limitations in time of war.

CHAPTER V. COURT-MARTIAL COMPOSITION AND PERSONNEL; CONVENING COURTS-MARTIAL

Rule 501. Composition and personnel of courts-martial

(a) *Composition of courts-martial.*

(1) *General courts-martial.*

(A) *Non-capital cases.* In non-capital cases, a general court-martial shall consist of:

(i) A military judge and eight members;

(ii) A military judge, eight members, and any alternate members authorized by the convening authority;

(iii) A military judge alone if trial by a military judge is requested and approved under R.C.M. 903; or

(iv) A military judge and six or seven members, but only if, after impanelment, the panel is reduced below eight members as a result of challenges or excusals.

(B) *Capital cases.* In capital cases, a general court-martial shall consist of:

(i) A military judge and twelve members; or

(ii) A military judge, twelve members, and any alternate members authorized by the convening authority.

(2) *Special courts-martial.* Special courts-martial shall consist of:

(A) A military judge and four members;

(B) A military judge, four members, and any alternate members authorized by the convening authority;

(C) A military judge alone if trial by a military judge is requested and approved under R.C.M. 903; or

(D) A military judge alone if the case is referred for trial by a special court-martial consisting of a military judge alone under Article 16(c)(2)(A).

Discussion

See R.C.M. 903 regarding the right of an enlisted accused to request a panel of at least one-third enlisted members or an all-officer panel.

See R.C.M. 912A regarding the impaneling of members and alternate members.

See R.C.M. 1301(a) concerning composition of summary courts-martial.

(b) *Counsel in general and special courts-martial.* Military trial and defense counsel shall be detailed to general and special courts-martial. Assistant trial and associate or assistant defense counsel may be detailed.

(c) *Other personnel.* Other personnel, such as interpreters, bailiffs, clerks, escorts, and orderlies, may be detailed or employed as appropriate but need not be detailed by the convening authority personally.

Rule 502. Qualifications and duties of personnel of courts-martial

(a) *Members.*

(1) *Qualifications.* The members detailed to a court-martial shall be those persons who in the opinion of the convening authority are best qualified for the duty by reason of their age, education, training, experience, length of service, and judicial temperament. Each member shall be on active duty with the armed forces and shall be:

(A) A commissioned officer;

(B) A warrant officer, except when the accused is a commissioned officer; or

(C) An enlisted person, except when the accused is either a commissioned or warrant officer.

Discussion

Retired members of any Regular component and members of Reserve components of the armed forces are eligible to serve as members if they are on active duty.

Members of the National Oceanic and Atmospheric Administration and of the Public Health Service are eligible to serve as members when assigned to and serving with an armed force. The Public Health Service includes both commissioned and warrant officers. The National Oceanic and Atmospheric Administration includes only commissioned officers.

---

(2) *Duties.*

(A) *Members.* The members of a court-martial shall determine whether the accused is proved guilty and, in a capital case in which the accused is unanimously found guilty of a capital offense, the members shall make a determination in accordance with Article 53(c)(1)(A). Each member has an equal voice and vote with other members in deliberating upon and deciding all matters submitted to them. No member may use rank or position to influence another member. No member of a court-martial may have access to or use in any open or closed session this Manual, reports of decided cases, or any other reference material.

(B) *Alternate members.* Members impaneled as alternate members shall have the same duties as members under subparagraph (A). However, an alternate member shall not vote or participate in deliberations on findings or sentencing unless the alternate member has become a member by replacing a member who was excused after impanelment under R.C.M. 912B.

Discussion

Members and alternate members should avoid any conduct or communication with the military judge, witnesses, or other trial personnel during the trial which might present an appearance of partiality. Except as provided in these rules, members and alternate members should not discuss any part of a case with anyone until the matter is submitted to them for determination. Members and alternate members should not on their own visit or conduct a view of the scene of the crime and should not investigate or gather evidence of the offense. Members and alternate members should not form an opinion on any matter in connection with a case until that matter has been submitted to them for determination.

(b) *President.*

(1) *Qualifications.* The president of a court-martial shall be the detailed member senior in rank then serving.

(2) *Duties.* The president shall have the same duties as the other members and shall also:

(A) Preside over closed sessions of the members of the court-martial during their deliberations; and

(B) Speak for the members of the court-martial when announcing the decision of the members or requesting instructions from the military judge

(c) *Qualifications of military judge and military magistrate.*

(1) *Military judge.* A military judge shall be a commissioned officer of the armed forces who is a member of the bar of a federal court or a member of the bar of the highest court of a State and who is certified to be qualified, by reason of education, training, experience, and judicial temperament, for duty as a military judge by the Judge Advocate General of the armed force of which such military judge is a member. In addition, the military judge of a general court-martial shall be designated for such duties by the Judge Advocate General or the Judge Advocate General's designee, certified to be qualified for duty as a military judge of a general court-martial, and assigned and directly responsible to the Judge Advocate General or the Judge Advocate General's designee. The Secretary concerned may prescribe additional qualifications for military judges in special courts-martial.

(2) *Military magistrate.* The Secretary concerned may establish a military magistrate program. A military magistrate shall be a commissioned officer of the armed forces who is a member of the bar of a federal court or a member of the bar of highest court of a State and who is certified to be qualified, by reason of education, training, experience, and judicial temperament, for duty as a military magistrate by the Judge Advocate General of the armed force of which such military magistrate is a member.

Discussion

See R.C.M. 801 for description of some of the general duties of the military judge and military magistrate.

Military judges assigned as general court-martial judges may perform duties in addition to the primary duty of judge of a general court-martial only when such duties are assigned or approved by the Judge Advocate General, or a designee, of the Department or Service of which the military judge is a member. Similar restrictions on other duties which a military judge in special courts-martial may perform may be prescribed in regulations of the Secretary concerned.

---

(3) *Minimum tour lengths.* A person assigned for duty as a military judge shall serve as a military judge for a term of not less than three years, subject to such provisions for reassignment as may be prescribed in regulations issued by the Secretary concerned.

(d) *Counsel.*

(1) *Qualifications of trial counsel.*

(A) *General courts-martial.* Only persons certified under Article 27(b) as competent to perform duties as counsel in courts-martial by the Judge Advocate General of the armed force of which the counsel is a member may be detailed as trial counsel in general courts-martial.

(B) *Trial counsel in special courts-martial and assistant trial counsel in general or special courts-martial.* Any commissioned officer may be detailed as trial counsel in special courts-martial, or as assistant trial counsel in general or special courts-martial if that person—

(i) is determined to be competent to perform such duties by the Judge Advocate General; and

(ii) takes an oath in accordance with Article 42(a), certifies to the court that the person has read and is familiar with the applicable rules of procedure, evidence, and professional responsibility, and meets any additional qualifications the Secretary concerned may establish.

(C) *Qualifications of special trial counsel.* Only judge advocates qualified, certified, and assigned as special trial counsel may be detailed as special trial counsel in general and special courts-martial. In accordance with regulations prescribed by the Secretary concerned, a special trial counsel shall be a judge advocate who is a member of the bar of a Federal court or a member of the bar of the highest court of a State; and is certified to be qualified, by reason of education, training, experience, and temperament, for duty as a special trial counsel by the Judge Advocate General of the armed force of which the officer is a member or, in the case of the Marine Corps, the Staff Judge Advocate to the Commandant of the Marine Corps. Special trial counsel shall be well-trained, experienced, highly-skilled and competent in handling cases involving covered offenses.

(2) *Qualifications of defense counsel.*

(A) *Detailed military counsel.* Only persons certified under Article 27(b) as competent to perform duties as counsel in courts-martial by the Judge Advocate General of the armed force of which the counsel is a member may be detailed as defense counsel, assistant defense counsel, or associate defense counsel in general or special courts-martial.

Discussion

When the accused has individual military or civilian defense counsel, the detailed counsel is "associate counsel" unless excused from the case. *See* R.C.M. 506(b)(3).

(B) *Individual military counsel and civilian defense counsel.* Individual military or civilian defense counsel who represents an accused in accordance with Article 38(b) in a court-martial shall be:

(i) a member of the bar of a federal court or of the bar of the highest court of a State; or

(ii) if not a member of such a bar, a lawyer who is authorized by a recognized licensing authority to practice law and is found by the military judge to be qualified to represent the accused upon a showing to the satisfaction of the military judge that the counsel has appropriate training and familiarity with the general principles of criminal law which apply in a court-martial.

Discussion

In making such a determination—particularly in the case of civilian defense counsel who are members only of a foreign bar—the military judge also should inquire into:

(i) the availability of the counsel at times at which sessions of the court-martial have been scheduled;

(ii) whether the accused wants the counsel to appear with military defense counsel;

(iii) the familiarity of the counsel with spoken English;

(iv) practical alternatives for discipline of the counsel in the event of misconduct;

(v) whether foreign witnesses are expected to testify with whom the counsel may more readily communicate than might military counsel; and

(vi) whether ethnic or other similarity between the accused and the counsel may facilitate communication and confidence between the accused and civilian defense counsel.

(C) *Counsel in capital cases.*

(i) *In general.* In any capital case, to the greatest extent practicable, at least one defense counsel shall, as determined by the Judge Advocate General, be learned in the law applicable to such cases. If necessary, this counsel may be a civilian and, if so, may be compensated in accordance with regulations prescribed by the Secretary of Defense.

(ii) *Qualifications.* A counsel learned in the law applicable to capital cases is an attorney whose background, knowledge, or experience would enable him or her to competently represent an accused in a capital case, with due consideration of the seriousness of the possible penalty and the unique and complex nature of the litigation.

Discussion

See Article 27(d). There exists no bright line or *per se* rule to determine the qualifications necessary for capital cases and unlike 18 U.S.C. § 3005 (2012), Article 27(d) requires detailing of at least one defense counsel learned in the law of capital cases to the greatest extent practicable and the Service Judge Advocate General determines whether the defense counsel is so qualified. Although the American Bar Association Guidelines for the Appointment and Performance of Defense Counsel in Death Penalty Cases (rev. ed. 2003), and federal civilian law, 18 U.S.C. § 3005 (2012), are instructive on the issue of whether counsel are qualified, neither authority, either individually or collectively, is dispositive of the issue.

---

(3) *Disqualifications.* No person shall act as trial counsel or assistant trial counsel or, except when expressly requested by the accused, as defense counsel or associate or assistant defense counsel in any case in which that person is or has been:

(A) The accuser, except that any determination by a special trial counsel to prefer or refer charges shall not disqualify that special trial counsel;

(B) An investigating or preliminary hearing officer;

(C) A military judge or appellate military judge; or

(D) A member.

Discussion

In the absence of evidence to the contrary, it is presumed that a person who, between referral and trial of a case, has been detailed as counsel for any party to the court-martial to which the case has been referred, has acted in that capacity. When a person has acted as counsel for a witness or victim, the issue of disqualification to serve as counsel for a party in the case is governed by the applicable rules of professional conduct.

---

(4) *Duties of trial and assistant trial counsel.* Trial counsel shall prosecute cases on behalf of the United States. Under the supervision of trial counsel an assistant trial counsel may perform any act or duty which trial counsel may perform under law, regulation, or custom of the Service.

Discussion

(A) *General duties before trial.* Immediately upon receipt of referred charges, the trial counsel should cause a copy of the charges to be served upon the accused. *See* R.C.M. 602.

The trial counsel should: examine the charge sheet and allied papers for completeness and correctness; correct (and initial) minor errors or obvious mistakes in the charges but may not without authority make any substantial changes (*see* R.C.M. 603); and ensure that the information about the accused on the charge sheet and any evidence of previous convictions are accurate.

(B) *Relationship with convening authority.* The trial counsel should: report to the convening authority any substantial irregularity in the convening orders, or allied papers; and report an actual or anticipated reduction of the number of members required under R.C.M. 501(a) to the convening authority. Except for offenses over which a special trial counsel has exercised authority and has not deferred, the trial counsel should report any substantial irregularity in the charges and bring to the attention of the convening authority any case in which the trial counsel finds trial inadvisable for lack of evidence or other reasons. For cases over which a special trial counsel has exercised authority and has not deferred, the special trial counsel is responsible for addressing irregularities in the charges.

(C) *Relationship with the accused and defense counsel.* The trial counsel must communicate with a represented accused only through the accused's defense counsel. *But see* R.C.M. 602.

(D) *Victim rights.* The trial counsel should ensure that the Government's responsibilities under Article 6b are fulfilled.

(E) *Preparation for trial.* The trial counsel should: ensure that a suitable room, a reporter (if authorized), and necessary equipment and supplies are provided for the court-martial; obtain copies of the charges and specifications and convening orders for each member and all personnel of the court-martial; give timely notice to the members, other parties, other personnel of the court-martial, and witnesses for the prosecution and (if known) defense of the date, time, place, and uniform of the meetings of the court-martial; ensure that any person having custody of the accused is also informed; comply with applicable disclosure and discovery rules (*see* R.C.M. 308, 405, and 701); prepare to make a prompt, full, and orderly presentation of the evidence at trial; consider the elements of proof of each offense charged, the burden of proof of guilt and the burdens of proof on motions which may be anticipated, and the Military Rules of Evidence; secure for use at trial such legal texts as may be available and necessary to sustain the prosecution's contentions; arrange for the presence of witnesses and evidence in accordance with R.C.M. 703; prepare to make an opening statement of the prosecution's case (*see* R.C.M. 913); prepare to conduct the examination and cross-examination of witnesses; and prepare to make final argument on the findings and, if necessary, on sentencing (*see* R.C.M. 919, 1001(h)).

(F) *Trial.* The trial counsel should bring to the attention of the military judge any substantial irregularity in the proceedings. The trial counsel should not allude to or disclose to the members any evidence not yet admitted or reasonably expected to be admitted in evidence or intimate, transmit, or purport to transmit to the military judge or members the views of the convening authority or others as to the guilt or innocence of the accused, an appropriate sentence, or any other matter within the discretion of the court-martial.

(G) *Post-trial duties.* The trial counsel should promptly provide written notice of the Statement of Trial Results to the convening authority or a designee, the accused's immediate commander, and (if applicable) the officer in charge of the confinement facility (*see* R.C.M. 1101(e)), and supervise the preparation, and distribution of copies of the record as required by these rules and regulations of the Secretary concerned (*see* R.C.M. 1112).

(H) *Assistant trial counsel.* An assistant trial counsel may act in that capacity only under the supervision of the detailed trial counsel. Responsibility for trial of a case may not devolve to an assistant not qualified to serve as trial counsel. Unless the contrary appears, all acts of an assistant trial counsel are presumed to have been done by the direction of the trial counsel. An assistant trial counsel may not act in the absence of the trial counsel at trial in a general court-martial unless the assistant has the qualifications required of a trial counsel. *See* R.C.M. 805(c).

---

(5) *Duties of defense and associate or assistant defense counsel.* Defense counsel shall represent the accused in matters under the UCMJ and these rules arising from the offenses of which the accused is then

suspected or charged. Under the supervision of defense counsel an associate or assistant defense counsel may perform any act or duty which a defense counsel may perform under law, regulation, or custom of the Service.

Discussion

(A) *Initial advice by military defense counsel.* Defense counsel should promptly explain to the accused the general duties of the defense counsel and inform the accused of the rights to request individual military counsel of the accused's own selection, and of the effect of such a request, and to retain civilian counsel. If the accused wants to request individual military counsel, the defense counsel should immediately inform the convening authority through trial counsel and, if the request is approved, serve as associate counsel if the accused requests and the request is approved. Unless the accused directs otherwise, military counsel will begin preparation of the defense immediately after being detailed without waiting for approval of a request for individual military counsel or retention of civilian counsel. *See* R.C.M. 506.

(B) *General duties of defense counsel.* Defense counsel must: guard the interests of the accused zealously within the bounds of the law without regard to personal opinion as to the guilt of the accused; disclose to the accused any interest defense counsel may have in connection with the case, any disqualification, and any other matter which might influence the accused in the selection of counsel; represent the accused with undivided fidelity and may not disclose the accused's secrets or confidences except as the accused may authorize (*see also* Mil. R. Evid. 502). A defense counsel designated to represent two or more co-accused in a joint or common trial or in allied cases must be particularly alert to conflicting interests of those accused. Defense counsel should bring such matters to the attention of the military judge so that the accused's understanding and choice may be made a matter of record. *See* R.C.M. 901(d)(4)(D).

Defense counsel must explain to the accused: the elections available as to composition of the court-martial and assist the accused to make any request necessary to effect the election (*see* R.C.M. 903); the right to plead guilty or not guilty and the meaning and effect of a plea of guilty; the rights to introduce evidence, to testify or remain silent, and to assert any available defense; and the rights to present evidence during presentencing proceedings and the rights of the accused to testify under oath, make an unsworn statement, and have counsel make a statement on behalf of the accused. These explanations must be made regardless of the intentions of the accused as to testifying and pleading.

Defense counsel should try to obtain complete knowledge of the facts of the case before advising the accused, and should give the accused a candid opinion of the merits of the case.

(C) *Preparation for trial.* Defense counsel may have the assistance of trial counsel in obtaining the presence of witnesses and evidence for the defense. *See* R.C.M. 703.

Defense counsel should consider the elements of proof of the offenses alleged and the pertinent rules of evidence to ensure that evidence that the defense plans to introduce is admissible and to be prepared to object to inadmissible evidence offered by the prosecution.

Defense counsel should: prepare to make an opening statement of the defense case (*see* R.C.M. 913(b)); and prepare to examine and cross-examine witnesses, and to make final argument on the findings and, if necessary, on sentencing (*see* R.C.M. 919; 1001(h)).

(D) *Trial.* Defense counsel should represent and protect the interests of the accused at trial.

(E) *Post-trial duties.*

(i) *Deferment of confinement.* If the accused is sentenced to confinement, the defense counsel must explain to the accused the right to request the convening authority to defer service of the sentence to confinement and assist the accused in making such a request if the accused chooses to make one. *See* R.C.M. 1103.

(ii) *Post-trial motions.* The defense counsel should file post-trial motions for any issue that is reasonably raised, to include corrections of the record and motions to set aside the findings based on legally insufficient evidence.

(iii) *Submission of matters.* If the accused is convicted, the defense counsel may submit to the convening authority matters for consideration in deciding whether to modify the findings or sentence, if authorized. *See* R.C.M. 1109-10. Defense counsel should discuss with the accused the right to submit matters to the convening authority and the powers of the convening authority in taking action on the case. *See* R.C.M. 1106. Defense counsel may also submit a brief of any matters counsel believes should be considered on further review.

(iv) *Appellate advice.* Defense counsel must explain to the accused the rights to appellate review that apply in the case, and advise the accused concerning the exercise of those rights. Defense counsel should explain the review authority of the Court of Criminal Appeals, advise the accused of the right to be represented by counsel before it, and if applicable, the time period allowed to file an appeal of right. *See* R.C.M. 1202 and 1203. Defense counsel should also explain the possibility of further review by the Court of Appeals for the Armed Forces and the Supreme Court. *See* R.C.M. 1204 and 1205.

If the case may be examined in the office of the Judge Advocate General under Article 65, defense counsel should explain the nature of such review to the accused. *See* R.C.M. 1201(d)(1) and (e).

Defense counsel must explain the consequences of waiver of appellate review, when applicable, and, if the accused elects to waive appellate review, defense counsel will assist in preparing the waiver. *See* R.C.M. 1115. If the accused waives appellate review, or if it is not available, defense counsel should explain that the case will be reviewed by an attorney designated by the Judge Advocate General. *See* R.C.M. 1201.

The accused should be advised of the right to apply to the Judge Advocate General for relief after final review under Article 69 when such review is available, the applicable time period for making such an application, and the opportunity for further review by the Court of Criminal Appeals. *See* R.C.M. 1201

(F) *Associate or assistant defense counsel.* Associate or assistant counsel may act in that capacity only under the supervision and by the general direction of the defense counsel. A detailed defense counsel becomes associate defense counsel when the accused has individual military or civilian counsel and detailed counsel is not excused. Although assistant and associate counsel act under the general supervision of the defense counsel, subject to R.C.M. 805(c), assistant and associate defense counsel may act without such supervision when circumstances require. *See, e.g.*, R.C.M. 805(c). Unless the contrary appears, all acts of an assistant or associate defense counsel are presumed to have been done under the supervision of the defense counsel.).

(e) *Interpreters, reporters, escorts, bailiffs, clerks, guards, and orderlies.*

(1) *Qualifications.* The qualifications of interpreters and reporters may be prescribed by the Secretary concerned. Any person who is not disqualified under paragraph (e)(2) of this rule may serve as escort, bailiff, clerk, guard, or orderly, subject to removal by the military judge.

(2) *Disqualifications.* In addition to any disqualifications which may be prescribed by the Secretary concerned, no person shall act as interpreter, reporter, escort, bailiff, clerk, guard, or orderly in any case in which that person is or has been in the same case:

(A) The accuser;

(B) A witness;

(C) An investigating or preliminary hearing officer;

(D) Counsel for any party; or

(E) A member of the court-martial or of any earlier court-martial of which the trial is a rehearing or new or other trial.

(3) *Duties.* In addition to such other duties as the Secretary concerned may prescribe, the following persons may perform the following duties.

(A) *Interpreters.* Interpreters shall interpret for the court-martial or for an accused who does not speak or understand English.

Discussion

The accused also may retain an unofficial interpreter without expense to the United States.

(B) *Reporters.* Reporters shall record the proceedings and testimony and shall transcribe them so as to comply with the requirements for the record of trial as prescribed in these rules.

(C) *Others.* Other personnel detailed for the assistance of the court-martial shall have such duties as may be imposed by the military judge.

(4) *Payment of reporters, interpreters.* The Secretary concerned may prescribe regulations for the payment of allowances, expenses, per diem, and compensation of reporters and interpreters.

Discussion

See R.C.M. 807 regarding oaths for reporters, interpreters, and escorts.

(f) *Action upon discovery of disqualification or lack of qualifications.* Any person who discovers that a person detailed to a court-martial is disqualified or lacks the qualifications specified by this rule shall cause a report of the matter to be made before the court-martial is first in session to the convening authority or, if discovered later, to the military judge.

Rule 503. Detailing members, military judge, and counsel, and designating military magistrates

(a) *Members.*

(1) *In general.* The convening authority shall—

(A) detail qualified persons as members for courts-martial in accordance with the criteria described in Article 25;

(B) state whether the military judge is—

(i) authorized to impanel a specified number of alternate members; or

(ii) authorized to impanel alternate members only if, after the exercise of all challenges, excess members remain; and

(C) provide a list of the detailed members to the military judge to randomize in accordance with R.C.M. 911.

Discussion

The following persons are subject to challenge under R.C.M. 912(f) and should not be detailed as members: any person who is, in the same case, an accuser, witness, preliminary hearing officer, or counsel for any party or witness; any person who, in the case of a new trial, other trial, or rehearing, was a member of any court-martial which previously heard the case; any person who is junior to the accused, unless this is unavoidable; or any person who is in arrest or confinement.

The convening authority should detail a sufficient number of qualified persons to allow for the randomization process in R.C.M. 911.

A military judge may not impanel alternate members unless expressly authorized by the convening authority. *See* Article 29. The procedure to be used by the military judge to impanel members and alternate members is specified in R.C.M. 912A.

(2) *Member election by enlisted accused.* An enlisted accused may, before assembly, request orally on the record or in writing that the membership of the court-

martial to which that accused's case has been referred be comprised entirely of officers or of at least one-third enlisted members. If such a request is made, the court-martial membership must be consistent with the accused's request unless eligible members cannot be obtained because of physical conditions or military exigencies. If the appropriate number of members cannot be obtained, the court-martial may be assembled and the members impaneled, and the trial may proceed without them, but the convening authority shall make a detailed written explanation why such members could not be obtained which must be appended to the record of trial.

Discussion

When an enlisted accused makes a request for either all-officer members or at least one-third enlisted members, the convening authority may need to:

(1) Detail an additional number of officers or enlisted members to the court-martial and, if appropriate, relieve an appropriate number of officers or enlisted persons previously detailed;

(2) Withdraw the charges from the court-martial to which they were originally referred and refer them to a court-martial which includes the proper proportion of officers or enlisted members; or

(3) Advise the court-martial before which the charges are then pending to proceed in the absence of officers or enlisted members if eligible officers or enlisted members cannot be detailed because of physical conditions or military exigencies.

When the accused elects one-third enlisted members, the military judge must ensure there are at least two enlisted members for a special court-martial and at least three enlisted members for a non-capital general court-martial. There must be at least two enlisted members in a general court-martial where the number of members falls to six as a result of excusals after impanelment. *See* Article 29.

---

(3) *Members from another command or armed force.* A convening authority may detail as members of general and special courts-martial persons under that convening authority's command or made available by their commander, even if those persons are members of an armed force different from that of the convening authority or accused.

Discussion

Concurrence of the proper commander may be oral and need not be shown by the record of trial.

Members should ordinarily be of the same armed force as the accused. When a court-martial composed of members of different armed forces is selected, at least a majority of the members should be of the same armed force as the accused unless impracticable. For purposes of this non-binding policy, members of the Department of the Air Force are treated as being in the same armed force.

---

(4) This subsection does not apply to charges referred to a special court-martial consisting of a military judge alone under Article 16(c)(2)(A).

(b) *Military judge.*

(1) *By whom detailed.* The military judge shall be detailed, in accordance with regulations of the Secretary concerned, by a person assigned as a military judge and directly responsible to the Judge Advocate General or the Judge Advocate General's designee. The authority to detail military judges may be delegated to persons assigned as military judges. If authority to detail military judges has been delegated to a military judge, that military judge may detail himself or herself as military judge for a court-martial.

(2) *Record of detail.* The order detailing a military judge shall be reduced to writing and included in the record of trial or announced orally on the record at the court-martial. The writing or announcement shall indicate by whom the military judge was detailed. The Secretary concerned may require that the order be reduced to writing.

(3) *Military judge from a different armed force.* A military judge from one armed force may be detailed to a court-martial convened in a different armed force, a combatant command or joint command when permitted by the Judge Advocate General of the armed force of which the military judge is a member. The Judge Advocate General may delegate authority to make military judges available for this purpose.

(4) *Military magistrate.* If authorized under regulations of the Secretary concerned, a detailed military judge may designate a military magistrate to perform pre-referral duties under R.C.M. 309, and, with the consent of the parties, to preside over a special court-martial consisting of a military judge alone under Article 16(c)(2)(A).

(c) *Counsel.*

(1) *By whom detailed.* Trial and defense counsel, assistant trial and defense counsel, and associate

defense counsel shall be detailed in accordance with these rules and the regulations of the Secretary concerned. If authority to detail counsel has been delegated to a person, that person may detail himself or herself as counsel for a court-martial. For each general and special court-martial for which charges and specifications were referred by special trial counsel, a special trial counsel shall be detailed as trial counsel, and, in accordance with regulations prescribed by the Secretary concerned, a special trial counsel may detail other trial counsel who are judge advocates. In a capital case, counsel learned in the law applicable to such cases under R.C.M. 502(d)(2)(C) shall be assigned in accordance with regulations of the Secretary concerned.

(2) *Record of detail.* The order detailing a counsel shall be reduced to writing and included in the record of trial or announced orally on the record at the court-martial. The writing or announcement shall indicate by whom the counsel was detailed. The Secretary concerned may require that the order be reduced to writing.

(3) *Counsel from a different armed force.* A person from one armed force may be detailed to serve as counsel in a court-martial in a different armed force, a combatant command or joint command when permitted by the Judge Advocate General of the armed force of which the counsel is a member. The Judge Advocate General may delegate authority to make persons available for this purpose.

Rule 504. Convening courts-martial

(a) *In general.* A court-martial is created by a convening order of the convening authority.

(b) *Who may convene courts-martial.*

(1) *General courts-martial.* Unless otherwise limited by superior competent authority, general courts-martial may be convened by persons occupying positions designated in Article 22(a) and by any commander designated by the Secretary concerned or empowered by the President. A commanding officer shall not be considered an accuser solely due to the role of the commanding officer in convening a special or general court-martial to which charges and specifications were referred by a special trial counsel.

Discussion

The authority to convene courts-martial is independent of rank and is retained as long as the convening authority remains a commander in one of the designated positions. The rules by which command devolves are found in regulations of the Secretary concerned.

---

(2) *Special courts-martial.* Unless otherwise limited by superior competent authority, special courts-martial may be convened by persons occupying positions designated in Article 23(a) and by commanders designated by the Secretary concerned.

Discussion

See the discussion accompanying R.C.M. 504(b)(1). Persons authorized to convene general courts-martial may also convene special courts-martial.

(A) *Definition.* For purposes of Articles 23 and 24, a command or unit is "separate or detached" when isolated or removed from the immediate disciplinary control of a superior in such manner as to make its commander the person held by superior commanders primarily responsible for discipline. "Separate or detached" is used in a disciplinary sense and not necessarily in a tactical or physical sense. A subordinate joint command or joint task force is ordinarily considered to be "separate or detached."

Discussion

The power of a commander of a separate or detached unit to convene courts-martial, like that of any other commander, may be limited by superior competent authority.

(B) *Determination.* If a commander is in doubt whether the command is separate or detached, the matter shall be determined:

(i) In the Army, Air Force, or Space Force, by the officer exercising general court-martial jurisdiction over the command; or

(ii) In the Naval Service or Coast Guard, by the flag or general officer in command or the senior officer present who designated the detachment; or

(iii) In a combatant command or joint command, by the officer exercising general court-martial jurisdiction over the command.

(3) *Summary courts-martial. See* R.C.M. 1302(a).

Discussion

See the discussion accompanying R.C.M. 504(b)(1).

(4) *Delegation prohibited.* The power to convene courts-martial may not be delegated.

(c) *Disqualification.*

(1) *Accuser.* An accuser may not convene a general or special court-martial for the trial of the person accused.

Discussion

See also Article 1(9); R.C.M. 307(a), 601(c). *But see* R.C.M. 1302(b) (accuser may convene a summary court-martial).

(2) *Other.* A convening authority junior in rank to an accuser may not convene a general or special court-martial for the trial of the accused unless that convening authority is superior in command to the accuser. A convening authority junior in command to an accuser may not convene a general or special court-martial for the trial of the accused.

(3) *Action when disqualified.* When a commander who would otherwise convene a general or special court-martial is disqualified in a case, the charges shall be forwarded to a superior competent authority for disposition. That authority may personally dispose of the charges or forward the charges to another convening authority who is superior in rank to the accuser, or, if in the same chain of command, who is superior in command to the accuser.

Discussion

See also R.C.M. 401(c).

(d) *Convening orders.*

(1) *General and special courts-martial.*

(A) A convening order for a general or special court-martial shall—

(i) designate the type of court-martial; and

(ii) detail the members, if any, in accordance with R.C.M. 503(a);

(B) A convening order may designate where the court-martial will meet.

(C) If the convening authority has been designated by the Secretary concerned, the convening order shall so state.

(2) *Summary courts-martial.* A convening order for a summary court-martial shall designate that it is a summary court-martial and detail the summary court-martial, and may designate where the court-martial will meet. If the convening authority has been designated by the Secretary concerned, the convening order shall so state.

Discussion

See also R.C.M. 1302(c).

(3) *Additional matters.* Additional matters to be included in convening orders may be prescribed by the Secretary concerned.

(e) *Place.* The convening authority shall ensure that an appropriate location and facilities for courts-martial are provided.

Rule 505. Changes of members, military judge, and counsel

(a) *In general.* Subject to this rule, the members, military judge, military magistrate, and counsel may be changed by an authority competent to detail or designate such persons. Members also may be excused as provided in clause (c)(1)(B)(ii) and subparagraph (c)(2)(A).

Discussion

Changes of the members of the court-martial should be kept to a minimum. If extensive changes are necessary and no session of the court-martial has begun, it may be appropriate to withdraw the charges from one court-martial and refer them to another. *See* R.C.M. 604

(b) *Procedure.* When new persons are added as members or counsel or when substitutions are made as to any members or counsel or the military judge or military magistrate, such persons shall be detailed or designated in accordance with R.C.M. 503. An order changing the members of the court-martial, except one which excuses members without replacement, shall be reduced to writing before certification of the record of trial.

Discussion

When members or counsel have been excused and the excusal is not reduced to writing, the excusal should be announced on the record. A member who has been temporarily excused need not be formally reappointed to the court-martial.

(c) *Changes of members.*

(1) *Before assembly.*

(A) *By convening authority.* Before the court-martial is assembled, the convening authority may change the members detailed to the court-martial without showing cause. New members shall be detailed in accordance with R.C.M. 503(a).

(B) *By convening authority's delegate.*

(i) *Delegation.* The convening authority may delegate, under regulations of the Secretary concerned, authority to excuse individual members to the staff judge advocate or legal officer or other principal assistant to the convening authority.

(ii) *Limitations.* Before the court-martial is assembled, the convening authority's delegate may excuse members without cause shown; however, no more than one-third of the total number of members detailed by the convening authority may be excused by the convening authority's delegate in any one court-martial. After assembly the convening authority's delegate may not excuse members.

(2) *After assembly.*

(A) *Excusal.* After assembly no member may be excused, except:

(i) By the convening authority for good cause shown on the record;

(ii) By the military judge for good cause shown on the record;

(iii) As a result of challenge under R.C.M. 912; or

(iv) By the military judge when the number of members is in excess of the number of members required for impanelment.

Discussion

R.C.M. 912A sets forth the procedures for excusing excess members.

(B) *New members.* In accordance with R.C.M. 503(a), new members may be detailed after assembly only when, as a result of excusals under R.C.M. 505(c)(2)(A), the number of members of the court-martial is reduced below the number of members required under R.C.M. 501(a), or the number of enlisted members, when the accused has made a timely written request for enlisted members, is reduced below one-third of the total membership.

(d) *Changes of detailed counsel.*

(1) *Trial counsel.* An authority competent to detail trial counsel may change trial counsel and any assistant trial counsel at any time without showing cause.

(2) *Defense counsel.*

(A) *Before formation of attorney-client relationship.* Before an attorney-client relationship has been formed between the accused and detailed defense counsel or associate or assistant defense counsel, an authority competent to detail defense counsel may excuse or change such counsel without showing cause.

(B) *After formation of attorney-client relationship.* After an attorney-client relationship has been formed between the accused and detailed defense counsel or associate or assistant defense counsel, an authority competent to detail such counsel may excuse or change such counsel only:

(i) Under R.C.M. 506(b)(3);

(ii) Upon request of the accused or application for withdrawal by such counsel under R.C.M. 506(c); or

(iii) For other good cause shown on the record

(e) *Change of military judge or military magistrate.*

(1) *Before assembly.* Before the court-martial is assembled, the military judge or military magistrate may be changed by an authority competent to detail the military judge or to designate the military magistrate, without cause shown on the record.

(2) *After assembly.* After the court-martial is assembled, the military judge or military magistrate may be changed by an authority competent to detail the military judge or to designate the military magistrate only when, as a result of disqualification under R.C.M. 902 or for good cause shown, the previously detailed military judge or previously designated military magistrate is unable to proceed.

Discussion

A change in the military magistrate after assembly does not require the consent of the parties. *See* R.C.M. 503.

(f) *Good cause*. For purposes of this rule, "good cause" includes physical disability, military exigency, and other extraordinary circumstances which render the member, counsel, or military judge or military magistrate unable to proceed with the court-martial within a reasonable time. "Good cause" does not include temporary inconveniences which are incident to normal conditions of military life.

Rule 506. Accused's rights to counsel

(a) *In general*.

(1) *Non-capital courts-martial*. The accused has the right to be represented before a non-capital general court-martial or a special court-martial by civilian counsel if retained by the accused at no expense to the Government, and either by the military counsel detailed under Article 27 or military counsel of the accused's own selection, if reasonably available. The accused is not entitled to be represented by more than one military counsel.

(2) *Capital courts-martial*. In a case referred with a special instruction that the case is to be tried as capital, the accused may be represented by more than one counsel. To the greatest extent practicable, in any capital case, at least one defense counsel shall, as determined by the Judge Advocate General, be learned in the law applicable to such cases under R.C.M. 502(d)(2)(C). If necessary, this counsel may be a civilian, and if so, may be compensated in accordance with regulations prescribed by the Secretary of Defense.

Discussion

The requirements of Article 27 are satisfied where an accused retains civilian counsel who is determined by the Judge Advocate General to be learned in the law applicable to capital cases in accordance with R.C.M. 502(d)(2)(C). Counsel learned in the law applicable to capital cases may be assigned prior to referral and should be considered for such assignment in a case in which a capital referral appears likely.

See R.C.M. 601(e) and 1004(b)(1) regarding special instructions for referral of capital cases.

(b) *Individual military counsel*.

(1) *Reasonably available*. Subject to this subsection, the Secretary concerned shall define "reasonably available." While so assigned, the following persons are not reasonably available to serve as individual military counsel because of the nature of their duties or positions:

(A) A general or flag officer;

(B) A trial or appellate military judge;

(C) A trial counsel;

(D) An appellate defense or government counsel;

(E) A principal legal advisor to a command, organization, or agency and, when such command, organization, or agency has general court-martial jurisdiction, the principal assistant of such an advisor;

(F) An instructor or student at a Service school or academy:

(G) A student at a college or university;

(H) A member of the staff of the Judge Advocate General of the Army, Navy, Air Force, Coast Guard, or the Staff Judge Advocate to the Commandant of the Marine Corps.

The Secretary concerned may determine other persons to be not reasonably available because of the nature or responsibilities of their assignments, geographic considerations, exigent circumstances, or military necessity. A person who is a member of an armed force different from that of which the accused is a member shall be reasonably available to serve as individual military counsel for such accused to the same extent as that person is available to serve as individual military counsel for an accused in the same armed force as the person requested. The Secretary concerned may prescribe circumstances under which exceptions may be made to the prohibitions in this subsection when merited by the existence of an attorney-client relationship regarding matters relating to a charge in question. However, if the attorney-client relationship arose solely because the counsel represented the accused on review under Article 70, this exception shall not apply.

(2) *Procedure*. Subject to this subsection, the Secretary concerned shall prescribe procedures for determining whether a requested person is "reasonably available" to act as individual military counsel. Requests for an individual military counsel shall be made by the accused or the detailed defense counsel through trial counsel to the convening authority. If the requested person is among those not reasonably available under paragraph (b)(1) of this rule or under regulations of the Secretary concerned, the convening authority shall deny the request and notify the accused, unless the accused asserts that there is an existing attorney-client relationship regarding a charge in

question or that the person requested will not, at the time of the trial or preliminary hearing for which requested, be among those so listed as not reasonably available. If the accused's request makes such a claim, or if the person is not among those so listed as not reasonably available, the convening authority shall forward the request to the commander or head of the organization, activity, or agency to which the requested person is assigned. That authority shall make an administrative determination whether the requested person is reasonably available in accordance with the procedure prescribed by the Secretary concerned. This determination is a matter within the sole discretion of that authority. An adverse determination may be reviewed upon request of the accused through that authority to the next higher commander or level of supervision, but no administrative review may be made which requires action at the departmental or higher level.

(3) *Excusal of detailed counsel.* If the accused is represented by individual military counsel, detailed defense counsel shall normally be excused. The authority who detailed defense counsel, as a matter of discretion, may approve a request from the accused that detailed defense counsel shall act as associate counsel. The action of the authority who detailed the counsel is subject to review only for abuse of discretion..

Discussion

A request under R.C.M. 506(b)(3) should be considered in light of the general statutory policy that the accused is not entitled to be represented by more than one military counsel. Among the factors that may be considered in the exercise of discretion are the seriousness of the case, retention of civilian defense counsel, complexity of legal or factual issues, and the detail of additional trial counsel.

See R.C.M. 905(b)(6) and 906(b)(2) as to motions concerning denial of a request for individual military counsel or retention of detailed counsel as associate counsel.

(c) *Excusal or withdrawal.* Except as otherwise provided in R.C.M. 505(d)(2) and paragraph (b)(3) of this rule, defense counsel may be excused only with the express consent of the accused, or by the military judge upon application for withdrawal by defense counsel for good cause shown.

(d) *Waiver.* The accused may expressly waive the right to be represented by counsel and may thereafter conduct the defense personally. Such waiver shall be accepted by the military judge only if the military judge finds that the accused is competent to understand the disadvantages of self-representation and that the waiver is voluntary and understanding. The military judge may require that a defense counsel remain present even if the accused waives counsel and conducts the defense personally. The right of the accused to conduct the defense personally may be revoked if the accused is disruptive or fails to follow basic rules of decorum and procedure.

(e) *Nonlawyer present.* Subject to the discretion of the military judge, the accused may have present and seated at the counsel table for purpose of consultation persons not qualified to serve as counsel under R.C.M. 502.

Discussion

See also Mil. R. Evid. 615 if the person is a potential witness in the case.

CHAPTER VI. REFERRAL, SERVICE, AMENDMENT, AND WITHDRAWAL OF CHARGES

Rule 601. Referral

(a) *In general.* Referral is the order of a convening authority or a special trial counsel that one or more charges and specifications against an accused will be tried by a specified court-martial.

Discussion

If a court-martial would be warranted but would be detrimental to the prosecution of a war or inimical to national security, see R.C.M. 401(d) and 407(b).

(b) *Who may refer.*

(1) Except as provided in R.C.M. 601(b)(2), any convening authority may refer charges to a court-martial convened by that convening authority or a predecessor, unless the power to do so has been withheld by superior competent authority.

(2) For charges over which a special trial counsel has exercised authority and has not deferred, only a special trial counsel may refer charges to a court-martial.

Discussion

See R.C.M. 306(a), 403, 404, 407, and 504.

The convening authority may be of any command, including a command different from that of the accused, but as a practical matter the accused must be subject to the orders of the convening authority or otherwise under the convening authority's control to assure the appearance of the accused at trial. The convening authority's power over the accused may be based upon agreements between the commanders concerned.

(c) *Disqualification.*

(1) Except as provided in R.C.M. 601(c)(2), an accuser may not refer charges to a general or special court-martial.

(2) A special trial counsel shall not be disqualified from referring charges to a general or special court-martial as a result of having preferred charges or having caused charges to be preferred.

Discussion

Convening authorities are not disqualified from referring charges by prior participation in the same case except when they have acted as accuser. For a definition of "accuser," see Article 1(9). A convening authority who is disqualified may forward the charges and allied papers for disposition by competent authority superior in rank or command. See R.C.M. 401(c) concerning actions which the superior may take.

See R.C.M. 1302 for rules relating to convening summary courts-martial.

(d) *When charges may be referred.*

(1) *Basis for referral.*

(A) Except as provided in R.C.M. 601(d)(1)(B), if the convening authority finds or is advised by a judge advocate that there is probable cause to believe that an offense triable by a court-martial has been committed and that the accused committed it, and that the specification alleges an offense, the convening authority may refer it. The finding may be based on hearsay in whole or in part. The convening authority or judge advocate may consider information from any source and shall not be limited to the information reviewed by any previous authority, but a case may not be referred to a general or special court-martial except in compliance with R.C.M. 601(d)(2) or (d)(3). The convening authority or judge advocate shall not be required before charges are referred to resolve legal issues, including objections to evidence, which may arise at trial.

(B) For offenses over which a special trial counsel has exercised authority and has not deferred, if a special trial counsel makes a written determination that each specification under a charge alleges an offense under the UCMJ, there is probable cause to believe that the accused committed the offense charged, and the court-martial would have jurisdiction over the accused and the offense, a special trial counsel may refer it. The finding may be based on hearsay in whole or in part. A special trial counsel may consider information from any source and shall not be limited to the information reviewed by any previous authority, but a case may not be referred to a general court-martial except in compliance with R.C.M. 601(d)(2) or (d)(3). A special trial counsel shall not be required before charges are referred to resolve legal issues, including objections to evidence, which may arise at trial.

Discussion

For a discussion of selection among alternative dispositions, see R.C.M. 306. The referral authority is not obliged to refer all charges that the evidence might support. The referral authority should consider the options and considerations under R.C.M. 306 and Appendix 2.1 (Disposition Guidance) in exercising the discretion to refer charges and specifications to court-martial.

---

(2) *Consideration.* Referral authorities shall consider whether the admissible evidence will probably be sufficient to obtain and sustain a conviction.

(3) *General courts-martial.* Charges may not be referred to a general court-martial unless there has been substantial compliance with the preliminary hearing requirements of R.C.M. 405 and:

(A) The convening authority has received the advice of the staff judge advocate required under R.C.M. 406(a)(1) and Article 34(a); or

(B) A special trial counsel has made a written determination as required under R.C.M. 406(b) and Article 34(c).

(4) *Special courts-martial.* Charges may not be referred to a special court-martial unless:

(A) The convening authority has consulted with a judge advocate as required under R.C.M. 406(a)(2) and Article 34(b); or

(B) A special trial counsel has made a written determination as required under R.C.M. 406(b) and Article 34(c).

Discussion

See R.C.M. 201(f)(2)(C) concerning limitations on referral of capital offenses to special courts-martial.

See R.C.M. 103(4) for the definition of the term "capital offense."

See R.C.M. 201(f)(2)(D)and (E) and R.C.M. 1301(c) concerning limitations on the referral of certain cases to special and summary courts-martial.

See R.C.M. 905(b)(1) and (e) for the rule regarding forfeiture for failure to object to a defect under this rule.

(e) *How charges shall be referred.*

(1) *Order, instructions.* Referral shall be by the personal order of the referral authority.

(A) *Capital cases.* If a case is to be tried as a capital case, the referral authority shall so indicate by including a special instruction on the charge sheet in accordance with R.C.M. 1004(b)(1).

(B) *Special court-martial consisting of a military judge alone.* If a case is to be tried as a special court-martial consisting of a military judge alone under Article 16(c)(2)(A), the referral shall so indicate by including a special instruction on the charge sheet prior to arraignment.

Discussion

Under the UCMJ as amended though the James M. Inhofe National Defense Authorization Act for Fiscal Year 2023, Pub. L. No. 117-263 136 Stat. 2395 (2022), a special trial counsel may not refer a charge to a special court-martial consisting of a military judge alone. *See* Article 16(c)(2)(A), 10 U.S.C. § 816(c)(2)(A) (2019) ("if the case is so referred by the *convening authority* . . . .") (emphasis added)."

(C) *Other instructions.* The referral authority may include any other additional instructions in the order as may be required.

Discussion

Referral is ordinarily evidenced by an indorsement on the charge sheet. Although the indorsement should be completed on all copies of the charge sheet, only the original must be signed. The signature may be that of a person acting by the order or direction of the referral authority. In such a case, the signature element or block should reflect the signer's authority.

If, for any reason, charges are referred to a court-martial different from that to which they were originally referred, the new referral is ordinarily made by a new indorsement attached to the original charge sheet. The previous indorsement should be lined out and initialed by the person signing the new referral. The original indorsement should not be obliterated. *See also* R.C.M. 604.

The failure to include a special instruction that a case is to be tried as a capital case at the time of the referral does not bar the referral authority from later adding the required special instruction, provided that the referral authority has otherwise complied with the applicable notice requirements. If the accused demonstrates specific prejudice from such failure to include the special instruction, a continuance or a recess is an adequate remedy. *See* R.C.M. 1004(b)(1).

For limitations regarding offenses that may be referred to a special court-martial consisting of a military judge alone, see R.C.M. 201(f)(2)(E).

If the only officer present in a command refers the charges to a summary court-martial and serves as the summary court-martial under R.C.M. 1302, the indorsement should be completed with the additional comments, "only officer present in the command."

Any special instructions must be stated in the referral indorsement.

When the charges have been referred to a court-martial, the indorsed charge sheet and allied papers should be promptly transmitted to the trial counsel.

---

(2) *Joinder of offenses.* In the discretion of the referral authority, two or more offenses charged against an accused may be referred to the same court-martial for trial, whether serious or minor offenses or both, regardless of whether the offenses are connected. Additional charges may be joined with other charges for a single trial at any time before arraignment if all necessary procedural requirements concerning the additional charges have been complied with. After arraignment of the accused upon charges, no additional charges may be referred to the same trial without consent of the accused.

(3) *Joinder of accused.* Allegations against two or more accused may be referred for joint trial if the accused are alleged to have participated in the same act or transaction or in the same series of acts or transactions constituting an offense or offenses. Such accused may be charged in one or more specifications together or separately, and every accused need not be charged in each specification. Related allegations against two or more accused which may be proved by substantially the same evidence may be referred to a common trial.

Discussion

A joint offense is one committed by two or more persons acting together with a common intent. Joint offenses may be referred for joint trial, along with all related offenses against each of the accused. A common trial may be used when the evidence of several offenses committed by several accused separately is essentially the same, even though the offenses were not jointly committed. See the Discussion accompanying R.C.M. 307(c)(5). Convening authorities should consider that joint and common trials may be complicated by procedural and evidentiary rules.

(f) *Superior convening authorities.* Except as otherwise provided in these rules, a superior competent authority may cause charges, whether or not referred, to be transmitted to the authority for further consideration, including, if appropriate, referral.

(g) *Parallel convening authorities.*

(1) Except as provided in R.C.M. 601(g)(2), if it is impracticable for the original convening authority to continue exercising authority over the charges, the convening authority may cause the charges, even if referred, to be transmitted to a parallel convening authority. This transmittal must be in writing and in accordance with such regulations as the Secretary concerned may prescribe. Subsequent actions taken by the parallel convening authority are within the sole discretion of that convening authority.

(2) For offenses over which a special trial counsel has exercised authority and has not deferred, a convening authority seeking to transfer charges to a parallel convening authority may do so in accordance with these rules and such regulations prescribed by the Secretary concerned.

Discussion

Parallel convening authorities are those convening authorities that possess the same court-martial jurisdiction authority. Examples of permissible transmittal of charges under this rule include the transmittal from a general court-martial convening authority to another general court-martial convening authority, or from one special court-martial convening authority to another special court-martial convening authority. It would be impracticable for an original convening authority to continue exercising authority over the charges, for example, when a command is being decommissioned or inactivated, or when deploying or redeploying and the accused is remaining behind. If charges have been referred, there is no requirement that the charges be withdrawn or dismissed prior to transfer. *See* R.C.M. 604. In the event that the case has been referred, the receiving convening authority may adopt the original court-martial convening order, including the court-martial panel selected to hear the case as indicated in that convening order. When charges are transmitted under this rule, no recommendation as to disposition may be made.

The transfer process is subject to the limitations contained in these rules, including the requirement that only a special trial counsel may withdraw, dismiss, or refer charges over which a special trial counsel has exercised authority and has not deferred.

Rule 602. Service of charges

(a) *Service of charges.* Trial counsel detailed to the court-martial to which charges have been referred for trial shall cause to be served upon each accused a copy of the charge sheet.

Discussion

Trial counsel should comply with this rule immediately upon receipt of the charges. Whenever after service the charges are amended or changed the trial counsel must give notice of the changes to the defense counsel. Whenever such amendments or changes add a new party, a new offense, or substantially new allegations, the charge sheet so amended or changed must be served anew. *See* R.C.M. 603.

Service may be made only upon the accused; substitute service upon defense counsel is insufficient. The trial counsel should promptly inform the defense counsel when charges have been served.

If the accused has questions when served with charges, the accused should be told to discuss the matter with defense counsel.

(b) *Commencement of trial.*

(1) Except in time of war, no person may, over objection, be brought to trial by general or special court-martial—including an Article 39(a) session—within the following time periods:

(A) In a general court-martial, from the time of service of charges under subsection (a) through the fifth day after the date of service.

(B) In a special court-martial, from the time of service of charges under subsection (a) through the third day after the date of service.

(2) If the first session of the court-martial occurs before the end of the applicable period under paragraph (1), the military judge shall, at the beginning of that session, inquire as to whether the defense objects to proceeding during the applicable period. If the defense objects, the trial may not proceed. If the defense does not object, the issue is waived.

Rule 603. Changes to charges and specifications

(a) *In general.* Any person forwarding, acting upon, or prosecuting charges on behalf of the United States except a preliminary hearing officer appointed under R.C.M. 405 may make major and minor changes to charges or specifications in accordance with this rule.

(b) *Major and minor changes defined.*

(1) *Major changes.* A major change is one that adds a party, an offense, or a substantial matter not fairly included in the preferred charge or specification, or that is likely to mislead the accused as to the offense charged.

(2) *Minor changes.* A minor change in a charge or specification is any change other than a major change.

Discussion

Minor changes include those necessary to correct inartfully drafted or redundant specifications; to correct a misnaming of the accused; to allege the proper article; or to correct other slight errors. Minor changes also include those which reduce the seriousness of an offense, as when the value of an allegedly stolen item in a larceny specification is reduced, or when a desertion specification is amended and alleges only unauthorized absence.

(c) *Major and minor changes before referral.* Before referral, subject to paragraph (d)(2), a major or minor change may be made to any charge or specification.

(d) *Major changes after referral or preliminary hearing.*

(1) After referral, a major change may not be made over the objection of the accused unless the charge or specification is withdrawn, amended, and referred anew.

(2) In the case of a general court-martial, a major change made to a charge or specification after the preliminary hearing may require reopening the preliminary hearing in accordance with R.C.M. 405.

Discussion

In the case of a general court-martial, a preliminary hearing under R.C.M. 405 will be necessary if the charge as amended or changed was not covered in a prior preliminary hearing. If the substance of the charge or specification as amended or changed has not been referred or, in the case of a general court-martial, considered at a preliminary hearing, a new referral and, if appropriate, preliminary hearing are necessary. When charges are re-referred, they must be served anew under R.C.M. 602.

(e) *Minor changes after referral.* Minor changes may be made to the charges and specifications after referral and before arraignment. After arraignment, the military judge may, upon motion, permit minor changes in the charges and specifications at any time before findings are announced if no substantial right of the accused is prejudiced.

Discussion

Charges and specifications forwarded or referred for trial should be free from defects of form and substance. Scriveners' errors may be corrected without the charge being sworn anew by the accuser. Other changes should be signed and sworn to by an accuser. All changes in the charges should be initialed by the person who makes the changes. Except for charges over which a special trial counsel has exercised authority and has not deferred, a trial counsel acting under this provision ordinarily should consult with the convening authority before making any changes that, even though minor, change the nature or seriousness of the offense.

Rule 604. Withdrawal of charges

(a) *Withdrawal.*

(1) Except as provided in R.C.M. 604(a)(2), the convening authority or a superior competent authority may for any reason cause any charge or specification to be withdrawn from a court-martial at any time before findings are announced.

(2) For charges over which a special trial counsel has exercised authority and has not deferred, only a special trial counsel may withdraw or cause to be withdrawn

any charge or specification from the court-martial at any time before findings are announced.

Discussion

Charges that are withdrawn from a court-martial should be dismissed (*see* R.C.M. 401(c)(1)) unless it is intended to refer them anew promptly or to forward them to another authority for disposition.

Charges should not be withdrawn from a court-martial arbitrarily or unfairly to an accused. *See also* R.C.M. 604 (b).

Some or all charges and specifications may be withdrawn. In a joint or common trial the withdrawal may be limited to charges against one or some of the accused.

Except for charges over which a special trial counsel has exercised authority and has not deferred, charges that have been properly referred to a court-martial may be withdrawn only by the direction of the convening authority or a superior competent authority in the exercise of that officer's independent judgment. The trial counsel may withdraw charges or specifications by lining out the affected charges or specifications, renumbering remaining charges or specifications as necessary, and initialing the changes. Charges and specifications withdrawn before commencement of trial will not be brought to the attention of the members. When charges or specifications are withdrawn after they have come to the attention of the members, the military judge must instruct them that the withdrawn charges or specifications may not be considered for any reason.

(b) *Referral of withdrawn charges*. Charges that have been withdrawn from a court-martial may be referred to another court-martial unless the withdrawal was for an improper reason. Charges withdrawn after the introduction of evidence on the general issue of guilt may be referred to another court-martial only if the withdrawal was necessitated by urgent and unforeseen military necessity.

Discussion

See also R.C.M. 915 (Mistrial).

When charges that have been withdrawn from a court-martial are referred to another court-martial, the reasons for the withdrawal and later referral should be included in the record of the later court-martial, if the later referral is more onerous to the accused. Therefore, if further prosecution is contemplated at the time of the withdrawal, the reasons for the withdrawal should be included in or attached to the record of the earlier proceeding.

Improper reasons for withdrawal include an intent to interfere with the free exercise by the accused of constitutional rights or rights provided under the UCMJ, or with the impartiality of a court-martial. A withdrawal is improper if it was not directed personally and independently by the convening authority, a special trial counsel, or a superior competent authority.

Whether the reason for a withdrawal is proper, for purposes of the propriety of a later referral, depends in part on the stage in the proceedings at which the withdrawal takes place. Before arraignment, there are many reasons for a withdrawal that will not preclude another referral. These include receipt of additional charges, absence of the accused, reconsideration by the convening authority, a special trial counsel, or a superior competent authority of the seriousness of the offenses, questions concerning the mental capacity of the accused, and routine duty rotation of the personnel constituting the court-martial. Charges withdrawn after arraignment may be referred to another court-martial under some circumstances. For example, it is permissible to refer charges that were withdrawn pursuant to a plea agreement if the accused fails to fulfill the terms of the agreement. *See* R.C.M. 705. Charges withdrawn after some evidence on the general issue of guilt is introduced may be re-referred only under the narrow circumstances described in the rule.

CHAPTER VII. PRETRIAL MATTERS

Rule 701. Discovery

(a) *Disclosure by trial counsel.* Except as otherwise provided in R.C.M. 701(f) and (g)(2), and unless previously disclosed to the defense, trial counsel shall provide the following to the defense:

(1) *Papers accompanying charges; convening orders; statements.* As soon as practicable after service of charges under R.C.M. 602, the trial counsel shall provide the defense with copies of, or, if extraordinary circumstances make it impracticable to provide copies, permit the defense to inspect:

Discussion

The purpose of this rule is to ensure the prompt, efficient, and fair administration of military justice by encouraging early and broad disclosure of information by the parties. Discovery in the military justice system is intended to eliminate pretrial gamesmanship, minimize pretrial litigation, and reduce the potential for surprise and delay at trial. Parties to a court-martial should consider these purposes when evaluating pretrial disclosure issues. In addition to this rule, other sources, to include other Rules for Courts-Martial, case law, and rules of professional conduct, may require disclosure of additional information or evidence.

(A) All papers that accompanied the charges presented to the convening authority;

(B) Any written determination made by a special trial counsel pursuant to Article 34;

(C) Any written recommendation from a commander as to disposition;

(D) Any papers sent with charges upon a rehearing or new trial;

(E) The convening order and any amending orders; and

(F) Any sworn or signed statement relating to an offense charged in the case that is in the possession of trial counsel.

(2) *Documents, tangible objects, reports.*

(A) After service of charges, upon request of the defense, the Government shall permit the defense to inspect any books, papers, documents, data, photographs, tangible objects, buildings, or places, or copies of portions of these items, if the item is within the possession, custody, or control of military authorities and—

(i) the item is relevant to defense preparation;

(ii) the Government intends to use the item in the case-in-chief at trial;

(iii) the Government anticipates using the item in rebuttal; or

(iv) the item was obtained from or belongs to the accused.

(B) After service of charges, upon request of the defense, the Government shall permit the defense to inspect the results or reports of physical or mental examinations, and of any scientific tests or experiments, or copies thereof, which are within the possession, custody, or control of military authorities, the existence of which is known or by the exercise of due diligence may become known to the trial counsel if

(i) the item is relevant to defense preparation;

(ii) the Government intends to use the item in the case-in-chief at trial; or

(iii) the Government anticipates using the item in rebuttal.

Discussion

For specific rules concerning certain mental examinations of the accused or third party patients, see R.C.M. 701(f), R.C.M. 706, Mil. R. Evid. 302 and Mil. R. Evid. 513.

---

(3) *Witnesses.* Before the beginning of trial on the merits, trial counsel shall notify the defense of the names and contact information of the witnesses the trial counsel intends to call:

(A) In the prosecution case-in-chief; and

(B) To rebut a defense of alibi, innocent ingestion, or lack of mental responsibility, when the trial counsel has received timely notice under R.C.M. 701(b)(1) or (2).

Discussion

Such notice should be in writing except when impracticable.

---

(4) *Prior convictions of accused offered on the merits.* Before arraignment, the trial counsel shall notify the defense of any records of prior civilian or

court-martial convictions of the accused of which the trial counsel is aware and which the trial counsel may offer on the merits for any purpose, including impeachment, and shall permit the defense to inspect such records when they are in the trial counsel's possession.

(5) *Information to be offered at sentencing.* Upon request of the defense, the trial counsel shall:

(A) Permit the defense to inspect such written material as will be presented by the prosecution at the presentencing proceedings; and

(B) Notify the defense of the names and contact information of the witnesses the trial counsel intends to call at the presentencing proceedings under R.C.M. 1001(b).

(6) *Evidence favorable to the defense.* The trial counsel shall, as soon as practicable, disclose to the defense the existence of evidence known to the trial counsel which reasonably tends to—

(A) Negate the guilt of the accused of an offense charged;

(B) Reduce the degree of guilt of the accused of an offense charged;

(C) Reduce the punishment; or

(D) Adversely affect the credibility of any prosecution witness or evidence.

Discussion

Nothing in this rule prohibits trial counsel or other Government counsel from disclosing information earlier than required by this rule or in addition to that required by this rule.

In addition to the matters required to be disclosed under subsection (a) of this rule, the Government is required to notify the defense of or provide to the defense certain information under other rules. Mil. R. Evid. 506 covers the disclosure of unclassified information which is under the control of the Government. Mil. R. Evid. 505 covers disclosure of classified information.

Other Rules for Courts-Martial and Military Rules of Evidence concern disclosure of other specific matters. *See* R.C.M. 308 (identification of accuser), 405 (report of Article 32 preliminary hearing), 706(c)(3)(B) (mental examination of accused), 914 (production of certain statements), and 1004(b)(1) (aggravating factors in capital cases); Mil.R. Evid. 301(d)(2) (notification of immunity or leniency to witnesses), 302 (mental examination of accused), 304(d) (statements by accused), 311(d)(1) (evidence seized from accused), 321(d)(1) (evidence based on lineups), 507 (identity of informants), 612 (memoranda used to refresh recollection), and 613(a) (prior inconsistent statements).

Requirements for notice of intent to use certain evidence are found in: Mil. R. Evid. 202(b) (judicial notice of foreign law), 301(d)(2) (notification of immunity or leniency to witnesses), 304(d) (notice of intent to use undisclosed confessions), 304(f)(3) (testimony of accused for limited purpose on confession), 311(d) (notice of intent to use undisclosed evidence seized), 311(d)(6) (testimony of accused for limited purpose on seizures), 321(d)(3)(notice of intent to use undisclosed line-up evidence), 321(d)(5) (testimony of accused for limited purpose of line-ups), 404(b) (intent to use evidence of other crimes, wrongs, or acts), 412(c)(1) and (2) (intent of defense to use evidence of sexual behavior or sexual predisposition of a victim); 505(i) (intent to disclose classified information), 506(h) (intent to disclose privileged government information), and 609(b) (intent to impeach with conviction over 10 years old).

In accordance with R.C.M. 701(d), trial counsel have a continuing duty to identify and disclose information that is favorable to the defense throughout the prosecution of the alleged offenses against the accused. In general, trial counsel should exercise due diligence and good faith in learning about any evidence favorable to the defense known to others acting on the Government's behalf in the case, including military, other governmental, and civilian law enforcement authorities.

In the spirit of eliminating "gamesmanship" from the discovery process, trial counsel should not avoid pursuit of information or evidence because the counsel believes it will damage the prosecution's case or aid the accused, nor should counsel intentionally attempt to obscure information identified pursuant to this subsection by disclosing it as part of a large volume of materials.

(b) *Disclosure by the defense.* Except as otherwise provided in subsection (f) and paragraph (g)(2) of this rule, the defense shall provide the following information to trial counsel:

(1) *Names of witnesses and statements.*

(A) Before the beginning of the trial on the merits, the defense shall notify trial counsel in writing of the names and contact information of all witnesses, other than the accused, whom the defense intends to call during the defense case in chief, and provide all sworn or signed statements known by the defense to have been made by such witnesses in connection with the case.

(B) Upon request of trial counsel, the defense shall also—

(i) Provide trial counsel with the names and contact information of any witnesses whom the defense intends to all at the presentencing proceedings under R.C.M. 1001(d); and

(ii) Permit trial counsel to inspect any written material that will be presented by the defense at the presentencing proceeding.

Discussion

See R.C.M. 701(f) for information that would not be subject to disclosure.

---

(2) *Notice of certain defenses.* The defense shall notify trial counsel in writing before the beginning of trial on the merits of its intent to offer the defense of alibi, innocent ingestion, or lack of mental responsibility, or its intent to introduce expert testimony as to the accused's mental condition. Such notice by the defense shall disclose, in the case of an alibi defense, the place or places at which the defense claims the accused to have been at the time of the alleged offense, and, in the case of an innocent ingestion defense, the place or places where, and the circumstances under which the defense claims the accused innocently ingested the substance in question, and the names and addresses of the witnesses upon whom the accused intends to rely to establish any such defenses.

Discussion

See R.C.M. 916(k) concerning the defense of lack of mental responsibility. See R.C.M. 706 concerning inquiries into the mental responsibility of the accused. See Mil. R. Evid. 302 concerning statements by the accused during such inquiries. If the defense needs more detail as to the time, date, or place of the offense to comply with this rule, it should request a bill of particulars. *See* R.C.M. 906(b)(6).

---

(3) *Documents and tangible items.* If the defense requests disclosure under subparagraph (a)(2)(A) of this rule, upon compliance with such request by the Government, the defense, on request of trial counsel, shall permit trial counsel to inspect and to copy or photograph books, papers, documents, data, photographs, tangible objects, or copies or portions of any of these items, or, in the case of buildings or places or portions thereof, inspect or photograph, if—

(A) the item is within the possession, custody, or control of the defense; and

(B) the defense intends to use the item in the defense case-in-chief at trial.

(4) *Reports of examination and tests.* If the defense requests disclosure under R.C.M. 701(a)(2)(B), upon compliance with such request by the Government, the defense, on request of the trial counsel, shall (except as provided in R.C.M. 706, Mil. R. Evid. 302, and Mil. R. Evid. 513) permit the trial counsel to inspect the results or reports, or copies thereof, of any physical or mental examinations and of any scientific tests or experiments made in connection with the particular case if the item is within the possession, custody, or control of the defense; and—

(A) the defense intends to use the item in the defense case-in-chief at trial; or

(B) the item was prepared by a witness whom the defense counsel intends to call at trial and the results or reports relate to that witness' testimony.

(5) *Inadmissibility of withdrawn defense.* If an intention to rely upon a defense under paragraph (b)(2) of this rule is withdrawn, evidence of such intention and disclosures by the accused or defense counsel made in connection with such intention is not, in any court-martial, admissible against the accused who gave notice of the intention.

Discussion

In addition to the matters covered in subsection (b) of this rule, defense counsel is required to give notice or disclose evidence under certain Military Rules of Evidence: Mil. R. Evid. 202(b) (judicial notice of foreign law), 304(f)(3) (testimony by the accused for a limited purpose in relation to a confession), 311(d)(6) (same, search), 321(d)(5) (same, lineup), 412(c)(1) and (2) (intent to offer evidence of sexual misconduct by a victim), 505(i) (intent to disclose classified information), 506(h) (intent to disclose privileged government information), 609(b) (intent to impeach a witness with a conviction older than 10 years), 612(a)(2) (writing used to refresh recollection), and 613(a) (prior inconsistent statements).

(c) *Failure to call witness.* The fact that a witness' name is on a list of expected or intended witnesses provided to an opposing party, whether required by this rule or not, shall not be ground for comment upon a failure to call the witness.

(d) *Continuing duty to disclose.* If, before or during the court-martial, a party discovers additional evidence or material previously requested or required to be produced, which is subject to discovery or inspection under this rule, that party shall promptly notify the other party or the military judge of the existence of the additional evidence or material.

Discussion

Trial counsel are encouraged to advise military authorities or other governmental agencies involved in the case of their continuing duty to identify, preserve, and disclose to the trial counsel or other Government counsel the information required to be disclosed under this rule.

(e) *Access to witnesses and evidence.* Each party shall have adequate opportunity to prepare its case and equal opportunity to interview witnesses and inspect evidence, subject to the limitations in paragraph (e)(1) of this rule. No party may unreasonably impede the access of another party to a witness or evidence.

(1) *Counsel for the Accused Interview of Victim of Alleged Offense.*

(A) Upon notice by counsel for the Government to counsel for the accused of the name of an alleged victim of an offense whom counsel for the Government intends to call as a witness at a proceeding, counsel for the accused, or that lawyer's representative, as defined in Mil. R. Evid. 502(b) (3), shall make any request to interview that victim through the special victims' counsel or other counsel for the victim, if applicable.

(B) If requested by an alleged victim who is subject to a request for interview under subparagraph (e)(1)(A) of this rule, any interview of the victim by counsel for the accused, or that lawyer's representative, as defined in Mil. R. Evid. 502(b)(3), shall take place only in the presence of counsel for the Government, counsel for the victim, or if applicable, a victim advocate.

(2) [Reserved]

(f) *Information not subject to disclosure.* Nothing in this rule shall be construed to require the disclosure of information protected from disclosure by the Military Rules of Evidence. Nothing in this rule shall require the disclosure or production of notes, memoranda, or similar working papers prepared by counsel and counsel's assistants and representatives.

(g) *Regulation of discovery.*

(1) *Time, place, and manner.* The military judge may, consistent with this rule, specify the time, place, and manner of making discovery and may prescribe such terms and conditions as are just.

(2) *Protective and modifying orders.* Upon a sufficient showing, the military judge may at any time order that the discovery or inspection be denied, restricted, or deferred, or make such other order as is appropriate. Subject to limitations in Part III of the Manual for Courts-Martial, if any rule requires, or upon motion by a party, the military judge may review any materials in camera, and permit the party to make such showing, in whole or in part, in writing to be inspected only by the military judge in camera. If the military judge reviews any materials in camera, the entirety of any materials examined by the military judge shall be attached to the record of trial as an appellate exhibit. The military judge shall seal any materials examined in camera and not disclosed and may seal other materials as appropriate. Such material may only be examined by reviewing or appellate authorities in accordance with R.C.M. 1113.

Discussion

In reviewing a motion under this paragraph, the military judge should consider the following: protection of witnesses and others from substantial risk of physical harm, bribes, economic reprisals, and other intimidation; maintenance of such secrecy regarding informants as is required for effective investigation of criminal activity; confidential information recognized by law, including protection of confidential relationships and privileges; and any other relevant considerations. If the military judge defers discovery or inspection, the military judge should ensure that all material and information to which a party is entitled are disclosed in sufficient time to permit counsel to make beneficial use of the disclosure. The terms of the sealing order may provide parameters for examination by or disclosure to those persons or entities whose interests are being protected.

---

(3) *Failure to comply.* If at any time during the court-martial it is brought to the attention of the military judge that a party has failed to comply with this rule, the military judge may take one or more of the following actions:

(A) Order the party to permit discovery;

(B) Grant a continuance;

(C) Prohibit the party from introducing evidence, calling a witness, or raising a defense not disclosed; and

(D) Enter such other order as is just under the circumstances. This rule shall not limit the right of the accused to testify in the accused's behalf.

Discussion

Factors to be considered in determining whether to grant an exception to exclusion under subsection (3)(C) include: the extent of disadvantage that resulted from a failure to disclose; the reason for the failure to disclose; the extent to which later events mitigated the disadvantage caused by the failure to disclose; and any other relevant factors.

The sanction of excluding the testimony of a defense witness should be used only upon finding that the defense counsel's failure to comply with this rule was willful and motivated by a desire to obtain a tactical advantage or to conceal a plan to present fabricated testimony. Moreover, the sanction of excluding the testimony of a defense witness should only be used if alternative sanctions could not have minimized the prejudice to the Government. Before imposing this sanction, the military judge must weigh the defendant's right to compulsory process against the countervailing public interests, including (1) the integrity of the adversary process; (2) the interest in the fair and efficient administration of military justice; and (3) the potential prejudice to the truth-determining function of the trial process.

Procedures governing refusal to disclose classified information are in Mil. R. Evid. 505. Procedures governing refusal to disclose other government information are in Mil. R. Evid. 506. Procedures governing refusal to disclose an informant's identity are in Mil. R. Evid. 507.

(h) *Inspect.* As used in this rule "inspect" includes the right to photograph and copy.

Rule 702. Depositions

(a) *In general.*

(1) A deposition may be ordered at the request of any party if the requesting party demonstrates that, due to exceptional circumstances, it is in the interest of justice that the testimony of a prospective witness be taken and preserved for use at trial.

(2) "Exceptional circumstances" under this rule includes circumstances under which the deponent is likely to be unavailable to testify at the time of trial.

(3) A victim's declination to testify at a preliminary hearing or a victim's declination to submit to pretrial interviews shall not, by themselves, be considered "exceptional circumstances" under this rule.

(4) A request for a written deposition may not be approved without the consent of the opposing party except when the deposition is ordered solely in lieu of producing a witness for sentencing under R.C.M. 1001 and the authority ordering the deposition determines that the interests of the parties and the court-martial can be adequately served by a written deposition.

(5) A request for an oral deposition may be approved without the consent of the opposing party.

Discussion

A deposition is the out-of-court testimony of a witness under oath in response to questions by the parties, which is reduced to writing or recorded on videotape or audiotape or similar material. A deposition taken on oral examination is an oral deposition, and a deposition taken on written interrogatories is a written deposition. Written interrogatories are questions, prepared by the prosecution, defense, or both, which are reduced to writing before submission to a witness whose testimony is to be taken by deposition. The answers, reduced to writing and properly sworn to, constitute the deposition testimony of the witness.

Note that under R.C.M. 702(j) a deposition may be taken by agreement of the parties without the necessity of an order.

Part or all of a deposition, so far as otherwise admissible under the Military Rules of Evidence, may be used on the merits or on an interlocutory question as substantive evidence if the witness is unavailable under Mil. R. Evid. 804(a) except that a deposition may be admitted in a capital case only upon offer by the defense. *See* Mil. R. Evid. 804(b)(1). In any case, a deposition may be used by any party for the purpose of contradicting or impeaching the testimony of the deponent as a witness. *See* Mil. R. Evid. 613. If only a part of a deposition is offered in evidence by a party, an adverse party may require the proponent to offer all which is relevant to the part offered, and any party may offer other parts. *See* Mil. R. Evid. 106.

A deposition which is transcribed is ordinarily read to the court-martial by the party offering it. *See also* R.C.M. 702(i)(1)(B). The transcript of a deposition may not be inspected by the members. Objections may be made to testimony in a written deposition in the same way that they would be if the testimony were offered through the personal appearance of a witness.

Part or all of a deposition so far as otherwise admissible under the Military Rules of Evidence may be used in presentencing proceedings as substantive evidence as provided in R.C.M. 1001.

DD Form 456 (Interrogatories and Deposition) may be used in conjunction with this rule.

See Article 6b(e)(2) concerning a victim's right to petition a Court of Criminal Appeals to quash an order to submit to a deposition.

(b) *Who may order.* Upon request of a party:

(1) Subject to R.C.M. 702(b)(2), before referral, a convening authority, or, after referral, the convening authority or the military judge, may order a deposition.

(2) For offenses over which special trial counsel exercises authority:

(i) Before referral, only a military judge may order a deposition, pursuant to R.C.M. 309(b)(3).

(ii) After referral, only a military judge may order a deposition.

(c) *Request to take deposition.* A party requesting a deposition shall do so in writing, and shall include in such written request—

(1) The name and contact information of the person whose deposition is requested, or, if the name of the person is unknown, a description of the office or position of the person;

(2) A statement of the matters on which the person is to be examined;

(3) A statement of the reasons for needing to preserve the testimony of the prospective witness; and

(4) Whether an oral or written deposition is requested.

Discussion

A copy of the request and any accompanying papers ordinarily should be served on the other party when the request is submitted.

(d) *Action on request.*

(1) *Prompt notification.* The authority under subsection (b) who acts on a request for deposition shall promptly inform the requesting party of the action on the request and, if the request is denied, the reasons for denial.

(2) *Action when request is denied.* If a request for deposition is denied by the convening authority, the requesting party may seek review of the decision by the military judge after referral.

(3) *Action when request is approved.*

(A) *Detail of deposition officer.* When a request for a deposition is approved, the convening authority shall detail a judge advocate certified under Article 27(b) to serve as deposition officer. In exceptional circumstances, when the appointment of a judge advocate as deposition officer is not practicable, the convening authority may detail an impartial commissioned officer or appropriate civil officer authorized to administer oaths, other than the accuser, to serve as deposition officer. If the deposition officer is not a judge advocate certified under Article 27(b), an impartial judge advocate so certified shall be made available to provide legal advice to the deposition officer.

Discussion

See Article 49(a)(4).

When a deposition will be at a point distant from the command, an appropriate authority may be requested to make available an officer to serve as deposition officer.

(B) *Assignment of counsel.* If charges have not yet been referred to a court-martial when a request to take a deposition is approved, the convening authority shall ensure that counsel qualified as required under R.C.M. 502(d) are assigned to represent each party.

Discussion

The counsel who represents the accused at a deposition ordinarily will form an attorney-client relationship with the accused, which will continue through a later court-martial. *See* R.C.M. 506.

If the accused has formed an attorney-client relationship with military counsel concerning the charges in question, ordinarily that counsel should be appointed to represent the accused.

(C) *Instructions.* The convening authority may give instructions not inconsistent with this rule to the deposition officer.

Discussion

Such instruction may include the time and place for taking the deposition.

(D) *Notice to other parties.* The requesting party shall give to every other party reasonable written notice of the time and place for the deposition and the name and address of each person to be examined. On motion of a party upon whom the notice is served, the deposition officer may for cause shown extend or shorten the time or change the place for taking the deposition, consistent with any instructions from the convening authority.

(e) *Duties of the deposition officer.* In accordance with this rule, and subject to any instructions under subparagraph (d)(3)(C), the deposition officer shall—

(1) Arrange a time and place for taking the deposition and, in the case of an oral deposition, notify the party who requested the deposition accordingly;

(2) Arrange for the presence of any witness whose deposition is to be taken in accordance with the procedures for production of witnesses and evidence under R.C.M. 703;

(3) Maintain order during the deposition and protect the parties and witnesses from annoyance, embarrassment, or oppression;

(4) Administer the oath to each witness, the reporter, and interpreter, if any;

(5) In the case of a written deposition, ask the questions submitted by counsel to the witness;

(6) Cause the proceedings to be recorded so that a verbatim transcript may be prepared;

(7) Record, but not rule upon, objections or motions and the testimony to which they relate;

(8) Certify the record of the deposition and forward it to the authority who ordered the deposition; and

(9) Report to the convening authority any substantial irregularity in the proceeding.

Discussion

When any unusual problem, such as improper conduct by counsel or a witness, prevents an orderly and fair proceeding, the deposition officer should adjourn the proceedings and inform the convening authority.

The authority who ordered the deposition should forward copies of the transcript of the deposition to the parties.

(f) *Rights of accused.*

(1) *Oral depositions.*

(A) At an oral deposition, the accused shall have the following rights:

(i) Except as provided in subparagraph (B), the right to be present.

(ii) The right to be represented by counsel as provided in R.C.M. 506.

(B) At an oral deposition, the accused shall not have the right to be present when—

(i) the accused, absent good cause shown, fails to appear after notice of time and place of the deposition;

(ii) the accused is disruptive within the meaning of R.C.M. 804(c)(2); or

(iii) the deposition is ordered in lieu of production of a witness on sentencing under R.C.M. 1001 and the authority ordering the deposition determines that the interests of the parties and the court-martial can be served adequately by an oral deposition without the presence of the accused.

(2) *Written depositions.* The accused shall have the right to be represented by counsel as provided in R.C.M. 506 for the purpose of taking a written deposition, except when the deposition is taken for use at a summary court-martial unless otherwise provided by the Secretary concerned.

(g) *Procedure.*

(1) *Oral depositions.*

(A) *Examination of witnesses.* Each witness giving an oral deposition shall be examined under oath. The scope and manner of examination and cross-examination shall be such as would be allowed in the trial itself. The Government shall make available to each accused for examination and use at the taking of the deposition any statement of the witness which is in the possession of the United States and to which the accused would be entitled at the trial.

Discussion

As to objections, see R.C.M. 702(e)(7) and (h). As to production of prior statements of witnesses, see R.C.M. 914; Mil. R. Evid. 612, 613.

A sample oath for a deposition follows:

"Do you (swear) (affirm) that the evidence you give shall be the truth, the whole truth, and nothing but the truth (so help you God)?"

(B) *How recorded.* In the discretion of the authority who ordered the deposition, a deposition may be recorded by a reporter or by other means including video and audio recording.

(2) *Written depositions.*

(A) *Presence of parties.* No party has a right to be present at a written deposition.

(B) *Submission of interrogatories to opponent.* The party requesting a written deposition shall submit to opposing counsel a list of written questions to be asked of the witness. Opposing counsel may examine the questions and shall be allowed a reasonable time to prepare cross-interrogatories and objections, if any.

Discussion

The interrogatories and cross-interrogatories should be sent to the deposition officer by the party who requested the deposition. See R.C.M. 702(h)(3) concerning objections.

(C) *Examination of witnesses.* The deposition officer shall swear the witness, read each question presented by the parties to the witness, and record each response. The testimony of the witness shall be recorded on videotape, audiotape, or similar material or shall be transcribed. When the testimony is transcribed, the deposition shall, except when impracticable, be submitted to the witness for examination. The deposition officer may enter additional matters then stated by the witness under oath. The deposition shall be signed by the witness if the witness is available. If the deposition is not signed by the witness, the deposition officer shall record the reason. The certificate of authentication shall then be executed.

(h) *Objections.*

(1) *In general.* A failure to object prior to the deposition to the taking of the deposition on grounds which may be corrected if the objection is made prior to the deposition forfeits such objection unless the

objection is affirmatively waived.

(2) *Oral depositions.* Objections to questions, testimony, or evidence at an oral deposition and the grounds for such objection shall be stated at the time of taking such deposition. If an objection relates to a matter which could have been corrected if the objection had been made during the deposition, the objection is forfeited if not made at the deposition.

Discussion

A party may show that an objection was made during the deposition but not recorded, but, in the absence of such evidence, the transcript of the deposition governs.

---

(3) *Written depositions.* Objections to any question in written interrogatories shall be served on the party who proposed the question before the interrogatories are sent to the deposition officer or the objection is forfeited. Objections to answers in a written deposition may be made at trial.

(i) *Admissibility and use as evidence.*

(1) *In general.*

(A) The ordering of a deposition under paragraph (a)(1) does not control the admissibility of the deposition at court-martial. Except as provided in paragraph (2), a party may use all or part of a deposition as provided by the rules of evidence.

(B) In the discretion of the military judge, audio or video recorded depositions may be played for the court-martial or may be transcribed and read to the court-martial.

(2) *Capital cases.* Testimony by deposition may be presented in capital cases only by the defense.

Discussion

A deposition read into evidence or one that is played during a court-martial is recorded and transcribed by the reporter in the same way as any other testimony. Such a deposition need not be included in the record of trial.

(j) *Deposition by agreement not precluded.*

(1) *Taking deposition.* Nothing in this rule shall preclude the taking of a deposition without cost to the United States, orally or upon written questions, by agreement of the parties.

(2) *Use of deposition.* Subject to Article 49, nothing in this rule shall preclude the use of a deposition at the court-martial by agreement of the parties unless the military judge forbids its use for good cause.

Rule 703. Production of witnesses and evidence

(a) *In general.* The prosecution, defense, and court-martial shall have equal opportunity to obtain witnesses and evidence, subject to the limitations set forth in R.C.M. 701, including the benefit of compulsory process.

Discussion

See also R.C.M. 801(c) concerning the opportunity of the court-martial to obtain witnesses and evidence.

(b) *Right to witnesses.*

(1) *On the merits or on interlocutory questions.* Each party is entitled to the production of any witness whose testimony on a matter in issue on the merits or on an interlocutory question would be relevant and necessary. With the consent of both the accused and Government, the military judge may authorize any witness to testify via remote means. Over a party's objection, the military judge may authorize any witness to testify on interlocutory questions via remote means or similar technology if the practical difficulties of producing the witness outweigh the significance of the witness' personal appearance (although such testimony will not be admissible over the accused's objection as evidence on the ultimate issue of guilt). Factors to be considered include, but are not limited to: the costs of producing the witness; the timing of the request for production of the witness; the potential delay in the interlocutory proceeding that may be caused by the production of the witness; the willingness of the witness to testify in person; the likelihood of significant interference with military operational deployment, mission accomplishment, or essential training; and, for child witnesses, the traumatic effect of providing in-court testimony

Discussion

See Mil. R. Evid. 401 concerning relevance.

Relevant testimony is necessary when it is not cumulative and when it would contribute to a party's presentation of the case in some positive way on a matter in issue. A matter is not in issue when it is stipulated as a fact.

The procedures for receiving testimony via remote means and the definition thereof are contained in R.C.M. 914B. An issue may arise as both an interlocutory question and a question that bears on the ultimate issue of guilt. *See* R.C.M. 801(e)(5). In such circumstances, this rule authorizes the admission of testimony by remote means or similar technology over the accused's objection only as evidence on the interlocutory question. In most instances, testimony taken over a party's objection will not be admissible as evidence on the question that bears on the ultimate issue of guilt; however, there may be certain limited circumstances where the testimony is admissible on the ultimate issue of guilt. Such determinations must be made based upon the relevant rules of evidence.

---

(2) *On sentencing.* Each party is entitled to the production of a witness whose testimony on sentencing is required under R.C.M. 1001(f).

(3) *Unavailable witness.* Notwithstanding paragraphs (b)(1) and (2) of this rule, a party is not entitled to the presence of a witness who is unavailable within the meaning of Mil. R. Evid. 804(a). However, if the testimony of a witness who is unavailable is of such central importance to an issue that it is essential to a fair trial, and if there is no adequate substitute for such testimony, the military judge shall grant a continuance or other relief in order to attempt to secure the witness' presence or shall abate the proceedings, unless the unavailability of the witness is the fault of or could have been prevented by the requesting party.

(c) *Determining which witnesses will be produced.*

(1) *Witnesses for the prosecution.* Trial counsel shall obtain the presence of witnesses whose testimony trial counsel considers relevant and necessary for the prosecution.

(2) *Witnesses for the defense.*

(A) *Request.* The defense shall submit to trial counsel a written list of witnesses whose production by the Government the defense requests.

(B) *Contents of request.*

(i) *Witnesses on merits or interlocutory questions.* A list of witnesses whose testimony the defense considers relevant and necessary on the merits or on an interlocutory question shall include the name, telephone number, if known, and address or location of the witness such that the witness can be found upon the exercise of due diligence and a synopsis of the expected testimony sufficient to show its relevance and necessity.

(ii) *Witnesses on sentencing.* A list of witnesses wanted for presentencing proceedings shall include the name, telephone number, if known, and address or location of the witness such that the witness can be found upon the exercise of due diligence, a synopsis of the testimony that it is expected the witness will give, and the reasons why the witness' personal appearance will be necessary under the standards set forth in R.C.M. 1001(f).

(C) *Time of request.* A list of witnesses under this subsection shall be submitted in time reasonably to allow production of each witness on the date when the witness' presence will be necessary. The military judge may set a specific date by which such lists must be submitted. Failure to submit the name of a witness in a timely manner shall permit denial of a motion for production of the witness, but relief from such denial may be granted for good cause shown.

(D) *Determination.* Trial counsel shall arrange for the presence of any witness listed by the defense unless trial counsel contends that the witness' production is not required under this rule. If trial counsel contends that the witness' production is not required by this rule, the matter may be submitted to the military judge. If the military judge grants a motion for a witness, trial counsel shall produce the witness or the proceedings shall be abated.

Discussion

When significant or unusual costs would be involved in producing witnesses, the trial counsel should inform the convening authority, as the convening authority may elect to dispose of the matter by means other than a court-martial. *See* R.C.M. 906(b)(7). *See also* R.C.M. 905(j).

(d) *Employment of expert witnesses and consultants.*

(1) *Funding experts for the prosecution.* When the employment of a prosecution expert witness or consultant is considered necessary, counsel for the Government shall, in advance of employment of the expert, and with notice to the defense, submit a request for funding of the expert in accordance with regulations prescribed by the Secretary concerned.

Discussion

See Mil. R. Evid. 702; 706.

---

(2) *Funding experts for the defense.* When the appointment or employment of a defense expert witness or consultant is considered necessary, the defense may submit a request for the appointment or funding of the expert in accordance with regulations

prescribed by the Secretary concerned.

(A) After referral of charges, a defense request for an expert witness or consultant may be raised before the military judge. Motions for expert consultants may be raised *ex parte*. The military judge shall determine:

(i) in the case of an expert witness, whether the testimony is relevant and necessary;

(ii) in the case of an expert consultant, whether the assistance is necessary for an adequate defense.

(B) If the military judge grants a motion for the appointment or employment of a defense expert witness or consultant, the expert witness or consultant, or an adequate substitute, shall be provided in accordance with regulations prescribed by the Secretary concerned. In the absence of advance approval by an official authorized to grant such approval under the regulations prescribed by the Secretary concerned, expert witnesses and consultants may not be paid fees other than those to which they are entitled under R.C.M. 207(g)(3)(E).

(3) *Notice of expert witnesses.*

(A) *Expert witnesses.*

(i) *Government.* In addition to the requirements of R.C.M. 701(a)(3), the Government shall provide the defense a written summary of the expected testimony from the expert witness.

(ii) *Defense.* After referral of charges, in addition to the requirements of R.C.M. 701(b)(1), the defense shall provide the Government a written summary of the expected testimony from the expert witness.

(B) *Timing.* The military judge shall set a date upon which notices under R.C.M. 703(d)(3)(A) are due to the opposing party.

(C) *Failure to comply.* If at any time it is brought to the attention of the military judge that a party has failed to comply with this rule, the military judge may take one or more of the following actions:

(i) Order the required notice;

(ii) Order the party to permit discovery;

(iii) Grant a continuance;

(iv) Prohibit the party from introducing evidence, calling a witness, or raising a defense not disclosed; and

(v) Enter such other order as is just under the circumstances.

Discussion

See R.C.M. 701(g)(3) Discussion.

Notice will include the name and contact information for the expert consultant or expert witness.

(e) *Right to evidence.*

(1) *In general.* Each party is entitled to the production of evidence which is relevant and necessary.

Discussion

Relevance is defined by Mil. R. Evid. 401. Relevant evidence is necessary when it is not cumulative and when it would contribute to a party's presentation of the case in some positive way on a matter in issue. A matter is not in issue when it is stipulated as a fact. The discovery and introduction of classified or other government information is controlled by Mil. R. Evid. 505 and 506.

---

(2) *Unavailable evidence.* Notwithstanding paragraph (e)(1), a party is not entitled to the production of evidence which is destroyed, lost, or otherwise not subject to compulsory process. However, if such evidence is of such central importance to an issue that it is essential to a fair trial, and if there is no adequate substitute for such evidence, the military judge shall grant a continuance or other relief in order to attempt to produce the evidence or shall abate the proceedings, unless the unavailability of the evidence is the fault of or could have been prevented by the requesting party.

(f) *Determining what evidence will be produced.* The procedures in subsection (c) shall apply to a determination of what evidence will be produced, except that any defense request for the production of evidence shall list the items of evidence to be produced and shall include a description of each item sufficient to show its relevance and necessity, a statement where it can be obtained, and, if known, the name, address, and telephone number of the custodian of the evidence.

(g) *Procedures for production of witnesses and evidence.*

(1) *Military witnesses.* The attendance of a military witness may be obtained by notifying the commander of the witness of the time, place, and date the presence of the witness is required and requesting the commander to issue any necessary orders to the witness.

Discussion

When military witnesses are located near the court-martial, their presence can usually be obtained through informal coordination with them and their commander. If the witness is not near the court-martial and attendance would involve travel at government expense, or if informal coordination is inadequate, the appropriate superior should be requested to issue the necessary order.

If practicable, a request for the attendance of a military witness should be made so that the witness will have at least 48 hours' notice before starting to travel to attend the court-martial.

The attendance of persons not on active duty should be obtained in the manner prescribed in R.C.M. 703(g)(3).

---

(2) *Evidence under the control of the Government.* Evidence under the control of the Government may be obtained by notifying the custodian of the evidence of the time, place, and date the evidence is required and requesting the custodian to send or deliver the evidence.

(3) *Civilian witnesses and evidence not under the control of the Government—subpoenas.*

(A) *In general.* The presence of witnesses not on active duty and evidence not under control of the Government may be obtained by subpoena.

Discussion

A subpoena is not necessary if the witness appears voluntarily at no expense to the United States.

Civilian employees of the Department of Defense may be directed by appropriate authorities to appear as witnesses in courts-martial as an incident of their employment. Appropriate travel orders may be issued for this purpose.

A subpoena may not be used to compel a civilian to travel outside the United States and its territories.

A witness must be subject to United States jurisdiction to be subject to a subpoena. Foreign nationals in a foreign country are not subject to subpoena. Their presence may be obtained through cooperation of the host nation.

(B) *Contents.* A subpoena shall state the command by which the proceeding or investigation is directed, and the title, if any, of the proceeding. A subpoena shall command each person to whom it is directed to attend and give testimony at the time and place specified therein, or to produce evidence—including books, papers, documents, data, writings, or other objects or electronically stored information designated therein at the proceeding or at an earlier time for inspection by the parties. A subpoena shall not command any person to attend or give testimony at an Article 32 preliminary hearing.

Discussion

A subpoena normally is prepared, signed, and issued in duplicate on official forms. See DD Form 453 for a template subpoena with certificate of service.

(C) *Investigative subpoenas.*

(i) *In general.* In the case of a subpoena issued before referral for the production of evidence for use in an investigation, the subpoena shall command each person to whom it is directed to produce the evidence requested for inspection by the Government counsel who issued the subpoena or for inspection in accordance with an order issued by the military judge under R.C.M. 309(b).

Discussion

A pre-referral investigative subpoena may be issued in accordance with R.C.M. 309 or subsection (g)(3)(D)(v) of this rule for the production of evidence not under control of the government for use at an Article 32 preliminary hearing. *See also* R.C.M. 405.

(ii) *Subpoenas for personal or confidential information about a victim.* After preferral, a subpoena requiring the production of personal or confidential information about a victim named in a specification may be served on an individual or organization by those authorized to issue a subpoena under R.C.M. 703(g)(3)(E) or with the consent of the victim. Before issuing a subpoena under this provision and unless there are exceptional circumstances, the victim must be given notice so that the victim can move for relief under R.C.M 703(g)(3)(I) or otherwise object.

Discussion

The term "victim" has the same meaning as the term "victim of an offense under this chapter" in Article 6b. A subpoena requiring the production of personal or confidential information of a named victim may be served on individuals, such as medical professionals, counselors, employers, or journalists, or upon an organization, such as a medical facility, school, treatment center, financial institution, news organization, or insurance company. Subpoenas to which R.C.M. 703(g)(3)(C) applies may also be subject to additional statutory requirements, *e.g.*, the Right to Financial Privacy Act, 12 USC §§ 3401-3422, which applies to financial records. Notice may be given to the victim or to a victim's representative such as a representative under R.C.M. 801(a)(6) or legal counsel. This provision is drawn from Fed. R. Crim. P. 17(c)(3) with differences to account for military justice circumstances. For a discussion of "exceptional circumstances," see Fed. R. Crim. P. 17 (Advisory Committee Notes, 2008 Amendments).

(D) *Ex parte request by defense.* Upon request by the defense after referral, including an *ex parte* request, the military judge shall issue a subpoena to compel the production of witnesses if the witness's testimony is determined to be relevant and necessary.

(E) *Who may issue.* A subpoena may be issued by:

(i) the military judge, after referral;

(ii) the summary court-martial;

(iii) the trial counsel of a general or special court-martial;

Discussion

When detailed to a general or special court-martial, a special trial counsel may issue a subpoena pursuant to R.C.M. 703(g)(3)(E)(iii). *See* R.C.M. 103(26).

(iv) the president of a court of inquiry;

(v) an officer detailed to take a deposition; or

(vi) in the case of a pre-referral investigative subpoena, a military judge or, when issuance of the subpoena is authorized by a general court-martial convening authority, the detailed trial counsel or counsel for the Government.

Discussion

If practicable, a subpoena should be issued in time to permit service at least 24 hours before the time the witness will have to travel to comply with the subpoena.

Informal service. Unless formal service is advisable, the person who issued the subpoena may mail it to the witness in duplicate, enclosing a postage-paid envelope bearing a return address, with the request that the witness sign the acceptance of service on the copy and return it in the envelope provided. The return envelope should be addressed to the person who issued the subpoena. The person who issued the subpoena should include with it a statement to the effect that the rights of the witness to fees and mileage will not be impaired by voluntary compliance with the request and that a voucher for fees and mileage will be delivered to the witness promptly on being discharged from attendance.

Formal service. Formal service is advisable whenever it is anticipated that the witness will not comply voluntarily with the subpoena. Appropriate fees and mileage must be paid or tendered. *See* Article 47. If formal service is advisable, the person who issued the subpoena must assure timely and economical service. That person may do so by serving the subpoena personally when the witness is in the vicinity. When the witness is not in the vicinity, the subpoena may be sent in duplicate to the commander of a military installation near the witness. Such commanders should give prompt and effective assistance, issuing travel orders for their personnel to serve the subpoena when necessary.

Service should ordinarily be made by a person subject to the UCMJ. The duplicate copy of the subpoena must have entered upon it proof of service as indicated on the form and must be promptly returned to the person who issued the subpoena. If service cannot be made, the person who issued the subpoena must be informed promptly. A stamped, addressed envelope should be provided for these purposes.

Hardship means any situation which would substantially preclude reasonable efforts to appear that could be solved by providing transportation or fees and mileage to which the witness is entitled for appearing at the hearing in question.

(F) *Notice.* Notice shall be given to all parties for any subpoena issued for a witness post-referral unless, for good cause, the military judge issues a protective order.

(G) *Service.* A subpoena may be served by the person authorized by this rule to issue it, a United States Marshal, or any other person who is not less than 18 years of age. Service shall be made by delivering a copy of the subpoena to the person named and, in the case of a subpoena of an individual to provide testimony, by providing to the person named travel orders and a means for reimbursement for fees and mileage as may be prescribed by the Secretary concerned, or in the case of hardship resulting in the subpoenaed witness's inability to comply with the subpoena absent initial Government payment, by providing to the person named travel orders, fees, and mileage sufficient to comply with the subpoena in rules prescribed by the Secretary concerned.

(H) *Place of service.*

(i) *In general.* A subpoena may be served at any place within the United States, its Territories, Commonwealths, or possessions.

Discussion

A warrant of attachment (DD Form 454) may be used when necessary to compel a witness to appear or produce evidence under this rule. A warrant of attachment is a legal order addressed to an official directing that official to have the person named in the order brought before a court.

Subpoenas issued under R.C.M. 703 are federal process and a person not subject to the UCMJ may be prosecuted in a federal civilian court under Article 47 for failure to comply with a subpoena issued in compliance with this rule and formally served.

Failing to comply with such a subpoena is a felony offense, and may result in a fine or imprisonment, or both, at the discretion of the district court. The different purposes of the warrant of attachment and criminal complaint under Article 47 should be borne in mind.

The warrant of attachment, available without the intervention of civilian judicial proceedings, has as its purpose the obtaining of the witness' presence, testimony, or documents. The criminal complaint, prosecuted through the federal civilian courts, has as its purpose punishment for failing to comply with process issued by military authority. It serves to vindicate the military interest in obtaining compliance with its lawful process.

A general court-martial convening authority may only issue a warrant of attachment to compel compliance with an investigative subpoena issued prior to referral. *See* Article 46(d).

(ii) *Foreign territory.* In foreign territory, the attendance of civilian witnesses and evidence not under the control of the Government may be obtained in accordance with existing agreements or, in the absence of agreements, with principles of international law.

(iii) *Occupied territory.* In occupied enemy territory, the appropriate commander may compel the attendance of civilian witnesses located within the occupied territory.

Discussion

In executing a warrant of attachment, no more force than necessary to bring the witness to the court-martial, deposition, or court of inquiry may be used.

(I) *Relief.* If a person subpoenaed requests relief on grounds that compliance is unreasonable, oppressive, or prohibited by law, the military judge or, if before referral, a military judge detailed under Article 30a, shall review the request and shall—

(i) order that the subpoena be modified or quashed, as appropriate; or

(ii) order the person to comply with the subpoena.

Discussion

See RCM 703(g)(3)(C)(ii) regarding the ability of a victim named in a specification to move for relief or otherwise object under R.C.M. 703(g)(3)(I).

(J) *Neglect or refusal to appear or produce evidence.*

(i) *Issuance of warrant of attachment.* If the person subpoenaed neglects or refuses to appear or produce evidence, the military judge or, if before referral, a military judge detailed under Article 30a or a general court-martial convening authority, may issue a warrant of attachment to compel the attendance of a witness or the production of evidence, as appropriate.

(ii) *Requirements.* A warrant of attachment may be issued only upon probable cause to believe that the witness or evidence custodian was duly served with a subpoena, that the subpoena was issued in accordance with these rules, that a means of reimbursement of fees and mileage, if applicable, was provided to the witness or advanced to the witness in cases of hardship, that the witness or evidence is material, that the witness or evidence custodian refused or willfully neglected to appear or produce the subpoenaed evidence at the time and place specified on the subpoena, and that no valid excuse is reasonably apparent for the witness' failure to appear or produce the subpoenaed evidence.

(iii) *Form.* A warrant of attachment shall be written. All documents in support of the warrant of attachment shall be attached to the warrant, together with the charge sheet and convening orders.

(iv) *Execution.* A warrant of attachment may be executed by a United States Marshal or such other person who is not less than 18 years of age as the authority issuing the warrant may direct. Only such non-deadly force as may be necessary to bring the witness before the court-martial or other proceeding or to compel production of the subpoenaed evidence may be used to execute the warrant. A witness attached under this rule shall be brought before the court-martial or proceeding without delay and shall testify or provide the subpoenaed evidence as soon as practicable and be released.

(v) *Definition.* For purposes of R.C.M. 703(g)(3)(J)(i), "military judge" does not include a summary court-martial.

Rule 703A. Warrant or order for wire or electronic communications

(a) *In general.* A military judge detailed in accordance with Article 26 or Article 30a, may, upon written application by a federal law enforcement officer, trial counsel, or other authorized counsel for the Government in connection with an ongoing investigation of an offense or offenses under the UCMJ, issue one or more of the following:

(1) A warrant for the disclosure by a provider of electronic communication service of the contents of

any wire or electronic communication.

(2) A warrant for the disclosure by a provider of remote computing service of the contents of any wire or electronic communication that is held or maintained on that service—

(A) on behalf of, and received by means of electronic transmission from (or created by means of computer processing of communications received by means of electronic transmission from), a subscriber or customer of such remote computing service; and

(B) solely for the purpose of providing storage or computer processing services to such subscriber or customer, if the provider is not authorized to access the contents of any such communications for purposes of providing any services other than storage or computer processing.

(3) A warrant or order for the disclosure by a provider of electronic communication service or remote computing service of a record or other information pertaining to a subscriber to or customer of such service (not including the contents of communications).

Discussion

See Article 46(d)(3) and 18 U.S.C. § 2703 concerning the authority for, and U.S. district court procedures concerning, warrants and court orders for electronically stored information.

(b) *Warrant procedures.*

(1) *Probable cause required.* A military judge shall issue a warrant authorizing the search for and seizure of information specified in subsection (a) of this rule if—

(A) The federal law enforcement officer, trial counsel, or other authorized counsel for the Government applying for the warrant presents an affidavit or sworn testimony, subject to examination by the military judge, in support of the application; and

(B) Based on the affidavit or sworn testimony, the military judge determines that there is probable cause to believe that the information sought contains evidence of a crime.

(2) *Issuing the warrant.* The military judge shall issue the warrant to the federal law enforcement officer, trial counsel, or other authorized counsel for the Government who applied for the warrant.

(3) *Contents of the warrant.* The warrant shall identify the property to be searched, identify any property or other information to be seized, and designate the military judge to whom the warrant must be returned.

(4) *Executing the warrant.* The presence of the federal law enforcement officer, trial counsel, or other authorized counsel for the Government identified in the warrant shall not be required for service or execution of a search warrant issued in accordance with this rule requiring disclosure by a provider of electronic communications service or remote computing service of the contents of communications or records or other information pertaining to a subscriber to or customer of such service.

(5) *Quashing or modifying the warrant.* A military judge issuing a warrant under subsection (a), on a motion made promptly by the service provider, may quash or modify such warrant, if the warrant is determined to be unreasonable or oppressive or prohibited by law.

(c) *Order procedures.*

(1) A military judge shall issue an order authorizing the disclosure of information specified in paragraph (a)(3) of this rule if the federal law enforcement officer, trial counsel, or other authorized counsel for the Government applying for the order offers specific and articulable facts showing that there are reasonable grounds to believe that the records or other information sought are relevant and material to an ongoing criminal investigation.

(2) *Quashing or modifying order.* A military judge issuing an order under paragraph (c)(1) of this rule, on a motion made promptly by the service provider, may quash or modify such order, if the order is determined to be unreasonable, oppressive, or prohibited by law.

Discussion

An order may be unreasonable or oppressive if the information or records requested are unusually voluminous in nature or compliance with such order otherwise would cause an undue burden on a provider.

(d) *Non-disclosure orders.*

(1) A federal law enforcement officer, trial counsel, or other authorized counsel for the Government acting under this rule may apply to a military judge for an order commanding a provider of electronic communications service or remote computing service

to whom a warrant or order under this rule is directed, for such period as the military judge deems appropriate, not to notify any other person of the existence of the warrant or order. The military judge shall issue the order if the military judge determines that there is reason to believe that notification of the existence of the warrant or order will result in an adverse result described in paragraph (d)(2) of this rule.

(2) An adverse result for purposes of paragraph (d)(1) of this rule is—

(A) endangering the life or physical safety of an individual;

(B) flight from prosecution;

(C) destruction of or tampering with evidence;

(D) intimidation of potential witnesses; or

(E) otherwise seriously jeopardizing an investigation or unduly delaying a trial.

(e) *No cause of action against a provider disclosing information under this rule.* As provided under 18 U.S.C. § 2703(e), no cause of action shall lie in any court against any provider of wire or electronic communication service, its officers, employees, agents, or other specified persons for providing information, facilities, or assistance in accordance with the terms of a warrant or order under this rule.

(f) *Requirement to preserve evidence.* To the same extent as provided in 18 U.S.C. § 2703(f)—

(1) A provider of wire or electronic communication services or a remote computing service, upon the request of a federal law enforcement officer, trial counsel, or other authorized counsel for the Government, shall take all necessary steps to preserve records and other evidence in its possession pending the issuance of an order or other process; and

(2) Shall retain such records and other evidence for a period of 90 days, which shall be extended for an additional 90-day period upon a renewed request by the governmental entity.

(g) *Definition.* As used in this rule, the term "federal law enforcement officer" includes an employee of the Army Criminal Investigation Command, the Naval Criminal Investigative Service, the Air Force Office of Special Investigations, or the Coast Guard Investigative Service who has authority to request a search warrant.

Rule 704. Immunity

(a) *Types of immunity.* Two types of immunity may be granted under this rule.

(1) *Transactional immunity.* A person may be granted transactional immunity from trial by court-martial for one or more offenses under the UCMJ.

(2) *Testimonial immunity.* A person may be granted immunity from the use of testimony, statements, and any information directly or indirectly derived from such testimony or statements by that person in a later court-martial.

Discussion

"Testimonial" immunity is also called "use" immunity.

Immunity ordinarily should be granted only when testimony or other information from the person is necessary to the public interest, including the needs of good order and discipline, and when the person has refused or is likely to refuse to testify or provide other information on the basis of the privilege against self-incrimination.

Testimonial immunity is preferred because it does not bar prosecution of the person for the offenses about which testimony or information is given under the grant of immunity.

In any trial of a person granted testimonial immunity after the testimony or information is given, the Government must meet a heavy burden to show that it has not used in any way for the prosecution of that person the person's statements, testimony, or information derived from them. In many cases this burden makes difficult a later prosecution of such a person for any offense that was the subject of that person's testimony or statements. Therefore, if it is intended to prosecute a person to whom testimonial immunity has been or will be granted for offenses about which that person may testify or make statements, it may be necessary to try that person before the testimony or statements are given.

(b) *Scope.* Nothing in this rule bars:

(1) A later court-martial for perjury, false swearing, making a false official statement, or failure to comply with an order to testify; or

(2) Use in a court-martial under paragraph (b)(1) of this rule of testimony or statements derived from such testimony or statements.

(c) *Authority to grant immunity.*

Discussion

Only general court-martial convening authorities or their designees are authorized to grant immunity. However, in some circumstances, when a person testifies or makes statements pursuant to a promise of immunity, or a similar promise, by a person with apparent authority to make it, such testimony or statements and evidence derived from them may be inadmissible in a later trial. Under some circumstances a promise of immunity by someone other than a general court-martial convening authority or designee may bar prosecution altogether.

Persons not authorized to grant immunity should exercise care when dealing with accused or suspects to avoid inadvertently causing statements to be inadmissible or prosecution to be barred.

When the victim of an alleged offense requests an expedited response to a request for immunity for misconduct that is collateral to the underlying offense, the convening authority should respond to the request as soon as practicable.

A convening authority who grants immunity to a prosecution witness in a court-martial may be disqualified from taking post-trial action in the case under some circumstances.

---

(1) Except as provided in R.C.M. 704(c)(2), a general court-martial convening authority, or designee, may grant immunity, and may do so only in accordance with this rule.

(2) For offenses over which a special trial counsel has exercised authority and has not deferred, a special trial counsel designated by the Secretary concerned, or that designated special trial counsel's designee, may grant immunity, and may do so only in accordance with this rule.

Discussion

Only special trial counsel designated by the Secretary concerned, general court-martial convening authorities, and their designees are authorized to grant immunity. However, in some circumstances, when a person testifies or makes statements pursuant to a promise of immunity, or a similar promise, by a person with apparent authority to make it, such testimony or statements and evidence derived from them may be inadmissible in a later trial. Under some circumstances, a promise of immunity by someone other than a general court-martial convening authority, special trial counsel designated by the Secretary concerned, or their designee may bar prosecution altogether. Persons not authorized to grant immunity should exercise care when dealing with accused or suspects to avoid inadvertently causing statements to be inadmissible or prosecution to be barred.

When the victim of an alleged offense requests an expedited response to a request for immunity for misconduct that is collateral to the underlying offense, the convening authority, special trial counsel designated by the Secretary concerned, or their designee should respond to the request as soon as practicable.

---

(3) *Persons subject to the UCMJ.* A general court-martial convening authority, a special trial counsel designated by the Secretary concerned, or their designees, may grant immunity to a person subject to the UCMJ. However, they may grant immunity to a person subject to the UCMJ extending to a prosecution in a United States District Court only when specifically authorized to do so by the Attorney General of the United States or other authority designated under chapter 601 of title 18 of the U.S. Code.

Discussion

When testimony or a statement for which a person subject to the UCMJ may be granted immunity may relate to an offense for which that person could be prosecuted in a United States District Court, immunity should not be granted without prior coordination with the Department of Justice. Ordinarily, coordination with the local United States Attorney is appropriate. Unless the Department of Justice indicates it has no interest in the case, authorization for the grant of immunity should be sought from the Attorney General. A request for such authorization should be forwarded through the office of the Judge Advocate General concerned. Service regulations may provide additional guidance. Even if the Department of Justice expresses no interest in the case, authorization by the Attorney General for the grant of immunity may be necessary to compel the person to testify or make a statement if such testimony or statement would make the person liable for a federal civilian offense.

---

(4) *Persons not subject to the UCMJ.* A general court-martial convening authority, a special trial counsel designated by the Secretary concerned, or their designees, may grant immunity to persons not subject to the UCMJ only when specifically authorized to do so by the Attorney General of the United States or other authority designated in chapter 601 of title 18 of the U.S. Code.

(5) *Limitations on delegation.*

(A) Subject to Service regulations, the authority to grant immunity under this rule may be delegated in writing at the discretion of the general court-martial convening authority to a subordinate special court-martial convening authority. Further delegation is not permitted. The authority to grant immunity or delegate the authority to grant immunity may be limited by superior authority.

(B) Subject to Service regulations, the authority to grant immunity under this rule may be delegated at the discretion of a special trial counsel designated by the Secretary concerned to a subordinate special trial counsel. The authority to grant immunity or delegate the authority to grant immunity may be limited by superior authority. Any delegation shall be in writing.

Discussion

A general court-martial convening authority has wide latitude under this section to exercise his or her discretion in delegating immunity authority. For example, a general court-martial convening authority may decide to delegate only the authority for a designee to grant immunity for certain offenses, such as a list of specific offenses or any offense not warranting a punitive discharge, while withholding authority to grant immunity for all others. A general court-martial convening authority may also delegate only authority for certain categories of grantees, such as victims of alleged sex-related offenses.

Department of Defense Instruction 5525.07 (March 5, 2020) provides: "A proposed grant of immunity in a case involving espionage, subversion, aiding the enemy, sabotage, spying, or violation of rules or statutes concerning classified information or the foreign relations of the United States, will be forwarded to the General Counsel of the Department of Defense for the purpose of consultation with the [Department of Justice (DOJ)]. The General Counsel of the Department of Defense will obtain the views of other appropriate elements of DoD that should be considered during consultation with DOJ."

(d) *Procedure.*

(1) A grant of immunity shall be written and signed by the individual convening authority, special trial counsel designated by the Secretary concerned, or designee who issues it. The grant shall include a statement of the authority under which it is made and shall identify the matters to which it extends.

(2) Subject to Service regulations, the convening authority shall order a person subject to the UCMJ who has received a grant of immunity, to answer questions by investigators or to testify or answer questions by counsel pursuant to that grant of immunity.

Discussion

A person who refuses to testify despite a valid grant of immunity may be prosecuted for such refusal. Persons subject to the UCMJ may be charged under Article 131d. A grant of immunity removes the right to refuse to testify or make a statement on self-incrimination grounds. It does not, however, remove other privileges against disclosure of information.

An immunity order or grant must not specify the contents of the testimony it is expected the witness will give.

When immunity is granted to a prosecution witness, the accused must be notified in accordance with Mil. R. Evid. 301(d)(2).

(e) *Decision to grant immunity.* Unless limited by superior competent authority, the decision to grant immunity is a matter within the sole discretion of the general court-martial convening authority, special trial counsel designated by the Secretary concerned, as applicable, or their designees. However, if a defense request to immunize a witness has been denied, the military judge may, upon motion by the defense, grant appropriate relief directing that either an appropriate convening authority or special trial counsel designated by the Secretary concerned, as applicable, grant testimonial immunity to a defense witness or, as to the affected charges and specifications, the proceedings against the accused be abated, upon findings that:

(1) The witness intends to invoke the right against self-incrimination to the extent permitted by law if called to testify;

(2) The Government has engaged in discriminatory use of immunity to obtain a tactical advantage, or the Government through its own overreaching, has forced the witness to invoke the privilege against self-incrimination; and

(3) The witness' testimony is material, clearly exculpatory, not cumulative, not obtainable from any other source, and does more than merely affect the credibility of other witnesses.

Rule 705. Plea agreements

(a) *In general.* Subject to such limitations as the Secretary concerned may prescribe, an accused and the convening authority or the accused and special trial counsel, as applicable, may enter into a plea agreement in accordance with this rule. In cases over which special trial counsel has exercised authority and has not deferred, an agreement may only be entered into between special trial counsel and the accused; however, any such agreement may bind convening authorities and other commanders subject to such limitations as prescribed by the Secretary concerned.

Discussion

The authority of convening authorities or special trial counsel to refer cases to trial and approve plea agreements extends only to trials by court-martial. To ensure that such actions do not preclude appropriate action by federal civilian authorities in cases likely to be prosecuted in the United States District Courts, convening authorities or special trial counsel, when applicable, shall ensure that appropriate consultation under the "Memorandum of Understanding Between the Departments of Justice and Defense Relating to the Investigation and Prosecution of Crimes Over Which the Two Departments Have Concurrent Jurisdiction" or its Coast Guard equivalent has taken place prior to trial by court-martial or approval of a plea agreement in cases where such consultation is required. *See* Appendix 3 and Appendix 4. Convening authorities and special trial counsel should also review and consider Appendix 2.1 (Disposition Guidance) for guidance concerning the disposition of charges and specifications through plea agreements.

(b) *Nature of agreement.* A plea agreement may include:

(1) A promise by the accused to plead guilty to, or to enter a confessional stipulation as to, one or more charges and specifications, and to fulfill such additional terms or conditions that may be included in

the agreement and that are not prohibited under this rule; and

(2) A promise by the convening authority or special trial counsel, as applicable, to do one or more of the following:

(A) Refer the charges to a certain type of court-martial;

(B) Refer a capital offense as noncapital;

(C) Withdraw one or more charges or specifications from the court-martial;

Discussion

A convening authority or special trial counsel may withdraw certain specifications and/or charges from a court-martial and dismiss them if the accused fulfills the accused's promises in the agreement. Except when jeopardy has attached (*see* R.C.M. 907(b)(2)(C)), such withdrawal and dismissal does not bar later reinstitution of the charges by special trial counsel or the same or different convening authority. A judicial determination that the accused breached the plea agreement is not required prior to reinstitution of withdrawn or dismissed specifications and/or charges. If the defense moves to dismiss the reinstituted specifications and/or charges on the grounds that the government remains bound by the terms of the plea agreement, the government will be required to prove, by a preponderance of the evidence that the accused has breached the terms of the plea agreement. If the agreement is intended to grant immunity to an accused, see R.C.M. 704.

(D) Have trial counsel present no evidence as to one or more specifications or portions thereof; and

(E) Limit the sentence that may be adjudged by the court-martial for one or more charges and specifications in accordance with R.C.M. 705(d); or

(3) A promise by either the convening authority or special trial counsel to take other action within their authority.

(c) *Terms and conditions.*

(1) *Prohibited terms and conditions.*

(A) *Not voluntary.* A term or condition in a plea agreement shall not be enforced if the accused did not freely and voluntarily agree to it.

(B) *Deprivation of certain rights.* A term or condition in a plea agreement shall not be enforced if it deprives the accused of: the right to counsel; the right to due process; the right to challenge the jurisdiction of the court-martial; the right to a speedy trial; the right to complete presentencing proceedings; the complete and effective exercise of post-trial and appellate rights.

Discussion

A plea agreement provision which prohibits the accused from making certain pretrial motions, such as for issues that are not waivable (*see* R.C.M. 905-907), is improper.

---

(2) *Permissible terms and conditions.* R.C.M. 705(c)(1)(A) and (1)(B) do not prohibit the convening authority, special trial counsel, or the accused from proposing the following additional conditions:

(A) A promise to enter into a stipulation of fact concerning offenses to which a plea of guilty or to which a confessional stipulation will be entered;

(B) A promise to testify as a witness in the trial of another person;

(C) A promise to provide restitution;

(D) A promise to conform the accused's conduct to certain conditions of probation before action by the convening authority in a summary court-martial or before entry of judgment in a general or special court-martial as well as during any period of suspension of the sentence, provided that the requirements of R.C.M. 1108 must be complied with before an alleged violation of such terms may relieve the Government of the obligation to fulfill the agreement;

(E) A promise to waive procedural requirements such as the Article 32 preliminary hearing, the right to trial by a court-martial composed of members, the right to request trial by military judge alone, the right to elect sentencing by members if applicable, or the opportunity to obtain the personal appearance of witnesses at presentencing proceedings;

Discussion

A plea agreement that includes a waiver of the accused's right to request trial by a court-martial composed of members necessarily waives the right to elect sentencing by members. *See* R.C.M. 1002.

A plea agreement that permits the accused to request trial by a court-martial composed of members necessarily preserves the accused's right to elect sentencing by military judge alone or members. In such cases, the accused will be sentenced for all offenses for which the accused was found guilty in accordance with the accused's election. *See* R.C.M. 1002.

(F) When applicable, a provision requiring that the sentences to confinement adjudged by the military judge for two or more charges or specifications be served concurrently or consecutively. Such an agreement shall identify the charges or specifications that will be served concurrently or consecutively; and

Discussion

A provision requiring the sentences to confinement be served concurrently or consecutively is applicable only to plea agreements in which the military judge determines the sentence under R.C.M. 1002(d)(2).

(G) Any other term or condition that is not contrary to or inconsistent with this rule.

(d) *Sentence limitations.*

(1) *In general.* Subject to such limitations as the Secretary concerned may prescribe pursuant to R.C.M. 705(a), a plea agreement that limits the sentence that can be imposed by the court-martial for one or more charges and specifications may contain:

(A) a limitation on the maximum punishment that can be imposed by the court-martial;

(B) a limitation on the minimum punishment that can be imposed by the court-martial;

(C) limitations on the maximum and minimum punishments that can be imposed by the court-martial; or,

(D) a specified sentence or portion of a sentence that shall be imposed by the court-martial.

(2) *Confinement and fines.*

(A) *General or special courts-martial.*

(i) In a plea agreement in which the accused waives the right to elect sentencing by members and agrees to a limitation on the confinement or the amount of a fine that may be imposed by the military judge for more than one charge or specification under paragraph (1), the agreement shall include separate limitations, as applicable, for each charge or specification.

(ii) In a plea agreement in which the convening authority and accused agree to sentencing by members, limitations on the sentence that may be adjudged shall be expressed as limitations on the total punishment that may be imposed by the members.

(B) *Summary court-martial.* A plea agreement involving limitations on the sentence that may be adjudged shall be expressed as limitations on the total punishment that may be imposed by the court-martial.

(3) *Other punishments.* A plea agreement may include a limitation as to other authorized punishments as set forth in R.C.M. 1003.

(4) *Capital cases.* A sentence limitation under paragraph (1) may not include the possibility of a sentence of death.

(5) *Mandatory minimum punishments for certain offenses.* A sentence limitation under paragraph (1) may not provide for a sentence less than the applicable mandatory minimum sentence for an offense referred to in Article 56(b)(2), except as follows:

(A) If the accused pleads guilty to the offense, the agreement may have the effect of reducing a mandatory dishonorable discharge to a bad-conduct discharge.

(B) Upon recommendation of trial counsel, in exchange for substantial assistance by the accused in the investigation or prosecution of another person who has committed an offense, a plea agreement may provide for a sentence that is less than the mandatory minimum sentence for the offense charged.

(e) *Procedure.*

(1) *Negotiation.* Plea agreement negotiations may be initiated by the accused, defense counsel, trial counsel, the staff judge advocate, convening authority, or their duly authorized representatives. Either the defense or the Government may propose any term or condition not prohibited by law or public policy. Government representatives shall negotiate with defense counsel unless the accused has waived the right to counsel.

(2) *Formal submission.* After negotiation, if any, under paragraph (1), if the accused elects to propose a plea agreement, the defense shall submit a written offer. All terms, conditions, and promises between the parties shall be written. The proposed agreement shall be signed by the accused and defense counsel, if any.

Discussion

The plea agreement ordinarily contains an offer to plead guilty and a description of the offenses to which the offer extends. It must also contain a complete and accurate statement of any other agreed terms or conditions. For example, if the convening authority or special trial counsel agrees to withdraw certain specifications, or if the accused agrees to waive the right to an Article 32 preliminary hearing or the right to elect sentencing by members, this should be stated. The written agreement should contain a statement by the accused that the accused enters it freely and voluntarily and may contain a statement that the accused has been advised of certain rights in connection with the agreement.

---

(3) *Acceptance by the convening authority or special trial counsel.*

(A) *In general.* The convening authority or special trial counsel, as applicable, may either accept or reject an offer of the accused to enter into a plea agreement or may propose by counteroffer any terms or conditions not prohibited by law or public policy. The decision whether to accept or reject an offer is within the sole discretion of the convening authority or special trial counsel, as applicable. When the convening authority has accepted a plea agreement, the agreement shall be signed by the convening authority or by a person, such as the staff judge advocate or trial counsel, who has been authorized by the convening authority to sign. When special trial counsel has accepted a plea agreement, the agreement shall be signed by special trial counsel.

Discussion

The convening authority should consult with the staff judge advocate or trial counsel and should review the applicable sections of Appendix 2.1 (Non-binding disposition guidance) before acting on an offer to enter into a plea agreement.

(B) *Victim consultation.* Prior to the convening authority or special trial counsel, as applicable, accepting a plea agreement, the convening authority or special trial counsel shall make the convening authority's or special trial counsel's best efforts to provide the victim an opportunity to submit views concerning the plea agreement terms and conditions in accordance with regulations prescribed by the Secretary concerned. The convening authority or special trial counsel, as applicable, shall consider any such views provided prior to accepting a plea agreement. For purposes of this rule, a "victim" is an individual who is alleged to have suffered direct physical, emotional, or pecuniary harm as a result of the matters set forth in a charge or specification under consideration and is named in one of the specifications under consideration.

(4) *Withdrawal.*

(A) *By accused.* The accused may withdraw from a plea agreement at any time prior to the sentence being announced. If the accused elects to withdraw from the plea agreement after the acceptance of the plea agreement but before the sentence is announced, the military judge shall permit the accused to withdraw only for good cause shown. Additionally, the accused may withdraw a plea of guilty or a confessional stipulation entered pursuant to a plea agreement only as provided in R.C.M. 910(h) or 811(d).

(B) *By convening authority or special trial counsel.* The convening authority or special trial counsel, as applicable, may withdraw from a plea agreement at any time:

(i) before substantial performance by the accused of promises contained in the agreement;

(ii) upon the failure by the accused to fulfill any material promise or condition in the agreement;

(iii) when inquiry by the military judge discloses a disagreement as to a material term in the agreement; or

(iv) if findings are set aside because a plea of guilty entered pursuant to the agreement is held improvident on appellate review.

(f) *Nondisclosure of existence of a plea agreement.* No court-martial member shall be informed of the existence of a plea agreement, except upon request of the accused or when the military judge finds that disclosure of the existence of the plea agreement is manifestly necessary in the interest of justice because of circumstances arising during the proceeding. In addition, except as provided in Mil. R. Evid. 410, the fact that an accused offered to enter into a plea agreement, and any statements made by an accused in connection therewith, whether during negotiations or during a providence inquiry, shall not be otherwise disclosed to the members.

Discussion

See R.C.M. 1002 and 1005.

Rule 706. Inquiry into the mental capacity or mental responsibility of the accused

(a) *Initial action.* If it appears to any commander who considers the disposition of charges, or to any preliminary hearing officer, trial counsel, defense counsel, military judge, or member that there is reason to believe that the accused lacked mental responsibility for any offense charged or lacks capacity to stand trial, that fact and the basis of the belief or observation shall be transmitted through appropriate channels to the officer authorized to order an inquiry into the mental condition of the accused. The submission may be accompanied by an application for a mental examination under this rule.

Discussion

See R.C.M. 909 concerning the capacity of the accused to stand trial and R.C.M. 916(k) concerning mental responsibility of the accused.

(b) *Ordering an inquiry.*

(1) *Before referral.* Before referral of charges, an inquiry into the mental capacity or mental responsibility of the accused may be ordered by any applicable convening authority, or by a military judge or magistrate in a proceeding conducted in accordance with R.C.M. 309.

(2) *After referral.* After referral of charges, an inquiry into the mental capacity or mental responsibility of the accused may be ordered by the military judge. The convening authority may order such an inquiry after referral of charges but before beginning of the first session of the court-martial (including any Article 39(a) session) when the military judge is not reasonably available. The military judge may order a mental examination of the accused regardless of any earlier determination by any authority.

(c) *Inquiry.*

(1) *By whom conducted.* When a mental examination is ordered under subsection (b) of this rule, the matter shall be referred to a board consisting of one or more persons. Each member of the board shall be either a physician or a clinical psychologist. Normally, at least one member of the board shall be either a psychiatrist or a clinical psychologist. The board shall report as to the mental capacity or mental responsibility or both of the accused.

(2) *Matters in inquiry.* When a mental examination is ordered under this rule, the order shall contain the reasons for doubting the mental capacity or mental responsibility, or both, of the accused, or other reasons for requesting the examination. In addition to other requirements, the order shall require the board to make separate and distinct findings as to each of the following questions:

(A) At the time of the alleged criminal conduct, did the accused have a severe mental disease or defect? (The term "severe mental disease or defect" does not include an abnormality manifested only by repeated criminal or otherwise antisocial conduct, or minor disorders such as nonpsychotic behavior disorders and personality defects.)

(B) What is the clinical psychiatric diagnosis?

(C) Was the accused, at the time of the alleged criminal conduct and as a result of such severe mental disease or defect, unable to appreciate the nature and quality or wrongfulness of his or her conduct?

(D) Is the accused presently suffering from a mental disease or defect rendering the accused unable to understand the nature of the proceedings against the accused or to conduct or cooperate intelligently in the defense?

Other appropriate questions may also be included.

(3) *Directions to board.* In addition to the requirements specified in paragraph (c)(2) of this rule, the order to the board shall specify:

(A) That upon completion of the board's investigation, a statement consisting only of the board's ultimate conclusions as to all questions specified in the order shall be submitted to the officer ordering the examination, the accused's commanding officer, the preliminary hearing officer, if any, appointed pursuant to Article 32, and to all government and defense counsel in the case, the convening authority, and, after referral, to the military judge.

(B) That the full report of the board may be released by the board or other medical personnel only to other medical personnel for medical purposes, unless otherwise authorized by the convening authority or, after referral of charges, by the military judge, except that a copy of the full report shall be furnished to the defense and, upon request, to the commanding officer of the accused; and

(C) That neither the contents of the full report nor any matter considered by the board during its investigation shall be released by the board or other medical personnel to any person not authorized to receive the full report, except pursuant to an order by the military judge.

Discussion

Based on the report, further action in the case may be suspended; the charges may be dismissed by the convening authority or special trial counsel; administrative action may be taken to discharge the accused from the service; or, subject to Mil. R. Evid. 302, the charges may be tried by court-martial."

---

(4) *Additional examinations.* Additional examinations may be directed under this rule at any stage of the proceedings as circumstances may require.

(5) *Disclosure to trial counsel.* No person, other than defense counsel, the accused, or, after referral of charges, the military judge may disclose to trial counsel any statement made by the accused to the board or any evidence derived from such statement.

Discussion

See Mil. R. Evid. 302.

Rule 707. Speedy trial

(a) *In general.* The accused shall be brought to trial within 120 days after the earlier of:

(1) Preferral of charges;

Discussion

Delay from the time of an offense to preferral of charges or the imposition of pretrial restraint is not considered for speedy trial purposes. *See also* Article 43 (statute of limitations). In some circumstances such delay may prejudice the accused and may result in dismissal of the charges or other relief.

---

(2) The imposition of restraint under R.C.M. 304(a)(2)–(4); or

(3) Entry on active duty under R.C.M. 204.

(b) *Accountability.*

(1) *In general.* The date of preferral of charges, the date on which pretrial restraint under R.C.M. 304 (a)(2)-(4) is imposed, or the date of entry on active duty under R.C.M. 204 shall not count for purpose of computing time under subsection (a) of this rule. The date on which the accused is brought to trial shall count. The accused is brought to trial within the meaning of this rule at the time of arraignment under R.C.M. 904.

(2) *Multiple Charges.* When charges are preferred at different times, accountability for each charge shall be determined from the appropriate date under subsection (a) of this rule for that charge.

(3) *Events which affect time periods.*

(A) *Dismissal or mistrial.* In the event of dismissal of charges or mistrial, a new 120-day period begins as follows:

(i) For an accused under pretrial restraint under R.C.M. 304(a)(2)-(4) at the time of the dismissal or mistrial, a new 120-day period begins on the date of the dismissal or mistrial.

(ii) For an accused not under pretrial restraint at the time of dismissal or mistrial, a new 120-day period begins on the earliest of:

(I) the date on which charges are preferred anew;

(II) the date of imposition of restraint under R.C.M. 304(a)(2)-(4); or

(III) in the case of a mistrial in which charges are not dismissed or preferred anew, the date of the mistrial.

(iii) In a case in which it is determined that charges were dismissed for an improper purpose or for subterfuge, the time period determined under subsection (a) shall continue to run.

(B) *Release from restraint.* If the accused is released from pretrial restraint for a significant period, the 120-day time period under this rule shall begin on the earlier of

(i) the date of preferral of charges;

(ii) the date on which restraint under R.C.M. 304(a) (2)-(4) is reimposed; or

(iii) date of entry on active duty under R.C.M. 204.

(C) *Government appeals.* If notice of appeal under R.C.M. 908 is filed, a new 120-day time period under this rule shall begin, for all charges neither proceeded on nor severed under R.C.M. 908(b)(4), on the date of notice to the parties under R.C.M. 908(b)(8) or 908(c)(3), unless it is determined that the appeal was filed solely for the purpose of delay with the knowledge that it was totally frivolous and without merit. After the decision of the Court of Criminal Appeals under R.C.M. 908, if there is a further appeal to the Court of Appeals for the Armed Forces or, subsequently, to the Supreme Court, a new 120-day time period under this rule shall begin on the date the parties are notified of the final decision of the Court of Appeals for the Armed Forces, or, if appropriate, the Supreme Court.

(D) *Rehearings.* If a rehearing is ordered or authorized by an appellate court, a new 120-day time period under this rule shall begin on the date that the responsible convening authority or, for charges and specifications referred by a special trial counsel, the special trial counsel receives the record of trial and the opinion authorizing or directing a rehearing. An accused is brought to trial within the meaning of this rule at the time of arraignment under R.C.M. 904 or, if arraignment is not required (such as in the case of a sentence-only rehearing), at the time of the first session under R.C.M. 803.

(E) *Commitment of the incompetent accused.* If the accused is committed to the custody of the Attorney General for hospitalization as provided in R.C.M. 909(f), all periods of such commitment shall be excluded when determining whether the period in subsection (a) of this rule has run. If, at the end of the period of commitment, the accused is returned to the custody of the general court-martial convening authority, a new 120-day time period under this rule shall begin on the date of such return to custody.

(c) *Excludable delay.* All periods of time during which appellate courts have issued stays in the proceedings, or the accused is absent without authority, or the accused is hospitalized due to incompetence, or is otherwise in the custody of the Attorney General, shall be excluded when determining whether the period in subsection (a) of this rule has run. All other pretrial delays approved by a military judge or the convening authority shall be similarly excluded.

(1) *Procedure.* Prior to referral, all requests for pretrial delay, together with supporting reasons and with notice to the defense, will be submitted to a convening authority with authority over the accused for resolution. The convening authority may delegate this authority to an Article 32 preliminary hearing officer. After referral, such requests for pretrial delay will be submitted to the military judge for resolution.

Discussion

The decision to grant or deny a reasonable delay is a matter within the sole discretion of the convening authority or a military judge. Reasons to grant a delay might include, for example, the need for: time to enable counsel to prepare for trial in complex cases; time to allow examination into the mental capacity of the accused; time to process a member of the reserve component to active duty for disciplinary action; time to complete other proceedings related to the case; time requested by the defense; time to secure the availability of the accused, substantial witnesses, or other evidence; time to obtain appropriate security clearances for access to classified information or time to declassify evidence; or additional time for other good cause. Pretrial delays should not be granted ex parte, and when practicable, the decision granting the delay, together with supporting reasons and the dates covering the delay, should be reduced to writing.

---

(2) *Motions.* Upon accused's timely motion to a military judge under R.C.M. 905 for speedy trial relief, counsel should provide the court a chronology detailing the processing of the case. This chronology should be made a part of the appellate record.

(d) *Remedy.* A failure to comply with this rule will result in dismissal of the affected charges, or, in a sentence-only rehearing, sentence relief as appropriate.

(1) *Dismissal.* Dismissal will be with or without prejudice to the Government's right to reinstitute court-martial proceedings against the accused for the same offense at a later date. The charges must be dismissed with prejudice where the accused has been deprived of his or her constitutional right to a speedy trial. In determining whether to dismiss charges with or without prejudice, the court shall consider, among others, each of the following factors: the seriousness of the offense; the facts and circumstances of the case that lead to dismissal; the impact of a re-prosecution on the administration of justice; and any prejudice to the accused resulting from the denial of a speedy trial.

(2) *Sentence relief.* In determining whether or how much sentence relief is appropriate, the military judge shall consider, among others, each of the following factors: the length of the delay, the reasons for the delay, the accused's demand for speedy trial, and any prejudice to the accused from the delay. Any sentence relief granted will be applied against the sentence approved by the convening authority.

Discussion

See R.C.M. 707(c)(1) and the accompanying Discussion concerning reasons for delay and procedures for parties to request delay.

(e) *Waiver.* Except as provided in R.C.M. 910(a)(2), a plea of guilty that results in a finding of guilty waives any speedy trial issue under this rule as to that offense.

(f) *Priority.* When considering the disposition of charges and the ordering of trials, a convening authority or special trial counsel shall give priority to cases in which the accused is held under those forms of pretrial restraint defined by R.C.M. 304(a)(3)-(4). Trial of or other disposition of charges against any accused held in arrest or confinement pending trial shall be given priority.

CHAPTER VIII. TRIAL PROCEDURE GENERALLY

Rule 801. Military judge's responsibilities; other matters

(a) *Responsibilities of military judge.* The military judge is the presiding officer in a court-martial. The military judge shall:

Discussion

The military judge is responsible for ensuring that court-martial proceedings are conducted in a fair and orderly manner, without unnecessary delay or waste of time or resources.

(1) Determine the time and uniform for each session of a court-martial;

Discussion

The military judge should consult with counsel concerning the scheduling of sessions and the uniform to be worn. The military judge recesses or adjourns the court-martial as appropriate. Subject to R.C.M. 504(d)(1), the military judge may also determine the place of trial. *See also* R.C.M. 906(b)(11).

(2) Ensure that the dignity and decorum of the proceedings are maintained;

Discussion

See generally R.C.M. 804 and 806. Courts-martial should be conducted in an atmosphere which is conducive to calm and detached deliberation and determination of the issues presented and which reflects the seriousness of the proceedings.

(3) Subject to the UCMJ and this Manual, exercise reasonable control over the proceedings to promote the purposes of these rules and this Manual;

Discussion

See R.C.M. 102. The military judge may, within the framework established by the code and this Manual, prescribe the manner and order in which the proceedings may take place. Thus, the military judge may determine: when, and in what order, motions will be litigated (*see* R.C.M. 905); the manner in which voir dire will be conducted and challenges made (*see* R.C.M. 902(d) and 912); the order in which witnesses may testify (*see* R.C.M. 913; Mil. R. Evid. 611); the order in which the parties may argue on a motion or objection; and the time limits for argument (*see* R.C.M. 905; 919; 1001(h)).

The military judge should prevent unnecessary waste of time and promote the ascertainment of truth, but must avoid undue interference with the parties' presentations or the appearance of partiality. The parties are entitled to a reasonable opportunity to properly present and support their contentions on any relevant matter.

(4) Rule on all interlocutory questions and all questions of law raised during the court-martial as provided under subsection (e);

(5) Instruct the members on questions of law and procedure which may arise; and

Discussion

The military judge instructs the members concerning findings (*see* R.C.M. 920) and, when applicable, sentence (*see* R.C.M. 1005), and when otherwise appropriate. For example, preliminary instructions to the members concerning their duties and the duties of other trial participants and other matters are normally appropriate. *See* R.C.M. 913. Other instructions (for example, instructions on the limited purpose for which evidence has been introduced, see Mil. R. Evid. 105) may be given whenever the need arises.

(6) At the military judge's discretion, in the case of a victim of an offense under the UCMJ who is under 18 years of age and not a member of the armed forces, or who is incompetent, incapacitated, or deceased, designate the legal guardian(s) of the victim or the representative(s) of the victim's estate, family members, or any other person deemed as suitable by the military judge to assume the victim's rights under the UCMJ.

(A) The military judge is not required to hold a hearing before determining whether a designation is required or before making such a designation under this rule.

(B) If the military judge determines a hearing under Article 39(a), UCMJ, is necessary, the victim shall be notified of the hearing and afforded the right to be present at the hearing.

(C) The individual designated shall not be the accused.

(D) At any time after appointment, a designee shall be excused upon request by the designee or a finding of good cause by the military judge.

(E) If the individual appointed to assume the

victim's rights is excused, the military may designate a successor consistent with this rule.

Discussion

The term "victim of an offense under the UCMJ" has the same meaning as the term "victim of an offense under this chapter" in Article 6b.

(b) *Rules of court; contempt.* The military judge may:

(1) Subject to R.C.M. 108, promulgate and enforce rules of court.

(2) Subject to R.C.M. 809, exercise contempt power.

(c) *Obtaining evidence.* The court-martial may act to obtain evidence in addition to that presented by the parties. The right of the members to have additional evidence obtained is subject to an interlocutory ruling by the military judge.

Discussion

The members may request and the military judge may require that a witness be recalled, or that a new witness be summoned, or other evidence produced. The members or military judge may direct trial counsel to make an inquiry along certain lines to discover and produce additional evidence. *See also* Mil. R. Evid. 614. In taking such action, the court-martial must not depart from an impartial role.

(d) *Uncharged offenses.* If during the trial there is evidence that the accused may be guilty of an untried offense not alleged in any specification before the court-martial, the court-martial shall proceed with the trial of the offense charged.

Discussion

A report of the matter may be made to the referral authority after trial.. If charges are preferred for an offense indicated by the evidence referred to in this subsection, no member of the court-martial who participated in the first trial should sit in any later trial. Such a member would ordinarily be subject to a challenge for cause. *See* R.C.M. 912. *See also* Mil. R. Evid. 105 concerning instructing the members on evidence of uncharged misconduct.

(e) *Interlocutory questions and questions of law.*

(1) *Rulings by the military judge.*

(A) *Finality of rulings.* Any ruling by the military judge upon a question of law, including a motion for a finding of not guilty, or upon any interlocutory question is final.

(B) *Changing a ruling.* The military judge may change a ruling made by that or another military judge in the case except a previously granted motion for a finding of not guilty, at any time during the trial.

(C) *Article 39(a) sessions.* When required by this Manual or otherwise deemed appropriate by the military judge, interlocutory questions or questions of law shall be presented and decided at sessions held without members under R.C.M. 803.

Discussion

Sessions without members are appropriate for interlocutory questions, questions of law, and instructions. *See also* Mil. R. Evid. 103, 304, 311, 321. Such sessions should be used to the extent possible consistent with the orderly, expeditious progress of the proceedings.

---

(2) [Reserved]

(3) [Reserved]

(4) *Standard of proof.* Questions of fact in an interlocutory question shall be determined by a preponderance of the evidence, unless otherwise stated in this Manual. In the absence of a rule in this Manual assigning the burden of persuasion, the party making the motion or raising the objection shall bear the burden of persuasion.

Discussion

A ruling on an interlocutory question should be preceded by any necessary inquiry into the pertinent facts and law. For example, the party making the objection, motion, or request may be required to furnish evidence or legal authority in support of the contention. An interlocutory issue may have a different standard of proof. See, for example, Mil. R. Evid. 314(e)(5), which requires consent for a search to be proved by clear and convincing evidence.

Most of the common motions are discussed in specific rules in this Manual, and the burden of persuasion is assigned therein. The prosecution usually bears the burden of persuasion (*see* Mil. R. Evid. 304(f)(6); 311(d)(5); *see also* R.C.M. 905 through 907) once an issue has been raised. What "raises" an issue may vary with the issue. Some issues may be raised by a timely motion or objection. *See, e.g.*, Mil. R. Evid. 304(f). Others may not be raised until the defense has made an offer of proof or presented evidence in support of its position. *See, e.g.*, Mil. R. Evid. 311(d)(4)(B). The rules in this Manual and relevant decisions should be consulted when a question arises as to whether an issue is raised, as well as which side has the burden of persuasion. The military judge may require a party to clarify a motion or objection or to make an offer of proof, regardless of the burden of persuasion, when it appears that the motion or objection is vague, inapposite, irrelevant, or spurious.

---

(5) *Scope.* Subsection (e) of this rule applies to the disposition of questions of law and interlocutory questions arising during trial except the question whether a challenge should be sustained.

Discussion

Questions of law and interlocutory questions include all issues which arise during trial other than the findings (that is, guilty or not guilty), sentence, and administrative matters such as declaring recesses and adjournments. A question may be both interlocutory and a question of law. Challenges are specifically covered in R.C.M. 902 and 912.

Questions of the applicability of a rule of law to an undisputed set of facts are normally questions of law. Similarly, the legality of an act is normally a question of law. For example, the legality of an order when disobedience of an order is charged, the legality of restraint when there is a prosecution for breach of arrest, or the sufficiency of warnings before interrogation are normally questions of law. It is possible, however, for such questions to be decided solely upon some factual issue, in which case they would be questions of fact. For example, the question of what warnings, if any, were given by an interrogator to a suspect would be a factual question.

A question is interlocutory unless the ruling on it would finally decide whether the accused is guilty. Questions which may determine the ultimate issue of guilt are not interlocutory. An issue may arise as both an interlocutory question and a question which may determine the ultimate issue of guilt. An issue is not purely interlocutory if an accused raises a defense or objection and the disputed facts involved determine the ultimate question of guilt. For example, if during a trial for desertion the accused moves to dismiss for lack of jurisdiction and presents some evidence that the accused is not a member of an armed force, the accused's status as a military person may determine the ultimate question of guilt because status is an element of the offense. If the motion is denied, the disputed facts must be resolved by each member in deliberation upon the findings. (The accused's status as a Servicemember would have to be proved by a preponderance of the evidence to uphold jurisdiction, *see* R.C.M. 907, but beyond a reasonable doubt to permit a finding of guilty.) If, on the other hand, the accused was charged with larceny and presented the same evidence as to military status, the evidence would bear only upon amenability to trial and the issue would be disposed of solely as an interlocutory question.

Interlocutory questions may be questions of fact or questions of law.

(f) *Rulings on record.* All sessions involving rulings or instructions made or given by the military judge shall be made a part of the record. All rulings and instructions shall be made or given in open session in the presence of the parties and the members, except as otherwise may be determined in the discretion of the military judge.

Discussion

See R.C.M. 808 and 1112 concerning preparation of the record of trial.

(g) *Effect of failure to raise defenses or objections.* Failure by a party to raise defenses or objections or to make requests or motions which must be made at the time set by this Manual or by the military judge under authority of this Manual, or prior to any extension thereof made by the military judge, shall constitute forfeiture unless the applicable rule provides that failure to raise the defense or objection constitutes waiver.

Rule 802. Conferences

(a) *In general.* The military judge may, upon request of any party or *sua sponte*, order one or more conferences with the parties to consider such matters as will promote a fair and expeditious trial. Such conferences may take place before or after referral, as applicable.

Discussion

The military judge may hold a conference when detailed to the court-martial following referral as well as after being detailed to conduct any pre-referral proceeding pursuant to Article 30a. *See* R.C.M. 309.

Conferences between the military judge and counsel may be held when necessary before or during trial. The purpose of such conference is to inform the military judge of anticipated issues and to expeditiously resolve matters on which the parties can agree, not to litigate or decide contested issues. No party may be compelled to resolve any matter at a conference. *See* R.C.M. 802(c).

A conference may be appropriate in order to resolve scheduling difficulties, so that witnesses and members are not unnecessarily inconvenienced. Matters which will ultimately be in the military judge's discretion, such as conduct of voir dire, seating arrangements in the courtroom, or procedures when there are multiple accused may be resolved at a conference. Conferences may be used to advise the military judge of issues or problems, such as unusual motions or objections, which are likely to arise during trial.

Occasionally it may be appropriate to resolve certain issues, in addition to routine or administrative matters, if this can be done with the consent of the parties. For example, a request for a witness which, if litigated and approved at trial, would delay the proceedings and cause expense or inconvenience, might be resolved at a conference. Note, however, that this could only be done by an agreement of the parties and not by a binding ruling of the military judge. Such a resolution must be included in the record. *See* R.C.M. 802(b).

A military judge may not participate in negotiations relating to pleas. *See* R.C.M. 705 and Mil. R. Evid. 410.

No place or method is prescribed for conducting a conference. A conference may be conducted by remote means or similar technology consistent with the definition in R.C.M. 914B.

(b) *Matters on record.* Conferences need not be made part of the record, but matters agreed upon at a conference shall be included in the record orally or in writing. Failure of a party to object at trial to failure to comply with this subsection shall waive this requirement.

(c) *Rights of parties.* No party may be prevented under this rule from presenting evidence or from making any argument, objection, or motion at trial.

(d) *Accused's presence.* The presence of the accused is neither required nor prohibited at a conference.

Discussion

Normally the defense counsel may be presumed to speak for the accused.

(e) *Admission.* No admissions made by the accused or defense counsel at a conference shall be used against the accused unless the admissions are reduced to writing and signed by the accused and defense counsel.

(f) *Limitations.* This rule shall not be invoked in the case of an accused who is not represented by counsel.

Rule 803. Court-martial sessions without members under Article 39(a)

A military judge who has been detailed to the court-martial may, under Article 39(a), after service of charges, call the court-martial into session without the presence of members. Such sessions may be held before and after assembly of the court-martial, and when authorized in these rules, after adjournment and before entry of the judgment in the record. All such sessions are a part of the trial and shall be conducted in the presence of the accused, defense counsel, and trial counsel, in accordance with R.C.M. 804 and 805, and shall be made a part of the record.

Discussion

The purpose of Article 39(a) is "to give statutory sanction to pretrial and other hearings without the presence of the members concerning those matters which are amenable to disposition on either a tentative or final basis by the military judge." The military judge may, and ordinarily should, call the court-martial into session without members to ascertain the accused's understanding of the right to counsel and forum selection, and the accused's choices with respect to these matters; dispose of interlocutory matters; hear objections and motions; rule upon other matters that may legally be ruled upon by the military judge, such as admitting evidence; and perform other procedural functions which do not require the presence of members. *See, e.g.,* R.C.M. 901–910. The military judge may hold the arraignment, receive pleas, enter findings of guilty upon an accepted plea of guilty, and conduct presentencing proceedings under R.C.M. 1001 without the members present.

Evidence may be admitted and process, including a subpoena, may be issued to compel attendance of witnesses and production of evidence at such sessions. *See* R.C.M. 703.

Article 39(a) authorizes sessions only after charges have been referred to trial and served on the accused, but the accused has an absolute right to object, in time of peace, to any session until the period prescribed by Article 35 has run.

See R.C.M. 804 concerning waiver by the accused of the right to be present. *See also* R.C.M. 802 concerning conferences.

See R.C.M. 309 concerning proceedings conducted before referral under Article 30a.

Rule 804. Presence at court-martial proceedings

(a) *Accused.*

(1) *Presence required.* The accused shall be present at the arraignment, the time of the plea, every stage of the trial including sessions conducted under Article 39(a), voir dire and challenges of members, the return of the findings, presentencing proceedings, and post-trial sessions, if any, except as otherwise provided by this rule. Attendance at these proceedings shall constitute the accused's appointed place of duty and, with respect to the accused's travel allowances, none of these proceedings shall constitute disciplinary action. This does not in any way limit authority to implement restriction, up to and including confinement, as necessary in accordance with R.C.M. 304 or R.C.M. 305.

(A) *Appearance.* The accused shall be properly attired in the uniform or dress prescribed by the military judge. An accused service member shall wear the insignia of grade and may wear any decorations, emblems, or ribbons to which the accused is entitled. The accused and defense counsel are responsible for ensuring that the accused is properly attired; however, upon request, the accused's commander shall render such assistance as may be reasonably necessary to ensure that the accused is properly attired.

Discussion

An accused has the right, as well as the obligation, to present a good military appearance at trial. An accused who refuses to present a proper military appearance before a court-martial may be compelled to do so.

(B) *Custody.* Responsibility for maintaining custody or control of an accused before and during trial may be assigned, subject to R.C.M. 304 and 305, and R.C.M. 804(c)(3), under such regulations as the Secretary concerned may prescribe.

(C) *Restraint.* Physical restraint shall not be imposed on the accused during open sessions of the court-martial unless prescribed by the military judge.

(2) *Continuation of proceeding without presence.* The further progress of the trial to and including the return of the findings and, if necessary, determination of a sentence shall not be prevented and the accused shall be considered to have waived the right to be present whenever an accused, initially present:

(A) Is voluntarily absent after arraignment (whether or not informed by the military judge of the obligation to remain during the trial); or

(B) After being warned by the military judge that disruptive conduct will cause the accused to be removed from the courtroom, persists in conduct which is such as to justify exclusion from the courtroom.

Discussion

Express waiver. The accused may expressly waive the right to be present at trial proceedings. There is no right to be absent, however, and the accused may be required to be present over objection. Thus, an accused cannot frustrate efforts to identify the accused at trial by waiving the right to be present. The right to be present is so fundamental, and the Government's interest in the attendance of the accused so substantial, that the accused should be permitted to waive the right to be present only for good cause, and only after the military judge explains to the accused the right, and the consequences of forgoing it, and secures the accused's personal consent to proceeding without the accused.

Voluntary absence. In any case the accused may forfeit the right to be present by being voluntarily absent after arraignment. "Voluntary absence" means voluntary absence from trial. For an absence from court-martial proceedings to be voluntary, the accused must have known of the scheduled proceedings and intentionally missed them. For example, although an accused service member might voluntarily be absent without authority, this would not justify proceeding with a court-martial in the accused's absence unless the accused was aware that the court-martial would be held during the period of the absence.

An accused who is in military custody or otherwise subject to military control at the time of trial or other proceeding may not properly be absent from the trial or proceeding without securing the permission of the military judge on the record.

The prosecution has the burden to establish by a preponderance of the evidence that the accused's absence from trial is voluntary. Voluntariness may not be presumed, but it may be inferred, depending on the circumstances. For example, it may be inferred, in the absence of evidence to the contrary, that an accused who was present when the trial recessed and who knew when the proceedings were scheduled to resume, but who nonetheless is not present when court reconvenes at the designated time, is absent voluntarily.

Where there is some evidence that an accused who is absent for a hearing or trial may lack mental capacity to stand trial, capacity to voluntarily waive the right to be present for trial must be shown. *See* R.C.M. 909.

Subsection (1) authorizes but does not require trial to proceed in the absence of the accused upon the accused's voluntary absence. When an accused is absent from trial after arraignment, a continuance or a recess may be appropriate, depending on all the circumstances.

Removal for disruption. Trial may proceed without the presence of an accused who has disrupted the proceedings, but only after at least one warning by the military judge that such behavior may result in removal from the courtroom. In order to justify removal from the proceedings, the accused's behavior should be of such a nature as to materially interfere with the conduct of the proceedings.

The military judge should consider alternatives to removal of a disruptive accused. Such alternatives include physical restraint (such as binding, shackling, and gagging) of the accused, or physically segregating the accused in the courtroom. Such alternatives need not be tried before removing a disruptive accused under subsection (2). Removal may be preferable to such an alternative as binding and gagging, which can be an affront to the dignity and decorum of the proceedings.

Disruptive behavior of the accused may also constitute contempt. *See* R.C.M. 809. When the accused is removed from the courtroom for disruptive behavior, the military judge should—

(A) Afford the accused and defense counsel ample opportunity to consult throughout the proceedings. To this end, the accused should be held or otherwise required to remain in the vicinity of the trial, and frequent recesses permitted to allow counsel to confer with the accused.

(B) Take such additional steps as may be reasonably practicable to enable the accused to be informed about the proceedings. Although not required, technological aids, such as closed-circuit television or audio transmissions, may be used for this purpose.

(C) Afford the accused a continuing opportunity to return to the courtroom upon assurance of good behavior. To this end, the accused should be brought to the courtroom at appropriate intervals, and offered the opportunity to remain upon good behavior.

(D) Ensure that the reasons for removal appear in the record.

---

(3) *Remote presence of the accused.*

(A) Except as provided in R.C.M. 804(a)(3)(B), for Article 39(a) sessions, the military judge may order the accused be present via remote means through the use of audiovisual technology. Use of such audiovisual technology will satisfy the "presence" requirement of the accused only when the accused has a defense counsel physically present at the accused's location or when the accused consents to presence by remote means with the opportunity for confidential consultation with defense counsel during the proceeding. Such technology may include two or more remote sites as long as all parties can see and hear each other.

(B) The accused may be present via remote means through the use of audiovisual technology for a plea inquiry under R.C.M. 910(d), (e) and (f), and presentencing proceedings before a military judge under R.C.M. 1001, only when there are exceptional circumstances that interfere with the normal administration of military justice, as determined by the military judge. The accused must consent to the use of audiovisual technology and defense counsel must be physically present at the accused's location for the hearing.

(4) *Voluntary absence for limited purpose of child testimony.*

(A) *Election by accused.* Following a determination by the military judge that remote live testimony of a child is appropriate pursuant to Mil. R. Evid. 611(d)(3), the accused may elect to be voluntarily absent from the courtroom in order to preclude the use of procedures described in R.C.M. 914A.

(B) *Procedure.* The accused's absence will be conditional upon the accused being able to view the witness' testimony from a remote location. Normally, transmission of the testimony will include a system that will transmit the accused's image and voice into the courtroom from a remote location as well as transmission of the child's testimony from the courtroom to the accused's location. A one-way transmission may be used if deemed necessary by the military judge. The accused will also be provided private, contemporaneous communication with his counsel. The procedures described herein shall be employed unless the accused has made a knowing and affirmative waiver of these procedures.

(C) *Effect on accused's rights generally.* An election by the accused to be absent pursuant to R.C.M. 804(a)(4)(A) shall not otherwise affect the accused's right to be present at the remainder of the trial in accordance with this rule.

Discussion

See paragraph 030706 of the Joint Travel Regulations Uniformed Service Members and DoD Civilian Employees, dated 1 September 2023.

(b) *Military judge.*

(1) No court-martial proceeding, except the deliberations of the members, may take place in the absence of the military judge. The military judge may attend Article 39(a) sessions via remote means through the use of audiovisual technology.

(2) When a new military judge is detailed under R.C.M. 505(e)(2) after the presentation of evidence on the merits has begun in a trial before a military judge alone, trial may not proceed unless the accused requests, and the new military judge approves, trial by military judge alone, and a verbatim record of the testimony and evidence or a stipulation thereof is read to or played for the new military judge in the presence of the accused and counsel for both sides, or the trial proceeds as if no evidence had been presented.

(c) *Members.*

(1) Unless the accused is tried or sentenced by military judge alone, no court-martial proceeding may take place in the absence of any detailed member except: Article 39(a) sessions under R.C.M. 803; temporary excusal under R.C.M. 911(b); examination of members under R.C.M. 912(d); when the member has been excused under R.C.M. 505, 912(f), or 912A; as otherwise provided in R.C.M. 1104(d)(1); or as otherwise provided in this Manual.

Discussion

See R.C.M. 501 and R.C.M. 505 concerning the minimum number of members and the procedures to follow when members are dismissed.

---

(2) When after presentation of evidence on the merits has begun, a new member is impaneled under R.C.M. 912A, trial may not proceed unless the testimony and evidence previously admitted on the merits, if recorded verbatim, is read to or played for the new member in the presence of the military judge, the accused, and counsel for both sides, or, if not recorded verbatim, and in the absence of a stipulation as to such testimony and evidence, the trial proceeds as if no evidence has been presented.

Discussion

When a new member is detailed, the military judge should give such instructions as may be appropriate. See also R.C.M. 912 concerning voir dire and challenges.

(d) *Counsel.* As long as at least one qualified counsel for each party is present, other counsel for each party may be absent from a court-martial session. In the case of a court-martial requiring the detailing of a special trial counsel, the presence of a special trial counsel is required unless a special trial counsel determines otherwise and another trial counsel, who is qualified according to Article 27(b), is also present. An assistant counsel who lacks the qualifications necessary to serve as counsel for a party may not act at a session in the absence of such qualified counsel. For purposes of Article 39(a) sessions and subject to R.C.M. 804(a)(3), the presence of counsel may be satisfied via remote means through the use of audiovisual technology.

Discussion

See R.C.M. 502(d) concerning qualifications of counsel.

Ordinarily, no court-martial proceeding should take place if any defense or assistant defense counsel is absent unless the accused expressly consents to the absence. The military judge may, however proceed in the absence of one or more defense counsel, without the consent of the accused, if the military judge finds that, under the circumstances, a continuance is not warranted and that the accused's right to be adequately represented would not be impaired.

See R.C.M. 502(d)(5), 505(d)(2), and 506(c) concerning withdrawal or substitution of counsel. See R.C.M. 506(d) concerning the right of the accused to proceed without counsel.

(e) *Victim and Victim's Counsel.* Subject to R.C.M. 914B, at the discretion of the military judge and for good cause, the victim and victim's counsel may be present through the use of audiovisual technology.

Discussion

The ability of a victim to attend a court-martial proceeding via remote means is not intended to circumvent an accused's constitutional rights.

Rule 805. [Reserved]

Rule 806. Public trial

(a) *In general.* Except as otherwise provided in this rule, courts-martial shall be open to the public. For purposes of this rule, "public" includes members of both the military and civilian communities.

Discussion

Because of the requirement for public trials, courts-martial must be conducted in facilities that can accommodate a reasonable number of spectators. Military exigencies may occasionally make attendance at courts-martial difficult or impracticable, as, for example, when a court-martial is conducted on a ship at sea or in a unit in a combat zone. These exigencies do not violate this rule. However, such exigencies should not be manipulated to prevent attendance at a court-martial. The requirements of this rule may be met even though only service members are able to attend a court-martial. Although not required, service members should be encouraged to attend courts-martial.

When public access to a court-martial is limited for some reason, including lack of space, special care must be taken to avoid arbitrary exclusion of specific groups or persons. This may include allocating a reasonable number of seats to members of the press and to relatives of the accused, and establishing procedures for entering and exiting from the courtroom. *See also* R.C.M. 806(b). There is no requirement that there actually be spectators at a court-martial.

The fact that a trial is conducted with members does not make it a public trial.

(b) *Control of spectators and closure.*

(1) *Limitation on number of spectators.* In order to maintain the dignity and decorum of the proceedings or for other good cause, the military judge may reasonably limit the number of spectators in, and the means of access to, the courtroom, and exclude specific persons from the courtroom.

Discussion

The military judge must ensure that the dignity and decorum of the proceedings are maintained and that the other rights and interests of the parties and society are protected. Public access to a session may be limited, specific persons may be excluded from the courtroom, and, under unusual circumstances, a session may be closed.

Exclusion of specific persons, if unreasonable under the circumstances, may violate the accused's right to a public trial, even though other spectators remain. Whenever specific persons or some members of the public are excluded, exclusion must be limited in time and scope to the minimum extent necessary to achieve the purpose for which it is ordered. Prevention of over-crowding or noise may justify limiting access to the courtroom. Disruptive or distracting appearance or conduct may justify excluding specific persons. Specific persons may be excluded when necessary to protect witnesses from harm or intimidation. Access may be reduced when no other means is available to relieve a witness' inability to testify due to embarrassment or extreme nervousness. Witnesses will ordinarily be excluded from the courtroom so that they cannot hear the testimony of other witnesses. *See* Mil. R. Evid. 615.

---

(2) *Exclusion of spectators.* When excluding specific persons, the military judge must make findings on the record establishing the reason for the exclusion, the basis for the military judge's belief that exclusion is necessary, and that the exclusion is as narrowly tailored as possible.

(3) *Right of victim not to be excluded.* A victim of an alleged offense committed by the accused may not be

excluded from any public hearing or proceeding in a court-martial relating to the offense unless the military judge, after receiving clear and convincing evidence, determines that testimony by the victim would be materially altered if the victim heard other testimony at that hearing or proceeding.

Discussion

Victims are also entitled to notice of all such proceedings, the right to confer with counsel for the Government, and the right to be reasonably protected from the accused. *See* Article 6b. For purposes of this rule, the term "victim of an alleged offense" has the same meaning as the term "victim of an offense under this chapter" in Article 6b.

---

(4) *Closure*. Courts-martial shall be open to the public unless (A) there is a substantial probability that an overriding interest will be prejudiced if the proceedings remain open; (B) closure is no broader than necessary to protect the overriding interest; (C) reasonable alternatives to closure were considered and found inadequate; and (D) the military judge makes case-specific findings on the record justifying closure.

Discussion

The military judge is responsible for protecting both the accused's right to, and the public's interest in, a public trial. A court-martial session is "closed" when no member of the public is permitted to attend. A court-martial is not "closed" merely because the exclusion of certain individuals results in there being no spectators present, as long as the exclusion is not so broad as to effectively bar everyone who might attend the sessions and is put into place for a proper purpose.

A session may be closed over the objection of the accused or the public upon meeting the constitutional standard set forth in this Rule. *See also* Mil. R. Evid. 412(c)(2), 505(k)(3), and 513(e)(2).

The accused may waive his right to a public trial. The fact that the prosecution and defense jointly seek to have a session closed does not, however, automatically justify closure, for the public has a right in attending courts-martial. Opening trials to public scrutiny reduces the chance of arbitrary and capricious decisions and enhances public confidence in the court-martial process.

The most likely reason for a defense request to close court-martial proceedings is to minimize the potentially adverse effect of publicity on the trial. For example, a pretrial Article 39(a) hearing at which the admissibility of a confession will be litigated may, under some circumstances, be closed, in accordance with this Rule, in order to prevent disclosure to the public (and hence to potential members) of the very evidence that may be excluded. When such publicity may be a problem, a session should be closed only as a last resort.

There are alternative means of protecting the proceedings from harmful effects of publicity, including a thorough *voir dire* (*see* R.C.M. 912), and, if necessary, a continuance to allow the harmful effects of publicity to dissipate (*see* R.C.M. 906(b)(1)). Alternatives that may occasionally be appropriate and are usually preferable to closing a session include: directing members not to read, listen to, or watch any accounts concerning the case; issuing a protective order (*see* R.C.M. 806(d)); selecting members from recent arrivals in the command, or from outside the immediate area (*see* R.C.M. 503(a)(3)); changing the place of trial (*see* R.C.M. 906(b)(11)); or sequestering the members.

(c) *Photography and broadcasting prohibited.* Video and audio recording and the taking of photographs—except for the purpose of preparing the record of trial—in the courtroom during the proceedings and radio or television broadcasting of proceedings from the courtroom shall not be permitted. However, the military judge may, as a matter of discretion permit contemporaneous closed-circuit video or audio transmission to permit viewing or hearing by an accused removed under R.C.M. 804 or by spectators when courtroom facilities are inadequate to accommodate a reasonable number of spectators.

(d) *Protective orders.* The military judge may, upon request of any party or *sua sponte*, issue an appropriate protective order, in writing, to prevent parties and witnesses from making extrajudicial statements that present a substantial likelihood of material prejudice to a fair trial by impartial members.

Discussion

A protective order may proscribe extrajudicial statements by counsel, parties, and witnesses that might divulge prejudicial matter not of public record in the case. Other appropriate matters may also be addressed by such a protective order. Before issuing a protective order, the military judge must consider whether other available remedies would effectively mitigate the adverse effects that any publicity might create, and consider such an order's likely effectiveness in ensuring an impartial court-martial panel. A military judge should not issue a protective order without first providing notice to the parties and an opportunity to be heard. The military judge must state on the record the reasons for issuing the protective order. If the reasons for issuing the order change, the military judge may reconsider the continued necessity for a protective order

---

Rule 807. Oaths

(a) *Definition.* "Oath" includes "affirmation."

(b) *Oaths in courts-martial.*

(1) *Who must be sworn.*

(A) *Court-martial personnel.* The military judge, members of a general or special court-martial, trial counsel, assistant trial counsel, defense counsel, associate defense counsel, assistant defense counsel, reporter, interpreter, and escort shall take an oath to perform their duties faithfully. For purposes of this rule, "defense counsel," "associate defense counsel," and "assistant defense counsel," include detailed and individual military and civilian counsel.

Discussion

Article 42(a) provides that regulations of the Secretary concerned shall prescribe: the form of the oath; the time and place of the taking thereof; the manner of recording it; and whether the oath shall be taken for all cases in which the duties are to be performed or in each case separately. In the case of certified legal personnel (Article 26(b); Article 27(b)), these regulations may provide for the administration of an oath on a one-time basis. *See also* R.C.M. 813 and 901 concerning the point in the proceedings at which it is ordinarily determined whether the required oaths have been taken or are then administered.

(B) *Witnesses.* Each witness before a court-martial shall be examined on oath.

Discussion

See R.C.M. 307 concerning the requirement for an oath in preferral of charges. *See* R.C.M. 405 and 702 concerning the requirements for an oath in Article 32 preliminary hearings and depositions.

An accused making an unsworn statement is not a "witness." *See* R.C.M. 1001(d)(2)(C).

A victim of an offense for which the accused has been found guilty is not a "witness" when making an unsworn statement during the presentencing phase of a court-martial. *See* R.C.M. 1001(c).

---

(2) *Procedure for administering oaths.* Any procedure which appeals to the conscience of the person to whom the oath is administered and which binds that person to speak the truth, or, in the case of one other than a witness, properly to perform certain duties, is sufficient.

Discussion

See Article 136 concerning persons authorized to administer oaths.

When the oath is administered in a session to the military judge, members, or any counsel, all persons in the courtroom should stand. In those rare circumstances in which the trial counsel testifies as a witness, the military judge administers the oath.

Unless otherwise prescribed by the Secretary concerned the forms in this Discussion may be used, as appropriate, to administer an oath.

(A) *Oath for military judge.* When the military judge is not previously sworn, the trial counsel will administer the following oath to the military judge:

"Do you (swear) (affirm) that you will faithfully and impartially perform, according to your conscience and the laws applicable to trial by court-martial, all the duties incumbent upon you as military judge of this court-martial (, so help you God)?"

(B) *Oath for members.* The following oath, as appropriate, will be administered to the members by the trial counsel:

"Do you (swear) (affirm) that you will answer truthfully the questions concerning whether you should serve as a member of this court-martial; that you will faithfully and impartially try, according to the evidence, your conscience, and the laws applicable to trial by court-martial, the case of the accused now before this court; and that you will not disclose or discover the vote or opinion of any particular member of the court (upon a challenge or) upon the findings or sentence unless required to do so in due course of law (, so help you God)?"

(C) *Oaths for counsel.* When counsel for either side, including any associate or assistant, is not previously sworn the following oath, as appropriate, will be administered by the military judge:

"Do you (swear) (affirm) that you will faithfully perform all the duties of (trial) (assistant trial) (defense) (associate defense) (assistant defense) counsel in the case now in hearing (, so help you God)?"

(D) *Oath for reporter.* The trial counsel will administer the following oath to every reporter of a court- martial who has not been previously sworn:

"Do you (swear) (affirm) that you will faithfully perform the duties of reporter to this court-martial (, so help you God)?"

(E) *Oath for interpreter.* The trial counsel or the summary court-martial shall administer the following oath to every interpreter in the trial of any case before a court-martial:

"Do you (swear) (affirm) that in the case now in hearing you will interpret truly the testimony you are called upon to interpret (, so help you God)?"

(F) *Oath for witnesses.* The trial counsel or the summary court-martial will administer the following oath to each witness before the witness first testifies in a case:

"Do you (swear) (affirm) that the evidence you shall give in the case now in hearing shall be the truth, the whole truth, and nothing but the truth (, so help you God)?"

(G) *Oath for escort.* The escort on views or inspections by the court-martial will, before serving, take the following oath, which will be administered by the trial counsel:

"Do you (swear) (affirm) that you will escort the court-martial and will well and truly point out to them (the place in which the offense charged in this case is alleged to have been committed) (_); and that you will not speak to the members concerning (the alleged offense) (________________________________),
except to describe (the place aforesaid) (________________) (, so help you God)?"

Rule 808. Record of trial

Trial counsel of a general or special court-martial shall take such action as may be necessary to ensure that a record that will meet the requirements of R.C.M. 1112 can be prepared.

Rule 809. Contempt proceedings

(a) *In general.* The contempt power under Article 48 may be exercised by a judicial officer specified under subsection (a) of that article.

Discussion

Under Article 48, the contempt power may be exercised by the following judicial officers: any judge of the Court of Appeals for the Armed Forces and any judge of a Court of Criminal Appeals under Article 66; any military judge detailed to a court-martial, a provost court, a military commission, or any other proceeding under the UCMJ; any military magistrate designated to preside under Article 19; and the president of a court of inquiry.

Article 48 makes punishable "direct" contempt, as well as "indirect" or "constructive" contempt. "Direct" contempt is that which is committed in the presence of the judicial officer during the proceeding or in the immediate proximity. "Presence" includes those places outside the courtroom itself, such as waiting areas, deliberation rooms, and other places set aside for the use of the court-martial or other proceeding while it is in session. "Indirect" or "constructive" contempt is non-compliance with lawful writs, processes, orders, rules, decrees, or commands of the judicial officer. A "direct" or "indirect" contempt may be actually seen or heard by the judicial officer, in which case it may be punished summarily. *See* subsection (b)(1) of this rule. A "direct" or "indirect" contempt may also be a contempt not actually observed by the judicial officer, for example, when an unseen person makes loud noises, whether inside or outside the courtroom, which impede the orderly progress of the proceedings. In such a case the procedures for punishing for contempt are more extensive. *See* R.C.M. 809(b)(2).

The words "any person," as used in Article 48, include all persons, whether or not subject to military law, except the military judge, members, and foreign nationals outside the territorial limits of the United States who are not subject to the UCMJ. The military judge may order the offender removed whether or not contempt proceedings are held. It may be appropriate to warn a person whose conduct is improper that persistence in a course of behavior may result in removal or punishment for contempt. *See* R.C.M. 804, 806.

Each contempt may be separately punished.

A person subject to the UCMJ who commits contempt may be tried by court-martial or otherwise disciplined under Article 134 for such misconduct in addition to or instead of punishment for contempt. *See* paragraph 85, Part IV; *see also* Article 131d. The 2011 amendment of Article 48 expanded the contempt power of military courts to enable them to enforce orders, such as discovery orders or protective orders regarding evidence, against military or civilian attorneys. Persons not subject to military jurisdiction under Article 2, having been duly subpoenaed, may be prosecuted in federal civilian court under Article 47 for neglect or refusal to appear or refusal to qualify as a witness or to testify or to produce evidence.

(b) *Method of disposition.*

(1) *Summary disposition.* When conduct constituting contempt is directly witnessed by the judicial officer during the proceeding, the conduct may be punished summarily; otherwise, the provisions of paragraph (b)(2) shall apply. If a contempt is punished summarily, the judicial officer shall ensure that the record accurately reflects the misconduct that was directly witnessed by the judicial officer during the proceeding.

(2) *Disposition upon notice and hearing.* When the conduct apparently constituting contempt is not directly witnessed by the judicial officer, the alleged offender shall be brought before the judicial officer outside the presence of any members and informed orally or in writing of the alleged contempt. The alleged offender shall be given a reasonable opportunity to present evidence, including calling witnesses. The alleged offender shall have the right to be represented by counsel and shall be so advised. The contempt must be proved beyond a reasonable doubt before it may be punished.

(c) *Procedure.* The judicial officer shall in all cases determine whether to punish for contempt and, if so, what the punishment shall be. The judicial officer shall also determine when during the court-martial or other proceeding the contempt proceedings shall be conducted. In the case of a court of inquiry, the judicial officer shall consult with the appointed legal advisor or a judge advocate before imposing punishment for contempt.

(d) *Record; review.*

(1) *Record.* A record of the contempt proceedings shall be part of the record of the court-martial or other proceeding during which it occurred. If the person was held in contempt, then a separate record of the contempt proceedings shall be prepared and forwarded for review in accordance with paragraph (2) or (3), as applicable.

(2) *Review by convening authority.* If the contempt punishment was imposed by a court of inquiry, the contempt proceedings shall be forwarded to the convening authority for review. The convening authority may approve or disapprove the contempt finding and all or part of the sentence. The action of the convening authority is not subject to further review or appeal.

(3) *Review by Court of Criminal Appeals.* If the contempt punishment was imposed by a military judge or military magistrate, the alleged offender may file an appeal to the Court of Criminal Appeals in accordance with the uniform rules of procedure for the Courts of Criminal Appeals. The Court of Criminal Appeals may set aside the finding or the sentence, in whole or in part.

Discussion

The appeal and defense of a contempt punishment will normally be handled by the Service appellate divisions. In unusual circumstances, the Judge Advocate General may appoint counsel to appeal and defend a contempt punishment.

Decisions of the Court of Criminal Appeals may be reviewed by the Court of Appeals for the Armed Forces and the Supreme Court of the United States in accordance with the rules of appellate procedure for each respective Court.

(e) *Sentence.*

(1) *In general.* The place of confinement for a civilian or military person who is held in contempt and is to be punished by confinement shall be designated by the judicial officer who imposed punishment for contempt, in accordance with regulations prescribed by the Secretary concerned. A judicial officer who imposes punishment for contempt may delay announcing the sentence after a finding of contempt to permit the person involved to continue to participate in the proceedings.

(2) *Maximum punishment.* If imposed by a court of inquiry, the maximum punishment that may be imposed for contempt is a fine of $500. Otherwise the maximum punishment that may be imposed for contempt is confinement for 30 days, a fine of $1,000, or both.

(3) *Execution of sentence when imposed by court of inquiry.* A sentence of a fine pursuant to a finding of contempt by a court of inquiry shall not become effective until approved by the convening authority.

(4) *Execution of sentence when imposed by military judge or magistrate.*

(A) A sentence of confinement pursuant to a finding of contempt by a military judge or military magistrate shall begin to run when it is announced unless—

(i) the person held in contempt notifies the judicial officer of an intent to file an appeal; and

(ii) the judicial officer, in the exercise of the judicial officer's discretion, defers the sentence pending action by the Court of Criminal Appeals under paragraph (d)(3).

(B) A sentence of a fine pursuant to a finding of contempt by a military judge or military magistrate shall become effective when it is announced.

Discussion

The immediate commander of the person held in contempt, or, in the case of a civilian, the convening authority should be notified immediately so that the necessary action on the sentence may be taken. *See* R.C.M. 1102.

(f) *Informing person held in contempt.* The person held in contempt shall be informed by the judicial officer in writing of the holding and sentence, if any, of the judicial officer, and of the applicable procedures and regulations concerning execution and review of the contempt punishment. The reviewing authority shall notify the person held in contempt and of the action of the reviewing authority upon the sentence.

Rule 810. Procedures for rehearings, new trials, other trials, and remands

(a) *In general.*

(1) *Rehearings in full and new or other trials.* In rehearings which require findings on all charges and specifications referred to a court-martial and in new or other trials, the procedure shall be the same as in an original trial except as otherwise provided in this rule.

(2) *Rehearings on sentence only.* In a rehearing on sentence only, the procedure shall be the same as in an original trial, except that the portion of the procedure which ordinarily occurs after challenges and through and including the findings is omitted, and except as otherwise provided in this rule.

(A) *Contents of the record.* The contents of the record of the original trial consisting of evidence properly admitted on the merits relating to each offense of which the accused stands convicted but not sentenced may be established by any party whether or not testimony so read is otherwise admissible under Mil. R. Evid. 804(b)(1) and whether or not it was given through an interpreter.

Discussion

The terms "rehearings," "new trials," "other trials," and "remands" generally have the following meanings: "rehearings" refers to a proceeding ordered by an appellate or reviewing authority on the findings and the sentence or on the sentence only; "new trials" refers to proceedings under Article 73 because of newly discovered evidence or fraud committed on the court; "other trials" refers to a proceeding ordered to consider new charges and specifications when the original proceedings are declared invalid because of a lack of jurisdiction or failure of a charge to state an offense; and "remands" connotes proceedings for determining issues raised on appeal which require additional inquiry. Matters excluded from the record of the original trial on the merits or improperly admitted on the merits must not be brought to the attention of the members as a part of the original record of trial.

(B) *Plea.* The accused at a rehearing only on sentence may not withdraw any plea of guilty upon which findings of guilty are based.

(3) *Combined rehearings.* When a rehearing on sentence is combined with a trial on the merits of one or more specifications referred to the court-martial, whether or not such specifications are being tried for the first time or reheard, the trial will proceed first on the merits. Reference to the offenses being reheard on sentence is permissible only as provided for by the Military Rules of Evidence. The presentencing proceedings procedure shall be the same as at an original trial, except as otherwise provided in this rule.

(4) *Additional charges.* A referral authority may refer additional charges for trial together with charges as to which a rehearing has been directed.

(5) *Rehearing impracticable.* If a rehearing was authorized on one or more findings, the convening authority, or in cases referred by a special trial counsel, a special trial counsel, may dismiss the affected charges if the referral authority determines that a rehearing is impracticable. If the referral authority dismisses such charges, a rehearing may proceed on any remaining charges not dismissed by the referral authority.

(6) *Forwarding.* When a rehearing, new trial, other trial, or remand is ordered, a military judge shall be detailed to the proceeding, and the matter forwarded to the military judge. In the case of a summary court-martial, when any proceeding is ordered, a new summary court-martial officer shall be detailed.

(b) *Composition.*

(1) *Members.* No member of the court-martial which previously heard the case may sit as a member of the court-martial at any rehearing, new trial, or other trial of the same case.

(2) *Military judge.* The military judge at a rehearing may be the same military judge who presided over a previous trial of the same case. The existence or absence of a request for trial by military judge alone at a previous hearing shall have no effect on the composition of a court-martial on rehearing.

(3) *Accused's election.* The accused at a rehearing or new or other trial shall have the same right to request enlisted members, an all-officer panel, or trial by military judge alone as the accused would have at an original trial.

Discussion

See R.C.M. 902; 903; and 1002(b).

(c) *Examination of record of former proceedings.* No member may, upon a rehearing or upon a new or other trial, examine the record of any former proceedings in the same case except when permitted to do so by the military judge after such matters have been received in evidence.

(d) *Sentence limitations.*

(1) *In general.* Sentences at rehearings, new trials, or other trials shall be adjudged within the limitations set forth in R.C.M. 1003. Except as otherwise provided in paragraph (d)(2), the new adjudged sentence for offenses on which a rehearing, new trial, or other trial has been ordered shall not exceed or be more severe than the original sentence as set forth in the judgment under R.C.M. 1111. When a rehearing or sentencing is combined with trial on new charges, the maximum punishment that may be imposed shall be the maximum punishment under R.C.M. 1003 for the offenses being reheard as limited in this rule, plus the total maximum punishment under R.C.M. 1003 for any new charges of which the accused has been found guilty.

(2) *Exceptions.* A rehearing, new trial, or other trial may adjudge any lawful sentence, without regard to the sentence of the previous hearing or trial when, as to any offense—

(A) the sentence prescribed for the offense is mandatory;

(B) in the case of an "other trial," the original trial was invalid because a summary or special court-martial tried an offense involving mandatory punishment, an offense for which only a general court-martial has jurisdiction, or one otherwise considered capital;

(C) the rehearing was ordered or authorized for any charge or specification for which a plea of guilty was entered at the first hearing or trial and a plea of not guilty was entered at the second hearing or trial to that same charge or specification;

(D) the rehearing was ordered or authorized for any charge or specification for which the sentence announced or adjudged by the first court-martial was in accordance with a plea agreement and, at the rehearing, the accused does not comply with the terms of the agreement; or

(E) the rehearing was ordered or authorized after an appeal by the Government under R.C.M. 1117.

(e) *Definition.* "Other trial" means another trial of a case in which the original proceedings were declared invalid because of lack of jurisdiction or failure of a charge to state an offense. The authority ordering an "other trial" shall state in the action the basis for declaring the proceedings invalid.

(f) *Remands.*

(1) *In general.* A Court of Criminal Appeals may order a remand for additional fact finding, or for other reasons, in order to address a substantial issue on appeal. A remand under this subsection is generally not appropriate to determine facts or investigate matters which could, through a party's exercise of reasonable diligence, have been investigated or considered at trial. Such orders shall be directed to the Chief Trial Judge. The Judge Advocate General, or the Judge Advocate General's delegate, shall designate a general court-martial convening authority who shall provide support for the hearing. In cases which were referred by a special trial counsel, a special trial counsel designated under regulations prescribed by the Secretary concerned shall be notified of any remand.

(2) *Detailing of military judge.* When the Court of Criminal Appeals orders a remand, the Chief Trial Judge shall detail an appropriate military judge to the matter and shall notify the commanding officer exercising general court-martial convening authority over the accused of the remand.

(3) *Remand impracticable.* If the general court-martial convening authority designated under R.C.M. 810(f)(1) or, in cases which were referred by a special trial counsel, a special trial counsel determines that the remand is impracticable due to military exigencies or other reasons, a Government appellate attorney shall notify the Court of Criminal Appeals. Upon receipt of such notification, the Court of Criminal Appeals may take any action authorized by law that does not materially prejudice the substantial rights of the accused.

Discussion

The Court of Criminal Appeals may direct that the remand proceed, or it may rescind the remand order and take any other appropriate action that resolves the issue that was to be settled at the remand. Such action may include modifying the findings or sentence. *See* Article 66(f).

Rule 811. Stipulations

(a) *In general.* The parties may make an oral or written stipulation to any fact, the contents of a document, or the expected testimony of a witness.

(b) *Authority to reject.* The military judge may, in the interest of justice, decline to accept a stipulation.

Discussion

Although the decision to stipulate should ordinarily be left to the parties, the military judge should not accept a stipulation if there is any doubt of the accused's or any other party's understanding of the nature and effect of the stipulation. The military judge should also refuse to accept a stipulation which is unclear or ambiguous. A stipulation of fact which amounts to a complete defense to any offense charged should not be accepted nor, if a plea of not guilty is outstanding, should one which practically amounts to a confession, except as described in the discussion under R.C.M. 811(c). If a stipulation is rejected, the parties may be entitled to a continuance.

(c) *Requirements.* Before accepting a stipulation in evidence, the military judge must be satisfied that the parties consent to its admission.

Discussion

Ordinarily, before accepting any stipulation the military judge should inquire to ensure that the accused understands the right not to stipulate, understands the stipulation, and consents to it.

If the stipulation practically amounts to a confession to an offense to which a not guilty plea is outstanding, it may not be accepted unless the military judge ascertains: (A) from the accused that the accused understands the right not to stipulate and that the stipulation will not be accepted without the accused's consent; that the accused understands the contents and effect of the stipulation; that a factual basis exists for the stipulation; and that the accused, after consulting with counsel, consents to the stipulation; and (B) from the accused and counsel for each party whether there are any agreements between the parties in connection with the stipulation, and, if so, what the terms of such agreements are.

A stipulation practically amounts to a confession when it is the equivalent of a guilty plea, that is, when it establishes, directly or by reasonable inference, every element of a charged offense and when the defense does not present evidence to contest any potential remaining issue of the merits. Thus, a stipulation which tends to establish, by reasonable inference, every element of a charged offense does not practically amount to a confession if the defense contests an issue going to guilt which is not foreclosed by the stipulation. For example, a stipulation of fact that contraband drugs were discovered in a vehicle owned by the accused would normally practically amount to a confession if no other evidence were presented on the issue, but would not if the defense presented evidence to show that the accused was unaware of the presence of the drugs. Whenever a stipulation establishes the elements of a charged offense, the military judge should conduct an inquiry as described in this rule.

If, during an inquiry into a confessional stipulation the military judge discovers that there is a plea agreement, the military judge must conduct an inquiry into the pretrial agreement. *See* R.C.M. 910(f). *See also* R.C.M. 705.

(d) *Withdrawal.* A party may withdraw from an agreement to stipulate or from a stipulation at any time before a stipulation is accepted; the stipulation may not then be accepted. After a stipulation has been accepted a party may withdraw from it only if permitted to do so in the discretion of the military judge.

Discussion

If a party withdraws from an agreement to stipulate or from a stipulation, before or after it has been accepted, the opposing party may be entitled to a continuance to obtain proof of the matters which were to have been stipulated.

If a party is permitted to withdraw from a stipulation previously accepted, the stipulation must be disregarded by the court-martial, and an instruction to that effect should be given.

(e) *Effect of stipulation.* Unless properly withdrawn or ordered stricken from the record, a stipulation of fact that has been accepted is binding on the court-martial and may not be contradicted by the parties thereto. The contents of a stipulation of expected testimony or of a document's contents may be attacked, contradicted, or explained in the same way as if the witness had actually so testified or the document had been actually admitted. The fact that the parties so stipulated does not admit the truth of the indicated testimony or document's contents, nor does it add anything to the evidentiary nature of the testimony or document. The Military Rules of Evidence apply to the contents of stipulations.

(f) *Procedure.* When offered, a written stipulation shall be presented to the military judge and shall be included in the record whether accepted or not. Once accepted, a written stipulation of expected testimony shall be read to the members, if any, but shall not be presented to them; a written stipulation of fact or of a document's contents may be read to the members, if any, presented to them, or both. Once accepted, an oral stipulation shall be announced to the members, if any.

Rule 812. Joint and common trials

In joint trials and in common trials, each accused shall be accorded the rights and privileges as if tried separately.

Discussion

A "joint trial" is one in which two or more accused are charged with a joint offense, that is, one in which they acted together with a common purpose. The offense is stated in a single specification and the accused are joined by the pleading. A "common trial" is one in which two or more accused are tried for an offense or offenses which, although not jointly committed, were committed at the same time and place and are provable by the same evidence. A common trial is ordered in the discretion of the referral authority by endorsement on the charge sheet. *See* R.C.M. 307(c)(5) concerning preparing charges and specifications for joint trials. *See* R.C.M. 601(e)(3) concerning referral of charges for joint or common trials, and the distinction between the two. *See* R.C.M. 906(b)(9) concerning motions to sever and other appropriate motions in joint or common trials.

In a joint or common trial, each accused may be represented by separate counsel; make challenges for cause; make peremptory challenges (*see* R.C.M. 912); cross-examine witnesses; elect whether to testify; introduce evidence; request that the membership of the court include enlisted persons or be limited to officer members, if an enlisted accused; and request trial by military judge alone.

In a joint or common trial, evidence which is admissible against only one or some of the joint or several accused may be considered only against the accused concerned. For example, when a stipulation is accepted which was made by only one or some of the accused, the stipulation does not apply to those accused who did not join it. *See also* Mil. R. Evid. 306. In such instances the members must be instructed that the stipulation or evidence may be considered only with respect to the accused with respect to whom it is accepted.

Rule 813. Announcing personnel of the court-martial and the accused

(a) *Opening sessions.* Except as noted in subsection (d), when the court-martial is called to order for the first time in a case, the military judge shall ensure that the following is announced:

(1) The order, including any amendment, by which the court is convened;

(2) The name, rank, and unit or address of the accused;

(3) The name and rank of the military judge presiding;

(4) The names and ranks of the members, if any, who are present;

(5) The names and ranks of members who are absent, if presence of members is required

(6) The names and ranks (if any) of counsel who are present;

(7) The names and ranks (if any) of counsel who are absent; and

(8) The name and rank (if any) of any detailed court reporter.

(b) *Later proceedings*. When the court-martial is called to order after a recess or adjournment or after it has been closed for any reason, the military judge shall ensure that the record reflects whether all parties and members who were present at the time of the adjournment or recess, or at the time the court-martial closed, are present.

(c) *Additions, replacement, and absences of personnel.* Whenever there is a replacement of the military judge, any member, or counsel, either through the appearance of new personnel or personnel previously absent or through the absence of personnel previously present, the military judge shall ensure the record reflects the change and the reason for it.

(d) Under R.C.M. 813(a)(1), the name, grade, and position of the convening authority, with the exception of the Secretary concerned, the Secretary of Defense, or the President, shall be omitted from announcement during the opening session of the court-martial.

CHAPTER IX. TRIAL PROCEDURES THROUGH FINDINGS

Rule 901. Opening session

(a) *Call to order*. A court-martial is in session when the military judge so declares.

Discussion

The military judge should examine the charge sheet, convening order, and any amending orders before calling the initial session to order.

See also R.C.M. 602(b)(1) concerning the waiting periods applicable after service of charges in general and special courts-martial.

(b) *Announcement of parties*. After the court-martial is called to order, the presence or absence of the parties, military judge, and members shall be announced.

Discussion

If the orders detailing the military judge and counsel have not been reduced to writing, an oral announcement of such detailing is required. *See* R.C.M. 503(b) and (c).

(c) *Swearing reporter and interpreter*. After the personnel have been accounted for as required in subsection (b) of this rule, trial counsel shall announce whether the reporter and interpreter, if any is present, have been properly sworn. If not sworn, the reporter and interpreter, if any, shall be sworn.

Discussion

See R.C.M. 807 concerning the oath to be administered to a court reporter or interpreter. If a reporter or interpreter is replaced at any time during trial, this should be noted for the record, and the procedures in this subsection should be repeated.

(d) *Counsel*.

(1) *Trial counsel*. Trial counsel shall announce the legal qualifications and status as to oaths of the members of the prosecution and whether any member of the prosecution has acted in any manner which might tend to disqualify that counsel.

(2) *Defense counsel*.

(A) *In general*. The detailed defense counsel shall announce the legal qualifications and status as to oaths of the detailed members of the defense and whether any member of the defense has acted in any manner that might tend to disqualify that counsel. Any defense counsel not detailed shall state that counsel's legal qualifications and whether that counsel has acted in any manner that might tend to disqualify the counsel.

(B) *Capital cases*. A defense counsel who has been detailed to a capital case as a counsel learned in the law applicable to such cases shall, in addition to the requirements of subparagraph (A), state such qualifications and assignment.

(3) *Disqualification*. If it appears that any counsel may be disqualified, the military judge shall decide the matter and take appropriate action.

Discussion

Counsel may be disqualified because of lack of necessary qualifications, or because of duties or actions which are inconsistent with the role of counsel. See R.C.M. 502(d) concerning qualifications of counsel.

If it appears that any counsel may be disqualified, the military judge should conduct an inquiry or hearing. If any detailed counsel is disqualified, the appropriate authority should be informed. If any defense counsel is disqualified, the accused should be so informed.

If the disqualification of trial or defense counsel is one which the accused may waive, the accused should be so informed by the military judge, and given the opportunity to decide whether to waive the disqualification. In the case of defense counsel, if the disqualification is not waivable or if the accused elects not to waive the disqualification, the accused should be informed of the choices available and given the opportunity to exercise such options.

If any counsel is disqualified, the military judge should ensure that the accused is not prejudiced by any actions of the disqualified counsel or any break in representation of the accused.

Disqualification of counsel is not a jurisdictional defect; such error must be tested for prejudice.

If the membership of the prosecution or defense changes at any time during the proceedings, the procedures in this subsection should be repeated as to the new counsel. In addition, the military judge should ascertain on the record whether the accused objects to a change of defense counsel. *See* R.C.M. 505(d)(2) and 506(c).

See R.C.M. 502(d)(2)(C) regarding qualifications of counsel learned in the law applicable to capital cases.

---

(4) *Inquiry*. The military judge shall, in open session:

(A) Inform the accused of the rights to be represented by military counsel detailed to the defense; or by individual military counsel requested by the accused, if such military counsel is reasonably available; and by civilian counsel, either alone or in association with military counsel, if such civilian counsel is provided at no expense to the United States;

(B) Inform the accused that, if afforded individual military counsel, the accused may request retention of detailed counsel as associate counsel, which request may be granted or denied in the sole discretion of the authority who detailed the counsel;

(C) Ascertain from the accused whether the accused understands these rights;

(D) Promptly inquire, whenever two or more accused in a joint or common trial are represented by the same detailed or individual military or civilian counsel, or by civilian counsel who are associated in the practice of law, with respect to such joint representation and shall personally advise each accused of the right to effective assistance of counsel, including separate representation. Unless it appears that there is good cause to believe no conflict of interest is likely to arise, the military judge shall take appropriate measures to protect each accused's right to counsel; and

Discussion

Whenever it appears that any defense counsel may face a conflict of interest, the military judge should inquire into the matter, advise the accused of the right to effective assistance of counsel, and ascertain the accused's choice of counsel. When defense counsel is aware of a potential conflict of interest, counsel should discuss the matter with the accused. If the accused elects to waive such conflict, counsel should inform the military judge of the matter at an Article 39(a) session so that an appropriate record can be made.

(E) Ascertain from the accused by whom the accused chooses to be represented.

(5) *Unsworn counsel.* The military judge shall administer the oath to any counsel not sworn.

Discussion

See R.C.M. 807.

(e) *Presence of members.* The procedures described in R.C.M. 901 through 910 shall be conducted without members present in accordance with the procedures set forth in R.C.M. 803.

Rule 902. Disqualification of military judge

(a) *In general.* Except as provided in subsection (e) of this rule, a military judge shall disqualify himself or herself in any proceeding in which that military judge's impartiality might reasonably be questioned.

(b) *Specific grounds.* A military judge shall also disqualify himself or herself in the following circumstances:

(1) Where the military judge has a personal bias or prejudice concerning a party or personal knowledge of disputed evidentiary facts concerning the proceeding.

(2) Where the military judge has acted as counsel, preliminary hearing officer, investigating officer, legal officer, staff judge advocate, or convening authority as to any offense charged or in the same case generally.

(3) Where the military judge has been or will be a witness in the same case; is the accuser; has forwarded charges in the case with a personal recommendation as to disposition; has referred charges in the case; or, except in the performance of duties as military judge in a previous trial of the same or a related case, has expressed an opinion concerning the guilt or innocence of the accused.

(4) Where the military judge is not eligible to act because the military judge is not qualified under R.C.M. 502(c) or not detailed under R.C.M. 503(b).

(5) Where the military judge, the military judge's spouse, or a person within the third degree of relationship to either of them or a spouse of such person:

(A) Is a party to the proceeding;

(B) Is known by the military judge to have an interest, financial or otherwise, that could be substantially affected by the outcome of the proceeding; or

(C) Is to the military judge's knowledge likely to be a material witness in the proceeding.

Discussion

A military judge should inform himself or herself about his or her financial interests, and make a reasonable effort to inform himself or herself about the financial interests of his or her spouse and minor children living in his or her household.

(c) *Definitions.* For the purposes of this rule the following words or phrases shall have the meaning indicated—

(1) "Proceeding" includes pretrial (to include pre-referral), trial, post-trial, appellate review, or other

stages of litigation.

(2) The "degree of relationship" is calculated according to the civil law system.

Discussion

Relatives within the third degree of relationship are children, grandchildren, great grandchildren, parents, grandparents, great grandparents, brothers, sisters, uncles, aunts, nephews, and nieces.

(d) *Procedure.*

(1) The military judge shall, upon motion of any party or *sua sponte*, decide whether the military judge is disqualified.

Discussion

There is no peremptory challenge against a military judge. A military judge should carefully consider whether any of the grounds for disqualification in this rule exist in each case. The military judge should broadly construe grounds for challenge but should not step down from a case unnecessarily.

Possible grounds for disqualification should be raised at the earliest reasonable opportunity. They may be raised at any time, and an earlier adverse ruling does not bar later consideration of the same issue, as, for example, when additional evidence is discovered.

---

(2) Each party shall be permitted to question the military judge and to present evidence regarding a possible ground for disqualification before the military judge decides the matter.

Discussion

Nothing in this rule prohibits the military judge from reasonably limiting the presentation of evidence, the scope of questioning, and argument on the subject so as to ensure that only matters material to the central issue of the military judge's possible disqualification are considered, thereby, preventing the proceedings from becoming a forum for unfounded opinion, speculation or innuendo.

---

(3) Except as provided under subsection (e) of this rule, if the military judge rules that the military judge is disqualified, the military judge shall recuse himself or herself.

(e) *Waiver.* No military judge shall accept from the parties to the proceeding a waiver of any ground for disqualification enumerated in subsection (b) of this rule. Where the ground for disqualification arises only under subsection (a) of this rule, waiver may be accepted provided it is preceded by a full disclosure on the record of the basis for disqualification.

Rule 903. Accused's elections on composition of court-martial

(a) *In general.*

(1) Except in a special court-martial consisting of a military judge alone under Article 16(c)(2)(A), before the end of the initial Article 39(a) session or, in the absence of such a session, before assembly, the military judge shall ascertain, as applicable:

(A) In the case of an enlisted accused, whether the accused elects to be tried by a court-martial composed of—

(i) at least one-third enlisted members; or

(ii) all officer members.

(B) In all noncapital cases, whether the accused requests trial by military judge alone.

(2) The accused may defer requesting trial by military judge alone until any time before assembly.

Discussion

Only an enlisted accused may request that enlisted members be detailed to a court-martial. Trial by military judge alone is not permitted in capital cases (*see* R.C.M. 201(f)(1)(C)).

If an accused makes no forum selection, the accused will be tried by a court-martial composed of a military judge and members, as specified in the convening order. When presenting the accused's forum options, the military judge should inform the accused of the effect of not making an election.

(b) *Form of election.* The accused's election or request, if any, under subsection (a), shall be in writing and signed by the accused or shall be made orally on the record.

(c) *Action on election.*

(1) *Request for specific panel composition.* If an enlisted accused makes a timely election under subparagraph (a)(1)(A), the convening authority, unless a sufficient number of members have already been detailed, shall detail a sufficient number of additional members to the court-martial in accordance with R.C.M. 503 or prepare a detailed written statement explaining why physical conditions or military exigencies prevented such detail. Proceedings that require the presence of members shall not proceed until either there is a sufficient number of additional members or the convening authority has prepared a written statement.

(2) *Request for military judge alone.* Upon receipt of a timely request for trial by military judge alone the military judge shall:

(A) Ascertain whether the accused has consulted with defense counsel and has been informed of the identity of the military judge and of the right to trial by members; and

Discussion

Ordinarily the military judge should inquire personally of the accused to ensure that the accused's waiver of the right to trial by members is knowing and understanding. The military judge should ensure the accused understands that the approval of a request for trial before military judge alone under Article 16(b)(3) or (c)(2)(B) means that the military judge will determine the findings and, if the accused is found guilty of any charge and specification, the sentence. *See* R.C.M. 1002. Failure to do so is not error, however, where such knowledge and understanding otherwise appear on the record.

DD Form 1722 (Request for Trial Before Military Judge Alone (Article 16, UCMJ)) should normally be used for the purpose of requesting trial by military judge alone under this rule, if a written request is used.

(B) Approve or disapprove the request, in the military judge's discretion.

Discussion

A timely request for trial by military judge alone should be granted unless there is substantial reason why, in the interest of justice, the military judge should not sit as factfinder. The military judge may hear arguments from counsel before acting on the request. The basis for denial of a request must be made a matter of record.

---

(3) *Composition.* Trial shall be by a court-martial composed of the members in accordance with the convening order, unless the case is referred for trial by military judge alone under Article 16(c)(2)(A), the military judge grants a request for trial by judge alone, or there is a request for a specific panel composition under subparagraph (a)(1)(A).

(d) *Right to withdraw request.*

(1) *Specific panel composition.* An election by an enlisted accused under subparagraph (a)(1)(A) may be withdrawn by the accused as a matter of right any time before the end of the initial Article 39(a) session, or, in the absence of such a session, before assembly.

(2) *Military judge.* A request for trial by military judge alone may be withdrawn by the accused as a matter of right any time before it is approved, or even after approval, if there is a change of the military judge

Discussion

Withdrawal of a request for enlisted members, all officer members, or trial by military judge alone should be shown in the record. The effect of such withdrawal is that the accused will be tried by a court-martial composed of members as specified by the convening order. *See* R.C.M. 505(c) concerning changing members prior to assembly.

(e) *Untimely requests.* Failure to request, or failure to withdraw a request for a specific panel composition or trial by military judge alone in a timely manner shall waive the right to submit or to withdraw such a request. However, the military judge may, until the beginning of the introduction of evidence on the merits, as a matter of discretion, approve an untimely request or withdrawal of a request.

Discussion

In exercising discretion whether to approve an untimely request or withdrawal of a request, the military judge should balance the reason for the request (for example, whether it is a mere change of tactics or results from a substantial change of circumstances) against any expense, delay, or inconvenience which would result from granting the request

---

Rule 904. Arraignment

Arraignment shall be conducted in a court-martial session and shall consist of reading the charges and specifications to the accused and calling on the accused to plead. The accused may waive the reading.

Discussion

Arraignment is complete when the accused is called upon to plead; the entry of pleas is not part of the arraignment.

The arraignment should be conducted at an Article 39(a) session. The accused may not be arraigned at a conference under R.C.M. 802.

Once the accused has been arraigned, no additional charges against that accused may be referred to that court-martial for trial with the previously referred charges. *See* R.C.M. 601(e)(2).

The defense should be asked whether it has any motions to make before pleas are entered. Some motions ordinarily must be made before a plea is entered. *See* R.C.M. 905(b).

Rule 905. Motions generally

(a) *Definitions and form.* A motion is an application to the military judge for particular relief. Motions may be oral or, at the discretion of the military judge, written. A motion shall state the grounds upon which it is made and shall set forth the ruling or relief sought. The substance of a motion, not its form or designation, shall control.

(b) *Pretrial motions.* Any defense, objection, or request which is capable of determination without the trial of the general issue of guilt may be raised before trial. The following must be raised before a plea is entered:

(1) Defenses or objections based on defects (other than jurisdictional defects) in the preferral, forwarding, or referral of charges, or in the preliminary hearing;

Discussion

Such nonjurisdictional defects include unsworn charges, inadequate Article 32 preliminary hearing, and inadequate pretrial advice. *See* R.C.M. 307, 401–407, 601–604, 906(b)(3).

---

(2) Defenses or objections based on defects in the charges and specifications (other than any failure to show jurisdiction or to charge an offense, which objections shall be resolved by the military judge at any time during the pendency of the proceedings);

Discussion

See R.C.M. 307, 906(b)(4).

---

(3) Motions to suppress evidence;

Discussion

Mil. R. Evid. 304(f), 311(d), and 321(d) deal with the admissibility of confessions and admissions, evidence obtained from unlawful searches and seizures, and eyewitness identification, respectively. Questions concerning the admissibility of evidence on other grounds may be raised by objection at trial or by motions in limine. *See* R.C.M. 906(b)(13), Mil. R. Evid. 103, 104(a) and (c).

---

(4) Motions for discovery under R.C.M. 701 or for production of witnesses or evidence;

Discussion

See R.C.M. 703, 1001(f).

---

(5) Motions for severance of charges or accused; or

Discussion

See R.C.M. 812, 906(b)(9) and (10).

---

(6) Objections based on denial of request for individual military counsel or for retention of detailed defense counsel when individual military counsel has been granted.

Discussion

See R.C.M. 506(b), 906(b)(2).

(c) *Burden of proof.*

(1) *Standard.* Unless otherwise provided in this Manual, the burden of proof on any factual issue the resolution of which is necessary to decide a motion shall be by a preponderance of the evidence.

Discussion

See Mil. R. Evid. 104(a) concerning the applicability of the Military Rules of Evidence to certain preliminary questions.

---

(2) *Assignment.*

(A) Except as otherwise provided in this Manual the burden of persuasion on any factual issue the resolution of which is necessary to decide a motion shall be on the moving party.

Discussion

See, for example, R.C.M. 905(c)(2)(B), R.C.M. 908 and Mil. R. Evid. 304(f), 311(d)(5), and 321(d)(6) for provisions specifically assigning the burden of proof.

(B) In the case of a motion to dismiss for lack of jurisdiction, denial of the right to speedy trial under R.C.M. 707, or the running of the statute of limitations, the burden of persuasion shall be upon the prosecution.

(d) *Ruling on motions.* A motion made before pleas are entered shall be determined before pleas are entered unless, if otherwise not prohibited by this Manual, the military judge for good cause orders that determination be deferred until trial of the general issue or after findings, but no such determination shall be deferred if a party's right to review or appeal is adversely affected. Where factual issues are involved in determining a motion, the military judge shall state the essential findings on the record.

Discussion

When trial cannot proceed further as the result of dismissal or other rulings on motions, the court-martial should adjourn and a record of the proceedings should be prepared. See R.C.M. 908(b)(4) regarding automatic stay of certain rulings and orders subject to appeal under that rule. Notwithstanding the dismissal of some specifications, trial may proceed in the normal manner as long as one or more charges and specifications remain. The judgment entered into the record should reflect the action taken by the court-martial on each charge and specification, including any of which were dismissed by the military judge on a motion. *See* R.C.M. 1111.

(e) *Effect of failure to raise defenses or objections.*

(1) Failure by a party to raise defenses or objections or to make motions or requests which must be made before pleas are entered under subsection (b) of this rule forfeits the defenses or objections absent an affirmative waiver. The military judge for good cause shown may permit a party to raise a defense or objection or make a motion or request outside of the timelines permitted under subsection (b) of this rule.

(2) Other motions, requests, defenses, or objections, except lack of jurisdiction, must be raised before the court-martial is adjourned for that case. Failure to raise such other motions, requests, defenses, or objections shall constitute forfeiture, absent an affirmative waiver.

Discussion

See also R.C.M. 910(j) concerning matters waived by a plea of guilty.

(f) *Reconsideration.* On request of any party or *sua sponte*, the military judge may, prior to entry of judgment, reconsider any ruling, other than one amounting to a finding of not guilty, made by the military judge.

Discussion

The military judge may reconsider any ruling that affects the legal sufficiency of any finding of guilt or the sentence. See R.C.M. 917(d) for the standard to be used to determine the legal sufficiency of evidence. See also R.C.M. 1104 concerning procedures for post-trial reconsideration. Different standards may apply depending on the nature of the ruling. *See United States v. Scaff*, 29 M.J. 60 (C.M.A. 1989).

(g) *Effect of final determinations.* Any matter put in issue and finally determined by a court-martial, reviewing authority, or appellate court which had jurisdiction to determine the matter may not be disputed by the United States in any other court-martial of the same accused, except that, when the offenses charged at one court-martial did not arise out of the same transaction as those charged at the court-martial at which the determination was made, a determination of law and the application of law to the facts may be disputed by the United States. This rule also shall apply to matters which were put in issue and finally determined in any other judicial proceeding in which the accused and the United States or a federal governmental unit were parties.

Discussion

See R.C.M. 907(b)(2)(C). Whether a matter has been finally determined in another judicial proceeding with jurisdiction to decide it, and whether such determination binds the United States in another proceeding are interlocutory questions. *See* R.C.M. 801(e). It does not matter whether the earlier proceeding ended in an acquittal, conviction, or otherwise, as long as the determination is final. Except for a ruling which is, or amounts to, a finding of not guilty, a ruling ordinarily is not final until action on the court-martial is completed. *See* Article 76; R.C.M. 1209. The accused is not bound in a court-martial by rulings in another court-martial. *But see* Article 3(b); R.C.M. 202.

The determination must have been made by a court-martial, reviewing authority, or appellate court, or by another judicial body, such as a United States court. A pretrial determination by a convening authority or a special trial counsel is not a final determination under this rule, although some decisions-may bind the Government under other rules.

The United States is bound by a final determination by a court of competent jurisdiction even if the earlier determination is erroneous, except when the offenses charged at the second proceeding arose out of a different transaction from those charged at the first and the ruling at the first proceeding was based on an incorrect determination of law.

A final determination in one case may be the basis for a motion to dismiss or a motion for appropriate relief in another case, depending on the circumstances. The nature of the earlier determination and the grounds for it will determine its effect in other proceedings.

Examples:

(1) The military judge dismissed a charge for lack of personal jurisdiction, on grounds that the accused was only 16 years old at the

time of enlistment and when the offenses occurred. At a second court-martial of the same accused for a different offense, the determination in the first case would require dismissal of the new charge unless the prosecution could show that since that determination the accused had effected a valid enlistment or constructive enlistment. *See* R.C.M. 202. Note, however, that if the initial ruling had been based on an error of law (for example, if the military judge had ruled the enlistment invalid because the accused was 18 at the time of enlistment) this would not require dismissal in the second court-martial for a different offense.

(2) The accused was tried in United States district court for assault on a federal officer. The accused defended solely on the basis of alibi and was acquitted. The accused is then charged in a court-martial with assault on a different person at the same time and place as the assault on a federal officer was alleged to have occurred. The acquittal of the accused in federal district court would bar conviction of the accused in the court-martial. In cases of this nature, the facts of the first trial must be examined to determine whether the finding of the first trial is logically inconsistent with guilt in the second case.

(3) At a court-martial for larceny, the military judge excluded evidence of a statement made by the accused relating to the larceny and other uncharged offenses because the statement was obtained by coercion. At a second court-martial for an unrelated offense, the statement excluded at the first trial would be inadmissible, based on the earlier ruling, if the first case had become final. If the earlier ruling had been based on an incorrect interpretation of law, however, the issue of admissibility could be litigated anew at the second proceeding.

(4) At a court-martial for absence without authority, the charge and specification were dismissed for failure to state an offense. At a later court-martial for the same offense, the earlier dismissal would be grounds for dismissing the same charge and specification, but would not bar further proceedings on a new specification not containing the same defect as the original specification.

(h) *Written motions.* Written motions may be submitted to the military judge after referral and when appropriate they may be supported by affidavits, with service and opportunity to reply to the opposing party. Such motions may be disposed of before arraignment and without a session. Either party may request an Article 39(a) session to present oral argument or have an evidentiary hearing concerning the disposition of written motions.

(i) *Service.* Written motions shall be served on all other parties. Unless otherwise directed by the military judge, the service shall be made upon counsel for each party.

(j) *Application to convening authority.* Except as otherwise provided in this Manual, any matters which may be resolved upon motion without trial of the general issue of guilt may be submitted by a party to the convening authority before trial for decision. Submission of such matter to the convening authority is not, except as otherwise provided in this Manual, required, and is, in any event, without prejudice to the renewal of the issue by timely motion before the military judge.

(k) *Production of statements on motion to suppress.* Except as provided in this subsection, R.C.M. 914 shall apply at a hearing on a motion to suppress evidence under paragraph (b)(3) of this rule. For purposes of this subsection, a law enforcement officer shall be deemed a witness called by the Government, and upon a claim of privilege the military judge shall excise portions of the statement containing privileged matter.

Rule 906. Motions for appropriate relief

(a) *In general.* A motion for appropriate relief is a request for a ruling to cure a defect which deprives a party of a right or hinders a party from preparing for trial or presenting its case.

(b) *Grounds for appropriate relief.* The following may be requested by motion for appropriate relief. This list is not exclusive.

(1) *Continuances.* A continuance may be granted only by the military judge.

Discussion

The military judge should, upon a showing of reasonable cause, grant a continuance to any party for as long and as often as is just. *See* Article 40. Whether a request for a continuance should be granted is a matter within the discretion of the military judge. Reasons for a continuance may include: insufficient opportunity to prepare for trial; unavailability of an essential witness; the interest of Government in the order of trial of related cases; and illness of an accused, counsel, military judge, or member. *See also* R.C.M. 602, 803.

---

(2) *Record of denial of individual military counsel or of denial of request to retain detailed counsel when a request for individual military counsel granted.* If a request for military counsel was denied, which denial was upheld on appeal (if available) or if a request to retain detailed counsel was denied when the accused is represented by individual military counsel, and if the accused so requests, the military judge shall ensure that a record of the matter is included in the record of trial, and may make findings. Trial counsel may request a continuance to inform the convening authority of those findings. The military judge may not dismiss the charges or otherwise effectively prevent further proceedings based on this issue. However, the military judge may grant reasonable continuances until the requested military counsel can be made available if the

unavailability results from temporary conditions or if the decision of unavailability is in the process of review in administrative channels.

(3) *Corrections.* Correction of defects in the Article 32 preliminary hearing, pretrial advice, or a written determination by special trial counsel.

Discussion

See R.C.M. 405, 406, 406A. If the motion is granted, the military judge should ordinarily grant a continuance so the defect may be corrected.

---

(4) *Amendment of charges or specifications.* After referral, a charge or specification may not be amended over the accused's objection except pursuant to R.C.M. 603(d) and (e).

Discussion

See also R.C.M. 307.

An amendment may be appropriate when a specification is unclear, redundant, inartfully drafted, misnames an accused, or is laid under the wrong article. A specification may be amended by striking surplusage, or substituting or adding new language. Surplusage may include irrelevant or redundant details or aggravating circumstances which are not necessary to enhance the maximum authorized punishment or to explain the essential facts of the offense. When a specification is amended after the accused has entered a plea to it, the accused should be asked to plead anew to the amended specification. A bill of particulars (*see* R.C.M. 906(b)(6)) may also be used when a specification is indefinite or ambiguous.

If a specification, although stating an offense, is so defective that the accused appears to have been misled, the accused should be given a continuance upon request, or, in an appropriate case, the specification may be dismissed. *See* R.C.M. 907(b)(3).

---

(5) *Severance of specifications.* Severance of a duplicitous specification into two or more specifications.

Discussion

Each specification may state only one offense. *See* R.C.M. 307(c)(4). A duplicitous specification is one which alleges two or more separate offenses. Lesser included offenses (*see* Part IV, paragraph 3; Appendix 12A) are not separate, nor is a continuing offense involving several separate acts. The sole remedy for a duplicitous specification is severance of the specification into two or more specifications, each of which alleges a separate offense contained in the duplicitous specification. However, if the duplicitousness is combined with or results in other defects, such as misleading the accused, other remedies may be appropriate. *See* R.C.M. 906(b)(3). *See also* R.C.M. 907(b)(3).

---

(6) *Bill of particulars.* A bill of particulars may be amended at any time, subject to such conditions as justice permits.

Discussion

The purposes of a bill of particulars are to inform the accused of the nature of the charge with sufficient precision to enable the accused to prepare for trial, to avoid or minimize the danger of surprise at the time of trial, and to enable the accused to plead the acquittal or conviction in bar of another prosecution for the same offense when the specification itself is too vague and indefinite for such purposes.

A bill of particulars should not be used to conduct discovery of the Government's theory of a case, to force detailed disclosure of acts underlying a charge, or to restrict the Government's proof at trial.

A bill of particulars need not be sworn because it is not part of the specification. A bill of particulars cannot be used to repair a specification which is otherwise not legally sufficient.

---

(7) *Discovery and Production.* Discovery and production of evidence and witnesses.

Discussion

See R.C.M. 701 concerning discovery. *See* R.C.M. 703, 914, and 1001(f) concerning production of evidence and witnesses.

---

(8) *Relief from pretrial confinement.* Upon a motion for release from pretrial confinement, a victim of an alleged offense committed by the accused has the right to reasonable, accurate, and timely notice of the motion and any hearing, the right to confer with counsel, and the right to be reasonably heard. Inability to reasonably afford a victim these rights shall not delay the proceedings. The right to be heard under this rule includes the right to be heard through counsel.

Discussion

See R.C.M. 305(j).

---

(9) *Severance of multiple accused.* Severance of multiple accused, if it appears that an accused or the Government is prejudiced by a joint or common trial. In a common trial, a severance shall be granted whenever any accused, other than the moving accused, faces charges unrelated to those charged against the moving accused.

Discussion

A motion for severance is a request that one or more accused against whom charges have been referred to a joint or common trial be tried separately. Such a request should be granted if good cause is shown. For example, a severance may be appropriate when: the moving party wishes to use the testimony of one or more of the coaccused or the spouse of a coaccused; a defense of a coaccused is antagonistic to the moving party; or evidence as to any other accused will improperly prejudice the moving accused.

If a severance is granted by the military judge, the military judge will decide which accused will be tried first. *See* R.C.M. 801(a). In the case of joint charges, the military judge will direct an appropriate amendment of the charges and specifications.

See also R.C.M. 307(c)(5), 601(e)(3), 604, 812.

---

(10) *Severance of offenses.*

(A) *In general.* Offenses may be severed, but only to prevent manifest injustice.

(B) *Capital cases.* In a capital case, if the joinder of unrelated non-capital offenses appears to prejudice the accused, the military judge may sever the non-capital offenses from the capital offenses.

Discussion

Joinder of minor and major offenses, or of unrelated offenses, is not alone a sufficient ground to sever offenses. For example, when an essential witness as to one offense is unavailable, it might be appropriate to sever that offense to prevent violation of the accused's right to a speedy trial.

---

(11) *Change of place of trial.* The place of trial may be changed when necessary to prevent prejudice to the rights of the accused or for the convenience of the Government if the rights of the accused are not prejudiced thereby.

Discussion

A change of the place of trial may be necessary when there exists in the place where the court-martial is pending so great a prejudice against the accused that the accused cannot obtain a fair and impartial trial there, or to obtain compulsory process over an essential witness.

When it is necessary to change the place of trial, the choice of places to which the court-martial will be transferred will be left to the convening authority, as long as the choice is not inconsistent with the ruling of the military judge.

---

(12) *Unreasonable multiplication of charges.* The military judge may provide a remedy, as described in this rule, if he or she finds there has been an unreasonable multiplication of charges as applied to findings or sentence.

(A) *As applied to findings.* Charges that arise from substantially the same transaction, while not legally multiplicious, may still be unreasonably multiplied as applied to findings. When the military judge finds, in his or her discretion, that the offenses have been unreasonably multiplied, the appropriate remedy shall be dismissal of the lesser offenses or merger of the offenses into one specification.

(B) *As applied to sentence.* Where the military judge finds that the unreasonable multiplication of charges requires a remedy that focuses more appropriately on punishment than on findings, the military judge may find that there is an unreasonable multiplication of charges as applied to sentence. If the military judge makes such a finding, the remedy shall be as set forth in R.C.M. 1002(d)(2). A ruling on this motion ordinarily should be deferred until after findings are entered.

Discussion

See RCM 1002(b) (providing for how the "military judge shall determine the sentence of a general or special court-martial . . . in all noncapital cases.")."

---

(13) *Admissibility.* Preliminary ruling on admissibility of evidence.

Discussion

See Mil. R. Evid. 104(c).

A request for a preliminary ruling on admissibility is a request that certain matters which are ordinarily decided during trial of the general issue be resolved before they arise, outside the presence of members. The purpose of such a motion is to avoid the prejudice which may result from bringing inadmissible matters to the attention of court members.

Whether to rule on an evidentiary question before it arises during trial is a matter within the discretion of the military judge. *But see* R.C.M. 905(b)(3) and (d); and Mil. R. Evid. 304(f)(5); 311(d)(7); 321(d)(7). Reviewability of preliminary rulings will be controlled by the Supreme Court's decision in *Luce v. United States*, 469 U.S. 38 (1984).

---

(14) *Mental capacity or responsibility.* Motions relating to mental capacity or responsibility of the accused.

Discussion

See R.C.M. 706, 909, and 916(k) regarding procedures and standards concerning the mental capacity or responsibility of the accused.

Rule 907. Motions to dismiss

(a) *In general.* A motion to dismiss is a request to terminate further proceedings as to one or more charges and specifications on grounds capable of resolution without trial of the general issue of guilt.

Discussion

Dismissal of a specification terminates the proceeding with respect to that specification unless the decision to dismiss is reconsidered and reversed by the military judge. *See* R.C.M. 905(f). Dismissal of a specification on grounds stated in R.C.M. 907(b)(1) or (b)(3)(A) does not ordinarily bar a later court-martial for the same offense if the grounds for dismissal no longer exist. *See also* R.C.M. 905(g) and R.C.M. 907(b)(2).

See R.C.M. 916 concerning defenses.

(b) *Grounds for dismissal.* Grounds for dismissal include the following—

(1) *Nonwaivable grounds.* A charge or specification shall be dismissed at any stage of the proceedings if the court-martial lacks jurisdiction to try the accused for the offense.

(2) *Waivable grounds.* A charge or specification shall be dismissed upon motion made by the accused before the final adjournment of the court-martial in that case if:

(A) Dismissal is required under R.C.M. 707;

(B) The statute of limitations (Article 43) has run, provided that, if it appears that the accused is unaware of the right to assert the statute of limitations in bar of trial, the military judge shall inform the accused of this right;

Discussion

Except for certain offenses for which there is either: no limitation as to time; or child abuse offenses for which a time limitation has been enacted and applies that is based upon the life of a child abuse victim, *see* Article 43(a) and (b)(2), a person charged with an offense under the UCMJ may not be tried by court-martial over objection if sworn charges have not been received by the officer exercising summary court-martial jurisdiction over the command within five years. *See* Article 43(b). This period may be tolled (Article 43(c) and (d)), extended (Article 43(e) and (g)), or suspended (Article 43(f)) under certain circumstances. The prosecution bears the burden of proving that the statute of limitations has been tolled, extended, or suspended if it appears that is has run.

Some offenses are continuing offenses and any period of the offense occurring within the statute of limitations is not barred. Absence without leave, desertion, and fraudulent enlistment are not continuing offenses and are committed, respectively, on the day the person goes absent, deserts, or first receives pay or allowances under the enlistment.

When computing the statute of limitations, periods in which the accused was fleeing from justice or periods when the accused was absent without leave or in desertion are excluded. The military judge must determine by a preponderance, as an interlocutory matter, whether the accused was absent without authority or fleeing from justice. It would not be necessary that the accused be charged with the absence offense. In cases where the accused is charged with both an absence offense and a non-absence offense, but is found not guilty of the absence offense, the military judge would reconsider, by a preponderance, his or her prior determination whether that period of time is excludable.

If sworn charges have been received by an officer exercising summary court-martial jurisdiction over the command within the period of the statute, minor amendments (*see* R.C.M. 603(a)) may be made to the specification after the statute of limitations has run. However, if new charges are drafted or a major amendment made (*see* R.C.M. 603(d)) after the statute of limitations has run, prosecution is barred. The date of receipt of sworn charges is excluded when computing the appropriate statutory period. The date of the offense is included in the computation of the elapsed time. Article 43(g) allows the Government time to reinstate charges dismissed as defective or insufficient for any cause. The Government would have up to six months to reinstate the charges if the original period of limitations has expired or will expire within six months of the dismissal.

In some cases, the issue whether the statute of limitations has run will depend on the findings on the general issue of guilt. For example, where the date of an offense is in dispute, a finding by the court-martial that the offense occurred at an earlier time may affect a determination as to the running of the statute of limitations.

When the statute of limitations has run as to a lesser included offense, but not as to the charged offense, see R.C.M. 920(e)(2) with regard to instructions on the lesser offense.

(C) The accused has previously been tried by court-martial or federal civilian court for the same offense, provided that:

(i) No court-martial proceeding is a trial in the sense of this rule unless—

(I) In the case of a trial by military judge alone, presentation of the evidence on the general issue of guilt has begun;

(II) In the case of a trial with a military judge and members, the members have been impaneled; or

(III) In the case of a summary court-martial, presentation of the evidence on the general issue of guilt has begun.

(ii) No court-martial proceeding which has been terminated under R.C.M. 604(b) or R.C.M. 915 shall bar later prosecution for the same offense or offenses, if so provided in those rules;

(iii) No court-martial proceeding in which an accused has been found guilty of any charge or specification is a trial in the sense of this rule until the finding of guilty has become final after review of the case has been fully completed; and

(iv) No court-martial proceeding which lacked jurisdiction to try the accused for the offense is a trial in the sense of this rule.

Discussion

R.C.M. 907(b)(2)(C)(i)(I) includes special courts-martial consisting of a military judge alone under Article 16(c)(2)(A).

(D) Prosecution is barred by:

(i) A pardon issued by the President;

(ii) Immunity from prosecution granted by a person authorized to do so; or

Discussion

See R.C.M. 704.

(iii) Prior punishment under Article 13 or 15 for the same offense, if that offense was punishable by confinement of one year or less.

Discussion

See Article 13 and Appendix 12, Maximum Punishment Chart.

(E) The specification fails to state an offense.

(3) *Permissible grounds.* A specification may be dismissed upon timely motion by the accused if one of the following is applicable:

(A) *Defective.* When the specification is so defective that it substantially misled the accused, and the military judge finds that, in the interest of justice, trial should proceed on any remaining charges and specifications without undue delay; or

(B) *Multiplicity.* When the specification is multiplicious with another specification, is unnecessary to enable the prosecution to meet the exigencies of proof through trial, review, and appellate action, and should be dismissed in the interest of justice. A charge is multiplicious if the proof of such charge also proves every element of another charge.

Discussion

Ordinarily, a specification should not be dismissed for multiplicity before trial unless it clearly alleges the same offense, or one necessarily included therein, as is alleged in another specification. It may be appropriate to dismiss the less serious of any multiplicious specifications after findings have been reached. Due consideration must be given, however, to possible post-trial or appellate action with regard to the remaining specification.

Rule 908. Appeal by the United States

(a) *In general.* The United States may appeal an order or ruling by a military judge that terminates the proceedings with respect to a charge or specification, or excludes evidence that is substantial proof of a fact material in the proceedings, or directs the disclosure of classified information, or that imposes sanctions for nondisclosure of classified information. The United States may also appeal a refusal by the military judge to issue a protective order sought by the United States to prevent the disclosure of classified information or to enforce such an order that has previously been issued by the appropriate authority. The United States may not appeal an order or ruling that is, or amounts to, a finding of not guilty with respect to the charge or specification except when the military judge enters a finding of not guilty with respect to a charge or specification following the return of a finding of guilty by the members.

Discussion

For the scope of these provisions, see Article 62(e). For rulings on a motion for a finding of not guilty, see R.C.M. 917.

(b) *Procedure.*

(1) *Delay.* After an order or ruling which may be subject to an appeal by the United States, the court-martial may not proceed, except as to matters unaffected by the ruling or order, if trial counsel requests a delay to determine whether to file notice of appeal under this rule. Trial counsel is entitled to no more than 72 hours under this subsection.

(2) *Decision to appeal.* The decision whether to file notice of appeal under this rule shall be made within 72 hours of the ruling or order to be appealed. If the Secretary concerned so prescribes, trial counsel shall not file notice of appeal unless authorized to do so by a person designated by the Secretary concerned.

(3) *Notice of appeal.* If the United States elects to appeal, trial counsel shall provide the military judge with written notice to this effect not later than 72 hours after the ruling or order. Such notice shall identify the ruling or order to be appealed and the charges and specifications affected. Trial counsel shall certify that the appeal is not taken for the purpose of delay and (if the order or ruling appealed is one which excludes evidence) that the evidence excluded is substantial proof of a fact material in the proceeding.

(4) *Effect on the court-martial.* Upon written notice to the military judge under paragraph (b)(3) of this rule, the ruling or order that is the subject of the appeal is automatically stayed and no session of the court-martial may proceed pending disposition by the Court of Criminal Appeals of the appeal, except that solely as to charges and specifications not affected by the ruling or order:

(A) Motions may be litigated, in the discretion of the military judge, at any point in the proceedings;

(B) When trial on the merits has not begun,

(i) a severance may be granted upon request of all the parties;

(ii) a severance may be granted upon request of the accused and when appropriate under R.C.M. 906(b)(10); or

(C) When trial on the merits has begun but has not been completed, a party may, on that party's request and in the discretion of the military judge, present further evidence on the merits.

(5) *Record.* Upon written notice to the military judge under paragraph (b)(3), trial counsel shall cause a record of the proceedings to be prepared. Such record shall be verbatim and complete to the extent necessary to resolve the issues appealed. The record shall be certified in accordance with R.C.M. 1112, and shall be reduced to a written transcript if required under R.C.M. 1114. The military judge or the Court of Criminal Appeals may direct that additional parts of the proceeding be included in the record.

(6) *Forwarding.* Upon written notice to the military judge under R.C.M. 908(b)(3), the trial counsel shall promptly and by expeditious means forward the appeal to a representative of the Government designated by the Judge Advocate General. The matter forwarded shall include: a statement of the issues appealed; the record of the proceedings or, if preparation of the record has not been completed, a summary of the evidence; and such other matters as the Secretary concerned may prescribe.

(7) *Appeal filed.*

(A) In cases over which a special trial counsel exercises authority, the decision to appeal shall be made by:

(i) if within the Department of Defense, a Lead Special Trial Counsel; or

(ii) if within the Coast Guard, a special trial counsel designated under regulations by the Secretary concerned.

(B) For all other cases, the person designated by the Judge Advocate General shall promptly decide whether to file the appeal with the Court of Criminal Appeals and notify trial counsel of that decision.

(C) If the United States elects to file an appeal, it shall be filed directly with the Court of Criminal Appeals, in accordance with the rules of that court.

(D) In all cases, a representative of the Government designated by the Judge Advocate General will be responsible for the substance and content of submissions to the Court of Criminal Appeals. For appeals in cases over which a special trial counsel exercises authority, the designated representative of the Government will consult with the special trial counsel who authorized the appeal or that special trial counsel's designee concerning the substance and content of appellate filings.

Discussion

When the Government files an appeal with the Court of Criminal Appeals under R.C.M. 908(b)(7), the Court maintains jurisdiction to review the case under Article 66(b) regardless of the sentence imposed.

(8) *Appeal not filed.* If the United States elects not to file an appeal, trial counsel promptly shall notify the military judge and the other parties.

(9) *Pretrial confinement of accused pending appeal.* If an accused is in pretrial confinement at the time the United States files notice of its intent to appeal under paragraph (b)(3) of this rule, the commander, in determining whether the accused should be confined pending the outcome of an appeal by the United States, should consider the same factors which would authorize the imposition of pretrial confinement under R.C.M. 305(h)(2)(B).

(c) *Appellate proceedings.*

(1) *Appellate counsel.* The parties shall be represented before appellate courts in proceedings under this rule as provided in R.C.M. 1202. Appellate Government counsel shall diligently prosecute an appeal under this rule.

(2) *Court of Criminal Appeals.* An appeal under Article 62 shall, whenever practicable, have priority over all other proceedings before the Court of Criminal Appeals. In determining an appeal under Article 62, the Court of Criminal Appeals may take action only with respect to matters of law.

(3) *Action following decision of Court of Criminal Appeals.* After the Court of Criminal Appeals has decided any appeal under Article 62, the accused may petition for review by the Court of Appeals for the Armed Forces, or the Judge Advocate General may certify a case to the Court of Appeals for the Armed Forces. The parties shall be notified of the decision of the Court of Criminal Appeals promptly. If the decision is adverse to the accused, the accused shall be notified of the decision and of the right to petition the Court of Appeals for the Armed Forces for review within 60 days. Such notification shall be made orally on the record at the court-martial or in accordance with R.C.M. 1203(d). If the accused is notified orally on the record, trial counsel shall forward by expeditious means a certificate that the accused was so notified to the Judge Advocate General, who shall forward a copy to the clerk of the Court of Appeals for the Armed Forces when required by the Court. If the decision by the Court of Criminal Appeals permits it, the court-martial may proceed as to the affected charges and specifications pending further review by the Court of Appeals for the Armed Forces or the Supreme Court, unless either court orders the proceedings stayed. Unless the case is reviewed by the Court of Appeals for the Armed Forces, it shall be returned to the military judge or the convening authority for appropriate action in accordance with the decision of the Court of Criminal Appeals. If the case is reviewed by the Court of Appeals for the Armed Forces, R.C.M. 1204 and 1205 shall apply.

Discussion

A special trial counsel may request that the applicable Judge Advocate General certify a case to the Court of Appeals for the Armed Forces. The United States may appeal a sentence in accordance with Article 56(d) and the procedures set forth in R.C.M. 1117.

Rule 909. Capacity of the accused to stand trial by court-martial

(a) *In general.* No person may be brought to trial by court-martial if that person is presently suffering from a mental disease or defect rendering him or her mentally incompetent to the extent that he or she is unable to understand the nature of the proceedings against them or to conduct or cooperate intelligently in the defense of the case.

Discussion

See also R.C.M. 916(k).

(b) *Presumption of capacity.* A person is presumed to have the capacity to stand trial unless the contrary is established.

(c) *Determination before referral.*

(1) For offenses over which special trial counsel has not exercised authority or has deferred, if an inquiry pursuant to R.C.M. 706 conducted before referral concludes that an accused is suffering from a mental disease or defect that renders him or her mentally incompetent to stand trial, the convening authority before whom the charges are pending for disposition may disagree with the conclusion and take any action authorized under R.C.M. 401, including referral of the charges to trial. If that convening authority concurs with the conclusion, the convening authority shall forward the charges to the general court-martial convening authority. If, upon receipt of the charges, the general court-martial convening authority similarly concurs, then the general court-martial convening authority shall commit the accused to the custody of the Attorney General. If the general court-martial

convening authority does not concur, that authority may take any action that he or she deems appropriate in accordance with R.C.M. 407, including referral of the charges to trial.

(2) For offenses over which special trial counsel has exercised authority and has not deferred, if an inquiry pursuant to R.C.M. 706 conducted before referral concludes that an accused is suffering from a mental disease or defect that renders him or her mentally incompetent to stand trial, the general court-martial convening authority may disagree with the conclusion and notify special trial counsel who may take any action authorized under R.C.M. 401A, including referral of charges. If the general court-martial convening authority concurs with the conclusion, that authority shall notify special trial counsel and commit the accused to the custody of the Attorney General.

(3) Upon request of the Government or the accused, a military judge may conduct a hearing to determine the mental capacity of the accused in accordance with R.C.M. 309 and R.C.M. 909(e) at any time prior to referral.

(d) *Determination after referral.* After referral, the military judge may conduct a hearing to determine the mental capacity of the accused, either *sua sponte* or upon request of either party. If an inquiry pursuant to R.C.M. 706 conducted before or after referral concludes that an accused is suffering from a mental disease or defect that renders him or her mentally incompetent to stand trial, the military judge shall conduct a hearing to determine the mental capacity of the accused. Any such hearing shall be conducted in accordance with subsection (e) of this rule.

(e) *Incompetence determination hearing.*

(1) *Nature of issue.* The mental capacity of the accused is an interlocutory question of fact.

(2) *Standard.* Trial may proceed unless it is established by a preponderance of the evidence that the accused is presently suffering from a mental disease or defect rendering him or her mentally incompetent to the extent that he or she is unable to understand the nature of the proceedings or to conduct or cooperate intelligently in the defense of the case. In making this determination, the military judge is not bound by the rules of evidence except with respect to privileges.

(3) If the military judge finds the accused is incompetent to stand trial, the judge shall report this finding to the general court-martial convening authority, who shall commit the accused to the custody of the Attorney General.

(f) *Hospitalization of the accused.* An accused who is found incompetent to stand trial under this rule shall be hospitalized by the Attorney General as provided in subsection 4241(d) of title 18, United States Code. If notified that the accused has recovered to such an extent that he or she is able to understand the nature of the proceedings and to conduct or cooperate intelligently in the defense of the case, then the general court-martial convening authority shall promptly take custody of the accused. If, at the end of the period of hospitalization, the accused's mental condition has not so improved, action shall be taken in accordance with section 4246 of title 18, United States Code.

Discussion

Under 18 U.S.C. § 4241(d), the initial period of hospitalization for an incompetent accused shall not exceed four months. However, in determining whether there is a substantial probability the accused will attain the capacity to permit the trial to proceed in the foreseeable future, the accused may be hospitalized for an additional reasonable period of time. This additional period of time ends either when the accused's mental condition is improved so that trial may proceed, or when the pending charges against the accused are dismissed. If charges are dismissed solely due to the accused's mental condition, the accused is subject to hospitalization as provided in 18 U.S.C. §4246.

(g) *Excludable delay.* All periods of commitment shall be excluded as provided by R.C.M. 707(c). The 120-day time period under R.C.M. 707 shall begin anew on the date the general court-martial convening authority takes custody of the accused at the end of any period of commitment. For offenses over which a special trial counsel has exercised authority and not deferred, the general court-martial convening authority shall immediately notify a special trial counsel in accordance with regulations prescribed by the Secretary concerned.

Rule 910. Pleas

(a) *Types of pleas.*

(1) *In general.* An accused may plead as follows:

(A) guilty;

(B) not guilty of an offense as charged, but guilty of a named lesser included offense;

(C) guilty with exceptions, with or without substitutions, not guilty of the exceptions, but guilty of the substitutions, if any; or

(D) not guilty.

Discussion

See paragraph 3, Part IV and Appendix 12A, concerning lesser included offenses. When the plea is to a lesser included offense without the use of exceptions and substitutions, the defense counsel should provide a written revised specification accurately reflecting the plea and request that the revised specification be included in the record as an appellate exhibit.

A plea of guilty to a lesser included offense does not bar the prosecution from proceeding on the offense as charged. *See also* R.C.M. 910(g).

A plea of guilty does not prevent the introduction of evidence, either in support of the factual basis for the plea, or, after findings are entered, in aggravation. *See* R.C.M. 1001(b)(4).

---

(2) *Conditional pleas.* With the approval of the military judge and the consent of the Government, an accused may enter a conditional plea of guilty, reserving the right, on further review or appeal, to review of the adverse determination of any specified pretrial motion. If the accused prevails on further review or appeal, the accused shall be allowed to withdraw the plea of guilty. The Secretary concerned may prescribe who may consent for Government; unless otherwise prescribed by the Secretary concerned, trial counsel may consent on behalf of the Government.

(b) *Refusal to plead; irregular plea.* If an accused fails or refuses to plead, or makes an irregular plea, the military judge shall enter a plea of not guilty for the accused.

Discussion

An irregular plea includes pleas such as guilty without criminality or guilty to a charge but not guilty to all specifications thereunder. When a plea is ambiguous, the military judge should have it clarified before proceeding further.

(c) *Advice to accused.* Before accepting a plea of guilty, the military judge shall address the accused personally and inform the accused of, and determine that the accused understands, the following:

(1) The nature of the offense to which the plea is offered, the mandatory minimum penalty, if any, provided by law, the maximum possible penalty provided by law, and if applicable, the effect of any sentence limitation(s) provided for in a plea agreement on the minimum or maximum possible penalty that may be adjudged including the effect of any concurrent or consecutive sentence limitations;

Discussion

The elements of each offense to which the accused has pleaded guilty should be described to the accused. *See also* R.C.M. 910(e). The term "maximum possible penalty" as used in this rule refers to the total penalty that may be adjudged for all offenses for which the accused is pleading guilty.

---

(2) In a general or special court-martial, if the accused is not represented by counsel, that the accused has the right to be represented by counsel at every stage of the proceedings;

(3) That the accused has the right to plead not guilty or to persist in that plea if already made, and that the accused has the right to be tried by a court-martial, and that at such trial the accused has the right to confront and cross-examine witnesses against the accused, and the right against self-incrimination;

(4) That if the accused pleads guilty, there will not be a trial of any kind as to those offenses to which the accused has so pleaded, so that by pleading guilty the accused waives the rights described in paragraph (c)(3) of this rule;

(5) That if the accused pleads guilty, the military judge will question the accused about the offenses to which the accused has pleaded guilty, and, if the accused answers these questions under oath, on the record, and in the presence of counsel, the accused's answers may later be used against the accused in a prosecution for perjury or false statement; and

Discussion

R.C.M. 910(c)(5) is inapplicable in a court-martial in which the accused is not represented by counsel.

---

(6) That if an election by the accused to be tried by military judge alone has been approved, the accused will be sentenced by the military judge.

Discussion

In a case in which the accused has not elected trial by military judge alone and has pleaded guilty to some offenses but not others, the case will proceed to trial on the merits on the remaining offenses before members. Following announcement of findings by the members on all offenses, the accused will be sentenced by the military judge unless the accused elects to be sentenced by members. *See* Articles 53(b) and 56, and R.C.M. 1002.

(d) *Ensuring that the plea is voluntary.* The military judge shall not accept a plea of guilty without first, by addressing the accused personally, determining that the plea is voluntary and not the result of force or threats or of promises apart from a plea agreement under R.C.M. 705. The military judge shall also inquire whether the accused's willingness to plead guilty results from prior discussions between the convening authority, a representative of the convening authority, or trial counsel, and the accused or defense counsel.

(e) *Determining accuracy of plea.* The military judge shall not accept a plea of guilty without making such inquiry of the accused as shall satisfy the military judge that there is a factual basis for the plea. The accused shall be questioned under oath about the offenses.

Discussion

A plea of guilty must be in accord with the truth. Before the plea is accepted, the accused must admit every element of the offense(s) to which the accused pleaded guilty. Ordinarily, the elements should be explained to the accused. If any potential defense is raised by the accused's account of the offense or by other matter presented to the military judge, the military judge should explain such a defense to the accused and should not accept the plea unless the accused admits facts which negate the defense. If the statute of limitations would otherwise bar trial for the offense, the military judge should not accept a plea of guilty to it without an affirmative waiver by the accused. *See* R.C.M. 907(b)(2)(B).

The accused need not describe from personal recollection all the circumstances necessary to establish a factual basis for the plea. Nevertheless the accused must be convinced of, and able to describe, all the facts necessary to establish guilt. For example, an accused may be unable to recall certain events in an offense, but may still be able to adequately describe the offense based on witness statements or similar sources which the accused believes to be true.

The accused should remain at the counsel table during questioning by the military judge.

(f) *Plea agreement inquiry.*

(1) *In general.* A plea agreement may not be accepted if it does not comply with R.C.M. 705.

(2) *Notice.* The parties shall inform the military judge if a plea agreement exists.

Discussion

The military judge should ask whether a plea agreement exists. *See* R.C.M. 910(d). Even if the military judge fails to so inquire or the accused answers incorrectly, counsel have an obligation to bring any agreements or understandings in connection with the plea to the attention of the military judge. However, the military judge may not participate in discussions between the parties concerning the prospective terms and conditions of the plea agreement. *See* Article 53a(a)(2).

---

(3) *Disclosure.* If a plea agreement exists, the military judge shall require disclosure of the entire agreement before the plea is accepted.

(4) *Inquiry.*

(A) The military judge shall inquire to ensure:

(i) that the accused understands the agreement; and

(ii) that the parties agree to the terms of the agreement.

(B) If the military judge determines that the accused does not understand the material terms of the agreement, or that the parties disagree as to such terms, the military judge shall:

(i) conform, with the consent of the Government, the agreement to the accused's understanding; or

(ii) permit the accused to withdraw the plea.

Discussion

If the plea agreement contains any unclear or ambiguous terms, the military judge should obtain clarification from the parties. If there is doubt about the accused's understanding of any terms in the agreement, including the maximum possible penalty that may be adjudged pursuant to any sentence limitation, the military judge should explain those terms to the accused. If the accused after entering a plea of guilty sets up a matter inconsistent with the plea, the military judge shall resolve the inconsistency or reject the plea. *See* Article 45.

---

(5) *Sentence limitations in plea agreements.* If a plea agreement contains limitations on the punishment that may be imposed, the court-martial, subject to subparagraph (4)(B) and R.C.M. 705, shall sentence the accused in accordance with the agreement.

(6) *Accepted plea agreement.* After the plea agreement inquiry, the military judge shall announce on the record whether the plea and the plea agreement are accepted. Upon acceptance by the military judge, a plea agreement shall bind the parties and the court-

martial.

(7) *Rejected plea agreement.* If the military judge does not accept a plea agreement, the military judge shall—

(A) issue a statement explaining the basis for the rejection;

(B) allow the accused to withdraw any plea; and

(C) inform the accused that if the plea is not withdrawn the court-martial may impose any lawful punishment.

(8) *Basis for rejecting a plea agreement.* The military judge of a general or special court-martial shall reject a plea agreement that—

(A) contains a provision that has not been accepted by both parties;

(B) contains a provision that is not understood by the accused;

(C) except as provided in Article 53a(c), contains a provision for a sentence that is less than the mandatory minimum sentence applicable to an offense referred to in Article 56(b)(2);

(D) is prohibited by law; or

(E) is contrary to, or is inconsistent with, these rules with respect to the terms, conditions, or other aspects of plea agreements.

Discussion

See Article 53a and R.C.M. 705 regarding the military judge's responsibility to review the terms and conditions of the plea agreement.

(g) *Findings.* Findings based on a plea of guilty may be entered immediately upon acceptance of the plea at an Article 39(a) session unless the plea is to a lesser included offense and the prosecution intends to proceed to trial on the offense as charged.

(h) *Later action.*

(1) *Withdrawal by the accused.* If after acceptance of the plea but before the sentence is announced the accused requests to withdraw a plea of guilty and substitute a plea of not guilty or a plea of guilty to a lesser included offense, the military judge shall permit the accused to do so only for good cause shown.

(2) *Statements by accused inconsistent with plea.* If after findings but before the sentence is announced the accused makes a statement to the court-martial, in testimony or otherwise, or presents evidence which is inconsistent with a plea of guilty on which a finding is based, the military judge shall inquire into the providence of the plea. If, following such inquiry, it appears that the accused entered the plea improvidently or through lack of understanding of its meaning and effect a plea of not guilty shall be entered as to the affected charges and specifications.

Discussion

When the accused withdraws a previously accepted plea for guilty or a plea of guilty is set aside, counsel should be given a reasonable time to prepare to proceed. In a trial by military judge alone, recusal of the military judge will ordinarily be necessary when a plea is rejected or withdrawn after findings; in trial with members, a mistrial will ordinarily be necessary.

(i) [Reserved]

(j) *Waiver.* Except as provided in paragraph (a)(2) of this rule, a plea of guilty that results in a finding of guilty waives any objection, whether or not previously raised, as to the factual issue of guilt of the offense(s) to which the plea was made and any non-jurisdictional defect as to the offense(s) to which the plea was made that occurred prior to the plea.

Discussion

Other errors with respect to the plea inquiry or acceptance of a plea under this rule are subject to waiver if not brought to the attention of the military judge.

Rule 911. Randomization and assembly of the court-martial panel

(a) Prior to assembly of the court-martial, at an open session of the court-martial, the military judge, or a designee thereof, shall randomly assign numbers to the members detailed by the convening authority.

(b) The military judge shall determine, after accounting for any excusals by the convening authority or designee, how many members detailed by the convening authority must be present at the initial session for which members are required. The required number of members shall be present, according to the randomly assigned order determined pursuant to R.C.M. 911(a). The military judge may temporarily excuse any member who has been detailed but is not required to be present.

(c) At the initial session for which members are required, the military judge shall cause the members who are present to be sworn, account on the record for any members who are temporarily excused, and then announce assembly of the court-martial.

(d) The military judge shall ensure any additional member is sworn at the first court session at which the member is present.

Discussion

The members are seated with the president, who is the senior member, in the center, and the other members alternately to the president's right and left according to rank. If the rank of a member is changed, or if the membership of the court-martial changes, the members should be reseated accordingly.

When an accused's request to be tried by military judge alone is approved, the court-martial is ordinarily assembled immediately following approval of the request.

In a special court-martial consisting of a military judge alone under Article 16(c)(2)(A), the court-martial is assembled prior to beginning of the trial on the merits.

Assembly of the court-martial is significant because it marks the point after which: substitution of the members and military judge may no longer take place without good cause (*see* Article 29, R.C.M. 505, 902, 912); the accused may no longer, as a matter of right, request trial by military judge alone or withdraw such a request previously approved (*see* Article 16, R.C.M. 903(d)); and the accused may no longer request members-even with the permission of the military judge, or withdraw from a request for members (*see* Article 25(c)(2); R.C.M. 903(d)).

Rule 912. Challenge of selection of members; examination and challenges of members

(a) *Pretrial matters.*

(1) *Questionnaires.* Before trial, trial counsel may, and shall upon request of defense counsel, submit to each member written questions requesting the following information:

(A) Date of birth;

(B) Sex;

(C) Race;

(D) Marital status and sex, age, and number of dependents;

(E) Home of record;

(F) Civilian and military education, including, when available, major areas of study, name of school or institution, years of education, and degrees received;

(G) Current unit to which assigned;

(H) Past duty assignments;

(I) Awards and decorations received;

(J) Date of rank; and

(K) Whether the member has acted as accuser, counsel, preliminary hearing officer, investigating officer, convening authority, or legal officer or staff judge advocate for the convening authority in the case, or has forwarded the charges with a recommendation as to disposition.

Additional information may be requested with the approval of the military judge. Each member's responses to the questions shall be written and signed by the member. For purposes of this rule, the term "members" includes any alternate members.

Discussion

Using questionnaires before trial may expedite voir dire and may permit more informed exercise of challenges.

If the questionnaire is marked or admitted as an exhibit at the court-martial it must be attached to or included in the record of trial. *See* R.C.M. 1112(b)(6).

---

(2) *Other materials.* A copy of any written materials considered by the convening authority in selecting the members detailed to the court-martial shall be provided to any party upon request, except that such materials pertaining solely to persons who were not selected for detail as members need not be provided unless the military judge, for good cause, so directs.

(b) *Challenge of selection of members.*

(1) *Motion.* Before the examination of members under subsection (d) of this rule begins, or at the next session after a party discovered or could have discovered by the exercise of diligence, the grounds therefor, whichever is earlier, that party may move to stay the proceedings on the ground that members were selected improperly.

Discussion

See R.C.M. 502(a) and 503(a) concerning selection of members. Members are also improperly selected when, for example, a certain group or class is arbitrarily excluded from consideration as members.

---

(2) *Procedure.* Upon a motion under paragraph (b)(1) of this rule containing an offer of proof of matters which, if true, would constitute improper selection of members, the moving party shall be entitled to present evidence, including any written materials considered by the convening authority in selecting the members. Any other party may also

present evidence on the matter. If the military judge determines that the members have been selected improperly, the military judge shall stay any proceedings requiring the presence of members until members are properly selected.

(3) *Forfeiture.* Failure to make a timely motion under this subsection shall forfeit the improper selection unless it constitutes a violation of R.C.M. 501(a), 502(a)(1), or 503(a)(2).

(c) *Stating grounds for challenge.* Trial counsel shall state any ground for challenge for cause against any member of which trial counsel is aware.

(d) *Examination of members.* The military judge may permit the parties to conduct examination of members or may personally conduct examination. In the latter event the military judge shall permit the parties to supplement the examination by such further inquiry as the military judge deems proper or the military judge shall submit to the members such additional questions by the parties as the military judge deems proper. A member may be questioned outside the presence of other members when the military judge so directs.

Discussion

Examination of the members is called "voir dire." If the members have not already been placed under oath for the purpose of voir dire (*see* R.C.M. 807(b)(2) Discussion (B)), they should be sworn before they are questioned.

The opportunity for voir dire should be used to obtain information for the intelligent exercise of challenges; counsel should not purposely use voir dire to present factual matter which will not be admissible or to argue the case.

The nature and scope of the examination of members is within the discretion of the military judge. Members may be questioned individually or collectively. Ordinarily, the military judge should permit counsel to personally question the members.

Trial counsel ordinarily conducts an inquiry before the defense. Whether trial counsel will question all the members before the defense begins or whether some other procedure will be followed depends on the circumstances. For example, when members are questioned individually outside the presence of other members, each party would ordinarily complete questioning that member before another member is questioned. The military judge and each party may conduct additional questioning, after initial questioning by a party, as necessary.

Ordinarily the members should be asked whether they are aware of any ground for challenge against them. This may expedite further questioning. The members should be cautioned, however, not to disclose information in the presence of other members which might disqualify them.

(e) *Evidence.* Any party may present evidence relating to whether grounds for challenge exist against a member.

(f) *Challenges and removal for cause.*

(1) *Grounds.* A member shall be excused for cause whenever it appears that the member:

(A) Is not competent to serve as a member under Article 25(a), (b), or (c);

(B) Has not been properly detailed as a member of the court-martial;

(C) Is an accuser as to any offense charged;

(D) Will be a witness in the court-martial;

(E) Has acted as counsel for any party as to any offense charged;

(F) Has been a preliminary hearing officer as to any offense charged;

(G) Has acted in the same case as convening authority or as the legal officer or staff judge advocate to the convening authority;

(H) Will act in the same case as reviewing authority or as the legal officer or staff judge advocate to the reviewing authority;

(I) Has forwarded charges in the case with a personal recommendation as to disposition;

(J) Upon a rehearing or new or other trial of the case, was a member of the court-martial which heard the case before;

(K) Is junior to the accused in grade or rank, unless it is established that this could not be avoided;

(L) Is in arrest or confinement;

(M) Has formed or expressed a definite opinion as to the guilt or innocence of the accused as to any offense charged;

(N) Should not sit as a member in the interest of having the court-martial free from substantial doubt as to legality, fairness, and impartiality.

Discussion

Examples of matters which may be grounds for challenge are that the member: has a direct personal interest in the result of the trial; is closely related to the accused, a counsel, or a witness in the case; has participated as a member or counsel in the trial of a closely related case; has a decidedly friendly or hostile attitude toward a party; or has an inelastic opinion concerning an appropriate sentence for the offenses charged.

---

(2) *When made.*

(A) *Upon completion of examination.* Upon completion of any examination under subsection (d) of this rule and the presentation of evidence, if any, on the matter, each party shall state any challenges for cause it elects to make.

(B) *Other times.* A challenge for cause may be made at any other time during trial when it becomes apparent that a ground for challenge may exist. Such examination of the member and presentation of evidence as may be necessary may be made in order to resolve the matter.

(3) *Procedure.* Each party shall be permitted to make challenges outside the presence of the members. The party making a challenge shall state the grounds for it. Ordinarily trial counsel shall enter any challenges for cause before defense counsel. The military judge shall rule finally on each challenge. The burden of establishing that grounds for a challenge exist is upon the party making the challenge. A member successfully challenged shall be excused.

(4) *Waiver.* The grounds for challenge in subparagraph (f)(1)(A) of this rule may not be waived. Notwithstanding the absence of a challenge or waiver of a challenge by the parties, the military judge may, in the interest of justice, excuse a member against whom a challenge for cause would lie. When a challenge for cause has been denied, the successful use of a peremptory challenge by either party, excusing the challenged member from further participation in the court-martial, shall preclude further consideration of the challenge of that excused member upon later review. Further, failure by the challenging party to exercise a peremptory challenge against any member shall constitute waiver of further consideration of the challenge upon later review.

Discussion

See Mil. R. Evid. 606 regarding when a member may be a witness.

Random numbers are assigned to the members in order to organize and identify the members to be impaneled under R.C.M. 912A.

(g) *Peremptory challenges.*

(1) *Procedure.* Each party may challenge one member peremptorily. Any member so challenged shall be excused. No party may be required to exercise a peremptory challenge before the examination of members and determination of any challenges for cause have been completed. Ordinarily, trial counsel shall enter any peremptory challenge before the defense. No member may be impaneled without being subject to peremptory challenge.

(2) *Additional Members.* If members not previously subject to peremptory challenge are required, the procedures in R.C.M. 912(g)(1) shall be followed with respect to such members.

Discussion

This rule allows for each party to exercise an additional preemptory challenge against a detailed member whose presence is directed in accordance with R.C.M. 912A, after examination and challenges for cause. *See* Article 41(c). If a military judge orders the presence of additional detailed members for examination in accordance with R.C.M. 911, those additional detailed members must be subject to a peremptory challenge prior to impanelment. If the convening authority details additional members, those additional detailed members must be subject to a peremptory challenge prior to impanelment.

Generally, no reason is necessary for a peremptory challenge. *But see Batson v. Kentucky*, 476 U.S. 79 (1986); *United States v. Tulloch*, 47 M.J. 283 (C.A.A.F. 1997); *United States v. Curtis*, 33 M.J. 101 (C.M.A. 1991), *cert. denied*, 502 U.S. 1097 (1992); *United States v. Moore*, 28 M.J. 366 (C.M.A. 1989); *United States v. Santiago-Davilla*, 26 M.J. 380 (C.M.A. 1988).

---

(3) *Waiver.* Failure to exercise a peremptory challenge when properly called upon to do so shall waive the right to make such a challenge. The military judge may, for good cause shown, grant relief from the waiver, but a peremptory challenge may not be made after the presentation of evidence before the members has begun. However, nothing in this subsection shall bar the exercise of a peremptory challenge against a member newly detailed under R.C.M. 505(c)(2)(B), even if presentation of evidence on the merits has begun.

Discussion

When the membership of the court-martial has been reduced below the number of members required under R.C.M. 501(a), as applicable, or, when enlisted members have been requested and the fraction of enlisted members has been reduced below one-third, the proceedings should be adjourned and the convening authority notified so that new members may be detailed. *See* R.C.M. 505. See also R.C.M. 805(d) concerning other procedures when new members are detailed.

(h) *Definitions.*

(1) *Witness.* For purposes of this rule, "witness"

includes one who testifies at a court-martial and anyone whose declaration is received in evidence for any purpose, including written declarations made by affidavit or otherwise.

Discussion

For example, a person who by certificate has attested or otherwise authenticated an official record or other writing introduced in evidence is a witness.

---

(2) *Preliminary hearing officer.* For purposes of this rule, "preliminary hearing officer" includes any person who has examined charges under R.C.M. 405 and any person who was counsel for a member of a court of inquiry, or otherwise personally has conducted an investigation of the general matter involving the offenses charged.

Rule 912A. Impaneling members and alternate members

(a) *In general.* After challenges for cause and peremptory challenges are exercised, the military judge of a general or special court-martial with members shall impanel the members based on the order assigned in R.C.M. 911(a), and, if authorized by the convening authority, alternate members, in accordance with the following numerical requirements:

(1) *Capital cases.* In a general court-martial in which the charges were referred with a special instruction that the case be tried as a capital case, the number of members impaneled, subject to R.C.M. 912A(a)(4), shall be twelve.

(2) *General courts-martial.* In a general court-martial other than as described in R.C.M. 912A(a)(1), the number of members impaneled, subject to R.C.M. 912A(a)(4), shall be eight.

(3) *Special courts-martial.* In a special court-martial, the number of members impaneled, subject to R.C.M. 912A(a)(4), shall be four.

(4) *Alternate members.* A convening authority may authorize the military judge to impanel alternate members. When authorized by the convening authority, the military judge shall designate which of the impaneled members are alternate members in accordance with these rules and consistent with the instructions of the convening authority. Alternate members shall not be notified that they are alternate members until they are excused prior to deliberations on findings.

(A) If the convening authority authorizes the military judge to impanel a specific number of alternate members, the number of members impaneled shall be the number of members required under R.C.M. 912A(a)(1), (2), or (3), as applicable, plus the number of alternate members specified by the convening authority. The military judge shall not impanel the court-martial until the specified number of alternate members has been identified. New members may be detailed in order to impanel the specified number of alternate members.

(B) If the convening authority does not authorize the military judge to impanel a specific number of alternate members, and instead authorizes the military judge to impanel alternate members only if, after the exercise of all challenges, excess members remain, the number of members impaneled shall be the number of members required under R.C.M. 912A(a)(1), (2), or (3) and no more than three alternate members. New members shall not be detailed in order to impanel alternate members.

Discussion

See Article 29(c), R.C.M. 503(a)(1), and R.C.M. 912A(d).

(b) *Enlisted accused.* In the case of an enlisted accused, the members shall be impaneled under R.C.M. 912A(a) in such numbers and proportion that—

(1) If the accused elected to be tried by a court-martial composed of at least one-third enlisted members, the membership of the panel includes at least one-third enlisted members; and

(2) If the accused elected to be tried by a court-martial composed of all officer members, the membership of the panel includes all officer members.

(c) *Number of members insufficient.*

(1) If, after challenges or excusals, the number of detailed members directed to be present by the military judge in accordance with R.C.M. 911(b) is:

(A) fewer than the number of members required for the court-martial under R.C.M. 912A(a), the military judge shall, according to the randomly assigned order determined pursuant to R.C.M. 911(a), determine how many additional detailed members are required and shall direct their presence for member examination in accordance with R.C.M. 912(d).

(B) fewer than the number of members required for the court-martial under R.C.M. 912A(b), the military judge shall, according to the randomly assigned order determined pursuant to R.C.M. 911(a), determine how many additional detailed enlisted members are required and shall direct their presence for member examination in accordance with R.C.M. 912(d).

(2) If, after challenges or excusals, the number of detailed members remaining is fewer than the number of members required for the court-martial under R.C.M. 912A(a) and (b), the convening authority shall detail new members under R.C.M. 503.

(d) *Impaneling members following the exercise of all challenges*. The military judge shall use the following procedures to identify the members who will be impaneled—

(1) In a case in which the accused has elected to be tried by a panel consisting of at least one-third enlisted members under R.C.M. 503(a)(2), the military judge shall:

(A) first identify the one-third enlisted members required under R.C.M. 912A(a) and (b) in numerical order beginning with the lowest random number assigned pursuant to R.C.M. 911(a); and

(B) then identify the remaining members required for the court-martial under R.C.M. 912A(a) and (b), in numerical order beginning with the lowest random number assigned pursuant to R.C.M. 911(a).

(2) For all other panels, the military judge shall identify the number of members required under R.C.M. 912A(a) and (b) in numerical order beginning with the lowest random number assigned pursuant to R.C.M. 911(a).

(3) If the convening authority:

(A) Authorizes the military judge to impanel a specific number of alternate members, the specified number of alternate members shall be identified in numerical order beginning with the lowest remaining random number assigned pursuant to R.C.M. 911(a), after first identifying members under R.C.M. 912A(d)(1) or (2).

(B) Does not authorize the military judge to impanel a specific number of alternate members, and instead authorizes the military judge to impanel alternate members only if, after the exercise of all challenges, excess members remain, alternate members shall be identified in numerical order beginning with the lowest remaining random number assigned pursuant to R.C.M. 911(a), after first identifying the members under 912A(d)(1) or (2). The military judge shall identify no more than three alternate members.

(C) In a case in which the accused has elected to be tried by a panel consisting of at least one-third enlisted members under R.C.M. 503(a)(2), the convening authority may instruct the military judge to prioritize impaneling a specific number of alternate enlisted members before impaneling alternate officer members. These members shall be identified in numerical order beginning with the lowest remaining random number assigned pursuant to R.C.M. 911(a), after first identifying members under 912A(d)(1).

(4) The military judge shall excuse any members not identified as members or alternate members, if any.

Discussion

When the accused has elected to be tried by a panel consisting of at least one-third enlisted members in accordance with R.C.M. 503(a)(2), the military judge is required to identify the minimum number of enlisted members before identifying the remaining members to ensure the number of members required under R.C.M. 501(a), as applicable, is reached. For example, in a general court-martial in which the accused has requested at least one-third enlisted members, there must be at least three enlisted members. If, after the exercise of all challenges, the number of enlisted members is greater than three, the military judge first seats the three enlisted members assigned the three lowest numbers during voir dire. The military judge then seats the next five members, regardless of grade, assigned the lowest numbers.

If the convening authority authorized the military judge to impanel alternate members, the military judge would follow this process to identify the authorized number of alternate members. For example, in a court-martial in which the convening authority has authorized the military judge to impanel alternate members, but has not directed that a specific number of alternate members be impaneled, the military judge first seats the number of members required for the court-martial. If three or fewer excess members remain, the military judge identifies all excess members as alternate members. If more than three excess members remain, the military judge then identifies the next three members, regardless of grade, assigned the next lowest numbers as alternate members.

All members not seated as members or identified as alternate members are then excused by the military judge.

(e) *Lowest number*. The lowest number is the number with the lowest numerical value.

Discussion

For example, the following numbers are listed numerically from lowest to highest: 1, 2, 3, and 4.

(f) *Announcement.* After identifying the members to be impaneled in accordance with this rule, and after excusing any excess members, the military judge shall announce that the members are impaneled.

Rule 912B. Excusal and replacement of members after impanelment

(a) *In general.* Prior to the start of deliberations, a member who has been excused after impanelment shall be replaced in accordance with this rule. Alternate members excused after impanelment shall not be replaced.

(b) *Alternate members impaneled.* Prior to the start of deliberations, an excused member shall be replaced with an impaneled alternate member. The alternate member with the lowest random number assigned pursuant to R.C.M. 911(a) shall replace the excused member, unless in the case of an enlisted accused, the use of such member would be inconsistent with the specific panel composition established under R.C.M. 903. Alternate members who have not replaced impaneled members prior to deliberations on findings shall be excused at the time the court closes for deliberations.

Discussion

When an accused has elected to be tried by a court-martial composed of at least one-third enlisted members, an officer member cannot replace an excused enlisted member unless the total panel membership remains at least one-third enlisted.

(c) *Alternate members not available.*

(1) *Detailing of new members not required.* In a general court-martial in which a sentence of death may not be adjudged, if, after impanelment, a court-martial member is excused and alternate members are not available, the court-martial may proceed if—

(A) There are at least six members; and

(B) In the case of an enlisted accused, the remaining panel composition is consistent with the specific panel composition established under R.C.M. 903.

(2) *Detailing of additional members required.* In all cases other than those described in paragraph (1), if an impaneled member is excused and no alternate member is available to replace the excused member, the court-martial may not proceed until the convening authority details sufficient additional new members.

(d) *After the start of deliberations.* Once the military judge has closed the court for deliberations, if the number of members is reduced below the requirements of Article 29, trial may not proceed and the military judge shall declare a mistrial.

Rule 913. Presentation of the case on the merits

(a) *Preliminary instructions.* The military judge may give such preliminary instructions as may be appropriate. If mixed pleas have been entered, the military judge should ordinarily defer informing the members of the offenses to which the accused pleaded guilty until after the findings on the remaining contested offenses have been entered.

Discussion

Preliminary instructions may include a description of the duties of members, procedures to be followed in the court-martial, and other appropriate matters.

Exceptions to the rule requiring the military judge to defer informing the members of an accused's prior pleas of guilty include cases in which the accused has specifically requested, on the record, that the military judge instruct the members of the prior pleas of guilty and cases in which a plea of guilty was to a lesser included offense within the contested offense charged in the specification. *See* R.C.M. 910(g), Discussion and R.C.M. 920(e), Discussion, paragraph 3.

(b) *Opening statements.* Each party may make one opening statement to the court-martial before presentation of evidence has begun. The defense may elect to make its statement after the prosecution has rested, before the presentation of evidence for the defense. The military judge may, as a matter of discretion, permit the parties to address the court-martial at other times.

Discussion

Counsel should confine their remarks to evidence they expect to be offered which they believe in good faith will be available and admissible and a brief statement of the issues in the case.

(c) *Presentation of evidence.* Each party shall have full opportunity to present evidence.

(1) *Order of presentation.* Ordinarily the following sequence shall be followed:

(A) Presentation of evidence for the prosecution;

(B) Presentation of evidence for the defense;

(C) Presentation of prosecution evidence in rebuttal;

(D) Presentation of defense evidence in surrebuttal;

(E) Additional rebuttal evidence in the discretion of the military judge; and

(F) Presentation of evidence requested by the military judge or members.

Discussion

See R.C.M. 801(a) and Mil. R. Evid. 611 concerning control by the military judge over the order of proceedings.

---

(2) *Taking testimony.* The testimony of witnesses shall be taken orally in open session, unless otherwise provided in this Manual.

Discussion

Each witness must testify under oath. *See* R.C.M. 807(b)(1)(B), Mil. R. Evid. 603. After a witness is sworn, the witness should be identified for the record (full name, rank, and unit, if military, or full name and address, if civilian). The party calling the witness conducts direct examination of the witness, followed by cross-examination of the witness by the opposing party. Redirect and re-cross-examination are conducted as necessary, followed by any questioning by the military judge and members. *See* Mil. R. Evid. 611, 614.

All documentary and real evidence (except marks or wounds on a person's body) should be marked for identification when first referred to in the proceedings and should be included in the record of trial whether admitted in evidence or not. *See* R.C.M. 1112. "Real evidence" include physical objects, such as clothing, weapons, and marks or wounds on a person's body. If it is impracticable to attach an item of real evidence to the record, the item should be clearly and accurately described by testimony, photographs, or other means so that it may be considered on review. Similarly, when documentary evidence is used, if the document cannot be attached to the record (as in the case of an original official record or a large map), a legible copy or accurate extract should be included in the record. When a witness points to or otherwise refers to certain parts of a map, photograph, diagram, chart, or other exhibit, the place to which the witness pointed or referred should be clearly identified for the record, either by marking the exhibit or by an accurate description of the witness' actions with regard to the exhibit.

---

(3) *Views and inspections.* The military judge may, as a matter of discretion, permit the court-martial to view or inspect premises or a place or an article or object. Such a view or inspection shall take place only in the presence of all parties, the members (if any), and the military judge. A person familiar with the scene may be designated by the military judge to escort the court-martial. Such person shall perform the duties of escort under oath. The escort shall not testify, but may point out particular features prescribed by the military judge. Any statement made at the view or inspection by the escort, a party, the military judge, or any member shall be made part of the record.

Discussion

The fact that a view or inspection has been made does not necessarily preclude the introduction in evidence of photographs, diagrams, maps, or sketches of the place or item viewed, if these are otherwise admissible.

---

(4) *Evidence subject to exclusion.* When offered evidence would be subject to exclusion upon objection, the military judge may, as a matter of discretion, bring the matter to the attention of the parties and may, in the interest of justice, exclude the evidence without an objection by a party.

Discussion

The military judge should not exclude evidence which is not objected to by a party except in extraordinary circumstances. Counsel should be permitted to try the case and present the evidence without unnecessary interference by the military judge. *See also* Mil. R. Evid. 103.

---

(5) *Reopening case.* The military judge may, as a matter of discretion, permit a party to reopen its case after it has rested.

Rule 914. Production of statements of witnesses

(a) *Motion for production.* After a witness other than the accused has testified on direct examination, the military judge, on motion of a party who did not call the witness, shall order the party who called the witness to produce, for examination and use by the moving party, any statement of the witness that relates to the subject matter concerning which the witness has testified, and that is:

(1) In the case of a witness called by trial counsel, in the possession of the United States; or

(2) In the case of a witness called by the defense, in the possession of the accused or defense counsel.

Discussion

See also R.C.M. 701.

Counsel should anticipate legitimate demands for statements under this and similar rules and avoid delays in the proceedings by voluntary disclosure before arraignment.

This rule does not apply to preliminary hearings under Article 32.

As to procedures for certain government information as to which a privilege is asserted, *see* Mil. R. Evid. 505, 506.

(b) *Production of entire statement.* If the entire contents of the statement relate to the subject matter concerning which the witness has testified, the military judge shall order that the statement be delivered to the moving party.

(c) *Production of excised statement.* If the party who called the witness claims that the statement contains matter that does not relate to the subject matter concerning which the witness has testified, the military judge shall order that it be delivered to the military judge. Upon inspection, the military judge shall excise the portions of the statement that do not relate to the subject matter concerning which the witness has testified, and shall order that the statement, with such material excised, be delivered to the moving party. Any portion of a statement that is withheld from an accused over objection shall be preserved by trial counsel, and, in the event of a conviction, shall be made available to the reviewing authorities for the purpose of determining the correctness of the decision to excise the portion of the statement.

(d) *Recess for examination of the statement.* Upon delivery of the statement to the moving party, the military judge may recess the trial for the examination of the statement and preparation for its use in the trial.

(e) *Remedy for failure to produce statement.*

(1) *Party refusal to comply.* If the other party elects not to comply with an order to deliver a statement to the moving party, the military judge shall order that the testimony of the witness be disregarded by the trier of fact and that the trial proceed, or, if it is the Government that elects not to comply, shall declare a mistrial if required in the interest of justice.

(2) *Exception.* In the event that the other party cannot comply with this rule because the statement is lost, and can prove, by a preponderance of evidence, that the loss of the witness statement was not attributable to bad faith or gross negligence, the military judge may exercise the sanctions set forth in paragraph (e)(1) of this rule only if—

(A) the statement is of such central importance to an issue that it is essential to a fair trial, and

(B) there is no adequate substitute for the statement.

(f) *Definition.* As used in this rule, a "statement" of a witness means:

(1) A written statement made by the witness that is signed or otherwise adopted or approved by the witness;

(2) A substantially verbatim recital of an oral statement made by the witness that is recorded contemporaneously with the making of the oral statement and contained in a recording or a transcription thereof; or

(3) A statement, however taken or recorded, or a transcription thereof, made by the witness to a federal grand jury.

914A. Use of remote live testimony of a child

(a) *General procedures.* A child shall be allowed to testify out of the presence of the accused after the military judge has determined that the requirements of Mil. R. Evid. 611(d)(3) have been satisfied. The procedure used to take such testimony will be determined by the military judge based upon the exigencies of the situation. At a minimum, the following procedures shall be observed:

(1) The witness shall testify from a remote location outside the courtroom;

(2) Attendance at the remote location shall be limited to the child, counsel for each side (not including an accused pro se), equipment operators, and other persons, such as an attendant for the child, whose presence is deemed necessary by the military judge;

(3) Sufficient monitors shall be placed in the courtroom to allow viewing and hearing of the testimony by the military judge, the accused, the members, the court reporter, and the public;

(4) The voice of the military judge shall be transmitted into the remote location to allow control of the proceedings; and

(5) The accused shall be permitted private, contemporaneous communication with his counsel.

(b) *Definition.* As used in this rule, "remote live testimony" includes, but is not limited to, testimony by video teleconference, closed circuit television, or similar technology.

(c) *Prohibitions.* The procedures described in this rule shall not be used where the accused elects to absent himself from the courtroom pursuant to R.C.M. 804(c)(1).

Discussion

For purposes of this rule, unlike R.C.M. 914B, remote means or similar technology does not include receiving testimony by telephone where the parties cannot see and hear each other.

Rule 914B. Use of remote testimony

(a) *General procedures.* The military judge shall determine the procedures used to take testimony via remote means. At a minimum, all parties shall be able to hear each other, those in attendance at the remote site shall be identified, and the accused shall be permitted private, contemporaneous communication with his counsel.

(b) *Definition.* As used in this rule, testimony via "remote means" includes, but is not limited to, testimony by video teleconference, closed circuit television, telephone, or similar technology.

Discussion

This rule applies for all witness testimony other than child witness testimony specifically covered by Mil. R. Evid. 611(d) and R.C.M. 914A. When utilizing testimony via remote means, military justice practitioners are encouraged to consult the procedure used in *In re San Juan Dupont Plaza Hotel Fire Litigation*, 129 F.R.D. 424 (D.P.R. 1989), and to read *United States v. Gigante*, 166 F.3d 75 (2d Cir. 1999), *cert. denied*, 528 U.S. 1114 (2000).

Rule 915. Mistrial

(a) *In general.* The military judge may, as a matter of discretion, declare a mistrial when such action is manifestly necessary in the interest of justice because of circumstances arising during the proceedings which cast substantial doubt upon the fairness of the proceedings. A mistrial may be declared as to some or all charges, and as to the entire proceedings or as to only the proceedings after findings.

Discussion

The power to grant a mistrial should be used with great caution, under urgent circumstances, and for plain and obvious reasons. As examples, a mistrial may be appropriate when inadmissible matters so prejudicial that a curative instruction would be inadequate are brought to the attention of the members or when members engage in prejudicial misconduct. Also, a mistrial is appropriate when the proceedings must be terminated because of a legal defect, such as a jurisdictional defect or a defective referral. See also R.C.M. 905(g) concerning the effect of rulings in one proceeding on later proceedings.

(b) *Procedure.* On motion for a mistrial or when it otherwise appears that grounds for a mistrial may exist, the military judge shall inquire into the views of the parties on the matter and then decide the matter as an interlocutory question.

(c) *Effect of declaration of mistrial.*

(1) *Withdrawal of charges.* A declaration of a mistrial shall have the effect of withdrawing the affected charges and specifications from the court-martial.

Discussion

Upon declaration of a mistrial, the affected charges are returned to the convening authority, or special trial counsel as applicable, who may refer them anew or otherwise dispose of them. *See* R.C.M. 401-407.

---

(2) *Further proceedings.* A declaration of a mistrial shall not prevent trial by another court-martial on the affected charges and specifications except when the mistrial was declared after jeopardy attached and before findings, and the declaration was:

(A) An abuse of discretion and without the consent of the defense; or

(B) The direct result of intentional prosecutorial misconduct designed to necessitate a mistrial.

Rule 916. Defenses

(a) *In general.* As used in this rule, "defenses" includes any special defense which, although not denying that the accused committed the objective acts constituting the offense charged, denies, wholly or partially, criminal responsibility for those acts.

Discussion

Special defenses are also called "affirmative defenses."

"Alibi" and "good character" are not special defenses, as they operate to deny that the accused committed one or more of the acts constituting the offense. As to evidence of the accused's good character, see Mil. R. Evid. 404. See R.C.M. 701(b)(2) concerning notice of alibi.

(b) *Burden of proof.*

(1) *General rule.* Except as listed in paragraphs (b)(2) and (3) of this rule, the prosecution shall have the burden of proving beyond a reasonable doubt that the defense did not exist.

(2) *Lack of mental responsibility.* The accused has the burden of proving the defense of lack of mental responsibility by clear and convincing evidence.

(3) *Mistake of fact as to age.* In the defense of mistake of fact as to age as described in Article 120b(d)(2) in a prosecution under Article 120b(b) (sexual assault of a child) or Article 120b(c) (sexual abuse of a child), the accused has the burden of proving mistake of fact as to age by a preponderance of the evidence.

Discussion

A defense may be raised by evidence presented by the defense, the prosecution, or the court-martial. For example, in a prosecution for assault, testimony by prosecution witnesses that the victim brandished a weapon toward the accused may raise a defense of self-defense. *See* R.C.M. 916(e). More than one defense may be raised as to a particular offense. The defenses need not necessarily be consistent.

See R.C.M. 920(e) concerning instructions on defenses.

(c) *Justification.* A death, injury, or other act caused or done in the proper performance of a legal duty is justified and not unlawful.

Discussion

The duty may be imposed by statute, regulation, or order. For example, the use of force by a law enforcement officer when reasonably necessary in the proper execution of a lawful apprehension is justified because the duty to apprehend is imposed by lawful authority. Also, killing an enemy combatant in battle is justified.

(d) *Obedience to orders.* It is a defense to any offense that the accused was acting pursuant to orders unless the accused knew the orders to be unlawful or a person of ordinary sense and understanding would have known the orders to be unlawful.

Discussion

Ordinarily, the lawfulness of an order is decided by the military judge. *See* R.C.M. 801(e). An exception might exist when the sole issue is whether the person who gave the order in fact occupied a certain position at the time.

An act performed pursuant to a lawful order is justified. *See* R.C.M. 916(c). An act performed pursuant to an unlawful order is excused unless the accused knew it to be unlawful or a person of ordinary sense and understanding would have known it to be unlawful.

(e) *Self-defense.*

(1) *Homicide or assault cases involving deadly force.* It is a defense to a homicide, assault involving deadly force, or battery involving deadly force that the accused:

(A) Apprehended, on reasonable grounds, that death or grievous bodily harm was about to be inflicted wrongfully on the accused; and

(B) Believed that the force the accused used was necessary for protection against death or grievous bodily harm.

Discussion

The words "involving deadly force" describe the factual circumstances of the case, not specific assault offenses. If the accused is charged with simple assault, battery, or any form of aggravated assault, or if simple assault, battery, or any form of aggravated assault is at issue as a lesser included offense, the accused may rely on this subparagraph if the test specified in subparagraphs (A) and (B) is satisfied.

The test for the first element of self-defense is objective. Thus, the accused's apprehension of death or grievous bodily harm must have been one which a reasonable, prudent person would have held under the circumstances. Because this test is objective, such matters as intoxication or emotional instability of the accused are irrelevant. On the other hand, such matters as the relative height, weight, and general build of the accused and the alleged victim, and the possibility of safe retreat are ordinarily among the circumstances which should be considered in determining the reasonableness of the apprehension of death or grievous bodily harm.

The test for the second element is entirely subjective. The accused is not objectively limited to the use of reasonable force. Accordingly, such matters as the accused's emotional control, education, and intelligence are relevant in determining the accused's actual belief as to the force necessary to repel the attack.

See also Mil. R. Evid. 404(a)(2) as to evidence concerning the character of the victim.

---

(2) *Certain aggravated offer-type assault cases.* It is a defense to aggravated assault that the accused:

(A) Apprehended, on reasonable grounds, that bodily harm was about to be inflicted wrongfully on the accused; and

(B) In order to deter the assailant, offered but did not actually inflict or attempt to inflict substantial or grievous bodily harm.

Discussion

The principles in the discussion of R.C.M. 916(e)(1) concerning reasonableness of the apprehension of bodily harm apply here.

---

(3) *Other assaults.* It is a defense to any assault punishable under Article 89, 91, 128, or 128b and not listed in paragraphs (e)(1) or (2) of this rule that the accused:

(A) Apprehended, upon reasonable grounds, that bodily harm was about to be inflicted wrongfully on the accused; and

(B) Believed that the force that the accused used was necessary for protection against bodily harm, provided that the force used by the accused was less than force reasonably likely to produce death or grievous bodily harm.

Discussion

The principles in the discussion under R.C.M. 916(e)(1) apply here.

If, in using only such force as the accused was entitled to use under this aspect of self-defense, death or serious injury to the victim results, this aspect of self-defense may operate in conjunction with the defense of accident (see subsection (f) of this rule) to excuse the accused's acts. The death or serious injury must have been an unintended and unexpected result of the accused's proper exercise of the right of self-defense.

---

(4) *Loss of right to self-defense.* The right to self-defense is lost and the defenses described in paragraphs (e)(1), (2), and (3) of this rule shall not apply if the accused was an aggressor, engaged in mutual combat, or provoked the attack which gave rise to the apprehension, unless the accused had withdrawn in good faith after the aggression, combat, or provocation and before the offense alleged occurred.

Discussion

A person does not become an aggressor or provocateur merely because that person approaches another to seek an interview, even if the approach is not made in a friendly manner. For example, one may approach another and demand an explanation of offensive words or redress of a complaint. If the approach is made in a nonviolent manner, the right to self-defense is not lost.

Failure to retreat, when retreat is possible, does not deprive the accused of the right to self-defense if the accused was lawfully present. The availability of avenues of retreat is one factor which may be considered in addressing the reasonableness of the accused's apprehension of bodily harm and the sincerity of the accused's belief that the force used was necessary for self-protection.

---

(5) *Defense of another.* The principles of self-defense under paragraphs (e)(1) through (4) of this rule apply to defense of another. It is a defense to homicide, attempted homicide, assault with intent to kill, or any assault under Article 89, 91, 128, or 128b that the accused acted in defense of another, provided that the accused may not use more force than the person defended was lawfully entitled to use under the circumstances.

Discussion

The accused acts at the accused's peril when defending another. Thus, if the accused goes to the aid of an apparent assault victim, the accused is guilty of any assault the accused commits on the apparent assailant if, unbeknownst to the accused, the apparent victim was in fact the aggressor and not entitled to use self-defense.

(f) *Accident.* A death, injury, or other event which occurs as the unintentional and unexpected result of doing a lawful act in a lawful manner is an accident and excusable.

Discussion

The defense of accident is not available when the act which caused the death, injury, or event was a negligent act.

(g) *Entrapment.* It is a defense that the criminal design or suggestion to commit the offense originated in the Government and the accused had no predisposition to commit the offense.

Discussion

The "Government" includes agents of the Government and persons cooperating with them (for example, informants). The fact that persons acting for the Government merely afford opportunities or facilities for the commission of the offense does not constitute entrapment. Entrapment occurs only when the criminal conduct is the product of the creative activity of law enforcement officials.

When the defense of entrapment is raised, evidence of uncharged misconduct by the accused of a nature similar to that charged is admissible to show predisposition. *See* Mil. R. Evid. 404(b).

(h) *Coercion or duress*. It is a defense to any offense except killing an innocent person that the accused's participation in the offense was caused by a reasonable apprehension that the accused or another innocent person would be immediately killed or would immediately suffer serious bodily injury if the accused did not commit the act. The apprehension must reasonably continue throughout the commission of the act. If the accused has any reasonable opportunity to avoid committing the act without subjecting the accused or another innocent person to the harm threatened, this defense shall not apply.

Discussion

The immediacy of the harm necessary may vary with the circumstances. For example, a threat to kill a person's wife the next day may be immediate if the person has no opportunity to contact law enforcement officials or otherwise protect the intended victim or avoid committing the offense before then.

(i) *Inability*. It is a defense to refusal or failure to perform a duty that the accused was, through no fault of the accused, not physically or financially able to perform the duty.

Discussion

The test of inability is objective in nature. The accused's opinion that a physical impairment prevented performance of the duty will not suffice unless the opinion is reasonable under all the circumstances.

If the physical or financial inability of the accused occurred through the accused's own fault or design, it is not a defense. For example, if the accused, having knowledge of an order to get a haircut, spends money on other nonessential items, the accused's inability to pay for the haircut would not be a defense.

(j) *Ignorance or mistake of fact*.

(1) *Generally*. Except as otherwise provided in this subsection, it is a defense to an offense that the accused held, as a result of ignorance or mistake, an incorrect belief of the true circumstances such that, if the circumstances were as the accused believed them, the accused would not be guilty of the offense. If the ignorance or mistake goes to an element requiring premeditation, specific intent, willfulness, or knowledge of a particular fact, the ignorance or mistake need only have existed in the mind of the accused. If the ignorance or mistake goes to any other element requiring only general intent or knowledge, the ignorance or mistake must have existed in the mind of the accused and must have been reasonable under all the circumstances. However, if the accused's knowledge or intent is immaterial as to an element, then ignorance or mistake is not a defense.

(2) *Child Sexual Offenses*. It is a defense to a prosecution under Article 120b(b), sexual assault of a child, and Article 120b(c), sexual abuse of a child, that, at the time of the offense, the child was at least 12 years of age, and the accused reasonably believed that the child had attained the age of 16 years. The accused must prove this defense by a preponderance of the evidence.

Discussion

Examples of ignorance or mistake which need only exist in fact include: ignorance of the fact that the person assaulted was an officer; belief that property allegedly stolen belonged to the accused; belief that a controlled substance was really sugar.

Examples of ignorance or mistake which must be reasonable as well as actual include: belief that the accused charged with unauthorized absence had permission to go; belief that the accused had a medical "profile" excusing shaving as otherwise required by regulation. Some offenses require special standards of conduct (*see, e.g.*, paragraph 94, Part IV, Check, worthless making and uttering – by dishonorably failing to maintain funds); the element of reasonableness must be applied in accordance with the standards imposed by such offenses.

Examples of offenses in which the accused's intent or knowledge is immaterial include: rape of a child, sexual assault of a child, or sexual abuse of a child (if the victim is under 12 years of age, knowledge or belief as to age is immaterial). However, such ignorance or mistake may be relevant in extenuation and mitigation.

See R.C.M. 916(l)(1) concerning ignorance or mistake of law.

(k) *Lack of mental responsibility*.

(1) *Lack of mental responsibility*. It is an affirmative defense to any offense that, at the time of the commission of the acts constituting the offense, the accused, as a result of a severe mental disease or defect, was unable to appreciate the nature and quality or the wrongfulness of his or her acts. Mental disease or defect does not otherwise constitute a defense.

Discussion

See R.C.M. 706 concerning sanity inquiries; R.C.M. 909 concerning the capacity of the accused to stand trial; and R.C.M. 1105 concerning any post-trial hearing for an accused found not guilty only by reason of lack of mental responsibility.

---

(2) *Partial mental responsibility*. A mental condition not amounting to a lack of mental responsibility under paragraph (k)(1) of this rule is not an affirmative defense.

Discussion

Evidence of a mental condition not amounting to a lack of mental responsibility may be admissible as to whether the accused entertained a state of mind necessary to be proven as an element of the offense. The defense must notify the trial counsel before the beginning of trial on the merits if the defense intends to introduce expert testimony as to the accused's mental condition. *See* R.C.M. 701(b)(2).

---

(3) *Procedure.*

(A) *Presumption.* The accused is presumed to have been mentally responsible at the time of the alleged offense. This presumption continues until the accused establishes, by clear and convincing evidence, that he or she was not mentally responsible at the time of the alleged offense.

Discussion

The accused is presumed to be mentally responsible, and this presumption continues throughout the proceedings unless the finder of fact determines that the accused has proven lack of mental responsibility by clear and convincing evidence. *See* R.C.M. 916(b).

(B) *Inquiry.* If a question is raised concerning the mental responsibility of the accused, the military judge shall rule finally whether to direct an inquiry under R.C.M. 706.

Discussion

If an inquiry is directed, priority should be given to it.

(C) *Determination.* The issue of mental responsibility shall not be considered as an interlocutory question.

(l) *Not defenses generally.*

(1) *Ignorance or mistake of law.* Ignorance or mistake of law, including general orders or regulations, ordinarily is not a defense.

Discussion

For example, ignorance that it is a crime to possess marijuana is not a defense to wrongful possession of marijuana.

Ignorance or mistake of law may be a defense in some limited circumstances. If the accused, because of a mistake as to a separate nonpenal law, lacks the criminal intent or state of mind necessary to establish guilt, this may be a defense. For example, if the accused, under mistaken belief that the accused is entitled to take an item under property law, takes an item, this mistake of law (as to the accused's legal right) would, if genuine, be a defense to larceny. On the other hand, if the accused disobeyed an order, under the actual but mistaken belief that the order was unlawful, this would not be a defense because the accused's mistake was as to the order itself, and not as to a separate nonpenal law. Also, mistake of law may be a defense when the mistake results from reliance on the decision or pronouncement of an authorized public official or agency. For example, if an accused, acting on the advice of an official responsible for administering benefits that the accused is entitled to those benefits, applies for and receives those benefits, the accused may have a defense even though the accused was not legally eligible for the benefits. On the other hand, reliance on the advice of counsel that a certain course of conduct is legal is not, of itself, a defense.

---

(2) *Voluntary intoxication.* Voluntary intoxication, whether caused by alcohol or drugs, is not a defense. However, evidence of any degree of voluntary intoxication may be introduced for the purpose of raising a reasonable doubt as to the existence of actual knowledge, specific intent, willfulness, or a premeditated design to kill, if actual knowledge, specific intent, willfulness, or premeditated design to kill is an element of the offense.

Discussion

Intoxication may reduce premeditated murder to unpremeditated murder, but it will not reduce murder to manslaughter or any other lesser offense. *See* paragraph 56.c.(2)(c), Part IV.

Although voluntary intoxication is not a defense, evidence of voluntary intoxication may be admitted in extenuation.

Rule 917. Motion for a finding of not guilty

(a) *In general.* The military judge, on motion by the accused or *sua sponte*, shall enter a finding of not guilty of one or more offenses charged at any time after the evidence on either side is closed but prior to entry of judgment if the evidence is insufficient to sustain a conviction of the offense affected. If a motion for a finding of not guilty at the close of the prosecution's case is denied, the defense may offer evidence on that offense without having reserved the right to do so.

Discussion

In a case with members, the military judge may reserve ruling on a motion until any time prior to entry of judgment, including after the members return with findings. See R.C.M. 908 on appeals by the United States when the military judge sets aside a panel's finding of guilty.

(b) *Form of motion.* The motion shall specifically indicate wherein the evidence is insufficient.

(c) *Procedure.* Before ruling on a motion for a finding of not guilty, whether made by counsel or *sua sponte*, the military judge shall give each party an opportunity to be heard on the matter.

Discussion

For a motion made under R.C.M. 917(a), the military judge ordinarily should permit the trial counsel to reopen the case as to the insufficiency specified in the motion before findings on the general issue of guilt are announced.

See R.C.M. 1104(b)(1)(B) regarding post-trial motions to set aside a finding of guilty.

(d) *Standard.* A motion for a finding of not guilty shall be granted only in the absence of some evidence which, together with all reasonable inferences and applicable presumptions, could reasonably tend to establish every essential element of an offense charged. The evidence shall be viewed in the light most favorable to the prosecution, without an evaluation of the credibility of witnesses.

(e) *Motion as to greater offense.* A motion for a finding of not guilty may be granted as to part of a specification and, if appropriate, the corresponding charge, as long as a lesser offense charged is alleged in the portion of the specification as to which the motion is not granted. In such cases, the military judge shall announce that a finding of not guilty has been granted as to specified language in the specification and, if appropriate, corresponding charge. In cases before members, the military judge shall instruct the members accordingly, so that any findings later announced will not be inconsistent with the granting of the motion.

(f) *Effect of ruling.* Except as provided in R.C.M. 908(a), a ruling granting a motion for a finding of not guilty is final when announced and may not be reconsidered. Such a ruling is a finding of not guilty of the affected specification, or affected portion thereof, and, when appropriate, of the corresponding charge. A ruling denying a motion for a finding of not guilty may be reconsidered at any time before entry of judgment.

(g) *Effect of denial on review.* If all the evidence admitted before findings, regardless by whom offered, is sufficient to sustain findings of guilty, the findings need not be set aside upon review solely because the motion for finding of not guilty should have been granted upon the state of the evidence when it was made.

Rule 918. Finding

(a) *General findings.* The general findings of a court-martial state whether the accused is guilty of each charge and specification. If two or more accused are tried together, separate findings as to each shall be made.

(1) *As to a specification.* General findings as to a specification may be:

(A) guilty;

(B) not guilty of an offense as charged, but guilty of a lesser included offense;

(C) guilty with exceptions, with or without substitutions, not guilty of the exceptions, but guilty of the substitutions, if any;

(D) not guilty only by reason of lack of mental responsibility; or

(E) not guilty.

Exceptions and substitutions may not be used to substantially change the nature of the offense or to increase the seriousness of the offense or the maximum punishment for it.

Discussion

Exceptions and substitutions. One or more words or figures may be excepted from a specification and, when necessary, others substituted, if the remaining language of the specification, with or without substitutions, states an offense by the accused which is punishable by court-martial. Changing the date or place of the offense may, but does not necessarily, change the nature or identity of an offense.

If A and B are joint accused and A is convicted but B is acquitted of the offense charged, A should be found guilty by excepting the name of B from the specification as well as any other words indicating the offense was a joint one.

Lesser included offenses. If the evidence fails to prove the offense charged but does prove an offense necessarily included in the offense charged, the factfinder may find the accused not guilty of the offense charged but guilty of the lesser included offense. See paragraph 3 of Part IV and Appendix 12A concerning lesser included offenses.

Offenses arising from the same act or transaction. The accused may be found guilty of two or more offenses arising from the same act or transaction, whether or not the offenses are separately punishable. *But see* R.C.M. 906(b)(12) and 907(b)(3)(B).

---

(2) *As to a charge.* General findings as to a charge may be:

(A) guilty;

(B) not guilty, but guilty of a violation of Article __________;

(C) not guilty only by reason of lack of mental responsibility; or

(D) not guilty.

Discussion

Where there are two or more specifications under one charge, conviction of any of those specifications requires a finding of guilty of the corresponding charge. Under such circumstances any findings of not guilty as to the other specifications do not affect that charge. If the accused is found guilty of one specification and of a lesser included offense prohibited by a different Article as to another specification under the same charge, the findings as to the corresponding charge should be: "Of the Charge as to specification 1: Guilty; as to specification 2: not guilty, but guilty of ____________, a violation of Article __________."

An attempt should be found as a violation of Article 80 unless the attempt is punishable under Articles 85, 94, 100, 103a, 103b, 119a, or 128, in which case it should be found as a violation of that Article.

A court-martial may not find an offense as a violation of an article under which it was not charged solely for the purpose of increasing the authorized punishment or for the purpose of adjudging less than the prescribed mandatory punishment.

(b) *Special findings.* In a trial by court-martial composed of military judge alone, the military judge shall make special findings upon request by any party. Special findings may be requested only as to matters of fact reasonably in issue as to an offense and need be made only as to offenses of which the accused was found guilty. Special findings may be requested at any time before general findings are announced. Only one set of special findings may be requested by a party in a case. If the request is for findings on specific matters, the military judge may require that the request be written. Special findings may be entered orally on the record at the court-martial or in writing during or after the court-martial, but in any event shall be made before entry of judgment and included in the record of trial.

Discussion

Special findings ordinarily include findings as to the elements of the offenses of which the accused has been found guilty, and any affirmative defense relating thereto.

See also R.C.M. 905(d); Mil. R. Evid. 304(f)(5), 311(d)(7), and 321(d)(7) concerning other findings to be made by the military judge.

Members may not make special findings. Special findings do not include, for example, the members' deliberation and voting on aggravating factors in a capital case under RCM 1004(c), or on the defense of lack of mental responsibility under R.C.M. 921(c)(4).

(c) *Basis of findings.* Findings may be based on direct or circumstantial evidence. Only matters properly before the court-martial on the merits of the case may be considered. A finding of guilty of any offense may be reached only when the factfinder is satisfied that guilt has been proved beyond a reasonable doubt.

Discussion

"Direct evidence" is evidence which tends directly to prove or disprove a fact in issue (for example, an element of the offense charged). "Circumstantial evidence" is evidence which tends directly to prove not a fact in issue but some other fact or circumstance from which, either alone or together with other facts or circumstances, one may reasonably infer the existence or non-existence of a fact in issue. There is no general rule for determining or comparing the weight to be given to direct or circumstantial evidence.

A reasonable doubt is a doubt based on reason and common sense. A reasonable doubt is not mere conjecture; it is an honest, conscientious doubt suggested by the evidence, or lack of it, in the case. An absolute or mathematical certainty is not required. The rule as to reasonable doubt extends to every element of the offense. It is not necessary that each particular fact advanced by the prosecution which is not an element be proved beyond a reasonable doubt.

The factfinder should consider the inherent probability or improbability of the evidence, using common sense and knowledge of human nature, and should weigh the credibility of witnesses. A fact finder may properly believe one witness and disbelieve others whose testimony conflicts with that of the one. A factfinder may believe part of the testimony of a witness and disbelieve other parts.

Rule 919. Argument by counsel on findings

(a) *In general.* After the closing of evidence, trial counsel shall be permitted to open the argument. Defense counsel shall be permitted to reply. Trial counsel shall then be permitted to reply in rebuttal.

(b) *Contents.* Arguments may properly include reasonable comment on the evidence in the case, including inferences to be drawn therefrom, in support of a party's theory of the case.

Discussion

The military judge may exercise reasonable control over argument. *See* R.C.M. 801(a)(3).

Argument may include comment about the testimony, conduct, motives, interests, and biases of witnesses to the extent supported by the evidence. Counsel should not express a personal belief or opinion as to the truth or falsity of any testimony or evidence or the guilt or innocence of the accused, nor should counsel make arguments calculated to inflame passions or prejudices. In argument, counsel may treat the testimony of witnesses as conclusively establishing the facts related by the witnesses. Counsel may not cite legal authorities or the facts of other cases when arguing to members on findings.

Trial counsel may not comment on the accused's exercise of the right against self-incrimination or the right to counsel. *See* Mil. R. Evid. 512. Trial counsel may not argue that the prosecution's evidence is unrebutted if the only rebuttal could come from the accused. When the accused is on trial for several offenses and testifies only as to some of the offenses, trial counsel may not comment on the accused's failure to testify as to the others. When the accused testifies on the merits regarding an offense charged, trial counsel may comment on the accused's failure in that testimony to deny or explain specific incriminating facts that the evidence for the prosecution tends to establish regarding that offense.

Trial counsel may not comment on the failure of the defense to call witnesses or of the accused to testify at the Article 32 preliminary hearing or upon the probable effect of the court-martial's findings on relations between the military and civilian communities.

The rebuttal argument of trial counsel is generally limited to matters argued by the defense. If trial counsel is permitted to introduce new matter in closing argument, the defense should be allowed to reply in rebuttal. However, this will not preclude trial counsel from presenting a final argument.

(c) *Forfeiture of objection to improper argument.* Failure to object to improper argument before the military judge begins to instruct the members on findings shall constitute forfeiture of the objection.

Discussion

If an objection that an argument is improper is sustained, the military judge should immediately instruct the members that the argument was improper and that they must disregard it. In extraordinary cases, improper argument may require a mistrial. *See* R.C.M. 915. The military judge should be alert to improper argument and take appropriate action when necessary.

Rule 920. Instructions on findings

(a) *In general.* The military judge shall give the members appropriate instructions on findings.

Discussion

Instructions consist of a statement of the issues in the case and an explanation of the legal standards and procedural requirements by which the members will determine findings. Instructions should be tailored to fit the circumstances of the case and should fairly and adequately cover the issues presented.

(b) *When given.* Instructions on findings shall be given before or after arguments by counsel, or at both times, and before the members close to deliberate on findings, but the military judge may, upon request of the members, any party, or *sua sponte*, give additional instructions at a later time.

Discussion

After members have reached a finding on a specification, instructions may not be given on an offense included therein which was not described in an earlier instruction unless the finding is illegal. This is true even if the finding has not been announced. When instructions are to be given is a matter within the sole discretion of the military trial judge.

(c) *Request for instructions.* At the close of the evidence or at such other time as the military judge may permit, any party may request that the military judge instruct the members on the law as set forth in the request. The military judge may require the requested instruction to be written. Each party shall be given the opportunity to be heard on any proposed instruction on findings before it is given. The military judge shall inform the parties of the proposed action on such requests before their closing arguments.

Discussion

Requests for and objections to instructions should be resolved at an Article 39(a) session. *See* R.C.M. 803.

If an issue has been raised, ordinarily the military judge must instruct on the issue when requested to do so. The military judge is not required to give the specific instruction requested by counsel, however, as long as the issue is adequately covered in the instructions.

The military judge should not identify the source of any instruction when addressing the members.

All written requests for instructions should be marked as appellate exhibits, whether or not they are given.

(d) *How given.* Instructions on findings shall be given orally on the record in the presence of all parties and the members. Written copies of the instructions, or, unless a party objects, portions of them, may also be given to the members for their use during deliberations.

Discussion

A copy of any written instructions delivered to the members should be marked as an appellate exhibit.

(e) *Required instructions.* Instructions on findings shall include:

(1) A description of the elements of each offense charged, unless findings on such offenses are unnecessary because they have been entered pursuant to a plea of guilty;

(2) A description of the elements of each lesser included offense in issue, unless trial of a lesser included offense is barred by the statute of limitations (Article 43) and the accused refuses to waive the bar;

(3) A description of any special defense under R.C.M. 916 in issue;

(4) A direction that only matters properly before the court-martial may be considered;

(5) A charge that—

(A) The accused must be presumed to be innocent until the accused's guilt is established by legal and competent evidence beyond reasonable doubt;

(B) In the case being considered, if there is a reasonable doubt as to the guilt of the accused, the doubt must be resolved in favor of the accused and the accused must be acquitted;

(C) If, when a lesser included offense is in issue, there is a reasonable doubt as to the degree of guilt of the accused, the finding must be in a lower degree as to which there is not reasonable doubt; and

(D) The burden of proof to establish the guilt of the accused is upon the Government. [When the issue of lack of mental responsibility is raised, add: The burden of proving the defense of lack of mental responsibility by clear and convincing evidence is upon the accused. When the issue of mistake of fact under R.C.M. 916(j)(2) is raised, add: The accused has the burden of proving the defense of mistake of fact as to consent or age by a preponderance of the evidence.]

(6) Directions on the procedures under R.C.M. 921 for deliberations and voting; and

(7) Such other explanations, descriptions, or directions as may be necessary and which are properly requested by a party or which the military judge determines, *sua sponte*, should be given.

Discussion

A matter is "in issue" when some evidence, without regard to its source or credibility, has been admitted upon which members might rely if they choose. An instruction on a lesser included offense is proper when (1) the offense is "necessarily included" in the charged offense in accordance with Article 79(b)(1); or (2) the offense is designated a lesser included offense by the President under Article 79(b)(2).

See R.C.M. 918(c) and the accompanying Discussion as to reasonable doubt and other matters relating to the basis for findings which may be the subject of an instruction.

Other matters which may be the subject of instruction in appropriate cases included: inferences (see the explanations in Part IV concerning inferences relating to specific offenses); the limited purpose for which evidence was admitted (regardless of whether such evidence was offered by the prosecution of defense) (*see* Mil. R. Evid. 105); the effect of character evidence (*see* Mil. R. Evid. 404, 405); the effect of judicial notice (*see* Mil. R. Evid. 201, 202); the weight to be given a pretrial statement (*see* Mil. R. Evid. 304(e)); the effect of stipulations (*see* R.C.M. 811); that, when a guilty plea to a lesser included offense has been accepted, the members should accept as proved the matters admitted by the plea, but must determine whether the remaining elements are established; that a plea of guilty to one offense may not be the basis for inferring the existence of a fact or element of another offense; the absence of the accused from trial should not be held against the accused; and that no adverse inferences may be drawn from an accused's failure to testify (*see* Mil. R. Evid. 301(f)).

The military judge may summarize and comment upon evidence in the case in instructions. In doing so, the military judge should present an accurate, fair, and dispassionate statement of what the evidence shows; not depart from an impartial role; not assume as true the existence or nonexistence of a fact in issue when the evidence is conflicting or disputed, or when there is no evidence to support the matter; and make clear that the members must exercise their independent judgment as to the facts.

(f) *Forfeiture and objections.* Failure to object to an instruction or to omission of an instruction before the members close to deliberate forfeits the objection. The parties shall be given the opportunity to be heard on any objection to or request for instructions outside the presence of the members. When a party objects to an instruction, the military judge may require the party objecting to specify in what respect the instructions given were improper.

(g) *Waiver.* Instructions on a lesser included offense shall not be given when both parties waive such an instruction. After receiving applicable notification of those lesser included offenses of which an accused may be convicted, the parties may waive a lesser included offense instruction. A written waiver is not required. The accused must affirmatively acknowledge that the accused understands the rights involved and affirmatively waive the instruction on the record. The accused's waiver must be made freely, knowingly, and intelligently. In the case of a joint or common trial, instructions on a lesser included offense shall not be given as to an individual accused when that accused and the Government agree to waive such an instruction.

Rule 921. Deliberations and voting on findings

(a) *In general.* After the military judge instructs the members on findings, the members shall deliberate and vote in a closed session. Only the members shall be present during deliberations and voting. Superiority in rank shall not be used in any manner in an attempt to control the independence of members in the exercise of their judgment.

(b) *Deliberations.* Deliberations properly include full and free discussion of the merits of the case. Unless otherwise directed by the military judge, members may take with them in deliberations their notes, if any, any exhibits admitted in evidence, and any written instructions. Members may request that the court-martial be reopened and that portions of the record be read to them or additional evidence introduced. The military judge may, in the exercise of discretion, grant such request.

(c) *Voting.*

(1) *Secret ballot.* Voting on the findings for each charge and specification shall be by secret written ballot. All members present shall vote.

(2) *Numbers of votes required to convict.* A finding of guilty results only if at least three-fourths of the members present vote for a finding of guilty.

Discussion

In computing the number of votes required to convict, any fraction of a vote is rounded up to the next whole number. For example, in a general court-martial with eight members, the concurrence of at least six members is required to convict. In the unusual case where a member has been excused after impanelment, resulting in a panel of seven members, the concurrence of at least six members is required to convict. Likewise, if there are only six members, the concurrence of at least five members is required to convict. In a case that was referred as capital with 12 members, the concurrence of at least nine members is required to convict. However, a sentence of death is not authorized without either the members' unanimous finding of guilty to a death eligible offense, or the military judge's acceptance of the accused's plea of guilty to such an offense, and the members' unanimous finding of at least one aggravating factor, unanimous finding that the extenuating and mitigating circumstances are substantially outweighed by any aggravating circumstances, and unanimous determination that the sentence for the offense shall be death. *See* R.C.M. 1004(a), (g). The military judge should instruct the members on the specific number of votes required to convict.

---

(3) *Acquittal.* If fewer than three-fourths of the members present vote for a finding of guilty, a finding of not guilty has resulted as to the charge or specification on which the vote was taken.

(4) *Not guilty only by reason of lack of mental responsibility.* When the defense of lack of mental responsibility is in issue under R.C.M. 916(k)(1), the members shall first vote on whether the prosecution has proven the elements of the offense beyond a reasonable doubt. If at least three-fourths of the members present vote for a finding of guilty, then the members shall vote on whether the accused has proven lack of mental responsibility. If a majority of the members present concur that the accused has proven lack of mental responsibility by clear and convincing evidence, a finding of not guilty only by reason of lack of mental responsibility results. If the vote on lack of mental responsibility does not result in a finding of not guilty only by reason of lack of mental responsibility, then the defense of lack of mental responsibility has been rejected and the finding of guilty stands.

Discussion

If lack of mental responsibility is in issue with regard to more than one specification, the members should determine the issue of lack of mental responsibility on each specification separately.

---

(5) *Included offenses.* Members shall not vote on a lesser included offense unless a finding of not guilty of the offense charged has been reached. If a finding of not guilty of an offense charged has been reached the members shall vote on each included offense on which they have been instructed, in order of severity beginning with the most severe. The members shall continue the vote on each included offense on which they have been instructed until a finding of guilty results or findings of not guilty have been reached as to each such offense.

(6) *Procedure for voting.*

(A) *Order.* Each specification shall be voted on separately before the corresponding charge. The order of voting on several specifications under a charge or on several charges shall be determined by the president unless a majority of the members object.

(B) *Counting votes*. The junior member shall collect the ballots and count the votes. The president shall check the count and inform the other members of the result.

Discussion

Once findings have been reached, they may be reconsidered only in accordance with R.C.M. 924.

(d) *Action after findings are reached.* After the members have reached findings on each charge and specification before them, the court-martial shall be opened and the president shall inform the military judge that findings have been reached. The military judge may, in the presence of the parties, examine any writing which the president intends to read to announce the findings and may assist the members in putting the findings in proper form. Neither that writing nor any oral or written clarification or discussion concerning it shall constitute announcement of the findings.

Discussion

Ordinarily a findings worksheet should be provided to the members as an aid to putting the findings in proper form. If the military judge examines any writing by the members or otherwise assists them to put findings in proper form, this must be done in an open session and counsel should be given the opportunity to examine such a writing and to be heard on any instructions the military judge may give. *See* Article 39(b).

The president should not disclose any specific number of votes for or against any finding.

Rule 922. Announcement of findings

(a) *In general*. Findings shall be announced in the presence of all parties promptly after they have been determined.

(b) *Findings by members*. The president shall announce the findings by the members. In a capital case, if a finding of guilty is unanimous with respect to a capital offense, the president shall so state.

Discussion

If the findings announced are ambiguous, the military judge should seek clarification. *See also* R.C.M. 924.

(c) *Findings by military judge*. The military judge shall announce the findings when trial is by military judge alone or in accordance with R.C.M. 910(g).

(d) *Erroneous announcement*. If an error was made in the announcement of the findings of the court-martial, the error may be corrected by a new announcement in accordance with this rule. The error must be discovered and the new announcement made before the final adjournment of the court-martial in the case.

Discussion

See R.C.M. 1104 concerning the action to be taken if the error in the announcement is discovered after final adjournment.

(e) *Polling prohibited.* Except as provided in Mil. R. Evid. 606, members may not be questioned about their deliberations and voting.

Rule 923. Impeachment of findings

Findings that are proper on their face may be impeached only when extraneous prejudicial information was improperly brought to the attention of a member, outside influence was improperly brought to bear upon any member, or unlawful command influence was brought to bear upon any member.

Discussion

Deliberations of the members ordinarily are not subject to disclosure. *See* Mil. R. Evid. 606. Unsound reasoning by a member, misconception of the evidence, or misapplication of the law is not a proper basis for challenging the findings. However, when a showing of a ground for impeaching the verdict has been made, members may be questioned about such a ground. The military judge determines, as an interlocutory matter, whether such an inquiry will be conducted and whether a finding has been impeached.

Rule 924. Reconsideration of findings

(a) *Time for reconsideration.* Members may reconsider any finding reached by them before such finding is announced in open session.

(b) *Procedure*. Any member may propose that a finding be reconsidered. If such a proposal is made in a timely manner, the question whether to reconsider shall be determined in closed session by secret written ballot. Any finding of not guilty shall be reconsidered if a majority vote for reconsideration. Any finding of guilty shall be reconsidered if more than one-fourth of the members vote for reconsideration. Any finding of not guilty only by reason of lack of mental responsibility shall be reconsidered on the issue of the finding of guilty of the elements if more than one-fourth of the members vote for reconsideration, and on the issue of mental responsibility if a majority vote for reconsideration. If a vote to reconsider a finding succeeds, the procedures in R.C.M. 921 shall apply.

Discussion

After the initial secret ballot vote on a finding in closed session, no other vote may be taken on that finding unless a vote to reconsider succeeds.

(c) *Military judge sitting alone.* In trial by military judge alone, the military judge may reconsider:

(1) any finding of guilty at any time before announcement of sentence; and

(2) the issue of the finding of guilty of the elements in a finding of not guilty only by reason of lack of mental responsibility at any time before announcement of sentence or, where there was no finding of guilty, entry of judgment.

Rule 925. Application of sentencing rules

(a) Only one set of sentencing rules shall apply in a court-martial.

(b) If convicted of any offense for which death may be adjudged, the accused shall be sentenced in accordance with R.C.M. 1004.

(c) Except as provided in R.C.M. 925(b):

(1) If convicted of any offense committed on or before December 27, 2023, the accused shall be sentenced in accordance with the Rules for Courts-Martial in effect prior to December 28, 2023. The military judge shall inquire into the accused's election of sentencing rules after the announcement of findings and before any matter is presented in the presentencing phase.

(2) If convicted of only offenses committed after December 27, 2023, the accused shall be sentenced by a military judge in accordance with R.C.M. 1002(a)(2).

(d) Any elections made by the accused pursuant to R.C.M. 925(c)(1) shall be made orally on the record or be in writing and signed by the accused. The military judge shall ascertain whether the accused has consulted with defense counsel and has been informed of the right to make the election of the applicable sentencing rules.

Discussion

This rule is applicable only to sentencing proceedings in which death may not be adjudged. See R.C.M. 1004 for capital sentencing procedures.

CHAPTER X. SENTENCING

Rule 1001. Presentencing procedure

(a) *In general.*

(1) *Procedure.* After findings of guilty have been announced, the Government and defense may present matters pursuant to this rule to aid the court-martial in determining an appropriate sentence. Such matters shall ordinarily be presented in the following sequence:

(A) Presentation by the trial counsel of:

(i) service data relating to the accused taken from the charge sheet;

(ii) personal data relating to the accused and of the character of the accused's prior service as reflected in the personnel records of the accused.

(B) Crime victim's right to be reasonably heard.

(C) Presentation by the defense of evidence in extenuation or mitigation or both.

(D) Rebuttal.

(E) Argument by the trial counsel on sentence.

(F) Argument by the defense counsel on sentence.

(G) Rebuttal argument in the discretion of the military judge.

(2) *Adjudging sentence.* A sentence shall be adjudged in all cases without unreasonable delay.

(3) *Advice and inquiry.*

(A) *Crime victim.* At the beginning of the presentencing proceeding, the military judge shall announce that any crime victim who is present at the presentencing proceeding has the right to be reasonably heard, including the right to make a sworn statement, unsworn statement, or both. Prior to the conclusion of the presentencing proceeding, the military judge shall ensure that any such crime victim was afforded the opportunity to be reasonably heard.

Discussion

In capital cases, the right to be reasonably heard does not include the right to make an unsworn statement. *See* R.C.M. 1001(c)(2)(D)(i).

(B) *Accused.* The military judge shall personally inform the accused of the right to present matters in extenuation and mitigation, including the right to make a sworn or unsworn statement or to remain silent, and shall ask whether the accused chooses to exercise those rights.

(b) *Matters to be presented by the prosecution.*

(1) *Service data from the charge sheet.* Trial counsel shall inform the court-martial of the data on the charge sheet relating to the pay and service of the accused and the duration and nature of any pretrial restraint. In the discretion of the military judge, this may be done by reading the material from the charge sheet or by giving the court-martial a written statement of such matter. If the defense objects to the data as being materially inaccurate or incomplete, or containing specified objectionable matter, the military judge shall determine the issue. Objections not asserted are forfeited.

(2) *Personal data and character of prior service of the accused.* Under regulations of the Secretary concerned, the trial counsel may obtain and introduce from the personnel records of the accused evidence of the accused's marital status; number of dependents, if any; and character of prior service. Such evidence includes copies of reports reflecting the past military efficiency, conduct, performance, and history of the accused and evidence of any disciplinary actions, including punishments under Article 15 and summary courts-martial after review has been completed pursuant to Article 64. "Personnel records of the accused" includes any records made or maintained in accordance with departmental regulations that reflect the past military efficiency, conduct, performance, and history of the accused. If the accused objects to a particular document as inaccurate or incomplete in a specified respect, or as containing matter that is not admissible under the Military Rules of Evidence, the matter shall be determined by the military judge. Objections not asserted are forfeited.

Discussion

Defense counsel may also, subject to the Military Rules of Evidence and this rule, present personnel records of the accused not introduced by trial counsel in accordance with R.C.M. 1001(b). A forfeited matter may be subject to review for plain error.

---

(3) *Evidence of prior convictions of the accused.*

(A) *In general.* Trial counsel may introduce evidence of prior military or civilian convictions of the accused. For purposes of this rule, there is a "conviction" in a court-martial case when a sentence has been adjudged. In a civilian case, a "conviction" includes any disposition following an initial judicial determination or assumption of guilt, such as when guilt has been established by guilty plea, trial, or plea of nolo contendere, regardless of the subsequent disposition, sentencing procedure, or final judgment. A "conviction" does not include a diversion from the judicial process without a finding or admission of guilt; expunged convictions; juvenile adjudications; minor traffic violations; foreign convictions; tribal court convictions; or convictions reversed, vacated, invalidated, or pardoned.

Discussion

A vacation of a suspended sentence (*see* R.C.M. 1108) is not a conviction and is not admissible as such, but may be admissible under R.C.M. 1001(b)(2) as reflective of the character of the prior service of the accused.

An accused may only be punished for the offenses of which he or she was convicted in that same court-martial.

(B) *Pendency of appeal.* The pendency of an appeal therefrom does not render evidence of a conviction inadmissible. Evidence of the pendency of an appeal is admissible.

(C) *Method of proof.* Previous convictions may be proved by any evidence admissible under the Military Rules of Evidence.

Discussion

Normally, previous convictions may be proved by use of the personnel records of the accused, by the record of the conviction, or by the judgment. *See* R.C.M. 1111 or DD Form 493 (Extract of Military Records of Previous Convictions).

---

(4) *Evidence in aggravation.* The trial counsel may present evidence as to any aggravating circumstance directly relating to or resulting from the offenses of which the accused has been found guilty. Evidence in aggravation includes, but is not limited to, evidence of financial, social, psychological, and medical impact on or cost to any person or entity who was the victim of an offense committed by the accused and evidence of significant adverse impact on the mission, discipline, or efficiency of the command directly and immediately resulting from the accused's offense. In addition, evidence in aggravation may include evidence that the accused intentionally selected any victim or any property as the object of the offense because of the actual or perceived race, color, religion, national origin, ethnicity, sex (including pregnancy), gender (including gender identity), disability, or sexual orientation of any person. Except in capital cases, a written or oral deposition taken in accordance with R.C.M. 702 is admissible in aggravation.

Discussion

See also R.C.M. 1004 concerning aggravating factors in capital cases.

---

(5) *Evidence of rehabilitative potential.* "Rehabilitative potential" refers to the accused's potential to be restored, through vocational, correctional, or therapeutic training or other corrective measures to a useful and constructive place in society.

(A) *In general.* Trial counsel may present, by testimony or oral deposition in accordance with R.C.M. 702(g)(1), evidence in the form of opinions concerning the accused's previous performance as a servicemember and potential for rehabilitation.

(B) *Foundation for opinion.* The witness or deponent providing opinion evidence regarding the accused's rehabilitative potential must possess sufficient information and knowledge about the accused to offer a rationally-based opinion that is helpful to the sentencing authority. Relevant information and knowledge include, but are not limited to, information and knowledge about the accused's character, performance of duty, moral fiber, determination to be rehabilitated, and nature and severity of the offense or offenses.

Discussion

See Mil. R. Evid. 701. See also Mil. R. Evid. 703 if the witness or deponent is testifying as an expert. The types of information and knowledge reflected in this subparagraph are illustrative only.

(C) *Bases for opinion.* An opinion regarding the accused's rehabilitative potential must be based upon relevant information and knowledge possessed by the witness or deponent, and must relate to the accused's personal circumstances. The opinion of the witness or deponent regarding the severity or nature of the accused's offense or offenses may not serve as the principal basis for an opinion of the accused's rehabilitative potential.

(D) *Scope of opinion.* An opinion offered under this rule is limited to whether the accused has rehabilitative potential and to the magnitude or quality of any such potential. A witness may not offer an opinion regarding the appropriateness of a punitive discharge or whether the accused should be returned to the accused's unit.

Discussion

On direct examination, a witness or deponent may respond affirmatively or negatively regarding whether the accused has rehabilitative potential. The witness or deponent may also opine succinctly regarding the magnitude or quality of the accused's rehabilitative potential; for example, the witness or deponent may opine that the accused has "great" or "little" rehabilitative potential. The witness or deponent, however, generally may not further elaborate on the accused's rehabilitative potential, such as describing the particular reasons for forming the opinion.

(E) *Cross-examination.* On cross-examination, inquiry is permitted into relevant and specific instances of conduct.

(F) *Redirect.* Notwithstanding any other provision in this rule, the scope of opinion testimony permitted on redirect may be expanded, depending upon the nature and scope of the cross-examination.

Discussion

For example, on redirect a witness or deponent may testify regarding specific instances of conduct when the cross-examination of the witness or deponent concerned specific instances of misconduct. Similarly, for example, on redirect a witness or deponent may offer an opinion on matters beyond the scope of the accused's rehabilitative potential if an opinion about such matters was elicited during cross-examination of the witness or deponent and is otherwise admissible.

(c) *Crime victim's right to be reasonably heard.*

(1) *In general.* After presentation by the trial counsel, a crime victim of an offense of which the accused has been found guilty has the right to be reasonably heard at the presentencing proceeding relating to that offense. A crime victim who makes an unsworn statement under R.C.M. 1001(c)(5) is not considered a witness for the purposes of Article 42(b). If the crime victim exercises the right to be reasonably heard, the crime victim shall be called by the court-martial. The exercise of the right is independent of whether the crime victim testified during findings or is called to testify by the Government or defense under this rule.

Discussion

If there are numerous victims, the military judge may reasonably limit the form of the statements provided. *See* R.C.M. 801(a)(3).

The method by which the opportunity to be reasonably heard was provided to any crime victim present at the proceedings should be included in the record orally or in writing.

---

(2) *Definitions.*

(A) *Crime victim.* For purposes of R.C.M. 1001(c), a crime victim is an individual who has suffered direct physical, emotional, or pecuniary harm as a result of the commission of an offense of which the accused was found guilty or the individual's lawful representative or designee appointed by the military judge under these rules.

(B) *Victim impact.* For purposes of R.C.M. 1001(c), victim impact includes any financial, social, psychological, or medical impact on the crime victim relating to or arising from the offense of which the accused has been found guilty.

(C) *Mitigation.* For the purposes of R.C.M. 1001(c), mitigation includes any matter that may lessen the punishment to be adjudged by the court-martial or furnish grounds for a recommendation of clemency.

(D) *Right to be reasonably heard.*

(i) *Capital cases.* In capital cases, for purposes of R.C.M. 1001(c), the "right to be reasonably heard" means the right to make a sworn statement. The statement may not recommend a specific sentence.

Discussion

See Booth v. Maryland, 482 U.S. 496, 501-502, 507, n.10 (1987) ("the Eighth Amendment prohibits a capital sentencing jury from considering victim impact evidence that does not relate to the circumstances of the crime."). *See also Bosse v. Oklahoma*, 580 U.S. 1, 3 (2016) (per curiam) (holding that a state court of appeals "remains bound by *Booth's* prohibition on characterizations and opinions from a victim's family members about the crime, the defendant, and the appropriate sentence unless this Court reconsiders that ban.").

(ii) *Noncapital cases.* In noncapital cases, for purposes of R.C.M. 1001(c), the "right to be reasonably heard" means the right to make a sworn statement, an unsworn statement, or both. This right includes the right to be heard on any objection to any unsworn statement.

(3) *Contents of statement.* The content of statements made under R.C.M. 1001(c)(4) or (5) may only include victim impact and matters in mitigation, except that, in a noncapital case, the victim may recommend a specific sentence.

(4) *Sworn statement.* The crime victim may make a sworn statement and shall be subject to cross-examination concerning it by the trial counsel and the defense counsel or examination on it by the court-martial.

(5) *Unsworn statement.* The crime victim may make an unsworn statement and may not be cross-examined by the trial counsel or the defense counsel or examined upon it by the court-martial. The Government or defense may, however, rebut any statements of fact therein. The unsworn statement may be oral, written, or both, and may be made by the crime victim, by counsel representing the crime victim, or both.

Discussion

A victim's statement should not exceed what is permitted under R.C.M. 1001(c)(3). A crime victim may also testify as a witness during presentencing proceedings in order to present evidence admissible under a rule other than R.C.M. 1001(c)(3). Upon objection by either party or *sua sponte*, a military judge may stop or interrupt a victim's statement that includes matters outside the scope of R.C.M. 1001(c)(3). A victim, victim's counsel, or designee has no separate right to present argument under R.C.M. 1001(h).

When the military judge waives the notice requirement under this rule, the military judge may conduct a session under Article 39(a) to ascertain the content of the victim's anticipated unsworn statement.

If the victim intends to submit a written statement, a copy of the statement satisfies the requirement for a written proffer.

(d) *Matter to be presented by the defense.*

(1) *In general.* The defense may present matters in rebuttal of any material presented by the prosecution and the crime victim, if any, and may present matters in extenuation and mitigation regardless whether the defense offered evidence before findings.

(A) *Matter in extenuation.* Matter in extenuation of an offense serves to explain the circumstances surrounding the commission of an offense, including those reasons for committing the offense which do not constitute a legal justification or excuse.

(B) *Matter in mitigation.* Matter in mitigation of an offense is introduced to lessen the punishment to be adjudged by the court-martial, or to furnish grounds for a recommendation of clemency. It includes the fact that nonjudicial punishment under Article 15 has been imposed for an offense growing out of the same act or omission that constitutes the offense of which the accused has been found guilty, particular acts of good conduct or bravery and evidence of the reputation or record of the accused in the service for efficiency, fidelity, subordination, temperance, courage, or any other trait that is desirable in a servicemember.

(2) *Statement by the accused.*

(A) *In general.* The accused may testify, make an unsworn statement, or both in extenuation, in mitigation, to rebut matters presented by the prosecution, or to rebut statements of fact contained in any crime victim's sworn or unsworn statement, whether or not the accused testified prior to findings. The accused may limit such testimony or statement to any one or more of the specifications of which the accused has been found guilty. The accused may make a request for a specific sentence. This subsection does not permit the filing of an affidavit of the accused.

(B) *Testimony of the accused.* The accused may give sworn oral testimony and shall be subject to cross-examination concerning it by trial counsel or examination on it by the court-martial, or both.

(C) *Unsworn statement.* The accused may make an unsworn statement and may not be cross-examined by trial counsel upon it or examined upon it by the court-martial. The prosecution may, however, rebut any statements of facts therein. The unsworn statement may be oral, written, or both, and may be made by the accused, by counsel, or both.

Discussion

An unsworn statement ordinarily should not include what is properly argument, but inclusion of such matter by the accused when personally making an oral statement normally should not be grounds for stopping the statement.

---

(3) *Rules of evidence relaxed.* The military judge may, with respect to matters in extenuation or mitigation or both, relax the rules of evidence. This may include admitting letters, affidavits, certificates of military and civil officers, and other writings of similar authenticity and reliability.

(e) *Rebuttal and surrebuttal.* The prosecution may rebut matters presented by the defense. The defense in surrebuttal may then rebut any rebuttal offered by the prosecution. Rebuttal and surrebuttal may continue, in the discretion of the military judge. If the Military Rules of Evidence were relaxed under paragraph (d)(3) of this rule, they may be relaxed during rebuttal and surrebuttal to the same degree.

(f) *Production of witnesses.*

(1) *In general.* During the presentencing proceedings, there shall be much greater latitude than on the merits to receive information by means other than testimony presented through the personal appearance of witnesses. During presentencing proceedings, a dispute as to the production of a witness at Government expense is a matter within the discretion of the military judge to resolve subject to the limitations in R.C.M. 1001(f)(2).

Discussion

See R.C.M. 703 concerning the procedures for production of witnesses for presentencing proceedings.

---

(2) *Limitations.* A witness may be produced to testify during presentencing proceedings through a subpoena or travel orders at Government expense only if—

(A) the testimony of the witness is necessary for consideration of a matter of substantial significance to a determination of an appropriate sentence;

(B) the weight or credibility of the testimony is of substantial significance to the determination of an appropriate sentence;

(C) the other party refuses to enter into a stipulation containing the matters to which the witness is expected to testify, except in an extraordinary case when such a stipulation would be an insufficient substitute for the testimony;

(D) other forms of evidence, such as oral depositions, written interrogatories, former testimony, or testimony by remote means would not be sufficient to meet the needs of the court-martial in the determination of an appropriate sentence; and

(E) the significance of the personal appearance of the witness to the determination of an appropriate sentence, when balanced against the practical difficulties of producing the witness, favors production of the witness. Factors to be considered include the costs of producing the witness, the timing of the request for production of the witness, the potential delay in the presentencing proceeding that may be caused by the production of the witness, and the likelihood of significant interference with military operational deployment, mission accomplishment, or essential training.

Discussion

The procedures for receiving testimony via remote means and the definition thereof are contained in R.C.M. 914B.

(g) *Additional matters to be considered.* In addition to matters introduced under this rule, the court-martial may consider—

(1) That a plea of guilty is a mitigating factor; and

(2) Any evidence properly introduced on the merits before findings, including:

(A) Evidence of other offenses or acts of misconduct even if introduced for a limited purpose; and

(B) Evidence relating to any mental impairment or deficiency of the accused.

Discussion

The fact that the accused is of low intelligence or that, because of a mental or neurological condition, the accused's ability to adhere to the right is diminished, may be extenuating. On the other hand, in determining the severity of a sentence, the court-martial may consider evidence tending to show that an accused has little regard for the rights of others.

(h) *Argument.* After introduction of matters relating to the sentence under this rule, counsel for the Government and defense may argue for an appropriate sentence. The trial counsel may not in argument purport to speak for the convening authority or any other higher authority or refer to the views of such authorities or any policy directive relative to punishment or to any punishment or quantum of punishment greater than the court-martial may adjudge. The trial counsel may, however, recommend a specific lawful sentence and may also refer to the sentencing considerations set forth in R.C.M. 1002(f). Failure to object to improper argument before the military judge begins deliberations, or before the military judge instructs the members on sentencing, shall constitute forfeiture of the objection.

Discussion

A victim, victims' counsel, or designee has no right to present argument under this rule. A forfeited matter may be subject to review for plain error.

Rule 1002. Sentencing determination

(a) *Generally*. Subject to limitations in this Manual, the sentence to be adjudged is a matter within the discretion of the court-martial. A court-martial may adjudge any punishment authorized in this Manual in order to achieve the purposes of sentencing under R.C.M. 1002(c), including the maximum punishment or any lesser punishment, or may adjudge a sentence of no punishment except as outlined below.

(1) *Mandatory minimum*. Unless otherwise authorized, when a mandatory minimum sentence is prescribed by the UCMJ, the sentence for an offense shall include any punishment that is made mandatory by law for that offense. The sentence for an offense may not be greater than the maximum sentence established by law or by the President for that offense.

Discussion

Under the UCMJ as amended though the James M. Inhofe National Defense Authorization Act for Fiscal Year 2023, Pub. L. No. 117-263 136 Stat. 2395 (2022), R.C.M. 1002(a)(1) prohibits a plea agreement for a term of imprisonment less than life, with the eligibility for parole, for convictions under Article 118(1) and 118(4). *See* Article 56 and R.C.M. 1003.

(2) *Parameters and criteria.*

(A) When an offense is subject to sentencing criteria, the military judge shall consider the applicable sentencing criteria in determining the sentence for that offense.

(B) When an offense is subject to sentencing parameters, the military judge shall sentence the accused for that offense within the applicable parameter, unless the military judge finds specific facts that warrant a sentence outside the applicable parameter. If the military judge imposes a sentence outside a sentencing parameter, the military judge shall include in the record a written statement of the factual basis for the sentence.

(3) If the military judge accepts a plea agreement with a sentence limitation, the court-martial shall sentence the accused in accordance with the limits established by the plea agreement. Subject to Article 53a(c), the military judge shall accept a plea agreement submitted by the parties, except that—

(A) in the case of an offense with a sentencing parameter, the military judge may reject a plea agreement that proposes a sentence that is outside the sentencing parameter if the military judge determines that the proposed sentence is plainly unreasonable; and

(B) in the case of an offense for which there is no sentencing parameter, the military judge may reject a plea agreement that proposes a sentence if the military judge determines that the proposed sentence is plainly unreasonable.

(b) *Noncapital cases*. The military judge shall determine the sentence of a general or special court-martial in accordance with this subsection in all noncapital cases.

(1) *Segmented sentencing for confinement and fines.* The military judge at a general or special court-martial shall determine an appropriate term of confinement and fine, if applicable, for each specification for which the accused was found guilty. Subject to R.C.M. 1002(a), such a determination may include a term of no confinement or no fine when appropriate for the offense.

(2) *Special court-martial.* The military judge shall, in a special court-martial, to the extent necessary, reduce the total confinement to the maximum confinement authorized under R.C.M. 201(f)(2).

(3) *Unitary sentencing for other forms of punishment.* All punishments other than confinement or a fine available under R.C.M. 1003, if any, shall be determined as a single, unitary component of the sentence, covering all of the guilty findings in their entirety. The military judge shall not segment those punishments among the guilty findings.

Discussion

The military judge should determine the appropriate amount of confinement or fine, if any, for each specification separately. The appropriate amount of confinement or fine that may be adjudged, if any, is at the discretion of the military judge subject to these rules.

Whether a term of confinement should run concurrently with another term of confinement should be determined only after determining the appropriate amount of confinement for each charge and specification. A military judge may exercise broad discretion in determining whether terms of confinement will run concurrently or consecutively consistent with R.C.M. 1002(c).

See R.C.M. 705(c)(2)(F) and 910(f)(5) regarding sentence limitations in plea agreements.

(c) *Imposition of sentence.* In sentencing an accused under this rule, the court-martial shall impose punishment that is sufficient, but not greater than necessary, to promote justice and to maintain good order and discipline in the United States Armed Forces, taking into consideration—

(1) the nature and circumstances of the offense and the history and characteristics of the accused;

(2) the impact of the offense on—

(A) the financial, social, psychological, or medical well-being of any victim of the offense; and

(B) the mission, discipline, or efficiency of the command of the accused and any victim of the offense;

(3) the need for the sentence to—

(A) reflect the seriousness of the offense;

(B) promote respect for the law;

(C) provide just punishment for the offense;

(D) promote adequate deterrence of misconduct;

(E) protect others from further crimes by the accused;

(F) rehabilitate the accused; and

(G) provide, in appropriate cases, the opportunity for retraining and returning to duty to meet the needs of the service; and

(4) the sentences available under these rules.

(d) *Information that may be considered.* The court-martial, in applying the factors listed in R.C.M. 1002(c) to the facts of a particular case, may consider—

(1) Any evidence admitted by the military judge during the presentencing proceeding under R.C.M. 1001; and

(2) Any evidence admitted by the military judge during the findings proceeding.

Rule 1003. Punishments

(a) *In general.* Subject to the limitations in this Manual, the punishments authorized in this rule may be adjudged in the case of any person found guilty of one or more charges and specifications by a court-martial.

Discussion

"Any person" includes officers, enlisted persons, person in custody of the armed forces serving a sentence imposed by a court-martial, and, insofar as the punishments are applicable, any other person subject to the UCMJ. *See* R.C.M. 202.

(b) *Authorized punishments.* Subject to the limitations in this Manual, a court-martial may adjudge only the following punishments:

(1) *Reprimand.* A court-martial shall not specify the terms or wording of a reprimand. A reprimand, if approved, shall be issued, in writing, by the convening authority.

Discussion

A reprimand adjudged by a court-martial is a punitive censure. Only the convening authority may specify the terms of the reprimand. When a court-martial adjudges a reprimand, the convening authority shall issue the reprimand in writing or may disapprove, reduce, commute, or suspend the reprimand in accordance with R.C.M. 1109 or R.C.M. 1110.

---

(2) *Forfeiture of pay and allowances.* Unless a total forfeiture is adjudged, a sentence to forfeiture shall state the exact amount in whole dollars to be forfeited each month and the number of months the forfeitures will last. Allowances shall be subject to forfeiture only when the sentence includes forfeiture of all pay and allowances. The maximum authorized amount of a partial forfeiture shall be determined by using the basic pay, retired pay, or retainer pay, as applicable, or, in the case of reserve component personnel on inactive duty, compensation for periods of inactive-duty training, authorized by the cumulative years of service of the accused, and, if no confinement is adjudged, any sea or hardship duty pay. If the sentence also includes reduction in grade, expressly or by operation of law, the maximum forfeiture shall be based on the grade to which the accused is reduced. Forfeitures of greater than two-thirds' pay per month may be imposed only during periods of confinement.

Discussion

A forfeiture deprives the accused of the amount of pay (and allowances) specified as it accrues. Forfeitures accrue to the United States.

Forfeitures of pay and allowances adjudged as part of a court-martial sentence, or occurring by operation of Article 58b, are effective 14 days after the sentence is adjudged or when the sentence of a summary court-martial is approved by the convening authority, whichever is earlier.

"Basic pay" does not include pay for special qualifications, such as diving pay, or incentive pay such as flying, parachuting, or duty on board a submarine.

Forfeiture of pay and allowances under Article 58b is not a part of the sentence, but is an administrative result thereof.

At a general court-martial, if both a punitive discharge and confinement are adjudged, then the operation of Article 58b results in total forfeiture of pay and allowances during that period of confinement. If only confinement is adjudged, and that confinement exceeds six months, the operation of Article 58b results in total forfeiture of pay and allowances during that period of confinement. If only a punitive discharge is adjudged, Article 58b has no effect on pay and allowances. A death sentence results in total forfeiture of pay and allowances.

At a special court-martial, if a bad-conduct discharge and confinement are adjudged, then the operation of Article 58b results in a forfeiture of two-thirds of pay only (not allowances) during that period of confinement. If only confinement is adjudged, and that confinement exceeds six months, then the operation of Article 58b results in a forfeiture of two-thirds of pay only (not allowances) during the period of confinement. If only a bad-conduct discharge is adjudged, Article 58b has no effect on pay.

If the sentence does not result in forfeitures by the operation of Article 58b, then only adjudged forfeitures are effective.

Article 58b has no effect on summary courts-martial.

---

(3) *Fine.* Any court-martial may adjudge a fine in lieu of or in addition to forfeitures. In the case of a member of the armed forces, summary and special courts-martial may not adjudge any fine or combination of fine and forfeitures in excess of the total amount of forfeitures that may be adjudged in that case. In the case of a person serving with or accompanying an armed force in the field, a summary court-martial may not adjudge a fine in excess of two-thirds of one month of the highest rate of enlisted pay, and a special court-martial may not adjudge a fine in excess of two-thirds of one year of the highest rate of officer pay. To enforce collection, a fine may be accompanied by a provision in the sentence that, in the event the fine is not paid, the person fined shall, in addition to any period of confinement adjudged, be further confined until a fixed period considered an equivalent punishment to the fine has expired. The total period of confinement so adjudged shall not exceed the jurisdictional limitations of the court-martial.

Discussion

A fine is in the nature of a judgment and, upon entry of judgment, makes the accused immediately liable to the United States for the entire amount of money specified in the sentence. A fine normally should not be adjudged against a member of the armed forces unless the accused was unjustly enriched as a result of the offense of which convicted. In the case of a civilian subject to military law, a fine, rather than a forfeiture, is the proper monetary penalty to be adjudged, regardless of whether unjust enrichment is present.

---

(4) *Reduction in pay grade.* Except as provided in R.C.M. 1301(d), a court-martial may sentence an enlisted member to be reduced to the lowest or any intermediate pay grade;

Discussion

Reduction under Article 58a is not a part of the sentence but is an administrative result thereof.

---

(5) *Restriction to specified limits.* Restriction may be adjudged for no more than 2 months for each month of authorized confinement and in no case for more than 2 months. Confinement and restriction may be adjudged in the same case, but they may not together exceed the maximum authorized period of confinement.

Discussion

Restriction does not exempt the person on whom it is imposed from any military duty. Restriction and hard labor without confinement may be adjudged in the same case provided they do not exceed the maximum limits for each. *See* R.C.M. 1003(c)(1)(A)(ii). The sentence adjudged should specify the limits of the restriction.

---

(6) *Hard labor without confinement.* Hard labor without confinement may be adjudged for no more than 1-1/2 months for each month of authorized confinement and in no case for more than three months. Hard labor without confinement may be adjudged only in the cases of enlisted members. The court-martial shall not specify the hard labor to be performed. Confinement and hard labor without confinement may be adjudged in the same case, but they may not together exceed the maximum authorized period of confinement, calculating the equivalency at the rate specified in this subsection.

Discussion

Hard labor without confinement is performed in addition to other regular duties and does not excuse or relieve a person from performing regular duties. Ordinarily, the immediate commander of the accused will designate the amount and character of the labor to be performed. Upon completion of the daily assignment, the accused should be permitted to take leave or liberty to which entitled.

See R.C.M. 1301(d) concerning limitations on hard labor without confinement in summary courts-martial.

---

(7) *Confinement.* The place of confinement shall not be designated by the court-martial. When confinement for life is authorized, it may be with or without eligibility for parole. A court-martial shall not adjudge a sentence to solitary confinement or to confinement without hard labor;

Discussion

The authority executing a sentence to confinement may require hard labor whether or not the words "at hard labor" are included in the sentence. *See* Article 58(b). To promote uniformity, the words "at hard labor" should be omitted in a sentence to confinement.

---

(8) *Punitive separation.* A court-martial may not adjudge an administrative separation from the service. There are three types of punitive separation.

(A) *Dismissal.* Dismissal applies only to commissioned officers, commissioned warrant officers, cadets, and midshipmen and may be adjudged only by a general court-martial. Regardless of the maximum punishment specified for an offense in Part IV of this Manual, a dismissal may be adjudged for any offense of which a commissioned officer, commissioned warrant officer, cadet, or midshipman has been found guilty;

(B) *Dishonorable discharge.* A dishonorable discharge applies only to enlisted persons and warrant officers who are not commissioned and may be adjudged only by a general court-martial. Regardless of the maximum punishment specified for an offense in Part IV of this Manual, a dishonorable discharge may be adjudged for any offense of which a warrant officer who is not commissioned has been found guilty. A dishonorable discharge should be reserved for those who should be separated under conditions of dishonor, after having been convicted of offenses usually recognized in civilian jurisdictions as felonies, or of offenses of a military nature requiring severe punishment; and

Discussion

See also R.C.M. 1003(d)(1) regarding when a dishonorable discharge is authorized as an additional punishment.

(C) *Bad-conduct discharge.* A bad-conduct discharge applies only to enlisted persons and may be adjudged by a general court-martial and by a special court-martial which has met the requirements of R.C.M. 201(f)(2)(B). A bad-conduct discharge is less severe than a dishonorable discharge and is designed as a punishment for bad-conduct rather than as a punishment for serious offenses of either a civilian or military nature. It is also appropriate for an accused who has been convicted repeatedly of minor offenses and whose punitive separation appears to be necessary;

Discussion

See also R.C.M. 1003(d)(2) and (3) regarding when a bad-conduct discharge is authorized as an additional punishment.

---

(9) *Death.* Death may be adjudged only in accordance with R.C.M. 1004; and

(10) *Punishments under the law of war.* In cases tried under the law of war, a general court-martial may adjudge any punishment not prohibited by the law of war.

(c) *Limits on punishments.*

(1) *Based on offenses.*

(A) *Offenses listed in Part IV.*

(i) *Maximum punishment.* The maximum limits for the authorized punishments of confinement, forfeitures, and punitive discharge (if any) are set forth for each offense listed in Part IV of this Manual. These limitations are for each separate offense, not for each charge, and apply notwithstanding any applicable sentencing parameter. When a dishonorable discharge is authorized, a bad-conduct discharge is also authorized.

(ii) *Other punishments.* Except as otherwise specifically provided in this Manual, the types of punishments listed in paragraphs (b)(1), (3), (4), (5), (6) and (7) of this rule may be adjudged in addition to or instead of confinement, forfeitures, a punitive discharge (if authorized), and death (if authorized).

(B) *Offenses not listed in Part IV.*

(i) *Included or closely related offenses.* For an offense not listed in Part IV of this Manual that is included in or closely related to an offense listed therein, the maximum punishment and the sentencing parameter or criteria shall be that or those of the offense listed; however, if an offense not listed is included in a listed offense, and is closely related to another or is equally closely related to two or more listed offenses, the maximum punishment and the sentencing parameter or criteria shall be the same as that or those of the least severe of the listed offenses.

(ii) *Not included or closely related offenses.* An offense not listed in Part IV and not included in or closely related to an offense listed therein is punishable as authorized by the United States Code or as authorized by the custom of the applicable service. When the United States Code provides for confinement for a specified period or not more than a specified period, the maximum punishment by court-martial shall include confinement for that period. If the period is 1 year or longer, the maximum punishment by court-martial also includes a dishonorable discharge and forfeiture of all pay and allowances; if the period is 6 months or more but less than 1 year, the maximum punishment by court-martial also includes a bad-conduct discharge and forfeiture of all pay and allowances; if the period is less than 6 months, the maximum punishment by court-martial also includes forfeiture of two-thirds pay per month for the authorized period of confinement.

(C) *Multiple Offenses.* When the accused is found guilty of two or more specifications, the maximum authorized punishment may be imposed for each separate specification, unless the military judge finds that the specifications are unreasonably multiplied.

Discussion

R.C.M. 906(b)(12) provides the available remedies for cases in which a military judge finds an unreasonable multiplication of charges.

---

(2) *Based on grade of accused.*

(A) *Commissioned or warrant officers, cadets, and midshipmen.*

(i) A commissioned or warrant officer or a cadet or midshipman may not be reduced in grade by any court-martial. However, in time of war or national emergency, the Secretary concerned, or such Under Secretary or Assistant Secretary as may be designated by the Secretary concerned, may commute a sentence of dismissal to reduction to any enlisted grade.

(ii) A commissioned or warrant officer or a cadet or midshipman may not be sentenced to hard labor without confinement.

(iii) Only a general court-martial, upon conviction of any offense in violation of the UCMJ, may sentence a commissioned or warrant officer or a cadet or midshipman to be separated from the service with a punitive separation. In the case of commissioned officers, cadets, midshipmen, and commissioned warrant officers, the separation shall be by dismissal. In the case of all other warrant officers, the separation shall be by dishonorable discharge.

(B) Enlisted persons. See paragraph (b)(9) of this rule and R.C.M. 1301(d).

(3) *Based on reserve status in certain circumstances.*

(A) *Restriction on liberty.* A member of a reserve component whose order to active duty is approved pursuant to Article 2(d)(5) may be required to serve any adjudged restriction on liberty during that period of active duty. Other members of a reserve component ordered to active duty pursuant to Article 2(d)(1) or tried by summary court-martial while on inactive duty training may not—

(i) be sentenced to confinement; or

(ii) be required to serve a court-martial punishment consisting of any other restriction on liberty except during subsequent periods of inactive-duty training or active duty.

(B) *Forfeiture.* A sentence to forfeiture of pay of a member not retained on active duty after completion of disciplinary proceedings may be collected from active duty and inactive-duty training pay during subsequent periods of duty.

Discussion

See R.C.M. 204. At the conclusion of nonjudicial punishment proceedings or final adjournment of the court-martial, the reserve component member who was ordered to active duty for the purpose of conducting disciplinary proceedings should be released from active duty within one working day unless the order to active duty was approved by the Secretary concerned and confinement or other restriction on liberty was adjudged. Unserved punishments may be carried over to subsequent periods of inactive-duty training or active duty.

---

(4) *Based on status as a person serving with or accompanying an armed force in the field.* In the case of a person serving with or accompanying an armed force in the field, no court-martial may adjudge forfeiture of pay and allowances, reduction in pay grade, hard labor without confinement, or a punitive separation.

(5) *Based on other rules.* The maximum limits on punishments in this rule may be further limited by other Rules for Courts-Martial.

Discussion

The maximum punishment may be limited by: the jurisdictional limits of the court-martial (*see* R.C.M. 201(f) and 1301(d)); the nature of the proceedings (*see* R.C.M. 810(d) (sentence limitations in rehearings, new trials, and other trials)); and by instructions by a convening authority (*see* R.C.M. 601(e)(1)).

(d) *Circumstances permitting increased punishments*.

(1) *Three or more convictions*. If an accused is found guilty of a specification or specifications for none of which a dishonorable discharge is otherwise authorized, proof of three or more previous convictions adjudged by a court-martial during the year next preceding the commission of any offense of which the accused stands convicted shall authorize a dishonorable discharge and forfeiture of all pay and allowances and, if the confinement otherwise authorized is less than 1 year, confinement for 1 year. In computing the 1-year period preceding the commission of any offense, periods of unauthorized absence shall be excluded. For purposes of this subsection, the court-martial convictions must be final.

(2) *Two or more convictions*. If an accused is found guilty of a specification or specifications for none of which a dishonorable or bad-conduct discharge is otherwise authorized, proof of two or more previous convictions adjudged by a court-martial during the 3 years next preceding the commission of any offense of which the accused stands convicted shall authorize a bad-conduct discharge and forfeiture of all pay and allowances and, if the confinement otherwise authorized is less than 3 months, confinement for 3 months. In computing the 3 year period preceding the commission of any offense, periods of unauthorized absence shall be excluded. For purposes of this subsection the court-martial convictions must be final.

(3) *Two or more specifications*. If an accused is found guilty of two or more specifications for none of which a dishonorable or bad-conduct discharge is otherwise authorized, the fact that the authorized confinement for these offenses totals 6 months or more shall, in addition, authorize a bad-conduct discharge and forfeiture of all pay and allowances.

Discussion

All of these increased punishments are subject to all other limitations on punishments set forth elsewhere in this rule. Convictions by summary court-martial may not be used to increase the maximum punishment under this rule. However, they may be admitted and considered under R.C.M. 1001.

Rule 1004. Capital cases

(a) *In general*. In addition to the provisions in R.C.M. 1001, the provisions in this rule shall apply in capital cases. Death may be adjudged only when—

(1) Death is expressly authorized under Part IV of this Manual for an offense of which the accused has been found guilty or is authorized under the law of war for an offense of which the accused has been found guilty under the law of war;

(2) The accused was properly notified that the case would be tried as a capital case and was properly notified of the aggravating factors the Government intended to prove;

(3) The accused was convicted of such an offense by either—

(A) the unanimous vote of all twelve members of the court-martial; or

(B) the military judge pursuant to the accused's plea of guilty to such an offense;

(4) The members unanimously find that at least one of the aggravating factors under R.C.M. 1004(c) existed beyond a reasonable doubt for that offense and notice of such factor was provided in accordance with R.C.M. 1004(b);

(5) The members unanimously find that the extenuating and mitigating circumstances are substantially outweighed by any aggravating circumstances, including any relevant aggravating factor(s); and

(6) The members unanimously determine that the sentence for that offense shall be death.

(b) *Notice*.

(1) *Referral*. The referral authority shall indicate that the case is to be tried as a capital case by including a special instruction on the charge sheet. Failure to include this special instruction at the time of the referral shall not bar the referral authority from later adding the required special instruction, provided that—

(A) the referral authority has otherwise complied with the notice requirement of R.C.M. 1004(b)(2); and

(B) if the accused demonstrates specific prejudice from such failure to include the special instruction, the military judge determines that a continuance or a recess is an adequate remedy.

(2) *Arraignment.* Before arraignment, the trial counsel shall give the defense written notice of which specific aggravating factor(s) under R.C.M. 1004(c) the Government intends to prove and to which offense(s) the aggravating factor(s) apply. Failure to provide timely notice under this subsection of any aggravating factors under R.C.M. 1004(c) shall not bar later notice and proof of such additional aggravating factors unless the accused demonstrates specific prejudice from such failure and that a continuance or a recess is not an adequate remedy.

(c) *Aggravating factors.* The trial counsel may present evidence in accordance with R.C.M. 1001(b)(4) tending to establish one or more of the aggravating factors enumerated below. Death may be adjudged only if the members find, beyond a reasonable doubt, one or more of the following aggravating factors:

(1) That the offense was committed before or in the presence of the enemy, except that this factor shall not apply in the case of a violation of Article 118;

Discussion

See paragraph 27, Part IV, for an explanation of "before or in the presence of the enemy."

---

(2) That in committing the offense the accused—

(A) Knowingly created a grave risk of substantial damage to the national security of the United States; or

(B) Knowingly created a grave risk of substantial damage to a mission, system, or function of the United States, provided that this subparagraph shall apply only if substantial damage to the national security of the United States would have resulted had the potential damage been effected;

(3) That the offense caused substantial damage to the national security of the United States, regardless of whether the accused intended such damage, except that this factor shall not apply in case of a violation of Article 118;

(4) That the offense was committed in such a way or under such circumstances that the life of one or more persons other than the victim was unlawfully and substantially endangered, except that this factor shall not apply to a violation of Articles 103a or 103b;

(5) That the accused committed the offense with the intent to avoid hazardous duty;

(6) That, only in the case of a violation of Article 118, the offense was committed in time of war and in territory in which the United States or an ally of the United States was then an occupying power or in which the United States Armed Forces were then engaged in active hostilities;

(7) That, only in the case of a violation of Article 118(1)—

(A) The accused was serving a sentence of confinement for 30 years or more or for life at the time of the murder;

(B) The murder was committed while the accused was engaged in the commission or attempted commission of a separate murder, or any robbery, rape, rape of a child, sexual assault, sexual assault of a child, aggravated sexual contact, sexual abuse of a child, aggravated arson, burglary, kidnapping, mutiny, sedition, or piracy of an aircraft or vessel; or while the accused was engaged in the commission or attempted commission of any offense involving the wrongful distribution, manufacture, or introduction or possession, with intent to distribute, of a controlled substance; or, while the accused was engaged in flight or attempted flight after the commission or attempted commission of any offense listed in this subparagraph (R.C.M. 1004(c)(7)(B)).

(C) The murder was committed for the purpose of receiving money or a thing of value;

(D) The accused procured another by means of compulsion, coercion, or a promise of an advantage, a service, or a thing of value to commit the murder;

(E) The murder was committed with the intent to avoid or to prevent lawful apprehension or effect an escape from custody or confinement;

(F) The victim was the President of the United States; the President-elect; the Vice President, or, if there was no Vice President, the next officer in the order of succession to the office of President of the United States; the Vice President-elect; any individual who is acting as President under the Constitution and laws of the United States; a Member of Congress (including a Delegate to, or Resident Commissioner in, the Congress) or Member of Congress-elect; a justice or judge of the United States; a chief of state or head of government (or the political equivalent) of a foreign nation; or a foreign official (as such term is defined in 18 U.S.C. § 1116(b)(3)(A)), if the official was on official business at the time of the offense and was in the United States or in a place described in Mil. R. Evid. 315(c)(2) or (c)(3);

(G) The accused then knew that the victim was any of the following persons in the execution of office: a commissioned, warrant, noncommissioned, or petty officer of the United States Armed Forces; a member of any law enforcement or security activity or agency, military or civilian, including correctional custody personnel; or any firefighter;

(H) The murder was committed with intent to obstruct justice;

(I) The murder was preceded by the intentional infliction of substantial physical harm or prolonged, substantial mental or physical pain and suffering to the victim. For purposes of this section, "substantial physical harm" means fractured or dislocated bones, deep cuts, torn members of the body, serious damage to internal organs, or other serious bodily injuries. The term "substantial physical harm" does not mean minor injuries, such as a black eye or bloody nose. The term "substantial mental or physical pain and suffering" is accorded its common meaning and includes torture.

(J) The accused has been found guilty in the same case of another violation of Article 118;

(K) The victim of the murder was under 15 years of age;

(8) That, only in the case of a violation of Article 118(4), the accused was the actual perpetrator of the killing or was a principal whose participation in the burglary, rape, rape of a child, sexual assault, sexual assault of a child, aggravated sexual contact, sexual abuse of a child, robbery, or aggravated arson was major and who manifested a reckless indifference for human life.

Discussion

Conduct amounts to "reckless indifference" when it evinces a wanton disregard of consequences under circumstances involving grave danger to the life of another, although no harm is necessarily intended. The accused must have had actual knowledge of the grave danger to others or knowledge of circumstances that would cause a reasonable person to realize the highly dangerous character of such conduct. In determining whether participation in the offense was major, the accused's presence at the scene and the extent to which the accused aided, abetted, assisted, encouraged, or advised the other participants should be considered. *See United States v. Berg*, 31 M.J. 38 (C.M.A. 1990); *United States v. McMonagle* 38 M.J. 53 (C.M.A. 1993).

---

(9) [Reserved]

(10) That, only in the case of a violation of the law of war, death is authorized under the law of war for the offense;

(11) That, only in the case of a violation of Article 103, 103a, or 103b—

(A) The accused has been convicted of another offense involving espionage, spying, or treason for which either a sentence of death or imprisonment for life was authorized by statute; or

(B) That in committing the offense, the accused knowingly created a grave risk of death to a person other than the individual who was the victim.

For purposes of R.C.M. 1004, "national security" means the national defense and foreign relations of the United States and specifically includes a military or defense advantage over any foreign nation or group of nations; a favorable foreign relations position; or a defense posture capable of successfully resisting hostile or destructive action from within or without.

Discussion

Examples of substantial damage to the national security of the United States include: impeding the performance of a combat mission or operation; impeding the performance of an important mission in a hostile fire or imminent danger pay area (*see* 37 U.S.C. § 310(a)); and disclosing military plans, capabilities, or intelligence such as to jeopardize any combat mission or operation of the armed services of the United States or its allies or to materially aid an enemy of the United States.

See also R.C.M. 1004(b)(5).

(d) *Evidence in extenuation and mitigation.* The accused shall be given broad latitude to present evidence in extenuation and mitigation.

Discussion

See R.C.M. 1001(d).

(e) *Basis for findings.* The findings specified by R.C.M. 1004(a)(4) and (a)(5) may be based on evidence introduced before or after findings under R.C.M. 921, or both.

(f) *Instructions.* Instructions shall be given after arguments by counsel and before the members close to deliberate on sentence, but the military judge may, upon request of the members, any party, or *sua sponte*, give additional instructions at a later time.

(1) *Requests for instructions*. During presentencing proceedings or at such other time as the military judge may permit, any party may request that the military judge instruct the members on the law as set forth in the request. The military judge may require the requested instruction to be written. Each party shall be given the opportunity to be heard on any proposed instruction before it is given. The military judge shall inform the parties of the proposed action on such requests before their arguments to the members.

Discussion

Requests for and objections to instructions should be resolved at an Article 39(a) session. *See* R.C.M. 801(e)(1)(C), 803.

The military judge is not required to give the specific instruction requested by counsel if the matter is adequately covered in the instructions.

The military judge should not identify the source of any instruction when addressing the members.

All written requests for instructions should be marked as appellate exhibits, whether or not they are given.

---

(2) *How given*. Instructions shall be given orally on the record in the presence of all parties and the members. Written copies of the instructions or, unless a party objects, portions of them may also be given to the members for their use during deliberations.

Discussion

A copy of any written instructions delivered to the members should be marked as an appellate exhibit.

---

(3) *Required instructions*. Instructions shall include—

(A) The charge(s) and specification(s) for which the members shall make a sentencing determination;

(B) The applicable aggravating factor or factors under R.C.M. 1004(c) and to which charge(s) and specification(s) the aggravating factor or factors apply;

(C) A statement of the procedures for deliberation and voting set out in R.C.M. 1004(g);

(D) A statement informing the members that they are solely responsible for selecting an appropriate determination and may not rely on the possibility of any mitigating action by the convening or higher authority;

(E) A statement that the members should consider all matters in aggravation, whether introduced before or after findings, and matters introduced under R.C.M. 1001(b)(1), (2), (3), and (5);

Discussion

For example, tailored instructions should reflect the considerations set forth in Article 56(c), including the reputation or record of the accused in the service for good conduct, efficiency, fidelity, courage, bravery, or other traits of good character, and any pretrial restraint imposed on the accused.

(F) A statement that the members may consider:

(i) Any evidence admitted by the military judge during the presentencing proceeding under R.C.M. 1001; and

(ii) Any evidence admitted by the military judge during the findings proceeding;

(G) A statement that the members shall consider all evidence in extenuation and mitigation before a sentence of death may be determined; and

(H) Such other explanations, descriptions, or directions that the military judge determines to be necessary, whether properly requested by a party or determined by the military judge *sua sponte*.

(4) *Failure to object*. After being afforded an opportunity to object, failure to object to an instruction or to omission of an instruction before the members close to deliberate shall constitute waiver of the objection. The military judge may require the party objecting to specify in what respect the instructions were improper. The parties shall be given the opportunity to be heard on any objection outside the presence of the members.

(g) *Deliberations and voting*.

(1) *In general*. With respect to each charge and specification for which a sentence of death may be determined, the members shall deliberate and vote after the military judge instructs the members. Only the members shall be present during deliberations and voting. Superiority in rank shall not be used in any manner to control the independence of members in the exercise of their judgment.

(2) *Deliberations*. Deliberations require a full and free discussion of the determination to be made in the

case. Unless otherwise directed by the military judge, members may take with them in deliberations their notes, if any; any exhibits admitted in evidence; and any written instructions. Members may request that the court-martial be reopened and that portions of the record be read to them or additional evidence introduced. The military judge may, in the exercise of discretion, grant such requests.

(3) *Voting generally.*

(A) *Duty of members.* Each member has the duty to vote on the necessary findings described in R.C.M. 1004(a)(4)-(6) as applicable. No member may abstain from voting.

(B) *Secret ballot.* Voting shall be by secret written ballot.

(4) *Procedure.*

(A) *Initial process.* The members shall employ the following process for each charge and specification for which death may be determined.

(i) The members shall vote separately on each aggravating factor under R.C.M. 1004(c) that applies to the offense and on which the members have been instructed. The members shall not proceed to R.C.M. 1004(g)(4)(A)(ii) unless the members unanimously find that at least one of the aggravating factors existed beyond a reasonable doubt.

(ii) The members shall vote on whether the extenuating and mitigating circumstances are substantially outweighed by any aggravating circumstances, including any relevant aggravating factor(s) under R.C.M. 1004(c). The members shall not proceed to R.C.M. 1004(g)(4)(B) unless the members unanimously find that any extenuating or mitigating circumstances are substantially outweighed by any aggravating circumstances.

(B) *Voting on a sentencing determination if death may be adjudged.*

(i) If the members unanimously find both that at least one aggravating factor exists and that the extenuating and mitigating circumstances are substantially outweighed by the aggravating circumstances, the members shall vote on the following sentencing determinations, which shall be binding on the military judge. Except as permitted under R.C.M. 1004(i), the members must vote on potential sentence determinations in the order listed below. The members must vote on each option separately from the other option, considering only one option at a time. During the voting on a particular option, each member may cast one vote for or against that option. The order of the options to be considered is:

(I) Death; or

(II) Life in prison without eligibility for parole.

(ii) If all 12 members vote for death, the sentencing determination of the members shall be death. If any member does not vote for death, the sentencing determination of the members shall not be death.

(iii) If the members' initial vote does not reach the required unanimous consensus for death, the members shall vote on life in prison without eligibility for parole. If three-fourths or more of the members vote for life in prison without eligibility for parole, the sentencing determination of the members shall be life in prison without eligibility for parole.

(iv) If the members' vote does not reach three-fourths for life in prison without eligibility for parole, the offense shall be returned to the military judge for imposition of a sentence of a lesser punishment in accordance with R.C.M. 1001.

(C) *Voting on a sentencing determination if death may not be adjudged.*

(i) If the members do not unanimously find that at least one aggravating factor exists or the members do not unanimously find that the aggravating circumstances substantially outweigh the extenuating and mitigating circumstances, the members shall vote on life in prison without eligibility for parole.

(ii) If the members' vote does not reach three-fourths for life in prison without eligibility for parole, the offense shall be returned to the military judge for imposition of a sentence of a lesser punishment in accordance with R.C.M. 1001.

(D) *Counting votes.* The junior member shall collect the ballots and count the votes. The president shall check the count and inform the other members of the result.

Discussion

A determination by the members may be reconsidered only in accordance with R.C.M. 1004(i).

(h) *Action after a sentence is reached.* After the members have agreed upon a determination by the required number of votes in accordance with this rule, the court-martial shall be opened, and the president shall inform the military judge that the members have reached a determination. The military judge may, in the presence of the parties, examine any writing used by the president to state the determination and may assist the members in putting the determination in proper form. If the members voted unanimously for a determination of death, the writing shall indicate which aggravating factor or factors under R.C.M. 1004(c) the members unanimously found to exist beyond a reasonable doubt. Neither that writing nor any oral or written clarification or discussion concerning it shall constitute announcement of the determination.

Discussion

Ordinarily a worksheet should be provided to the members as an aid to putting the determination in proper form. If a worksheet has been provided, the military judge should examine it before announcing the determination. If the military judge intends to instruct the members after such examination, counsel should be permitted to examine the worksheet and to be heard on any instructions the military judge may give.

The president should not disclose any specific number of votes for or against any sentence.

If the sentence is ambiguous or apparently illegal, see R.C.M. 1004(i).

If the members voted unanimously for a sentence of death, the sentence worksheet shall indicate which aggravating factor or factors under R.C.M. 1004(c) the members unanimously found to exist beyond a reasonable doubt. *See* R.C.M. 1004(b)(8).

(i) *Reconsideration.* Subject to this rule, a sentence may be reconsidered at any time before it is announced in open session of the court.

(1) *Clarification of determination.* A sentence determination may be clarified at any time before entry of judgment. When a determination by the members in a capital case is ambiguous, the military judge shall bring the matter to the attention of the members if the matter is discovered before the court-martial is adjourned. If the matter is discovered after adjournment, the military judge may call a session for clarification by the members as soon as practicable after the ambiguity is discovered, or the military judge may resolve the ambiguity.

(2) *Action by the convening authority.*

(A) Prior to entry of judgment, if a convening authority becomes aware that the sentence of the court-martial is ambiguous, the convening authority shall return the matter to the court-martial for clarification. When the sentence of the court-martial appears to be illegal, the convening authority shall return the matter to the court-martial for correction.

(B) Prior to entry of judgment in a case in which a special trial counsel has exercised authority—

(i) if the special trial counsel becomes aware that the sentence of a court-martial is ambiguous, the special trial counsel shall make a binding determination that the convening authority return the matter to the court-martial for clarification; or

(ii) if the sentence of the court-martial appears to be illegal, the special trial counsel shall make a binding determination that the convening authority shall return the matter to the court-martial for correction.

(3) *Reconsideration procedure.* Any member of the court-martial may propose that a determination of the members in a capital case be reconsidered.

(A) *Instructions.* When reconsideration has been requested, the military judge shall instruct the members on the procedure for reconsideration.

(B) *Voting.* The members shall vote by secret written ballot in closed session whether to reconsider a determination.

(C) *Number of votes required for aggravating factors in capital cases.* Members may reconsider a unanimous vote under R.C.M. 1004(g)(4)(A) (i) that an aggravating factor was proven beyond a reasonable doubt if at least one member votes to reconsider. Members may reconsider a unanimous vote under R.C.M. 1004(g)(4)(A)(ii) that any extenuating and mitigating circumstances are substantially outweighed by any aggravating circumstances admissible under R.C.M. 1001(b)(4), including the factors under R.C.M. 1004(c), if at least one member votes to reconsider. In all other circumstances, a vote under R.C.M. 1004(g)(4)(A)(i) or (ii) may be reconsidered only if at least a majority of the members vote for reconsideration.

(D) *Number of votes required for determinations.*

(i) *With a view toward increasing.* Members may reconsider a determination with a view toward increasing the severity of the determination only if at least a majority votes for reconsideration. However, members may not reconsider a non-unanimous vote for a determination of death.

(ii) *With a view toward decreasing.* Members may reconsider a determination with a view toward decreasing the severity of the determination only if—

(I) In the case of a death determination, at least one member votes to reconsider; or

(II) In the case of a determination of life in prison without eligibility for parole, more than one-fourth of the members vote to reconsider.

Discussion

After a determination has been adopted by secret ballot in closed session, no other vote may be taken on the sentence unless a vote to reconsider succeeds.

(E) *Successful vote.* If a vote to reconsider succeeds, the members will revote in accordance with R.C.M. 1001(g)(3) and (4).

(j) *Sentencing by military judge.*

(1) The military judge shall sentence the accused in accordance with the binding determination of the members under R.C.M. 1004(g). The military judge may include in any sentence to death or life in prison without eligibility for parole any other authorized lesser punishment. When the military judge's sentence includes confinement or fines, the military judge shall determine an appropriate term of confinement and fine for each specification for which the accused was found guilty.

(2) Where there is a finding of guilty for a specification for which death may be adjudged and a finding of guilty for a specification for which death may not be adjudged—

(A) The members shall make a determination for each specification for which death may be adjudged in accordance with subsection (g);

(B) The military judge shall determine the sentence for any specification returned by the members for sentencing of a lesser punishment than death or life in prison without eligibility for parole; and

(C) The military judge shall determine the sentence for all charges and specifications for which death may not be adjudged. If the sentence includes more than one term of confinement, the military judge shall determine whether the terms of confinement will run concurrently or consecutively.

Discussion

A sentence of death may not be ordered executed until approved by the President. *See* R.C.M. 1207. A sentence of death which has been finally ordered executed will be carried out in the manner prescribed by the Secretary concerned. *See* R.C.M. 1102(b)(5).

(k) *Other penalties.* When death is an authorized punishment for an offense, all other punishments authorized under R.C.M. 1003 are also authorized for that offense, including confinement for life, with or without eligibility for parole, and may be adjudged in lieu of death, subject to limitations specifically prescribed in this Manual. A sentence of death includes a dishonorable discharge or dismissal as appropriate. Confinement is a necessary incident of a sentence of death, but not a part of it.

(l) *Impeachment of determination.* A determination that is proper on its face may be impeached only when extraneous prejudicial information was improperly brought to the attention of any member, outside influence was improperly brought to bear upon any member, or unlawful command influence was brought to bear upon any member.

Rule 1005. Reconsideration of sentence in noncapital cases

(a) *Reconsideration.* Subject to this rule, a sentence may be reconsidered at any time before such sentence is announced in open session of the court.

(b) *Exceptions.*

(1) If the sentence announced in open session was less than the mandatory minimum prescribed for an offense of which the accused has been found guilty, the court that announced the sentence may reconsider such sentence.

(2) If the sentence announced in open session exceeds the maximum permissible punishment for the offense or the jurisdictional limitation of the court-martial, the court that announced the sentence may reconsider such sentence.

(3) If the sentence announced in open session is not in accordance with a sentence limitation in the plea agreement, if any, the court that announced the sentence may reconsider such sentence.

(c) *Clarification of sentence.* A sentence may be clarified at any time before entry of judgment. When a sentence determined by the military judge is ambiguous, the military judge shall call a session for clarification as soon as practicable after the ambiguity is discovered.

(d) *Action by the convening authority or special trial*

counsel.

(1) Prior to entry of judgment, if a convening authority becomes aware that the sentence of the court-martial is ambiguous, the convening authority shall return the matter to the court-martial for clarification. When the sentence of the court-martial appears to be illegal, the convening authority shall return the matter to the court-martial for correction.

(2) Prior to entry of judgment in a case in which a special trial counsel has exercised authority—

(A) if the special trial counsel becomes aware that the sentence of a court-martial is ambiguous, the special trial counsel shall make a binding determination that the convening authority return the matter to the court-martial for clarification.

(B) if the sentence of the court-martial appears to be illegal, the special trial counsel shall make a binding determination that the convening authority shall return the matter to the court-martial for correction.

(e) *Limitation.* A military judge may reconsider a sentence once announced only under the circumstances described in R.C.M. 1005(b).

Discussion

See R.C.M. 1111(c) for correcting errors after entry of judgment.

Rule 1006. [Reserved]

Rule 1007. Announcement of sentence

(a) *In general.* The sentence shall be announced in the presence of all parties promptly after it has been determined.

Discussion

The date that the sentence is announced is the date a sentence is adjudged. *See* Articles 53 and 57.

(b) *Announcement.*

(1) In a capital case, the determination of the members shall be announced by the military judge. If the members voted unanimously for death, the military judge shall announce which aggravating factor or factors under R.C.M. 1004(c) the members unanimously found to exist beyond a reasonable doubt.

(2) In all other cases, the military judge shall announce the sentence and shall specify—

(A) the term of confinement, if any, and the amount of fine, if any, determined for each offense;

(B) for each term of confinement announced under subparagraph (A), whether the term of confinement is to run concurrently or consecutively with any other term or terms of confinement adjudged; and

(C) any other punishments under R.C.M. 1003 as a single, unitary sentence.

Discussion

If the sentence announced by the military judge includes death, the military judge must also announce which aggravating factor or factors under R.C.M. 1004(c) the members unanimously found to exist beyond a reasonable doubt. *See* R.C.M. 1004(h).

(c) *Erroneous announcement.* If the announced sentence is not the one actually determined by the court-martial, the error may be corrected by a new announcement made before entry of the judgment into the record. This action shall not constitute reconsideration of the sentence. If the court-martial is adjourned before the error is discovered, the military judge may call the court-martial into session to correct the announcement.

(d) *Polling prohibited.* Except as provided in Mil. R. Evid. 606, members may not otherwise be questioned about their deliberations and voting.

Rule 1008. Impeachment of sentence

A sentence that is proper on its face may be impeached only when extraneous prejudicial information was improperly brought to the attention of the military judge, outside influence was improperly brought to bear upon the military judge, or unlawful command influence was brought to bear upon the military judge.

Discussion

See R.C.M. 923 Discussion concerning impeachment of findings.

Rule 1009. [Reserved]

Rule 1010. Notice concerning post-trial and appellate rights

In each general and special court-martial, prior to

adjournment, the military judge shall ensure that defense counsel has informed the accused orally and in writing of:

(a) The right to submit matters to the convening authority to consider before taking action;

(b) The right to appellate review, and the effect of waiver or withdrawal of such right, or failure to file an appeal, as applicable;

(c) The right to apply for relief from the Judge Advocate General if the case is not reviewed by a Court of Criminal Appeals under Article 66; and

(d) The right to the advice and assistance of counsel in the exercise of the foregoing rights or any decision to waive them.

The written advice to the accused concerning post-trial and appellate rights shall be signed by the accused and defense counsel and inserted in the record of trial as an appellate exhibit.

Discussion

The post-trial duties of the defense counsel concerning the appellate rights of the accused are set forth in paragraph (E)(iv) of the Discussion accompanying R.C.M. 502(d)(5). The defense counsel shall explain the appellate rights to the accused and prepare the written document of such advisement prior to or during trial.

Rule 1011. Adjournment

The military judge may adjourn the court-martial at the end of the trial of an accused or proceed to trial of other cases referred to that court-martial. Such an adjournment may be for a definite or indefinite period.

Discussion

A court-martial and its personnel have certain powers and responsibilities following the trial. *See, e.g.*, R.C.M. 502(d)(4) Discussion (G), 502(d)(5) Discussion (E), 808, 1007, Chapter XI.

CHAPTER XI. POST-TRIAL PROCEDURE

Rule 1101. Statement of trial results

(a) *Content.* After final adjournment of a general or special court-martial, the military judge shall sign and include in the record of trial a Statement of Trial Results. The Statement of Trial Results shall consist of the following—

(1) *Findings.* For each charge and specification referred to trial—

(A) a summary of each charge and specification;

(B) the plea(s) of the accused; and

(C) the finding or other disposition of each charge and specification.

(2) *Sentence.* The sentence of the court-martial and the date the sentence was announced by the court-martial, and the amount of credit, if any, applied to the sentence for pretrial confinement or for other reasons. If the accused was convicted of more than one specification and any part of the sentence was determined by a military judge, the Statement of Trial Results shall also specify—

(A) the confinement and fine for each specification, if any;

(B) whether any term of confinement is to run consecutively or concurrently with any other term(s) of confinement;

(C) the total amount of any fine(s) and the total amount of any confinement, after accounting for any credit and any terms of confinement that are to run consecutively or concurrently.

Discussion

The date that the sentence is adjudged is the date the sentence was announced. *See* Articles 53 and 57. The adjudged sentence may be modified by the convening authority or the military judge. *See generally* R.C.M.s 1104, 1109, and 1110.

See R.C.M. 1002(b) for military judge alone sentencing and R.C.M. 1004 for sentencing in capital cases by military judge and members.

---

(3) *Forum.* The type of court-martial and the command by which it was convened.

(4) *Plea agreements.* In a case with a plea agreement, the statement shall specify any limitations on the punishment as set forth in the plea agreement.

(5) *Suspension recommendation.* If the military judge recommends that any portion of the sentence should be suspended, the statement shall specify—

(A) the portion(s) of the sentence to which the recommendation applies;

(B) the minimum duration of the suspension; and

(C) the facts supporting the suspension recommendation.

Discussion

The convening authority may only suspend a sentence of dishonorable discharge, bad-conduct discharge, or confinement in excess of six months if the military judge includes a recommendation for suspension in the Statement of Trial Results. *See* R.C.M. 1109(f). When the accused is sentenced by members, the members may recommend suspension of punitive discharge or confinement in excess of six months, but the convening authority may only act to suspend these punishments if the military judge adopts the suspension recommendation and includes it in the Statement of Trial Results.

---

(6) *Other information.* Any additional information directed by the military judge or required under regulations prescribed by the Secretary concerned.

(b) *Not guilty only by reason of lack of mental responsibility.* If an accused was found not guilty only by reason of lack of mental responsibility of any charge or specification, the military judge shall sign the Statement of Trial Results only after a hearing is conducted under R.C.M. 1105.

(c) *Abatement.* If the military judge abated the proceedings and the court-martial adjourned without a disposition as to at least one specification, the military judge shall include a brief explanation as to the reasons for abatement in the record of trial. If all charges are subsequently withdrawn, dismissed, or otherwise disposed of, the military judge shall sign a Statement of Trial Results in accordance with this rule.

Discussion

The issuance of an explanation of the reasons for abatement does not prevent a later termination of the abatement.

(d) *Distribution.* Trial counsel shall promptly provide a copy of the Statement of Trial Results to the accused's immediate commander, the convening authority or the convening authority's designee, and, if appropriate, the officer in charge of the confinement facility. A copy of the Statement of Trial Results shall be provided to the accused or to the accused's defense counsel. If the statement is served on defense counsel, defense counsel shall, by expeditious means, provide the accused with a copy. A copy of the Statement of Trial Results shall be provided to any crime victim or victim's counsel in the case, without regard to whether the accused was convicted or acquitted of any offense.

(e) *Modification.* The Statement of Trial Results may be modified as follows:

(1) The military judge may modify the Statement of Trial Results to correct any errors prior to certification of the record of trial under R.C.M. 1112.

(2) The Court of Criminal Appeals, the Court of Appeals for the Armed Forces, and the Judge Advocate General or the Judge Advocate General's designee may modify the Statement of Trial Results in the performance of their duties and responsibilities.

(3) If a case is remanded to a military judge, the military judge may modify the Statement of Trial Results consistent with the purposes of the remand.

(4) Any modification to the Statement of Trial Results must be included in the record of trial.

Discussion

Correcting the Statement of Trial Results after the convening authority makes a decision under R.C.M. 1109 or R.C.M. 1110 should not ordinarily trigger the need for the convening authority to reconsider clemency unless the original Statement of Trial Results prejudiced the accused's ability to obtain relief under R.C.M. 1109 or R.C.M. 1110.

Rule 1102. Execution and effective date of sentences

(a) *In general.* Except as provided in subsection (b), a sentence is executed and takes effect as follows:

(1) *General and special courts-martial.* In the case of a general or special court-martial, a sentence is executed and takes effect when the judgment is entered into the record under R.C.M. 1111.

Discussion

Except for a punishment of death or dismissal, the sentence of a general or special court-martial is not required to be approved or ordered executed in order to take effect.

---

(2) *Summary courts-martial.* In the case of a summary court-martial, a sentence is executed and takes effect when the convening authority acts on the sentence.

(b) *Exceptions.*

(1) *Forfeiture.* Unless deferred under R.C.M. 1103 or suspended under R.C.M. 1107, that part of an adjudged sentence that includes forfeitures is executed and takes effect as follows:

(A) Generally. Subject to subparagraph (B), if a sentence includes forfeitures in pay or allowances, or, if forfeiture is required by Article 58b, that part of the sentence shall take effect on the earlier of—

(i) 14 days after the sentence is announced under R.C.M. 1007; or

(ii) in the case of a summary court-martial, the date on which the sentence is approved by the convening authority.

(B) *Accused Not in Confinement.* If an accused is not confined and is performing military duties, that portion of the sentence that provides for forfeiture of more than two-thirds' pay per month shall not be executed.

Discussion

The date that the sentence is adjudged is the date the sentence was announced. *See* Articles 53 and 57.

Discussion

An accused who is required to perform duties may not, as a result of a court-martial sentence, be deprived of more than two-thirds of pay while in such a status. This rule does not prohibit other deductions or withholdings from an accused's pay and allowances.

---

(2) *Confinement.*

(A) *In general.* A commander shall deliver the accused into post-trial confinement when the sentence of the court-martial includes death or confinement, unless a sentence of confinement is deferred under R.C.M. 1103.

(B) *Calculation.* Any period of confinement

included in the sentence of a court-martial begins to run from the date the sentence is announced by the court-martial. If the accused was earlier ordered into confinement under R.C.M. 305, the accused's sentence shall be credited one day for each day of confinement already served.

(C) *Exclusions in calculating confinement.* The following periods shall be excluded in computing the service of the term of confinement:

(i) Periods during which the sentence to confinement is suspended or deferred;

(ii) Periods during which the accused is in custody of civilian authorities under Article 14 from the time of the delivery to the return to military custody, if the accused was convicted in the civilian court;

(iii) Periods during which the accused is in custody of civilian or foreign authorities after the convening authority, pursuant to Article 57(b)(2), has postponed the service of a sentence to confinement;

(iv) Periods during which the accused has escaped, or is absent without authority, or is absent under a parole that a proper authority has later revoked, or is released from confinement through misrepresentation or fraud on the part of the prisoner, or is released from confinement upon the prisoner's petition for a writ under a court order that is later reversed; and

(v) Periods during which another sentence by court-martial to confinement is being served. When a prisoner serving a court-martial sentence to confinement is later convicted by a court-martial of another offense and sentenced to confinement, the later sentence interrupts the running of the earlier sentence. Any unremitted remaining portion of the earlier sentence will be served after the later sentence is fully executed.

(D) *Multiple sentences of confinement.* If a court-martial sentence includes more than one term of confinement, each term of confinement shall be served consecutively or concurrently as determined by the military judge.

Discussion

When an accused is convicted of two or more charges or specifications and sentencing is conducted in accordance with R.C.M. 1002(b) or 1004, the military judge must specifically state whether multiple terms of confinement for such offenses are to run concurrently or consecutively. *See* R.C.M. 1101.

Whether two or more terms of confinement should run concurrently is a matter of judicial discretion. *See* R.C.M. 1002.

(E) *Nature of the confinement.* The omission of hard labor from any sentence of a court-martial which has adjudged confinement shall not prohibit an appropriate authority from requiring hard labor as part of the punishment.

(F) *Place of confinement.* The place of confinement for persons sentenced to confinement by courts-martial shall be determined by regulations prescribed by the Secretary concerned. Under such regulations as the Secretary concerned may prescribe, a sentence to confinement adjudged by a court-martial or other military tribunal, regardless whether the sentence includes a punitive discharge or dismissal and regardless whether the punitive discharge or dismissal has been executed, may be ordered to be served in any place of confinement under the control of any of the armed forces or in any penal or correctional institution under the control of the United States or which the United States may be allowed to use. Persons so confined in a penal or correctional institution not under the control of one of the armed forces are subject to the same discipline and treatment as persons confined or committed by the courts of the United States or of the State, Territory, District of Columbia, or place in which the institution is situated. No member of the armed forces, or person serving with or accompanying an armed force in the field, may be placed in confinement in immediate association with enemy prisoners, or with individuals who are detained under the law of war and are foreign nationals and not members of the armed forces. The Secretary concerned may prescribe regulations governing the conditions of confinement.

(3) *Dishonorable or a bad-conduct discharge, self-executing.* A bad-conduct or dishonorable discharge shall be executed under regulations prescribed by the Secretary concerned after an appropriate official designated by those regulations has certified that the accused's case is final within the meaning of R.C.M. 1209. Upon completion of the certification, the official shall forward the certification to the accused's personnel office for preparation of a final discharge order and certificate.

(4) *Dismissal of a commissioned officer, cadet, or midshipman.* Dismissal of a commissioned officer, cadet, or midshipman shall be executed under regulations prescribed by the Secretary concerned—

(A) after the conviction is final within the meaning of R.C.M. 1209 and Article 57(c)(1) as certified by the approval authority designated pursuant to Article 57(a)(4); and

(B) only after the approval by the Secretary concerned or such Under Secretary or Assistant Secretary as the Secretary concerned may designate.

(5) *Sentences extending to death.* A punishment of death shall be carried out in a manner prescribed by the Secretary concerned—

(A) after the conviction is final within the meaning of R.C.M. 1209; and

(B) only after the approval of the President under R.C.M. 1207.

(6) *Reduction in Enlisted Grade.*

(A) *Adjudged Reduction.* Unless deferred under R.C.M. 1103 or suspended under R.C.M. 1107, that part of an adjudged sentence that includes reduction in enlisted grade shall take effect on the earlier of—

(i) 14 days after the sentence is announced under R.C.M. 1007; or

(ii) in the case of a summary court-martial, the date on which the sentence is approved by the convening authority.

(B) *Automatic Reduction.* An enlisted accused in a pay grade above E-1 whose sentence as set forth in the judgment of a court-martial includes a dishonorable or bad-conduct discharge, confinement, or hard labor without confinement may be reduced automatically to pay grade E-1 if permitted by, and under circumstances provided in, regulations prescribed by the Secretary concerned.

(c) *Other considerations concerning the execution of certain sentences.*

(1) *Death; action when accused lacks mental capacity.* An accused lacking the mental capacity to understand the punishment to be suffered or the reason for imposition of the death sentence may not be put to death during any period when such incapacity exists. The accused is presumed to possess the mental capacity to understand the punishment to be suffered and the reason for imposition of the death sentence. If a substantial question is raised as to whether the accused lacks capacity, the convening authority then exercising general court-martial jurisdiction over the accused shall order a hearing on the question. A military judge, counsel for the Government, and defense counsel shall be detailed. The convening authority shall direct an examination of the accused in accordance with R.C.M. 706, but the examination may be limited to determining whether the accused understands the punishment to be suffered and the reason therefor. The military judge shall consider all evidence presented, including evidence provided by the accused. The accused has the burden of proving such lack of capacity by a preponderance of the evidence. The military judge shall make findings of fact, which will then be forwarded to the convening authority ordering the hearing. If the accused is found to lack capacity, the convening authority shall stay the execution until the accused regains appropriate capacity.

(2) *Restriction; hard labor without confinement.* When restriction and hard labor without confinement are included in the same sentence, they shall, unless one is suspended, be executed concurrently.

Rule 1103. Deferment of confinement, forfeitures, and reduction in grade; waiver of Article 58b forfeitures

(a) *In general.*

(1) After a sentence is announced, the convening authority may defer a sentence to confinement, forfeitures, or reduction in grade in accordance with this rule. Deferment may be at the request of the accused as provided in subsection (b), or without a request of the accused as provided in subsection (c).

(2) Deferment of a sentence to confinement, forfeitures, or reduction in grade is a postponement of the running of the sentence.

(b) *Deferment requested by an accused.* The convening authority or, if the accused is no longer in the convening authority's jurisdiction, the officer exercising general court-martial jurisdiction over the command to which the accused is assigned, may, upon written application of the accused, at any time after the adjournment of the court-martial and before the entry of judgment, defer the accused's service of a sentence to confinement, forfeitures, and reduction in grade.

(c) *Deferment without a request from the accused.*

(1) In a case in which a court-martial sentences to confinement an accused referred to in paragraph (2), the convening authority may defer service of the sentence to confinement, without the consent of the accused, until after the accused has been permanently released to the armed forces by a State or foreign country.

(2) Paragraph (1) applies to an accused who, while

in custody of a State or foreign country, is temporarily returned by that State or foreign country to the armed forces for trial by court-martial and, after the court-martial, is returned to that State or foreign country under the authority of a mutual agreement or treaty, as the case may be.

(3) As used in this subsection, the term "State" means a State of the United States, the District of Columbia, a territory, and a possession of the United States.

(d) *Action on deferment request.*

(1) The authority acting on the deferment request may, in that authority's discretion, defer service of a sentence to confinement, forfeitures, or reduction in grade.

(2) In a case in which the accused requests deferment, the accused shall have the burden of showing that the interests of the accused and the community in deferral outweigh the community's interests in imposition of the punishment on its effective date. Factors that the authority acting on a deferment request may consider in determining whether to grant the deferment request include, where applicable: the probability of the accused's flight; the probability of the accused's commission of other offenses, intimidation of witnesses, or interference with the administration of justice; the nature of the offenses (including the effect on the victim) of which the accused was convicted; the sentence adjudged; the command's immediate need for the accused; the effect of deferment on good order and discipline in the command; the accused's character, mental condition, family situation, and service record. The decision of the authority acting on the deferment request shall be subject to judicial review only for abuse of discretion. The action of the authority acting on the deferment request shall be in writing. A copy of the action on the deferment request, to include any rescission, shall be included in the record of trial and a copy shall be provided to the accused and to the military judge.

(e) *Restraint when deferment is granted.* When deferment of confinement is granted, no form of restraint or other limitation on the accused's liberty may be ordered as a substitute form of punishment. An accused may, however, be restricted to specified limits or conditions may be placed on the accused's liberty during the period of deferment for any other proper reason, including a ground for restraint under R.C.M. 304.

(f) *End of deferment.* Deferment of a sentence to confinement, forfeitures, or reduction in grade ends:

(1) In a case where the accused requested deferment under subsection (b)—

(A) When the military judge of a general or special court-martial enters the judgment into the record of trial under R.C.M. 1111; or

(B) When the convening authority of a summary court-martial acts on the sentence of the court-martial;

(2) In a case where the deferment was granted under subsection (c), when the accused has been permanently released to the armed forces by a State or foreign country;

(3) When the deferred confinement, forfeitures, or reduction in grade are suspended;

(4) When the deferment expires by its own terms; or

(5) When the deferment is otherwise rescinded in accordance with subsection (g).

(g) *Rescission of deferment.*

(1) *Who may rescind.* The authority who granted the deferment or, if the accused is no longer within that authority's jurisdiction, the officer exercising general court-martial jurisdiction over the command to which the accused is assigned, may rescind the deferment.

(2) *Action.* Deferment of confinement, forfeitures, or reduction in grade may be rescinded when additional information is presented to a proper authority which, when considered with all other information in the case, that authority finds, in that authority's discretion, is grounds for denial of deferment under paragraph (d)(2). The accused and the military judge shall promptly be informed of the basis for the rescission. The accused shall also be informed of the right to submit written matters and to request that the rescission be reconsidered. The accused may be required to serve the sentence to confinement, forfeitures, or reduction in grade pending this action.

(3) *Orders.* Rescission of a deferment before or concurrently with the entry of judgment shall be noted in the judgment that is entered into the record of trial under R.C.M. 1111.

(h) *Waiving forfeitures resulting from a sentence to confinement to provide for dependent support.*

(1) With respect to forfeiture of pay and allowances resulting only by operation of law and not adjudged by the court, the convening authority may waive, for a period not to exceed six months, all or part of the forfeitures for the purpose of providing support to the accused's dependent(s). The convening authority may

waive and direct payment of any such forfeitures when they become effective by operation of Article 58(b).

(2) Factors that may be considered by the convening authority in determining the amount of forfeitures, if any, to be waived include, but are not limited to, the length of the accused's confinement, the number and age(s) of the accused's family members, whether the accused requested waiver, any debts owed by the accused, the ability of the accused's family members to find employment, and the availability of transitional compensation for abused dependents permitted under 10 U.S.C. 1059.

(3) For the purposes of this rule, a "dependent" means any person qualifying as a "dependent" under 37 U.S.C. 401.

Discussion

Forfeitures resulting by operation of law, rather than those adjudged as part of a sentence, may be waived for six months or for the duration of the period of confinement, whichever is less. The waived forfeitures are paid as support to dependent(s) designated by the convening authority. When directing waiver and payment, the convening authority should identify by name the dependent(s) to whom the payments will be made and state the number of months for which the waiver and payment shall apply. In cases where the amount to be waived and paid is less than the jurisdictional limit of the court, the monthly dollar amount of the waiver and payment should be stated.

Reductions in grade resulting by operation of law may not be deferred.

Rule 1104. Post-trial motions and proceedings

(a) *Post-trial Article 39(a) sessions.*

(1) *In general.* Upon motion of either party or *sua sponte,* the military judge may direct a post-trial Article 39(a) session at any time before the entry of judgment under R.C.M. 1111 and, when necessary, after a case has been returned to the military judge by a higher court. Counsel for the accused shall be present in accordance with R.C.M. 804 and R.C.M. 805.

Discussion

A post-trial session with members requires calling the court to order, and is not a post-trial Article 39(a) session.

---

(2) *Purpose.* The purpose of post-trial Article 39(a) sessions is to inquire into, and, when appropriate, to resolve any matter that arises after trial that substantially affects the legal sufficiency of any findings of guilty or the sentence.

(3) *Scope.* A military judge at a post-trial Article 39(a) session may reconsider any trial ruling that substantially affects the legal sufficiency of any findings of guilty or the sentence. Prior to entering such a finding or findings, the military judge shall give each party an opportunity to be heard on the matter in a post-trial Article 39(a) session. The military judge may *sua sponte*, at any time prior to the entry of judgment, take one or both of the following actions:

(i) enter a finding of not guilty of one or more offenses charged; or

(ii) enter a finding of not guilty of a part of a specification as long as a lesser offense charged is alleged in the remaining portion of the specification.

(b) *Post-trial motions.*

(1) *Matters.* Post-trial motions may be filed by either party or when directed by the military judge to address such matters as—

(A) An allegation of error in the acceptance of a plea of guilty;

(B) A motion to set aside one or more findings because the evidence is legally insufficient;

(C) A motion to correct a computational, technical, or other clear error in the sentence;

(D) An allegation of error in the Statement of Trial Results;

(E) An allegation of error in the post-trial processing of the court-martial; and

(F) An allegation of error in the convening authority's action under R.C.M. 1109 or 1110.

(2) *Timing.*

(A) Except as provided in subparagraphs (B) and (C), post-trial motions shall be filed not later than 14 days after defense counsel receives the Statement of Trial Results. The military judge may extend the time to submit such matters by not more than an additional 30 days for good cause.

(B) A motion to correct an error in the action of the convening authority shall be filed within five days after the party receives the convening authority's action. If any post-trial action by the convening authority is incomplete, irregular, or contains error, the military judge shall—

(i) return the action to the convening authority for correction; or

(ii) with the agreement of all parties, correct the

action of the convening authority in the entry of judgment.

(C) A motion to correct a clerical or computational error in a judgment entered by the military judge shall be made within five days after a party is provided a copy of the judgment.

(c) *Matters not subject to post-trial sessions.* A post-trial session may not be directed:

(1) For reconsideration of a finding of not guilty of any specification, or a ruling which amounts to a finding of not guilty;

(2) For reconsideration of a finding of not guilty of any charge, unless the record shows a finding of guilty under a specification laid under that charge, which sufficiently alleges a violation of some article of the code; or

(3) For increasing the severity of the sentence unless the sentence prescribed for the offense is mandatory.

(d) *Procedure.*

(1) *Personnel.* The requirements of R.C.M. 505 and 805 shall apply at post-trial sessions except that, for good cause, a different military judge may be detailed, subject to R.C.M. 502(c) and 902.

(2) *Record.* All post-trial sessions shall be held in open session. The record of the post-trial sessions shall be prepared, certified, and provided in accordance with R.C.M. 1112 and shall be included in the record of the prior proceedings.

(e) *Notice to Victims.* A victim must be notified of any post-trial motion, filing, or hearing that may address:

(1) the findings or sentence of a court-martial with respect to the accused;

(2) the unsealing of privileged or private information of a victim; or

(3) any action resulting in the release of an accused.

Discussion

The notification process under R.C.M. 1104(e) is addressed through such regulations as the Secretary concerned may prescribe.

Rule 1105. Post-trial hearing for person found not guilty only by reason of lack of mental responsibility

(a) *In general.* The military judge shall conduct a hearing not later than forty days following the finding that an accused is not guilty only by reason of a lack of mental responsibility.

(b) *Psychiatric or psychological examination and report.* Prior to the hearing, the military judge or convening authority shall order a psychiatric or psychological examination of the accused, with the resulting psychiatric or psychological report transmitted to the military judge for use in the post-trial hearing.

(c) *Post-trial hearing.*

(1) The accused shall be represented by defense counsel and shall have the opportunity to testify, present evidence, call witnesses on his or her behalf, and to confront and cross-examine witnesses who appear at the hearing.

(2) The military judge is not bound by the rules of evidence except with respect to privileges.

(3) An accused found not guilty only by reason of a lack of mental responsibility of an offense involving bodily injury to another, or serious damage to the property of another, or involving a substantial risk of such injury or damage, has the burden of proving by clear and convincing evidence that his or her release would not create a substantial risk of bodily injury to another person or serious damage to property of another due to a present mental disease or defect. With respect to any other offense, the accused has the burden of such proof by a preponderance of the evidence.

(4) If, after the hearing, the military judge finds the accused has satisfied the standard specified in paragraph (3), the military judge shall inform the general court-martial convening authority of this result and the accused shall be released. If, however, the military judge finds after the hearing that the accused has not satisfied the standard specified in paragraph (3), then the military judge shall inform the general court-martial convening authority of this result and that authority may commit the accused to the custody of the Attorney General.

Rule 1106. Matters submitted by the accused

(a) *In general.* After a sentence is announced in a court-martial, the accused may submit matters to the convening authority for consideration in the exercise of the convening authority's powers under R.C.M. 1109, 1110, or 1306.

(b) *Matters submitted by the accused.*

(1) Subject to paragraph (2), the accused may submit to the convening authority any matters that may reasonably tend to inform the convening authority's

exercise of discretion under R.C.M. 1109 or 1110. The convening authority is only required to consider written submissions. Submissions are not subject to the Military Rules of Evidence.

(2) Submissions under this rule may not include matters that relate to the character of a crime victim unless such matters were admitted as evidence at trial.

Discussion

See also R.C.M. 1109(d)(3)(C)(ii). For purposes of this provision, the term "crime victim" has the same meaning as the term "victim of an offense under this chapter" in Article 6b.

(c) *Access to court-martial record.* Upon request by the defense, trial counsel shall provide the accused or counsel for the accused a copy of the recording of all open sessions of the court-martial, and copies of, or access to, the evidence admitted at the court-martial, and the appellate exhibits. Such access shall not include sealed or classified court-martial material or recordings unless authorized by a military judge upon a showing of good cause. A military judge shall issue appropriate protective orders when authorizing such access.

Discussion

The record of trial is not certified until after entry of judgment. This rule allows the defense to have access to the court-martial recordings and evidence in a timely manner in order to submit matters to the convening authority for consideration in deciding whether to take action on either the findings or sentence. *See* R.C.M. 1109 and 1110.

(d) *Time periods.*

(1) *General and special courts-martial.* After a trial by general or special court-martial, the accused may submit matters to the convening authority under this rule within ten days after the sentence is announced.

(2) *Summary courts-martial.* After a trial by summary court-martial, the accused may submit matters under this rule within seven days after the sentence is announced.

(3) *Rebuttal.* In a case where a crime victim has submitted matters under R.C.M. 1106A, the accused shall have five days from receipt of those matters to submit any matters in rebuttal. Such a response shall be limited to addressing matters raised in the crime victim's submissions.

(4) *Extension of time.*

(A) If, within the period described in paragraph (1) or (2), the accused shows that additional time is required for the accused to submit matters, the convening authority may, for good cause, extend the period for not more than 20 days.

(B) For purposes of this rule, good cause for an extension ordinarily does not include the need to obtain matters that reasonably could have been presented at the court-martial.

Discussion

If at the time a victim makes a submission under R.C.M. 1106A the accused has not yet made a submission, the accused's submission may include any matters permitted by R.C.M. 1106(b) in addition to matters in rebuttal under R.C.M. 1106(d)(1)(3).

(e) *Waiver.*

(1) *Failure to submit matters.* Failure to submit matters within the time prescribed by this rule waives the right to submit such matters.

(2) *Submission of matters.* Submission of any matters under this rule shall be deemed a waiver of the right to submit additional matters unless the right to submit additional matters within the prescribed time limits is expressly reserved in writing.

(3) *Written waiver.* The accused may expressly waive, in writing, the right to submit matters under this rule. Once submitted, such a waiver may not be revoked.

(4) *Absence of accused.* If the accused does not submit matters under this rule as a result of an unauthorized absence, the accused shall be deemed to have waived the right to submit matters under this rule.

Rule 1106A. Matters submitted by crime victim

(a) *In general.* In a case with a crime victim, after a sentence is announced in a court-martial any crime victim of an offense may submit matters to the convening authority for consideration in the exercise of the convening authority's powers under R.C.M. 1109, 1110, or 1306.

(b) *Notice to a crime victim.*

(1) *In general.* Subject to such regulations as the Secretary concerned may prescribe, trial counsel, or in the case of a summary court-martial, the summary court-martial officer, shall make reasonable efforts to

inform crime victims, through counsel, if applicable, of their rights under this rule, and shall advise such crime victims on the procedure for making submissions.

(2) *Crime victim defined.* As used in this rule, the term "crime victim" means an individual who has suffered direct physical, emotional, or pecuniary harm as a result of the commission of an offense of which the accused was found guilty, and on which the convening authority may take action under R.C.M. 1109 or 1110, or the individual's lawful representative or designee appointed by the military judge under these rules.

(c) *Matters submitted by a crime victim.*

(1) Subject to paragraph (2), a crime victim may submit to the convening authority any matters that may reasonably tend to inform the convening authority's exercise of discretion under R.C.M. 1109 or 1110. The convening authority is only required to consider written submissions. Submissions are not subject to the Military Rules of Evidence.

(2) *Limitations on submissions.*

(A) Submissions under this rule may not include matters that relate to the character of the accused unless such matters were admitted as evidence at trial.

Discussion

See R.C.M. 1109(d)(3)(C)(i).

(B) The crime victim is entitled to one opportunity to submit matters to the convening authority under this rule.

Discussion

A convening authority is not required to consider matters submitted outside the single submission or outside the prescribed time limitations, and may not consider matters adverse to the accused without providing the accused an opportunity to respond. *See* R.C.M. 1109(d)(3)(C)(i).

(3) The convening authority shall ensure any matters submitted by a crime victim under this subsection be provided to the accused as soon as practicable.

Discussion

See R.C.M. 1106(d)(3).

(d) *Access to court-martial record.* Upon request by a crime victim or crime victim's counsel, trial counsel shall provide a copy of the recording of all open sessions of the court-martial, and copies of, or access to, the evidence admitted at the court-martial, and the appellate exhibits. Such access shall not include sealed or classified court-martial material or recordings unless authorized by a military judge upon a showing of good cause. A military judge shall issue appropriate protective orders when authorizing such access.

Discussion

The record of trial is not certified until after entry of judgment. This rule allows the victim to have access to the court-martial recordings and evidence in a timely manner in order to submit matters to the convening authority for consideration.

(e) *Time periods.*

(1) *General and special courts-martial.* After a trial by general or special court-martial, a crime victim may submit matters to the convening authority under this rule within ten days after the sentence is announced.

(2) *Summary courts-martial.* After a trial by summary court-martial, a crime victim may submit matters under this rule within seven days after the sentence is announced.

(3) *Extension of time.*

(A) If, within the period described in paragraph (1) or (2), the crime victim shows that additional time is required for the crime victim to submit matters, the convening authority may, for good cause, extend the period for not more than 20 days.

(B) For purposes of this rule, good cause for an extension ordinarily does not include the need to obtain matters that reasonably could have been obtained prior to the conclusion of the court-martial.

(f) *Waiver.*

(1) *Failure to submit matters.* Failure to submit matters within the time prescribed by this rule waives the right to submit such matters.

(2) *Written waiver.* A crime victim may expressly waive, in writing, the right to submit matters under this rule. Once filed, such a waiver may not be revoked.

Rule 1107. Suspension of execution of sentence; remission

(a) *In general.* Suspension of a sentence grants the

accused a probationary period during which the suspended part of a sentence is not executed, and upon the accused's successful completion of which the suspended part of the sentence shall be remitted. Remission cancels the unexecuted part of a sentence to which it applies. The unexecuted part of a sentence is that part of the sentence that has not been carried out.

(b) *Who may suspend and remit.*

(1) *Suspension when acting on sentence.* The convening authority may suspend the execution of a court-martial sentence as authorized under R.C.M. 1109 or 1110.

(2) *Suspension after entry of judgment.* The convening authority who convened the original court-martial, the convening authority's successor in command, or a convening authority otherwise designated by the Secretary concerned may suspend any part of the unexecuted part of any sentence except a sentence of death, dishonorable discharge, bad-conduct discharge, dismissal, or confinement for more than six months.

(3) *Remission of sentence.* The commander of the accused who has the authority to convene a court-martial of the type that imposed the sentence on the accused may remit any unexecuted part of the sentence, except a sentence of death, dishonorable discharge, bad-conduct discharge, dismissal, or confinement for more than six months.

(4) *Secretarial authority.* The Secretary concerned and, when designated by the Secretary concerned, any Under Secretary, Assistant Secretary, Judge Advocate General, or commanding officer may suspend or remit any part or amount of the unexecuted part of any sentence other than a sentence approved by the President or a sentence of confinement for life without eligibility for parole. The Secretary concerned may, however, suspend or remit the unexecuted part of a sentence of confinement for life without eligibility for parole only after the service of a period of confinement of not less than 20 years.

(c) *Conditions of suspension.* The authority who suspends the execution of the sentence of a court-martial shall:

(1) Specify in writing the conditions of the suspension;

(2) Cause a copy of the conditions of the suspension to be served on the probationer; and

(3) Cause a receipt to be secured from the probationer for service of the conditions of the suspension.

Unless otherwise stated, an action suspending a sentence includes as a condition that the probationer not violate any punitive article of the Uniform Code of Military Justice.

(d) *Limitations on suspension.*

(1) A sentence of death may not be suspended.

(2) A sentence of dishonorable discharge, bad-conduct discharge, dismissal, or confinement for more than six months may be suspended only as provided by paragraph (b)(4) and R.C.M. 1109(f).

(3) Suspension shall be for a stated period or until the occurrence of an anticipated future event. The period shall not be unreasonably long. The Secretary concerned may further limit by regulation the period for which the execution of a sentence may be suspended. The convening authority shall provide in the action that, unless the suspension is sooner vacated, the expiration of the period of suspension shall remit the suspended portion of the sentence.

(e) *Termination of suspension by remission.* Expiration of the period provided in the action suspending a sentence or part of a sentence shall remit the suspended sentence portion unless the suspension is sooner vacated. Death or separation which terminates status as a person subject to the UCMJ will result in remission of the suspended portion of the sentence.

Rule 1108. Vacation of suspension of sentence

(a) *In general.* Suspension of execution of the sentence of a court-martial may be vacated for violation of any condition of the suspension as provided in this rule.

(b) *Timeliness.*

(1) *Violation of conditions.* Vacation shall be based on a violation of any condition of suspension which occurs within the period of suspension.

(2) *Vacation proceedings.* Vacation proceedings under this rule shall be completed within a reasonable time.

(3) *Order vacating the suspension.* The order vacating the suspension shall be issued before the expiration of the period of suspension.

(4) *Interruptions to the period of suspension.* Unauthorized absence of the probationer or the commencement of proceedings under this rule to vacate suspension interrupts and tolls the running of the period of suspension.

(c) *Confinement of probationer pending vacation*

proceedings.

(1) *In general.* A probationer under a suspended sentence to confinement may be confined pending action under subsection (e) of this rule, in accordance with the procedures in this subsection.

(2) *Who may order confinement.* Any person who may order pretrial restraint under R.C.M. 304(b) may order confinement of a probationer under a suspended sentence to confinement.

(3) *Basis for confinement.* A probationer under a suspended sentence to confinement may be ordered into confinement upon probable cause to believe the probationer violated any conditions of the suspension.

(4) *Preliminary review of confinement.* Unless vacation proceedings under subsection (d) of this rule are completed within 7 days of imposition of confinement of the probationer (not including any delays requested by probationer), a preliminary review of the confinement shall be conducted by a neutral and detached officer appointed in accordance with regulations of the Secretary concerned.

(A) *Rights of confined probationer.* Before the preliminary review, the probationer shall be notified in writing of:

(i) The time, place, and purpose of the preliminary review, including the alleged violation(s) of the conditions of suspension;

(ii) The right to be present at the preliminary review;

(iii) The right to be represented at the preliminary review by civilian counsel provided by the probationer or, upon request, by military counsel detailed for this purpose; and

(iv) The opportunity to be heard, to present witnesses who are reasonably available and other evidence, and the right to confront and cross-examine adverse witnesses unless the officer conducting the preliminary review determines that this would subject these witnesses to risk or harm. For purposes of this subsection, a witness is not reasonably available if the witness requires reimbursement by the United States for cost incurred in appearing, cannot appear without unduly delaying the proceedings or, if a military witness, cannot be excused from other important duties. Witness testimony may be provided in person, by video teleconference, by telephone, or by similar means of remote testimony.

(B) *Rules of evidence.* Only Mil. R. Evid. 301, 302, 303, 305, 412, and Section V (Privileges) apply to proceedings under this rule, except Mil. R. Evid. 412(b)(1)(C) does not apply. In applying these rules to a preliminary review, the term "military judge," as used in these rules, shall mean the officer conducting the preliminary review, who shall assume the military judge's authority to exclude evidence from the hearing, and who shall, in discharging this duty, follow the procedures set forth in these rules.

(C) *Decision.* The officer conducting the preliminary review shall determine whether there is probable cause to believe that the probationer violated the conditions of the probationer's suspension. If the officer conducting the preliminary review determines that probable cause is lacking, the officer shall issue a written order directing that the probationer be released from confinement. If the officer determines that there is probable cause to believe that the probationer violated a condition of suspension, the officer shall set forth this determination in a written memorandum that details therein the evidence relied upon and reasons for making the decision. The officer shall forward the original memorandum or release order to the probationer's commander and forward a copy to the probationer and the officer in charge of the confinement facility.

(d) *Vacation proceedings.*

(1) *In general.* The purpose of the vacation hearing is to determine whether there is probable cause to believe that the probationer violated a condition of the probationer's suspension.

(A) *Sentence of general courts-martial and certain special courts-martial.* In the case of vacation proceedings for a suspended sentence of any general court-martial or a suspended sentence of a special court-martial that adjudged either a bad-conduct discharge or confinement for more than six months, the officer having special court-martial jurisdiction over the probationer shall either personally hold the hearing or detail a judge advocate to preside at the hearing. If there is no officer having special court-martial jurisdiction over the probationer who is subordinate to the officer having general court-martial jurisdiction over the probationer, the officer exercising general court-martial jurisdiction over the probationer shall either personally hold a hearing under this subsection or detail a judge advocate to conduct the hearing.

(B) *Special court-martial wherein a bad-conduct discharge or confinement for more than six months was not adjudged.* In the case of vacation proceedings for a sentence from a special court-martial that did not include a bad-conduct discharge or confinement for more than six months, the officer having special court-martial jurisdiction over the probationer shall either personally hold the hearing or detail a judge advocate to conduct the hearing.

(C) *Sentence of summary court-martial.* In the case of vacation proceedings for a suspended sentence of a summary court-martial, the officer having summary court-martial jurisdiction over the probationer shall either personally hold the hearing or detail a commissioned officer to conduct the hearing.

(2) *Notice to probationer.* Before the hearing, the officer conducting the hearing shall cause the probationer to be notified in writing of:

(A) The time, place, and purpose of the hearing;

(B) The right to be present at the hearing;

(C) The alleged violation(s) of the conditions of suspension and the evidence expected to be relied on;

(D) The right to be represented at the hearing by civilian counsel provided by the probationer or, upon request, by military counsel detailed for this purpose; and

(E) The opportunity to be heard, to present witnesses who are reasonably available and other evidence, and the right to confront and cross-examine adverse witnesses unless the officer conducting the preliminary review determines that this would subject these witnesses to risk or harm.

(3) *Procedure.*

(A) *Generally.* The hearing shall begin with the hearing officer informing the probationer of the probationer's rights. The Government will then present evidence. Upon the conclusion of the Government's presentation of evidence, the probationer may present evidence. The probationer shall have full opportunity to present any matters in defense, extenuation, or mitigation. Both the Government and probationer shall be afforded an opportunity to cross-examine adverse witnesses. The hearing officer may also question witnesses called by the parties.

(B) *Rules of evidence.* The Military Rules of Evidence applicable to vacation proceedings are the same as those set forth in subparagraph (c)(4)(B) of this rule.

(C) *Production of witnesses and other evidence.* The procedure for the production of witnesses and other evidence shall follow that prescribed in R.C.M. 405(h), except that R.C.M. 405(h)(3)(B) shall not apply. The hearing officer shall only consider testimony and other evidence that is relevant to the limited purpose of the hearing.

Discussion

A hearing officer may not order the production of any privileged matters.

(D) *Presentation of testimony.* Witness testimony may be provided in person, by video teleconference, by telephone, or by similar means of remote testimony. All testimony shall be taken under oath, except that the probationer may make an unsworn statement.

Discussion

See R.C.M. 807. The hearing officer is required to include in the record of the hearing, at a minimum, a summary of the substance of all testimony.

(E) *Other evidence.* If relevant to the limited purpose of the hearing, and not cumulative, a hearing officer may consider other evidence, in addition to or in lieu of witness testimony, including statements, tangible evidence, or reproductions thereof, offered by either side, that the hearing officer determines is reliable. This other evidence need not be sworn.

(F) *Protective order for release of privileged information.* If the Government agrees to disclose to the probationer information to which the protections afforded by Mil. R. Evid. 505 or 506 may apply, the convening authority, or other person designated by regulation of the Secretary of the service concerned, may enter an appropriate protective order, in writing, to guard against the compromise of information disclosed to the probationer. The terms of any such protective order may include prohibiting the disclosure of the information except as authorized by the authority.

(G) *Presence of probationer.* The taking of evidence shall not be prevented and the probationer shall be considered to have waived the right to be present whenever the probationer:

(i) After being notified of the time and place of the proceeding is voluntarily absent; or

(ii) After being warned by the hearing officer that disruptive conduct will cause removal from the proceeding, persists in conduct that is such as to justify exclusion from the proceeding.

(H) *Objections.* Any objection alleging failure to comply with these rules shall be made to the convening authority via the hearing officer. The hearing officer shall include a record of all objections in the written recommendations to the convening authority.

(I) *Access by spectators.* The procedures for access by spectators shall follow those prescribed in R.C.M. 405(j)(3).

(J) *Victims' rights.* Any victim of the underlying offense for which the probationer received the suspended sentence, or any victim of the alleged offense that is the subject of the vacation hearing, has the right to reasonable, accurate, and timely notice of the vacation hearing.

Discussion

The term "victim" has the same meaning as the term "victim of an offense under this chapter" in Article 6b.

---

(4) *Record and recommendation.* The officer conducting the hearing shall make a summarized record of the hearing. If the hearing is not personally conducted by the officer having the authority to take action under subsection (e) of this rule, the officer who conducted the hearing shall forward the record and that officer's written recommendation concerning vacation to such authority. The record shall include the recommendation, the evidence relied upon, and the rationale supporting the recommendation.

(5) *Release from confinement.* If the hearing is not personally conducted by the officer having the authority to take action under subsection (e) of this rule and the officer conducting the hearing finds there is not probable cause to believe that the probationer violated any condition of the suspension, the officer shall order the release of the probationer from any confinement ordered under subsection (c) of this rule, and forward the record and recommendation to the officer having the authority to take action under subsection (e) of this rule.

(e) *Action.*

(1) *General courts-martial and certain special courts-martial.* In a case of a suspended sentence from any general court-martial or a suspended sentence from a special court-martial that adjudged either a bad-conduct discharge or confinement for more than six months, unless the officer exercising general court-martial jurisdiction over the probationer personally conducted the hearing, the officer exercising general court-martial jurisdiction over the probationer shall review the record and the recommendation produced by the officer who conducted the hearing on the alleged violation of the conditions of suspension, decide whether the probationer violated a condition of suspension, and, if so, decide whether to vacate the suspended sentence. If the officer exercising general court-martial jurisdiction decides to vacate the suspended sentence, that officer shall prepare a written statement of the evidence relied on and the reasons for vacating the suspended sentence.

(2) *Special courts-martial wherein a bad-conduct discharge and confinement for more than six months was not adjudged.* In a case of a suspended sentence from a special court-martial that did not include a bad-conduct discharge or confinement for more than six months, unless the officer having special court-martial jurisdiction over the probationer personally conducted the hearing, the officer having special court-martial jurisdiction over the probationer shall review the record and the recommendation produced by the officer who conducted the hearing, decide whether the probationer violated a condition of suspension, and, if so, decide whether to vacate the suspended sentence. If the officer exercising special court-martial jurisdiction decides to vacate the suspended sentence, that officer shall prepare a written statement of the evidence relied on and the reasons for vacating the suspended sentence. The authority holding the same or higher court-martial authority as the officer who originally suspended the probationer's sentence may withhold the authority to take action under this paragraph to that officer.

(3) *Vacation of a suspended sentence from a summary court-martial.* In a case of a suspended sentence from a summary court-martial, unless the officer having summary court-martial jurisdiction over the probationer personally conducted the hearing, the officer having summary court-martial jurisdiction over the probationer shall review the record and the recommendation produced by the officer who conducted the hearing, and decide whether the probationer violated a condition of suspension, and, if so, decide whether to vacate the suspended sentence. If the officer exercising summary court-martial jurisdiction decides to vacate the suspended sentence, that officer shall prepare a written statement of the evidence relied on and the reasons for vacating the suspended sentence. The authority holding the same or higher court-martial authority as the officer who

originally suspended the probationer's sentence may withhold the authority to take action under this paragraph to that officer.

(4) *Execution.* Any unexecuted part of a suspended sentence ordered vacated under this subsection shall be executed.

Rule 1109. Reduction of sentence, general and special courts-martial

(a) *In general.* This rule applies to the post-trial actions of the convening authority in any general or special court-martial in which—

(1) The court-martial found the accused guilty of—

(A) An offense for which the maximum authorized sentence to confinement is more than two years, without considering the jurisdictional maximum of the court;

(B) A violation of Article 120(a) or (b);

(C) A violation of Article 120b; or

(D) A violation of such other offense as the Secretary of Defense has specified by regulation; or

(2) The sentence of the court-martial includes—

(A) A bad-conduct discharge, dishonorable discharge, or dismissal;

(B) A term of confinement, or terms of confinement running consecutively, more than six months; or

Discussion

The applicability of R.C.M. 1109(a)(2)(B) is determined by assessing the total amount of confinement that is to be served. In a case where the military judge determined the sentence of the accused, the total amount of confinement is based upon the military judge's determination as to whether any terms of confinement are to run concurrently or consecutively. For instance, if the military judge determines that all terms of confinement are to be served concurrently and the total amount of confinement is six months or less, R.C.M. 1109(a)(2)(B) does not apply. If, however, the military judge determines that two or more terms of confinement are to be served consecutively and the total amount of confinement is more than six months, R.C.M. 1109(a)(2)(B) applies.

(C) Death.

(b) *Limitation of authority on findings.* For any court-martial described under subsection (a), the convening authority may not set aside, disapprove, or take any other action on the findings of the court-martial.

(c) *Limited authority to act on sentence.* For any court-martial described under subsection (a), the convening authority may—

(1) Modify a bad-conduct discharge, dishonorable discharge, or dismissal only as provided in subsections (e) and (f);

(2) Modify a term of confinement of more than six months, or terms of confinement that running consecutively are more than six months, only as provided in subsections (e) and (f);

Discussion

See the Discussion following R.C.M. 1109(a)(2)(B).

---

(3) Reduce or commute a punishment of death only as provided in subsection (e);

(4) Reduce, commute, or suspend, in whole or in part, any punishment adjudged for an offense tried under the law of war other than the punishments specified in paragraphs (1), (2), and (3);

(5) Reduce, commute, or suspend, in whole or in part, the following punishments:

(A) The confinement portion of a sentence if the confinement portion of the sentence is six months or less, to include terms of confinement that running consecutively total six months or less;

Discussion

See the Discussion following R.C.M. 1109(a)(2)(B).

(B) A reprimand;

(C) Forfeiture of pay or allowances;

(D) A fine;

(E) Reduction in pay grade;

(F) Restriction to specified limits; and

(G) Hard labor without confinement.

(d) *General Considerations.*

(1) *Who may take action.* If it is impracticable for the convening authority to act under this rule, the convening authority shall, in accordance with such regulations as the Secretary concerned may prescribe, forward the case to an officer exercising general court-martial jurisdiction who may take action under this rule.

(2) *Legal advice.* In determining whether to take action, or to decline taking action under this rule, the convening authority shall consult with the staff judge advocate or legal advisor.

(3) *Consideration of matters.*

(A) *Matters submitted by accused and crime victim.* Before taking or declining to take any action on the sentence under this rule, the convening authority shall consider matters timely submitted under R.C.M. 1106 and 1106A, if any, by the accused and any crime victim.

(B) *Additional matters.* Before taking action the convening authority may consider—

(i) The Statement of Trial Results;

Discussion

See R.C.M. 1104(b) addressing post-trial motions and proceedings to resolve allegations of error in a Statement of Trial Results.

(ii) The evidence introduced at the court-martial, any appellate exhibits, and the recording or transcription of the proceedings, subject to the provisions of R.C.M. 1113 and subparagraph (C);

(iii) The personnel records of the accused; and

(iv) Such other matters as the convening authority deems appropriate.

(C) *Prohibited matters.*

(i) *Accused.* The convening authority may not consider matters adverse to the accused that were not admitted at the court-martial, with knowledge of which the accused is not chargeable, unless the accused is first notified and given an opportunity to rebut.

(ii) *Crime victim.* The convening authority shall not consider any matters that relate to the character of a crime victim unless such matters were presented as evidence at trial and not excluded at trial.

Discussion

For purposes of this provision, the term "crime victim" has the same meaning as "victim of an offense under this chapter" in Article 6b.

---

(3) *Timing.* Except as provided in subsection (e), any action taken by the convening authority under this rule shall be taken prior to entry of judgment. If the convening authority decides to take no action, that decision shall be transmitted promptly to the military judge as provided under subsection (g).

(e) *Reduction of sentence for substantial assistance by accused.*

(1) *In general.* A convening authority may reduce, commute, or suspend the sentence of an accused, in whole or in part, if the accused has provided substantial assistance in the criminal investigation or prosecution of another person.

(2) *Trial counsel.* A convening authority may reduce the sentence of an accused under this subsection only upon the recommendation of trial counsel who prosecuted the accused. If the person who served as trial counsel is no longer serving in that position, or is not reasonably available, the attorney who is primarily responsible for the investigation or prosecution in which the accused has provided substantial assistance, and who represents the United States, is trial counsel for the purposes of this subsection. The recommendation of trial counsel is the decision of trial counsel alone. No person may direct trial counsel to make or not make such a recommendation.

(3) *Who may act.*

(A) Before entry of judgment, the convening authority who convened the original court-martial or the convening authority's successor in command may act on the recommendation of trial counsel under paragraph (2).

(B) After entry of judgment, the convening authority who convened the original court-martial or the convening authority's successor in command or a convening authority otherwise designated by the Secretary concerned may act on the recommendation of trial counsel under paragraph (2).

(4) *Scope of authority.* A convening authority authorized to act under paragraph (3) may accept the recommendation of trial counsel under paragraph (2) of this subsection, and may reduce, commute, or suspend a sentence in whole or in part, including any mandatory minimum sentence.

(5) *Limitations.*

(A) A sentence of death may not be suspended under this subsection.

(B) In the case of a recommendation by trial counsel under paragraph (2) of this subsection made more than one year after entry of judgment, the convening authority who convened the original court-martial or the convening authority's successor in command or a convening authority otherwise designated by the Secretary concerned may reduce a sentence only if the substantial assistance of the accused involved—

(i) Information not known to the accused until one year or more after sentencing;

(ii) Information the usefulness of which could not reasonably have been anticipated by the accused until more than one year after sentencing and which was promptly provided to the Government after its usefulness was reasonably apparent to the accused; or

(iii) Information provided by the accused to the Government within one year of sentencing, but which did not become useful to the Government until more than one year after sentencing.

(6) *Evaluating substantial assistance.* In evaluating whether the accused has provided substantial assistance, the trial counsel and convening authority may consider the presentence assistance of the accused.

(7) *Action after entry of judgment.* If the convening authority who convened the original court-martial or the convening authority's successor in command or a convening authority otherwise designated by the Secretary concerned acts on the sentence of an accused after entry of judgment, the action shall be forwarded to the chief trial judge. The chief trial judge, or a military judge detailed by the chief trial judge, shall modify the judgment of the court-martial to reflect the action. The action and the modified judgment shall be forwarded to the Judge Advocate General and shall be included in the original record of trial. The reduction of a sentence under this rule shall not abridge any right of the accused to appellate review.

(f) *Suspension.*

(1) The convening authority may suspend a sentence of a dishonorable discharge, bad-conduct discharge, dismissal, or confinement in excess of six months, if—

(A) The Statement of Trial Results filed under R.C.M. 1101 includes a recommendation by the military judge that the convening authority suspend the sentence, in whole or in part; and

(B) The military judge includes a statement explaining the basis for the suspension recommendation.

(2) If the convening authority suspends a sentence under this subsection—

(A) The portion of the sentence that is to be suspended may not exceed the portion of the sentence that the military judge recommended be suspended;

(B) The duration of the suspension may not be less than that recommended by the military judge; and

(C) The suspended portion of the sentence may be terminated by remission only as provided in R.C.M. 1107(e).

(3) A sentence that is suspended under this rule shall comply with the procedures prescribed in R.C.M. 1107(c), (d), and (e).

(g) *Decision; forwarding of decision and related matters.*

(1) *No action.* If the convening authority decides to take no action on the sentence under this rule, the staff judge advocate or legal advisor shall notify the military judge of this decision.

(2) *Action on sentence.* If the convening authority decides to act on the sentence under this rule, such action shall be in writing and shall include a written statement explaining the action. If any part of the sentence is disapproved, reduced, commuted, or suspended, the action shall clearly state which part or parts are disapproved, reduced, commuted, or suspended. The convening authority's staff judge advocate or legal advisor shall forward the action with the written explanation to the military judge to be attached to the record of trial.

(h) *Service on accused and crime victim.* If the convening authority took any action on the sentence under this rule, a copy of such action shall be served on the accused, crime victim, or on their respective counsel. If the action is served on counsel, counsel shall, by expeditious means, provide the accused or crime victim with a copy. If the judgment is entered expeditiously, service of the judgment will satisfy the requirements of this subsection.

Discussion

See R.C.M. 1104(b) addressing post-trial motions and proceedings to resolve allegations of error in the convening authority's action under R.C.M. 1109. For purposes of this provision, the term "crime victim" has the same meaning as in R.C.M. 1106A(b)(2).

Rule 1110. Action by convening authority in certain general and special courts-martial

(a) *In general.* This rule applies to the post-trial actions of the convening authority in any general or special court-martial not specified in R.C.M. 1109(a).

(b) *Action on findings.* In any court-martial subject to this rule, action on findings is not required; however, the convening authority may—

(1) Change a finding of guilty to a charge or specification to a finding of guilty to an offense that is a lesser included offense of the offense stated in the charge or specification; or

(2) Set aside any finding of guilty and—

(A) Dismiss the specification and, if appropriate, the charge; or

(B) Order a rehearing in accordance with the procedures set forth in R.C.M. 810.

A rehearing may not be ordered as to findings of guilty when there is a lack of sufficient evidence in the record to support the findings of guilty of the offense charged or of any lesser included offense. A rehearing may be ordered, however, if the proof of guilt consisted of inadmissible evidence for which there is available an admissible substitute. A rehearing may be ordered as to any lesser offense included in an offense of which the accused was found guilty, provided there is sufficient evidence in the record to support the lesser included offense.

(c) *Action on sentence.*

(1) In any court-martial subject to this rule, action on the sentence is not required; however, the convening authority may disapprove, reduce, commute, or suspend, in whole or in part, the court-martial sentence. If the sentence is disapproved, the convening authority may order a rehearing on the sentence.

(2) In any court-martial subject to this rule, the convening authority, after entry of judgment, may reduce a sentence for substantial assistance in accordance with the procedures under R.C.M. 1109(e).

(d) *Procedures.* The convening authority shall use the same procedures as in subsections (d) and (h) of R.C.M. 1109 for any post-trial action on findings and sentence under this rule.

(e) *Decision; forwarding of decision and related matters.*

(1) *No action.* If the convening authority decides to take no action on the findings or sentence under this rule, the convening authority's staff judge advocate or legal advisor shall notify the military judge of the decision.

(2) *Action on findings.* If the convening authority decides to act on the findings under this rule, the action of the convening authority shall be in writing and shall include a written statement explaining the reasons for the action. If a rehearing is not ordered, the affected charges and specifications shall be dismissed by the convening authority in the action. The convening authority's staff judge advocate or legal advisor shall forward the action with the written explanation to the military judge to be attached to the record of trial.

(3) *Action on sentence.* If the convening authority decides to act on the sentence under this rule, the action of the convening authority on the sentence shall be in writing and shall include a written statement explaining the reasons for the action. If any part of the sentence is disapproved, the action shall clearly state which part or parts are disapproved. The convening authority's staff judge advocate or legal advisor shall forward the action with the written explanation to the military judge to be attached to the record of trial.

Discussion

See R.C.M. 1104(b) addressing post-trial motions and proceedings to resolve allegations of error in the convening authority's action under R.C.M. 1110.

Rule 1111. Entry of judgment

(a) *In general.*

(1) *Scope.* Under regulations prescribed by the Secretary concerned, the military judge of a general or special court-martial shall enter into the record of trial the judgment of the court. If the Chief Trial Judge determines that the military judge is not reasonably available, the Chief Trial Judge may detail another military judge to enter the judgment.

(2) *Purpose.* The judgment reflects the result of the court-martial, as modified by any post-trial actions, rulings, or orders. The entry of judgment terminates the trial proceedings and initiates the appellate process.

(3) *Summary courts-martial.* In a summary court-martial, the findings and sentence of the court-martial, as modified or approved by the convening authority, constitute the judgment of the court-martial. A separate document need not be issued.

(b) *Contents.* The judgment of the court shall be signed and dated by the military judge and shall consist of—

(1) *Findings.* For each charge and specification referred to trial—

(A) a summary of each charge and specification;

(B) the plea of the accused; and

(C) the findings or other disposition of each charge and specification accounting for any modifications made by reason of any post-trial action by the convening authority or any post-trial ruling, order, or other determination by the military judge;

(2) *Sentence.* The sentence, accounting for any modifications made by reason of any post-trial action by the convening authority or any post-trial ruling, order, or other determination by the military judge, as well as the total amount of sentence credit, if any, to be applied to the accused's sentence to confinement. If the accused was convicted of more than one specification and any part of the sentence was determined by a military judge, the judgment shall also specify—

(A) the confinement and fine for each specification, if any;

(B) whether any term of confinement shall run consecutively or concurrently with any other term(s) of confinement; and

(C) the total amount of any fine(s) and the total duration of confinement to be served, after accounting for the following—

(i) any terms of confinement that are to run consecutively or concurrently; and

(ii) any modifications to the sentence made by reason of any post-trial action by the convening authority or any post-trial ruling, order, or other determination by the military judge.

Discussion

The date that the sentence is adjudged is the date the sentence was announced. *See* Articles 53 and 57. The adjudged sentence may be modified by the convening authority or the military judge. *See generally* R.C.M. 1104, R.C.M. 1107, R.C.M. 1109, and R.C.M. 1110.

See R.C.M. 1002(b) for military judge alone sentencing and R.C.M. 1004 for sentencing in capital cases by military judge and members.

---

(3) *Additional information.*

(A) *Deferment.* If the accused requested that any portion of the sentence be deferred, the judgment shall specify the nature of the request, the convening authority's action, the effective date if approved, and, if the deferment ended prior to the entry of judgment, the date the deferment ended.

(B) *Waiver of automatic forfeitures.* If the accused requested that automatic forfeitures be waived by the convening authority under Article 58b, the judgment shall specify the nature of the request, the convening authority's action, and the effective date and length, if approved.

(C) *Suspension.* If the Statement of Trial Results included a recommendation by the military judge that a portion of the sentence be suspended, the judgment shall specify the action of the convening authority on the recommendation.

(D) *Reprimand.* If the sentence included a reprimand, the judgment shall contain the reprimand issued by the convening authority.

(E) *Rehearing.* If the judgment is entered after a rehearing, new trial or other trial, the judgment shall specify any sentence limitation applicable by operation of Article 63.

(F) *Other information.* Any additional information that the Secretary concerned may require by regulation.

(4) *Statement of Trial Results.* The Statement of Trial Results shall be included in the judgment in accordance with regulations prescribed by the Secretary concerned.

Discussion

See Article 60 and R.C.M. 1101. The judgment of the court entered under this rule should provide a complete statement of the findings and the sentence reflecting the effect of any post-trial modifications. The judgment of the court should avoid using phrases such as "exceptions" and "substitutions" to reflect post-trial actions. Such a formulation is not an appropriate substitute for a complete statement of the findings and sentence.

(c) *Modification of judgment.* The judgment may be modified as follows—

(1) The military judge who entered a judgment may issue a modified judgment to correct any errors prior to certification of the record of trial under R.C.M. 1112.

(2) The Court of Criminal Appeals, the Court of Appeals for the Armed Forces, and the Judge Advocate General or the Judge Advocate General's designee may modify a judgment in the performance of their duties and responsibilities.

(3) If a case is remanded to a military judge, the military judge may modify the judgment consistent with the purposes of the remand.

(4) Any modification to the judgment of a court-martial must be included in the record of trial.

(d) *Rehearings, new trials, and other trials.* In the case of a rehearing, new trial, or other trial, the military judge shall enter a new judgment into the record of trial to reflect the results of the rehearing, new trial, or other trial.

(e) *When judgment is entered.*

(1) *Courts-martial without a finding of guilty.* When a court-martial results in a full acquittal or when a court-martial terminates before findings, the judgment shall be entered as soon as practicable. When a court-martial results in a finding of not guilty only by reason of lack of mental responsibility of all charges and specifications, the judgment shall be entered as soon as practicable after a hearing is conducted under R.C.M. 1105.

(2) *Courts-martial with a finding of guilty.* If a court-martial includes a finding of guilty to any specification or charge, the judgment shall be entered as soon as practicable after the staff judge advocate or legal advisor notifies the military judge of the convening authority's post-trial action or decision to take no action under R.C.M. 1109 or 1110, as applicable.

(f) *Publication.*

(1) The judgment shall be entered into the record of trial.

(2) A copy of the judgment shall be provided to the accused or to the accused's defense counsel. If the judgment is served on defense counsel, defense counsel shall, by expeditious means, provide the accused with a copy.

(3) A copy of the judgment shall be provided upon request to any crime victim or crime victim's counsel in the case, without regard to whether the accused was convicted or acquitted of any offense.

Discussion

For the definition of "crime victim," see R.C.M. 1001(c)(2)(A). However, in this provision, a copy of the Statement of Trial Results shall be provided to any crime victim without regard to whether the accused was convicted or acquitted of any offense.

---

(4) The commander of the accused or the convening authority may publish the judgment of the court-martial to their respective commands.

(5) Under regulations prescribed by the Secretary of Defense, court-martial judgments shall be made available to the public.

Rule 1112. Certification of record of trial; general and special courts-martial

(a) *In general.* Each general and special court-martial shall keep a separate record of the proceedings in each case brought before it. The record shall be independent of any other document and shall include a recording of the court-martial. Court-martial proceedings may be recorded by videotape, audiotape, or other technology from which sound images may be reproduced to accurately depict the court-martial.

Discussion

Video and audio recording and the taking of photographs in the courtroom are permitted only for the purpose of preparing the record of trial or as permitted by R.C.M. 806(c). Spectators, witnesses, counsel for the accused and counsel for victims are not permitted to make video or audio recordings or to take photographs in the courtroom.

(b) *Contents of the record of trial.* The record of trial contains the court-martial proceedings and includes any evidence or exhibits considered by the court-martial in determining the findings or sentence. The record of trial in every general and special court-martial shall include:

(1) A substantially verbatim recording of the court-martial proceedings except sessions closed for deliberations and voting;

(2) The original charge sheet or a duplicate;

(3) A copy of the convening order and any amending order;

(4) The request, if any, for trial by military judge alone; the accused's election, if any, of members under R.C.M. 903; and, when applicable, any statement by the convening authority required under R.C.M. 503(a)(2);

(5) Exhibits, or, if permitted by the military judge, copies, photographs, or descriptions of any exhibits that were received in evidence and any appellate exhibits;

(6) The Statement of Trial Results;

(7) Any action by the convening authority under R.C.M. 1109 or 1110; and

(8) The judgment entered into the record by the military judge.

(c) *Certification.* A court reporter shall prepare and certify that the record of trial includes all items required under subsection (b). If the court reporter cannot certify the record of trial because of the court reporter's death, disability, or absence, the military judge shall certify the record of trial.

(1) *Timing of certification.* The record of trial shall be certified as soon as practicable after the judgment has been entered into the record.

(2) *Additional proceedings.* If additional proceedings are held after the court reporter certifies the record, a record of those proceedings shall be included in the record of trial, and a court reporter shall prepare a supplemental certification.

(d) *Loss of record, incomplete record, and correction of record.*

(1) If the certified record of trial is lost or destroyed, a court reporter shall, if practicable, certify another record of trial.

(2) A record of trial is complete if it complies with the requirements of subsection (b). If the record is incomplete or defective, a court reporter or any party may raise the matter to the military judge for appropriate corrective action. A record of trial found to be incomplete or defective before or after certification may be corrected to make it accurate. A superior competent authority may return a record of trial to the military judge for correction under this rule. The military judge shall give notice of the proposed correction to all parties and permit them to examine and respond to the proposed correction. All parties shall be given reasonable access to any court reporter notes or recordings of the proceedings.

(3) The military judge may take corrective action by any of the following means—

(A) reconstructing the portion of the record affected;

(B) dismissing affected specifications;

(C) reducing the sentence of the accused; or

(D) if the error was raised by motion or on appeal by the defense, declaring a mistrial as to the affected specifications.

Discussion

Where there is an electronic or digital recording failure or loss of court reporter notes, the record should be reconstructed as completely as possible. If the interruption is discovered during trial, the military judge should summarize or reconstruct the portion of the proceedings which has not been recorded. If both parties agree to the summary or reconstruction of the proceedings, the proceedings may continue. If either party objects to the summary or reconstruction, the trial should proceed anew, and the proceedings repeated from the point where the interruption began.

(e) *Copies of the record of trial.*

(1) *Accused and victim.* Any victim entitled to a copy of the certified record of trial shall be notified of the opportunity to receive a copy of the certified record of trial. Following certification of the record of trial under subsection (c), in every general and special court-martial, subject to paragraphs (3) and (4), a court reporter shall, in accordance with regulations issued by the Secretary concerned, provide a copy of the certified record of trial free of charge to—

(A) The accused;

(B) The victim of an offense of which the accused was charged if the victim testified during the proceedings; and

(C) Any victim named in a specification of which the accused was charged, upon request, without regard to the findings of the court-martial.

Discussion

The term "victim" has the same meaning as the term "victim of an offense under this chapter" in Article 6b. The record of trial includes only those items listed in R.C.M. 1112(b).

---

(2) *Providing copy impracticable.* If it is impracticable to provide the record of trial to an individual entitled to receive a copy under paragraph (1) because of the unauthorized absence of the individual, or military exigency, or if the individual so requests on the record at the court-martial or in writing, the individual's copy of the record shall be forwarded to the individual's counsel, if any.

(3) *Sealed exhibits; classified information; closed sessions.* Any copy of the record of trial provided to an individual under paragraph (1) shall not contain classified information, information under seal, or recordings of closed sessions of the court-martial, and shall be handled as follows:

(A) *Classified information.*

(i) *Forwarding to convening authority.* If the copy of the record of trial prepared for an individual under this rule contains classified information, trial counsel, unless directed otherwise by the convening authority, shall forward the individual's copy to the convening authority, before it is provided to the individual.

(ii) *Responsibility of the convening authority.* The convening authority shall:

(I) cause any classified information to be deleted or withdrawn from the individual's copy of the record of trial;

(II) cause a certificate indicating that classified information has been deleted or withdrawn to be attached to the record of trial; and

(III) cause the expurgated copy of the record of trial and the attached certificate regarding classified information to be provided to the individual as provided in subparagraphs (1)(A), (B), and (C).

(iii) *Contents of certificate.* The certificate regarding deleted or withdrawn classified information shall indicate:

(I) that the original record of trial may be inspected in the Office of the Judge Advocate General under such regulations as the Secretary concerned may prescribe;

(II) the locations in the record of trial from which matter has been deleted;

(III) the locations in the record of trial which have been entirely deleted; and

(IV) the exhibits which have been withdrawn.

(B) *Sealed exhibits and closed sessions.* The court reporter shall delete or withdraw from an individual's copy of the record of trial—

(i) any matter ordered sealed by the military judge under R.C.M. 1113; and

(ii) any recording or transcript of a session that was ordered closed by the military judge, to include closed sessions held pursuant to Mil. R. Evid. 412, 513, and 514.

Discussion

Once classified information, sealed exhibits, and closed sessions are removed, the record of trial should ordinarily consist of the public proceedings of a court-martial, and should ordinarily contain public matters not subject to further redaction. In all cases, redactions should be in compliance with R.C.M. 1112(e)(4). If the terms of the sealing order permit, the court reporter may disclose to the individual being provided the record of trial those portions that the military judge has deemed appropriate for such disclosure in the sealing order.

---

(4) *Portions of the record protected by the Privacy Act.* Any copy of the record of trial provided to a victim under paragraph (1) shall not contain any portion of the record the release of which would unlawfully violate the privacy interests of any person other than that victim, to include those privacy interests recognized by 5 U.S.C. § 552a, the Privacy Act of 1974.

(5) *Additional copies.* The convening or higher authority may direct that additional copies of the record of trial of any general or special court-martial be prepared.

(f) *Attachments for appellate review.* In accordance with regulations prescribed by the Secretary concerned, a court reporter shall attach the following matters to the record before the certified record of trial is forwarded to the office of the Judge Advocate General for appellate review:

(1) If not used as exhibits—

(A) The preliminary hearing report under Article 32, if any;

(B) The pretrial advice under Article 34, if any;

(C) If the trial was a rehearing or new or other trial of the case, the record of any former hearings; and

(D) Written special findings, if any, by the military judge;

(2) Exhibits or, with the permission of the military judge, copies, photographs, or descriptions of any exhibits which were marked for and referred to on the record but not received in evidence;

(3) Any matter filed by the accused or victim under R.C.M. 1106 or 1106A, or any written waiver of the right to submit such matters;

(4) Any deferment request and the action on it;

(5) Conditions of suspension, if any, and proof of service on probationer under R.C.M. 1107;

(6) Any waiver or withdrawal of appellate review under R.C.M. 1115;

(7) Records of any proceedings in connection with a vacation of suspension of the sentence under R.C.M. 1108;

(8) Any transcription of the court-martial proceedings created pursuant to R.C.M. 1114; and

(9) Any redacted materials.

Discussion

The record of trial and attachments may include electronic versions of any matters.

(g) *Security classification.* If the record of trial contains matters that must be classified under applicable security regulations, trial counsel shall cause a proper security classification to be assigned to the record of trial and on each page thereof on which classified material appears.

Rule 1113. Sealed exhibits, proceedings, and other materials

(a) *In general.* If the report of preliminary hearing or record of trial contains exhibits, proceedings, or other materials ordered sealed by the preliminary hearing officer or military judge, counsel for the Government, the court reporter, or trial counsel shall cause such materials to be sealed so as to prevent unauthorized examination or disclosure. Counsel for the Government, the court reporter, or trial counsel shall ensure that such materials are properly marked, including an annotation that the material was sealed by order of the preliminary hearing officer or military judge, and inserted at the appropriate place in the record of trial. Copies of the report of preliminary hearing or record of trial shall contain appropriate annotations that materials were sealed by order of the preliminary hearing officer or military judge and have been inserted in the report of preliminary hearing or record of trial. This rule shall be implemented in a manner consistent with Executive Order 13526, concerning classified national security information.

Discussion

Upon request or otherwise for good cause, a military judge may seal matters at his or her discretion. The terms "examination" and "disclosure" are defined in R.C.M. 1113(b)(4) and (5).

(b) *Examination and disclosure of sealed materials.* Except as provided in this rule, sealed materials may not be examined or disclosed.

Discussion

The terms of the sealing order may provide parameters for examination by or disclosure to those persons or entities whose interests are being protected.

---

(1) *Prior to referral.* Prior to referral of charges, the following individuals may examine and disclose sealed materials only if necessary for proper fulfillment of their responsibilities under the UCMJ, this Manual, governing directives, instructions, regulations, applicable rules for practice and procedure, or rules of professional conduct: the judge advocate advising the convening authority who directed the Article 32 preliminary hearing; the convening authority who directed the Article 32 preliminary hearing; the staff judge advocate to the general court-martial convening authority; a military judge detailed to an Article 30a proceeding; the general court-martial convening authority; and special trial counsel for the purposes of making a determination on referral.

(2) *Referral through certification.* After referral of charges and prior to certification of the record under R.C.M. 1112(c), sealed materials may not be examined or disclosed in the absence of an order from the military judge based upon good cause.

Discussion

A convening authority who has granted clemency based upon review of sealed materials in the record of trial is not permitted to disclose the contents of the sealed materials when providing a written explanation of the reason for such action, as directed under R.C.M. 1109 or 1110.

---

(3) *Reviewing and appellate authorities; appellate counsel.*

(A) *Examination by reviewing and appellate authorities.* Reviewing and appellate authorities may examine sealed matters when those authorities determine that examination is reasonably necessary to a proper fulfillment of their responsibilities under the UCMJ, this Manual, governing directives, instructions, regulations, applicable rules for practice and procedure, or rules of professional conduct.

(B) *Examination by appellate counsel.* Appellate counsel may examine sealed materials subject to the following procedures.

(i) *Sealed materials released to trial counsel or defense counsel.* Materials presented or reviewed at trial and sealed, as well as materials reviewed in camera, released to trial counsel or defense counsel, and sealed, may be examined by appellate counsel upon a colorable showing to the reviewing or appellate authority that examination is reasonably necessary to a proper fulfillment of the appellate counsel's responsibilities under the UCMJ, this Manual, governing directives, instructions, regulations, applicable rules for practice and procedure, or rules of professional conduct.

(ii) *Sealed materials reviewed in camera but not released to trial counsel or defense counsel.* Materials reviewed in camera by a military judge, not released to trial counsel or defense counsel, and sealed may be examined by reviewing or appellate authorities. After examination of said materials, the reviewing or appellate authority may permit examination by appellate counsel for good cause.

Discussion

For disclosure procedures, *see* R.C.M. 1113(b)(3)(C).

(C) *Disclosure.* Appellate counsel shall not disclose sealed materials in the absence of:

(i) prior authorization of the Judge Advocate General in the case of review under R.C.M. 1201 or 1210; or

(ii) prior authorization of the appellate court before which a case is pending review under R.C.M. 1203 or 1204; or

(iii) prior authorization of the Judge Advocate General for a case eligible for review under R.C.M. 1203 or 1204.

Discussion

In general, the Judge Advocate General or an appellate court should authorize disclosure of sealed material when such disclosure is necessary for review. Authorizations may place conditions on disclosure.

(D) For purposes of this rule, reviewing and appellate authorities are limited to:

(i) Judge advocates reviewing records pursuant to R.C.M. 1307;

(ii) Officers and attorneys in the office of the Judge Advocate General reviewing records pursuant to R.C.M. 1201 and 1210;

(iii) Officers and attorneys designated by the Judge Advocate General;

(iv) Appellate judges of the Courts of Criminal Appeals and their professional staffs;

(v) The judges of the United States Court of Appeals for the Armed Forces and their professional staffs;

(vi) The Justices of the United States Supreme Court and their professional staffs; and

(vii) Any other court of competent jurisdiction.

(4) *Examination of sealed materials.* For purposes of this rule, "examination" includes reading, inspecting, and viewing.

(5) *Disclosure of sealed materials.* For purposes of this rule, "disclosure" includes photocopying, photographing, disseminating, releasing, manipulating, or communicating the contents of sealed materials in any way.

(6) Notwithstanding any other provision of this rule, in those cases in which review is sought or pending before the United States Supreme Court, authorization to disclose sealed materials or information shall be obtained under that Court's rules of practice and procedure.

Rule 1114. Transcription of proceedings

(a) *Transcription of complete record.* A certified verbatim transcript of the record of trial shall be prepared—

(1) When the judgment entered into the record includes a sentence of death, dismissal of a commissioned officer, cadet, or midshipman, a dishonorable or bad-conduct discharge, or confinement for more than six months; or

(2) As otherwise required by court rule, court order, or under regulations prescribed by the Secretary concerned.

Discussion

See R.C.M. 1116(b) regarding transcription of the record when a case is forwarded to appellate defense counsel.

(b) *Transcription of portions of the record.* A certified verbatim transcript of relevant portions of the record of trial shall be prepared—

(1) Upon application of a party as approved by the military judge, any court, or the Judge Advocate General; or

(2) As otherwise required under regulations prescribed by the Secretary concerned.

Discussion

See R.C.M. 1106 and 1106A regarding providing the record to the accused, a victim, or their counsel. When a certified transcript is prepared, the accused, counsel, or victim may request or be provided a copy to the same extent and under the same criteria as the applicable portion of the record.

(c) *Cost.* Any certified transcript required by this rule shall be prepared without cost to the accused.

(d) *Inclusion in the record of trial.* If a certified transcript is made under this rule, it shall be attached to the record of trial.

(e) *Authority.* The Secretary concerned shall prescribe by regulation the procedure for preparing and certifying a transcript under this rule.

Rule 1115. Waiver or withdrawal of appellate review

(a) *In general.* After any general court-martial, except one in which the judgment entered into the record includes a sentence of death, and after any special court-martial in which the judgment entered into the record includes a finding of guilt, the accused may waive or withdraw the right to appellate review by a Court of Criminal Appeals. The accused may sign a waiver of the right to appeal at any time after entry of judgment and may withdraw an appeal at any time before such review is completed.

Discussion

All general court-martial cases in which the judgment entered into the record includes a sentence of death and all other general and special courts-martial in which an accused does not affirmatively waive or withdraw an appeal in accordance with this rule and the judgment entered into the record includes a sentence of dismissal of a commissioned officer, cadet, or midshipman; dishonorable discharge or bad-conduct discharge; or confinement for two years or more receive automatic appellate review by a Court of Criminal Appeals. *See* Article 66(b)(3). All general and special courts-martial not subject to automatic appellate review are eligible for direct appellate review by a Court of Criminal Appeals upon the appeal of the accused if the judgment entered into the record includes a finding of guilt. *See* Article 66(b)(1). General and special courts-martial in which appellate review is waived or withdrawn or an appeal is not filed under Article 66(b)(1) are reviewed by an attorney under R.C.M. 1201. After the attorney's review under R.C.M. 1201, such cases may also be submitted to the Judge Advocate General by application of the accused for post-final review. *See* R.C.M. 1201(h).

(b) *Right to counsel.*

(1) *In general.* The accused shall have the right to consult with qualified counsel before submitting a waiver or withdrawal of appellate review.

(2) *Waiver.*

(A) *Counsel who represented the accused at the court-martial.* The accused shall have the right to consult with any civilian, individual military, or detailed counsel who represented the accused at the court-martial concerning whether to waive appellate review unless such counsel has been excused under R.C.M. 505(d)(2)(B).

(B) *Associate counsel.* If counsel who represented the accused at the court-martial has not been excused but is not immediately available to consult with the accused because of physical separation or other reasons, associate defense counsel shall be detailed to the accused upon request by the accused. Such counsel shall communicate with the counsel who represented the accused at the court-martial, and shall advise the accused concerning whether to waive appellate review.

(C) *Substitute counsel.* If counsel who represented the accused at the court-martial has been excused under R.C.M. 505(d)(2)(B), substitute defense counsel shall be detailed to advise the accused concerning waiver of appellate rights.

(3) *Withdrawal.*

(A) *Appellate defense counsel.* If the accused is represented by appellate defense counsel, the accused shall have the right to consult with such counsel concerning whether to withdraw an appeal.

(B) *Associate defense counsel.* If the accused is represented by appellate defense counsel, and such counsel is not immediately available to consult with the accused because of physical separation or other reasons, associate defense counsel shall be detailed to the accused, upon request by the accused. Such counsel shall communicate with appellate defense counsel and shall advise the accused whether to withdraw an appeal.

(C) *No counsel.* If appellate defense counsel has not been assigned to the accused, defense counsel shall be detailed for the accused. Such counsel shall advise the accused concerning whether to withdraw an appeal.

(4) *Civilian counsel.* Whether or not the accused was represented by civilian counsel at the court-martial, the accused may consult with civilian counsel, at no expense to the United States, concerning whether to waive or withdraw appellate review.

(5) *Record of trial.* Any defense counsel with whom the accused consults under this rule shall be given reasonable opportunity to examine the record of trial and any attachments.

Discussion

See R.C.M. 1112(f) for required attachments to the record of trial.

---

(6) *Right to consult.* The right to consult with counsel, as used in this rule, does not require communication in the presence of one another.

(c) *Compulsion, coercion, and inducement prohibited.* No person may compel, coerce, or induce an accused by force, promises of clemency, or otherwise to waive or withdraw appellate review.

(d) *Form of waiver or withdrawal.* A waiver or withdrawal of appellate review shall:

(1) Be written;

(2) State that the accused and defense counsel have discussed the accused's rights to appellate review and the effect of waiver or withdrawal of appellate review and that the accused understands these matters;

(3) State that the waiver or withdrawal is submitted voluntarily; and

(4) Be signed by the accused and by defense counsel.

(e) *To whom submitted.*

(1) *Waiver.* A waiver of appellate review shall be filed with the convening authority or the Judge Advocate General. The waiver shall be attached to the record of trial.

(2) *Withdrawal.* A withdrawal of appellate review may be filed with the authority exercising general court-martial jurisdiction over the accused, who shall promptly forward it to the Judge Advocate General, or directly with the Judge Advocate General. The withdrawal shall be attached to the record of trial.

(f) *Effect of waiver or withdrawal; substantial compliance required.*

(1) *In general.* A valid waiver or withdrawal of appellate review under this rule shall bar review by the Court of Criminal Appeals. Once submitted, a waiver or withdrawal in compliance with this rule may not be revoked.

(2) *Waiver.* If the accused files a waiver of appellate review in accordance with this rule, the record of trial and attachments shall be forwarded for review by a judge advocate under R.C.M. 1201.

(3) *Withdrawal.* Action on a withdrawal of appellate review shall be carried out in accordance with procedures established by the Judge Advocate General, or if the case is pending before a Court of Criminal Appeals, in accordance with the rules of such court. If the appeal is withdrawn, the record of trial and attachments shall be forwarded for review in accordance with R.C.M. 1201.

(4) *Substantial compliance required.* A purported waiver or withdrawal of an appeal which does not substantially comply with this rule shall have no effect.

Rule 1116. Transmittal of records of trial for general and special courts-martial

(a) *Cases forwarded to the Judge Advocate General.* In all general and special courts-martial in which the judgment includes a finding of guilty, the certified record of trial and attachments required under R.C.M. 1112(f) shall be sent directly to the Judge Advocate General concerned. Forwarding an electronic copy of the certified record of trial and attachments satisfies the requirements under this rule. The records of trial in general and special courts-martial without a finding of guilty shall be disposed of in accordance with the regulations of the Secretary concerned.

(b) *Transmittal of records for cases eligible for appellate review by a Court of Criminal Appeals.*

(1) *Automatic review.* Except when the accused has waived or withdrawn the right to appellate review, if the court-martial judgment includes a sentence of death, dismissal of a commissioned officer, cadet, or midshipman, a dishonorable or bad-conduct discharge, or confinement for 2 years or more, the Judge Advocate General shall forward the certified record of trial and attachments required under R.C.M. 1112(f) to the Court of Criminal Appeals for automatic review under Article 66(b)(3).

Discussion

See R.C.M. 1203(b).

(A) A copy of the record of trial and attachments shall be forwarded to appellate defense counsel in accordance with rules prescribed by the Secretary concerned. If the record forwarded does not include a written transcript of the proceedings, the Government shall provide appellate defense counsel with appropriate equipment for playback of the recording and with either—

(i) the means to transform the recording into a text format through voice recognition software or similar means; or

(ii) a transcription of the record in either printed or digital format.

(B) Upon written request of the accused, a copy of the record and attachments shall be forwarded to a civilian counsel provided by the accused.

(C) Copies of the record provided under subparagraph (b)(1)(A) of this rule shall not include sealed exhibits, recordings or transcriptions of closed sessions, or classified matters.

Discussion

An accused may not waive or withdraw the right to appellate review before the Court of Criminal Appeals of any general court-martial in which the judgment includes a sentence of death. *See* Article 61, R.C.M. 1115.

See R.C.M. 1114 regarding the procedure for preparing and obtaining certified transcripts of all or a portion of the record. If a transcription is provided in digital format, the Government shall ensure that the recipient has an appropriate means of reading the transcription.

See R.C.M. 1112 and 1113 regarding access to classified and sealed matters. See R.C.M. 1201(a)(2) for review by an attorney of those cases eligible for appellate review by the Court of Criminal Appeals, but where the accused waives the right to appeal, withdraws an appeal, or fails to file a timely appeal. See R.C.M. 1202 concerning representation of the accused by appellate counsel before the appellate courts. See R.C.M. 1203 concerning review by the Court of Criminal Appeals and the powers and responsibilities of the Judge Advocate General after such review.

---

(2) *Cases eligible for direct appeal by the accused.* Except when the accused has waived or withdrawn the right to appeal under Article 61, if a general and special court-martial is not subject to automatic review under Article 66(b)(3) but is eligible for review under Article 66(b)(1), the Judge Advocate General shall provide notice to the accused of the right to file an appeal either by depositing the notice in the United States mails for delivery by first class certified mail to the accused at an address provided by the accused, or, if the accused has not provided an address, to the latest address listed for the accused in the official service record of the accused. Proof of service shall be attached to the record of trial.

Discussion

See R.C.M. 1115 for rules regarding the waiver or withdrawal of appellate review. See R.C.M. 1203 for rules concerning appellate review by a Court of Criminal Appeals.

(A) The Judge Advocate General shall forward a copy of the record of trial and attachments required under R.C.M. 1112(f) to an appellate defense counsel who shall be detailed to review the case, and upon request of the accused, to represent the accused before the Court of Criminal Appeals.

(B) The record of trial and attachments required under R.C.M. 1112(f) shall be forwarded in accordance with the procedures set forth in subparagraphs (b)(1)(A)–(C) of this rule.

(c) *General and special courts-martial not reviewed by a Court of Criminal Appeals.* General and special courts-martial with a finding of guilty not reviewed by a Court of Criminal Appeals under Article 66(b)(1) or (3) shall be reviewed under Article 65(d)(2).

Discussion

See R.C.M. 1201(a)(1); and R.C.M. 1203(b) and (c).

(d) *Review when appellate review by a Court of Criminal Appeals is waived, withdrawn, or not filed.* In a general or special court-martial in which the accused waives the right to appellate review or withdraws an appeal under Article 61, or fails to file a timely appeal in a case eligible for review by the Court of Criminal Appeals under Article 66(b)(1), the case shall be reviewed under Article 65(d)(3).

Discussion

See R.C.M. 1115, R.C.M. 1201(a)(2), and R.C.M. 1203(c).

Rule 1117. Appeal of sentence by the United States

(a) *In general.* With the approval of the Judge Advocate General concerned, the Government may appeal a sentence announced under R.C.M. 1007 to the Court of Criminal Appeals on the grounds that—

(1) The sentence violates the law;

(2) The sentence is a result of an incorrect application of sentencing parameters or criteria established under Article 56(c); or

(3) The sentence is plainly unreasonable.

(b) *Timing.*

(1) An appeal under this rule must be filed within 60 days after the date on which the judgment of the court-martial is entered into the record under R.C.M. 1111.

(2) Any request for approval must be submitted in sufficient time to obtain and consider submissions under R.C.M. 1117(c)(5).

(c) *Approval process.*

(1) A request from the Government to the Judge Advocate General for approval of an appeal under this rule shall include a statement of reasons in support of an appeal under R.C.M. 1117(a)(1), (a)(2), or (a)(3), as applicable, based upon the information contained in the record before the sentencing authority at the time the sentence was announced under R.C.M. 1007.

(2) A statement of reasons in support of an appeal under R.C.M. 1117(a)(1) shall identify the specific provisions of law at issue and the facts in the record demonstrating a violation of the law in the announced sentence under R.C.M. 1007.

(3) A statement of reasons in support of an appeal under R.C.M. 1117(a)(2) shall identify parameters or criteria at issue and the facts supporting how parameters or criteria were applied incorrectly.

(4) A statement of reasons in support of an appeal under R.C.M. 1117(a)(3) shall identify the facts in the record that demonstrate by clear and convincing evidence that the sentence announced under R.C.M. 1007 was plainly unreasonable.

(5) Prior to acting on a request from the Government, the Judge Advocate General shall transmit the request to the military judge who presided over the presentencing proceeding for purposes of providing the military judge, the parties, and any person who, at the time of sentencing, was a crime victim as defined by R.C.M. 1001(c)(2)(A), with an opportunity to make a submission addressing the statement of reasons in the Government's request.

(A) The military judge shall establish the time for the parties and crime victims to provide such a submission to the military judge and for the military judge to forward all submissions to the Judge Advocate General. The military judge shall ensure that the parties have not less than 7 days to prepare, review, and transmit such submissions.

(B) Submissions under this paragraph (R.C.M. 1117(c)(5)) shall not include facts beyond the record established at the time the sentence was announced under R.C.M. 1007.

(6) The decision of the Judge Advocate General as to whether to approve a request shall be based on the information developed under this rule.

(7) If an appeal is approved by the Judge Advocate General and submitted to the Court of Criminal Appeals under this rule, the following shall be included with the appeal: the statement of approval, the Government's request and statement of reasons under R.C.M. 1117(c), and any submissions under R.C.M. 1117(c)(5).

(d) *Contents of the record of trial.* Unless the record has been forwarded to the Court of Criminal Appeals for review under R.C.M. 1116(b), the record of trial for an appeal under this rule shall consist of—

(1) Any portion of the record in the case that is designated as pertinent by either of the parties;

(2) The information submitted during the presentencing proceeding; and

(3) Any information required by rule or order of the Court of Criminal Appeals.

Discussion

For Appellant's right to counsel in cases reviewed by a Court of Criminal Appeals, see R.C.M. 1202. For action on cases following review by a Court of Criminal Appeals, see R.C.M. 1203(e).

CHAPTER XII. APPEALS AND REVIEW

Rule 1201. Review by the Judge Advocate General

(a) *Review of certain general and special courts-martial.* Except as provided in subsection (b), an attorney designated by the Judge Advocate General shall review:

(1) Each general and special court-martial case that is not eligible for appellate review by a Court of Criminal Appeals under Article 66(b)(1) or (3); and

Discussion

See R.C.M. 1203(b) and (c).

---

(2) Each general or special court-martial eligible for appellate review by a Court of Criminal Appeals in which the Court of Criminal Appeals does not review the case because:

(A) In a case under Article 66(b)(3), other than one in which the sentence includes death, the accused withdraws direct appeal or waives the right to appellate review.

Discussion

See R.C.M. 1203(b).

(B) In a case under Article 66(b)(1), the accused does not file a timely appeal, or files a timely appeal and then withdraws it.

Discussion

See R.C.M. 1307 for judge advocate review of summary courts-martial.

(b) *Exception.* If the accused was found not guilty or not guilty only by reason of lack of mental responsibility of all offenses, or if the convening authority set aside all findings of guilty, no review under this rule is required.

(c) *By whom.*

(1) A review conducted under this rule may be conducted by an attorney within the Office of the Judge Advocate General or another attorney designated by the Judge Advocate General under regulations prescribed by the Secretary concerned.

(2) No person may review a case under this rule if that person has acted in the same case as an accuser, preliminary hearing officer, member of the court-martial, military judge, or counsel, or has otherwise acted on behalf of the prosecution or defense.

(d) *Form and content for review of cases not eligible for appellate review at the Court of Criminal Appeals.* The review referred to in paragraph (a)(1) shall include a written conclusion as to each of the following:

(1) Whether the court had jurisdiction over the accused and the offense;

(2) Whether each charge and specification stated an offense;

(3) Whether the sentence was within the limits prescribed as a matter of law; and

(4) When applicable, a response to each allegation of error made in writing by the accused.

(e) *Form and content for review of cases in which the accused has waived or withdrawn appellate review or failed to file an appeal.* The review referred to in paragraph (a)(2) shall include a written conclusion as to each of the following:

(1) Whether the court had jurisdiction over the accused and the offense;

(2) Whether each charge and specification stated an offense; and

(3) Whether the sentence was within the limits prescribed as a matter of law.

(f) *Remedies.*

(1) If the attorney conducting the review under subsection (a) believes corrective action is required, the attorney shall forward the matter to the Judge Advocate General, who may modify or set aside the findings or sentence, in whole or in part.

(2) In setting aside the findings or sentence, the Judge Advocate General may order a rehearing, except that a rehearing may not be ordered where the evidence was legally insufficient at the trial to support the findings.

(3) If the Judge Advocate General sets aside findings and sentence and does not order a rehearing, the Judge Advocate General shall dismiss the charges.

(4) If the Judge Advocate General sets aside findings

and orders a rehearing and the convening authority determines that a rehearing would be impractical, the convening authority shall dismiss the charges.

Discussion

See R.C.M. 1111 for modification of the judgment to reflect any action by the Judge Advocate General or convening authority under this rule.

(g) *Notification.* After a case is reviewed under subsection (a), the accused shall be notified of the results of the review and any action taken by the Judge Advocate General or convening authority by means of depositing a copy of the review and any modified judgment in the United States mails for delivery by first-class certified mail to the accused at an address provided by the accused or, if no such address has been provided by the accused, at the latest address listed for the accused in the accused's official service record. Proof of service shall be attached to the record of trial.

(h) *Application for relief to the Judge Advocate General after final review.*

(1) *In general.* Notwithstanding R.C.M. 1209, the Judge Advocate General may, upon application of the accused or a person with authority to act for the accused or receipt of the record pursuant to R.C.M. 1307(g):

(A) With respect to a summary court-martial previously reviewed under R.C.M. 1307, modify or set aside, in whole or in part, the findings and sentence; or

(B) With respect to a general or special court-martial previously reviewed under paragraph (a)(1) or (2), order such a court-martial to be reviewed under R.C.M. 1203 by the Court of Criminal Appeals.

(2) *Timing.* To qualify for consideration under this subsection, an accused must submit an application not later than one year after—

(A) In the case of a summary court-martial, the date of completion of review under R.C.M. 1307; or

(B) In the case of a general or special court-martial, the end of the 90-day period beginning on the date the accused is provided notice of appellate rights under R.C.M. 1116(b)(2).

(3) *Extension.* The Judge Advocate General may, for good cause shown, extend the period for submission of an application under paragraph (h)(2) for a time period not to exceed three additional years. The Judge Advocate General may not consider an application submitted more than three years after the applicable expiration date specified in paragraph (h)(2).

(4) *Scope.*

(A) In a case previously reviewed under R.C.M. 1307 or paragraph (a)(1), the Judge Advocate General may act on the grounds of newly discovered evidence, fraud on the court, lack of jurisdiction over the accused or the offense, error prejudicial to the substantial rights of the accused, or the appropriateness of the sentence.

(B) In a case previously reviewed under paragraph (a)(2), the Judge Advocate General's review is limited to the issue of whether the waiver, withdrawal, or failure to file an appeal was invalid under the law.

Discussion

If the Judge Advocate General determines that the waiver or withdrawal of an appeal was invalid, the Judge Advocate General may order any corrective action, including forwarding the case to the Court of Criminal Appeals for appropriate appellate review.

See also R.C.M. 1210 concerning a petition for a new trial in any case, including a case where the accused waived or withdrew from appellate review, or failed to file an appeal.

Review of a case by a Judge Advocate General under this subsection is not part of appellate review within the meaning of Article 76 or R.C.M. 1209.

Review of a finding of not guilty only by reason of lack of mental responsibility under this rule may not extend to the determination of lack of mental responsibility. Thus, modification of a finding of not guilty only by reason of lack of mental responsibility under this rule is limited to changing the finding to not guilty or not guilty only by reason of lack of mental responsibility of a lesser included offense.

---

(5) *Procedure.* Each Judge Advocate General shall provide procedures for considering all cases properly submitted under this rule and may prescribe the manner by which an application for relief under this rule may be made and, if submitted by a person other than the accused, may require that the applicant show authority to act on behalf of the accused.

(i) *Remission and suspension.* The Judge Advocate General may, when so authorized by the Secretary concerned under Article 74, at any time remit or suspend the unexecuted part of any sentence, other than a sentence approved by the President.

(j) *Mandatory review of summary courts-martial forwarded under R.C.M. 1307.* The Judge Advocate General shall review summary courts-martial if the record of trial and the action thereon are forwarded under R.C.M. 1307(g). On such review, the Judge

Advocate General may vacate or modify, in whole or in part, the findings or sentence, or both, of the court-martial on the ground of newly discovered evidence, fraud on the court-martial, lack of jurisdiction over the accused or the offense, error prejudicial to the substantial rights of the accused, or the appropriateness of the sentence.

(k) *Cases referred or submitted to the Court of Criminal Appeals.*

(1) *In general.* Action taken by the Judge Advocate General under subsections (h) or (j) may be reviewed by the Court of Criminal Appeals under Article 69(d) as follows:

(A) The Judge Advocate General may forward a case to the Court of Criminal Appeals. If the case is forwarded to a Court of Criminal Appeals, the accused shall be informed and shall have the rights to appellate defense counsel afforded under R.C.M. 1202(b)(2).

(B) The accused may submit an application for review to the Court of Criminal Appeals. The Court of Criminal Appeals may grant such an application only if the application demonstrates a substantial basis for concluding that the Judge Advocate General's action under this rule constituted prejudicial error, and the application is filed not later than the earlier of—

(i) 60 days after the date on which the accused is notified of the decision of the Judge Advocate General; or

(ii) 60 days after the date on which a copy of the decision of the Judge Advocate General is deposited in the United States mails for delivery by first-class certified mail to the accused at an address provided by the accused or, if no such address has been provided by the accused, at the latest address listed for the accused in the accused's official service record. Proof of service shall be attached to the record of trial.

Discussion

See R.C.M. 1203.

---

(2) The submission of an application for review under subparagraph (k)(1)(B) does not constitute a proceeding before the Court of Criminal Appeals for purposes of representation by appellate defense counsel under Article 70(c)(1).

(3) In any case reviewed by a Court of Criminal Appeals under this subsection, the Court may take action only with respect to matters of law.

Rule 1202. Appellate counsel

(a) *In general.* The Judge Advocate General concerned shall detail one or more commissioned officers as appellate Government counsel and one or more commissioned officers as appellate defense counsel who are qualified under Article 27(b)(1).

(b) *Duties.*

(1) *Appellate Government counsel.* Appellate Government counsel shall represent the United States before the Court of Criminal Appeals or the United States Court of Appeals for the Armed Forces when directed to do so by the Judge Advocate General concerned. Appellate Government counsel may represent the United States before the United States Supreme Court when requested to do so by the Attorney General.

(2) *Appellate defense counsel.*

(A) In every general and special court-martial that includes a finding of guilty, an appellate defense counsel shall be detailed to review the case, unless the accused has waived the right to appeal under Article 61 or submits a written statement declining representation. Upon request, the detailed appellate defense counsel shall represent the accused in accordance with subparagraph (B).

Discussion

See R.C.M. 1203(c) and R.C.M. 1115.

(B) Appellate defense counsel shall represent the accused before the Court of Criminal Appeals, the Court of Appeals for the Armed Forces, or the Supreme Court when the accused is a party in the case before such court and:

(i) The accused requests to be represented by appellate defense counsel;

Discussion

See Article 65(b) and Article 61.

(ii) The United States is represented by counsel; or

(iii) The Judge Advocate General has sent the case to the United States Court of Appeals for the Armed Forces. Appellate defense counsel is authorized to communicate directly with the accused. The accused is a party in the case when named as a party in pleadings before the court or, even if not so named, when the military judge is named as respondent in a petition by the Government for extraordinary relief from a ruling in favor of the accused at trial.

Discussion

For a discussion of the accused's right to detailed appellate defense counsel in any case eligible for review at the Court of Criminal Appeals, see R.C.M. 1202. See R.C.M. 1204(b)(1) concerning detailing counsel with respect to the right to appeal to the Court of Appeals for the Armed Forces for review. For a discussion of the duties of the trial defense counsel concerning post-trial and appellate matters, see R.C.M. 502(d)(5) Discussion (E). Appellate defense counsel may communicate with trial defense counsel concerning the case. *See also* Mil. R. Evid. 502 (privileges).

If all or part of the findings and sentence are affirmed by the Court of Criminal Appeals, appellate defense counsel should advise the accused whether the accused should petition for further review in the United States Court of Appeals for the Armed Forces and concerning which issues should be raised.

The accused may be represented by civilian counsel before the Court of Criminal Appeals, the Court of Appeals for the Armed Forces, and the Supreme Court. Civilian counsel may represent the accused before these courts in addition to or instead of military counsel.

If, after any decision of the Court of Appeals for the Armed Forces, the accused may apply for a writ of certiorari (*see* R.C.M. 1205), appellate defense counsel should advise the accused whether to apply for review by the Supreme Court and which issues might be raised. If authorized to do so by the accused, appellate defense counsel may prepare and file a petition for a writ of certiorari on behalf of the accused.

The accused has no right to select appellate defense counsel. Under some circumstances, however, the accused may be entitled to request that the detailed appellate defense counsel be replaced by another appellate defense counsel.

(c) *Counsel in capital cases.* To the greatest extent practicable, in any case in which death is adjudged, at least one appellate defense counsel shall, as determined by the Judge Advocate General, be learned in the law applicable to capital cases. Such counsel may, if necessary, be a civilian, and, if so, may be compensated in accordance with regulations prescribed by the Secretary of Defense or the Secretary of Homeland Security, as applicable.

Discussion

See R.C.M. 502(d)(2)(C) concerning the qualifications for counsel learned in the law applicable to capital cases.

Rule 1203. Review by a Court of Criminal Appeals

(a) *In general.* Each Judge Advocate General shall establish a Court of Criminal Appeals composed of appellate military judges who shall serve for a tour of not less than three years, subject to such provision for reassignment as may be prescribed in regulations issued by the Secretary concerned.

Discussion

See Article 66 concerning the composition of the Courts of Criminal Appeals, the qualifications of appellate military judges, the grounds for their ineligibility, and restrictions upon the official relationship of the members of the court to other members. Uniform rules of court for the Courts of Criminal Appeals are prescribed by the Judge Advocates General.

(b) *Cases reviewed by a Court of Criminal Appeals—Automatic Review.* A Court of Criminal Appeals shall review cases forwarded to it by the Judge Advocate General under Article 65(b)(1).

Discussion

See R.C.M. 1116(b)(1).

Except for when an accused waives or withdraws the right to appellate review, a Court of Criminal Appeals automatically reviews cases in which the judgment entered into the record includes a sentence of death; dismissal of a commissioned officer, cadet, or midshipman; dishonorable discharge or bad-conduct discharge; or confinement for 2 years or more. *See* Article 65(b)(1), Article 66(b)(3), R.C.M. 1116(b)(1).

An accused may not waive the right to appellate review or withdraw an appeal before the Court of Criminal Appeals in any general court-martial in which the judgment includes a sentence of death. *See* R.C.M. 1115.

(c) *Cases eligible for review by a Court of Criminal Appeals—Appeal by the accused.* A Court of Criminal Appeals shall review a timely appeal from the judgment of the court-martial in accordance with the standards set forth in Article 66(b)(1) and the rules prescribed under Article 66(h).

Discussion

The Court of Criminal Appeals may specify additional issues for briefing, argument, and decision, and may review eligible cases for plain error. See R.C.M. 1115 for waiver of appellate review or withdrawal of an appeal. In those cases in which an accused chooses not to file an appeal, the case will be reviewed by an attorney under R.C.M. 1201(a)(2).

If a Court of Criminal Appeals sets aside any finding of guilty or the sentence, it may, except as to findings set aside for lack of sufficient evidence in the record to support the findings, authorize an appropriate type of rehearing or reassess the sentence as appropriate. See R.C.M. 810 concerning rehearings. If the Court of Criminal Appeals sets aside all the findings and the sentence and does not authorize a rehearing, it must order the charges dismissed. *See* Article 59(a) and Article 66.

A Court of Criminal Appeals may on petition for extraordinary relief issue all writs necessary or appropriate in aid of its jurisdiction and agreeable to the usages and principles of law. Any party may petition a Court of Criminal Appeals for extraordinary relief.

See R.C.M. 908 concerning procedures for interlocutory appeals by the Government. See R.C.M. 1117 concerning Government appeals of certain sentences.

(d) *Timeliness*. In order for an appeal under subsection (c) to be timely, it must be filed in accordance with Article 66(c) and the rules prescribed under Article 66(h).

(e) *Action on cases reviewed by a Court of Criminal Appeals*.

(1) *Forwarding by the Judge Advocate General to the Court of Appeals for the Armed Forces*. The Judge Advocate General may forward the decision of the Court of Criminal Appeals to the Court of Appeals for the Armed Forces for review with respect to any matter of law. In such a case, the Judge Advocate General shall cause a copy of the decision of the Court of Criminal Appeals and the order forwarding the case to be served on the accused and on appellate defense counsel. While a review of a forwarded case is pending, the Secretary concerned may defer further service of a sentence to confinement that has been ordered executed in such a case.

Discussion

Prior to forwarding a case to the Court of Appeals for the Armed Forces for review, the Judge Advocate General concerned is required to provide appropriate notification to the other Judge Advocates General and the Staff Judge Advocate to the Commandant of the Marine Corps. *See* Article 67(a)(2) and R.C.M. 1204(a)(2).

When a decision of the Court of Criminal Appeals has the effect of setting aside confinement the appellant is serving, and the Judge Advocate General has decided to forward the decision of the Court of Criminal Appeals to the Court of Appeals for the Armed Forces for review under this rule, a new R.C.M. 305 review may be required if continued confinement is sought.

---

(2) *Action when findings are set aside*. In a case reviewed by the Court of Criminal Appeals under this rule in which it has set aside the findings and which is not forwarded to the Court of Appeals for the Armed Forces under R.C.M. 1203(e)(1), the Judge Advocate General shall instruct an appropriate authority to take action in accordance with the decision of the Court of Criminal Appeals. If the Court of Criminal Appeals has authorized a rehearing on findings, the record shall be sent to an appropriate referral authority.

(A) If the Court has authorized a rehearing, but the convening authority to whom the record is transmitted finds a rehearing impracticable, the convening authority shall dismiss the charges.

(B) If the Court has authorized a rehearing, but the special trial counsel to whom the record is transmitted finds a rehearing impracticable, special trial counsel shall dismiss the charges.

Discussion

If charges are dismissed, see R.C.M. 1208 concerning restoration of rights, privileges, and property. See R.C.M. 1111 concerning the entry of judgment.

---

(3) *Action when sentence is set aside*. In a case reviewed by the Court of Criminal Appeals under this rule in which it has set aside the sentence and which is not forwarded to the Court of Appeals for the Armed Forces under R.C.M. 1203(e)(1), the Judge Advocate General shall instruct an appropriate authority to modify the judgment in accordance with the decision of the Court of Criminal Appeals. If the Court of Criminal Appeals has authorized a rehearing on sentence, the record shall be sent to an appropriate referral authority.

(A) If the convening authority finds a rehearing impracticable, the applicable convening authority shall order either that a sentence of no punishment be imposed or that the applicable charges be dismissed.

(B) If special trial counsel finds a rehearing impracticable, special trial counsel may dismiss the applicable charges. If special trial counsel makes a determination not to dismiss the applicable charges, the convening authority shall order that a sentence of no punishment be imposed.

(4) *Action when sentence is affirmed in whole or part*.

(A) *Sentence including death*. If the Court of Criminal Appeals affirms any sentence which includes death, the Judge Advocate General shall transmit the record of trial and the decision of the Court of Criminal Appeals directly to the Court of Appeals for the Armed Forces when any period for reconsideration provided by the rules of the Courts of Criminal Appeals has expired.

(B) *Other cases.* If the Court of Criminal Appeals affirms any sentence other than one which includes death, the Judge Advocate General shall cause a copy of the decision of the Court of Criminal Appeals to be served on the accused in accordance with R.C.M. 1203(f).

Discussion

If charges are dismissed, see R.C.M. 1208 concerning restoration of rights, privileges, and property. See R.C.M. 1111 concerning the entry of judgment.

---

(5) *Remission or suspension.* If the Judge Advocate General believes that a sentence as affirmed by the Court of Criminal Appeals, other than one which includes death, should be remitted or suspended in whole or part, the Judge Advocate General may, before taking action under R.C.M. 1203(e)(1) or (4), transmit the record of trial and the decision of the Court of Criminal Appeals to the Secretary concerned with a recommendation for action under Article 74 or may take such action as may be authorized by the Secretary concerned under Article 74(a).

(6) *Action when accused lacks mental capacity.* In a review conducted under R.C.M. 1203(b) or (c), the Court of Criminal Appeals may not affirm the proceedings while the accused lacks mental capacity to understand and to conduct or cooperate intelligently in the appellate proceedings. In the absence of substantial evidence to the contrary, the accused is presumed to have the capacity to understand and to conduct or cooperate intelligently in the appellate proceedings. If a substantial question is raised as to the requisite mental capacity of the accused, the Court of Criminal Appeals may direct an examination of the accused in accordance with R.C.M. 706, but the examination may be limited to determining the accused's present capacity to understand and cooperate in the appellate proceedings. The Court may further order a remand under R.C.M. 810(f) as may be necessary. If the record is thereafter returned to the Court of Criminal Appeals, the Court of Criminal Appeals may affirm part or all of the findings or sentence unless it is established, by a preponderance of the evidence—including matters outside the record of trial—that the accused does not have the requisite mental capacity. If the accused does not have the requisite mental capacity, the Court of Criminal Appeals shall stay the proceedings until the accused regains appropriate capacity or take other appropriate action. Nothing in this subsection shall prohibit the Court of Criminal Appeals from making a determination in favor of the accused which will result in the setting aside of a conviction.

(f) *Notification to accused.*

(1) *Notification of decision.* The accused shall be notified of the decision of the Court of Criminal Appeals in accordance with regulations prescribed by the Secretary concerned.

Discussion

The accused may be notified personally, or a copy of the decision may be sent, after service on appellate counsel of record, if any, by first class certified mail to the accused at an address provided by the accused or, if no such address has been provided by the accused, at the latest address listed for the accused in the accused's official service record.

If the Judge Advocate General has forwarded the case to the Court of Appeals for the Armed Forces, the accused should be so notified.

---

(2) *Notification of right to petition the Court of Appeals for the Armed Forces for review.* If the accused has the right to petition the Court of Appeals for the Armed Forces for review, the accused shall be provided with a copy of the decision of the Court of Criminal Appeals bearing an endorsement notifying the accused of this right. The endorsement shall inform the accused that such a petition:

(A) May be filed only within 60 days from the time the accused was in fact notified of the decision of the Court of Criminal Appeals or the mailed copy of the decision was postmarked, whichever is earlier; and

(B) May be forwarded through the officer immediately exercising general court-martial jurisdiction over the accused and through the appropriate Judge Advocate General or filed directly with the Court of Appeals for the Armed Forces.

Discussion

See Article 67(c); *see also* R.C.M. 1204(b).

---

(3) *Receipt by the accused—disposition.* When the accused has the right to petition the Court of Appeals for the Armed Forces for review, the receipt of the accused for the copy of the decision of the Court of Criminal Appeals, a certificate of service on the accused, or the postal receipt for delivery of certified mail shall be transmitted in duplicate by expeditious means to the appropriate Judge Advocate General. If the accused is personally served, the receipt or certificate of service shall show the date of service. The Judge Advocate General shall forward one copy of the receipt, certificate, or postal receipt to the clerk of the Court of Appeals for the Armed Forces when required by the court.

(g) *Cases not reviewed by the Court of Appeals for the Armed Forces.* If the decision of the Court of Criminal Appeals is not subject to review by the Court of Appeals for the Armed Forces, or if the Judge Advocate General has not forwarded the case to the Court of Appeals for the Armed Forces and the accused has not filed or the Court of Appeals for the Armed Forces has denied a petition for review, then either:

(1) The Judge Advocate General shall, if the sentence affirmed by the Court of Criminal Appeals includes a dismissal, transmit the record, the decision of the Court of Criminal Appeals, and the Judge Advocate General's recommendation to the Secretary concerned for action under R.C.M. 1206; or

(2) If the sentence affirmed by the Court of Criminal Appeals does not include a dismissal, the unexecuted portion of the sentence affirmed by the Court of Criminal Appeals shall be executed in accordance with R.C.M. 1102.

Discussion

See R.C.M. 1102, 1206, and Article 74(a) concerning the authority of the Secretary and others to take action.

Rule 1204. Review by the Court of Appeals for the Armed Forces

(a) *Cases reviewed by the Court of Appeals for the Armed Forces.* Under such rules as it may prescribe, the Court of Appeals for the Armed Forces shall review the record in all cases:

(1) in which the sentence, as affirmed by a Court of Criminal Appeals, extends to death;

(2) reviewed by a Court of Criminal Appeals which the Judge Advocate General, after appropriate notification to the other Judge Advocate Generals and the Staff Judge Advocate to the Commandant of the Marine Corps, orders sent to the Court of Appeals for the Armed Forces for review; and

(3) reviewed by a Court of Criminal Appeals in which, upon petition of the accused and on good cause shown, the Court of Appeals for the Armed Forces has granted a review.

Discussion

See Article 67(a)(2) on the notification requirement when the Judge Advocate General orders a case sent to the Court under R.C.M. 1204(a)(2). Notification ensures that the views of each of the Judge Advocates General and the Staff Judge Advocate to the Commandant of the Marine Corps are taken into consideration before the certification process is used to present a case to the Court of Appeals for the Armed Forces.

(b) *Petition by the accused for review by the Court of Appeals for the Armed Forces.*

(1) *Counsel.* When the accused is notified of the right to forward a petition for review by the Court of Appeals for the Armed Forces, if requested by the accused, associate counsel qualified under R.C.M. 502(d)(2) shall be detailed to advise and assist the accused in connection with preparing a petition for further appellate review.

Discussion

See R.C.M. 1202 for duties of appellate defense counsel.

---

(2) *Forwarding petition.* The accused shall file any petition for review by the Court of Appeals for the Armed Forces under paragraph (a)(3) of this rule directly with the Court of Appeals for the Armed Forces.

Discussion

See Article 67(b) and R.C.M. 1203(f)(2) concerning notifying the accused of the right to petition the Court of Appeals for the Armed Forces for review and the time limits for submitting a petition. See also the rules of the Court of Appeals for the Armed Forces concerning when the time for filing a petition begins to run and when a petition is now timely.

(c) *Action on decision by the Court of Appeals for the Armed Forces.*

(1) *In general.* After it has acted on a case, the Court of Appeals for the Armed Forces may direct the Judge Advocate General to return the record to the Court of Criminal Appeals for further proceedings in accordance with the decision of the court. Otherwise, unless the decision is subject to review by the Supreme Court, or there is to be further action by the President or the Secretary concerned, the Judge Advocate General shall instruct the appropriate authority to take action in accordance with that decision. If the Court has authorized a rehearing, but the convening authority to whom the record is transmitted finds a rehearing impracticable, the convening authority may dismiss the charges. If a special trial counsel referred the affected charges, the special trial counsel shall determine if a rehearing is impracticable. If a special trial counsel determines a rehearing is impracticable, the special trial counsel shall dismiss the charges.

Discussion

See R.C.M. 1111 concerning modification of the judgment in the case. *See also* R.C.M. 1206 and Article 74(a).

---

(2) *Sentence requiring approval of the President.*

(A) If the Court of Appeals for the Armed Forces has affirmed a sentence that must be approved by the President before it may be executed, the Judge Advocate General shall transmit the record of trial, the decision of the Court of Criminal Appeals, the decision of the Court of Appeals for the Armed Forces, and the recommendation of the Judge Advocate General to the Secretary concerned.

(B) If the Secretary concerned is the Secretary of a military department, the Secretary concerned shall forward the material received under subparagraph (A) to the Secretary of Defense, together with the recommendation of the Secretary concerned. The Secretary of Defense shall forward the material, with the recommendation of the Secretary concerned and the recommendation of the Secretary of Defense, to the President for the action of the President.

(C) If the Secretary concerned is the Secretary of Homeland Security, the Secretary concerned shall forward the material received under subparagraph (A) to the President, together with the recommendation of the Secretary concerned, for action of the President.

Discussion

See Article 57(a)(3) and R.C.M. 1207.

---

(3) *Sentence requiring approval of the Secretary concerned.* If the Court of Appeals for the Armed Forces has affirmed a sentence which requires approval of the Secretary concerned before it may be executed, the Judge Advocate General shall follow the procedure in R.C.M. 1203(e)(3).

Discussion

See Article 57(a)(4) and R.C.M. 1206.

---

(4) *Decisions subject to review by the Supreme Court.* If the decision of the Court of Appeals for the Armed Forces is subject to review by the Supreme Court, the Judge Advocate General shall take no action under R.C.M. 1204(c)(1), (2), or (3) until:

(A) the time for filing a petition for a writ of certiorari with the Supreme Court has expired; or

(B) the Supreme Court has denied any petitions for writ of certiorari filed in the case.

(5) Upon the occurrence of an event described by R.C.M. 1204(c)(4)(A) or (B), the Judge Advocate General shall take action in accordance with R.C.M. 1204(c)(1), (2), or (3). If the Supreme Court issues a writ of certiorari, the Judge Advocate General shall take action under R.C.M. 1205(b).

Rule 1205. Review by the Supreme Court

(a) *Cases subject to review by the Supreme Court.* Under 28 U.S.C. § 1259 and Article 67a, decisions of the Court of Appeals for the Armed Forces may be reviewed by the Supreme Court by writ of certiorari in the following cases:

(1) Cases reviewed by the Court of Appeals for the Armed Forces under Article 67(a)(1);

(2) Cases certified to the Court of Appeals for the Armed Forces by the Judge Advocate General under Article 67(a)(2);

(3) Cases in which the Court of Appeals for the Armed Forces granted a petition for review under Article 67(a)(3); and

(4) Cases other than those described in paragraphs (a)(1), (2), and (3) of this rule in which the Court of Appeals for the Armed Forces granted relief.

The Supreme Court may not review by writ of certiorari any action of the Court of Appeals for the Armed Forces in refusing to grant a petition for review.

(b) *Action by the Supreme Court.* After the Supreme Court has taken action, other than denial of a petition for writ of certiorari, in any case, the Judge Advocate General shall, unless the case is returned to the Court of Appeals for the Armed Forces for further proceedings, forward the case to the President or the Secretary concerned in accordance with R.C.M. 1204(c)(2) or (3) when appropriate, or take action in accordance with the decision.

Rule 1206. Powers and responsibilities of the Secretary

(a) *Sentences requiring approval by the Secretary.* No part of a sentence extending to dismissal of a commissioned officer, cadet, or midshipman may be executed until approved by the Secretary concerned or such Under Secretary or Assistant Secretary as may be designated by the Secretary.

Discussion

See Article 57(a)(4).

(b) *Remission and suspension.*

(1) *In general.* The Secretary concerned and, when designated by the Secretary concerned, any Under Secretary, Assistant Secretary, Judge Advocate General, or commander may remit or suspend any part or amount of the unexecuted part of any sentence, including all uncollected forfeitures, other than a sentence approved by the President.

(2) *Substitution of discharge.* The Secretary concerned may, for good cause, substitute an administrative discharge for a discharge or dismissal executed in accordance with the sentence of a court-martial.

(3) *Sentence commuted by the President.* When the President has commuted a death sentence to a lesser punishment, the Secretary concerned may remit or suspend any remaining part or amount of the unexecuted portion of the sentence of a person convicted by a military tribunal under the Secretary's jurisdiction.

Rule 1207. Sentences requiring approval by the President

No part of a court-martial sentence extending to death may be executed until approved by the President.

Discussion

See Article 57(a)(3). See also R.C.M. 1203 and 1204 concerning review by the Court of Criminal Appeals and Court of Appeals for the Armed Forces in capital cases.

Rule 1208. Restoration

(a) *New trial.* All rights, privileges, and property affected by an executed portion of a court-martial sentence—except an executed dismissal or discharge—which has not again been adjudged upon a new trial or which, after the new trial, has not been sustained upon the action of any reviewing authority, shall be restored. So much of the findings and so much of the sentence adjudged at the earlier trial shall be set aside as may be required by the findings and sentence at the new trial. Ordinarily, action taken under this subsection shall be reflected in the new judgment entered in the case.

Discussion

See Article 75(b) and (c) concerning the action to be taken on an executed dismissal or discharge which is not imposed at a new trial.

(b) *Other cases.* In cases other than those in subsection (a), all rights, privileges, and property affected by an executed part of a court-martial sentence that has been set aside or disapproved by any competent authority shall be restored unless a new trial, other trial, or rehearing is ordered and such executed part is included in a sentence imposed at the new trial, other trial, or rehearing. Ordinarily, any restoration shall be reflected in the new judgment entered in the case. In accordance with regulations established by the Secretary concerned, for the period after the date on which an executed part of a court-martial sentence is set aside, an accused who is pending a rehearing, new trial, or other trial shall receive the pay and allowances due at the restored grade.

(c) *Effective date of sentences.* Once a sentence has been set aside or disapproved, the effective date of a sentence that relates to that portion which was set aside or disapproved shall be calculated from the date a new sentence relating to that portion is adjudged at a new trial, other trial, or rehearing and shall be in accordance with R.C.M. 1102.

Discussion

See R.C.M. 1111 concerning entry of a new judgment in the case.

Rule 1209. Finality of courts-martial

(a) *When a conviction is final.*

(1) *General and special courts-martial.* A conviction in a general or special court-martial is final when—

(A) Review is completed under R.C.M. 1201(a) (Article 65);

(B) Review is completed by a Court of Criminal Appeals and—

(i) The accused does not file a timely petition for review by the Court of Appeals for the Armed Forces and the case is not otherwise under review by that court;

(ii) A petition for review is denied or otherwise rejected by the Court of Appeals for the Armed Forces; or

(iii) Review is completed in accordance with the judgment of the Court of Appeals for the Armed Forces and—

(I) A petition for a writ of certiorari is not filed within the time limits prescribed by the Supreme Court;

(II) A petition for writ of certiorari is denied or otherwise rejected by the Supreme Court; or

(III) Review is otherwise completed in accordance with the judgment of the Supreme Court.

Discussion

See R.C.M. 1201, 1203, 1204, and 1205 concerning cases subject to review by a Court of Criminal Appeals, the Court of Appeals for the Armed Forces, and the Supreme Court. See also R.C.M. 1115 for waiver or withdrawal of appellate review.

---

(2) *Summary courts-martial.* A conviction in a summary court-martial is final when a judge advocate completes review under R.C.M. 1307(d) and no further action is required under R.C.M. 1307(e).

Discussion

Although a summary court-martial conviction is final under R.C.M. 1209(a)(2), an accused may petition for post-final review pursuant to R.C.M. 1307(h). *See also* R.C.M. 1201(h).

(b) *Effect of finality.* The appellate review of records of trial provided by the UCMJ, the proceedings, findings, and sentences of courts-martial as approved, reviewed, or affirmed as required by the UCMJ, and all dismissals and discharges carried into execution under sentences by courts-martial following approval, review, or affirmation as required by the UCMJ, are final and conclusive. The judgment of a court-martial and orders publishing the proceedings of courts-martial and all action taken pursuant to those proceedings are binding upon all departments, courts, agencies, and officers of the United States, subject only to action upon a petition for a new trial under Article 73, to action under Article 69, to action by the Secretary concerned as provided in Article 74, and the authority of the President.

Rule 1210. New trial

(a) *In general.* At any time within three years after the date of entry of judgment, the accused may petition the Judge Advocate General for a new trial on the ground of newly discovered evidence or fraud on the court-martial. A petition may not be submitted after the death of the accused. A petition for a new trial of the facts may not be submitted on the basis of newly discovered evidence when the petitioner was found guilty of the relevant offense pursuant to a guilty plea.

(b) *Who may petition.* A petition for a new trial may be submitted by the accused personally, or by accused's counsel, regardless whether the accused has been separated from the Service.

(c) *Form of petition.* A petition for a new trial shall be written and shall be signed under oath or affirmation by the accused, by a person possessing the power of attorney of the accused for that purpose, or by a person with the authorization of an appropriate court to sign the petition as the representative of the accused. The petition shall contain the following information, or an explanation why such matters are not included:

(1) The name, service number, and current address of the accused;

(2) The date and location of the trial;

(3) The type of court-martial and the title or position

of the convening authority;

(4) The request for the new trial;

(5) The sentence or a description thereof as reflected in the judgment of the case, with any later reduction thereof by clemency or otherwise;

(6) A brief description of any finding or sentence believed to be unjust;

(7) A full statement of the newly discovered evidence or fraud on the court-martial which is relied upon for the remedy sought;

(8) Affidavits pertinent to the matters in paragraph (c)(7) of this rule; and

(9) The affidavit of each person whom the accused expects to present as a witness in the event of a new trial. Each such affidavit should set forth briefly the relevant facts within the personal knowledge of the witness.

(d) *Effect of petition.* The submission of a petition for a new trial does not stay the execution of a sentence.

(e) *Who may act on petition.* If the accused's case is pending before a Court of Criminal Appeals or the Court of Appeals for the Armed Forces, the Judge Advocate General shall refer the petition to the appropriate court for action. Otherwise, the Judge Advocate General of the armed force which reviewed the previous trial shall act on the petition, except that petitions submitted by persons who, at the time of trial and sentence from which the petitioner seeks relief, were members of the Coast Guard, and who were members of the Coast Guard at the time the petition is submitted, shall be acted on in the Department in which the Coast Guard is serving at the time the petition is so submitted.

(f) *Grounds for new trial.*

(1) *In general.* A new trial may be granted only on grounds of newly discovered evidence or fraud on the court-martial.

(2) *Newly discovered evidence.* A new trial shall not be granted on the grounds of newly discovered evidence unless the petition shows that:

(A) The evidence was discovered after the trial;

(B) The evidence is not such that it would have been discovered by the petitioner at the time of trial in the exercise of due diligence; and

(C) The newly discovered evidence, if considered by a court-martial in the light of all other pertinent evidence, would probably produce a substantially more favorable result for the accused.

(3) *Fraud on court-martial.* No fraud on the court-martial warrants a new trial unless it had a substantial contributing effect on a finding of guilty or the sentence adjudged.

Discussion

Examples of fraud on a court-martial which may warrant granting a new trial are: confessed or proved perjury in testimony or forgery of documentary evidence that clearly had a substantial contributing effect on a finding of guilty and without which there probably would not have been a finding of guilty of the offense; willful concealment by the prosecution from the defense of evidence favorable to the defense that, if presented to the court-martial, would probably have resulted in a finding of not guilty; and willful concealment of a material ground for challenge of the military judge or any member or of the disqualification of counsel or the convening authority, when the basis for challenge or disqualification was not known to the defense at the time of trial.

(g) *Action on petition.*

(1) *In general.* The authority considering the petition may cause such additional investigation to be made and such additional information to be secured as that authority believes appropriate. Upon written request, and in its discretion, the authority considering the petition may permit oral argument on the matter.

(2) *Courts of Criminal Appeals; Court of Appeals for the Armed Forces.* The Courts of Criminal Appeals and the Court of Appeals for the Armed Forces shall act on a petition for a new trial in accordance with their respective rules.

(3) *The Judge Advocates General.* When a petition is considered by the Judge Advocate General, any hearing may be before the Judge Advocate General or before an officer or officers designated by the Judge Advocate General. If the Judge Advocate General believes meritorious grounds for relief under Article 74 have been established but that a new trial is not appropriate, the Judge Advocate General may act under Article 74 if authorized to do so, or transmit the petition and related papers to the Secretary concerned with a recommendation. The Judge Advocate General may also, in cases which have been finally reviewed but have not been reviewed by a Court of Criminal Appeals, act under Article 69.

Discussion

See also R.C.M. 1201(h).

(h) *Action when new trial is granted.*

(1) *Forwarding to appropriate authority.* When a petition for a new trial is granted, the Judge Advocate General shall select and forward the case to an appropriate authority for disposition.

(2) *Charges at new trial.* At a new trial, the accused may not be tried for any offense of which the accused was found not guilty or upon which the accused was not tried at the earlier court-martial.

(3) *Action by convening authority.* The convening authority's action on the record of a new trial is the same as in other courts-martial.

(4) *Disposition of record.* The disposition of the record of a new trial is the same as for other courts-martial.

(5) *Judgment.* After a new trial, a new judgment shall be entered in accordance with R.C.M. 1111.

Discussion

See Article 75 and R.C.M. 1208.

---

(6) *Action by persons charged with execution of the sentence.* Persons charged with the administrative duty of executing a sentence adjudged upon a new trial shall credit the accused with any executed portion or amount of the original sentence included in the new sentence in computing the term or amount of punishment actually to be executed pursuant to the sentence.

CHAPTER XIII. SUMMARY COURTS-MARTIAL

Rule 1301. Summary courts-martial

(a) *Composition.* A summary court-martial is composed of one commissioned officer on active duty. Unless otherwise prescribed by the Secretary concerned, a summary court-martial shall be of the same armed force as the accused. Summary courts-martial shall be conducted in accordance with the regulations of the military Service to which the accused belongs. Whenever practicable, a summary court-martial should be an officer whose grade is not below lieutenant of the Navy or Coast Guard or captain of the Army, Marine Corps, Air Force, or Space Force. When only one commissioned officer is present with a command or detachment, that officer shall be the summary court-martial of that command or detachment. When more than one commissioned officer is present with a command or detachment, the convening authority may not be the summary court-martial of that command or detachment.

(b) *Function.* The function of the summary court-martial is to promptly adjudicate minor offenses under a simple disciplinary proceeding. A finding of guilt by the summary court-martial does not constitute a criminal conviction as it is not a criminal forum. However, a summary court-martial shall constitute a trial for purposes of determining former jeopardy under Article 44. The summary court-martial shall thoroughly and impartially inquire into both sides of the matter and shall ensure that the interests of both the Government and the accused are safeguarded and that justice is done. A summary court-martial may seek advice from a judge advocate or legal officer on questions of law, but the summary court-martial may not seek advice from any person on factual conclusions that should be drawn from evidence or the sentence that should be imposed, as the summary court-martial has the independent duty to make these determinations.

Discussion

For a definition of "minor offenses," see subparagraph 1.e, Part V. See R.C.M. 1209(a)(2) for the finality of a finding of guilty at a summary court-martial.

(c) *Jurisdiction.*

[Note: R.C.M. 1301(c) applies to offenses committed on or after 24 June 2014.]

(1) Subject to Chapter II and R.C.M. 1301(c)(2), summary courts-martial have the power to try persons subject to the UCMJ, except commissioned officers, warrant officers, cadets, aviation cadets, and midshipmen, for any non-capital offense made punishable by the UCMJ.

Discussion

See R.C.M. 103(4) for the definition of the term "capital offense."

---

(2) Notwithstanding paragraph (c)(1), summary courts-martial do not have jurisdiction over offenses under Articles 120(a), 120(b), 120b(a), 120b(b), and attempts thereof under Article 80. Such offenses shall not be referred to a summary court-martial.

Discussion

Only a general court-martial has jurisdiction to try penetrative sex offenses under subsections (a) and (b) of Article 120, subsections (a) and (b) of Article 120b, and attempts to commit such penetrative sex offenses under Article 80.

(d) *Punishments.*

(1) *Limitations—amount.* Subject to R.C.M. 1003, summary courts-martial may impose any punishment not forbidden by the UCMJ except death, dismissal, dishonorable or bad-conduct discharge, confinement for more than 1 month, hard labor without confinement for more than 45 days, restriction to specified limits for more than 2 months, or forfeiture of more than two-thirds of 1 month's pay.

Discussion

The maximum penalty that can be adjudged in a summary court-martial is confinement for 30 days, forfeiture of two-thirds pay per month for one month, and reduction to the lowest pay grade. See R.C.M. 1301(d)(2) for additional limits on sentences that may be adjudged where the accused is serving in a pay grade above the fourth enlisted pay grade.

A summary court-martial may not suspend all or part of a sentence, although the summary court-martial may recommend to the convening authority that all or part of a sentence be suspended. If a sentence includes both reduction in grade and forfeitures, the maximum forfeiture is calculated at the reduced pay grade. See also R.C.M. 1003 concerning other punishments which may be imposed, the effects of certain types of punishment, and the combination of certain types of punishment.

(2) *Limitations—pay grade.* In the case of enlisted members above the fourth enlisted pay grade, summary courts-martial may not adjudge confinement, hard labor without confinement, or reduction except to the next pay grade.

Discussion

The provisions of this subsection apply to an accused in the fifth enlisted pay grade who is reduced to the fourth enlisted pay grade by the summary court-martial.

(e) *Counsel.* The accused at a summary court-martial does not have the right to counsel. If the accused has counsel qualified under R.C.M. 502(d)(2), that counsel may be permitted to represent the accused at the summary court-martial if such appearance will not unreasonably delay the proceedings and if military exigencies do not preclude it.

Discussion

Neither the Constitution nor any statute establishes any right to counsel at summary courts-martial. Therefore, it is not error to deny an accused the opportunity to be represented by counsel at a summary court-martial. However, appearance of counsel is not prohibited. The detailing authority may, as a matter of discretion, detail, or otherwise make available, a military attorney to represent the accused at a summary court-martial.

(f) *Power to obtain witnesses and evidence.* A summary court-martial may obtain evidence pursuant to R.C.M. 703.

Discussion

The summary court-martial must obtain witnesses for the prosecution and the defense pursuant to the standards in R.C.M. 703. The summary court-martial rules on any request by the accused for witnesses or evidence in accordance with the procedure in R.C.M. 703(c) and (e).

(g) *Secretarial limitations.* The Secretary concerned may prescribe procedural or other rules for summary courts-martial not inconsistent with this Manual or the UCMJ.

Rule 1302. Convening a summary court-martial

(a) *Who may convene summary courts-martial.* Unless limited by competent authority summary courts-martial may be convened by:

(1) Any person who may convene a general or special court-martial;

(2) The commander of a detached company or other detachment of the Army;

(3) The commander of a detached squadron or other detachment of the Air Force or a corresponding unit of the Space Force.

(4) The commander or officer in charge of any other command when empowered by the Secretary concerned; or

(5) A superior competent authority to any of the above.

(b) *When convening authority is accuser.* If the convening authority or the summary court-martial is the accuser, it is discretionary with the convening authority whether to forward the charges to a superior authority with a recommendation to convene the summary court-martial. If the convening authority or the summary court-martial is the accuser, the jurisdiction of the summary court-martial is not affected.

(c) *Procedure.* After the requirements of Chapters III and IV of this Part have been satisfied, summary courts-martial shall be convened in accordance with R.C.M. 504(d)(2). The convening order may be by notation signed by the convening authority on the charge sheet. Charges shall be referred to summary courts-martial in accordance with R.C.M. 601.

Discussion

When the convening authority is the summary court-martial because the convening authority is the only commissioned officer present with the command or detachment, see R.C.M. 1301(a), that fact should be noted on the charge sheet.

Rule 1303. Right to object to trial by summary court-martial

No person who objects thereto before arraignment may be tried by summary court-martial even if that person also refused punishment under Article 15 and demanded trial by court-martial for the same offenses.

Rule 1304. Trial procedure

(a) *Pretrial duties*.

(1) *Examination of file*. The summary court-martial shall carefully examine the charge sheet, allied papers, and immediately available personnel records of the accused before trial.

Discussion

"Personnel records" are those personnel records of the accused that are maintained locally and are immediately available. "Allied papers" in a summary court-martial include convening orders, investigative reports, correspondence relating to the case, and witness statements.

(2) *Report of irregularity*. The summary court-martial shall report to the convening authority any substantial irregularity in the charge sheet, allied papers, or personnel records.

Discussion

The summary court-martial should examine the charge sheet, allied papers, and personnel records to ensure that they are complete and free from errors or omissions which might affect admissibility. The summary court-martial should check the charges and specifications to ensure that each alleges personal jurisdiction over the accused (*see* R.C.M. 202) and an offense under the UCMJ (*see* R.C.M. 203 and Part IV). Substantial defects or errors in the charges and specifications must be reported to the convening authority, because such defects cannot be corrected except by preferring and referring the affected charge and specification anew in proper form. A defect or error is substantial if correcting it would state an offense not otherwise stated, or include an offense, person, or matter not fairly included in the specification as preferred. See R.C.M. 1304(a)(3) concerning minor errors.

(3) *Correction and amendment*. The summary court-martial may, subject to R.C.M. 603, correct errors on the charge sheet and amend charges and specifications. Any such corrections or amendments shall be initialed.

(4) *Rights of victims at summary courts-martial*. Pursuant to Article 6b, a victim at summary court-martial is entitled to the following rights:

(A) To be reasonably protected from the accused;

(B) To reasonable, accurate, and timely notice of the summary court-martial;

(C) To not be excluded from the summary court-martial unless the summary court-martial officer, after receiving clear and convincing evidence, determines that testimony by the victim of an offense under this chapter would be materially altered if the victim heard other testimony at the summary court-martial;

(D) To be reasonably heard during sentencing in accordance with R.C.M. 1001(c); and

(E) The reasonable right to confer with the representative of the command and counsel for the government, if any.

Discussion

The term "victim" has the same meaning as the term "victim of an offense under this chapter" in Article 6b.

(b) *Summary court-martial procedure*.

Discussion

The Guide for Summary Courts-Martial is found at Appendix 8.

(1) *Preliminary proceeding*. After complying with R.C.M. 1304(a), the summary court-martial shall hold a preliminary proceeding during which the accused shall be given a copy of the charge sheet and informed of the following:

(A) The general nature of the charges;

(B) The fact that the charges have been referred to a summary court-martial for trial and the date of referral;

(C) The identity of the convening authority;

(D) The name(s) of the accuser(s);

(E) The names of the witnesses who could be called to testify and any documents or physical evidence which the summary court-martial expects to introduce into evidence;

(F) The accused's right to inspect the allied papers and immediately available personnel records;

(G) That during the trial the summary court-martial will not consider any matters, including statements previously made by the accused to the officer detailed as summary court-martial unless admitted in accordance with the Military Rules of Evidence;

(H) The accused's right to plead not guilty or guilty;

(I) The accused's right to cross-examine witnesses and have the summary court-martial cross-examine witnesses on behalf of the accused;

(J) The accused's right to call witnesses and produce evidence with the assistance of the summary court-martial as necessary;

(K) The accused's right to testify on the merits, or to remain silent with the assurance that no adverse inference will be drawn by the summary court-martial from such silence;

(L) If any findings of guilty are announced, the accused's rights to remain silent, to make an unsworn statement, oral or written or both, and to testify, and to introduce evidence in extenuation or mitigation;

(M) The maximum sentence which the summary court-martial may adjudge if the accused is found guilty of the offense or offenses alleged; and

(N) The accused's right to object to trial by summary court-martial.

(2) *Trial proceeding.*

(A) *Objection to trial.* The summary court-martial shall give the accused a reasonable period of time to decide whether to object to trial by summary court-martial. The summary court-martial shall thereafter record the response. If the accused objects to trial by summary court-martial, the summary court-martial shall return the charge sheet, allied papers, and personnel records to the convening authority. If the accused fails to object to trial by summary court-martial, trial shall proceed.

(B) *Arraignment.* After complying with R.C.M. 1304(b)(1) and (2)(A), the summary court-martial shall read and show the charges and specifications to the accused and, if necessary, explain them. The accused may waive the reading of the charges. The summary court-martial shall then ask the accused to plead to each specification and charge.

(C) *Motions.* Before receiving pleas the summary court-martial shall allow the accused to make motions to dismiss or for other relief. The summary court-martial shall take action on behalf of the accused, if requested by the accused, or if it appears necessary in the interests of justice.

(D) *Pleas.*

(i) *Not guilty pleas.* When a not guilty plea is entered, the summary court-martial shall proceed to trial.

(ii) *Guilty pleas.* If the accused pleads guilty to any offense, the summary court-martial shall comply with R.C.M. 910.

(iii) *Rejected guilty pleas.* If the summary court-martial is in doubt that the accused's pleas of guilty are voluntarily and understandingly made, or if at any time during the trial any matter inconsistent with pleas of guilty arises, which inconsistency cannot be resolved, the summary court-martial shall enter not guilty pleas as to the affected charges and specifications.

(iv) *No plea.* If the accused refuses to plead, the summary court-martial shall enter not guilty pleas.

(v) *Changed pleas.* The accused may change any plea at any time before findings are announced. The accused may change pleas from guilty to not guilty after findings are announced only for good cause.

(E) *Presentation of evidence.*

(i) The Military Rules of Evidence (Part III) apply to summary courts-martial.

(ii) The summary court-martial shall arrange for the attendance of necessary witnesses for the prosecution and defense, including those requested by the accused.

Discussion

See R.C.M. 703. Ordinarily witnesses should be excluded from the courtroom until called to testify. *See* Mil. R. Evid. 615.

(iii) Witnesses for the prosecution shall be called first and examined under oath. The accused shall be permitted to cross-examine these witnesses. The summary court-martial shall aid the accused in cross-examination if such assistance is requested or appears necessary in the interests of justice. The witnesses for the accused shall then be called and similarly examined under oath.

(iv) The summary court-martial shall obtain evidence which tends to disprove the accused's guilt or establishes extenuating circumstances.

Discussion

See R.C.M. 703 and 1001.

(F) *Findings and sentence.*

(i) The summary court-martial shall apply the principles in R.C.M. 918 in determining the findings. The summary court-martial shall announce the findings to the accused in open session.

(ii) The summary court-martial shall follow the procedures in R.C.M. 1001 and 1002 and apply the principles in the remainder of Chapter X in determining a sentence, except as follows:

(I) If an accused is found guilty of more than one offense, a summary court-martial shall determine the appropriate confinement and fine, if any, for all offenses of which the accused was found guilty. The summary court-martial shall not determine or announce separate terms of confinement or fines for each offense; and

(II) The summary court-martial shall announce the sentence to the accused in open session.

(iii) If the sentence includes confinement, the summary court-martial shall advise the accused of the right to apply to the convening authority for deferment of the service of the confinement.

(iv) If the accused is found guilty, the summary court-martial shall advise the accused of the rights under R.C.M. 1306(a) and (h) and R.C.M. 1307(h) after the sentence is announced.

(v) The summary court-martial shall, as soon as practicable, inform the convening authority of the findings, sentence, recommendations, if any, for suspension of the sentence, and any deferment request.

(vi) If the sentence includes confinement, the summary court-martial shall cause the delivery of the accused to the accused's commanding officer or the commanding officer's designee.

Discussion

If the accused's immediate commanding officer is not the convening authority, the summary court-martial should ensure that the immediate commanding officer is informed of the findings, sentence, and any recommendations pertaining thereto. See R.C.M. 1102 concerning post-trial confinement.

Rule 1305. Record of trial

(a) *In general.* The record of trial of a summary court-martial shall be prepared as prescribed in subsection (b) of this rule. The convening or higher authority may prescribe additional requirements for the record of trial.

Discussion

DD Form 2329 provides a sample Record of Trial by Summary Court-Martial.

Any matters submitted under R.C.M. 1306(a) should be appended to the record of trial.

(b) *Contents.* The summary court-martial shall prepare a written record of trial, which shall include:

(1) The pleas, findings, and sentence, and if the accused was represented by counsel at the summary court-martial, a notation to that effect;

(2) The fact that the accused was advised of the matters set forth in R.C.M. 1304(b)(1);

(3) If the summary court-martial is the convening authority, a notation to that effect.

(c) *Certification.* The summary court-martial shall certify the record by signing the record of trial. An electronic record of trial may be certified with the electronic signature of the summary court-martial.

Discussion

Certification means attesting that the record accurately reports the proceedings and includes any matters prescribed by the Secretary concerned.

(d) *Forwarding copies of the record.*

(1) *Accused's copy.*

(A) *Service.* The summary court-martial shall cause a copy of the record of trial to be served on the accused as soon as it is certified. Service of a certified electronic copy of the record of trial with a means to review the record of trial satisfies the requirement of service under this rule.

(B) *Receipt.* The summary court-martial shall cause the accused's receipt for the copy of the record of trial to be obtained and attached to the original record of trial or shall attach to the original record of trial a certificate that the accused was served a copy of the record. If the record of trial was not served on the accused personally, the summary court-martial shall attach a statement explaining how and when such service was accomplished. If the accused was represented by counsel, such counsel may be served with the record of trial.

(C) *Classified information.* If classified information is included in the record of trial of a summary court-martial, R.C.M. 1112(e)(3)(A) shall apply.

(2) *Forwarding to the convening authority.* The original and one copy of the record of trial shall be

forwarded to the convening authority after compliance with paragraph (d)(1) of this rule.

(3) *Further disposition.* After compliance with R.C.M. 1306(b) and (h) and R.C.M. 1307(h), if applicable, the record of trial shall be disposed of under regulations prescribed by the Secretary concerned.

(e) *Loss of record; defective record; correction of record.*

(1) *Loss of record.* If the certified record of trial is lost or destroyed, the summary court-martial shall, if practicable, cause another record of trial to be prepared for certification. The new record of trial shall become the record of trial in the case if the requirements of this rule are met.

(2) *Defective record.* A record of trial found to be defective after certification may be returned to the summary court-martial to be corrected. The summary court-martial shall give notice of the proposed correction to the parties and permit them to examine and respond to the proposed correction before issuing a certificate of correction. The parties shall be given reasonable access to any recording of the proceedings.

Discussion

The type of opportunity to respond depends on the nature and scope of the proposed correction. In many instances an adequate opportunity can be provided by allowing the parties to present affidavits and other documentary evidence to the person issuing the certificate of correction or by a conference telephone call among the summary court-martial, the parties, and the reporter, if any. In other instances, an evidentiary hearing with witnesses may be required. The accused need not be present at any hearing on a certificate of correction.

(3) C*ertificate of correction; service on the accused.* The certificate of correction shall be certified as provided in subsection (c) of this rule and a copy served on the accused as provided in paragraph (d)(1) of this rule. The certificate of correction and the accused's receipt for the certificate of correction shall be attached to each copy of the record of trial required to be prepared under this rule.

Rule 1306. Post-trial procedure, summary court-martial

(a) *Matters submitted.* After a sentence is adjudged by a summary court-martial, the accused and any crime victim may submit matters to the convening authority in accordance with R.C.M. 1106 and R.C.M. 1106A.

Discussion

For the definition of "crime victim," see R.C.M. 1106A(b)(2).

(b) *Convening authority's action.*

(1) *In general.* The convening authority shall take action on the sentence of a summary court-martial and, in the discretion of the convening authority, the findings of a summary court-martial.

(2) *Action on findings.* Action on the findings is not required. With respect to findings, the convening authority may:

(A) change a finding of guilty to a charge or specification to a finding of guilty to an offense that is a lesser included offense of the offense stated in the charge or specification; or

(B) set aside any finding of guilty and:

(i) dismiss the specification and, if appropriate, the charge; or

(ii) direct a rehearing in accordance with R.C.M. 810 and subsection (e).

(3) *Action on sentence.* The convening authority shall take action on the sentence. The convening authority may approve the sentence as adjudged or disapprove, commute, or suspend, in whole or in part, any portion of an adjudged sentence. The convening authority shall approve the sentence that is warranted by the circumstances of the offense and appropriate for the accused.

Discussion

In determining what sentence should be approved, the convening authority should consider the sentencing guidance in R.C.M. 1002(f) and all matters relating to clemency, such as pretrial confinement.

See R.C.M. 910(f)(5) on the effect of a plea agreement on the sentence of a summary court-martial.

A sentence adjudged by a court-martial may be approved if it was within the jurisdiction of the court-martial to adjudge (*see* R.C.M. 201(f)) and did not exceed the maximum limits prescribed in Part IV and Chapter X of this Part for the offense(s) of which the accused legally has been found guilty.

See also R.C.M. 1003(b).

See R.C.M. 1103(c) for the convening authority's ability to defer service of a sentence to confinement in a summary court-martial where the accused is in the custody of a state or foreign country.

(4) *When proceedings resulted in finding of not guilty.* The convening authority shall not take action

disapproving a finding of not guilty, a finding of not guilty only by reason of lack of mental responsibility, or a ruling amounting to a finding of not guilty. When an accused is found not guilty only by reason of lack of mental responsibility, the convening authority, however, shall commit the accused to a suitable facility pending a hearing and disposition in accordance with R.C.M. 1105.

(5) *Action when accused lacks mental capacity.* The convening authority may not approve a sentence while the accused lacks mental capacity to understand and to conduct or cooperate intelligently in the post-trial proceedings. If, before the convening authority takes action, a substantial question is raised as to the requisite mental capacity of the accused, the convening authority shall either—

(A) direct an examination of the accused in accordance with R.C.M. 706 to determine the accused's present capacity to understand and cooperate in the post-trial proceedings; or

(B) disapprove the findings and sentence.

Discussion

See R.C.M. 909 regarding presumptions and standards governing issues of mental competence.

(c) *Ordering rehearing or other trial.* The convening authority may, in the convening authority's discretion, order a rehearing. A rehearing may be ordered as to some or all offenses of which findings of guilty were entered and the sentence, or as to sentence only. A rehearing may not be ordered as to findings of guilty when there is a lack of sufficient evidence in the record to support the findings of guilty of the offense charged or of any lesser included offense. A rehearing may be ordered, however, if the proof of guilt consisted of inadmissible evidence for which there is available an admissible substitute. A rehearing may be ordered as to any lesser offense included in an offense of which the accused was found guilty, provided there is sufficient evidence in the record to support the lesser included offense.

Discussion

See R.C.M. 810 regarding procedures for rehearings and limitations on sentence at rehearings.

(d) *Contents of action and related matters.*

(1) *In general.* The convening authority shall state in writing and insert in the record of trial the convening authority's decision as to the sentence, whether any findings of guilty are disapproved, whether any charges or specifications are changed or dismissed and an explanation for such action, and any orders as to further disposition. The action shall be signed by the convening authority. The convening authority's authority to sign shall appear below the signature. The convening authority may recall and modify any action taken by that convening authority at any time before it has been published, or, if the action is favorable to the accused, at any time prior to forwarding the record for review or before the accused has been officially notified.

(2) *Sentence.* The action shall state whether the sentence adjudged by the court-martial is approved. If only part of the sentence is approved, the action shall state which parts are approved. A rehearing may not be directed if any sentence is approved.

(3) *Suspension.* The action shall indicate, when appropriate, whether an approved sentence is to be executed or whether the execution of all or any part of the sentence is to be suspended. No reasons need be stated.

(4) *Deferment of service of sentence to confinement.* Whenever the service of the sentence to confinement is deferred by the convening authority under R.C.M. 1103 before or concurrently with the initial action in the case, the action shall include the date on which the deferment became effective. The reason for the deferment need not be stated in the action.

(e) *Incomplete, ambiguous, or erroneous action.* When the action of the convening authority or of a higher authority is incomplete, ambiguous, or contains error, the authority who took the incomplete, ambiguous, or erroneous action may be instructed by an authority acting under Article 64, 66, 67, 67a, or 69 to withdraw the original action and substitute a corrected action.

(f) *Service.* A copy of the convening authority's action shall be served on the accused or on defense counsel and, upon the victim's request, the victim. If the action is served on defense counsel, defense counsel shall, by expeditious means, provide the accused with a copy.

Discussion

The term "victim" has the same meaning as "crime victim" in R.C.M. 1106A(b)(2).

(g) *Subsequent action.* Any action taken on a summary court-martial after the initial action by the convening authority shall be in writing, signed by the authority taking the action, and promulgated in appropriate orders.

(h) *Review by a judge advocate.* A judge advocate shall review each summary court-martial in which there is a finding of guilty pursuant to R.C.M. 1307.

Rule 1307. Review of summary courts-martial by a judge advocate

(a) *In general.* Except as provided in subsection (b) of this rule, under regulations of the Secretary concerned, a judge advocate shall review each summary court-martial in which there is a finding of guilty.

(b) *Exception.* If the accused is found not guilty or not guilty only by reason of lack of mental responsibility of all offenses or if the convening authority disapproved all findings of guilty, no review under this rule is required.

(c) *Disqualification.* No person may review a case under this rule if that person has acted in the same case as an accuser, preliminary hearing officer, summary court-martial officer, or counsel, or has otherwise acted on behalf of the prosecution or defense.

(d) *Form and content of review.* The judge advocate's review shall be in writing and shall contain the following:

(1) Conclusions as to whether—

(A) the court-martial had jurisdiction over the accused and each offense as to which there is a finding of guilty that has not been disapproved;

(B) each specification as to which there is a finding of guilty that has not been disapproved stated an offense; and

(C) the sentence was legal.

(2) A response to each allegation of error made in writing by the accused. Such allegations may be filed under R.C.M. 1106 or directly with the judge advocate who reviews the case; and

(3) If the case is sent for action to the officer exercising general court-martial jurisdiction under subsection (e) of this rule, a recommendation as to the appropriate action to be taken and an opinion as to whether corrective action is required as a matter of law.

A copy of the judge advocate's review under this rule shall be attached to the record of trial. A copy of the review shall also be forwarded to the accused.

(e) *Forwarding to officer exercising general court-martial jurisdiction.* In cases reviewed under this rule, the record of trial shall be sent for action to the officer exercising general court-martial convening authority over the accused at the time the court-martial was held (or to that officer's successor) when:

(1) The judge advocate who reviewed the case recommends corrective action; or

(2) Such action is otherwise required by regulations of the Secretary concerned.

(f) *Action by officer exercising general court-martial jurisdiction.*

(1) *Action.* The officer exercising general court-martial jurisdiction who receives a record under subsection (e) of this rule may—

(A) Disapprove or approve the findings or sentence in whole or in part;

(B) Remit, commute, or suspend the sentence in whole or in part;

(C) Except where the evidence was insufficient at the trial to support the findings, order a rehearing on the findings, on the sentence, or on both; or

(D) Dismiss the charges.

Discussion

See R.C.M. 1102(a) concerning when the officer exercising general court-martial jurisdiction may order parts of the sentence executed. See R.C.M. 1111(a)(3) explaining that the findings and sentence of the court-martial, as modified or approved by the convening authority, constitute the judgment in summary courts-martial.

(2) *Rehearing.* If the officer exercising general court-martial jurisdiction orders a rehearing, but the convening authority finds a rehearing impracticable, the convening authority shall dismiss the charges.

(3) *Notification.* After the officer exercising general court-martial jurisdiction has taken action, the accused shall be notified of the action and the accused shall be provided with a copy of the action.

(g) *Records forwarded to the Judge Advocate General.* If the judge advocate who reviews the case under this rule states that corrective action is required as a matter of law, and the officer exercising general court-martial jurisdiction does not take action that is at least as favorable to the accused as that recommended by the judge advocate, the record of trial and the action thereon shall be forwarded to the Judge Advocate General for review under R.C.M. 1201(j).

(h) *Application for post-final review by the Judge Advocate General.* Not later than one year after completion of the judge advocate's review of the case under this rule, the accused may apply for review by the Judge Advocate General under R.C.M. 1201(h) on the grounds of newly discovered evidence, fraud on the court-martial, lack of jurisdiction over the accused or offense, error prejudicial to the substantial rights of the accused, or the appropriateness of the sentence.

(i) *Review by a Court of Criminal Appeals.* After the Judge Advocate General reviews a summary court-martial under R.C.M. 1201(h) or (j), the case may be sent to the Court of Criminal Appeals by order of the Judge Advocate General, or the accused may submit an application for review to the Court of Criminal Appeals in accordance with R.C.M. 1201(k).

(j) *Other records.* Records reviewed under this rule that are not forwarded under subsection (g) shall be disposed of as prescribed by the Secretary concerned.

PART III
MILITARY RULES OF EVIDENCE:

SECTION I
GENERAL PROVISIONS

Rule 101. Scope

(a) *Scope.* These rules apply to courts-martial proceedings to the extent and with the exceptions stated in Mil. R. Evid. 1101.

(b) *Sources of Law.* In the absence of guidance in this Manual or these rules, courts-martial will apply:

(1) First, the Federal Rules of Evidence and the case law interpreting them; and

(2) Second, when not inconsistent with subdivision (b)(1), the rules of evidence at common law.

(c) *Rule of Construction.*

(1) Except as otherwise provided in these rules, the term "military judge" includes:

(A) a military magistrate designated to preside at a special court-martial or pre-referral judicial proceeding; and

(B) a summary court-martial officer.

(2) A reference in these rules to any kind of written material or any other medium includes electronically stored information.

Discussion

Discussion was added to these Rules in 2013. The Discussion itself does not have the force of law, even though it may describe legal requirements derived from other sources. It is in the nature of a treatise, and may be used as secondary authority. If a matter is included in a rule, it is intended that the matter be binding, unless it is clearly expressed as precatory. The Discussion will be revised from time to time as warranted by changes in applicable law. *See* Composition of the Manual for Courts-Martial in Appendix 15

Practitioners should also refer to the Analysis of the Military Rules of Evidence contained in Appendix 16 of this Manual. The Analysis is similar to Committee Notes accompanying the Federal Rules of Evidence and is intended to address the basis of the rule, deviation from the Federal Rules of Evidence, relevant precedent, and drafters' intent.

Rule 102. Purpose

These rules should be construed so as to administer every proceeding fairly, eliminate unjustifiable expense and delay, and promote the development of evidence law, to the end of ascertaining the truth and securing a just determination.

Rule 103. Rulings on evidence

(a) *Preserving a Claim of Error.* A party may claim error in a ruling to admit or exclude evidence only if the error materially prejudices a substantial right of the party and:

(1) if the ruling admits evidence, a party, on the record:

(A) timely objects or moves to strike; and

(B) states the specific ground, unless it was apparent from the context; or

(2) if the ruling excludes evidence, a party informs the military judge of its substance by an offer of proof, unless the substance was apparent from the context.

(b) *Not Needing to Renew an Objection or Offer of Proof.* Once the military judge rules definitively on the record admitting or excluding evidence, either before or at trial, a party need not renew an objection or offer of proof to preserve a claim of error for appeal.

(c) *Review of Constitutional Error.* The standard provided in subdivision (a)(2) does not apply to errors implicating the United States Constitution as it applies to members of the Armed Forces, unless the error arises under these rules and subdivision (a)(2) provides a standard that is more advantageous to the accused than the constitutional standard.

(d) *Military Judge's Statement about the Ruling; Directing an Offer of Proof.* The military judge may make any statement about the character or form of the evidence, the objection made, and the ruling. The military judge may direct that an offer of proof be made in question-and-answer form.

(e) *Preventing the Members from Hearing Inadmissible Evidence.* In a court-martial composed of a military judge and members, to the extent practicable, the military judge must conduct a trial so that inadmissible evidence is not suggested to the members by any means.

(f) *Taking Notice of Plain Error.* A military judge may take notice of a plain error that materially prejudices a substantial right, even if the claim of error was not properly preserved.

Rule 104. Preliminary questions

(a) *In general.* The military judge must decide any preliminary question about whether a witness is available or qualified, a privilege exists, a continuance should be granted, or evidence is admissible. In so deciding, the military judge is not bound by evidence rules, except those on privilege.

(b) *Relevance that Depends on a Fact.* When the relevance of evidence depends on whether a fact exists, proof must be introduced sufficient to support a finding that the fact does exist. The military judge may admit the proposed evidence on the condition that the proof be introduced later. A ruling on the sufficiency of evidence to support a finding of fulfillment of a condition of fact is the sole responsibility of the military judge, except where these rules or this Manual provide expressly to the contrary.

(c) *Conducting a Hearing so that the Members Cannot Hear It.* The military judge must conduct any hearing on a preliminary question so that the members cannot hear it if:

(1) the hearing involves the admissibility of a statement of the accused under Mil. R. Evid. 301-306;

(2) the accused is a witness and so requests; or

(3) justice so requires.

(d) *Cross-Examining the Accused.* By testifying on a preliminary question, the accused does not become subject to cross-examination on other issues in the case.

(e) *Evidence Relevant to Weight and Credibility.* This rule does not limit a party's right to introduce before the members evidence that is relevant to the weight or credibility of other evidence.

Rule 105. Limiting evidence that is not admissible against other parties or for other purposes

If the military judge admits evidence that is admissible against a party or for a purpose - but not against another party or for another purpose - the military judge, on timely request, must restrict the evidence to its proper scope and instruct the members accordingly.

Rule 106. Remainder of or related writings or recorded statements

If a party introduces all or part of a writing or recorded statement, an adverse party may require the introduction, at that time, of any other part - or any other writing or recorded statement - that in fairness ought to be considered at the same time.

SECTION II
JUDICIAL NOTICE

Rule 201. Judicial notice of adjudicative facts

(a) *Scope.* This rule governs judicial notice of an adjudicative fact only, not a legislative fact.

(b) *Kinds of Facts that May Be Judicially Noticed.* The military judge may judicially notice a fact that is not subject to reasonable dispute because it:

(1) is generally known universally, locally, or in the area pertinent to the event; or

(2) can be accurately and readily determined from sources whose accuracy cannot reasonably be questioned.

(c) *Taking Notice.* The military judge:

(1) may take judicial notice whether requested or not; or

(2) must take judicial notice if a party requests it and the military judge is supplied with the necessary information.

The military judge must inform the parties in open court when, without being requested, he or she takes judicial notice of an adjudicative fact essential to establishing an element of the case.

(d) *Timing.* The military judge may take judicial notice at any stage of the proceeding.

(e) *Opportunity to Be Heard.* On timely request, a party is entitled to be heard on the propriety of taking judicial notice and the nature of the fact to be noticed. If the military judge takes judicial notice before notifying a party, the party, on request, is still entitled to be heard.

(f) *Instructing the Members.* The military judge must instruct the members that they may or may not accept the noticed fact as conclusive.

Rule 202. Judicial notice of law

(a) *Domestic Law.* The military judge may take judicial notice of domestic law. If a domestic law is a fact that is of consequence to the determination of the action, the procedural requirements of Mil. R. Evid. 201—except Rule 201(f)—apply.

(b) *Foreign Law.* A party who intends to raise an issue concerning the law of a foreign country must give reasonable written notice. The military judge, in determining foreign law, may consider any relevant material or source, in accordance with Mil. R. Evid. 104. Such a determination is a ruling on a question of law.

SECTION III

EXCLUSIONARY RULES AND RELATED MATTERS CONCERNING SELF-INCRIMINATION, SEARCH AND SEIZURE, AND EYEWITNESS IDENTIFICATION

Rule 301. Privilege concerning compulsory self-incrimination

(a) *General Rule.* An individual may claim the most favorable privilege provided by the Fifth Amendment to the United States Constitution, Article 31, or these rules. The privileges against self-incrimination are applicable only to evidence of a testimonial or communicative nature.

(b) *Standing.* The privilege of a witness to refuse to respond to a question that may tend to incriminate the witness is a personal one that the witness may exercise or waive at his or her discretion.

(c) *Limited Waiver.* An accused who chooses to testify as a witness waives the privilege against self-incrimination only with respect to the matters about which he or she testifies. If the accused is on trial for two or more offenses and on direct examination testifies about only one or some of the offenses, the accused may not be cross-examined as to guilt or innocence with respect to the other offenses unless the cross-examination is relevant to an offense concerning which the accused has testified. This waiver is subject to Mil. R. Evid. 608(b).

Discussion

A military judge is not required to provide Article 31 warnings. If a witness who seems uninformed of the privileges under this rule, appears likely to incriminate himself or herself, the military judge may advise the witness of the right to decline to make any answer that might tend to incriminate the witness and that any self-incriminating answer the witness might make can later be used as evidence against the witness. Counsel for any party or for the witness may ask the military judge to so advise a witness if such a request is made out of the hearing of the witness and the members, if present. Failure to so advise a witness does not make the testimony of the witness inadmissible.

(d) *Exercise of the Privilege.* If a witness states that the answer to a question may tend to incriminate him or her, the witness cannot be required to answer unless the military judge finds that the facts and circumstances are such that no answer the witness might make to the question would tend to incriminate the witness or that the witness has, with respect to the question, waived the privilege against self-incrimination. A witness may not assert the privilege if he or she is not subject to criminal penalty as a result of an answer by reason of immunity, running of the statute of limitations, or similar reason.

(1) *Immunity Requirements.* The minimum grant of immunity adequate to overcome the privilege is that which under either R.C.M. 704 or other proper authority provides that neither the testimony of the witness nor any evidence obtained from that testimony may be used against the witness at any subsequent trial other than in a prosecution for perjury, false swearing, the making of a false official statement, or failure to comply with an order to testify after the military judge has ruled that the privilege may not be asserted by reason of immunity.

(2) *Notification of Immunity or Leniency.* When a prosecution witness before a court-martial has been granted immunity or leniency in exchange for testimony, the grant must be reduced to writing and must be served on the accused prior to arraignment or within a reasonable time before the witness testifies. If notification is not made as required by this rule, the military judge may grant a continuance until notification is made, prohibit or strike the testimony of the witness, or enter such other order as may be required.

(e) *Waiver of the Privilege.* A witness who answers a self-incriminating question without having asserted the privilege against self-incrimination may be required to answer questions relevant to the disclosure, unless the questions are likely to elicit additional self-incriminating information.

(1) If a witness asserts the privilege against self-incrimination on cross-examination, the military judge, upon motion, may strike the direct testimony of the witness in whole or in part, unless the matters to which the witness refuses to testify are purely collateral.

(2) Any limited waiver of the privilege under subdivision (e) applies only at the trial in which the answer is given, does not extend to a rehearing or new or other trial, and is subject to Mil. R. Evid. 608(b).

(f) *Effect of Claiming the Privilege.*

(1) *No Inference to Be Drawn.* The fact that a witness has asserted the privilege against self-incrimination

cannot be considered as raising any inference unfavorable to either the accused or the government.

(2) *Pretrial Invocation Not Admissible.* The fact that the accused during official questioning and in exercise of rights under the Fifth Amendment to the United States Constitution or Article 31 remained silent, refused to answer a certain question, requested counsel, or requested that the questioning be terminated, is not admissible against the accused.

(3) *Instructions Regarding the Privilege.* When the accused does not testify at trial, defense counsel may request that the members of the court be instructed to disregard that fact and not to draw any adverse inference from it. Defense counsel may request that the members not be so instructed. Defense counsel's election will be binding upon the military judge except that the military judge may give the instruction when the instruction is necessary in the interests of justice.

Rule 302. Privilege concerning mental examination of an accused

(a) *General rule.* The accused has a privilege to prevent any statement made by the accused at a mental examination ordered under R.C.M. 706 and any derivative evidence obtained through use of such a statement from being received into evidence against the accused on the issue of guilt or innocence or during sentencing proceedings. This privilege may be claimed by the accused notwithstanding the fact that the accused may have been warned of the rights provided by Mil. R. Evid. 305 at the examination.

(b) *Exceptions.*

(1) There is no privilege under this rule when the accused first introduces into evidence such statements or derivative evidence.

(2) If the court-martial has allowed the defense to present expert testimony as to the mental condition of the accused, an expert witness for the prosecution may testify as to the reasons for his or her conclusions, but such testimony may not extend to statements of the accused except as provided in subdivision (b)(1).

(c) *Release of Evidence from an R.C.M. 706 Examination.* If the defense offers expert testimony concerning the mental condition of the accused, the military judge, upon motion, must order the release to the prosecution of the full contents, other than any statements made by the accused, of any report prepared pursuant to R.C.M. 706. If the defense offers statements made by the accused at such examination, the military judge, upon motion, may order the disclosure of such statements made by the accused and contained in the report as may be necessary in the interests of justice.

(d) *Noncompliance by the Accused.* The military judge may prohibit an accused who refuses to cooperate in a mental examination authorized under R.C.M. 706 from presenting any expert medical testimony as to any issue that would have been the subject of the mental examination.

(e) *Procedure.* The privilege in this rule may be claimed by the accused only under the procedure set forth in Mil. R. Evid. 304 for an objection or a motion to suppress.

Rule 303. Degrading questions

Statements and evidence are inadmissible if they are not material to the issue and may tend to degrade the person testifying.

Rule 304. Confessions and admissions

(a) *General rule.* If the accused makes a timely motion or objection under this rule, an involuntary statement from the accused, or any evidence derived therefrom, is inadmissible at trial except as provided in subdivision (e).

(1) *Definitions.* As used in this rule:

(A) "Involuntary statement" means a statement obtained in violation of the self-incrimination privilege or Due Process Clause of the Fifth Amendment to the United States Constitution, Article 31, or through the use of coercion, unlawful influence, or unlawful inducement.

(B) "Confession" means an acknowledgment of guilt.

(C) "Admission" means a self-incriminating statement falling short of an acknowledgment of guilt, even if it was intended by its maker to be exculpatory.

(2) Failure to deny an accusation of wrongdoing is not an admission of the truth of the accusation if at the time of the alleged failure the person was under investigation or was in confinement, arrest, or custody for the alleged wrongdoing.

(b) *Evidence Derived from a Statement of the Accused.* When the defense has made an appropriate and timely motion or objection under this rule, evidence allegedly derived from a statement of the accused may not be admitted unless the military judge finds by a preponderance of the evidence that:

(1) the statement was made voluntarily,

(2) the evidence was not obtained by use of the accused's statement, or

(3) the evidence would have been obtained even if the statement had not been made.

(c) *Corroboration of a Confession or Admission.*

(1) An admission or a confession of the accused may be considered as evidence against the accused on the question of guilt or innocence only if independent evidence, either direct or circumstantial, has been admitted into evidence that would tend to establish the trustworthiness of the admission or confession.

(2) Other uncorroborated confessions or admissions of the accused that would themselves require corroboration may not be used to supply this independent evidence. If the independent evidence raises an inference of the truth of the admission or confession, then it may be considered as evidence against the accused. Not every element or fact contained in the confession or admission must be independently proven for the confession or admission to be admitted into evidence in its entirety.

(3) Corroboration is not required for a statement made by the accused before the court by which the accused is being tried, for statements made prior to or contemporaneously with the act, or for statements offered under a rule of evidence other than that pertaining to the admissibility of admissions or confessions.

(4) *Quantum of Evidence Needed.* The independent evidence necessary to establish corroboration need not be sufficient of itself to establish beyond a reasonable doubt the truth of facts stated in the admission or confession. The independent evidence need raise only an inference of the truth of the admission or confession. The amount and type of evidence introduced as corroboration is a factor to be considered by the trier of fact in determining the weight, if any, to be given to the admission or confession.

(5) *Procedure.* The military judge alone is to determine when adequate evidence of corroboration has been received. Corroborating evidence must be introduced before the admission or confession is introduced unless the military judge allows submission of such evidence subject to later corroboration.

(d) *Disclosure of Statements by the Accused and Derivative Evidence.* Before arraignment, the prosecution must disclose to the defense the contents of all statements, oral or written, made by the accused that are relevant to the case, known to trial counsel, and within the control of the Armed Forces, and all evidence derived from such statements, that the prosecution intends to offer against the accused.

(e) *Limited Use of an Involuntary Statement.* A statement obtained in violation of Article 31 or Mil. R. Evid. 305(b)-(c) may be used only:

(1) to impeach by contradiction the in-court testimony of the accused; or

(2) in a later prosecution against the accused for perjury, false swearing, or the making of a false official statement.

(f) *Motions and Objections.*

(1) Motions to suppress or objections under this rule, or Mil. R. Evid. 302 or 305, to any statement or derivative evidence that has been disclosed must be made by the defense prior to submission of a plea. In the absence of such motion or objection, the defense may not raise the issue at a later time except as permitted by the military judge for good cause shown. Failure to so move or object constitutes a waiver of the objection.

(2) If the prosecution seeks to offer a statement made by the accused or derivative evidence that was not disclosed before arraignment, the prosecution must provide timely notice to the military judge and defense counsel. The defense may object at that time, and the military judge may make such orders as are required in the interests of justice.

(3) The defense may present evidence relevant to the admissibility of evidence as to which there has been an objection or motion to suppress under this rule. An accused may testify for the limited purpose of denying that the accused made the statement or that the statement was made voluntarily.

(A) Prior to the introduction of such testimony by the accused, the defense must inform the military judge that the testimony is offered under subdivision (f)(3).

(B) When the accused testifies under subdivision (f)(3), the accused may be cross-examined only as to the matter on which he or she testifies. Nothing said by the accused on either direct or cross-examination may be used against the accused for any purpose other than in a prosecution for perjury, false swearing, or the making of a false official statement.

(4) *Specificity.* The military judge may require the defense to specify the grounds upon which the defense

moves to suppress or object to evidence. If defense counsel, despite the exercise of due diligence, has been unable to interview adequately those persons involved in the taking of a statement, the military judge may make any order required in the interests of justice, including authorization for the defense to make a general motion to suppress or general objection.

(5) *Rulings.* The military judge must rule, prior to plea, upon any motion to suppress or objection to evidence made prior to plea unless, for good cause, the military judge orders that the ruling be deferred for determination at trial or after findings. The military judge may not defer ruling if doing so adversely affects a party's right to appeal the ruling. The military judge must state essential findings of fact on the record when the ruling involves factual issues.

(6) *Burden of Proof.* When the defense has made an appropriate motion or objection under this rule, the prosecution has the burden of establishing the admissibility of the evidence. When the military judge has required a specific motion or objection under subdivision (f)(4), the burden on the prosecution extends only to the grounds upon which the defense moved to suppress or object to the evidence.

(7) *Standard of Proof.* The military judge must find by a preponderance of the evidence that a statement by the accused was made voluntarily before it may be received into evidence.

(8) *Effect of Guilty Plea.* Except as otherwise expressly provided in R.C.M. 910(a)(2), a plea of guilty to an offense that results in a finding of guilty waives all privileges against self-incrimination and all motions and objections under this rule with respect to that offense regardless of whether raised prior to plea.

(g) *Weight of the Evidence.* If a statement is admitted into evidence, the military judge must permit the defense to present relevant evidence with respect to the voluntariness of the statement and must instruct the members to give such weight to the statement as it deserves under all the circumstances.

(h) *Completeness.* If only part of an alleged admission or confession is introduced against the accused, the defense, by cross-examination or otherwise, may introduce the remaining portions of the statement.

(i) *Evidence of an Oral Statement.* A voluntary oral confession or admission of the accused may be proved by the testimony of anyone who heard the accused make it, even if it was reduced to writing and the writing is not accounted for.

(j) *Refusal to Obey an Order to Submit a Body Substance.* If an accused refuses a lawful order to submit for chemical analysis a sample of his or her blood, breath, urine or other body substance, evidence of such refusal may be admitted into evidence on:

(1) a charge of violating an order to submit such a sample; or

(2) any other charge on which the results of the chemical analysis would have been admissible.

Rule 305. Warnings about rights

(a) *General rule.* A statement obtained in violation of this rule is involuntary and will be treated under Mil. R. Evid. 304.

(b) *Definitions.* As used in this rule:

(1) "Person subject to the code" means a person subject to the Uniform Code of Military Justice as contained in Chapter 47 of Title 10, United States Code. This term includes, for purposes of subdivision (c) of this rule, a knowing agent of any such person or of a military unit.

(2) "Interrogation" means any formal or informal questioning in which an incriminating response either is sought or is a reasonable consequence of such questioning.

(3) "Custodial interrogation" means questioning that takes place while the accused or suspect is in custody, could reasonably believe himself or herself to be in custody, or is otherwise deprived of his or her freedom of action in any significant way.

(c) *Warnings Concerning the Accusation, Right to Remain Silent, and Use of Statements.*

(1) *Article 31 Rights Warnings.* A statement obtained from the accused in violation of the accused's rights under Article 31 is involuntary and therefore inadmissible against the accused except as provided in subdivision (d). Pursuant to Article 31, a person subject to the code may not interrogate or request any statement from an accused or a person suspected of an offense without first:

(A) informing the accused or suspect of the nature of the accusation;

(B) advising the accused or suspect that the accused or suspect has the right to remain silent; and

(C) advising the accused or suspect that any statement made may be used as evidence against the accused or suspect in a trial by court-martial.

(2) *Fifth Amendment Right to Counsel.* If a person suspected of an offense and subjected to custodial interrogation requests counsel, any statement made in the interrogation after such request, or evidence derived from the interrogation after such request, is inadmissible against the accused unless counsel was present for the interrogation.

(3) *Sixth Amendment Right to Counsel.* If an accused against whom charges have been preferred is interrogated on matters concerning the preferred charges by anyone acting in a law enforcement capacity, or the agent of such a person, and the accused requests counsel, or if the accused has appointed or retained counsel, any statement made in the interrogation, or evidence derived from the interrogation, is inadmissible unless counsel was present for the interrogation.

(4) *Exercise of Rights.* If a person chooses to exercise the privilege against self-incrimination, questioning must cease immediately. If a person who is subjected to interrogation under the circumstances described in subdivisions (c)(2) or (c)(3) of this rule chooses to exercise the right to counsel, questioning must cease until counsel is present.

(d) *Presence of Counsel.* When a person entitled to counsel under this rule requests counsel, a judge advocate or an individual certified in accordance with Article 27(b) will be provided by the United States at no expense to the person and without regard to the person's indigency and must be present before the interrogation may proceed. In addition to counsel supplied by the United States, the person may retain civilian counsel at no expense to the United States. Unless otherwise provided by regulations of the Secretary concerned, an accused or suspect does not have a right under this rule to have military counsel of his or her own selection.

(e) *Waiver.*

(1) *Waiver of the Privilege Against Self-Incrimination.* After receiving applicable warnings under this rule, a person may waive the rights described therein and in Mil. R. Evid. 301 and make a statement. The waiver must be made freely, knowingly, and intelligently. A written waiver is not required. The accused or suspect must affirmatively acknowledge that he or she understands the rights involved, affirmatively decline the right to counsel, and affirmatively consent to making a statement.

(2) *Waiver of the Right to Counsel.* If the right to counsel is applicable under this rule and the accused or suspect does not affirmatively decline the right to counsel, the prosecution must demonstrate by a preponderance of the evidence that the individual waived the right to counsel.

(3) *Waiver After Initially Invoking the Right to Counsel.*

(A) *Fifth Amendment Right to Counsel.* If an accused or suspect subjected to custodial interrogation requests counsel, any subsequent waiver of the right to counsel obtained during a custodial interrogation concerning the same or different offenses is invalid unless the prosecution can demonstrate by a preponderance of the evidence that:

(i) the accused or suspect initiated the communication leading to the waiver; or

(ii) the accused or suspect has not continuously had his or her freedom restricted by confinement, or other means, during the period between the request for counsel and the subsequent waiver.

(B) *Sixth Amendment Right to Counsel.* If an accused or suspect interrogated after preferral of charges as described in subdivision (c)(3) requests counsel, any subsequent waiver of the right to counsel obtained during an interrogation concerning the same offenses is invalid unless the prosecution can demonstrate by a preponderance of the evidence that the accused or suspect initiated the communication leading to the waiver.

(f) *Standards for Nonmilitary Interrogations.*

(1) *United States Civilian Interrogations.* When a person subject to the code is interrogated by an official or agent of the United States, of the District of Columbia, or of a State, Commonwealth, or possession of the United States, or any political subdivision of such a State, Commonwealth, or possession, the person's entitlement to rights warnings and the validity of any waiver of applicable rights will be determined by the principles of law generally recognized in the trial of criminal cases in the United States district courts involving similar interrogations.

(2) *Foreign Interrogations.* Warnings under Article 31 and the Fifth and Sixth Amendments to the United States Constitution are not required during an interrogation conducted outside of a State, district, Commonwealth, territory, or possession of the United States by officials of a foreign government or their agents unless such interrogation is conducted, instigated, or participated in by military personnel or their agents or by those officials or agents listed in

subdivision (f)(1). A statement obtained from a foreign interrogation is admissible unless the statement is obtained through the use of coercion, unlawful influence, or unlawful inducement. An interrogation is not "participated in" by military personnel or their agents or by the officials or agents listed in subdivision (f)(1) merely because such a person was present at an interrogation conducted in a foreign nation by officials of a foreign government or their agents, or because such a person acted as an interpreter or took steps to mitigate damage to property or physical harm during the foreign interrogation.

Rule 306. Statements by one of several accused

When two or more accused are tried at the same trial, evidence of a statement made by one of them which is admissible only against him or her or only against some but not all of the accused may not be received in evidence unless all references inculpating an accused against whom the statement is inadmissible are deleted effectively or the maker of the statement is subject to cross-examination.

Rule 311. Evidence obtained from unlawful searches and seizures

(a) *General rule.* Evidence obtained as a result of an unlawful search or seizure made by a person acting in a governmental capacity is inadmissible against the accused if:

(1) the accused makes a timely motion to suppress or an objection to the evidence under this rule;

(2) the accused had a reasonable expectation of privacy in the person, place, or property searched;

the accused had a legitimate interest in the property or evidence seized when challenging a seizure; or the accused would otherwise have grounds to object to the search or seizure under the Constitution of the United States as applied to members of the Armed Forces; and

(3) exclusion of the evidence results in appreciable deterrence of future unlawful searches or seizures and the benefits of such deterrence outweigh the costs to the justice system.

(b) *Definition.* As used in this rule, a search or seizure is "unlawful" if it was conducted, instigated, or participated in by:

(1) military personnel or their agents and was in violation of the Constitution of the United States as applied to members of the Armed Forces, a federal statute applicable to trials by court-martial that requires exclusion of evidence obtained in violation thereof, or Mil. R. Evid. 312-317;

(2) other officials or agents of the United States, of the District of Columbia, or of a State, Commonwealth, or possession of the United States or any political subdivision of such a State, Commonwealth, or possession, and was in violation of the Constitution of the United States, or is unlawful under the principles of law generally applied in the trial of criminal cases in the United States district courts involving a similar search or seizure; or

(3) officials of a foreign government or their agents, where evidence was obtained as a result of a foreign search or seizure that subjected the accused to gross and brutal maltreatment. A search or seizure is not "participated in" by a United States military or civilian official merely because that person is present at a search or seizure conducted in a foreign nation by officials of a foreign government or their agents, or because that person acted as an interpreter or took steps to mitigate damage to property or physical harm during the foreign search or seizure.

(c) *Exceptions.*

(1) *Impeachment.* Evidence that was obtained as a result of an unlawful search or seizure may be used to impeach by contradiction the in-court testimony of the accused.

(2) *Inevitable Discovery.* Evidence that was obtained as a result of an unlawful search or seizure may be used when the evidence would have been obtained even if such unlawful search or seizure had not been made.

(3) *Good Faith Exception of a Warrant or Search Authorization*: Evidence that was obtained as a result of an unlawful search or seizure may be used if:

(A) the search or seizure resulted from an authorization to search, seize, or apprehend issued by an individual competent to issue the authorization under Mil. R. Evid. 315(d) or from a search warrant or arrest warrant issued by competent civilian authority, or from such an authorization or warrant issued by an individual whom the officials seeking and executing the authorization or warrant reasonably and with good faith believed was competent to issue the authorization or warrant;

(B) the individual issuing the authorization or warrant had a substantial basis for determining the existence of probable cause or the officials seeking and executing the authorization or warrant reasonably and with good faith believed that the individual issuing the authorization or warrant had a substantial basis for determining the existence of probable cause; and

(C) the officials seeking and executing the authorization or warrant reasonably and with good faith relied on the issuance of the authorization or warrant. Good faith is to be determined using an objective standard.

Discussion

See U.S. v. Perkins, 78 M.J. 381 (C.A.A.F. 2019).

---

(4) *Reliance on Statute or Binding Precedent.* Evidence that was obtained as a result of an unlawful search or seizure may be used when the official seeking the evidence acted in objectively reasonable reliance on a statute or on binding precedent later held violative of the Fourth Amendment.

(d) *Motions to Suppress and Objections.*

(1) *Disclosure.* Prior to arraignment, the prosecution must disclose to the defense all evidence seized from the person or property of the accused, or believed to be owned by the accused, or evidence derived therefrom, that it intends to offer into evidence against the accused at trial.

(2) *Time Requirements.*

(A) When evidence has been disclosed prior to arraignment under subdivision (d)(1), the defense must make any motion to suppress or objection under this rule prior to submission of a plea. In the absence of such motion or objection, the defense may not raise the issue at a later time except as permitted by the military judge for good cause shown. Failure to so move or object constitutes a waiver of the motion or objection.

(B) If the prosecution intends to offer evidence described in subdivision (d)(1) that was not disclosed prior to arraignment, the prosecution must provide timely notice to the military judge and to counsel for the accused. The defense may enter an objection at that time and the military judge may make such orders as are required in the interest of justice.

(3) *Specificity.* The military judge may require the defense to specify the grounds upon which the defense moves to suppress or object to evidence described in subdivision (d)(1). If defense counsel, despite the exercise of due diligence, has been unable to interview adequately those persons involved in the search or seizure, the military judge may enter any order required by the interests of justice, including authorization for the defense to make a general motion to suppress or a general objection.

(4) *Challenging Probable Cause.*

(A) *Relevant Evidence.* If the defense challenges evidence seized pursuant to a search warrant or search authorization on the ground that the warrant or authorization was not based upon probable cause, the evidence relevant to the motion is limited to evidence concerning the information actually presented to or otherwise known by the authorizing officer, except as provided in subdivision (d)(4)(B).

(B) *False Statements.* If the defense makes a substantial preliminary showing that a government agent knowingly and intentionally or with reckless disregard for the truth included a false statement or omitted a material fact in the information presented to the authorizing officer, and if the allegedly false statement or omitted material fact is necessary to the finding of probable cause, the defense, upon request, is entitled to a hearing. At the hearing, the defense has the burden of establishing by a preponderance of the evidence the allegation of knowing and intentional falsity or reckless disregard for the truth. If the defense meets its burden, the prosecution has the burden of proving by a preponderance of the evidence, with the false information set aside, that the remaining information presented to the authorizing officer is sufficient to establish probable cause. If the prosecution does not meet its burden, the objection or motion must be granted unless the search is otherwise lawful under these rules."

(5) *Burden and Standard of Proof.*

(A) *In general.* When the defense makes an appropriate motion or objection under subdivision (d), the prosecution has the burden of proving by a preponderance of the evidence that the evidence was not obtained as a result of an unlawful search or seizure; that the evidence would have been obtained even if the unlawful search or seizure had not been made; that the evidence was obtained by officials who reasonably and with good faith relied on the issuance of an authorization to search, seize, or apprehend or a search warrant or an arrest warrant; that the evidence was obtained by officials in objectively reasonable reliance on a statute or on binding precedent later held violative of the Fourth Amendment; or that the deterrence of future unlawful searches or seizures is not appreciable or such deterrence does not outweigh the costs to the justice system of excluding the evidence.

(B) *Statement Following Apprehension.* In addition to subdivision (d)(5)(A), a statement obtained from a person apprehended in a dwelling in violation of R.C.M. 302(d)(2) and (e), is admissible if the prosecution shows by a preponderance of the evidence that the apprehension was based on probable cause, the statement was made at a location outside the dwelling subsequent to the apprehension, and the statement was otherwise in compliance with these rules.

(C) *Specific Grounds of Motion or Objection.* When the military judge has required the defense to make a specific motion or objection under subdivision (d)(3), the burden on the prosecution extends only to the grounds upon which the defense moved to suppress or objected to the evidence.

(6) *Defense Evidence.* The defense may present evidence relevant to the admissibility of evidence as to which there has been an appropriate motion or objection under this rule. An accused may testify for the limited purpose of contesting the legality of the search or seizure giving rise to the challenged evidence. Prior to the introduction of such testimony by the accused, the defense must inform the military judge that the testimony is offered under subdivision (d). When the accused testifies under subdivision (d), the accused may be cross-examined only as to the matter on which he or she testifies. Nothing said by the accused on either direct or cross-examination may be used against the accused for any purpose other than in a prosecution for perjury, false swearing, or the making of a false official statement.

(7) *Rulings.* The military judge must rule, prior to plea, upon any motion to suppress or objection to evidence made prior to plea unless, for good cause, the military judge orders that the ruling be deferred for determination at trial or after findings. The military judge may not defer ruling if doing so adversely affects a party's right to appeal the ruling. The military judge must state essential findings of fact on the record when the ruling involves factual issues.

(8) *Informing the Members.* If a defense motion or objection under this rule is sustained in whole or in part, the court-martial members may not be informed of that fact except when the military judge must instruct the members to disregard evidence.

(e) *Effect of Guilty Plea.* Except as otherwise expressly provided in R.C.M. 910(a)(2), a plea of guilty to an offense that results in a finding of guilty waives all issues under the Fourth Amendment to the Constitution of the United States and Mil. R. Evid. 311-317 with respect to the offense, whether or not raised prior to plea.

Rule 312. Body views and intrusions

(a) *General rule.* Evidence obtained from body views and intrusions conducted in accordance with this rule is admissible at trial when relevant and not otherwise inadmissible under these rules.

(b) *Visual examination of the body.*

(1) *Consensual Examination.* Evidence obtained from a visual examination of the unclothed body is admissible if the person consented to the inspection in accordance with Mil. R. Evid. 314(e).

(2) *Involuntary Examination.* Evidence obtained from an involuntary display of the unclothed body, including a visual examination of body cavities, is admissible only if the inspection was conducted in a reasonable fashion and authorized under the following provisions of the Military Rules of Evidence:

(A) inspections and inventories under Mil. R. Evid. 313;

(B) searches under Mil. R. Evid. 314(b) and 314(c) if there is a reasonable suspicion that weapons, contraband, or evidence of crime is concealed on the body of the person to be searched;

(C) searches incident to lawful apprehension under Mil. R. Evid. 314(g);

(D) searches within a jail, confinement facility, or similar facility under Mil. R. Evid. 314(h) if reasonably necessary to maintain the security of the institution or its personnel;

(E) emergency searches under Mil. R. Evid. 314(i); and

(F) probable cause searches under Mil. R. Evid. 315.

Discussion

An examination of the unclothed body under this rule should be conducted whenever practicable by a person of the same sex as that of the person being examined; however, failure to comply with this requirement does not make an examination an unlawful search within the meaning of Mil. R. Evid. 311.

(c) *Intrusion into Body Cavities.*

(1) *Mouth, Nose, and Ears*. Evidence obtained from a reasonable nonconsensual physical intrusion into the mouth, nose, and ears is admissible under the same standards that apply to a visual examination of the body under subdivision (b).

(2) *Other Body Cavities*. Evidence obtained from nonconsensual intrusions into other body cavities is admissible only if made in a reasonable fashion by a person with appropriate medical qualifications and if:

(A) at the time of the intrusion there was probable cause to believe that a weapon, contraband, or other evidence of crime was present;

(B) conducted to remove weapons, contraband, or evidence of crime discovered under subdivisions (b) or (c)(2)(A) of this rule;

(C) conducted pursuant to Mil. R. Evid. 316(c)(5)(C);

(D) conducted pursuant to a search warrant or search authorization under Mil. R. Evid. 315; or

(E) conducted pursuant to Mil. R. Evid. 314(h) based on a reasonable suspicion that the individual is concealing a weapon, contraband, or evidence of crime.

(d) *Extraction of Body Fluids*. Evidence obtained from nonconsensual extraction of body fluids is admissible if seized pursuant to a search warrant or a search authorization under Mil. R. Evid. 315. Evidence obtained from nonconsensual extraction of body fluids made without such a warrant or authorization is admissible, notwithstanding Mil. R. Evid. 315(g), only when probable cause existed at the time of extraction to believe that evidence of crime would be found and that the delay necessary to obtain a search warrant or search authorization could have resulted in the destruction of the evidence. Evidence obtained from nonconsensual extraction of body fluids is admissible only when executed in a reasonable fashion by a person with appropriate medical qualifications.

(e) *Other Intrusive Searches*. Evidence obtained from a nonconsensual intrusive search of the body, other than searches described in subdivisions (c) or (d), conducted to locate or obtain weapons, contraband, or evidence of crime is admissible only if obtained pursuant to a search warrant or search authorization under Mil. R. Evid. 315 and conducted in a reasonable fashion by a person with appropriate medical qualifications in such a manner so as not to endanger the health of the person to be searched.

(f) *Intrusions for Valid Medical Purposes*. Evidence or contraband obtained in the course of a medical examination or an intrusion conducted for a valid medical purpose is admissible. Such an examination or intrusion may not, for the purpose of obtaining evidence or contraband, exceed what is necessary for the medical purpose.

Discussion

Nothing in this rule will be deemed to interfere with the lawful authority of the Armed Forces to take whatever action may be necessary to preserve the health of a service member.

Compelling a person to ingest substances for the purposes of locating the property described above or to compel the bodily elimination of such property is a search within the meaning of this section.

(g) *Medical Qualifications*. The Secretary concerned may prescribe appropriate medical qualifications for persons who conduct searches and seizures under this rule.

Rule 313. Inspections and inventories in the Armed Forces

(a) *General Rule*. Evidence obtained from lawful inspections and inventories in the Armed Forces is admissible at trial when relevant and not otherwise inadmissible under these rules. An unlawful weapon, contraband, or other evidence of a crime discovered during a lawful inspection or inventory may be seized and is admissible in accordance with this rule.

(b) *Lawful Inspections*. An "inspection" is an examination of the whole or part of a unit, organization, installation, vessel, aircraft, or vehicle, including an examination conducted at entrance and exit points, conducted as an incident of command the primary purpose of which is to determine and to ensure the security, military fitness, or good order and discipline of the unit, organization, installation, vessel, aircraft, or vehicle. Inspections must be conducted in a reasonable fashion and, if applicable, must comply with Mil. R. Evid. 312. Inspections may utilize any reasonable natural or technological aid and may be conducted with or without notice to those inspected.

(1) *Purpose of Inspections*. An inspection may include, but is not limited to, an examination to determine and to ensure that any or all of the following requirements are met: that the command is properly equipped, functioning properly, maintaining proper

standards of readiness, sea or airworthiness, sanitation and cleanliness; and that personnel are present, fit, and ready for duty. An order to produce body fluids, such as urine, is permissible in accordance with this rule.

(2) *Searches for Evidence.* An examination made for the primary purpose of obtaining evidence for use in a trial by court-martial or in other disciplinary proceedings is not an inspection within the meaning of this rule.

(3) *Examinations to Locate and Confiscate Weapons or Contraband.*

(A) An inspection may include an examination to locate and confiscate unlawful weapons and other contraband provided that the criteria set forth in subdivision (b)(3)(B) are not implicated.

(B) The prosecution must prove by clear and convincing evidence that the examination was an inspection within the meaning of this rule if a purpose of an examination is to locate weapons or contraband, and if:

(i) the examination was directed immediately following a report of a specific offense in the unit, organization, installation, vessel, aircraft, or vehicle and was not previously scheduled;

(ii) specific individuals are selected for examination; or

(iii) persons examined are subjected to substantially different intrusions during the same examination.

(c) *Lawful Inventories.* An "inventory" is a reasonable examination, accounting, or other control measure used to account for or control property, assets, or other resources. It is administrative and not prosecutorial in nature, and if applicable, the inventory must comply with Mil. R. Evid. 312. An examination made for the primary purpose of obtaining evidence for use in a trial by court-martial or in other disciplinary proceedings is not an inventory within the meaning of this rule.

Rule 314. Searches not requiring probable cause

(a) *General Rule.* Evidence obtained from reasonable searches not requiring probable cause is admissible at trial when relevant and not otherwise inadmissible under these rules or the Constitution of the United States as applied to members of the Armed Forces.

(b) *Border Searches.* Evidence from a border search for customs or immigration purposes authorized by a federal statute is admissible.

(c) *Searches Upon Entry to or Exit from United States Installations, Aircraft, and Vessels Abroad.* In addition to inspections under Mil. R. Evid. 313(b), evidence is admissible when a commander of a United States military installation, enclave, or aircraft on foreign soil, or in foreign or international airspace, or a United States vessel in foreign or international waters, has authorized appropriate personnel to search persons or the property of such persons upon entry to or exit from the installation, enclave, aircraft, or vessel to ensure the security, military fitness, or good order and discipline of the command. A search made for the primary purpose of obtaining evidence for use in a trial by court-martial or other disciplinary proceeding is not authorized by subdivision (c).

Discussion

Searches under subdivision (c) may not be conducted at a time or in a manner contrary to an express provision of a treaty or agreement to which the United States is a party; however, failure to comply with a treaty or agreement does not render a search unlawful within the meaning of Mil. R. Evid. 311.

(d) *Searches of Government Property.* Evidence resulting from a search of government property without probable cause is admissible under this rule unless the person to whom the property is issued or assigned has a reasonable expectation of privacy therein at the time of the search. Normally a person does not have a reasonable expectation of privacy in government property that is not issued for personal use. Wall or floor lockers in living quarters issued for the purpose of storing personal possessions normally are issued for personal use, but the determination as to whether a person has a reasonable expectation of privacy in government property issued for personal use depends on the facts and circumstances at the time of the search.

(e) *Consent Searches.*

(1) *General Rule.* Evidence of a search conducted without probable cause is admissible if conducted with lawful consent.

(2) *Who May Consent.* A person may consent to a search of his or her person or property, or both, unless control over such property has been given to another. A person may grant consent to search property when the person exercises control over that property.

Discussion

Where a co-occupant of property is physically present at the time of the requested search and expressly states his refusal to consent to the search, a warrantless search is unreasonable as to that co-occupant and evidence from the search is inadmissible as to that co-occupant. *Georgia v. Randolph*, 547 U.S. 103 (2006).

---

(3) *Scope of Consent.* Consent may be limited in any way by the person granting consent, including limitations in terms of time, place, or property, and may be withdrawn at any time.

(4) *Voluntariness.* To be valid, consent must be given voluntarily. Voluntariness is a question to be determined from all the circumstances. Although a person's knowledge of the right to refuse to give consent is a factor to be considered in determining voluntariness, the prosecution is not required to demonstrate such knowledge as a prerequisite to establishing a voluntary consent. Mere submission to the color of authority of personnel performing law enforcement duties or acquiescence in an announced or indicated purpose to search is not a voluntary consent.

(5) *Burden and Standard of Proof.* The prosecution must prove consent by clear and convincing evidence. The fact that a person was in custody while granting consent is a factor to be considered in determining the voluntariness of consent, but it does not affect the standard of proof.

(f) *Searches Incident to a Lawful Stop.*

(1) *Lawfulness.* A stop is lawful when conducted by a person authorized to apprehend under R.C.M. 302(b) or others performing law enforcement duties and when the person making the stop has information or observes unusual conduct that leads him or her reasonably to conclude in light of his or her experience that criminal activity may be afoot. The stop must be temporary and investigatory in nature.

(2) *Stop and Frisk.* Evidence is admissible if seized from a person who was lawfully stopped and who was frisked for weapons because he or she was reasonably suspected to be armed and dangerous. Contraband or evidence that is located in the process of a lawful frisk may be seized.

Discussion

Mil. R. Evid. 314(f)(2) requires that the official making the stop have a reasonable suspicion based on specific and articulable facts that the person being frisked is armed and dangerous. Officer safety is a factor, and the officer need not be absolutely certain that the individual detained is armed for the purposes of frisking or patting down that person's outer clothing for weapons. The test is whether a reasonably prudent person in similar circumstances would be warranted in a belief that his or her safety was in danger. The purpose of a frisk is to search for weapons or other dangerous items, including but not limited to: firearms, knives, needles, or razor blades. A limited search of outer clothing for weapons serves to protect both the officer and the public; therefore, a frisk is reasonable under the Fourth Amendment.

---

(3) *Vehicles.* Evidence is admissible if seized in the course of a search for weapons in the areas of the passenger compartment of a vehicle in which a weapon may be placed or hidden, so long as the person lawfully stopped is the driver or a passenger and the official who made the stop has a reasonable suspicion that the person stopped is dangerous and may gain immediate control of a weapon.

Discussion

The scope of the search is similar to the "stop and frisk" defined in Mil. R. Evid. 314(f)(2). During the search for weapons, the official may seize any item that is immediately apparent as contraband or as evidence related to the offense serving as the basis for the stop. As a matter of safety, the official may, after conducting a lawful stop of a vehicle, order the driver and any passengers out of the car without any additional suspicion or justification.

(g) *Searches Incident to Apprehension.*

(1) *General Rule.* Evidence is admissible if seized in a search of a person who has been lawfully apprehended or if seized as a result of a reasonable protective sweep.

(2) *Search for Weapons and Destructible Evidence.* A lawful search incident to apprehension may include a search for weapons or destructible evidence in the area within the immediate control of a person who has been apprehended. "Immediate control" means that area in which the individual searching could reasonably believe that the person apprehended could reach with a sudden movement to obtain such property.

Discussion

The scope of the search for weapons is limited to that which is necessary to protect the arresting official. The official may not search a vehicle for weapons if there is no possibility that the arrestee could reach into the searched area, for example, after the arrestee is handcuffed and removed from the vehicle. The scope of the search is broader for destructible evidence related to the offense for which the individual is being arrested. Unlike a search for weapons, the search for destructible offense-related evidence may take place after the arrestee is handcuffed and removed from a vehicle. If, however, the official cannot expect to find destructible offense-related evidence, this exception does not apply.

---

(3) *Protective Sweep for Other Persons.*

(A) *Area of Potential Immediate Attack.* Apprehending officials may, incident to apprehension, as a precautionary matter and without probable cause or reasonable suspicion, look in closets and other spaces immediately adjoining the place of apprehension from which an attack could be immediately launched.

(B) *Wider Protective Sweep.* When an apprehension takes place at a location in which another person might be present who might endanger the apprehending officials or others in the area of the apprehension, a search incident to arrest may lawfully include a reasonable examination of those spaces where a person might be found. Such a reasonable examination is lawful under subdivision (g) if the apprehending official has a reasonable suspicion based on specific and articulable facts that the area to be examined harbors an individual posing a danger to those in the area of the apprehension.

(h) *Searches within Jails, Confinement Facilities, or Similar Facilities.* Evidence obtained from a search within a jail, confinement facility, or similar facility is admissible even if conducted without probable cause provided that it was authorized by persons with authority over the institution.

(i) *Emergency Searches to Save Life or for Related Purposes.* Evidence obtained from emergency searches of persons or property conducted to save life, or for a related purpose, is admissible provided that the search was conducted in a good faith effort to render immediate medical aid, to obtain information that will assist in the rendering of such aid, or to prevent immediate or ongoing personal injury.

(j) *Searches of Open Fields or Woodlands.* Evidence obtained from a search of an open field or woodland is admissible provided that the search was not unlawful within the meaning of Mil. R. Evid. 311.

Rule 315. Probable cause searches

(a) *General rule.* Evidence obtained from reasonable searches conducted pursuant to a search warrant or search authorization, or under the exigent circumstances described in this rule, is admissible at trial when relevant and not otherwise inadmissible under these rules or the Constitution of the United States as applied to members of the Armed Forces.

(b) *Definitions.* As used in these rules:

(1) "Search authorization" means express permission, written or oral, issued by competent military authority to search a person or an area for specified property or evidence or for a specific person and to seize such property, evidence, or person. It may contain an order directing subordinate personnel to conduct a search in a specified manner.

(2) "Search warrant" means express permission to search and seize issued by competent civilian authority or under R.C.M. 703A.

(3) "Warrant for wire or electronic communications" means a warrant issued by a military judge pursuant to 18 U.S.C. §§ 2703(a), (b)(1)(A), or (c)(1)(A) in accordance with 10 U.S.C. § 846(d)(3) and R.C.M. 309(b)(2) and R.C.M. 703A.

(c) *Scope of Search Authorization.* A search authorization may be valid under this rule for a search of:

(1) the physical person of anyone subject to military law or the law of war wherever found;

(2) military property of the United States or of nonappropriated fund activities of an Armed force of the United States wherever located;

(3) persons or property situated on or in a military installation, encampment, vessel, aircraft, vehicle, or any other location under military control, wherever located; or

(4) nonmilitary property within a foreign country.

Discussion

If nonmilitary property within a foreign country is owned, used, occupied by, or in the possession of an agency of the United States other than the Department of Defense, a search should be conducted in coordination with an appropriate representative of the agency concerned, although failure to obtain such coordination would not render a search unlawful within the meaning of Mil. R. Evid. 311. If other nonmilitary property within a foreign country is to be searched, the search should be conducted in accordance with any relevant treaty or agreement or in coordination with an appropriate representative of the foreign country, although failure to obtain such coordination or noncompliance with a treaty or agreement would not render a search unlawful within the meaning of Mil. R. Evid. 311.

(d) *Who May Authorize.* A search authorization under this rule is valid only if issued by an impartial individual in one of the categories set forth in paragraphs (d)(1), (d)(2), and (d)(3) of this rule. Only a military judge may issue a warrant for wire or electronic communications under this rule. An otherwise impartial authorizing official does not lose impartiality merely because the official is present at the scene of a search or is otherwise readily available to persons who may seek the issuance of a search authorization; nor does such an official lose impartial character merely because the official previously and impartially authorized investigative activities when such previous authorization is similar in intent or function to a pretrial authorization made by the United States district courts.

(1) *Commander.* A commander or other person serving in a position designated by the Secretary concerned as either a position analogous to an officer in charge or a position of command, who has control over the place where the property or person to be searched is situated or found, or, if that place is not under military control, having control over persons subject to military law or the law of war;

(2) *Military Judge or Magistrate.* A military judge or magistrate if authorized under regulations prescribed by the Secretary of Defense or the Secretary concerned; or

(3) *Other competent search authority.* A competent, impartial official as designated under regulations by the Secretary of Defense or the Secretary concerned as an individual authorized to issue search authorizations under this rule.

(e) *Who May Search.*

(1) *Search Authorization.* Any commissioned officer, warrant officer, petty officer, noncommissioned officer, and, when in the execution of guard or police duties, any criminal investigator, member of the Air Force security forces, military police, or shore patrol, or person designated by proper authority to perform guard or police duties, or any agent of any such person, may conduct or authorize a search when a search authorization has been granted under this rule or a search would otherwise be proper under subdivision (g).

(2) *Search Warrants.* Any civilian or military criminal investigator authorized to request search warrants pursuant to applicable law or regulation is authorized to serve and execute search warrants. The execution of a search warrant affects admissibility only insofar as exclusion of evidence is required by the Constitution of the United States or an applicable federal statute.

(f) *Basis for Search Authorizations.*

(1) *Probable Cause Requirement.* A search authorization issued under this rule must be based upon probable cause.

(2) *Probable Cause Determination.* Probable cause to search exists when there is a reasonable belief that the person, property, or evidence sought is located in the place or on the person to be searched. A search authorization may be based upon hearsay evidence in whole or in part. A determination of probable cause under this rule will be based upon any or all of the following:

(A) written statements communicated to the authorizing official;

(B) oral statements communicated to the authorizing official in person, via telephone, or by other appropriate means of communication; or

(C) such information as may be known by the authorizing official that would not preclude the officer from acting in an impartial fashion. The Secretary of Defense or the Secretary concerned may prescribe additional requirements through regulation.

(g) *Exigencies.* Evidence obtained from a probable cause search is admissible without a search warrant or search authorization when there is a reasonable belief that the delay necessary to obtain a search warrant or search authorization would result in the removal, destruction, or concealment of the property or evidence sought. Military operational necessity may create an exigency by prohibiting or preventing communication with a person empowered to grant a search authorization.

Rule 316. Seizures

(a) *General rule.* Evidence obtained from reasonable seizures is admissible at trial when relevant and not otherwise inadmissible under these rules or the Constitution of the United States as applied to members of the Armed Forces.

(b) *Apprehension.* Apprehension is governed by R.C.M. 302.

(c) *Seizure of Property or Evidence.*

(1) Based on Probable Cause. Evidence is admissible when seized based on a reasonable belief that the property or evidence is an unlawful weapon, contraband, evidence of crime, or might be used to resist apprehension or to escape.

(2) *Abandoned Property*. Abandoned property may be seized without probable cause and without a search warrant or search authorization. Such seizure may be made by any person.

(3) *Consent*. Property or evidence may be seized with consent consistent with the requirements applicable to consensual searches under Mil. R. Evid. 314.

(4) *Government Property*. Government property may be seized without probable cause and without a search warrant or search authorization by any person listed in subdivision (d), unless the person to whom the property is issued or assigned has a reasonable expectation of privacy therein, as provided in Mil. R. Evid. 314(d), at the time of the seizure.

(5) *Other Property*. Property or evidence not included in subdivisions (c)(1)-(4) may be seized for use in evidence by any person listed in subdivision (d) if:

(A) *Authorization*. The person is authorized to seize the property or evidence by a search warrant or a search authorization under Mil. R. Evid. 315;

(B) *Exigent Circumstances*. The person has probable cause to seize the property or evidence and under Mil. R. Evid. 315(g) a search warrant or search authorization is not required; or

(C) *Plain View*. The person while in the course of otherwise lawful activity observes in a reasonable fashion property or evidence that the person has probable cause to seize.

(6) *Temporary Detention*. Nothing in this rule prohibits temporary detention of property on less than probable cause when authorized under the Constitution of the United States.

(d) *Who May Seize*. Any commissioned officer, warrant officer, petty officer, noncommissioned officer, and, when in the execution of guard or police duties, any criminal investigator, member of the Air Force security forces, military police, or shore patrol, or individual designated by proper authority to perform guard or police duties, or any agent of any such person, may seize property pursuant to this rule.

(e) *Other Seizures*. Evidence obtained from a seizure not addressed in this rule is admissible provided that its seizure was permissible under the Constitution of the United States as applied to members of the Armed Forces.

Rule 317. Interception of wire and oral communications

(a) *General rule*. Wire or oral communications constitute evidence obtained as a result of an unlawful search or seizure within the meaning of Mil. R. Evid. 311 when such evidence must be excluded under the Fourth Amendment to the Constitution of the United States as applied to members of the Armed Forces or if such evidence must be excluded under a federal statute applicable to members of the Armed Forces.

(b) *When Authorized by Court Order*. Evidence from the interception of wire or oral communications is admissible when authorized pursuant to an application to a federal judge of competent jurisdiction under the provisions of a federal statute.

Discussion

Pursuant to 18 U.S.C. § 2516(1), the Attorney General, Deputy Attorney General, Associate Attorney General, or any Assistant Attorney General, any acting Assistant Attorney General, or any Deputy Assistant Attorney General or acting Deputy Assistant Attorney General in the Criminal Division or National Security Division specially designated by the Attorney General, may authorize an application to a Federal judge of competent jurisdiction for, and such judge may grant in conformity with 18 U.S.C. § 2518, an order authorizing or approving the interception of wire or oral communications by the Federal Bureau of Investigation, or a Federal agency having responsibility for the investigation of the offense as to which the application is made, for purposes of obtaining evidence concerning the offenses enumerated in 18 U.S.C. § 2516(1), to the extent such offenses are punishable under the Uniform Code of Military Justice.

(c) *Regulations*. Notwithstanding any other provision of these rules, evidence obtained by members of the Armed Forces or their agents through interception of wire or oral communications for law enforcement purposes is not admissible unless such interception:

(1) takes place in the United States and is authorized under subdivision (b);

(2) takes place outside the United States and is authorized under regulations issued by the Secretary of Defense or the Secretary concerned; or

(3) is authorized under regulations issued by the Secretary of Defense or the Secretary concerned and is not unlawful under applicable federal statutes.

Rule 321. Eyewitness identification

(a) *General rule*. Testimony concerning a relevant out-of-court identification by any person is admissible, subject to an appropriate objection under this rule, if such testimony is otherwise admissible under these rules. The witness making the identification and any person who has observed the previous identification may testify concerning it. When in testimony a witness identifies the accused as being, or not being, a participant in an offense or makes any other relevant identification concerning a person in the courtroom, evidence that on a previous occasion the witness made a similar identification is admissible to corroborate the witness' testimony as to identity even if the credibility of the witness has not been attacked directly, subject to appropriate objection under this rule.

(b) *When Inadmissible.* An identification of the accused as being a participant in an offense, whether such identification is made at the trial or otherwise, is inadmissible against the accused if:

(1) The identification is the result of an unlawful lineup or other unlawful identification process, as defined in subdivision (c), conducted by the United States or other domestic authorities and the accused makes a timely motion to suppress or an objection to the evidence under this rule; or

(2) Exclusion of the evidence is required by the Due Process Clause of the Fifth Amendment to the Constitution of the United States as applied to members of the Armed Forces. Evidence other than an identification of the accused that is obtained as a result of the unlawful lineup or unlawful identification process is inadmissible against the accused if the accused makes a timely motion to suppress or an objection to the evidence under this rule and if exclusion of the evidence is required under the Constitution of the United States as applied to members of the Armed Forces.

(c) *Unlawful Lineup or Identification Process.*

(1) *Unreliable.* A lineup or other identification process is unreliable, and therefore unlawful, if the lineup or other identification process is so suggestive as to create a substantial likelihood of misidentification.

(2) *In Violation of Right to Counsel.* A lineup is unlawful if it is conducted in violation of the accused's rights to counsel.

(A) *Military Lineups.* An accused or suspect is entitled to counsel if, after preferral of charges or imposition of pretrial restraint under R.C.M. 304 for the offense under investigation, the accused is required by persons subject to the code or their agents to participate in a lineup for the purpose of identification. When a person entitled to counsel under this rule requests counsel, a judge advocate or a person certified in accordance with Article 27(b) will be provided by the United States at no expense to the accused or suspect and without regard to indigency or lack thereof before the lineup may proceed. The accused or suspect may waive the rights provided in this rule if the waiver is freely, knowingly, and intelligently made.

(B) *Nonmilitary Lineups.* When a person subject to the code is required to participate in a lineup for purposes of identification by an official or agent of the United States, of the District of Columbia, or of a State, Commonwealth, or possession of the United States, or any political subdivision of such a State, Commonwealth, or possession, and the provisions of subdivision (c)(2)(A) do not apply, the person's entitlement to counsel and the validity of any waiver of applicable rights will be determined by the principles of law generally recognized in the trial of criminal cases in the United States district courts involving similar lineups.

(d) *Motions to Suppress and Objections.*

(1) *Disclosure.* Prior to arraignment, the prosecution must disclose to the defense all evidence of, or derived from, a prior identification of the accused as a lineup or other identification process that it intends to offer into evidence against the accused at trial.

(2) *Time Requirement.* When such evidence has been disclosed, any motion to suppress or objection under this rule must be made by the defense prior to submission of a plea. In the absence of such motion or objection, the defense may not raise the issue at a later time except as permitted by the military judge for good cause shown. Failure to so move constitutes a waiver of the motion or objection.

(3) *Continuing Duty.* If the prosecution intends to offer such evidence and the evidence was not disclosed prior to arraignment, the prosecution must provide timely notice to the military judge and counsel for the accused. The defense may enter an objection at that time, and the military judge may make such orders as are required in the interests of justice.

(4) *Specificity.* The military judge may require the defense to specify the grounds upon which the defense moves to suppress or object to evidence. If defense counsel, despite the exercise of due diligence, has been unable to interview adequately those persons involved in the lineup or other identification process, the military judge may enter any order required by the interests of justice, including authorization for the

defense to make a general motion to suppress or a general objection.

(5) *Defense Evidence*. The defense may present evidence relevant to the issue of the admissibility of evidence as to which there has been an appropriate motion or objection under this rule. An accused may testify for the limited purpose of contesting the legality of the lineup or identification process giving rise to the challenged evidence. Prior to the introduction of such testimony by the accused, the defense must inform the military judge that the testimony is offered under subdivision (d). When the accused testifies under subdivision (d), the accused may be cross-examined only as to the matter on which he or she testifies. Nothing said by the accused on either direct or cross-examination may be used against the accused for any purpose other than in a prosecution for perjury, false swearing, or the making of a false official statement.

(6) *Burden and Standard of Proof*. When the defense has raised a specific motion or objection under subdivision (d)(3), the burden on the prosecution extends only to the grounds upon which the defense moved to suppress or object to the evidence.

(A) *Right to Counsel*.

(i) *Initial Violation of Right to Counsel at a Lineup*. When the accused raises the right to presence of counsel under this rule, the prosecution must prove by a preponderance of the evidence that counsel was present at the lineup or that the accused, having been advised of the right to the presence of counsel, voluntarily and intelligently waived that right prior to the lineup.

(ii) *Identification Subsequent to a Lineup Conducted in Violation of the Right to Counsel*. When the military judge determines that an identification is the result of a lineup conducted without the presence of counsel or an appropriate waiver, any later identification by one present at such unlawful lineup is also a result thereof unless the military judge determines that the contrary has been shown by clear and convincing evidence.

(B) *Unreliable Identification*.

(i) *Initial Unreliable Identification*. When an objection raises the issue of an unreliable identification, the prosecution must prove by a preponderance of the evidence that the identification was reliable under the circumstances.

(ii) *Identification Subsequent to an Unreliable Identification*. When the military judge determines that an identification is the result of an unreliable identification, a later identification may be admitted if the prosecution proves by clear and convincing evidence that the later identification is not the result of the inadmissible identification.

(7) *Rulings*. A motion to suppress or an objection to evidence made prior to plea under this rule will be ruled upon prior to plea unless the military judge, for good cause, orders that it be deferred for determination at the trial of the general issue or until after findings, but no such determination will be deferred if a party's right to appeal the ruling is affected adversely. Where factual issues are involved in ruling upon such motion or objection, the military judge will state his or her essential findings of fact on the record.

(e) *Effect of Guilty Pleas*. Except as otherwise expressly provided in R.C.M. 910(a)(2), a plea of guilty to an offense that results in a finding of guilty waives all issues under this rule with respect to that offense whether or not raised prior to the plea.

SECTION IV
RELEVANCY AND ITS LIMITS

Rule 401. Test for relevant evidence

Evidence is relevant if:

(a) it has any tendency to make a fact more or less probable than it would be without the evidence; and

(b) the fact is of consequence in determining the action.

Rule 402. General admissibility of relevant evidence

(a) Relevant evidence is admissible unless any of the following provides otherwise:

(1) the United States Constitution as it applies to members of the Armed Forces;

(2) a federal statute applicable to trial by courts-martial;

(3) these rules; or

(4) this Manual.

(b) Irrelevant evidence is not admissible.

Rule 403. Excluding relevant evidence for prejudice, confusion, waste of time, or other reasons

The military judge may exclude relevant evidence if its probative value is substantially outweighed by a danger of one or more of the following: unfair prejudice, confusing the issues, misleading the members, undue delay, wasting time, or needlessly presenting cumulative evidence.

Rule 404. Character evidence, crimes or other acts

(a) *Character Evidence.*

(1) *Prohibited Uses.* Evidence of a person's character or character trait is not admissible to prove that on a particular occasion the person acted in accordance with the character or trait.

(2) *Exceptions for an Accused or Victim.*

(A) The accused may offer evidence of the accused's pertinent trait and, if the evidence is admitted, the prosecution may offer evidence to rebut it. General military character is not a pertinent trait for the purposes of showing the probability of innocence of the accused for the following offenses under the UCMJ:

(i) Article 105;

(ii) Articles 120-122;

(iii) Articles 123a-124;

(iv) Articles 126-127;

(v) Articles 129-131;

(vi) Any other offense in which evidence of general military character of the accused is not relevant to any element of an offense for which the accused has been charged; or

(vii) An attempt or conspiracy to commit one of the above offenses.

(B) Subject to the limitations in Mil. R. Evid. 412, the accused may offer evidence of an alleged victim's pertinent trait, and if the evidence is admitted, the prosecution may:

(i) offer evidence to rebut it; and

(ii) offer evidence of the accused's same trait; and

(C) in a homicide or assault case, the prosecution may offer evidence of the alleged victim's trait of peacefulness to rebut evidence that the victim was the first aggressor.

(3) *Exceptions for a Witness.* Evidence of a witness' character may be admitted under Mil R. Evid. 607, 608, and 609.

(b) *Other Crimes, Wrongs, or Acts.*

(1) *Prohibited Uses.* Evidence of any other crime, wrong, or act is not admissible to prove a person's character in order to show that on a particular occasion the person acted in accordance with the character.

(2) *Permitted Uses.* This evidence may be admissible for another purpose, such as proving motive, opportunity, intent, preparation, plan, knowledge, identity, absence of mistake, or lack of accident.

(3) *Notice in a Criminal Case.* In a criminal case, the trial counsel must:

(A) provide reasonable notice of any such evidence that the trial counsel intends to offer at trial, so the accused has a fair opportunity to meet it;

(B) articulate in the notice the permitted purpose for which the trial counsel intends to offer the evidence and the reasoning that supports the purpose; and

(C) do so in writing before trial—or in any form during trial if the court, for good cause, excuses lack of pretrial notice.

Rule 405. Methods of proving character

(a) *By Reputation or Opinion.* When evidence of a person's character or character trait is admissible, it may be proved by testimony about the person's reputation or by testimony in the form of an opinion. On cross-examination of the character witness, the military judge may allow an inquiry into relevant specific instances of the person's conduct.

(b) *By Specific Instances of Conduct.* When a person's character or character trait is an essential element of a charge, claim, or defense, the character or trait may also be proved by relevant specific instances of the person's conduct.

(c) *By Affidavit.* The defense may introduce affidavits or other written statements of persons other than the accused concerning the character of the accused. If the defense introduces affidavits or other written statements under this subdivision, the prosecution may, in rebuttal, also introduce affidavits or other written statements regarding the character of the accused. Evidence of this type may be introduced by the defense or prosecution only if, aside from being contained in an affidavit or other written statement, it would otherwise be admissible under these rules.

(d) *Definitions.* "Reputation" means the estimation in which a person generally is held in the community in which the person lives or pursues a business or profession. "Community" in the Armed Forces includes a post, camp, ship, station, or other military organization regardless of size.

Rule 406. Habit; routine practice

Evidence of a person's habit or an organization's routine practice may be admitted to prove that on a particular occasion the person or organization acted in accordance with the habit or routine practice. The military judge may admit this evidence regardless of whether it is corroborated or whether there was an eyewitness.

Rule 407. Subsequent remedial measures

(a) When measures are taken that would have made an earlier injury or harm less likely to occur, evidence of the subsequent measures is not admissible to prove:

(1) negligence;

(2) culpable conduct;

(3) a defect in a product or its design; or

(4) a need for a warning or instruction.

(b) The military judge may admit this evidence for another purpose, such as impeachment or—if disputed—proving ownership, control, or the feasibility of precautionary measures.

Rule 408. Compromise offers and negotiations

(a) *Prohibited Uses.* Evidence of the following is not admissible—on behalf of any party—either to prove or disprove the validity or amount of a disputed claim or to impeach by a prior inconsistent statement or a contradiction:

(1) furnishing, promising, or offering—or accepting, promising to accept, or offering to accept—a valuable consideration in order to compromise the claim; and

(2) conduct or a statement made during compromise negotiations about the claim - except when the negotiations related to a claim by a public office in the exercise of its regulatory, investigative, or enforcement authority.

(b) *Exceptions.* The military judge may admit this evidence for another purpose, such as proving witness bias or prejudice, negating a contention of undue delay, or proving an effort to obstruct a criminal investigation or prosecution.

Rule 409. Offers to pay medical and similar expenses

Evidence of furnishing, promising to pay, or offering to pay medical, hospital, or similar expenses resulting from an injury is not admissible to prove liability for the injury.

Rule 410. Pleas, plea discussions, and related statements

(a) *Prohibited Uses.* Evidence of the following is not admissible against the accused who made the plea or participated in the plea discussions:

(1) a guilty plea that was later withdrawn;

(2) a nolo contendere plea;

(3) any statement made in the course of any judicial inquiry regarding either of the foregoing pleas; or

(4) any statement made during plea discussions with the convening authority, staff judge advocate, trial counsel or other counsel for the government if the discussions did not result in a guilty plea or they resulted in a later-withdrawn guilty plea.

(b) *Exceptions.* The military judge may admit a statement described in subdivision (a)(3) or (a)(4):

(1) when another statement made during the same plea or plea discussions has been introduced, if in fairness the statements ought to be considered together; or

(2) in a proceeding for perjury or false statement, if the accused made the statement under oath, on the record, and with counsel present.

(c) *Request for Administrative Disposition.* A "statement made during plea discussions" includes a statement made by the accused solely for the purpose of requesting disposition under an authorized procedure for administrative action in lieu of trial by court-martial; "on the record" includes the written statement submitted by the accused in furtherance of such request.

Rule 411. Liability insurance

Evidence that a person was or was not insured against liability is not admissible to prove whether the person acted negligently or otherwise wrongfully. The military judge may admit this evidence for another purpose, such as proving witness bias or prejudice or proving agency, ownership, or control.

Rule 412. Sex offense cases: The victim's sexual behavior or predisposition

(a) *Evidence generally inadmissible.* The following evidence is not admissible in any proceeding involving an alleged sexual offense except as provided in subdivisions (b) and (c):

(1) Evidence offered to prove that a victim engaged in other sexual behavior; or

(2) Evidence offered to prove a victim's sexual predisposition.

(b) *Exceptions.* In a proceeding, the following evidence is admissible, if otherwise admissible under these rules:

(1) evidence of specific instances of a victim's sexual behavior, if offered to prove that someone other than the accused was the source of semen, injury, or other physical evidence;

(2) evidence of specific instances of a victim's sexual behavior with respect to the person accused of the sexual misconduct, if offered by the accused to prove consent or if offered by the prosecution; and

(3) evidence the exclusion of which would violate the accused's constitutional rights.

(c) *Procedure to determine admissibility.*

(1) A party intending to offer evidence under subdivision (b) must—

(A) file a written motion at least 5 days prior to entry of pleas specifically describing the evidence and stating the purpose for which it is offered unless the military judge, for good cause shown, requires a different time for filing or permits filing during trial; and

(B) serve the motion on the opposing party and the military judge and notify the victim or, when appropriate, the victim's guardian or representative.

(2) Before admitting evidence under this rule, the military judge must conduct a hearing, which shall be closed. At this hearing, the parties may call witnesses, including the victim, and offer relevant evidence. The victim must be afforded a reasonable opportunity to attend and be heard. However, the hearing may not be unduly delayed for this purpose. The right to be heard under this rule includes the right to be heard through counsel, including Special Victims' Counsel under section 1044e of title 10, United States Code. In a case before a court-martial composed of a military judge and members, the military judge shall conduct the hearing outside the presence of the members pursuant to Article 39(a). The motion, related papers, and the record of the hearing must be sealed in accordance with R.C.M. 1113 and remain under seal unless the military judge, the Judge Advocate General, or an appellate court orders otherwise.

(3) If the military judge determines on the basis of the hearing described in paragraph (2) of this subdivision that the evidence that the accused seeks to offer is relevant for a purpose under subdivision (b)(1) or (2) of this rule and that the probative value of such evidence outweighs the danger of unfair prejudice to the victim's privacy, or that the evidence is described by subdivision (b)(3) of this rule, such evidence shall be admissible under this rule to the extent an order made by the military judge specifies evidence that may be offered and areas with respect to which the victim may be examined or cross-examined. Any evidence introduced under this rule is subject to challenge under Mil. R. Evid. 403.

(d) *Definitions.* For purposes of this rule, the term "sexual offense" includes any sexual misconduct punishable under the Uniform Code of Military Justice, federal law or state law. "Sexual behavior" includes any sexual behavior not encompassed by the alleged offense. The term "sexual predisposition" refers to a victim's mode of dress, speech, or lifestyle that does not directly refer to sexual activities or thoughts but that may have a sexual connotation for the fact finder. For purposes of this rule, the term "victim" includes an alleged victim.

Rule 413. Similar crimes in sexual offense cases

(a) *Permitted Uses.* In a court-martial proceeding for a sexual offense, the military judge may admit evidence that the accused committed any other sexual offense. The evidence may be considered on any matter to which it is relevant.

(b) *Disclosure to the Accused.* If the prosecution intends to offer this evidence, the prosecution must disclose it to the accused, including any witnesses' statements or a summary of the expected testimony. The prosecution must do so at least 5 days prior to entry of pleas or at a later time that the military judge allows for good cause.

(c) *Effect on Other Rules.* This rule does not limit the admission or consideration of evidence under any other rule.

(d) *Definition.* As used in this rule, "sexual offense" means an offense punishable under the Uniform Code of Military Justice, or a crime under federal or state law (as "state" is defined in 18 U.S.C. § 513), involving:

(1) any conduct prohibited by Article 120;

(2) any conduct prohibited by 18 U.S.C. chapter 109A;

(3) contact, without consent, between any part of the accused's body, or an object held or controlled by the accused, and another person's genitals or anus;

(4) contact, without consent, between the accused's genitals or anus and any part of another person's body;

(5) contact with the aim of deriving sexual pleasure or gratification from inflicting death, bodily injury, or physical pain on another person; or

(6) an attempt or conspiracy to engage in conduct described in subdivisions (d)(1)-(5).

Rule 414. Similar crimes in child-molestation cases

(a) *Permitted Uses.* In a court-martial proceeding in which an accused is charged with an act of child molestation, the military judge may admit evidence that the accused committed any other offense of child molestation. The evidence may be considered on any matter to which it is relevant.

(b) *Disclosure to the Accused.* If the prosecution intends to offer this evidence, the prosecution must disclose it to the accused, including witnesses' statements or a summary of the expected testimony. The prosecution must do so at least 5 days prior to entry of pleas or at a later time that the military judge allows for good cause.

(c) *Effect on Other Rules.* This rule does not limit the admission or consideration of evidence under any other rule.

(d) *Definitions.* As used in this rule:

(1) "Child" means a person below the age of 16; and

(2) "Child molestation" means an offense punishable under the Uniform Code of Military Justice, or a crime under federal law or under state law (as "state" is defined in 18 U.S.C. § 513), that involves:

(A) any conduct prohibited by Article 120 and committed with a child, or prohibited by Article 120b.

(B) any conduct prohibited by 18 U.S.C. chapter 109A and committed with a child;

(C) any conduct prohibited by 18 U.S.C. chapter 110;

(D) contact between any part of the accused's body, or an object held or controlled by the accused, and a child's genitals or anus;

(E) contact between the accused's genitals or anus and any part of a child's body;

(F) contact with the aim of deriving sexual pleasure or gratification from inflicting death, bodily injury, or physical pain on a child; or

(G) an attempt or conspiracy to engage in conduct described in subdivisions (d)(2)(A)-(F).

SECTION V
PRIVILEGES

Rule 501. Privilege in general

(a) A person may not claim a privilege with respect to any matter except as required by or provided for in:

(1) the United States Constitution as applied to members of the Armed Forces;

(2) a federal statute applicable to trials by courts-martial;

(3) these rules;

(4) this Manual; or

(5) the principles of common law generally recognized in the trial of criminal cases in the United States district courts under rule 501 of the Federal Rules of Evidence, insofar as the application of such principles in trials by courts-martial is practicable and not contrary to or inconsistent with the Uniform Code of Military Justice, these rules, or this Manual.

(b) A claim of privilege includes, but is not limited to, the assertion by any person of a privilege to:

(1) refuse to be a witness;

(2) refuse to disclose any matter;

(3) refuse to produce any object or writing; or

(4) prevent another from being a witness or disclosing any matter or producing any object or writing.

(c) The term "person" includes an appropriate representative of the Federal Government, a State, or political subdivision thereof, or any other entity claiming to be the holder of a privilege.

(d) Notwithstanding any other provision of these rules, information not otherwise privileged does not become privileged on the basis that it was acquired by a medical officer or civilian physician in a professional capacity.

Rule 502. Lawyer-client privilege

(a) *General Rule.* A client has a privilege to refuse to disclose and to prevent any other person from disclosing confidential communications made for the purpose of facilitating the rendition of professional legal services to the client:

(1) between the client or the client's representative and the lawyer or the lawyer's representative;

(2) between the lawyer and the lawyer's representative;

(3) by the client or the client's lawyer to a lawyer representing another in a matter of common interest;

(4) between representatives of the client or between the client and a representative of the client; or

(5) between lawyers representing the client.

(b) *Definitions.* As used in this rule:

(1) "Client" means a person, public officer, corporation, association, organization, or other entity, either public or private, who receives professional legal services from a lawyer, or who consults a lawyer with a view to obtaining professional legal services from the lawyer.

(2) "Lawyer" means a person authorized, or reasonably believed by the client to be authorized, to practice law; or a member of the Armed Forces detailed, assigned, or otherwise provided to represent a person in a court-martial case or in any military investigation or proceeding. The term "lawyer" does not include a member of the Armed Forces serving in a capacity other than as a judge advocate, legal officer, or law specialist as defined in Article 1, unless the member:

(A) is detailed, assigned, or otherwise provided to represent a person in a court-martial case or in any military investigation or proceeding;

(B) is authorized by the Armed Forces, or reasonably believed by the client to be authorized, to render professional legal services to members of the Armed Forces; or

(C) is authorized to practice law and renders professional legal services during off-duty employment.

(3) "Lawyer's representative" means a person employed by or assigned to assist a lawyer in providing professional legal services.

(4) A communication is "confidential" if not intended to be disclosed to third persons other than those to whom disclosure is in furtherance of the rendition of professional legal services to the client or those reasonably necessary for the transmission of the communication.

(c) *Who May Claim the Privilege.* The privilege may be claimed by the client, the guardian or conservator of the client, the personal representative of a deceased client, or the successor, trustee, or similar representative of a corporation, association, or other organization, whether or not in existence. The lawyer or the lawyer's representative who received the communication may claim the privilege on behalf of the client. The authority of the lawyer to do so is presumed in the absence of evidence to the contrary.

(d) *Exceptions.* There is no privilege under this rule under any of the following circumstances:

(1) *Crime or Fraud.* If the communication clearly contemplated the future commission of a fraud or crime or if services of the lawyer were sought or obtained to enable or aid anyone to commit or plan to commit what the client knew or reasonably should have known to be a crime or fraud;

(2) *Claimants through Same Deceased Client.* As to a communication relevant to an issue between parties who claim through the same deceased client, regardless of whether the claims are by testate or intestate succession or by inter vivos transaction;

(3) *Breach of Duty by Lawyer or Client.* As to a communication relevant to an issue of breach of duty by the lawyer to the client or by the client to the lawyer;

(4) *Document Attested by the Lawyer.* As to a communication relevant to an issue concerning an attested document to which the lawyer is an attesting witness; or

(5) *Joint Clients.* As to a communication relevant to a matter of common interest between two or more clients if the communication was made by any of them to a lawyer retained or consulted in common, when offered in an action between any of the clients.

Rule 503. Communications to clergy

(a) *General Rule.* A person has a privilege to refuse to disclose and to prevent another from disclosing a confidential communication by the person to a clergy member or to a clergy member's assistant, if such communication is made either as a formal act of religion or as a matter of conscience.

(b) *Definitions.* As used in this rule:

(1) "Clergy member" means a minister, priest, rabbi, imam, chaplain, or other similar functionary of a religious organization, or an individual reasonably believed to be so by the person consulting the clergy member.

(2) "Clergy member's assistant" means a person employed or assigned to assist a clergy member in the clergy member's capacity as a spiritual advisor.

(3) A communication is "confidential" if made to a clergy member in the clergy member's capacity as a spiritual advisor or to a clergy member's assistant in the assistant's official capacity and is not intended to be disclosed to third persons other than those to whom disclosure is in furtherance of the purpose of the communication or to those reasonably necessary for the transmission of the communication.

(c) *Who May Claim the Privilege.* The privilege may be claimed by the person, guardian, or conservator, or by a personal representative if the person is deceased. The clergy member or clergy member's assistant who received the communication may claim the privilege on behalf of the person. The authority of the clergy member or clergy member's assistant to do so is presumed in the absence of evidence to the contrary.

Rule 504. Marital privilege

(a) *Spousal Incapacity.* A person has a privilege to refuse to testify against his or her spouse. There is no privilege under subdivision (a) when, at the time of the testimony, the parties are divorced, or the marriage has been annulled.

(b) *Confidential Communication Made During the Marriage.*

(1) *General Rule.* A person has a privilege during and after the marital relationship to refuse to disclose, and to prevent another from disclosing, any confidential communication made to the spouse of the person while they were married and not separated as provided by law.

(2) *Who May Claim the Privilege.* The privilege may be claimed by the spouse who made the communication or by the other spouse on his or her behalf. The authority of the latter spouse to do so is presumed in the absence of evidence of a waiver. The privilege will not prevent disclosure of the communication at the request of the spouse to whom the communication was made if that spouse is an accused regardless of whether the spouse who made the communication objects to its disclosure.

(c) *Exceptions.*

(1) *To Confidential Communications Only.* Where both parties have been substantial participants in illegal activity, those communications between the spouses during the marriage regarding the illegal activity in which they have jointly participated are not marital communications for purposes of the privilege in subdivision (b) and are not entitled to protection under the privilege in subdivision (b).

(2) *To Spousal Incapacity and Confidential Communications.* There is no privilege under subdivisions (a) or (b):

(A) In proceedings in which one spouse is charged with a crime against the person or property of the other spouse or a child of either, or with a crime against the person or property of a third person committed in the course of committing a crime against the other spouse;

(B) When the marital relationship was entered into with no intention of the parties to live together as spouses, but only for the purpose of using the purported marital relationship as a sham, and with respect to the privilege in subdivision (a), the relationship remains a sham at the time the testimony or statement of one of the parties is to be introduced against the other, or with respect to the privilege in subdivision (b), the relationship was a sham at the time of the communication; or

(C) In proceedings in which a spouse is charged, in accordance with Article 133 or 134, with importing the other spouse as an alien for prostitution or other immoral purpose in violation of 8 U.S.C. § 1328 with transporting the other spouse in interstate commerce for prostitution, immoral purposes, or another offense in violation of 18 U.S.C. §§ 2421-2424; or with violation of such other similar statutes under which such privilege may not be claimed in the trial of criminal cases in the United States district courts.

(d) *Definitions.* As used in this rule:

(1) "A child of either" means a biological child, adopted child, or ward of one of the spouses and includes a child who is under the permanent or temporary physical custody of one of the spouses, regardless of the existence of a legal parent-child relationship. For purposes of this rule only, a child is:

(A) an individual under the age of 18; or

(B) an individual with a mental handicap who functions under the age of 18.

(2) "Temporary physical custody" means a parent has entrusted his or her child with another. There is no minimum amount of time necessary to establish temporary physical custody, nor is a written agreement required. Rather, the focus is on the parent's agreement with another for assuming parental responsibility for the child. For example, temporary physical custody may include instances where a parent entrusts another with the care of his or her child for recurring care or during absences due to temporary duty or deployments.

(3) As used in this rule, a communication is "confidential" if made privately by any person to the spouse of the person and is not intended to be disclosed to third persons other than those reasonably necessary for transmission of the communication.

Rule 505. Classified information

(a) *General Rule.* Classified information must be protected and is privileged from disclosure if disclosure would be detrimental to the national security. Under no circumstances may a military judge order the release of classified information to any person not authorized to receive such information. The Secretary of Defense may prescribe security procedures for protection against the compromise of classified information submitted to courts-martial and appellate authorities.

(b) *Definitions.* As used in this rule:

(1) "Classified information" means any information or material that has been determined by the United States Government pursuant to an executive order, statute, or regulations, to require protection against unauthorized disclosure for reasons of national security, and any restricted data, as defined in 42 U.S.C. §2014(y).

(2) "National security" means the national defense and foreign relations of the United States.

(3) "In camera hearing" means a session under Article 39(a) from which the public is excluded.

(4) "In camera review" means an inspection of documents or other evidence conducted by the military judge alone in chambers and not on the record.

(5) "Ex parte" means a discussion between the military judge and either defense counsel or prosecution, without the other party or the public present. This discussion can be on or off the record, depending on the circumstances. The military judge will grant a request for an ex parte discussion or hearing only after finding that such discussion or hearing is necessary to protect classified information or other good cause. Prior to granting a request from one party for an ex parte discussion or hearing, the military judge must provide notice to the opposing party on the record. If the ex parte discussion is conducted off the record, the military judge should later state on the record that such ex parte discussion took place and generally summarize the subject matter of the discussion, as appropriate.

(c) *Access to Evidence.* Any information admitted into evidence pursuant to any rule, procedure, or order by the military judge must be provided to the accused.

(d) *Declassification.* Trial counsel should, when practicable, seek declassification of evidence that may be used at trial, consistent with the requirements of national security. A decision not to declassify evidence under this section is not subject to review by a military judge or upon appeal.

(e) *Action Prior to Referral of Charges.*

(1) Prior to referral of charges, upon a showing by the accused that the classified information sought is relevant and necessary to an element of the offense or a legally cognizable defense, the convening authority must respond in writing to a request by the accused for classified information if the privilege in this rule is claimed for such information. In response to such a request, the convening authority may:

(A) delete specified items of classified information from documents made available to the accused;

(B) substitute a portion or summary of the information for such classified documents;

(C) substitute a statement admitting relevant facts that the classified information would tend to prove;

(D) provide the document subject to conditions that will guard against the compromise of the information disclosed to the accused; or

(E) withhold disclosure if actions under (A) through (D) cannot be taken without causing identifiable damage to the national security.

(2) An Article 32 preliminary hearing officer may not rule on any objection by the accused to the release of documents or information protected by this rule.

(3) Any objection by the accused to the withholding of information or to the conditions of disclosure must be raised through a motion for appropriate relief at a pretrial conference.

(f) *Actions after Referral of Charges.*

(1) *Pretrial Conference.* At any time after referral of charges, any party may move for a pretrial conference under Article 39(a) to consider matters relating to classified information that may arise in connection with the trial. Following such a motion, or when the military judge recognizes the need for such conference, the military judge must promptly hold a pretrial conference under Article 39(a).

(2) *Ex Parte Permissible.* Upon request by either party and with a showing of good cause, the military judge must hold such conference ex parte to the extent necessary to protect classified information from disclosure.

(3) *Matters to be Established at Pretrial Conference.*

(A) *Timing of Subsequent Actions.* At the pretrial conference, the military judge must establish the timing of:

(i) requests for discovery;

(ii) the provision of notice required by subdivision (i) of this rule; and

(iii) established by subdivision (j) of this rule.

(B) *Other Matters.* At the pretrial conference, the military judge may also consider any matter that relates to classified information or that may promote a fair and expeditious trial.

(4) *Convening Authority and Special Trial Counsel Notice and Action.* If a claim of privilege has been made under this rule with respect to classified information that apparently contains evidence that is relevant and necessary to an element of the offense or a legally cognizable defense and is otherwise admissible in evidence in the court-martial proceeding, the matter must be reported to the convening authority and special trial counsel, as applicable.

(A) The convening authority may institute action to obtain the classified information for use by the military judge in making a determination under Mil. R. Evid. 505(j).

(B) The convening authority or special trial counsel, as applicable, may:

(i) dismiss the charges;

(ii) dismiss the charges or specifications or both to which the information relates; or

(iii) take such other action as may be required in the interests of justice.

(5) *Remedies.* If, after a reasonable period of time, the information is not provided to the military judge in circumstances where proceeding with the case without such information would materially prejudice a substantial right of the accused, the military judge must dismiss the charges or specifications or both to which the classified information relates.

(g) *Protective Orders.* Upon motion of trial counsel, the military judge must issue an order to protect against the disclosure of any classified information that has been disclosed by the United States to any accused in any court-martial proceeding or that has otherwise been provided to, or obtained by, any such accused in any such court-martial proceeding. The terms of any such protective order may include, but are not limited to, provisions:

(1) prohibiting the disclosure of the information except as authorized by the military judge;

(2) requiring storage of material in a manner appropriate for the level of classification assigned to the documents to be disclosed;

(3) requiring controlled accesses to the material during normal business hours and at other times upon reasonable notice;

(4) mandating that all persons requiring security clearances will cooperate with investigatory personnel in any investigations that are necessary to obtain a security clearance;

(5) requiring the maintenance of logs regarding access by all persons authorized by the military judge to have access to the classified information in connection with the preparation of the defense;

(6) regulating the making and handling of notes taken from material containing classified information; or

(7) requesting the convening authority to authorize the assignment of government security personnel and the provision of government storage facilities.

(h) *Discovery and Access by the Accused.*

(1) *Limitations.*

(A) *Government Claim of Privilege.* In a court-martial proceeding in which the government seeks to delete, withhold, or otherwise obtain other relief with respect to the discovery of or access to any classified information, trial counsel must submit a declaration invoking the United States' classified information privilege and setting forth the damage to the national security that the discovery of or access to such information reasonably could be expected to cause. The declaration must be signed by the head, or designee, of the executive or military department or government agency concerned.

(B) *Standard for Discovery or Access by the Accused.* Upon the submission of a declaration under subdivision (h)(1)(A), the military judge may not authorize the discovery of or access to such classified information unless the military judge determines that such classified information would be noncumulative and relevant to a legally cognizable defense, rebuttal of the prosecution's case, or to sentencing. If the discovery of or access to such classified information is authorized, it must be addressed in accordance with the requirements of subdivision (h)(2).

(2) *Alternatives to Full Discovery.*

(A) *Substitutions and Other Alternatives.* The military judge, in assessing the accused's right to discover or access classified information under subdivision (h), may authorize the government:

(i) to delete or withhold specified items of classified information;

(ii) to substitute a summary for classified information; or

(iii) to substitute a statement admitting relevant facts that the classified information or material would tend to prove, unless the military judge determines that disclosure of the classified information itself is necessary to enable the accused to prepare for trial.

(B) *In Camera Review.* The military judge must, upon the request of the prosecution, conduct an in camera review of the prosecution's motion and any materials submitted in support thereof and must not disclose such information to the accused.

(C) *Action by Military Judge.* The military judge must grant the request of trial counsel to substitute a summary or to substitute a statement admitting relevant facts, or to provide other relief in accordance with subdivision (h)(2)(A), if the military judge finds that the summary, statement, or other relief would provide the accused with substantially the same ability to make a defense as would discovery of or access to the specific classified information.

(3) *Reconsideration.* An order of a military judge authorizing a request of trial counsel to substitute, summarize, withhold, or prevent access to classified information under subdivision (h) is not subject to a motion for reconsideration by the accused, if such order was entered pursuant to an ex parte showing under subdivision (h).

(i) *Disclosure by the Accused.*

(1) *Notification to Trial Counsel and Military Judge.* If an accused reasonably expects to disclose, or to cause the disclosure of, classified information in any manner in connection with any trial or pretrial proceeding involving the prosecution of such accused, the accused must, within the time specified by the military judge or, where no time is specified, prior to arraignment of the accused, notify trial counsel and the military judge in writing.

(2) *Content of Notice.* Such notice must include a brief description of the classified information.

(3) *Continuing Duty to Notify.* Whenever the accused learns of additional classified information the accused reasonably expects to disclose, or to cause the disclosure of, at any such proceeding, the accused must notify trial counsel and the military judge in writing as soon as possible thereafter and must include a brief description of the classified information.

(4) *Limitation on Disclosure by Accused.* The accused may not disclose, or cause the disclosure of, any information known or believed to be classified in connection with a trial or pretrial proceeding until:

(A) notice has been given under subdivision (i); and

(B) the government has been afforded a reasonable opportunity to seek a determination pursuant to the procedure set forth in subdivision (j).

(5) *Failure to comply.* If the accused fails to comply with the requirements of subdivision (i), the military judge:

(A) may preclude disclosure of any classified information not made the subject of notification; and

(B) may prohibit the examination by the accused of any witness with respect to any such information.

(j) *Procedure for Use of Classified Information in Trials and Pretrial Proceedings.*

(1) *Hearing on Use of Classified Information.*

(A) *Motion for Hearing.* Within the time specified by the military judge for the filing of a motion under this rule, either party may move for a hearing concerning the use at any proceeding of any classified information. Upon a request by either party, the military judge must conduct such a hearing and must rule prior to conducting any further proceedings.

(B) *Request for In Camera Hearing.* Any hearing held pursuant to subdivision (j) (or any portion of such hearing specified in the request of a knowledgeable United States official) must be held in camera if a knowledgeable United States official possessing authority to classify information submits to the military judge a declaration that a public proceeding may result in the disclosure of classified information.

(C) *Notice to Accused.* Before the hearing, trial counsel must provide the accused with notice of the classified information that is at issue. Such notice must identify the specific classified information at issue whenever that information previously has been made available to the accused by the United States. When the United States has not previously made the information available to the accused in connection with the case the information may be described by generic category, in such forms as the military judge may approve, rather than by identification of the specific information of concern to the United States.

(D) *Standard for Disclosure.* Classified information is not subject to disclosure under subdivision (j) unless the information is relevant and necessary to an element of the offense or a legally cognizable defense and is otherwise admissible in evidence. In presenting proceedings, relevant and material classified information pertaining to the appropriateness of, or the appropriate degree of, punishment must be admitted only if no unclassified version of such information is available.

(E) *Written Findings.* As to each item of classified information, the military judge must set forth in writing the basis for the determination.

(2) *Alternatives to Full Disclosure.*

(A) *Motion by the Prosecution.* Upon any determination by the military judge authorizing the disclosure of specific classified information under the procedures established by subdivision (j), trial counsel may move that, in lieu of the disclosure of such specific classified information, the military judge order:

(i) the substitution for such classified information of a statement admitting relevant facts that the specific classified information would tend to prove:

(ii) the substitution for such classified information of a summary of the specific classified information; or

(iii) any other procedure or redaction limiting the disclosure of specific classified information.

(B) *Declaration of Damage to National Security.* Trial counsel may, in connection with a motion under subdivision (j), submit to the military judge a declaration signed by the head, or designee, of the executive or military department or government agency concerned certifying that disclosure of classified information would cause identifiable damage to the national security of the United States and explaining the basis for the classification of such information. If so requested by trial counsel, the military judge must examine such declaration during an in camera review.

(C) *Hearing.* The military judge must hold a hearing on any motion under subdivision (j). Any such hearing must be held in camera at the request of a knowledgeable United States official possessing authority to classify information.

(D) *Standard for Use of Alternatives.* The military judge must grant such a motion of trial counsel if the military judge finds that the statement, summary, or other procedure or redaction will provide the accused with substantially the same ability to make his or her defense as would disclosure of the specific classified information.

(3) *Sealing of Records of In Camera Hearings.* If at the close of an in camera hearing under subdivision (j) (or any portion of a hearing under subdivision (j) that is held in camera), the military judge determines that the classified information at issue may not be disclosed or elicited at the trial or pretrial proceeding, the record of such in camera hearing must be sealed in accordance with R.C.M. 1113 and preserved for use in the event of an appeal. The accused may seek reconsideration of the military judge's determination prior to or during trial.

(4) *Remedies.*

(A) If the military judge determines that alternatives to full disclosure may not be used and the prosecution continues to object to disclosure of the information, the military judge must issue any order that the interests of justice require, including but not limited to, an order:

(i) striking or precluding all or part of the testimony of a witness;

(ii) declaring a mistrial;

(iii) finding against the government on any issue as to which the evidence is relevant and material to the defense;

(iv) dismissing the charges, with or without prejudice; or

(v) dismissing the charges or specifications or both to which the information relates.

(B) The government may avoid the sanction for nondisclosure by permitting the accused to disclose the information at the pertinent court-martial proceeding.

(5) *Disclosure of Rebuttal Information.* Whenever the military judge determines that classified information may be disclosed in connection with a trial or pretrial proceeding, the military judge must, unless the interests of fairness do not so require, order the prosecution to provide the accused with the information it expects to use to rebut the classified information.

(A) *Continuing Duty.* The military judge may place the prosecution under a continuing duty to disclose such rebuttal information.

(B) *Sanction for Failure to Comply.* If the prosecution fails to comply with its obligation under subdivision (j), the military judge:

(i) may exclude any evidence not made the subject of a required disclosure; and

(ii) may prohibit the examination by the prosecution of any witness with respect to such information.

(6) *Disclosure at Trial of Previous Statements by a Witness.*

(A) *Motion for Production of Statements in Possession of the Prosecution.* After a witness called by trial counsel has testified on direct examination, the military judge, on motion of the accused, may order production of statements of the witness in the possession of the prosecution that relate to the subject matter as to which the witness has testified. This paragraph does not preclude discovery or assertion of a privilege otherwise authorized.

(B) *Invocation of Privilege by the Government.* If the government invokes a privilege, trial counsel may provide the prior statements of the witness to the military judge for in camera review to the extent necessary to protect classified information from disclosure.

(C) *Action by Military Judge.* If the military judge finds that disclosure of any portion of the statement identified by the government as classified would be detrimental to the national security in the degree required to warrant classification under the applicable Executive Order, statute, or regulation, that such portion of the statement is consistent with the testimony of the witness, and that the disclosure of such portion is not necessary to afford the accused a fair trial, the military judge must excise that portion from the statement. If the military judge finds that such portion of the statement is inconsistent with the testimony of the witness or that its disclosure is necessary to afford the accused a fair trial, the military judge must, upon the request of trial counsel, consider alternatives to disclosure in accordance with subdivision (j)(2).

(k) *Introduction into Evidence of Classified Information.*

(1) *Preservation of Classification Status.* Writings, recordings, and photographs containing classified information may be admitted into evidence in court-martial proceedings under this rule without change in their classification status.

(A) *Precautions.* The military judge in a trial by court-martial, in order to prevent unnecessary disclosure of classified information, may order admission into evidence of only part of a writing, recording, or photograph, or may order admission into evidence of the whole writing, recording, or photograph with excision of some or all of the classified information contained therein, unless the whole ought in fairness be considered.

(B) *Classified Information Kept Under Seal.* The military judge must allow classified information offered or accepted into evidence to remain under seal during the trial, even if such evidence is disclosed in the court-martial proceeding, and may upon motion by the government, seal exhibits containing classified information in accordance with R.C.M. 1113 for any period after trial as necessary to prevent a disclosure of classified information when a knowledgeable United States official possessing authority to classify information submits to the military judge a declaration setting forth the damage to the national security that the disclosure of such information reasonably could be expected to cause.

(2) *Testimony.*

(A) *Objection by Trial Counsel.* During the examination of a witness, trial counsel may object to any question or line of inquiry that may require the witness to disclose classified information not previously found to be admissible.

(B) *Action by Military Judge.* Following an objection under subdivision (k), the military judge must take such suitable action to determine whether the response is admissible as will safeguard against the compromise of any classified information. Such action may include requiring trial counsel to provide the military judge with a proffer of the witness' response to the question or line of inquiry and requiring the accused to provide the military judge with a proffer of the nature of the information sought to be elicited by the accused. Upon request, the military judge may accept an ex parte proffer by trial counsel to the extent necessary to protect classified information from disclosure.

(3) *Closed session.* The military judge may, subject to the requirements of the United States Constitution, exclude the public during that portion of the presentation of evidence that discloses classified information.

(l) *Record of Trial.* If under this rule any information is reviewed in camera by the military judge and withheld from the accused, the accused objects to such withholding, and the trial continues to an adjudication of guilt of the accused, the entire unaltered text of the relevant documents as well as any motions and any materials submitted in support thereof must be sealed in accordance with R.C.M. 701(g)(2) or R.C.M. 1113 and attached to the record of trial as an appellate exhibit. Such material will be made available to reviewing and appellate authorities in accordance with R.C.M. 1113. The record of trial with respect to any classified matter will be prepared under R.C.M. 1112(e)(3).

Discussion

In addition to the Sixth Amendment right of an accused to a public trial, the Supreme Court has held that the press and general public have a constitutional right under the First Amendment to access to criminal trials. *United States v. Hershey*, 20 M.J. 433, 436 (C.M.A. 1985) (citing *Richmond Newspapers, Inc. v. Virginia*, 448 U.S. 555 (1980)). The test that must be met before closure of a criminal trial to the public is set out in *Press-Enterprise Co. v. Superior Court*, 464 U.S. 501 (1984), to wit: the presumption of openness "may be overcome only by an overriding interest based on findings that closure is essential to preserve higher values and is narrowly tailored to serve that interest." *Id.* at 510.

The military judge must consider reasonable alternatives to closure and must make adequate findings supporting the closure to aid in review.

Rule 506. Government information

(a) *Protection of Government Information.* Except where disclosure is required by a federal statute, government information is privileged from disclosure if disclosure would be detrimental to the public interest.

(b) *Scope.* "Government information" includes official communication and documents and other information within the custody or control of the Federal Government. This rule does not apply to the identity of an informant (Mil. R. Evid. 507).

Discussion

For additional procedures concerning information contained in safety investigations, consult Service regulations and DoD Instruction 6055.07, "Mishap Notification, Investigation, Reporting, and Record Keeping.

(c) *Definitions.* As used in this rule:

(1) "In camera hearing" means a session under Article 39(a) from which the public is excluded.

(2) "In camera review" means an inspection of documents or other evidence conducted by the military judge alone in chambers and not on the record.

(3) "Ex parte" means a discussion between the military judge and either defense counsel or prosecution, without the other party or the public present. This discussion can be on or off the record, depending on the circumstances. The military judge will grant a request for an ex parte discussion or hearing only after finding that such discussion or hearing is necessary to protect government information or other good cause. Prior to granting a request from one party for an ex parte discussion or hearing, the military judge must provide notice to the opposing party on the record. If the ex parte discussion is conducted off the record, the military judge should later state on the record that such ex parte discussion took place and generally summarize the subject matter of the discussion, as appropriate.

(d) *Who May Claim the Privilege.* The privilege may be claimed by the head, or designee, of the executive or military department or government agency concerned. The privilege for records and information of the Inspector General may be claimed by the immediate superior of the inspector general officer responsible for creation of the records or information, the Inspector General, or any other superior authority. A person who may claim the privilege may authorize a witness or trial counsel to claim the privilege on his or her behalf. The authority of a witness or trial counsel to do so is presumed in the absence of evidence to the contrary.

(e) *Action Prior to Referral of Charges.*

(1) Prior to referral of charges, upon a showing by the accused that the government information sought is relevant and necessary to an element of the offense or a legally cognizable defense, the convening authority must respond in writing to a request by the accused for government information if the privilege in this rule is

claimed for such information. In response to such a request, the convening authority may:

(A) delete specified items of government information claimed to be privileged from documents made available to the accused;

(B) substitute a portion or summary of the information for such documents;

(C) substitute a statement and admitting relevant facts that the government information would tend to prove;

(D) provide the document subject to conditions similar to those set forth in subdivision (g) of this rule; or

(E) withhold disclosure if actions under subdivisions (e)(1)(A)-(D) cannot be taken without causing identifiable damage to the public interest.

(2) Any objection by the accused to withholding of information or to the conditions of disclosure must be raised through a motion for appropriate relief at a pretrial conference.

(f) *Action After Referral of Charges.*

(1) *Pretrial Conference.* At any time after referral of charges, any party may move for a pretrial conference under Article 39(a) to consider matters relating to government information that may arise in connection with the trial. Following such a motion, or when the military judge recognizes the need for such conference, the military judge must promptly hold a pretrial conference under Article 39(a).

(2) *Ex Parte Permissible.* Upon request by either party and with a showing of good cause, the military judge must hold such conference ex parte to the extent necessary to protect government information from disclosure.

(3) *Matters to be Established at Pretrial Conference.*

(A) *Timing of Subsequent Actions.* At the pretrial conference, the military judge must establish the timing of:

(i) requests for discovery;

(ii) the provision of notice required by subdivision (i) of this rule; and

(iii) the initiation of the procedure established by subdivision (j) of this rule.

(B) *Other Matters.* At the pretrial conference, the military judge may also consider any matter which relates to government information or which may promote a fair and expeditious trial.

(4) *Convening Authority and Special Trial Counsel Notice and Action.* If a claim of privilege has been made under this rule with respect to government information that apparently contains evidence that is relevant and necessary to an element of the offense or a legally cognizable defense and is otherwise admissible in evidence in the court-martial proceeding, the matter must be reported to the convening authority and special trial counsel, as applicable.

(A) The convening authority may institute action to obtain the information for use by the military judge in making a determination under Mil. R. Evid. 505(j).

(B) The convening authority or special trial counsel, as applicable, may:

(i) dismiss the charges;

(ii) dismiss the charges or specifications or both to which the information relates; or

(iii) take such other action as may be required in the interests of justice.

(5) *Remedies.* If after a reasonable period of time the information is not provided to the military judge in circumstances where proceeding with the case without such information would materially prejudice a substantial right of the accused, the military judge must dismiss the charges or specifications or both to which the information relates.

(g) *Protective Orders.* Upon motion of trial counsel, the military judge must issue an order to protect against the disclosure of any government information that has been disclosed by the United States to any accused in any court-martial proceeding or that has otherwise been provided to, or obtained by, any such accused in any such court-martial proceeding. The terms of any such protective order may include, but are not limited to, provisions:

(1) prohibiting the disclosure of the information except as authorized by the military judge;

(2) requiring storage of the material in a manner appropriate for the nature of the material to be disclosed;

(3) requiring controlled access to the material during normal business hours and at other times upon reasonable notice;

(4) requiring the maintenance of logs recording access by persons authorized by the military judge to have access to the government information in connection with the preparation of the defense;

(5) regulating the making and handling of notes taken from material containing government information; or

(6) requesting the convening authority to authorize the assignment of government security personnel and the provision of government storage facilities.

(h) *Discovery and Access by the Accused.*

(1) *Limitations.*

(A) *Government Claim of Privilege.* In a court-martial proceeding in which the government seeks to delete, withhold, or otherwise obtain other relief with respect to the discovery of or access to any government information subject to a claim of privilege, trial counsel must submit a declaration invoking the United States' government information privilege and setting forth the detriment to the public interest that the discovery of or access to such information reasonably could be expected to cause. The declaration must be signed by a knowledgeable United States official as described in subdivision (d) of this rule.

(B) *Standard for Discovery or Access by the Accused.* Upon the submission of a declaration under subdivision (h)(1)(A), the military judge may not authorize the discovery of or access to such government information unless the military judge determines that such government information would be noncumulative, relevant, and helpful to a legally cognizable defense, rebuttal of the prosecution's case, or to sentencing. If the discovery of or access to such governmental information is authorized, it must be addressed in accordance with the requirements of subdivision (h)(2).

(2) *Alternatives to Full Disclosure.*

(A) *Substitutions and Other Alternatives.* The military judge, in assessing the accused's right to discovery or access government information under subdivision (h), may authorize the government:

(i) to delete or withhold specified items of government information;

(ii) to substitute a summary for government information; or

(iii) to substitute a statement admitting relevant facts that the government information or material would tend to prove, unless the military judge determines that disclosure of the government information itself is necessary to enable the accused to prepare for trial.

(B) *In Camera Review.* The military judge must, upon the request of the prosecution, conduct an in camera review of the prosecution's motion and any materials submitted in support thereof and must not disclose such information to the accused.

(C) *Action by Military Judge.* The military judge must grant the request of trial counsel to substitute a summary or to substitute a statement admitting relevant facts, or to provide other relief in accordance with subdivision (h)(2)(A), if the military judge finds that the summary, statement, or other relief would provide the accused with substantially the same ability to make a defense as would discovery of or access to the specific government information.

(i) *Disclosure by the Accused.*

(1) *Notification to Trial Counsel and Military Judge.* If an accused reasonably expects to disclose, or to cause the disclosure of, government information subject to a claim of privilege in any manner in connection with any trial or pretrial proceeding involving the prosecution of such accused, the accused must, within the time specified by the military judge or, where no time is specified, prior to arraignment of the accused, notify trial counsel and the military judge in writing.

(2) *Content of Notice.* Such notice must include a brief description of the government information.

(3) *Continuing Duty to Notify.* Whenever the accused learns of additional government information the accused reasonably expects to disclose, or to cause the disclosure of, at any such proceeding, the accused must notify trial counsel and the military judge in writing as soon as possible thereafter and must include a brief description of the government information.

(4) *Limitation on Disclosure by Accused.* The accused may not disclose, or cause the disclosure of, any information known or believed to be subject to a claim of privilege in connection with a trial or pretrial proceeding until:

(A) notice has been given under subdivision (i); and

(B) the government has been afforded a reasonable opportunity to seek a determination pursuant to the procedure set forth in subdivision (j).

(5) *Failure to Comply.* If the accused fails to comply with the requirements of subdivision (i), the military judge:

(A) may preclude disclosure of any government information not made the subject of notification; and

(B) may prohibit the examination by the accused of any witness with respect to any such information.

(j) *Procedure for Use of Government Information Subject to a Claim of Privilege in Trials and Pretrial Proceedings.*

(1) *Hearing on Use of Government Information.*

(A) *Motion for Hearing.* Within the time specified by the military judge for the filing of a motion under this rule, either party may move for an in camera hearing concerning the use at any proceeding of any government information that may be subject to a claim of privilege. Upon a request by either party, the military judge must conduct such a hearing and must rule prior to conducting any further proceedings.

(B) *Request for In Camera Hearing.* Any hearing held pursuant to subdivision (j) must be held in camera if a knowledgeable United States official described in subdivision (d) of this rule submits to the military judge a declaration that disclosure of the information reasonably could be expected to cause identifiable damage to the public interest.

(C) *Notice to Accused.* Subject to subdivision (j)(2) below, the prosecution must disclose government information claimed to be privileged under this rule for the limited purpose of litigating, in camera, the admissibility of the information at trial. The military judge must enter an appropriate protective order to the accused and all other appropriate trial participants concerning the disclosure of the information according to subdivision (g), above. The accused may not disclose any information provided under subdivision (j) unless, and until, such information has been admitted into evidence by the military judge. In the in camera hearing, both parties may have the opportunity to brief and argue the admissibility of the government information at trial.

(D) *Standard for Disclosure.* Government information is subject to disclosure at the court-martial proceeding under subdivision (j) if the party making the request demonstrates a specific need for information containing evidence that is relevant to the guilt or innocence or to punishment of the accused, and is otherwise admissible in the court-martial proceeding.

(E) *Written Findings.* As to each item of government information, the military judge must set forth in writing the basis for the determination.

(2) *Alternatives to Full Disclosure.*

(A) *Motion by the Prosecution.* Upon any determination by the military judge authorizing disclosure of specific government information under the procedures established by subdivision (j), the prosecution may move that, in lieu of the disclosure of such information, the military judge order:

(i) the substitution for such government information of a statement admitting relevant facts that the specific government information would tend to prove;

(ii) the substitution for such government information of a summary of the specific government information; or

(iii) any other procedure or redaction limiting the disclosure of specific government information.

(B) *Hearing.* The military judge must hold a hearing on any motion under subdivision (j). At the request of trial counsel, the military judge will conduct an in camera hearing.

(C) *Standard for Use of Alternatives.* The military judge must grant such a motion of trial counsel if the military judge finds that the statement, summary, or other procedure or redaction will provide the accused with substantially the same ability to make his or her defense as would disclosure of the specific government information.

(3) *Sealing of Records of In Camera Hearings.* If at the close of an in camera hearing under subdivision (j) (or any portion of a hearing under subdivision (j) that is held in camera), the military judge determines that the government information at issue may not be disclosed or elicited at the trial or pretrial proceeding, the record of such in camera hearing must be sealed in accordance with R.C.M. 1113 and preserved for use in the event of an appeal. The accused may seek reconsideration of the military judge's determination prior to or during trial.

(4) *Remedies.*

(A) If the military judge determines that alternatives to full disclosure may not be used and the prosecution continues to object to disclosure of the information, the military judge must issue any order that the interests of justice require, including but not limited to, an order:

(i) striking or precluding all or part of the testimony of a witness;

(ii) declaring a mistrial;

(iii) finding against the government on any issue as to which the evidence is relevant and necessary to the defense;

(iv) dismissing the charges, with or without prejudice; or

(v) dismissing the charges or specifications or both to which the information relates.

(B) The government may avoid the sanction for nondisclosure by permitting the accused to disclose the information at the pertinent court-martial proceeding.

(5) *Disclosure of Rebuttal Information.* Whenever the military judge determines that government information may be disclosed in connection with a trial or pretrial proceeding, the military judge must, unless the interests of fairness do not so require, order the prosecution to provide the accused with the information it expects to use to rebut the government information.

(A) *Continuing Duty.* The military judge may place the prosecution under a continuing duty to disclose such rebuttal information.

(B) *Sanction for Failure to Comply.* If the prosecution fails to comply with its obligation under subdivision (j), the military judge may make such ruling as the interests of justice require, to include:

(i) excluding any evidence not made the subject of a required disclosure; and

(ii) prohibiting the examination by the prosecution of any witness with respect to such information.

(k) *Appeals of Orders and Rulings.* In a court-martial in which a punitive discharge may be adjudged, the government may appeal an order or ruling of the military judge that terminates the proceedings with respect to a charge or specification, directs the disclosure of government information, or imposes sanctions for nondisclosure of government information. The government may also appeal an order or ruling in which the military judge refuses to issue a protective order sought by the United States to prevent the disclosure of government information, or to enforce such an order previously issued by appropriate authority. The government may not appeal an order or ruling that is, or amounts to, a finding of not guilty with respect to the charge or specification.

(l) *Introduction into Evidence of Government Information Subject to a Claim of Privilege.*

(1) *Precautions.* The military judge in a trial by court-martial, in order to prevent unnecessary disclosure of government information after there has been a claim of privilege under this rule, may order admission into evidence of only part of a writing, recording, or photograph or admit into evidence the whole writing, recording, or photograph with excision of some or all of the government information contained therein, unless the whole ought in fairness to be considered.

(2) *Government Information Kept Under Seal.* The military judge must allow government information offered or accepted into evidence to remain under seal during the trial, even if such evidence is disclosed in the court-martial proceeding, and may, upon motion by the prosecution, seal exhibits containing government information in accordance with R.C.M. 1113 for any period after trial as necessary to prevent a disclosure of government information when a knowledgeable United States official described in subdivision (d) submits to the military judge a declaration setting forth the detriment to the public interest that the disclosure of such information reasonably could be expected to cause.

(3) *Testimony.*

(A) *Objection by Trial Counsel.* During examination of a witness, trial counsel may object to any question or line of inquiry that may require the witness to disclose government information not previously found admissible if such information has been or is reasonably likely to be the subject of a claim of privilege under this rule.

(B) *Action by Military Judge.* Following such an objection, the military judge must take such suitable action to determine whether the response is admissible as will safeguard against the compromise of any government information. Such action may include requiring trial counsel to provide the military judge with a proffer of the witness' response to the question or line of inquiry and requiring the accused to provide the military judge with a proffer of the nature of the information sought to be elicited by the accused. Upon request, the military judge may accept an ex parte proffer by trial counsel to the extent necessary to protect government information from disclosure.

(m) *Record of Trial.* If under this rule any information is reviewed in camera by the military judge and withheld from the accused, the accused objects to such withholding, and the trial continues to an adjudication of guilt of the accused, the entire unaltered text of the relevant documents as well as any motions and any materials submitted in support thereof must be sealed in accordance with R.C.M. 701(g)(2) or 1113 and attached to the record of trial as an appellate exhibit.

Such material will be made available to reviewing and appellate authorities in accordance with R.C.M. 1113.

Rule 507. Identity of informants

(a) *General Rule*. The United States or a State or subdivision thereof has a privilege to refuse to disclose the identity of an informant. Unless otherwise privileged under these rules, the communications of an informant are not privileged except to the extent necessary to prevent the disclosure of the informant's identity.

(b) *Definitions*. As used in this rule:

(1) "Informant" means a person who has furnished information relating to or assisting in an investigation of a possible violation of law to a person whose official duties include the discovery, investigation, or prosecution of crime.

(2) "In camera review" means an inspection of documents or other evidence conducted by the military judge alone in chambers and not on the record.

(c) *Who May Claim the Privilege*. The privilege may be claimed by an appropriate representative of the United States, regardless of whether information was furnished to an officer of the United States or a State or subdivision thereof. The privilege may be claimed by an appropriate representative of a State or subdivision if the information was furnished to an officer thereof, except the privilege will not be allowed if the prosecution objects.

(d) *Exceptions*.

(1) *Voluntary Disclosures; Informant as a Prosecution Witness*. No privilege exists under this rule:

(A) if the identity of the informant has been disclosed to those who would have cause to resent the communication by a holder of the privilege or by the informants own action; or

(B) if the informant appears as a witness for the prosecution.

(2) *Informant as a Defense Witness*. If a claim of privilege has been made under this rule, the military judge must, upon motion by the accused, determine whether disclosure of the identity of the informant is necessary to the accused's defense on the issue of guilt or innocence. Whether such a necessity exists will depend on the particular circumstances of each case, taking into consideration the offense charged, the possible defense, the possible significance of the informant's testimony, and other relevant factors. If it appears from the evidence in the case or from other showing by a party that an informant may be able to give testimony necessary to the accused's defense on the issue of guilt or innocence, the military judge may make any order required by the interests of justice.

(3) *Informant as a Witness regarding a Motion to Suppress Evidence*. If a claim of privilege has been made under this rule with respect to a motion under Mil. R. Evid. 311, the military judge must, upon motion of the accused, determine whether disclosure of the identity of the informant is required by the United States Constitution as applied to members of the Armed Forces. In making this determination, the military judge may make any order required by the interests of justice.

(e) *Procedures*.

(1) *In Camera Review*. If the accused has articulated a basis for disclosure under the standards set forth in this rule, the prosecution may ask the military judge to conduct an in camera review of affidavits or other evidence relevant to disclosure.

(2) *Order by the Military Judge*. If a claim of privilege has been made under this rule, the military judge may make any order required by the interests of justice.

(3) *Action by the Convening Authority or Special Trial Counsel*. If the military judge determines that disclosure of the identity of the informant is required under the standards set forth in this rule, and the prosecution elects not to disclose the identity of the informant, the matter must be reported to the convening authority. The convening authority or the special trial counsel, as applicable, may institute action to secure disclosure of the identity of the informant, terminate the proceedings, or take such other action as may be appropriate under the circumstances.

(4) *Remedies*. If, after a reasonable period of time disclosure is not made, the military judge, sua sponte or upon motion of either counsel and after a hearing if requested by either party, may dismiss the charge or specifications or both to which the information regarding the informant would relate if the military judge determines that further proceedings would materially prejudice a substantial right of the accused.

Rule 508. Political vote

A person has a privilege to refuse to disclose the tenor of the person's vote at a political election conducted by secret ballot unless the vote was cast illegally.

Rule 509. Deliberations of courts and juries

Except as provided in Mil. R. Evid. 606, the deliberations of courts, courts-martial, military judges, and grand and petit juries are privileged to the extent that such matters are privileged in trial of criminal cases in the United States district courts, but the results of the deliberations are not privileged.

Rule 510. Waiver of privilege by voluntary disclosure

(a) A person upon whom these rules confer a privilege against disclosure of a confidential matter or communication waives the privilege if the person or the person's predecessor while holder of the privilege voluntarily discloses or consents to disclosure of any significant part of the matter or communication under such circumstances that it would be inappropriate to allow the claim of privilege. This rule does not apply if the disclosure is itself a privileged communication.

(b) Unless testifying voluntarily concerning a privileged matter or communication, an accused who testifies in his or her own behalf or a person who testifies under a grant or promise of immunity does not, merely by reason of testifying, waive a privilege to which he or she may be entitled pertaining to the confidential matter or communication.

Rule 511. Privileged matter disclosed under compulsion or without opportunity to claim privilege

(a) *General Rule.*

Evidence of a statement or other disclosure of privileged matter is not admissible against the holder of the privilege if disclosure was compelled erroneously or was made without an opportunity for the holder of the privilege to claim the privilege.

(b) *Use of Communications Media.*

The telephonic transmission of information otherwise privileged under these rules does not affect its privileged character. Use of electronic means of communication other than the telephone for transmission of information otherwise privileged under these rules does not affect the privileged character of such information if use of such means of communication is necessary and in furtherance of the communication.

Rule 512. Comment upon or inference from claim of privilege; instruction

(a) *Comment or Inference not permitted.*

(1) The claim of a privilege by the accused whether in the present proceeding or upon a prior occasion is not a proper subject of comment by the military judge or counsel for any party. No inference may be drawn therefrom.

(2) The claim of a privilege by a person other than the accused whether in the present proceeding or upon a prior occasion normally is not a proper subject of comment by the military judge or counsel for any party. An adverse inference may not be drawn therefrom except when determined by the military judge to be required by the interests of justice.

(b) *Claiming a Privilege Without the Knowledge of the Members.* In a trial before a court-martial with members, proceedings must be conducted, to the extent practicable, so as to facilitate the making of claims of privilege without the knowledge of the members.

(c) *Instruction.* Upon request, any party against whom the members might draw an adverse inference from a claim of privilege is entitled to an instruction that no inference may be drawn therefrom except as provided in subdivision (a)(2).

Rule 513. Psychotherapist—patient privilege

(a) *General Rule.* A patient has a privilege to refuse to disclose and to prevent any other person from disclosing a confidential communication made between the patient and a psychotherapist or an assistant to the psychotherapist, in a case arising under the Uniform Code of Military Justice, if such communication was made for the purpose of facilitating diagnosis or treatment of the patient's mental or emotional condition.

(b) *Definitions.* As used in this rule:

(1) "Patient" means a person who consults with or is examined or interviewed by a psychotherapist for purposes of advice, diagnosis, or treatment of a mental or emotional condition.

(2) "Psychotherapist" means a psychiatrist, clinical psychologist, clinical social worker, or other mental health professional who is licensed in any State,

territory, possession, the District of Columbia, or Puerto Rico to perform professional services as such, or who holds credentials to provide such services as such, or who holds credentials to provide such services from any military health care facility, or is a person reasonably believed by the patient to have such license or credentials.

(3) "Assistant to a psychotherapist" means a person directed by or assigned to assist a psychotherapist in providing professional services, or is reasonably believed by the patient to be such.

(4) A communication is "confidential" if not intended to be disclosed to third persons other than those to whom disclosure is in furtherance of the rendition of professional services to the patient or those reasonably necessary for such transmission of the communication.

(5) "Evidence of a patient's records or communications" means testimony of a psychotherapist, or assistant to the same, or patient records that pertain to communications by a patient to a psychotherapist, or assistant to the same, for the purposes of diagnosis or treatment of the patient's mental or emotional condition.

(c) *Who May Claim the Privilege*. The privilege may be claimed by the patient or the guardian or conservator of the patient. A person who may claim the privilege may authorize trial counsel, defense counsel, or any counsel representing the patient to claim the privilege on his or her behalf. The psychotherapist or assistant to the psychotherapist who received the communication may claim the privilege on behalf of the patient. The authority of such a psychotherapist, assistant, guardian, or conservator to so assert the privilege is presumed in the absence of evidence to the contrary.

(d) *Exceptions*. There is no privilege under this rule:

(1) when the patient is dead;

(2) when the communication is evidence of child abuse or of neglect, or in a proceeding in which one spouse is charged with a crime against a child of either spouse;

(3) when federal law, state law, or service regulation imposes a duty to report information contained in a communication;

(4) when a psychotherapist or assistant to a psychotherapist believes that a patient's mental or emotional condition makes the patient a danger to any person, including the patient;

(5) if the communication clearly contemplated the future commission of a fraud or crime or if the services of the psychotherapist are sought or obtained to enable or aid anyone to commit or plan to commit what the patient knew or reasonably should have known to be a crime or fraud;

(6) when necessary to ensure the safety and security of military personnel, military dependents, military property, classified information, or the accomplishment of a military mission; or

(7) when an accused offers statements or other evidence concerning his mental condition in defense, extenuation, or mitigation, under circumstances not covered by R.C.M. 706 or Mil. R. Evid. 302. In such situations, the military judge may, upon motion, order disclosure of any statement made by the accused to a psychotherapist as may be necessary in the interests of justice.

(e) *Procedure to Determine Admissibility of Patient Records or Communications*.

(1) In any case in which the production or admission of records or communications of a patient other than the accused is a matter in dispute, a party may seek an interlocutory ruling by the military judge. In order to obtain such a ruling, the party must:

(A) file a written motion at least 5 days prior to entry of pleas specifically describing the evidence and stating the purpose for which it is sought or offered, or objected to, unless the military judge, for good cause shown, requires a different time for filing or permits filing during trial; and

(B) serve the motion on the opposing party, the military judge and, if practical, notify the patient or the patient's guardian, conservator, or representative that the motion has been filed and that the patient has an opportunity to be heard as set forth in subdivision (e)(2).

(2) Before ordering the production or admission of evidence of a patient's records or communication, the military judge must conduct a hearing, which shall be closed. At the hearing, the parties may call witnesses, including the patient, and offer other relevant evidence. The patient must be afforded a reasonable opportunity to attend the hearing and be heard. However, the hearing may not be unduly delayed for this purpose. The right to be heard under this rule includes the right to be heard through counsel, including Special Victims' Counsel under section 1044e of title 10, United States Code. In a case before a court-martial composed of a military judge and members, the

military judge must conduct the hearing outside the presence of the members.

(3) The military judge may examine the evidence or a proffer thereof in camera, if such examination is necessary to rule on the production or admissibility of protected records or communications. Prior to conducting an in-camera review, the military judge must find by a preponderance of the evidence that the moving party showed:

(A) a specific, credible factual basis demonstrating a reasonable likelihood that the records or communications would contain or lead to the discovery of evidence admissible under an exception to the privilege;

(B) that the requested information meets one of the enumerated exceptions under subdivision (d) of this rule;

(C) that the information sought is not merely cumulative of other information available; and

(D) that the party made reasonable efforts to obtain the same or substantially similar information through non-privileged sources.

(4) Any production or disclosure permitted by the military judge under this rule must be narrowly tailored to only the specific records or communications, or portions of such records or communications, that meet the requirements for one of the enumerated exceptions to the privilege under subdivision (d) of this Rule and are included in the stated purpose for which the records or communications are sought under subdivision (e)(1)(A) of this Rule.

(5) To prevent unnecessary disclosure of a patient's records or communications, the military judge may issue protective orders or may admit only portions of the evidence.

(6) The motion, related papers, and the record of the hearing must be sealed in accordance with R.C.M. 701(g)(2) or 1113 and must remain under seal unless the military judge, the Judge Advocate General, or an appellate court orders otherwise.

Rule 514. Victim advocate—victim privilege

(a) *General Rule.* A victim has a privilege to refuse to disclose and to prevent any other person from disclosing a confidential communication made between the alleged victim and a victim advocate or between the alleged victim and Department of Defense Safe Helpline staff, in a case arising under the UCMJ, if such communication was made for the purpose of facilitating advice or assistance to the alleged victim.

(b) *Definitions.* As used in this rule:

(1) "Victim" means any person who is alleged to have suffered direct physical or emotional harm as the result of a sexual or violent offense.

(2) "Victim advocate" means a person, other than a prosecutor, trial counsel, any victims' counsel, law enforcement officer, or military criminal investigator in the case, who:

(A) is designated in writing as a victim advocate in accordance with service regulation;

(B) is authorized to perform victim advocate duties in accordance with service regulation and is acting in the performance of those duties; or

(C) is certified as a victim advocate pursuant to federal or state requirements.

(3) "Department of Defense Safe Helpline staff" are persons who are designated by competent authority in writing as Department of Defense Safe Helpline staff.

(4) A communication is "confidential" if made in the course of the victim advocate-victim relationship or Department of Defense Safe Helpline staff-victim relationship and not intended to be disclosed to third persons other than those to whom disclosure is made in furtherance of the rendition of advice or assistance to the alleged victim or those reasonably necessary for such transmission of the communication.

(5) "Evidence of a victim's records or communications" means testimony of a victim advocate or Department of Defense Safe Helpline staff, or records that pertain to communications by a victim to a victim advocate or Department of Defense Safe Helpline staff, for the purposes of advising or providing assistance to the victim.

(c) *Who May Claim the Privilege.* The privilege may be claimed by the victim or the guardian or conservator of the victim. A person who may claim the privilege may authorize trial counsel or a counsel representing the victim to claim the privilege on his or her behalf. The victim advocate or Department of Defense Safe Helpline staff who received the communication may claim the privilege on behalf of the victim. The authority of such a victim advocate, Department of Defense Safe Helpline staff, guardian, conservator, or a counsel representing the victim to so assert the privilege is presumed in the absence of evidence to the contrary.

(d) *Exceptions.* There is no privilege under this rule:

(1) when the victim is dead;

(2) when federal law, state law, Department of Defense regulation, or service regulation imposes a duty to report information contained in a communication;

(3) when a victim advocate or Department of Defense Safe Helpline staff believes that a victim's mental or emotional condition makes the victim a danger to any person, including the victim;

(4) if the communication clearly contemplated the future commission of a fraud or crime, or if the services of the victim advocate or Department of Defense Safe Helpline staff are sought or obtained to enable or aid anyone to commit or plan to commit what the victim knew or reasonably should have known to be a crime or fraud;

(5) when necessary to ensure the safety and security of military personnel, military dependents, military property, classified information, or the accomplishment of a military mission; or

(6) when admission or disclosure of a communication is constitutionally required.

(e) *Procedure to Determine Admissibility of Victim Records or Communications.*

(1) In any case in which the production or admission of records or communications of a victim is a matter in dispute, a party may seek an interlocutory ruling by the military judge. In order to obtain such a ruling, the party must:

(A) file a written motion at least 5 days prior to entry of pleas specifically describing the evidence and stating the purpose for which it is sought or offered, or objected to, unless the military judge, for good cause shown, requires a different time for filing or permits filing during trial; and

(B) serve the motion on the opposing party, the military judge and, if practicable, notify the victim or the victim's guardian, conservator, or representative that the motion has been filed and that the victim has an opportunity to be heard as set forth in subdivision (e)(2).

(2) Before ordering the production or admission of evidence of a patient's records or communication, the military judge must conduct a hearing, which shall be closed. At the hearing, the parties may call witnesses, including the victim, and offer other relevant evidence. The victim must be afforded a reasonable opportunity to attend the hearing and be heard. However, the hearing may not be unduly delayed for this purpose. The right to be heard under this rule includes the right to be heard through counsel, including Special Victims' Counsel under section 1044e of title 10, United States Code. In a case before a court-martial composed of a military judge and members, the military judge must conduct the hearing outside the presence of the members.

(3) The military judge may examine the evidence or a proffer thereof in camera, if such examination is necessary to rule on the production or admissibility of protected records or communications. Prior to conducting an in camera review, the military judge must find by a preponderance of the evidence that the moving party showed:

(A) a specific, credible factual basis demonstrating a reasonable likelihood that the records or communications would contain or lead to the discovery of evidence admissible under an exception to the privilege;

(B) that the requested information meets one of the enumerated exceptions under subdivision (d) of this rule;

(C) that the information sought is not merely cumulative of other information available; and

(D) that the party made reasonable efforts to obtain the same or substantially similar information through non-privileged sources.

(4) Any production of disclosure permitted by the military judge under this rule must be narrowly tailored to only the specific records or communications, or portions of such records or communications, that meet the requirements for one of the enumerated exceptions to the privilege under subdivision (d) of this Rule and are included in the stated purpose for which the records or communications are sought under subdivision (e)(1)(A) of this rule.

(5) To prevent unnecessary disclosure of evidence of a victim's records or communications, the military judge may issue protective orders or may admit only portions of the evidence.

(6) The motion, related papers, and the record of the hearing must be sealed in accordance with R.C.M. 701(g)(2) or 1113 and must remain under seal unless the military judge, the Judge Advocate General, or an appellate court orders otherwise.

SECTION VI
WITNESSES

Rule 601. Competency to testify in general

Every person is competent to be a witness unless these rules provide otherwise.

Rule 602. Need for personal knowledge

A witness may testify to a matter only if evidence is introduced sufficient to support a finding that the witness has personal knowledge of the matter. Evidence to prove personal knowledge may consist of the witness' own testimony. This rule does not apply to a witness' expert testimony under Mil. R. Evid. 703.

Rule 603. Oath or affirmation to testify truthfully

Before testifying, a witness must give an oath or affirmation to testify truthfully. It must be in a form designed to impress that duty on the witness' conscience.

Rule 604. Interpreter

An interpreter must be qualified and must give an oath or affirmation to make a true translation.

Rule 605. Military judge's competency as a witness

(a) The presiding military judge may not testify as a witness at any proceeding of that court-martial. A party need not object to preserve the issue.

(b) This rule does not preclude the military judge from placing on the record matters concerning docketing of the case.

Rule 606. Member's competency as a witness

(a) *At the Trial by Court-Martial.* A member of a court-martial may not testify as a witness before the other members at any proceeding of that court-martial. If a member is called to testify, the military judge must give the opposing party an opportunity to object outside the presence of the members.

(b) *During an Inquiry into the Validity of a Finding or Sentence.*

(1) Prohibited Testimony or Other Evidence. During an inquiry into the validity of a finding or sentence, a member of a court-martial may not testify about any statement made or incident that occurred during the deliberations of that court-martial; the effect of anything on that member's or another member's vote; or any member's mental processes concerning the finding or sentence. The military judge may not receive a member's affidavit or evidence of a member's statement on these matters.

(2) *Exceptions.* A member may testify about whether:

(A) extraneous prejudicial information was improperly brought to the members' attention;

(B) unlawful command influence or any other outside influence was improperly brought to bear on any member; or

(C) a mistake was made in entering the finding or sentence on the finding or sentence forms.

Rule 607. Who may impeach a witness

Any party, including the party that called the witness, may attack the witness' credibility.

Rule 608. A witness' character for truthfulness or untruthfulness

(a) *Reputation or Opinion Evidence.* A witness' credibility may be attacked or supported by testimony about the witness' reputation for having a character for truthfulness or untruthfulness, or by testimony in the form of an opinion about that character. Evidence of truthful character is admissible only after the witness' character for truthfulness has been attacked.

(b) *Specific Instances of Conduct.* Except for a criminal conviction under Mil. R. Evid. 609, extrinsic evidence is not admissible to prove specific instances of a witness' conduct in order to attack or support the witness' character for truthfulness. The military judge may, on cross-examination, allow them to be inquired into if they are probative of the character for truthfulness or untruthfulness of:

(1) the witness; or

(2) another witness whose character the witness being cross-examined has testified about. By testifying on another matter, a witness does not waive any privilege against self-incrimination for testimony that relates only to the witness' character for truthfulness.

(c) *Evidence of Bias.* Bias, prejudice, or any motive to misrepresent may be shown to impeach the witness either by examination of the witness or by evidence otherwise adduced.

Rule 609. Impeachment by evidence of a criminal conviction or finding of guilty by summary court-martial

(a) *In General.* The following rules apply to attacking a witness' character for truthfulness by evidence of a criminal conviction or finding of guilty by summary court-martial.

(1) For an offense that, in the convicting jurisdiction, was punishable by death, dishonorable discharge, or by imprisonment for more than one year, the evidence:

(A) must be admitted, subject to Mil. R. Evid. 403, in a court-martial in which the witness is not the accused; and

(B) must be admitted in a court-martial in which the witness is the accused, if the probative value of the evidence outweighs its prejudicial effect to that accused; and

(2) For any offense regardless of the punishment, the evidence must be admitted if the court can readily determine that establishing the elements of the crime required proving – or the witness' admitting – a dishonest act or false statement.

(3) In determining whether an offense tried by court-martial was punishable by death, dishonorable discharge, or imprisonment in excess of one year, the maximum punishment prescribed by the President under Article 56 at the time of the conviction applies without regard to whether the case was tried by general, special, or summary court-martial.

(b) *Limit on Using the Evidence After 10 Years.* Subdivision (b) applies if more than 10 years have passed since the witness' conviction or finding of guilty by summary court-martial or release from confinement for it, whichever is later. Evidence of the conviction or finding of guilty by summary court-martial is admissible only if:

(1) its probative value, supported by specific facts and circumstances, substantially outweighs its prejudicial effect; and

(2) the proponent gives an adverse party reasonable written notice of the intent to use it so that the party has a fair opportunity to contest its use.

(c) *Effect of a Pardon, Annulment, or Certificate of Rehabilitation.* Evidence of a conviction or finding of guilty by summary court-martial is not admissible if:

(1) the conviction or finding of guilty by summary court-martial has been the subject of a pardon, annulment, certificate of rehabilitation, or other equivalent procedure based on a finding that the person has been rehabilitated, and the person has not been convicted of a later crime punishable by death, dishonorable discharge, or imprisonment for more than one year; or

(2) the conviction or finding of guilty by summary court-martial has been the subject of a pardon, annulment, or other equivalent procedure based on a finding of innocence.

(d) *Juvenile Adjudications.* Evidence of a juvenile adjudication is admissible under this rule only if:

(1) the adjudication was of a witness other than the accused;

(2) an adult's conviction for that offense would be admissible to attack the adult's credibility; and

(3) admitting the evidence is necessary to fairly determine guilt or innocence.

(e) *Limit on use of a finding of guilty by summary court-martial.* A finding of guilty by summary court-martial may not be used for purposes of impeachment unless the accused at the summary court-martial proceeding was represented by military or civilian defense counsel.

(f) *Pendency of an Appeal.* A conviction that satisfies this rule is admissible even if an appeal is pending, except that a finding of guilty by summary court-martial may not be used for purposes of impeachment until review has been completed under Article 64. Evidence of the pendency is also admissible.

(g) *Definition.* For purposes of this rule, there is a conviction in a general or special court-martial when a sentence has been adjudged.

Rule 610. Religious beliefs or opinions

Evidence of a witness' religious beliefs or opinions is not admissible to attack or support the witness' credibility.

Rule 611. Mode and order of examining witnesses and presenting evidence

(a) *Control by the Military Judge; Purposes.*

The military judge should exercise reasonable control over the mode and order of examining witnesses and presenting evidence so as to:

(1) make those procedures effective for determining the truth;

(2) avoid wasting time; and

(3) protect witnesses from harassment or undue embarrassment.

(b) *Scope of Cross-Examination.* Cross-examination should not go beyond the subject matter of the direct examination and matters affecting the witness' credibility. The military judge may allow inquiry into additional matters as if on direct examination.

(c) *Leading Questions.* Leading questions should not be used on direct examination except as necessary to develop the witness' testimony. Ordinarily, the military judge should allow leading questions:

(1) on cross-examination; and

(2) when a party calls a hostile witness or a witness identified with an adverse party.

(d) *Remote live testimony of a child.*

(1) In a case involving domestic violence or a case involving the abuse of a child, the military judge must, subject to the requirements of subdivision (d)(3) of this rule, allow a child victim or child witness to testify from an area outside the courtroom as prescribed in R.C.M. 914A.

(2) *Definitions.*

As used in this rule:

(A) "Child" means a person who is under the age of 16 at the time of his or her testimony.

(B) "Abuse of a child" means the physical or mental injury, sexual abuse or exploitation, or negligent treatment of a child.

(C) "Exploitation" means child pornography or child prostitution.

(D) "Negligent treatment" means the failure to provide, for reasons other than poverty, adequate food, clothing, shelter, or medical care so as to endanger seriously the physical health of the child.

(E) "Domestic violence" means conduct that may constitute an offense under Article 128b.

(3) Remote live testimony will be used only where the military judge makes the following three findings on the record:

(A) that it is necessary to protect the welfare of the particular child witness;

(B) that the child witness would be traumatized, not by the courtroom generally, but by the presence of the accused; and

(C) that the emotional distress suffered by the child witness in the presence of the accused is more than *de minimis.*

(4) Remote live testimony of a child will not be used when the accused elects to absent himself from the courtroom in accordance with R.C.M. 804(d).

(5) In making a determination under subdivision (d)(3), the military judge may question the child in chambers, or at some comfortable place other than the courtroom, on the record for a reasonable period of time, in the presence of the child, a representative of the prosecution, a representative of the defense, and the child's attorney or guardian ad litem.

Rule 612. Writing used to refresh a witness' memory

(a) *Scope.* This rule gives an adverse party certain options when a witness uses a writing to refresh memory:

(1) while testifying; or

(2) before testifying, if the military judge decides that justice requires the party to have those options.

(b) *Adverse Party's Options; Deleting Unrelated Matter.* An adverse party is entitled to have the writing produced at the hearing, to inspect it, to cross-examine the witness about it, and to introduce in evidence any portion that relates to the witness' testimony. If the producing party claims that the writing includes unrelated or privileged matter, the military judge must examine the writing in camera, delete any unrelated or privileged portion, and order that the rest be delivered to the adverse party. Any portion deleted over objection must be preserved for the record.

(c) *Failure to Produce or Deliver the Writing.* If a writing is not produced or is not delivered as ordered, the military judge may issue any appropriate order. If the prosecution does not comply, the military judge must strike the witness' testimony or - if justice so requires - declare a mistrial.

(d) *No Effect on Other Disclosure Requirements.* This rule does not preclude disclosure of information required to be disclosed under other provisions of these rules or this Manual.

Rule 613. Witness' prior statement

(a) *Showing or Disclosing the Statement During Examination.* When examining a witness about the witness' prior statement, a party need not show it or disclose its contents to the witness. The party must, on request, show it or disclose its contents to an adverse party's attorney.

(b) *Extrinsic Evidence of a Prior Inconsistent Statement.* Extrinsic evidence of a witness' prior inconsistent statement is admissible only if the witness is given an opportunity to explain or deny the statement and an adverse party is given an opportunity to examine the witness about it, or if justice so requires. Subdivision (b) does not apply to an opposing party's statement under Mil R. Evid. 801(d)(2).

Rule 614. Court-martial's calling or examining a witness

(a) *Calling.* The military judge may—sua sponte or at the request of the members or the suggestion of a party—call a witness. Each party is entitled to cross-examine the witness. When the members wish to call or recall a witness, the military judge must determine whether the testimony would be relevant and not barred by any rule or provision of this Manual.

(b) *Examining.* The military judge or members may examine a witness regardless of who calls the witness. Members must submit their questions to the military judge in writing. Following the opportunity for review by both parties, the military judge must rule on the propriety of the questions, and ask the questions in an acceptable form on behalf of the members. When the military judge or the members call a witness who has not previously testified, the military judge may conduct the direct examination or may assign the responsibility to counsel for any party.

(c) *Objections.* Objections to the calling of witnesses by the military judge or the members or to the interrogation by the military judge or the members may be made at the time or at the next available opportunity when the members are not present.

Rule 615. Excluding witnesses

At a party's request, the military judge must order witnesses excluded so that they cannot hear other witnesses' testimony, or the military judge may do so sua sponte. This rule does not authorize excluding:

(a) the accused;

(b) a member of an Armed service or an employee of the United States after being designated as a representative of the United States by trial counsel;

(c) a person whose presence a party shows to be essential to presenting the party's case;

(d) a person authorized by statute to be present; or

(e) a victim of an offense from the trial of an accused for that offense, unless the military judge, after receiving clear and convincing evidence, determines that testimony by the victim would be materially altered if the victim heard other testimony at that hearing or proceeding.

SECTION VII
OPINIONS AND EXPERT TESTIMONY

Rule 701. Opinion testimony by lay witnesses

If a witness is not testifying as an expert, testimony in the form of an opinion is limited to one that is:

(a) rationally based on the witness' perception;

(b) helpful to clearly understanding the witness' testimony or to determining a fact in issue; and

(c) not based on scientific, technical, or other specialized knowledge within the scope of Mil. R. Evid. 702.

Rule 702. Testimony by expert witnesses

A witness who is qualified as an expert by knowledge, skill, experience, training, or education may testify in the form of an opinion or otherwise if:

(a) the expert's scientific, technical, or other specialized knowledge will help the trier of fact to understand the evidence or to determine a fact in issue;

(b) the testimony is based on sufficient facts or data;

(c) the testimony is the product of reliable principles and methods; and

(d) the expert has reliably applied the principles and methods to the facts of the case.

Rule 703. Bases of an expert's opinion testimony

An expert may base an opinion on facts or data in the case that the expert has been made aware of or personally observed. If experts in the particular field would reasonably rely on those kinds of facts or data in forming an opinion on the subject, they need not be admissible for the opinion to be admitted. If the facts or data would otherwise be inadmissible, the proponent of the opinion may disclose them to the members of a court-martial only if the military judge finds that their probative value in helping the members evaluate the opinion substantially outweighs their prejudicial effect.

Rule 704. Opinion on an ultimate issue

An opinion is not objectionable just because it embraces an ultimate issue.

Rule 705. Disclosing the facts or data underlying an expert's opinion

Unless the military judge orders otherwise, an expert may state an opinion - and give the reasons for it – without first testifying to the underlying facts or data. The expert may be required to disclose those facts or data on cross-examination.

Rule 706. Court-appointed expert witnesses

(a) *Appointment Process.* Trial counsel, defense counsel, and the court-martial have equal opportunity to obtain expert witnesses under Article 46 and R.C.M. 703.

(b) *Compensation.* The compensation of expert witnesses is governed by R.C.M. 703.

(c) *Accused's Choice of Experts.* This rule does not limit an accused in calling any expert at the accused's own expense.

Rule 707. Polygraph examinations

(a) *Prohibitions.* Notwithstanding any other provision of law, the result of a polygraph examination, the polygraph examiner's opinion, or any reference to an offer to take, failure to take, or taking of a polygraph examination is not admissible.

(b) *Statements Made During a Polygraph Examination.* This rule does not prohibit admission of an otherwise admissible statement made during a polygraph examination.

SECTION VIII
HEARSAY

Rule 801. Definitions that apply to this section; exclusions from hearsay

(a) *Statement.* "Statement" means a person's oral assertion, written assertion, or nonverbal conduct, if the person intended it as an assertion.

(b) *Declarant.* "Declarant" means the person who made the statement.

(c) *Hearsay.* "Hearsay" means a statement that:

(1) the declarant does not make while testifying at the current trial or hearing; and

(2) a party offers in evidence to prove the truth of the matter asserted in the statement.

(d) *Statements that Are Not Hearsay.* A statement that meets the following conditions is not hearsay:

(1) *A Declarant-Witness' Prior Statement.* The declarant testifies and is subject to cross-examination about a prior statement, and the statement:

(A) is inconsistent with the declarant's testimony and was given under penalty of perjury at a trial, hearing, or other proceeding or in a deposition;

(B) is consistent with the declarant's testimony and is offered:

(i) to rebut an express or implied charge that the declarant recently fabricated it or acted from a recent improper influence or motive in so testifying; or

(ii) to rehabilitate the declarant's credibility as a witness when attacked on another ground; or

(C) identifies a person as someone the declarant perceived earlier.

(2) *An Opposing Party's Statement.* The statement is offered against an opposing party and:

(A) was made by the party in an individual or representative capacity;

(B) is one the party manifested that it adopted or believed to be true;

(C) was made by a person whom the party authorized to make a statement on the subject;

(D) was made by the party's agent or employee on a matter within the scope of that relationship and while it existed; or

(E) was made by the party's co-conspirator during and in furtherance of the conspiracy. The statement must be considered but does not by itself establish the declarant's authority under (C); the existence or scope of the relationship under (D); or the existence of the conspiracy or participation in it under (E).

Rule 802. The rule against hearsay

Hearsay is not admissible unless any of the following provides otherwise:

(a) a federal statute applicable in trial by courts-martial; or

(b) these rules.

Rule 803. Exceptions to the rule against hearsay – regardless of whether the declarant is available as a witness

The following are not excluded by the rule against hearsay, regardless of whether the declarant is available as a witness:

(1) *Present Sense Impression.* A statement describing or explaining an event or condition, made while or immediately after the declarant perceived it.

(2) *Excited Utterance.* A statement relating to a startling event or condition, made while the declarant was under the stress of excitement that it caused.

(3) *Then-Existing Mental, Emotional, or Physical Condition.* A statement of the declarant's then-existing state of mind (such as motive, intent, or plan) or emotional, sensory, or physical condition (such as mental feeling, pain, or bodily health), but not including a statement of memory or belief to prove the fact remembered or believed unless it relates to the validity or terms of the declarant's will.

(4) *Statement Made for Medical Diagnosis or Treatment.* A statement that—

(A) is made for—and is reasonably pertinent to—medical diagnosis or treatment; and

(B) describes medical history; past or present symptoms or sensations; their inception; or their general cause.

(5) *Recorded Recollection.* A record that—

(A) is on a matter the witness once knew about but now cannot recall well enough to testify fully and accurately;

(B) was made or adopted by the witness when the matter was fresh in the witness's memory; and

(C) accurately reflects the witness' knowledge.

If admitted, the record may be read into evidence but may be received as an exhibit only if offered by an adverse party.

(6) *Records of a Regularly Conducted Activity.* A record of an act, event, condition, opinion, or diagnosis if:

(A) the record was made at or near the time by - or from information transmitted by - someone with knowledge;

(B) the record was kept in the course of a regularly conducted activity of a uniformed service, business, institution, association, profession, organization, occupation, or calling of any kind, whether or not conducted for profit;

(C) making the record was a regular practice of that activity;

(D) all these conditions are shown by the testimony of the custodian or another qualified witness, or by a certification that complies with Mil. R. Evid. 902(11) or with a statute permitting certification in a criminal proceeding in a court of the United States; and

(E) the opponent does not show that the source of information or the method or circumstance of preparation indicate a lack of trustworthiness. Records of regularly conducted activities include, but are not limited to, enlistment papers, physical examination papers, fingerprint cards, forensic laboratory reports, chain of custody documents, morning reports and other personnel accountability documents, service records, officer and enlisted qualification records, logs, unit personnel diaries, individual equipment records, daily strength records of prisoners, and rosters of prisoners.

(7) *Absence of a Record of a Regularly Conducted Activity.* Evidence that a matter is not included in a record described in paragraph (6) if:

(A) the evidence is admitted to prove that the matter did not occur or exist;

(B) a record was regularly kept for a matter of that kind; and

(C) the opponent does not show that the possible source of the information or other circumstances indicate a lack of trustworthiness.

(8) *Public Records.* A record or statement of a public office if:

(A) it sets out:

(i) the office's activities;

(ii) a matter observed while under a legal duty to report, but not including a matter observed by law-enforcement personnel and other personnel acting in a law enforcement capacity; or

(iii) against the government, factual findings from a legally authorized investigation; and

(B) the opponent does not show that the source of information or other circumstances indicate a lack of trustworthiness. Notwithstanding subdivision (8)(A)(ii), the following are admissible as a record of a fact or event if made by a person within the scope of the person's official duties and those duties included a duty to know or to ascertain through appropriate and trustworthy channels of information the truth of the fact or event and to record such fact or event: enlistment papers, physical examination papers, fingerprint cards, forensic laboratory reports, chain of custody documents, morning reports and other personnel accountability documents, service records, officer and enlisted qualification records, court-martial conviction records, logs, unit personnel diaries, individual equipment records, daily strength records of prisoners, and rosters of prisoners.

(9) *Public Records of Vital Statistics.* A record of a birth, death, or marriage, if reported to a public office in accordance with a legal duty.

(10) *Absence of a Public Record.*

Testimony - or a certification under Rule 902 - that a diligent search failed to disclose a public record or statement if:

(A) the testimony or certification is admitted to prove that

(i) the record or statement does not exist; or

(ii) a matter did not occur or exist, if a public office regularly kept a record or statement for a matter of that kind; and

(B) a counsel for the government who intends to offer a certification provides written notice of that intent at least 14 days before trial, and the accused does not object in writing within 7 days of receiving the notice - unless the military judge sets a different time for the notice or the objection.

(11) *Records of Religious Organizations Concerning Personal or Family History.* A statement of birth, legitimacy, ancestry, marriage, divorce, death, relationship by blood or marriage, or similar facts of personal or family history, contained in a regularly kept record of a religious organization.

(12) *Certificates of Marriage, Baptism, and Similar Ceremonies.* A statement of fact contained in a certificate:

(A) made by a person who is authorized by a religious organization or by law to perform the act certified;

(B) attesting that the person performed a marriage or similar ceremony or administered a sacrament; and

(C) purporting to have been issued at the time of the act or within a reasonable time after it.

(13) *Family Records.* A statement of fact about personal or family history contained in a family record, such as a Bible, genealogy, chart, engraving on a ring, inscription on a portrait, or engraving on an urn or burial marker.

(14) *Records of Documents that Affect an Interest in Property.* The record of a document that purports to establish or affect an interest in property if:

(A) the record is admitted to prove the content of the original recorded document, along with its signing and its delivery by each person who purports to have signed it;

(B) the record is kept in a public office; and

(C) a statute authorizes recording documents of that kind in that office.

(15) *Statements in Documents that Affect an Interest in Property.* A statement contained in a document that purports to establish or affect an interest in property if the matter stated was relevant to the document's purpose unless later dealings with the property are inconsistent with the truth of the statement or the purport of the document.

(16) *Statements in Ancient Documents.* A statement in a document that was prepared before January 1, 1998, and whose authenticity is established.

(17) *Market Reports and Similar Commercial Publications.* Market quotations, lists (including government price lists), directories, or other compilations that are generally relied on by the public or by persons in particular occupations.

(18) *Statements in Learned Treatises, Periodicals, or Pamphlets.* A statement contained in a treatise, periodical, or pamphlet if:

(A) the statement is called to the attention of an expert witness on cross-examination or relied on by the expert on direct examination; and

(B) the publication is established as a reliable authority by the expert's admission or testimony, by another expert's testimony, or by judicial notice.

If admitted, the statement may be read into evidence but not received as an exhibit.

(19) *Reputation Concerning Personal or Family History.* A reputation among a person's family by blood, adoption, or marriage - or among a person's associates or in the community - concerning the person's birth, adoption, legitimacy, ancestry, marriage, divorce, death, relationship by blood, adoption, or marriage, or similar facts of personal or family history, age, ancestry, or other similar fact of the person's personal or family history.

(20) *Reputation Concerning Boundaries or General History.* A reputation in a community - arising before the controversy - concerning boundaries of land in the

community or customs that affect the land, or concerning general historical events important to that community, State, or nation.

(21) *Reputation Concerning Character.* A reputation among a person's associates or in the community concerning the person's character.

(22) *Judgment of a Previous Conviction.* Evidence of a final judgment of conviction if:

(A) the judgment was entered after a trial or guilty plea, but not a nolo contendere plea;

(B) the conviction was for a crime punishable by death, dishonorable discharge, or imprisonment for more than a year;

(C) the evidence is admitted to prove any fact essential to the judgment; and

(D) when offered by the prosecution for a purpose other than impeachment, the judgment was against the accused.

The pendency of an appeal may be shown but does not affect admissibility. In determining whether a crime tried by court-martial was punishable by death, dishonorable discharge, or imprisonment for more than one year, the maximum punishment prescribed by the President under Article 56 of the Uniform Code of Military Justice at the time of the conviction applies without regard to whether the case was tried by general, special, or summary court-martial.

(23) *Judgments Involving Personal, Family, or General History, or a Boundary.* A judgment that is admitted to prove a matter of personal, family, or general history, or boundaries, if the matter:

(A) was essential to the judgment; and

(B) could be proved by evidence of reputation.

Rule 804. Exceptions to the rule against hearsay – when the declarant is unavailable as a witness

(a) *Criteria for Being Unavailable.* A declarant is considered to be unavailable as a witness if the declarant:

(1) is exempted from testifying about the subject matter of the declarant's statement because the military judge rules that a privilege applies;

(2) refuses to testify about the subject matter despite the military judge's order to do so;

(3) testifies to not remembering the subject matter;

(4) cannot be present or testify at the trial or hearing because of death or a then-existing infirmity, physical illness, or mental illness; or

(5) is absent from the trial or hearing and the statement's proponent has not been able, by process or other reasonable means, to procure:

(A) the declarant's attendance, in the case of a hearsay exception under subdivision (b)(1) or (b)(5);

(B) the declarant's attendance or testimony, in the case of a hearsay exception under subdivision (b)(2), (b)(3), or (b)(4); or

(6) has previously been deposed about the subject matter and is absent due to military necessity, age, imprisonment, non-amenability to process, or other reasonable cause.

Subdivision (a) does not apply if the statement's proponent procured or wrongfully caused the declarant's unavailability as a witness in order to prevent the declarant from attending or testifying.

(b) *The Exceptions.* The following are exceptions to the rule against hearsay, and are not excluded by that rule if the declarant is unavailable as a witness:

(1) *Former Testimony.* Testimony that:

(A) was given by a witness at a trial, hearing, or lawful deposition, whether given during the current proceeding or a different one; and

(B) is now offered against a party who had an opportunity and similar motive to develop it by direct, cross-, or redirect examination.

Subject to the limitations in Articles 49 and 50, a record of testimony given before a court-martial, court of inquiry, military commission, other military tribunal, or preliminary hearing under Article 32 is admissible under subdivision (b)(1) if the record of the testimony is a verbatim record.

(2) *Statement under the Belief of Imminent Death.* In a prosecution for any offense resulting in the death of the alleged victim, a statement that the declarant, while believing the declarant's death to be imminent, made about its cause or circumstances.

(3) *Statement against Interest.* A statement that:

(A) a reasonable person in the declarant's position would have made only if the person believed it to be true because, when made, it was so contrary to the declarant's proprietary or pecuniary interest or had so great a tendency to invalidate the declarant's claim against someone else or to expose the declarant to civil or criminal liability; and

(B) is supported by corroborating circumstances that clearly indicate its trustworthiness, if it tends to expose the declarant to criminal liability and is offered to exculpate the accused.

(4) *Statement of Personal or Family History.* A statement about:

(A) the declarant's own birth, adoption, legitimacy, ancestry, marriage, divorce, relationship by blood or marriage, or similar facts of personal or family history, even though the declarant had no way of acquiring personal knowledge about that fact; or

(B) another person concerning any of these facts, as well as death, if the declarant was related to the person by blood, adoption, or marriage or was so intimately associated with the person's family that the declarant's information is likely to be accurate

(5) *Other Exceptions.* [Transferred to Mil. R. Evid. 807]

(6) *Statement Offered against a Party that Wrongfully Caused the Declarant's Unavailability.* A statement offered against a party that wrongfully caused or acquiesced in wrongfully causing the declarant's unavailability as a witness, and did so intending that result.

Rule 805. Hearsay within hearsay

Hearsay within hearsay is not excluded by the rule against hearsay if each part of the combined statements conforms with an exception or exclusion to the rule.

Rule 806. Attacking and supporting the declarant's credibility

When a hearsay statement - or a statement described in Mil. R. Evid. 801(d)(2)(C), (D), or (E) - has been admitted in evidence, the declarant's credibility may be attacked, and then supported, by any evidence that would be admissible for those purposes if the declarant had testified as a witness. The military judge may admit evidence of the declarant's inconsistent statement or conduct, regardless of when it occurred or whether the declarant had an opportunity to explain or deny it. If the party against whom the statement was admitted calls the declarant as a witness, the party may examine the declarant on the statement as if on cross-examination.

Rule 807. Residual exception

(a) *In General.* Under the following conditions, a hearsay statement is not excluded by the rule against hearsay even if the statement is not admissible under a hearsay exception in Mil. R. Evid. 803 or 804:

(1) the statement is supported by sufficient guarantees of trustworthiness—after considering the totality of the circumstances under which it is made and evidence, if any, corroborating the statement; and

(2) the statement is more probative on the point for which it is offered than any other evidence that the proponent can obtain through reasonable efforts.

(b) *Notice.* The statement is admissible only if the proponent gives an adverse party reasonable notice of the intent to offer the statement—including its substance and the declarant's name—so that the party has a fair opportunity to meet it. The notice must be provided in writing before the trial or hearing—or in any form during the trial or hearing if the court, for good cause, excuses a lack of earlier notice.

SECTION IX
AUTHENTICATION AND IDENTIFICATION

Rule 901. Authenticating or identifying evidence

(a) *In General.* To satisfy the requirement of authenticating or identifying an item of evidence, the proponent must produce evidence sufficient to support a finding that the item is what the proponent claims it is.

(b) *Examples.* The following are examples only - not a complete list - of evidence that satisfies the requirement:

(1) *Testimony of a Witness with Knowledge.* Testimony that an item is what it is claimed to be.

(2) *Nonexpert Opinion about Handwriting.* A nonexpert's opinion that handwriting is genuine, based on a familiarity with it that was not acquired for the current litigation.

(3) *Comparison by an Expert Witness or the Trier of Fact.* A comparison with an authenticated specimen by an expert witness or the trier of fact.

(4) *Distinctive Characteristics and the Like.* The appearance, contents, substance, internal patterns, or other distinctive characteristics of the item, taken together with all the circumstances.

(5) *Opinion about a Voice.* An opinion identifying a person's voice—whether heard firsthand or through mechanical or electronic transmission or recording—based on hearing the voice at any time under circumstances that connect it with the alleged speaker.

(6) *Evidence about a Telephone Conversation.* For a telephone conversation, evidence that a call was made to the number assigned at the time to:

(A) a particular person, if circumstances, including self-identification, show that the person answering was the one called; or

(B) a particular business, if the call was made to a business and the call related to business reasonably transacted over the telephone.

(7) *Evidence about Public Records.* Evidence that:

(A) a document was recorded or filed in a public office as authorized by law; or

(B) a purported public record or statement is from the office where items of this kind are kept.

(8) *Evidence about Ancient Documents or Data Compilations.* For a document or data compilation, evidence that it:

(A) is in a condition that creates no suspicion about its authenticity;

(B) was in a place where, if authentic, it would likely be; and

(C) is at least 20 years old when offered.

(9) *Evidence about a Process or System.* Evidence describing a process or system and showing that it produces an accurate result.

(10) *Methods Provided by a Statute or Rule.* Any method of authentication or identification allowed by a federal statute, a rule prescribed by the Supreme Court, or an applicable regulation prescribed pursuant to statutory authority.

Rule 902. Evidence that is self-authenticating

The following items of evidence are self-authenticating; they require no extrinsic evidence of authenticity in order to be admitted:

(1) *Domestic Public Documents that are Sealed and Signed.* A document that bears:

(A) a seal purporting to be that of the United States; any State, district, Commonwealth, territory, or insular possession of the United States; the former Panama Canal Zone; the Trust Territory of the Pacific Islands; a political subdivision of any of these entities; or a department, agency, or officer of any entity named above; and

(B) a signature purporting to be an execution or attestation.

(2) *Domestic Public Documents that are Not Sealed but are Signed and Certified.* A document that bears no seal if:

(A) it bears the signature of an officer or employee of an entity named in subdivision (1)(A) above; and

(B) another public officer who has a seal and official duties within that same entity certifies under seal—or its equivalent—that the signer has the official capacity and that the signature is genuine.

(3) *Foreign Public Documents.* A document that purports to be signed or attested by a person who is authorized by a foreign country's law to do so. The document must be accompanied by a final certification that certifies the genuineness of the signature and official position of the signer or attester - or of any foreign official whose certificate of genuineness relates to the signature or attestation or is in a chain of certificates of genuineness relating to the signature or attestation. The certification may be made by a secretary of a United States embassy or legation; by a consul general, vice consul, or consular agent of the United States; or by a diplomatic or consular official of the foreign country assigned or accredited to the United States. If all parties have been given a reasonable opportunity to investigate the document's authenticity and accuracy, the military judge may, for good cause, either:

(A) order that it be treated as presumptively authentic without final certification; or

(B) allow it to be evidenced by an attested summary with or without final certification.

(4) *Certified Copies of Public Records.* A copy of an official record - or a copy of a document that was recorded or filed in a public office as authorized by law - if the copy is certified as correct by:

(A) the custodian or another person authorized to make the certification; or

(B) a certificate that complies with subdivision (1), (2), or (3) above, a federal statute, a rule prescribed by the Supreme Court, or an applicable regulation prescribed pursuant to statutory authority.

(4a) Documents or Records of the United States Accompanied by Attesting Certificates. Documents or records kept under the authority of the United States by any department, bureau, agency, office, or court thereof when attached to or accompanied by an attesting certificate of the custodian of the document or record without further authentication.

(5) *Official Publications.* A book, pamphlet, or other publication purporting to be issued by a public authority.

(6) *Newspapers and Periodicals.* Printed material purporting to be a newspaper or periodical.

(7) *Trade Inscriptions and the Like.* An inscription, sign, tag, or label purporting to have been affixed in the course of business and indicating origin, ownership, or control.

(8) *Acknowledged Documents.* A document accompanied by a certificate of acknowledgment that is lawfully executed by a notary public or another officer who is authorized to take acknowledgments.

(9) *Commercial Paper and Related Documents.* Commercial paper, a signature on it, and related documents, to the extent allowed by general commercial law.

(10) *Presumptions under a Federal Statute or Regulation.* A signature, document, or anything else that a federal statute, or an applicable regulation prescribed pursuant to statutory authority, declares to be presumptively or prima facie genuine or authentic.

(11) *Certified Domestic Records of a Regularly Conducted Activity.* The original or a copy of a domestic record that meets the requirements of Mil. R. Evid. 803(6)(A)-(C), as shown by a certification of the custodian or another qualified person that complies with a federal statute or a rule prescribed by the Supreme Court. Before the trial or hearing, or at a later time that the military judge allows for good cause, the proponent must give an adverse party reasonable written notice of the intent to offer the record and must make the record and certification available for inspection so that the party has a fair opportunity to challenge them.

(12) Reserved.

(13) *Certified Records Generated by an Electronic Process or System.* A record generated by an electronic process or system that produces an accurate result, as shown by a certification of a qualified person that complies with the certification requirements of Mil. R. Evid. 902(11). The proponent also must meet the notice requirements of Mil. R. Evid. Rule 902(11).

(14) *Certified Data Copied from an Electronic Device, Storage Medium, or File.* Data copied from an electronic device, storage medium, or file, if authenticated by a process of digital identification, as shown by a certification of a qualified person that complies with the certification requirements of Mil. R. Evid. 902(11). The proponent also must meet the notice requirements of Mil. R. Evid. 902(11).

Rule 903. Subscribing witness' testimony

A subscribing witness' testimony is necessary to authenticate a writing only if required by the law of the jurisdiction that governs its validity.

SECTION X
CONTENTS OF WRITINGS, RECORDINGS, AND PHOTOGRAPHS

Rule 1001. Definitions that apply to this section

In this section:

(a) A "writing" consists of letters, words, numbers, or their equivalent set down in any form.

(b) A "recording" consists of letters, words, numbers, or their equivalent recorded in any manner.

(c) A "photograph" means a photographic image or its equivalent stored in any form.

(d) An "original" of a writing or recording means the writing or recording itself or any counterpart intended to have the same effect by the person who executed or issued it. For electronically stored information, "original" means any printout or other output readable by sight if it accurately reflects the information. An "original" of a photograph includes the negative or a print from it.

(e) A "duplicate" means a counterpart produced by a mechanical, photographic, chemical, electronic, or other equivalent process or technique that accurately reproduces the original.

Rule 1002. Requirement of the original

An original writing, recording, or photograph is required in order to prove its content unless these rules, this Manual, or a federal statute provides otherwise.

Rule 1003. Admissibility of duplicates

A duplicate is admissible to the same extent as the original unless a genuine question is raised about the original's authenticity or the circumstances make it unfair to admit the duplicate.

Rule 1004. Admissibility of other evidence of content

An original is not required and other evidence of the content of a writing, recording, or photograph is admissible if:

(a) *Originals lost or destroyed.* All the originals are lost or destroyed, and not by the proponent acting in bad faith;

(b) *Original not obtainable.* An original cannot be obtained by any available judicial process;

(c) *Original in possession of opponent.* The party against whom the original would be offered had control of the original; was at that time put on notice, by pleadings or otherwise, that the original would be a subject of proof at the trial or hearing; and fails to produce it at the trial or hearing; or

(d) *Collateral matters.* The writing, recording, or photograph is not closely related to a controlling issue.

Rule 1005. Copies of public records to prove content

The proponent may use a copy to prove the content of an official record—or of a document that was recorded or filed in a public office as authorized by law—if these conditions are met: the record or document is otherwise admissible; and the copy is certified as correct in accordance with Mil. R. Evid. 902(4) or is testified to be correct by a witness who has compared it with the original. If no such copy can be obtained by reasonable diligence, then the proponent may use other evidence to prove the content.

Rule 1006. Summaries to prove content

The proponent may use a summary, chart, or calculation to prove the content of voluminous writings, recordings, or photographs that cannot be conveniently examined in court. The proponent must make the originals or duplicates available for examination or copying, or both, by other parties at a reasonable time or place. The military judge may order the proponent to produce them in court.

Rule 1007. Testimony or statement of a party to prove content

The proponent may prove the content of a writing, recording, or photograph by the testimony, deposition, or written statement of the party against whom the evidence is offered. The proponent need not account for the original.

Rule 1008. Functions of the military judge and the members

Ordinarily, the military judge determines whether the proponent has fulfilled the factual conditions for admitting other evidence of the content of a writing, recording, or photograph under Mil. R. Evid. 1004 or 1005. When a court-martial is composed of a military judge and members, the members determine - in accordance with Mil. R. Evid. 104(b) - any issue about whether:

(a) an asserted writing, recording, or photograph ever existed;

(b) another one produced at the trial or hearing is the original; or

(c) other evidence of content accurately reflects the content.

SECTION XI
MISCELLANEOUS RULES

Rule 1101. Applicability of these rules

(a) *In General.* Except as otherwise provided in this Manual, these rules apply generally to all courts-martial, including summary courts-martial, Article 39(a) sessions, Article 30a proceedings, remands, proceedings in revision, and contempt proceedings other than contempt proceedings in which the judge may act summarily.

(b) *Rules Relaxed.* The application of these rules may be relaxed in presentencing proceedings as provided under R.C.M. 1001 and otherwise as provided in this Manual.

(c) *Rules on Privilege.* The rules on privilege apply at all stages of a case or proceeding.

(d) Exceptions. Unless otherwise provided for in this Manual, these rules—except for Mil. R. Evid. 412 and those on privilege—do not apply to the following:

(1) the military judge's determination, under Rule 104(a), on a preliminary question of fact governing admissibility;

(2) preliminary hearings under Article 32;

(3) proceedings for vacation of suspension of sentence under Article 72; and

(4) miscellaneous actions and proceedings related to search authorizations, pretrial restraint, pretrial confinement, or other proceedings authorized under the Uniform Code of Military Justice or this Manual that are not listed in subdivision (a).

Rule 1102. Amendments

(a) *General Rule.* Amendments to the Federal Rules of Evidence—other than Articles III and V—will amend parallel provisions of the Military Rules of Evidence by operation of law 18 months after the effective date of such amendments, unless action to the contrary is taken by the President.

(b) *Rules Determined Not to Apply.* The President has determined that the following Federal Rules of Evidence do not apply to the Military Rules of Evidence: Rules 301, 302, 415, and 902(12).

Rule 1103. Title

These rules may be cited as the Military Rules of Evidence.

Part IV
PUNITIVE ARTICLES
(Statutory text of each Article is in bold)

Discussion

Part IV of the Manual addresses the punitive articles, 10 U.S.C.§§ 877-934. Part IV is organized by paragraph beginning with Article 77; therefore, each paragraph number is associated with an article. For example, paragraph 60 addresses Article 120, Rape and sexual assault generally. Article 77, Principals, and Article 79, Lesser included offenses, are located in the punitive article subchapter of Title 10 but are not chargeable offenses as such.

Other than Articles 77 and 79, the punitive articles of the code are discussed using the following sequence:

a. Text of the article

b. Elements of the offense or offenses

c. Explanation

d. Maximum punishment

e. Sample specifications

Presidentially prescribed lesser included offenses, as authorized under Article 79(b)(2), are established in Appendix 12A. For offenses not listed in Appendix 12A that may or may not be lesser included offenses, see R.C.M. 307(c)(3) and its accompanying Discussion regarding charging in the alternative. Practitioners are advised to read and comply with *United States v. Jones*, 68 M.J. 465 (C.A.A.F. 2010).

Sample specifications are provided in subparagraph e of each paragraph in Part IV and are meant to serve as a guide. The specifications may be varied in form and content as necessary.

R.C.M. 307 prescribes rules for preferral of charges and for drafting specifications. The discussion under that rule explains how to allege violations under the code using the format of charge and specification; however, practitioners are advised to read and comply with *United States v. Fosler*, 70 M.J. 225 (C.A.A.F. 2011) and *United States v. Jones*, 68 M.J. 465 (C.A.A.F. 2010).

The term "elements," as used in Part IV, includes both the statutory elements of the offense and any aggravating factors listed under the President's authority which increases the maximum permissible punishment when specified aggravating factors are pled and proven.

The prescriptions of maximum punishments in subparagraph d of each paragraph of Part IV must be read in conjunction with R.C.M. 1003, which prescribes additional punishments that may be available and additional limitations on punishments.

---

1. Article 77 (10 U.S.C. 877)—Principals

a. *Text of statute.*

Any person punishable under this chapter who—

(1) commits an offense punishable by this chapter, or aids, abets, counsels, commands, or procures its commission; or

(2) causes an act to be done which if directly performed by him would be punishable by this chapter;

is a principal.

b. *Explanation.*

(1) *Purpose.* Article 77 does not define an offense. Its purpose is to make clear that a person need not personally perform the acts necessary to constitute an offense to be guilty of it. A person who aids, abets, counsels, commands, or procures the commission of an offense, or who causes an act to be done which, if done by that person directly would be an offense, is equally guilty of the offense as one who commits it directly, and may be punished to the same extent.

Article 77 eliminates the common law distinctions between principal in the first degree ("perpetrator"); principal in the second degree (one who aids, counsels, commands, or encourages the commission of an offense and who is present at the scene of the crime—commonly known as an "aider and abettor"); and accessory before the fact (one who aids, counsels, commands, or encourages the commission of an offense and who is not present at the scene of the crime). All of these are now "principals."

(2) *Who may be liable for an offense.*

(a) *Perpetrator.* A perpetrator is one who actually commits the offense, either by the perpetrator's own hand, or by causing an offense to be committed by knowingly or intentionally inducing or setting in motion acts by an animate or inanimate agency or instrumentality which result in the commission of an offense. For example, a person who knowingly conceals contraband drugs in an automobile, and then induces another person, who is unaware and has no reason to know of the presence of drugs, to drive the automobile onto a military installation, is, although not present in the automobile, guilty of wrongful introduction of drugs onto a military installation. (On these facts, the driver would be guilty of no crime.) Similarly, if, upon orders of a superior, a soldier shot a person who appeared to the soldier to be an enemy, but was known to the superior as a friend, the superior would be guilty of murder (but the soldier would be guilty of no offense).

(b) *Other Parties*. If one is not a perpetrator, to be guilty of an offense committed by the perpetrator, the person must:

(i) Assist, encourage, advise, instigate, counsel, command, or procure another to commit, or assist, encourage, advise, counsel, or command another in the commission of the offense; and

(ii) Share in the criminal purpose or design.

One who, without knowledge of the criminal venture or plan, unwittingly encourages or renders assistance to another in the commission of an offense is not guilty of a crime. See the parentheticals in the examples in subparagraph 1.b.(2)(a) of this paragraph. In some circumstances, inaction may make one liable as a party, where there is a duty to act. If a person (for example, a security guard) has a duty to interfere in the commission of an offense, but does not interfere, that person is a party to the crime if such a noninterference is intended to and does operate as an aid or encouragement to the actual perpetrator.

(3) *Presence*.

(a) *Not necessary*. Presence at the scene of the crime is not necessary to make one a party to the crime and liable as a principal. For example, one who, knowing that a person intends to shoot another person and intending that such an assault be carried out, provides the person with a pistol, is guilty of assault when the offense is committed, even though not present at the scene.

(b) *Not sufficient*. Mere presence at the scene of a crime does not make one a principal unless the requirements of subparagraph 1.b.(2)(a) or (b) have been met.

(4) *Parties whose intent differs from the perpetrator's*. When an offense charged requires proof of a specific intent or particular state of mind as an element, the evidence must prove that the accused had that intent or state of mind, whether the accused is charged as a perpetrator or an "other party" to crime. It is possible for a party to have a state of mind more or less culpable than the perpetrator of the offense. In such a case, the party may be guilty of a more or less serious offense than that committed by the perpetrator. For example, when a homicide is committed, the perpetrator may act in the heat of sudden passion caused by adequate provocation and be guilty of manslaughter, while the party who, without such passion, hands the perpetrator a weapon and encourages the perpetrator to kill the victim, would be guilty of murder. On the other hand, if a party assists a perpetrator in an assault on a person who, known only to the perpetrator, is an officer, the party would be guilty only of assault, while the perpetrator would be guilty of assault on an officer.

(5) *Responsibility for other crimes*. A principal may be convicted of crimes committed by another principal if such crimes are likely to result as a natural and probable consequence of the criminal venture or design. For example, the accused who is a party to a burglary is guilty as a principal not only of the offense of burglary, but also, if the perpetrator kills an occupant in the course of the burglary, of murder. (See also paragraph 5, Conspiracy, concerning liability for offenses committed by co-conspirators.)

(6) *Principals independently liable*. One may be a principal, even if the perpetrator is not identified or prosecuted, or is acquitted.

(7) *Withdrawal*. A person may withdraw from a common venture or design and avoid liability for any offenses committed after the withdrawal. To be effective, the withdrawal must meet the following requirements:

(a) It must occur before the offense is committed;

(b) The assistance, encouragement, advice, instigation, counsel, command, or procurement given by the person must be effectively countermanded or negated; and

(c) The withdrawal must be clearly communicated to the would-be perpetrators or to appropriate law enforcement authorities in time for the perpetrators to abandon the plan or for law enforcement authorities to prevent the offense.

2. Article 78 (10 U.S.C. 878)—Accessory after the fact

a. *Text of statute*.

Any person subject to this chapter who, knowing that an offense punishable by this chapter has been committed, receives, comforts, or assists the offender in order to hinder or prevent his apprehension, trial, or punishment shall be punished as a court-martial may direct.

b. *Elements*.

(1) That an offense punishable by the UCMJ was committed by a certain person;

(2) That the accused knew that this person had committed such offense;

(3) That thereafter the accused received, comforted, or assisted the offender; and

(4) That the accused did so for the purpose of hindering or preventing the apprehension, trial, or punishment of the offender.

c. *Explanation.*

(1) *In general.* The assistance given a principal by an accessory after the fact is not limited to assistance designed to effect the escape or concealment of the principal, but also includes acts performed to conceal the commission of the offense by the principal (for example, by concealing evidence of the offense).

(2) *Failure to report offense.* The mere failure to report a known offense will not make one an accessory after the fact. Such failure may violate a general order or regulation, however, and thus constitute an offense under Article 92. *See* paragraph 18. If the offense involved is a serious offense, and the accused does anything to conceal it, failure to report it may constitute the offense of misprision of a serious offense, under Article 131c. *See* paragraph 84.

(3) *Offense punishable by the UCMJ.* The term "offense punishable by this chapter" in the text of the article means any offense described in the UCMJ.

(4) *Status of principal.* The principal who committed the offense in question need not be subject to the UCMJ, but the offense committed must be punishable by the UCMJ.

(5) *Conviction or acquittal of principal.* The prosecution must prove that a principal committed the offense to which the accused is allegedly an accessory after the fact. However, evidence of the conviction or acquittal of the principal in a separate trial is not admissible to show that the principal did or did not commit the offense. Furthermore, an accused may be convicted as an accessory after the fact despite the acquittal in a separate trial of the principal whom the accused allegedly comforted, received, or assisted.

(6) *Accessory after the fact not a lesser included offense.* The offense of being an accessory after the fact is not a lesser included offense of the primary offense.

(7) *Actual knowledge.* Actual knowledge is required but may be proved by circumstantial evidence.

d. *Maximum punishment.* Any person subject to the UCMJ who is found guilty as an accessory after the fact to an offense punishable under the UCMJ shall be subject to the maximum punishment authorized for the principal offense, except that in no case shall the death penalty nor more than one-half of the maximum confinement authorized for that offense be adjudged, nor shall the period of confinement exceed 10 years in any case, including offenses for which life imprisonment may be adjudged.

e. *Sample specification.*

In that __________ (personal jurisdiction data), knowing that (at/on board—location), on or about _____ 20 __, had committed an offense punishable by thc Uniform Code of Military Justice, to wit: __________, did, (at/on board—location) (subject-matter jurisdiction data, if required), on or about _____ 20 __, in order to (hinder) (prevent) the (apprehension) (trial) (punishment) of the said __________, (receive) (comfort) (assist) the said __________ by __________.

3. Article 79 (10 U.S.C. 879)—Conviction of offense charged, Lesser included offenses, and attempts

a. *Text of statute.*

(a) IN GENERAL.—An accused may be found guilty of any of the following:

(1) The offense charged.

(2) A lesser included offense.

(3) An attempt to commit the offense charged.

(4) An attempt to commit a lesser included offense, if the attempt is an offense in its own right.

(b) LESSER INCLUDED OFFENSE DEFINED.—In this section (article), the term "lesser included offense" means—

(1) an offense that is necessarily included in the offense charged; and

(2) any lesser included offense so designated by regulation prescribed by the President.

(c) REGULATORY AUTHORITY.—Any designation of a lesser included offense in a regulation referred to in subsection (b) shall be reasonably included in the greater offense.

b. *Explanation.*

(1) *In general.* Article 79 contains two provisions concerning notice of Lesser included offenses: (1) offenses that are "necessarily included" in the charged offense in accordance with Article 79(b)(1); and (2) offenses designated as Lesser included offenses by the President under Article 79(b)(2). Each provision sets forth an independent basis for providing notice of a lesser included offense.

(2) *"Necessarily included" offenses.* Under Article 79(b)(1), an offense is "necessarily included" in a charged offense when the elements of the lesser offense are a subset of the elements of the charged offense, thereby putting the accused on notice to be prepared to defend against the lesser offense in addition to the offense specifically charged. A lesser offense is "necessarily included" when:

(a) All of the elements of the lesser offense are included in the greater offense, and the common elements are identical (for example, wrongful appropriation as a lesser included offense of larceny);

(b) All of the elements of the lesser offense are included in the greater offense, but at least one element is a subset by being legally less serious (for example, unlawful entry as a lesser included offense of burglary); or

(c) All of the elements of the lesser offense are "included and necessary" parts of the greater offense, but the mental element is a subset by being legally less serious (for example, voluntary manslaughter as a lesser included offense of premeditated murder).

(3) *Offenses designated by the President.* Under Article 79(b)(2), Congress has authorized the President to designate Lesser included offenses by regulation.

(a) The President may designate an offense as a lesser included offense under Article 79(b)(2), subject to the requirement in Article 79(c) that the designated lesser included offense "shall be reasonably included in the greater offense."

(b) Appendix 12A sets forth the list of Lesser included offenses designated by the President under Article 79(b)(2).

(c) The President may include a "necessarily included offense" in the list of offenses prescribed under Article 79(b)(2), but is not required to do so. A court may identify an offense as a "necessarily included" offense under Article 79(b)(1) regardless of whether the offense has been designated under Article 79(b)(2).

Discussion

For offenses that may or may not be lesser included offenses, see R.C.M. 307(c)(3) and its accompanying Discussion regarding charging in the alternative.

---

(4) *Sua sponte duty.* Subject to R.C.M. 920(g), a military judge must instruct panel members on lesser included offenses reasonably raised by the evidence.

(5) *Multiple Lesser included offenses.* When the offense charged is a compound offense comprising two or more Lesser included offenses, an accused may be found guilty of any or all of the offenses included in the offense charged.

(6) *Findings of guilty to a lesser included offense.* A court-martial may find an accused not guilty of the offense charged, but guilty of a lesser included offense by the process of exception and substitution. The court-martial may except (that is, delete) the words in the specification that pertain to the offense charged and, if necessary, substitute language appropriate to the lesser included offense. For example, the accused is charged with murder in violation of Article 118, but found guilty of voluntary manslaughter in violation of Article 119. Such a finding may be worded as follows:

Of the Specification: Guilty, except the word "murder" substituting therefor the words "willfully and unlawfully kill," of the excepted word, not guilty, of the substituted words, guilty.

Of the Charge: Not guilty, but guilty of a violation of Article 119.

If a court-martial finds an accused guilty of a lesser included offense, the finding as to the charge shall state a violation of the specific punitive article violated and not a violation of Article 79.

4. Article 80 (10 U.S.C. 880)—Attempts

a. *Text of statute.*

(a) An act, done with specific intent to commit an offense under this chapter, amounting to more than mere preparation and tending, even though failing to effect its commission, is an attempt to commit that offense.

(b) Any person subject to this chapter who attempts to commit any offense punishable by this chapter shall be punished as a court-martial may direct, unless otherwise specifically prescribed.

(c) Any person subject to this chapter may be convicted of an attempt to commit an offense although it appears on the trial that the offense was consummated.

b. *Elements.*

(1) That the accused did a certain overt act;

(2) That the act was done with the specific intent to commit a certain offense under the UCMJ;

(3) That the act amounted to more than mere preparation; and

(4) That the act apparently tended to effect the commission of the intended offense.

c. *Explanation.*

(1) *In general.* To constitute an attempt there must be a specific intent to commit the offense accompanied by an overt act which directly tends to accomplish the unlawful purpose.

(2) *More than preparation.* Preparation consists of devising or arranging the means or measures necessary for the commission of the offense. The overt act required goes beyond preparatory steps and is a direct movement toward the commission of the offense. For example, a purchase of matches with the intent to burn a haystack is not an attempt to commit arson, but it is an attempt to commit arson to apply a burning match to a haystack, even if no fire results. The overt act need not be the last act essential to the consummation of the offense. For example, an accused could commit an overt act, and then voluntarily decide not to go through with the intended offense. An attempt would nevertheless have been committed, for the combination of a specific intent to commit an offense, plus the commission of an overt act directly tending to accomplish it, constitutes the offense of attempt. Failure to complete the offense, whatever the cause, is not a defense.

(3) *Factual impossibility.* A person who purposely engages in conduct which would constitute the offense if the attendant circumstances were as that person believed them to be is guilty of an attempt. For example, if A, without justification or excuse and with intent to kill B, points a gun at B and pulls the trigger, A is guilty of attempt to murder, even though, unknown to A, the gun is defective and will not fire. Similarly, a person who reaches into the pocket of another with the intent to steal that person's billfold is guilty of an attempt to commit larceny, even though the pocket is empty.

(4) *Voluntary abandonment.* It is a defense to an attempt offense that the person voluntarily and completely abandoned the intended crime, solely because of the person's own sense that it was wrong, prior to the completion of the crime. The voluntary abandonment defense is not allowed if the abandonment results, in whole or in part, from other reasons, for example, the person feared detection or apprehension, decided to await a better opportunity for success, was unable to complete the crime, or encountered unanticipated difficulties or unexpected resistance. A person who is entitled to the defense of voluntary abandonment may nonetheless be guilty of a lesser included, completed offense. For example, a person who voluntarily abandoned an attempted armed robbery may nonetheless be guilty of assault with a dangerous weapon.

(5) *Solicitation.* Soliciting another to commit an offense does not constitute an attempt. See paragraph 6 for a discussion of Article 82, Solicitation.

(6) *Attempts not under Article 80.* While most attempts should be charged under Article 80, the following attempts are specifically addressed by some other article, and should be charged accordingly:

(a) Article 85—Desertion

(b) Article 94—Mutiny or sedition

(c) Article 100—Subordinate compelling surrender

(d) Article 103a—Espionage

(e) Article 103b—Aiding the enemy

(f) Article 119a—Death or injury of an unborn child

(g) Article 128—Assault

(7) *Regulations.* An attempt to commit conduct which would violate a lawful general order or regulation under Article 92 (*see* paragraph 18) should be charged under Article 80. It is not necessary in such cases to prove that the accused intended to violate the order or regulation, but it must be proved that the accused intended to commit the prohibited conduct.

d. *Maximum punishment.* Any person subject to the UCMJ who is found guilty of an attempt under Article 80 to commit any offense punishable by the UCMJ shall be subject to the same maximum punishment authorized for the commission of the offense attempted, except that in no case shall the death penalty be adjudged, and in no case, other than attempted murder, shall confinement exceeding 20 years be adjudged. Except in the cases of attempts of rape and sexual assault under Article 120(a) or (b), and rape and sexual assault of a child under Article 120b(a) or (b), mandatory minimum punishment provisions shall not apply.

e. *Sample specification.*

In that __________ (personal jurisdiction data) did, (at/on board—location) (subject-matter jurisdiction data, if required), on or about _____ 20 __, attempt to (describe offense with sufficient detail to include expressly or by necessary implication every element).

5. Article 81 (10 U.S.C. 881)—Conspiracy

a. *Text of statute.*

(a) Any person subject to this chapter who conspires with any other person to commit an offense under this chapter shall, if one or more of the conspirators does an act to effect the object of the conspiracy, be punished as a court-martial may direct.

(b) Any person subject to this chapter who conspires with any other person to commit an offense under the law of war, and who knowingly does an overt act to effect the object of the conspiracy, shall be punished, if death results to one or more of the victims, by death or such other punishment as a court-martial or military commission may direct, and, if death does not result to any of the victims, by such punishment, other than death, as a court-martial or military commission may direct.

b. *Elements.*

(1) *Conspiracy.*

(a) That the accused entered into an agreement with one or more persons to commit an offense under the UCMJ; and

(b) That, while the agreement continued to exist, and while the accused remained a party to the agreement, the accused or at least one of the co-conspirators performed an overt act for the purpose of bringing about the object of the conspiracy.

(2) *Conspiracy when offense is an offense under the law of war resulting in the death of one or more victims.*

(a) That the accused entered into an agreement with one or more persons to commit an offense under the law of war;

(b) That, while the agreement continued to exist, and while the accused remained a party to the agreement, the accused knowingly performed an overt act for the purpose of bringing about the object of the conspiracy; and

(c) That death resulted to one or more victims.

c. *Explanation.*

(1) *Co-conspirators.* Two or more persons are required in order to have a conspiracy. Knowledge of the identity of co-conspirators and their particular connection with the criminal purpose need not be established. The accused must be subject to the UCMJ, but the other co-conspirators need not be. A person may be guilty of conspiracy although incapable of committing the intended offense. For example, a bedridden conspirator may knowingly furnish the car to be used in a robbery. The joining of another conspirator after the conspiracy has been established does not create a new conspiracy or affect the status of the other conspirators. However, the conspirator who joined an existing conspiracy can be convicted of this offense only if, at or after the time of joining the conspiracy, an overt act in furtherance of the object of the agreement is committed.

(2) *Agreement.* The agreement in a conspiracy need not be in any particular form or manifested in any formal words. It is sufficient if the minds of the parties arrive at a common understanding to accomplish the object of the conspiracy, and this may be shown by the conduct of the parties. The agreement need not state the means by which the conspiracy is to be accomplished or what part each conspirator is to play.

(3) *Object of the agreement.* The object of the agreement must, at least in part, involve the commission of one or more offenses under the UCMJ. An agreement to commit several offenses is ordinarily but a single conspiracy. Some offenses require two or more culpable actors acting in concert. There can be no conspiracy where the agreement exists only between the persons necessary to commit such an offense. Examples include dueling, bigamy, extramarital sexual conduct, and bribery.

(4) *Overt act.*

(a) The overt act must be independent of the agreement to commit the offense; must take place at the time of or after the agreement; must be done by one or more of the conspirators, but not necessarily the accused; and must be done to effectuate the object of the agreement.

(b) The overt act need not be in itself criminal, but it must be a manifestation that the agreement is being executed. Although committing the intended offense may constitute the overt act, it is not essential that the object offense be committed. Any overt act is enough, no matter how preliminary or preparatory in nature, as long as it is a manifestation that the agreement is being executed.

(c) An overt act by one conspirator becomes the act of all without any new agreement specifically directed to that act and each conspirator is equally guilty even though each does not participate in, or have knowledge of, all of the details of the execution of the conspiracy.

(5) *Liability for offenses*. Each conspirator is liable for all offenses committed pursuant to the conspiracy by any of the co-conspirators while the conspiracy continues and the person remains a party to it.

(6) *Withdrawal*. A party to the conspiracy who abandons or withdraws from the agreement to commit the offense before the commission of an overt act by any conspirator is not guilty of conspiracy. An effective withdrawal or abandonment must consist of affirmative conduct which is wholly inconsistent with adherence to the unlawful agreement and which shows that the party has severed all connection with the conspiracy. A conspirator who effectively abandons or withdraws from the conspiracy after the performance of an overt act by one of the conspirators remains guilty of conspiracy and of any offenses committed pursuant to the conspiracy up to the time of the abandonment or withdrawal. However, a person who has abandoned or withdrawn from the conspiracy is not liable for offenses committed thereafter by the remaining conspirators. The withdrawal of a conspirator from the conspiracy does not affect the status of the remaining members.

(7) *Factual impossibility*. It is not a defense that the means adopted by the conspirators to achieve their object, if apparently adapted to that end, were actually not capable of success, or that the conspirators were not physically able to accomplish their intended object.

(8) *Conspiracy as a separate offense*. A conspiracy to commit an offense is a separate and distinct offense from the offense which is the object of the conspiracy, and both the conspiracy and the consummated offense which was its object may be charged, tried, and punished. The commission of the intended offense may also constitute the overt act which is an element of the conspiracy to commit that offense.

(9) *Special conspiracies under Article 134*. The United States Code prohibits conspiracies to commit certain specific offenses which do not require an overt act. These conspiracies should be charged under Article 134. Examples include conspiracies to impede or injure any federal officer in the discharge of duties under 18 U.S.C. § 372, conspiracies against civil rights under 18 U.S.C. § 241, and certain drug conspiracies under 21 U.S.C. § 846. *See* subparagraph 91.c.(4)(a)(1)(iii).

d. *Maximum punishment*.

(1) *Offenses under the UCMJ*. Any person subject to the UCMJ who is found guilty of conspiracy shall be subject to the maximum punishment authorized for the offense that is the object of the conspiracy, except that in no case shall the death penalty be imposed, subject to subparagraph d.(2) of this paragraph.

(2) *Offenses under the law of war resulting in the death of one or more victims*. Any person subject to the UCMJ who conspires with any other person to commit an offense under the law of war, and who knowingly does an overt act to effect the object of the conspiracy, shall be punished, if death results to one or more of the victims, by death or such other punishment as a court-martial or military commission may direct, and, if death does not result to any of the victims, by such punishment, other than death, as a court-martial or military commission may direct.

e. *Sample specification*.

(1) *Conspiracy*.

In that ________ (personal jurisdiction data), did, (at/on board—location) (subject-matter jurisdiction data, if required), on or about _____20__, conspire with _______ (and______) to commit an offense under the Uniform Code of Military Justice, to wit: (larceny of______, of a value of (about) $____, the property of _____), and in order to effect the object of the conspiracy the said ______ (and _____) did _____.

(2) *Conspiracy when an offense is an offense under the law of war resulting in the death of one or more victims*.

In that ________ (personal jurisdiction data), did, (at/on board—location) (subject-matter jurisdiction data, if required), on or about _____20__, conspire with _______ (and______) to commit an offense under the law of war, to wit: (murder of ________), and in order to effect the object of the conspiracy the said _______ knowingly did ______ resulting in the death of _______.

6. Article 82 (10 U.S.C. 882)—Soliciting commission of offenses

a. *Text of statute*.

(a) SOLICITING COMMISSION OF OFFENSES GENERALLY.—Any person subject to this chapter who solicits or advises another to commit an offense under this chapter (other than an offense specified in subsection (b)) shall be punished as a court-martial may direct.

(b) SOLICITING DESERTION, MUTINY, SEDITION, OR MISBEHAVIOR BEFORE THE ENEMY.—Any person subject to this chapter who solicits or advises another to violate section 885 of this title (article 85), section 894 of this title (article 94), or section 899 of this title (article 99)—

(1) if the offense solicited or advised is attempted or is committed, shall be punished with the punishment provided for the commission of the offense; and

(2) if the offense solicited or advised is not attempted or committed, shall be punished as a court-martial may direct.

b. *Elements.*

(1) That the accused solicited or advised a certain person or persons to commit a certain offense under the UCMJ; and

(2) That the accused did so with the intent that the offense actually be committed.

[Note: If the offense solicited or advised was attempted or committed, add the following element]

(3) That the offense solicited or advised was (committed) (attempted) as the proximate result of the solicitation.

c. *Explanation.*

(1) *Instantaneous offense.* The offense is complete when a solicitation is made or advice is given with the specific wrongful intent to influence another or others to commit any offense under the UCMJ. It is not necessary that the person or persons solicited or advised agree to or act upon the solicitation or advice.

(2) *Form of solicitation.* Solicitation may be by means other than word of mouth or writing. Any act or conduct which reasonably may be construed as a serious request or advice to commit any offense under the UCMJ may constitute solicitation. It is not necessary that the accused act alone in the solicitation or in the advising; the accused may act through other persons in committing this offense.

(3) *Solicitations as an element in another offense.* Some offenses require, as an element of proof, some act of solicitation by the accused. These offenses are separate and distinct from solicitations under Article 82. When the accused's act of solicitation constitutes, by itself, a separate offense, the accused should be charged with that separate, distinct offense—for example, pandering and obstructing justice.

d. *Maximum punishment.*

(1) *Solicitation of espionage.* Such punishment that a court-martial may direct, other than death.

(2) *Solicitation of desertion; mutiny or sedition; misbehavior before the enemy.* If the offense solicited or advised is committed or attempted, then the accused shall be punished with the punishment provided for the commission of the offense solicited or advised. If the offense solicited or advised is not committed or attempted, then the following punishment may be imposed: dishonorable discharge, forfeiture of all pay and allowances, and confinement for 15 years, or the maximum punishment of the underlying offense, whichever is lesser.

(3) *Solicitation of all other offenses.* Any person subject to the UCMJ who is found guilty of soliciting or advising another person to commit an offense not specified in subparagraph d.(1)-(2) of this paragraph that, if committed by one subject to the UCMJ, would be punishable under the UCMJ, shall be subject to the following maximum punishment: dishonorable discharge, forfeiture of all pay and allowances, and confinement for 10 years, or the maximum punishment of the underlying offense, whichever is lesser.

e. *Sample specifications.*

(1) *For soliciting another to commit an offense.*

In that __________ (personal jurisdiction data), did, (at/on board—location) (subject-matter jurisdiction data, if required), on or about _____ 20 __, wrongfully (solicit) (advise) __________ (to disobey a general regulation, to wit: __________) (to steal __________, of a value of (about) $__________, the property of __________) (to __________), by_____________.

(2) *For soliciting desertion (Article 85) or mutiny (Article 94(a)).*

In that __________ (personal jurisdiction data), did, (at/on board—location), on or about _____ 20 __, (a time of war) by (here state the manner and form of solicitation or advice), (solicit) (advise) __________ (and __________) to (desert in violation of Article 85) (mutiny in violation of Article 94(a)) [*and, as a result of such (solicitation) (advice), the offense (solicited) (advised) was, on or about __________, 20 __, (at/on board—location), (attempted) (committed) by __________ (and __________)].

[*Note: This language should be added to the end of the specification if the offense solicited or advised is actually committed.]

(3) *For soliciting sedition (Article 94(a)) or misbehavior before or in the presence of the enemy (Article 99).*

In that __________ (personal jurisdiction data) did, (at/on board—location), on or about _____ 20 __, (a time of war) by (here state the manner and form of solicitation or advice), (solicit) (advise) __________ (and __________) to commit (an act of misbehavior before the enemy in violation of Article 99) (sedition in violation of Article 94(a)) [*and, as a result of such (solicitation) (advice), the offense (solicited) (advised) was, on or about _____ 20 __, (at/on board—location), committed by __________ (and __________)].

[*Note: This language should be added to the end of the specification if the offense solicited or advised is actually committed.]

7. Article 83 (10 U.S.C. 883)—Malingering

a. *Text of statute.*

Any person subject to this chapter who, with the intent to avoid work, duty, or service—

(1) feigns illness, physical disablement, mental lapse, or mental derangement; or

(2) intentionally inflicts self-injury;

shall be punished as a court-martial may direct.

b. *Elements.*

(1) That the accused was assigned to, or was aware of prospective assignment to, or availability for, the performance of work, duty, or service;

(2) That the accused feigned illness, physical disablement, mental lapse, mental derangement, or intentionally inflicted injury upon himself or herself; and

(3) That the accused's purpose or intent in doing so was to avoid the work, duty, or service.

[Note: If the offense was committed in time of war or in a hostile fire pay zone, add the following element]

(4) That the offense was committed (in time of war) (in a hostile fire pay zone).

c. *Explanation.*

(1) *Nature of offense.* The essence of this offense is the design to avoid performance of any work, duty, or service which may properly or normally be expected of one in the military service. Whether to avoid all duty, or only a particular job, it is the purpose to shirk which characterizes the offense. Hence, the nature or permanency of a self-inflicted injury is not material on the question of guilt. The seriousness of a sham physical or mental disability is also not material on the question of guilt. Evidence of the extent of the self-inflicted injury or feigned disability may, however, be relevant as a factor indicating the presence or absence of the purpose.

(2) *How injury inflicted.* The injury may be inflicted by nonviolent as well as by violent means and may be accomplished by any act or omission which produces, prolongs, or aggravates any sickness or disability. Thus, voluntary starvation which results in debility is a self-inflicted injury and when done for the purpose of avoiding work, duty, or service constitutes a violation of this article.

Discussion

Bona fide suicide attempts should not be charged as criminal offenses. When making a determination whether the injury by the Servicemember was a bona fide suicide attempt, the convening authority should consider factors including, but not limited to, health conditions, personal stressors, and DoD policy related to suicide prevention.

d. *Maximum punishment.*

(1) *Feigning illness, physical disablement, mental lapse, or mental derangement.* Dishonorable discharge, forfeiture of all pay and allowances, and confinement for 1 year.

(2) *Feigning illness, physical disablement, mental lapse, or mental derangement in a hostile fire pay zone or in time of war.* Dishonorable discharge, forfeiture of all pay and allowances, and confinement for 3 years.

(3) *Intentional self-inflicted injury.* Dishonorable discharge, forfeiture of all pay and allowances, and confinement for 5 years.

(4) *Intentional self-inflicted injury in a hostile fire pay zone or in time of war.* Dishonorable discharge, forfeiture of all pay and allowances, and confinement for 10 years.

e. *Sample specification.*

In that __________ (personal jurisdiction data), did, (at/on board—location) (in a hostile fire pay zone) (subject-matter jurisdiction data, if required) (on or about _____ 20 __) (from about _____ 20 __ to about _____ 20 __), (a time of war) for the purpose of avoiding ((his) (her) duty as officer of the day) ((his) (her) duty as aircraft mechanic) (work in the mess hall) (service as an enlisted person) (__________) (feign (a headache) (a sore back) (illness) (mental lapse) (mental derangement) (__)) (intentionally injure himself/herself by __________).

8. Article 84 (10 U.S.C. 884)—Breach of medical quarantine

a. *Text of statute.*

Any person subject to this chapter—

(1) who is ordered into medical quarantine by a person authorized to issue such order; and

(2) who, with knowledge of the quarantine and the limits of the quarantine, goes beyond those limits before being released from the quarantine by proper authority;

shall be punished as a court-martial may direct.

b. *Elements.*

(1) That a certain person ordered the accused into medical quarantine;

(2) That the person was authorized to order the accused into medical quarantine;

(3) That the accused knew of this medical quarantine and the limits thereof; and

(4) That the accused went beyond the limits of the medical quarantine before being released therefrom by proper authority.

[Note: If the offense involved violation of a medical quarantine imposed in response to emergence of a "quarantinable communicable disease" as defined in 42 C.F.R. § 70.1, add the following element]

(5) That the medical quarantine was imposed in reference to a quarantinable communicable disease (to wit:__________) as defined in 42 C.F.R. § 70.1.

c. *Explanation.*

(1) *Distinguishing "quarantine" from "quarters" orders.* Putting a person "on quarters" or other otherwise excusing a person from duty because of illness does not of itself constitute a medical quarantine.

d. *Maximum punishment.*

(1) *Breach of medical quarantine involving a quarantinable communicable disease defined by 42 C.F.R. § 70.1.* Dishonorable discharge, forfeiture of all pay and allowances, and confinement for 1 year.

(2) *Breach of medical quarantine—all other cases.* Bad-conduct discharge, forfeiture of two-thirds pay per month for 6 months, and confinement for 6 months.

e. *Sample specification.*

In that __________ (personal jurisdiction data) having been placed in medical quarantine by a person authorized to order the accused into medical quarantine (for a quarantinable communicable disease as defined in 42 C.F.R. § 70.1, to wit: _________), having knowledge of the quarantine and the limits of the quarantine, did, (at/on board—location) (subject-matter jurisdiction data, if required), on or about _____ 20 __, break said medical quarantine.

9. Article 85 (10 U.S.C. 885)—Desertion

a. *Text of statute.*

(a) Any member of the armed forces who—

(1) without authority goes or remains absent from his unit, organization, or place of duty with intent to remain away therefrom permanently;

(2) quits his unit, organization, or place of duty with intent to avoid hazardous duty or to shirk important service; or

(3) without being regularly separated from one of the armed forces enlists or accepts an appointment in the same or another one of the armed forces without fully disclosing the fact that he has not been regularly separated, or enters any foreign armed service except when authorized by the United States;

is guilty of desertion.

(b) Any commissioned officer of the armed forces who, after tender of his resignation and before notice of its acceptance, quits his post or proper duties without leave and with intent to remain away therefrom permanently is guilty of desertion.

(c) Any person found guilty of desertion or attempt to desert shall be punished, if the offense is committed in time of war, by death or such other punishment as a court-martial may direct, but if the desertion or attempt to desert occurs at any other time, by such punishment, other than death, as a court-martial may direct.

b. *Elements.*

(1) *Desertion with intent to remain away permanently.*

(a) That the accused absented himself or herself from his or her unit, organization, or place of duty;

(b) That such absence was without authority;

(c) That the accused, at the time the absence began or at some time during the absence, intended to remain away from his or her unit, organization, or place of duty permanently; and

(d) That the accused remained absent until the date alleged.

[Note: If the absence was terminated by apprehension, add the following element]

(e) That the accused's absence was terminated by apprehension.

(2) *Desertion with intent to avoid hazardous duty or to shirk important service.*

(a) That the accused quit his or her unit, organization, or other place of duty;

(b) That the accused did so with the intent to avoid a certain duty or shirk a certain service;

(c) That the duty to be performed was hazardous or the service important;

(d) That the accused knew that he or she would be required for such duty or service; and

(e) That the accused remained absent until the date alleged.

(3) *Desertion before notice of acceptance of resignation.*

(a) That the accused was a commissioned officer of an armed force of the United States, and had tendered his or her resignation;

(b) That before he or she received notice of the acceptance of the resignation, the accused quit his or her post or proper duties;

(c) That the accused did so with the intent to remain away permanently from his or her post or proper duties; and

(d) That the accused remained absent until the date alleged.

[Note: If the absence was terminated by apprehension, add the following element]

(e) That the accused's absence was terminated by apprehension.

(4) *Attempted desertion.*

(a) That the accused did a certain overt act;

(b) That the act was done with the specific intent to desert;

(c) That the act amounted to more than mere preparation; and

(d) That the act apparently tended to effect the commission of the offense of desertion.

c. *Explanation.*

(1) *Desertion with intent to remain away permanently.*

(a) *In general.* Desertion with intent to remain away permanently is complete when the person absents himself or herself without authority from his or her unit, organization, or place of duty, with the intent to remain away therefrom permanently. A prompt repentance and return, while material in extenuation, is no defense. It is not necessary that the person be absent entirely from military jurisdiction and control.

(b) *Absence without authority*—inception, duration, termination. *See* subparagraph 10.c.

(c) *Intent to remain away permanently.*

(i) The intent to remain away permanently from the unit, organization, or place of duty may be formed any time during the unauthorized absence. The intent need not exist throughout the absence, or for any particular period of time, as long as it exists at some time during the absence.

(ii) The accused must have intended to remain away permanently from the unit, organization, or place of duty. When the accused had such an intent, it is no defense that the accused also intended to report for duty elsewhere, or to enlist or accept an appointment in the same or a different armed force.

(iii) The intent to remain away permanently may be proved by circumstantial evidence. Among the circumstances from which an inference may be drawn that an accused intended to remain absent permanently are: that the period of absence was lengthy; that the accused attempted to, or did, dispose of uniforms or other military property; that the accused purchased a ticket for a distant point or was arrested, apprehended, or surrendered a considerable distance from the accused's station; that the accused could have conveniently surrendered to military control but did not; that the accused was dissatisfied with the accused's unit, ship, or with military service; that the accused made remarks indicating an intention to desert; that the accused was under charges or had escaped from confinement at the time of the absence; that the accused made preparations indicative of an intent not to return (for example, financial arrangements); or that the accused enlisted or accepted an appointment in the same or another armed force without disclosing the fact that the accused had not been regularly separated, or entered any foreign armed service without being authorized by the United States. On the other hand, the following are included in the circumstances which may tend to negate an inference that the accused intended to remain away permanently: previous long and excellent service; that the accused left valuable personal property in the unit or on the ship; or that the accused was under the influence of alcohol or drugs during the absence. These lists are illustrative only.

(iv) Entries on documents, such as personnel accountability records, which administratively refer to an accused as a "deserter" are not evidence of intent to desert.

(v) Proof of, or a plea of guilty to, an unauthorized absence, even of extended duration, does not, without more, prove guilt of desertion.

(d) *Effect of enlistment or appointment in the same or a different armed force.* Article 85(a)(3) does not state a separate offense. Rather, it is a rule of evidence by which the prosecution may prove intent to remain away permanently. Proof of an enlistment or acceptance of an appointment in a Service without disclosing a preexisting duty status in the same or a different service provides the basis from which an inference of intent to permanently remain away from the earlier unit, organization, or place of duty may be drawn. Furthermore, if a person, without being regularly separated from one of the armed forces, enlists or accepts an appointment in the same or another armed force, the person's presence in the military service under such an enlistment or appointment is not a return to military control and does not terminate any desertion or absence without authority from the earlier unit or organization, unless the facts of the earlier period of service are known to military authorities. If a person, while in desertion, enlists or accepts an appointment in the same or another armed force, and deserts while serving the enlistment or appointment, the person may be tried and convicted for each desertion.

(2) *Quitting unit, organization, or place of duty with intent to avoid hazardous duty or to shirk important service.*

(a) *Hazardous duty or important service.* "Hazardous duty" or "important service" may include service such as duty in a combat or other dangerous area; embarkation for certain foreign or sea duty; movement to a port of embarkation for that purpose; entrainment for duty on the border or coast in time of war or threatened invasion or other disturbances; strike or riot duty; or employment in aid of the civil power in, for example, protecting property, or quelling or preventing disorder in times of great public disaster. Such services as drill, target practice, maneuvers, and practice marches are not ordinarily "hazardous duty or important service." Whether a duty is hazardous or a service is important depends upon the circumstances of the particular case, and is a question of fact for the court-martial to decide.

(b) *Quits.* "Quits" in Article 85 means "goes absent without authority."

(c) *Actual knowledge.* Article 85(a)(2) requires proof that the accused actually knew of the hazardous duty or important service. Actual knowledge may be proved by circumstantial evidence.

(3) *Attempting to desert.* Once the attempt is made, the fact that the person desists, voluntarily or otherwise, does not cancel the offense. The offense is complete, for example, if the person, intending to desert, hides in an empty freight car on a military reservation, intending to escape by being taken away in the car. Entering the car with the intent to desert is the overt act. For a more detailed discussion of attempts, see paragraph 4. For an explanation concerning intent to remain away permanently, see paragraph 9.c.(1)(c).

(4) *Prisoner with executed punitive discharge.* A prisoner whose dismissal or dishonorable or bad-conduct discharge has been executed is not a "member of the armed forces" within the meaning of Articles 85 or 86, although the prisoner may still be subject to military law under Article 2(a)(7). If the facts warrant, such a prisoner could be charged with escape from confinement under Article 87a or an offense under Article 134.

d. *Maximum punishment.*

(1) *Completed or attempted desertion with intent to avoid hazardous duty or to shirk important service.* Dishonorable discharge, forfeiture of all pay and allowances, and confinement for 5 years.

(2) *Other cases of completed or attempted desertion.*

(a) *Terminated by apprehension.* Dishonorable discharge, forfeiture of all pay and allowances, and confinement for 3 years.

(b) *Terminated otherwise.* Dishonorable discharge, forfeiture of all pay and allowances, and confinement for 2 years.

(3) *In time of war.* Death or such other punishment as a court-martial may direct.

e. *Sample specifications.*

(1) *Desertion with intent to remain away permanently.*

In that __________ (personal jurisdiction data), did, on or about _____ 20 __, (a time of war) without authority and with intent to remain away therefrom permanently, absent himself/herself from (his) (her) (unit) (organization) (place of duty), to wit: __________, located at (__________), and did remain so absent in desertion until ((he) (she) was apprehended) on or about _____ 20 __.

(2) *Desertion with intent to avoid hazardous duty or shirk important service.*

In that __________ (personal jurisdiction data), knowing that (he) (she) would be required to perform (hazardous duty) (important service), namely: __________, did, on or about _____ 20 __, (a time of war) with intent to (avoid said hazardous duty) (shirk said important service), quit (his) (her) (unit) (organization) (place of duty), to wit: __________, located at (__________), and did remain so absent in desertion until on or about _____ 20 __.

(3) *Desertion prior to acceptance of resignation.*

In that __________ (personal jurisdiction data) having tendered (his) (her) resignation and prior to due notice of the acceptance of the same, did, on or about _____ 20 __, (a time of war) without leave and with intent to remain away therefrom permanently, quit (his) (her) (post) (proper duties), to wit: __________, and did remain so absent in desertion until ((he) (she) was apprehended) on or about _____ 20 __.

(4) *Attempted desertion.*

In that __________ (personal jurisdiction data), did (at/on board—location), on or about _____ 20 __, (a time of war) attempt to (absent himself/herself from (his) (her) (unit) (organization) (place of duty) to wit: __________, without authority and with intent to remain away therefrom permanently) (quit (his) (her) (unit) (organization) (place of duty), to wit: __________, located at __________, with intent to (avoid hazardous duty) (shirk important service) namely ____) (_____).

10. Article 86 (10 U.S.C. 886)—Absence without leave

a. *Text of statute.*

Any member of the armed forces who, without authority—

(1) fails to go to his appointed place of duty at the time prescribed;

(2) goes from that place; or

(3) absents himself or remains absent from his unit, organization, or place of duty at which he is required to be at the time prescribed;

shall be punished as a court-martial may direct.

b. *Elements.*

(1) *Failure to go to appointed place of duty.*

(a) That a certain authority appointed a certain time and place of duty for the accused;

(b) That the accused knew of that time and place; and

(c) That the accused, without authority, failed to go to the appointed place of duty at the time prescribed.

(2) *Going from appointed place of duty.*

(a) That a certain authority appointed a certain time and place of duty for the accused;

(b) That the accused knew of that time and place; and

(c) That the accused, without authority, went from the appointed place of duty after having reported at such place.

(3) *Absence from unit, organization, or place of duty.*

(a) That the accused absented himself or herself from his or her unit, organization, or place of duty at which he or she was required to be;

(b) That the absence was without authority from anyone competent to give him or her leave; and

(c) That the absence was for a certain period of time.

[Note: if the absence was terminated by apprehension, add the following element]

(d) That the absence was terminated by apprehension.

(4) *Abandoning watch or guard.*

(a) That the accused was a member of a guard, watch, or duty;

(b) That the accused absented himself or herself from his or her guard, watch, or duty section;

(c) That absence of the accused was without authority; and

[Note: If the absence was with intent to abandon the accused's guard, watch, or duty section, add the following element]

(d) That the accused intended to abandon his or her guard, watch, or duty section.

(5) *Absence from unit, organization, or place of duty with intent to avoid maneuvers or field exercises.*

(a) That the accused absented himself or herself from his or her unit, organization, or place of duty at which he or she was required to be;

(b) That the absence of the accused was without authority;

(c) That the absence was for a certain period of time;

(d) That the accused knew that the absence would occur during a part of a period of maneuvers or field exercises; and

(e) That the accused intended to avoid all or part of a period of maneuvers or field exercises.

c. *Explanation.*

(1) *In general.* This article is designed to cover every case not elsewhere provided for in which any member of the armed forces is through the member's own fault not at the place where the member is required to be at a prescribed time. It is not necessary that the person be absent entirely from military jurisdiction and control. The first part of this article—relating to the appointed place of duty—applies whether the place is appointed as a rendezvous for several or for one only.

(2) *Actual knowledge.* The offenses of failure to go to and going from appointed place of duty require proof that the accused actually knew of the appointed time and place of duty. The offense of absence from unit, organization, or place of duty with intent to avoid maneuvers or field exercises requires proof that the accused actually knew that the absence would occur during a part of a period of maneuvers or field exercises. Actual knowledge may be proved by circumstantial evidence.

(3) *Intent.* Specific intent is not an element of unauthorized absence. Specific intent is an element for certain aggravated unauthorized absences.

(4) *Aggravated forms of unauthorized absence.* There are variations of unauthorized absence under Article 86(3) which are more serious because of aggravating circumstances such as duration of the absence, a special type of duty from which the accused absents himself or herself, and a particular specific intent which accompanies the absence. These circumstances are not essential elements of a violation of Article 86. They simply constitute special matters in aggravation. The following are aggravated unauthorized absences:

(a) Unauthorized absence for more than 3 days (duration).

(b) Unauthorized absence for more than 30 days (duration).

(c) Unauthorized absence from a guard, watch, or duty (special type of duty).

(d) Unauthorized absence from guard, watch, or duty section with the intent to abandon it (special type of duty and specific intent).

(e) Unauthorized absence with the intent to avoid maneuvers or field exercises (special type of duty and specific intent).

(5) *Control by civilian authorities.* A member of the armed forces turned over to the civilian authorities upon request under Article 14 (*see* R.C.M. 106) is not absent without leave while held by them under that delivery. When a member of the armed forces, being absent with leave, or absent without leave, is held, tried, and acquitted by civilian authorities, the member's status as absent with leave, or absent without leave, is not thereby changed, regardless how long held. The fact that a member of the armed forces is convicted by the civilian authorities, or adjudicated to be a juvenile offender, or the case is "diverted" out of the regular criminal process for a probationary period does not excuse any unauthorized absence, because the member's inability to return was the result of willful misconduct. If a member is released by the civilian authorities without trial, and was on authorized leave at the time of arrest or detention, the member may be found guilty of unauthorized absence only if it is proved that the member actually committed the offense for which detained, thus establishing that the absence was the result of the member's own misconduct.

(6) *Inability to return.* The status of absence without leave is not changed by an inability to return through sickness, lack of transportation facilities, or other disabilities. But the fact that all or part of a period of unauthorized absence was in a sense enforced or involuntary is a factor in extenuation and should be given due weight when considering the initial disposition of the offense. When, however, a person on authorized leave, without fault, is unable to return at the expiration thereof, that person has not committed the offense of absence without leave.

(7) *Determining the unit or organization of an accused.* A person undergoing transfer between

activities is ordinarily considered to be attached to the activity to which ordered to report. A person on temporary additional duty continues as a member of the regularly assigned unit and if the person is absent from the temporary duty assignment, the person becomes absent without leave from both units, and may be charged with being absent without leave from either unit.

(8) *Duration.* Unauthorized absence under Article 86(3) is an instantaneous offense. It is complete at the instant an accused absents himself or herself without authority. Duration of the absence is a matter in aggravation for the purpose of increasing the maximum punishment authorized for the offense. Even if the duration of the absence is not over 3 days, it is ordinarily alleged in an Article 86(3) specification. If the duration is not alleged or if alleged but not proved, an accused can be convicted of and punished for only 1 day of unauthorized absence.

(9) *Computation of duration.* In computing the duration of an unauthorized absence, any one continuous period of absence found that totals not more than 24 hours is counted as 1 day; any such period that totals more than 24 hours and not more than 48 hours is counted as 2 days, and so on. The hours of departure and return on different dates are assumed to be the same if not alleged and proved. For example, if an accused is found guilty of unauthorized absence from 0600 hours, 4 April, to 1000 hours, 7 April of the same year (76 hours), the maximum punishment would be based on an absence of 4 days. However, if the accused is found guilty simply of unauthorized absence from 4 April to 7 April, the maximum punishment would be based on an absence of 3 days.

(10) *Termination—methods of return to military control.*

(a) *Surrender to military authority.* A surrender occurs when a person presents himself or herself to any military authority, whether or not a member of the same armed force, notifies that authority of his or her unauthorized absence status, and submits or demonstrates a willingness to submit to military control. Such a surrender terminates the unauthorized absence.

(b) *Apprehension by military authority.* Apprehension by military authority of a known absentee terminates an unauthorized absence.

(c) *Delivery to military authority.* Delivery of a known absentee by anyone to military authority terminates the unauthorized absence.

(d) *Apprehension by civilian authorities at the request of the military.* When an absentee is taken into custody by civilian authorities at the request of military authorities, the absence is terminated.

(e) *Apprehension by civilian authorities without prior military request.* When an absentee is in the hands of civilian authorities for other reasons and these authorities make the absentee available for return to military control, the absence is terminated when the military authorities are informed of the absentee's availability.

(11) *Findings of more than one absence under one specification.* An accused may properly be found guilty of two or more separate unauthorized absences under one specification, provided that each absence is included within the period alleged in the specification and provided that the accused was not misled. If an accused is found guilty of two or more unauthorized absences under a single specification, the maximum authorized punishment shall not exceed that authorized if the accused had been found guilty as charged in the specification.

d. *Maximum punishment.*

(1) *Failing to go to, or going from, the appointed place of duty.* Confinement for 1 month and forfeiture of two-thirds pay per month for 1 month.

(2) *Absence from unit, organization, or other place of duty.*

(a) *For not more than 3 days.* Confinement for 1 month and forfeiture of two-thirds pay per month for 1 month.

(b) *For more than 3 days but not more than 30 days.* Confinement for 6 months and forfeiture of two-thirds pay per month for 6 months.

(c) *For more than 30 days.* Dishonorable discharge, forfeiture of all pay and allowances, and confinement for 1 year.

(d) *For more than 30 days and terminated by apprehension.* Dishonorable discharge, forfeiture of all pay and allowances, and confinement for 18 months.

(3) *From guard or watch.* Confinement for 3 months and forfeiture of two-thirds pay per month for 3 months.

(4) *From guard or watch with intent to abandon.* Bad-conduct discharge, forfeiture of all pay and allowances, and confinement for 6 months.

(5) *With intent to avoid maneuvers or field exercises.* Bad-conduct discharge, forfeiture of all pay and allowances, and confinement for 6 months.

e. *Sample specifications.*

(1) *Failing to go or leaving place of duty.*

In that _____ (personal jurisdiction data), did (at/on board—location), on or about _____ 20 __, without authority, (fail to go at the time prescribed to) (go from) (his) (her) appointed place of duty, to wit: (here set forth the appointed place of duty).

(2) *Absence from unit, organization, or place of duty.*

In that __________ (personal jurisdiction data), did, on or about _____ 20 __, without authority, absent himself/herself from (his) (her) (unit) (organization) (place of duty at which (he) (she) was required to be), to wit: __________, located at __________, and did remain so absent until ((he) (she) was apprehended) on or about _____ 20 __.

(3) *Absence from unit, organization, or place of duty with intent to avoid maneuvers or field exercises.*

In that _____ (personal jurisdiction data), did, on or about _____ 20 __, without authority and with intent to avoid (maneuvers) (field exercises), absent himself/herself from (his) (her) (unit) (organization) (place of duty at which (he) (she) was required to be), to wit: _____ located at (_____), and did remain so absent until on or about _____ 20 __.

(4) *Abandoning watch or guard.*

In that __________ (personal jurisdiction data), being a member of the __________ (guard) (watch) (duty section), did, (at/on board—location), on or about _____ 20 __, without authority, go from (his) (her) (guard) (watch) (duty section) (with intent to abandon the same).

11. Article 87 (10 U.S.C. 887)—Missing movement; jumping from vessel

a. *Text of statute.*

(a) MISSING MOVEMENT.—Any person subject to this chapter who, through neglect or design, misses the movement of a ship, aircraft, or unit with which the person is required in the course of duty to move shall be punished as a court-martial may direct.

(b) JUMPING FROM VESSEL INTO THE WATER.—Any person subject to this chapter who wrongfully and intentionally jumps into the water from a vessel in use by the armed forces shall be punished as a court-martial may direct.

b. *Elements.*

(1) *Missing movement.*

(a) That the accused was required in the course of duty to move with a ship, aircraft, or unit;

(b) That the accused knew of the prospective movement of the ship, aircraft, or unit; and

(c) That the accused missed the movement through design or neglect.

(2) *Jumping from vessel into the water.*

(a) That the accused jumped from a vessel in use by the armed forces into the water; and

(b) That such act by the accused was wrongful and intentional.

c. *Explanation.*

(1) *Missing movement.*

(a) *Movement.* "Movement" as used in Article 87 includes a move, transfer, or shift of a ship, aircraft, or unit involving a substantial distance and period of time. Whether a particular movement is substantial is a question to be determined by the court-martial considering all the circumstances. Changes which do not constitute a "movement" include practice marches of a short duration with a return to the point of departure, and minor changes in location of ships, aircraft, or units, as when a ship is shifted from one berth to another in the same shipyard or harbor or when a unit is moved from one barracks to another on the same post.

(b) *Mode of movement.*

(i) *Unit.* If a person is required in the course of duty to move with a unit, the mode of travel is not important, whether it be military or commercial, and includes travel by ship, train, aircraft, truck, bus, or walking. The word "unit" is not limited to any specific technical category such as those listed in a table of organization and equipment, but also includes units which are created before the movement with the intention that they have organizational continuity upon arrival at their destination regardless of their technical designation, and units intended to be disbanded upon arrival at their destination.

(ii) *Ship, aircraft.* If a person is assigned as a crew member or is ordered to move as a passenger aboard a particular ship or aircraft, military or chartered, then missing the particular sailing or flight is essential to establish the offense of missing movement.

(c) *Design.* "Design" means on purpose, intentionally, or according to plan and requires specific intent to miss the movement.

(d) *Neglect.* "Neglect" means the omission to take such measures as are appropriate under the circumstances to assure presence with a ship, aircraft, or unit at the time of a scheduled movement, or doing some act without giving attention to its probable consequences in connection with the prospective movement, such as a departure from the vicinity of the prospective movement to such a distance as would make it likely that one could not return in time for the movement.

(e) *Actual knowledge.* In order to be guilty of the offense, the accused must have actually known of the prospective movement that was missed. Knowledge of the exact hour or even of the exact date of the scheduled movement is not required. It is sufficient if the approximate date was known by the accused as long as there is a causal connection between the conduct of the accused and the missing of the scheduled movement. Knowledge may be proved by circumstantial evidence.

(f) *Proof of absence.* That the accused actually missed the movement may be proved by documentary evidence, as by a proper entry or absence of entry in a log or a morning report. This fact may also be proved by the testimony of personnel of the ship, aircraft, or unit (or by other evidence) that the movement occurred at a certain time, together with evidence that the accused was physically elsewhere at that time.

(2) *Jumping from vessel into the water.* The phrase "in use by" means any vessel operated by or under the control of the armed forces. This offense may be committed at sea, at anchor, or in port.

Discussion

Bona fide suicide attempts should not be charged as criminal offenses. When making a determination whether an action by the Servicemember was a bona fide suicide attempt, the convening authority should consider factors including, but not limited to, health conditions, personal stressors, and DoD policy related to suicide prevention.

---

d. *Maximum punishment.*

(1) *Missing movement.*

(a) *Design.* Dishonorable discharge, forfeiture of all pay and allowances, and confinement for 2 years.

(b) *Neglect.* Bad-conduct discharge, forfeiture of all pay and allowances, and confinement for 1 year.

(2) *Jumping from vessel into the water.* Bad-conduct discharge, forfeiture of all pay and allowances, and confinement for 6 months.

e. *Sample specifications.*

(1) *Missing movement.*

In that __________ (personal jurisdiction data), did, (at/on board—location), on or about _____ 20 __, through (neglect) (design) miss the movement of (Aircraft No. __________) (Flight __________) (the USS __________) (Company A, 1st Battalion, 7th Infantry) (__________) with which (he) (she) was required in the course of duty to move.

(2) *Jumping from vessel into the water.*

In that __________ (personal jurisdiction data), did, on board __________, at (location), on or about _____ 20 __, wrongfully and intentionally jump from __________, a vessel in use by the armed forces, into the (sea) (lake) (river).

12. Article 87a (10 U.S.C. 887a)—Resistance, flight, breach of arrest, and escape

a. *Text of statute.*

Any person subject to this chapter who—

(1) resists apprehension;

(2) flees from apprehension;

(3) breaks arrest; or

(4) escapes from custody or confinement;

shall be punished as a court-martial may direct.

b. *Elements.*

(1) *Resisting apprehension.*

(a) That a certain person attempted to apprehend the accused;

(b) That said person was authorized to apprehend the accused; and

(c) That the accused actively resisted the apprehension.

(2) *Flight from apprehension.*

(a) That a certain person attempted to apprehend the accused;

(b) That said person was authorized to apprehend the accused; and

(c) That the accused fled from the apprehension.

(3) *Breaking arrest.*

(a) That a certain person ordered the accused into arrest;

(b) That said person was authorized to order the accused into arrest; and

(c) That the accused went beyond the limits of arrest before being released from that arrest by proper authority.

(4) *Escape from custody.*

(a) That a certain person apprehended the accused;

(b) That said person was authorized to apprehend the accused; and

(c) That the accused freed himself or herself from custody before being released by proper authority.

(5) *Escape from confinement.*

(a) That a certain person ordered the accused into confinement;

(b) That said person was authorized to order the accused into confinement; and

(c) That the accused freed himself or herself from confinement before being released by proper authority.

[Note: If the escape was post-trial confinement, add the following element]

(d) That the confinement was the result of a court-martial conviction.

c. *Explanation.*

(1) *Resisting apprehension.*

(a) *Apprehension.* Apprehension is the taking of a person into custody. *See* R.C.M. 302.

(b) *Authority to apprehend.* See R.C.M. 302(b) concerning who may apprehend. Whether the status of a person authorized that person to apprehend the accused is a question of law to be decided by the military judge. Whether the person who attempted to make an apprehension had such a status is a question of fact to be decided by the factfinder.

(c) *Nature of the resistance.* The resistance must be active, such as assaulting the person attempting to apprehend. Mere words of opposition, argument, or abuse, and attempts to escape from custody after the apprehension is complete, do not constitute the offense of resisting apprehension although they may constitute other offenses.

(d) *Mistake.* It is a defense that the accused held a reasonable belief that the person attempting to apprehend did not have authority to do so. However, the accused's belief at the time that no basis exists for the apprehension is not a defense.

(e) *Illegal apprehension.* A person may not be convicted of resisting apprehension if the attempted apprehension is illegal, but may be convicted of other offenses, such as assault, depending on all the circumstances. An attempted apprehension by a person authorized to apprehend is presumed to be legal in the absence of evidence to the contrary. Ordinarily the legality of an apprehension is a question of law to be decided by the military judge.

(2) *Flight from apprehension.* The flight must be active, such as running or driving away.

(3) *Breaking arrest.*

(a) *Arrest.* There are two types of arrest: pretrial arrest under Article 9 (see R.C.M. 304) and arrest under Article 15 (see subparagraph 5.c.(3), Part V, MCM). This article prohibits breaking any arrest.

(b) *Authority to order arrest.* See R.C.M. 304(b) and paragraph 2 and subparagraph 5.b., Part V, MCM concerning authority to order arrest.

(c) *Nature of restraint imposed by arrest.* In arrest, the restraint is moral restraint imposed by orders fixing the limits of arrest.

(d) *Breaking.* Breaking arrest is committed when the person in arrest infringes the limits set by orders. The reason for the infringement is immaterial. For example, innocence of the offense with respect to which an arrest may have been imposed is not a defense.

(e) *Illegal arrest.* A person may not be convicted of breaking arrest if the arrest is illegal. An arrest ordered by one authorized to do so is presumed to be legal in the absence of some evidence to the contrary. Ordinarily, the legality of an arrest is a question of law to be decided by the military judge.

(4) *Escape from custody.*

(a) *Custody.* Custody is restraint of free locomotion imposed by lawful apprehension. The restraint may be physical or, once there has been a submission to apprehension or a forcible taking into custody, it may consist of control exercised in the presence of the prisoner by official acts or orders. Custody is temporary restraint intended to continue until other restraint (arrest, restriction, confinement) is imposed or the person is released.

(b) *Authority to apprehend.* See subparagraph (1)(b) of this paragraph.

(c) *Escape*. For a discussion of escape, see subparagraph c.(5)(c) of this paragraph.

(d) *Illegal custody*. A person may not be convicted of this offense if the custody was illegal. An apprehension effected by one authorized to apprehend is presumed to be lawful in the absence of evidence to the contrary. Ordinarily, the legality of an apprehension is a question of law to be decided by the military judge.

(e) *Correctional custody*. *See* paragraph 13.

(5) *Escape from confinement*.

(a) *Confinement*. Confinement is physical restraint imposed under R.C.M. 305, 1102, or subparagraph 5.b., Part V, MCM. For purposes of the element of post-trial confinement (subparagraph b.(5)(d)) and increased punishment therefrom (subparagraph e.(4)), the confinement must have been imposed pursuant to an adjudged sentence of a court-martial and not as a result of pretrial restraint or nonjudicial punishment.

(b) *Authority to order confinement*. See R.C.M. 304(b), 1102(b)(2); and paragraph 2 and subparagraph 5.b., Part V, MCM concerning who may order confinement.

(c) *Escape*. An escape may be either with or without force or artifice, and either with or without the consent of the custodian. However, where a prisoner is released by one with apparent authority to do so, the prisoner may not be convicted of escape from confinement. *See also* subparagraph 24.c.(2)(b). Any completed casting off of the restraint of confinement, before release by proper authority, is an escape, and lack of effectiveness of the restraint imposed is immaterial. An escape is not complete until the prisoner is momentarily free from the restraint. If the movement toward escape is opposed, or before it is completed, an immediate pursuit follows, there is no escape until opposition is overcome or pursuit is eluded.

(d) *Status when temporarily outside confinement facility*. A prisoner who is temporarily escorted outside a confinement facility for a work detail or other reason by a guard, who has both the duty and means to prevent that prisoner from escaping, remains in confinement.

(e) *Legality of confinement*. A person may not be convicted of escape from confinement if the confinement is illegal. Confinement ordered by one authorized to do so is presumed to be lawful in the absence of evidence to the contrary. Ordinarily, the legality of confinement is a question of law to be decided by the military judge.

d. *Maximum punishment*.

(1) *Resisting apprehension*. Bad-conduct discharge, forfeiture of all pay and allowances, and confinement for 1 year.

(2) *Flight from apprehension*. Bad-conduct discharge, forfeiture of all pay and allowances, and confinement for 1 year.

(3) *Breaking arrest*. Bad-conduct discharge, forfeiture of all pay and allowances, and confinement for 6 months.

(4) *Escape from custody, pretrial confinement, or confinement pursuant to Article 15*. Dishonorable discharge, forfeiture of all pay and allowances, and confinement for 1 year.

(5) *Escape from post-trial confinement*. Dishonorable discharge, forfeiture of all pay and allowances, and confinement for 5 years.

e. *Sample specifications*.

(1) *Resisting apprehension*.

In that __________ (personal jurisdiction data), did, (at/on board—location) (subject-matter jurisdiction data, if required), on or about _____ 20 __, resist being apprehended by __________, (an armed force policeman) (__________), a person authorized to apprehend the accused.

(2) *Flight from apprehension*.

In that __________ (personal jurisdiction data), did, (at/on board—location) (subject-matter jurisdiction data, if required), on or about _____ 20 __, flee apprehension by __________, (an armed force policeman) (__________), a person authorized to apprehend the accused.

(3) *Breaking arrest*.

In that __________ (personal jurisdiction data), having been placed in arrest (in quarters) (in (his) (her) company area) (__________) by a person authorized to order the accused into arrest, did, (at/on board—location) on or about _____ 20 __, break said arrest.

(4) *Escape from custody*.

In that __________ (personal jurisdiction data), did, (at/on board—location) (subject-matter jurisdiction data, if required), on or about _____ 20 __, escape from the custody of __________, a person authorized to apprehend the accused.

(5) *Escape from confinement*.

In that __________ (personal jurisdiction data), having been placed in (post-trial) confinement in (place of confinement), by a person authorized to order said accused into confinement did, (at/on board—location) (subject-matter jurisdiction data, if required), on or about _____ 20 __, escape from confinement.

13. Article 87b (10 U.S.C. 887b)—Offenses against correctional custody and restriction

a. *Text of statute.*

(a) ESCAPE FROM CORRECTIONAL CUSTODY.—Any person subject to this chapter—

(1) who is placed in correctional custody by a person authorized to do so;

(2) who, while in correctional custody, is under physical restraint; and

(3) who escapes from the physical restraint before being released from the physical restraint by proper authority

shall be punished as a court-martial may direct.

(b) BREACH OF CORRECTIONAL CUSTODY.—Any person subject to this chapter—

(1) who is placed in correctional custody by a person authorized to do so;

(2) who, while in correctional custody, is under restraint other than physical restraint; and

(3) who goes beyond the limits of the restraint before being released from the correctional custody or relieved of the restraint by proper authority;

shall be punished as a court-martial may direct.

(c) BREACH OF RESTRICTION.—Any person subject to this chapter—

(1) who is ordered to be restricted to certain limits by a person authorized to do so; and

(2) who, with knowledge of the limits of the restriction, goes beyond those limits before being released by proper authority;

shall be punished as a court-martial may direct.

b. *Elements.*

(1) *Escape from correctional custody.*

(a) That the accused was placed in correctional custody by a person authorized to do so;

(b) That, while in such correctional custody, the accused was under physical restraint; and

(c) That the accused freed himself or herself from the physical restraint of this correctional custody before being released therefrom by proper authority.

(2) *Breach of correctional custody.*

(a) That the accused was placed in correctional custody by a person authorized to do so;

(b) That, while in correctional custody, a certain restraint was imposed upon the accused; and

(c) That the accused went beyond the limits of the restraint imposed before having been released from the correctional custody or relieved of the restraint by proper authority.

(3) *Breach of restriction.*

(a) That a certain person ordered the accused to be restricted to certain limits;

(b) That said person was authorized to order said restriction;

(c) That the accused knew of the restriction and the limits thereof; and

(d) That the accused went beyond the limits of the restriction before being released therefrom by proper authority.

c. *Explanation.*

(1) *Escape from correctional custody.* Escape from correctional custody is the act of a person undergoing the punishment of correctional custody pursuant to Article 15, who, before being set at liberty by proper authority, casts off any physical restraint imposed by the custodian or by the place or conditions of custody.

(2) *Breach of correctional custody.* Breach of restraint during correctional custody is the act of a person undergoing the punishment who, in the absence of physical restraint imposed by a custodian or by the place or conditions of custody, breaches any form of restraint imposed during this period.

(3) *Authority to impose correctional custody.* See Part V concerning who may impose correctional custody. Whether the status of a person authorized that person to impose correctional custody is a question of law to be decided by the military judge. Whether the person who imposed correctional custody had such a status is a question of fact to be decided by the factfinder.

(4) *Breach of restriction.* Restriction is the moral restraint of a person imposed by an order directing a person to remain within certain specified limits. "Restriction" includes restriction under R.C.M. 304(a)(2), restriction resulting from imposition of

either nonjudicial punishment (see Part V) or the sentence of a court-martial (see R.C.M. 1003(b)(5)), and administrative restriction in the interest of training, operations, security, or safety.

d. *Maximum punishment.*

(1) *Escape from correctional custody.* Dishonorable discharge, forfeiture of all pay and allowances, and confinement for 1 year.

(2) *Breach of correctional custody.* Bad-conduct discharge, forfeiture of all pay and allowances, and confinement for 6 months.

(3) *Breach of restriction.* Confinement for 1 month and forfeiture of two-thirds pay per month for 1 month.

e. *Sample specifications.*

(1) *Escape from correctional custody.*

In that _____ (personal jurisdiction data), while undergoing the punishment of correctional custody imposed by a person authorized to do so, did, (at/on board—location), on or about _____ 20 __, escape from correctional custody.

(2) *Breach of correctional custody.*

In that __________ (personal jurisdiction data), while duly undergoing the punishment of correctional custody imposed by a person authorized to do so, did, (at/on board—location), on or about ______ 20 __, breach the restraint imposed thereunder by __________.

(3) *Breach of restriction.*

In that __________ (personal jurisdiction data), having been restricted to the limits of __________, by a person authorized to do so, did, (at/on board—location), on or about _____ 20 __, break said restriction.

14. Article 88 (10 U.S.C. 888)—Contempt toward officials

a. *Text of statute.*

Any commissioned officer who uses contemptuous words against the President, the Vice President, Congress, the Secretary of Defense, the Secretary of a military department, the Secretary of Homeland Security, or the Governor or legislature of any State, Commonwealth, or possession in which he is on duty or present shall be punished as a court-martial may direct.

b. *Elements.*

(1) That the accused was a commissioned officer of the United States armed forces;

(2) That the accused used certain words against an official or legislature named in the article;

(3) That by an act of the accused these words came to the knowledge of a person other than the accused; and

(4) That the words used were contemptuous, either in themselves or by virtue of the circumstances under which they were used.

[Note: If the words were against a Governor or legislature, add the following element]

(5) That the accused was then present in the State, Commonwealth, or possession of the Governor or legislature concerned.

c. *Explanation.*

The official or legislature against whom the words are used must be occupying one of the offices or be one of the legislatures named in Article 88 at the time of the offense. Neither "Congress" nor "legislature" includes its members individually. "Governor" does not include "lieutenant governor." It is immaterial whether the words are used against the official in an official or private capacity. If not personally contemptuous, adverse criticism of one of the officials or legislatures named in the article in the course of a political discussion, even though emphatically expressed, may not be charged as a violation of the article. Similarly, expressions of opinion made in a purely private conversation should not ordinarily be charged. Giving broad circulation to a written publication containing contemptuous words of the kind made punishable by this article, or the utterance of contemptuous words of this kind in the presence of military subordinates, aggravates the offense. The truth or falsity of the statements is immaterial.

d. *Maximum punishment.* Dismissal, forfeiture of all pay and allowances, and confinement for 1 year.

e. *Sample specification.*

In that __________ (personal jurisdiction data), did, (at/on board—location), on or about _____ 20 __, [use (orally and publicly) (_____) the following contemptuous words] [in a contemptuous manner, use (orally and publicly) (__________) the following words] against the [(President) (Vice President) (Congress) (Secretary of _____)] [(Governor) (legislature) of the (State of _____) (________), a (State) (__________) in which (he) (she), the said

__________, was then (on duty), (present)], to wit: "__________," or words to that effect.

15. Article 89 (10 U.S.C. 889)—Disrespect toward superior commissioned officer; assault of superior commissioned officer

a. *Text of statute.*

(a) DISRESPECT.—Any person subject to this chapter who behaves with disrespect toward that person's superior commissioned officer shall be punished as a court-martial may direct.

(b) ASSAULT.—Any person subject to this chapter who strikes that person's superior commissioned officer or draws or lifts up any weapon or offers any violence against that officer while the officer is in the execution of the officer's office shall be punished—

(1) if the offense is committed in time of war, by death or such other punishment as a court-martial may direct; and

(2) if the offense is committed at any other time, by such punishment, other than death, as a court-martial may direct.

b. *Elements.*

(1) *Disrespect toward superior commissioned officer.*

(a) That the accused did or omitted certain acts or used certain language to or concerning a certain commissioned officer;

(b) That such behavior or language was directed toward that officer;

(c) That the officer toward whom the acts, omissions, or words were directed was the superior commissioned officer of the accused;

(d) That the accused then knew that the commissioned officer toward whom the acts, omissions, or words were directed was the accused's superior commissioned officer; and

(e) That, under the circumstances, the behavior or language was disrespectful to that commissioned officer.

(2) *Striking or assaulting superior commissioned officer.*

(a) That the accused struck, drew, or lifted up a weapon against, or offered violence against, a certain commissioned officer;

(b) That the officer was the superior commissioned officer of the accused;

(c) That the accused then knew that the officer was the accused's superior commissioned officer; and

(d) That the superior commissioned officer was then in the execution of office.

[Note: if the offense was committed in time of war, add the following element]

(e) That the offense was committed in time of war.

c. *Explanation.*

(1) *Superior Commissioned Officer. See* 10 U.S.C. § 801(5) ("The term 'superior commissioned officer' means a commissioned officer superior in rank or command.").

(2) *Disrespect toward superior commissioned officer.*

(a) *Knowledge.* If the accused did not know that the person against whom the acts or words were directed was the accused's superior commissioned officer, the accused may not be convicted of a violation of this article. Knowledge may be proved by circumstantial evidence.

(b) *Disrespect.* Disrespectful behavior is that which detracts from the respect due the authority and person of a superior commissioned officer. It may consist of acts or language, however expressed, and it is immaterial whether they refer to the superior as an officer or as a private individual. Disrespect by words may be conveyed by abusive epithets or other contemptuous or denunciatory language. Truth is no defense. Disrespect by acts includes neglecting the customary salute, or showing a marked disdain, indifference, insolence, impertinence, undue familiarity, or other rudeness in the presence of the superior officer.

(c) *Presence.* It is not essential that the disrespectful behavior be in the presence of the superior, but ordinarily one should not be held accountable under this article for what was said or done in a purely private conversation.

(d) *Special defense—unprotected victim.* A superior commissioned officer whose conduct in relation to the accused under all the circumstances departs substantially from the required standards appropriate to that officer's rank or position under similar circumstances loses the protection of this article. That accused may not be convicted of being disrespectful to the officer who has so lost the entitlement to respect protected by Article 89.

(3) *Striking or assaulting superior commissioned officer.*

(a) *Superior commissioned officer.* The definition in subparagraph 15.c.(1) of this paragraph, applies here.

(b) *Knowledge.* The explanation in subparagraph 15.c.(2)(a) of this paragraph applies here.

(c) *Strikes.* "Strikes" means an intentional contact and includes any offensive touching of the person of an officer, however slight.

(d) *Draws or lifts up any weapon against.* The phrase "draws or lifts up any weapon against" covers any simple assault committed in the manner stated. The drawing of any weapon in an aggressive manner or the raising or brandishing of the same in a threatening manner in the presence of and at the superior is the sort of act proscribed. The raising in a threatening manner of a firearm, whether or not loaded, of a club, or of anything by which a serious blow or injury could be given is included in "lifts up."

(e) *Offers any violence against.* The phrase "offers any violence against" includes any form of battery or of mere assault not embraced in the preceding more specific terms "strikes" and "draws or lifts up." If not executed, the violence must be physically attempted or menaced. A mere threatening in words is not an offering of violence in the sense of this article.

(f) *Execution of office.* An officer is in the execution of office when engaged in any act or service required or authorized by treaty, statute, regulation, the order of a superior, or military usage. In general, any striking or use of violence against any superior commissioned officer by a person over whom it is the duty of that officer to maintain discipline at the time, would be striking or using violence against the officer in the execution of office. The commanding officer on board a ship or the commanding officer of a unit in the field is generally considered to be on duty at all times.

(g) *Defenses.* In a prosecution for striking or assaulting a superior commissioned officer in violation of this article, it is a defense that the accused acted in the proper discharge of some duty, or that the victim behaved in a manner toward the accused such as to lose the protection of this article (*see* subparagraph 15.c.(2)(d)). For example, if the victim initiated an unlawful attack on the accused, this would deprive the victim of the protection of this article, and, in addition, could excuse any lesser included offense of assault as done in self-defense, depending on the circumstances (*see* subparagraph 77.c.; R.C.M. 916(e)).

d. *Maximum punishment.*

(1) *Disrespect toward superior commissioned officer in command.* Bad-conduct discharge, forfeiture of all pay and allowances, and confinement for 1 year.

(2) *Disrespect toward superior commissioned officer superior in rank.* Bad-conduct discharge, forfeiture of all pay and allowances, and confinement for 6 months.

(3) *Striking, drawing or lifting up a weapon or offering any violence to superior commissioned officer in execution of office in time of war.* Death or such other punishment as a court-martial may direct.

(4) *Striking, drawing or lifting up a weapon or offering any violence to superior commissioned officer in execution of office at any other time.* Dishonorable discharge, forfeiture of all pay and allowances, and confinement for 10 years.

e. *Sample specifications.*

(1) *Disrespect toward superior commissioned officer.*

In that ________ (personal jurisdiction data), did, (at/on board—location) (subject-matter jurisdiction data, if required), on or about _____ 20 __, behave himself/herself with disrespect toward _______ , (his) (her) superior commissioned officer (in command) (in rank), then known by the said ________ to be (his) (her) superior commissioned officer (in command) (in rank), by (saying to (him) (her) "________," or words to that effect) (contemptuously turning from and leaving (him) (her) while (he) (she), the said ________, was talking to (him) (her), the said ________) (________).

(2) *Striking superior commissioned officer.*

In that ________ (personal jurisdiction data), did, (at/on board—location) (subject-matter jurisdiction data, if required), on or about ________ 20 ________, (a time of war) strike ________, (his) (her) superior commissioned officer (in command) (in rank), then known by the said ________ to be (his) (her) superior commissioned officer (in command) (in rank), who was then in the execution of (his) (her) office, (in) (on) the ________ with (a) ((his) (her)) ________.

(3) *Drawing or lifting up a weapon against superior commissioned officer.*

In that ________ (personal jurisdiction data), did, (at/on board—location) (subject-matter jurisdiction data, if required), on or about ________ 20 __, (a time of war) (draw) (lift up) a weapon, to wit: a ________, against ________, (his) (her) superior commissioned officer (in command) (in rank), then known by the said

________ to be (his) (her) superior commissioned officer (in command) (in rank), who was then in the execution of (his) (her) office.

(4) *Offering violence to superior commissioned officer.*

In that ________ (personal jurisdiction data), did, (at/on board—location) (subject-matter jurisdiction data, if required), on or about ________ 20 __, (a time of war) offer violence against ________, his/ her superior commissioned officer (in command) (in rank), then known by the said ________ to be (his) (her) superior commissioned officer (in command) (in rank), who was then in the execution of (his) (her) office, by ________.

16. Article 90 (10 U.S.C. 890)—Willfully disobeying superior commissioned officer

a. *Text of statute.*

Any person subject to this chapter who willfully disobeys a lawful command of that person's superior commissioned officer shall be punished—

(1) if the offense is committed in time of war, by death or such other punishment as a court-martial may direct; and

(2) if the offense is committed at any other time, by such punishment, other than death, as a court-martial may direct.

b. *Elements.*

(1) That the accused received a lawful command from a superior commissioned officer;

(2) That this officer was the superior commissioned officer of the accused;

(3) That the accused then knew that this officer was the accused's superior commissioned officer; and

(4) That the accused willfully disobeyed the lawful command.

[Note: if the offense was committed in time of war, add the following element]

(5) That the offense was committed in time of war.

c. *Explanation.*

(1) *Superior commissioned officer.* The definition in subparagraph 15.c.(1) applies here.

(2) *Disobeying superior commissioned officer.*

(a) *Lawfulness of the order.*

(i) *Inference of lawfulness.* An order requiring the performance of a military duty or act may be inferred to be lawful, and it is disobeyed at the peril of the subordinate. This inference does not apply to a patently illegal order, such as one that directs the commission of a crime.

(ii) *Determination of lawfulness.* The lawfulness of an order is a question of law to be determined by the military judge.

(iii) *Authority of issuing officer.* The commissioned officer issuing the order must have authority to give such an order. Authorization may be based on law, regulation, custom of the Service, or applicable order to direct, coordinate, or control the duties, activities, health, welfare, morale, or discipline of the accused.

(iv) *Relationship to military duty.* The order must relate to military duty, which includes all activities reasonably necessary to accomplish a military mission, or safeguard or promote the morale, discipline, and usefulness of members of a command and directly connected with the maintenance of good order in the Service. The order may not, without such a valid military purpose, interfere with private rights or personal affairs. However, the dictates of a person's conscience, religion, or personal philosophy cannot justify or excuse the disobedience of an otherwise lawful order. Disobedience of an order which has for its sole object the attainment of some private end, or which is given for the sole purpose of increasing the penalty for an offense which it is expected the accused may commit, is not punishable under this article.

(v) *Relationship to statutory or constitutional rights.* The order must not conflict with the statutory or constitutional rights of the person receiving the order.

(b) *Personal nature of the order.* The order must be directed specifically to the subordinate. Violations of regulations, standing orders or directives, or failure to perform previously established duties are not punishable under this article, but may violate Article 92.

(c) *Form and transmission of the order.* As long as the order is understandable, the form of the order is immaterial, as is the method by which it is transmitted to the accused.

(d) *Specificity of the order.* The order must be a specific mandate to do or not to do a specific act. An exhortation to "obey the law" or to perform one's military duty does not constitute an order under this article.

(e) *Knowledge*. The accused must have actual knowledge of the order and of the fact that the person issuing the order was the accused's superior commissioned officer. Actual knowledge may be proved by circumstantial evidence.

(f) *Nature of the disobedience*. "Willful disobedience" is an intentional defiance of authority. Failure to comply with an order through heedlessness, remissness, or forgetfulness is not a violation of this article but may violate Article 92.

(g) *Time for compliance*. When an order requires immediate compliance, an accused's declared intent not to obey and the failure to make any move to comply constitutes disobedience. Immediate compliance is required for any order that does not explicitly or implicitly indicate that delayed compliance is authorized or directed. If an order requires performance in the future, an accused's present statement of intention to disobey the order does not constitute disobedience of that order, although carrying out that intention may.

(3) *Civilians and discharged prisoners*. A discharged prisoner or other civilian subject to military law (*see* Article 2) and under the command of a commissioned officer is subject to the provisions of this article.

d. *Maximum punishment*.

(1) *Willfully disobeying a lawful order of superior commissioned officer in time of war*. Death or such other punishment as a court-martial may direct.

(2) *At any other time*. Dishonorable discharge, forfeiture of all pay and allowances, and confinement for 5 years.

e. *Sample specification*.

In that __________ (personal jurisdiction data), having received a lawful command from __________, (his) (her) superior commissioned officer, then known by the said __________ to be (his) (her) superior commissioned officer, to __________, or words to that effect, did, (at/on board—location), on or about _____ 20 __, willfully disobey the same.

17. Article 91 (10 U.S.C. 891)—Insubordinate conduct toward warrant officer, noncommissioned officer, or petty officer

a. *Text of statute*.

Any warrant officer or enlisted member who—

(1) strikes or assaults a warrant officer, noncommissioned officer, or petty officer, while that officer is in the execution of his office;

(2) willfully disobeys the lawful order of a warrant officer, noncommissioned officer, or petty officer; or

(3) treats with contempt or is disrespectful in language or deportment toward a warrant officer, noncommissioned officer, or petty officer, while that officer is in the execution of his office;

shall be punished as a court-martial may direct.

b. *Elements*.

(1) *Striking or assaulting warrant, noncommissioned, or petty officer*.

(a) That the accused was a warrant officer or enlisted member;

(b) That the accused struck or assaulted a certain warrant, noncommissioned, or petty officer;

(c) That the striking or assault was committed while the victim was in the execution of office; and

(d) That the accused then knew that the person struck or assaulted was a warrant, noncommissioned, or petty officer.

[Note: If the victim was the superior noncommissioned or petty officer of the accused, add the following elements]

(e) That the victim was the superior noncommissioned, or petty officer of the accused; and

(f) That the accused then knew that the person struck or assaulted was the accused's superior noncommissioned, or petty officer.

(2) *Disobeying a warrant, noncommissioned, or petty officer*.

(a) That the accused was a warrant officer or enlisted member;

(b) That the accused received a certain lawful order from a certain warrant, noncommissioned, or petty officer;

(c) That the accused then knew that the person giving the order was a warrant, noncommissioned, or petty officer;

(d) That the accused had a duty to obey the order; and

(e) That the accused willfully disobeyed the order.

(3) *Treating with contempt or being disrespectful in language or deportment toward a warrant, noncommissioned, or petty officer*.

(a) That the accused was a warrant officer or enlisted member;

(b) That the accused did or omitted certain acts, or used certain language;

(c) That such behavior or language was used toward and within sight or hearing of a certain warrant, noncommissioned, or petty officer;

(d) That the accused then knew that the person toward whom the behavior or language was directed was a warrant, noncommissioned, or petty officer;

(e) That the victim was then in the execution of office; and

(f) That under the circumstances the accused, by such behavior or language, treated with contempt or was disrespectful to said warrant, noncommissioned, or petty officer.

[Note: If the victim was the superior noncommissioned, or petty officer of the accused, add the following elements]

(g) That the victim was the superior noncommissioned, or petty officer of the accused; and

(h) That the accused then knew that the person toward whom the behavior or language was directed was the accused's superior noncommissioned, or petty officer.

c. *Explanation.*

(1) *In general.* Article 91 has the same general objects with respect to warrant, noncommissioned, and petty officers as Articles 89 and 90 have with respect to commissioned officers, namely, to ensure obedience to their lawful orders, and to protect them from violence, insult, or disrespect. Unlike Articles 89 and 90, however, this article does not require a superior-subordinate relationship as an element of any of the offenses denounced. This article does not protect an acting noncommissioned officer or acting petty officer, nor does it protect military police or members of the shore patrol who are not warrant, noncommissioned, or petty officers.

(2) *Knowledge.* All of the offenses prohibited by Article 91 require that the accused have actual knowledge that the victim was a warrant, noncommissioned, or petty officer. Actual knowledge may be proved by circumstantial evidence.

(3) *Striking or assaulting a warrant, noncommissioned, or petty officer.* For a discussion of "strikes" and "in the execution of office," see subparagraph 15.c. For a discussion of "assault," see subparagraph 77.c. An assault by a prisoner who has been discharged from the Service, or by any other civilian subject to military law, upon a warrant, noncommissioned, or petty officer should be charged under Article 128 or 134.

(4) *Disobeying a warrant, noncommissioned, or petty officer.* See subparagraph 16.c for a discussion of lawfulness, personal nature, form, transmission, and specificity of the order, nature of the disobedience, and time for compliance with the order.

(5) *Treating with contempt or being disrespectful in language or deportment toward a warrant, noncommissioned, or petty officer.* "Toward" requires that the behavior and language be within the sight or hearing of the warrant, noncommissioned, or petty officer concerned. For a discussion of "in the execution of his office," see subparagraph 15.c. For a discussion of "disrespect," see subparagraph 15.c.

d. *Maximum punishment.*

(1) *Striking or assaulting warrant officer.* Dishonorable discharge, forfeiture of all pay and allowances, and confinement for 5 years.

(2) *Striking or assaulting superior noncommissioned or petty officer.* Dishonorable discharge, forfeiture of all pay and allowances, and confinement for 3 years.

(3) *Striking or assaulting other noncommissioned or petty officer.* Dishonorable discharge, forfeiture of all pay and allowances, and confinement for 1 year.

(4) *Willfully disobeying the lawful order of a warrant officer.* Dishonorable discharge, forfeiture of all pay and allowances, and confinement for 2 years.

(5) *Willfully disobeying the lawful order of a noncommissioned or petty officer.* Bad-conduct discharge, forfeiture of all pay and allowances, and confinement for 1 year.

(6) *Contempt or disrespect to warrant officer.* Bad-conduct discharge, forfeiture of all pay and allowances, and confinement for 9 months.

(7) *Contempt or disrespect to superior noncommissioned or petty officer.* Bad-conduct discharge, forfeiture of all pay and allowances, and confinement for 6 months.

(8) *Contempt or disrespect to other noncommissioned or petty officer.* Forfeiture of two-thirds pay per month for 3 months, and confinement for 3 months.

e. *Sample specifications.*

(1) *Striking or assaulting warrant, noncommissioned, or petty officer.*

In that __________ (personal jurisdiction data), did, (at/on board—location) (subject-matter jurisdiction data, if required), on or about _____ 20 __, (strike) (assault) __________, a __________ officer, then known to the said __________ to be a (superior) __________ officer who was then in the execution of (his) (her) office, by __________ (him) (her) (in) (on) (the __________) with (a) __________ ((his) (her)) _____________.

(2) *Willful disobedience of warrant, noncommissioned, or petty officer.*

In that __________ (personal jurisdiction data), having received a lawful order from __________, a _____ officer, then known by the said _____ to be a _____ officer, to _____, an order which it was (his) (her) duty to obey, did (at/on board—location) (subject-matter jurisdiction data, if required), on or about _____ 20 __, willfully disobey the same.

(3) *Contempt or disrespect toward warrant, noncommissioned, or petty officer.*

In that __________ (personal jurisdiction data) (at/on board—location) (subject-matter jurisdiction data, if required), on or about _____ 20 __, [did treat with contempt] [was disrespectful in (language) (deportment) toward] __________, a __________ officer, then known by the said __________ to be a (superior) __________ officer, who was then in the execution of (his) (her) office, by (saying to (him) (her), "__________," or words to that effect) (spitting at (his) (her) feet) (__________).

18. Article 92 (10 U.S.C. 892)—Failure to obey order or regulation

a. *Text of statute.*

Any person subject to this chapter who—

(1) violates or fails to obey any lawful general order or regulation;

(2) having knowledge of any other lawful order issued by a member of the armed forces, which it is his duty to obey, fails to obey the order; or

(3) is derelict in the performance of his duties;

shall be punished as a court-martial may direct.

b. *Elements.*

(1) *Violation of or failure to obey a lawful general order or regulation.*

(a) That there was in effect a certain lawful general order or regulation;

(b) That the accused had a duty to obey it; and

(c) That the accused violated or failed to obey the order or regulation.

(2) *Failure to obey other lawful order.*

(a) That a member of the armed forces issued a certain lawful order;

(b) That the accused had knowledge of the order;

(c) That the accused had a duty to obey the order; and

(d) That the accused failed to obey the order.

(3) *Dereliction in the performance of duties.*

(a) That the accused had certain duties;

(b) That the accused knew or reasonably should have known of the duties; and

(c) That the accused was (willfully) (through neglect or culpable inefficiency) derelict in the performance of those duties.

[Note: In cases where the dereliction of duty resulted in death or grievous bodily harm, add the following element as applicable]

(d) That such dereliction of duty resulted in death or grievous bodily harm to a person other than the accused.

c. *Explanation.*

(1) *Violation of or failure to obey a lawful general order or regulation.*

(a) *Authority to issue general orders and regulations.* General orders or regulations are those orders or regulations generally applicable to an armed force which are properly published by the President or the Secretary of Defense, of Homeland Security, or of a military department, and those orders or regulations generally applicable to the command of the officer issuing them throughout the command or a particular subdivision thereof which are issued by:

(i) an officer having general court-martial jurisdiction;

(ii) a general or flag officer in command; or

(iii) a commander superior to (i) or (ii).

(b) *Effect of change of command on validity of order.* A general order or regulation issued by a commander with authority under Article 92(1) retains its character as a general order or regulation when another officer takes command, until it expires by its own terms or is rescinded by separate action, even if it is issued by an officer who is a general or flag officer in command and command is assumed by another officer who is not a general or flag officer.

(c) *Lawfulness.* A general order or regulation is lawful unless it is contrary to the Constitution, the laws of the United States, or lawful superior orders or for some other reason is beyond the authority of the official issuing it. See the discussion of lawfulness in subparagraph 16.c.

(d) *Knowledge.* Knowledge of a general order or regulation need not be alleged or proved as knowledge is not an element of this offense and a lack of knowledge does not constitute a defense.

(e) *Enforceability.* Not all provisions in general orders or regulations can be enforced under Article 92(1). Regulations which only supply general guidelines or advice for performing military functions may not be enforceable under Article 92(1).

(2) *Violation of or failure to obey other lawful order.*

(a) *Scope.* Article 92(2) includes all other lawful orders which may be issued by a member of the armed forces, violations of which are not chargeable under Article 90, 91, or 92(1). It includes the violation of written regulations which are not general regulations. See also subparagraph (1)(e) of this paragraph as applicable.

(b) *Knowledge.* In order to be guilty of this offense, a person must have had actual knowledge of the order or regulation. Knowledge of the order may be proved by circumstantial evidence.

(c) *Duty to obey order.*

(i) *From superior.* A member of one armed force who is senior in rank to a member of another armed force is the superior of that member with authority to issue orders which that member has a duty to obey under the same circumstances as a commissioned officer of one armed force is the superior commissioned officer of a member of another armed force for the purposes of Articles 89 and 90. *See* subparagraph 13.c.(1).

(ii) *From one not a superior.* Failure to obey the lawful order of one not a superior is an offense under Article 92(2), provided the accused had a duty to obey the order, such as one issued by a sentinel or a member of the armed forces police. See subparagraph 17.b.(2) if the order was issued by a warrant, noncommissioned, or petty officer in the execution of office.

(3) *Dereliction in the performance of duties.*

(a) *Duty.* A duty may be imposed by treaty, statute, regulation, lawful order, standard operating procedure, or custom of the Service.

(b) *Knowledge.* Actual knowledge of duties may be proved by circumstantial evidence. Actual knowledge need not be shown if the individual reasonably should have known of the duties. This may be demonstrated by regulations, training or operating manuals, customs of the Service, academic literature or testimony, testimony of persons who have held similar or superior positions, or similar evidence.

(c) *Derelict.* A person is derelict in the performance of duties when that person willfully or negligently fails to perform that person's duties or when that person performs them in a culpably inefficient manner. "Willfully" means intentionally. It refers to the doing of an act knowingly and purposely, specifically intending the natural and probable consequences of the act. "Negligently" means an act or omission of a person who is under a duty to use due care which exhibits a lack of that degree of care which a reasonably prudent person would have exercised under the same or similar circumstances. Culpable inefficiency is inefficiency for which there is no reasonable or just excuse.

(d) *Ineptitude.* A person is not derelict in the performance of duties if the failure to perform those duties is caused by ineptitude rather than by willfulness, negligence, or culpable inefficiency, and may not be charged under this article, or otherwise punished. For example, a recruit who has tried earnestly during rifle training and throughout record firing is not derelict in the performance of duties if the recruit fails to qualify with the weapon.

(e) *Grievous bodily harm.* For purposes of this offense, the term "grievous bodily harm" has the same meaning ascribed to it in Article 128 (paragraph 77).

(f) Where the dereliction of duty resulted in death or grievous bodily harm, the intent to cause death or grievous bodily harm is not required.

d. *Maximum punishment.*

(1) *Violation of or failure to obey lawful general order or regulation.* Dishonorable discharge, forfeiture of all pay and allowances, and confinement for 2 years.

(2) *Violation of or failure to obey other lawful order.* Bad-conduct discharge, forfeiture of all pay and allowances, and confinement for 6 months.

(3) *Dereliction in the performance of duties.*

(a) *Through neglect or culpable inefficiency.* Forfeiture of two-thirds pay per month for 3 months and confinement for 3 months.

(b) *Through neglect or culpable inefficiency resulting in death or grievous bodily harm.* Bad-conduct discharge, forfeiture of all pay and allowances, and confinement for 18 months.

(c) *Willful.* Bad-conduct discharge, forfeiture of all pay and allowances, and confinement for 6 months.

(d) *Willful dereliction of duty resulting in death or grievous bodily harm.* Dishonorable discharge, forfeiture of all pay and allowances, and confinement for 2 years.

[Note: For (1) and (2) of this rule, the punishment set forth does not apply in the following cases: if, in the absence of the order or regulation which was violated or not obeyed, the accused would on the same facts be subject to conviction for another specific offense for which a lesser punishment is prescribed; or if the violation or failure to obey is a breach of restraint imposed as a result of an order. In these instances, the maximum punishment is that specifically prescribed elsewhere for that particular offense.]

e. *Sample specifications.*

(1) *Violation or failure to obey lawful general order or regulation.*

In that __________ (personal jurisdiction data), did, (at/on board—location) (subject-matter jurisdiction data, if required), on or about _____ 20 __, (violate) (fail to obey) a lawful general (order) (regulation) which was (his)(her) duty to obey, to wit: paragraph __ (Army) (Air Force) Regulation, dated ____) (Article, U.S. Navy Regulations, dated __) (General Order No.__, U.S. Navy, dated ____) (_______), by (wrongfully_______).

(2) *Violation or failure to obey other lawful written order.*

In that __________ (personal jurisdiction data), having knowledge of a lawful order issued by _____, to wit: (paragraph, (the Combat Group Regulation No. __) (USS_____, Regulation ______), dated____) (_________), an order which it was (his) (her) duty to obey, did, (at/on board—location) (subject-matter jurisdiction data, if required), on or about _____ 20 __, fail to obey the same by (wrongfully) ________________________.

(3) *Failure to obey other lawful order.*

In that__________ (personal jurisdiction data) having knowledge of a lawful order issued by __________ (to submit to certain medical treatment) (to) (not to ____________) (__________________), an order which it was (his) (her) duty to obey (at/on board—location) (subject-matter jurisdiction data, if required), on or about__20__, fail to obey the same (by (wrongfully) ________________________.

(4) *Dereliction in the performance of duties.*

In that, _________ (personal jurisdiction data), who (knew) (should have known) of (his) (her) duties (at/on board—location) (subject-matter jurisdiction data, if required), (on or about ____ 20__) (from about ____ 20__ to about _____ 20__), was derelict in the performance of those duties in that (he) (she) (negligently) (willfully) (by culpable inefficiency) failed _______, as it was (his) (her) duty to do, [and that such dereliction of duty resulted in (grievous bodily harm, to wit: (broken leg) (deep cut) (fractured skull) (______) to _______) (the death of ____________)].

19. Article 93 (10 U.S.C. 893)—Cruelty and maltreatment

a. *Text of statute.*

Any person subject to this chapter who is guilty of cruelty toward, or oppression or maltreatment of, any person subject to his orders shall be punished as a court-martial may direct.

b. *Elements.*

(1) That a certain person was subject to the orders of the accused; and

(2) That the accused was cruel toward, or oppressed, or maltreated that person.

c. *Explanation.*

(1) *Nature of victim.* "Any person subject to his orders" means not only those persons under the direct or immediate command of the accused but extends to all persons, subject to the UCMJ or not, who by reason of some duty are required to obey the lawful orders of the accused, regardless whether the accused is in the direct chain of command over the person.

(2) *Nature of act.* The cruelty, oppression, or maltreatment, although not necessarily physical, must be measured by an objective standard. Assault, improper punishment, and sexual harassment may constitute this offense if the conduct meets the elements of this offense. Sexual harassment under this paragraph includes influencing, offering to influence, or threatening the career, pay, or job of another person

in exchange for sexual favors, and deliberate or repeated offensive comments or gestures of a sexual nature. The imposition of necessary or proper duties and the exaction of their performance does not constitute this offense even though the duties are arduous or hazardous or both.

d. *Maximum punishment.* Dishonorable discharge, forfeiture of all pay and allowances, and confinement for 3 years.

e. *Sample specification.*

In that (personal jurisdiction data), (at/on board—location) (subject-matter jurisdiction data, if required), on or about _________ 20__, (was cruel toward) did (oppress) (maltreat) ____________), a person subject to (his) (her) orders, by (kicking (him) (her) in the stomach) (confining (him) (her) for twenty-four hours without water) (________________).

20. Article 93a (10 U.S.C. 893a)—Prohibited activities with military recruit or trainee by person in position of special trust

a. *Text of statute.*

(a) ABUSE OF TRAINING LEADERSHIP POSITION.—Any person subject to this chapter—

(1) who is an officer, a noncommissioned officer, or a petty officer;

(2) who is in a training leadership position with respect to a specially protected junior member of the armed forces; and

(3) who engages in prohibited sexual activity with such specially protected junior member of the armed forces;

shall be punished as a court-martial may direct.

(b) ABUSE OF POSITION AS MILITARY RECRUITER.—Any person subject to this chapter—

(1) who is a military recruiter and engages in prohibited sexual activity with an applicant for military service; or

(2) who is a military recruiter and engages in prohibited sexual activity with a specially protected junior member of the armed forces who is enlisted under a delayed entry program;

shall be punished as a court-martial may direct.

(c) CONSENT.—Consent is not a defense for any conduct at issue in a prosecution under this section (article).

(d) DEFINITIONS.—In this section (article):

(1) SPECIALLY PROTECTED JUNIOR MEMBER OF THE ARMED FORCES.—The term "specially protected junior member of the armed forces" means—

(A) a member of the armed forces who is assigned to, or is awaiting assignment to, basic training or other initial active duty for training, including a member who is enlisted under a delayed entry program;

(B) a member of the armed forces who is a cadet, a midshipman, an officer candidate, or a student in any other officer qualification program; and

(C) a member of the armed forces in any program that, by regulation prescribed by the Secretary concerned, is identified as a training program for initial career qualification.

(2) TRAINING LEADERSHIP POSITION.—The term "training leadership position" means, with respect to a specially protected junior member of the armed forces, any of the following:

(A) Any drill instructor position or other leadership position in a basic training program, an officer candidate school, a reserve officers' training corps unit, a training program for entry into the armed forces, or any program that, by regulation prescribed by the Secretary concerned, is identified as a training program for initial career qualification.

(B) Faculty and staff of the United States Military Academy, the United States Naval Academy, the United States Air Force Academy, and the United States Coast Guard Academy.

(3) APPLICANT FOR MILITARY SERVICE.—The term "applicant for military service" means a person who, under regulations prescribed by the Secretary concerned, is an applicant for original enlistment or appointment in the armed forces.

(4) MILITARY RECRUITER.—The term "military recruiter" means a person who, under regulations prescribed by the Secretary concerned, has the primary duty to recruit persons for military service.

(5) PROHIBITED SEXUAL ACTIVITY.—The term "prohibited sexual activity" means, as specified in regulations prescribed by the Secretary

concerned, inappropriate physical intimacy under circumstances described in such regulations.

b. *Elements.*

(1) *Abuse of training leadership position.*

(a) That the accused was a commissioned, warrant, noncommissioned, or petty officer;

(b) That the accused was in a training leadership position with respect to a specially protected member of the armed forces; and

(c) That the accused engaged in prohibited sexual activity with a person the accused knew was a specially protected junior member of the armed forces.

(2) *Abuse of position as a military recruiter.*

(a) That the accused was a commissioned, warrant, noncommissioned, or petty officer;

(b) That the accused was performing duties as a military recruiter; and

(c) That the accused engaged in prohibited sexual activity with a person the accused knew was an applicant for military service or a specially protected junior member of the armed forces who is enlisted under a delayed entry program.

c. *Explanation.*

(1) *In general.* The prevention of inappropriate sexual activity by trainers, recruiters, and drill instructors with recruits, trainees, students attending service academies, and other potentially vulnerable persons in the initial training environment is crucial to the maintenance of good order and military discipline. Military law, regulation, and custom invest officers, non-commissioned officers, drill instructors, recruiters, cadre, and others with the right and obligation to exercise control over those they supervise. In this context, inappropriate sexual activity between those potentially vulnerable persons and those with authority to exercise control over them is inherently destructive to good order and discipline.

(2) *Prohibited activity.* The responsibility for identifying relationships subject to this offense and those outside the scope of this offense is entrusted to the individual Services to determine and specify by appropriate regulations. This offense is intended to cover those situations that involve the improper use of authority by virtue of an individual's position in either a training or recruiting environment. Not all contact or associations are prohibited by this article. Service regulations must consider circumstances where pre-existing relationships (for example, marriage relationships) exist. Additionally, this offense criminalizes only activity occurring when there is a training or recruiting relationship between the accused and the alleged victim of this offense.

(3) *Knowledge.* The accused must have actual or constructive knowledge that a person was a "specially protected junior member of the armed forces" or an "applicant for military service" (as those terms are defined in this offense). Knowledge may be proved by circumstantial evidence.

(4) *Consent.* Consent is not a defense to this offense.

d. *Maximum punishment.* Dishonorable discharge, forfeiture of all pay and allowances, and confinement for 5 years.

e. *Sample specifications.*

(1) *Prohibited act with specially protected junior member of the armed forces.*

In that ___ (personal jurisdiction data), a (commissioned) (warrant) (noncommissioned) (petty) officer, while in a training leadership position over ___, did (at/on board—location) (subject-matter jurisdiction data, if required), on or about ___ 20__, engage in a prohibited act, to wit: _____________ with _____________, whom the accused knew was a specially protected junior Servicemember in initial active duty training.

(2) *Prohibited act with an applicant for military service.*

In that ___ (personal jurisdiction data), a (commissioned) (warrant) (noncommissioned) (petty) officer, while in a training leadership position over ___, did (at/on board—location) (subject-matter jurisdiction data, if required), on or about ___ 20__, engage in a prohibited act, to wit: ____________ with _________________, whom the accused knew was (an applicant for military service) (a specially protected junior member of the armed forces who is enlisted under a delayed entry program).

21. Article 94 (10 U.S.C. 894)—Mutiny or sedition

a. *Text of statute.*

(a) Any person subject to this chapter who—

(1) with intent to usurp or override lawful military authority, refuses, in concert with any other person, to obey orders or otherwise do his duty or creates any violence or disturbance is guilty of mutiny;

(2) with intent to cause the overthrow or destruction of lawful civil authority, creates, in concert with any other person, revolt, violence, or other disturbance against that authority is guilty of sedition;

(3) fails to do his utmost to prevent and suppress a mutiny or sedition being committed in his presence, or fails to take all reasonable means to inform his superior commissioned officer or commanding officer of a mutiny or sedition which he knows or has reason to believe is taking place, is guilty of a failure to suppress or report a mutiny or sedition.

(b) A person who is found guilty of attempted mutiny, mutiny, sedition, or failure to suppress or report a mutiny or sedition shall be punished by death or such other punishment as a court-martial may direct.

b. *Elements.*

(1) *Mutiny by creating violence or disturbance.*

(a) That the accused created violence or a disturbance; and

(b) That the accused created this violence or disturbance with intent to usurp or override lawful military authority.

(2) *Mutiny by refusing to obey orders or perform duty.*

(a) That the accused refused to obey orders or otherwise do the accused's duty;

(b) That the accused in refusing to obey orders or perform duty acted in concert with another person or persons; and

(c) That the accused did so with intent to usurp or override lawful military authority.

(3) *Sedition.*

(a) That the accused created revolt, violence, or disturbance against lawful civil authority;

(b) That the accused acted in concert with another person or persons; and

(c) That the accused did so with the intent to cause the overthrow or destruction of that authority.

(4) *Failure to prevent and suppress a mutiny or sedition.*

(a) That an offense of mutiny or sedition was committed in the presence of the accused; and

(b) That the accused failed to do the accused's utmost to prevent and suppress the mutiny or sedition.

(5) *Failure to report a mutiny or sedition.*

(a) That an offense of mutiny or sedition occurred;

(b) That the accused knew or had reason to believe that the offense was taking place; and

(c) That the accused failed to take all reasonable means to inform the accused's superior commissioned officer or commander of the offense.

(6) *Attempted mutiny.*

(a) That the accused committed a certain overt act;

(b) That the act was done with specific intent to commit the offense of mutiny;

(c) That the act amounted to more than mere preparation; and

(d) That the act apparently tended to effect the commission of the offense of mutiny.

c. *Explanation.*

(1) *Mutiny.* Article 94(a)(1) defines two types of mutiny, both requiring an intent to usurp or override military authority.

(a) *Mutiny by creating violence or disturbance.* Mutiny by creating violence or disturbance may be committed by one person acting alone or by more than one acting together.

(b) *Mutiny by refusing to obey orders or perform duties.* Mutiny by refusing to obey orders or perform duties requires collective insubordination and necessarily includes some combination of two or more persons in resisting lawful military authority. This concert of insubordination need not be preconceived, nor is it necessary that the insubordination be active or violent. It may consist simply of a persistent and concerted refusal or omission to obey orders, or to do duty, with an insubordinate intent, that is, with an intent to usurp or override lawful military authority. The intent may be declared in words or inferred from acts, omissions, or surrounding circumstances.

(2) *Sedition.* Sedition requires a concert of action in resistance to civil authority. This differs from mutiny by creating violence or disturbance. *See* subparagraph c.(1)(a) of this paragraph.

(3) *Failure to prevent and suppress a mutiny or sedition.* "Utmost" means taking those measures to prevent and suppress a mutiny or sedition which may properly be called for by the circumstances, including the rank, responsibilities, or employment of the person concerned. "Utmost" includes the use of such force, including deadly force, as may be reasonably necessary

under the circumstances to prevent and suppress a mutiny or sedition.

(4) *Failure to report a mutiny or sedition.*

(a) *In general.* Failure to "take all reasonable means to inform" includes failure to take the most expeditious means available. When the circumstances known to the accused would have caused a reasonable person in similar circumstances to believe that a mutiny or sedition was occurring, this may establish that the accused had such "reason to believe" that mutiny or sedition was occurring. Failure to report an impending mutiny or sedition is not an offense in violation of Article 94. *But see* subparagraph 18.c.(3) (dereliction of duty).

(b) *Superior commissioned officer.* For purposes of this paragraph, "a superior commissioned officer" means a superior commissioned officer in the chain of command.

(5) *Attempted mutiny.* For a discussion of attempts, see paragraph 4.

d. *Maximum punishment.* Death or such other punishment as a court-martial may direct.

e. *Sample specifications.*

(1) *Mutiny by creating violence or disturbance.*

In that __________ (personal jurisdiction data), with intent to (usurp) (override) (usurp and override) lawful military authority, did, (at/on board—location) (subject-matter jurisdiction data, if required), on or about _____ 20 __, create (violence) (a disturbance) by (attacking the officers of the said ship) (barricading himself/herself in Barracks T7, firing (his) (her) rifle at __________, and exhorting other persons to join (him) (her) in defiance of _____) (_____).

(2) *Mutiny by refusing to obey orders or perform duties.*

In that __________ (personal jurisdiction data), with intent to (usurp) (override) (usurp and override) lawful military authority, did, (at/on board—location) (subject-matter jurisdiction data, if required), on or about _____ 20 __, refuse, in concert with __________ (and __________) (others whose names are unknown), to (obey the orders of __________ to __________) (perform (his) (her) duty as __________).

(3) *Sedition.*

In that __________ (personal jurisdiction data), with intent to cause the (overthrow) (destruction) (overthrow and destruction) of lawful civil authority, to wit: __________, did, (at/on board—location) (subject-matter jurisdiction data, if required), on or about _____ 20 __, in concert with (__________) and (__________) (others whose names are unknown), create (revolt) (violence) (a disturbance) against such authority by (entering the Town Hall of __________ and destroying property and records therein) (marching upon and compelling the surrender of the police of __________) (__________).

(4) *Failure to prevent and suppress a mutiny or sedition.*

In that __________ (personal jurisdiction data), did, (at/on board—location) (subject-matter jurisdiction data, if required), on or about _____ 20 __, fail to do (his) (her) utmost to prevent and suppress a (mutiny) (sedition) among the (Soldiers) (Sailors) Airmen) (Marines) (__________) of __________, which (mutiny) (sedition) was being committed in (his) (her) presence, in that ((he) (she) took no means to compel the dispersal of the assembly) ((he) (she) made no effort to assist __________ who was attempting to quell the mutiny) (__________).

(5) *Failure to report a mutiny or sedition.*

In that __________ (personal jurisdiction data), did, (at/on board—location) (subject-matter jurisdiction data, if required), on or about _____ 20 __, fail to take all reasonable means to inform (his) (her) superior commissioned officer or (his) (her) commander of a (mutiny) (sedition) among the (Soldiers) (Sailors) (Airmen) (Marines) (__________) of __________, which (mutiny) (sedition) (he) (she), the said __________ (knew) (had reason to believe) was taking place.

(6) *Attempted mutiny.*

In that __________ (personal jurisdiction data), with intent to (usurp) (override) (usurp and override) lawful military authority, did, (at/on board—location) (subject-matter jurisdiction data, if required), on or about _____ 20 __, attempt to (create (violence) (a disturbance) by _____) (_____).

22. Article 95 (10 U.S.C. 895)—Offenses by sentinel or lookout

a. *Text of statute.*

(a) DRUNK OR SLEEPING ON POST, OR LEAVING POST BEFORE BEING RELIEVED.—Any sentinel or lookout who is drunk on post, who sleeps on post, or who leaves post before being regularly relieved, shall be punished—

(1) if the offense is committed in time of war, by death or such other punishment as a court-martial may direct; and

(2) if the offense is committed other than in time of war, by such punishment, other than death, as a court-martial may direct.

(b) LOITERING OR WRONGFULLY SITTING ON POST.—Any sentinel or lookout who loiters or wrongfully sits down on post shall be punished as a court-martial may direct.

b. *Elements.*

(1) *Drunk or sleeping on post, or leaving post before being relieved.*

(a) That the accused was posted or on post as a sentinel or lookout;

(b) That the accused was drunk while on post, was sleeping while on post, or left post before being regularly relieved.

[Note: If the offense was committed in time of war or while the accused was receiving special pay under 37 U.S.C. § 310, add the following element:]

(c) That the offense was committed (in time of war) (while the accused was receiving special pay under 37 U.S.C. § 310).

(2) *Loitering or wrongfully sitting on post.*

(a) That the accused was posted as a sentinel or lookout; and

(b) That while so posted, the accused loitered or wrongfully sat down on post.

[Note: If the offense was committed in time of war or while the accused was receiving special pay under 37 U.S.C. § 310, add the following element:]

(c) That the accused was so posted (in time of war) (while receiving special pay under 37 U.S.C. § 310).

c. *Explanation.*

(1) *Drunk or sleeping on post, or leaving post before being relieved.*

(a) *In general.* Article 95(a) defines three kinds of misbehavior committed by sentinels or lookouts: being drunk on post, sleeping on post, or leaving it before being regularly relieved. Article 95(a) does not include an officer or enlisted person of the guard, or of a ship's watch, not posted or performing the duties of a sentinel or lookout, nor does it include a person whose duties as a watchman or attendant do not require constant alertness.

(b) *Post.* "Post" is the area where the sentinel or lookout is required to be for the performance of duties. It is not limited by an imaginary line, but includes, according to orders or circumstances, such surrounding area as may be necessary for the proper performance of the duties for which the sentinel or lookout was posted. The offense of leaving post is not committed when a sentinel or lookout goes an immaterial distance from the post, unless it is such a distance that the ability to fully perform the duty for which posted is impaired.

(c) *On post.* A sentinel or lookout becomes "on post" after having been given a lawful order to go "on post" as a sentinel or lookout and being formally or informally posted. The fact that a sentinel or lookout is not posted in the regular way is not a defense. It is sufficient, for example, if the sentinel or lookout has taken the post in accordance with proper instruction, whether or not formally given. A sentinel or lookout is "on post" within the meaning of the article not only when at a post physically defined, as is ordinarily the case in garrison or aboard ship, but also, for example, when stationed in observation against the approach of an enemy, or detailed to use any equipment designed to locate friend, foe, or possible danger, or at a designated place to maintain internal discipline, or to guard stores, or to guard prisoners while in confinement or at work.

(d) *Sentinel or lookout.* A "sentinel" or a "lookout" is a person whose duties include the requirement to maintain constant alertness, be vigilant, and remain awake, in order to observe for the possible approach of the enemy, or to guard persons, property, or a place and to sound the alert, if necessary.

(e) *Drunk.* For an explanation of "drunk," see subparagraph 51.c.(6).

(f) *Sleeping.* As used in this article, "sleeping" is that condition of insentience which is sufficient sensibly to impair the full exercise of the mental and physical faculties of a sentinel or lookout. It is not necessary to show that the accused was in a wholly comatose condition. The fact that the accused's sleeping resulted from a physical incapacity caused by disease or accident is an affirmative defense. *See* R.C.M. 916(i).

(2) *Loitering or wrongfully sitting on post by a sentinel or lookout.*

(a) *In general.* The discussion set forth in subparagraph 22.c.(1) applies to loitering or sitting down while posted as a sentinel or lookout in violation of Article 95(b) as well.

(b) *Loiter*. "Loiter" means to stand around, to move about slowly, to linger, or to lag behind when that conduct is in violation of known instructions or accompanied by a failure to give complete attention to duty.

d. *Maximum punishment.*

(1) *Drunk or sleeping on post, or leaving post before being relieved.*

(a) *In time of war*. Death or such other punishment as a court-martial may direct.

(b) *While receiving special pay under 37 U.S.C. § 310*. Dishonorable discharge, forfeiture of all pay and allowances, and confinement for 10 years.

(c) *In all other places*. Dishonorable discharge, forfeiture of all pay and allowances, and confinement for 1 year.

(2) *Loitering or wrongfully sitting on post by a sentinel or lookout.*

(a) *In time of war or while receiving special pay under 37 U.S.C. § 310*. Dishonorable discharge, forfeiture of all pay and allowances, and confinement for 2 years.

(b) *Other cases*. Bad-conduct discharge, forfeiture of all pay and allowances, and confinement for 6 months.

e. *Sample specifications.*

(1) *Drunk or sleeping on post, or leaving post before being relieved.*

In that __________ (personal jurisdiction data), on or about _____ 20 __ (a time of war) (at/on board—location), (while receiving special pay under 37 U.S.C. § 310), being (posted) (on post) as a (sentinel) (lookout) at (warehouse no. 7) (post no. 11) (for radar observation) (__________) (was (drunk) (sleeping) upon (his) (her) post) (did leave (his) (her) post before (he) (she) was regularly relieved).

(2) *Loitering or wrongfully sitting down on post by a sentinel or lookout.*

In that __________ (personal jurisdiction data), while posted as a (sentinel) (lookout), did, (at/on board—location) (while receiving special pay under 37 U.S.C. § 310) on or about _____ 20 __, (a time of war) (loiter) (wrongfully sit down) on (his) (her) post.

23. Article 95a (10 U.S.C. 895a)—Disrespect toward sentinel or lookout

a. *Text of statute.*

(a) DISRESPECTFUL LANGUAGE TOWARD SENTINEL OR LOOKOUT.—Any person subject to this chapter who, knowing that another person is a sentinel or lookout, uses wrongful and disrespectful language that is directed toward and within the hearing of the sentinel or lookout, who is in the execution of duties as a sentinel or lookout, shall be punished as a court-martial may direct.

(b) DISRESPECTFUL BEHAVIOR TOWARD SENTINEL OR LOOKOUT.—Any person subject to this chapter who, knowing that another person is a sentinel or lookout, behaves in a wrongful and disrespectful manner that is directed toward and within the sight of the sentinel or lookout, who is in the execution of duties as a sentinel or lookout, shall be punished as a court-martial may direct.

b. *Elements.*

(1) *Disrespectful language toward sentinel or lookout.*

(a) That a certain person was a sentinel or lookout;

(b) That the accused knew that said person was a sentinel or lookout;

(c) That the accused used certain disrespectful language;

(d) That such language was wrongful;

(e) That such language was directed toward and within the hearing of the sentinel or lookout; and

(f) That said person was at the time in the execution of duties as a sentinel or lookout.

(2) *Disrespectful behavior toward sentinel or lookout.*

(a) That a certain person was a sentinel or lookout;

(b) That the accused knew that said person was a sentinel or lookout;

(c) That the accused behaved in a certain disrespectful manner;

(d) That such behavior was wrongful;

(e) That such behavior was directed toward and within the sight of the sentinel or lookout; and

(f) That said person was at the time in the execution of duties as a sentinel or lookout.

c. *Explanation.* See subparagraph 15.c.(2)(b) for a discussion of "disrespect."

d. *Maximum punishment.* Confinement for 3 months and forfeiture of two-thirds pay per month for 3 months.

e. *Sample specification.*

(1) *Disrespectful language toward sentinel or lookout.*

In that __________ (personal jurisdiction data), did, (at/on board—location) (subject-matter jurisdiction, if required), on or about _____ 20 __, then knowing that __________ was a sentinel or lookout, wrongfully use the following disrespectful language "__________," or words to that effect, to __________, and that such language was directed toward and within the hearing of __________, the (sentinel) (lookout) in the execution of (his) (her) duty.

(2) *Disrespectful behavior toward sentinel or lookout.*

In that __________ (personal jurisdiction data), did, (at/on board—location) (subject-matter jurisdiction, if required), on or about _____ 20 __, then knowing that __________ was a sentinel or lookout, wrongfully behave in a disrespectful manner toward __________, by __________, and that such behavior was directed toward and within the sight of ________, the (sentinel) (lookout) in the execution of (his) (her) duty.

24. Article 96 (10 U.S.C. 896)—Release of prisoner without authority; drinking with prisoner

a. *Text of statute.*

(a) RELEASE OF PRISONER WITHOUT AUTHORITY.—Any person subject to this chapter—

(1) who, without authority to do so, releases a prisoner; or

(2) who, through neglect or design, allows a prisoner to escape; shall be punished as a court-martial may direct, whether or not the prisoner was committed in strict compliance with the law.

(b) DRINKING WITH PRISONER.—Any person subject to this chapter who unlawfully drinks any alcoholic beverage with a prisoner shall be punished as a court-martial may direct.

b. *Elements.*

(1) *Releasing a prisoner without authority.*

(a) That a certain person was a prisoner; and

(b) That the accused released the prisoner without authority.

(2) *Allowing a prisoner to escape through neglect.*

(a) That a certain person was a prisoner;

(b) That the prisoner escaped;

(c) That the accused did not take such care to prevent the escape as a reasonably careful person, acting in the capacity in which the accused was acting, would have taken in the same or similar circumstances; and

(d) That the escape was the proximate result of the neglect.

(3) *Allowing a prisoner to escape through design.*

(a) That a certain person was a prisoner;

(b) That the design of the accused was to allow the escape of that prisoner; and

(c) That the prisoner escaped as a result of the carrying out of the design of the accused.

(4) *Drinking with prisoner.*

(a) That a certain person was a prisoner; and

(b) That the accused unlawfully drank any alcoholic beverage with that prisoner.

c. *Explanation.*

(1) *Prisoner.* A prisoner is a person who is in confinement or custody imposed under R.C.M. 302, 304, or 305, or under sentence of a court-martial who has not been set free by a person with authority to release the prisoner.

(2) *Releasing a prisoner without authority.*

(a) *Release.* The release of a prisoner is removal of restraint by the custodian rather than by the prisoner.

(b) *Authority to release.* See R.C.M. 305(g) as to who may release pretrial prisoners. Normally, the lowest authority competent to order release of a post-trial prisoner is the commander who convened the court-martial that sentenced the prisoner or the officer exercising general court-martial jurisdiction over the prisoner. *See also* R.C.M. 1103.

(3) *Allowing a prisoner to escape through neglect.*

(a) *Allow.* "Allow" means to permit; not to forbid or hinder.

(b) *Neglect.* "Neglect" is a relative term. It is the absence of conduct that would have been taken by a reasonably careful custodian in the same or similar circumstances.

(c) *Escape.* "Escape" is defined in subparagraph 12.c.(5)(c).

(d) *Status of prisoner after escape not a defense.* After escape, the fact that a prisoner returns, is captured, killed, or otherwise dies is not a defense.

(4) *Allowing a prisoner to escape through design.* An escape is allowed through design when it is

intended by the custodian. Such intent may be inferred from conduct so wantonly devoid of care that the only reasonable inference which may be drawn is that the escape was contemplated as a probable result.

(5) *Drinking with prisoner.* For purposes of this section, "unlawful" is synonymous with "wrongful." That is, it is unlawful to drink an alcoholic beverage with a prisoner unless the accused had a legal justification or excuse to do so. In this context, any consumption of alcohol with a prisoner would be unlawful unless the accused had been granted specific authority to do so by competent authority (e.g., a commander of a confinement facility authorizing limited alcohol consumption by prisoners on a holiday or special occasion).

d. *Maximum punishment.*

(1) *Releasing a prisoner without authority.* Dishonorable discharge, forfeiture of all pay and allowances, and confinement for 2 years.

(2) *Allowing a prisoner to escape through neglect.* Bad-conduct discharge, forfeiture of all pay and allowances, and confinement for 2 years.

(3) *Allowing a prisoner to escape through design.* Dishonorable discharge, forfeiture of all pay and allowances, and confinement for 5 years.

(4) *Drinking with prisoner.* Confinement for 1 year and forfeiture of two-thirds pay per month for 1 year.

e. *Sample specifications.*

(1) *Releasing a prisoner without authority.*

In that __________ (personal jurisdiction data), did, (at/on board—location) (subject-matter jurisdiction, if required), on or about _____ 20 __, without authority, release __________, a prisoner.

(2) *Allowing a prisoner to escape through neglect or design.*

In that __________ (personal jurisdiction data), did, (at/on board—location) (subject-matter jurisdiction, if required), on or about _____ 20 __, through (neglect) (design), allow __________, a prisoner, to escape.

(3) *Drinking with prisoner.*

In that _____ (personal jurisdiction data), did, (at/on board—location) (subject-matter jurisdiction, if required), on or about _____ 20 __, unlawfully drink alcohol with __________, a prisoner.

25. Article 97 (10 U.S.C. 897)—Unlawful detention

a. *Text of statute.*

Any person subject to this chapter who, except as provided by law, apprehends, arrests, or confines any person shall be punished as a court-martial may direct.

b. *Elements.*

(1) That the accused apprehended, arrested, or confined a certain person; and

(2) That the accused unlawfully exercised the accused's authority to do so.

c. *Explanation.*

(1) *Scope.* This article prohibits improper acts by those empowered by the UCMJ to arrest, apprehend, or confine. *See* Articles 7 and 9; R.C.M. 302, 304, 305, and 1103, and paragraph 2 and subparagraph 5.b., Part V. It does not apply to private acts of false imprisonment or unlawful restraint of another's freedom of movement by one not acting under such a delegation of authority under the UCMJ.

(2) *No force required.* The apprehension, arrest, or confinement must be against the will of the person restrained, but force is not required.

(3) *Defense.* A reasonable belief held by the person imposing restraint that it is lawful is a defense.

d. *Maximum punishment.* Dishonorable discharge, forfeiture of all pay and allowances, and confinement for 3 years.

e. *Sample specification.*

In that __________ (personal jurisdiction data) (subject-matter jurisdiction, if required), did, (at/on board—location), on or about _____ 20 __, unlawfully (apprehend __________) (place __________ in arrest) (confine __________ in __________).

26. Article 98 (10 U.S.C. 898)—Misconduct as prisoner

a. *Text of statute.*

Any person subject to this chapter who, while in the hands of the enemy in time of war—

(1) for the purpose of securing favorable treatment by his captors acts without proper authority in a manner contrary to law, custom, or regulation, to the detriment of others of whatever nationality held by the enemy as civilian or military prisoners; or

(2) while in a position of authority over such persons maltreats them without justifiable cause;

shall be punished as a court-martial may direct.

b. *Elements.*

(1) *Acting without authority to the detriment of another for the purpose of securing favorable treatment.*

(a) That without proper authority the accused acted in a manner contrary to law, custom, or regulation;

(b) That the act was committed while the accused was in the hands of the enemy in time of war;

(c) That the act was done for the purpose of securing favorable treatment of the accused by the captors; and

(d) That other prisoners held by the enemy, either military or civilian, suffered some detriment because of the accused's act.

(2) *Maltreating prisoners while in a position of authority.*

(a) That the accused maltreated a prisoner held by the enemy;

(b) That the act occurred while the accused was in the hands of the enemy in time of war;

(c) That the accused held a position of authority over the person maltreated; and

(d) That the act was without justifiable cause.

c. *Explanation.*

(1) *Enemy.* For a discussion of "enemy," see subparagraph 27.c.(1)(b).

(2) *In time of war. See* R.C.M. 103(21).

(3) *Acting without authority to the detriment of another for the purpose of securing favorable treatment.*

(a) *Nature of offense.* Unauthorized conduct by a prisoner of war must be intended to result in improvement by the enemy of the accused's condition and must operate to the detriment of other prisoners either by way of closer confinement, reduced rations, physical punishment, or other harm. Examples of this conduct include reporting plans of escape being prepared by others or reporting secret food caches, equipment, or arms. The conduct of the prisoner must be contrary to law, custom, or regulation.

(b) *Escape.* Escape from the enemy is authorized by custom. An escape or escape attempt which results in closer confinement or other measures against fellow prisoners still in the hands of the enemy is not an offense under this article.

(4) *Maltreating prisoners while in a position of authority.*

(a) *Authority.* The source of authority is not material. It may arise from the military rank of the accused or—despite Service regulations or customs to the contrary—designation by the captor authorities, or voluntary election or selection by other prisoners for their self-government.

(b) *Maltreatment.* The maltreatment must be real, although not necessarily physical, and it must be without justifiable cause. Abuse of an inferior by inflammatory and derogatory words may, through mental anguish, constitute this offense.

d. *Maximum punishment.* Any punishment other than death that a court-martial may direct.

e. *Sample specifications.*

(1) *Acting without authority to the detriment of another for the purpose of securing favorable treatment.*

In that __________ (personal jurisdiction data), while in the hands of the enemy, did, (at/on board—location) (subject-matter jurisdiction, if required), on or about _____ 20 __, a time of war, without proper authority and for the purpose of securing favorable treatment by (his) (her) captors, (report to the commander of Camp __________ the preparations by __________, a prisoner at said camp, to escape, as a result of which report the said _____ was placed in solitary confinement) (_____).

(2) *Maltreating prisoner while in a position of authority.*

In that __________ (personal jurisdiction data), did, (at/on board—location) (subject-matter jurisdiction, if required), on or about _____ 20 __, a time of war, while in the hands of the enemy and in a position of authority over __________, a prisoner at __________, as (officer in charge of prisoners at _____) (_____), maltreat the said _____ by (depriving (him) (her) of _____) (_____), without justifiable cause.

27. Article 99 (10 U.S.C. 899)—Misbehavior before the enemy

a. *Text of statute.*

Any member of the armed forces who before or in the presence of the enemy—

(1) runs away;

(2) shamefully abandons, surrenders, or delivers up any command, unit, place, or military property which it is his duty to defend;

(3) through disobedience, neglect, or intentional misconduct endangers the safety of any such command, unit, place, or military property;

(4) casts away his arms or ammunition;

(5) is guilty of cowardly conduct;

(6) quits his place of duty to plunder or pillage;

(7) causes false alarms in any command, unit, or place under control of the armed forces;

(8) willfully fails to do his utmost to encounter, engage, capture, or destroy any enemy troops, combatants, vessels, aircraft, or any other thing, which it is his duty so to encounter, engage, capture, or destroy; or

(9) does not afford all practicable relief and assistance to any troops, combatants, vessels, or aircraft of the armed forces belonging to the United States or their allies when engaged in battle;

shall be punished by death or such other punishment as a court-martial may direct.

b. *Elements.*

(1) *Running away.*

(a) That the accused was before or in the presence of the enemy;

(b) That the accused misbehaved by running away; and

(c) That the accused intended to avoid actual or impending combat with the enemy by running away.

(2) *Shamefully abandoning, surrendering, or delivering up command.*

(a) That the accused was charged by orders or circumstances with the duty to defend a certain command, unit, place, ship, or military property;

(b) That, without justification, the accused shamefully abandoned, surrendered, or delivered up that command, unit, place, ship, or military property; and

(c) That this act occurred while the accused was before or in the presence of the enemy.

(3) *Endangering safety of a command, unit, place, ship, or military property.*

(a) That it was the duty of the accused to defend a certain command, unit, place, ship, or certain military property;

(b) That the accused committed certain disobedience, neglect, or intentional misconduct;

(c) That the accused thereby endangered the safety of the command, unit, place, ship, or military property; and

(d) That this act occurred while the accused was before or in the presence of the enemy.

(4) *Casting away arms or ammunition.*

(a) That the accused was before or in the presence of the enemy; and

(b) That the accused cast away certain arms or ammunition.

(5) *Cowardly conduct.*

(a) That the accused committed an act of cowardice;

(b) That this conduct occurred while the accused was before or in the presence of the enemy; and

(c) That this conduct was the result of fear.

(6) *Quitting place of duty to plunder or pillage.*

(a) That the accused was before or in the presence of the enemy;

(b) That the accused quit the accused's place of duty; and

(c) That the accused's intention in quitting was to plunder or pillage public or private property.

(7) *Causing false alarms.*

(a) That an alarm was caused in a certain command, unit, or place under control of the armed forces of the United States;

(b) That the accused caused the alarm;

(c) That the alarm was caused without any reasonable or sufficient justification or excuse; and

(d) That this act occurred while the accused was before or in the presence of the enemy.

(8) *Willfully failing to do utmost to encounter enemy.*

(a) That the accused was serving before or in the presence of the enemy;

(b) That the accused had a duty to encounter, engage, capture, or destroy certain enemy troops, combatants, vessels, aircraft, or a certain other thing; and

(c) That the accused willfully failed to do the utmost to perform that duty.

(9) *Failing to afford relief and assistance.*

(a) That certain troops, combatants, vessels, or aircraft of the armed forces belonging to the United States or an ally of the United States were engaged in battle and required relief and assistance;

(b) That the accused was in a position and able to render relief and assistance to these troops, combatants, vessels, or aircraft, without jeopardy to the accused's mission;

(c) That the accused failed to afford all practicable relief and assistance; and

(d) That, at the time, the accused was before or in the presence of the enemy.

c. *Explanation.*

(1) *Running away.*

(a) *Running away.* "Running away" means an unauthorized departure to avoid actual or impending combat. It need not, however, be the result of fear, and there is no requirement that the accused literally run.

(b) *Enemy.* Enemy includes organized forces of the enemy in time of war, any hostile body that our forces may be opposing, such as a rebellious mob or a band of renegades, and includes civilians as well as members of military organizations. Enemy is not restricted to the enemy government or its armed forces. All the citizens of one belligerent are enemies of the government and all the citizens of the other.

(c) *Before or in the presence of the enemy.* Whether a person is before or in the presence of the enemy is a question of tactical relation, not distance. For example, a member of an antiaircraft gun crew charged with opposing anticipated attack from the air, or a member of a unit about to move into combat may be before the enemy although miles from the enemy lines. On the other hand, an organization some distance from the front or immediate area of combat which is not a part of a tactical operation then going on or in immediate prospect is not "before or in the presence of the enemy" within the meaning of this article.

(2) *Shamefully abandoning, surrendering, or delivering up of command.*

(a) *Scope.* This provision concerns primarily commanders chargeable with responsibility for defending a command, unit, place, ship or military property. Abandonment by a subordinate would ordinarily be charged as running away.

(b) *Shameful.* Surrender or abandonment without justification is shameful within the meaning of this article.

(c) *Surrender; deliver up.* "Surrender" and "deliver up" are synonymous for the purposes of this article.

(d) *Justification.* Surrender or abandonment of a command, unit, place, ship, or military property by a person charged with its defense can be justified only by the utmost necessity or extremity.

(3) *Endangering safety of a command, unit, place, ship, or military property.*

(a) *Neglect.* Neglect is the absence of conduct which would have been taken by a reasonably careful person in the same or similar circumstances.

(b) *Intentional misconduct.* Intentional misconduct does not include a mere error in judgment.

(4) *Casting away arms or ammunition.* Self-explanatory.

(5) *Cowardly conduct.*

(a) *Cowardice.* Cowardice is misbehavior motivated by fear.

(b) *Fear.* Fear is a natural feeling of apprehension when going into battle. The mere display of apprehension does not constitute this offense.

(c) *Nature of offense.* Refusal or abandonment of a performance of duty before or in the presence of the enemy as a result of fear constitutes this offense.

(d) *Defense.* Genuine and extreme illness, not generated by cowardice, is a defense.

(6) *Quitting place of duty to plunder or pillage.*

(a) *Place of duty.* Place of duty includes any place of duty, whether permanent or temporary, fixed or mobile.

(b) *Plunder or pillage.* "Plunder or pillage" means to seize or appropriate public or private property unlawfully.

(c) *Nature of offense.* The essence of this offense is quitting the place of duty with intent to plunder or pillage. Merely quitting with that purpose is sufficient, even if the intended misconduct is not done.

(7) *Causing false alarms.* This provision covers spreading of false or disturbing rumors or reports, as well as the false giving of established alarm signals.

(8) *Willfully failing to do utmost to encounter enemy.* Willfully refusing a lawful order to go on a combat patrol may violate this provision.

(9) *Failing to afford relief and assistance.*

(a) *All practicable relief and assistance.* "All practicable relief and assistance" means all relief and assistance which should be afforded within the limitations imposed upon a person by reason of that person's own specific tasks or mission.

(b) *Nature of offense.* This offense is limited to a failure to afford relief and assistance to forces engaged in battle.

d. *Maximum punishment.* All offenses under Article 99. Death or such other punishment as a court-martial may direct.

e. *Sample specifications.*

(1) *Running away.*

In that __________ (personal jurisdiction data), did, (at/on board—location) (subject-matter jurisdiction, if required), on or about _____ 20 __, (before) (in the presence of) the enemy, run away (from (his) (her) company) (and hide) (_____), (and did not return until after the engagement had been concluded) (__________).

(2) *Shamefully abandoning, surrendering, or delivering up command.*

In that __________ (personal jurisdiction data), did, (at/on board—location) (subject-matter jurisdiction, if required), on or about _____ 20 __, (before) (in the presence of) the enemy, shamefully (abandon) (surrender) (deliver up) __________, which it was (his) (her) duty to defend.

(3) *Endangering safety of a command, unit, place, ship, or military property.*

In that __________ (personal jurisdiction data), did, (at/on board—location) (subject-matter jurisdiction, if required), on or about _____ 20 __, (before) (in the presence of) the enemy, endanger the safety of __________, which it was (his) (her) duty to defend, by (disobeying an order from __________ to engage the enemy) (neglecting (his) (her) duty as a sentinel by engaging in a card game while on (his) (her) post) (intentional misconduct in that (he) (she) became drunk and fired flares, thus revealing the location of (his) (her) unit) (_____).

(4) *Casting away arms or ammunition.*

In that __________ (personal jurisdiction data), did, (at/on board—location) (subject-matter jurisdiction, if required), on or about _____ 20 __, (before) (in the presence of) the enemy, cast away (his) (her) (rifle) (ammunition) (_____).

(5) *Cowardly conduct.*

In that __________ (personal jurisdiction data), (at/on board—location) (subject-matter jurisdiction, if required), on or about _____ 20 __, (before) (in the presence of) the enemy, was guilty of cowardly conduct as a result of fear, in that ____________.

(6) *Quitting place of duty to plunder or pillage.*

In that __________ (personal jurisdiction data), did, (at/on board—location) (subject-matter jurisdiction, if required), on or about _____ 20 __, (before) (in the presence of) the enemy, quit (his) (her) place of duty for the purpose of (plundering) (pillaging) (plundering and pillaging).

(7) *Causing false alarms.*

In that __________ (personal jurisdiction data), did, (at/on board—location) (subject-matter jurisdiction, if required), on or about _____ 20 __, (before) (in the presence of) the enemy, cause a false alarm in (Fort _____) (the said ship) (the camp) (_____) by (needlessly and without authority (causing the call to arms to be sounded) (sounding the general alarm) (_____).

(8) *Willfully failing to do utmost to encounter enemy.*

In that __________ (personal jurisdiction data), being (before) (in the presence of) the enemy, did, (at/on board—location) (subject-matter jurisdiction, if required), on or about _____ 20 __, by, (ordering (his) (her) troops to halt their advance) (__________), willfully fail to do (his) (her) utmost to (encounter) (engage) (capture) (destroy), as it was (his) (her) duty to do, (certain enemy troops which were in retreat) (__________).

(9) *Failing to afford relief and assistance.*

In that __________ (personal jurisdiction data), did, (at/on board—location) (subject-matter jurisdiction, if required), on or about _____ 20 __, (before) (in the presence of) the enemy, fail to afford all practicable relief and assistance to (the USS __________, which was engaged in battle and had run aground, in that (he) (she) failed to take her in tow) (certain troops of the ground forces of __________, which were engaged in battle and were pinned down by enemy fire, in that (he) (she) failed to furnish air cover) (__________) as (he) (she) properly should have done.

28. Article 100 (10 U.S.C. 900)—Subordinate compelling surrender

a. *Text of statute.*

Any person subject to this chapter who compels or attempts to compel the commander of any place, vessel, aircraft, or other military property, or of any

body of members of the armed forces, to give it up to an enemy or to abandon it, or who strikes the colors or flag to an enemy without proper authority, shall be punished by death or such other punishment as a court-martial may direct.

b. *Elements.*

(1) *Compelling surrender.*

(a) That a certain person was in command of a certain place, vessel, aircraft, or other military property or of a body of members of the armed forces;

(b) That the accused did an overt act which was intended to and did compel that commander to give it up to the enemy or abandon it; and

(c) That the place, vessel, aircraft, or other military property or body of members of the armed forces was actually given up to the enemy or abandoned.

(2) *Attempting to compel surrender.*

(a) That a certain person was in command of a certain place, vessel, aircraft, or other military property or of a body of members of the armed forces;

(b) That the accused did a certain overt act;

(c) That the act was done with the intent to compel that commander to give up to the enemy or abandon the place, vessel, aircraft, or other military property or body of members of the armed forces;

(d) That the act amounted to more than mere preparation; and

(e) That the act apparently tended to bring about the compelling of surrender or abandonment.

(3) *Striking the colors or flag.*

(a) That there was an offer of surrender to an enemy;

(b) That this offer was made by striking the colors or flag to the enemy or in some other manner;

(c) That the accused made or was responsible for the offer; and

(d) That the accused did not have proper authority to make the offer.

c. *Explanation.*

(1) *Compelling surrender.*

(a) *Nature of offense.* The offenses under this article are similar to mutiny or attempted mutiny designed to bring about surrender or abandonment. Unlike some cases of mutiny, however, concert of action is not an essential element of the offenses under this article. The offense is not complete until the place, military property, or command is actually abandoned or given up to the enemy.

(b) *Surrender.* "Surrender" and "to give it up to an enemy" are synonymous.

(c) *Acts required.* The surrender or abandonment must be compelled or attempted to be compelled by acts rather than words.

(2) *Attempting to compel surrender.* The offense of attempting to compel a surrender or abandonment does not require actual abandonment or surrender, but there must be some act done with this purpose in view, even if it does not accomplish the purpose.

(3) *Striking the colors or flag.*

(a) *In general.* To "strike the colors or flag" is to haul down the colors or flag in the face of the enemy or to make any other offer of surrender. It is traditional wording for an act of surrender.

(b) *Nature of offense.* The offense is committed when one assumes the authority to surrender a military force or position when not authorized to do so either by competent authority or by the necessities of battle. If continued battle has become fruitless and it is impossible to communicate with higher authority, those facts will constitute proper authority to surrender. The offense may be committed whenever there is sufficient contact with the enemy to give the opportunity of making an offer of surrender and it is not necessary that an engagement with the enemy be in progress. It is unnecessary to prove that the offer was received by the enemy or that it was rejected or accepted. The sending of an emissary charged with making the offer or surrender is an act sufficient to prove the offer, even though the emissary does not reach the enemy.

(4) *Enemy.* For a discussion of "enemy," see subparagraph 27.c.(1)(b).

d. *Maximum punishment.* All offenses under Article 100. Death or such other punishment as a court-martial may direct.

e. *Sample specifications.*

(1) *Compelling surrender or attempting to compel surrender.*

In that __________ (personal jurisdiction data), did, (at/on board—location) (subject-matter jurisdiction, if required), on or about _____ 20 __, (attempt to) compel __________, the commander of __________, (to give up to the enemy) (to abandon) said __________, by __________.

(2) *Striking the colors or flag.*

In that __________ (personal jurisdiction data), did, (at/on board—location) (subject-matter jurisdiction, if required), on or about _____ 20 __, without proper authority, offer to surrender to the enemy by (striking the (colors) (flag)) (_____).

29. Article 101 (10 U.S.C. 901)—Improper use of countersign

a. *Text of statute.*

Any person subject to this chapter who in time of war discloses the parole or countersign to any person not entitled to receive it or who gives to another who is entitled to receive and use the parole or countersign a different parole or countersign from that which, to his knowledge, he was authorized and required to give, shall be punished by death or such other punishment as a court-martial may direct.

b. *Elements.*

(1) *Disclosing the parole or countersign to one not entitled to receive it.*

(a) That, in time of war, the accused disclosed the parole or countersign to a person, identified or unidentified; and

(b) That this person was not entitled to receive it.

(2) *Giving a parole or countersign different from that authorized.*

(a) That, in time of war, the accused knew that the accused was authorized and required to give a certain parole or countersign; and

(b) That the accused gave to a person entitled to receive and use this parole or countersign a different parole or countersign from that which the accused was authorized and required to give.

c. *Explanation.*

(1) *Countersign.* A countersign is a word, signal, or procedure given from the principal headquarters of a command to aid guards and sentinels in their scrutiny of persons who apply to pass the lines. It consists of a secret challenge and a password, signal, or procedure.

(2) *Parole.* A parole is a word used as a check on the countersign; it is given only to those who are entitled to inspect guards and to commanders of guards.

(3) *Who may receive countersign.* The class of persons entitled to receive the countersign or parole will expand and contract under the varying circumstances of war. Who these persons are will be determined largely, in any particular case, by the general or special orders under which the accused was acting. Before disclosing such a word, a person subject to military law must determine at that person's peril that the recipient is a person authorized to receive it.

(4) *Intent, motive, negligence, mistake, ignorance not defense.* The accused's intent or motive in disclosing the countersign or parole is immaterial to the issue of guilt, as is the fact that the disclosure was negligent or inadvertent. It is no defense that the accused did not know that the person to whom the countersign or parole was given was not entitled to receive it.

(5) *How accused received countersign or parole.* It is immaterial whether the accused had received the countersign or parole in the regular course of duty or whether it was obtained in some other way.

(6) *In time of war. See* R.C.M. 103(21).

d. *Maximum punishment.* Death or such other punishment as a court-martial may direct.

e. *Sample specifications.*

(1) *Disclosing the parole or countersign to one not entitled to receive it.*

In that __________ (personal jurisdiction data), did, (at/on board—location) (subject-matter jurisdiction, if required), on or about _____ 20 __, a time of war, disclose the (parole) (countersign), to wit: __________, to __________, a person who was not entitled to receive it.

(2) *Giving a parole or countersign different from that authorized.*

In that __________ (personal jurisdiction data), did, (at/on board—location) (subject-matter jurisdiction, if required), on or about _____ 20 __, a time of war, give to __________, a person entitled to receive and use the (parole) (countersign), a (parole) (countersign), namely: __________ which was different from that which, to (his) (her) knowledge, (he) (she) was authorized and required to give, to wit: __________.

30. Article 102 (10 U.S.C. 902)—Forcing a safeguard

a. *Text of statute.*

Any person subject to this chapter who forces a safeguard shall suffer death or such other punishment as a court-martial may direct.

b. *Elements.*

(1) That a safeguard had been issued or posted for the protection of a certain person or persons, place, or property;

(2) That the accused knew or should have known of the safeguard; and

(3) That the accused forced the safeguard.

c. *Explanation.*

(1) *Safeguard.* A safeguard is a detachment, guard, or detail posted by a commander for the protection of persons, places, or property of the enemy, or of a neutral affected by the relationship of belligerent forces in their prosecution of war or during circumstances amounting to a state of belligerency. The term also includes a written order left by a commander with an enemy subject or posted upon enemy property for the protection of that person or property. A safeguard is not a device adopted by a belligerent to protect its own property or nationals or to ensure order within its own forces, even if those forces are in a theater of combat operations, and the posting of guards or of off-limits signs does not establish a safeguard unless a commander takes those actions to protect enemy or neutral persons or property. The effect of a safeguard is to pledge the honor of the nation that the person or property shall be respected by the national armed forces.

(2) *Forcing a safeguard.* "Forcing a safeguard" means to perform an act or acts in violation of the protection of the safeguard.

(3) *Nature of offense.* Any trespass on the protection of the safeguard will constitute an offense under this article, whether the safeguard was imposed in time of war or in circumstances amounting to a state of belligerency short of a formal state of war.

(4) *Knowledge.* Actual knowledge of the safeguard is not required. It is sufficient if an accused should have known of the existence of the safeguard.

d. *Maximum punishment.* Death or such other punishment as a court-martial may direct.

e. *Sample specification.*

In that ________ (personal jurisdiction data), did, (at/on board—location) (subject-matter jurisdiction, if required), on or about _____ 20 __, force a safeguard, (known by (him) (her) to have been placed over the premises occupied by __________ at __________ by (overwhelming the guard posted for the protection of the same) (__________)) (__________).

31. Article 103 (10 U.S.C. 903)—Spies

a. *Text of statute.*

Any person who in time of war is found lurking as a spy or acting as a spy in or about any place, vessel, or aircraft, within the control or jurisdiction of any of the armed forces, or in or about any shipyard, any manufacturing or industrial plant, or any other place or institution engaged in work in aid of the prosecution of the war by the United States, or elsewhere, shall be tried by a general court-martial or by a military commission and on conviction shall be punished by death or such other punishment as a court-martial or a military commission may direct. This section does not apply to a military commission established under chapter 47A of this title.

b. *Elements.*

(1) That the accused was found in, about, or in and about a certain place, vessel, or aircraft within the control or jurisdiction of an armed force of the United States, or a shipyard, manufacturing or industrial plant, or other place or institution engaged in work in aid of the prosecution of the war by the United States, or elsewhere;

(2) That the accused was lurking, acting clandestinely or under false pretenses;

(3) That the accused was collecting or attempting to collect certain information;

(4) That the accused did so with the intent to convey this information to the enemy; and

(5) That this was done in time of war.

c. *Explanation.*

(1) *In time of war. See* R.C.M. 103(21).

(2) *Enemy.* For a discussion of "enemy," *see* subparagraph 27.c.(1)(b).

(3) *Scope of offense.* The words "any person" bring within the jurisdiction of general courts-martial and military commissions all persons of whatever nationality or status who commit spying.

(4) *Nature of offense.* A person can be a spy only when, acting clandestinely or under false pretenses, that person obtains or seeks to obtain information with the intent to convey it to a hostile party. It is not essential that the accused obtain the information sought or that it be communicated. The offense is complete with lurking or acting clandestinely or under false pretenses with intent to accomplish these objects.

(5) *Intent.* It is necessary to prove an intent to convey information to the enemy. This intent may be inferred from evidence of a deceptive insinuation of the accused among our forces, but evidence that the person had come within the lines for a comparatively innocent purpose, as to visit family or to reach friendly lines by assuming a disguise, is admissible to rebut this inference.

(6) *Persons not included under "spying."*

(a) Members of a military organization not wearing a disguise, dispatch drivers, whether members of a military organization or civilians, and persons in ships or aircraft who carry out their missions openly and who have penetrated enemy lines are not spies because, while they may have resorted to concealment, they have not acted under false pretenses.

(b) A spy who, after rejoining the armed forces to which the spy belongs, is later captured by the enemy incurs no responsibility for previous acts of spying.

(c) A person living in occupied territory who, without lurking, or acting clandestinely or under false pretenses, merely reports what is seen or heard through agents to the enemy may be charged under Article 103a with giving intelligence to or communicating with the enemy, but may not be charged under this article as being a spy.

d. *Maximum punishment.* Death or such other punishment as a court-martial or military commission may direct.

e. *Sample specification.*

In that _____ (personal jurisdiction data), was, (at/on board—location) (subject-matter jurisdiction, if required), on or about _____ 20 __, a time of war, found (lurking) (acting) as a spy (in) (about) (in and about) __________, (a (fortification) (port) (base) (vessel) (aircraft) (__________) within the (control) (jurisdiction) (control and jurisdiction) of an armed force of the United States, to wit: __________) (a (shipyard) (manufacturing plant) (industrial plant) (__________) engaged in work in aid of the prosecution of the war by the United States) (__________), for the purpose of (collecting) (attempting to collect) information in regard to the [(numbers) (resources) (operations) (__) of the armed forces of the United States] [(military production) (_____) of the United States] [_____], with intent to impart the same to the enemy.

32. Article 103a (10 U.S.C. 903a)—Espionage

a. *Text of statute.*

(a)(1) Any person subject to this chapter who, with intent or reason to believe that it is to be used to the injury of the United States or to the advantage of a foreign nation, communicates, delivers, or transmits, or attempts to communicate, deliver, or transmit, to any entity described in paragraph (2), either directly or indirectly, anything described in paragraph (3) shall be punished as a court-martial may direct, except that if the accused is found guilty of an offense that directly concerns (A) nuclear weaponry, military spacecraft or satellites, early warning systems, or other means of defense or retaliation against large scale attack, (B) war plans, (C) communications intelligence or cryptographic information, or (D) any other major weapons system or major element of defense strategy, the accused shall be punished by death or such other punishment as a court-martial may direct.

(2) An entity referred to in paragraph (1) is—

(A) a foreign government;

(B) a faction or party or military or naval force within a foreign country, whether recognized or unrecognized by the United States; or

(C) a representative, officer, agent, employee, subject, or citizen of such a government, faction, party, or force.

(3) A thing referred to in paragraph (1) is a document, writing, code book, signal book, sketch, photograph, photographic negative, blueprint, plan, map, model, note, instrument, appliance, or information relating to the national defense.

(b)(1) No person may be sentenced by court-martial to suffer death for an offense under this section (article) unless—

(A) the members of the court-martial unanimously find at least one of the aggravating factors set out in subsection (c); and

(B) the members unanimously determine that any extenuating or mitigating circumstances are substantially outweighed by any aggravating circumstances, including the aggravating factors set out in subsection (c).

(2) Findings under this subsection may be based on—

(A) evidence introduced on the issue of guilt or innocence;

(B) evidence introduced during the sentencing proceeding; or

(C) all such evidence.

(3) The accused shall be given broad latitude to present matters in extenuation and mitigation.

(c) A sentence of death may be adjudged by a court-martial for an offense under this section (article) only if the members unanimously find, beyond a reasonable doubt, one or more of the following aggravating factors:

(1) The accused has been convicted of another offense involving espionage or treason for which either a sentence of death or imprisonment for life was authorized by statute.

(2) In the commission of the offense, the accused knowingly created a grave risk of substantial damage to the national security.

(3) In the commission of the offense, the accused knowingly created a grave risk of death to another person.

(4) Any other factor that may be prescribed by the President by regulations under section 836 of this title (article 36).

b. *Elements.*

(1) *Espionage.*

(a) That the accused communicated, delivered, or transmitted any document, writing, code book, signal book, sketch, photograph, photographic negative, blueprint, plan, map, model, note, instrument, appliance, or information relating to the national defense;

(b) That this matter was communicated, delivered, or transmitted to any foreign government, or to any faction or party or military or naval force within a foreign country, whether recognized or unrecognized by the United States, or to any representative, officer, agent, employee, subject or citizen thereof, either directly or indirectly; and

(c) That the accused did so with intent or reason to believe that such matter would be used to the injury of the United States or to the advantage of a foreign nation.

(2) *Attempted espionage.*

(a) That the accused did a certain overt act;

(b) That the act was done with the intent to commit the offense of espionage;

(c) That the act amounted to more than mere preparation; and

(d) That the act apparently tended to bring about the offense of espionage.

(3) *Espionage as a capital offense.*

(a) That the accused committed espionage or attempted espionage; and

(b) That the offense directly concerned (1) nuclear weaponry, military spacecraft or satellites, early warning systems, or other means of defense or retaliation against large scale attack, (2) war plans, (3) communications intelligence or cryptographic information, or (4) any other major weapons system or major element of defense strategy.

c. *Explanation.*

(1) *Intent.* "Intent or reason to believe that the information is to be used to the injury of the United States or to the advantage of a foreign nation" means that the accused acted in bad faith and without lawful authority with respect to information that is not lawfully accessible to the public.

(2) *National defense information.* "Instrument, appliance, or information relating to the national defense" includes the full range of modern technology and matter that may be developed in the future, including chemical or biological agents, computer technology, and other matter related to the national defense.

(3) *Espionage as a capital offense.* Capital punishment is authorized if the government alleges and proves that the offense directly concerned (1) nuclear weaponry, military spacecraft or satellites, early warning systems, or other means of defense or retaliation against large scale attack, (2) war plans, (3) communications intelligence or cryptographic information, or (4) any other major weapons system or major element of defense strategy. See R.C.M. 1004 concerning presentencing proceedings in capital cases.

d. *Maximum punishment.*

(1) *Espionage as a capital offense.* Death or such other punishment as a court-martial may direct.

(2) *Espionage or attempted espionage.* Any punishment, other than death, that a court-martial may direct.

e. *Sample specification.*

In that __________ (personal jurisdiction data), did, (at/on board—location) (subject-matter jurisdiction, if required), on or about _____ 20 __, with intent or reason to believe it would be used to the injury of the United States or to the advantage of __________, a foreign nation, (attempt to) (communicate) (deliver) (transmit) __________ (description of item), (a document) (a writing) (a code book) (a sketch) (a photograph) (a photographic negative) (a blueprint) (a plan) (a map) (a model) (a note) (an instrument) (an appliance) (information) relating to the national defense, [(which directly concerned (nuclear weaponry) (military spacecraft) (military satellites) (early warning systems) (__________, a means of defense or retaliation against a large scale attack) (war plans) (communications intelligence) (cryptographic information) (_____, a major weapons system) (_____, a major element of defense strategy)] to __________ ((a representative of) (an officer of) (an agent of) (an employee of) (a subject of) (a citizen of)) ((a foreign government) (a faction within a foreign country) (a party within a foreign country) (a military force within a foreign country) (a naval force within a foreign country)) (indirectly by __________).

33. Article 103b (10 U.S.C. 903b)—Aiding the enemy

a. *Text of statute.*

Any person who—

(1) aids, or attempts to aid, the enemy with arms, ammunition, supplies, money, or other things; or

(2) without proper authority, knowingly harbors or protects or gives intelligence to, or communicates or corresponds with or holds any intercourse with the enemy, either directly or indirectly;

shall suffer death or such other punishment as a court-martial or military commission may direct. This section does not apply to a military commission established under chapter 47A of this title.

b. *Elements.*

(1) *Aiding the enemy.*

(a) That the accused aided the enemy; and

(b) That the accused did so with certain arms, ammunition, supplies, money, or other things.

(2) *Attempting to aid the enemy.*

(a) That the accused did a certain overt act;

(b) That the act was done with the intent to aid the enemy with certain arms, ammunition, supplies, money, or other things;

(c) That the act amounted to more than mere preparation; and

(d) That the act apparently tended to bring about the offense of aiding the enemy with certain arms, ammunition, supplies, money, or other things.

(3) *Harboring or protecting the enemy.*

(a) That the accused, without proper authority, harbored or protected a person;

(b) That the person so harbored or protected was the enemy; and

(c) That the accused knew that the person so harbored or protected was an enemy.

(4) *Giving intelligence to the enemy.*

(a) That the accused, without proper authority, knowingly gave intelligence information to the enemy; and

(b) That the intelligence information was true, or implied the truth, at least in part.

(5) *Communicating with the enemy.*

(a) That the accused, without proper authority, communicated, corresponded, or held intercourse with the enemy; and

(b) That the accused knew that the accused was communicating, corresponding, or holding intercourse with the enemy.

c. *Explanation.*

(1) *Scope of Article 103b.* This article denounces offenses by all persons whether or not otherwise subject to military law. Offenders may be tried by court-martial or by military commission.

(2) *Enemy.* For a discussion of "enemy," *see* subparagraph 27.c.(1)(b).

(3) *Aiding or attempting to aid the enemy.* It is not a violation of this article to furnish prisoners of war subsistence, quarters, and other comforts or aid to which they are lawfully entitled.

(4) *Harboring or protecting the enemy.*

(a) *Nature of offense.* An enemy is harbored or protected when, without proper authority, that enemy is shielded, either physically or by use of any artifice, aid, or representation from any injury or misfortune which in the chance of war may occur.

(b) *Knowledge.* Actual knowledge is required, but may be proved by circumstantial evidence.

(5) *Giving intelligence to the enemy.*

(a) *Nature of offense.* Giving intelligence to the enemy is a particular case of corresponding with the enemy made more serious by the fact that the communication contains intelligence that may be useful to the enemy for any of the many reasons that make information valuable to belligerents. This intelligence may be conveyed by direct or indirect means.

(b) *Intelligence.* Intelligence imports that the information conveyed is true or implies the truth, at least in part.

(c) *Knowledge.* Actual knowledge is required but may be proved by circumstantial evidence.

(6) *Communicating with the enemy.*

(a) *Nature of the offense.* No unauthorized communication, correspondence, or intercourse with the enemy is permissible. The intent, content, and method of the communication, correspondence, or intercourse are immaterial. No response or receipt by the enemy is required. The offense is complete the moment the communication, correspondence, or intercourse issues from the accused. The communication, correspondence, or intercourse may be conveyed directly or indirectly. A prisoner of war may violate this Article by engaging in unauthorized communications with the enemy. *See* also subparagraph 26.c.(3).

(b) *Knowledge.* Actual knowledge is required but may be proved by circumstantial evidence.

(c) *Citizens of neutral powers.* Citizens of neutral powers resident in or visiting invaded or occupied territory can claim no immunity from the customary laws of war relating to communication with the enemy. 12A.

d. *Maximum punishment.*

Death or such other punishment as a court-martial or military commission may direct.

e. *Sample specifications.*

(1) *Aiding or attempting to aid the enemy.*

In that __________ (personal jurisdiction data), did, (at/on board—location) (subject-matter jurisdiction, if required), on or about _____ 20 __, (attempt to) aid the enemy with (arms) (ammunition) (supplies) (money) (_____), by (furnishing and delivering to _____, members of the enemy's armed forces _____) (____).

(2) *Harboring or protecting the enemy.*

In that __________ (personal jurisdiction data), did, (at/on board—location) (subject-matter jurisdiction, if required), on or about _____ 20 __, without proper authority, knowingly (harbor) (protect) __________, an enemy, by (concealing the said _____ in (his) (her) house) (_____).

(3) *Giving intelligence to the enemy.*

In that __________ (personal jurisdiction data), did, (at/on board—location) (subject-matter jurisdiction, if required), on or about _____ 20 __, without proper authority, knowingly give intelligence to the enemy, by (informing a patrol of the enemy's forces of the whereabouts of a military patrol of the United States forces) (____).

(4) *Communicating with the enemy.*

In that __________ (personal jurisdiction data), did, (at/on board—location) (subject-matter jurisdiction, if required), on or about _____ 20 __, without proper authority, knowingly (communicate with) (correspond with) (hold intercourse with) the enemy (by writing and transmitting secretly through the lines to one __________, whom (he) (she), the said __________, knew to be (an officer of the enemy's armed forces) (_____) a communication in words and figures substantially as follows, to wit: _____) (indirectly by publishing in _____, a newspaper published at _____, a communication in words and figures as follows, to wit: _____, which communication was intended to reach the enemy) (_____).

34. Article 104 (10 U.S.C. 904)—Public records offenses

a. *Text of statute.*

Any person subject to this chapter who, willfully and unlawfully—

(1) alters, conceals, removes, mutilates, obliterates, or destroys a public record; or

(2) takes a public record with the intent to alter, conceal, remove, mutilate, obliterate, or destroy the public record;

shall be punished as a court-martial may direct.

b. *Elements.*

(1) That the accused altered, concealed, removed, mutilated, obliterated, destroyed, or took with the intent to alter, conceal, remove, mutilate, obliterate, or destroy, a certain public record; and

(2) That the act of the accused was willful and unlawful.

c. *Explanation.* "Public records" include records, reports, statements, or data compilations, in any form, of public offices or agencies, setting forth the activities of the office or agency, or matters observed pursuant to duty imposed by law as to which matters there was a duty to report. "Public records" include classified matters.

d. *Maximum punishment.* Dishonorable discharge, forfeiture of all pay and allowances, and confinement for 3 years.

e. *Sample specification.*

In that __________ (personal jurisdiction data), did, (at/on board—location) (subject-matter jurisdiction data, if required), on or about _____ 20 __, willfully and unlawfully [(alter) (conceal) (remove) (mutilate) (obliterate) (destroy)] [take with intent to (alter) (conceal) (remove) (mutilate) (obliterate) (destroy)] a public record, to wit: __________.

35. Article 104a (10 U.S.C. 904a)—Fraudulent enlistment, appointment, or separation

a. *Text of statute.*

Any person who—

(1) procures his own enlistment or appointment in the armed forces by knowingly false representation or deliberate concealment as to his qualifications for that enlistment or appointment and receives pay or allowances thereunder; or

(2) procures his own separation from the armed forces by knowingly false representation or deliberate concealment as to his eligibility for that separation;

shall be punished as a court-martial may direct.

b. *Elements.*

(1) *Fraudulent enlistment or appointment.*

(a) That the accused was enlisted or appointed in an armed force;

(b) That the accused knowingly misrepresented or deliberately concealed a certain material fact or facts regarding qualifications of the accused for enlistment or appointment;

(c) That the accused's enlistment or appointment was obtained or procured by that knowingly false representation or deliberate concealment; and

(d) That under this enlistment or appointment that accused received pay or allowances or both.

(2) *Fraudulent separation.*

(a) That the accused was separated from an armed force;

(b) That the accused knowingly misrepresented or deliberately concealed a certain material fact or facts about the accused's eligibility for separation; and

(c) That the accused's separation was obtained or procured by that knowingly false representation or deliberate concealment.

c. *Explanation.*

(1) *In general.* A fraudulent enlistment, appointment, or separation is one procured by either a knowingly false representation as to any of the qualifications prescribed by law, regulation, or orders for the specific enlistment, appointment, or separation, or a deliberate concealment as to any of those disqualifications. Matters that may be material to an enlistment, appointment, or separation include any information used by the recruiting, appointing, or separating officer in reaching a decision as to enlistment, appointment, or separation in any particular case, and any information that normally would have been so considered had it been provided to that officer.

(2) *Receipt of pay or allowances.* A member of the armed forces who enlists or accepts an appointment without being regularly separated from a prior enlistment or appointment should be charged under Article 104a only if that member has received pay or allowances under the fraudulent enlistment or appointment. Acceptance of food, clothing, shelter, or transportation from the Government constitutes receipt of allowances. However, whatever is furnished the accused while in custody, confinement, arrest, or other restraint pending trial for fraudulent enlistment or appointment is not considered an allowance. The receipt of pay or allowances may be proved by circumstantial evidence.

(3) *One offense.* One who procures one's own enlistment, appointment, or separation by several misrepresentations or concealment as to qualifications for the one enlistment, appointment, or separation so procured, commits only one offense under Article 104a.

d. *Maximum punishment.*

(1) Fraudulent enlistment or appointment. Dishonorable discharge, forfeiture of all pay and allowances, and confinement for 2 years.

(2) Fraudulent separation. Dishonorable discharge, forfeiture of all pay and allowances, and confinement for 5 years.

e. *Sample specifications.*

(1) *For fraudulent enlistment or appointment.*

In that __________ (personal jurisdiction data), did, (at/on board—location) (subject-matter jurisdiction, if required), on or about _____ 20 __, by means of [knowingly false representations that (here state the fact or facts material to qualification for enlistment or appointment which were represented), when in fact (here state the true fact or facts)] [deliberate concealment of the fact that (here state the fact or facts disqualifying the accused for enlistment or appointment which were concealed)], procure himself/herself to be (enlisted as a __________) (appointed as a __________) in the (here state the armed force in which the accused procured the enlistment or appointment), and did thereafter, (at/on board—location), receive (pay) (allowances) (pay and allowances) under the enlistment) (appointment) so procured.

(2) *For fraudulent separation.*

In that __________ (personal jurisdiction data), did, (at/on board—location) (subject-matter jurisdiction, if required), on or about _____ 20 __, by means of [knowingly false representations that (here state the fact or facts material to eligibility for separation which were represented), when in fact (here state the true fact or facts)] [deliberate concealment of the fact that (here state the fact or facts concealed which made the accused ineligible for separation)], procure himself/herself to be separated from the (here state the armed force from which the accused procured (his) (her) separation).

36. Article 104b (10 U.S.C. 904b)—Unlawful enlistment, appointment, or separation

a. *Text of statute.*

Any person subject to this chapter who effects an enlistment or appointment in or a separation from the armed forces of any person who is known to him to be ineligible for that enlistment, appointment, or separation because it is prohibited by law, regulation, or order shall be punished as a court-martial may direct.

b. *Elements.*

(1) That the accused effected the enlistment, appointment, or separation of the person named;

(2) That this person was ineligible for this enlistment, appointment, or separation because it was prohibited by law, regulation, or order; and

(3) That the accused knew of the ineligibility at the time of the enlistment, appointment, or separation.

c. *Explanation.* It must be proved that the enlistment, appointment, or separation was prohibited by law, regulation, or order when effected and that the accused then knew that the person enlisted, appointed, or separated was ineligible for the enlistment, appointment, or separation.

d. *Maximum punishment.* Dishonorable discharge, forfeiture of all pay and allowances, and confinement for 5 years.

e. *Sample specification.*

In that __________ (personal jurisdiction data), did, (at/on board—location) (subject-matter jurisdiction, if required), on or about _____ 20 __, effect [the (enlistment) (appointment) of __________ as a __________ in (here state the armed force in which the person was enlisted or appointed)] [the separation of __________ from (here state the armed force from which the person was separated)], then well knowing that the said __________ was ineligible for such (enlistment) (appointment) (separation) because (here state facts whereby the enlistment, appointment, or separation was prohibited by law, regulation, or order).

37. Article 105 (10 U.S.C. 905)—Forgery

a. *Text of statute.*

Any person subject to this chapter who, with intent to defraud—

(1) falsely makes or alters any signature to, or any part of, any writing which would, if genuine, apparently impose a legal liability on another or change his legal right or liability to his prejudice; or

(2) utters, offers, issues, or transfers such a writing, known by him to be so made or altered;

is guilty of forgery and shall be punished as a court-martial may direct.

b. *Elements.*

(1) *Forgery—making or altering.*

(a) That the accused falsely made or altered a certain signature or writing;

(b) That the signature or writing was of a nature which would, if genuine, apparently impose a legal liability on another or change another's legal rights or liabilities to that person's prejudice; and

(c) That the false making or altering was with the intent to defraud.

(2) *Forgery—uttering.*

(a) That a certain signature or writing was falsely made or altered;

(b) That the signature or writing was of a nature which would, if genuine, apparently impose a legal liability on another or change another's legal rights or liabilities to that person's prejudice;

(c) That the accused uttered, offered, issued, or transferred the signature or writing;

(d) That at such time the accused knew that the signature or writing had been falsely made or altered; and

(e) That the uttering, offering, issuing or transferring was with the intent to defraud.

c. *Explanation.*

(1) *In general.* Forgery may be committed either by falsely making a writing or by knowingly uttering a falsely made writing. There are three elements common to both aspects of forgery: a writing falsely made or altered; an apparent capability of the writing as falsely made or altered to impose a legal liability on another or to change another's legal rights or liabilities to that person's prejudice; and an intent to defraud.

(2) *False.* "False" refers not to the contents of the writing or to the facts stated therein but to the making or altering of it. Hence, forgery is not committed by the genuine making of a false instrument even when made with intent to defraud. A person who, with intent to defraud, signs that person's own signature as the maker of a check drawn on a bank in which that person does not have money or credit does not commit forgery. Although the check falsely represents the existence of the account, it is what it purports to be, a check drawn by the actual maker, and therefore it is not falsely made. *But see* paragraph 70. Likewise, if a person makes a false signature of another to an instrument, but adds the word "by" with that person's own signature thus indicating authority to sign, the offense is not forgery even if no such authority exists. False recitals of fact in a genuine document, as an aircraft flight report which is "padded" by the one preparing it, do not make the writing a forgery. *But see* paragraph 41 concerning false official statements.

(3) *Signatures.* Signing the name of another to an instrument having apparent legal efficacy without authority and with intent to defraud is forgery as the signature is falsely made. The distinction is that in this case the falsely made signature purports to be the act of one other than the actual signer. Likewise, a forgery may be committed by a person signing that person's own name to an instrument. For example, when a check payable to the order of a certain person comes into the hands of another of the same name, forgery is committed if, knowing the check to be another's, that person indorses it with that person's own name intending to defraud. Forgery may also be committed by signing a fictitious name, as when Roe makes a check payable to Roe and signs it with a fictitious name—Doe—as drawer.

(4) *Nature of writing.* The writing must be one which would, if genuine, apparently impose a legal liability on another, as a check or promissory note, or change that person's legal rights or liabilities to that person's prejudice, as a receipt. Some other instruments which may be the subject of forgery are orders for the delivery of money or goods, railroad tickets, and military orders directing travel. A writing falsely "made" includes an instrument that may be partially or entirely printed, engraved, written with a pencil, or made by photography or other device. A writing may be falsely "made" by materially altering an existing writing, by filling in a paper signed in blank, or by signing an instrument already written. With respect to the apparent legal efficacy of the writing falsely made or altered, the writing must appear either on its face or from extrinsic facts to impose a legal liability on another, or to change a legal right or liability to the prejudice of another. If under all the circumstances the instrument has neither real nor apparent legal efficacy, there is no forgery. Thus, the false making with intent to defraud of an instrument affirmatively invalid on its face is not forgery nor is the false making or altering, with intent to defraud, of a writing which could not impose a legal liability, as a mere letter of introduction. However, the false making of another's signature on an instrument with intent to defraud is forgery, even if there is no resemblance to the genuine signature and the name is misspelled.

(5) *Intent to defraud. See* subparagraph 70.c.(14). The intent to defraud need not be directed toward anyone in particular nor be for the advantage of the offender. It is immaterial that nobody was actually defrauded, or that no further step was made toward carrying out the intent to defraud other than the false making or altering of a writing.

(6) *Alteration.* The alteration must effect a material change in the legal tenor of the writing. Thus, an alteration which apparently increases, diminishes, or discharges any obligation is material. Examples of material alterations in the case of a promissory note are changing the date, amount, or place of payment. If a genuine writing has been delivered to the accused and while in the accused's possession is later found to be

altered, it may be inferred that the writing was altered by the accused.

(7) *Uttering. See* subparagraph 70.c.(4).

d. *Maximum punishment.* Dishonorable discharge, forfeiture of all pay and allowances, and confinement for 5 years.

e. *Sample specifications.*

(1) *Forgery—making or altering.*

In that __________ (personal jurisdiction data), did, (at/on board—location) (subject-matter jurisdiction data, if required), on or about _____ 20 __, with intent to defraud, falsely [make (in its entirety) (the signature of __________ as an indorsement to) (the signature of _____ to) (_____) a certain (check) (writing) (_____) in the following words and figures, to wit: _____] [alter a certain (check) (writing) (_____) in the following words and figures, to wit: _____, by (adding thereto _____) (_____)], which said (check) (writing) (_____) would, if genuine, apparently operate to the legal harm of another [*and which _____ (could be) (was) used to the legal harm of _____, in that _____].

[*Note: This allegation should be used when the document specified is not one which by its nature would clearly operate to the legal prejudice of another—for example, an insurance application. The manner in which the document could be or was used to prejudice the legal rights of another should be alleged in the last blank.]

(2) *Forgery—uttering.*

In that __________ (personal jurisdiction data), did, (at/on board—location) (subject-matter jurisdiction data, if required), on or about _____ 20 __, with intent to defraud, (utter) (offer) (issue) (transfer) a certain (check) (writing) (__________) in the following words and figures, to wit: __________, a writing which would, if genuine, apparently operate to the legal harm of another, (which said (check) (writing) (_____)) (the signature to which said (check) (writing) (_____)) (_____) was, as (he) (she), the said _____, then well knew, falsely (made) (altered) (*and which _____ (could be) (was) used to the legal harm of _____, in that _____).

[*Note: *See* the note following (1), of subparagraph e.]

38. Article 105a (10 U.S.C. 905a)—False or unauthorized pass offenses

a. *Text of statute.*

(a) WRONGFUL MAKING, ALTERING, ETC.—Any person subject to this chapter who, wrongfully and falsely, makes, alters, counterfeits, or tampers with a military or official pass, permit, discharge certificate, or identification card shall be punished as a court-martial may direct.

(b) WRONGFUL SALE, ETC.—Any person subject to this chapter who wrongfully sells, gives, lends, or disposes of a false or unauthorized military or official pass, permit, discharge certificate, or identification card, knowing that the pass, permit, discharge certificate, or identification card is false or unauthorized, shall be punished as a court-martial may direct.

(c) WRONGFUL USE OR POSSESSION.—Any person subject to this chapter who wrongfully uses or possesses a false or unauthorized military or official pass, permit, discharge certificate, or identification card, knowing that the pass, permit, discharge certificate, or identification card is false or unauthorized, shall be punished as a court-martial may direct.

b. *Elements.*

(1) *Wrongful making, altering, counterfeiting, or tampering with a military or official pass, permit, discharge certificate, or identification card.*

(a) That the accused wrongfully and falsely made, altered, counterfeited, or tampered with a certain military or official pass, permit, discharge certificate, or identification card; and

(b) That the accused then knew that the pass, permit, discharge certificate, or identification card was false or unauthorized.

(2) *Wrongful sale, gift, loan, or disposition of a military or official pass, permit, discharge certificate, or identification card.*

(a) That the accused wrongfully sold, gave, loaned, or disposed of a certain military or official pass, permit, discharge certificate, or identification card;

(b) That the pass, permit, discharge certificate, or identification card was false or unauthorized; and

(c) That the accused then knew that the pass, permit, discharge certificate, or identification card was false or unauthorized.

(3) *Wrongful use or possession of a false or unauthorized military or official pass, permit, discharge certificate, or identification card.*

(a) That the accused wrongfully used or possessed a certain military or official pass, permit, discharge certificate, or identification card;

(b) That the pass, permit, discharge certificate, or identification card was false or unauthorized; and

(c) That the accused then knew that the pass, permit, discharge certificate, or identification card was false or unauthorized.

[Note: When there is intent to defraud or deceive, add the following element:]

(d) That the accused used or possessed the pass, permit, discharge certificate, or identification card with intent to defraud or deceive.

c. *Explanation.*

(1) *In general.* Military or official pass, permit, discharge certificate, or identification card includes, as well as the more usual forms of these documents, all documents issued by any governmental agency for the purpose of identification and copies thereof.

(2) *Intent to defraud or deceive. See* subparagraphs 70.c.(14) and (15).

d. *Maximum punishment.*

(1) *Possessing or using with intent to defraud or deceive, or making, altering, counterfeiting, tampering with, or selling.* Dishonorable discharge, forfeiture of all pay and allowances, and confinement for 3 years.

(2) *All other cases.* Bad-conduct discharge, forfeiture of all pay and allowances, and confinement for 6 months.

e. *Sample specifications.*

(1) *Wrongful making, altering, counterfeiting, or tampering with military or official pass, permit, discharge certificate, or identification card.*

In that __________ (personal jurisdiction data), did, (at/on board—location) (subject-matter jurisdiction data, if required), on or about _____ 20 __, wrongfully and falsely (make) (forge) (alter by __________) (counterfeit) (tamper with by __________) (a certain instrument purporting to be) (a) (an) (another's) (naval) (military) (official) (pass) (permit) (discharge certificate) (identification card) (__________) in words and figures as follows _________.

(2) *Wrongful sale, gift, loan, or disposition of a military or official pass, permit, discharge certificate, or identification card.*

In that __________ (personal jurisdiction data), did, (at/on board—location) (subject-matter jurisdiction data, if required), on or about _____ 20 __, wrongfully (sell to _____) (give to _____) (loan to _____) (dispose of by _____) (a certain instrument purporting to be) (a) (an) (another's) (naval) (military) (official) (pass) (permit) (discharge certificate) (identification card) (_____) in words and figures as follows: _____, (he) (she), the said _____, then well knowing the same to be (false) (unauthorized).

(3) *Wrongful use or possession of a false or unauthorized military or official pass, permit, discharge certificate, or identification card.*

In that __________ (personal jurisdiction data), did (at/on board—location) (subject-matter jurisdiction data, if required), on or about _____ 20 __, wrongfully (use) (possess) (with intent to (defraud) (deceive)) (a certain instrument purporting to be) (a) (an) (another's) (naval) (military) (official) (pass) (permit) (discharge certificate) (identification card) (__________), (he) (she), the said __________, then well knowing the same to be (false) (unauthorized).

39. Article 106 (10 U.S.C. 906)—Impersonation of officer, noncommissioned or petty officer, or agent or official

a. *Text of statute.*

(a) IN GENERAL.—Any person subject to this chapter who, wrongfully and willfully, impersonates—

(1) an officer, a noncommissioned officer, or a petty officer;

(2) an agent of superior authority of one of the armed forces; or

(3) an official of a government; shall be punished as a court-martial may direct.

(b) IMPERSONATION WITH INTENT TO DEFRAUD.—Any person subject to this chapter who, wrongfully, willfully, and with intent to defraud, impersonates any person referred to in paragraph (1), (2), or (3) of subsection (a) shall be punished as a court-martial may direct.

(c) IMPERSONATION OF GOVERNMENT OFFICIAL WITHOUT INTENT TO DEFRAUD.—Any person subject to this chapter who, wrongfully, willfully, and without intent to defraud, impersonates an official of a government by committing an act that exercises or asserts the authority of the office that the person claims to have shall be punished as a court-martial may direct.

b. *Elements.*

(1) That the accused impersonated an officer, noncommissioned officer, or petty officer, or an agent of superior authority of one of the armed forces, or an official of a certain government, in a certain manner; and

(2) That the impersonation was wrongful and willful.

[Note 1: If intent to defraud is in issue, add the following element:]

(3) That the accused did so with the intent to defraud a certain person or organization in a certain manner.

[Note 2: If the accused is charged with impersonating an official of a certain government without an intent to defraud, use the following element:]

(3) That the accused committed one or more acts which exercised or asserted the authority of the office the accused claimed to have.

c. *Explanation.*

(1) *Nature of offense.* Impersonation does not depend upon the accused deriving a benefit from the deception or upon some third party being misled, although this is an aggravating factor.

(2) *Officer.* The term "officer" has the same meaning as that term carries in 10 U.S.C. § 101(b)(1).

(3) *Willfulness.* "Willful" means with the knowledge that one is falsely holding one's self out as such.

(4) *Intent to defraud. See* subparagraph 70.c.(14).

d. *Maximum punishment.*

(1) With intent to defraud. Dishonorable discharge, forfeiture of all pay and allowances, and confinement for 3 years.

(2) All other cases. Bad-conduct discharge, forfeiture of all pay and allowances, and confinement for 6 months.

f. *Sample specification.*

In that __________ (personal jurisdiction data), did, (at/on board—location) (subject-matter jurisdiction data, if required), on or about _____ 20 __, wrongfully and willfully impersonate (a(n) (officer) (noncommissioned officer) (petty officer) (agent of superior authority) of the (Army) (Navy) (Marine Corps) (Air Force) (Coast Guard)) (an official of the Government of __________) by (publicly wearing the uniform and insignia of rank of a (lieutenant of the __________) (_____)) (showing the credentials of __________) (_____) [*with intent to defraud _____ by _____] [**and (exercised) (asserted) the authority of _____ by _____].

[**See* subparagraph b note 1.]

[***See* subparagraph b note 2.]

40. Article 106a (10 U.S.C. 906a)—Wearing unauthorized insignia, decoration, badge, ribbon, device, or lapel button

a. *Text of statute.*

Any person subject to this chapter—

(1) who is not authorized to wear an insignia, decoration, badge, ribbon, device, or lapel button; and

(2) who wrongfully wears such insignia, decoration, badge, ribbon, device, or lapel button upon the person's uniform or civilian clothing;

shall be punished as a court-martial may direct.

b. *Elements.*

(1) That the accused wore a certain insignia, decoration, badge, ribbon, device, or lapel button upon the accused's uniform or civilian clothing;

(2) That the accused was not authorized to wear the item; and

(3) That the wearing was wrongful.

[Note: If applicable, add the following element]

(4) That the accused wore any of the following decorations: (Medal of Honor); (Distinguished Service Cross); (Navy Cross); (Air Force Cross); (Silver Star); (Purple Heart) (or any valor device on any personal award).

c. *Explanation.*

(1) *In general.* Authorization of the wearing of a military insignia, decoration, badge, ribbon, device, or lapel pin is governed by Department of Defense and Service regulations. The wearing of an item is "wrongful" where it is intentional and the accused knew that the accused was not entitled to wear it.

(2) *Scope of "unauthorized" wearing.* The wearing of an item is not unauthorized if the circumstances reveal it to be in jest or for an innocent or legitimate purpose—for instance, as part of a costume for dramatic or other reasons, or for legitimate law enforcement activities.

(3) *Wrongful.* Conduct is wrongful when it is done without legal justification or excuse. Actual knowledge that the accused was not authorized to wear the item in question is required. Knowledge may be proved by circumstantial evidence.

d. *Maximum punishment.*

(1) *Wrongful wearing of the Medal of Honor; Distinguished Service Cross; Navy Cross; Air Force Cross; Silver Star; Purple Heart; or a valor device on any personal award.* Bad-conduct discharge, forfeiture of all pay and allowances, and confinement for 1 year.

(2) *All other cases.* Bad-conduct discharge, forfeiture of all pay and allowances, and confinement for 6 months.

e. *Sample specification.*

In that __________ (personal jurisdiction data), did, (at/on board—location) (subject-matter jurisdiction, if required), on or about ______ 20 __, wrongfully, without authority, wear upon (his) (her) (uniform) (civilian clothing) (the insignia or grade of a (master sergeant of __________) (chief gunner's mate of __________)) (Combat Infantryman Badge) (the Distinguished Service Cross) (the ribbon representing the Silver Star) (the lapel button representing the Legion of Merit) (__________).

41. Article 107 (10 U.S.C. 907)—False official statements; false swearing

a. *Text of statute.*

(a) FALSE OFFICIAL STATEMENTS.—Any person subject to this chapter who, with intent to deceive—

(1) signs any false record, return, regulation, order, or other official document, knowing it to be false; or

(2) makes any other false official statement knowing it to be false; shall be punished as a court-martial may direct.

(b) FALSE SWEARING.—Any person subject to this chapter—

(1) who takes an oath that—

(A) is administered in a matter in which such oath is required or authorized by law; and

(B) is administered by a person with authority to do so; and

(2) who, upon such oath, makes or subscribes to a statement; if the statement is false and at the time of taking the oath, the person does not believe the statement to be true, shall be punished as a court-martial may direct.

b. *Elements.*

(1) *False official statements.*

(a) That the accused signed a certain official document or made a certain official statement;

(b) That the document or statement was false in certain particulars;

(c) That the accused knew it to be false at the time of signing it or making it; and

(d) That the false document or statement was made with the intent to deceive.

(2) *False swearing.*

(a) That the accused took an oath or equivalent;

(b) That the oath or equivalent was administered to the accused in a matter in which such oath or equivalent was required or authorized by law;

(c) That the oath or equivalent was administered by a person having authority to do so;

(d) That upon this oath or equivalent the accused made or subscribed a certain statement;

(e) That the statement was false; and

(f) That the accused did not then believe the statement to be true.

c. *Explanation.*

(1) *False official statements.*

(a) *Statements.* Statements may be made orally or in writing and include records, returns, regulations, orders, or other documents.

(b) *Official statements.* Official statements are those that affect military functions, which encompass matters within the jurisdiction of the military departments and Services. There are three broad categories of official statements under this offense:

(i) where the accused makes a statement while acting in the line of duty or where the statement bears a clear and direct relationship to the accused's official duties;

(ii) where the accused makes a statement to a military member who is carrying out a military duty at the time the statement is made; or

(iii) where the accused makes a statement to a civilian who is necessarily performing a military function at the time the accused makes the statement.

(c) *Status of victim of deception.* The rank or status of any person intended to be deceived is immaterial if that person was authorized in the execution of a particular duty to require or receive the statement from the accused. The Government may be the victim of this offense.

(d) *Intent to deceive.* The false representation must be made with the intent to deceive. It is not necessary that the false statement be material to the issue inquiry. If, however, the falsity is in respect to a material matter, it may be considered as some evidence of the intent to deceive, while immateriality may tend to show an absence of this intent.

(e) *Material gain.* The expectation of material gain is not an element of this offense. Such expectation or lack of it, however, is circumstantial evidence bearing on the element of intent to deceive.

(f) *Knowledge that the statement was false.* The false representation must be one which the accused actually knew was false. Actual knowledge may be proved by circumstantial evidence. An honest, although erroneous, belief that a statement made is true, is a defense.

(2) *False swearing.*

(a) *Nature of offense.* False swearing is the making under a lawful oath or equivalent of any false statement, oral or written, not believing the statement to be true. It does not include such statements made in a judicial proceeding or course of justice, as those are under Article 131, perjury (see paragraph 81). Unlike a false official statement, there is no requirement that the statement be made with an intent to deceive or that the statement be official.

(b) *Oath. See* Article 136 and R.C.M. 807 as to the authority to administer oaths, and *see* Section IX of Part III (Military Rules of Evidence) concerning proof of the signatures of persons authorized to administer oaths. An oath includes an affirmation when authorized in lieu of an oath.

d. *Maximum punishment.*

(1) *False official statement.* Dishonorable discharge, forfeiture of all pay and allowances, and confinement for 5 years.

(2) *False swearing.* Dishonorable discharge, forfeiture of all pay and allowances, and confinement for 3 years.

e. *Sample specifications.*

(1) *False official statements.*

In that __________ (personal jurisdiction data), did, (at/on board—location), (subject-matter jurisdiction data, if required), on or about _____ 20 __, with intent to deceive, [sign an official (record) (return) (_____), to wit: _____] [make to _____, an official statement, to wit: _____], which (record) (return) (statement) (_____) was (totally false) (false in that _____), and was then known by the said _____ to be so false.

(2) *False swearing.*

In that __________ (personal jurisdiction data), did, (at/on board—location) (subject-matter jurisdiction data, if required), on or about _____ 20 __, (in an affidavit) (in __________), (make) (subscribe) under lawful (oath) (affirmation) a false statement in substance as follows: __________, which statement (he) (she) did not then believe to be true.

42. Article 107a (10 U.S.C. 907a)—Parole violation

a. *Text of statute.*

Any person subject to this chapter—

(1) who, having been a prisoner as the result of a court-martial conviction or other criminal proceeding, is on parole with conditions; and

(2) who violates the conditions of parole;

shall be punished as a court-martial may direct.

b. *Elements.*

(1) That the accused was a prisoner as the result of a court-martial conviction or other criminal proceeding;

(2) That the accused was on parole;

(3) That there were certain conditions of parole that the parolee was bound to obey; and

(4) That the accused violated the conditions of parole by doing an act or failing to do an act.

c. *Explanation.*

(1) *"Prisoner"* refers only to those in confinement resulting from conviction at a court-martial or other criminal proceeding.

(2) *"Parole" is defined as "word of honor."* A prisoner on parole, or parolee, has agreed to adhere to a parole plan and conditions of parole. A parole plan is a written or oral agreement made by the prisoner prior to parole to do or refrain from doing certain acts or activities. A parole plan may include a residence requirement stating where and with whom a parolee will live, and a requirement that the prisoner have an offer of guaranteed employment. Conditions of parole include the parole plan and other reasonable and appropriate conditions of parole, such as paying restitution, beginning or continuing treatment for alcohol or drug abuse, or paying a fine ordered executed as part of the prisoner's court-martial sentence. In return for giving his or her word of honor

to abide by a parole plan and conditions of parole, the prisoner is granted parole.

d. *Maximum punishment.* Bad-conduct discharge, confinement for 6 months, and forfeiture of two-thirds pay per month for 6 months.

e. *Sample specification.*

In that __________ (personal jurisdiction data), a prisoner on parole, did, (at/on board—location) (subject-matter jurisdiction, if required), on or about _____ 20 __, violate the conditions of (his) (her) parole by __________.

43. Article 108 (10 U.S.C. 908)—Military property of United States—Loss, damage, destruction, or wrongful disposition

a. *Text of statute.*

Any person subject to this chapter who, without proper authority—

(1) sells or otherwise disposes of;

(2) willfully or through neglect damages, destroys, or loses; or

(3) willfully or through neglect suffers to be lost, damaged, destroyed, sold, or wrongfully disposed of; any military property of the United States,

shall be punished as a court-martial may direct.

b. *Elements.*

(1) *Selling or otherwise disposing of military property.*

(a) That the accused sold or otherwise disposed of certain property (which was a firearm or explosive);

(b) That the sale or disposition was without proper authority;

(c) That the property was military property of the United States; and

(d) That the property was of a certain value.

(2) *Damaging, destroying, or losing military property.*

(a) That the accused, without proper authority, damaged or destroyed certain property in a certain way, or lost certain property;

(b) That the property was military property of the United States;

(c) That the damage, destruction, or loss was willfully caused by the accused or was the result of neglect by the accused; and

(d) That the property was of a certain value or the damage was of a certain amount.

(3) *Suffering military property to be lost, damaged, destroyed, sold, or wrongfully disposed of.*

(a) That certain property (which was a firearm or explosive) was lost, damaged, destroyed, sold, or wrongfully disposed of;

(b) That the property was military property of the United States;

(c) That the loss, damage, destruction, sale, or wrongful disposition was suffered by the accused, without proper authority, through a certain omission of duty by the accused;

(d) That the omission was willful or negligent; and

(e) That the property was of a certain value or the damage was of a certain amount.

c. *Explanation.*

(1) *Military property.* Military property is all property, real or personal, owned, held, or used by one of the armed forces of the United States. Military property is a term of art, and should not be confused with Government property. The terms are not interchangeable. While all military property is Government property, not all Government property is military property. An item of Government property is not military property unless the item in question meets the definition provided in this paragraph. It is immaterial whether the property sold, disposed, destroyed, lost, or damaged had been issued to the accused, to someone else, or even issued at all. If it is proved by either direct or circumstantial evidence that items of individual issue were issued to the accused, it may be inferred, depending on all the evidence, that the damage, destruction, or loss proved was due to the neglect of the accused. Retail merchandise of Service exchange stores is not military property under this article.

(2) *Suffering military property to be lost, damaged, destroyed, sold, or wrongfully disposed of.* "To suffer" means to allow or permit. The willful or negligent sufferance specified by this article includes: deliberate violation or intentional disregard of some specific law, regulation, or order; reckless or unwarranted personal use of the property; causing or allowing it to remain exposed to the weather, insecurely housed, or not guarded; permitting it to be consumed, wasted, or injured by other persons; or loaning it to a person, known to be irresponsible, by whom it is damaged.

(3) *Value and damage.* In the case of loss, destruction, sale, or wrongful disposition, the value of the property controls the maximum punishment which may be adjudged. In the case of damage, the amount of damage controls. As a general rule, the amount of damage is the estimated or actual cost of repair by the Government agency normally employed in such work, or the cost of replacement, as shown by Government price lists or otherwise, whichever is less.

(4) *Firearm or explosive.* For purposes of determining the maximum punishment for this offense (*see* subparagraphs d.(1)(b) and d.(3)(b)), the term "explosive" includes ammunition. See generally R.C.M. 103(11), (12).

d. *Maximum punishment.*

(1) Selling or otherwise disposing of military property.

(a) Of a value of $1,000 or less. Bad-conduct discharge, forfeiture of all pay and allowances, and confinement for 1 year.

(b) Of a value of more than $1,000 or any firearm or explosive. Dishonorable discharge, forfeiture of all pay and allowances, and confinement for 10 years.

(2) Through neglect damaging, destroying, or losing, or through neglect suffering to be lost, damaged, destroyed, sold, or wrongfully disposed of, military property.

(a) Of a value or damage of $1,000 or less. Confinement for 6 months, and forfeiture of two-thirds pay per month for 6 months.

(b) Of a value or damage of more than $1,000. Bad-conduct discharge, forfeiture of all pay and allowances, and confinement for 1 year.

(3) Willfully damaging, destroying, or losing, or willfully suffering to be lost, damaged, destroyed, sold, or wrongfully disposed of, military property.

(a) Of a value or damage of $1,000 or less. Bad-conduct discharge, forfeiture of all pay and allowances, and confinement for 1 year.

(b) Of a value or damage of more than $1,000, or of any firearm or explosive. Dishonorable discharge, forfeiture of all pay and allowances, and confinement for 10 years.

e. *Sample specifications.*

(1) Selling or disposing of military property.

In that __________ (personal jurisdiction data), did, (at/on board—location) (subject-matter jurisdiction data, if required), on or about _____ 20 __, without proper authority, (sell to __________) (dispose of by __________) __________, [(a firearm) (an explosive)] of a value of (about) $__________, military property of the United States.

(2) Damaging, destroying, or losing military property.

In that __________ (personal jurisdiction data), did, (at/on board—location) (subject-matter jurisdiction data, if required), on or about _____ 20 __, without proper authority, (willfully) (through neglect) (damage by __________) (destroy by __________) (lose) __________, of a value of (about) $__________, military property of the United States (the amount of said damage being in the sum of (about) $__________).

(3) Suffering military property to be lost, damaged, destroyed, sold, or wrongfully disposed of.

In that __________ (personal jurisdiction data), did, (at/on board—location) (subject-matter jurisdiction data, if required), on or about _____ 20 __, without proper authority, (willfully) (through neglect) suffer __________, [(a firearm) (an explosive)] (of a value of (about) $__________) military property of the United States, to be (lost) (damaged by __________) (destroyed by __________) (sold to __________) (wrongfully disposed of by __________) (the amount of said damage being in the sum of (about $__________).

44. Article 108a (10 U.S.C. 908a)—Captured or abandoned property

a. *Text of statute.*

(a) All persons subject to this chapter shall secure all public property taken from the enemy for the service of the United States, and shall give notice and turn over to the proper authority without delay all captured or abandoned property in their possession, custody, or control.

(b) Any person subject to this chapter who—

(1) fails to carry out the duties prescribed in subsection (a);

(2) buys, sells, trades, or in any way deals in or disposes of captured or abandoned property, whereby he receives or expects any profit, benefit, or advantage to himself or another directly or indirectly connected with himself; or

(3) engages in looting or pillaging; shall be punished as a court-martial may direct.

b. *Elements*.

(1) *Failing to secure public property taken from the enemy*.

(a) That certain public property was taken from the enemy;

(b) That this property was of a certain value; and

(c) That the accused failed to do what was reasonable under the circumstances to secure this property for the service of the United States.

(2) *Failing to report and turn over captured or abandoned property*.

(a) That certain captured or abandoned public or private property came into the possession, custody, or control of the accused;

(b) That this property was of a certain value; and

(c) That the accused failed to give notice of its receipt and failed to turn over to proper authority, without delay, the captured or abandoned public or private property.

(3) *Dealing in captured or abandoned property*.

(a) That the accused bought, sold, traded, or otherwise dealt in or disposed of certain public or private captured or abandoned property;

(b) That this property was of certain value; and

(c) That by so doing the accused received or expected some profit, benefit, or advantage to the accused or to a certain person or persons connected directly or indirectly with the accused.

(4) *Looting or pillaging*.

(a) That the accused engaged in looting, pillaging, or looting and pillaging by unlawfully seizing or appropriating certain public or private property;

(b) That this property was located in enemy or occupied territory, or that it was on board a seized or captured vessel; and

(c) That this property was:

(i) left behind, owned by, or in the custody of the enemy, an occupied state, an inhabitant of an occupied state, or a person under the protection of the enemy or occupied state, or who, immediately prior to the occupation of the place where the act occurred, was under the protection of the enemy or occupied state; or

(ii) part of the equipment of a seized or captured vessel; or

(iii) owned by, or in the custody of the officers, crew, or passengers on board a seized or captured vessel.

c. *Explanation*.

(1) *Failing to secure public property taken from the enemy*.

(a) *Nature of property*. Unlike the remaining offenses under this article, failing to secure public property taken from the enemy involves only public property. Immediately upon its capture from the enemy public property becomes the property of the United States. Neither the person who takes it nor any other person has any private right in this property.

(b) *Nature of duty*. Every person subject to military law has an immediate duty to take such steps as are reasonably within that person's power to secure public property for the service of the United States and to protect it from destruction or loss.

(2) *Failing to report and turn over captured or abandoned property*.

(a) *Reports*. Reports of receipt of captured or abandoned property are to be made directly or through such channels as are required by current regulations, orders, or the customs of the Service.

(b) *Proper authority*. "Proper authority" is any authority competent to order disposition of the property in question.

(3) *Dealing in captured or abandoned property*. "Disposed of" includes destruction or abandonment.

(4) *Looting or pillaging*. "Looting or pillaging" means unlawfully seizing or appropriating property which is located in enemy or occupied territory.

(5) *Enemy*. For a discussion of "enemy," see subparagraph 27.c.(1)(b).

(6) *Firearms or explosive*. For purposes of determining the maximum punishment for this offense (*see* subparagraph d.(1)(b)), the term "explosive" includes ammunition. *See generally* R.C.M. 103(11), (12).

d. *Maximum punishment*.

(1) *Failing to secure public property taken from the enemy; failing to secure, give notice and turn over, selling, or otherwise wrongfully dealing in or disposing of captured or abandoned property*:

(a) *Of a value of $1,000 or less*. Bad-conduct discharge, forfeiture of all pay and allowances, and confinement for 6 months.

(b) *Of a value of more than $1,000 or any firearm or explosive*. Dishonorable discharge, forfeiture of all pay and allowances, and confinement for 5 years.

(2) *Looting or pillaging.* Any punishment, other than death, that a court-martial may direct.

e. *Sample specifications.*

(1) *Failing to secure public property taken from the enemy.*

In that __________ (personal jurisdiction data), did, (at/on board—location) (subject-matter jurisdiction, if required), on or about _____ 20 __, fail to secure for the service of the United States certain public property taken from the enemy, to wit: __, of a value of (about) $_____.

(2) *Failing to report and turn over captured or abandoned property.*

In that __________ (personal jurisdiction data), did, (at/on board—location) (subject-matter jurisdiction, if required), on or about _____ 20 __, fail to give notice and turn over to proper authority without delay certain (captured) (abandoned) property which had come into (his) (her) (possession) (custody) (control), to wit: __________, of a value of (about) $__________.

(3) *Dealing in captured or abandoned property.*

In that __________ (personal jurisdiction data), did, (at/on board—location) (subject-matter jurisdiction, if required), on or about _____ 20 __, (buy) (sell) (trade) (deal in) (dispose of) (__) certain (captured) (abandoned) property, to wit: _____, (a firearm) (an explosive), of a value of (about) $__________, thereby (receiving) (expecting) a (profit) (benefit) (advantage) to (himself/herself) (_____, (his) (her) accomplice) (_____, (his) (her) brother) (__________).

(4) *Looting or pillaging.*

In that (personal jurisdiction data), did, (at/onboard—location) (subject-matter jurisdiction, if required), on or about (date), engage in (looting) (and) (pillaging) by unlawfully (seizing) (appropriating) __________, (property which had been left behind) (the property of __________), [(an inhabitant of __________) (__________)].

45. Article 109 (10 U.S.C. 909)—Property other than military property of United States—waste, spoilage, or destruction

a. *Text of statute.*

Any person subject to this chapter who willfully or recklessly wastes, spoils, or otherwise willfully and wrongfully destroys or damages any property other than military property of the United States shall be punished as a court-martial may direct.

b. *Elements.*

(1) *Wasting or spoiling of non-military property.*

(a) That the accused willfully or recklessly wasted or spoiled certain real property in a certain manner;

(b) That the property was that of another person; and

(c) That the property was of a certain value.

(2) *Damaging non-military property.*

(a) That the accused willfully and wrongfully damaged certain personal property in a certain manner;

(b) That the property was that of another person; and

(c) that the damage inflicted on the property was of a certain amount.

(3) *Destroying non-military property.*

(a) That the accused willfully and wrongfully destroyed certain personal property in a certain manner;

(b) That the property was that of another person; and

(c) That the property was of a certain value.

c. *Explanation.*

(1) *Wasting or spoiling non-military property.* This portion of Article 109 proscribes willful or reckless waste or spoliation of the real property of another. The terms "wastes" and "spoils" as used in this article refer to such wrongful acts of voluntary destruction of or permanent damage to real property as burning down buildings, burning piers, tearing down fences, or cutting down trees. This destruction is punishable whether done willfully, that is intentionally, recklessly, or is through a culpable disregard of the foreseeable consequences of some voluntary act.

(2) *Destroying or damaging non-military property.* This portion of Article 109 proscribes the willful and wrongful destruction or damage of the personal property of another. To be destroyed, the property need not be completely demolished or annihilated, but must be sufficiently injured to be useless for its intended purpose. Damage consists of any physical injury to the property. To constitute an offense under this section, the destruction or damage of the property must have been willful and wrongful. As used in this section "willfully" means intentionally and "wrongfully" means contrary to law, regulation, lawful order, or custom. Willfulness may be proved by circumstantial evidence, such as the manner in which the acts were done.

(3) *Value and damage.* In the case of destruction, the value of the property destroyed controls the maximum punishment which may be adjudged. In the case of damage, the amount of the damage controls. As a general rule, the amount of damage is the estimated or actual cost of repair by artisans employed in this work who are available to the community wherein the owner resides, or the replacement cost, whichever is less. See also subparagraph 64.c.(1)(g).

d. *Maximum punishment.*

(1) *Wasting or spoiling, non-military property—real property.*

(a) *Of property valued at $1,000 or less.* Bad-conduct discharge, forfeiture of all pay and allowances, and confinement for 1 year.

(b) *Of property valued at more than $1,000.* Dishonorable discharge, forfeiture of all pay and allowances, and confinement for 5 years.

(2) *Damaging any property other than military property of the United States.*

(a) *Inflicting damage of $1,000 or less.* Bad-conduct discharge, forfeiture of all pay and allowances, and confinement for 1 year.

(b) *Inflicting damage of more than $1,000.* Dishonorable discharge, forfeiture of all pay and allowances, and confinement for 5 years.

(3) *Destroying any property other than military property of the United States.*

(a) *Destroying property valued at $1,000 or less.* Bad-conduct discharge, forfeiture of all pay and allowances, and confinement for 1 year.

(b) *Destroying property valued at more than $1,000.* Dishonorable discharge; forfeiture of all pay and allowances, and confinement for 5 years.

e. *Sample specifications.*

(1) *Wasting or spoiling real property other than military property of the United States.*

In that __________ (personal jurisdiction data), did, (at/on board—location) (subject-matter jurisdiction data, if required), on or about _____ 20 __, [(willfully) recklessly) waste _______] [(willfully) (recklessly) spoil______] (of a value of (about) $__________) (the amount of said damage being in the sum of (about) $__________), the property of __________.

(2) *Damaging any property other than military property of the United States.*

In that __________ (personal jurisdiction data), did, (at/on board—location) (subject-matter jurisdiction data, if required), on or about _____ 20 __, willfully and wrongfully damage by (method of damage) (identify property damaged__________) (the amount of said damage being in the sum of (about) $__________), the property of __________.

(3) *Destroying personal property other than military property of the United States.*

In that __________ (personal jurisdiction data), did, (at/on board—location) (subject-matter jurisdiction data, if required), on or about _____ 20 __, willfully and wrongfully destroy (identify property destroyed __________), of a value of (about) $__________ the property of __________.

46. Article 109a (10 U.S.C. 909a)—Mail matter: wrongful taking, opening, etc.

a. *Text of statute.*

(a) TAKING.—Any person subject to this chapter who, with the intent to obstruct the correspondence of, or to pry into the business or secrets of, any person or organization, wrongfully takes mail matter before the mail matter is delivered to or received by the addressee shall be punished as a court-martial may direct.

(b) OPENING, SECRETING, DESTROYING, STEALING.—Any person subject to this chapter who wrongfully opens, secretes, destroys, or steals mail matter before the mail matter is delivered to or received by the addressee shall be punished as a court-martial may direct.

b. *Elements.*

(1) *Taking.*

(a) That the accused took certain mail matter;

(b) That such taking was wrongful;

(c) That the mail matter was taken by the accused before it was delivered to or received by the addressee; and

(d) That such taking was with the intent to obstruct the correspondence or pry into the business or secrets of any person or organization.

(2) *Opening, secreting, destroying, or stealing.*

(a) That the accused opened, secreted, destroyed, or stole certain mail matter;

(b) That such opening, secreting, destroying, or stealing was wrongful; and

(c) That the mail matter was opened, secreted, destroyed, or stolen by the accused before it was delivered to or received by the addressee.

c. *Explanation.* These offenses are intended to protect the mail and mail system. "Mail matter" means any matter deposited in a postal system of any government or any authorized depository thereof or in official mail channels of the United States or an agency thereof including the armed forces. The value of the mail matter is not an element. *See* subparagraph 64.c.(1) concerning "steal."

d. *Maximum punishment.* Dishonorable discharge, forfeiture of all pay and allowances, and confinement for 5 years.

e. *Sample specifications.*

(1) *Taking.*

In that __________ (personal jurisdiction data), did, (at/on board—location) (subject-matter jurisdiction data, if required), on or about _____ 20 __, wrongfully take certain mail matter, to wit: (a) (letter(s)) (postal card(s)) (package(s)), addressed to __________, (out of the (__________ Post Office __________) (orderly room of __________) (unit mail box of __________) (__________) (from __________) before (it) (they) (was) (were) (delivered) (actually received) (to) (by) the (addressee) with intent to (obstruct the correspondence) (pry into the (business) (secrets)) of __________.

(2) *Opening, secreting, destroying, or stealing.*

In that __________ (personal jurisdiction data), did, (at/on board—location) (subject-matter jurisdiction data, if required), on or about _____, 20 __, (wrongfully (open) (secret) (destroy)) (steal) certain mail matter, to wit: (a) (letter(s)) (postal card(s)) (package(s)) addressed to __________, which said (letters(s)) (__________) (was) (were) then (in (the __________ Post Office __________) (orderly room of __________) (unit mail box of __________) (custody of __________) (__________) (had previously been committed to __________, (a representative of __________,) (an official agency for the transmission of communications)) before said (letter(s)) (__________) (was) (were) (delivered) (actually received) (to) (by) the (addressee).

47. Article 110 (10 U.S.C. 910)—Improper hazarding of vessel or aircraft

a. *Text of statute.*

(a) WILLFUL AND WRONGFUL HAZARDING.—Any person subject to this chapter who, willfully and wrongfully, hazards or suffers to be hazarded any vessel or aircraft of the armed forces shall be punished by death or such other punishment as a court-martial may direct.

(b) NEGLIGENT HAZARDING.—Any person subject to this chapter who negligently hazards or suffers to be hazarded any vessel or aircraft of the armed forces shall be punished as a court-martial may direct.

b. *Elements.*

(1) That a vessel or aircraft of the armed forces was hazarded in a certain manner; and

(2) That the accused by certain acts or omissions, willfully and wrongfully, or negligently, caused or suffered the vessel or aircraft to be hazarded.

c. *Explanation.*

(1) *Hazard.* "Hazard" means to put in danger of loss or injury. Actual damage to, or loss of, a vessel or aircraft of the armed forces by collision, stranding, running upon a shoal or a rock, or by any other cause, is conclusive evidence that the vessel or aircraft was hazarded but not of the fact of culpability on the part of any particular person. "Strand" means run a vessel aground so that the vessel is fast for a time.

(2) *Willfully and wrongfully.* As used in this article, "willfully" means intentionally and "wrongfully" means contrary to law, regulation, lawful order, or custom.

(3) *Negligence.* "Negligence" as used in this article means the failure to exercise the care, prudence, or attention to duties which the interests of the Government require a prudent and reasonable person to exercise under the circumstances. This negligence may consist of the omission to do something the prudent and reasonable person would have done, or the doing of something which such a person would not have done under the circumstances. No person is relieved of culpability who fails to perform such duties as are imposed by the general responsibilities of that person's grade or rank, or by the customs of the Service for the safety and protection of vessels and aircraft of the armed forces, simply because these duties are not specifically enumerated in a regulation or order. However, a mere error in judgment that a reasonably able person might have committed under the same circumstances does not constitute an offense under this article.

(4) *Suffer*. "To suffer" means to allow or permit. A ship or aircraft is willfully suffered to be hazarded by one who, although not in direct control of the vessel or aircraft, knows a danger to be imminent but takes no steps to prevent it, for example, as by a navigator of a ship under way who fails to report to the officer of the deck a radar target which is observed to be on a collision course with, and dangerously close to, the ship, or an aircraft's copilot or navigator who similarly fails to report an imminent danger. A suffering through neglect implies an omission to take such measures as were appropriate under the circumstances to prevent a foreseeable danger.

(5) *Vessel. See* 1 U.S.C. § 3.

(6) *Aircraft. See* 18 U.S.C. § 31(a)(1). Additionally, aircraft includes remotely piloted aircraft and unmanned aerial vehicles.

d. *Maximum punishment.*

(1) *Willfully and wrongfully*. Death or such other punishment as a court-martial may direct.

(2) *Negligently*. Dishonorable discharge, forfeiture of all pay and allowances, and confinement for 2 years.

e. *Sample specifications*.

(1) *Hazarding or suffering to be hazarded any vessel or aircraft, willfully and wrongfully.*

In that __________ (personal jurisdiction data) (subject-matter jurisdiction, if required), did, on _____ 20 __, while serving as _____ (aboard) (on) the ________ in the vicinity of _______, willfully and wrongfully (hazard the said (vessel) (aircraft)) (suffer the said (vessel) (aircraft)) to be hazarded) by (causing the said (vessel) (aircraft) to collide with __________) (allowing the said vessel to run aground) (allowing said aircraft to) (_____________).

(2) *Hazarding of vessel or aircraft, negligently.*

(a) *Example 1.*

In that __________ (personal jurisdiction data) (subject-matter jurisdiction, if required), on _____ 20 __, while serving (in command of the __________) (as the pilot of _________), (making entrance to (Boston Harbor)) (approaching (______ Air Force Base) (______ Air Field)) did negligently hazard the said (vessel) (aircraft) by failing and neglecting to maintain or cause to be maintained an accurate (running plot of the true position) (location) of said (vessel) (aircraft) while making said approach, as a result of which neglect the said __________, at or about __________, hours on the day aforesaid, became (stranded) (_____________) in the vicinity of (Channel Buoy Number Three) (__________ runway) (________________________).

(b) *Example 2.*

In that __________ (personal jurisdiction data) (subject-matter jurisdiction, if required), on _____ 20 __, while serving as navigator of the __________, cruising on special service in the __________ Ocean off the coast of __________, notwithstanding the fact that at about midnight, _____ 20 __, the northeast point of _____ Island bore abeam and was about six miles distant, the said ship being then under way and making a speed of about ten knots, and well knowing the position of the said ship at the time stated, and that the charts of the locality were unreliable and the currents thereabouts uncertain, did then and there negligently hazard the said vessel or aircraft by failing and neglecting to exercise proper care and attention in navigating said ship while approaching __________ Island, in that (he) (she) neglected and failed to lay a course that would carry said ship clear of the last aforesaid island, and to change the course in due time to avoid disaster; and the said ship, as a result of said negligence on the part of said __________, ran upon a rock off the southwest coast of __________ Island, at about _____ hours, _____, 20 __, in consequence of which the said __________ was lost.

(c) *Example 3.*

In that __________ (personal jurisdiction data) (subject-matter jurisdiction, if required), on _____ 20 __, while serving as navigator of the __________ and well knowing that at about sunset of said day the said ship had nearly run her estimated distance from the __________ position, obtained and plotted by (him) (her), to the position of __________, and well knowing the difficulty of sighting __________, from a safe distance after sunset, did then and there negligently hazard the said vessel by failing and neglecting to advise (his) (her) commanding officer to lay a safe course for said ship to the northward before continuing on a westerly course, as it was the duty of said __________ to do; in consequence of which the said ship was, at about __________ hours on the day above mentioned, run upon _____ bank in the __________ Sea, about latitude __ degrees, __ minutes, north, and longitude __ degrees, __ minutes, west, and seriously injured.

(3) *Suffering a vessel or aircraft to be hazarded, negligently.*

(a) *Example 1.*

In that __________ (personal jurisdiction data) (subject-matter jurisdiction, if required), while serving as combat intelligence center officer on board the __________, making passage from Boston to Philadelphia, and having, between _____ and _____ hours on _____, 20 __, been duly informed of decreasing radar ranges and constant radar bearing indicating that the said __________ was upon a collision course approaching a radar target, did then and there negligently suffer the said vessel or aircraft to be hazarded by failing and neglecting to report said collision course with said radar target to the officer of the deck, as it was (his) (her) duty to do, and (he) (she), the said __________, through negligence, did cause the said __________ to collide with the __________ at or about __________ hours on said date, with resultant damage to ________.

(b) *Example 2.*

In that __________ (personal jurisdiction data) (subject-matter jurisdiction, if required), while serving as (navigator) (________) on ______________, transiting from (_________ Air Force Base) to (__________ Air Force Base), and having, between ______ and ________ hours on ________, 20 ___, becoming aware of (inclement weather conditions) (inaccurate fuel calculations) threatening said aircraft, did then and there negligently suffer the said aircraft to be hazarded by failing and neglecting to report said (weather conditions) (inaccurate fuel calculations) to the (pilot) (copilot), as it was (his) (her) duty to do, the said (navigator) (________), through negligence, did cause the said aircraft to ________, at or about _________ hours on said date, with resultant damage to wit: ____________.

48. Article 111 (10 U.S.C. 911)—Leaving scene of vehicle accident

a. *Text of statute.*

(a) DRIVER.—Any person subject to this chapter—

(1) who is the driver of a vehicle that is involved in an accident that results in personal injury or property damage; and

(2) who wrongfully leaves the scene of the accident—

(A) without providing assistance to an injured person; or

(B) without providing personal identification to others involved in the accident or to appropriate authorities;

shall be punished as a court-martial may direct.

(b) SENIOR PASSENGER.—Any person subject to this chapter—

(1) who is a passenger in a vehicle that is involved in an accident that results in personal injury or property damage;

(2) who is the superior commissioned or noncommissioned officer of the driver of the vehicle or is the commander of the vehicle; and

(3) who wrongfully and unlawfully orders, causes, or permits the driver to leave the scene of the accident—

(A) without providing assistance to an injured person; or

(B) without providing personal identification to others involved in the accident or to appropriate authorities;

shall be punished as a court-martial may direct.

b. *Elements.*

(1) *Driver.*

(a) That the accused was the driver of a vehicle;

(b) That while the accused was driving the vehicle was involved in an accident;

(c) That the accused knew that the vehicle had been in an accident;

(d) That the accused left the scene of the accident without (providing assistance to the victim who had been struck (and injured) by the said vehicle) or (providing identification); and

(e) That such leaving was wrongful.

(2) *Senior passenger.*

(a) That the accused was a passenger in a vehicle which was involved in an accident;

(b) That the accused knew that said vehicle had been in an accident; and

(c) That the accused was the superior commissioned or noncommissioned officer of the driver, or commander of the vehicle, and wrongfully and unlawfully ordered, caused, or permitted the driver to leave the scene of the accident without (providing assistance to the victim who had been struck (and injured) by the said vehicle) (or) (providing identification).

c. *Explanation.*

(1) *Nature of offense.* This offense covers "hit and run" situations where there is damage to property other than the driver's vehicle or injury to someone other than the driver or a passenger in the driver's vehicle. It also covers accidents caused by the accused, even if the accused's vehicle does not contact other people, vehicles, or property.

(2) *Knowledge.* Actual knowledge that an accident has occurred is an essential element of this offense. Actual knowledge may be proved by circumstantial evidence.

(3) *Passenger.* A passenger other than a senior passenger may also be liable under this paragraph. *See* paragraph 1 of this Part.

d. *Maximum punishment.* Bad-conduct discharge, forfeiture of all pay and allowances, and confinement for 6 months.

e. *Sample specification.*

In that __________ (personal jurisdiction data), [the driver of)][*a passenger in] [the senior officer/noncommissioned officer in] (_____ in) a vehicle at the time of an accident in which said vehicle was involved, and having knowledge of said accident, did, at _____ (subject-matter jurisdiction data, if required), on or about _____ 20 __ [wrongfully leave] [*by _____, assist the driver of the said vehicle in wrongfully leaving] [wrongfully order, cause, or permit the driver to leave] the scene of the accident without (providing assistance to _____, who had been struck (and injured) by the said vehicle) (making (his) (her) (the driver's) identity known).

[*Note: This language should be used when the accused was a passenger and is charged as a principal. *See* paragraph 1 of this Part.]

49. Article 112 (10 U.S.C. 912)—Drunkenness and other incapacitation offenses

a. *Text of statute.*

(a) DRUNK ON DUTY.—Any person subject to this chapter who is drunk on duty shall be punished as a court-martial may direct.

(b) INCAPACITATION FOR DUTY FROM DRUNKENNESS OR DRUG USE.—Any person subject to this chapter who, as a result of indulgence in any alcoholic beverage or any drug, is incapacitated for the proper performance of duty shall be punished as a court-martial may direct.

(c) DRUNK PRISONER.—Any person subject to this chapter who is a prisoner and, while in such status, is drunk shall be punished as a court-martial may direct.

b. *Elements.*

(1) *Drunk on duty.*

(a) That the accused was on a certain duty; and

(b) That the accused was drunk while on this duty.

(2) *Incapacitation for duty from drunkenness or drug use.*

(a) That the accused had certain duties to perform;

(b) That the accused was incapacitated for the proper performance of such duties; and

(c) That such incapacitation was the result of previous indulgence in intoxicating liquor or any drug.

(3) *Drunk prisoner.*

(a) That the accused was a prisoner; and

(b) That while in such status the accused was drunk.

c. *Explanation.*

(1) *Drunk on duty.*

(a) *Drunk.* "Drunk" means—

(i) the state of intoxication by alcohol that is sufficient to impair the rational and full exercise of mental or physical faculties; or

(ii) the state of meeting or exceeding a blood alcohol content limit with respect to alcohol concentration in a person's blood of 0.08 grams of alcohol per 100 milliliters of blood and with respect to alcohol concentration in a person's breath of 0.08 grams of alcohol per 210 liters of breath, as shown by chemical analysis.

(b) *Duty.* "Duty" as used in this article means military duty. Every duty which an officer or enlisted person may legally be required by superior authority to execute is necessarily a military duty. Within the meaning of this article, when in the actual exercise of command, the commander of a post, or of a command, or of a detachment in the field is constantly on duty, as is the commanding officer on board a ship. In the case of other officers or enlisted persons, "on duty" relates to duties or routine or detail, in garrison, at a station, or in the field, and does not relate to those periods when, no duty being required of them by orders or regulations, officers and enlisted persons occupy the status of leisure known as "off duty" or "on liberty." In a region of active hostilities, the circumstances are often such that all members of a command may properly be considered as being continuously on duty within the meaning of this article. So also, an officer of the day and members of the guard, or of the watch, are on duty during their entire tour within the meaning of this article.

(c) *Nature of offense.* It is necessary that the accused be drunk while actually on the duty alleged, and the fact the accused became drunk before going on duty, although material in extenuation, does not affect the question of guilt. If, however, the accused does not undertake the responsibility or enter upon the duty at all, the accused's conduct does not fall within the terms of this article, nor does that of a person who absents himself or herself from duty and is drunk while so absent. Included within the article is drunkenness while on duty of an anticipatory nature such as that of an aircraft crew ordered to stand by for flight duty, or of an enlisted person ordered to stand by for guard duty.

(d) *Defenses.* If the accused is known by superior authorities to be drunk at the time a duty is assigned, and the accused is thereafter allowed to assume that duty anyway, or if the drunkenness results from an accidental over dosage administered for medicinal purposes, the accused will have a defense to this offense.

(2) *Incapacitation for duty from drunkenness or drug use.*

(a) *Incapacitated.* "Incapacitated" means unfit or unable to properly perform duties as a result of previous alcohol consumption or drug use. Illness resulting from previous indulgence is an example of being "unable" to perform duties.

(b) *Affirmative defense.* The accused's lack of knowledge of the duties assigned is an affirmative defense to this offense.

(3) *Drunk prisoner.*

(a) *Prisoner. See* subparagraph 24.c.(1).

(b) *Drunk. See* subparagraph 49.c.(1)(a).

d. *Maximum punishment.*

(1) *Drunk on duty.* Bad-conduct discharge, forfeiture of all pay and allowances, and confinement for 9 months.

(2) *Incapacitation for duty from drunkenness or drug use.* Confinement for 3 months and forfeiture of two-thirds pay per month for 3 months.

(3) *Drunk prisoner.* Confinement for 3 months and forfeiture of two-thirds pay per month for 3 months.

e. *Sample specifications.*

(1) *Drunk on duty.*

In that __________ (personal jurisdiction data), was, (at/on board—location) (subject-matter jurisdiction, if required), on or about _____ 20 __, found drunk while on duty as __________.

(2) *Incapacitation for duty from drunkenness or drug use.*

In that _________ (personal jurisdiction data), was, (at/on board—location) (subject-matter jurisdiction, if required), on or about _____ 20 __, as a result of previous overindulgence in intoxicating liquor or drugs incapacitated for the proper performance of (his) (her) duties.

(3) *Drunk prisoner.*

In that __________ (personal jurisdiction data), a prisoner, was (at/on board—location) (subject-matter jurisdiction, if required), on or about _____ 20 __, found drunk.

50. Article 112a (10 U.S.C. 912a)—Wrongful use, possession, etc., of controlled substances

a. *Text of statute.*

(a) Any person subject to this chapter who wrongfully uses, possesses, manufactures, distributes, imports into the customs territory of the United States, exports from the United States, or introduces into an installation, vessel, vehicle, or aircraft used by or under the control of the armed forces a substance described in subsection (b) shall be punished as a court-martial may direct.

(b) The substances referred to in subsection (a) are the following:

(1) Opium, heroin, cocaine, amphetamine, lysergic acid diethylamide, methamphetamine, phencyclidine, barbituric acid, and marijuana and any compound or derivative of any such substance.

(2) Any substance not specified in clause (1) that is listed on a schedule of controlled substances prescribed by the President for the purposes of this article.

(3) Any other substance not specified in clause (1) or contained on a list prescribed by the President under clause (2) that is listed in schedules I through V of section 202 of the Controlled Substances Act (21 U.S.C. § 812).

b. *Elements.*

(1) *Wrongful possession of controlled substance.*

(a) That the accused possessed a certain amount of a controlled substance; and

(b) That the possession by the accused was wrongful.

(2) *Wrongful use of controlled substance.*

(a) That the accused used a controlled substance; and

(b) That the use by the accused was wrongful.

(3) *Wrongful distribution of controlled substance.*

(a) That the accused distributed a certain amount of a controlled substance; and

(b) That the distribution by the accused was wrongful.

(4) *Wrongful introduction of a controlled substance.*

(a) That the accused introduced onto a vessel, aircraft, vehicle, or installation used by the armed forces or under the control of the armed forces a certain amount of a controlled substance; and

(b) That the introduction was wrongful.

(5) *Wrongful manufacture of a controlled substance.*

(a) That the accused manufactured a certain amount of a controlled substance; and

(b) That the manufacture was wrongful.

(6) *Wrongful possession, manufacture, or introduction of a controlled substance with intent to distribute.*

(a) That the accused (possessed) (manufactured) (introduced) a certain amount of a controlled substance;

(b) That the (possession) (manufacture) (introduction) was wrongful; and

(c) That the (possession) (manufacture) (introduction) was with the intent to distribute.

(7) *Wrongful importation or exportation of a controlled substance.*

(a) That the accused (imported into the customs territory of) (exported from) the United States a certain amount of a controlled substance; and

(b) That the (importation) (exportation) was wrongful.

[Note: When any of the aggravating circumstances listed in subparagraph d. is alleged, it must be listed as an element.]

c. *Explanation.*

(1) *Controlled substance.* "Controlled substance" means amphetamine, cocaine, heroin, lysergic acid diethylamide, marijuana, methamphetamine, opium, phencyclidine, and barbituric acid, including phenobarbital and secobarbital. "Controlled substance" also means any substance that is included in Schedules I through V established by the Controlled Substances Act of 1970 (21 U.S.C. § 812).

(2) *Possess.* "Possess" means to exercise control of something. Possession may be direct physical custody like holding an item in one's hand, or it may be constructive, as in the case of a person who hides an item in a locker or car to which that person may return to retrieve it. Possession must be knowing and conscious. Possession inherently includes the power or authority to preclude control by others. It is possible, however, for more than one person to possess an item simultaneously, as when several people share control of an item. An accused may not be convicted of possession of a controlled substance if the accused did not know that the substance was present under the accused's control. Awareness of the presence of a controlled substance may be inferred from circumstantial evidence.

(3) *Distribute, deliver.* "Distribute" means to deliver to the possession of another. "Deliver" means the actual, constructive, or attempted transfer of an item, whether or not there exists an agency relationship.

(4) *Manufacture.* "Manufacture" means the production, preparation, propagation, compounding, or processing of a drug or other substance, either directly or indirectly or by extraction from substances of natural origin, or independently by means of chemical synthesis or by a combination of extraction and chemical synthesis, and includes any packaging or repackaging of such substance or labeling or relabeling of its container. Production, as used in this subparagraph, includes the planting, cultivating, growing, or harvesting of a drug or other substance.

(5) *Wrongfulness.* To be punishable under Article 112a, possession, use, distribution, introduction, or manufacture of a controlled substance must be wrongful. Possession, use, distribution, introduction, or manufacture of a controlled substance is wrongful if it is without legal justification or authorization. Possession, distribution, introduction, or manufacture of a controlled substance is not wrongful if such act or acts are: (A) done pursuant to legitimate law enforcement activities (for example, an informant who receives drugs as part of an undercover operation is not

in wrongful possession); (B) done by authorized personnel in the performance of medical duties; or (C) without knowledge of the contraband nature of the substance (for example, a person who possesses cocaine, but actually believes it to be sugar, is not guilty of wrongful possession of cocaine). Possession, use, distribution, introduction, or manufacture of a controlled substance may be inferred to be wrongful in the absence of evidence to the contrary. The burden of going forward with evidence with respect to any such exception in any court-martial or other proceeding under the UCMJ shall be upon the person claiming its benefit. If such an issue is raised by the evidence presented, then the burden of proof is upon the United States to establish that the use, possession, distribution, manufacture, or introduction was wrongful.

(6) *Intent to distribute*. Intent to distribute may be inferred from circumstantial evidence. Examples of evidence which may tend to support an inference of intent to distribute are: possession of a quantity of substance in excess of that which one would be likely to have for personal use; market value of the substance; the manner in which the substance is packaged; and that the accused is not a user of the substance. On the other hand, evidence that the accused is addicted to or is a heavy user of the substance may tend to negate an inference of intent to distribute.

(7) *Certain amount*. When a specific amount of a controlled substance is believed to have been possessed, distributed, introduced, or manufactured by an accused, the specific amount should ordinarily be alleged in the specification. It is not necessary to allege a specific amount, however, and a specification is sufficient if it alleges that an accused possessed, distributed, introduced, or manufactured "some," "traces of," or "an unknown quantity of" a controlled substance.

(8) *Missile launch facility*. A missile launch facility includes the place from which missiles are fired and launch control facilities from which the launch of a missile is initiated or controlled after launch.

(9) *Customs territory of the United States*. Customs territory of the United States includes only the States, the District of Columbia, and Puerto Rico.

(10) *Use*. "Use" means to inject, ingest, inhale, or otherwise introduce into the human body, any controlled substance. Knowledge of the presence of the controlled substance is a required component of use. Knowledge of the presence of the controlled substance may be inferred from the presence of the controlled substance in the accused's body or from other circumstantial evidence. This permissive inference may be legally sufficient to satisfy the Government's burden of proof as to knowledge.

(11) *Deliberate ignorance*. An accused who consciously avoids knowledge of the presence of a controlled substance or the contraband nature of the substance is subject to the same criminal liability as one who has actual knowledge.

d. *Maximum punishment*.

(1) *Wrongful use, possession, manufacture, or introduction of controlled substance*.

(a) *Amphetamine, cocaine, heroin, lysergic acid diethylamide, marijuana (except possession of less than 30 grams or use of marijuana), methamphetamine, opium, phencyclidine, secobarbital, and Schedule I, II, III controlled substances*. Dishonorable discharge, forfeiture of all pay and allowances, and confinement for 5 years.

(b) *Marijuana (possession of less than 30 grams or use), phenobarbital, and Schedule IV and V controlled substances*. Dishonorable discharge, forfeiture of all pay and allowances, and confinement for 2 years.

(2) *Wrongful distribution, possession, manufacture, or introduction of controlled substance with intent to distribute, or wrongful importation or exportation of a controlled substance*.

(a) *Amphetamine, cocaine, heroin, lysergic acid diethylamide, marijuana, methamphetamine, opium, phencyclidine, secobarbital, and Schedule I, II, and III controlled substances*. Dishonorable discharge, forfeiture of all pay and allowances, and confinement for 15 years.

(b) *Phenobarbital and Schedule IV and V controlled substances*. Dishonorable discharge, forfeiture of all pay and allowances, and confinement for 10 years.

When any offense under this paragraph is committed; while the accused is on duty as a sentinel or lookout; on board a vessel or aircraft used by or under the control of the armed forces; in or at a missile launch facility used by or under the control of the armed forces; while receiving special pay under 37 U.S.C. § 310; in time of war; or in a confinement facility used by or under the control of the armed forces, the maximum period of confinement authorized for such offense shall be increased by 5 years.

e. *Sample specifications*.

(1) *Wrongful possession, manufacture, or distribution of controlled substance.*

In that __________ (personal jurisdiction data) did, (at/on board—location) (subject-matter jurisdiction data, if required), on or about _____, 20 __, wrongfully (possess) (distribute) (manufacture) _____ (grams) (ounces) (pounds) (_____) of _____ (a schedule (_____) controlled substance), (with the intent to distribute the said controlled substance) (while on duty as a sentinel or lookout) (while (on board a vessel/aircraft) (in or at a missile launch facility) used by the armed forces or under the control of the armed forces, to wit: _____) (while receiving special pay under 37 U.S.C. § 310) (during time of war).

(2) *Wrongful use of controlled substance.*

In that __________ (personal jurisdiction data), did, (at/on board—location) (subject-matter jurisdiction data, if required), on or about _____, 20 __, wrongfully use __________ (a Schedule __ controlled substance) (while on duty as a sentinel or lookout) (while (on board a vessel/aircraft) (in or at a missile launch facility) used by the armed forces or under the control of the armed forces, to wit: __________) (while receiving special pay under 37 U.S.C. § 310) (during time of war).

(3) *Wrongful introduction of controlled substance.*

In that __________ (personal jurisdiction data) did, (at/on board—location) (subject-matter jurisdiction data, if required), on or about _____, 20 __, wrongfully introduce __________ (grams) (ounces) (pounds) (__________) of __________ (a Schedule (__________) controlled substance) onto a vessel, aircraft, vehicle, or installation used by the armed forces or under control of the armed forces, to wit: __________ (with the intent to distribute the said controlled substance) (while on duty as a sentinel or lookout) (while receiving special pay under 37 U.S.C. § 310) (during a time of war).

(4) *Wrongful importation or exportation of controlled substance.*

In that __________ (personal jurisdiction data) did, (at/on board—location) (subject-matter jurisdiction data, if required), on or about _____, 20 __, wrongfully (import) (export) _____ (grams) (ounces) (pounds) (__________) of __________ (a Schedule (__) controlled substance) (into the customs territory of) (from) the United States (while on board a vessel/aircraft used by the armed forces or under the control of the armed forces, to wit: __________) (during time of war).

51. Article 113 (10 U.S.C. 913)—Drunken or reckless operation of a vehicle, aircraft, or vessel

a. *Text of statute.*

(a) Any person subject to this chapter who—

(1) operates or physically controls any vehicle, aircraft, or vessel in a reckless or wanton manner or while impaired by a substance described in section 912a(b) of this title (article 112a(b)), or

(2) operates or is in actual physical control of any vehicle, aircraft, or vessel while drunk or when the alcohol concentration in the person's blood or breath is equal to or exceeds the applicable limit under subsection (b), shall be punished as a court-martial may direct.

(b)(1) For purposes of subsection (a), the applicable limit on the alcohol concentration in a person's blood or breath is as follows:

(A) In the case of the operation or control of a vehicle, aircraft, or vessel in the United States, such limit is the lesser of—

(i) the blood alcohol content limit under the law of the State in which the conduct occurred, except as may be provided under paragraph (2) for conduct on a military installation that is in more than one State; or

(ii) the blood alcohol content limit specified in paragraph (3).

(B) In the case of the operation or control of a vehicle, aircraft, or vessel outside the United States, the applicable blood alcohol content limit is the blood alcohol content limit specified in paragraph (3) or such lower limit as the Secretary of Defense may by regulation prescribe.

(2) In the case of a military installation that is in more than one State, if those States have different blood alcohol content limits under their respective State laws, the Secretary may select one such blood alcohol content limit to apply uniformly on that installation.

(3) For purposes of paragraph (1), the blood alcohol content limit with respect to alcohol concentration in a person's blood is 0.08 grams of alcohol per 100 milliliters of blood and with respect to alcohol concentration in a person's breath is 0.08 grams of alcohol per 210 liters of breath, as shown by chemical analysis. The Secretary may by regulation prescribe limits that are lower than the

limits specified in the preceding sentence, if such lower limits are based on scientific developments, as reflected in Federal law of general applicability.

(4) In this subsection:

(A) The term "blood alcohol content limit" means the amount of alcohol concentration in a person's blood or breath at which operation or control of a vehicle, aircraft, or vessel is prohibited.

(B) The term "United States" includes the District of Columbia, the Commonwealth of Puerto Rico, the Virgin Islands, Guam, and American Samoa and the term "State" includes each of those jurisdictions.

b. *Elements.*

(1) That the accused was operating or in physical control of a vehicle, aircraft, or vessel; and

(2) That while operating or in physical control of a vehicle, aircraft, or vessel, the accused—

(a) did so in a wanton or reckless manner; or

(b) was drunk or impaired; or

(c) the alcohol concentration in the accused's blood or breath equaled or exceeded the applicable limit under Article 113(b).

[Note: Add the following if applicable]

(3) That the accused thereby caused the vehicle, aircraft, or vessel to injure a person.

c. *Explanation.*

(1) *Vehicle. See* 1 U.S.C. § 4.

(2) *Vessel. See* 1 U.S.C. § 3.

(3) *Aircraft. See* 18 U.S.C. § 31(a)(1).

(4) *Operates.* Operating a vehicle, aircraft, or vessel includes not only driving or guiding a vehicle, aircraft, or vessel while it is in motion, either in person or through the agency of another, but also setting of its motive power in action or the manipulation of its controls so as to cause the particular vehicle, aircraft, or vessel to move.

(5) *Physical control and actual physical control.* These terms as used in the statute are synonymous. They describe the present capability and power to dominate, direct, or regulate the vehicle, vessel, or aircraft, either in person or through the agency of another, regardless of whether such vehicle, aircraft, or vessel is operated. For example, the intoxicated person seated behind the steering wheel of a vehicle with the keys of the vehicle in or near the ignition but with the engine not turned on could be deemed in actual physical control of that vehicle. However, the person asleep in the back seat with the keys in his or her pocket would not be deemed in actual physical control. Physical control necessarily encompasses operation.

(6) *Drunk or impaired.* Drunk and impaired mean any intoxication which is sufficient to impair the rational and full exercise of the mental or physical faculties. The term drunk is used in relation to intoxication by alcohol. The term impaired is used in relation to intoxication by a substance described in Article 112(a).

(7) *Reckless.* The operation or physical control of a vehicle, vessel, or aircraft is reckless when it exhibits a culpable disregard of foreseeable consequences to others from the act or omission involved. Recklessness is not determined solely by reason of the happening of an injury, or the invasion of the rights of another, nor by proof alone of excessive speed or erratic operation, but all these factors may be admissible and relevant as bearing upon the ultimate question: whether, under all the circumstances, the accused's manner of operation or physical control of the vehicle, vessel, or aircraft was of that heedless nature which made it actually or imminently dangerous to the occupants, or to the rights or safety of others. It is operating or physically controlling a vehicle, vessel, or aircraft with such a high degree of negligence that if death were caused, the accused would have committed involuntary manslaughter, at least. The nature of the conditions in which the vehicle, vessel, or aircraft is operated or controlled, the time of day or night, the proximity and number of other vehicles, vessels, or aircraft and the condition of the vehicle, vessel, or aircraft, are often matters of importance in the proof of an offense charged under this article and, where they are of importance, may properly be alleged.

(8) *Wanton.* Wanton includes "reckless," but in describing the operation or physical control of a vehicle, vessel, or aircraft, wanton may, in a proper case, connote willfulness, or a disregard of probable consequences, and thus describe a more aggravated offense.

(9) *Causation.* The accused's drunken or reckless driving must be a proximate cause of injury for the accused to be guilty of drunken or reckless driving resulting in personal injury. To be proximate, the accused's actions need not be the sole cause of the injury, nor must they be the immediate cause of the injury, that is, the latest in time and space preceding the

injury. A contributing cause is deemed proximate only if it plays a material role in the victim's injury.

(10) *Separate offenses*. While the same course of conduct may constitute violations of both paragraphs (a)(1) and (2) of Article 113, e.g., both drunken and reckless operation or physical control, this article proscribes the conduct described in both paragraphs (a)(1) and (2) as separate offenses, which may be charged separately. However, as recklessness is a relative matter, evidence of all the surrounding circumstances that made the operation dangerous, whether alleged or not, may be admissible. Thus, on a charge of reckless driving, for example, evidence of drunkenness might be admissible as establishing one aspect of the recklessness, and evidence that the vehicle exceeded a safe speed, at a relevant prior point and time, might be admissible as corroborating other evidence of the specific recklessness charged. Similarly, on a charge of drunken driving, relevant evidence of recklessness might have probative value as corroborating other proof of drunkenness.

d. *Maximum punishment*.

(1) *Resulting in personal injury*. Dishonorable discharge, forfeiture of all pay and allowances, and confinement for 18 months.

(2) *No personal injury involved*. Bad-conduct discharge, forfeiture of all pay and allowances, and confinement for 6 months.

e. *Sample specification*.

In that __________ (personal jurisdiction data), did (at/on board—location) (subject-matter jurisdiction data, if required), on or about _____, 20 __, (in the motor pool area) (near the Officers' Club) (at the intersection of __________ and __________) (while in the Gulf of Mexico) (while in flight over North America) physically control [a vehicle, to wit: (a truck) (a passenger car) (_____)] [an aircraft, to wit: (an AH-64 helicopter) (an F-14A fighter) (a KC-135 tanker) (_____)] [a vessel, to wit: (the aircraft carrier USS __________) (the Coast Guard Cutter __________) (__________)], [while drunk] [while impaired by __________] [while the alcohol concentration in (his) (her) (blood or breath) equaled or exceeded the applicable limit under subsection (b) of the text of the statute in paragraph 51 as shown by chemical analysis] [in a (reckless) (wanton) manner by (attempting to pass another vehicle on a sharp curve) (ordering that the aircraft be flown below the authorized altitude)] [and did thereby cause said (vehicle) (aircraft) (vessel) to (strike and) (injure __________)].

52. Article 114 (10 U.S.C. 914)—Endangerment offenses

a. *Text of statute*.

(a) RECKLESS ENDANGERMENT.—Any person subject to this chapter who engages in conduct that—

(1) is wrongful and reckless or is wanton; and

(2) is likely to produce death or grievous bodily harm to another person;

shall be punished as a court-martial may direct.

(b) DUELING.—Any person subject to this chapter—

(1) who fights or promotes, or is concerned in or connives at fighting, a duel; or

(2) who, having knowledge of a challenge sent or about to be sent, fails to report the facts promptly to the proper authority;

shall be punished as a court-martial may direct.

(c) FIREARM DISCHARGE, ENDANGERING HUMAN LIFE.—Any person subject to this chapter who, willfully and wrongly, discharges a firearm, under circumstances such as to endanger human life shall be punished as a court-martial may direct.

(d) CARRYING CONCEALED WEAPON.—Any person subject to this chapter who unlawfully carries a dangerous weapon concealed on or about his person shall be punished as a court-martial may direct.

b. *Elements*.

(1) *Reckless endangerment*.

(a) That the accused did engage in conduct;

(b) That the conduct was wrongful and reckless or wanton; and

(c) That the conduct was likely to produce death or grievous bodily harm to another person.

(2) *Dueling*.

(a) That the accused fought another person with deadly weapons;

(b) That the combat was for private reasons; and

(c) That the combat was by prior agreement.

(3) *Promoting a duel*.

(a) That the accused promoted a duel between certain persons; and

(b) That the accused did so in a certain manner.

(4) *Conniving at fighting a duel.*

(a) That certain persons intended to and were about to engage in a duel;

(b) That the accused had knowledge of the planned duel; and

(c) That the accused connived at the fighting of the duel in a certain manner.

(5) *Failure to report a duel.*

(a) That a challenge to fight a duel had been sent or was about to be sent;

(b) That the accused had knowledge of this challenge; and

(c) That the accused failed to report this fact promptly to proper authority.

(6) *Firearm discharge, endangering human life.*

(a) That the accused discharged a firearm;

(b) That the discharge was willful and wrongful; and

(c) That the discharge was under circumstances such as to endanger human life.

(7) *Carrying concealed weapon.*

(a) That the accused carried a certain weapon concealed on or about the accused's person;

(b) That the carrying was unlawful; and

(c) That the weapon was a dangerous weapon.

Discussion

For negligent discharge of a firearm, see paragraph 100.

---

c. *Explanation.*

(1) *Reckless endangerment.*

(a) *In general.* This offense is intended to prohibit and therefore deter reckless or wanton conduct that wrongfully creates a substantial risk of death or grievous bodily harm to others.

(b) *Wrongfulness.* Conduct is wrongful when it is without legal justification or excuse.

(c) *Recklessness.* "Reckless" conduct is conduct that exhibits a culpable disregard of foreseeable consequences to others from the act or omission involved. The accused need not intentionally cause a resulting harm or know that his conduct is substantially certain to cause that result. The ultimate question is whether, under all the circumstances, the accused's conduct was of that heedless nature that made it actually or imminently dangerous to the rights or safety of others.

(d) *Wantonness.* "Wanton" includes "reckless" but may connote willfulness, or a disregard of probable consequences, and thus describe a more aggravated offense.

(e) *Likely to produce.* When the natural or probable consequence of particular conduct would be death or grievous bodily harm, it may be inferred that the conduct is likely to produce that result.

(f) *Grievous bodily harm.* This phrase has the same meaning given it in subparagraph 77.c.(1)(c).

(g) *Death or injury not required.* It is not necessary that death or grievous bodily harm be actually inflicted to prove reckless endangerment.

(2) *Dueling.*

(a) *Duel.* A duel is combat between two persons for private reasons fought with deadly weapons by prior agreement.

(b) *Promoting a duel.* Urging or taunting another to challenge or to accept a challenge to duel, acting as a second or as carrier of a challenge or acceptance, or otherwise furthering or contributing to the fighting of a duel are examples of promoting a duel.

(c) *Conniving at fighting a duel.* Anyone who has knowledge that steps are being taken or have been taken toward arranging or fighting a duel and who fails to take reasonable preventive action thereby connives at the fighting of a duel.

(3) *Firearm discharge, endangering human life.* "Under circumstances such as to endanger human life" refers to a reasonable potentiality for harm to human beings in general. The test is not whether the life was in fact endangered but whether, considering the circumstances surrounding the wrongful discharge of the weapon, the act was unsafe to human life in general.

(4) *Carrying concealed weapon.*

(a) *Concealed weapon.* A weapon is concealed when it is carried by a person and intentionally covered or kept from sight.

(b) *Dangerous weapon.* For purposes of this paragraph, a weapon is dangerous if it was specifically designed for the purpose of doing grievous bodily harm, or it was used or intended to be used by the accused to do grievous bodily harm.

(c) *On or about*. "On or about" means the weapon was carried on the accused's person or was within the immediate reach of the accused.

d. *Maximum punishment*. Dishonorable discharge, forfeiture of all pay and allowances, and confinement for 1 year.

e. *Sample specifications*.

(1) *Reckless endangerment.*

In that __________ (personal jurisdiction data), did, (at/on board—location)

(subject-matter jurisdiction data, if required), on or about ______ 20 __, wrongfully and (recklessly) (wantonly) engage in conduct, to wit: ________, conduct likely to cause death or grievous bodily harm to __________.

(2) *Dueling.*

(a) *Dueling.*

In that___________ (personal jurisdiction data) (and___________), did, (at/onboard—location) (subject-matter jurisdiction data, if required), on or about_____20_____, fight a duel (with ______), using as weapons therefor (pistols) (swords) (______).

(b) *Promoting a duel.*

In that_________ (personal jurisdiction data), did, (at/on board—location) (subject-matter jurisdiction data, if required), on or about _______20____, promote a duel between ___________ and ________ by (telling said ________ (he) (she) would be a coward if (he) (she) failed to challenge said _______ to a duel) (knowingly carrying from said _______ to said _______ a challenge to fight a duel).

(c) *Conniving at fighting a duel.*

In that __________ (personal jurisdiction data), having knowledge that ______ and ______ were about to engage in a duel, did (at/onboard—location) (subject-matter jurisdiction data, if required), on or about ______ 20____, connive at the fighting of said duel by (failing to take reasonable preventive action) (_________).

(d) *Failure to report a duel.*

In that _________ (personal jurisdiction data), having knowledge that a challenge to fight a duel (had been sent) (was about to be sent) by ______ to _______, did, (at/on board—location) (subject-matter jurisdiction data, if required), on or about _____ 20_____, fail to report that fact promptly to the proper authority.

(3) *Firearm discharge, endangering human life.*

In that __________ (personal jurisdiction data), did, (at/on board—location) (subject-matter jurisdiction data, if required), on or about _____ 20 __, wrongfully and willfully discharge a firearm, to wit: _____, (in the mess hall of _____) (_____), under circumstances such as to endanger human life.

(4) *Carrying concealed weapon.*

In that __________ (personal jurisdiction data), did, (at/on board—location) (subject-matter jurisdiction data, if required), on or about _____ 20 __, unlawfully carry on or about (his) (her) person a concealed weapon, to wit: a __________.

53. Article 115 (10 U.S.C. 915)—Communicating threats

a. *Text of statute.*

(a) COMMUNICATING THREATS GENERALLY.—Any person subject to this chapter who wrongfully communicates a threat to injure the person, property, or reputation of another shall be punished as a court-martial may direct.

(b) COMMUNICATING THREAT TO USE EXPLOSIVE, ETC.—Any person subject to this chapter who wrongfully communicates a threat to injure the person or property of another by use of (1) an explosive, (2) a weapon of mass destruction, (3) a biological or chemical agent, substance, or weapon, or (4) a hazardous material, shall be punished as a court-martial may direct.

(c) COMMUNICATING FALSE THREAT CONCERNING USE OF EXPLOSIVE, ETC.—Any person subject to this chapter who maliciously communicates a false threat concerning injury to the person or property of another by use of (1) an explosive, (2) a weapon of mass destruction, (3) a biological or chemical agent, substance, or weapon, or (4) a hazardous material, shall be punished as a court-martial may direct. As used in the preceding sentence, the term "false threat" means a threat that, at the time the threat is communicated, is known to be false by the person communicating the threat.

b. *Elements.*

(1) *Threats generally.*

(a) That the accused communicated certain language expressing a present determination or intent to injure the person, property, or reputation of another person, presently or in the future;

(b) That the communication was made known to that person or to a third person; and

(c) That the communication was wrongful.

(2) *Threat to use explosive, etc.*

(a) That the accused communicated certain language;

(b) That the information communicated amounted to a threat;

(c) That the harm threatened was to be done by means of an explosive; weapon of mass destruction; biological or chemical agent, substance, or weapon; or hazardous material; and

(d) That the communication was wrongful.

(3) *False threats concerning use of explosives, etc.*

(a) That the accused communicated or conveyed certain information;

(b) That the information communicated or conveyed concerned an attempt being made or to be made by means of an explosive; weapon of mass destruction; biological or chemical agent, substance, or weapon; or hazardous material, to unlawfully kill, injure, or intimidate a person or to unlawfully damage or destroy certain property;

(c) That the information communicated or conveyed by the accused was false and that the accused then knew it to be false; and

(d) That the communication of the information by the accused was malicious.

c. *Explanation.*

(1) *Threat.* A "threat" means an expressed present determination or intent to kill, injure, or intimidate a person or to damage or destroy certain property presently or in the future. The communication must be one that a reasonable person would understand as expressing a present determination or intent to wrongfully injure the person, property, or reputation of another person, presently or in the future. Proof that the accused actually intended to kill, injure, intimidate, damage or destroy is not required.

(2) *Wrongful.* A communication must be wrongful in order to constitute this offense. The wrongfulness of the communication relates to the accused's subjective intent. For purposes of this paragraph, the mental state requirement is satisfied if the accused transmitted the communication for the purpose of issuing a threat or with knowledge that the communication will be viewed as a threat. A statement made under circumstances that reveal it to be in jest or for an innocent or legitimate purpose that contradicts the expressed intent to commit the act is not wrongful. Nor is the offense committed by the mere statement of intent to commit an unlawful act not involving a threat.

(3) *Explosive.* "Explosive" means gunpowder, powders used for blasting, all forms of high explosives, blasting materials, fuses (other than electrical circuit breakers), detonators, and other detonating agents, smokeless powders, any explosive bomb, grenade, missile, or similar device, and any incendiary bomb or grenade, fire bomb, or similar device, and any other explosive compound, mixture, or similar material.

(4) *Weapon of mass destruction.* A "weapon of mass destruction" means any device, explosive or otherwise, that is intended, or has the capability, to cause death or serious bodily injury to a significant number of people through the release, dissemination, or impact of: toxic or poisonous chemicals, or their precursors; a disease organism; or radiation or radioactivity.

(5) *Biological agent.* The term "biological agent" means any microorganism (including bacteria, viruses, fungi, rickettsiac, or protozoa), pathogen, or infectious substance, and any naturally occurring, bioengineered, or synthesized component of any such micro-organism, pathogen, or infectious substance, whatever its origin or method of production, that is capable of causing—

(a) death, disease, or other biological malfunction in a human, an animal, a plant, or another living organism;

(b) deterioration of food, water, equipment, supplies, or materials of any kind; or

(c) deleterious alteration of the environment.

(6) *Chemical agent, substance, or weapon.* A "chemical agent, substance, or weapon" refers to a toxic chemical and its precursors or a munition or device, specifically designed to cause death or other harm through toxic properties of those chemicals that would be released as a result of the employment of such munition or device, and any equipment specifically designed for use directly in connection with the employment of such munitions or devices.

(7) *Hazardous material.* A substance or material (including explosive, radioactive material, etiologic agent, flammable or combustible liquid or solid, poison, oxidizing or corrosive material, and compressed gas, or mixture thereof) or a group or class of material designated as hazardous by the Secretary of Transportation.

(8) *Malicious*. A communication is malicious if the accused believed that the information would probably interfere with the peaceful use of the building, vehicle, aircraft, or other property concerned, or would cause fear or concern to one or more persons.

d. *Maximum punishment.*

(1) *Threats and false threats generally*. Dishonorable discharge, forfeiture of all pay and allowances, and confinement for 3 years.

(2) *Threats and false threats concerning use of explosives, etc.* Dishonorable discharge, forfeitures of all pay and allowances, and confinement for 10 years.

e. *Sample specifications.*

(1) *Threats generally.*

In that __________ (personal jurisdiction data), did, (at/on board—location) (subject-matter jurisdiction data, if required), on or about _____ 20 __, wrongfully communicate to __________ a threat (to injure _____ by _____) (to accuse _____ of having committed the offense of _____) (_____).

(2) *Threats concerning use of explosives, etc.*

In that __________ (personal jurisdiction data) did, (at/on board—location) (subject-matter jurisdiction data, if required), on or about _____ 20 __, wrongfully communicate certain information, to wit: __________, which language constituted a threat to harm a person or property by means of a(n) [explosive; weapon of mass destruction; biological agent, substance, or weapon; chemical agent, substance, or weapon; and/or (a) hazardous material(s)].

(3) *False threats concerning use of explosives, etc.*

In that __________ (personal jurisdiction data) did, (at/on board—location) (subject-matter jurisdiction data, if required), on or about _____ 20 __, maliciously (communicate) (convey) certain information concerning an attempt being made or to be made to unlawfully [(kill) (injure) (intimidate) __________] [(damage) (destroy) __________] by means of a(n) [explosive; weapon of mass destruction; biological agent, substance, or weapon; chemical agent, substance, or weapon; and/or (a) hazardous material(s)], to wit: __________, which information was false and which the accused then knew to be false.

54. Article 116 (10 U.S.C. 916)—Riot or breach of peace

a. *Text of statute.*

Any person subject to this chapter who causes or participates in any riot or breach of the peace shall be punished as a court-martial may direct.

b. *Elements.*

(1) *Riot.*

(a) That the accused was a member of an assembly of three or more persons;

(b) That the accused and at least two other members of this group mutually intended to assist one another against anyone who might oppose them in doing an act for some private purpose;

(c) That the group or some of its members, in furtherance of such purpose, unlawfully committed a tumultuous disturbance of the peace in a violent or turbulent manner; and

(d) That these acts terrorized the public in general in that they caused or were intended to cause public alarm or terror.

(2) *Breach of the peace.*

(a) That the accused caused or participated in a certain act of a violent or turbulent nature; and

(b) That the peace was thereby unlawfully disturbed.

c. *Explanation.*

(1) *Riot.* A riot is a tumultuous disturbance of the peace by three or more persons assembled together in furtherance of a common purpose to execute some enterprise of a private nature by concerted action against anyone who might oppose them, committed in such a violent and turbulent manner as to cause or be calculated to cause public terror. The gravamen of the offense of riot is terrorization of the public. It is immaterial whether the act intended was lawful. Furthermore, it is not necessary that the common purpose be determined before the assembly. It is sufficient if the assembly begins to execute in a tumultuous manner a common purpose formed after it assembled.

(2) *Breach of the peace.* A breach of the peace is an unlawful disturbance of the peace by an outward demonstration of a violent or turbulent nature. The acts or conduct contemplated by this article are those which disturb the public tranquility or impinge upon the peace and good order to which the community is entitled. Engaging in an affray and unlawful discharge of firearms in a public street are examples of conduct which may constitute a breach of the peace. Loud speech and unruly conduct may also constitute a breach

of the peace by the speaker. A speaker may also be guilty of causing a breach of the peace if the speaker uses language which can reasonably be expected to produce a violent or turbulent response and a breach of the peace results. The fact that the words are true or used under provocation is not a defense, nor is tumultuous conduct excusable because incited by others.

(3) *Community and public.* Community and public include a military organization, post, camp, ship, aircraft, or station.

d. *Maximum punishment.*

(1) *Riot.* Dishonorable discharge, forfeiture of all pay and allowances, and confinement for 10 years.

(2) *Breach of the peace.* Confinement for 6 months and forfeiture of two-thirds pay per month for 6 months.

e. *Sample specifications.*

(1) *Riot.*

In that __________ (personal jurisdiction data), did, (at/on board—location) (subject-matter jurisdiction data, if required), on or about _____ 20 __, (cause) (participate in) a riot by unlawfully assembling with _____ (and _____) (and) (others to the number of about _____ whose names are unknown) for the purpose of (resisting the police of _____) (assaulting passers-by) (_____), and in furtherance of said purpose did (fight with said police) (assault certain persons, to wit: _____) (_____), to the terror and disturbance of _____.

(2) *Breach of the peace.*

In that __________ (personal jurisdiction data), did, (at/on board—location) (subject-matter jurisdiction data, if required), on or about _____ 20 __, (cause) (participate in) a breach of the peace by (wrongfully engaging in a fist fight in the dayroom with __________) (using the following provoking language (toward _____), to wit: "_____," or words to that effect) (wrongfully shouting and singing in a public place, to wit: _____) (_____).

55. Article 117 (10 U.S.C. 917)—Provoking speeches or gestures

a. *Text of statute.*

Any person subject to this chapter who uses provoking or reproachful words or gestures towards any other person subject to this chapter shall be punished as a court-martial may direct.

b. *Elements.*

(1) That the accused wrongfully used words or gestures toward a certain person;

(2) That the words or gestures used were provoking or reproachful; and

(3) That the person toward whom the words or gestures were used was a person subject to the UCMJ.

c. *Explanation.*

(1) *In general.* As used in this article, provoking and reproachful describe those words or gestures which are used in the presence of the person to whom they are directed and which a reasonable person would expect to induce a breach of the peace under the circumstances. These words and gestures do not include reprimands, censures, reproofs and the like which may properly be administered in the interests of training, efficiency, or discipline in the armed forces.

(2) *Knowledge.* It is not necessary that the accused have knowledge that the person toward whom the words or gestures are directed is a person subject to the UCMJ.

d. *Maximum punishment.* Confinement for 6 months and forfeiture of two-thirds pay per month for 6 months.

e. *Sample specification.*

In that __________ (personal jurisdiction data), did, (at/on board—location) (subject-matter jurisdiction data, if required), on or about _____ 20 __, wrongfully use (provoking) (reproachful) (words, to wit: "__________" or words to that effect) (and) (gestures, to wit: __________) towards (Sergeant __________, U.S. Air Force) (__________).

55a. Article 117a (10 U.S.C. 917a)—Wrongful broadcast or distribution of intimate visual images

a. *Text of statute.*

(a) PROHIBITION.—Any person subject to this chapter—

(1) who knowingly and wrongfully broadcasts or distributes an intimate visual image of another person or a visual image of sexually explicit conduct involving a person who—

(A) is at least 18 years of age at the time the intimate visual image or visual image of sexually explicit conduct was created;

(B) is identifiable from the intimate visual image or visual image of sexually explicit conduct itself, or from information displayed in connection with the intimate visual image or visual image of sexually explicit conduct; and

(C) does not explicitly consent to the broadcast or distribution of the intimate visual image or visual image of sexually explicit conduct;

(2) who knows or reasonably should have known that the intimate visual image or visual image of sexually explicit conduct was made under circumstances in which the person depicted in the intimate visual image or visual image of sexually explicit conduct retained a reasonable expectation of privacy regarding any broadcast or distribution of the intimate visual image or visual image of sexually explicit conduct;

(3) who knows or reasonably should have known that the broadcast or distribution of the intimate visual image or visual image of sexually explicit conduct is likely—

(A) to cause harm, harassment, intimidation, emotional distress, or financial loss for the person depicted in the intimate visual image or visual image of sexually explicit conduct; or

(B) to harm substantially the depicted person with respect to that person's health, safety, business, calling, career, financial condition, reputation, or personal relationships; and

(4) whose conduct, under the circumstances, had a reasonably direct and palpable connection to a military mission or military environment,

is guilty of wrongful distribution of intimate visual images or visual images of sexually explicit conduct and shall be punished as a court-martial may direct.

(b) DEFINITIONS.—In this section:

(1) BROADCAST.—The term "broadcast" means to electronically transmit a visual image with the intent that it be viewed by a person or persons.

(2) DISTRIBUTE.—The term "distribute" means to deliver to the actual or constructive possession of another person, including transmission by mail or electronic means.

(3) INTIMATE VISUAL IMAGE.—The term "intimate visual image" means a visual image that depicts a private area of a person.

(4) PRIVATE AREA. —The term "private area" means the naked or underwear-clad genitalia, anus, buttocks, or female areola or nipple.

(5) REASONABLE EXPECTATION OF PRIVACY. — The term "reasonable expectation of privacy" means circumstances in which a reasonable person would believe that a private

area of the person, or sexually explicit conduct involving the person, would not be visible to the public.

(6) SEXUALLY EXPLICIT CONDUCT. —The term "sexually explicit conduct" means actual or simulated genital-genital contact, oral-genital contact, anal-genital contact, or oral-anal contact, whether between persons of the same or opposite sex, bestiality, masturbation, or sadistic or masochistic abuse.

(7) VISUAL IMAGE. —The term "visual image" means the following:

(A) Any developed or undeveloped photograph, picture, film, or video.

(B) Any digital or computer image, picture, film, or video made by any means, including those transmitted by any means, including streaming media, even if not stored in a permanent format.

(C) Any digital or electronic data capable of conversion into a visual image.

b. *Elements.*

(1) That the accused knowingly and wrongfully broadcasted or distributed a visual image;

(2) That the visual image is an intimate visual image of another person or a visual image of sexually explicit conduct involving another person;

(3) That the person depicted in the intimate visual image or visual image of sexually explicit conduct—

(a) is at least 18 years of age at the time the intimate visual image or visual image of sexually explicit conduct was created;

(b) is identifiable from the intimate visual image or visual image of sexually explicit conduct itself or from information displayed in connection with the intimate visual image or visual image of sexually explicit conduct; and

(c) does not explicitly consent to the broadcast or distribution of the intimate visual image or visual image of sexually explicit conduct;

(4) That the accused knew or reasonably should have known that the intimate visual image or visual image

of sexually explicit conduct was made under circumstances in which the person depicted retained a reasonable expectation of privacy regarding any broadcast or distribution of the intimate visual image or visual image of sexually explicit conduct;

(5) That the accused knew or reasonably should have known that the broadcast or distribution of the intimate visual image or visual image of sexually explicit conduct was likely to—

(a) cause harm, harassment, intimidation, emotional distress, or financial loss for the person depicted in the intimate visual image or visual image of sexually explicit conduct; or

(b) harm substantially the depicted person with respect to that person's health, safety, business, calling, career, financial condition, reputation, or personal relationships; and

(6) That the conduct of the accused, under the circumstances, had a reasonably direct and palpable connection to a military mission or military environment.

c. *Explanation.* See Paragraph 55a.a.(b) for definitions.

(1) *Wrongful.* Wrongful means without legal justification or excuse. This paragraph shall not apply in the case of a visual image the disclosure of which is in the bona fide public interest. For example, this paragraph does not prohibit any lawful law enforcement, correctional, or intelligence activity; shall not apply to the reporting of unlawful activity; and shall not apply to a subpoena or court order for use in a legal proceeding.

(2) *Reasonable Expectation of Privacy.* A reasonable expectation of privacy is determined based on the totality of the circumstances.

(3) *A reasonably direct and palpable connection to a military mission or military environment.* The connection between the conduct and a military mission or military environment is contextually oriented and cannot be evidenced by conduct that is connected only in a remote or indirect sense. To constitute an offense under the UCMJ, the conduct must have a measurably divisive effect on unit or organization discipline, morale, or cohesion, or must be clearly detrimental to the authority or stature of or respect toward a Servicemember.

d. *Maximum punishment.* Dishonorable discharge, forfeiture of all pay and allowances, and confinement for 2 years.

e. *Sample specification.*

In that ____ (personal jurisdiction data), did (at/on board-location), on or about __ 20 _, knowingly and wrongfully [(distribute) (broadcast)] [(an intimate visual image of _______) (a visual image of sexually explicit conduct involving ________)], a person who was at least 18 years of age when the image was created, is identifiable from (the image itself) (information conveyed in connection with the image), and did not explicitly consent to the (broadcast) (distribution) of the image, when the accused (knew) (reasonably should have known) the image was made under circumstances in which ___________ retained a reasonable expectation of privacy regarding any (broadcast) (distribution) of the image, and where the accused (knew) (reasonably should have known) that the (broadcast) (distribution) of the image was likely to [cause (harm) (harassment) (intimidation) (emotional distress) (financial loss), to wit: ____] [harm substantially the (health) (safety) (business) (calling) (career) (financial condition) (reputation) (personal relationships), to wit: ______] and that, under the circumstances, such conduct had a reasonably direct and palpable connection to a (military mission) (military environment)."

56. Article 118 (10 U.S.C. 918)—Murder

a. *Text of statute.*

Any person subject to this chapter who, without justification or excuse, unlawfully kills a human being, when he—

(1) has a premeditated design to kill;

(2) intends to kill or inflict great bodily harm;

(3) is engaged in an act which is inherently dangerous to another and evinces a wanton disregard of human life; or

(4) is engaged in the perpetration or attempted perpetration of burglary, rape, rape of a child, sexual assault, sexual assault of a child, aggravated sexual contact, sexual abuse of a child, robbery or aggravated arson;

is guilty of murder, and shall suffer such punishment as a court-martial may direct, except that if found guilty under clause (1) or (4), he shall suffer death or imprisonment for life as a court-martial may direct.

b. *Elements.*

(1) *Premeditated murder.*

(a) That a certain named or described person is dead;

(b) That the death resulted from the act or omission of the accused;

(c) That the killing was unlawful; and

(d) That, at the time of the killing, the accused had a premeditated design to kill.

(2) *Intent to kill or inflict great bodily harm.*

(a) That a certain named or described person is dead;

(b) That the death resulted from the act or omission of the accused;

(c) That the killing was unlawful; and

(d) That, at the time of the killing, the accused had the intent to kill or inflict great bodily harm upon a person.

(3) *Act inherently dangerous to another.*

(a) That a certain named or described person is dead;

(b) That the death resulted from the intentional act of the accused;

(c) That this act was inherently dangerous to another and showed a wanton disregard for human life;

(d) That the accused knew that death or great bodily harm was a probable consequence of the act; and

(e) That the killing was unlawful.

(4) *During certain offenses.*

(a) That a certain named or described person is dead;

(b) That the death resulted from the act or omission of the accused;

(c) That the killing was unlawful; and

(d) That, at the time of the killing, the accused was engaged in the perpetration or attempted perpetration of burglary, rape, rape of a child, sexual assault, sexual assault of a child, aggravated sexual contact, sexual abuse of a child, robbery, or aggravated arson.

c. *Explanation.*

(1) *In general.* Killing a human being is unlawful when done without justification or excuse. *See* R.C.M. 916. Whether an unlawful killing constitutes murder or a lesser offense depends upon the circumstances. The offense is committed at the place of the act or omission although the victim may have died elsewhere. Whether death occurs at the time of the accused's act or omission, or at some time thereafter, it must have followed from an injury received by the victim which resulted from the act or omission.

(2) *Premeditated murder.*

(a) *Premeditation.* A murder is not premeditated unless the thought of taking life was consciously conceived and the act or omission by which it was taken was intended. Premeditated murder is murder committed after the formation of a specific intent to kill someone and consideration of the act intended. It is not necessary that the intention to kill have been entertained for any particular or considerable length of time. When a fixed purpose to kill has been deliberately formed, it is immaterial how soon afterwards it is put into execution. The existence of premeditation may be inferred from the circumstances.

(b) *Transferred premeditation.* When an accused with a premeditated design attempted to unlawfully kill a certain person, but, by mistake or inadvertence, killed another person, the accused is still criminally responsible for a premeditated murder, because the premeditated design to kill is transferred from the intended victim to the actual victim.

(c) *Intoxication.* Voluntary intoxication (*see* R.C.M. 916(l)(2)) not amounting to legal insanity may reduce premeditated murder (Article 118(1)) to unpremeditated murder (Article 118(2) or (3)) but it does not reduce either premeditated murder or unpremeditated murder to manslaughter (Article 119) or any other lesser offense.

(3) *Intent to kill or inflict great bodily harm.*

(a) *Intent.* An unlawful killing without premeditation is also murder when the accused had either an intent to kill or inflict great bodily harm. It may be inferred that a person intends the natural and probable consequences of an act purposely done. Hence, if a person does an intentional act likely to result in death or great bodily injury, it may be inferred that death or great bodily injury was intended. The intent need not be directed toward the person killed, or exist for any particular time before commission of the act, or have previously existed at all. It is sufficient that it existed at the time of the act or omission (except if death is inflicted in the heat of a sudden passion caused by adequate provocation – *see* paragraph 57). For example, a person committing housebreaking who strikes and kills the householder attempting to prevent flight can be guilty of murder even if the householder was not seen until the moment before striking the fatal blow.

(b) *Great bodily harm*. "Great bodily harm" means serious injury; it does not include minor injuries such as a black eye or a bloody nose, but it does include fractured or dislocated bones, deep cuts, torn members of the body, serious damage to internal organs, and other serious bodily injuries. It is synonymous with the term "grievous bodily harm."

(c) *Intoxication*. Voluntary intoxication not amounting to legal insanity does not reduce unpremeditated murder to manslaughter (Article 119) or any other lesser offense.

(4) *Act inherently dangerous to others*.

(a) *Wanton disregard of human life*. Intentionally engaging in an act inherently dangerous to another—although without an intent to cause the death of or great bodily harm to any particular person, or even with a wish that death will not be caused—may also constitute murder if the act shows wanton disregard of human life. Such disregard is characterized by heedlessness of the probable consequences of the act or omission, or indifference to the likelihood of death or great bodily harm. Examples include throwing a live grenade toward another in jest or flying an aircraft very low over one or more persons to cause alarm.

(b) *Knowledge*. The accused must know that death or great bodily harm was a probable consequence of the inherently dangerous act. Such knowledge may be proved by circumstantial evidence.

(5) *During certain offenses*.

(a) *In general*. The commission or attempted commission of any of the offenses listed in Article 118(4) is likely to result in homicide, and when an unlawful killing occurs as a consequence of the perpetration or attempted perpetration of one of these offenses, the killing is murder. Under these circumstances it is not a defense that the killing was unintended or accidental.

(b) *Separate offenses*. The perpetration or attempted perpetration of burglary, rape, rape of a child, sexual assault, sexual assault of a child, aggravated sexual contact, sexual abuse of a child, robbery, or aggravated arson may be charged separately from the homicide.

d. *Maximum punishment*.

(1) Article 118(1) or (4)—death. Mandatory minimum—imprisonment for life with the eligibility for parole.

(2) Article 118(2) or (3)—such punishment other than death as a court-martial may direct.

e. *Sample specification*.

In that ______________ (personal jurisdiction data), did, (at/on board—location) (subject-matter jurisdiction data, if required), on or about ______ 20___, (with premeditation) (while (perpetrating) (attempting to perpetrate)__________) murder __________________ by means of (shooting (him) (her) with a rifle) (__________).

57. Article 119 (10 U.S.C. 919)—Manslaughter

a. *Text of statute*.

(a) Any person subject to this chapter who, with an intent to kill or inflict great bodily harm, unlawfully kills a human being in the heat of sudden passion caused by adequate provocation is guilty of voluntary manslaughter and shall be punished as a court-martial may direct.

(b) Any person subject to this chapter who, without an intent to kill or inflict great bodily harm, unlawfully kills a human being—

(1) by culpable negligence; or

(2) while perpetrating or attempting to perpetrate an offense, other than those named in clause (4) of section 918 of this title (article 118), directly affecting the person;

is guilty of involuntary manslaughter and shall be punished as a court-martial may direct.

b. *Elements*.

(1) *Voluntary manslaughter*.

(a) That a certain named or described person is dead;

(b) That the death resulted from the act or omission of the accused;

(c) That the killing was unlawful; and

(d) That, at the time of the killing, the accused had the intent to kill or inflict great bodily harm upon the person killed.

[Note: Add the following if applicable]

(e) That the person killed was a child under the age of 16 years.

(2) *Involuntary manslaughter*.

(a) That a certain named or described person is dead;

(b) That the death resulted from the act or omission of the accused;

(c) That the killing was unlawful; and

(d) That this act or omission of the accused constituted culpable negligence, or occurred while the accused was perpetrating or attempting to perpetrate an offense directly affecting the person other than burglary, rape, rape of a child, sexual assault, sexual assault of a child, aggravated sexual contact, sexual abuse of a child, robbery, or aggravated arson.

[Note: Add the following if applicable]

(e) That the person killed was a child under the age of 16 years.

c. *Explanation.*

(1) *Voluntary manslaughter.*

(a) *Nature of offense.* An unlawful killing, although done with an intent to kill or inflict great bodily harm, is not murder but voluntary manslaughter if committed in the heat of sudden passion caused by adequate provocation. Heat of passion may result from fear or rage. A person may be provoked to such an extent that in the heat of sudden passion caused by the provocation, although not in necessary defense of life or to prevent bodily harm, a fatal blow may be struck before self-control has returned. Although adequate provocation does not excuse the homicide, it does preclude conviction of murder.

(b) *Nature of provocation.* The provocation must be adequate to excite uncontrollable passion in a reasonable person, and the act of killing must be committed under and because of the passion. However, the provocation must not be sought or induced as an excuse for killing or doing harm. If, judged by the standard of a reasonable person, sufficient cooling time elapses between the provocation and the killing, the offense is murder, even if the accused's passion persists. Examples of acts which may, depending on the circumstances, constitute adequate provocation are the unlawful infliction of great bodily harm, unlawful imprisonment, and the sight by one spouse of an act of adultery committed by the other spouse. Insulting or abusive words or gestures, a slight blow with the hand or fist, and trespass or other injury to property are not, standing alone, adequate provocation.

(c) *When committed upon a child under 16 years of age.* The maximum punishment is increased when voluntary manslaughter is committed upon a child under 16 years of age. The accused's knowledge that the child was under 16 years of age at the time of the offense is not required for the increased maximum punishment.

(2) *Involuntary manslaughter.*

(a) *Culpable negligence.*

(i) Nature of culpable negligence. Culpable negligence is a degree of carelessness greater than simple negligence. It is a negligent act or omission accompanied by a culpable disregard for the foreseeable consequences to others of that act or omission. Thus, the basis of a charge of involuntary manslaughter may be a negligent act or omission which, when viewed in the light of human experience, might foreseeably result in the death of another, even though death would not necessarily be a natural and probable consequence of the act or omission. Acts which may amount to culpable negligence include negligently conducting target practice so that the bullets go in the direction of an inhabited house within range; pointing a pistol in jest at another and pulling the trigger, believing, but without taking reasonable precautions to ascertain, that it would not be dangerous; and carelessly leaving poisons or dangerous drugs where they may endanger life.

(ii) Legal duty required. When there is no legal duty to act there can be no neglect. Thus, when a stranger makes no effort to save a drowning person, or a person allows a beggar to freeze or starve to death, no crime is committed.

(b) *Offense directly affecting the person.* An "offense directly affecting the person" means an offense affecting some particular person as distinguished from an offense affecting society in general. Among offenses directly affecting the person are the various types of assault, battery, false imprisonment, voluntary engagement in an affray, and maiming.

(c) *When committed upon a child under 16 years of age.* The maximum punishment is increased when involuntary manslaughter is committed upon a child under 16 years of age. The accused's knowledge that the child was under 16 years of age at the time of the offense is not required for the increased maximum punishment.

d. *Maximum punishment.*

(1) *Voluntary manslaughter.* Dishonorable discharge, forfeiture of all pay and allowances, and confinement for 15 years.

(2) *Involuntary manslaughter.* Dishonorable discharge, forfeiture of all pay and allowances, and confinement for 10 years.

(3) *Voluntary manslaughter of a child under 16 years of age.* Dishonorable discharge, forfeiture of all pay and allowances, and confinement for 20 years.

(4) *Involuntary manslaughter of a child under 16 years of age.* Dishonorable discharge, forfeiture of all pay and allowances, and confinement for 15 years.

e. *Sample specification.*

(1) *Voluntary manslaughter.*

In that _________ (personal jurisdiction data), did, (at/on board—location) (subject-matter jurisdiction data, if required), on or about _____ 20 ___, willfully and unlawfully kill ___________, (a child under 16 years of age) by ___________ (him) (her) (in) (on) the ___________ with a __________.

(2) *Involuntary manslaughter.*

In that _________ (personal jurisdiction data), did, (at/on board—location) (subject-matter jurisdiction data, if required), on or about _____ 20 ___, (by culpable negligence) (while (perpetrating) (attempting to perpetrate) an offense directly affecting the person of __________, to wit: (maiming) (a battery) (_______)) unlawfully kill __________, (a child under 16 years of age) by ___________ (him) (her) (in) (on) the ___________ with a __________.

58. Article 119a (10 U.S.C. 919a)—Death or injury of an unborn child

a. *Text of statute.*

(a)(1) Any person subject to this chapter who engages in conduct that violates any of the provisions of law listed in subsection (b) and thereby causes the death of, or bodily injury (as defined in section 1365 of title 18) to, a child, who is in utero at the time the conduct takes place, is guilty of a separate offense under this section and shall, upon conviction, be punished by such punishment, other than death, as a court-martial may direct, which shall be consistent with the punishments prescribed by the President for that conduct had that injury or death occurred to the unborn child's mother.

(2) An offense under this section does not require proof that—

(i) the person engaging in the conduct had knowledge or should have had knowledge that the victim of the underlying offense was pregnant; or

(ii) the accused intended to cause the death of, or bodily injury to, the unborn child.

(3) If the person engaging in the conduct thereby intentionally kills or attempts to kill the unborn child, that person shall, instead of being punished under paragraph (1), be punished as provided under sections 880, 918, and 919(a) of this title (articles 80, 118, and 119(a)) for intentionally killing or attempting to kill a human being.

(4) Notwithstanding any other provision of law, the death penalty shall not be imposed for an offense under this section.

(b) The provisions referred to in subsection (a) are sections 918, 919(a), 919(b)(2), 920(a), 922, 926, 928, and 928a of this title (articles 118, 119(a), 119(b)(2), 120(a), 122, 126, 128, and 128a).

(c) Nothing in this section shall be construed to permit the prosecution—

(1) of any person for conduct relating to an abortion for which the consent of the pregnant woman, or a person authorized by law to act on her behalf, has been obtained or for which such consent is implied by law;

(2) of any person for any medical treatment of the pregnant woman or her unborn child; or

(3) of any woman with respect to her unborn child.

(d) In this section, the term "unborn child" means a child in utero, and the term "child in utero" or "child, who is in utero" means a member of the species homo sapiens, at any stage of development, who is carried in the womb.

b. *Elements.*

(1) *Injuring an unborn child.*

(a) That the accused was engaged in the [(murder (article 118)), (voluntary manslaughter (article 119(a))), (involuntary manslaughter (article 119(b)(2))), (rape (article 120(a))), (robbery (article 122)), (maiming (article 128a)), (assault (article 128)), of] or [burning or setting afire, as arson (article 126), of (a dwelling inhabited by) (a structure or property (known to be occupied by) (belonging to))] a woman;

(b) That the woman was then pregnant; and

(c) That the accused thereby caused bodily injury to the unborn child of that woman.

(2) *Killing an unborn child.*

(a) That the accused was engaged in the [(murder (article 118)), (voluntary manslaughter (article 119(a))), (involuntary manslaughter (article 119(b)(2))), (rape (article 120(a))), (robbery (article

122)), (maiming (article 128a)), (assault (article 128)), of] or [burning or setting afire, as arson (article 126), of (a dwelling inhabited by) (a structure or property (known to be occupied by) (belonging to))] a woman;

(b) That the woman was then pregnant; and

(c) That the accused thereby caused the death of the unborn child of that woman.

(3) *Attempting to kill an unborn child.*

(a) That the accused was engaged in the [(murder (article 118)), (voluntary manslaughter (article 119(a))), (involuntary manslaughter (article 119(b)(2))), (rape (article 120(a))), (robbery (article 122)), (maiming (article 128a)), (assault (article 128)), of] or [burning or setting afire, as arson (article 126), of (a dwelling inhabited by) (a structure or property (known to be occupied by) (belonging to))] a woman;

(b) That the woman was then pregnant; and

(c) That the accused thereby intended and attempted to kill the unborn child of that woman.

(4) *Intentionally killing an unborn child.*

(a) That the accused was engaged in the [(murder (article 118)), (voluntary manslaughter (article 119(a))), (involuntary manslaughter (article 119(b)(2))), (rape (article 120(a))), (robbery (article 122)), (maiming (article 128a)), (assault (article 128)), of] or [burning or setting afire, as arson (article 126), of (a dwelling inhabited by) (a structure or property (known to be occupied by) (belonging to))] a woman;

(b) That the woman was then pregnant; and

(c) That the accused thereby intentionally killed the unborn child of that woman.

c. *Explanation.*

(1) *Nature of offense.* This article makes it a separate, punishable crime to cause the death of or bodily injury to an unborn child while engaged in arson (article 126, UCMJ); murder (article 118, UCMJ); voluntary manslaughter (article 119(a), UCMJ); involuntary manslaughter (article 119(b)(2), UCMJ); rape (article 120(a), UCMJ); robbery (article 122, UCMJ); maiming (article 128a, UCMJ); or assault (article 128, UCMJ) against a pregnant woman. For all underlying offenses, except arson, this article requires that the victim of the underlying offense be the pregnant mother. For purposes of arson, the pregnant mother must have some nexus to the arson such that she sustained some bodily injury due to the arson. For the purposes of this article the term "woman" means a female of any age. This article does not permit the prosecution of any—

(a) person for conduct relating to an abortion for which the consent of the pregnant woman, or a person authorized by law to act on her behalf, has been obtained or for which such consent is implied by law;

(b) person for any medical treatment of the pregnant woman or her unborn child; or

(c) woman with respect to her unborn child.

(2) *The offenses of injuring an unborn child and killing an unborn child do not require proof that—*

(a) the accused had knowledge or should have had knowledge that the victim of the underlying offense was pregnant; or

(b) the accused intended to cause the death of, or bodily injury to, the unborn child.

(3) The offense of attempting to kill an unborn child requires that the accused intended by his conduct to cause the death of the unborn child (*see* subparagraph b.(3)(c) of this paragraph).

(4) *Bodily injury.* For the purpose of this offense, the term "bodily injury" is that which is provided by section 1365 of title 18, to wit: a cut, abrasion, bruise, burn, or disfigurement; physical pain; illness; impairment of the function of a bodily member, organ, or mental faculty; or any other injury to the body, no matter how temporary.

(5) *Unborn child.* "Unborn child" means a child in utero or a member of the species homo sapiens who is carried in the womb, at any stage of development, from conception to birth.

d. *Maximum punishment.* The maximum punishment for (1) Injuring an unborn child; (2) Killing an unborn child; (3) Attempting to kill an unborn child; or (4) Intentionally killing an unborn child is such punishment, other than death, as a court-martial may direct, but shall be consistent with the punishment had the bodily injury, death, attempt to kill, or intentional killing occurred to the unborn child's mother.

d. Sample specifications.

(1) *Injuring an unborn child.*

In that ____________ (personal jurisdiction data), did (at/on board—location), (subject-matter jurisdiction data, if required), on or about _________ 20 ____, cause bodily injury to the unborn child of a pregnant woman, by engaging in the [(murder) (voluntary manslaughter) (involuntary manslaughter) (rape) (robbery) (maiming) (assault) of] [(burning) (setting afire) of (a dwelling inhabited by) (a structure or property known to (be occupied by) (belong to))] that woman.

(2) *Killing an unborn child.*

In that ____________ (personal jurisdiction data), did (at/on board—location), (subject-matter jurisdiction data, if required), on or about ________ 20 ____, cause the death of the unborn child of a pregnant woman, by engaging in the [(murder) (voluntary manslaughter) (involuntary manslaughter) (rape) (robbery) (maiming) (assault) of] [(burning) (setting afire) of (a dwelling inhabited by) (a structure or property known to (be occupied by) (belong to))] that woman.

(3) *Attempting to kill an unborn child.*

In that ____________ (personal jurisdiction data), did (at/on board—location), (subject-matter jurisdiction data, if required), on or about ________ 20 ____, attempt to kill the unborn child of a pregnant woman, by engaging in the [(murder) (voluntary manslaughter) (involuntary manslaughter) (rape) (robbery) (maiming) (assault) of] [(burning) (setting afire) of (a dwelling inhabited by) (a structure or property known to (be occupied by) (belong to))] that woman.

(4) *Intentionally killing an unborn child.*

In that ____________ (personal jurisdiction data), did (at/on board—location), (subject-matter jurisdiction data, if required), on or about ________ 20 ____, intentionally kill the unborn child of a pregnant woman, by engaging in the [(murder) (voluntary manslaughter) (involuntary manslaughter) (rape) (robbery) (maiming) (assault) of] [(burning) (setting afire) of (a dwelling inhabited by) (a structure or property known to (be occupied by) (belong to))] that woman.

59. Article 119b (10 U.S.C. 919b)—Child endangerment

a. *Text of statute.*

Any person subject to this chapter—

(1) who has a duty for the care of a child under the age of 16 years; and

(2) who, through design or culpable negligence, endangers the child's mental or physical health, safety, or welfare;

shall be punished as a court-martial may direct.

b. *Elements.*

(1) That the accused had a duty for the care of a certain child;

(2) That the child was under the age of 16 years; and

(3) That the accused endangered the child's mental or physical health, safety, or welfare through design or culpable negligence.

c. *Explanation.*

(1) *Design.* "Design" means on purpose, intentionally, or according to plan and requires specific intent to endanger the child.

(2) *Culpable negligence.* Culpable negligence is a degree of carelessness greater than simple negligence. It is a negligent act or omission accompanied by a culpable disregard for the foreseeable consequences to others of that act or omission. In the context of this offense, culpable negligence may include acts that, when viewed in the light of human experience, might foreseeably result in harm to a child. The age and maturity of the child, the conditions surrounding the neglectful conduct, the proximity of assistance available, the nature of the environment in which the child may have been left, the provisions made for care of the child, and the location of the parent or adult responsible for the child relative to the location of the child, among others, may be considered in determining whether the conduct constituted culpable negligence.

(3) *Harm.* Actual physical or mental harm to the child is not required. The offense requires that the accused's actions reasonably could have caused physical or mental harm or suffering. However, if the accused's conduct does cause actual physical or mental harm, the potential maximum punishment increases. See subparagraph 77.c.(1)(c) for an explanation of grievous bodily harm.

(4) *Endanger.* "Endanger" means to subject one to a reasonable probability of harm.

(5) *Age of victim as a factor.* While this offense may be committed against any child under 16, the age of the victim is a factor in the culpable negligence determination. Leaving a teenager alone for an evening may not be culpable (or even simple) negligence; leaving an infant or toddler for the same period might constitute culpable negligence. On the other hand, leaving a teenager without supervision for an extended period while the accused was on temporary duty outside commuting distance might constitute culpable negligence.

(6) *Duty required.* The duty of care is determined by the totality of the circumstances and may be

established by statute, regulation, legal parent-child relationship, mutual agreement, or assumption of control or custody by affirmative act. When there is no duty of care of a child, there is no offense under this paragraph. Thus, there is no offense when a stranger makes no effort to feed a starving child or an individual not charged with the care of a child does not prevent the child from running and playing in the street.

d. *Maximum punishment.*

(1) *Endangerment by design resulting in grievous bodily harm.* Dishonorable discharge, forfeiture of all pay and allowances, and confinement for 8 years.

(2) *Endangerment by design resulting in harm.* Dishonorable discharge, forfeiture of all pay and allowances, and confinement for 5 years.

(3) *Other cases by design.* Dishonorable discharge, forfeiture of all pay and allowances and confinement for 4 years.

(4) *Endangerment by culpable negligence resulting in grievous bodily harm.* Dishonorable discharge, forfeiture of all pay and allowances, and confinement for 3 years.

(5) *Endangerment by culpable negligence resulting in harm.* Bad-conduct discharge, forfeiture of all pay and allowances, and confinement for 2 years.

(6) *Other cases by culpable negligence.* Bad-conduct discharge, forfeiture of all pay and allowances, and confinement for 1 year.

e. *Sample specifications.*

(1) *Resulting in grievous bodily harm.*

In that____________(personal jurisdiction data), (at/on board—location) (subject-matter jurisdiction data, if required) on or about _____ 20 __, had a duty for the care of ________, a child under the age of 16 years and did endanger the (mental health) (physical health) (safety) (welfare) of said ____________, by (leaving the said _________ unattended in (his) (her) quarters for over _________ (hours) (days) with no adult present in the home) (by failing to obtain medical care for the said ________'s diabetic condition) (_________), and that such conduct (was by design) (constituted culpable negligence) (which resulted in grievous bodily harm, to wit:________________) (broken leg) (deep cut) (fractured skull)).

(2) *Resulting in harm.*

In that _________ (personal jurisdiction data), (at/on board—location) (subject-matter jurisdiction data, if required) on or about _________ 20 __, had a duty for the care of _________, a child under the age of 16 years, and did endanger the (mental health) (physical health) (safety) (welfare) of said _________, by (leaving the said _________unattended in (his) (her) quarters for over _________ (hours) (days) with no adult present in the home) (by failing to obtain medical care for the said _________'s diabetic condition) (______________), and that such conduct (was by design) (constituted culpable negligence) (which resulted in (harm, to wit:________) (a black eye) (bloody nose) (minor cut)).

(3) *Other cases.*

In that __________(personal jurisdiction data), (at/on board—location) (subject-matter jurisdiction data, if required) on or about ______ 20 __, was responsible for the care of __________, a child under the age of 16 years, and did endanger the (mental health) (physical health) (safety) (welfare) of said________, by (leaving the said _____________ unattended in (his) (her) quarters for over _________ (hours) (days) with no adult present in the home) (by failing to obtain medical care for the said ___________'s diabetic condition) (___________), and that such conduct (was by design) (constituted culpable negligence).

60. Article 120 (10 U.S.C. 920)—Rape and sexual assault generally

[Note: This statute applies to offenses committed on or after 1 January 2019. Previous versions of Article 120 are located as follows: for offenses committed on or before 30 September 2007, *see* Appendix 20; for offenses committed during the period 1 October 2007 through 27 June 2012, *see* Appendix 21; for offenses committed during the period 28 June 2012 through 31 December 2018, *see* Appendix 22.]

a. *Text of statute.*

(a) RAPE.—Any person subject to this chapter who commits a sexual act upon another person by—

(1) using unlawful force against that other person;

(2) using force causing or likely to cause death or grievous bodily harm to any person;

(3) threatening or placing that other person in fear that any person will be subjected to death, grievous bodily harm, or kidnapping;

(4) first rendering that other person unconscious; or

(5) administering to that other person by force or threat of force, or without the knowledge or consent of that person, a drug, intoxicant, or other similar substance and thereby substantially impairing the ability of that other person to appraise or control conduct;

is guilty of rape and shall be punished as a court-martial may direct.

(b) SEXUAL ASSAULT.—Any person subject to this chapter who—

(1) commits a sexual act upon another person by—

(A) threatening or placing that other person in fear;

(B) making a fraudulent representation that the sexual act serves a professional purpose; or

(C) inducing a belief by any artifice, pretense, or concealment that the person is another person;

(2) commits a sexual act upon another person—

(A) without the consent of the other person; or

(B) when the person knows or reasonably should know that the other person is asleep, unconscious, or otherwise unaware that the sexual act is occurring;

(3) commits a sexual act upon another person when the other person is incapable of consenting to the sexual act due to—

(A) impairment by any drug, intoxicant, or other similar substance, and that condition is known or reasonably should be known by the person; or

(B) a mental disease or defect, or physical disability, and that condition is known or reasonably should be known by the person;

is guilty of sexual assault and shall be punished as a court-martial may direct.

(c) AGGRAVATED SEXUAL CONTACT.—Any person subject to this chapter who commits or causes sexual contact upon or by another person, if to do so would violate subsection (a) (rape) had the sexual contact been a sexual act, is guilty of aggravated sexual contact and shall be punished as a court-martial may direct.

(d) ABUSIVE SEXUAL CONTACT.—Any person subject to this chapter who commits or causes sexual contact upon or by another person, if to do so would violate subsection (b) (sexual assault) had the sexual contact been a sexual act, is guilty of abusive sexual contact and shall be punished as a court-martial may direct.

(e) PROOF OF THREAT.—In a prosecution under this section, in proving that a person made a threat, it need not be proven that the person actually intended to carry out the threat or had the ability to carry out the threat.

(f) DEFENSES.—An accused may raise any applicable defenses available under this chapter or the Rules for Court-Martial. Marriage is not a defense for any conduct in issue in any prosecution under this section.

(g) DEFINITIONS.—In this section:

(1) SEXUAL ACT.—The term "sexual act" means—

(A) the penetration, however slight, of the penis into the vulva or anus or mouth;

(B) contact between the mouth and the penis, vulva, scrotum, or anus; or

(C) the penetration, however slight, of the vulva or penis or anus of another by any part of the body or any object, with an intent to abuse, humiliate, harass, or degrade any person or to arouse or gratify the sexual desire of any person.

(2) SEXUAL CONTACT.—The term "sexual contact" means touching, or causing another person to touch, either directly or through the clothing, the vulva, penis, scrotum, anus, groin, breast, inner thigh, or buttocks of any person, with an intent to abuse, humiliate, harass, or degrade any person or to arouse or gratify the sexual desire of any person. Touching may be accomplished by any part of the body or an object.

(3) GRIEVOUS BODILY HARM.—The term "grievous bodily harm" means serious bodily injury. It includes fractured or dislocated bones, deep cuts, torn members of the body, serious damage to internal organs, and other severe bodily injuries. It does not include minor injuries such as a black eye or a bloody nose.

(4) FORCE.—The term "force" means—

(A) the use of a weapon;

(B) the use of such physical strength or violence as is sufficient to overcome, restrain, or injure a person; or

(C) inflicting physical harm sufficient to coerce or compel submission by the victim.

(5) UNLAWFUL FORCE.—The term "unlawful force" means an act of force done without legal justification or excuse.

(6) THREATENING OR PLACING THAT OTHER PERSON IN FEAR.—The term "threatening or placing that other person in fear" means a communication or action that is of sufficient consequence to cause a reasonable fear that non-compliance will result in the victim or another person being subjected to the wrongful action contemplated by the communication or action.

(7) CONSENT.—

(A) The term "consent" means a freely given agreement to the conduct at issue by a competent person. An expression of lack of consent through words or conduct means there is no consent. Lack of verbal or physical resistance does not constitute consent. Submission resulting from the use of force, threat of force, or placing another person in fear also does not constitute consent. A current or previous dating or social or sexual relationship by itself or the manner of dress of the person involved with the accused in the conduct at issue does not constitute consent.

(B) A sleeping, unconscious, or incompetent person cannot consent. A person cannot consent to force causing or likely to cause death or grievous bodily harm or to being rendered unconscious. A person cannot consent while under threat or in fear or under the circumstances described in subparagraph (B) or (C) of subsection (b)(1).

(C) All the surrounding circumstances are to be considered in determining whether a person gave consent.

(8) INCAPABLE OF CONSENTING.—The term "incapable of consenting" means the person is—

(A) incapable of appraising the nature of the conduct at issue; or

(B) physically incapable of declining participation in, or communicating unwillingness to engage in, the sexual act at issue.

b. *Elements.*

(1) *Rape.*

(a) *By unlawful force.*

(i) That the accused committed a sexual act upon another person; and

(ii) That the accused did so with unlawful force.

(b) *By force causing or likely to cause death or grievous bodily harm.*

(i) That the accused committed a sexual act upon another person; and

(ii) That the accused did so by using force causing or likely to cause death or grievous bodily harm to any person.

(c) *By threatening or placing that other person in fear that any person would be subjected to death, grievous bodily harm, or kidnapping.*

(i) That the accused committed a sexual act upon another person; and

(ii) That the accused did so by threatening or placing that other person in fear that any person would be subjected to death, grievous bodily harm, or kidnapping.

(d) *By first rendering that other person unconscious.*

(i) That the accused committed a sexual act upon another person; and

(ii) That the accused did so by first rendering that other person unconscious.

(e) *By administering a drug, intoxicant, or other similar substance.*

(i) That the accused committed a sexual act upon another person; and

(ii) That the accused did so by administering to that other person by force or threat of force, or without the knowledge or consent of that person, a drug, intoxicant, or other similar substance and thereby substantially impairing the ability of that other person to appraise or control conduct.

(2) *Sexual assault.*

(a) *By threatening or placing that other person in fear.*

(i) That the accused committed a sexual act upon another person; and

(ii) That the accused did so by threatening or placing that other person in fear.

(b) *By fraudulent representation.*

(i) That the accused committed a sexual act upon another person; and

(ii) That the accused did so by making a fraudulent representation that the sexual act served a professional purpose.

(c) *By artifice, pretense, or concealment.*

(i) That the accused committed a sexual act upon another person; and

(ii) That the accused did so by inducing a belief by any artifice, pretense, or concealment that the accused was another person.

(d) *Without consent.*

(i) That the accused committed a sexual act upon another person; and

(ii) That the accused did so without the consent of the other person.

(e) *Of a person who is asleep, unconscious, or otherwise unaware the act is occurring.*

(i) That the accused committed a sexual act upon another person;

(ii) That the other person was asleep, unconscious, or otherwise unaware that the sexual act was occurring; and

(iii) That the accused knew or reasonably should have known that the other person was asleep, unconscious, or otherwise unaware that the sexual act was occurring.

(f) *When the other person is incapable of consenting.*

(i) That the accused committed a sexual act upon another person;

(ii) That the other person was incapable of consenting to the sexual act due to:

(A) Impairment by any drug, intoxicant or other similar substance; or

(B) A mental disease or defect, or physical disability; and

(iii) That the accused knew or reasonably should have known of that condition.

(3) *Aggravated sexual contact.*

(a) *By force.*

(i) That the accused committed sexual contact upon or by another person; and

(ii) That the accused did so with unlawful force.

(b) *By force causing or likely to cause death or grievous bodily harm.*

(i) That the accused committed sexual contact upon another person; and

(ii) That the accused did so by using force causing or likely to cause death or grievous bodily harm to any person.

(c) *By threatening or placing that other person in fear that any person would be subjected to death, grievous bodily harm, or kidnapping.*

(i) That the accused committed sexual contact upon another person; and

(ii) That the accused did so by threatening or placing that other person in fear that any person would be subjected to death, grievous bodily harm, or kidnapping.

(d) *By first rendering that other person unconscious.*

(i) That the accused committed sexual contact upon another person; and

(ii) That the accused did so by first rendering that other person unconscious.

(e) *By administering a drug, intoxicant, or other similar substance.*

(i) That the accused committed sexual contact upon another person; and

(ii) That the accused did so by administering to that other person by force or threat of force, or without the knowledge or consent of that person, a drug, intoxicant, or other similar substance and thereby substantially impairing the ability of that other person to appraise or control conduct.

(4) *Abusive sexual contact.*

(a) *By threatening or placing that other person in fear.*

(i) That the accused committed sexual contact upon or by another person; and

(ii) That the accused did so by threatening or placing that other person in fear.

(b) *By fraudulent representation.*

(i) That the accused committed sexual contact upon another person; and

(ii) That the accused did so by making a fraudulent representation that the sexual act served a professional purpose.

(c) *By artifice, pretense, or concealment.*

(i) That the accused committed sexual contact upon another person; and

(ii) That the accused did so by inducing a belief by any artifice, pretense, or concealment that the accused was another person.

(d) *Without consent.*

(i) That the accused committed sexual contact upon another person; and

(ii) That the accused did so without the consent of the other person.

(e) *Of a person who is asleep, unconscious, or otherwise unaware the contact is occurring.*

(i) That the accused committed sexual contact upon another person;

(ii) That the other person was asleep, unconscious, or otherwise unaware that the sexual contact was occurring; and

(iii) That the accused knew or reasonably should have known that the other person was asleep, unconscious, or otherwise unaware that the sexual contact was occurring.

(f) *When the other person is incapable of consenting.*

(i) That the accused committed sexual contact upon another person;

(ii) That the other person was incapable of consenting to the sexual contact due to:

(A) Impairment by any drug, intoxicant or other similar substance; or

(B) A mental disease or defect, or physical disability; and

(iii) That the accused knew or reasonably should have known of that condition.

c. *Explanation.*

(1) *In general.* Sexual offenses have been separated into three statutes: offenses against adults (Art. 120), offenses against children (Art. 120b), and other offenses (Art. 120c).

(2) *Definitions.* The terms are defined in subparagraph 60.a.(g).

(3) *Victim sexual behavior or predisposition and privilege. See* Mil. R. Evid. 412 concerning rules of evidence relating to the sexual behavior or predisposition of the victim of an alleged sexual offense. *See* Mil. R. Evid. 514 concerning rules of evidence relating to privileged communications between the victim and victim advocate.

(4) *Scope of "threatening or placing that other person in fear."* For purposes of this offense, the phrase "wrongful action" within Article 120(g)(6) (defining "threatening or placing that other person in fear") includes an abuse of military rank, position, or authority in order to engage in a sexual act or sexual contact with a victim. This includes, but is not limited to, threats to initiate an adverse personnel action unless the victim submits to the accused's requested sexual act or contact; and threats to withhold a favorable personnel action unless the victim submits to the accused's requested sexual act or sexual contact. Superiority in rank is a factor in, but not dispositive of, whether a reasonable person in the position of the victim would fear that his or her noncompliance with the accused's desired sexual act or sexual contact would result in the threatened wrongful action contemplated by the communication or action.

d. *Maximum punishment.*

(1) *Rape.* Forfeiture of all pay and allowances and confinement for life without eligibility for parole. Mandatory minimum—Dismissal or dishonorable discharge.

(2) *Sexual assault.* Forfeiture of all pay and allowances, and confinement for 30 years. Mandatory minimum—Dismissal or dishonorable discharge.

(3) *Aggravated sexual contact.* Dishonorable discharge, forfeiture of all pay and allowances, and confinement for 20 years.

(4) *Abusive sexual contact.* Dishonorable discharge, forfeiture of all pay and allowances, and confinement for 7 years.

e. *Sample specifications.*

(1) *Rape.*

(a) *By force.*

In that ________ (personal jurisdiction data), did (at/on board—location) (subject-matter jurisdiction data, if required), on or about________ 20__, commit a sexual act upon _______________ by [penetrating __________'s (vulva) (anus) (mouth) with __________'s penis] [causing contact between _______'s mouth and __________'s (penis) (vulva) (scrotum) (anus)] [penetrating _______'s (vulva) (penis) (anus) with (______'s body part) (an object) to wit:__________, with an intent to [(abuse) (humiliate) (harass) (degrade) _______] [(arouse) (gratify) the sexual desire of_________]], by using unlawful force.

(b) *By force causing or likely to cause death or grievous bodily harm.*

In that ___________ (personal jurisdiction data), did (at/on board—location) (subject-matter jurisdiction data, if required), on or about __________ 20__, commit a sexual act upon __________ by [penetrating ___________'s (vulva) (anus) (mouth) with __________'s penis] [causing contact between _______'s mouth and ____________'s (penis) (vulva) (scrotum) (anus)] [penetrating _______'s (vulva) (penis) (anus) with (__________'s body part) (an object) to wit:___________, with an intent to [(abuse) (humiliate) (harass) (degrade) _______] [(arouse) (gratify) the sexual desire of _________]], by using force likely to cause death or grievous bodily harm to _______, to wit:______________.

(c) *By threatening or placing that other person in fear that any person would be subjected to death, grievous bodily harm, or kidnapping.*

In that __________ (personal jurisdiction data), did (at/on board—location) (subject-matter jurisdiction data, if required), on or about ___________ 20______, commit a sexual act upon __________ by [penetrating ___________'s (vulva) (anus) (mouth) with __________'s penis] [causing contact between _______'s mouth and ____________'s (penis) (vulva) (scrotum) (anus)] [penetrating _______'s (vulva) (penis) (anus) with (___________'s body part) (an object) to wit:______, with an intent to [(abuse) (humiliate) (harass) (degrade) _______] [(arouse) (gratify) the sexual desire of _________]], by (threatening ______) (placing ______ in fear) that __________ would be subjected to (death) (grievous bodily harm) (kidnapping).

(d) *By first rendering that other person unconscious.*

In that __________ (personal jurisdiction data), did (at/on board—location) (subject-matter jurisdiction data, if required), on or about _________ 20____, commit a sexual act upon __________ by [penetrating ___________'s (vulva) (anus) (mouth) with __________'s penis] [causing contact between _______'s mouth and _____________'s (penis) (vulva) (scrotum) (anus)] [penetrating _______'s (vulva) (penis) (anus) with (______'s body part) (an object) to wit:______, with an intent to [(abuse) (humiliate) (harass) (degrade) _______] [(arouse) (gratify) the sexual desire of _________]], by first rendering __________ unconscious by____________.

(e) *By administering a drug, intoxicant, or other similar substance.*

In that ___________ (personal jurisdiction data), did (at/on board—location) (subject-matter jurisdiction data, if required), on or about _________ 20__, commit a sexual act upon ___________ by [penetrating ___________'s (vulva) (anus) (mouth) with __________'s penis] [causing contact between _______'s mouth and ________'s (penis) (vulva) (scrotum) (anus)] [penetrating _______'s (vulva) (penis) (anus) with (__________'s body part) (an object) to wit:___________, with an intent to [(abuse) (humiliate) (harass) (degrade) _______] [(arouse) (gratify) the sexual desire of _________]], by administering to __________ (by force) (by threat of force) (without the knowledge or permission of __________) a (drug) (intoxicant) (list other similar substance), to wit: ___________, thereby substantially impairing the ability of __________to appraise or control (his) (her) conduct.

(2) *Sexual assault.*

(a) *By threatening or placing that other person in fear.*

In that _________ (personal jurisdiction data), did (at/on board—location) (subject-matter jurisdiction data, if required), on or about ________20__, commit a sexual act upon _________, by [penetrating ___________'s (vulva) (anus) (mouth) with __________'s penis] [causing contact between _______'s mouth and ____________'s (penis) (vulva) (scrotum) (anus)] [penetrating _______'s (vulva) (penis) (anus) with (__________'s body part) (an object) to wit:______, with an intent to [(abuse) (humiliate) (harass) (degrade) _______] [(arouse) (gratify) the sexual desire of _________]], by (threatening _______) (placing_______ in fear).

(b) *By fraudulent representation.*

In that _________ (personal jurisdiction data), did (at/on board—location) (subject-matter jurisdiction data, if required), on or about __________20__, commit a sexual act upon ___________, by [penetrating ___________'s (vulva) (anus) (mouth) with __________'s penis] [causing contact between _______'s mouth and _________'s (penis) (vulva) (scrotum) (anus)] [penetrating _______'s (vulva) (penis) (anus) with (______'s body part) (an object) to wit:______, with an intent to [(abuse) (humiliate) (harass) (degrade) _______] [(arouse) (gratify) the sexual desire of __________]], by making a fraudulent representation that the sexual act served a professional purpose, to wit:_______________.

(c) *By false pretense.*

In that ___________ (personal jurisdiction data), did (at/on board—location) (subject-matter jurisdiction data, if required), on or about ________20__, commit a sexual act upon __________, by [penetrating ___________'s (vulva) (anus) (mouth) with __________'s penis] [causing contact between _______'s mouth and ________'s (penis) (vulva) (scrotum) (anus)] [penetrating _______'s (vulva) (penis) (anus) with (______'s body part) (an object) to wit:______, with an intent to [(abuse) (humiliate) (harass) (degrade) _______] [(arouse) (gratify) the sexual desire of _________]], by inducing a belief by (artifice) (pretense) (concealment) that the said accused was another person.

(d) *Without consent.*

In that _________ (personal jurisdiction data), did (at/on board—location) (subject-matter jurisdiction data, if required), on or about ________20__, commit a sexual act upon _________, by [penetrating __________'s (vulva) (anus) (mouth) with __________'s penis] [causing contact between _______'s mouth and ________'s (penis) (vulva) (scrotum) (anus),] [penetrating _______'s (vulva) (penis) (anus) with (______'s body part) (an object) to wit:______, with an intent to [(abuse) (humiliate) (harass) (degrade) _______] [(arouse) (gratify) the sexual desire of _________]], without the consent of ___________.

(e) *Of a person who is asleep, unconscious, or otherwise unaware the act is occurring.*

In that _________ (personal jurisdiction data), did (at/on board—location) (subject-matter jurisdiction data, if required), on or about ______20__, commit a sexual act upon_________, by [penetrating ___________'s (vulva) (anus) (mouth) with __________'s penis] [causing contact between _______'s mouth and ________'s (penis) (vulva) (scrotum) (anus)] [penetrating _______'s (vulva) (penis) (anus) with (______'s body part) (an object) to wit:______, with an intent to [(abuse) (humiliate) (harass) (degrade) _______] [(arouse) (gratify) the sexual desire of _________]], when (he) (she) knew or reasonably should have known that _______ was (asleep) (unconscious) (unaware the sexual act was occurring due to _________).

(f) *When the other person is incapable of consenting.*

In that _________ (personal jurisdiction data), did (at/on board—location) (subject-matter jurisdiction data, if required), on or about ________ 20__, commit a sexual act upon _______, by [penetrating ___________'s (vulva) (anus) (mouth) with __________'s penis] [causing contact between _______'s mouth and ________'s (penis) (vulva) (scrotum) (anus)] [penetrating _______'s (vulva) (penis) (anus) with (______'s body part) (an object) to wit:______, with an intent to [(abuse) (humiliate) (harass) (degrade) _______] [(arouse) (gratify) the sexual desire of _________]], when ________was incapable of consenting to the sexual act because (he) (she) [was impaired by (a drug, to wit: __________) (an intoxicant, to wit:_________) (________)] [had a (mental disease, to wit:___________) (mental defect, to wit:___________) (physical disability, to wit:__________)], and the accused (knew) (reasonably should have known) of that condition.

(3) *Aggravated sexual contact.*

(a) *By force.*

In that _________ (personal jurisdiction data), did (at/on board—location) (subject-matter jurisdiction data, if required), on or about _______ 20___, [(touch) (cause ____ to touch)] [(directly) (through the clothing)] the (vulva) (penis) (scrotum) (anus) (groin) (breast) (inner thigh) (buttocks) of ________, with [(______'s body part) (an object), to wit: _______] with an intent to [(abuse) (humiliate) (harass) (degrade) _______] [(arouse) (gratify) the sexual desire of _________] by using unlawful force.

(b) *By force causing or likely to cause death or grievous bodily harm.*

In that ________ (personal jurisdiction data), did (at/on board—location) (subject-matter jurisdiction data, if required), on or about _______ 20__, [(touch) (cause ____ to touch)] [(directly) (through the clothing)] the (vulva) (penis) (scrotum) (anus) (groin) (breast) (inner thigh) (buttocks) of ________, with [(______'s body part) (an object), to wit: _______] with an intent to [(abuse) (humiliate) (harass) (degrade) _______] [(arouse) (gratify) the sexual desire of _________], by using force likely to cause death or grievous bodily harm to ________, to wit: ___________.

(c) *By threatening or placing that other person in fear that any person would be subjected to death, grievous bodily harm, or kidnapping.*

In that ________ (personal jurisdiction data), did (at/on board—location) (subject-matter jurisdiction data, if required), on or about __________ 20__, [(touch) (cause ____ to touch)] [(directly) (through the clothing)] the (vulva) (penis) (scrotum) (anus) (groin) (breast) (inner thigh) (buttocks) of ________, with [(______'s body part) (an object), to wit: _______] with an intent to [(abuse) (humiliate) (harass) (degrade) _______] [(arouse) (gratify) the sexual desire of _________], by (threatening _________) (placing __________ in fear) that ___________ would be subjected to (death) (grievous bodily harm) (kidnapping).

(d) *By first rendering that other person unconscious.*

In that _________ (personal jurisdiction data), did (at/on board—location) (subject-matter jurisdiction data, if required), on or about ________ 20___, [(touch) (cause ____ to touch)] [(directly) (through the clothing)] the (vulva) (penis) (scrotum) (anus) (groin) (breast) (inner thigh) (buttocks) of ________, with [(______'s body part) (an object), to wit: _______] with an intent to [(abuse) (humiliate) (harass) (degrade) _______] [(arouse) (gratify) the sexual desire of _________], by rendering _________ unconscious by_________________.

(e) *By administering a drug, intoxicant, or other similar substance.*

In that _________ (personal jurisdiction data), did (at/on board—location) (subject-matter jurisdiction data, if required), on or about __________ 20___, [(touch) (cause ____ to touch)] [(directly) (through the clothing)] the (vulva) (penis) (scrotum) (anus) (groin) (breast) (inner thigh) (buttocks) of ________, with [(______'s body part) (an object), to wit: _______] with an intent to [(abuse) (humiliate) (harass) (degrade) _______] [(arouse) (gratify) the sexual desire of_________], by administering to _______ (by force) (by threat of force) (without the knowledge or permission of _________) a (drug) (intoxicant) (______) thereby substantially impairing the ability of _______ to appraise or control (his) (her) conduct..

(4) *Abusive sexual contact.*

(a) *By threatening or placing that other person in fear.*

In that ________ (personal jurisdiction data), did (at/on board—location) (subject-matter jurisdiction data, if required), on or about _________ 20__, [(touch) (cause ____ to touch)] [(directly) (through the clothing)] the (vulva) (penis) (scrotum) (anus) (groin) (breast) (inner thigh) (buttocks) of ________, with [(______'s body part) (an object), to wit: _______] with an intent to [(abuse) (humiliate) (harass) (degrade) _______] [(arouse) (gratify) the sexual desire of _________], by (threatening _______) (placing __________ in fear).

(b) *By fraudulent representation.*

In that ___________ (personal jurisdiction data), did (at/on board—location) (subject-matter jurisdiction data, if required), on or about ________ 20__, [(touch) (cause ____ to touch)] [(directly) (through the clothing)] the (vulva) (penis) (scrotum) (anus) (groin) (breast) (inner thigh) (buttocks) of ________, with [(______'s body part) (an object), to wit: _______] with an intent to [(abuse) (humiliate) (harass) (degrade) _______] [(arouse) (gratify) the sexual desire of _________], by making a fraudulent representation that the sexual contact served a professional purpose, to wit: __________.

(c) *By false pretense.*

In that _________ (personal jurisdiction data), did (at/on board—location) (subject-matter jurisdiction data, if required), on or about _________ 20__, [(touch) (cause ____ to touch)] [(directly) (through the clothing)] the (vulva) (penis) (scrotum) (anus) (groin) (breast) (inner thigh) (buttocks) of ________, with [(______'s body part) (an object), to wit: _______] with an intent to [(abuse) (humiliate) (harass) (degrade) _______] [(arouse) (gratify) the sexual desire of_________], by inducing a belief by (artifice) (pretense) (concealment) that the said accused was another person.

(d) *Without consent.*

In that ______(personal jurisdiction data), did (at/on board—location) (subject-matter jurisdiction data, if required), on or about ________ 20___, [(touch) (cause ____ to touch)] [(directly) (through the clothing)] the (vulva) (penis) (scrotum) (anus) (groin) (breast) (inner thigh) (buttocks) of ________, with [(______'s body part) (an object), to wit: _______] with an intent to [(abuse) (humiliate) (harass) (degrade) ______] [(arouse) (gratify) the sexual desire of ________] without the consent of_____.

(e) *Of a person who is asleep, unconscious, or otherwise unaware the act is occurring.*

In that ______(personal jurisdiction data), did (at/on board—location) (subject-matter jurisdiction data, if required), on or about __________ 20____, [(touch) (cause ____ to touch)] [(directly) (through the clothing)] the (vulva) (penis) (scrotum) (anus) (groin) (breast) (inner thigh) (buttocks) of ________, with [(______'s body part) (an object), to wit: _______] with an intent to [(abuse) (humiliate) (harass) (degrade) _______] [(arouse) (gratify) the sexual desire of _________], when (he) (she) (knew) (reasonably should have known) that __________ was (asleep) (unconscious) (unaware the sexual contact was occurring due to ___________).

(f) *When that person is incapable of consenting.*

In that _______ (personal jurisdiction data), did (at/on board—location) (subject-matter jurisdiction data, if required), on or about _______ 20_____, [(touch) (cause ____ to touch)] [(directly) (through the clothing)] the (vulva) (penis) (scrotum) (anus) (groin) (breast) (inner thigh) (buttocks) of ________, with [(______'s body part) (an object), to wit: _______] with an intent to [(abuse) (humiliate) (harass) (degrade) _______] [(arouse) (gratify) the sexual desire of _________], when _________ was incapable of consenting to the sexual contact because (he) (she) [was impaired by (a drug, to wit: ____________) (an intoxicant, to wit: __________) (_________)] [had a (mental disease, to wit: _________) (mental defect, to wit: _____________) (physical disability, to wit: ____________)] and the accused (knew) (reasonably should have known) of that condition..

61. Article 120a (10 U.S.C. 920a)—Mails: deposit of obscene matter

a. *Text of statute.*

Any person subject to this chapter who, wrongfully and knowingly, deposits obscene matter for mailing and delivery shall be punished as a court-martial may direct.

b. *Elements.*

(1) That the accused deposited or caused to be deposited in the mails certain matter for mailing and delivery;

(2) That the act was done wrongfully and knowingly; and

(3) That the matter was obscene.

c. *Explanation.* Whether something is obscene is a question of fact. Obscene is synonymous with indecent as the latter is defined in subparagraph 104.c. The matter must violate community standards of decency or obscenity and must go beyond customary limits of expression. "Knowingly" means the accused deposited the material with knowledge of its nature. Knowingly depositing obscene matter in the mails is wrongful if it is done without legal justification or authorization.

d. *Maximum punishment.* Dishonorable discharge, forfeiture of all pay and allowances, and confinement for 3 years.

e. *Sample specification.*

In that _____________ (personal jurisdiction data), did, (at/on board—location) (subject-matter jurisdiction data, if required), on or about __ 20____, wrongfully and knowingly (deposit) (cause to be deposited) in the (United States) (________) mails, for mailing and delivery a (letter) (picture) (_________) (containing) (portraying) (suggesting) (__________) certain obscene matters, to wit: __________.

62. Article 120b (10 U.S.C. 920b)—Rape and sexual assault of a child

[Note: This statute applies to offenses committed on or after 1 January 2019. Previous versions of child sexual offenses are located as follows: for offenses committed on or before 30 September 2007, see Appendix 20; for offenses committed during the period 1 October 2007 through 27 June 2012, see Appendix 21; for offenses committed during the period 28 June 2012 through 31 December 2018, see Appendix 22.]

a. *Text of statute.*

(a) RAPE OF A CHILD.—Any person subject to this chapter who—

(1) commits a sexual act upon a child who has not attained the age of 12 years; or

(2) commits a sexual act upon a child who has attained the age of 12 years by—

(A) using force against any person;

(B) threatening or placing that child in fear;

(C) rendering that child unconscious; or

(D) administering to that child a drug, intoxicant, or other similar substance;

is guilty of rape of a child and shall be punished as a court-martial may direct.

(b) SEXUAL ASSAULT OF A CHILD.—Any person subject to this chapter who commits a sexual act upon a child who has attained the age of 12 years is guilty of sexual assault of a child and shall be punished as a court-martial may direct.

(c) SEXUAL ABUSE OF A CHILD.—Any person subject to this chapter who commits a lewd act upon a child is guilty of sexual abuse of a child and shall be punished as a court-martial may direct.

(d) AGE OF CHILD.—

(1) UNDER 12 YEARS.—In a prosecution under this section, it need not be proven that the accused knew the age of the other person engaging in the sexual act or lewd act. It is not a defense that the accused reasonably believed that the child had attained the age of 12 years.

(2) UNDER 16 YEARS.—In a prosecution under this section, it need not be proven that the accused knew that the other person engaging in the sexual act or lewd act had not attained the age of 16 years, but it is a defense in a prosecution under subsection (b) (sexual assault of a child) or subsection (c) (sexual abuse of a child), which the accused must prove by a preponderance of the evidence, that the accused reasonably believed that the child had attained the age of 16 years, if the child had in fact attained at least the age of 12 years.

(e) PROOF OF THREAT.—In a prosecution under this section, in proving that a person made a threat, it need not be proven that the person actually intended to carry out the threat or had the ability to carry out the threat.

(f) MARRIAGE.—In a prosecution under subsection (b) (sexual assault of a child) or subsection (c) (sexual abuse of a child), it is a defense, which the accused must prove by a preponderance of the evidence, that the persons engaging in the sexual act or lewd act were at that time married to each other, except where the accused commits a sexual act upon the person when the accused knows or reasonably should know that the other person is asleep, unconscious, or otherwise unaware that the sexual act is occurring or when the other person is incapable of consenting to the sexual act due to impairment by any drug, intoxicant, or other similar substance, and that condition was known or reasonably should have been known by the accused.

(g) CONSENT.—Lack of consent is not an element and need not be proven in any prosecution under this section. A child not legally married to the person committing the sexual act, lewd act, or use of force cannot consent to any sexual act, lewd act, or use of force.

(h) DEFINITIONS.—In this section:

(1) SEXUAL ACT AND SEXUAL CONTACT.—The terms "sexual act" and "sexual contact" have the meanings given those terms in section 920(g) of this title (article 120(g)), except that the term "sexual act" also includes the intentional touching, not through the clothing, of the genitalia of another person who has not attained the age of 16 years with an intent to abuse, humiliate, harass, degrade, or arouse or gratify the sexual desire of any person.

(2) FORCE.—The term "force" means—

(A) the use of a weapon;

(B) the use of such physical strength or violence as is sufficient to overcome, restrain, or injure a child; or

(C) inflicting physical harm.

In the case of a parent-child or similar relationship, the use or abuse of parental or similar authority is sufficient to constitute the use of force.

(3) THREATENING OR PLACING THAT CHILD IN FEAR.—The term "threatening or placing that child in fear" means a communication or action that is of sufficient consequence to cause the child to fear that non-compliance will result in the child or another person being subjected to the action contemplated by the communication or action.

(4) CHILD.—The term "child" means any person who has not attained the age of 16 years.

(5) LEWD ACT.—The term "lewd act" means—

(A) any sexual contact with a child;

(B) intentionally exposing one's genitalia, anus, buttocks, or female areola or nipple to a child by any means, including via any communication technology, with an intent to abuse, humiliate, or degrade any person, or to arouse or gratify the sexual desire of any person;

(C) intentionally communicating indecent language to a child by any means, including via any communication technology, with an intent to abuse, humiliate, or degrade any person, or to arouse or gratify the sexual desire of any person; or

(D) any indecent conduct, intentionally done with or in the presence of a child, including via any communication technology, that amounts to a form of immorality relating to sexual impurity which is grossly vulgar, obscene, and repugnant to common propriety, and tends to excite sexual desire or deprave morals with respect to sexual relations.

b. *Elements.*

(1) *Rape of a child.*

(a) *Rape of a child who has not attained the age of 12.*

(i) That the accused committed a sexual act upon a child; and

(ii) That at the time of the sexual act the child had not attained the age of 12 years.

(b) *Rape by force of a child who has attained the age of 12.*

(i) That the accused committed a sexual act upon a child;

(ii) That at the time of the sexual act the child had attained the age of 12 years but had not attained the age of 16 years; and

(iii) That the accused did so by using force against that child or any other person.

(c) *Rape by threatening or placing in fear a child who has attained the age of 12.*

(i) That the accused committed a sexual act upon a child;

(ii) That at the time of the sexual act the child had attained the age of 12 years but had not attained the age of 16 years; and

(iii) That the accused did so by threatening the child or another person or placing that child in fear.

(d) *Rape by rendering unconscious a child who has attained the age of 12.*

(i) That the accused committed a sexual act upon a child;

(ii) That at the time of the sexual act the child had attained the age of 12 years but had not attained the age of 16 years; and

(iii) That the accused did so by rendering that child unconscious.

(e) *Rape by administering a drug, intoxicant, or other similar substance to a child who has attained the age of 12.*

(i) That the accused committed a sexual act upon a child;

(ii) That at the time of the sexual act the child had attained the age of 12 years but had not attained the age of 16 years; and

(iii) That the accused did so by administering to that child a drug, intoxicant, or other similar substance.

(2) *Sexual assault of a child.*

(a) *Sexual assault of a child who has attained the age of 12.*

(i) That the accused committed a sexual act upon a child; and

(ii) That at the time of the sexual act the child had attained the age of 12 years but had not attained the age of 16 years.

(3) *Sexual abuse of a child.* That the accused committed a lewd act upon a child.

c. *Explanation.*

(1) *In general.* Sexual offenses have been separated into three statutes: offenses against adults (120), offenses against children (120b), and other offenses (120c).

(2) *Definitions.* Terms not defined in this paragraph are defined in subparagraph 60.a.(g), supra, except that the term "sexual act" also includes the intentional touching, not through the clothing, of the genitalia of another person who has not attained the age of 16 years with an intent to abuse, humiliate, harass, degrade, or arouse or gratify the sexual desire of any person.

d. *Maximum punishment.*

(1) *Rape of a child.* Forfeiture of all pay and allowances, and confinement for life without eligibility for parole. Mandatory minimum—Dismissal or dishonorable discharge.

(2) *Sexual assault of a child.* Forfeiture of all pay and allowances, and confinement for 30 years. Mandatory minimum—Dismissal or dishonorable discharge.

(3) *Sexual abuse of a child.*

(a) *Cases involving sexual contact.* Dishonorable discharge, forfeiture of all pay and allowances, and confinement for 20 years.

(b) *Other cases.* Dishonorable discharge, forfeiture of all pay and allowances, and confinement for 15 years.

e. *Sample specifications.*

(1) *Rape of a child.*

(a) *Rape of a child who has not attained the age of 12.*

In that ________ (personal jurisdiction data), did (at/on board—location) (subject-matter jurisdiction, if required), on or about________ 20__, commit a sexual act upon ________________, a child who had not attained the age of 12 years, by [penetrating ___________'s (vulva) (anus) (mouth) with __________'s penis] [causing contact between _______'s mouth and ________'s (penis) (vulva) (scrotum) (anus)] [penetrating _______'s (vulva) (penis) (anus) with (______'s body part) (an object) to wit:______, with an intent to [(abuse) (humiliate) (harass) (degrade) _______] [(arouse) (gratify) the sexual desire of _________]] [intentionally touching, not through the clothing, the genitalia of _________, with an intent to [(abuse) (humiliate) (harass) (degrade) _______] [(arouse) (gratify) the sexual desire of _________]].

(b) *Rape by force of a child who has attained the age of 12 years.*

In that ___________ (personal jurisdiction data), did (at/on board—location) (subject-matter jurisdiction, if required), on or about _______ 20__, commit a sexual act upon __________, a child who had attained the age of 12 years but had not attained the age of 16 years, by [penetrating ___________'s (vulva) (anus) (mouth) with __________'s penis] [causing contact between _______'s mouth and ________'s (penis) (vulva) (scrotum) (anus)] [penetrating _______'s (vulva) (penis) (anus) with (______'s body part) (an object) to wit:______, with an intent to [(abuse) (humiliate) (harass) (degrade) _______] [(arouse) (gratify) the sexual desire of _________]] [intentionally touching, not through the clothing, the genitalia of _________, with an intent to [(abuse) (humiliate) (harass) (degrade) _______] [(arouse) (gratify) the sexual desire of _________]], by using force against ________, to wit: ______________.

(c) *Rape by threatening or placing in fear a child who has attained the age of 12 years.*

In that ________ (personal jurisdiction data), did (at/on board—location) (subject-matter jurisdiction, if required), on or about ______ 20__, commit a sexual act upon __________, a child who had attained the age of 12 years but had not attained the age of 16 years, by [penetrating ___________'s (vulva) (anus) (mouth) with __________'s penis] [causing contact between _______'s mouth and ________'s (penis) (vulva) (scrotum) (anus)] [penetrating _______'s (vulva) (penis) (anus) with (______'s body part) (an object) to wit:______, with an intent to [(abuse) (humiliate) (harass) (degrade) _______] [(arouse) (gratify) the sexual desire of _________]] [intentionally touching, not through the clothing, the genitalia of _________, with an intent to [(abuse) (humiliate) (harass) (degrade) _______] [(arouse) (gratify) the sexual desire of _________]], by (threatening ______) (placing _______ in fear).

(d) *Rape by rendering unconscious of a child who has attained the age of 12 years.*

In that __________ (personal jurisdiction data), did (at/on board—location) (subject-matter jurisdiction, if required), on or about _____ 20__, commit a sexual act upon ________, a child who had attained the age of 12 years but had not attained the age of 16 years, by [penetrating ___________'s (vulva) (anus) (mouth) with __________'s penis] [causing contact between _______'s mouth and ________'s (penis) (vulva) (scrotum) (anus)] [penetrating _______'s (vulva) (penis) (anus) with (______'s body part) (an object) to wit:______, with an intent to [(abuse) (humiliate) (harass) (degrade) _______] [(arouse) (gratify) the sexual desire of _________]] [intentionally touching, not through the clothing, the genitalia of _________, with an intent to [(abuse) (humiliate) (harass) (degrade) _______] [(arouse) (gratify) the sexual desire of _________]], by rendering __________ unconscious by __________________.

(e) *Rape by administering a drug, intoxicant, or other similar substance to a child who has attained the age of 12 years.*

In that ___________ (personal jurisdiction data), did (at/on board—location) (subject-matter jurisdiction, if required), on or about ______ 20__, commit a sexual act upon __________, a child who had attained the age of 12 years but had not attained the age of 16 years, by [penetrating ___________'s (vulva) (anus) (mouth) with __________'s penis] [causing contact between _______'s mouth and ________'s (penis) (vulva) (scrotum) (anus)] [penetrating _______'s (vulva) (penis) (anus) with (______'s body part) (an object) to wit:______, with an intent to [(abuse) (humiliate) (harass) (degrade) _______] [(arouse) (gratify) the sexual desire of _________]] [intentionally touching, not through the clothing, the genitalia of _________, with an intent to [(abuse) (humiliate) (harass) (degrade) _______] [(arouse) (gratify) the sexual desire of _________]], by administering to ___________ a (drug) (intoxicant) (____), to wit: _____________.

(2) *Sexual assault of a child.*

(a) *Sexual assault of a child who has attained the age of 12 years.*

In that __________ (personal jurisdiction data), did (at/on board—location) (subject-matter jurisdiction, if required), on or about _____ 20__, commit a sexual act upon _______, a child who had attained the age of 12 years but had not attained the age of 16 years, by [penetrating ___________'s (vulva) (anus) (mouth) with __________'s penis] [causing contact between _______'s mouth and ________'s (penis) (vulva) (scrotum) (anus)] [penetrating _______'s (vulva) (penis) (anus) with (______'s body part) (an object) to wit:______, with an intent to [(abuse) (humiliate) (harass) (degrade) _______] [(arouse) (gratify) the sexual desire of _________]] [intentionally touching, not through the clothing, the genitalia of ________, with an intent to [(abuse) (humiliate) (harass) (degrade) _______] [(arouse) (gratify) the sexual desire of _________]].

(3) *Sexual abuse of a child.*

(a) *Sexual abuse of a child involving sexual contact.*

In that _________ (personal jurisdiction data), did (at/on board—location) (subject-matter jurisdiction, if required), on or about ______ 20__, commit a lewd act upon __________, a child who had not attained the age of 16 years, by (touching) (causing _____ to touch) the (vulva) (penis) (scrotum) (anus) (groin) (breast) (inner thigh) (buttocks) of________, with [(______'s body part) (an object) to wit: _______], with an intent to [(abuse) (humiliate) (harass) (degrade) __________] [(arouse) (gratify) the sexual desire of __________].

(b) *Sexual abuse of a child involving indecent exposure.*

In that _________ (personal jurisdiction data), did (at/on board—location) (subject-matter jurisdiction, if required), on or about ____ 20__, commit a lewd act upon _______, a child who had not attained the age of 16 years, by intentionally exposing [his (genitalia) (anus) (buttocks)] [her (genitalia) (anus) (buttocks) (areola) (nipple)] to __________, with an intent to [(abuse) (humiliate) (degrade) ______] [(arouse) (gratify) the sexual desire of __________].

(c) *Sexual abuse of a child involving indecent communication.*

In that ________ (personal jurisdiction data), did (at/on board—location) (subject-matter jurisdiction, if required), on or about _______ 20__, commit a lewd act upon __________, a child who had not attained the age of 16 years, by intentionally communicating to ________ indecent language to wit: ___________, with an intent to [(abuse) (humiliate) (degrade)_____] [(arouse) (gratify) the sexual desire of _________].

(d) *Sexual abuse of a child involving indecent conduct.*

In that ________ (personal jurisdiction data), did (at/on board—location) (subject-matter jurisdiction, if required), on or about _______ 20__, commit a lewd act upon __________, a child who had not attained the age of 16 years, by engaging in indecent conduct, to wit: _________, intentionally done (with) (in the presence of) _______, which conduct amounted to a form of immorality relating to sexual impurity which is grossly vulgar, obscene, and repugnant to common propriety, and tends to excite sexual desire or deprave morals with respect to sexual relations.

63. Article 120c (10 U.S.C. 920c)—Other sexual misconduct

[Previous versions of offenses included in Article 120c are located as follows: for the offense of indecent exposure committed on or before 30 September 2007, a previous version of Article 134, indecent exposure, applies and is located at Appendix 20; for the offense of forcible pandering committed on or before 30 September 2007, a previous version of Article 134, pandering and prostitution, applies and is located at Appendix 20; for Article 120c offenses committed during the period 1 October 2007 through 27 June 2012, see Appendix 21; for Article 120c offenses committed during the period 28 June 2012 through 31 December 2018, the previous version of Article 120c applies and is located at Appendix 22.]

a. *Text of statute.*

(a) INDECENT VIEWING, VISUAL RECORDING, OR BROADCASTING.—Any person subject to this chapter who, without legal justification or lawful authorization—

(1) knowingly and wrongfully views the private area of another person, without that other person's consent and under circumstances in which that other person has a reasonable expectation of privacy;

(2) knowingly photographs, videotapes, films, or records by any means the private area of another person, without that other person's consent and under circumstances in which that other person has a reasonable expectation of privacy; or

(3) knowingly broadcasts or distributes any such recording that the person knew or reasonably should have known was made under the circumstances proscribed in paragraphs (1) and (2);

is guilty of an offense under this section and shall be punished as a court-martial may direct.

(b) FORCIBLE PANDERING.—Any person subject to this chapter who compels another person to engage in an act of prostitution with any person is guilty of forcible pandering and shall be punished as a court-martial may direct.

(c) INDECENT EXPOSURE.—Any person subject to this chapter who intentionally exposes, in an indecent manner, the genitalia, anus, buttocks,

or female areola or nipple is guilty of indecent exposure and shall by punished as a court-martial may direct.

(d) DEFINITIONS.—In this section:

(1) ACT OF PROSTITUTION.—The term "act of prostitution" means a sexual act or sexual contact (as defined in section 920(g) of this title (article 120(g))) on account of which anything of value is given to, or received by, any person.

(2) PRIVATE AREA.—The term "private area" means the naked or underwear-clad genitalia, anus, buttocks, or female areola or nipple.

(3) REASONABLE EXPECTATION OF PRIVACY.—The term "under circumstances in which that other person has a reasonable expectation of privacy" means—

(A) circumstances in which a reasonable person would believe that he or she could disrobe in privacy, without being concerned that an image of a private area of the person was being captured; or

(B) circumstances in which a reasonable person would believe that a private area of the person would not be visible to the public.

(4) BROADCAST.—The term "broadcast" means to electronically transmit a visual image with the intent that it be viewed by a person or persons.

(5) DISTRIBUTE.—The term "distribute" means delivering to the actual or constructive possession of another, including transmission by electronic means.

(6) INDECENT MANNER.—The term "indecent manner" means conduct that amounts to a form of immorality relating to sexual impurity which is grossly vulgar, obscene, and repugnant to common propriety, and tends to excite sexual desire or deprave morals with respect to sexual relations.

b. *Elements.*

(1) *Indecent viewing.*

(a) That the accused, without legal justification or lawful authorization, knowingly and wrongfully viewed the private area of another person;

(b) That said viewing was without the other person's consent; and

(c) That said viewing took place under circumstances in which the other person had a reasonable expectation of privacy.

(2) *Indecent recording.*

(a) That the accused, without legal justification or lawful authorization, knowingly recorded (photographed, videotaped, filmed, or recorded by any means) the private area of another person;

(b) That said recording was without the other person's consent; and

(c) That said recording was made under circumstances in which the other person had a reasonable expectation of privacy.

(3) *Broadcasting of an indecent recording.*

(a) That the accused, without legal justification or lawful authorization, knowingly broadcast a certain recording of another person's private area;

(b) That said recording was made without the other person's consent;

(c) That the accused knew or reasonably should have known that the recording was made without the other person's consent;

(d) That said recording was made under circumstances in which the other person had a reasonable expectation of privacy; and

(e) That the accused knew or reasonable should have known that said recording was made under circumstances in which the other person had a reasonable expectation of privacy.

(4) *Distribution of an indecent recording.*

(a) That the accused, without legal justification or lawful authorization, knowingly distributed a certain recording of another person's private area;

(b) That said recording was made without the other person's consent;

(c) That the accused knew or reasonably should have known that said recording was made without the other person's consent;

(d) That said recording was made under circumstances in which the other person had a reasonable expectation of privacy; and

(e) That the accused knew or reasonably should have known that said recording was made under circumstances in which the other person had a reasonable expectation of privacy.

(5) *Forcible pandering.*

That the accused compelled another person to engage in an act of prostitution with any person.

(6) *Indecent exposure.*

(a) That the accused exposed the accused's genitalia, anus, buttocks, or female areola or nipple;

(b) That the exposure was in an indecent manner; and

(c) That the exposure was intentional.

c. *Explanation.*

(1) *In general.* Sexual offenses have been separated into three statutes: offenses against adults (120), offenses against children (120b), and other offenses (120c).

(2) *Definitions.*

(a) *Recording.* A recording is a still or moving visual image captured or recorded by any means.

(b) Other terms are defined in subparagraph 60.a.(g), supra.

d. *Maximum punishment.*

(1) Indecent viewing. Dishonorable discharge, forfeiture of all pay and allowances, and confinement for 1 year.

(2) Indecent recording. Dishonorable discharge, forfeiture of all pay and allowances, and confinement for 5 years.

(3) Broadcasting or distribution of an indecent recording. Dishonorable discharge, forfeiture of all pay and allowances, and confinement for 7 years.

(4) Forcible pandering. Dishonorable discharge, forfeiture of all pay and allowances, and confinement for 20 years.

(5) Indecent exposure. Dishonorable discharge, forfeiture of all pay and allowances, and confinement for 1 year.

e. *Sample specifications.*

(1) *Indecent viewing, recording, or broadcasting.*

(a) *Indecent viewing.*

In that ________ (personal jurisdiction data), did (at/on board—location) (subject-matter jurisdiction, if required), on or about _______ 20__, without legal justification or lawful authorization, knowingly and wrongfully view the private area of __________, without (his) (her) consent and under circumstances in which (he) (she) had a reasonable expectation of privacy.

(b) *Indecent recording.*

In that ________ (personal jurisdiction data), did (at/on board—location) (subject-matter jurisdiction, if required), on or about _______ 20__, without legal justification or lawful authorization, knowingly (photograph) (videotape) (film) (make a recording of) the private area of __________, without (his) (her) consent and under circumstances in which (he) (she) had a reasonable expectation of privacy.

(c) *Broadcasting or distributing an indecent recording.*

In that _________ (personal jurisdiction data), did (at/on board—location) (subject-matter jurisdiction, if required), on or about _______ 20__, without legal justification or lawful authorization, knowingly (broadcast) (distribute) a recording of the private area of __________, when the said accused knew or reasonably should have known that the said recording was made without the consent of _____________ and under circumstances in which (he) (she) had a reasonable expectation of privacy.

64. Article 121 (10 U.S.C. 921)—Larceny and wrongful appropriation

a. *Text of statute.*

(a) Any person subject to this chapter who wrongfully takes, obtains, or withholds, by any means, from the possession of the owner or of any other person any money, personal property, or article of value of any kind—

(1) with intent permanently to deprive or defraud another person of the use and benefit of property or to appropriate it to his own use or the use of any person other than the owner, steals that property and is guilty of larceny; or

(2) with intent temporarily to deprive or defraud another person of the use and benefit of property or to appropriate it to his own use or the use of any person other than the owner,

is guilty of wrongful appropriation.

(b) Any person found guilty of larceny or wrongful appropriation shall be punished as a court-martial may direct.

b. *Elements.*

(1) *Larceny.*

(a) That the accused wrongfully took, obtained, or withheld certain property from the possession of the owner or of any other person;

(b) That the property belonged to a certain person;

(c) That the property was of a certain value, or of some value; and

(d) That the taking, obtaining, or withholding by the accused was with the intent permanently to deprive or defraud another person of the use and benefit of the property or permanently to appropriate the property for the use of the accused or for any person other than the owner.

[Note: If the property is alleged to be military property, as defined in subparagraph 64.c.(1)(h), add the following element]

(e) That the property was military property.

(2) *Wrongful appropriation.*

(a) That the accused wrongfully took, obtained, or withheld certain property from the possession of the owner or of any other person;

(b) That the property belonged to a certain person;

(c) That the property was of a certain value, or of some value; and

(d) That the taking, obtaining, or withholding by the accused was with the intent temporarily to deprive or defraud another person of the use and benefit of the property or temporarily to appropriate the property for the use of the accused or for any person other than the owner.

c. *Explanation.*

(1) *Larceny.*

(a) *In general.* A wrongful taking with intent permanently to deprive includes the common law offense of larceny; a wrongful obtaining with intent permanently to defraud includes the offense formerly known as obtaining by false pretense; and a wrongful withholding with intent permanently to appropriate includes the offense formerly known as embezzlement. Any of the various types of larceny under Article 121 may be charged and proved under a specification alleging that the accused did steal the property in question.

(b) *Taking, obtaining, or withholding.* There must be a taking, obtaining, or withholding of the property by the thief. For instance, there is no taking if the property is connected to a building by a chain and the property has not been disconnected from the building; property is not obtained by merely acquiring title thereto without exercising some possessory control over it. As a general rule, however, any movement of the property or any exercise of dominion over it is sufficient if accompanied by the requisite intent. Thus, if an accused enticed another's horse into the accused's stable without touching the animal, or procured a railroad company to deliver another's trunk by changing the check on it, or obtained the delivery of another's goods to a person or place designated by the accused, or had the funds of another transferred to the accused's bank account, the accused is guilty of larceny if the other elements of the offense have been proved. A person may obtain the property of another by acquiring possession without title, and one who already has possession of the property of another may obtain it by later acquiring title to it. A withholding may arise as a result of a failure to return, account for, or deliver property to its owner when a return, accounting, or delivery is due, even if the owner has made no demand for the property, or it may arise as a result of devoting property to a use not authorized by its owner. Generally, this is so whether the person withholding the property acquired it lawfully or unlawfully. *See* subparagraph c.(1)(f) of this paragraph. However, acts which constitute the offense of unlawfully receiving, buying, or concealing stolen property or of being an accessory after the fact are not included within the meaning of withholds. Therefore, neither a receiver of stolen property nor an accessory after the fact can be convicted of larceny on that basis alone. The taking, obtaining, or withholding must be of specific property. A debtor does not withhold specific property from the possession of a creditor by failing or refusing to pay a debt, for the relationship of debtor and creditor does not give the creditor a possessory right in any specific money or other property of the debtor.

(c) *Ownership of the property.*

(i) *In general.* Article 121 requires that the taking, obtaining, or withholding be from the possession of the owner or of any other person. Care, custody, management, and control are among the definitions of possession.

(ii) *Owner.* "Owner" refers to the person who, at the time of the taking, obtaining, or withholding, had the superior right to possession of the property in the light of all conflicting interests therein which may be involved in the particular case. For instance, an organization is the true owner of its funds as against the custodian of the funds charged with the larceny thereof.

(iii) *Any other person.* "Any other person" means any person—even a person who has stolen the property—who has possession or a greater right to possession than the accused. In pleading a violation of this article, the ownership of the property may be alleged to have been in any person, other than the accused, who at the time of the theft was a general owner or a special owner thereof. A general owner of property is a person who has title to it, whether or not that person has possession of it; a special owner, such as a borrower or hirer, is one who does not have title but who does have possession, or the right of possession, of the property.

(iv) *Person*. Person, as used in referring to one from whose possession property has been taken, obtained, or withheld, and to any owner of property, includes (in addition to a natural person) a government, a corporation, an association, an organization, and an estate. Such a person need not be a legal entity.

(d) *Wrongfulness of the taking, obtaining, or withholding*. The taking, obtaining, or withholding of the property must be wrongful. As a general rule, a taking or withholding of property from the possession of another is wrongful if done without the consent of the other, and an obtaining of property from the possession of another is wrongful if the obtaining is by false pretense. However, such an act is not wrongful if it is authorized by law or apparently lawful superior orders, or, generally, if done by a person who has a right to the possession of the property either equal to or greater than the right of one from whose possession the property is taken, obtained, or withheld. An owner of property who takes or withholds it from the possession of another, without the consent of the other, or who obtains it therefrom by false pretense, does so wrongfully if the other has a superior right—such as a lien—to possession of the property. A person who takes, obtains, or withholds property as the agent of another has the same rights and liabilities as does the principal, but may not be charged with a guilty knowledge or intent of the principal which that person does not share.

(e) *False pretense*. With respect to obtaining property by false pretense, the false pretense may be made by means of any act, word, symbol, or token. The pretense must be in fact false when made and when the property is obtained, and it must be knowingly false in the sense that it is made without a belief in its truth. A false pretense is a false representation of past or existing fact. In addition to other kinds of facts, the fact falsely represented by a person may be that person's or another's power, authority, or intention. Thus, a false representation by a person that the person presently intends to perform a certain act in the future is a false representation of an existing fact—the intention—and thus a false pretense. Although the pretense need not be the sole cause inducing the owner to part with the property, it must be an effective and intentional cause of the obtaining. A false representation made after the property was obtained will not result in a violation of Article 121. A larceny is committed when a person obtains the property of another by false pretense and with intent to steal, even though the owner neither intended nor was requested to part with title to the property. Thus, a person who gets another's watch by pretending that it will be borrowed briefly and then returned, but who really intends to sell it, is guilty of larceny.

(f) *Intent*.

(i) *In general*. The offense of larceny requires that the taking, obtaining, or withholding by the thief be accompanied by an intent permanently to deprive or defraud another of the use and benefit of property or permanently to appropriate the property to the thief's own use or the use of any person other than the owner. These intents are collectively called an intent to steal. Although a person gets property by a taking or obtaining which was not wrongful or which was without a concurrent intent to steal, a larceny is nevertheless committed if an intent to steal is formed after the taking or obtaining and the property is wrongfully withheld with that intent. For example, if a person rents another's vehicle, later decides to keep it permanently, and then either fails to return it at the appointed time or uses it for a purpose not authorized by the terms of the rental, larceny has been committed, even though at the time the vehicle was rented, the person intended to return it after using it according to the agreement.

(ii) *Inference of intent*. An intent to steal may be proved by circumstantial evidence. Thus, if a person secretly takes property, hides it, and denies knowing anything about it, an intent to steal may be inferred; if the property was taken openly and returned, this would tend to negate such an intent. Proof of sale of the property may show an intent to steal, and therefore, evidence of such a sale may be introduced to support a charge of larceny. An intent to steal may be inferred from a wrongful and intentional dealing with the property of another in a manner likely to cause that person to suffer a permanent loss thereof.

(iii) *Special situations*.

(A) *Motive does not negate intent*. The accused's purpose in taking an item ordinarily is irrelevant to the accused's guilt as long as the accused had the intent required under subparagraph c.(1)(f)(i) of this paragraph. For example, if the accused wrongfully took property as a joke or "to teach the owner a lesson" this would not be a defense, although if the accused intended to return the property, the accused would be guilty of wrongful appropriation, not larceny. When a person takes property intending only to return it to its lawful owner, as when stolen property is taken from a thief in order to return it to its owner, larceny or wrongful appropriation is not committed.

(B) *Intent to pay for or replace property not a defense.* An intent to pay for or replace the stolen property is not a defense, even if that intent existed at the time of the theft. If, however, the accused takes money or a negotiable instrument having no special value above its face value, with the intent to return an equivalent amount of money, the offense of larceny is not committed although wrongful appropriation may be.

(C) *Return of property not a defense.* Once a larceny is committed, a return of the property or payment for it is no defense. See subparagraph c.(2) of this paragraph when the taking, obtaining, or withholding is with the intent to return.

(g) *Value.*

(i) *In general.* Value is a question of fact to be determined on the basis of all of the evidence admitted.

(ii) *Government property.* When the stolen property is an item issued or procured from Government sources, the price listed in an official publication for that property at the time of the theft is admissible as evidence of its value. *See* Mil. R. Evid. 803(17). However, the stolen item must be shown to have been, at the time of the theft, in the condition upon which the value indicated in the official price list is based. The price listed in the official publication is not conclusive as to the value of the item, and other evidence may be admitted on the question of its condition and value.

(iii) *Other property.* As a general rule, the value of other stolen property is its legitimate market value at the time and place of the theft. If this property, because of its character or the place where it was stolen, had no legitimate market value at the time and place of the theft or if that value cannot readily be ascertained, its value may be determined by its legitimate market value in the United States at the time of the theft, or by its replacement cost at that time, whichever is less. Market value may be established by proof of the recent purchase price paid for the article in the legitimate market involved or by testimony or other admissible evidence from any person who is familiar through training or experience with the market value in question. The owner of the property may testify as to its market value if familiar with its quality and condition. The fact that the owner is not an expert of the market value of the property goes only to the weight to be given that testimony, and not to its admissibility. *See* Mil. R. Evid. 701. When the character of the property clearly appears in evidence—for instance, when it is exhibited to the court-martial—the court-martial, from its own experience, may infer that it has some value. If as a matter of common knowledge the property is obviously of a value substantially in excess of $1,000, the court-martial may find a value of more than $1,000. Writings representing value may be considered to have the value—even though contingent—which they represented at the time of the theft.

(iv) *Limited interest in property.* If an owner of property or someone acting in the owner's behalf steals it from a person who has a superior, but limited, interest in the property, such as a lien, the value for punishment purposes shall be that of the limited interest.

(h) *Military property.* Military property is all property, real or personal, owned, held, or used by one of the armed forces of the United States. Military property is a term of art, and should not be confused with Government property. The terms are not interchangeable. While all military property is Government property, not all Government property is military property. An item of Government property is not military property unless the item in question meets the definition provided in this paragraph. Retail merchandise of Service exchange stores is not military property under this article.

(i) *Miscellaneous considerations.*

(i) *Lost property.* A taking or withholding of lost property by the finder is larceny if accompanied by an intent to steal and if a clue to the identity of the general or special owner, or through which such identity may be traced, is furnished by the character, location, or marketing of the property, or by other circumstances.

(ii) *Multiple article larceny.* When a larceny of several articles is committed at substantially the same time and place, it is a single larceny even though the articles belong to different persons. Thus, if a thief steals a suitcase containing the property of several persons or goes into a room and takes property belonging to various persons, there is but one larceny, which should be alleged in but one specification.

(iii) *Special kinds of property which may also be the subject of larceny.* Included in property which may be the subject of larceny is property which is taken, obtained, or withheld by severing it from real estate and writings which represent value such as commercial paper.

(iv) *Services.* Theft of services may not be charged under this paragraph. *But see* paragraph 66.

(v) *Credit, debit, and electronic transactions.* Wrongfully engaging in a credit, debit, or electronic transaction to obtain goods or money ordinarily should be charged under paragraph 65.

(2) *Wrongful appropriation.*

(a) *In general.* Wrongful appropriation requires an intent to temporarily—as opposed to permanently—deprive the owner of the use and benefit of, or appropriate to the use of another, the property wrongfully taken, withheld, or obtained. In all other respects wrongful appropriation and larceny are identical.

(b) *Examples.* Wrongful appropriation includes: taking another's automobile without permission or lawful authority with intent to drive it a short distance and then return it or cause it to be returned to the owner; obtaining a service weapon by falsely pretending to be about to go on guard duty with intent to use it on a hunting trip and later return it; and while driving a Government vehicle on a mission to deliver supplies, withholding the vehicle from Government service by deviating from the assigned route without authority, to visit a friend in a nearby town and later restore the vehicle to its lawful use. An inadvertent exercise of control over the property of another will not result in wrongful appropriation. For example, a person who fails to return a borrowed boat at the time agreed upon because the boat inadvertently went aground is not guilty of this offense.

d. *Maximum punishment.*

(1) *Larceny.*

(a) *Property of a value of $1,000 or less.* Bad-conduct discharge, forfeiture of all pay and allowances, and confinement for 1 year.

(b) *Military property of a value of more than $1,000 or of any military motor vehicle, aircraft, vessel, firearm, or explosive.* Dishonorable discharge, forfeiture of all pay and allowances, and confinement for 10 years.

(c) *Property other than military property of a value of more than $1,000 or any motor vehicle, aircraft, vessel, firearm, or explosive not included in subparagraph d.(1)(b).* Dishonorable discharge, forfeiture of all pay and allowances, and confinement for 5 years."

(2) *Wrongful appropriation.*

(a) *Of a value of $1,000 or less.* Confinement for 3 months, and forfeiture of two-thirds pay per month for 3 months.

(b) *Of a value of more than $1,000.* Bad-conduct discharge, forfeiture of all pay and allowances, and confinement for 1 year.

(c) *Of any motor vehicle, aircraft, vessel, firearm, explosive, or military property of a value of more than $1,000.* Dishonorable discharge, forfeiture of all pay and allowances, and confinement for 2 years.

e. *Sample specifications.*

(1) *Larceny.*

In that ______________ (personal jurisdiction data), did, (at/on board—location) (subject-matter jurisdiction data, if required), on or about ______ 20___, steal ______________, (military property), of a value of (about) $_________, the property of ______________.

(2) *Wrongful appropriation.*

In that ___________ (personal jurisdiction data), did, (at/on board—location) (subject-matter jurisdiction data, if required), on or about _______ 20___, wrongfully appropriate ______________, of a value of (about) $__________, the property of _____________.

65. Article 121a (10 U.S.C. 921a)—Fraudulent use of credit cards, debit cards, and other access devices

a. *Text of statute.*

(a) IN GENERAL.—Any person subject to this chapter who, knowingly and with intent to defraud, uses—

(1) a stolen credit card, debit card, or other access device;

(2) a revoked, cancelled, or otherwise invalid credit card, debit card, or other access device; or

(3) a credit card, debit card, or other access device without the authorization of a person whose authorization is required for such use; to obtain money, property, services, or anything else of value

shall be punished as a court-martial may direct.

(b) ACCESS DEVICE DEFINED.—In this section (article), the term "access device" has the meaning given that term in section 1029 of title 18.

b. *Elements.*

(1) That the accused knowingly used a stolen credit card, debit card, or other access device; or

(2) That the accused knowingly used a revoked, cancelled, or otherwise invalid credit card, debit card; or

(3) That the accused knowingly used a credit card, debit card, or other access device without the authorization of a person whose authorization was required for such use;

(4) That the use was to obtain money, property, services, or anything else of value; and

(5) The use by the accused was with the intent to defraud.

c. *Explanation.*

(1) *In general.* This offense focuses on the intent of the accused and the technology used by the accused.

(2) *Intent to defraud.* See subparagraph 70.c.(14).

(3) *Inference of intent.* An intent to defraud may be proved by circumstantial evidence.

(4) *Use of a credit card, debit card, or other access device without the authorization of a person whose authorization was required for such use.* This provision applies to situations where an accused has no authorization to use the access device from a person whose authorization is required for such use, as well as situations where an accused exceeds the authorization of a person whose authorization is required for such use.

d. *Maximum punishment.*

(1) *Fraudulent use of a credit card, debit card, or other access device to obtain property of a value of $1,000 or less.* Bad-conduct discharge, forfeiture of all pay and allowances, and confinement for 10 years.

(2) *Fraudulent use during any 1-year period of a credit card, debit card, or other access device to obtain property the aggregate value of which is more than $1,000.* Dishonorable discharge, forfeiture of all pay and allowances, and confinement for 15 years.

e. *Sample specification.*

In that __________ (personal jurisdiction data), did, (at/on board—location) (subject matter jurisdiction data, if required), on or about _____ 20 __, knowingly and with the intent to defraud, use a (debit card) (credit card) (access device, to wit:________) (that was stolen) (that was revoked, cancelled, or otherwise invalid) (without the authorization of __________, a person whose authorization was required for such use), to obtain (money) (property) (services) (________) (of a value of about $________).

66. Article 121b (10 U.S.C. 921b)—False pretenses to obtain services

a. *Text of statute.*

Any person subject to this chapter who, with intent to defraud, knowingly uses false pretenses to obtain services shall be punished as a court-martial may direct.

b. *Elements.*

(1) That the accused wrongfully obtained certain services;

(2) That the obtaining was done by using false pretenses;

(3) That the accused then knew of the falsity of the pretenses;

(4) That the obtaining was with intent to defraud; and

(5) That the services were of a certain value, or of some value.

c. *Explanation.* This offense is similar to the offenses of larceny and wrongful appropriation by false pretenses, except that the object of the obtaining is services (for example, telephone service) rather than money, personal property, or articles of value of any kind as under Article 121. *See* paragraph 64.c. See paragraph 70.c.(14) for a definition of intent to defraud.

d. *Maximum punishment.* Obtaining services under false pretenses.

(1) *Of a value of $1,000 or less.* Bad-conduct discharge, forfeiture of all pay and allowances, and confinement for 1 year.

(2) *Of a value of more than $1,000.* Dishonorable discharge, forfeiture of all pay and allowances, and confinement for 5 years.

e. *Sample specification.*

In that __________ (personal jurisdiction data), did, (at/on board—location) (subject-matter jurisdiction data, if required), on or about _____ 20 __, with intent to defraud, falsely pretend to __________ that __________, then knowing that the pretenses were false, and by means thereof did wrongfully obtain from__________ services, of a value of (about) $__________, to wit: __________.

67. Article 122 (10 U.S.C. 922)—Robbery

a. *Text of statute.*

Any person subject to this chapter who takes anything of value from the person or in the presence of another, against his will, by means of force or violence or fear of immediate or future injury to his person or property or to the person or property of a relative or member of his family or of anyone in his company at the time of the robbery, is guilty of robbery and shall be punished as a court-martial may direct.

b. *Elements.*

(1) That the accused wrongfully took certain property from the person or from the possession and in the presence of a person named or described;

(2) That the taking was against the will of that person;

(3) That the taking was by means of force, violence, or force and violence, or putting the person in fear of immediate or future injury to that person, a relative, a member of the person's family, anyone accompanying the person at the time of the robbery, the person's property, or the property of a relative, family member, or anyone accompanying the person at the time of the robbery;

(4) That the property belonged to a person named or described; and

(5) That the property was of a certain or of some value.

[Note: If the robbery was committed with a dangerous weapon, add the following element]

(6) That the means of force or violence or of putting the person in fear was a dangerous weapon.

c. *Explanation.*

(1) *Taking in the presence of the victim.* It is not necessary that the property taken be located within any certain distance of the victim. If persons enter a house and force the owner by threats to disclose the hiding place of valuables in an adjoining room, and, leaving the owner tied, go into that room and steal the valuables, they have committed robbery.

(2) *Force or violence.* For a robbery to be committed by force or violence, there must be actual force or violence to the person, preceding or accompanying the taking against the person's will, and it is immaterial that there is no fear engendered in the victim. Any amount of force is enough to constitute robbery if the force overcomes the actual resistance of the person robbed, puts the person in such a position that no resistance is made, or suffices to overcome the resistance offered by a chain or other fastening by which the article is attached to the person. The offense is not robbery if an article is merely snatched from the hand of another or a pocket is picked by stealth, no other force is used, and the owner is not put in fear. But if resistance is overcome in snatching the article, there is sufficient violence, as when an earring is torn from a person's ear. There is sufficient violence when a person's attention is diverted by being jostled by a confederate of a pickpocket, who is thus enabled to steal the person's watch, even though the person had no knowledge of the act; or when a person is knocked insensible and that person's pockets rifled; or when a guard steals property from the person of a prisoner in the guard's charge after handcuffing the prisoner on the pretext of preventing escape.

(3) *Fear.* For a robbery to be committed by putting the victim in fear, there need be no actual force or violence, but there must be a demonstration of force or menace by which the victim is placed in such fear that the victim is warranted in making no resistance. The fear must be a reasonable apprehension of present or future injury, and the taking must occur while the apprehension exists. The injury apprehended may be death or bodily injury to the person or to a relative or family member, or to anyone in the person's company at the time, or it may be the destruction of the person's habitation or other property or that of a relative or family member or anyone in the person's company at the time of sufficient gravity to warrant giving up the property demanded by the assailant.

(4) *Multiple-victim robberies.* Robberies of different persons at the same time and place are separate offenses and each such robbery should be alleged in a separate specification.

(5) *Dangerous weapon.* For purposes of qualifying for the maximum punishment for this offense as specified in subparagraph d.(1), the term "dangerous weapon" has the same meaning as that ascribed to the term in subparagraph 77.c.(5)(a)(iii).

d. *Maximum punishment.*

(1) *When committed with a dangerous weapon.* Dishonorable discharge, forfeiture of all pay and allowances, and confinement for 15 years.

(2) *All other cases.* Dishonorable discharge, forfeiture of all pay and allowances, and confinement for 10 years.

e. *Sample specification.*

In that ___________________ (personal jurisdiction data), did, (at/on board—location) (subject-matter jurisdiction data, if required), on or about _______ 20____, by means of (force) (violence) (force and violence) (and) (putting (him) (her) in fear) [with a dangerous weapon, to wit: ______________] seize from the (person) (presence) of ______________, against (his) (her) will, (a watch) (__________) of value of (about) $__________, the property of ______________.

68. Article 122a (10 U.S.C. 922a)—Receiving stolen property

a. *Text of statute.*

Any person subject to this chapter who wrongfully receives, buys, or conceals stolen property, knowing the property to be stolen property, shall be punished as a court-martial may direct.

b. *Elements.*

(1) That the accused wrongfully received, bought, or concealed certain property of some value;

(2) That the property belonged to another person;

(3) That the property had been stolen; and

(4) That the accused knew that the property had been stolen.

c. *Explanation.*

(1) *In general.* The actual thief is not criminally liable for receiving the property stolen; however a principal to the larceny (see paragraph 1), when not the actual thief, may be found guilty of knowingly receiving the stolen property but may not be found guilty of both the larceny and receiving the property.

(2) *Knowledge.* Actual knowledge that the property was stolen is required. Knowledge may be proved by circumstantial evidence.

(3) *Wrongfulness.* Receiving stolen property is wrongful if it is without justification or excuse. For example, it would not be wrongful for a person to receive stolen property for the purpose of returning it to its rightful owner, or for a law enforcement officer to seize it as evidence.

d. *Maximum punishment.*

(1) *Receiving, buying, or concealing stolen property of a value of $1,000 or less.* Bad-conduct discharge, forfeiture of all pay and allowances, and confinement for 1 year.

(2) *Receiving, buying, or concealing stolen property of a value of more than $1,000.* Dishonorable discharge, forfeiture of all pay and allowances, and confinement for 3 years.

e. *Sample specification.*

In that __________ (personal jurisdiction data), did, (at/on board—location) (subject-matter jurisdiction data, if required), on or about _____ 20 __, wrongfully (receive) (buy) (conceal) __________, of a value of (about) $__________, the property of __________ which property, as (he) (she), the said _____________, then knew, had been stolen.

69. Article 123 (10 U.S.C. 923)—Offenses concerning Government computers

a. *Text of statute.*

(a) IN GENERAL.—Any person subject to this chapter who—

(1) knowingly accesses a Government computer, with an unauthorized purpose, and by doing so obtains classified information, with reason to believe such information could be used to the injury of the United States, or to the advantage of any foreign nation, and intentionally communicates, delivers, transmits, or causes to be communicated, delivered, or transmitted such information to any person not entitled to receive it;

(2) intentionally accesses a Government computer, with an unauthorized purpose, and thereby obtains classified or other protected information from any such Government computer; or

(3) knowingly causes the transmission of a program, information, code, or command, and as a result of such conduct, intentionally causes damage without authorization to a Government computer;

shall be punished as a court-martial may direct.

(b) DEFINITIONS.—In this section:

(1) The term "computer" has the meaning given that term in section 1030 of title 18.

(2) The term "Government computer" means a computer owned or operated by or on behalf of the United States Government.

(3) The term "damage" has the meaning given that term in section 1030 of title 18.

b. *Elements.*

(1) *Unauthorized distribution of classified information obtained from a Government computer.*

(a) That the accused knowingly accessed a Government computer with an unauthorized purpose;

(b) That the accused obtained classified information;

(c) That the accused had reason to believe the information could be used to injure the United States or benefit a foreign nation; and

(d) That the accused intentionally communicated, delivered, transmitted, or caused to be communicated, delivered, or transmitted, such information to any person not entitled to receive it.

(2) *Unauthorized access of a Government computer and obtaining classified or other protected information.*

(a) That the accused intentionally accessed a Government computer with an unauthorized purpose; and

(b) That the accused thereby obtained classified or other protected information from any such Government computer.

(3) *Causing damage to a Government computer.*

(a) That the accused knowingly caused the transmission of a program, information, code, or command; and

(b) That the accused, as a result, intentionally and without authorization caused damage to a Government computer.

c. *Explanation.*

(1) *Access.* "Access" means to gain entry to, instruct, cause input to, cause output from, cause data processing with, or communicate with, the logical, arithmetical, or memory function resources of a computer, computer system, or computer network.

(2) *With an unauthorized purpose.* The phrase "with an unauthorized purpose" may refer to more than one unauthorized purpose, or an unauthorized purpose in conjunction with an authorized purpose. The phrase covers persons accessing Government computers without any authorization, i.e., "outsiders," as well as persons with authorization who access Government computers for an improper purpose or who exceed their authorization, i.e., "insiders." The key criterion to determine criminality is whether the person intentionally used the computer for a purpose that was clearly contrary to the interests or intent of the authorizing party.

(3) *Classified Information. See* 10 U.S.C. § 801(15).

(4) *Protected Information.* Non-classified protected information includes Personally Identifiable Information (PII), as well as information designated as Controlled Unclassified Information (CUI) by the Secretary of Defense, and information designated as For Official Use Only (FOUO), Law Enforcement Sensitive (LES), Unclassified Nuclear Information (UCNI), and Limited Distribution.

(5) *Damage.* The definition of "damage" is taken from 18 U.S.C. § 1030 and means any impairment to the integrity or availability of data, a program, a system, or information.

(6) *Computer.* The definition of "computer" is taken from 18 U.S.C. § 1030 and means an electronic, magnetic, optical, electrochemical, or other high speed data processing device performing logical, arithmetic, or storage functions, and includes any data storage facility or communications facility directly related to or operating in conjunction with such device, but such term does not include an automated typewriter or typesetter, a portable hand held calculator, or other similar device. A portable computer, including a smartphone, is a computer.

d. *Maximum punishment.*

(1) *Unauthorized distribution of classified information obtained from a Government computer.* Dishonorable discharge, forfeiture of all pay and allowances, and confinement for 10 years.

(2) *Unauthorized access of a Government computer and obtaining classified or other protected information.* Dishonorable discharge, forfeiture of all pay and allowances, and confinement for 5 years.

(3) *Causing damage to a Government computer.* Dishonorable discharge, forfeiture of all pay and allowances, and confinement for 10 years.

e. *Sample specifications.*

(1) *Unauthorized distribution of classified information obtained from a Government computer.*

In that __________ (personal jurisdiction data), did (at/on board—location), (subject-matter jurisdiction data, if required), (on or about _____ 20 __) (from about _____ to about _____ 20 __), knowingly access a government computer with an unauthorized purpose and obtained classified information, to wit:_____, with reason to believe the information could be used to injure the United States or benefit a foreign nation, and intentionally (communicated) (delivered) (transmitted) (caused to be communicated/delivered/transmitted) such information to ______, a person not entitled to receive it.

(2) *Accessing a computer and obtaining information.*

In that __________ (personal jurisdiction data), did (at/on board—location), (subject-matter jurisdiction data, if required), (on or about _____ 20 __) (from about _____ to about _____ 20 __), intentionally access a government computer with an unauthorized purpose and thereby knowingly obtained (classified) (protected) information, to wit:______ from such government computer.

(3) *Causing damage by computer contaminant.*

In that __________ (personal jurisdiction data), did (at/on board—location), (subject-matter jurisdiction data, if required), (on or about _____ 20 __) (from about _____ to about _____ 20 __), knowingly cause the transmission of a program, information, code, or command, and as a result, intentionally and without authorization caused damage to a government computer.

70. Article 123a (10 U.S.C. 923a)—Making, drawing, or uttering check, draft, or order without sufficient funds

a. *Text of statute.*

Any person subject to this chapter who—

(1) for the procurement of any article or thing of value, with intent to defraud; or

(2) for the payment of any past due obligation, or for any other purpose, with intent to deceive;

makes, draws, utters, or delivers any check, draft, or order for the payment of money upon any bank or other depository, knowing at the time that the maker or drawer has not or will not have sufficient funds in, or credit with, the bank or other depository for the payment of that check, draft, or order in full upon its presentment, shall be punished as a court-martial may direct. The making, drawing, uttering, or delivering by a maker or drawer of a check, draft, or order, payment of which is refused by the drawee because of insufficient funds of the maker or drawer in the drawee's possession or control, is prima facie evidence of his intent to defraud or deceive and of his knowledge of insufficient funds in, or credit with, that bank or other depository, unless the maker or drawer pays the holder the amount due within five days after receiving notice, orally or in writing, that the check, draft, or order was not paid on presentment. In this section, the word "credit" means an arrangement or understanding, express or implied, with the bank or other depository for the payment of that check, draft, or order.

b. *Elements.*

(1) *For the procurement of any article or thing of value, with intent to defraud.*

(a) That the accused made, drew, uttered, or delivered a check, draft, or order for the payment of money payable to a named person or organization;

(b) That the accused did so for the purpose of procuring an article or thing of value;

(c) That the act was committed with intent to defraud; and

(d) That at the time of making, drawing, uttering, or delivery of the instrument the accused knew that the accused or the maker or drawer had not or would not have sufficient funds in, or credit with, the bank or other depository for the payment thereof upon presentment.

(2) *For the payment of any past due obligation, or for any other purpose, with intent to deceive.*

(a) That the accused made, drew, uttered, or delivered a check, draft, or order for the payment of money payable to a named person or organization;

(b) That the accused did so for the purpose or purported purpose of effecting the payment of a past due obligation or for some other purpose;

(c) That the act was committed with intent to deceive; and

(d) That at the time of making, drawing, uttering, or delivering of the instrument, the accused knew that the accused or the maker or drawer had not or would not have sufficient funds in, or credit with, the bank or other depository for the payment thereof upon presentment.

c. *Explanation.*

(1) *Written instruments.* The written instruments covered by this article include any check, draft (including share drafts), or order for the payment of money drawn upon any bank or other depository, whether or not the drawer bank or depository is actually in existence. It may be inferred that every check, draft, or order carries with it a representation that the instrument will be paid in full by the bank or other depository upon presentment by a holder when due.

(2) *Bank or other depository.* Bank or other depository includes any business regularly but not necessarily exclusively engaged in public banking activities.

(3) *Making or drawing.* Making and drawing are synonymous and refer to the act of writing and signing the instrument.

(4) *Uttering or delivering.* Uttering and delivering have similar meanings. Both mean transferring the instrument to another, but uttering has the additional meaning of offering to transfer. A person need not personally be the maker or drawer of an instrument in order to violate this article if that person utters or delivers it. For example, if a person holds a check which that person knows is worthless, and utters or delivers the check to another, that person may be guilty of an offense under this article despite the fact that the person did not personally draw the check.

(5) *For the procurement.* "For the procurement" means for the purpose of obtaining any article or thing of value. It is not necessary that an article or thing of value actually be obtained, and the purpose of the obtaining may be for the accused's own use or benefit or for the use or benefit of another.

(6) *For the payment.* "For the payment" means for the purpose or purported purpose of satisfying in whole or in part any past due obligation. Payment need not be legally effected.

(7) *For any other purpose.* For any other purpose includes all purposes other than the payment of a past due obligation or the procurement of any article or thing of value. For example, it includes paying or purporting to pay an obligation which is not yet past due. The check, draft, or order, whether made or negotiated for the procurement of an article or thing of value or for the payment of a past due obligation or for some other purpose, need not be intended or represented as payable immediately. For example, the making of a postdated check, delivered at the time of entering into an installment purchase contract and intended as payment for a future installment, would, if made with the requisite intent and knowledge, be a violation of this article.

(8) *Article or thing of value.* Article or thing of value extends to every kind of right or interest in property, or derived from contract, including interests and rights which are intangible or contingent or which mature in the future.

(9) *Past due obligation.* A past due obligation is an obligation to pay money, which obligation has legally matured before making, drawing, uttering, or delivering the instrument.

(10) *Knowledge.* The accused must have knowledge, at the time the accused makes, draws, utters, or delivers the instrument, that the maker or drawer, whether the accused or another, has not or will not have sufficient funds in, or credit with, the bank or other depository for the payment of the instrument in full upon its presentment. Such knowledge may be proved by circumstantial evidence.

(11) *Sufficient funds.* "Sufficient funds" refers to a condition in which the account balance of the maker or drawer in the bank or other depository at the time of the presentment of the instrument for payment is not less than the face amount of the instrument and has not been rendered unavailable for payment by garnishment, attachment, or other legal procedures.

(12) *Credit.* "Credit" means an arrangement or understanding, express or implied, with the bank or other depository for the payment of the check, draft, or order. An absence of credit includes those situations in which an accused writes a check on a nonexistent bank or on a bank in which the accused has no account.

(13) *Upon its presentment.* "Upon its presentment" refers to the time the demand for payment is made upon presentation of the instrument to the bank or other depository on which it was drawn.

(14) *Intent to defraud.* "Intent to defraud" means an intent to obtain, through a misrepresentation, an article or thing of value and to apply it to one's own use and benefit or to the use and benefit of another, either permanently or temporarily.

(15) *Intent to deceive.* "Intent to deceive" means an intent to mislead, cheat, or trick another by means of a misrepresentation made for the purpose of gaining an advantage for oneself or for a third person, or of bringing about a disadvantage to the interests of the person to whom the representation was made or to interests represented by that person.

(16) *The relationship of time and intent.* Under this article, two times are involved: (a) when the accused makes, draws, utters, or delivers the instrument; and (b) when the instrument is presented to the bank or other depository for payment. With respect to (a), the accused must possess the requisite intent and must know that the maker or drawer does not have or will not have sufficient funds in, or credit with, the bank or the depository for payment of the instrument in full upon its presentment when due. With respect to (b), if it can otherwise be shown that the accused possessed

the requisite intent and knowledge at the time the accused made, drew, uttered, or delivered the instrument, neither proof of presentment nor refusal of payment is necessary, as when the instrument is one drawn on a nonexistent bank.

(17) *Statutory rule of evidence.* The provision of this article with respect to establishing prima facie evidence of knowledge and intent by proof of notice and nonpayment within 5 days is a statutory rule of evidence. The failure of an accused who is a maker or drawer to pay the holder the amount due within 5 days after receiving either oral or written notice from the holder of a check, draft, or order, or from any other person having knowledge that such check, draft, or order was returned unpaid because of insufficient funds, is prima facie evidence (a) that the accused had the intent to defraud or deceive as alleged; and (b) that the accused knew at the time the accused made, drew, uttered, or delivered the check, draft, or order that the accused did not have or would not have sufficient funds in, or credit with, the bank or other depository for the payment of such check, draft, or order upon its presentment for payment. Prima facie evidence is that evidence from which the accused's intent to defraud or deceive and the accused's knowledge of insufficient funds in or credit with the bank or other depository may be inferred, depending on all the circumstances. The failure to give notice referred to in the article, or payment by the accused, maker, or drawer to the holder of the amount due within 5 days after such notice has been given, precludes the prosecution from using the statutory rule of evidence but does not preclude conviction of this offense if all the elements are otherwise proved.

(18) *Affirmative defense.* Honest mistake is an affirmative defense to offenses under this article. *See* R.C.M. 916(j).

d. *Maximum punishment.*

(1) *For the procurement of any article or thing of value, with intent to defraud, in the face amount of:*

(a) *$1,000 or less.* Bad-conduct discharge, forfeiture of all pay and allowances, and confinement for 6 months.

(b) *More than $1,000.* Dishonorable discharge, forfeiture of all pay and allowances, and confinement for 5 years.

(2) *For the payment of any past due obligation, or for any other purpose, with intent to deceive.* Bad-conduct discharge, forfeiture of all pay and allowances, and confinement for 6 months.

e. *Sample specifications.*

(1) *For the procurement of any article or thing of value, with intent to defraud.*

In that ______________ (personal jurisdiction data), did, (at/on board—location) (subject-matter jurisdiction data, if required), on or about __________ 20___, with intent to defraud and for the procurement of (lawful currency) (and) (________ (an article) (a thing) of value), wrongfully and unlawfully ((make (draw)) (utter) (deliver) to __________,) a certain (check) (draft) (money order) upon the (_________ Bank) (__________ depository) in words and figures as follows, to wit: __________________, then knowing that (he) (she) (___________), the (maker) (drawer) thereof, did not or would not have sufficient funds in or credit with such (bank) (depository) for the payment of the said (check) (draft) (order) in full upon its presentment.

(2) *For the payment of any past due obligation, or for any other purpose, with intent to deceive.*

In that _____________ (personal jurisdiction data), did, (at/on board—location) (subject-matter jurisdiction data, if required), on or about _________ 20____, with intent to deceive and for the payment of a past due obligation, to wit: _______________ (for the purpose of ___________) wrongfully and unlawfully ((make) (draw)) (utter) (deliver) to ______________, a certain (check) (draft) (money order) for the payment of money upon (_____ Bank) (______ depository), in words and figures as follows, to wit: __________, then knowing that (he) (she) (__________), the (maker) (drawer) thereof, did not or would not have sufficient funds in or credit with such (bank) (depository) for the payment of the said (check) (draft) (order) in full upon its presentment.

71. Article 124 (10 U.S.C. 924)—Frauds against the United States

a. *Text of statute.*

Any person subject to this chapter—

(1) who, knowing it to be false or fraudulent—

(A) makes any claim against the United States or any officer thereof; or

(B) presents to any person in the civil or military service thereof, for approval or payment, any claim against the United States or any officer thereof;

(2) who, for the purpose of obtaining the approval, allowance, or payment of any claim against the United States or any officer thereof—

(A) makes or uses any writing or other paper knowing it to contain any false or fraudulent statements;

(B) makes any oath to any fact or to any writing or other paper knowing the oath to be false; or

(C) forges or counterfeits any signature upon any writing or other paper, or uses any such signature knowing it to be forged or counterfeited;

(3) who, having charge, possession, custody or control of any money, or other property of the United States, furnished or intended for the armed forces thereof, knowingly delivers to any person having authority to receive it, any amount thereof less than that for which he receives a certificate or receipt; or

(4) who, being authorized to make or deliver any paper certifying the receipt of any property of the United States furnished or intended for the armed forces thereof, makes or delivers to any person such writing without having full knowledge of the truth of the statements therein contained and with intent to defraud the United States;

shall, upon conviction, be punished as a court-martial may direct.

b. *Elements.*

(1) *Making a false or fraudulent claim.*

(a) That the accused made a certain claim against the United States or an officer thereof;

(b) That the claim was false or fraudulent in certain particulars; and

(c) That the accused then knew that the claim was false or fraudulent in these particulars.

(2) *Presenting for approval or payment a false or fraudulent claim.*

(a) That the accused presented for approval or payment to a certain person in the civil or military service of the United States having authority to approve or pay it a certain claim against the United States or an officer thereof;

(b) That the claim was false or fraudulent in certain particulars; and

(c) That the accused then knew that the claim was false or fraudulent in these particulars.

(3) *Making or using a false writing or other paper in connection with a claim.*

(a) That the accused made or used a certain writing or other paper;

(b) That certain material statements in the writing or other paper were false or fraudulent;

(c) That the accused then knew the statements were false or fraudulent; and

(d) That the act of the accused was for the purpose of obtaining the approval, allowance, or payment of a certain claim or claims against the United States or an officer thereof.

(4) *False oath in connection with a claim.*

(a) That the accused made an oath to a certain fact or to a certain writing or other paper;

(b) That the oath was false in certain particulars;

(c) That the accused then knew it was false; and

(d) That the act was for the purpose of obtaining the approval, allowance, or payment of a certain claim or claims against the United States or an officer thereof.

(5) *Forgery of signature in connection with a claim.*

(a) That the accused forged or counterfeited the signature of a certain person on a certain writing or other paper; and

(b) That the act was for the purpose of obtaining the approval, allowance, or payment of a certain claim against the United States or an officer thereof.

(6) *Using forged signature in connection with a claim.*

(a) That the accused used the forged or counterfeited signature of a certain person;

(b) That the accused then knew that the signature was forged or counterfeited; and

(c) That the act was for the purpose of obtaining the approval, allowance, or payment of a certain claim against the United States or an officer thereof.

(7) *Delivering less than amount called for by receipt.*

(a) That the accused had charge, possession, custody, or control of certain money or property of the United States furnished or intended for the armed forces thereof;

(b) That the accused obtained a certificate or receipt for a certain amount or quantity of that money or property;

(c) That for the certificate or receipt the accused knowingly delivered to a certain person having authority to receive it, an amount or quantity of money or property less than the amount or quantity thereof specified in the certificate or receipt; and

(d) That the undelivered money or property was of a certain value.

(8) *Making or delivering receipt without having full knowledge that it is true.*

(a) That the accused was authorized to make or deliver a paper certifying the receipt from a certain person of certain property of the United States furnished or intended for the armed forces thereof;

(b) That the accused made or delivered to that person a certificate or receipt;

(c) That the accused made or delivered the certificate without having full knowledge of the truth of a certain material statement or statements therein;

(d) That the act was done with intent to defraud the United States; and

(e) That the property certified as being received was of a certain value.

c. *Explanation.*

(1) *Making a false or fraudulent claim.*

(a) *Claim.* A claim is a demand for a transfer of ownership of money or property and does not include requisitions for the mere use of property. This article applies only to claims against the United States or any officer thereof as such, and not to claims against an officer of the United States in that officer's private capacity.

(b) *Making a claim.* Making a claim is a distinct act from presenting it. A claim may be made in one place and presented in another. The mere writing of a paper in the form of a claim, without any further act to cause the paper to become a demand against the United States or an officer thereof, does not constitute making a claim. However, any act placing the claim in official channels constitutes making a claim, even if that act does not amount to presenting a claim. It is not necessary that the claim be allowed or paid or that it be made by the person to be benefited by the allowance or payment. *See also* subparagraph c.(2).

(c) *Knowledge.* The claim must be made with knowledge of its fictitious or dishonest character. This article does not proscribe claims, however groundless they may be, that the maker believes to be valid, or claims that are merely made negligently or without ordinary prudence.

(2) *Presenting for approval or payment a false or fraudulent claim.*

(a) *False and fraudulent.* False and fraudulent claims include not only those containing some material false statement, but also claims that the claimant knows to have been paid or for some other reason the claimant knows the claimant is not authorized to present or upon which the claimant knows the claimant has no right to collect.

(b) *Presenting a claim.* The claim must be presented, directly or indirectly, to some person having authority to pay it. The person to whom the claim is presented may be identified by position or authority to approve the claim, and need not be identified by name in the specification. A false claim may be tacitly presented, as when a person who knows that there is no entitlement to certain pay accepts it nevertheless without disclosing a disqualification, even though the person may not have made any representation of entitlement to the pay. For example, a person cashing a pay check that includes an amount for a dependency allowance, knowing at the time that the entitlement no longer exists because of a change in that dependency status, has tacitly presented a false claim. See also subparagraph (1) of this paragraph.

(3) *Making or using a false writing or other paper in connection with a claim.* The false or fraudulent statement must be material, that is, it must have a tendency to mislead governmental officials in their consideration or investigation of the claim. The offense of making a writing or other paper known to contain a false or fraudulent statement for the purpose of obtaining the approval, allowance, or payment of a claim is complete when the writing or paper is made for that purpose, whether or not any use of the paper has been attempted and whether or not the claim has been presented. See also the explanation in subparagraphs (1) and (2) of this paragraph.

(4) *False oath in connection with a claim.* See subparagraphs (1) and (2) of this paragraph.

(5) *Forgery of signature in connection with a claim.* Any fraudulent making of the signature of another is forging or counterfeiting, whether or not an attempt is made to imitate the handwriting. See subparagraph 37.c. and subparagraphs (1) and (2) of this paragraph.

(6) *Delivering less than amount called for by receipt.* It is immaterial by what means—whether deceit,

collusion, or otherwise—the accused effected the transaction, or what was the accused's purpose.

(7) *Making or delivering receipt without having full knowledge that it is true.* When an officer or other person subject to military law is authorized to make or deliver any paper certifying the receipt of any property of the United States furnished or intended for the armed forces thereof, and a receipt or other paper is presented for signature stating that a certain amount of supplies has been furnished by a certain contractor, it is that person's duty before signing the paper to know that the full amount of supplies therein stated to have been furnished has in fact been furnished, and that the statements contained in the paper are true. If the person signs the paper with intent to defraud the United States and without that knowledge, that person is guilty of a violation of this section of the article. If the person signs the paper with knowledge that the full amount was not received, it may be inferred that the person intended to defraud the United States.

d. *Maximum punishment.*

(1) *Article 124 (1) and (2).* Dishonorable discharge, forfeiture of all pay and allowances, and confinement for 5 years.

(2) *Article 124 (3) and (4).*

(a) *When amount is $1,000 or less.* Bad-conduct discharge, forfeiture of all pay and allowances, and confinement for 6 months.

(b) *When amount is more than $1,000.* Dishonorable discharge, forfeiture of all pay and allowances, and confinement for 5 years.

e. *Sample specifications.*

(1) *Making false claim.*

In that ______________ (personal jurisdiction data), did, (at/on board—location) (subject-matter jurisdiction data, if required), on or about ______ 20___, (by preparing (a voucher) (_______) for presentation for approval or payment) (_____), make a claim against the (United States) (finance officer at _____) (________) in the amount of $________ for (private property alleged to have been (lost) (destroyed) in the military service) (____________), which claim was (false) (fraudulent) (false and fraudulent) in the amount of $________ in that _______ and was then known by the said _______ to be (false) (fraudulent) (false and fraudulent).

(2) *Presenting false claim.*

In that ______________ (personal jurisdiction data), did, (at/on board—location) (subject-matter jurisdiction data, if required), on or about ______ 20___, by presenting (a voucher) (________) to ______, an officer of the United States duly authorized to (approve) (pay) (approve and pay) such claim, present for (approval) (payment) (approval and payment) a claim against the (United States) (finance officer at _________) (________) in the amount of $________ for (services alleged to have been rendered to the United States by ___________ during ___________) (____________), which claim was (false) (fraudulent) (false and fraudulent) in the amount of $________ in that _______, and was then known by the said _______ to be (false) (fraudulent) (false and fraudulent).

(3) *Making or using false writing.*

In that _______________ (personal jurisdiction data), for the purpose of obtaining the (approval) (allowance) (payment) (approval, allowance, and payment) of a claim against the United States in the amount of $______, did (at/on board—location) (subject-matter jurisdiction data, if required), on or about ________ 20____, (make) (use) (make and use) a certain (writing) (paper), to wit:___________, which said (writing) (paper), as (he) (she), the said _______, then knew, contained a statement that ____________, which statement was (false) (fraudulent) (false and fraudulent) in that ___________, and was then known by the said ___________ to be (false) (fraudulent) (false and fraudulent).

(4) *Making false oath.*

In that _______________ (personal jurisdiction data), for the purpose of obtaining the (approval) (allowance) (payment) (approval, allowance, and payment) of a claim against the United States, did (at/on board—location) (subject-matter jurisdiction data, if required), on or about ________ 20____, make an oath (to the fact that ___________) (to a certain (writing) (paper), to wit: _____________), to the effect that ___________, which said oath was false in that ___________, and was then known by the said ___________ to be false.

(5) *Forging or counterfeiting signature.*

In that _______________ (personal jurisdiction data), for the purpose of obtaining the (approval) (allowance) (payment) (approval, allowance, and payment) of a claim against the United States, did (at/on board—location) (subject-matter jurisdiction data, if required), on or about ________ 20____, (forge) (counterfeit) (forge and counterfeit) the signature of _______ upon a ___________ in words and figures as follows: __________.

(6) *Using forged signature.*

In that _______________ (personal jurisdiction data), for the purpose of obtaining the (approval) (allowance) (payment) (approval, allowance, and payment) of a claim against the United States, did (at/on board—location) (subject-matter jurisdiction data, if required), on or about ________ 20____, use the signature of ___________ on a certain (writing) (paper), to wit: __________, then knowing such signature to be (forged) (counterfeited) (forged and counterfeited).

(7) *Paying amount less than called for by a receipt.*

In that _______________ (personal jurisdiction data), having (charge) (possession) (custody) (control) of (money) (________) of the United States, (furnished) (intended) (furnished and intended) for the armed forces thereof, did, (at/on board—location) (subject-matter jurisdiction data, if required), on or about ________ 20____, knowingly deliver to _____, the said __________ having authority to receive the same, (an amount) (_____), which, as (he) (she), ________, then knew, was ($______) (____________) less than the (amount) (______) for which (he) (she) received a (certificate) (receipt) from the said __________.

(8) *Making receipt without knowledge of the facts.*

In that _______________ (personal jurisdiction data), being authorized to (make) (deliver) (make and deliver) a paper certifying the receipt of property of the United States (furnished) (intended) (furnished and intended) for the armed forces thereof, did, (at/on board—location) (subject-matter jurisdiction data, if required), on or about ________ 20____, without having full knowledge of the statement therein contained and with intent to defraud the United States, (make) (deliver) (make and deliver) to ___________, such a writing, in words and figures as follows: ____________, the property therein certified as received being of a value of about $_________.

72. Article 124a (10 U.S.C. 924a)—Bribery

a. *Text of statute.*

(a) ASKING, ACCEPTING, OR RECEIVING THING OF VALUE.—Any person subject to this chapter—

(1) who occupies an official position or who has official duties; and

(2) who wrongfully asks, accepts, or receives a thing of value with the intent to have the person's decision or action influenced with respect to an official matter in which the United States is interested;

shall be punished as a court-martial may direct.

(b) PROMISING, OFFERING, OR GIVING THING OF VALUE.—Any person subject to this chapter who wrongfully promises, offers, or gives a thing of value to another person, who occupies an official position or who has official duties, with the intent to influence the decision or action of the other person with respect to an official matter in which the United States is interested, shall be punished as a court-martial may direct.

b. *Elements.*

(1) *Asking, accepting, or receiving.*

(a) That the accused wrongfully asked, accepted, or received a thing of value from a certain person or organization;

(b) That the accused then occupied a certain official position or had certain official duties;

(c) That the accused asked, accepted, or received this thing of value with the intent to have the accused's decision or action influenced with respect to a certain matter; and

(d) That this certain matter was an official matter in which the United States was interested.

(2) *Promising, offering, or giving.*

(a) That the accused wrongfully promised, offered, or gave a thing of value to a certain person;

(b) That this person then occupied a certain official position or had certain official duties;

(c) That this thing of value was promised, offered, or given with the intent to influence the decision or action of this person; and

(d) That this matter was an official matter in which the United States was interested.

c. *Explanation.* Bribery requires an intent to influence or be influenced in an official matter.

d. *Maximum punishment.* Dishonorable discharge, forfeiture of all pay and allowances, and confinement for 5 years.

e. *Sample specifications.*

(1) *Asking, accepting, or receiving.*

In that __________ (personal jurisdiction data), being at the time (a contracting officer for _____) (the personnel officer of _____) (_____), did, (at/on board—location) (subject-matter jurisdiction data, if required), on or about _____ 20 __, wrongfully (ask) (accept) (receive) from _____, (a contracting company engaged in _____) (_____), (the sum of $_____) (_________, of a value of (about) $_____) (_____), (with intent to have (his) (her) (decision) (action) influenced with respect to) ((as compensation for) (in recognition of)) service (rendered) (to be rendered).

(2) *Promising, offering, or giving.*

In that __________ (personal jurisdiction data), did (at/on board—location) (subject-matter jurisdiction data, if required), on or about _____ 20 __, wrongfully (promise) (offer) (give) to __________, ((his) (her) commanding officer) (the claims officer of _____) (_____), (the sum of $_____) (_____, of a value of (about) $_____) (_____), (with intent to influence the (decision) (action) of the said _____ with respect to) ((as compensation for) (in recognition of)) services (rendered) (to be rendered).

73. Article 124b (10 U.S.C. 924b)—Graft

a. *Text of statute.*

(a) ASKING, ACCEPTING, OR RECEIVING THING OF VALUE.—Any person subject to this chapter—

(1) who occupies an official position or who has official duties; and

(2) who wrongfully asks, accepts, or receives a thing of value as compensation for or in recognition of services rendered or to be rendered by the person with respect to an official matter in which the United States is interested;

shall be punished as a court-martial may direct.

(b) PROMISING, OFFERING, OR GIVING THING OF VALUE.—Any person subject to this chapter who wrongfully promises, offers, or gives a thing of value to another person, who occupies an official position or who has official duties, as compensation for or in recognition of services rendered or to be rendered by the other person with respect to an official matter in which the United States is interested, shall be punished as a court-martial may direct.

b. *Elements.*

(1) *Asking, accepting, or receiving.*

(a) That the accused wrongfully asked, accepted, or received a thing of value from a certain person or organization;

(b) That the accused then occupied a certain official position or had certain official duties;

(c) That the accused asked, accepted, or received this thing of value as compensation for or in recognition of services rendered, to be rendered, or both, by the accused in relation to a certain matter; and

(d) That this certain matter was an official matter in which the United States was interested.

(2) *Promising, offering, or giving.*

(a) That the accused wrongfully promised, offered, or gave a thing of value to a certain person;

(b) That this person then occupied a certain official position or had certain official duties;

(c) That this thing of value was promised, offered, or given as compensation for or in recognition of services rendered, to be rendered, or both, by this person in relation to a certain matter; and

(d) That this matter was an official matter in which the United States was interested.

c. *Explanation.* Graft does not require an intent to influence or be influenced in an official matter. Graft involves compensation for services performed in an official matter when no compensation is due.

d. *Maximum punishment.* Dishonorable discharge, forfeiture of all pay and allowances, and confinement for 3 years.

e. *Sample specifications.*

(1) *Asking, accepting, or receiving.*

In that __________ (personal jurisdiction data), being at the time (a contracting officer for _____) (the personnel officer of _____) (_____), did,(at/on board—location) (subject-matter jurisdiction data, if required), on or about _____ 20 __, wrongfully (ask) (accept) (receive) from _____, (a contracting company engaged in _____) (_____), (the sum of $_____) (_________, of a value of (about) $_____) (_____), (rendered or to be rendered) by (him) (her) the said _____ in relation to) an official matter in which the United States was interested, to wit: (the purchasing of military supplies from _____) (the transfer of _____ to duty with _____) (_____).

(2) *Promising, offering, or giving.*

In that __________ (personal jurisdiction data), did (at/on board—location) (subject-matter jurisdiction data, if required), on or about _____ 20 __, wrongfully (promise) (offer) (give) to __________, ((his) (her) commanding officer) (the claims officer of _____) (_____), (the sum of $_____) (_____, of a value of (about) $_____) (_____, (rendered or to be rendered) by the said _____ in relation to) an official matter in which the United States was interested, to wit: (the granting of leave to _____) (the processing of a claim against the United States in favor of _____) (_____).

74. Article 125 (10 U.S.C. 925)—Kidnapping

a. *Text of statute.*

Any person subject to this chapter who wrongfully—

(1) seizes, confines, inveigles, decoys, or carries away another person; and

(2) holds the other person against that person's will;

shall be punished as a court-martial may direct.

b. *Elements.*

(1) That the accused seized, confined, inveigled, decoyed, or carried away a certain person;

(2) That the accused then held such person against that person's will; and

(3) That the accused did so wrongfully.

c. *Explanation.*

(1) *Inveigle, decoy.* "Inveigle" means to lure, lead astray, or entice by false representations or other deceitful means. For example, a person who entices another to ride in a car with a false promise to take the person to a certain destination has inveigled the passenger into the car. "Decoy" means to entice or lure by means of some fraud, trick, or temptation. For example, one who lures a child into a trap with candy has decoyed the child.

(2) *Held.* "Held" means detained. The holding must be more than a momentary or incidental detention. For example, a robber who holds the victim at gunpoint while the victim hands over a wallet, or a rapist who throws his victim to the ground, does not, by such acts, commit kidnapping. On the other hand, if, before or after such robbery or rape, the victim is involuntarily transported some substantial distance, as from a housing area to a remote area of the base or post, this may be kidnapping, in addition to robbery or rape.

(3) *Against the will.* "Against that person's will" means that the victim was held involuntarily. The involuntary nature of the detention may result from force, mental or physical coercion, or from other means, including false representations. If the victim is incapable of having a recognizable will, as in the case of a very young child or a mentally incompetent person, the holding must be against the will of the victim's parents or legal guardian. Evidence of the availability or nonavailability to the victim of means of exit or escape is relevant to the voluntariness of the detention, as is evidence of threats or force, or lack thereof, by the accused to detain the victim.

(4) *Financial or personal gain.* The holding need not have been for financial or personal gain or for any other particular purpose. It may be an aggravating circumstance that the kidnapping was for ransom, however. *See* R.C.M. 1001(b)(4).

(5) *Wrongfully.* "Wrongfully" means without justification or excuse. For example, a law enforcement official may justifiably apprehend and detain, by force if reasonably necessary (*see* R.C.M. 302(d)(3)), a person reasonably believed to have committed an offense. An official who unlawfully uses the official's authority to apprehend someone is not guilty of kidnapping, but may be guilty of unlawful detention. *See* paragraph 25.

d. *Maximum punishment.* Dishonorable discharge, forfeiture of all pay and allowances, and confinement for life without eligibility for parole.

e. *Sample specification.*

In that _____, (personal jurisdiction data), did, (at/on board—location) (subject-matter jurisdiction data, if required), on or about _____ 20 __, wrongfully (seize) (confine) (inveigle) (decoy) (carry away) and hold _____ (a minor whose parent or legal guardian the accused was not) (a person not a minor) against (his) (her) will.

75. Article 126 (10 U.S.C. 926)—Arson; burning property with intent to defraud

a. *Text of statute.*

(a) AGGRAVATED ARSON.—Any person subject to this chapter who, willfully and maliciously, burns or sets on fire an inhabited dwelling, or any other structure, movable or immovable, wherein, to the knowledge of that person, there is at the time a human being, is guilty of aggravated arson and shall be punished as a court-martial may direct.

(b) SIMPLE ARSON.—Any person subject to this chapter who, willfully and maliciously, burns or sets fire to the property of another is guilty of simple arson and shall be punished as a court-martial may direct.

(c) BURNING PROPERTY WITH INTENT TO DEFRAUD.—Any person subject to this chapter who, willfully, maliciously, and with intent to defraud, burns or sets fire to any property shall be punished as a court-martial may direct.

b. *Elements.*

(1) *Aggravated arson.*

(a) *Inhabited dwelling.*

(i) That the accused burned or set on fire an inhabited dwelling; and

(ii) That the act was willful and malicious.

(b) *Structure.*

(i) That the accused burned or set on fire a certain structure;

(ii) That the act was willful and malicious;

(iii) That there was a human being in the structure at the time; and

(iv) That the accused knew that there was a human being in the structure at the time.

(2) *Simple arson.*

(a) That the accused burned or set fire to certain property of another; and

(b) That the act was willful and malicious.

[Note: if the property is of a value of more than $1,000, add the following element:]

(c) That the property is of a value of more than $1,000.

(3) *Burning with the intent to defraud.*

(a) That the accused burned or set fire to certain property; and

(b) That the act was willful and malicious; and

(c) That such burning or setting on fire was with the intent to defraud a certain person or organization.

c. *Explanation.*

(1) *In general.* In aggravated arson, danger to human life is the essential element; in simple arson, it is injury to the property of another. In either case, it is immaterial that no one is, in fact, injured. It must be shown that the accused set the fire willfully and maliciously, that is, not merely by negligence or accident. In burning with intent to defraud, it is the fraudulent intent motivating the burning of any property that is the essential element. It is immaterial to whom the property belonged; the focus is that the burning of that property was for a fraudulent purpose (e.g., the intent to file a false insurance claim for the property burned by the accused).

(2) *Aggravated arson.*

(a) *Inhabited dwelling.* "An inhabited dwelling" means the structure must be used for habitation, not that a human being must be present therein at the time the dwelling is burned or set on fire. It includes the outbuildings that form part of the cluster of buildings used as a residence. A shop or store is not an inhabited dwelling unless occupied as such, nor is a house that has never been occupied or that has been temporarily abandoned. A person may be guilty of aggravated arson of the person's dwelling, whether as owner or tenant.

(b) *Structure.* Aggravated arson may also be committed by burning or setting on fire any other structure, movable or immovable, such as a theater, church, boat, trailer, tent, auditorium, or any other sort of shelter or edifice, whether public or private, when the offender knows that there is a human being inside at the time. It may be that the offender had this knowledge when the nature of the structure—as a department store or theater during hours of business, or other circumstances—are shown to have been such that a reasonable person would have known that a human being was inside at the time.

(c) *Damage to property.* It is not necessary that the dwelling or structure be consumed or materially injured; it is enough if fire is actually communicated to any part thereof. Any actual burning or charring is sufficient, but a mere scorching or discoloration by heat is not.

(d) *Value and ownership of property.* For the offense of aggravated arson, the value and ownership of the dwelling or other structure are immaterial, but may be alleged and proved to permit the finding in an appropriate case of the included offense of simple arson.

(3) *Simple arson.* Simple arson is the willful and malicious burning or setting fire to the property of another under circumstances not amounting to aggravated arson. The offense includes burning or setting fire to real or personal property of someone other than the offender. See subparagraph 75.c.(1) for discussion of willful and malicious.

(4) *Burning with the intent to defraud.* See subparagraph 70.c.(14) for a discussion of intent to defraud.

d. *Maximum punishment.*

(1) *Aggravated arson.* Dishonorable discharge, forfeiture of all pay and allowances, and confinement for 25 years.

(2) *Simple arson—*

(a) *Where the property is of some value.* Dishonorable discharge, forfeiture of all pay and allowances, and confinement for 5 years.

(b) *Where the property is of a value of more than $1,000.* Dishonorable discharge, forfeiture of all pay and allowances, and confinement for 10 years.

(3) *Burning with intent to defraud.* Dishonorable discharge, forfeiture of all pay and allowances, and confinement for 10 years.

e. *Sample specifications.*

(1) *Aggravated arson.*

(a) *Inhabited dwelling.*

In that __________ (personal jurisdiction data), did, (at/on board—location) (subject-matter jurisdiction data, if required), on or about _____ 20 __, willfully and maliciously (burn) (set on fire) an inhabited dwelling, to wit: (a house) (an apartment) (__________).

(b) *Structure.*

In that __________ (personal jurisdiction data), did, (at/on board—location) (subject-matter jurisdiction data, if required), on or about _____ 20 __, willfully and maliciously (burn) (set on fire), knowing that a human being was therein at the time, (the Post Theater) (__________).

(2) *Simple arson.*

In that __________ (personal jurisdiction data), did, (at/on board—location) (subject-matter jurisdiction data, if required), on or about _____ 20 __, willfully and maliciously (burn) (set fire to) (an automobile) (__________), (of some value) (of a value of more than $1,000), the property of another.

(3) *Burning with intent to defraud.*

In that __________ (personal jurisdiction data), did, (at/on board—location) (subject-matter jurisdiction data, if required), on or about _____ 20 __, willfully and maliciously (burn) (set fire to) (a dwelling) (a barn) (an automobile) (_________), with intent to defraud (the insurer thereof, to wit: ________) (________).

76. Article 127 (10 U.S.C. 927)—Extortion

a. *Text of statute.*

Any person subject to this chapter who communicates threats to another person with the intention thereby to obtain anything of value or any acquittance, advantage, or immunity is guilty of extortion and shall be punished as a court-martial may direct.

b. *Elements.*

(1) That the accused communicated a certain threat to another; and

(2) That the accused intended to unlawfully obtain something of value, or any acquittance, advantage, or immunity.

c. *Explanation.*

(1) *In general.* Extortion is complete upon communication of the threat with the requisite intent. The actual or probable success of the extortion need not be proved.

(2) *Threat.* A threat may be communicated by any means but must be received by the intended victim. The threat may be: a threat to do any unlawful injury to the person or property of the person threatened or to any member of that person's family or any other person held dear to that person; a threat to accuse the person threatened, or any member of that person's family or any other person held dear to that person, of any crime; a threat to expose or impute any deformity or disgrace to the person threatened or to any member of that person's family or any other person held dear to that person; a threat to expose any secret affecting the person threatened or any member of that person's family or any other person held dear to that person; or a threat to do any other harm.

(3) *Acquittance.* An acquittance is a release or discharge from an obligation.

(4) *Advantage or immunity.* Unless it is clear from the circumstances, the advantage or immunity sought should be described in the specification. An intent to make a person do an act against that person's will is not, by itself, sufficient to constitute extortion.

d. *Maximum punishment.* Dishonorable discharge, forfeiture of all pay and allowances, and confinement for 3 years.

e. *Sample specifications.*

In that __________ (personal jurisdiction data), did, (at/on board—location) (subject-matter jurisdiction data, if required), on or about _____ 20 __, with intent unlawfully to obtain (something of value, to wit: ________) (an acquittance) (an advantage, to wit: __________) (an immunity, to wit: __________), communicate to __________ a threat to (here describe the threat).

77. Article 128 (10 U.S.C. 928)—Assault

a. *Text of statute.*

(a) ASSAULT.—Any person subject to this chapter who, unlawfully and with force

or violence—

(1) attempts to do bodily harm to another person;

(2) offers to do bodily harm to another person; or

(3) does bodily harm to another person;

is guilty of assault and shall be punished as a court-martial may direct.

(b) AGGRAVATED ASSAULT.—Any person subject to this chapter—

(1) who, with the intent to do bodily harm, offers to do bodily harm with a

dangerous weapon;

(2) who, in committing an assault, inflicts substantial bodily harm or grievous bodily

harm on another person; or

(3) who commits an assault by strangulation or suffocation;

is guilty of aggravated assault and shall be punished as a court-martial may direct.

(c) ASSAULT WITH INTENT TO COMMIT SPECIFIED OFFENSES.—

(1) IN GENERAL.—Any person subject to this chapter who commits assault with intent to commit an offense specified in paragraph (2) shall be punished as a court-martial may direct.

(2) OFFENSES SPECIFIED.—The offenses referred to in paragraph (1) are murder, voluntary manslaughter, rape, sexual assault, rape of a child, sexual assault of a child, robbery, arson, burglary, and kidnapping.

b. *Elements.*

(1) *Simple assault.*

(a) That the accused attempted to do or offered to do bodily harm to a certain person;

(b) That the attempt or offer was done unlawfully; and

(c) That the attempt or offer was done with force or violence.

(2) *Assault consummated by a battery.*

(a) That the accused did bodily harm to a certain person;

(b) That the bodily harm was done unlawfully; and

(c) That the bodily harm was done with force or violence.

(3) *Assaults permitting increased punishment based on status of victim.*

(a) *Assault upon a commissioned, warrant, noncommissioned, or petty officer.*

(i) That the accused attempted to do, offered to do, or did bodily harm to a certain person;

(ii) That the attempt, offer, or bodily harm was done unlawfully;

(iii) That the attempt, offer, or bodily harm was done with force or violence;

(iv) That the person was a commissioned, warrant, noncommissioned, or petty officer; and

(v) That the accused then knew that the person was a commissioned, warrant, noncommissioned, or petty officer.

(b) *Assault upon a sentinel or lookout in the execution of duty, or upon a person in the execution of law enforcement duties.*

(i) That the accused attempted to do, offered to do, or did bodily harm to a certain person;

(ii) That the attempt, offer, or bodily harm was done unlawfully;

(iii) That the attempt, offer, or bodily harm was done with force or violence;

(iv) That the person was a sentinel or lookout in the execution of duty or was a person who then had and was in the execution of security police, military police, shore patrol, master at arms, or other military or civilian law enforcement duties; and

(v) That the accused then knew that the person was a sentinel or lookout in the execution of duty or was a person who then had and was in the execution of security police, military police, shore patrol, master at arms, or other military or civilian law enforcement duties.

(c) *Assault consummated by a battery upon a child under 16 years.*

(i) That the accused did bodily harm to a certain person;

(ii) That the bodily harm was done unlawfully;

(iii) That the bodily harm was done with force or violence; and

(iv) That the person was then a child under the age of 16 years.

(4) *Aggravated assault.*

(a) *Assault with a dangerous weapon.*

(i) That the accused offered to do bodily harm to a certain person;

(ii) The offer was made with the intent to do bodily harm; and

(iii) That the accused did so with a dangerous weapon.

[Note: Add any of the following elements as applicable:]

(iv) That the dangerous weapon was a loaded firearm.

(v) That the person was a child under the age of 16 years.

(b) *Assault in which substantial bodily harm is inflicted.*

(i) That the accused assaulted a certain person; and

(ii) That substantial bodily harm was thereby inflicted upon such person.

[Note: Add any of the following elements as applicable:]

(iii) That the injury was inflicted with a loaded firearm.

(iv) That the person was a child under the age of 16 years.

(c) *Assault in which grievous bodily harm is inflicted.*

(i) That the accused assaulted a certain person; and

(ii) That grievous bodily harm was thereby inflicted upon such person.

[Note: Add any of the following elements as applicable:]

(iii) That the injury was inflicted with a loaded firearm.

(iv) That the person was a child under the age of 16 years.

(d) *Aggravated Assault by strangulation or suffocation.*

(i) That the accused assaulted a certain person;

(ii) That the accused did so by strangulation or suffocation; and;

(iii) That the strangulation or suffocation was done with unlawful force or

violence;

[Note: Add the following as applicable]

(iv) That the person was a child under the age of 16 years.

(5) *Assault with intent to commit specified offenses.*

(a) That the accused assaulted a certain person; and

(b) That the accused, at the time of the assault, intended to: kill (as required for murder or voluntary manslaughter), or commit rape, rape of a child, sexual assault, sexual assault of a child, robbery, arson, burglary, or kidnapping.

c. *Explanation.*

(1) *Definitions of bodily harm.*

(a) "Bodily harm" means an offensive touching of another, however slight.

(b) "Substantial bodily harm" means a bodily injury that involves:

(i) a temporary but substantial disfigurement, or

(ii) a temporary but substantial loss or impairment of function of any bodily member, organ, or mental faculty.

(c) "Grievous bodily harm" means a bodily injury that involves:

(i) a substantial risk of death;

(ii) extreme physical pain;

(iii) protracted and obvious disfigurement; or

(iv) protracted loss or impairment of the function of a bodily member, organ, or mental faculty.

(2) *Simple assault.*

(a) *Definition of assault.* An assault is an unlawful attempt or offer, made with force or violence, to do bodily harm to another, whether or not the attempt or offer is consummated. It must be done without legal justification or excuse and without the lawful consent of the person affected.

(b) *Difference between attempt and offer type assaults.*

(i) *Attempt-type assault.* An attempt-type assault requires a specific intent to inflict bodily harm, and an overt act—that is, an act that amounts to more than mere preparation and apparently tends to effect the intended bodily harm. An attempt-type assault may be committed even though the victim had no knowledge of the incident at the time.

(ii) *Offer-type assault.* An offer-type assault is an unlawful demonstration of violence, either by an intentional or by a culpably negligent act or omission, which creates in the mind of another a reasonable apprehension of receiving immediate bodily harm. Specific intent to inflict bodily harm is not required.

(iii) *Examples.*

(A) If Doe swings a fist at Roe's head intending to hit Roe but misses, Doe has committed an attempt-type assault, whether or not Roe is aware of the attempt.

(B) If Doe swings a fist in the direction of Roe's head either intentionally or as a result of culpable negligence, and Roe sees the blow coming and is thereby put in apprehension of being struck, Doe has committed an offer-type assault whether or not Doe intended to hit Roe.

(C) If Doe swings at Roe's head, intending to hit it, and Roe sees the blow coming and is thereby put in apprehension of being struck, Doe has committed both on offer- and an attempt-type assault.

(D) If Doe swings at Roe's head simply to frighten Roe, not intending to hit Roe, and Roe does not see the blow and is not placed in fear, then no assault of any type has been committed.

(c) *Situations not amounting to assault.*

(i) *Mere preparation.* Preparation not amounting to an overt act, such as picking up a stone without any attempt or offer to throw it, does not constitute an assault.

(ii) *Threatening words.* The use of threatening words alone does not constitute an assault. However, if the threatening words are accompanied by a menacing act or gesture, there may be an assault, since the combination constitutes a demonstration of violence.

(iii) *Circumstances negating intent to harm.* If the circumstances known to the person menaced clearly negate an intent to do bodily harm, there is no assault. Thus, if a person accompanies an apparent attempt to strike another by an unequivocal announcement in some form of an intention not to strike, there is no assault. For example, if Doe raises a stick and shakes it at Roe within striking distance saying, "If you weren't an old man, I would knock you down," Doe has committed no assault. However, an offer to inflict bodily injury upon another instantly if that person does not comply with a demand that the assailant has no lawful right to make is an assault. Thus, if Doe points a pistol at Roe and says, "If you don't hand over your watch, I will shoot you," Doe has committed an assault upon Roe. See also paragraph 67 (Robbery) of this Part.

(d) *Situations not constituting defenses to assault.*

(i) *Assault attempt fails.* It is not a defense to a charge of assault that for some reason unknown to the assailant, an assault attempt was bound to fail. Thus, if a person loads a rifle with what is believed to be a good cartridge and, pointing it at another, pulls the trigger, that person may be guilty of assault although the cartridge was defective and did not fire. Likewise, if a person in a house shoots through the roof at a place where a policeman is believed to be, that person may be guilty of assault even though the policeman is at another place on the roof.

(ii) *Retreating victim.* An assault is complete if there is a demonstration of violence and an apparent ability to inflict bodily injury causing the person at whom it was directed to reasonably apprehend that unless the person retreats bodily harm will be inflicted. This is true even though the victim retreated and was never within actual striking distance of the assailant. There must, however, be an apparent present ability to inflict the injury. Thus, to aim a pistol at a person at such a distance that it clearly could not injure would not be an assault.

(3) *Battery.*

(a) *In general.* A battery is an assault in which the attempt or offer to do bodily harm is consummated by the infliction of that harm.

(b) *Application of force.* The force applied in a battery may have been directly or indirectly applied. Thus, a battery can be committed by inflicting bodily injury on a person through striking the horse on which the person is mounted causing the horse to throw the person, as well as by striking the person directly.

(c) *Examples of battery.* It may be a battery to spit on another, push a third person against another, set a dog at another that bites the person, cut another's clothes while the person is wearing them though without touching or intending to touch the person, shoot a person, cause a person to take poison, or drive an automobile into a person. A person who, although excused in using force, uses more force than is required, commits a battery. Throwing an object into a crowd may be a battery on anyone whom the object hits.

(d) *Situations not constituting battery.* If bodily harm is inflicted unintentionally and without culpable negligence, there is no battery. It is also not a battery to touch another to attract the other's attention or to prevent injury.

(4) *Assaults permitting increased punishment based on status of victims.*

(a) *Assault upon a commissioned, warrant, noncommissioned, or petty officer.* The maximum punishment is increased when assault is committed upon a commissioned officer of the armed forces of the United States, or of a friendly foreign power, or upon a warrant, noncommissioned, or petty officer of the armed forces of the United States. Knowledge of the status of the victim is an essential element of the offense and may be proved by circumstantial evidence. It is not necessary that the victim be superior in rank or command to the accused, that the victim be in the same armed force, or that the victim be in the execution of office at the time of the assault.

(b) *Assault upon a sentinel or lookout in the execution of duty, or upon a person in the execution of law enforcement duties.* The maximum punishment is increased when assault is committed upon a sentinel or lookout in the execution of duty or upon a person who was then performing security police, military police, shore patrol, master at arms, or other military or civilian law enforcement duties. Knowledge of the status of the victim is an essential element of this offense and may be proved by circumstantial evidence. See subparagraph 22.c.(1)(d) for the definition of sentinel or lookout.

(c) *Assault consummated by a battery upon a child under 16 years of age.* The maximum punishment is increased when assault consummated by a battery is committed upon a child under 16 years of age. Knowledge that the person assaulted was under 16 years of age is not an element of this offense.

(5) *Aggravated assault.*

(a) *Assault with a dangerous weapon.*

(i) *In general.* It must be proved that the accused specifically intended to do bodily harm. Culpable negligence will not suffice.

(ii) *Proving intent.* Specific intent may be proved by circumstantial evidence. When bodily harm has been inflicted by means of intentionally using force in a manner capable of achieving that result, it may be inferred that bodily harm was intended.

(iii) *Dangerous weapon.* A weapon is dangerous when used in a manner capable of inflicting death or grievous bodily harm. What constitutes a dangerous weapon depends not on the nature of the object itself but on its capacity, given the manner of its use, to kill or inflict grievous bodily harm. Thus, a bottle, beer glass, a rock, a bunk adaptor, a piece of pipe, a piece of wood, boiling water, drugs, or a rifle butt may be used in a manner capable of inflicting death or grievous bodily harm. Furthermore, under the appropriate circumstances, fists, teeth, feet, elbows, etc. may be considered a dangerous weapon when employed in a manner capable of inflicting death or grievous bodily harm.

(iv) *Injury not required.* It is not necessary that bodily harm be actually inflicted to prove assault with a dangerous weapon.

(v) *When committed upon a child under 16 years of age.* The maximum punishment is increased when assault with a dangerous weapon is committed upon a child under 16 years of age. Knowledge that the person assaulted was under the age of 16 years is not an element of the offense.

(b) *Assault in which substantial or grievous bodily harm is inflicted.*

(i) *In general.* Assault in which substantial or grievous bodily harm is inflicted is a general intent crime which requires that the accused assaulted another person and that the assault resulted in substantial or grievous bodily harm. The offense does not require specific intent to cause substantial or grievous bodily harm. The focus of the offense is the degree of bodily harm resulting from an assault. This contrasts with the offense of assault with a dangerous weapon, where the focus of the offense is the accused's intent to do bodily harm and the use of a dangerous weapon, regardless of whether any bodily harm results.

(ii) *When committed on a child under 16 years of age.* The maximum punishment is increased when assault involving infliction of substantial or grievous bodily harm is inflicted upon a child under 16 years of age. Knowledge that the person assaulted was under the age of 16 years is not an element of the offense.

(c) *Aggravated Assault by strangulation or suffocation.*

(i) *In general.* Assault by strangulation or suffocation is an assault committed intentionally, knowingly, or recklessly, regardless of whether that conduct results in any visible injury or whether there is any intent to kill or protractedly injure the victim.

(ii) *Assault. See* paragraph 77.c.(2)(a).

(iii) *Strangulation.* Intentionally, knowingly, or recklessly impeding the normal breathing or circulation of the blood of a person by applying pressure to the throat or neck, regardless of whether that conduct results in any visible injury or whether there is any intent to kill or protractedly injure the victim.

(iv) *Suffocation.* Intentionally, knowingly, or recklessly impeding the normal breathing of a person by covering the mouth of the person, the nose of the person, or both, regardless of whether that conduct results in any visible injury or whether there is any intent to kill or protractedly injure the victim.

(v) *When committed upon a child under 16 years of age.* The maximum punishment is increased when aggravated assault by strangulation or suffocation is inflicted upon a child under 16 years of age. Knowledge that the person assaulted was under the age of 16 years is not an element of the offense.

(6) *Assault with intent to commit specified offenses.*

(a) *In general.* An assault with intent to commit any of the offenses referenced below is not necessarily the equivalent of an attempt to commit the intended offense, for an assault can be committed with intent to commit an offense without achieving that proximity to consummation of an intended offense that is essential to an attempt. See paragraph 4 of this Part.

(b) *Assault with intent to murder.* Assault with intent to commit murder is assault with the specific intent to kill. Actual infliction of injury is not necessary. To constitute an assault with intent to murder with a firearm, it is not necessary that the weapon be discharged. When the intent to kill exists, the fact that for some unknown reason the actual consummation of the murder by the means employed is impossible is not a defense if the means are apparently adapted to the end in view. The intent to kill need not be directed against the person assaulted if the assault is committed with intent to kill some person. For example, if a person, intending to kill Jones, shoots Smith, mistaking Smith for Jones, that person is guilty of assaulting Smith with intent to murder. If a person fires into a group with intent to kill anyone in the group, that person is guilty of an assault with intent to murder each member of the group.

(c) *Assault with intent to commit voluntary manslaughter.* Assault with intent to commit voluntary manslaughter is an assault committed with a specific intent to kill under such circumstances that, if death resulted therefrom, the offense of voluntary manslaughter would have been committed. There can be no assault with intent to commit involuntary manslaughter, for it is not a crime capable of being intentionally committed.

(d) *Assault with intent to commit rape, rape of a child, sexual assault, and sexual assault of a child.* In assault with intent to commit any rape or sexual assault, the accused must have intended to complete the offense. Any lesser intent will not suffice. No actual touching is necessary. Once an assault with intent to commit rape is made, it is no defense that the accused voluntarily desisted.

(e) *Assault with intent to rob.* For assault with intent to rob, the fact that the accused intended to take money and that the person the accused intended to rob had none is not a defense.

d. *Maximum punishment.*

(1) *Simple assault.*

(a) *Generally.* Confinement for 3 months and forfeiture of two-thirds pay per month for 3 months.

(b) *When committed with a firearm or other dangerous weapon.* Dishonorable discharge, forfeiture of all pay and allowances, and confinement for 2 years.

(c) *When committed with a loaded firearm.* Dishonorable discharge, forfeiture of all pay and allowances, and confinement for 4 years.

(2) *Battery.*

(a) *Assault consummated by a battery.* Bad-conduct discharge, forfeiture of all pay and allowances, and confinement for 6 months.

(b) *Assault consummated by a battery upon a child under 16 years.* See paragraph 77.d.(3)(e).

(3) *Assaults permitting increased punishments based upon status of victim.*

(a) *Assault upon a commissioned officer of the armed forces of the United States or of a friendly foreign power, not in the execution of office.* Dishonorable discharge, forfeiture of all pay and allowances, and confinement for 3 years.

(b) *Assault upon a warrant officer, not in the execution of office.* Dishonorable discharge, forfeiture of all pay and allowances, and confinement for 18 months.

(c) *Assault upon a noncommissioned or petty officer, not in the execution of office*. Bad conduct discharge, forfeiture of all pay and allowances, and confinement for 6 months.

(d) *Assault upon a sentinel or lookout in the execution of duty, or upon any person who, in the execution of office, is performing security policy, military police, shore patrol, master at arms, or other military or civilian law enforcement duties*. Dishonorable discharge, forfeiture of all pay and allowances, and confinement for 3 years.

(e) *Assault consummated by a battery upon a child under 16 years*. Dishonorably discharge, forfeiture of all pay and allowances, and confinement for 2 years.

(4) *Aggravated assault*.

(a) *Aggravated assault with a dangerous weapon*.

(i) *When committed with a loaded firearm*. Dishonorable discharge, forfeiture of all pay and allowances, and confinement for 8 years.

(ii) *When committed upon a child under the age of 16 years*. Dishonorable discharge, forfeiture of all pay and allowances, and confinement for 5 years.

(iii) *Other cases*. Dishonorable discharge, forfeiture of all pay and allowances, and confinement for 3 years.

(b) *Aggravated assault in which substantial bodily harm is inflicted*.

(i) *When the injury is inflicted with a loaded firearm*. Dishonorable discharge, forfeiture of all pay and allowances, and confinement for 8 years.

(ii) *When the injury is inflicted upon a child under the age of 16 years*. Dishonorable discharge, forfeiture of all pay and allowances, and confinement for 6 years.

(iii) *Other cases*. Dishonorable discharge, forfeiture of all pay and allowances, and confinement for 3 years.

(c) *Aggravated assault in which grievous bodily harm is inflicted.*

(i) *When the injury is inflicted with loaded firearm*. Dishonorable discharge, forfeiture of all pay and allowance, and confinement for 10 years.

(ii) *When the injury is inflicted upon a child under the age of 16 years*. Dishonorable, forfeiture of all pay and allowances, and confinement for 8 years.

(iii) *Other cases*. Dishonorable discharge, forfeiture of all pay and allowances, and confinement for 5 years.

(d) *Aggravated Assault by strangulation or suffocation*.

(i) *Aggravated assault by strangulation or suffocation when committed upon a child under the age of 16 years*. Dishonorable discharge, forfeiture of all pay and allowances, and confinement for 8 years.

(ii) *Other cases*. Dishonorable discharge, forfeiture of all pay and allowances, and confinement for 5 years.

(5) *Assault with intent to commit specified offenses*.

(a) *Assault with intent to commit murder, rape, or rape of a child*. Dishonorable discharge, forfeiture of all pay and allowances, and confinement for 20 years.

(b) *Assault with intent to commit voluntary manslaughter, robbery, arson, burglary, kidnapping, sexual assault, or sexual assault of a child*. Dishonorable discharge, forfeiture of all pay and allowances, and confinement for 10 years.

e. *Sample specifications*.

(1) *Simple assault*.

In that __________ (personal jurisdiction data), did, (at/on board—location), (subject-matter jurisdiction data, if required), on or about _____ 20 __, assault __________ by (striking at (him) (her) with a __________) (__________).

(2) *Assault consummated by a battery*.

In that __________ (personal jurisdiction data), did, (at/on board—location) (subject-matter jurisdiction data, if required), on or about _____ 20 __, unlawfully (strike) (__________) __________ (on) (in) the __________ with __________.

(3) *Assault upon a commissioned officer*.

In that __________ (personal jurisdiction data), did, (at/on board—location) (subject-matter jurisdiction data, if required), on or about _____ 20 __, assault _____, who then was and was then known by the accused to be a commissioned officer of (_____, a friendly foreign power) [the United States (Army) (Navy) (Marine Corps) (Air Force) (Coast Guard) (______)] by ______________.

(4) *Assault upon a warrant, noncommissioned, or petty officer*.

In that __________ (personal jurisdiction data), did, (at/on board—location) (subject-matter jurisdiction data, if required), on or about _____ 20 __, assault __________, who then was and was then known by the accused to be a (warrant) (noncommissioned) (petty) officer of the [the United States (Army) (Navy)

(Marine Corps) (Air Force) (Coast Guard) (______)] by ______________.

(5) *Assault upon a sentinel or lookout.*

In that __________ (personal jurisdiction data), did, (at/on board—location) (subject-matter jurisdiction data, if required), on or about _____ 20 __, assault __________, who then was and was then known by the accused to be a (sentinel) (lookout) in the execution of (his) (her) duty, ((in) (on) the __________) by __________.

(6) *Assault upon a person in the execution of law enforcement duties.*

In that __________ (personal jurisdiction data), did, (at/on board—location) (subject-matter jurisdiction data, if required), on or about _____ 20 __, assault __________, who then was and was then known by the accused to be a person then having and in the execution of (Air Force security police) (military police) (shore patrol) (master at arms) ((military) (civilian) law enforcement)) duties, by __________.

(7) *Assault consummated by a battery upon a child under 16 years.*

In that __________ (personal jurisdiction data), did, (at/on board-location) (subject-matter jurisdiction data, if required), on or about _____ 20 __, unlawfully (strike) (_______) _________ (a child under the age of 16 years) (in) (on) the _____ with ____________.

(8) *Assault, aggravated—with a dangerous weapon.*

In that __________ (personal jurisdiction data), did, (at/on board-location) (subject matter jurisdiction data, if required), on or about _____ 20 __, with the intent to inflict bodily harm, commit an assault upon __________ (a child under the age of 16 years) by (shooting) (pointing) (striking) (cutting) (_____) (at (him) (her)) with a dangerous weapon, to wit: a (loaded firearm) (pickax) (bayonet) (club) (_________).

(9) *Assault, aggravated—inflicting substantial bodily harm.*

In that __________ (personal jurisdiction data), did, (at/on board-location) (subject matter jurisdiction data, if required), on or about _____ 20 __, commit an assault upon _____ (a child under the age of 16 years) by (shooting) (striking) (cutting) (___) (him) (her) (on) the _____ with a (loaded firearm) (club) (rock) (brick) (________) and did thereby inflict substantial bodily harm upon (him) (her), to wit: (severe bruising of the face) (head concussion) (temporary blindness) (__________).

(10) *Assault, aggravated—inflicting grievous bodily harm.*

In that __________ (personal jurisdiction data), did, (at/on board-location) (subject matter jurisdiction data, if required), on or about _____ 20 __, commit an assault upon _____ (a child under the age of 16 years) by (shooting) (striking) (cutting) (___) (him) (her) (on) the _____ with a (loaded firearm) (club) (rock) (brick) (_________) and did thereby inflict grievous bodily harm upon (him) (her), to wit: a (broken leg) (deep cut) (fractured skull) (__________).

(11) *Assault, aggravated—by strangulation or suffocation.*

In that __________ (personal jurisdiction data), did, (at/on board-location) (subject matter jurisdiction data, if required), on or about _____ 20 __, commit an assault upon __________ (a child under the age of 16 years) by unlawfully (strangling) (suffocating) (him) (her) (with/by __________).

(12) *Assault with intent to commit specified offenses.*

In that __________ (personal jurisdiction data), did, (at/on board-location) (subject matter jurisdiction data, if required), on or about _____ 20 __, with intent to commit (murder) (voluntary manslaughter) (rape) (rape of a child) (sexual assault) (sexual assault of a child) (robbery) (arson) (burglary) (kidnapping), assault____________ by (striking at (him) (her) with a __________) (__________).

78. Article 128a (10 U.S.C. 928a)—Maiming

a. *Text of statute.*

Any person subject to this chapter who, with intent to injure, disfigure, or disable, inflicts upon the person of another an injury which—

(1) seriously disfigures his person by any mutilation thereof;

(2) destroys or disables any member or organ of his body; or

(3) seriously diminishes his physical vigor by the injury of any member or organ;

is guilty of maiming and shall be punished as a court-martial may direct.

b. *Elements.*

(1) That the accused inflicted a certain injury upon a certain person;

(2) That this injury seriously disfigured the person's body, destroyed or disabled an organ or member, or

seriously diminished the person's physical vigor by the injury to an organ or member; and

(3) That the accused inflicted this injury with an intent to cause some injury to a person.

c. *Explanation.*

(1) *Nature of offense.* It is maiming to put out a person's eye, to cut off a hand, foot, or finger, or to knock out a tooth, as these injuries destroy or disable those members or organs. It is also maiming to injure an internal organ so as to seriously diminish the physical vigor of a person. Likewise, it is maiming to cut off an ear or to scar a face with acid, as these injuries seriously disfigure a person. A disfigurement need not mutilate any entire member to come within the article, or be of any particular type, but must be such as to impair perceptibly and materially the victim's comeliness. The disfigurement, diminishment of vigor, or destruction or disablement of any member or organ must be a serious injury of a substantially permanent nature. However, the offense is complete if such an injury is inflicted even though there is a possibility that the victim may eventually recover the use of the member or organ, or that the disfigurement may be cured by surgery.

(2) *Means of inflicting injury.* To prove the offense it is not necessary to prove the specific means by which the injury was inflicted. However, such evidence may be considered on the question of intent.

(3) *Intent.* Maiming requires a specific intent to injure generally but not a specific intent to maim. Thus, one commits the offense who intends only a slight injury, if in fact there is infliction of an injury of the type specified in this article. Infliction of the type of injuries specified in this article upon the person of another may support an inference of the intent to injure, disfigure, or disable.

d. *Maximum punishment.* Dishonorable discharge, forfeiture of all pay and allowances, and confinement for 20 years.

e. *Sample specification.*

In that __________ (personal jurisdiction data), did, (at/on board—location) (subject-matter jurisdiction data, if required) on or about _____ 20 __, maim __________ by (crushing (his) (her) foot with a sledge hammer) (__________).

78a. Article 128b (10 U.S.C. 928b) – Domestic Violence

a. *Text of statute.*

Any person who—

(1) commits a violent offense against a spouse, an intimate partner, or an immediate family member of that person;

(2) with intent to threaten or intimidate a spouse, an intimate partner, or an immediate family member of that person—

(A) commits an offense under this chapter against any person; or

(B) commits an offense under this chapter against any property, including an animal;

(3) with intent to threaten or intimidate a spouse, an intimate partner, or an immediate family member of that person, violates a protection order;

(4) with intent to commit a violent offense against a spouse, an intimate partner, or an immediate family member of that person, violates a protection order; or

(5) assaults a spouse, an intimate partner, or an immediate family member of that person by strangling or suffocating; shall be punished as a court-martial may direct.

b. *Elements.*

(1) *Commission of a violent offense against a spouse, intimate partner, or immediate family member of that person.*

(a) That the accused committed a violent offense; and

(b) That the violent offense was committed against a spouse, intimate partner, or immediate family member of the accused.

[Note: Add the following as applicable]

(c) That the immediate family member was a child under the age of 16 years.

(2) *Commission of a violation of the UCMJ against any person with intent to threaten or intimidate a spouse, an intimate partner, or an immediate family member of that person.*

(a) That the accused committed an act in violation of the UCMJ;

(b) That the accused committed the act against any person; and

(c) That the accused committed the act with the intent to threaten or intimidate a spouse, an intimate partner, or an immediate family member of the accused.

(3) *Commission of a violation of the UCMJ against any property, including an animal, with the intent to*

threaten or intimidate a spouse, intimate partner, or an immediate family member of that person.

(a) That the accused committed an act in violation of the UCMJ;

(b) That the accused committed the act against any property, including an animal; and

(c) That the accused committed the act with the intent to threaten or intimidate a spouse, an intimate partner, or an immediate family member of the accused.

(4) *Violation of a protection order with the intent to threaten or intimidate a spouse, an intimate partner, or an immediate family member of that person.*

(a) That a lawful protection order was in place;

(b) That the accused committed an act in violation of that lawful protection order; and

(c) That the accused committed the act with the intent to threaten or intimidate a spouse, an intimate partner, or an immediate family member of the accused.

(5) *Violation of a protection order with the intent to commit a violent offense against a spouse, an intimate partner, or an immediate family member of that person.*

(a) That a lawful protection order was in place;

(b) That the accused committed an act in violation of that lawful protection order; and

(c) That the accused committed the act with the intent to commit a violent offense against a spouse, an intimate partner, or an immediate family member of the accused.

(6) *Assaulting a spouse, an intimate partner, or an immediate family member of that person by strangulation or suffocation.*

(a) That the accused assaulted a spouse, an intimate partner, or an immediate family member of the accused;

(b) That the accused did so by strangulation or suffocation; and

(c) That the strangulation or suffocation was done with unlawful force or violence;

[Note: Add the following as applicable]

(d) That the person was a child under the age of 16 years.

c. *Explanation.*

(1) *Violent Offense.* The term "violent offense" means a violation of the following:

(a) 10 U.S.C. § 918 (article 118)

(b) 10 U.S.C. § 919(a) (article 119(a))

(c) 10 U.S.C. § 919a (article 119a)

(d) 10 U.S.C. § 920 (article 120)

(e) 10 U.S.C. § 920b (article 120b)

(f) 10 U.S.C. § 922 (article 122)

(g) 10 U.S.C. § 925 (article 125)

(h) 10 U.S.C. § 926 (article 126)

(i) 10 U.S.C. § 928 (article 128)

(j) 10 U.S.C. § 928a (article 128a)

(k) 10 U.S.C. § 930 (article 130)

(l) Any other offense that has an element that includes the use, attempted use, or threatened use of physical force against the person or property of another.

(2) *Spouse.* The term "spouse" means one's husband or wife by lawful marriage.

(3) *Intimate partner.* The term "intimate partner" means—

(a) one's former spouse, a person with whom one shares a child in common, or a person with whom one cohabits or with whom one has cohabited as a spouse; or

(b) a person with whom one has been in a social relationship of a romantic or intimate nature, as determined by the length of the relationship, the type of relationship, and the frequency of interaction between the persons involved in the relationship.

(4) *Immediate family.* The term "immediate family" means—

(a) one's spouse, parent, brother or sister, child, or other person to whom he or she stands in loco parentis; or

(b) any other person living in one's household to whom he or she is related by blood or marriage.

(5) Strangulation. The term "strangulation" has the same meaning ascribed to that term in subparagraph 77.c.(5)(c)(iii).

(6) Suffocation. The term "suffocation" has the same meaning ascribed to that term in subparagraph 77.c.(5)(c)(iv).

(7) *Protection order.* The term "protection order" means—

(a) a military protective order enforceable under 10 U.S.C. § 892 (article 92); or

(b) a protection order, as defined in 18 U.S.C. § 2266 and, if issued by a State, tribal, or territorial court, is in accordance with the standards specified in 18 U.S.C. § 2265.

(8) *Mandatory Minimum Punishments.* In accordance with 10 U.S.C. § 856 (article 56), for a conviction of an offense under this paragraph, mandatory minimum punishment provisions

shall not apply.

d. *Maximum punishment.* Dishonorable discharge, forfeiture of all pay and allowances, and confinement as follows:

(1) *Commission of a violent offense against a spouse, an intimate partner, or an immediate family member of that person.* Any person subject to the UCMJ who is found guilty of violating Article 128b by committing a violent offense against a spouse, an intimate partner, or an immediate family member of that person shall be subject to the same maximum period of confinement authorized for the commission of the underlying offense plus an additional 3 years of confinement except for those violent offenses for which the maximum punishment includes death, confinement for life without eligibility for parole, or confinement for life.

(2) *Commission of a violation of the UCMJ against any person with intent to threaten or intimidate a spouse, an intimate partner, or an immediate family member of that person.* Any person subject to the UCMJ who is found guilty of violating Article 128b by committing an offense punishable under the UCMJ with intent to threaten or intimidate a spouse, an intimate partner, or an immediate family member of that person shall be subject to the same maximum period of confinement authorized for the commission of the underlying offense plus an additional 3 years, with the exception of those offenses for which the maximum punishment includes death, confinement for life without eligibility for parole, or confinement for life.

(3) *Commission of a violation of the UCMJ against any property, including an animal, with the intent to threaten or intimidate a spouse, intimate partner, or an immediate family member of that person.* Any person subject to the UCMJ who is found guilty of violating Article 128b by committing an offense punishable under the UCMJ against any property, including an animal, with the intent to threaten or intimidate a spouse, an intimate partner, or an immediate family member of that person shall be subject to the same maximum period of confinement authorized for the commission of the underlying offense plus an additional 3 years, with the exception of those offenses for which the maximum punishment includes death, confinement for life without eligibility for parole, or confinement for life.

(4) *Violation of a protection order with the intent to threaten or intimidate a spouse, an intimate partner, or an immediate family member of that person.* Confinement for 3 years.

(5) *Violation of a protection order with the intent to commit a violent offense against a spouse, an intimate partner, or an immediate family member of that person.* Confinement for 5 years.

(6) *Assaulting a spouse, an intimate partner, or an immediate family member of that person by strangulation or suffocation.*

(a) *Aggravated assault by strangulation or suffocation when committed upon a child under the age of 16 years.* Confinement for 11 years.

(b) *Other cases.* Confinement for 8 years.

e. *Sample Specifications.*

(1) In that __________ (personal jurisdiction data), did, (at/on board-location) (subject matter jurisdiction data, if required), on or about _____ 20 __, commit a violent offense against __________, the (spouse) (intimate partner) (immediate family member) (immediate family member under the age of 16 years) of the accused, to wit: (describe offense with sufficient detail to include expressly or by necessary implication every element and any applicable sentence enhancer from the underlying offense).

(2) In that __________ (personal jurisdiction data), did, (at/on board-location) (subject matter jurisdiction data, if required), on or about _____ 20 __, with the intent to (threaten) (intimidate) the (spouse) (intimate partner) (immediate family member) of the accused, commit an offense in violation of the UCMJ against (any person) (a child under the age of 16 years), to wit: (describe offense with sufficient detail to include expressly or by necessary implication every element and any applicable sentence enhancer from the underlying offense).

(3) In that __________ (personal jurisdiction data), did, (at/on board-location) (subject matter jurisdiction data, if required), on or about _____ 20 __, with the intent to (threaten) (intimidate) the (spouse) (intimate partner) (immediate family member) of the accused, commit an offense in violation of the UCMJ against

any property, to wit: (describe offense with sufficient detail to include expressly or by necessary implication every element and any applicable sentence enhancer from the underlying offense).

(4) In that __________ (personal jurisdiction data), did, (at/on board-location) (subject matter jurisdiction data, if required), on or about _____ 20 __, with the intent to (threaten) (intimidate) the (spouse) (intimate partner) (immediate family member) of the accused, wrongfully violate a protection order by ______________________.

(5) In that __________ (personal jurisdiction data), did, (at/on board-location) (subject matter jurisdiction data, if required), on or about _____ 20 __, violate a protection order, to wit: _______________, with the intent to commit a violent offense, to wit: (describe offense with sufficient detail to include expressly or by necessary implication every element), against the (spouse) (intimate partner) (immediate family member) of the accused.

(6) In that __________ (personal jurisdiction data), did, (at/on board-location) (subject matter jurisdiction data, if required), on or about _____ 20 __, commit an assault upon ____________, the (spouse) (intimate partner) (immediate family member) (immediate family member under the age of 16 years) of the accused, by unlawfully (strangling) (suffocating) him/her (with/by __________)."

79. Article 129 (10 U.S.C. 929)—Burglary; unlawful entry

a. *Text of statute.*

(a) BURGLARY.—Any person subject to this chapter who, with intent to commit an offense under this chapter, breaks and enters the building or structure of another shall be punished as a court-martial may direct.

(b) UNLAWFUL ENTRY.—Any person subject to this chapter who unlawfully enters—

(1) the real property of another; or

(2) the personal property of another which amounts to a structure usually used for habitation or storage;

shall be punished as a court-martial may direct.

b. *Elements.*

(1) *Burglary.*

(a) That the accused unlawfully broke and entered the building or structure of another; and

(b) That the breaking and entering were done with the intent to commit an offense punishable under the UCMJ.

[Note: If the breaking and entering were with the intent to commit an offense punishable under sections 918-920, 920b-921, 922, 925-928a, and 930 of this title (Article 118-120, 120b-121, 122, 125-128a, and 130), add the following element:]

(c) That the breaking and entering were with the intent to commit an offense punishable under Article 118-120, 120b-121, 122, 125-128a, and 130.

(2) *Unlawful entry.*

(a) That the accused entered—

(i) the real property of another; or

(ii) certain personal property of another which amounts to a structure usually used for habitation or storage; and

(b) That the entry was unlawful.

c. *Explanation.*

(1) *In general.* This article combines and consolidates the crimes of burglary, housebreaking, and unlawful entry. There is no requirement that an accused break and enter in the nighttime or that the structure entered constitute the dwelling house of another to commit the offense of burglary.

(2) *Breaking.* There must be a breaking, actual or constructive. Merely entering through a hole left in the wall or roof or through an open window or door will not constitute a breaking; but if a person moves any obstruction to entry of the house without which movement the person could not have entered, the person has committed a breaking. Opening a closed door or window or other similar fixture, opening wider a door or window already partly open but insufficient for the entry, or cutting out the glass of a window or the netting of a screen is a sufficient breaking. The breaking of an inner door by one who has entered the house without breaking, or by a person lawfully within the house who has no authority to enter the particular room, is a sufficient breaking, but unless such a breaking is followed by an entry into the particular room with the requisite intent, burglary is not committed. There is a constructive breaking when the entry is gained by a trick, such as concealing oneself in a box; under false pretense, such as impersonating a gas or telephone inspector; by intimidating the occupants through violence or threats into opening the door; through collusion with a confederate, an occupant of the house; or by descending a chimney,

even if only a partial descent is made and no room is entered.

(3) *Entry.* An entry must be effected before the offense is complete, but the entry of any part of the body, even a finger, is sufficient. Insertion into the house of a tool or other instrument is also a sufficient entry, unless the insertion is solely to facilitate the breaking or entry. An entry is unlawful if made without consent of any person authorized to consent to entry or without other lawful authority.

(4) *Building, structure.* Building includes room, shop, store, office, or apartment in a building. Structure refers only to those structures that are in the nature of a building or dwelling. Examples of these structures are a stateroom, hold, or other compartment of a vessel, an inhabitable trailer, an enclosed truck or freight car, a tent, and a houseboat. It is not necessary that the building or structure be in use at the time of the entry.

(5) *Intent to commit offense.*

(a) *Burglary.* Both the breaking and entry must be done with the intent to commit an offense punishable under the UCMJ in the building or structure. If, after the breaking and entering, the accused commits one or more of these offenses, it may be inferred that the accused intended to commit the offense or offenses at the time of the breaking and entering. If the evidence warrants, the intended offense may be separately charged. It is immaterial whether the offense intended is committed or even attempted. If the offense is intended, it is no defense that its commission was impossible. For example, if an accused enters a house with intent to murder a resident, but the resident is not present in the house, the accused may still be found guilty of burglary.

(b) *Unlawful entry.* Neither specific intent to commit an offense, nor breaking is required for this offense.

(6) *Property protected from unlawful entry.* The property protected against unlawful entry includes real property and the sort of personal property that amounts to a structure usually used for habitation or storage, which would usually include vehicles expressly used for habitation, such as mobile homes and recreational vehicles. It would usually not include an aircraft, automobile, tracked vehicle, or a person's locker, even though used for storage purposes. However, depending on the circumstances, an intrusion into such property may be punishable under Article 134, UCMJ as conduct prejudicial to good order and discipline or of a nature to bring discredit upon the armed forces.

(7) *Unlawfulness of entry.* An entry is unlawful if made without the consent of any person authorized to consent to entry or without other lawful authority.

d. *Maximum punishment.*

(1) *Burglary* (with the intent to commit an offense punishable under Article 118-120, 120b-121, 122, 125-128a, or 130). Dishonorable discharge, forfeiture of all pay and allowances, and confinement for 10 years.

(2) *Burglary* (with intent to commit any other offense punishable under the UCMJ). Dishonorable discharge, forfeiture of all pay and allowances, and confinement for 5 years.

(3) *Unlawful entry.* Bad-conduct discharge, forfeiture of all pay and allowances, and confinement for 6 months.

e. *Sample specifications.*

(1) *Burglary*

In that __________ (personal jurisdiction data), did, (at/on board—location) (subject-matter jurisdiction data, if required), on or about _____ 20 __, unlawfully break and enter the (building) (structure) of __________, to wit _______, with intent to commit an offense under the Uniform Code of Military Justice therein, to wit: ________________.

(2) *Unlawful entry.*

In that __________, (personal jurisdiction data), did, (at/on board—location) (subject-matter jurisdiction data, if required), on or about _____ 20 __, unlawfully enter the (real property) (personal property) (a structure usually used for habitation or storage) of ____________, to wit ____________.

80. Article 130 (10 U.S.C. 930)—Stalking

a. *Text of statute.*

(a) IN GENERAL.—Any person subject to this chapter—

(1) who wrongfully engages in a course of conduct directed at a specific person that would cause a reasonable person to fear death or bodily harm, including sexual assault, to himself or herself, to a member of his or her immediate family, or to his or her intimate partner;

(2) who has knowledge, or should have knowledge, that the specific person will be placed in reasonable fear of death or bodily harm, including sexual assault, to himself or herself, to a member of his or her immediate family, or to his or her intimate partner; and

(3) whose conduct induces reasonable fear in the specific person of death or bodily harm, including sexual assault, to himself or herself, to a member of his or her immediate family, or to his or her intimate partner;

is guilty of stalking and shall be punished as a court-martial may direct.

(b) DEFINITIONS.—In this section:

(1) The term "conduct" means conduct of any kind, including use of surveillance, the mails, an interactive computer service, an electronic communication service, or an electronic communication system.

(2) The term "course of conduct" means—

(A) a repeated maintenance of visual or physical proximity to a specific person;

(B) a repeated conveyance of verbal threat, written threats, or threats implied by conduct, or a combination of such threats, directed at or toward a specific person; or

(C) a pattern of conduct composed of repeated acts evidencing a continuity of purpose.

(3) The term "repeated", with respect to conduct, means two or more occasions of such conduct.

(4) The term "immediate family", in the case of a specific person, means—

(A) that person's spouse, parent, brother or sister, child, or other person to whom he or she stands in loco parentis; or

(B) any other person living in his or her household and related to him or her by blood or marriage.

(5) The term "intimate partner", in the case of a specific person, means—

(A) a former spouse of the specific person, a person who shares a child in common with the specific person, or a person who cohabits with or has cohabited as a spouse with the specific person; or

(B) a person who has been in a social relationship of a romantic or intimate nature with the specific person, as determined by the length of the relationship, the type of relationship, and the frequency of interaction between the persons involved in the relationship.

b. *Elements.*

(1) That the accused wrongfully engaged in a course of conduct directed at a specific person that would cause a reasonable person to fear death or bodily harm, including sexual assault, to himself or herself, to a member of his or her immediate family, or to his or her intimate partner;

(2) That the accused had knowledge, or should have had knowledge, that the specific person would be placed in reasonable fear of death or bodily harm, including sexual assault, to himself or herself, to a member of his or her immediate family, or to his or her intimate partner; and

(3) That the accused's conduct induced reasonable fear in the specific person of death or bodily harm, including sexual assault, to himself or herself, to a member of his or her immediate family, or to his or her intimate partner.

c. *Explanation.*

(1) *Bodily Harm.* "Bodily harm" means any offensive touching of another, however slight, including sexual assault. See subparagraph 77.c.(1).

(2) *Threat.* "Threat" means a communication, by words or conduct, of a present determination or intent to cause bodily harm to a specific person, an immediate family member of that person, or intimate partner of that person, presently or in the future. The threat may be made directly to or in the presence of the person it is directed at or towards, or the threat may be conveyed to such person in some manner. Actual intent to cause bodily harm is not required.

d. *Maximum punishment.* Dishonorable discharge, forfeiture of all pay and allowances, and confinement for 3 years.

e. *Sample specifications.*

In that __________ (personal jurisdiction data), did (at/on board—location) (subject-matter jurisdiction, if required), (on or about _____ 20 __) (from about _____ to about _____ 20 __), engage in a course of conduct directed at ________, that would cause a reasonable person to fear (death) (bodily harm, to wit:_______), to (himself) (herself) (a member of (his) (her) immediate family) ((his) (her) intimate partner); that the accused knew or should have known that the course of conduct would place ______ in reasonable fear of (death) (bodily harm, to wit _____) to (himself) (herself) (a member of (his) (her) immediate family) ((his) (her) intimate partner); and that the accused's conduct placed ______ in reasonable fear of (death) (bodily harm, to wit:_____) to (himself) (herself) (a member of (his) (her) immediate family) ((his) (her) intimate partner).

81. Article 131 (10 U.S.C. 931)—Perjury

a. *Text of statute.*

Any person subject to this chapter who in a judicial proceeding or in a course of justice willfully and corruptly—

(1) upon a lawful oath or in any form allowed by law to be substituted for an oath, gives any false testimony material to the issue or matter of inquiry; or

(2) in any declaration, certificate, verification, or statement under penalty of perjury as permitted under section 1746 of title 28, subscribes any false statement material to the issue or matter of inquiry;

is guilty of perjury and shall be punished as a court-martial may direct.

b. *Elements.*

(1) *Giving false testimony.*

(a) That the accused took an oath or affirmation in a certain judicial proceeding or course of justice;

(b) That the oath or affirmation was administered to the accused in a matter in which an oath or affirmation was required or authorized by law;

(c) That the oath or affirmation was administered by a person having authority to do so;

(d) That upon the oath or affirmation that accused willfully gave certain testimony;

(e) That the testimony was material;

(f) That the testimony was false; and

(g) That the accused did not then believe the testimony to be true.

(2) *Subscribing false statement.*

(a) That the accused subscribed a certain statement in a judicial proceeding or course of justice;

(b) That in the declaration, certification, verification, or statement under penalty of perjury, the accused declared, certified, verified, or stated the truth of that certain statement;

(c) That the accused willfully subscribed the statement;

(d) That the statement was material;

(e) That the statement was false; and

(f) That the accused did not then believe the statement to be true.

c. *Explanation.*

(1) *In general.* Judicial proceeding includes a trial by court-martial, and course of justice includes preliminary hearings conducted under Article 32. If the accused is charged with having committed perjury before a court-martial, it must be shown that the court-martial was duly constituted.

(2) *Giving false testimony.*

(a) *Nature.* The testimony must be false and must be willfully and corruptly given; that is, it must be proved that the accused gave the false testimony willfully and did not believe it to be true. A witness may commit perjury by testifying to the truth of a matter when in fact the witness knows nothing about it at all or is not sure about it, whether the thing is true or false in fact. A witness may also commit perjury in testifying falsely as to a belief, remembrance, or impression, or as to a judgment or opinion. It is no defense that the witness voluntarily appeared, that the witness was incompetent as a witness, or that the testimony was given in response to questions that the witness could have declined to answer.

(b) *Material matter.* The false testimony must be with respect to a material matter, but that matter need not be the main issue in the case. Thus, perjury may be committed by giving false testimony with respect to the credibility of a material witness or in an affidavit in support of a request for a continuance, as well as by giving false testimony with respect to a fact from which a legitimate inference may be drawn as to the existence or nonexistence of a fact in issue.

(c) *Proof.* The falsity of the allegedly perjured statement cannot be proved by circumstantial evidence alone, except with respect to matters which by their nature are not susceptible of direct proof. The falsity of the statement cannot be proved by the testimony of a single witness unless that testimony directly contradicts the statement and is corroborated by other evidence either direct or circumstantial, tending to prove the falsity of the statement. However, documentary evidence directly disproving the truth of the statement charged to have been perjured need not be corroborated if: the document is an official record shown to have been well known to the accused at the time the oath was taken; or the documentary evidence originated from the accused—or had in any manner been recognized by the accused as containing the truth—before the allegedly perjured statement was made.

(d) *Oath.* The oath must be one recognized or authorized by law and must be duly administered by one authorized to administer it. When a form of oath has been prescribed, a literal following of that form is not essential; it is sufficient if the oath administered conforms in substance to the prescribed form. Oath includes an affirmation when the latter is authorized in lieu of an oath.

(c) *Belief of accused.* The fact that the accused did not believe the statement to be true may be proved by testimony of one witness without corroboration or by circumstantial evidence.

(3) *Subscribing false statement.* See subparagraphs (1) and (2), above, as applicable. Section 1746 of title 28, United States Code, provides for subscribing to the truth of a document by signing it expressly subject to the penalty for perjury. The signing must take place in a judicial proceeding or course of justice—for example, if a witness signs under penalty of perjury summarized testimony given at an Article 32 preliminary hearing. It is not required that the document be sworn before a third party. Section 1746 does not change the requirement that a deposition be given under oath or alter the situation where an oath is required to be taken before a specific person.

d. *Maximum punishment.* Dishonorable discharge, forfeiture of all pay and allowances, and confinement for 5 years.

e. *Sample specifications.*

(1) *Giving false testimony.*

In that __________ (personal jurisdiction data), having taken a lawful (oath) (affirmation) in a (trial by __________ court-martial of __________) (trial by a court of competent jurisdiction, to wit: __________ of __________) (deposition for use in a trial by __________ of __________) (__________) that (he) (she) would (testify) (depose) truly, did, (at/on board—location) (subject-matter jurisdiction data, if required), on or about _____ 20 __, willfully, corruptly, and contrary to such (oath) (affirmation), (testify) (depose) falsely in substance that __________, which (testimony) (deposition) was upon a material matter and which (he) (she) did not then believe to be true.

(2) *Subscribing false statement.*

In that __________ (personal jurisdiction data), did (at/on board—location) (subject-matter jurisdiction data, if required), on or about _____ 20 __, in a (judicial proceeding) (course of justice), and in a (declaration) (certification) (verification) (statement) under penalty of perjury pursuant to section 1746 of title 28, United States Code, willfully and corruptly subscribed a false statement material to the (issue) (matter of inquiry), to wit: __________, which statement was false in that __________, and which statement (he) (she) did not then believe to be true.

82. Article 131a (10 U.S.C. 931a)—Subornation of perjury

a. *Text of statute.*

(a) IN GENERAL.—Any person subject to this chapter who induces and procures another person—

(1) to take an oath; and

(2) to falsely testify, depose, or state upon such oath;

shall, if the conditions specified in subsection (b) are satisfied, be punished as a court-martial may direct.

(b) CONDITIONS.—The conditions referred to in subsection (a) are the following:

(1) The oath is administered with respect to a matter for which such oath is required or authorized by law.

(2) The oath is administered by a person having authority to do so.

(3) Upon the oath, the other person willfully makes or subscribes a statement.

(4) The statement is material.

(5) The statement is false.

(6) When the statement is made or subscribed, the person subject to this chapter and the other person do not believe that the statement is true.

b. *Elements.*

(1) That the accused induced and procured a certain person to take an oath or its equivalent and to falsely testify, depose, or state upon such oath or its equivalent concerning a certain matter;

(2) That the oath or its equivalent was administered to said person in a matter in which an oath or its equivalent was required or authorized by law;

(3) That the oath or its equivalent was administered by a person having authority to do so;

(4) That upon the oath or its equivalent said person willfully made or subscribed a certain statement;

(5) That the statement was material;

(6) That the statement was false; and

(7) That the accused and the said person did not then believe that the statement was true.

c. *Explanation.*

(1) See subparagraph 81.c for applicable principles.

(2) "Induce and procure" means to influence, persuade, or cause.

(3) The word "oath" includes affirmation, and sworn includes affirmed. *See* 1 U.S.C. § 1.

d. *Maximum punishment.* Dishonorable discharge, forfeiture of all pay and allowances, and confinement for 5 years.

e. *Sample specification.*

In that __________ (personal jurisdiction data), did, (at/on board—location) (subject-matter jurisdiction data, if required), on or about _____ 20 __, procure __________ to commit perjury by inducing (him) (her), the said _____, to take a lawful (oath) (affirmation) in a (trial by court-martial of _____) (trial by a court of competent jurisdiction, to wit: _____ of _____) (deposition for use in a trial by _____ of __________) (_____) that (he) (she), the said _____, would (testify) (depose) (_____) truly, and to (testify) (depose) (_____) willfully, corruptly, and contrary to such (oath) (affirmation) in substance that _____, which (testimony) (deposition) (_____) was upon a material matter and which the accused and the said _____ did not then believe to be true.

83. Article 131b (10 U.S.C. 931b)—Obstructing justice

a. *Text of statute.*

Any person subject to this chapter who engages in conduct in the case of a certain person against whom the accused had reason to believe there were or would be criminal or disciplinary proceedings pending, with intent to influence, impede, or otherwise obstruct the due administration of justice shall be punished as a court-martial may direct.

b. *Elements.*

(1) That the accused wrongfully did a certain act;

(2) That the accused did so in the case of a certain person against whom the accused had reason to believe there were or would be criminal or disciplinary proceedings pending; and

(3) That the act was done with the intent to influence, impede, or otherwise obstruct the due administration of justice.

c. *Explanation.*

This offense may be based on conduct that occurred before preferral of charges. Actual obstruction of justice is not an element of this offense. Criminal proceedings include general courts-martial, special courts-martial, and all other criminal proceedings. For purposes of this paragraph, disciplinary proceedings include summary courts-martial as well as nonjudicial punishment proceedings under Part V of this Manual. Examples of obstruction of justice include wrongfully influencing, intimidating, impeding, or injuring a witness, a person acting on charges under this chapter, a preliminary hearing officer, or a party; and by means of bribery, intimidation, misrepresentation, or force or threat of force delaying or preventing communication of information relating to a violation of any criminal statute of the United States to a person authorized by a department, agency, or armed force of the United States to conduct or engage in investigations or prosecutions of such offenses; or endeavoring to do so. *See also* paragraph 87 and Article 37.

d. *Maximum punishment.* Dishonorable discharge, forfeiture of all pay and allowances, and confinement for 5 years.

e. *Sample specification.*

In that __________ (personal jurisdiction data), did, (at/on board—location) (subject-matter jurisdiction data, if required), on or about _____ 20 __, wrongfully do a certain act, to wit: ______________, with intent to (influence) (impede) (obstruct) the due administration of justice in the case of ____________, against whom the accused had reason to believe that there were or would be (criminal) (disciplinary) proceedings pending.

84. Article 131c (10 U.S.C. 931c)—Misprision of serious offense

a. *Text of statute.*

IN GENERAL.—Any person subject to this chapter—

(1) who knows that another person has committed a serious offense; and

(2) wrongfully conceals the commission of the offense and fails to make the commission of the offense known to civilian or military authorities as soon as possible;

shall be punished as a court-martial may direct.

b. *Elements.*

(1) That a certain serious offense was committed by a certain person;

(2) That the accused knew that the said person had committed the serious offense; and

(3) That, thereafter, the accused wrongfully concealed the serious offense and failed to make it known to civilian or military authorities as soon as possible.

c. *Explanation.*

(1) *In general.* Misprision of a serious offense is the offense of concealing a serious offense committed by another but without such previous concert with or subsequent assistance to the principal as would make the accused an accessory. *See* paragraph 2. An intent to benefit the principal is not necessary to this offense.

(2) *Serious offense.* For purposes of this paragraph, a serious offense is any offense punishable under the authority of the UCMJ by death or by confinement for a term exceeding 1 year.

(3) *Positive act of concealment.* A mere failure or refusal to disclose the serious offense without some positive act of concealment does not make one guilty of this offense. Making a false entry in an account book for the purpose of concealing a theft committed by another is an example of a positive act of concealment.

d. *Maximum punishment.* Dishonorable discharge, forfeiture of all pay and allowances, and confinement for 3 years.

e. *Sample specification.*

In that __________ (personal jurisdiction data), having knowledge that __________ had actually committed a serious offense to wit: (the murder of __________) (__________), did, (at/on board—location) (subject-matter jurisdiction data, if required), from about _____ 20 __, to about _____ 20 __, wrongfully conceal such serious offense by __________ and fail to make the same known to the civil or military authorities as soon as possible.

85. Article 131d (10 U.S.C. 931d)—Wrongful refusal to testify

a. *Text of statute.*

Any person subject to this chapter who, in the presence of a court-martial, a board of officers, a military commission, a court of inquiry, preliminary hearing, or an officer taking a deposition, of or for the United States, wrongfully refuses to qualify as a witness or to answer a question after having been directed to do so by the person presiding shall be punished as a court-martial may direct.

b. *Elements.*

(1) That the accused was in the presence of a court-martial, board of officers, military commission, court of inquiry, an officer conducting a preliminary hearing under Article 32, or an officer taking a deposition, of or for the United States, at which a certain person was presiding;

(2) That the said person presiding directed the accused to qualify as a witness or, having so qualified, to answer a certain question;

(3) That the accused refused to qualify as a witness or answer said question; and

(4) That the refusal was wrongful.

c. *Explanation.* "To qualify as a witness" means that the witness declares that the witness will testify truthfully. *See* R.C.M. 807; Mil. R. Evid. 603. A good faith but legally incorrect belief in the right to remain silent does not constitute a defense to a charge of wrongful refusal to testify. *See also* Mil. R. Evid. 301 and Section V of the Military Rules of Evidence.

d. *Maximum punishment.* Dishonorable discharge, forfeiture of all pay and allowances, and confinement for 5 years.

e. *Sample specification.*

In that __________ (personal jurisdiction data), being in the presence of (a) (an) ((general) (special) (summary) court-martial) (board of officers) (military commission) (court of inquiry) (officer conducting a preliminary hearing under Article 32, Uniform Code of Military Justice) (officer taking a deposition) (_____) (of) (for) the United States, of which _____ was (military judge) (president), (_____), (and having been directed by the said _____ to qualify as a witness) (and having qualified as a witness and having been directed by the said _____ to answer the following question(s) put to (him) (her) as a witness, "_____"), did, (at/on board—location) (subject-matter jurisdiction, if required), on or about _____ 20 __, wrongfully refuse (to qualify as a witness) (to answer said question(s)).

86. Article 131e (10 U.S.C. 931e)—Prevention of authorized seizure of property

a. *Text of statute.*

Any person subject to this chapter who, knowing that one or more persons authorized to make

searches and seizures are seizing, are about to seize, or are endeavoring to seize property, destroys, removes, or otherwise disposes of the property with intent to prevent the seizure thereof shall be punished as a court-martial may direct.

b. *Elements.*

(1) That one or more persons authorized to make searches and seizures were seizing, about to seize, or endeavoring to seize certain property;

(2) That the accused destroyed, removed, or otherwise disposed of that property with intent to prevent the seizure thereof; and

(3) That the accused then knew that person(s) authorized to make searches were seizing, about to seize, or endeavoring to seize the property.

c. *Explanation.* See Mil. R. Evid. 316 concerning military personnel who may make seizures. It is not a defense that a search or seizure was technically defective.

d. *Maximum punishment.* Dishonorable discharge, forfeiture of all pay and allowances, and confinement for 5 years.

e. *Sample specification.*

In that __________ (personal jurisdiction data), did, (at/on board—location) (subject matter jurisdiction data, if required), on or about _____ 20 __, with intent to prevent its seizure, (destroy) (remove) (dispose of) __________, property which, as __________ then knew, (a) person(s) authorized to make searches and seizures were (seizing) (about to seize) (endeavoring to seize).

87. Article 131f (10 U.S.C. 931f)—Noncompliance with procedural rules

a. *Text of statute.*

Any person subject to this chapter who—

(1) is responsible for unnecessary delay in the disposition of any case of a person accused of an offense under this chapter; or

(2) knowingly and intentionally fails to enforce or comply with any provision of this chapter regulating the proceedings before, during, or after trial of an accused;

shall be punished as a court-martial may direct.

b. *Elements.*

(1) *Unnecessary delay in disposing of case.*

(a) That the accused was charged with a certain duty in connection with the disposition of a case of a person accused of an offense under the UCMJ;

(b) That the accused knew that the accused was charged with this duty;

(c) That delay occurred in the disposition of the case;

(d) That the accused was responsible for the delay; and

(e) That, under the circumstances, the delay was unnecessary.

(2) *Knowingly and intentionally failing to enforce or comply with provisions of the UCMJ.*

(a) That the accused failed to enforce or comply with a certain provision of the UCMJ regulating a proceeding before, during, or after a trial;

(b) That the accused had the duty of enforcing or complying with that provision of the UCMJ;

(c) That the accused knew that the accused was charged with this duty; and

(d) That the accused's failure to enforce or comply with that provision was intentional.

c. *Explanation.*

(1) *Unnecessary delay in disposing of case.* The purpose of section (1) of Article 131f is to ensure expeditious disposition of cases of persons accused of offenses under the UCMJ. A person may be responsible for delay in the disposition of a case only when that person's duties require action with respect to the disposition of that case.

(2) *Knowingly and intentionally failing to enforce or comply with provisions of the UCMJ.* Section (2) of Article 131f does not apply to errors made in good faith before, during, or after trial. It is designed to punish intentional failure to enforce or comply with the provisions of the UCMJ regulating the proceedings before, during, and after trial. Unlawful command influence under Article 37 may be prosecuted under this Article. See also Article 31 and R.C.M. 104.

d. *Maximum punishment.*

(1) *Unnecessary delay in disposing of case.* Bad-conduct discharge, forfeiture of all pay and allowances, and confinement for 6 months.

(2) *Knowingly and intentionally failing to enforce or comply with provisions of the UCMJ.* Dishonorable discharge, forfeiture of all pay and allowances, and confinement for 5 years.

e. *Sample specifications.*

(1) *Unnecessary delay in disposing of case.*

In that __________ (personal jurisdiction data), being charged with the duty of ((investigating) (taking immediate steps to determine the proper disposition of) charges preferred against __________, a person accused of an offense under the Uniform Code of Military Justice) (__________), was, (at/on board—location) (subject-matter jurisdiction, if required), on or about _____ 20 __, responsible for unnecessary delay in (investigating said charges) (determining the proper disposition of said charges (_____), in that (he) (she) (did _____) (failed to _____) (_____).

(2) *Knowingly and intentionally failing to enforce or comply with provisions of the UCMJ.*

In that __________ (personal jurisdiction data), being charged with the duty of __________, did, (at/on board—location) (subject-matter jurisdiction, if required), on or about _____ 20 __, knowingly and intentionally fail to (enforce) (comply with) Article __________, Uniform Code of Military Justice, in that (he) (she) __________.

88. Article 131g (10 U.S.C. 931g)—Wrongful interference with adverse administrative proceeding

a. *Text of statute.*

Any person subject to this chapter who, having reason to believe that an adverse administrative proceeding is pending against any person subject to this chapter, wrongfully acts with the intent—

(1) to influence, impede, or obstruct the conduct of the proceeding; or

(2) otherwise to obstruct the due administration of justice;

shall be punished as a court-martial may direct.

b. *Elements.*

(1) That the accused wrongfully did a certain act;

(2) That the accused did so in the case of a certain person against whom the accused had reason to believe there was or would be an adverse administrative proceeding pending; and

(3) That the act was done with the intent to influence, impede, or obstruct the conduct of such administrative proceeding, or otherwise obstruct the due administration of justice.

c. *Explanation.* For purposes of this paragraph an adverse administrative proceeding includes any administrative proceeding or action, initiated against a Servicemember, that could lead to discharge, loss of special or incentive pay, administrative reduction in grade, loss of a security clearance, bar to reenlistment, or reclassification. Examples of wrongful interference include wrongfully influencing, intimidating, impeding, or injuring a witness, an investigator, or other person acting on an adverse administrative action; by means of bribery, intimidation, misrepresentation, or force or threat of force delaying or preventing communication of information relating to such administrative proceeding; and the wrongful destruction or concealment of information relevant to such adverse administrative proceeding.

d. *Maximum punishment.* Dishonorable discharge, forfeiture of all pay and allowances, and confinement for 5 years.

e. *Sample specification.*

In that __________ (personal jurisdiction data), did (at/on board—location) (subject-matter jurisdiction data, if required), on or about _____ 20 __, (wrongfully endeavor to) [impede (an adverse administrative proceeding) (an investigation) (_____)] [influence the actions of _____, (an officer responsible for making a recommendation concerning the adverse administrative action) (an individual responsible for making a decision concerning an adverse administrative proceeding) (an individual responsible for processing an adverse administrative proceeding) (_____)] [(influence) (alter) the testimony of _____ a witness before (a board established to consider an administrative proceeding or elimination) (an investigating officer) (_____)] in the case of _____, by](promising) (offering) (giving) to the said _____, (the sum of $_____) (_____, of a value of (about) $_____)] [communicating to the said _____ a threat to _____] [_____], (if) (unless) the said _____, would [recommend dismissal of the action against said _____] [(wrongfully refuse to testify) (testify falsely concerning _____) (_____)] [(at such administrative proceeding) (before such investigating officer) (before such administrative board)] [_____].

89. Article 132 (10 U.S.C. 932)—Retaliation

a. *Text of statute.*

(a) IN GENERAL.—Any person subject to this chapter who, with the intent to retaliate against any person for reporting or planning to report a criminal offense, or making or planning to make a protected communication, or with the intent to discourage any person from reporting a criminal offense or making or planning to make a protected communication—

(1) wrongfully takes or threatens to take an adverse personnel action against any person; or

(2) wrongfully withholds or threatens to withhold a favorable personnel action with respect to any person;

shall be punished as a court-martial may direct.

(b) DEFINITIONS.—In this section:

(1) The term "protected communication" means the following:

(A) A lawful communication to a Member of Congress or an Inspector General.

(B) A communication to a covered individual or organization in which a member of the armed forces complains of, or discloses information that the member reasonably believes constitutes evidence of, any of the following:

(i) A violation of law or regulation, including a law or regulation prohibiting sexual harassment or unlawful discrimination.

(ii) Gross mismanagement, a gross waste of funds, an abuse of authority, or a substantial and specific danger to public health or safety.

(2) The term "Inspector General" has the meaning given that term in section 1034(j) of this title.

(3) The term "covered individual or organization" means any recipient of a communication specified in clauses (i) through (v) of section 1034(b)(1)(B) of this title.

(4) The term "unlawful discrimination" means discrimination on the basis of race, color, religion, sex, or national origin.

b. *Elements.*

(1) Retaliation

(a) That the accused wrongfully

(i) took or threatened to take an adverse personnel action against any person, or

(ii) withheld or threatened to withhold a favorable personnel action with respect to any person; and

(b) That, at the time of the action, the accused intended to retaliate against any person for reporting or planning to report a criminal offense, or for making or planning to make a protected communication.

(2) Discouraging a report of criminal offense or protected communication.

(a) That the accused wrongfully

(i) took or threatened to take an adverse personnel action against any person, or

(ii) withheld or threatened to withhold a favorable personnel action with respect to any person; and

(b) That, at the time of the action, the accused intended to discourage any person from reporting a criminal offense or making a protected communication.

c. *Explanation.*

(1) *In general.* This offense focuses upon the abuse of otherwise lawful military authority for the purpose of retaliating against any person for reporting or planning to report a criminal offense or for making or planning to make a protected communication or to discourage any person from reporting a criminal offense or for making or planning to make a protected communication. The offense prohibits personnel actions, either favorable or adverse, taken or withheld, or threatened to be taken or withheld, with the specific intent to retaliate against any person for reporting or planning to report a criminal offense or for making or planning to make a protected communication or to discourage any person from reporting a criminal offense or for making or planning to make a protected communication. The offense may be committed by any person subject to the UCMJ with the authority to initiate, forward, recommend, decide, or otherwise act on a favorable or adverse personnel action who takes such action wrongfully and with the requisite specific intent. This offense does not prohibit the lawful and appropriate exercise of command authority to discipline or reward Servicemembers.

(2) *Personnel action.* For purposes of this offense, "personnel action" means—

(a) any action taken on a Servicemember that affects, or has the potential to affect, that Servicemember's current position or career, including promotion; disciplinary or other corrective action;

transfer or reassignment; performance evaluations; decisions concerning pay, benefits, awards, or training; relief and removal; separation; discharge; referral for mental health evaluations; and any other personnel actions as defined by law or regulation, such as 5 U.S.C. § 2302 and DoD Directive 7050.06 (17 April 2015); or,

(b) any action taken on a civilian employee that affects, or has the potential to affect, that person's current position or career, including promotion; disciplinary or other corrective action; transfer or reassignment; performance evaluations; decisions concerning pay benefits, awards, or training; relief and removal; discharge; and any other personnel actions as defined by law or regulation such as 5 U.S.C. § 2302.

(3) *Intent to retaliate.* An action is taken with the intent to retaliate when the personnel action taken or withheld, or threatened to be taken or withheld, is done for the purpose of reprisal, retribution, or revenge for reporting or planning to report a criminal offense or for making or planning to make a protected communication.

(4) *Threatens to take or withhold.* This offense requires that the accused had the intent to retaliate, but proof that the accused actually intended to take an adverse personnel action, or to withhold a favorable personnel action, is not required. A declaration made under circumstances which reveal it to be in jest or for an innocent or legitimate purpose, or which contradict the expressed intent to commit the act, does not constitute this offense. Nor is the offense committed by the mere statement of intent to commit an unlawful act not involving a favorable or adverse personnel action.

(5) *Criminal offense.* Criminal offense for purposes of this offense includes violations of the UCMJ, the United States Code, or state law.

(6) *Wrongful.* Taking or threatening to take adverse personnel action, or withholding or threatening to withhold favorable personnel action, is wrongful when used for the purpose of reprisal, rather than for purposes of lawful personnel administration.

(7) *Other retaliatory actions.* This offense does not prohibit the Secretary of Defense and Secretaries of the Military Services from proscribing other types or categories of prohibited retaliatory actions by regulation, which may be punished as violations of Article 92.

d. *Maximum punishment.* Dishonorable discharge, forfeiture of all pay and allowances, and confinement for 3 years.

e. *Sample specifications.*

(1) *Retaliation*

In that __________ (personal jurisdiction data), did, (at/on board—location) (subject matter jurisdiction data, if required), on or about _____ 20 __, with intent to retaliate against _______________for [(reporting) (planning to report) a criminal offense] [(making) (planning to make) a protected communication], wrongfully [(took) (threatened to take) an adverse personnel action against _______________ to wit:_______________][(withheld) (threatened to withhold) a favorable personnel action with respect to _____________ to wit:___________].

(2) *Discouraging a report of criminal offense or protected communication*

In that __________ (personal jurisdiction data), did, (at/on board—location) (subject matter jurisdiction data, if required), on or about _____ 20 __, with intent to discourage __________________ from (reporting a criminal offense) (making a protected communication), wrongfully [(took) (threatened to take) an adverse personnel action against _______________, to wit :_______________][(withheld) (threatened to withhold) a favorable personnel action with respect to _____________, to wit:___________].

90. Article 133 (10 U.S.C. 933)—Conduct unbecoming an officer

a. Text of statute.

Any commissioned officer, cadet, or midshipman who is convicted of conduct unbecoming an officer shall be punished as a court-martial may direct.

b. *Elements.*

(1) That the accused was a commissioned officer, cadet, or midshipman;

(2) That the accused did or omitted to do certain acts; and

(3) That, under the circumstances, these acts or omissions constituted conduct unbecoming an officer.

c. *Explanation.*

(1) *Officership generally.* As used in the phrase "conduct unbecoming an officer" in this article, "officer" refers to a "commissioned officer, cadet, or midshipman..

(2) *Nature of the offense.* The focus of this article is conduct that is likely to seriously compromise the

accused's standing as an officer. A military officer holds a particular position of responsibility in the armed forces, and one critically important responsibility of a military officer is to inspire the trust and respect of the personnel who must obey the officer's orders. Conduct violative of this article is action or behavior in an official capacity that, in dishonoring or disgracing the person as an officer, seriously compromises the officer's character, or action or behavior in an unofficial or private capacity that, in dishonoring or disgracing the officer personally, seriously compromises the person's standing as an officer. This article includes misconduct that approximates, but may not meet every element of, another enumerated offense. An officer's conduct need not violate other provisions of the UCMJ or be otherwise criminal to violate Article 133. The gravamen of the offense is that the officer's conduct disgraces the officer personally or brings dishonor to the military profession in a manner that affects the officer's fitness to command the obedience of the officer's subordinates so as to effectively complete the military mission. The absence of a "custom of the service," statute, regulation, or order expressly prohibiting certain conduct is not dispositive of whether the officer was on sufficient notice that such conduct was unbecoming.

(3) *Examples of offenses.* Instances of violation of this article include knowingly making a false official statement; dishonorable failure to pay a debt; cheating on an exam; opening and reading a letter of another without authority; using insulting or defamatory language to another officer in that officer's presence or about that officer to other military persons; being drunk and disorderly in a public place; committing or attempting to commit a crime involving moral turpitude; and failing without good cause to support the officer's family.

(4) *Relation to Other Punitive Articles*: conduct unbecoming an officer. Thus, a commissioned officer who steals property violates both this article and Article 121. Whenever the offense charged is the same as a specific offense set forth in this Manual, the elements of proof are the same as those set forth in the paragraph that treats that specific offense, with the additional requirement that the act or omission constitutes conduct unbecoming an officer.

d. *Maximum punishment.* Dismissal, forfeiture of all pay and allowances, and confinement for a period not in excess of that authorized for the most analogous offense for which a punishment is prescribed in this Manual, or, if none is prescribed, for 1 year.

e. *Sample specifications.*

(1) *Copying or using examination paper.*

In that __________ (personal jurisdiction data), did, (at/on board—location) (subject-matter jurisdiction data, if required), on or about _____ 20 __, while undergoing a written examination on the subject of __________, wrongfully and dishonorably (receive) (request) unauthorized aid by ((using) (copying) the examination paper of __)).

(2) *Drunk or disorderly.*

In that __________ (personal jurisdiction data), was, (at/on board—location) (subject-matter jurisdiction data, if required), on or about _____ 20 __, in a public place, to wit: __________, (drunk) (disorderly) (drunk and disorderly) while in uniform, to the disgrace of the armed forces.

91. Article 134 (10 U.S.C. 934)—General article

a. *Text of statute.*

Though not specifically mentioned in this chapter, all disorders and neglects to the prejudice of good order and discipline in the armed forces, all conduct of a nature to bring discredit upon the armed forces, and crimes and offenses not capital, of which persons subject to this chapter may be guilty, shall be taken cognizance of by a general, special, or summary court-martial, according to the nature and degree of the offense, and shall be punished at the discretion of that court. As used in the preceding sentence, the term "crimes and offenses not capital" includes any conduct engaged in outside the United States, as defined in section 5 of title 18, that would constitute a crime or offense not capital if the conduct had been engaged in within the special maritime and territorial jurisdiction of the United States, as defined in section 7 of title 18.

Discussion

The terminal element is merely the expression of one of the clauses under Article 134. See subparagraph c. for an explanation of the clauses and rules for drafting specifications. More than one clause may be alleged and proven; however, proof of only one clause will satisfy the terminal element. For clause 3 offenses, the military judge may judicially notice whether an offense is capital. *See* Mil. R. Evid. 202.

b. *Elements*. The proof required for conviction of an offense under Article 134 depends upon the nature of the misconduct charged. If the conduct is punished as a crime or offense not capital, the proof must establish every element of the crime or offense as required by the applicable law. All offenses under Article 134 require proof of a single terminal element.

(1) For clause 1 offenses under Article 134, the following proof is required:

(a) That the accused did or failed to do certain acts; and

(b) That, under the circumstances, the accused's conduct was to the prejudice of good order and discipline in the armed forces

(2) For clause 2 offenses under Article 134, the following proof is required:

(a) That the accused did or failed to do certain acts; and

(b) That, under the circumstances, the accused's conduct was of a nature to bring discredit upon the armed forces.

(3) For clause 3 offenses under Article 134, the following proof is required:

(a) That the accused did or failed to do certain acts that satisfy each element of the federal statute (including, in the case of a prosecution under 18 U.S.C. § 13, each element of the assimilated State, Territory, Possession, or District law); and

(b) That the offense charged was an offense not capital.

c. *Explanation*.

(1) *In general*. Article 134 makes punishable acts in three categories of offenses not specifically covered in any other article of the UCMJ. These are referred to as "clauses 1, 2, and 3" of Article 134. Clause 1 offenses involve disorders and neglects to the prejudice of good order and discipline in the armed forces. Clause 2 offenses involve conduct of a nature to bring discredit upon the armed forces. Clause 3 offenses involve noncapital crimes or offenses which violate federal civilian law including law made applicable through the Federal Assimilative Crimes Act, see subparagraph c.(4). If any conduct of this nature is specifically made punishable by another article of the UCMJ, it must be charged as a violation of that article. See subparagraph c.(5)(a). However, see subparagraph 90.c for offenses committed by commissioned officers, cadets, and midshipmen.

(2) *Disorders and neglects to the prejudice of good order and discipline in the armed forces (clause 1)*.

(a) *To the prejudice of good order and discipline*. To the prejudice of good order and discipline refers only to acts directly prejudicial to good order and discipline and not to acts which are prejudicial only in a remote or indirect sense. Almost any irregular or improper act on the part of a member of the military service could be regarded as prejudicial in some indirect or remote sense; however, this article does not include these distant effects. It is confined to cases in which the prejudice is reasonably direct and palpable. An act in violation of a local civil law or of a foreign law may be punished if it constitutes a disorder or neglect to the prejudice of good order and discipline in the armed forces. However, see R.C.M. 203 concerning subject-matter jurisdiction.

(b) *Breach of custom of the Service*. A breach of a custom of the Service may result in a violation of clause 1 of Article 134. In its legal sense, "custom" means more than a method of procedure or a mode of conduct or behavior which is merely of frequent or usual occurrence. Custom arises out of long established practices which by common usage have attained the force of law in the military or other community affected by them. No custom may be contrary to existing law or regulation. A custom which has not been adopted by existing statute or regulation ceases to exist when its observance has been generally abandoned. Many customs of the Service are now set forth in regulations of the various armed forces. Violations of these customs should be charged under Article 92 as violations of the regulations in which they appear if the regulation is punitive. See subparagraph 18.b.(1).

(3) *Conduct of a nature to bring discredit upon the armed forces (clause 2)*. "Discredit" means to injure the reputation of. This clause of Article 134 makes punishable conduct which has a tendency to bring the service into disrepute or which tends to lower it in public esteem. Acts in violation of a local civil law or a foreign law may be punished if they are of a nature to bring discredit upon the armed forces. However, see R.C.M. 203 concerning subject-matter jurisdiction.

(4) *Crimes and offenses not capital (Article 134, clause 3)*.

(a) *In general*. For the purpose of court-martial jurisdiction, the laws that may be applied under clause 3 of Article 134 are divided into two categories:

(1) Federal crimes and offenses according to the terms of jurisdiction set forth in the applicable federal criminal statute.

(i) Noncapital crimes and offenses prohibited by the United States Code that are punishable regardless where the wrongful act or omission occurred.

Discussion

Counterfeiting is an example of a crime punishable regardless where the wrongful act or omission occurred. *See* 18 U.S.C. § 471.

(ii) Noncapital crimes and offenses prohibited by the United States Code within a limited jurisdiction that are punishable when committed within a specified area.

(iii) The Federal Assimilative Crimes Act (18 U.S.C. § 13) is an adoption by Congress of state criminal laws for areas of exclusive or concurrent federal jurisdiction, provided federal criminal law, including the UCMJ, has not defined an applicable offense for the misconduct committed. The Act applies to state laws validly existing at the time of the offense without regard to when these laws were enacted, whether before or after passage of the Act, and whether before or after the acquisition of the land where the offense was committed. For example, if a person committed an act on a military installation in the United States as a certain location over which the United States had either exclusive or concurrent jurisdiction, and it was not an offense specifically defined by federal law (including the UCMJ), that person could be punished for that act by a court-martial if it was a violation of a noncapital offense under the law of the State where the military installation was located. This is possible because the Act adopts the criminal law of the State wherein the military installation is located and applies it as though it were federal law. The text of the Act's first paragraph is as follows: "Whoever within or upon any of the places now existing or hereafter reserved or acquired as provided in section 7 of this title, or on, above, or below any portion of the territorial sea of the United States not within the jurisdiction of any State, Commonwealth, territory, possession, or district is guilty of any act or omission which, although not made punishable by any enactment of Congress, would be punishable if committed or omitted within the jurisdiction of the State, Territory, Possession, or District in which such place is situated, by the laws thereof in force at the time of such act or omission, shall be guilty of a like offense and subject to a like punishment."

Discussion

If the direct prosecution of state and federal crimes under Article 134, clause 3 is unavailable because the offense is committed outside of otherwise applicable areas of jurisdiction, the substance of these crimes may still be prosecuted, in an appropriate case, under clause 1 or clause 2 of Article 134. In such a case, the Government would be required to prove the terminal element under clause 1 or clause 2 that the underlying misconduct was either prejudicial to good order and discipline; of a nature to bring discredit upon the armed forces; or both.

18 U.S.C. § 5 provides, "The term 'United States', as used in this title in a territorial sense, includes all places and waters, continental or insular, subject to the jurisdiction of the United States, except the Canal Zone."

18 U.S.C. § 7 provides, "The term "special maritime and territorial jurisdiction of the United States", as used in this title, includes:

(1) The high seas, any other waters within the admiralty and maritime jurisdiction of the United States and out of the jurisdiction of any particular State, and any vessel belonging in whole or in part to the United States or any citizen thereof, or to any corporation created by or under the laws of the United States, or of any State, Territory, District, or possession thereof, when such vessel is within the admiralty and maritime jurisdiction of the United States and out of the jurisdiction of any particular State.

(2) Any vessel registered, licensed, or enrolled under the laws of the United States, and being on a voyage upon the waters of any of the Great Lakes, or any of the waters connecting them, or upon the Saint Lawrence River where the same constitutes the International Boundary Line.

(3) Any lands reserved or acquired for the use of the United States, and under the exclusive or concurrent jurisdiction thereof, or any place purchased or otherwise acquired by the United States by consent of the legislature of the State in which the same shall be, for the erection of a fort, magazine, arsenal, dockyard, or other needful building.

(4) Any island, rock, or key containing deposits of guano, which may, at the discretion of the President, be considered as appertaining to the United States.

(5) Any aircraft belonging in whole or in part to the United States, or any citizen thereof, or to any corporation created by or under the laws of the United States, or any State, Territory, district, or possession thereof, while such aircraft is in flight over the high seas, or over any other waters within the admiralty and maritime jurisdiction of the United States and out of the jurisdiction of any particular State.

(6) Any vehicle used or designed for flight or navigation in space and on the registry of the United States pursuant to the Treaty on Principles Governing the Activities of States in the Exploration and Use of Outer Space, Including the Moon and Other Celestial Bodies and the Convention on Registration of Objects Launched into Outer Space, while that vehicle is in flight, which is from the moment when all external doors are closed on Earth following embarkation until the moment when one such door is

opened on Earth for disembarkation or in the case of a forced landing, until the competent authorities take over the responsibility for the vehicle and for persons and property aboard.

(7) Any place outside the jurisdiction of any nation with respect to an offense by or against a national of the United States.

(8) To the extent permitted by international law, any foreign vessel during a voyage having a scheduled departure from or arrival in the United States with respect to an offense committed by or against a national of the United States.

(9) With respect to offenses committed by or against a national of the United States as that term is used in section 101 of the Immigration and Nationality Act—

(a) the premises of United States diplomatic, consular, military or other United States Government missions or entities in foreign States, including the buildings, parts of buildings, and land appurtenant or ancillary thereto or used for purposes of those missions or entities, irrespective of ownership; and

(b) residences in foreign States and the land appurtenant or ancillary thereto, irrespective of ownership, used for purposes of those missions or entities or used by United States personnel assigned to those missions or entities.

Nothing in this paragraph shall be deemed to supersede any treaty or international agreement with which this paragraph conflicts. This paragraph does not apply with respect to an offense committed by a person described in section 3261(a) of this title."

---

(5) *Limitations on Article 134.*

(a) *Preemption doctrine.* The preemption doctrine prohibits application of Article 134 to conduct covered by Articles 80 through 132. For example, larceny is covered in Article 121, and if an element of that offense is lacking—for example, intent—there can be no larceny or larceny-type offense, either under Article 121 or, because of preemption, under Article 134. Article 134 cannot be used to create a new kind of larceny offense, one without the required intent, where Congress has already set the minimum requirements for such an offense in Article 121.

Discussion

Although the preemption doctrine generally does not preclude charging Article 134, clause 3 offenses (crimes or offense, not capital), the preemption doctrine does preclude charging a federal "crime or offense, not capital" under Article 134 clause 3 where either direct legislative language or direct legislative history demonstrate that Congress intended a factually similar UCMJ punitive article to cover a class of offenses in a complete way.

(b) *Capital offense.* A capital offense may not be tried under Article 134.

(6) *Drafting specifications for Article 134 offenses.*

(a) *Specifications under clause 1 or 2.* When alleging a clause 1 or 2 violation, the specification must expressly allege that the conduct was "to the prejudice of good order and discipline" or that it was "of a nature to bring discredit upon the armed forces." The same conduct may be prejudicial to good order and discipline in the armed forces and at the same time be of a nature to bring discredit upon the armed forces. Both clauses may be alleged; however, only one must be proven to satisfy the terminal element. If conduct by an accused does not fall under any of the enumerated Article 134 offenses (paragraphs 92 through 109 of this Part), a specification not listed in this Manual may be used to allege the offense.

Discussion

Clauses 1 and 2 are theories of liability that must be expressly alleged in a specification so that the accused will have notice as to which clause or clauses to defend against. The words "to the prejudice of good order and discipline in the armed forces" encompass both subparagraph c.(2)(a), prejudice to good order and discipline, and subparagraph c.(2)(b), breach of custom of the Service.

If clauses 1 and 2 are alleged together in the terminal element, the word "and" should be used to separate them. Any clause not proven beyond a reasonable doubt should be excepted from the specification at findings. *See* R.C.M. 918(a)(1). *See also* Appendix 17 of this Manual, Art. 79.

Although using the conjunctive "and" to connect the two theories of liability is recommended, a specification connecting the two theories with the disjunctive "or" is sufficient to provide the accused reasonable notice of the charge against him. *See* Appendix 11 of this Manual, Art. 134. However, use of the term "or" as a charging mechanism for alleging the terminal element in an Article 134 specification (i.e. "such conduct was prejudicial to good order and discipline or of a nature to bring discredit upon the armed forces") is not recommended due to the risk of creating a vague and duplicitous specification, which may lead to uncertainty as to which theory of liability the members convicted the accused. To avoid ambiguity, an Article 134 clause 1 or 2 violation should be alleged as follows: (1) the conduct was prejudicial to good order and discipline; (2) the conduct was of a nature to bring discredit upon the armed forces; or (3) the conduct was prejudicial to good order and discipline and of a nature to bring discredit upon the armed forces.

See Appendix 12A for a chart of lesser included offenses.

(b) *Specifications under clause 3.* When alleging a clause 3 violation, each element of the federal statute (including, in the case of a prosecution under 18 U.S.C. § 13, each element of the assimilated State, Territory, Possession, or District law) must be alleged expressly or by necessary implication, and the specification must expressly allege that the conduct was "an offense not capital." In addition, any applicable statutes should be identified in the specification.

92. Article 134—(Animal abuse)

a. *Text of statute.* See paragraph 91.

b. *Elements.*

(1) Abuse, neglect, or abandonment of an animal.

(a) That the accused wrongfully abused, neglected, or abandoned a certain (public*) animal (and the accused caused serious injury or death of the animal*); and

(b) That, under the circumstances, the conduct of the accused was either: (i) to the prejudice of good order and discipline in the armed forces; (ii) was of a nature to bring discredit upon the armed forces; or (iii) to the prejudice of good order and discipline in the armed forces and of a nature to bring discredit upon the armed forces.

[Note: Add these elements as applicable.]

(2) Sexual act with an animal.

(a) That the accused engaged in a sexual act with a certain animal; and

(b) That, under the circumstances, the conduct of the accused was either: (i) to the prejudice of good order and discipline in the armed forces; (ii) was of a nature to bring discredit upon the armed forces; or (iii) to the prejudice of good order and discipline in the armed forces and of a nature to bring discredit upon the armed forces.

c. *Explanation.*

(1) *In general.* This offense prohibits intentional abuse, culpable neglect, and abandonment of an animal. This offense does not include legal hunting, trapping, or fishing; reasonable and recognized acts of training, handling, or disciplining of an animal; normal and accepted farm or veterinary practices; research or testing conducted in accordance with approved governmental protocols; protection of person or property from an unconfined animal; or authorized military operations or military training.

(2) *Definitions.* As used in this paragraph:

(a) "Abuse" means intentionally and unjustifiably overdriving, overloading, overworking, tormenting, beating, depriving of necessary sustenance, allowing to be housed in a manner that results in chronic or repeated serious physical harm, carrying or confining in or upon any vehicles in a cruel or reckless manner, or otherwise mistreating an animal. Abuse may include any sexual touching of an animal if not included in the definition of sexual act with an animal below.

(b) "Neglect" means knowingly allowing another to abuse an animal, or, having the charge or custody of any animal, knowingly, or through culpable negligence, failing to provide it with proper food, drink, or protection from the weather consistent with the species, breed, and type of animal involved.

(c) "Abandon" means, while having the charge or custody of an animal, knowingly or through culpable negligence leaving of that animal at a location without providing minimum care for the animal.

(d) "Animal" means pets and animals of the type that are raised by individuals for resale to others, including: cattle, horses, sheep, pigs, goats, chickens, dogs, cats, and similar animals owned or under the control of any person. Animal does not include reptiles, insects, arthropods, or any animal defined or declared to be a pest by the administrator of the United States Environmental Protection Agency.

(e) "Public animal" means any animal owned or used by the United States or any animal owned or used by a local or State government in the United States, its territories or possessions. This would include, for example, drug detector dogs used by the Government.

(f) "Sexual act with an animal" means

(i) contact between the sex organ or anus of a person and the sex organ, anus, or mouth of an animal; or

(ii) contact between the sex organ or anus of an animal and a person or object manipulated by a person, if done with an intent to arouse or gratify the sexual desire of any person.

(g) "Serious injury of an animal" means physical harm that involves a temporary but substantial disfigurement; causes a temporary but substantial loss or impairment of the function of any bodily part or organ; causes a fracture of any bodily part; causes permanent maiming; causes acute pain of a duration that results in suffering; or carries a substantial risk of death. Serious injury includes burning, torturing, poisoning, or maiming.

d. *Maximum punishment.*

(1) *Abuse, neglect, or abandonment of an animal.* Bad-conduct discharge, forfeiture of all pay and allowances, and confinement for 1 year.

(2) *Abuse, neglect, or abandonment of a public animal.* Bad-conduct discharge, forfeiture of all pay and allowances, and confinement for 2 years.

(3) *Sexual act with an animal or cases where the accused caused the serious injury or death of the*

animal. Dishonorable discharge, forfeiture of all pay and allowances, and confinement for 5 years.

e. *Sample specification.*

In that _________, (personal jurisdiction data), did, (at/on board—location) (subject-matter jurisdiction data, if required), on or about _____ 20 __ (date), (wrongfully [abuse] [neglect] [abandon]) (*engage in a sexual act, to wit: _________, with) a certain (*public) animal (*and caused [serious injury to] [the death of] the animal), and that said conduct was (to the prejudice of good order and discipline in the armed forces) (of a nature to bring discredit upon the armed forces) (to the prejudice of good order and discipline in the armed forces and was of a nature to bring discredit upon the armed forces).

93. Article 134—(Bigamy)

a. *Text of statute*. See paragraph 91.

b. *Elements.*

(1) That the accused had a living lawful spouse;

(2) That while having such spouse the accused wrongfully married another person; and

(3) That, under the circumstances, the conduct of the accused was either: (i) to the prejudice of good order and discipline in the armed forces; (ii) was of a nature to bring discredit upon the armed forces; or (iii) to the prejudice of good order and discipline in the armed forces and of a nature to bring discredit upon the armed forces.

c. *Explanation*. Bigamy is contracting another marriage by one who already has a living lawful spouse. If a prior marriage was void, it will have created no status of "lawful spouse." A belief that a prior marriage has been terminated by divorce, death of the other spouse, or otherwise, constitutes a mistake of fact defense only if the belief was reasonable. See R.C.M. 916(j)(1).

d. *Maximum punishment*. Dishonorable discharge, forfeiture of all pay and allowances, and confinement for 2 years.

e. *Sample specification.*

In that ____________ (personal jurisdiction data), did, at, (subject-matter jurisdiction data, if required), on or about _____ 20 __, wrongfully marry ____________, having at the time of (his) (her) said marriage to a lawful spouse then living, to wit:____________________ , and that such conduct was (to the prejudice of good order and discipline in the armed forces) (of a nature to bring discredit upon the armed forces) (to the prejudice of good order and discipline in the armed forces and of a nature to bring discredit upon the armed forces).

94. Article 134—(Check, worthless making and uttering – by dishonorably failing to maintain funds)

a. *Text of statute*. See paragraph 91.

b. *Elements.*

(1) That the accused made and uttered a certain check;

(2) That the check was made and uttered for the purchase of a certain thing, in payment of a debt, or for a certain purpose;

(3) That the accused subsequently failed to place or maintain sufficient funds in or credit with the drawee bank for payment of the check in full upon its presentment for payment;

(4) That this failure was dishonorable; and

(5) That, under the circumstances, the conduct of the accused was either: (i) to the prejudice of good order and discipline in the armed forces; (ii) was of a nature to bring discredit upon the armed forces; or (iii) to the prejudice of good order and discipline in the armed forces and of a nature to bring discredit upon the armed forces.

c. *Explanation*. This offense differs from an Article 123a offense (paragraph 70) in that there need be no intent to defraud or deceive at the time of making, drawing, uttering, or delivery, and that the accused need not know at that time that the accused did not or would not have sufficient funds for payment. The gist of the offense lies in the conduct of the accused after uttering the instrument. Mere negligence in maintaining one's bank balance is insufficient for this offense, for the accused's conduct must reflect bad faith or gross indifference in this regard. As in the offense of dishonorable failure to pay debts (see paragraph 96), dishonorable conduct of the accused is necessary, and the other principles discussed in paragraph 96 also apply here.

d. *Maximum punishment*. Bad-conduct discharge, forfeiture of all pay and allowances, and confinement for 6 months.

e. *Sample specification.*

In that _________ (personal jurisdiction data), did, (at/on board—location) (subject-matter jurisdiction data, if required), on or about _____ 20 __, make and utter to __________ a certain check, in words and figures as follows, to wit: __________, (for the purchase of __________) (in payment of a debt) (for the purpose of __________), and did thereafter dishonorably fail to (place) (maintain) sufficient funds in the __________ Bank for payment of such check in full upon its presentment for payment, and that said conduct was (to the prejudice of good order and discipline in the armed forces) (of a nature to bring discredit upon the armed forces) (to the prejudice of good order and discipline in the armed forces and was of a nature to bring discredit upon the armed forces).

95. Article 134—(Child pornography)

a. *Text of statute.* See paragraph 91.

b. *Elements.*

(1) *Possessing, receiving, or viewing child pornography.*

(a) That the accused knowingly and wrongfully possessed, received, or viewed child pornography; and

(b) That, under the circumstances, the conduct of the accused was either: (i) to the prejudice of good order and discipline in the armed forces; (ii) was of a nature to bring discredit upon the armed forces; or (iii) to the prejudice of good order and discipline in the armed forces and of a nature to bring discredit upon the armed forces.

(2) *Possessing child pornography with intent to distribute.*

(a) That the accused knowingly and wrongfully possessed child pornography;

(b) That the possession was with the intent to distribute; and

(c) That, under the circumstances, the conduct of the accused was either: (i) to the prejudice of good order and discipline in the armed forces; (ii) was of a nature to bring discredit upon the armed forces; or (iii) to the prejudice of good order and discipline in the armed forces and of a nature to bring discredit upon the armed forces.

(3) *Distributing child pornography.*

(a) That the accused knowingly and wrongfully distributed child pornography to another; and

(b) That, under the circumstances, the conduct of the accused was either: (i) to the prejudice of good order and discipline in the armed forces; (ii) was of a nature to bring discredit upon the armed forces; or (iii) to the prejudice of good order and discipline in the armed forces and of a nature to bring discredit upon the armed forces.

(4) *Producing child pornography.*

(a) That the accused knowingly and wrongfully produced child pornography; and

(b) That, under the circumstances, the conduct of the accused was either: (i) to the prejudice of good order and discipline in the armed forces; (ii) was of a nature to bring discredit upon the armed forces; or (iii) to the prejudice of good order and discipline in the armed forces and of a nature to bring discredit upon the armed forces.

c. *Explanation.*

(1) *In general.* The Article 134 offense of child pornography is broader than the federal and state statutes referenced below and extends to visual depictions of what appear to be minors. That is, the images include sexually explicit images that may not actually involve minors, but either resemble or are staged to appear so. Article 134—Child pornography is not intended to preempt prosecution of other federal and state law child pornography and obscenity offenses which may be amenable to courts-martial via Article 134 clauses 2 and 3.

(2) *Federal "Child pornography" and "Obscenity" offenses.* Practitioners are advised that the Title 18, United States Code, criminalizes the production, distribution, possession with intent to distribute, possession, and receipt of sexually explicit images of actual children under the age of 18. See 18 U.S.C. §§ 2251; 2252A. Practitioners may charge these offenses utilizing Article 134, clause 3 (crimes and offenses not capital). Practitioners are further advised that Title 18 United States Code, Chapter 71, criminalizes the production of "obscene images," that is, visual depictions of any kind, including a drawing, cartoon, sculpture, or painting. Such images are considered obscene under federal law when they depict minors involved in sexually explicit activity, and/or engaging in bestiality, sadistic or masochistic abuse. See 18 U.S.C. § 1466A. These federal obscenity offenses may likewise be prosecuted at courts-martial via Article 134, clause 3.

(3) *State "child pornography" and "obscenity" offenses.* If a Servicemember violates an applicable state child pornography or obscenity statute within the jurisdiction of a given state, the substance of that state child pornography and obscenity law may be charged via Article 134, clause 2 as conduct "of a nature to

bring discredit upon the armed forces." When so charged, the Article 134 charge should recite every applicable element under the state statute. The maximum punishment for such offenses is the applicable maximum punishment prescribed for such an offense under state law.

(4) "Child pornography" means material that contains either an obscene visual depiction of a minor engaging in sexually explicit conduct or a visual depiction of an actual minor engaging in sexually explicit conduct.

(5) An accused may not be convicted of possessing, receiving, viewing, distributing, or producing child pornography if he was not aware that the images were of minors, or what appeared to be minors, engaged in sexually explicit conduct. Awareness may be inferred from circumstantial evidence such as the name of a computer file or folder, the name of the host website from which a visual depiction was viewed or received, search terms used, and the number of images possessed.

(6) "Distributing" means delivering to the actual or constructive possession of another.

(7) "Minor" means any person under the age of 18 years.

(8) "Possessing" means exercising control of something. Possession may be direct physical custody like holding an item in one's hand, or it may be constructive, as in the case of a person who hides something in a locker or a car to which that person may return to retrieve it. Possession must be knowing and conscious. Possession inherently includes the power or authority to preclude control by others. It is possible for more than one person to possess an item simultaneously, as when several people share control over an item.

(9) "Producing" means creating or manufacturing. As used in this paragraph, it refers to making child pornography that did not previously exist. It does not include reproducing or copying.

(10) "Sexually explicit conduct" means actual or simulated:

(a) sexual intercourse or sodomy, including genital to genital, oral to genital, anal to genital, or oral to anal, whether between persons of the same or opposite sex;

(b) bestiality;

(c) masturbation;

(d) sadistic or masochistic abuse; or

(e) lascivious exhibition of the genitals or pubic area of any person.

(11) Visual depiction includes any developed or undeveloped photograph, picture, film, or video; any digital or computer image, picture, film, or video made by any means, including those transmitted by any means including streaming media, even if not stored in a permanent format; or any digital or electronic data capable of conversion into a visual image.

(12) *Wrongfulness*. Any facts or circumstances that show that a visual depiction of child pornography was unintentionally or inadvertently acquired are relevant to wrongfulness, including, but not limited to, the method by which the visual depiction was acquired, the length of time the visual depiction was maintained, and whether the visual depiction was promptly, and in good faith, destroyed or reported to law enforcement.

(13) On motion of the Government, in any prosecution under this paragraph, except for good cause shown, the name, address, social security number, or other nonphysical identifying information, other than the age or approximate age, of any minor who is depicted in any child pornography or visual depiction or copy thereof shall not be admissible and may be redacted from any otherwise admissible evidence, and the panel shall be instructed, upon request of the Government, that it can draw no inference from the absence of such evidence.

d. *Maximum punishment*.

(1) *Possessing, receiving, or viewing child pornography*. Dishonorable discharge, forfeiture of all pay and allowances, and confinement for 10 years.

(2) *Possessing child pornography with intent to distribute*. Dishonorable discharge, forfeiture of all pay and allowances, and confinement for 15 years.

(3) *Distributing child pornography*. Dishonorable discharge, forfeiture of all pay and allowances, and confinement for 20 years.

(4) *Producing child pornography*. Dishonorable discharge, forfeiture of all pay and allowances, and confinement for 30 years.

e. *Sample specification*.

In that _____ (personal jurisdiction data), did (at/on board—location) (subject-matter jurisdiction data, if required), on or about _____ 20 __ knowingly and wrongfully (possess) (receive) (view) (distribute) (produce) child pornography, to wit: a (photograph) (picture) (film) (video) (digital image) (computer image) of a minor, or what appears to be a minor, engaging in sexually explicit conduct (with intent to distribute the said child pornography), and that said conduct was (to the prejudice of good order and discipline in the armed forces) (of a nature to bring discredit upon the armed forces) (to the prejudice of good order and discipline in the armed forces and was of a nature to bring discredit upon the armed forces).

96. Article 134—(Debt, dishonorably failing to pay)

a. *Text of statute.* See paragraph 91.

b. *Elements.*

(1) That the accused was indebted to a certain person or entity in a certain sum;

(2) That this debt became due and payable on or about a certain date;

(3) That while the debt was still due and payable the accused dishonorably failed to pay this debt; and

(4) That, under the circumstances, the conduct of the accused was either: (i) to the prejudice of good order and discipline in the armed forces; (ii) was of a nature to bring discredit upon the armed forces; or (iii) to the prejudice of good order and discipline in the armed forces and of a nature to bring discredit upon the armed forces.

c. *Explanation.* More than negligence in nonpayment is necessary. The failure to pay must be characterized by deceit, evasion, false promises, or other distinctly culpable circumstances indicating a deliberate nonpayment or grossly indifferent attitude toward one's just obligations. For a debt to form the basis of this offense, the accused must not have had a defense, or an equivalent offset or counterclaim, either in fact or according to the accused's belief, at the time alleged. The offense should not be charged if there was a genuine dispute between the parties as to the facts or law relating to the debt which would affect the obligation of the accused to pay. The offense is not committed if the creditor or creditors involved are satisfied with the conduct of the debtor with respect to payment. The length of the period of nonpayment and any denial of indebtedness which the accused may have made may tend to prove that the accused's conduct was dishonorable, but the court-martial may convict only if it finds from all of the evidence that the conduct was in fact dishonorable.

d. *Maximum punishment.* Bad-conduct discharge, forfeiture of all pay and allowances, and confinement for 6 months.

e. *Sample specification.*

In that __________ (personal jurisdiction data), being indebted to _____ in the sum of $_____ for _____, which amount became due and payable (on) (about) (on or about) _____ 20 __, did (at/on board—location) (subject-matter jurisdiction data, if required), from _____ 20 __, to _____ 20 __, dishonorably fail to pay said debt, and that said conduct was (to the prejudice of good order and discipline in the armed forces) (of a nature to bring discredit upon the armed forces) (to the prejudice of good order and discipline in the armed forces and of a nature to bring discredit upon the armed forces).

97. Article 134—(Disloyal statements)

a. *Text of statute.* See paragraph 91.

b. *Elements.*

(1) That the accused made a certain statement;

(2) That the statement was communicated to another person;

(3) That the statement was disloyal to the United States;

(4) That the statement was made with the intent to promote disloyalty or disaffection toward the United States by any member of the armed forces or to interfere with or impair the loyalty to the United States or good order and discipline of any member of the armed forces; and

(5) That, under the circumstances, the conduct of the accused was either: (i) to the prejudice of good order and discipline in the armed forces; (ii) was of a nature to bring discredit upon the armed forces; or (iii) to the prejudice of good order and discipline in the armed forces and of a nature to bring discredit upon the armed forces.

c. *Explanation.* Certain disloyal statements by military personnel may not constitute an offense under 18 U.S.C. §§ 2385, 2387, and 2388, but may, under the circumstances, be punishable under this article. Examples include praising the enemy, attacking the war aims of the United States, or denouncing our form of government with the intent to promote disloyalty or disaffection among members of the armed Services. A declaration of personal belief can amount to a disloyal statement if it disavows allegiance owed to the United States by the declarant. The disloyalty involved for this offense must be to the United States as a political entity and not merely to a department or other agency that is a part of its administration.

d. *Maximum punishment.* Dishonorable discharge, forfeiture of all pay and allowances, and confinement for 3 years.

e. *Sample specification.*

In that __________ (personal jurisdiction data), did, (at/on board—location) (subject-matter jurisdiction), on or about _____ 20 __, with intent to (promote (disloyalty) (disaffection) (disloyalty and disaffection)) ((interfere with) (impair) the (loyalty) (good order and discipline)) of any member of the armed forces of the United States communicate to __________, a statement, to wit: "__________," or words to that effect, which statement was disloyal to the United States, and that such conduct was (to the prejudice of good order and discipline in the armed forces) (of a nature to bring discredit upon the armed forces) (to the prejudice of good order and discipline in the armed forces and of a nature to bring discredit upon the armed forces).

98. Article 134—(Disorderly conduct, drunkenness)

a. *Text of statute.* See paragraph 91.

b. *Elements.*

(1) That the accused was drunk, disorderly, or drunk and disorderly on board ship or in some other place; and

(2) That, under the circumstances, the conduct of the accused was either: (i) to the prejudice of good order and discipline in the armed forces; (ii) was of a nature to bring discredit upon the armed forces; or (iii) to the prejudice of good order and discipline in the armed forces and of a nature to bring discredit upon the armed forces.

c. *Explanation.*

(1) *Drunkenness.* See subparagraph 49.c.(1)(a) for a discussion of drunk.

(2) *Disorderly.* Disorderly conduct is conduct of such a nature as to affect the peace and quiet of persons who may witness it and who may be disturbed or provoked to resentment thereby. It includes conduct that endangers public morals or outrages public decency and any disturbance of a contentious or turbulent character.

(3) *Service discrediting.* Conduct of a nature to bring discredit upon the armed forces must be included in the specification and proved in order to authorize the higher maximum punishment when the offense is Service discrediting.

d. *Maximum punishment.*

(1) *Disorderly conduct.*

(a) Under such circumstances as to bring discredit upon the military Service. Confinement for 4 months and forfeiture of two-thirds pay per month for 4 months.

(b) Other cases. Confinement for 1 month and forfeiture of two-thirds pay per month for 1 month.

(2) *Drunkenness.*

(a) Aboard ship or under such circumstances as to bring discredit upon the military Service. Confinement for 3 months and forfeiture of two-thirds pay per month for 3 months.

(b) Other cases. Confinement for 1 month and forfeiture of two-thirds pay per month for 1 month.

(3) *Drunk and disorderly.*

(a) Aboard ship. Bad-conduct discharge, forfeiture of all pay and allowances, and confinement for 6 months.

(b) Under such circumstances as to bring discredit upon the military Service. Confinement for 6 months and forfeiture of two-thirds pay per month for 6 months.

(c) Other cases. Confinement for 3 months and forfeiture of two-thirds pay per month for 3 months.

e. *Sample specification.*

In that __________ (personal jurisdiction data), was, (at/on board—location) (subject-matter jurisdiction data, if required), on or about _____ 20 __, (drunk) (disorderly) (drunk and disorderly) (which conduct was of a nature to bring discredit upon the armed forces), and that said conduct was (to the prejudice of good order and discipline in the armed forces) (of a nature to bring discredit upon the armed forces) (to the prejudice of good order and discipline in the armed forces and was of a nature to bring discredit upon the armed forces).

99. Article 134—(Extramarital sexual conduct)

a. *Text of statute.* See paragraph 91.

b. *Elements.*

(1) That the accused wrongfully engaged in extramarital conduct as described in subparagraph c.(2) with a certain person;

(2) That, at the time, the accused knew that the accused or the other person was married to someone else; and

(3) That, under the circumstances, the conduct of the accused was either: (i) to the prejudice of good order and discipline in the armed forces; (ii) was of a nature to bring discredit upon the armed forces; or (iii) to the prejudice of good order and discipline in the armed forces and of a nature to bring discredit upon the armed forces.

c. *Explanation.*

(1) *Conduct prejudicial to good order and discipline or of a nature to bring discredit upon the armed forces.* To constitute an offense under the UCMJ, the extramarital conduct must either be directly prejudicial to good order and discipline or service discrediting or both. Extramarital conduct that is directly prejudicial to good order and discipline includes conduct that has an obvious, and measurably divisive effect on unit or organization discipline, morale, or cohesion, or is clearly detrimental to the authority or stature of or respect toward a Servicemember, or both. Extramarital conduct may be Service discrediting, even though the conduct is only indirectly or remotely prejudicial to good order and discipline. "Discredit" means to injure the reputation of the armed forces and includes extramarital conduct that has a tendency, because of its open or notorious nature, to bring the Service into disrepute, make it subject to public ridicule, or lower it in public esteem. While extramarital conduct that is private and discreet in nature may not be service discrediting by this standard, under the circumstances, it may be determined to be conduct prejudicial to good order and discipline. Commanders should consider all relevant circumstances, including but not limited to the following factors, when determining whether extramarital conduct is prejudicial to good order and discipline or is of a nature to bring discredit upon the armed forces, or both:

(a) The accused's marital status, military rank, grade, or position

(b) The co-actor's marital status, military rank, grade, and position, or relationship to the armed forces

(c) The military status of the accused's spouse or the spouse of the co-actor, or their relationship to the armed forces;

(d) The impact, if any, of the extramarital conduct on the ability of the accused, the co-actor, or the spouse of either to perform their duties in support of the armed forces;

(e) The misuse, if any, of Government time and resources to facilitate the commission of the conduct;

(f) Whether the conduct persisted despite counseling or orders to desist; the flagrancy of the conduct, such as whether any notoriety ensued; and whether the extramarital conduct was accompanied by other violations of the UCMJ;

(g) The negative impact of the conduct on the units or organizations of the accused, the co-actor or the spouse of either of them, such as a detrimental effect on unit or organization morale, teamwork, and efficiency;

(h) Whether the accused's or co-actor's marriage was pending legal dissolution, which is defined as an action with a view towards divorce proceedings, such as the filing of a petition for divorce; and

(i) Whether the extramarital conduct involves an ongoing or recent relationship or is remote in time.

(2) *Extramarital conduct.* The conduct covered under this paragraph means any of the following acts engaged in by persons of the same or opposite sex:

(a) genital to genital sexual intercourse;

(b) oral to genital sexual intercourse;

(c) anal to genital sexual intercourse; and

(d) oral to anal sexual intercourse.

(3) *Marriage.* A marriage exists until it is dissolved in accordance with the laws of a competent state or foreign jurisdiction.

(4) *Legal Separation.* It is an affirmative defense to the offense of Extramarital sexual conduct that the accused, co-actor, or both were legally separated by order of a court of competent jurisdiction. The affirmative defense does not apply unless all parties to the conduct are either legally separated or unmarried at the time of the conduct.

(5) *Mistake of fact*: A defense of mistake of fact exists if the accused had an honest and reasonable belief either that the accused and the co-actor were both unmarried or legally separated, or that they were lawfully married to each other. If this defense is raised by the evidence, then the burden of proof is upon the United States to establish that the accused's belief was unreasonable or not honest.

d. *Maximum punishment.* Dishonorable discharge, forfeiture of all pay and allowances, and confinement for 1 year.

e. *Sample specification.*

In that ____________ (personal jurisdiction data), (a married person), did, (at/on board—location) (subject-matter jurisdiction data, if required), on or about

________ 20 ___, wrongfully engage in extramarital conduct, (to wit: ____________) with ____________, (a person the accused knew was married to a person other than the accused) (a person the accused knew was not the accused's spouse), and that such conduct was (to the prejudice of good order and discipline in the armed forces) (of a nature to bring discredit upon the armed forces) (to the prejudice of good order and discipline in the armed forces and of a nature to bring discredit upon the armed forces).

100. Article 134—(Firearm, discharging—through negligence)

a. *Text of statute.* See paragraph 91.

b. *Elements.*

(1) That the accused discharged a firearm;

(2) That such discharge was caused by the negligence of the accused; and

(3) That, under the circumstances, the conduct of the accused was either: (i) to the prejudice of good order and discipline in the armed forces; (ii) was of a nature to bring discredit upon the armed forces; or (iii) to the prejudice of good order and discipline in the armed forces and of a nature to bring discredit upon the armed forces.

c. *Explanation.* For a discussion of negligence, see subparagraph 103.c.(2).

d. *Maximum punishment.* Confinement for 3 months and forfeiture of two-thirds pay per month for 3 months.

e. *Sample specification.*

In that __________ (personal jurisdiction data), did, (at/on board—location) (subject-matter jurisdiction data, if required), on or about _____ 20 __, through negligence, discharge a (service rifle) (__) in the (squadron) (tent) (barracks) (_____) of _____, and that said conduct was (to the prejudice of good order and discipline in the armed forces) (of a nature to bring discredit upon the armed forces) (to the prejudice of good order and discipline in the armed forces and was of a nature to bring discredit upon the armed forces).

101. Article 134—(Fraternization)

a. *Text of statute.* See paragraph 91.

b. *Elements.*

(1) That the accused was a commissioned or warrant officer;

(2) That the accused fraternized on terms of military equality with one or more certain enlisted member(s) in a certain manner;

(3) That the accused then knew the person(s) to be (an) enlisted member(s);

(4) That such fraternization violated the custom of the accused's Service that officers shall not fraternize with enlisted members on terms of military equality; and

(5) That, under the circumstances, the conduct of the accused was either: (i) to the prejudice of good order and discipline in the armed forces; (ii) was of a nature to bring discredit upon the armed forces; or (iii) to the prejudice of good order and discipline in the armed forces and of a nature to bring discredit upon the armed forces.

c. *Explanation.*

(1) *In general.* The gist of this offense is a violation of the custom of the armed forces against fraternization. Not all contact or association between officers and enlisted persons is an offense. Whether the contact or association in question is an offense depends on the surrounding circumstances. Factors to be considered include whether the conduct has compromised the chain of command, resulted in the appearance of partiality, or otherwise undermined good order, discipline, authority, or morale. The facts and circumstances must be such as to lead a reasonable person experienced in the problems of military leadership to conclude that the good order and discipline of the armed forces has been prejudiced by their tendency to compromise the respect of enlisted persons for the professionalism, integrity, and obligations of an officer.

(2) *Regulations.* Regulations, directives, and orders may also govern conduct between officer and enlisted personnel on both a Service-wide and a local basis. Relationships between enlisted persons of different ranks, or between officers of different ranks may be similarly covered. Violations of such regulations, directives, or orders may be punishable under Article 92. See paragraph 18.

d. *Maximum punishment.* Dismissal, forfeiture of all pay and allowances, and confinement for 2 years.

e. *Sample specification.*

In that __________ (personal jurisdiction data), did, (at/on board—location) (subject-matter jurisdiction data, if required), on or about _____ 20 __, knowingly fraternize with __________, an enlisted person, on terms of military equality, to wit: __________, in violation of the custom of (the Naval Service of the United States) (the United States Army) (the United States Air Force) (the United States Coast Guard) that officers shall not fraternize with enlisted persons on terms of military equality, and that said conduct was (to the prejudice of good order and discipline in the armed forces) (of a nature to bring discredit upon the armed forces) (to the prejudice of good order and discipline in the armed forces and was of a nature to bring discredit upon the armed forces).

102. Article 134—(Gambling with subordinate)

a. *Text of statute.* See paragraph 91.

b. *Elements.*

(1) That the accused gambled with a certain Servicemember;

(2) That the accused was then a noncommissioned or petty officer;

(3) That the Servicemember was not then a noncommissioned or petty officer and was subordinate to the accused;

(4) That the accused knew that the Servicemember was not then a noncommissioned or petty officer and was subordinate to the accused; and

(5) That, under the circumstances, the conduct of the accused was either: (i) to the prejudice of good order and discipline in the armed forces; (ii) was of a nature to bring discredit upon the armed forces; or (iii) to the prejudice of good order and discipline in the armed forces and of a nature to bring discredit upon the armed forces.

c. *Explanation.* This offense can only be committed by a noncommissioned or petty officer gambling with an enlisted person of less than noncommissioned or petty officer rank. Gambling by an officer with an enlisted person may be a violation of Article 133. See also paragraph 90.

d. *Maximum punishment.* Confinement for 3 months and forfeiture of two-thirds pay per month for 3 months.

e. *Sample specification.*

In that __________ (personal jurisdiction data), did (at/on board—location) (subject-matter jurisdiction data, if required), on or about _____ 20 __, gamble with __________, then knowing that the said __________ was not a noncommissioned or petty officer and was subordinate to the said ______, and that said conduct was (to the prejudice of good order and discipline in the armed forces) (of a nature to bring discredit upon the armed forces) (to the prejudice of good order and discipline in the armed forces and was of a nature to bring discredit upon the armed forces).

103. Article 134—(Homicide, negligent)

a. *Text of statute.* See paragraph 91.

b. *Elements.*

(1) That a certain person is dead;

(2) That this death resulted from the act or failure to act of the accused;

(3) That the killing by the accused was unlawful;

(4) That the act or failure to act of the accused which caused the death amounted to simple negligence; and

(5) That, under the circumstances, the conduct of the accused was either: (i) to the prejudice of good order and discipline in the armed forces; (ii) was of a nature to bring discredit upon the armed forces; or (iii) to the prejudice of good order and discipline in the armed forces and of a nature to bring discredit upon the armed forces.

c. *Explanation.*

(1) *Nature of offense.* Negligent homicide is any unlawful homicide which is the result of simple negligence. An intent to kill or injure is not required.

(2) *Simple negligence.* Simple negligence is the absence of due care, that is, an act or omission of a person who is under a duty to use due care which exhibits a lack of that degree of care of the safety of others which a reasonably careful person would have exercised under the same or similar circumstances. Simple negligence is a lesser degree of carelessness than culpable negligence. See subparagraph 57.c.(2)(a).

d. *Maximum punishment.* Dishonorable discharge, forfeiture of all pay and allowances, and confinement for 3 years.

e. *Sample specification.*

In that __________ (personal jurisdiction data), did, (at/on board—location) (subject-matter jurisdiction data, if required), on or about _____ 20 __, unlawfully kill _____, (by negligently _____ the said _____ (in) (on) the _____ with a _____) (by driving a (motor vehicle) (_____) against the said _____ in a negligent manner) (_____), and that said conduct was (to the prejudice of good order and discipline in the armed forces) (of a nature to bring discredit upon the armed forces) (to the prejudice of good order and discipline in the armed forces and was of a nature to bring discredit upon the armed forces).

104. Article 134—(Indecent conduct)

a. *Text of statute.* See paragraph 91.

b. *Elements.*

(1) That the accused engaged in certain conduct;

(2) That the conduct was indecent; and

(3) That, under the circumstances, the conduct of the accused was either: (i) to the prejudice of good order and discipline in the armed forces; (ii) was of a nature to bring discredit upon the armed forces; or (iii) to the prejudice of good order and discipline in the armed forces and of a nature to bring discredit upon the armed forces.

c. *Explanation.*

(1) "Indecent" means that form of immorality relating to sexual impurity which is grossly vulgar, obscene, and repugnant to common propriety, and tends to excite sexual desire or deprave morals with respect to sexual relations.

(2) Indecent conduct includes offenses previously proscribed by "Indecent acts with another" except that the presence of another person is no longer required. For purposes of this offense, the words "conduct" and "act" are synonymous. For child offenses, some indecent conduct may be included in the definition of lewd act and preempted by Article 120b(c). See subparagraph 91.c.(5)(a).

d. *Maximum punishment.* Dishonorable discharge, forfeiture of all pay and allowances, and confinement for 5 years.

e. *Sample specification.*

In that ______ (personal jurisdiction data), did (at/on board—location) (subject-matter jurisdiction data, if required), on or about ________20___ , commit indecent conduct, to wit: _________, and that said conduct was (to the prejudice of good order and discipline in the armed forces) (of a nature to bring discredit upon the armed forces) (to the prejudice of good order and discipline in the armed forces and was of a nature to bring discredit upon the armed forces).

105. Article 134—(Indecent language)

a. *Text of statute.* See paragraph 91.

b. *Elements.*

(1) That the accused orally or in writing communicated to another person certain language;

(2) That such language was indecent; and

(3) That, under the circumstances, the conduct of the accused was either: (i) to the prejudice of good order and discipline in the armed forces; (ii) was of a nature to bring discredit upon the armed forces; or (iii) to the prejudice of good order and discipline in the armed forces and of a nature to bring discredit upon the armed forces.

[Note: If applicable, add the following additional element:]

(4) That the person to whom the language was communicated was a child under the age of 16.

c. *Explanation.* Indecent language is that which is grossly offensive to modesty, decency, or propriety, or shocks the moral sense, because of its vulgar, filthy, or disgusting nature, or its tendency to incite lustful thought. Language is indecent if it tends reasonably to corrupt morals or incite libidinous thoughts. The language must violate community standards. See paragraph 62 if the communication was made in the physical presence of a child.

d. *Maximum punishment.*

(1) *Communicated to any child under the age of 16 years.* Dishonorable discharge, forfeiture of all pay and allowances, and confinement for 2 years.

(2) *Other cases.* Bad-conduct discharge; forfeiture of all pay and allowances, and confinement for 6 months.

e. *Sample specification.*

In that __________ (personal jurisdiction data), did (at/on board—location) (subject-matter jurisdiction data, if required), on or about _____ 20 __, (orally) (in writing) communicate to __________, (a child under the age of 16 years), certain indecent language, to wit: __________, and that such conduct was (to the prejudice of good order and discipline in the armed forces) (of a nature to bring discredit upon the armed forces) (to the prejudice of good order and discipline in the armed forces and of a nature to bring discredit upon the armed forces).

106. Article 134—(Pandering and prostitution)

a. *Text of statute.* See paragraph 91.

b. *Elements.*

(1) *Prostitution.*

(a) That the accused engaged in a sexual act with another person not the accused's spouse;

(b) That the accused did so for the purpose of receiving money or other compensation;

(c) That this act was wrongful; and

(d) That, under the circumstances, the conduct of the accused was either: (i) to the prejudice of good order and discipline in the armed forces; (ii) was of a nature to bring discredit upon the armed forces; or (iii) to the prejudice of good order and discipline in the armed forces and of a nature to bring discredit upon the armed forces.

(2) *Patronizing a prostitute.*

(a) That the accused engaged in a sexual act with another person not the accused's spouse;

(b) That the accused compelled, induced, enticed, or procured such person to engage in a sexual act in exchange for money or other compensation;

(c) That this act was wrongful; and

(d) That, under the circumstances, the conduct of the accused was either: (i) to the prejudice of good order and discipline in the armed forces; (ii) was of a nature to bring discredit upon the armed forces; or (iii) to the prejudice of good order and discipline in the armed forces and of a nature to bring discredit upon the armed forces.

(3) *Pandering by inducing, enticing, or procuring act of prostitution.*

(a) That the accused induced, enticed, or procured a certain person to engage in a sexual act for hire and reward with a person to be directed to said person by the accused;

(b) That this inducing, enticing, or procuring was wrongful;

(c) That, under the circumstances, the conduct of the accused was either: (i) to the prejudice of good order and discipline in the armed forces; (ii) was of a nature to bring discredit upon the armed forces; or (iii) to the prejudice of good order and discipline in the armed forces and of a nature to bring discredit upon the armed forces.

(4) *Pandering by arranging or receiving consideration for arranging for a sexual act.*

(a) That the accused arranged for, or received valuable consideration for arranging for, a certain person to engage in a sexual act;

(b) That the arranging (and receipt of consideration) was wrongful; and

(c) That, under the circumstances, the conduct of the accused was either: (i) to the prejudice of good order and discipline in the armed forces; (ii) was of a nature to bring discredit upon the armed forces; or (iii) to the prejudice of good order and discipline in the armed forces and of a nature to bring discredit upon the armed forces.

c. *Explanation.*

(1) *Sexual act.* Sexual act as used in this paragraph shall be as defined in paragraph 60.a.(g)(1).

(2) *Other regulations.* This offense does not preempt any other lawful regulations or orders prescribed by a proper authority that proscribe other forms of sexual conduct for compensation by military personnel. Violations of such regulations or orders may be punishable under Article 92. See paragraph 18.

d. *Maximum punishment.*

(1) *Prostitution and patronizing a prostitute.* Dishonorable discharge, forfeiture of all pay and allowances, and confinement for 1 year.

(2) *Pandering.* Dishonorable discharge, forfeiture of all pay and allowances, and confinement for 5 years.

e. *Sample specifications.*

(1) *Prostitution.*

In that __________ (personal jurisdiction data), did, (at/on board—location) (subject-matter jurisdiction data, if required), on or about _____ 20 __, wrongfully engage in (a sexual act) (sexual acts), to wit:_________, with _____, a person not (his) (her) spouse, for the purpose of receiving (money) (_____), and that such conduct was (to the prejudice of good order and discipline in the armed forces) (of a nature to bring discredit upon the armed forces) (to the prejudice of good order and discipline in the armed forces and of a nature to bring discredit upon the armed forces).

(2) *Patronizing a prostitute.*

In that __________ (personal jurisdiction data), did, (at/on board—location) (subject-matter jurisdiction data, if required), on or about _____ 20 __, wrongfully (compel) (induce) (entice) (procure) __________, a person not (his) (her) spouse, to engage in (a sexual act) (sexual acts), to wit:_________, with the accused in exchange for (money) (__________), and that such conduct was (to the prejudice of good order and discipline in the armed forces) (of a nature to bring discredit upon the armed forces) (to the prejudice of good order and discipline in the armed forces and of a nature to bring discredit upon the armed forces).

(3) *Inducing, enticing, or procuring act of prostitution.*

In that __________ (personal jurisdiction data), did (at/on board—location) (subject-matter jurisdiction data, if required), on or about _____ 20 __, wrongfully (induce) (entice) (procure) __________ to engage in (a sexual act) (sexual acts), to wit:_________, for hire and reward with persons to be directed to (him) (her) by the said __________, and that such conduct was (to the prejudice of good order and discipline in the armed forces) (of a nature to bring discredit upon the armed forces) (to the prejudice of good order and discipline in the armed forces and of a nature to bring discredit upon the armed forces).

(4) *Arranging, or receiving consideration for arranging for a sexual act.*

In that __________ (personal jurisdiction data), did, (at/on board—location) (subject-matter jurisdiction data, if required), on or about _____ 20 __, wrongfully (arrange for) (receive valuable consideration, to wit: __________ on account of arranging for) __________ to engage in (a sexual act) (sexual acts) to wit:_________, with __________, and that such conduct was (to the prejudice of good order and discipline in the armed forces) (of a nature to bring discredit upon the armed forces) (to the prejudice of good order and discipline in the armed forces and of a nature to bring discredit upon the armed forces).

107. Article 134—(Self-injury without intent to avoid service)

a. *Text of statute.* See paragraph 91.

b. *Elements.*

(1) That the accused intentionally inflicted injury upon himself or herself;

(2) That, under the circumstances, the conduct of the accused was either: (i) to the prejudice of good order and discipline in the armed forces; (ii) was of a nature to bring discredit upon the armed forces; or (iii) to the prejudice of good order and discipline in the armed forces and of a nature to bring discredit upon the armed forces.

[Note: If the offense was committed in time of war or in a hostile fire pay zone, add the following element:]

(3) That the offense was committed (in time of war) (in a hostile fire pay zone).

c. *Explanation.*

(1) *Nature of offense.* This offense differs from malingering (see paragraph 7) in that for this offense, the accused need not have harbored a design to avoid performance of any work, duty, or service which may properly or normally be expected of one in the military service. This offense is characterized by intentional self-injury under such circumstances as prejudice good order and discipline or discredit the armed forces. It is not required that the accused be unable to perform duties, or that the accused actually be absent from his or her place of duty as a result of the injury. For example, the accused may inflict the injury while on leave or pass. The circumstances and extent of injury, however, are relevant to a determination that the accused's conduct was prejudicial to good order and discipline, or Service discrediting.

(2) *How injury inflicted.* The injury may be inflicted by nonviolent as well as by violent means and may be accomplished by any act or omission that produces, prolongs, or aggravates a sickness or disability. Thus, voluntary starvation that results in debility is a self-inflicted injury. Similarly, the injury may be inflicted by another at the accused's request.

Discussion

Bona fide suicide attempts should not be charged as criminal offenses. When making a determination whether the injury by the Servicemember was a bona fide suicide attempt, the convening authority should consider factors including, but not limited to, health conditions, personal stressors, and DoD policy related to suicide prevention.

---

d. *Maximum punishment.*

(1) *Intentional self-inflicted injury.* Dishonorable discharge, forfeiture of all pay and allowances, and confinement for 2 years.

(2) *Intentional self-inflicted injury in time of war or in a hostile fire pay zone.* Dishonorable discharge, forfeiture of all pay and allowances, and confinement for 5 years.

e. *Sample specification.*

In that __________ (personal jurisdiction data), did, (at/on board—location) (subject-matter jurisdiction data, if required) (in a hostile fire pay zone) on or about _____ 20 __, (a time of war,) intentionally injure (himself) (herself) by __________ (nature and circumstances of injury), and that such conduct was (to the prejudice of good order and discipline in the armed forces) (of a nature to bring discredit upon the armed forces) (to the prejudice of good order and discipline in the armed forces and of a nature to bring discredit upon the armed forces).

107a. Article 134—(Sexual Harassment)

a. *Text of statute.* See paragraph 91.

b. *Elements.*

(1) That the accused knowingly made sexual advances, demands or requests for sexual

favors, or knowingly engaged in other conduct of a sexual nature;

(2) That such conduct was unwelcome;

(3) That, under the circumstances, such conduct:

(a) Would cause a reasonable person to believe, and a certain person did believe, that submission to such conduct would be made, either explicitly or implicitly, a term or condition of a person's job, pay, career, benefits, or entitlements;

(b) Would cause a reasonable person to believe, and a certain person did believe, that submission to, or rejection of, such conduct would be used as a basis for decisions affecting that person's job, pay, career, benefits, or entitlements; or

(c) Was so severe, repetitive, or pervasive that a reasonable person would perceive, and a certain person did perceive, an intimidating, hostile, or offensive working environment; and

(4) That, under the circumstances, the conduct of the accused was either: (i) to the prejudice of good order and discipline in the armed forces; (ii) of a nature to bring discredit upon the armed forces; or (iii) to the prejudice of good order and discipline in the armed forces and of a nature to bring discredit upon the armed forces.

c. *Explanation.*

(1) Whether "other conduct" is "of a sexual nature" is dependent upon the circumstances of the act or acts alleged and may include conduct that, without context, would not appear to be sexual in nature.

(2) *Nature of victim.* "A certain person" extends to any person, regardless of gender or seniority, and regardless of whether subject to the UCMJ, who by some duty or military-related reason may work or associate with the accused.

(3) *Timing and location of act.* The act constituting sexual harassment can occur at any location, regardless of whether the victim or accused is on or off duty at the time of the alleged act or acts. Physical proximity is not required, and the acts may be committed through online or other electronic means.

(4) *Mens Rea.* The accused must have actual knowledge that he or she is making a sexual advance or a demand or request for sexual favors, or engaging in other conduct of a sexual nature. Actual knowledge is not required for the other elements of the offense.

(5) *A certain person's belief or perception.* For purposes of the portions of the elements dealing with a certain person's belief or perception, that belief or perception may be satisfied by such a belief or perception being formed at any time; the belief or perception need not be formed contemporaneously with the actions that gave rise to that belief or perception.

d. *Maximum punishment.* Dishonorable discharge, forfeiture of all pay and allowances, and confinement for 2 years.

e. *Sample specification.*

In that __________ (personal jurisdiction data), did, (at/on board-location) (subject-matter jurisdiction data, if required), on or about _____ 20__, knowingly (make sexual advances)

(demand or request sexual favors) (engage in conduct of a sexual nature), to wit (by saying to (him) (her), "__________," or words to that effect) (by __________); that such conduct was unwelcome; and under the circumstances (would cause a reasonable person to believe, and _________ did believe, that submission to such conduct would be made, either explicitly or implicitly, a term or condition of a person's job, pay, career, benefits or entitlements) (would cause a reasonable person to believe, and _________ did believe, that submission to, or rejection of, such conduct would be used as a basis for career or employment decisions affecting _________) (was so severe, repetitive, or pervasive that a reasonable person would perceive, and _________ did perceive, an intimidating, hostile, or offensive working environment); and that such conduct was (to the prejudice of good order and discipline in the armed forces) (of a nature to bring discredit upon the armed forces) (to the prejudice of good order and discipline in the armed forces and of a nature to bring discredit upon the armed forces).

108. Article 134—(Straggling)

a. *Text of statute.* See paragraph 91.

b. *Elements.*

(1) That the accused, while accompanying the accused's organization on a march, maneuvers, or similar exercise, straggled;

(2) That the straggling was wrongful; and

(3) That, under the circumstances, the conduct of the accused was either: (i) to the prejudice of good order and discipline in the armed forces; (ii) was of a nature to bring discredit upon the armed forces; or (iii) to the prejudice of good order and discipline in the armed forces and of a nature to bring discredit upon the armed forces.

c. *Explanation.* "Straggle" means to wander away, to stray, to become separated from, or to lag or linger behind.

d. *Maximum punishment.* Confinement for 3 months and forfeiture of two-thirds pay per month for 3 months.

e. *Sample specification.*

In that __________ (personal jurisdiction data) (subject-matter jurisdiction data, if required), did, at __________, on or about _____ 20 __, while accompanying (his) (her) organization on (a march) (maneuvers) (__________), wrongfully straggle, and that such conduct was (to the prejudice of good order and discipline in the armed forces) (of a nature to bring discredit upon the armed forces) (to the prejudice of good order and discipline in the armed forces and of a nature to bring discredit upon the armed forces).

PART V
NONJUDICIAL PUNISHMENT PROCEDURE

1. General

a. *Authority*. Nonjudicial punishment in the United States Armed Forces is authorized by Article 15.

b. *Nature*. Nonjudicial punishment is a disciplinary measure more serious than the administrative corrective measures discussed in paragraph 1g, but less serious than trial by court-martial.

c. *Purpose*. Nonjudicial punishment provides commanders with an essential and prompt means of maintaining good order and discipline and also promotes positive behavior changes in Servicemembers without the stigma of a court-martial conviction.

d. *Policy*.

(1) *Commander's responsibility*. Commanders are responsible for good order and discipline in their commands. Generally, discipline can be maintained through effective leadership including, when necessary, administrative corrective measures. Nonjudicial punishment is ordinarily appropriate when administrative corrective measures are inadequate due to the nature of the minor offense or the record of the Servicemember, unless it is clear that only trial by court-martial will meet the needs of justice and discipline. Nonjudicial punishment shall be considered on an individual basis. Commanders considering nonjudicial punishment should consider the nature of the offense, the record of the Servicemember, the needs for good order and discipline, and the effect of nonjudicial punishment on the Servicemember and the Servicemember's record.

(2) *Commander's discretion*. A commander who is considering a case for disposition under Article 15 will exercise personal discretion in evaluating each case, both as to whether nonjudicial punishment is appropriate, and, if so, as to the nature and amount of punishment appropriate. No superior may direct that a subordinate authority impose nonjudicial punishment in a particular case, issue regulations, orders, or "guides" which suggest to subordinate authorities that certain categories of minor offenses be disposed of by nonjudicial punishment instead of by court-martial or administrative corrective measures, or that predetermined kinds or amounts of punishments be imposed for certain classifications of offenses that the subordinate considers appropriate for disposition by nonjudicial punishment.

(3) *Commander's suspension authority*. Commanders should consider suspending all or part of any punishment selected under Article 15, particularly in the case of first offenders or when significant extenuating or mitigating matters are present. Suspension provides an incentive to the offender and gives an opportunity to the commander to evaluate the offender during the period of suspension.

e. *Minor offenses*. Nonjudicial punishment may be imposed for acts or omissions that are minor offenses under the punitive article (*see* Part IV). Whether an offense is minor depends on several factors: the nature of the offense and the circumstances surrounding its commission; the offender's age, rank, duty assignment, record and experience; and the maximum sentence imposable for the offense if tried by general court-martial. Ordinarily, a minor offense is an offense for which the maximum sentence imposable would not include a dishonorable discharge or confinement for longer than 1 year if tried by general court-martial. The decision whether an offense is "minor" is a matter of discretion for the commander imposing nonjudicial punishment, but nonjudicial punishment for an offense other than a minor offense (even though thought by the commander to be minor) is not a bar to trial by court-martial for the same offense. *See* R.C.M. 907(b)(2)(D)(iii). However, the accused may show at trial that nonjudicial punishment was imposed, and if the accused does so, this fact must be considered in determining an appropriate sentence. *See* Article 15(f); R.C.M. 1001(d)(1)(B).

f. *Limitations on nonjudicial punishment*.

(1) *Double punishment prohibited*. When nonjudicial punishment has been imposed for an offense, punishment may not again be imposed for the same offense under Article 15. *But see* paragraph 1e concerning trial by court-martial.

(2) *Increase in punishment prohibited*. Once nonjudicial punishment has been imposed, it may not be increased, upon appeal or otherwise.

(3) *Multiple punishment prohibited*. When a commander determines that nonjudicial punishment is appropriate for a particular Servicemember, all known offenses determined to be appropriate for disposition by nonjudicial punishment and ready to be considered at that time, including all such offenses arising from a single incident or course of conduct, shall ordinarily be

considered together, and not made the basis for multiple punishments.

(4) *Statute of limitations.* Except as provided in Article 43(c) and (d), nonjudicial punishment may not be imposed for offenses which were committed more than 2 years before the date of imposition, unless knowingly and voluntarily waived by the member. *See* Article 43(b)(3)."

(5) *Civilian courts.* Nonjudicial punishment may not be imposed for an offense tried by a court which derives its authority from the United States. Nonjudicial punishment may not be imposed for an offense tried by a State or foreign court unless authorized by regulations of the Secretary concerned.

g. *Relationship of nonjudicial punishment to administrative corrective measures.* Article 15 and Part V of this Manual do not apply to, include, or limit use of administrative corrective measures that promote efficiency and good order and discipline such as counseling, admonitions, reprimands, exhortations, disapprovals, criticisms, censures, reproofs, rebukes, extra military instruction, and administrative withholding of privileges. *See also* R.C.M. 306. Administrative corrective measures are not punishment and they may be used for acts or omissions which are not offenses under the code and for acts or omissions which are offenses under the code.

h. *Burden of proof.* The burden of proof to be utilized by commanders throughout the nonjudicial punishment process shall be a preponderance of the evidence. This means the commanding officer must determine it is "more likely than not" the member committed the offense defined by the UCMJ. Each element of each offense, as defined in the Manual for Courts-Martial, must be supported by a preponderance of the evidence (*i.e.*, "more likely than not"). This standard is more rigorous than a "probable cause" standard of proof used by law enforcement to obtain a warrant but a lower standard of proof than the "beyond a reasonable doubt" standard used at a court-martial.

i. *Effect of errors.* Failure to comply with any of the procedural provisions of Part V of this Manual shall not invalidate a punishment imposed under Article 15, unless the error materially prejudiced a substantial right of the Servicemember on whom the punishment was imposed.

j. *Service regulations and procedures.* Unless otherwise provided, the Service regulations and procedures of the Servicemember shall apply.

2. Who may impose nonjudicial punishment

The following persons may serve as a nonjudicial punishment authority for the purposes of administering nonjudicial punishment proceedings under this Part:

a. *Commander.* As provided by regulations of the Secretary concerned, a commander may impose nonjudicial punishment upon any military personnel of that command. "Commander" means a commissioned or warrant officer who, by virtue of rank and assignment, exercises primary command authority over a military organization or prescribed territorial area, which under pertinent official directives is recognized as a "command." "Commander" includes a commander of a joint command. Subject to subparagraph 1d(2) and any regulations of the Secretary concerned, the authority of a commander to impose nonjudicial punishment as to certain types of offenses, certain categories of persons, or in specific cases, or to impose certain types of punishment, may be limited or withheld by a superior commander or by the Secretary concerned.

b. *Officer in charge.* If authorized by regulations of the Secretary concerned, an officer in charge may impose nonjudicial punishment upon enlisted persons assigned to that unit.

c. *Principal assistant.* If authorized by regulations of the Secretary concerned, a commander exercising general court-martial jurisdiction or an officer of general or flag rank in command may delegate that commander's powers under Article 15 to a principal assistant. The Secretary concerned may define "principal assistant."

3. Right to demand trial

Except in the case of a person attached to or embarked in a vessel, punishment may not be imposed under Article 15 upon any member of the armed forces who has, before the imposition of nonjudicial punishment, demanded trial by court-martial in lieu of nonjudicial punishment. This right may also be granted to a person attached to or embarked in a vessel if so authorized by regulations of the Secretary concerned. A person is "attached to" or "embarked in" a vessel if, at the time nonjudicial punishment is imposed, that person is assigned or attached to the vessel, is on board for passage, or is assigned or attached to an embarked staff, unit, detachment, squadron, team, air group, or other regularly organized body.

4. Procedure

a. *Notice.* If, after a preliminary inquiry (*see* R.C.M. 303), the nonjudicial punishment authority determines that disposition by nonjudicial punishment proceedings is appropriate (*see* R.C.M. 306; paragraph 1 of this Part), the nonjudicial punishment authority shall cause the Servicemember to be notified. The notice shall include:

(1) a statement that the nonjudicial punishment authority is considering the imposition of nonjudicial punishment;

(2) a statement describing the alleged offenses—including the article of the code—which the member is alleged to have committed;

(3) a brief summary of the information upon which the allegations are based or a statement that the member may, upon request, examine available statements and evidence;

(4) a statement of the rights that will be accorded to the Servicemember under subparagraphs 4c(1) and (2) of this Part;

(5) unless the right to demand trial is not applicable (*see* paragraph 3 of this Part), a statement that the member may demand trial by court-martial in lieu of nonjudicial punishment, a statement of the maximum punishment which the nonjudicial punishment authority may impose by nonjudicial punishment; a statement that, if trial by court-martial is demanded, charges could be referred for trial by summary, special, or general court-martial; that the member may not be tried by summary court-martial over the member's objection; and that at a special or general court-martial the member has the right to be represented by counsel.

b. *Decision by Servicemember.*

(1) *Demand for trial by court-martial.* If the Servicemember demands trial by court-martial (when this right is applicable), the nonjudicial proceedings shall be terminated. It is within the discretion of the commander whether to forward or refer charges for trial by court-martial (*see* R.C.M. 306; 307; 401–407) in such a case, but in no event may nonjudicial punishment be imposed for the offenses affected unless the demand is voluntarily withdrawn.

(2) *No demand for trial by court-martial.* If the Servicemember does not demand trial by court-martial within a reasonable time after notice under paragraph 4a of this Part, or if the right to demand trial by court-martial is not applicable, the nonjudicial punishment authority may proceed under paragraph 4c of this Part.

c. *Nonjudicial punishment proceeding accepted.*

(1) *Personal appearance requested; procedure.* Before nonjudicial punishment may be imposed, the Servicemember shall be entitled to appear personally before the nonjudicial punishment authority who offered nonjudicial punishment, except when appearance is prevented by the unavailability of the nonjudicial punishment authority or by extraordinary circumstances, in which case the Servicemember shall be entitled to appear before a person designated by the nonjudicial punishment authority who shall prepare a written summary of any proceedings before that person and forward it and any written matter submitted by the Servicemember to the nonjudicial punishment authority. If the Servicemember requests personal appearance, the Servicemember shall be entitled to:

(A) Be informed in accordance with Article 31(b);

(B) Be accompanied by a spokesperson provided or arranged for by the member unless the punishment to be imposed will not exceed extra duty for 14 days, restriction for 14 days, and an oral reprimand. Such a spokesperson need not be qualified under R.C.M. 502(d); such spokesperson is not entitled to travel or similar expenses, and the proceedings need not be delayed to permit the presence of a spokesperson; the spokesperson may speak for the Servicemember, but may not question witnesses except as the nonjudicial punishment authority may allow as a matter of discretion;

(C) Be informed orally or in writing of the information against the Servicemember and relating to the offenses alleged;

(D) Be allowed to examine documents or physical objects against the Servicemember that the nonjudicial punishment authority has examined in connection with the case and on which the nonjudicial punishment authority intends to rely in deciding whether and how much nonjudicial punishment to impose;

(E) Present matters in defense, extenuation, and mitigation orally, or in writing, or both;

(F) Have present witnesses, including those adverse to the Servicemember, upon request, if their statements will be relevant and they are reasonably available. For purposes of this subparagraph, a witness is not reasonably available if the witness requires reimbursement by the United States for any cost incurred in appearing, cannot appear without unduly delaying the proceedings, or, if a military witness, cannot be excused from other important duties;

(G) Have the proceeding open to the public unless the nonjudicial punishment authority determines that the proceeding should be closed for good cause, such as military exigencies or security interests, or unless the punishment to be imposed will not exceed extra duty for 14 days, restriction for 14 days, and an oral reprimand; however, nothing in this subparagraph requires special arrangements to be made to facilitate access to the proceeding.

(2) *Personal appearance waived; procedure.* Subject to the approval of the nonjudicial punishment authority, the Servicemember may request not to appear personally under subparagraph 4c(1) of this Part. If such request is granted, the Servicemember may submit written matters for consideration by the nonjudicial punishment authority before such authority's decision under subparagraph 4c(4) of this Part. The Servicemember shall be informed of the right to remain silent and that matters submitted may be used against the member in a trial by court-martial.

(3) *Evidence.* The Military Rules of Evidence (Part III), other than with respect to privileges, do not apply at nonjudicial punishment proceedings. Any relevant matter may be considered, after compliance with subparagraphs 4c(1)(C) and (D) of this Part.

(4) *Decision.* After considering all relevant matters presented by a preponderance of the evidence standard, if the nonjudicial punishment authority—

(A) does not conclude that the Servicemember committed the offenses alleged, the nonjudicial punishment authority shall so inform the member and terminate the proceedings;

(B) concludes that the Servicemember committed one or more of the offenses alleged, the nonjudicial punishment authority shall:

(i) so inform the Servicemember;

(ii) inform the Servicemember of the punishment imposed; and

(iii) inform the Servicemember of the right to appeal (see paragraph 7 of this Part).

d. *Nonjudicial punishment based on record of court of inquiry or other investigative body.* Nonjudicial punishment may be based on the record of a court of inquiry or other investigative body, in which proceeding the member was accorded the rights of a party. No additional proceeding under subparagraph 4c(1) of this Part is required. The Servicemember shall be informed in writing that nonjudicial punishment is being considered based on the record of the proceedings in question, and given the opportunity, if applicable, to refuse nonjudicial punishment. If the Servicemember does not demand trial by court-martial or has no option, the Servicemember may submit, in writing, any matter in defense, extenuation, or mitigation, to the officer considering imposing nonjudicial punishment, for consideration by that officer to determine whether the member committed the offenses in question, and, if so, to determine an appropriate punishment.

5. Punishments

a. *General limitations.* The Secretary concerned may limit the power granted by Article 15 with respect to the kind and amount of the punishment authorized. Subject to paragraphs 1 and 4 of this Part and to regulations of the Secretary concerned, the kinds and amounts of punishment authorized by Article 15(b) may be imposed upon Servicemembers as provided in this paragraph.

b. *Authorized maximum punishments.* In addition to or in lieu of admonition or reprimand, the following disciplinary punishments, subject to the limitation of paragraph 5d of this Part, may be imposed upon Servicemembers:

(1) *Upon commissioned officers and warrant officers—*

(A) By any commanding officer—restriction to specified limits, with or without suspension from duty for not more than 30 consecutive days;

(B) If imposed by an officer exercising general court-martial jurisdiction, an officer of general or flag rank in command, or a principal assistant as defined in paragraph 2c of this Part—

(i) arrest in quarters for not more than 30 consecutive days;

(ii) forfeiture of not more than one-half of one month's pay per month for 2 months;

(iii) restriction to specified limits, with or without suspension from duty, for not more than 60 consecutive days;

(2) *Upon other military personnel of the command—*

(A) By any nonjudicial punishment authority—

(i) if imposed upon a person attached to or embarked in a vessel, confinement for not more than 3 consecutive days;

(ii) correctional custody for not more than 7 consecutive days;

(iii) forfeiture of not more than 7 days' pay;

(iv) reduction to the next inferior grade, if the grade from which demoted is within the promotion authority of the officer imposing the reduction or any officer subordinate to the one who imposes the reduction;

(v) extra duties, including fatigue or other duties, for not more than 14 consecutive days;

(vi) restriction to specified limits with or without suspension from duty, for not more than 14 consecutive days;

(B) If imposed by a commanding officer of the grade of major or lieutenant commander or above or a principal assistant as defined in paragraph 2c of this Part—

(i) if imposed upon a person attached to or embarked in a vessel, confinement for not more than 3 consecutive days;

(ii) correctional custody for not more than 30 consecutive days;

(iii) forfeiture of not more than one-half of 1 month's pay per month for 2 months;

(iv) reduction to the lowest or any intermediate pay grade, if the grade from which demoted is within the promotion authority of the officer imposing the reduction or any officer subordinate to the one who imposes the reduction, but enlisted members in pay grades above E-4 may not be reduced more than one pay grade, except that during time of war or national emergency this category of persons may be reduced two grades if the Secretary concerned determines that circumstances require the removal of this limitation;

(v) extra duties, including fatigue or other duties, for not more than 45 consecutive days;

(vi) restrictions to specified limits, with or without suspension from duty, for not more than 60 consecutive days.

c. *Nature of punishment.*

(1) *Admonition and reprimand.* Admonition and reprimand are two forms of censure intended to express adverse reflection upon or criticism of a person's conduct. A reprimand is a more severe form of censure than an admonition. When imposed as nonjudicial punishment, the admonition or reprimand is considered to be punitive, unlike the nonpunitive admonition and reprimand provided for in paragraph 1g of this Part. In the case of commissioned officers and warrant officers, admonitions and reprimands given as nonjudicial punishment must be administered in writing. In other cases, unless otherwise prescribed by the Secretary concerned, they may be administered either orally or in writing.

(2) *Restriction.* Restriction is the least severe form of deprivation of liberty. Restriction involves moral rather than physical restraint. The severity of this type of restraint depends on its duration and the geographical limits specified when the punishment is imposed. A person undergoing restriction may be required to report to a designated place at specified times if reasonably necessary to ensure that the punishment is being properly executed. Unless otherwise specified by the nonjudicial punishment authority, a person in restriction may be required to perform any military duty.

(3) *Arrest in quarters.* As in the case of restriction, the restraint involved in arrest in quarters is enforced by a moral obligation rather than by physical means. This punishment may be imposed only on officers. An officer undergoing this punishment may be required to perform those duties prescribed by the Secretary concerned. However, an officer so punished is required to remain within that officer's quarters during the period of punishment unless the limits of arrest are otherwise extended by appropriate authority. The quarters of an officer may consist of a military residence, whether a tent, stateroom, or other quarters assigned, or a private residence when government quarters have not been provided.

(4) *Correctional custody.* Correctional custody is the physical restraint of a person during duty or nonduty hours, or both, imposed as a punishment under Article 15, and may include extra duties, fatigue duties, or hard labor as an incident of correctional custody. A person may be required to serve correctional custody in a confinement facility, but, if practicable, not in immediate association with persons awaiting trial or held in confinement pursuant to trial by court-martial. A person undergoing correctional custody may be required to perform those regular military duties, extra duties, fatigue duties, and hard labor which may be assigned by the authority charged with the administration of the punishment. The conditions under which correctional custody is served shall be prescribed by the Secretary concerned. In addition, the Secretary concerned may limit the categories of enlisted members upon whom correctional custody may be imposed. The authority competent to order the release of a person from correctional custody shall be as designated by the Secretary concerned.

(5) *Confinement.* Confinement may be imposed upon a person attached to or embarked on a vessel. Confinement involves confinement for not more than three consecutive days in places where the person so confined may communicate only with authorized personnel. The categories of enlisted personnel upon whom this type of punishment may be imposed may be limited by the Secretary concerned.

(6) *Extra duties.* Extra duties involve the performance of duties in addition to those normally assigned to the person undergoing the punishment. Extra duties may include fatigue duties. Military duties of any kind may be assigned as extra duty. However, no extra duty may be imposed which constitutes a known safety or health hazard to the member or which constitutes cruel or unusual punishment or which is not sanctioned by customs of the Service concerned. Extra duties assigned as punishment of noncommissioned officers, petty officers, or any other enlisted persons of equivalent grades or positions designated by the Secretary concerned, should not be of a kind which demeans their grades or positions.

(7) *Reduction in grade.* Reduction in grade is one of the most severe forms of nonjudicial punishment and it should be used with discretion. As used in Article 15, the phrase "if the grade from which demoted is within the promotion authority of the officer imposing the reduction or any officer subordinate to the one who imposes the reduction," does not refer to the authority to promote the person concerned but to the general authority to promote to the grade held by the person to be punished.

(8) *Forfeiture of pay.* "Forfeiture" means a permanent loss of entitlement to the pay forfeited. "Pay," as used with respect to forfeiture of pay under Article 15, refers to the basic pay of the person or, in the case of reserve component personnel on inactive-duty, compensation for periods of inactive-duty training, plus any sea or hardship duty pay. "Basic pay" includes no element of pay other than the basic pay fixed by statute for the grade and length of service of the person concerned and does not include special pay for a special qualification, incentive pay for the performance of hazardous duties, proficiency pay, subsistence and quarters allowances, and similar types of compensation. If the punishment includes both reduction, whether or not suspended, and forfeiture of pay, the forfeiture must be based on the grade to which reduced. The amount to be forfeited will be expressed in whole dollar amounts only and not in a number of day's pay or fractions of monthly pay. If the forfeiture is to be applied for more than 1 month, the amount to be forfeited per month and the number of months should be stated. Forfeiture of pay may not extend to any pay accrued before the date of its imposition.

d. *Limitations on combination of punishments.*

(1) Arrest in quarters may not be imposed in combination with restriction;

(2) Confinement may not be imposed in combination with correctional custody, extra duties, or restriction;

(3) Correctional custody may not be imposed in combination with restriction or extra duties;

(4) Restriction and extra duties may be combined to run concurrently, but the combination may not exceed the maximum imposable for extra duties;

(5) Subject to the limits in subparagraphs 5d(1) through (4) all authorized punishments may be imposed in a single case in the maximum amounts.

e. *Punishments imposed on reserve component personnel while on inactive-duty training.* When a punishment under Article 15 amounting to a deprivation of liberty (for example, restriction, correctional custody, extra duties, or arrest in quarters) is imposed on a member of a reserve component during a period of inactive-duty training, the punishment may be served during one or both of the following:

(1) A normal period of inactive-duty training; or

(2) A subsequent period of active duty (not including a period of active duty under Article 2(d)(1), unless such active duty was approved by the Secretary concerned).

Unserved punishments may be carried over to subsequent periods of inactive-duty training or active duty. A sentence to forfeiture of pay may be collected from active duty and inactive-duty training pay during subsequent periods of duty.

f. *Punishments imposed on reserve component personnel when ordered to active duty for disciplinary purposes.* When a punishment under Article 15 is imposed on a member of a reserve component during a period of active duty to which the reservist was ordered pursuant to R.C.M. 204 and which constitutes a deprivation of liberty (for example, restriction, correctional custody, extra duties, or arrest in quarters), the punishment may be served during any or all of the following:

(1) That period of active duty to which the reservist was ordered pursuant to Article 2(d), but only where

the order to active duty was approved by the Secretary concerned;

(2) A subsequent normal period of inactive-duty training; or

(3) A subsequent period of active duty (not including a period of active duty pursuant to R.C.M. 204 which was not approved by the Secretary concerned).

Unserved punishments may be carried over to subsequent periods of inactive-duty training or active duty. A sentence to forfeiture of pay may be collected from active duty and inactive-duty training pay during subsequent periods of duty.

g. *Effective date and execution of punishments.* Reduction and forfeiture of pay, if unsuspended, take effect on the date the commander imposes the punishments. Other punishments, if unsuspended, will take effect and be carried into execution as prescribed by the Secretary concerned.

6. Suspension, mitigation, remission, and setting aside

a. *Suspension.* The nonjudicial punishment authority who imposed nonjudicial punishment, the commander who imposes nonjudicial punishment, or a successor in command over the person punished, may, at any time, suspend any part or amount of the unexecuted punishment imposed and may suspend a reduction in grade or a forfeiture, whether or not executed, subject to the following rules:

(1) An executed punishment of reduction or forfeiture of pay may be suspended only within a period of 4 months after the date of execution.

(2) Suspension of a punishment may not be for a period longer than 6 months from the date of the suspension, and the expiration of the current enlistment or term of service of the Servicemember involved automatically terminates the period of suspension.

(3) Unless the suspension is sooner vacated, suspended portions of the punishment are remitted, without further action, upon the termination of the period of suspension.

(4) Unless otherwise stated, an action suspending a punishment includes a condition that the Servicemember not violate any punitive article of the code. The nonjudicial punishment authority may specify in writing additional conditions of the suspension.

(5) A suspension may be vacated by any nonjudicial punishment authority or commander competent to impose upon the Servicemember concerned punishment of the kind and amount involved in the vacation of suspension. Vacation of suspension may be based only on a violation of the conditions of suspension which occurs within the period of suspension. Before a suspension may be vacated, the Servicemember ordinarily shall be notified and given an opportunity to respond. Although a hearing is not required to vacate a suspension, if the punishment is of the kind set forth in Article 15(e)(1)-(7), the Servicemember should, unless impracticable, be given an opportunity to appear before the officer authorized to vacate suspension of the punishment to present any matters in defense, extenuation, or mitigation of the violation on which the vacation action is to be based. Vacation of a suspended nonjudicial punishment is not itself nonjudicial punishment, and additional action to impose nonjudicial punishment for a violation of a punitive article of the code upon which the vacation action is based is not precluded thereby.

b. *Mitigation.* Mitigation is a reduction in either the quantity or quality of a punishment, its general nature remaining the same. Mitigation is appropriate when the offender's later good conduct merits a reduction in the punishment, or when it is determined that the punishment imposed was disproportionate. The nonjudicial punishment authority who imposes nonjudicial punishment, the commander who imposes nonjudicial punishment, or a successor in command may, at any time, mitigate any part or amount of the unexecuted portion of the punishment imposed. The nonjudicial punishment authority who imposes nonjudicial punishment, the commander who imposes nonjudicial punishment, or a successor in command may also mitigate reduction in grade, whether executed or unexecuted, to forfeiture of pay, but the amount of the forfeiture may not be greater than the amount that could have been imposed by the officer who initially imposed the nonjudicial punishment. Reduction in grade may be mitigated to forfeiture of pay only within 4 months after the date of execution.

When mitigating—

(1) arrest in quarters to restriction;

(2) confinement to correctional custody;

(3) correctional custody or confinement to extra duties or restriction, or both; or

(4) extra duties to restriction, the mitigated punishment may not be for a greater period than the

punishment mitigated. As restriction is the least severe form of deprivation of liberty, it may not be mitigated to a lesser period of another form of deprivation of liberty, as that would mean an increase in the quality of the punishment.

c. *Remission.* Remission is an action whereby any portion of the unexecuted punishment is cancelled. Remission is appropriate under the same circumstances as mitigation. The nonjudicial punishment authority who imposes punishment, the commander who imposes nonjudicial punishment, or a successor in command may, at any time, remit any part or amount of the unexecuted portion of the punishment imposed. The expiration of the current enlistment or term of service of the Servicemember automatically remits any unexecuted punishment imposed under Article 15.

d. *Setting aside.* Setting aside is an action whereby the punishment, or any part or amount thereof, whether executed or unexecuted, is set aside and any property, privileges, or rights affected by the portion of the punishment set aside are restored. The nonjudicial punishment authority who imposed punishment, the commander who imposes nonjudicial punishment, or a successor in command may set aside punishment. The power to set aside punishments and restore rights, privileges, and property affected by the executed portion of a punishment should ordinarily be exercised only when the authority considering the case believes that, under all circumstances of the case, the punishment has resulted in clear injustice. Also, the power to set aside an executed punishment should ordinarily be exercised only within a reasonable time after the punishment has been executed. In this connection, 4 months is a reasonable time in the absence of unusual circumstances.

7. Appeals

a. *In general.* Any Servicemember punished under Article 15 who considers the punishment to be unjust or disproportionate to the offense may appeal through the proper channels to the next superior authority.

b. *Who may act on appeal.* A "superior authority," as prescribed by the Secretary concerned, may act on an appeal. When punishment has been imposed under delegation of a commander's authority to administer nonjudicial punishment (*see* paragraph 2c of this Part), the appeal may not be directed to the commander who delegated the authority.

c. *Format of appeal.* Appeals shall be in writing and may include the appellant's reasons for regarding the punishment as unjust or disproportionate.

d. *Time limit.* An appeal shall be submitted within 5 days of imposition of punishment, or the right to appeal shall be waived in the absence of good cause shown. A Servicemember who has appealed may be required to undergo any punishment imposed while the appeal is pending, except that if action is not taken on the appeal within 5 days after the appeal was submitted, and if the Servicemember so requests, any unexecuted punishment involving restraint or extra duty shall be stayed until action on the appeal is taken.

e. *Legal review.* Before acting on an appeal from any punishment of the kind set forth in Article 15(e)(1)-(7), the authority who is to act on the appeal shall refer the case to a judge advocate or to a lawyer of the Department of Homeland Security for consideration and advice, and may so refer the case upon appeal from any punishment imposed under Article 15. When the case is referred, the judge advocate or lawyer is not limited to an examination of any written matter comprising the record of proceedings and may make any inquiries and examine any additional matter deemed necessary.

f. *Action by superior authority.*

(1) *In general.* In acting on an appeal, the superior authority may exercise the same power with respect to the punishment imposed as may be exercised under Article 15(d) and paragraph 6 of this Part by the officer who imposed the punishment. The superior authority may take such action even if no appeal has been filed.

(2) *Matters considered.* When reviewing the action of an officer who imposed nonjudicial punishment, the superior authority may consider the record of the proceedings, any matters submitted by the Servicemember, any matters considered during the legal review, if any, and any other appropriate matters.

(3) *Additional proceedings.* If the superior authority sets aside a nonjudicial punishment due to a procedural error, that authority may authorize additional proceedings under Article 15, to be conducted by the officer who imposed the nonjudicial punishment, the commander, or a successor in command, for the same offenses involved in the original proceedings. Any punishment imposed as a result of these additional proceedings may be no more severe than that originally imposed.

(4) *Notification.* Upon completion of action by the superior authority, the Servicemember upon whom

punishment was imposed shall be promptly notified of the result.

(5) *Delegation to principal assistant.* If authorized by regulation of the Secretary concerned a superior authority who is a commander exercising general court-martial jurisdiction, or is an officer of general or flag rank in command, may delegate the power under Article 15(e) and this paragraph to a principal assistant.

8. Records of nonjudicial punishment

The content, format, use, and disposition of records of nonjudicial punishment may be prescribed by regulations of the Secretary concerned.

APPENDIX 1
CONSTITUTION OF THE UNITED STATES—1787

We the People of the United States, in Order to form a more perfect Union, establish Justice, insure domestic Tranquility, provide for the common defence, promote the general Welfare, and secure the Blessings of Liberty to ourselves and our Posterity, do ordain and establish this Constitution of the United States of America.

ARTICLE I

Section 1. All legislative Powers herein granted shall be vested in a Congress of the United States, which shall consist of a Senate and a House of Representatives.

Section 2. The House of Representatives shall be composed of Members chosen every second year by the people of the several states, and the Electors in each State shall have the Qualifications requisite for Electors of the most numerous Branch of the State Legislature.

No person shall be a Representative who shall not have attained to the Age of twenty-five Years, and been seven Years a Citizen of the United States, and who shall not, when elected, be an Inhabitant of that State in which he shall be chosen.

[1] Representative and direct Taxes shall be apportioned among the several States which may be included within this Union, according to their respective Numbers, which shall be determined by adding to the whole Number of free Persons, including those bound to Service for a Term of Years, and excluding Indians not taxed, three fifths of all other Persons. The actual Enumeration shall be made within three Years after the first Meeting of the Congress of the United States, and within every subsequent Term of ten Years in such Manner as they shall by Law direct. The Number of Representative shall not exceed one for every thirty Thousand, but each state shall have at Least one Representative; and until such enumeration shall be made, the state of New Hampshire shall be entitled to choose three, Massachusetts eight, Rhode Island and Providence Plantations one, Connecticut five, New York six, New Jersey four, Pennsylvania eight, Delaware one, Maryland six, Virginia ten, North Carolina five, South Carolina five, and Georgia three.

When vacancies happen in the Representation from any state, the Executive Authority thereof shall issue Writs of Election to fill such Vacancies.

The House of Representatives shall choose the Speaker and other officers; and shall have the sole power of Impeachment.

Section 3. [2] The Senate of the United States shall be composed of two Senators from each State chosen by the Legislature thereof, for six Years and each Senator shall have one Vote.

Immediately after they shall be assembled in Consequence of the first Election, they shall be divided as equally as may be into three Classes. The Seats of the Senators of the first Class shall be vacated at the Expiration of the second Year, of the second Class at the Expiration of the fourth Year, and of the third Class at the Expiration of the sixth Year, so that one third may be chosen every second Year; and if Vacancies happen by Resignation, or otherwise during the Recess of the Legislature of any State, the Executive thereof may make temporary Appointments until the next Meeting of the Legislature, which shall then fill such Vacancies.

No person shall be a Senator who shall not have attained to the Age of thirty Years, and been nine Years a Citizen of the United States, who shall not, when elected, be an Inhabitant of that State for which he shall be chosen.

The Vice-President of the United States shall be President of the Senate, but shall have no Vote unless they be equally divided.

The Senate shall choose their other Officers, and also a President pro tempore, in the Absence of the Vice-President, or when he shall exercise the Office of President of the United States.

The Senate shall have the sole Power to try all Impeachments. When sitting for that Purpose, they shall be on Oath or Affirmation. When the President of the United States is tried, the Chief Justice shall preside: And no Person shall be convicted without the Concurrence of two-thirds of the Members present.

Judgement in Cases of Impeachment shall not extend further than to removal from Office and disqualification to hold and enjoy any Office of honor, Trust or Profit under the United States; but the Party convicted shall nevertheless be liable and subject to Indictment, Trial, Judgment and Punishment, according to Law.

Section 4. The Times, Places and Manner of holding Elections for Senators and Representatives, shall be prescribed in each State by the Legislature thereof: but the Congress may at any time by Law make or alter such Regulations, except as to the Places of choosing Senators.

[3] The Congress shall assemble at least once in every Year, and such Meeting shall be on the first Monday in December, unless they shall by Law appoint a different Day.

Section 5. Each House shall be the Judge of the Elections, Returns and Qualifications of its own Members, and a Majority of each shall constitute a Quorum to do Business; but a smaller Number may adjourn from day to day, and may be authorized to compel the Attendance of absent Members, in such Manner, and under such Penalties as each House may provide.

Each House may determine the Rules of its Proceedings, punish its Members for disorderly Behaviour, and with the Concurrence of two-thirds, expel a Member.

Each House shall keep a Journal of its Proceedings, and from time to time publish the same, excepting such Parts as may in their Judgment require Secrecy; and the Yeas and Nays of the Members either House on any question shall, at the Desire of one fifth of those Present be entered on the Journal.

Neither House, during the Session of Congress shall, without the Consent of the other, adjourn for more than three days, nor to any other Place than that in which the two Houses shall be sitting.

Section 6. The Senators and Representatives shall receive a Compensation for their Services, to be ascertained by Law, and paid

---

[1] This clause has been affected by the 14th and 16th amendments.
[2] This section has been affected by the 17th amendment.
[3] This clause has been affected by the 20th amendment.

out of the Treasury of the United States. They shall in all Cases, except Treason, Felony and Breach of the Peace, be privileged from Arrest during their Attendance at the Session of their respective Houses, and in going to and returning from the same; and for any Speech or Debate in either House, they shall not be questioned in any other Place.

No Senator or Representative shall, during the Time for which he is elected, be appointed to any Civil Office under the Authority of the United States, which shall have been created, or the Emoluments whereof shall have been increased during such time; and no Person holding any Office under the United States, shall be a Member of either House during his Continuance in Office.

Section 7. All Bills for raising Revenue shall originate in the House of Representatives; but the Senate may propose or concur with Amendments as on other Bills.

Every Bill which shall have passed the House of Representatives and the Senate, shall, before it become a Law, be presented to the President of the United States; if he approve he shall sign it, but if not he shall return it, with his Objections to that House in which it shall have originated, who shall enter the Objections at large on their Journal, and proceed to reconsider it. If after such Reconsideration two-thirds of that House shall agree to pass the Bill, it shall be sent, together with the Objections, to the other House, by which is shall likewise be reconsidered, and if approved by two-thirds of that House, it shall become a Law. But in all such Cases the Votes of Both Houses shall be determined by Yeas and Nays, and the Names of the Persons voting for and against the Bill shall be entered on the Journal of each House respectively. If any Bill shall not be returned by the President within ten Days (Sundays excepted) after it shall have been presented to him, the Same shall be a Law, in like Manner as if he had signed it, unless the Congress by their Adjournment prevent its Return, in which Case it shall not be a Law.

Every Order, Resolution, or Vote to which the Concurrence of the Senate and House of Representative may be necessary (except on a question of Adjournment) shall be presented to the President of the United States; and before the Same shall take Effect, shall be approved by him, or being disapproved by him, shall be repassed by two thirds of the Senate and House of Representatives, according to the Rules and Limitations prescribed in the Case of a Bill.

Section 8. The Congress shall have Power To lay and collect Taxes, Duties, Imposts and Excises, to pay the Debts and provide for the common Defence and general Welfare of the United States; but all Duties, Imposts and Excises shall be uniform throughout the United States.

To borrow Money on the credit of the United States;

To regulate Commerce with foreign Nations, and among the several States, and with the Indian Tribes;

To establish an uniform rule of Naturalization, and uniform Laws on the subject of Bankruptcies throughout the United States;

To coin Money, regulate the Value thereof, and of foreign coin, and fix the Standard of Weights and Measures;

To provide for the Punishment of counterfeiting the Securities and current Coin of the United States;

To establish Post Offices and post Roads;

To promote the Progress of Science and useful Arts, by securing for limited Times to Authors and Inventors the exclusive Right to their respective Writings and Discoveries;

To constitute Tribunals inferior to the Supreme Court;

To define and punish Piracies and Felonies committed on the high Seas, and Offenses against the Law of Nations;

To declare War, grant Letters of Marque and Reprisal, and make Rules concerning Captures on Land and Water;

To raise and support Armies, but no Appropriation of Money to that use shall be for a longer Term than two Years;

To provide and maintain a Navy;

To make Rules for the Government and Regulation of the land and naval Forces;

To provide for calling forth the Militia to execute the Laws of the Union, suppress Insurrections and repel Invasions;

To provide for organizing, arming, and disciplining, the Militia, and for governing such Part of them as may be employed in the Service of the United States, reserving to the States respectively, the Appointment of the Officers, and the Authority of training the Militia according to the discipline prescribed by Congress;

To exercise exclusive Legislation in all Cases whatsoever, over such District (not exceeding ten Miles square) as may, by Cession of particular States, and the Acceptance of Congress, become the Seat of the Government of the United States, and to exercise like Authority over all Places purchased by the Consent of the Legislature of the States in which the Same shall be, for the Erection of Forts, Magazines, Arsenals, dock-Yards, and other needful Buildings; And

To make all Laws which shall be necessary and proper for carrying into Execution the foregoing Powers, and all other Powers vested by the Constitution in the Government of the United States, or in any Department or Officer thereof.

Section 9. The Migration or Importation of such Persons as any of the States now existing shall think proper to admit, shall not be prohibited by the Congress prior to the Year one thousand eight hundred and eight, but a Tax or duty may be imposed on such Importation, not exceeding ten dollars for each Person.

Privilege of the Writ of Habeas Corpus shall not be suspended, unless when in Cases of Rebellion or Invasion the public Safety require it.

No Bill of Attainder or ex post facto Law shall be passed. No Capitation, or other direct, Tax shall be laid, unless in Proportion to the Census or Enumeration herein before directed to be taken.

No Tax or Duty shall be laid on Articles exported from any State.

No Preference shall be given by any Regulation of Commerce or Revenue to the Ports of one State over those of another: nor shall Vessels bound to, or from, one State, be obliged to enter, clear, or pay Duties in another.

No Money shall be drawn from the Treasury, but in Consequence of Appropriations made by Law; and a regular Statement and Account of the Receipts and Expenditures of all public Money shall be published from time to time.

No Title of Nobility shall be granted by the United States: And no Person holding any Office of Profit or Trust under them, shall, without the Consent of the Congress, accept of any present, Emolument, Office, or Title, of any kind whatever, from any King, Prince, or foreign State.

Section 10. No State shall enter into any Treaty, Alliance, or Confederation; grant Letters of Marque and Reprisal; coin Money;

emit Bills of Credit; make any Thing but gold and silver Coin a Tender in Payment of Debts; pass any Bill of Attainder, ex post facto Law, or Law impairing the Obligation of Contracts, or grant any Title of Nobility.

No State shall, without the Consent of the Congress, lay any Imposts or Duties on Imports or Exports, except what may be absolutely necessary for executing its inspection Laws; and the net Produce of all Duties and Imports, laid by any State on Imports or Exports, shall be for the Use of the Treasury of the United States; all such Laws shall be subject to the Revision and Control of the Congress.

No State shall, without the Consent of Congress, lay any Duty of Tonnage, keep Troops, or Ships of War in time of Peace, enter into any Agreement or Compact with another State, or with a foreign Power, or engage in War, unless actually invaded, or in such imminent Danger as will not admit of delay.

ARTICLE II

Section 1. The executive Power shall be vested in a President of the United States and, together with the Vice President, chosen for the same Term, be elected as follows.

Each State shall appoint, in such Manner as the Legislature thereof may direct, a Number of Electors, equal to the whole Number of Senators and Representatives to which the State may be entitled in the Congress: but no Senator or Representative, or Person holding an Office of Trust or Profit under the United States, shall be appointed an Elector.

[4] The Electors shall meet in their respective States, and vote by Ballot for two Persons, of whom one at least shall not be an Inhabitant of the same State with themselves. And they shall make a List of all the Persons voted for, and of the Number of Votes for each; which List they shall sign and certify, and transmit sealed to the Seat of the Government of the United States, directed to the President of the Senate. The President of the Senate shall, in the Presence of the Senate and House of Representatives, open all the Certificates, and the Votes shall then be counted. The Person having the greatest Number of Votes shall be the President, if such Number be a Majority of the whole Number of Electors appointed; and if there be more than one who have such Majority, and have an equal Number of Electors appointed; and if there be more than one who have such Majority, and have an equal Number of Votes, then the House of Representatives shall immediately choose by Ballot one of them for President; and if no Person have a Majority, then from the five highest on the List the said House shall in like Manner choose the President. But in choosing the President, the Votes shall be taken by States, the Representation from each State having one Vote; a quorum for this Purpose shall consist of a Member or Members from two thirds of the States, and a Majority of all the states shall be necessary to a choice. In every case, after the Choice of the President, the Person having the greatest Number of Votes of the Electors shall be the Vice President. But if there should remain two or more who have equal Votes, the Senate shall choose from them by Ballot the Vice President.

The Congress may determine the Time of the choosing the Electors, and the Day on which they shall give their Votes; which Day shall be the same throughout the United States.

No Person except a natural born Citizen, or a Citizen of the United States, at the time of the Adoption of this Constitution, shall be eligible to the Office of President; neither shall any Person be eligible to that Office who shall not have attained to the Age of thirty five Years, and been fourteen Years a Resident within the United States.

In Case of the Removal of the President from Office, or his Death, Resignation, or Inability to discharge the Powers and Duties of the said Office, the Same shall devolve on the Vice President, and the Congress may by Law provide for the Case of Removal, Death, Resignation or Inability, both of the President and Vice President, declaring what Officer shall then act as Pres dent, and such Officer shall act accordingly, until the Disability be removed, or a President be elected.

The President shall, at stated Times, receive for his Services, a Compensation, which shall neither be increased nor diminished during the Period for which he shall have been elected, and he hall not receive within a Period any other Emolument from the United States, or any of them.

Before he enter on the Execution of his Office, he shall take the following Oath or Affirmation: "I do solemnly swear (or affirm) that I will faithfully execute the Office of President of the United States, and will to the best of my Ability, preserve, protect and defend the Constitution of the United States. "

Section 2. The President shall be Commander in Chief of the Army and Navy of the United States, and of the Militia of the several States, when called into the actual Service of the United States; he may require the Opinion, in writing of the principal Officer in each of the executive Departments, upon any Subject relating to the Duties of their respective Offices, and he shall have power to grant Reprieves and Pardons for Offenses against the United States, except in Cases of Impeachment.

He shall have Power, by and with the Advice and Consent of the Senate, to make Treaties, provided two thirds of the Senators present concur; and he shall nominate, and by and with the Advice and Consent of the Senate, shall appoint Ambassadors, other public Ministers and Consuls, Judges of the supreme Court, and all other Officers of the United States, whose Appointments are not herein otherwise provided for, and which shall be established by Law. But the Congress may by law vest the Appointment of such inferior Officers, as they think proper, in the President alone, in the Courts of Law, or in the Heads of Departments.

The President shall have Power to fill up all Vacancies that may happen during the Recess of the Senate, by granting Commissions which shall expire at the End of their next Session.

Section 3. He shall from time to time give to the Congress Information of the State of the Union, and recommend to their Consideration such Measures as he shall judge necessary and expedient; he may, on extraordinary Occasions, convene both Houses, or either of them, and in Case of Disagreement between them, with Respect to the Time of Adjournment, he may adjourn them to such Time as he shall think proper; he shall receive Ambassadors and other public Ministers; he shall take Care that the Laws be faithfully executed, and shall Commission all the Officers of the United States.

Section 4. The President, Vice President and all civil Officers of the United States, shall be removed from Office on Impeachment for,

[4] This clause has been affected by the 12th amendment.

and Conviction of, Treason, Bribery, or other high Crimes and Misdemeanors.

ARTICLE III

Section 1. The judicial Power of the United States shall be vested in one Supreme Court, and in such inferior courts as the Congress may from time to time ordain and establish. The Judges, both of the Supreme and inferior Courts, shall hold their Offices during good Behavior, and shall, at stated Times, receive for their Services a Compensation which shall not be diminished during their Continuance in Office.

Section 2. The judicial Power shall extend to all Cases, in Law and Equity, arising under this Constitution, the Laws of the United States, and Treaties made, or which shall be made, under their Authority; to all Cases affecting Ambassadors, other public Ministers, and Consuls; to all Cases of admiralty and maritime Jurisdiction; to Controversies to which the United States shall be a Party; to Controversies between two or more States, between a State and Citizens of another State, between Citizens of different States, between Citizens of the same State claiming Lands under Grants of different States, and between a State or the Citizens thereof, and foreign States, Citizens, or Subjects.

In all Cases affecting Ambassadors, other public Ministers and Consuls, and those in which a State shall be a Party, the Supreme Court shall have original Jurisdiction. In all the other Cases before mentioned, the Supreme Court shall have appellate Jurisdiction, both as to Law and Fact, with such Exceptions and under such Regulations as the Congress shall make.

The Trial of all Crimes, except in Cases of Impeachment, shall be by Jury; and such Trial shall be held in the State where the said Crimes shall have been committed; but when not committed within any State the Trial shall be at such Place or Places as the Congress may by Law have directed.

Section 3. Treason against the United States shall consist only in levying War against them, or in adhering to their Enemies, giving them Aid and Comfort. No Person shall be convicted of Treason unless on the Testimony of two Witnesses to the same overt Act, or on Confession in open Court.

The Congress shall have Power to declare the Punishment of Treason, but no Attainder of Treason shall work Corruption of Blood, or Forfeiture except during the Life of the Person attained.

ARTICLE IV

Section 1. Full Faith and Credit shall be given in each State to the public Act, Records, and judicial Proceedings of every other State. And the Congress may, by general Laws, prescribe the Manner in which such Acts, Records, and Proceedings shall be proved, and the Effect thereof.

Section 2. The Citizens of each State shall be entitled to all Privileges and Immunities of Citizens in the several States.

A Person charged in any State with Treason, Felony, or other Crime, who shall flee from Justice, and be found in another State, shall, on Demand of the executive Authority of the State from which he fled, be delivered up, to be removed to the State having Jurisdiction of the Crime.

No Person held to Service or Labor in one State, under the Laws thereof, escaping into another, shall, in Consequence of any Law or Regulation therein, be discharged from such Service or Labor, but shall be delivered up on Claim of the Party to whom such Service or Labor may be due.

Section 3. New States may be admitted by the Congress into this Union; but no new State shall be formed or erected within the Jurisdiction of any other State, nor any State be formed by the Junction of two or more States, or Parts of States, without the Consent of the Legislatures of the States concerned as well as of the Congress.

The Congress shall have Power to dispose of and make all needful Rules and Regulations respecting the Territory or other Property belonging to the United States; and nothing in this Constitution shall be so construed as to Prejudice any Claims of the United States, or of any particular State.

Section 4. The United States shall guarantee to every State in this Union a Republican Form of Government, and shall protect each of them against Invasion; and on Application of the Legislature, or of the Executive (when the Legislature cannot be convened), against domestic Violence.

ARTICLE V

The Congress, whenever two thirds of both House shall deem it necessary, shall propose Amendments to this Constitution, or, on the Application of the Legislatures of two thirds of the several States, shall call a Convention for proposing Amendments, which, in either Case, shall be valid, to all intents and Purposes, as Part of this Constitution, when ratified by the Legislatures of three fourths of the several States, or by Conventions in three fourths thereof, as the one or the other Mode of Ratification may be proposed by the Congress; Provided that no Amendment which may be made prior to the Year One thousand eight hundred and eight shall in any Manner affect the first and fourth Clauses in the Ninth Section of the first Article; and that no State, without its Consent, shall be deprived of its equal Suffrage in the Senate.

ARTICLE VI

All Debts contracted and Engagements entered into, before the Adoption of this Constitution, shall be as valid against the United States under this Constitution, as under the Confederation.

This Constitution, and the Laws of the United States which shall be made in Pursuance thereof, and all Treaties made, or which shall be made, under the Authority of the United States, shall be the supreme Law of the Land; and the Judges in every State shall be bound thereby, Anything in the Constitution or Laws of any State to the Contrary notwithstanding.

The Senators and Representatives before mentioned, and the Members of the several State Legislatures, and all executive and judicial Officers, both of the United States and of the several States, shall be bound, by Oath or Affirmation, to support this Constitution; but no religious Test shall ever be required as a Qualification to any Office or public Trust under the United States.

ARTICLE VII

The Ratification of the Conventions of nine States shall be sufficient for the Establishment of this Constitution between the States so ratifying the Same.

Articles in Addition to, and Amendment of, the Constitution of the United States of America, Proposed by Congress, and Ratified by the Legislatures of the Several States Pursuant to the Fifth Article of the Original Constitution

AMENDMENT I

Congress shall make no law respecting an establishment of religion, or prohibiting the free exercise thereof; or abridging the freedom of speech, or of the press; or the right of the people peaceably to assemble, and to petition the Government for a redress of grievances.

AMENDMENT II

A well-regulated Militia being necessary to the security of a free State, the right of the people to keep and bear Arms, shall not be infringed.

AMENDMENT III

No Soldier shall, in time of peace, be quartered in any house, without the consent of the Owner; nor in time of war, but in a manner to be prescribed by law.

AMENDMENT IV

The right of the people to be secure in their persons, houses, papers, and effects, against unreasonable searches and seizures, shall not be violated; and no Warrants shall issue, but upon probable cause, supported by Oath or affirmation, and particularly describing the place to be searched and the persons or things to be seized.

AMENDMENT V

No person shall be held to answer for a capital, or otherwise infamous, crime, unless on a presentment or indictment of a Grand Jury, except in cases arising in the land or naval forces, or in the Militia, when in actual service, in time of War, or public danger; nor shall any person be subject, for the same offence, to be twice put in jeopardy of life or limb; nor shall be compelled in any criminal case to be a witness against himself nor be deprived of life, liberty, or property, without due process of law; nor shall private property be taken for public use, without just compensation.

AMENDMENT VI

In all criminal prosecutions, the accused shall enjoy the right to a speedy and public trial, by an impartial jury of the State and district wherein the crime shall have been committed, which district shall have been previously ascertained by law; and to be informed of the nature and cause of the accusation; to be confronted with the witnesses against him; to have compulsory process for obtaining witnesses in his favor; and to have the Assistance of Counsel for his defence.

AMENDMENT VII

In Suits at common law, where the value in controversy shall exceed twenty dollars, the right of trial by jury shall be preserved; and no fact, tried by a jury, shall be otherwise reexamined in any Court of the United States than according to the rules of the common law.

AMENDMENT VIII

Excessive bail shall not be required, nor excessive fines imposed, nor cruel and unusual punishment inflicted.

AMENDMENT IX

The enumeration in the Constitution of certain rights shall not be construed to deny or disparage others retained by the people.

AMENDMENT X

The powers not delegated to the United States by the Constitution, nor prohibited by it to the States, are reserved to the States respectively or to the people.

AMENDMENT XI

The Judicial power of the United States shall not be construed to extend to any suit in law or equity, commenced or prosecuted against one of the United States by Citizens of another State or by Citizens or Subjects of any Foreign State.

AMENDMENT XII

The Electors shall meet in their respective States, and vote by ballot for President and Vice-President, one of whom, at least, shall not be an inhabitant of the same State with themselves; they shall name in their ballots the person voted for as President, and in distinct ballots the person voted for as Vice-President; and they shall make distinct lists of all persons voted for as President, and of all persons voted for as Vice-President, and of the number of votes for each, which lists they shall sign, and certify, and transmit, sealed, to the seat of the government of the United States, directed to the President of the Senate; the President of the Senate shall, in the presence of the Senate and the House of Representatives, open all the certificates, and the votes shall then be counted; the person having the greatest number of votes for President shall be the President, if such number be a majority of the whole number of Electors appointed; and if no person have such a majority, then, from the persons having the highest numbers, not exceeding three, on the list of those voted for a President, the House of Representatives shall choose immediately, by ballot, the President. But in choosing the President, the votes shall be taken by States, the representation from each State having one vote; a quorum for this purpose shall consist of a member or members from two-thirds of the States, and a majority of all the States shall be necessary to a choice. And if the House of Representatives shall not choose a President, whenever the right of choice shall devolve upon them, before the fourth day of March next following, the Vice-President shall act as President, as in case of death, or other constitutional disability of the President. The person having the greatest number of votes as Vice-President, shall be the Vice-President, if such number be a majority of the whole number of Electors appointed; and if no person have a majority, then, from the two highest numbers on the list, the Senate shall choose the Vice-President; a quorum for the purpose shall consist of two-thirds of the whole number of Senators; a majority of the whole number shall be necessary to a choice. But no person constitutionally ineligible to the office of President shall be eligible to that of Vice-President of the United States.

AMENDMENT XIII

Section 1. Neither slavery nor involuntary servitude, except as a punishment for crime, whereof the party shall have been duly convicted, shall exist within the United States, or any place subject to their jurisdiction.

Section 2. Congress shall have power to enforce this article by appropriate legislation.

AMENDMENT XIV

Section 1. All persons born or naturalized in the United States, and subject to the jurisdiction thereof, are citizens of the United States and of the State wherein they reside. No State shall make or enforce any law which shall abridge the privileges or immunities of citizens of the United States; nor shall any State deprive any person of life, liberty, or property, without due process of law, nor deny any person within its jurisdiction the equal protection of the laws.

Section 2. Representatives shall be apportioned among the several States according to their respective numbers, counting the whole number of persons in each State, excluding Indians not taxed. But when the right to vote at any election for the choice of electors for President and Vice-President of the United States, Representatives in Congress, the Executive and Judicial officers of a State, or the members of the Legislature thereof, is denied to any of the male inhabitants of such State, being twenty one years of age, and citizens of the United States, or in any way abridged, except for participation in rebellion or other crime, the basis of representation therein shall be reduced in the proportion which the number of such male citizens shall bear to the whole number of male citizens twenty one years of age in such State.

Section 3. No person shall be a Senator or Representative in Congress, or elector of President and Vice President, or hold any office, civil or military, under the United States, or under any State, who, having previously taken an oath, as a Member of Congress, or as an officer of the United States, or as a member of any State legislature, or as an executive or judicial officer of any State, to support the Constitution of the United States, shall have engaged in insurrection or rebellion against the same, or given aid or comfort to the enemies thereof. But Congress may, by a vote of two thirds of each House, remove such disability.

Section 4. The validity of the public debt of the United States, authorized by law, including debts incurred for payment of pensions and bounties for services in suppressing insurrection or rebellion, shall not be questioned. But neither the United States nor any State shall assume or pay any debt or obligation incurred in aid of insurrection or rebellion against the United States, or any claim for the loss or emancipation of any slave; but all such debts, obligations, and claims shall be held illegal and void.

Section 5. The Congress shall have power to enforce, by appropriate legislation, the provisions of this article.

AMENDMENT XV

Section 1. The right of citizens of the United States to vote shall not be denied or abridged by the United States or by any State on account of race, color, or previous condition of servitude.

Section 2. The Congress shall have power to enforce this article by appropriate legislation.

AMENDMENT XVI

The Congress shall have power to lay and collect taxes on incomes, from whatever source derived, without apportionment among the several States and without regard to any census or enumeration.

AMENDMENT XVII

The Senate of the United States shall be composed of two Senators from each State, elected by the people thereof, for six years; and each Senator shall have one vote. The electors in each State shall have the qualifications requisite for electors of the most numerous branch of the State legislatures.

When vacancies happen in the representation of any State in the Senate, the executive authority of such State shall issue writs of election to fill such vacancies: Provided, That the legislature of any State may empower the executive thereof to make temporary appointment until the people fill the vacancies by election as the legislature may direct.

This amendment shall not be so construed as to affect the election or term of any Senator chosen before it becomes valid as part of the Constitution.

AMENDMENT XVIII

[5]

Section 1. After one year from the ratification of this article the manufacture, sale or transportation of intoxicating liquors within, the importation thereof into, or the exportation thereof from the United States and all territory subject to the jurisdiction thereof for beverage purposes is hereby prohibited.

Section 2. The Congress and the several States shall have concurrent power to enforce this article by appropriate legislation.

Section 3. This article shall be inoperative unless it shall have been ratified as an amendment to the Constitution by the legislatures of the several States, as provided in the Constitution, within seven years of the date of the submission hereof to the States by Congress.

[5] This article was replaced by the 21st amendment.

AMENDMENT XIX

The right of citizens of the United States to vote shall not be denied or abridged by the United States or by any State on account of sex.

Congress shall have power to enforce this article by appropriate legislation.

AMENDMENT XX

Section 1. The terms of the President and Vice President shall end at noon on the 20th day of January, and the terms of Senators and Representatives at noon on the 3d day of January, of the years in which such terms would have ended if this article had not been ratified; and the terms of their successors shall then begin.

Section 2. The Congress shall assemble at least once in every year, and such meeting shall begin at noon on the 3d day of January, unless they shall by law appoint a different day.

Section 3. If, at the time fixed for the beginning of the term of the President, the President-elect shall have died, the Vice President-elect shall become President. If a President shall not have been chosen before the time fixed for the beginning of his term, or if the President-elect shall have failed to qualify, then the Vice President-elect shall act as President until a President shall have qualified; and the Congress may by law provide for the case wherein neither a President-elect nor a Vice President-elect shall have qualified, declaring who shall then act as President, or the manner in which one who is to act shall be selected, and such person shall act accordingly until a President or Vice President shall have qualified.

Section 4. The Congress may by law provide for the case of the death of any of the persons from whom the House of Representatives may choose a President whenever the right of choice shall have devolved upon them, and for the case of the death of any of the persons from whom the Senate may choose a Vice President whenever the right of choice shall have devolved upon them.

Section 5. Sections 1 and 2 shall take effect on the 15th day of October following the ratification of this article.

Section 6. This article shall be inoperative unless it shall have been ratified as an amendment to the Constitution by three fourths of the several States within seven years from the date of its submission.

AMENDMENT XXI

Section 1. The eighteenth article of amendment to the Constitution of the United States is hereby repealed.

Section 2. The transportation or importation into any State, Territory, or possession of the United States for delivery or use therein of intoxicating liquors, in violation of the laws thereof, is hereby prohibited.

Section 3. This article shall be inoperative unless it shall have been ratified as an amendment to the Constitution by conventions in the several States, as provided in the Constitution, within seven years from the date of the submission hereof to the States by the Congress.

AMENDMENT XXII

Section 1. No person shall be elected to the office of the President more than twice, and no person who has held the office of President, or acted as President, for more than two years of a term to which some other person was elected President shall be elected to the office of the President more than once. But this Article shall not apply to any person holding the office of President when this Article was proposed by the Congress, and shall not prevent any person who may be holding the office of President, or acting as President, during the term within which his Article becomes operative from holding the office of President or acting as President during the remainder of such term.

Section 2. This article shall be inoperative unless it shall have been ratified as an amendment to the Constitution by the legislatures of three-fourths of the several States within seven years from the date of its submission to the States by the Congress.

AMENDMENT XXIII

Section 1. The District constituting the seat of Government of the United States shall appoint in such manner as the Congress may direct:

A number of electors of President and Vice President equal to the whole number of Senators and Representative in Congress to which the District would be entitled if it were a State, but in no event more than the least populous State; they shall be considered, for the purposes of the election of President and Vice President, to be electors appointed by a State; and they shall meet in the District and perform such duties as provided by the twelfth article of amendment.

Section 2. The Congress shall have power to enforce this article by appropriate legislation.

AMENDMENT XXIV

Section 1. The right of citizens of the United States to vote in any primary or other election for President or Vice President, for electors for President or Vice President, or for Senator or Representative in Congress, shall not be denied or abridged by the United States or any State by reason of failure to pay any poll tax or other tax.

Section 2. The Congress shall have power to enforce this article by appropriate legislation.

AMENDMENT XXV

Section 1. In case of the removal of the President from office or of his death or resignation, the Vice President shall become President.

Section 2. Whenever there is a vacancy in the office of the Vice President, the President shall nominate a Vice President who shall take office upon confirmation by a majority vote of both Houses of Congress.

Section 3. Whenever the President transmits to the President pro tempore of the Senate and the Speakers of the House of Representatives his written declaration that he is unable to discharge the powers and duties of his office, and until he transmits to them a written declaration to the contrary, such powers and duties shall be discharged by the Vice President as Acting President.

Section 4. Whenever the Vice President and a majority of either the principal officers of the Executive departments or of such other body as Congress may by law provide, transmit to the President pro tempore of the Senate and the Speaker of the House of Representatives their written declaration that the President is unable to discharge the powers and duties of his office, the Vice President shall immediately assume the powers and duties of the office as Acting President.

Thereafter, when the President transmits to the President pro tempore of the Senate and the Speaker of the House of Representatives his written declaration that no inability exists, he shall resume the powers and duties of his office unless the Vice President and a majority of either principal officers of the executive department or of such other body as Congress may by law provide, transmit within four days to the President pro tempore of the Senate and the Speaker of the House of Representatives their written declaration that the President is unable to discharge the powers and duties of his office. Thereupon Congress shall decide the issue, assembling within forty-eight hours for that purpose if not in session. If the Congress, within twenty one days after Congress is required to assemble, determines by two thirds vote of both Houses that the President is unable to discharge the powers and duties of his office, the Vice President shall continue to discharge the same as Acting President; otherwise, the President shall resume the powers and duties of his office.

AMENDMENT XXVI

Section 1. The right of citizens of the United States, who are eighteen years of age or older, to vote shall not be denied or abridged by the United States or by any State on account of age.

Section 2. The Congress shall have the power to enforce this article by appropriate legislation.

AMENDMENT XXVII

No law, varying the compensation for the services of the Senators and Representatives, shall take effect, until an election of Representatives shall have intervened.

APPENDIX 2
UNIFORM CODE OF MILITARY JUSTICE

Note: Text contains those laws within chapter 47 of title 10, United States Code, that are in effect as of December 27, 2023. It does not include any amendments made after the enactment of the James M. Inhofe National Defense Authorization Act for Fiscal Year 2023, Pub. L. No. 117-263, 136 Stat. 2395 (2022). While this publication does not represent the official version of any Federal law, substantial efforts have been made to ensure the accuracy of its contents. The official and most up-to-date version of chapter 47 can be found in the United States Code as published by the Office of the Law Revision Counsel and available online at https://uscode.house.gov.

CHAPTER 47. UNIFORM CODE OF MILITARY JUSTICE

SUBCHAPTER I—GENERAL PROVISIONS

§801. Art. 1. Definitions

In this chapter (the Uniform Code of Military justice):

(1) The term "Judge Advocate General" means, severally, the Judge Advocates General of the Army, Navy, and Air Force and, except when the Coast Guard is operating as a service in the Navy, an official designated to serve as Judge Advocate General of the Coast Guard by the Secretary of Homeland Security.

(2) The Navy, the Marine Corps, and the Coast Guard when it is operating as a service in the Navy, shall be considered as one armed force.

(3) The term "commanding officer" includes only commissioned officers.

(4) The term "officer in charge" means a member of the Navy, the Marine Corps, or the Coast Guard designated as such by appropriate authority.

(5) The term "superior commissioned officer" means a commissioned officer superior in rank or command.

(6) The term "cadet" means a cadet of the United States Military Academy, the United States Air Force Academy, or the United States Coast Guard Academy.

(7) The term "midshipman" means a midshipman of the United States Naval Academy and any other midshipman on active duty in the naval service.

(8) The term "military" refers to any or all of the armed forces.

(9) The term "accuser" means a person who signs and swears to charges, any person who directs that charges nominally be signed and sworn to by another, and any other person who has an interest other than an official interest in the prosecution of the accused.

(10) The term "military judge" means a judge advocate designated under section 826(c) of this title (article 26(c)) who is detailed under section 826(a) or section 830a of this title (article 26(a) or 30a)).

(11) The term 'military magistrate' means a commissioned officer certified for duty as a military magistrate in accordance with section 826a of this title (article 26a).

(12) The term "legal officer" means any commissioned officer of the Navy, Marine Corps, or Coast Guard designated to perform legal duties for a command.

(13) The term "judge advocate" means—

(A) an officer of the Judge Advocate General's Corps of the Army, the Navy, or the Air Force;

(B) an officer of the Marine Corps who is designated as a judge advocate; or

(C) a commissioned officer of the Coast Guard designated for special duty (law).

(14) The term "record", when used in connection with the proceedings of a court-martial, means—

(A) an official written transcript, written summary, or other writing relating to the proceedings; or

(B) an official audiotape, videotape, or similar material from which sound, or sound and visual images, depicting the proceedings may be reproduced.

(15) The term "classified information" means (A) any information or material that has been determined by an official of the United States pursuant to law, an Executive order, or regulation to require protection against unauthorized disclosure for reasons of national security, and (B) any restricted data, as defined in section 11(y) of the Atomic Energy Act of 1954 (42 U.S.C. 2014(y)).

(16) The term "national security" means the national defense and foreign relations of the United States.

(17) The term "covered offense" means—

(A) an offense under section 917a (article 117a), section 918 (article 118), section 919 (article 119), section 119a (article 119a), section 920 (article 120), section 920a (article 120a), section 920b (article 120b), section 920c (article 120c), section 925 (article 125), section 928b (article 128b), section 930 (article 130), section 932 (article 132), or the standalone offense of child pornography punishable under section 934 (article 134) of this title;

(B) a conspiracy to commit an offense specified in subparagraph (A) as punishable under section 881 of this title (article 81);

(C) a solicitation to commit an offense specified in subparagraph (A) as punishable under section 882 of this title (article 82); or

(D) an attempt to commit an offense specified in subparagraph (A), (B), or (C) as punishable under section 880 of this title (article 80).

(18) The term "special trial counsel" means a judge advocate detailed as a special trial counsel in accordance with section 824a of this title (article 24a) and includes a judge advocate appointed as a lead special trial counsel pursuant to section 1044f(a)(2) of this title.

Office of Law Revision Counsel, United States Code, *18 USC 801: Article 1. Definitions* (Sep. 13, 2023, 5:17 PM), https://uscode.house.gov/view.xhtml?req=(title:10%20section:801%20edition:prelim) provides:

"Pub. L. 117-263, div, title V, § 541(b), Dec. 23, 2022, 136 Stat. 2580, provided that, effective Jan. 1, 2025, and applicable with respect to offenses that occur after that date, paragraph (17)(A) of this second is amended:

(1) by striking "or"; and

(2) by striking "of this title" and inserting ", or the standalone offense of sexual harassment punishable under section 934 (article 134) of this title in each instance in which a formal complaint is made and such formal complaint is substantiated in accordance with regulations prescribed by the Secretary concerned."

§802. Art. 2. Persons subject to this chapter

(a) The following persons are subject to this chapter:

(1) Members of a regular component of the armed forces, including those awaiting discharge after expiration of their terms of enlistment; volunteers from the time of their muster or acceptance into the armed forces; inductees from the time of their actual induction into the armed forces; and other persons lawfully called or ordered into, or to duty in or for training in, the armed forces, from the dates when they are required by the terms of the call or order to obey it.

(2) Cadets, aviation cadets, and midshipmen.

(3)(A) While on inactive-duty training and during any of the periods specified in subparagraph (B)—

(i) members of a reserve component; and

(ii) members of the Army National Guard of the United States or the Air National Guard of the United States, but only when in Federal service.

(B) The periods referred to in subparagraph (A) are the following:

(i) Travel to and from the inactive-duty training site of the member, pursuant to orders or regulations.

(ii) Intervals between consecutive periods of inactive-duty training on the same day, pursuant to orders or regulations.

(iii) Intervals between inactive-duty training on consecutive days, pursuant to orders or regulations.

(4) Retired members of a regular component of the armed forces who are entitled to pay.

(5) Retired members of a reserve component who are receiving hospitalization from an armed force.

(6) Members of the Fleet Reserve and Fleet Marine Corps Reserve.

(7) Persons in custody of the armed forces serving a sentence imposed by a court-martial.

(8) Members of the National Oceanic and Atmospheric Administration, Public Health Service, and other organizations, when assigned to and serving with the armed forces.

(9) Prisoners of war in custody of the armed forces.

(10) In time of declared war or a contingency operation, persons serving with or accompanying an armed force in the field.

(11) Subject to any treaty or agreement to which the United States is or may be a party or to any accepted rule of international law, persons serving with, employed by, or accompanying the armed forces outside the United States and outside the Commonwealth of Puerto Rico, Guam, and the Virgin Islands.

(12) Subject to any treaty or agreement to which the United States is or may be a party or to any accepted rule of international law, persons within an area leased by or otherwise reserved or acquired for the use of the United States which is under the control of the Secretary concerned and which is outside the United States and outside the Commonwealth of Puerto Rico, Guam, and the Virgin Islands.

(13) Individuals belonging to one of the eight categories enumerated in Article 4 of the Convention Relative to the Treatment of Prisoners of War, done at Geneva August 12, 1949 (6 UST 3316), who violate the law of war.

(b) The voluntary enlistment of any person who has the capacity to understand the significance of enlisting in the armed forces shall be valid for purposes of jurisdiction under subsection (a) and a change of status from civilian to member of the armed forces shall be effective upon the taking of the oath of enlistment.

(c) Notwithstanding any other provision of law, a person serving with an armed force who—

(1) submitted voluntarily to military authority;

(2) met the mental competency and minimum age qualifications of sections 504 and 505 of this title at the time of voluntary submission to military authority;

(3) received military pay or allowances; and

(4) performed military duties;

is subject to this chapter until such person's active service has been terminated in accordance with law or regulations promulgated by the Secretary concerned.

(d)(1) A member of a reserve component who is not on active duty and who is made the subject of proceedings under section 815 (article 15) or section 830 (article 30) with respect to an offense against this chapter may be ordered to active duty involuntarily for the purpose of—

(A) a preliminary hearing under section 832 of this title (article 32);

(B) trial by court-martial; or

(C) nonjudicial punishment under section 815 of this title (article 15).

(2) A member of a reserve component may not be ordered to active duty under paragraph (1) except with respect to an offense committed while the member was—

(A) on active duty; or

(B) on inactive-duty training, but in the case of members of the Army National Guard of the United States or the Air National Guard of the United States only when in Federal service.

(3) Authority to order a member to active duty under paragraph (1) shall be exercised under regulations prescribed by the President.

(4) A member may be ordered to active duty under paragraph (1) only by a person empowered to convene general courts-martial in a regular component of the armed forces.

(5) A member ordered to active duty under paragraph (1), unless the order to active duty was approved by the Secretary concerned, may not—

(A) be sentenced to confinement; or

(B) be required to serve a punishment consisting of any restriction on liberty during a period other than a period of inactive-duty training or active duty (other than active duty ordered under paragraph (1)).

(e) The provisions of this section are subject to section 876b(d)(2) of this title (article 76b(d)(2)).

§803. Art. 3. Jurisdiction to try certain personnel

(a) Subject to section 843 of this title (article 43), a person who is in a status in which the person is subject to this chapter and who committed an offense against this chapter while formerly in a status in which the person was subject to this chapter is not relieved from amenability to the jurisdiction of this chapter for that offense by reason of a termination of that person's former status.

(b) Each person discharged from the armed forces who is later charged with having fraudulently obtained his discharge is, subject to section 843 of this title (article 43), subject to trial by court-martial on that charge and is after apprehension subject to this chapter while in the custody of the armed forces for that trial. Upon conviction of that charge he is subject to trial by court-martial for all offenses under this chapter committed before the fraudulent discharge.

(c) No person who has deserted from the armed forces may be relieved from amenability to the jurisdiction of this chapter by virtue of a separation from any later period of service.

(d) A member of a reserve component who is subject to this chapter is not, by virtue of the termination of a period of active duty or inactive-duty training, relieved from amenability to the jurisdiction of this chapter for an offense against this chapter committed during such period of active duty or inactive-duty training.

§804. Art. 4. Dismissed officer's right to trial by court-martial

(a) If any commissioned officer, dismissed by order of the President, makes a written application for trial by court-martial, setting forth, under oath, that he has been wrongfully dismissed, the President, as soon as practicable, shall convene a general court-martial to try that officer on the charges on which he was dismissed. A court-martial so convened has jurisdiction to try the dismissed officer on those charges, and he shall be considered to have waived the right to plead any statute of limitations applicable to any offense with which he is charged. The court-martial may, as part of its sentence, adjudge the affirmance of the dismissal, but if the court-martial acquits the accused or if the sentence adjudged, as finally approved or affirmed, does not include dismissal or death, the Secretary concerned shall substitute for the dismissal ordered by the President a form of discharge authorized for administrative issue.

(b) If the President fails to convene a general court-martial within six months from the presentation of an application for trial under this article, the Secretary concerned shall substitute for the dismissal ordered by the President a form of discharge authorized for administrative issue.

(c) If a discharge is substituted for a dismissal under this article, the President alone may reappoint the officer to such commissioned grade and with such rank as, in the opinion of the President, that former officer would have attained had he not been dismissed. The reappointment of such a former officer shall be without regard to the existence of a vacancy and shall affect the promotion status of other officers only insofar as the President may direct. All time between the dismissal and the reappointment shall be considered as actual service for all purposes, including the right to pay and allowances.

(d) If an officer is discharged from any armed force by administrative action or is dropped from the rolls by order of the President, he has no right to trial under this article.

§805. Art. 5. Territorial applicability of this chapter

This chapter applies in all places.

§806. Art. 6. Judge advocates and legal officers

(a) The assignment for duty of judge advocates of the Army, Navy, Air Force, and Coast Guard shall be made upon the recommendation of the Judge Advocate General of the armed force of which they are members. The assignment for duty of judge advocates of the Marine Corps shall be made by direction of the Commandant of the Marine Corps. The Judge Advocates General, and within the Marine Corps the Staff Judge Advocate to the Commandant of the Marine Corps, or senior members of their staffs, shall make frequent inspections in the field in supervision of the administration of military justice.

(b) Convening authorities shall at all times communicate directly with their staff judge advocates or legal officers in matters relating to the administration of military justice; and the staff judge advocate or legal officer of any command is entitled to communicate directly with the staff judge advocate or legal officer of a superior or subordinate command, or with the Judge Advocate General.

(c)(1) No person who, with respect to a case, serves in a capacity specified in paragraph (2) may later serve as a staff judge advocate or legal officer to any reviewing or convening authority upon the same case.

(2) The capacities referred to in paragraph (1) are, with respect to the case involved, any of the following:

(A) Preliminary hearing officer, court member, military judge, military magistrate, or appellate judge.

(B) Counsel who have acted in the same case or appeared in any proceeding before a military judge, military magistrate, preliminary hearing officer, or appellate court.

(d)(1) A judge advocate who is assigned or detailed to perform the functions of a civil office in the Government of the United States under section 973(b)(2)(B) of this title may perform such duties as may be requested by the agency concerned, including representation of the United States in civil and criminal cases.

(2) The Secretary of Defense, and the Secretary of Homeland Security with respect to the Coast Guard when it is not operating as a service in the Navy, shall prescribe regulations providing that reimbursement may be a condition of assistance by judge advocates assigned or detailed under section 973(b)(2)(B) of this title.

§806a. Art. 6a. Investigation and disposition of matters pertaining to the fitness of military judges

(a) The President shall prescribe procedures for the investigation and disposition of charges, allegations, or information pertaining to the fitness of a military appellate judge, military judge, or military magistrate to perform the duties of the position involved. To the extent practicable, the procedures shall be uniform for all armed forces.

(b) The President shall transmit a copy of the procedures prescribed pursuant to this section to the Committee on Armed Services of the Senate and the Committee on Armed Services of the House of Representatives.

§806b. Art. 6b. Rights of the victim of an offense under this chapter

(a) RIGHTS OF A VICTIM OF AN OFFENSE UNDER THIS CHAPTER.—A victim of an offense under this chapter has the following rights:

(1) The right to be reasonably protected from the accused.

(2) The right to reasonable, accurate, and timely notice of any of the following:

(A) A public hearing concerning the continuation of confinement prior to trial of the accused.

(B) A preliminary hearing under section 832 of this title (article 32) relating to the offense.

(C) A court-martial relating to the offense.

(D) A post-trial motion, filing, or hearing that may address the finding or sentence of a court-martial with respect to the accused, unseal privileged or private information of the victim, or result in the release of the accused.

(E) A public proceeding of the service clemency and parole board relating to the offense.

(F) The release or escape of the accused, unless such notice may endanger the safety of any person.

(3) The right not to be excluded from any public hearing or proceeding described in paragraph (2) unless the military judge or preliminary hearing officer, as applicable, after receiving clear and convincing evidence, determines that testimony by the victim of an offense under this chapter would be materially altered if the victim heard other testimony at that hearing or proceeding.

(4) The right to be reasonably heard at any of the following:

(A) A public hearing concerning the continuation of confinement prior to trial of the accused.

(B) A sentencing hearing relating to the offense.

(C) A public proceeding of the service clemency and parole board relating to the offense.

(5) The reasonable right to confer with the counsel representing the Government at any proceeding described in paragraph (2).

(6) The right to receive restitution as provided in law.

(7) The right to proceedings free from unreasonable delay.

(8) The right to be informed in a timely manner of any plea agreement, separation-in-lieu-of-trial agreement, or non-prosecution agreement relating to the offense, unless providing such information would jeopardize a law enforcement proceeding or would violate the privacy concerns of an individual other than the accused.

(9) The right to be treated with fairness and with respect for the dignity and privacy of the victim of an offense under this chapter.

(b) VICTIM OF AN OFFENSE UNDER THIS CHAPTER DEFINED.—In this section, the term "victim of an offense under this chapter" means an individual who has suffered direct physical, emotional, or pecuniary harm as a result of the commission of an offense under this chapter.

(c) APPOINTMENT OF INDIVIDUALS TO ASSUME RIGHTS FOR CERTAIN VICTIMS.—In the case of a victim of an offense under this chapter who is under 18 years of age (but who is not a member of the armed forces), incompetent, incapacitated, or deceased, the legal guardians of the victim or the representatives of the victim's estate, family members, or any other person designated as suitable by the military judge, may assume the rights of the victim under this section. However, in no event may the individual so designated be the accused.

(d) RULE OF CONSTRUCTION.—Nothing in this section (article) shall be construed—

(1) to authorize a cause of action for damages;

(2) to create, to enlarge, or to imply any duty or obligation to any victim of an offense under this chapter or other person for the breach of which the United States or any of its officers or employees could be held liable in damages; or

(3) to impair the exercise of discretion under sections 830 and 834 of this title (articles 30 and 34).

(e) ENFORCEMENT BY COURT OF CRIMINAL APPEALS.—

(1) If the victim of an offense under this chapter believes that a preliminary hearing ruling under section 832 of this title (article 32) or a court-martial ruling violates the rights of the victim afforded by a section (article) or rule specified in paragraph (4), the victim may petition the Court of Criminal Appeals for a writ of mandamus to require the preliminary hearing officer or the court-martial to comply with the section (article) or rule.

(2) If the victim of an offense under this chapter is subject to an order to submit to a deposition, notwithstanding the availability of the victim to testify at the court-martial trying the accused for the offense, the victim may petition the Court of Criminal Appeals for a writ of mandamus to quash such order.

(3)(A) A petition for a writ of mandamus described in this subsection shall be forwarded directly to the Court of Criminal Appeals, by such means as may be prescribed by the President, subject to section 830a of this title (article 30a).

(B) To the extent practicable, a petition for a writ of mandamus described in this subsection shall have priority over all proceedings before the Court of Criminal Appeals.

(C) Review of any decision of the Court of Criminal Appeals on a petition for a writ of mandamus described in this subsection shall have priority in the Court of Appeals for the Armed Forces, as determined under the rules of the Court of Appeals for the Armed Forces.

(4) Paragraph (1) applies with respect to the protections afforded by the following:

(A) This section (article).

(B) Section 832 (article 32) of this title.

(C) Military Rule of Evidence 412, relating to the admission of evidence regarding a victim's sexual background.

(D) Military Rule of Evidence 513, relating to the psychotherapist-patient privilege.

(E) Military Rule of Evidence 514, relating to the victim advocate-victim privilege.

(F) Military Rule of Evidence 615, relating to the exclusion of witnesses.

(f) COUNSEL FOR ACCUSED INTERVIEW OF VICTIM OF ALLEGED OFFENSE.—

(1) Upon notice by counsel for the Government to counsel for the accused of the name of an alleged victim of an offense under this chapter who counsel for the Government intends to call as a witness at a proceeding under this chapter, counsel for the accused shall make any request to interview the victim through the Special Victim's Counsel or other counsel for the victim, if applicable.

(2) If requested by an alleged victim who is subject to a request for interview under paragraph (1), any interview of the victim by counsel for the accused shall take place only in the presence of the counsel for the Government, a counsel for the victim, or, if applicable, a victim advocate.

SUBCHAPTER II—APPREHENSION AND RESTRAINT

§807. Art. 7. Apprehension

(a) Apprehension is the taking of a person into custody.

(b) Any person authorized under regulations governing the armed forces to apprehend persons subject to this chapter or to trial thereunder may do so upon reasonable belief that an offense has been committed and that the person apprehended committed it.

(c) Commissioned officers, warrant officers, petty officers, and noncommissioned officers have authority to quell quarrels, frays, and disorders among persons subject to this chapter and to apprehend persons subject to this chapter who take part therein.

§808. Art. 8. Apprehension of deserters

Any civil officer having authority to apprehend offenders under the laws of the United States or of a State, Commonwealth, possession, or the District of Columbia may summarily apprehend a deserter from the armed forces and deliver him into the custody of those forces.

§809. Art. 9. Imposition of restraint

(a) Arrest is the restraint of a person by an order, not imposed as a punishment for an offense, directing him to remain within certain specified limits. Confinement is the physical restraint of a person.

(b) An enlisted member may be ordered into arrest or confinement by any commissioned officer by an order, oral or written, delivered in person or through other persons subject to this chapter. A commanding officer may authorize warrant officers, petty officers, or noncommissioned officers to order enlisted members of his command or subject to his authority into arrest or confinement.

(c) A commissioned officer, a warrant officer, or a civilian subject to this chapter or to trial thereunder may be ordered into arrest or confinement only by a commanding officer to whose authority he is subject, by an order, oral or written, delivered in person or by another commissioned officer. The authority to order such persons into arrest or confinement may not be delegated.

(d) No person may be ordered into arrest or confinement except for probable cause.

(e) Nothing in this article limits the authority of persons authorized to apprehend offenders to secure the custody of an alleged offender until proper authority may be notified.

§810. Art. 10. Restraint of persons charged

(a) IN GENERAL.—

(1) Subject to paragraph (2), any person subject to this chapter who is charged with an offense under this chapter may be ordered into arrest or confinement as the circumstances require.

(2) When a person subject to this chapter is charged only with an offense that is normally tried by summary court-martial, the person ordinarily shall not be ordered into confinement.

(b) NOTIFICATION TO ACCUSED AND RELATED PROCEDURES.—

(1) When a person subject to this chapter is ordered into arrest or confinement before trial, immediate steps shall be taken—

(A) to inform the person of the specific offense of which the person is accused; and

(B) to try the person or to dismiss the charges and release the person.

(2) To facilitate compliance with paragraph (1), the President shall prescribe regulations setting forth procedures relating to referral for trial, including procedures for prompt forwarding of the charges and specifications and, if applicable, the preliminary hearing report submitted under section 832 of this title (article 32).

§811. Art. 11. Reports and receiving of prisoners

(a) No provost marshal, commander of a guard, or master at arms may refuse to receive or keep any prisoner committed to his charge by a commissioned officer of the armed forces, when the committing officer furnishes a statement, signed by him, of the offense charged against the prisoner.

(b) Every commander of a guard or master at arms to whose charge a prisoner is committed shall, within twenty-four hours after that commitment or as soon as he is relieved from guard, report to the commanding officer the name of the prisoner, the offense charged against him, and the name of the person who ordered or authorized the commitment.

§812. Art. 12. Prohibition of confinement of members of the armed forces with enemy prisoners and certain others

No member of the armed forces may be placed in confinement in immediate association with—

(1) enemy prisoners; or

(2) other individuals—

(A) who are detained under the law of war and are foreign nationals; and

(B) who are not members of the armed forces.

§813. Art. 13. Punishment prohibited before trial

No person, while being held for trial, may be subjected to punishment or penalty other than arrest or confinement upon the charges pending against him, nor shall the arrest or confinement imposed upon him be any more rigorous than the circumstances require to insure his presence, but he may be subjected to minor punishment during that period for infractions of discipline.

§814. Art. 14. Delivery of offenders to civil authorities

(a) Under such regulations as the Secretary concerned may prescribe, a member of the armed forces accused of an offense against civil authority may be delivered, upon request, to the civil authority for trial.

(b) When delivery under this article is made to any civil authority of a person undergoing sentence of a court-martial, the delivery, if followed by conviction in a civil tribunal, interrupts the execution of the sentence of the court-martial, and the offender after having answered to the civil authorities for his offense shall, upon the request of competent military authority, be returned to military custody for the completion of his sentence.

SUBCHAPTER III. NON-JUDICIAL PUNISHMENT

§815. Art. 15. Commanding officer's non-judicial punishment

(a) Under such regulations as the President may prescribe, and under such additional regulations as may be prescribed by the Secretary concerned, limitations may be placed on the powers granted by this article with respect to the kind and amount of punishment authorized, the categories of commanding officers and warrant officers exercising command authorized to exercise those powers, the applicability of this article to an accused who demands trial by court-martial, and the kinds of courts-martial to which the case may be referred upon such a demand. However, except in the case of a member attached to or embarked in a vessel, punishment may not be imposed upon any member of the armed forces under this article if the member has, before the imposition of such punishment, demanded trial by court-martial in lieu of such punishment. Under similar regulations, rules may be prescribed with respect to the suspension of punishments authorized hereunder. If authorized by regulations of the Secretary concerned, a commanding officer exercising general court-martial jurisdiction or an officer of general or flag rank in command may delegate his powers under this article to a principal assistant.

(b) Subject to subsection (a), any commanding officer may, in addition to or in lieu of admonition or reprimand, impose one or more of the following disciplinary punishments for minor offenses without the intervention of a court-martial—

(1) upon officers of his command—

(A) restriction to certain specified limits, with or without suspension from duty, for not more than 30 consecutive days;

(B) if imposed by an officer exercising general court-martial jurisdiction or an officer of general or flag rank in command—

(i) arrest in quarters for not more than 30 consecutive days;

(ii) forfeiture of not more than one-half of one month's pay per month for two months;

(iii) restriction to certain specified limits, with or without suspension from duty, for not more than 60 consecutive days;

(iv) detention of not more than one-half of one month's pay per month for three months;

(2) upon other personnel of his command—

(A) if imposed upon a person attached to or embarked in a vessel, confinement for not more than three consecutive days;

(B) correctional custody for not more than seven consecutive days;

(C) forfeiture of not more than seven days' pay;

(D) reduction to the next inferior pay grade, if the grade from which demoted is within the promotion authority of the officer imposing the reduction or any officer subordinate to the one who imposes the reduction;

(E) extra duties, including fatigue or other duties, for not more than 14 consecutive days;

(F) restriction to certain specified limits, with or without suspension from duty, for not more than 14 consecutive days;

(G) detention of not more than 14 days' pay;

(H) if imposed by an officer of the grade of major or lieutenant commander, or above—

(i) the punishment authorized under clause (A);

(ii) correctional custody for not more than 30 consecutive days;

(iii) forfeiture of not more than one-half of one month's pay per month for two months;

(iv) reduction to the lowest or any intermediate pay grade, if the grade from which demoted is within the promotion authority of the officer imposing the reduction or any officer subordinate to the one who imposes the reduction, but an enlisted member in a pay grade above E–4 may not be reduced more than two pay grades;

(v) extra duties, including fatigue or other duties, for not more than 45 consecutive days;

(vi) restrictions to certain specified limits, with or without suspension from duty, for not more than 60 consecutive days;

(vii) detention of not more than one-half of one month's pay per month for three months. Detention of pay shall be for a stated period of not more than one year but if the offender's term of service expires earlier, the detention shall terminate upon that expiration. No two or more of the punishments of arrest in quarters, confinement, correctional custody, extra duties, and restriction may be combined to run consecutively in the maximum amount imposable for each.

Whenever any of those punishments are combined to run consecutively, there must be an apportionment. In addition, forfeiture of pay may not be combined with detention of pay without an apportionment. For the purposes of this subsection, "correctional custody" is the physical restraint of a person during duty or nonduty hours and may include extra duties, fatigue duties, or hard labor. If practicable, correctional custody will not be served in immediate association with persons awaiting trial or held in confinement pursuant to trial by court-martial.

(c) An officer in charge may impose upon enlisted members assigned to the unit of which he is in charge such of the punishments authorized under subsection (b)(2)(A)–(G) as the Secretary concerned may specifically prescribe by regulation.

(d) The officer who imposes the punishment authorized in subsection (b), or his successor in command, may, at any time, suspend probationally any part or amount of the unexecuted punishment imposed and may suspend probationally a reduction in grade or a forfeiture imposed under subsection (b), whether or not executed. In addition, he may, at any time, remit or mitigate any part or amount of the unexecuted punishment imposed and may set aside in whole or in part the punishment, whether executed or unexecuted, and restore all rights, privileges, and property affected. He may also mitigate reduction in grade to forfeiture or detention of pay. When mitigating—

(1) arrest in quarters to restriction;

(2) confinement to correctional custody;

(3) correctional custody or confinement to extra duties or restriction, or both; or

(4) extra duties to restriction; the mitigated punishment shall not be for a greater period than the punishment mitigated. When mitigating forfeiture of pay to detention of pay, the amount of the detention shall not be greater than the amount of the forfeiture. When mitigating reduction in grade to forfeiture or detention of pay, the amount of the forfeiture or detention shall not be greater than the amount that could have been imposed initially under this article by the officer who imposed the punishment mitigated.

(e) A person punished under this article who considers his punishment unjust or disproportionate to the offense may, through the proper channel, appeal to the next superior authority. The appeal shall be promptly forwarded and decided, but the person punished may in the meantime be required to undergo the punishment adjudged. The superior authority may exercise the same powers with respect to the punishment imposed as may be exercised under subsection (d) by the officer who imposed the punishment. Before acting on an appeal from a punishment of—

(1) arrest in quarters for more than seven days;

(2) correctional custody for more than seven days;

(3) forfeiture of more than seven days' pay;

(4) reduction of one or more pay grades from the fourth or a higher pay grade;

(5) extra duties for more than 14 days;

(6) restriction for more than 14 days; or

(7) detention of more than 14 days' pay; the authority who is to act on the appeal shall refer the case to a judge advocate or a lawyer of the Department of Homeland Security for consideration and advice, and may so refer the case upon appeal from any punishment imposed under subsection (b).

(f) The imposition and enforcement of disciplinary punishment under this article for any act or omission is not a bar to trial by court-martial for a serious crime or offense growing out of the same act or omission, and not properly punishable under this article; but the fact that a disciplinary punishment has been enforced may be shown by the accused upon trial, and when so shown shall be considered in determining the measure of punishment to be adjudged in the event of a finding of guilty.

(g) The Secretary concerned may, by regulation, prescribe the form of records to be kept of proceedings under this article and may also prescribe that certain categories of those proceedings shall be in writing.

SUBCHAPTER IV. COURT-MARTIAL JURISDICTION

§816. Art. 16. Courts-martial classified

(a) IN GENERAL.—The three kinds of courts-martial in each of the armed forces are the following:

(1) General courts-martial, as described in subsection (b).

(2) Special courts-martial, as described in subsection (c).

(3) Summary courts-martial, as described in subsection (d).

(b) GENERAL COURTS-MARTIAL.—General courts-martial are of the following three types:

(1) A general court-martial consisting of a military judge and eight members, subject to sections 825(e)(3) and 829 of this title (articles 25(e)(3) and 29).

(2) In a capital case, a general court-martial consisting of a military judge and the number of members determined under section 825a of this title (article 25a), subject to sections 825(e)(3) and 829 of this title (articles 25(e)(3) and 29).

(3) A general court-martial consisting of a military judge alone, if, before the court is assembled, the accused, knowing the identity of the military judge and after consultation with defense counsel, requests, orally on the record or in writing, a court composed of a military judge alone and the military judge approves the request.

(c) SPECIAL COURTS-MARTIAL.—Special courts-martial are of the following two types:

(1) A special court-martial, consisting of a military judge and four members, subject to sections 825(e)(3) and 829 of this title (articles 25(e)(3) and 29.

(2) A special court-martial consisting of a military judge alone—

(A) if the case is so referred by the convening authority, subject to section 819 of this title (article 19) and such limitations as the President may prescribe by regulation; or

(B) if the case is referred under paragraph (1) and, before the court is assembled, the accused, knowing the identity of the military judge and after consultation with defense counsel, requests, orally on the record or in writing, a court composed of a military judge alone and the military judge approves the request.

(d) SUMMARY COURT-MARTIAL.—A summary court-martial consists of one commissioned officer.

§817. Art. 17. Jurisdiction of courts-martial in general

(a) Each armed force has court-martial jurisdiction over all persons subject to this chapter. The exercise of jurisdiction by one armed force over personnel of another armed force shall be in accordance with regulations prescribed by the President.

(b) In all cases, departmental review after that by the officer with authority to convene a general court-martial for the command which held the trial, where that review is required under this chapter, shall be carried out by the department that includes the armed force of which the accused is a member.

§818. Art. 18. Jurisdiction of general courts-martial

(a) Subject to section 817 of this title (article 17), general courts-martial have jurisdiction to try persons subject to this chapter for any offense made punishable by this chapter and may, under such limitations as the President may prescribe, adjudge any punishment not forbidden by this chapter, including the penalty of death when specifically authorized by this chapter. General courts-martial also have jurisdiction to try any person who by the law of war is subject to trial by a military tribunal and may adjudge any punishment permitted by the law of war.

(b) A general court-martial of the kind specified in section 816(b)(3) of this title (article 16(b)(3)) shall not have jurisdiction to try any person for any offense for which the death penalty may be adjudged unless the case has been previously referred to trial as a noncapital case.

(c) Consistent with sections 819 and 820 of this title (articles 19 and 20), only general courts-martial have jurisdiction over the following offenses:

(1) A violation of subsection (a) or (b) of section 920 of this title (article 120).

(2) A violation of subsection (a) or (b) of section 920b of this title (article 120b).

(3) An attempt to commit an offense specified in paragraph (1) or (2) that is punishable under section 880 of this title (article 80).

§819. Art. 19. Jurisdiction of special courts-martial

(a) IN GENERAL.—Subject to section 817 of this title (article 17), special courts-martial have jurisdiction to try persons subject to this chapter for any noncapital offense made punishable by this chapter and, under such regulations as the President may prescribe, for capital offenses. Special courts-martial may, under such limitations as the President may prescribe, adjudge any punishment not forbidden by this chapter except death, dishonorable discharge, dismissal, confinement for more than one year, hard labor without confinement for more than three months, forfeiture of pay exceeding two-thirds pay per month, or forfeiture of pay for more than one year.

(b) ADDITIONAL LIMITATION.—Neither a bad-conduct discharge, nor confinement for more than six months, nor forfeiture of pay for more than six months may be adjudged if charges and specifications are referred to a special court-martial consisting of a military judge alone under section 816(c)(2)(A) of this title (article 16(c)(2)(A)).

(c) MILITARY MAGISTRATE.—If charges and specifications are referred to a special court-martial consisting of a military judge alone under section 816(c)(2)(A) of this title (article 16(c)(2)(A)), the military judge, with the consent of the parties, may designate a military magistrate to preside over the special court-martial.

§820. Art. 20. Jurisdiction of summary courts-martial

(a) IN GENERAL.—Subject to section 817 of this title (article 17), summary courts-martial have jurisdiction to try persons subject to this chapter, except officers, cadets, aviation cadets, and midshipmen, for any noncapital offense made punishable by this chapter. No person with respect to whom summary courts-martial have jurisdiction may be brought to trial before a summary court-martial if he objects thereto. If objection to trial by summary court-martial is made by an accused, trial may be ordered by special or general court-martial as may be appropriate. Summary courts-martial may, under such limitations as the President may prescribe, adjudge any punishment not forbidden by this chapter except death, dismissal, dishonorable or bad-conduct discharge, confinement for more than one month, hard-labor without confinement for more than 45 days, restriction to specified limits for more than two months, or forfeiture of more than two-thirds of one month's pay.

(b) NON-CRIMINAL FORUM.—A summary court-martial is a non-criminal forum. A finding of guilty at a summary court-martial does not constitute a criminal conviction.

§821. Art. 21. Jurisdiction of courts-martial not exclusive

The provisions of this chapter conferring jurisdiction upon courts-martial do not deprive military commissions, provost courts, or other military tribunals of concurrent jurisdiction with respect to offenders or offenses that by statute or by the law of war may be tried by military commissions, provost courts, or other military tribunals. This section does not apply to a military commission established under chapter 47A of this title.

SUBCHAPTER V. COMPOSITION OF COURTS-MARTIAL

§822. Art. 22. Who may convene general courts-martial

(a) General courts-martial may be convened by—

(1) the President of the United States;

(2) the Secretary of Defense;

(3) the commanding officer of a unified or specified combatant command;

(4) the Secretary concerned;

(5) the commanding officer of an Army Group, an Army, an Army Corps, a division, a separate brigade, or a corresponding unit of the Army or Marine Corps;

(6) the commander of a fleet; the commanding officer of a naval station or larger shore activity of the Navy beyond the United States;

(7) the commanding officer of an air command, an air force, an air division, or a separate wing of the Air Force or Marine Corps, or the commanding officer of a corresponding unit of the Space Force;

(8) any other commanding officer designated by the Secretary concerned; or

(9) any other commanding officer in any of the armed forces when empowered by the President.

(b)(1) If any such commanding officer is an accuser, the court shall be convened by superior competent authority, and may in any case be convened by such authority if considered desirable by him.

(2) A commanding officer shall not be considered an accuser solely due to the role of the commanding officer in convening a general court-martial to which charges and specifications were referred by a special trial counsel in accordance with this chapter.

§823. Art. 23. Who may convene special courts-martial

(a) Special courts-martial may be convened by—

(1) any person who may convene a general court-martial;

(2) the commanding officer of a district, garrison, fort, camp, station, Air Force or Space Force military installation, auxiliary air field, or other place where members of the Army, the Air Force, or the Space Force are on duty;

(3) the commanding officer of a brigade, regiment, detached battalion, or corresponding unit of the Army;

(4) the commanding officer of a wing, group, or separate squadron of the Air Force or a corresponding unit of the Space Force;

(5) the commanding officer of any naval or Coast Guard vessel, shipyard, base, or station; the commanding officer of any Marine brigade, regiment, detached battalion, or corresponding unit; the commanding officer of any Marine barracks, wing, group, separate squadron, station, base, auxiliary air field, or other place where members of the Marine Corps are on duty;

(6) the commanding officer of any separate or detached command or group of detached units of any of the armed forces placed under a single commander for this purpose; or

(7) the commanding officer or officer in charge of any other command when empowered by the Secretary concerned.

(b)(1) If any such officer is an accuser, the court shall be convened by superior competent authority, and may in any case be convened by such authority if considered advisable by him.

(2) A commanding officer shall not be considered an accuser solely due to the role of the commanding officer in convening a special court-martial to which charges and specifications were referred by a special trial counsel in accordance with this chapter.

§824. Art. 24. Who may convene summary courts-martial

(a) Summary courts-martial may be convened by—

(1) any person who may convene a general or special court-martial;

(2) the commanding officer of a detached company, or other detachment of the Army;

(3) the commanding officer of a detached squadron or other detachment of the Air Force or a corresponding unit of the Space Force; or

(4) the commanding officer or officer in charge of any other command when empowered by the Secretary concerned.

(b) When only one commissioned officer is present with a command or detachment he shall be the summary court-martial of that command or detachment and shall hear and determine all summary court-martial cases brought before him. Summary courts-martial may, however, be convened in any case by superior competent authority when considered desirable by him.

§824a. Art. 24a. Special trial counsel

(a) DETAIL OF SPECIAL TRIAL COUNSEL.—Each Secretary concerned shall promulgate regulations for the detail of commissioned officers to serve as special trial counsel.

(b) QUALIFICATIONS.—A special trial counsel shall be a commissioned officer who—

(1)(A) is a member of the bar of a Federal court or a member of the bar of the highest court of a State; and

(B) is certified to be qualified, by reason of education, training, experience, and temperament, for duty as special trial counsel by—

(i) the Judge Advocate General of the armed force of which the officer is a member; or

(ii) in the case of the Marine Corps, the Staff Judge Advocate to the Commandant of the Marine Corps; and

(2) in the case of a lead special trial counsel appointed pursuant to section 1044f(a)(2) of this title, is in a grade no lower than O-7.

(c) DUTIES AND AUTHORITIES.—

(1) IN GENERAL.—Special trial counsel shall carry out the duties described in this chapter and any other duties prescribed by the Secretary concerned, by regulation.

(2) DETERMINATION OF COVERED OFFENSE; RELATED CHARGES.—

(A) AUTHORITY.—A special trial counsel shall have exclusive authority to determine if a reported offense is a covered offense and shall exercise authority over any such offense in accordance with this chapter. Any determination to prefer or refer charges shall not act to disqualify the special trial counsel as an accuser.

(B) KNOWN AND RELATED OFFENSES.—If a special trial counsel determines that a reported offense is a covered offense, the special trial counsel may also exercise authority over any offense that the special trial counsel determines to be related to the covered offense and any other offense alleged to have been committed by a person alleged to have committed the covered offense.

(3) DISMISSAL; REFERRAL; PLEA BARGAINS.—Subject to paragraph (5), with respect to changes and specifications alleging any offense over which a special trial counsel exercises authority, a special trial counsel shall have exclusive authority to, in accordance with this chapter—

(A) on behalf of the Government, withdraw or dismiss the charges and specifications or make a motion to withdraw or dismiss the charges and specifications;

(B) refer the charges and specifications for trial by a special or general court-martial;

(C) enter into a plea agreement; and

(D) determine if an authorized rehearing is impracticable.

(4) BINDING DETERMINATION.—The determination of a special trial counsel to refer charges and specifications to a court-martial for trial shall be binding on any applicable convening authority for the referral of such charges and specifications.

(5) DEFERRAL TO COMMANDER OR CONVENING AUTHORITY.—If a special trial counsel exercises authority over an offense and elects not to prefer charges and specifications for such offense or, with respect to charges and specifications for such offense preferred by a person other than a special trial counsel, elects not to refer such charges and specifications, a commander or convening authority may exercise any of the authorities of such commander or convening authority under this chapter with respect to such offense, except that such commander or convening authority may not refer charges and specifications for a covered offense for trial by special or general court-martial.

§825. Art. 25. Who may serve on courts-martial

(a) Any commissioned officer on active duty is eligible to serve on all courts-martial for the trial of any person who may lawfully be brought before such courts for trial.

(b) Any warrant officer on active duty is eligible to serve on general and special courts-martial for the trial of any person, other than a commissioned officer, who may lawfully be brought before such courts for trial.

(c)(1) Any enlisted member on active duty is eligible to serve on a general or special court-martial for the trial of any other enlisted member.

(2) Before a court-martial with a military judge and members is assembled for trial, an enlisted member who is an accused may personally request, orally on the record or in writing, that—

(A) the membership of the court-martial be comprised entirely of officers; or

(B) enlisted members comprise at least one-third of the membership of the court-martial, regardless of whether enlisted members have been detailed to the court-martial.

(3) Except as provided in paragraph (4), after such a request, the accused may not be tried by a general or special court-martial if the membership of the court-martial is inconsistent with the request.

(4) If, because of physical conditions or military exigencies, a sufficient number of eligible officers or enlisted members, as the case may be, is not available to carry out paragraph (2), the trial may nevertheless be held. In that event, the convening authority shall make a detailed written statement of the reasons for nonavailability. The statement shall be appended to the record.

(d)(1) Except as provided in paragraph (2) for capital offenses, the accused in a court-martial with a military judge and members may, after the findings are announced and before any matter is presented in the sentencing phase, request, orally on the record or in writing, sentencing by members.

(2) In a capital case, the accused shall be sentenced by the members for all offenses for which the court-martial may sentence the accused to death in accordance with section 853(c) of this title (article 53(c)).

(3) In a capital case, if the accused is convicted of a non-capital offense, the accused shall be sentenced for such non-capital offense in accordance with section 853(b) of this title (article 53(b)), regardless of whether the accused is convicted of an offense for which the court-martial may sentence the accused to death.

(e)(1) When it can be avoided, no member of an armed force may be tried by a court-martial any member of which is junior to him in rank or grade.

(2) When convening a court-martial, the convening authority shall detail as members thereof such members of the armed forces as, in his opinion, are best qualified for the duty by reason of age, education, training, experience, length of service, and judicial temperament. No member of an armed force is eligible to serve as a member of a general or special court-martial when he is the accuser or a witness for the prosecution or has acted as preliminary hearing officer or as counsel in the same case.

(3) The convening authority shall detail not less than the number of members necessary to impanel the court-martial under section 829 of this title (article 29).

(f) Before a court-martial is assembled for the trial of a case, the convening authority may excuse a member of the court from participating in the case. Under such regulations as the Secretary concerned may prescribe, the convening authority may delegate his authority under this subsection to his staff judge advocate or legal officer or to any other principal assistant.

Office of Law Revision Counsel, United States Code, *10 U.S.C. 825: Art. 25. Who may serve on courts-martial* (Sep. 13, 2023, 5:24 PM) (https://uscode.house.gov (go to "Jump to" and insert "10" in "Title" and "825" in "Section")) provides:

"Pub. L. 117-263, div. A. title V, § 543(a), (b), Dec. 23, 2022, 136 Stat. 2582, provided that, effective on the date that is two years after Dec. 23, 2022, and applicable with respect to courts-martial convened on or after that date, section (e) of this section is amended by adding at the end the following new paragraph:

(4) When convening a court-martial, the convening authority shall detail as members thereof members of the armed forces under such regulations as the President may prescribe for the randomized selection of qualified personnel, to the maximum extent practicable."

§825a. Art. 25a. Number of court-martial members in capital cases

(a) IN GENERAL.—In a case in which the accused may be sentenced to death, the number of members shall be 12.

(b) CASE NO LONGER CAPITAL.—Subject to section 829 of this title (article 29)—

(1) if a case is referred for trial as a capital case and, before the members are impaneled, the accused may no longer be sentenced to death, the number of members shall be eight; and

(2) if a case is referred for trial as a capital case and, after the members are impaneled, the accused may no longer be sentenced to death, the number of members shall remain 12.

§826. Art. 26. Military judge of a general or special court-martial

(a) A military judge shall be detailed to each general and special court-martial. The Secretary concerned shall prescribe regulations providing for the manner in which military judges are detailed for such courts-martial and for the persons who are authorized to detail military judges for such courts-martial. The military judge shall preside over each open session of the court-martial to which he has been detailed.

(b) A military judge shall be a commissioned officer of the armed forces who is a member of the bar of a Federal court or a member of the bar of the highest court of a State and who is certified to be qualified, by reason of education, training, experience, and judicial temperament, for duty as a military judge by the Judge Advocate General of the armed force of which such military judge is a member.

(c)(1) In accordance with regulations prescribed under subsection (a), a military judge of a general or special court-martial shall be designated for detail by the Judge Advocate General of the armed force of which the military judge is a member.

(2) Neither the convening authority nor any member of the staff of the convening authority shall prepare or review any report concerning the effectiveness, fitness, or efficiency of the military judge so detailed, which relates to the military judge's performance of duty as a military judge.

(3) A commissioned officer who is certified to be qualified for duty as a military judge of a general court-martial—

(A) may perform such duties only when the officer is assigned and directly responsible to the Judge Advocate General of the armed force of which the military judge is a member; and

(B) may perform duties of a judicial or nonjudicial nature other than those relating to the officer's primary duty as a military judge of a general court-martial when such duties are assigned to the officer by or with the approval of that Judge Advocate General.

(4) In accordance with regulations prescribed by the President, assignments of military judges under this section (article) shall be for appropriate minimum periods, subject to such exceptions as may be authorized in the regulations.

(d) No person is eligible to act as military judge in a case if he is the accuser or a witness for the prosecution or has acted as preliminary hearing officer or a counsel in the same case.

(e) The military judge of a court-martial may not consult with the members of the court except in the presence of the accused, trial counsel, and defense counsel, nor may he vote with the members of the court.

(f) A military judge may be detailed under subsection (a) to a court-martial or a proceeding under section 830a of this title (article 30a) that is convened in a different armed force, when so permitted by the Judge Advocate General of the armed force of which the military judge is a member.

(g) In accordance with regulations prescribed by the President, each Judge Advocate General shall designate a chief trial judge from among the members of the applicable trial judiciary.

§826a. Art. 26a. Military magistrates

(a) QUALIFICATIONS.—A military magistrate shall be a commissioned officer of the armed forces who—

(1) is a member of the bar of a Federal court or a member of the bar of the highest court of a State; and

(2) is certified to be qualified, by reason of education, training, experience, and judicial temperament, for duty as a military magistrate by the Judge Advocate General of the armed force of which the officer is a member.

(b) DUTIES.—In accordance with regulations prescribed by the Secretary concerned, in addition to duties when designated under section 819 of this title or section 830a of this title (articles 19 or 30a), a military magistrate may be assigned to perform other duties of a nonjudicial nature.

§827. Art. 27. Detail of trial counsel and defense counsel

(a)(1) Trial counsel and defense counsel shall be detailed for each general and special court-martial. Assistant trial counsel and assistant and associate defense counsel may be detailed for each general and special court-martial. The Secretary concerned shall prescribe regulations providing for the manner in which counsel are detailed for such courts-martial and for the persons who are authorized to detail counsel for such courts-martial.

(2) No person who, with respect to a case, has served as a preliminary hearing officer, court member, military judge, military magistrate, or appellate judge, may later serve as trial counsel, assistant trial counsel, or, unless expressly requested by the accused, as defense counsel or assistant or associate defense counsel in the same case. No person who has acted for the prosecution may act later in the same case for the defense, nor may any person who has acted for the defense act later in the same case for the prosecution.

(b) Trial counsel, defense counsel, or assistant defense counsel detailed for a general court-martial—

(1) must be a judge advocate who is a graduate of an accredited law school or is a member of the bar of a Federal court or of the highest court of a State; or must be a member of the bar of a Federal court or of the highest court of a State; and

(2) must be certified as competent to perform such duties by the Judge Advocate General of the armed force of which he is a member.

(c)(1) Defense counsel and assistant defense counsel detailed for a special court-martial shall have the qualifications set forth in subsection (b).

(2) Trial counsel and assistant trial counsel detailed for a special court-martial and assistant trial counsel detailed for a general court-martial must be determined to be competent to perform such duties by the Judge Advocate General, under such rules as the President may prescribe.

(d) To the greatest extent practicable, in any capital case, at least one defense counsel shall, as determined by the Judge Advocate General, be learned in the law applicable to such cases. If necessary, this counsel may be a civilian and, if so, may be compensated in accordance with regulations prescribed by the Secretary of Defense.

(e) For each general and special court-martial for which charges and specifications were referred by a special trial counsel—

(1) a special trial counsel shall be detailed as trial counsel; and

(2) a special trial counsel may detail other trial counsel as necessary who are judge advocates.

§828. Art. 28. Detail or employment of reporters and interpreters

Under such regulations as the Secretary concerned may prescribe, the convening authority of a court-martial, military commission, or court of inquiry shall detail or employ qualified court reporters, who shall record the proceedings of and testimony taken before that court or commission. Under like regulations the convening authority of a court-martial, military commission, or court of inquiry may detail or employ interpreters who shall interpret for the court or commission. This section does not apply to a military commission established under chapter 47A of this title.

§829. Art. 29. Assembly and impaneling of members; detail of new members and military judges

(a) ASSEMBLY.—The military judge shall announce the assembly of a general or special court-martial with members. After such a court-martial is assembled, no member may be absent, unless the member is excused—

(1) as a result of a challenge;

(2) under subsection (b)(1)(B); or

(3) by order of the military judge or the convening authority for disability or other good cause.

(b) IMPANELING.—

(1) Under rules prescribed by the President, the military judge of a general or special court-martial with members shall—

(A) after determination of challenges, impanel the court-martial; and

(B) excuse the members who, having been assembled, are not impaneled.

(2) In a general court-martial, the military judge shall impanel—

(A) 12 members in a capital case; and

(B) eight members in a noncapital case.

(3) In a special court-martial, the military judge shall impanel four members.

(c) ALTERNATE MEMBERS.—In addition to members under subsection (b), the military judge shall impanel alternate members, if the convening authority authorizes alternate members.

(d) DETAIL OF NEW MEMBERS.—

(1) If, after members are impaneled, the membership of the court-martial is reduced to—

(A) fewer than 12 members with respect to a general court-martial in a capital case;

(B) fewer than six members with respect to a general court-martial in a noncapital case; or

(C) fewer than four members with respect to a special court-martial; the trial may not proceed unless the convening authority details new members and, from among the members so detailed, the military judge impanels new members sufficient in number to provide the membership specified in paragraph (2).

(2) The membership referred to in paragraph (1) is as follows:

(A) 12 members with respect to a general court-martial in a capital case.

(B) At least six but not more than eight members with respect to a general court-martial in a noncapital case.

(C) Four members with respect to a special court-martial.

(e) DETAIL OF NEW MILITARY JUDGE.—If the military judge is unable to proceed with the trial because of disability or otherwise, a new military judge shall be detailed to the court-martial.

(f) EVIDENCE.—

(1) In the case of new members under subsection (d), the trial may proceed with the new members present after the evidence previously introduced is read or, in the case of audiotape, videotape, or similar recording, is played, in the presence of the new members, the military judge, the accused, and counsel for both sides.

(2) In the case of a new military judge under subsection (e), the trial shall proceed as if no evidence had been introduced, unless the evidence previously introduced is read or, in the case of audiotape, videotape, or similar recording, is played, in the presence of the new military judge, the accused, and counsel for both sides.

SUBCHAPTER VI—PRE-TRIAL PROCEDURE

§830. Art. 30. Charges and specifications

(a) IN GENERAL.—Charges and specifications—

(1) may be preferred only by a person subject to this chapter; and

(2) shall be preferred by presentment in writing, signed under oath before a commissioned officer of the armed forces who is authorized to administer oaths.

(b) REQUIRED CONTENT.—The writing under subsection (a) shall state that—

(1) the signer has personal knowledge of, or has investigated, the matters set forth in the charges and specifications; and

(2) the matters set forth in the charges and specifications are true, to the best of the knowledge and belief of the signer.

(c) DUTY OF PROPER AUTHORITY.—When charges and specifications are preferred under subsection (a), the proper authority shall, as soon as practicable—

(1) inform the person accused of the charges and specifications; and

(2) determine what disposition should be made of the charges and specifications in the interest of justice and discipline.

§830a. Art. 30a. Proceedings conducted before referral

(a) IN GENERAL.—

(1) The President shall prescribe regulations for matters relating to proceedings conducted before referral of charges and specifications to court-martial for trial, including the following:

(A) Pre-referral investigative subpoenas.

(B) Pre-referral warrants or orders for electronic communications.

(C) Pre-referral matters referred by an appellate court.

(D) Pre-referral matters under subsection (c) or (e) of section 806b of this title (article 6b).

(E) Pre-referral matters relating to the following:

(i) Pre-trial confinement of an accused.

(ii) The mental capacity or mental responsibility of an accused.

(iii) A request for an individual military counsel.

(2) In addition to the matters specified in paragraph (1), the regulations prescribed under that paragraph shall—

(A) set forth the matters that a military judge may rule upon in such proceedings;

(B) include procedures for the review of such rulings;

(C) include appropriate limitations to ensure that proceedings under this section extend only to matters that would be subject to consideration by a military judge in a general or special court-martial; and

(D) provide such limitations on the relief that may be ordered under this section as the President considers appropriate.

(3) If any matter in a proceeding under this section becomes a subject at issue with respect to charges that have been referred to a general or special court-martial, the matter shall be transferred to the military judge detailed to the court-martial.

(b) DETAIL OF MILITARY JUDGE.—The Secretary concerned shall prescribe regulations providing for the manner in which military judges are detailed to proceedings under subsection (a)(1).

(c) DISCRETION TO DESIGNATE MAGISTRATE TO PRESIDE.—In accordance with regulations prescribed by the Secretary concerned, a military judge detailed to a proceeding under subsection (a)(1), other than a proceeding described in subparagraph (B) of that subsection, may designate a military magistrate to preside over the proceeding.

§831. Art. 31. Compulsory self-incrimination prohibited

(a) No person subject to this chapter may compel any person to incriminate himself or to answer any question the answer to which may tend to incriminate him.

(b) No person subject to this chapter may interrogate, or request any statement from, an accused or a person suspected of an offense without first informing him of the nature of the accusation and advising him that he does not have to make any statement regarding the offense of which he is accused or suspected and that any statement made by him may be used as evidence against him in a trial by court-martial.

(c) No person subject to this chapter may compel any person to make a statement or produce evidence before any military tribunal if the statement or evidence is not material to the issue and may tend to degrade him.

(d) No statement obtained from any person in violation of this article, or through the use of coercion, unlawful influence, or unlawful inducement may be received in evidence against him in a trial by court-martial.

§832. Art. 32. Preliminary hearing required before referral to general court-martial

(a) IN GENERAL.—

(1)(A) Except as provided in subparagraph (B), a preliminary hearing shall be held before referral of charges and specifications for trial by general court-martial. The preliminary hearing shall be conducted by an impartial hearing officer detailed in accordance with subparagraph (C).

(B) Under regulations prescribed by the President, a preliminary hearing need not be held if the accused submits a written waiver to—

(i) except as provided in clause (ii), the convening authority and the convening authority determines that a hearing is not required, and

(ii) with respect to charges and specifications over which the special trial counsel is exercising authority in accordance with section 824a of this title (article 24a), the special trial counsel and the special trial counsel determines that a hearing is not required.

(C)(i) Except as provided in clause (ii), the convening authority shall detail a hearing officer.

(ii) If a special trial counsel is exercising authority over the charges and specifications subject to a preliminary hearing under this section (article), the special trial counsel shall request a hearing officer and a hearing officer shall be provided by the convening authority, in accordance with regulations prescribed by the President.

(2) The purpose of the preliminary hearing shall be limited to determining the following:

(A) Whether or not the specification alleges an offense under this chapter.

(B) Whether or not there is probable cause to believe that the accused committed the offense charged.

(C) Whether or not the convening authority has court-martial jurisdiction over the accused and over the offense.

(D) A recommendation as to the disposition that should be made of the case.

(b) HEARING OFFICER.—

(1) A preliminary hearing under this section shall be conducted by an impartial hearing officer, who—

(A) whenever practicable, shall be a judge advocate who is certified under section 827(b)(2) of this title (article 27(b)(2)); or

(B) when it is not practicable to appoint a judge advocate because of exceptional circumstances, is not a judge advocate so certified.

(2) In the case of a hearing officer under paragraph (1)(B), a judge advocate who is certified under section 827(b)(2) of this title (article 27(b)(2)) shall be available to provide legal advice to the hearing officer.

(3) Whenever practicable, the hearing officer shall be equal in grade or senior in grade to military counsel who are detailed to represent the accused or the Government at the preliminary hearing.

(c) REPORT TO CONVENING AUTHORITY OR SPECIAL TRIAL COUNSEL.—After a preliminary hearing under this section, the hearing officer shall submit to the convening authority or, in the case of a preliminary hearing in which the hearing officer is provided at the request of a special trial counsel to the special trial counsel, a written report (accompanied by a recording of the preliminary hearing under subsection (e)) that includes the following:

(1) For each specification, a statement of the reasoning and conclusions of the hearing officer with respect to determinations under subsection (a)(2), including a summary of relevant witness testimony and documentary evidence presented at the hearing and

any observations of the hearing officer concerning the testimony of witnesses and the availability and admissibility of evidence at trial.

(2) Recommendations for any necessary modifications to the form of the charges or specifications.

(3) An analysis of any additional information submitted after the hearing by the parties or by a victim of an offense, that, under such rules as the President may prescribe, is relevant to disposition under sections 830 and 834 of this title (articles 30 and 34).

(4) A statement of action taken on evidence adduced with respect to uncharged offenses, as described in subsection (f).

(d) RIGHTS OF ACCUSED AND VICTIM.—(1) The accused shall be advised of the charges against the accused and of the accused's right to be represented by counsel at the preliminary hearing under this section. The accused has the right to be represented at the preliminary hearing as provided in section 838 of this title (article 38) and in regulations prescribed under that section.

(2) The accused may cross-examine witnesses who testify at the preliminary hearing and present additional evidence that is relevant to the issues for determination under subsection (a)(2).

(3) A victim may not be required to testify at the preliminary hearing. A victim who declines to testify shall be deemed to be not available for purposes of the preliminary hearing. A declination under this paragraph shall not serve as the sole basis for ordering a deposition under section 849 of this title (article 49).

(4) The presentation of evidence and examination (including cross-examination) of witnesses at a preliminary hearing shall be limited to the matters relevant to determinations under subsection (a)(2).

(e) RECORDING OF PRELIMINARY HEARING.—A preliminary hearing under subsection (a) shall be recorded by a suitable recording device. The victim may request the recording and shall have access to the recording under such rules as the President may prescribe.

(f) EFFECT OF EVIDENCE OF UNCHARGED OFFENSE.—If evidence adduced in a preliminary hearing under subsection (a) indicates that the accused committed an uncharged offense, the hearing officer may consider the subject matter of that offense without the accused having first been charged with the offense if the accused—

(1) is present at the preliminary hearing;

(2) is informed of the nature of each uncharged offense considered; and

(3) is afforded the opportunities for representation, cross-examination, and presentation consistent with subsection (d).

(g) EFFECT OF VIOLATION.—The requirements of this section are binding on all persons administering this chapter, but failure to follow the requirements does not constitute jurisdictional error. A defect in a report under subsection (c) is not a basis for relief if the report is in substantial compliance with that subsection.

(h) VICTIM DEFINED.—In this section, the term "victim" means a person who—

(1) is alleged to have suffered a direct physical, emotional, or pecuniary harm as a result of the matters set forth in a charge or specification being considered; and

(2) is named in one of the specifications.

§833. Art. 33. Disposition guidance

The President shall direct the Secretary of Defense to issue, in consultation with the Secretary of the department in which the Coast Guard is operating when it is not operating as a service in the Navy, non-binding guidance regarding factors that commanders, convening authorities, staff judge advocates, and judge advocates should take into account when exercising their duties with respect to disposition of charges and specifications in the interest of justice and discipline under sections 830 and 834 of this title (articles 30 and 34). Such guidance shall take into account, with appropriate consideration of military requirements, the principles contained in official guidance of the Attorney General to attorneys for the Government with respect to disposition of Federal criminal cases in accordance with the principle of fair and evenhanded administration of Federal criminal law.

§834. Art. 34. Advice to convening authority before referral for trial

(a) GENERAL COURT-MARTIAL.—

(1) STAFF JUDGE ADVOCATE ADVICE REQUIRED BEFORE REFERRAL.—Subject to subsection (c), before referral of charges and specifications to a general court-martial for trial, the convening authority shall submit the matter to the staff judge advocate for advice, which the staff judge advocate shall provide to the convening authority in writing. The convening authority may not refer a specification under a charge to a general court-martial unless the staff judge advocate advises the convening authority in writing that—

(A) the specification alleges an offense under this chapter;

(B) there is probable cause to believe that the accused committed the offense charged; and

(C) a court-martial would have jurisdiction over the accused and the offense.

(2) STAFF JUDGE ADVOCATE RECOMMENDATION AS TO DISPOSITION.—Together with the written advice provided under paragraph (1), the staff judge advocate shall provide a written recommendation to the convening authority as to the disposition that should be made of the specification in the interest of justice and discipline.

(3) STAFF JUDGE ADVOCATE ADVICE AND RECOMMENDATION TO ACCOMPANY REFERRAL.—When a convening authority makes a referral for trial by general court-martial, the written advice of the staff judge advocate under paragraph (1) and the written recommendation of the staff judge advocate under paragraph (2) with respect to each specification shall accompany the referral.

(b) SPECIAL COURT-MARTIAL; CONVENING AUTHORITY CONSULTATION WITH JUDGE ADVOCATE.—Subject to subsection (c), before referral of charges and specifications to a special court-martial for trial, the convening authority shall consult a judge advocate on relevant legal issues.

(c) COVERED OFFENSES.——A referral to a general or special court-martial for trial of charges and specifications over which a special trial counsel exercises authority may only be made—

(1) by a special trial counsel, subject to a special trial counsel's written determination accompanying the referral that—

(A) each specification under a charge alleges an offense under this chapter;

(B) there is probable cause to believe that the accused committed the offense charged; and

(C) a court-martial would have jurisdiction over the accused and the offense; or

(2) in the case of charges and specifications that do not allege a covered offense and as to which a special trial counsel declines to

prefer or, in the case of charges and specifications preferred by a person other than a special trial counsel, refer charges, by the convening authority in accordance with this section.

(d) GENERAL AND SPECIAL COURTS-MARTIAL; CORRECTION OF CHARGES AND SPECIFICATIONS BEFORE REFERRAL.—Before referral for trial by general court-martial or special court-martial, changes may be made to charges and specifications—

(1) to correct errors in form; and

(2) when applicable, to conform to the substance of the evidence contained in a report under section 832(c) of this title (article 32(c)).

(e) REFERRAL DEFINED.—In this section, the term "referral" means the order of a convening authority or, with respect to charges and specifications over which a special trial counsel exercises authority in accordance with section 824a of this title (article 24a), a special trial counsel, that charges and specifications against an accused be tried by a specified court-martial.

§835. Art. 35. Service of charges; commencement of trial

(a) IN GENERAL.—Trial counsel detailed for a court-martial under section 827 of this title (article 27) shall cause to be served upon the accused a copy of the charges and specifications referred for trial.

(b) COMMENCEMENT OF TRIAL.—

(1) Subject to paragraphs (2) and (3), no trial or other proceeding of a general court-martial or a special court-martial (including any session under section 839(a) of this title (article 39(a)) may be held over the objection of the accused—

(A) with respect to a general court-martial, from the time of service through the fifth day after the date of service; or

(B) with respect to a special court-martial, from the time of service through the third day after the date of service.

(2) An objection under paragraph (1) may be raised only at the first session of the trial or other proceeding and only if the first session occurs before the end of the applicable period under paragraph (1)(A) or (1)(B). If the first session occurs before the end of the applicable period, the military judge shall, at that session, inquire as to whether the defense objects under this subsection.

(3) This subsection shall not apply in time of war.

SUBCHAPTER VII—TRIAL PROCEDURE

§836. Art. 36. President may prescribe rules

(a) Pretrial, trial, and post-trial procedures, including modes of proof, for cases arising under this chapter triable in courts-martial, military commissions and other military tribunals, and procedures for courts of inquiry, may be prescribed by the President by regulations which shall, so far as he considers practicable, apply the principles of law and the rules of evidence generally recognized in the trial of criminal cases in the United States district courts, but which may not, except as provided in chapter 47A of this title, be contrary to or inconsistent with this chapter.

(b) All rules and regulations made under this article shall be uniform insofar as practicable, except insofar as applicable to military commissions established under chapter 47A of this title.

§837. Art. 37. Command influence

(a)(1) No court-martial convening authority, nor any other commanding officer, may censure, reprimand, or admonish the court or any member, military judge, or counsel thereof, with respect to the findings or sentence adjudged by the court, or with respect to any other exercise of its or his functions in the conduct of the proceeding.

(2) No court-martial convening authority, nor any other commanding officer, may deter or attempt to deter a potential witness from participating in the investigatory process or testifying at a court-martial. The denial of a request to travel at government expense or refusal to make a witness available shall not by itself constitute unlawful command influence.

(3) No person subject to this chapter may attempt to coerce or, by any unauthorized means, attempt to influence the action of a court-martial or any other military tribunal or any member thereof, in reaching the findings or sentence in any case, or the action of any convening, approving, or reviewing authority or preliminary hearing officer with respect to such acts taken pursuant to this chapter as prescribed by the President.

(4) Conduct that does not constitute a violation of paragraphs (1) through (3) may include, for example—

(A) general instructional or informational courses in military justice if such courses are designed solely for the purpose of instructing persons on the substantive and procedural aspects of courts-martial;

(B) statements regarding criminal activity or a particular criminal offense that do not advocate a particular disposition, or a particular court-martial finding or sentence, or do not relate to a particular accused; or

(C) statements and instructions given in open court by the military judge or counsel.

(5)(A) Notwithstanding paragraphs (1) through (3), but subject to subparagraph (B)-

(i) a superior convening authority or officer may generally discuss matters to consider regarding the disposition of alleged violations of this chapter with a subordinate convening authority or officer; and

(ii) a subordinate convening authority or officer may seek advice from a superior convening authority or officer regarding the disposition of an alleged offense under this chapter.

(B) No superior convening authority or officer may direct a subordinate convening authority or officer to make a particular disposition in a specific case or otherwise substitute the discretion of such authority or such officer for that of the subordinate convening authority or officer.

(b) In the preparation of an effectiveness, fitness, or efficiency report, or any other report or document used in whole or in part for the purpose of determining whether a member of the armed forces is qualified to be advanced in grade, or in determining the assignment or transfer of a member of the armed forces or in determining whether a member of the armed forces should be retained on active duty, no person subject to this chapter may, in preparing any such report (1) consider or evaluate the performance of duty of any such member as a member of a court-martial, or (2) give a less favorable rating or evaluation of any member of the armed forces because of the zeal with which such member, as counsel, represented any person in a court-martial proceeding.

(c) No finding or sentence of a court-martial may be held incorrect on the ground of a violation of this section unless the violation materially prejudices the substantial rights of the accused.

(d)(1) A superior convening authority or commanding officer may withhold the authority of a subordinate convening authority or officer to dispose of offenses in individual cases, types of cases, or generally.

(2) Except as provided in paragraph (1) or as otherwise authorized by this chapter, a superior convening authority or commanding officer may not limit the discretion of a subordinate convening authority or officer to act with respect to a case for which the subordinate convening authority or officer has authority to dispose of the offenses.

§838. Art. 38. Duties of trial counsel and defense counsel

(a) The trial counsel of a general or special court-martial shall prosecute in the name of the United States, and shall, under the direction of the court, prepare the record of the proceedings.

(b)(1) The accused has the right to be represented in his defense before a general or special court-martial or at a preliminary hearing under section 832 of this title (article 32) as provided in this subsection.

(2) The accused may be represented by civilian counsel if provided by him.

(3) The accused may be represented—

(A) by military counsel detailed under section 827 of this title (article 27); or

(B) by military counsel of his own selection if that counsel is reasonably available (as determined under regulations prescribed under paragraph (7)).

(4) If the accused is represented by civilian counsel, military counsel detailed or selected under paragraph (3) shall act as associate counsel unless excused at the request of the accused.

(5) Except as provided under paragraph (6), if the accused is represented by military counsel of his own selection under paragraph (3)(B), any military counsel detailed under paragraph (3)(A) shall be excused.

(6) The accused is not entitled to be represented by more than one military counsel. However, the person authorized under regulations prescribed under section 827 of this title (article 27) to detail counsel, in his sole discretion—

(A) may detail additional military counsel as assistant defense counsel; and

(B) if the accused is represented by military counsel of his own selection under paragraph (3)(B), may approve a request from the accused that military counsel detailed under paragraph (3)(A) act as associate defense counsel.

(7) The Secretary concerned shall, by regulation, define "reasonably available" for the purpose of paragraph (3)(B) and establish procedures for determining whether the military counsel selected by an accused under that paragraph is reasonably available. Such regulations may not prescribe any limitation based on the reasonable availability of counsel solely on the grounds that the counsel selected by the accused is from an armed force other than the armed force of which the accused is a member. To the maximum extent practicable, such regulations shall establish uniform policies among the armed forces while recognizing the differences in the circumstances and needs of the various armed forces. The Secretary concerned shall submit copies of regulations prescribed under this paragraph to the Committee on Armed Services of the Senate and the Committee on Armed Services of the House of Representatives.

(c) In any court-martial proceeding resulting in a conviction, the defense counsel—

(1) may forward for attachment to the record of proceedings a brief of such matters as he determines should be considered in behalf of the accused on review (including any objection to the contents of the record which he considers appropriate);

(2) may assist the accused in the submission of any matter under section 860, 860a, or 860b of this title (article 60,60a, or 60b); and

(3) may take other action authorized by this chapter.

(d) An assistant trial counsel of a general court-martial may, under the direction of the trial counsel or when he is qualified to be a trial counsel as required by section 827 of this title (article 27), perform any duty imposed by law, regulation, or the custom of the service upon the trial counsel of the court. An assistant trial counsel of a special court-martial may perform any duty of the trial counsel.

(e) An assistant defense counsel of a general or special court-martial may-perform any duty imposed by law, regulation, or the custom of the service upon counsel for the accused.

§839. Art. 39. Sessions

(a) At any time after the service of charges which have been referred for trial to a court-martial composed of a military judge and members, the military judge may, subject to section 835 of this title (article 35), call the court into session without the presence of the members for the purpose of—

(1) hearing and determining motions raising defenses or objections which are capable of determination without trial of the issues raised by a plea of not guilty;

(2) hearing and ruling upon any matter which may be ruled upon by the military judge under this chapter, whether or not the matter is appropriate for later consideration or decision by the members of the court;

(3) holding the arraignment and receiving the pleas of the accused;

(4) conducting a sentencing proceeding and sentencing the accused under section 853(b)(1) of this title (article 53(b)(1)); and

(5) performing any other procedural function which may be performed by the military judge under this chapter or under rules prescribed pursuant to section 836 of this title (article 36) and which does not require the presence of the members of the court.

(b) Proceedings under subsection (a) shall be conducted in the presence of the accused, the defense counsel, and the trial counsel and shall be made a part of the record. These proceedings may be conducted notwithstanding the number of members of the court and without regard to section 829 of this title (article 29). If authorized by regulations of the Secretary concerned, and if at least one defense counsel is physically in the presence of the accused, the presence required by this subsection may otherwise be established by audiovisual technology (such as video teleconferencing technology).

(c) When the members of a court-martial deliberate or vote, only the members may be present. All other proceedings, including any other consultation of the members of the court with counsel or the military judge, shall be made a part of the record and shall be in the presence of the accused, the defense counsel, the trial counsel, and the military judge.

(d) The findings, holdings, interpretations, and other precedents of military commissions under chapter 47A of this title—

(1) may not be introduced or considered in any hearing, trial, or other proceeding of a court-martial under this chapter; and

(2) may not form the basis of any holding, decision, or other determination of a court-martial.

§840. Art. 40. Continuances

The military judge or a summary court-martial may, for reasonable cause, grant a continuance to any party for such time, and as often, as may appear to be just.

§841. Art. 41. Challenges

(a)(1) The military judge and members of a general or special court-martial may be challenged by the accused or the trial counsel for cause stated to the court. The military judge shall determine the relevancy and validity of challenges for cause, and may not receive a challenge to more than one person at a time. Challenges by the trial counsel shall ordinarily be presented and decided before those by the accused are offered.

(2) If exercise of a challenge for cause reduces the court below the number of members required by section 816 of this title (article 16), all parties shall (notwithstanding section 829 of this title (article 29)) either exercise or waive any challenge for cause then apparent against the remaining members of the court before additional members are detailed to the court. However, peremptory challenges shall not be exercised at that time.

(b)(1) Each accused and the trial counsel are entitled initially to one peremptory challenge of members of the court. The military judge may not be challenged except for cause.

(2) If exercise of a peremptory challenge reduces the court below the number of members required by section 816 of this title (article 16), the parties shall (notwithstanding section 829 of this title (article 29)) either exercise or waive any remaining peremptory challenge (not previously waived) against the remaining members of the court before additional members are detailed to the court.

(c) Whenever additional members are detailed to the court, and after any challenges for cause against such additional members are presented and decided, each accused and the trial counsel are entitled to one peremptory challenge against members not previously subject to peremptory challenge.

§842. Art. 42. Oaths

(a) Before performing their respective duties, military judges, members of general and special courts-martial, trial counsel, assistant trial counsel, defense counsel, assistant or associate defense counsel, reporters, and interpreters shall take an oath to perform their duties faithfully. The form of the oath, the time and place of the taking thereof, the manner of recording the same, and whether the oath shall be taken for all cases in which these duties are to be performed or for a particular case, shall be as prescribed in regulations of the Secretary concerned. These regulations may provide that an oath to perform faithfully duties as a military judge, trial counsel, assistant trial counsel, defense counsel, or assistant or associate defense counsel may be taken at any time by any judge advocate or other person certified to be qualified or competent for the duty, and if such an oath is taken it need not again be taken at the time the judge advocate or other person is detailed to that duty.

(b) Each witness before a court-martial shall be examined on oath.

§843. Art. 43. Statute of limitations

(a) NO LIMITATIONS FOR CERTAIN OFFENSES.—A person charged with absence without leave or missing movement in time of war, with murder, rape or sexual assault, or rape or sexual assault of a child, maiming of a child, kidnapping of a child, or with any other offense punishable by death, may be tried and punished at any time without limitation.

(b) FIVE-YEAR LIMITATION FOR TRIAL BY COURT-MARTIAL.—

(1) Except as otherwise provided in this section (article), a person charged with an offense is not liable to be tried by court-martial if the offense was committed more than five years before the receipt of sworn charges and specifications by an officer exercising summary court-martial jurisdiction over the command.

(2)(A) A person charged with having committed a child abuse offense against a child is liable to be tried by court-martial if the sworn charges and specifications are received during the life of the child or within ten years after the date on which the offense was committed, whichever provides a longer period, by an officer exercising summary court-martial jurisdiction with respect to that person.

(B) In subparagraph (A), the term "child abuse offense" means an act that involves abuse of a person who has not attained the age of 16 years and constitutes any of the following offenses:

(i) Any offense in violation of section 920, 920a, 920b, 920c, or 930 of this title (article 120, 120a, 120b, 120c, or 130), unless the offense is covered by subsection (a).

(ii) Aggravated assault, assault consummated by a battery, or assault with intent to commit specified offenses in violation of section 928 of this title (article 128).

(C) In subparagraph (A), the term "child abuse offense" includes an act that involves abuse of a person who has not attained the age of 18 years and would constitute an offense under chapter 110 or 117 of title 18 or under section 1591 of that title.

(3) A person charged with an offense is not liable to be punished under section 815 of this title (article 15) if the offense was committed more than two years before the imposition of punishment.

(c) TOLLING FOR ABSENCE WITHOUT LEAVE OR FLIGHT FROM JUSTICE.—Periods in which the accused is absent without authority or fleeing from justice shall be excluded in computing the period of limitation prescribed in this section (article).

(d) TOLLING FOR ABSENCE FROM US OR MILITARY JURISDICTION.—Periods in which the accused was absent from territory in which the United States has the authority to apprehend him, or in the custody of civil authorities, or in the hands of the enemy, shall be excluded in computing the period of limitation prescribed in this article.

(e) EXTENSION FOR OFFENSES IN TIME OF WAR DETRIMENTAL TO PROSECUTION OF WAR.—For an offense the trial of which in time of war is certified to the President by the Secretary concerned to be detrimental to the prosecution of the war or inimical to the national security, the period of limitation prescribed in this article is extended to six months after the termination of hostilities as proclaimed by the President or by a joint resolution of Congress.

(f) EXTENSION FOR OTHER OFFENSES IN TIME OF WAR.—When the United States is at war, the running of any statute of limitations applicable to any offense under this chapter—

(1) involving fraud or attempted fraud against the United States or any agency thereof in any manner, whether by conspiracy or not;

(2) committed in connection with the acquisition, care, handling, custody, control, or disposition of any real or personal property of the United States; or

(3) committed in connection with the negotiation, procurement, award, performance, payment, interim financing, cancellation, or other termination or settlement, of any contract, subcontract, or purchase order which is connected with or related to the prosecution of the war, or with any disposition of termination inventory by any war contractor or Government agency;

is suspended until three years after the termination of hostilities as proclaimed by the President or by a joint resolution of Congress.

(g) DEFECTIVE OR INSUFFICIENT CHARGES.—

(1) If charges or specifications are dismissed as defective or insufficient for any cause and the period prescribed by the applicable statute of limitations—

(A) has expired; or

(B) will expire within 180 days after the date of dismissal of the charges and specifications, trial and punishment under new charges and specifications are not barred by the statute of limitations if the conditions specified in paragraph (2) are met.

(2) The conditions referred to in paragraph (1) are that the new charges and specifications must—

(A) be received by an officer exercising summary court-martial jurisdiction over the command within 180 days after the dismissal of the charges or specifications; and

(B) allege the same acts or omissions that were alleged in the dismissed charges or specifications (or allege acts or omissions that were included in the dismissed charges or specifications).

(h) FRAUDULENT ENLISTMENT OR APPOINTMENT.—A person charged with fraudulent enlistment or fraudulent appointment under section 904a(1) of this title (article 104a(1)) may be tried by court-martial if the sworn charges and specifications are received by an officer exercising summary court-martial jurisdiction with respect to that person, as follows:

(1) In the case of an enlisted member, during the period of the enlistment or five years, whichever provides a longer period.

(2) In the case of an officer, during the period of the appointment or five years, whichever provides a longer period.

(i) DNA EVIDENCE.—If DNA testing implicates an identified person in the commission of an offense punishable by confinement for more than one year, no statute of limitations that would otherwise preclude prosecution of the offense shall preclude such prosecution until a period of time following the implication of the person by DNA testing has elapsed that is equal to the otherwise applicable limitation period.

§844. Art. 44. Former jeopardy

(a) No person may, without his consent, be tried a second time for the same offense.

(b) No proceeding in which an accused has been found guilty by a court-martial upon any charge or specification is a trial in the sense of this article until the finding of guilty has become final after review of the case has been fully completed.

(c)(1) A court-martial with a military judge alone is a trial in the sense of this section (article) if, without fault of the accused—

(A) after introduction of evidence; and

(B) before announcement of findings under section 853 of this title (article 53); the case is dismissed or terminated by the convening authority or the special trial counsel or on motion of the prosecution for failure of available evidence or witnesses.

(2) A court-martial with a military judge and members is a trial in the sense of this section (article) if, without fault of the accused—

(A) after the members, having taken an oath as members under section 842 of this title (article 42) and after completion of challenges under section 841 of this title (article 41), are impaneled; and

(B) before announcement of findings under section 853 of this title (article 53); the case is dismissed or terminated by the convening authority or the special trial counsel or on motion of the prosecution for failure of available evidence or witnesses.

§845. Art. 45. Pleas of the accused

(a) IRREGULAR AND SIMILAR PLEAS.—If an accused after arraignment makes an irregular pleading, or after a plea of guilty sets up matter inconsistent with the plea, or if it appears that he has entered the plea of guilty improvidently or through lack of understanding of its meaning and effect, or if he fails or refuses to plead, a plea of not guilty shall be entered in the record, and the court shall proceed as though he had pleaded not guilty.

(b) PLEAS OF GUILTY.—A plea of guilty by the accused may not be received to any charge or specification alleging an offense for which the death penalty is mandatory. With respect to any other charge or specification to which a plea of guilty has been made by the accused and accepted by the military judge, a finding of guilty of the charge or specification may be entered immediately without vote. This finding shall constitute the finding of the court unless the plea of guilty is withdrawn prior to announcement of the sentence, in which event the proceedings shall continue as though the accused had pleaded not guilty.

(c) HARMLESS ERROR.—A variance from the requirements of this article is harmless error if the variance does not materially prejudice the substantial rights of the accused.

§846. Art. 46. Opportunity to obtain witnesses and other evidence in trial by court-martial

(a) OPPORTUNITY TO OBTAIN WITNESSES AND OTHER EVIDENCE.—In a case referred for trial by court-martial, the trial counsel, the defense counsel, and the court-martial shall have equal opportunity to obtain witnesses and other evidence in accordance with such regulations as the President may prescribe.

(b) SUBPOENA AND OTHER PROCESS GENERALLY.—Any subpoena or other process issued under this section (article)—

(1) shall be similar to that which courts of the United States having criminal jurisdiction may issue;

(2) shall be executed in accordance with regulations prescribed by the President; and

(3) shall run to any part of the United States and to the Commonwealths and possessions of the United States.

(c) SUBPOENA AND OTHER PROCESS FOR WITNESSES.—A subpoena or other process may be issued to compel a witness to appear and testify—

(1) before a court-martial, military commission, or court of inquiry;

(2) at a deposition under section 849 of this title (article 49); or

(3) as otherwise authorized under this chapter.

(d) SUBPOENA AND OTHER PROCESS FOR EVIDENCE.—

(1) IN GENERAL.—A subpoena or other process may be issued to compel the production of evidence—

(A) for a court-martial, military commission, or court of inquiry;

(B) for a deposition under section 849 of this title (article 49);

(C) for an investigation of an offense under this chapter; or

(D) as otherwise authorized under this chapter.

(2) INVESTIGATIVE SUBPOENA.—An investigative subpoena under paragraph (1)(C) may be issued before referral of charges to a court-martial only if a general court-martial convening authority has authorized counsel for the Government to issue such a subpoena or a military judge issues such a subpoena pursuant to section 830a of this title (article 30a).

(3) WARRANT OR ORDER FOR WIRE OR ELECTRONIC COMMUNICATIONS.—With respect to an investigation of an offense under this chapter, a military judge detailed in accordance with section 826 or 830a of this title (article 26 or 30a), may issue warrants or court orders for the contents of, and records concerning, wire or electronic communications in the same manner as such warrants and orders may be issued by a district court of the United States under chapter 121 of title 18, subject to such limitations as the President may prescribe by regulation.

(e) REQUEST FOR RELIEF FROM SUBPOENA OR OTHER PROCESS.—If a person requests relief from a subpoena or other process under this section (article) on grounds that compliance is unreasonable or oppressive or is prohibited by law, a military judge detailed in accordance with section 826 or 830a of this title (article 26 or 30a) shall review the request and shall—

(1) order that the subpoena or other process be modified or withdrawn, as appropriate; or

(2) order the person to comply with the subpoena or other process.

§ 847. Art. 47. Refusal of person not subject to chapter to appear, testify, or produce evidence

(a) IN GENERAL.—

(1) Any person described in paragraph (2) who—

(A) willfully neglects or refuses to appear; or

(B) willfully refuses to qualify as a witness or to testify or to produce any evidence which that person is required to produce; is guilty of an offense against the United States.

(2) The persons referred to in paragraph (1) are the following:

(A) Any person not subject to this chapter who—

(i) is issued a subpoena or other process described in subsection (c) of section 846 of this title (article 46); and

(ii) is provided a means for reimbursement from the Government for fees and mileage at the rates allowed to witnesses attending the courts of the United States or, in the case of extraordinary hardship, is advanced such fees and mileage.

(B) Any person not subject to this chapter who is issued a subpoena or other process described in subsection (d) of section 846 of this title (article 46).

(b) Any person who commits an offense named in subsection (a) shall be tried on indictment or information in a United States district court or in a court of original criminal jurisdiction in any of the Commonwealths or possessions of the United States, and jurisdiction is conferred upon those courts for that purpose. Upon conviction, such a person shall be fined or imprisoned, or both, at the court's discretion.

(c) The United States attorney or the officer prosecuting for the United States in any such court of original criminal jurisdiction shall, upon the certification of the facts to him by the military court, commission, court of inquiry, board, or convening authority, file an information against and prosecute any person violating this article.

(d) The fees and mileage of witnesses shall be advanced or paid out of the appropriations for the compensation of witnesses.

§848. Art. 48. Contempt

(a) AUTHORITY TO PUNISH.—

(1) With respect to any proceeding under this chapter, a judicial officer specified in paragraph (2) may punish for contempt any person who—

(A) uses any menacing word, sign, or gesture in the presence of the judicial officer during the proceeding;

(B) disturbs the proceeding by any riot or disorder; or

(C) willfully disobeys a lawful writ, process, order, rule, decree, or command issued with respect to the proceeding.

(2) A judicial officer referred to in paragraph (1) is any of the following:

(A) Any judge of the Court of Appeals for the Armed Forces and any judge of a Court of Criminal Appeals under section 866 of this title (article 66).

(B) Any military judge detailed to a court-martial, a provost court, a military commission, or any other proceeding under this chapter.

(C) Any military magistrate designated to preside under section 819 of this title (article 19).

(D) The president of a court of inquiry.

(b) PUNISHMENT.—The punishment for contempt under subsection (a) may not exceed confinement for 30 days, a fine of $1,000, or both.

(c) REVIEW.—A punishment under this section—

(1) if imposed by a military judge or military magistrate, may be reviewed by the Court of Criminal Appeals in accordance with the uniform rules of procedure for the Courts of Criminal Appeals under section 866(h) of this title (article 66(h));

(2) if imposed by a judge of the Court of Appeals for the Armed Forces or a judge of a Court of Criminal Appeals, shall constitute a judgment of the court, subject to review under the applicable provisions of section 867 or 867a of this title (article 67 or 67a); and

(3) if imposed by a court of inquiry, shall be subject to review by the convening authority in accordance with rules prescribed by the President.

(d) INAPPLICABILITY TO MILITARY COMMISSIONS UNDER CHAPTER 47A.—This section does not apply to a military commission established under chapter 47A of this title.

§849. Art. 49. Depositions

(a) IN GENERAL.—

(1) Subject to paragraph (2), a convening authority or a military judge may order depositions at the request of any party.

(2) A deposition may be ordered under paragraph (1) only if the requesting party demonstrates that, due to exceptional circumstances, it is in the interest of justice that the testimony of a prospective witness be preserved for use at a court-martial, military commission, court of inquiry, or other military court or board.

(3) A party who requests a deposition under this section shall give to every other party reasonable written notice of the time and place for the deposition.

(4) A deposition under this section shall be taken before, and authenticated by, an impartial officer, as follows:

(A) Whenever practicable, by an impartial judge advocate certified under section 827(b) of this title (article 27(b)).

(B) In exceptional circumstances, by an impartial military or civil officer authorized to administer oaths by (i) the laws of the United States or (ii) the laws of the place where the deposition is taken.

(b) REPRESENTATION BY COUNSEL.—Representation of the parties with respect to a deposition shall be by counsel detailed in the same manner as trial counsel and defense counsel are detailed under section 827 of this title (article 27). In addition, the accused shall have the right to be represented by civilian or military counsel in the same manner as such counsel are provided for in section 838(b) of this title (article 38(b)).

(c) ADMISSIBILITY AND USE AS EVIDENCE.—A deposition order under subsection (a) does not control the admissibility of the deposition in a court-martial or other proceeding under this chapter. Except as provided by subsection (d), a party may use all or part of a deposition as provided by the rules of evidence.

(d) CAPITAL CASES.—Testimony by deposition may be presented in capital cases only by the defense.

§850. Art. 50. Admissibility of sworn testimony from records of courts of inquiry

(a) USE AS EVIDENCE BY ANY PARTY— In any case not capital and not extending to the dismissal of a commissioned officer, the sworn testimony, contained in the duly authenticated record of proceedings of a court of inquiry, of a person whose oral testimony cannot be obtained, may, if otherwise admissible under the rules of evidence, be read in evidence by any party before a court-martial or military commission if the accused was a party before the court of inquiry and if the same issue was involved or if the accused consents to the introduction of such evidence. This section does not apply to a military commission established under chapter 47A of this title.

(b) USE AS EVIDENCE BY DEFENSE— Such testimony may be read in evidence only by the defense in capital cases or cases extending to the dismissal of a commissioned officer.

(c) USE IN COURTS OF INQUIRY AND MILITARY BOARDS— Such testimony may also be read in evidence before a court of inquiry or a military board.

(d) AUDIOTAPE OR VIDEOTAPE.—Sworn testimony that—

(1) is recorded by audiotape, videotape, or similar method; and

(2) is contained in the duly authenticated record of proceedings of a court of inquiry;

is admissible before a court-martial, military commission, court of inquiry, or military board, to the same extent as sworn testimony may be read in evidence before any such body under subsection (a), (b), or (c).

§850a. Art. 50a. Defense of lack of mental responsibility

(a) It is an affirmative defense in a trial by court-martial that, at the time of the commission of the acts constituting the offense, the accused, as a result of a severe mental disease or defect, was unable to appreciate the nature and quality or the wrongfulness of the acts. Mental disease or defect does not otherwise constitute a defense.

(b) The accused has the burden of proving the defense of lack of mental responsibility by clear and convincing evidence.

(c) Whenever lack of mental responsibility of the accused with respect to an offense is properly at issue, the military judge shall instruct the members of the court as to the defense of lack of mental responsibility under this section and charge them to find the accused—

(1) guilty;

(2) not guilty; or

(3) not guilty only by reason of lack of mental responsibility.

(d) Subsection (c) does not apply to a court-martial composed of a military judge only. In the case of a court-martial composed of a military judge only, whenever lack of mental responsibility of the accused with respect to an offense is properly at issue, the military judge shall find the accused—

(1) guilty;

(2) not guilty; or

(3) not guilty only by reason of lack of mental responsibility.

(e) Notwithstanding the provisions of section 852 of this title (article 52), the accused shall be found not guilty only by reason of lack of mental responsibility if—

(1) a majority of the members of the court-martial present at the time the vote is taken determines that the defense of lack of mental responsibility has been established; or

(2) in the case of a court-martial composed of a military judge only, the military judge determines that the defense of lack of mental responsibility has been established.

§851. Art. 51. Voting and rulings

(a) Voting by members of a general or special court martial on the findings and on the sentence shall be by secret written ballot. The junior member of the court shall count the votes. The count shall be checked by the president, who shall forthwith announce the result of the ballot to the members of the court.

(b) The military judge shall rule upon all questions of law and all interlocutory questions arising during the proceedings. Any such ruling made by the military judge upon any question of law or any interlocutory question other than the factual issue of mental responsibility of the accused is final and constitutes the ruling of the court, except that the military judge may change a ruling at any time during trial.

(c) Before a vote is taken on the findings, the military judge shall, in the presence of the accused and counsel, instruct the members of the court as to the elements of the offense and charge them—

(1) that the accused must be presumed to be innocent until his guilt is established by legal and competent evidence beyond reasonable doubt;

(2) that in the case being considered, if there is a reasonable doubt as to the guilt of the accused, the doubt must be resolved in favor of the accused and he must be acquitted;

(3) that, if there is a reasonable doubt as to the degree of guilt, the finding must be in a lower degree as to which there is no reasonable doubt; and

(4) that the burden of proof to establish the guilt of the accused beyond reasonable doubt is upon the United States.

(d) Subsections (a), (b), and (c) do not apply to a court-martial composed of a military judge only. The military judge of such a court-martial shall determine all questions of law and fact arising during the proceedings and, if the accused is convicted, adjudge an appropriate sentence. The military judge of such a court-martial shall make a general finding and shall in addition on request find the facts specially. If an opinion or memorandum of decision is filed, it will be sufficient if the findings of fact appear therein.

§852. Art. 52. Votes required for conviction, sentencing, and other matters

(a) IN GENERAL.—No person may be convicted of an offense in a general or special court-martial, other than—

(1) after a plea of guilty under section 845(b) of this title (article 45(b));

(2) by a military judge in a court-martial with a military judge alone, under section 816 of this title (article 16); or

(3) in a court-martial with members under section 816 of this title (article 16), by the concurrence of at least three-fourths of the members present when the vote is taken.

(b) LEVEL OF CONCURRENCE REQUIRED.—

(1) IN GENERAL—Except as provided in subsection (a) and in paragraph (2), all matters to be decided by members of a general or special court-martial shall be determined by a majority vote, but a reconsideration of a finding of guilty or reconsideration of a sentence, with a view toward decreasing the sentence, may be made by any lesser vote which indicates that the reconsideration is not opposed by the number of votes required for that finding or sentence.

(2) SENTENCING.—A sentence of death requires (A) a unanimous finding of guilty of an offense in this chapter expressly made punishable by death and (B) a unanimous determination by the members that the sentence for that offense shall include death. All other sentences imposed by members shall be determined by the concurrence of at least three-fourths of the members present when the vote is taken.

§853. Art. 53. Findings and sentencing

(a) ANNOUNCEMENT.—A court-martial shall announce its findings and sentence to the parties as soon as determined.

(b) SENTENCING GENERALLY.—

(1) GENERAL AND SPECIAL COURTS-MARTIAL.—Except as provided in subsection (c) for capital offenses, if the accused is convicted of an offense in a trial by general or special court martial, the military judge shall sentence the accused. The sentence determined by the military judge constitutes the sentence of the court-martial.

(A) SENTENCING BY MILITARY JUDGE.—Except as provided in subparagraph (B), and in subsection (c) for capital offenses, if the accused is convicted of an offense in a trial by general or special court-martial, the military judge shall sentence the accused.

(B) SENTENCING BY MEMBERS.—If the accused is convicted of an offense by general or special court-martial consisting of a military judge and members and the accused elects sentencing by members under section 825 of this title (article 25), the members shall sentence the accused.

(C) SENTENCE OF THE ACCUSED.—The sentence determined pursuant to this paragraph constitutes the sentence of the accused.

(2) SUMMARY COURTS-MARTIAL. —If the accused is convicted of an offense in a trial by summary court-martial, the court-martial shall sentence the accused.

(c) SENTENCING FOR CAPITAL OFFENSES.—

(1) IN GENERAL.—In a capital case, if the accused is convicted of an offense for which the court-martial may sentence the accused to death—

(A) the members shall determine—

(i) whether the sentence for that offense shall be death or life in prison without eligibility for parole; or

(ii) whether the matter shall be returned to the military judge for determination of a lesser punishment; and

(B) the military judge shall sentence the accused for that offense in accordance with the determination of the members under subparagraph (A).

(2) LESSER AUTHORIZED PUNISHMENT.—In accordance with regulations prescribed by the President, the military judge may include in any sentence to death or life in prison without eligibility for parole other lesser punishments authorized under this chapter.

(3) OTHER NON-CAPITAL OFFENSES.—In a capital case, if the accused is convicted of a non-capital offense, the accused shall be sentenced for such non-capital offense in accordance with subsection (b), regardless of whether the accused is convicted of an offense for which the court-martial may sentence the accused to death.

§853a. Art. 53a. Plea agreements

(a) IN GENERAL.—

(1) Subject to paragraph (3), at any time before the announcement of findings under section 853 of this title (article 53), the convening authority and the accused may enter into a plea agreement with respect to such matters as—

(A) the manner in which the convening authority will dispose of one or more charges and specifications; and

(B) limitations on the sentence that may be adjudged for one or more charges and specifications.

(2) The military judge of a general or special court-martial may not participate in discussions between the parties concerning prospective terms and conditions of a plea agreement.

(3) With respect to charges and specifications over which a special trial counsel exercises authority pursuant to section 824a of this title (article 24a), a plea agreement under this section may only be entered into between a special trial counsel and the accused. Such agreement shall be subject to the same limitations and conditions applicable to other plea agreements under this section (article).

(b) ACCEPTANCE OF PLEA AGREEMENT.—Subject to subsection (c), the military judge of a general or special court-martial shall accept a plea agreement submitted by the parties, except that—

(1) in the case of an offense with a sentencing parameter set forth in regulations prescribed by the President pursuant to section 539E(e) of the National Defense Authorization Act for Fiscal Year 2022, the military judge may reject a plea agreement that proposes a sentence that is outside the sentencing parameter if the military judge determines that the proposed sentence is plainly unreasonable; and

(2) in the case of an offense for which the President has not established a sentencing parameter pursuant to section 539E(e) of the National Defense Authorization Act for Fiscal Year 2022, the military judge may reject a plea agreement that proposes a sentence if the military judge determines that the proposed sentence is plainly unreasonable.

(c) LIMITATION ON ACCEPTANCE OF PLEA AGREEMENTS.—The military judge of a general or special court-martial shall reject a plea agreement that—

(1) contains a provision that has not been accepted by both parties;

(2) contains a provision that is not understood by the accused;

(3) except as provided in subsection (c), contains a provision for a sentence that is less than the mandatory minimum sentence applicable to an offense referred to in section 856(b)(2) of this title (article 56(b)(2));

(4) is prohibited by law; or

(5) is contrary to, or is inconsistent with, a regulation prescribed by the President with respect to terms, conditions, or other aspects of plea agreements.

(d) LIMITED CONDITIONS FOR ACCEPTANCE OF PLEA AGREEMENT FOR SENTENCE BELOW MANDATORY MINIMUM FOR CERTAIN OFFENSES.—With respect to an offense referred to in section 856(b)(2) of this title (article 56(b)(2))—

(1) the military judge may accept a plea agreement that provides for a sentence of bad conduct discharge; and

(2) upon recommendation of the trial counsel, in exchange for substantial assistance by the accused in the investigation or prosecution of another person who has committed an offense, the military judge may accept a plea agreement that provides for a sentence that is less than the mandatory minimum sentence for the offense charged.

(e) BINDING EFFECT OF PLEA AGREEMENT.—Upon acceptance by the military judge of a general or special court-martial, a plea agreement shall bind the parties (including the convening authority and the special trial counsel in the case of a plea agreement entered into under subsection (a)(3)) and the court-martial.

§854. Art. 54. Record of trial

(a) GENERAL AND SPECIAL COURTS-MARTIAL.—Each general or special court-martial shall keep a separate record of the proceedings in each case brought before it. The record shall be certified by a court-reporter, except that in the case of death, disability, or absence of a court reporter, the record shall be certified by an official selected as the President may prescribe by regulation.

(b) SUMMARY COURT-MARTIAL.—Each summary court-martial shall keep a separate record of the proceedings in each case, and the record shall be certified in the manner required by such regulations as the President may prescribe.

(c) CONTENTS OF RECORD.—

(1) Except as provided in paragraph (2), the record shall contain such matters as the President may prescribe by regulation.

(2) In accordance with regulations prescribed by the President, a complete record of proceedings and testimony shall be prepared in any case of a sentence of death, dismissal, discharge, confinement for more than six months, or forfeiture of pay for more than six months.

(d) COPY TO ACCUSED.— A copy of the record of the proceedings of each general and special court-martial shall be given to the accused as soon as it is certified.

(e) COPY TO VICTIM.—In the case of a general or special court-martial, upon request, a copy of all prepared records of the proceedings of the court-martial shall be given to the victim of the offense if the victim testified during the proceedings. The records of the proceedings shall be provided without charge and as soon as the records are certified. The victim shall be notified of the opportunity to receive the records of the proceedings.

SUBCHAPTER VIII—SENTENCES

§855. Art. 55. Cruel and unusual punishments prohibited

Punishment by flogging, or by branding, marking, or tattooing on the body, or any other cruel or unusual punishment, may not be adjudged by any court-martial or inflicted upon any person subject to this chapter. The use of irons, single or double, except for the purpose of safe custody, is prohibited.

§856. Art. 56. Sentencing

(a) SENTENCE MAXIMUMS.—The punishment which a court-martial may direct for an offense may not exceed such limits as the President may prescribe for that offense.

(b) SENTENCE MINIMUMS FOR CERTAIN OFFENSES.—(1) Except as provided in subsection (c) of section 853a of this title (article 53a), punishment for any offense specified in paragraph (2) shall include dismissal or dishonorable discharge, as applicable.

(2) The offenses referred to in paragraph (1) are as follows:

(A) Rape under subsection (a) of section 920 of this title (article 120).

(B) Sexual assault under subsection (b) of such section (article).

(C) Rape of a child under subsection (a) of section 920b of this title (article 120b).

(D) Sexual assault of a child under subsection (b) of such section (article).

(E) An attempt to commit an offense specified in subparagraph (A), (B), (C), or (D) that is punishable under section 880 of this title (article 80).

(F) Conspiracy to commit an offense specified in subparagraph (A), (B), (C), or (D) that is punishable under section 881 of this title (article 81).

(c) IMPOSITION OF SENTENCE.—

(1) IN GENERAL.—In sentencing an accused under section 853 of this title (article 53), a court-martial shall impose punishment that is sufficient, but not greater than necessary, to promote justice and to maintain good order and discipline in the armed forces, taking into consideration—

(A) the nature and circumstances of the offense and the history and characteristics of the accused;

(B) the impact of the offense on—

(i) the financial, social, psychological, or medical well-being of any victim of the offense; and

(ii) the mission, discipline, or efficiency of the command of the accused and any victim of the offense;

(C) the need for the sentence—

(i) to reflect the seriousness of the offense;

(ii) to promote respect for the law;

(iii) to provide just punishment for the offense;

(iv) to promote adequate deterrence of misconduct;

(v) to protect others from further crimes by the accused;

(vi) to rehabilitate the accused; and

(vii) to provide, in appropriate cases, the opportunity for retraining and return to duty to meet the needs of the service;

(D) the sentences available under this chapter; and

(E) the applicable sentencing parameters or sentencing criteria set forth in regulations prescribed by the President pursuant to section 539E(e) of the National Defense Authorization Act for Fiscal Year 2022.

(2) APPLICATION OF SENTENCING PARAMETERS IN GENERAL AND SPECIAL COURTS-MARTIAL.—

(A) REQUIREMENT TO SENTENCE WITHIN PARAMETERS.—Except as provided in subparagraph (B), in a general or special court-martial in which the accused is convicted of an offense for which the President has established a sentencing parameter pursuant to section 539E(e) of the National Defense Authorization Act for Fiscal Year 2022, the military judge shall sentence the accused for that offense within the applicable parameter.

(B) EXCEPTION.—The military judge may impose a sentence outside a sentencing parameter upon finding specific facts that warrant such a sentence. If the military judge imposes a sentence outside a sentencing parameter under this subparagraph, the military judge shall include in the record a written statement of the factual basis for the sentence.

(3) USE OF SENTENCING CRITERIA IN GENERAL AND SPECIAL COURTS-MARTIAL.—In a general or special court-martial in which the accused is convicted of an offense for which the President has established sentencing criteria pursuant to section 539E(e) of the National Defense Authorization Act for Fiscal Year 2022, the military judge shall consider the applicable sentencing criteria in determining the sentence for that offense.

(4) OFFENSE-BASED SENTENCING IN GENERAL AND SPECIAL COURTS MARTIAL.—In announcing the sentence under section 853 of this title (article 53) in a general or special court-martial, the military judge shall, with respect to each offense of which the accused is found guilty, specify the term of confinement, if any, and the amount of the fine, if any. If the accused is sentenced to confinement for more than one offense, the military judge shall specify whether the terms of confinement are to run consecutively or concurrently.

(5) INAPPLICABILITY TO DEATH PENALTY.—Sentencing parameters and sentencing criteria shall not apply to a determination of whether an offense should be punished by death.

(6) SENTENCE OF CONFINEMENT FOR LIFE WITHOUT ELIGIBILITY FOR PAROLE.—

(A) IN GENERAL.—If an offense is subject to a sentence of confinement for life, a court-martial may impose a sentence of confinement for life without eligibility for parole.

(B) TERM OF CONFINEMENT.—An accused who is sentenced to confinement for life without eligibility for parole shall be confined for the remainder of the accused's life unless—

(i) the sentence is set aside or otherwise modified as a result of—

(I) action taken by the convening authority or the Secretary concerned; or

(II) any other action taken during post-trial procedure or review under any other provision of subchapter IX of this chapter;

(ii) the sentence is set aside or otherwise modified as a result of action taken by a court of competent jurisdiction; or

(iii) the accused receives a pardon or another form of Executive clemency.

(d) APPEAL OF SENTENCE BY THE UNITED STATES.—

(1) With the approval of the Judge Advocate General concerned, and consistent with standards and procedures set forth in regulations prescribed by the President, the Government may appeal a sentence to the Court of Criminal Appeals, on the grounds that—

(A) the sentence violates the law;

(B) in the case of a sentence for an offense for which the President has established a sentencing parameter pursuant to section 539E(e) of the National Defense Authorization Act for Fiscal Year 2022, the sentence is a result of an incorrect application of the parameter; or

(C) the sentence is plainly unreasonable.

(2) An appeal under this subsection must be filed within 60 days after the date on which the judgment of a court-martial is entered into the record under section 860c of this title (article 60c).

§857. Art. 57. Effective date of sentences

(a) EXECUTION OF SENTENCES.—A court-martial sentence shall be executed and take effect as follows:

(1) FORFEITURE AND REDUCTION.—A forfeiture of pay or allowances shall be applicable to pay and allowances accruing on and after the date on which the sentence takes effect. Any forfeiture of pay or allowances or reduction in grade that is included in a sentence of a court-martial takes effect on the earlier of—

(A) the date that is 14 days after the date on which the sentence is adjudged; or

(B) in the case of a summary court-martial, the date on which the sentence is approved by the convening authority.

(2) CONFINEMENT.—Any period of confinement included in a sentence of a court-martial begins to run from the date the sentence is adjudged by the court-martial, but periods during which the sentence to confinement is suspended or deferred shall be excluded in computing the service of the term of confinement.

(3) APPROVAL OF SENTENCE OF DEATH.—If the sentence of the court-martial extends to death, that part of the sentence providing for death may not be executed until approved by the President. In such a case, the President may commute, remit, or suspend the sentence, or any part thereof, as the President sees fit. That part of the sentence providing for death may not be suspended.

(4) APPROVAL OF DISMISSAL.—If in the case of a commissioned officer, cadet, or midshipman, the sentence of a court-martial extends to dismissal, that part of the sentence providing for dismissal may not be executed until approved by the Secretary concerned or such Under Secretary or Assistant Secretary as may be designated by the Secretary concerned. In such a case, the Secretary, Under Secretary, or Assistant Secretary, as the case may be, may commute, remit, or suspend the sentence, or any part of the sentence, as the Secretary sees fit. In time of war or national emergency he may commute a sentence of dismissal to reduction to any enlisted grade. A person so reduced may be required to serve for the duration of the war or emergency and six months thereafter.

(5) COMPLETION OF APPELLATE REVIEW.—If a sentence extends to death, dismissal, or a dishonorable or bad-conduct discharge, that part of the sentence extending to death, dismissal, or a dishonorable or bad-conduct discharge may be executed, in accordance with service regulations, after completion of appellate review (and, with respect to death or dismissal, approval under paragraph (3) or (4), as appropriate).

(6) OTHER SENTENCES.—Except as otherwise provided in this subsection, a general or special court-martial sentence is effective upon entry of judgment and a summary court-martial sentence is effective when the convening authority acts on the sentence.

(b) DEFERRAL OF SENTENCES.—

(1) IN GENERAL.—On application by an accused, the convening authority or, if the accused is no longer under his or her jurisdiction, the officer exercising general court-martial jurisdiction over the command to which the accused is currently assigned, may, in his or her sole discretion, defer the effective date of a sentence of confinement, reduction, or forfeiture. The deferment shall terminate upon entry of judgment or, in the case of a summary court-martial, when the convening authority acts on the sentence. The deferment may be rescinded at any time by the officer who granted it or, if the accused is no longer under his jurisdiction, by the officer exercising general court-martial jurisdiction over the command to which the accused is currently assigned.

(2) DEFERRAL OF CERTAIN PERSONS SENTENCED TO CONFINEMENT.—In any case in which a court-martial sentences a person referred to in paragraph (3) to confinement, the convening authority may defer the service of the sentence to confinement, without the consent of that person, until after the person has been permanently released to the armed forces by a State or foreign country referred to in that paragraph.

(3) COVERED PERSONS.—Paragraph (2) applies to a person subject to this chapter who—

(A) while in the custody of a State or foreign country is temporarily returned by that State or foreign country to the armed forces for trial by court-martial; and

(B) after the court-martial, is returned to that State or foreign country under the authority of a mutual agreement or treaty, as the case may be.

(4) STATE DEFINED.—In this subsection, the term "State" includes the District of Columbia and any Commonwealth, territory, or possession of the United States.

(5) DEFERRAL WHILE REVIEW PENDING.—In any case in which a court-martial sentences a person to confinement, but in which review of the case under section 867(a)(2) of this title (article 67(a)(2)) is pending, the Secretary concerned may defer further service of the sentence to confinement while that review is pending.

(c) APPELLATE REVIEW.—

(1) COMPLETION OF APPELLATE REVIEW.—Appellate review is complete under this section when—

(A) a review under section 865 of this title (article 65) is completed; or

(B) a review under section 866 of this title (article 66) is completed by a Court of Criminal Appeals and—

(i) the time for the accused to file a petition for review by the Court of Appeals for the Armed Forces has expired and the accused has not filed a timely petition for such review and the case is not otherwise under review by that Court;

(ii) such a petition is rejected by the Court of Appeals for the Armed Forces; or

(iii) review is completed in accordance with the judgment of the Court of Appeals for the Armed Forces and—

(I) a petition for a writ of certiorari is not filed within the time limits prescribed by the Supreme Court;

(II) such a petition is rejected by the Supreme Court; or

(III) review is otherwise completed in accordance with the judgment of the Supreme Court.

(2) COMPLETION AS FINAL JUDGMENT OF LEGALITY OF PROCEEDINGS.—The completion of appellate review shall constitute a final judgment as to the legality of the proceedings.

§858. Art. 58. Execution of confinement

(a) Under such instructions as the Secretary concerned may prescribe, a sentence of confinement adjudged by a court-martial or other military tribunal, whether or not the sentence includes discharge or dismissal, and whether or not the discharge or dismissal has been executed, may be carried into execution by confinement in any place of confinement under the control of any of the armed forces or in any penal or correctional institution under the control of the United States, or which the United States may be allowed to use. Persons so confined in a penal or correctional institution not under the control of one of the armed forces are subject to the same discipline and treatment as persons confined or committed by the courts of the United States or of the State, District of Columbia, or place in which the institution is situated.

(b) The omission of the words "hard labor" from any sentence of a court-martial adjudging confinement does not deprive the authority executing that sentence of the power to require hard labor as a part of the punishment.

§858a. Art. 58a. Sentences: reduction in enlisted grade

(a) A court-martial sentence of an enlisted member in a pay grade above E–1, as set forth in the judgment of the court-martial entered into the record under section 860c of this title (article 60c), that includes—

(1) a dishonorable or bad-conduct discharge;

(2) confinement; or

(3) hard labor without confinement;

reduces that member to pay grade E–1, if such reduction is authorized by regulation prescribed by the President. The reduction in pay grade shall take effect on the date on which the judgment is so entered.

(b) If the sentence of a member who is reduced in pay grade under subsection (a) is set aside or reduced, or, as finally affirmed, does not include any punishment named in subsection (a)(1), (2), or (3), the rights and privileges of which he was deprived because of that reduction shall be restored to him and he is entitled to the pay and allowances to which he would have been entitled, for the period the reduction was in effect, had he not been so reduced.

§858b. Art. 58b. Sentences: forfeiture of pay and allowances during confinement

(a)(1) A court-martial sentence described in paragraph (2) shall result in the forfeiture of pay, or of pay and allowances, due that member during any period of confinement or parole. The forfeiture pursuant to this section shall take effect on the date determined under section 857 of this title (article 57) and may be deferred as provided in that section. The pay and allowances forfeited, in the case of a general court-martial, shall be all pay and allowances due that member during such period and, in the case of a special court-martial, shall be two-thirds of all pay due that member during such period.

(2) A sentence covered by this section is any sentence that includes—

(A) confinement for more than six months or death; or

(B) confinement for six months or less and a dishonorable or bad-conduct discharge or dismissal.

(b) In a case involving an accused who has dependents, the convening authority or other person acting under section 860a or 860b of this title (article 60a or 60b) may waive any or all of the forfeitures of pay and allowances required by subsection (a) for a period not to exceed six months. Any amount of pay or allowances that, except for a waiver under this subsection, would be forfeited shall be paid, as the convening authority or other person taking action directs, to the dependents of the accused.

(c) If the sentence of a member who forfeits pay and allowances under subsection (a) is set aside or disapproved or, as finally approved, does not provide for a punishment referred to in subsection (a)(2), the member shall be paid the pay and allowances which the member would have been paid, except for the forfeiture, for the period during which the forfeiture was in effect.

SUBCHAPTER IX. POST-TRIAL PROCEDURE AND REVIEW OF COURTS-MARTIAL

§859. Art. 59. Error of law; lesser included offense

(a) A finding or sentence of a court-martial may not be held incorrect on the ground of an error of law unless the error materially prejudices the substantial rights of the accused.

(b) Any reviewing authority with the power to approve or affirm a finding of guilty may approve or affirm, instead, so much of the finding as includes a lesser included offense.

§860. Art. 60. Post-trial processing in general and special courts-martial

(a) STATEMENT OF TRIAL RESULTS.—

(1) The military judge of a general or special court-martial shall enter into the record of trial a document entitled "Statement of Trial Results", which shall set forth—

(A) each plea and finding;

(B) the sentence, if any; and

(C) such other information as the President may prescribe by regulation.

(2) Copies of the Statement of Trial Results shall be provided promptly to the convening authority, the accused, and any victim of the offense.

(b) POST-TRIAL MOTIONS.—In accordance with regulations prescribed by the President, the military judge in a general or special court-martial shall address all post-trial motions and other post-trial matters that—

(1) may affect a plea, a finding, the sentence, the Statement of Trial Results, the record of trial, or any post-trial action by the convening authority; and

(2) are subject to resolution by the military judge before entry of judgment.

§860a. Art. 60a. Limited authority to act on sentence in specified post-trial circumstances

(a) IN GENERAL.—

(1) The convening authority of a general or special court-martial described in paragraph (2)—

(A) may act on the sentence of the court-martial only as provided in subsection (b), (c), or (d); and

(B) may not act on the findings of the court-martial.

(2) The courts-martial referred to in paragraph (1) are the following:

(A) A general or special court-martial in which the maximum sentence of confinement established under subsection (a) of section 856 of this title (article 56) for any offense of which the accused is found guilty is more than two years.

(B) A general or special court-martial in which the total of the sentences of confinement imposed, running consecutively, is more than six months.

(C) A general or special court-martial in which the sentence imposed includes a dismissal, dishonorable discharge, or bad-conduct discharge.

(D) A general or special court-martial in which the accused is found guilty of a violation of subsection (a) or (b) of section 920 of this title (article 120), section 920b of this title (article 120b), or such other offense as the Secretary of Defense may specify by regulation.

(3) Except as provided in subsection (d), the convening authority may act under this section only before entry of judgment.

(4) Under regulations prescribed by the Secretary concerned, a commissioned officer commanding for the time being, a successor in command, or any person exercising general court-martial jurisdiction may act under this section in place of the convening authority.

(b) REDUCTION, COMMUTATION, AND SUSPENSION OF SENTENCES GENERALLY.—

(1) Except as provided in subsection (c) or (d), the convening authority may not reduce, commute, or suspend any of the following sentences:

(A) A sentence of confinement, if the total period of confinement imposed for all offenses involved, running consecutively, is greater than six months.

(B) A sentence of dismissal, dishonorable discharge, or bad-conduct discharge.

(C) A sentence of death.

(2) The convening authority may reduce, commute, or suspend any sentence not specified in paragraph (1).

(c) SUSPENSION OF CERTAIN SENTENCES UPON RECOMMENDATION OF MILITARY JUDGE.—

(1) Upon recommendation of the military judge, as included in the Statement of Trial Results, together with an explanation of the facts supporting the recommendation, the convening authority may suspend—

(A) a sentence of confinement, in whole or in part; or

(B) a sentence of dismissal, dishonorable discharge, or bad-conduct discharge.

(2) The convening authority may not, under paragraph (1)—

(A) suspend a mandatory minimum sentence; or

(B) suspend a sentence to an extent in excess of the suspension recommended by the military judge.

(d) REDUCTION OF SENTENCE FOR SUBSTANTIAL ASSISTANCE BY ACCUSED.—

(1) Upon a recommendation by the trial counsel, if the accused, after sentencing and before entry of judgment, provides substantial assistance in the investigation or prosecution of another person, the convening authority may reduce, commute, or suspend a sentence, in whole or in part, including any mandatory minimum sentence.

(2) Upon a recommendation by a trial counsel, designated in accordance with rules prescribed by the President, if the accused, after entry of judgment, provides substantial assistance in the investigation or prosecution of another person, a convening authority, designated under such regulations, may reduce, commute, or suspend a sentence, in whole or in part, including any mandatory minimum sentence.

(3) In evaluating whether the accused has provided substantial assistance under this subsection, the convening authority may consider the presentence assistance of the accused.

(e) SUBMISSIONS BY ACCUSED AND VICTIM.—

(1) In accordance with rules prescribed by the President, in determining whether to act under this section, the convening authority shall consider matters submitted in writing by the accused or any victim of an offense. Such rules shall include—

(A) procedures for notice of the opportunity to make such submissions;

(B) the deadlines for such submissions; and

(C) procedures for providing the accused and any victim of an offense with a copy of the recording of any open sessions of the court-martial and copies of, or access to, any admitted, unsealed exhibits.

(2) The convening authority shall not consider under this section any submitted matters that relate to the character of a victim unless such matters were presented as evidence at trial and not excluded at trial.

(f) DECISION OF CONVENING AUTHORITY.—

(1) The decision of the convening authority under this section shall be forwarded to the military judge, with copies provided to the accused and to any victim of the offense.

(2) If, under this section, the convening authority reduces, commutes, or suspends the sentence, the decision of the convening authority shall include a written explanation of the reasons for such action.

(3) If, under subsection (d)(2), the convening authority reduces, commutes, or suspends the sentence, the decision of the convening authority shall be forwarded to the chief trial judge for appropriate modification of the entry of judgment, which shall be transmitted to the Judge Advocate General for appropriate action.

§860b. Art. 60b. Post-trial actions in summary courts-martial and certain general and special courts-martial

(a) IN GENERAL.—

(1) In a court-martial not specified in section 860a(a)(2) of this title (article 60a(a)(2)), the convening authority may—

(A) dismiss any charge or specification by setting aside the finding of guilty;

(B) change a finding of guilty to a charge or specification to a finding of guilty to a lesser included offense;

(C) disapprove the findings and the sentence and dismiss the charges and specifications;

(D) disapprove the findings and the sentence and order a rehearing as to the findings and the sentence;

(E) disapprove, commute, or suspend the sentence, in whole or in part; or

(F) disapprove the sentence and order a rehearing as to the sentence.

(2) In a summary court-martial, the convening authority shall approve the sentence or take other action on the sentence under paragraph (1).

(3) Except as provided in paragraph (4), the convening authority may act under this section only before entry of judgment.

(4) The convening authority may act under this section after entry of judgment in a general or special court-martial in the same manner as the convening authority may act under section 860a(d)(2) of this title (article 60a(d)(2)). Such action shall be forwarded to the chief trial judge, who shall ensure appropriate modification to the entry of judgment and shall transmit the entry of judgment to the Judge Advocate General for appropriate action.

(5) Under regulations prescribed by the Secretary concerned, a commissioned officer commanding for the time being, a successor in command, or any person exercising general court-martial jurisdiction may act under this section in place of the convening authority.

(b) LIMITATIONS ON REHEARINGS.—The convening authority may not order a rehearing under this section—

(1) as to the findings, if there is insufficient evidence in the record to support the findings;

(2) to reconsider a finding of not guilty of any specification or a ruling which amounts to a finding of not guilty; or

(3) to reconsider a finding of not guilty of any charge, unless there has been a finding of guilty under a specification laid under that charge, which sufficiently alleges a violation of some article of this chapter.

(c) SUBMISSIONS BY ACCUSED AND VICTIM.—In accordance with rules prescribed by the President, in determining whether to act under this section, the convening authority shall consider matters submitted in writing by the accused or any victim of the offense. Such rules shall include the matter required by section 860a(e) of this title (article 60a(e)).

(d) DECISION OF CONVENING AUTHORITY.—

(1) In a general or special court-martial, the decision of the convening authority under this section shall be forwarded to the military judge, with copies provided to the accused and to any victim of the offense.

(2) If the convening authority acts on the findings or the sentence under subsection (a)(1), the decision of the convening authority shall include a written explanation of the reasons for such action.

§860c. Art 60c. Entry of judgment

(a) ENTRY OF JUDGMENT OF GENERAL OR SPECIAL COURT-MARTIAL.—

(1) In accordance with rules prescribed by the President, in a general or special court-martial, the military judge shall enter into the record of trial the judgment of the court. The judgment of the court shall consist of the following:

(A) The Statement of Trial Results under section 860 of this title (article 60).

(B) Any modifications of, or supplements to, the Statement of Trial Results by reason of—

(i) any post-trial action by the convening authority; or

(ii) any ruling, order, or other determination of the military judge that affects a plea, a finding, or the sentence.

(2) Under rules prescribed by the President, the judgment under paragraph (1) shall be—

(A) provided to the accused and to any victim of the offense; and

(B) made available to the public.

(b) SUMMARY COURT-MARTIAL JUDGMENT.—The findings and sentence of a summary court-martial, as modified by any post-trial action by the convening authority under section 860b of this title (article 60b), constitutes the judgment of the court-martial and shall be recorded and distributed under rules prescribed by the President.

§861. Art. 61. Waiver of right to appeal; withdrawal of appeal

(a) WAIVER OF RIGHT TO APPEAL.—After entry of judgment in a general or special court-martial, under procedures prescribed by the Secretary concerned, the accused may waive the right to appellate review in each case subject to such review under section 866 of this title (article 66). Such a waiver shall be—

(1) signed by the accused and by defense counsel; and

(2) attached to the record of trial.

(b) WITHDRAWAL OF APPEAL.—In a general or special court-martial, the accused may withdraw an appeal at any time.

(c) DEATH PENALTY CASE EXCEPTION.—Notwithstanding subsections (a) and (b), an accused may not waive the right to appeal or withdraw an appeal with respect to a judgment that includes a sentence of death.

(d) WAIVER OR WITHDRAWAL AS BAR. Except as provided by section 869(c)(2) of this title (article 69(c)(2)), a waiver or withdrawal under this section bars review under section 866 of this title (article 66).

§862. Art. 62. Appeal by the United States

(a)(1) In a trial by general or special court-martial, or in a pretrial proceeding under section 830a of this title (article 30a), the United States may appeal the following:

(A) An order or ruling of the military judge which terminates the proceedings with respect to a charge or specification.

(B) An order or ruling which excludes evidence that is substantial proof of a fact material in the proceeding.

(C) An order or ruling which directs the disclosure of classified information.

(D) An order or ruling which imposes sanctions for nondisclosure of classified information.

(E) A refusal of the military judge to issue a protective order sought by the United States to prevent the disclosure of classified information.

(F) A refusal by the military judge to enforce an order described in subparagraph (E) that has previously been issued by appropriate authority.

(G) An order or ruling of the military judge entering a finding of not guilty with respect to a charge or specification following the return of a finding of guilty by the members.

(2)(A) An appeal of an order or ruling may not be taken unless the trial counsel provides the military judge with written notice of appeal from the order or ruling within 72 hours of the order or ruling. Such notice shall include a certification by the trial counsel that the appeal is not taken for the purpose of delay and (if the order or ruling appealed is one which excludes evidence) that the evidence excluded is substantial proof of a fact material in the proceeding.

(B) An appeal of an order or ruling may not be taken when prohibited by section 844 of this title (article 44).

(3) An appeal under this section shall be diligently prosecuted by appellate Government counsel.

(b) An appeal under this section shall be forwarded by a means prescribed under regulations of the President directly to the Court of Criminal Appeals and shall, whenever practicable, have priority over all other proceedings before that court. In ruling on an appeal under this section, the Court of Criminal Appeals may act only with respect to matters of law.

(c) Any period of delay resulting from an appeal under this section shall be excluded in deciding any issue regarding denial of a speedy trial unless an appropriate authority determines that the appeal was filed solely for the purpose of delay with the knowledge that it was totally frivolous and without merit.

(d) The United States may appeal a ruling or order of a military magistrate in the same manner as had the ruling or order been made by a military judge, except that the issue shall first be presented to the military judge who designated the military magistrate or to a military judge detailed to hear the issue.

(e) The provisions of this article shall be liberally construed to effect its purposes.

§863. Art. 63. Rehearings

(a) Each rehearing under this chapter shall take place before a court-martial composed of members not members of the court-martial which first heard the case. Upon a rehearing the accused may not be tried for any offense of which he was found not guilty by the first court-martial, and no sentence in excess of or more severe than the original sentence may be adjudged, unless the sentence is based upon a finding of guilty of an offense not considered upon the merits in the original proceedings, or unless the sentence prescribed for the offense is mandatory.

(b) If the sentence adjudged by the first court-martial was in accordance with a plea agreement under section 853a of this title (article 53a) and the accused at the rehearing does not comply with the agreement, or if a plea of guilty was entered for an offense at the first court-martial and a plea of not guilty was entered at the rehearing, the sentence as to those charges or specifications may include any punishment not in excess of that which could have been adjudged at the first court-martial, subject to limitations as the President may prescribe by regulation.

(c) If, after appeal by the Government under section 856(d) of this title (article 56(d)), the sentence adjudged is set aside and a rehearing on sentence is ordered by the Court of Criminal Appeals or Court of Appeals for the Armed Forces, the court-martial may impose any sentence that is in accordance with the order or ruling setting aside the adjudged sentence, subject to such limitations as the President may prescribe by regulation.

§864. Art. 64. Judge advocate review of finding of guilty in summary court-martial

(a) IN GENERAL.—Under regulations prescribed by the Secretary concerned, each summary court-martial in which there is a finding of guilty shall be reviewed by a judge advocate. A judge advocate may not review a case under this subsection if the judge advocate has acted in the same case as an accuser, preliminary hearing officer, member of the court, military judge, or counsel or has otherwise acted on behalf of the prosecution or defense. The judge advocate's review shall be in writing and shall contain the following:

(1) Conclusions as to whether—

(A) the court had jurisdiction over the accused and the offense;

(B) the charge and specification stated an offense; and

(C) the sentence was within the limits prescribed as a matter of law.

(2) A response to each allegation of error made in writing by the accused.

(3) If the case is sent for action under subsection (b), a recommendation as to the appropriate action to be taken and an opinion as to whether corrective action is required as a matter of law.

(b) RECORD.—The record of trial and related documents in each case reviewed under subsection (a) shall be sent for action to the person exercising general court-martial jurisdiction over the accused at the time the court was convened (or to that person's successor in command) if—

(1) the judge advocate who reviewed the case recommends corrective action; or

(2) such action is otherwise required by regulations of the Secretary concerned.

(c)(1) The person to whom the record of trial and related documents are sent under subsection (b) may—

(A) disapprove or approve the findings or sentence, in whole or in part;

(B) remit, commute, or suspend the sentence in whole or in part;

(C) except where the evidence was insufficient at the trial to support the findings, order a rehearing on the findings, on the sentence, or on both; or

(D) dismiss the charges.

(2) If a rehearing is ordered but the convening authority finds a rehearing impracticable, he shall dismiss the charges.

(3) If the opinion of the judge advocate in the judge advocate's review under subsection (a) is that corrective action is required as a matter of law and if the person required to take action under subsection (b) does not take action that is at least as favorable to the accused as that recommended by the judge advocate, the record of trial and action thereon shall be sent to the Judge Advocate General for review under section 869 of this title (article 69).

§865. Art. 65. Transmittal and review of records

(a) TRANSMITTAL OF RECORDS.—

(1) FINDING OF GUILTY IN GENERAL OR SPECIAL COURT-MARTIAL.—If the judgment of a general or special court-martial entered under section 860c of this title (article 60c) includes a finding of guilty, the record shall be transmitted to the Judge Advocate General.

(2) OTHER CASES.—In all other cases, records of trial by court-martial and related documents shall be transmitted and disposed of as the Secretary concerned may prescribe by regulation.

(b) CASES FOR DIRECT APPEAL.—

(1) AUTOMATIC REVIEW.—If the judgment includes a sentence of death, dismissal of a commissioned officer, cadet, or midshipman, dishonorable discharge or bad-conduct discharge, or confinement for 2 years or more, the Judge Advocate General shall forward the record of trial to the Court of Criminal Appeals for review under section 866(b)(3) of this title (article 66(b)(3)).

(2) CASES ELIGIBLE FOR DIRECT APPEAL REVIEW.—

(A) IN GENERAL.—If the case is eligible for direct review under section 866(b)(1) of this title (article 66(b)(1)), the Judge Advocate General shall—

(i) forward a copy of the record of trial to an appellate defense counsel who shall be detailed to review the case and, upon request of the accused, to represent the accused before the Court of Criminal Appeals; and

(ii) upon written request of the accused, forward a copy of the record of trial to civilian counsel provided by the accused.

(B) INAPPLICABILITY.—Subparagraph (A) shall not apply if the accused—

(i) waives the right to appeal under section 861 of this title (article 61); or

(ii) declines in writing the detailing of appellate defense counsel under subparagraph (A)(i).

(c) NOTICE OF RIGHT TO APPEAL.—

(1) IN GENERAL.—The Judge Advocate General shall provide notice to the accused of the right to file an appeal under section 866(b)(1) of this title (article 66(b)(1)) by means of depositing in the United States mails for delivery by first class certified mail to the accused at an address provided by the accused or, if no such address has been provided by the accused, at the latest address listed for the accused in the official service record of the accused.

(2) INAPPLICABILITY UPON WAIVER OF APPEAL.—Paragraph (1) shall not apply if the accused waives the right to appeal under section 861 of this title (article 61).

(d) REVIEW BY JUDGE ADVOCATE GENERAL.—

(1) BY WHOM.—A review conducted under this subsection may be conducted by an attorney within the Office of the Judge Advocate General or another attorney designated under regulations prescribed by the Secretary concerned.

(2) REVIEW OF CASES NOT ELIGIBLE FOR DIRECT APPEAL.—

(A) IN GENERAL.—A review under subparagraph (B) shall be completed in each general and special court-martial that is not eligible for direct appeal under paragraph (1) or (3) of section 866(b) of this title (article 66(b)).

(B) SCOPE OF REVIEW.—A review referred to in subparagraph (A) shall include a written decision providing each of the following:

(i) A conclusion as to whether the court had jurisdiction over the accused and the offense.

(ii) A conclusion as to whether the charge and specification stated an offense.

(iii) A conclusion as to whether the sentence was within the limits prescribed as a matter of law.

(iv) A response to each allegation of error made in writing by the accused.

(3) REVIEW WHEN DIRECT APPEAL IS WAIVED, WITHDRAWN, OR NOT FILED.—

(A) IN GENERAL.—A review under subparagraph (B) shall be completed in each general and special court-martial if—

(i) the accused waives the right to appeal or withdraws appeal under section 861 of this title (article 61); or

(ii) the accused does not file a timely appeal in a case eligible for direct appeal under subparagraph (A), (B), or (C) of section 866(b)(1) of this title (article 66(b)(1)).

(B) SCOPE OF REVIEW.—A review referred to in subparagraph (A) shall include a written decision limited to providing conclusions on the matters specified in clauses (i), (ii), and (iii) of paragraph (2)(B).

(e) REMEDY.—

(1) IN GENERAL.—If after a review of a record under subsection (d), the attorney conducting the review believes corrective action may be required, the record shall be forwarded to the Judge Advocate General, who may set aside the findings or sentence, in whole or in part.

(2) REHEARING.—In setting aside findings or sentence, the Judge Advocate General may order a rehearing, except that a rehearing may not be ordered in violation of section 844 of this title (article 44).

(3) REMEDY WITHOUT REHEARING.—

(A) DISMISSAL WHEN NO REHEARING ORDERED.—If the Judge Advocate General sets aside findings and sentence and does not order a rehearing, the Judge Advocate General shall dismiss the charges.

(B) DISMISSAL WHEN REHEARING IMPRACTICABLE.—

(i) IN GENERAL.—Subject to clause (ii), if the Judge Advocate General sets aside findings and orders a rehearing and the convening authority determines that a rehearing would be impracticable, the convening authority shall dismiss the charges.

(ii) CASES REFERRED BY SPECIAL TRIAL COUNSEL.—If a case was referred to trial by a special trial counsel, a special trial counsel shall determine if a rehearing is impracticable and shall dismiss the charges if the special trial counsel so determines.

§866. Art. 66. Courts of Criminal Appeals

(a) COURTS OF CRIMINAL APPEALS.—

(1) IN GENERAL.— Each Judge Advocate General shall establish a Court of Criminal Appeals which shall be composed of one or more panels, and each such panel shall be composed of not less than three appellate military judges. For the purpose of reviewing court-martial cases, the court may sit in panels or as a whole in accordance with rules prescribed under subsection (h). Any decision of a panel may be reconsidered by the court sitting as a whole in accordance with such rules. Appellate military judges who are assigned to a Court of Criminal Appeals may be commissioned officers or civilians, each of whom must be a member of a bar of a Federal court or of the highest court of a State and must be certified by the Judge Advocate General as qualified, by reason of education, training, experience, and judicial temperament, for duty as an appellate military judge. The Judge Advocate General shall designate as chief judge one of the appellate military judges of the Court of Criminal Appeals established by him. The chief judge shall determine on which panels of the court the appellate judges assigned to the court will serve and which military judge assigned to the court will act as the senior judge on each panel. In accordance with regulations prescribed by the President, assignments of appellate military judges under this section (article) shall be for appropriate minimum periods, subject to such exceptions as may be authorized in the regulations.

(2) ADDITIONAL QUALIFICATIONS.—In addition to any other qualifications specified in paragraph (1), any commissioned officer or civilian assigned as an appellate military judge to a Court of Criminal Appeals shall have not fewer than 12 years of experience in the practice of law before such assignment.

(b) REVIEW.—

(1) APPEALS BY ACCUSED.—A Court of Criminal Appeals shall have jurisdiction over—

(A) a timely appeal from the judgment of a court-martial, entered into the record under section 860c(a) of this title (article 60c(a)), that includes a finding of guilty; and

(B) a summary court-martial case in which the accused filed an application for review with the Court under section 869(d)(1) of this title (article 69(d)(1)) and for which the application has been granted by the Court.

(2) REVIEW OF CERTAIN SENTENCES. —A Court of Criminal Appeals shall have jurisdiction over all cases that the Judge Advocate General orders sent to the Court for review under section 856(d) of this title (article 56(d)).

(3) AUTOMATIC REVIEW. —A Court of Criminal Appeals shall have jurisdiction over a court-martial in which the judgment entered into the record under section 860(c) of this title (article 60c) includes a sentence of death, dismissal of a commissioned officer, cadet, or midshipman, dishonorable discharge or bad-conduct discharge, or confinement for 2 years or more.

(c) TIMELINESS.—An appeal under subsection (b)(1) is timely if—

(1) in the case of an appeal under subparagraph (A) of such subsection, it is filed before the later of—

(A) the end of the 90-day period beginning on the date the accused is provided notice of appellate rights under section 865(c) of this title (article 65(c)); or

(B) the date set by the Court of Criminal Appeals by rule or order; and

(2) in the case of an appeal under subparagraph (B) of such subsection, an application for review with the Court is filed not later than the earlier of the dates established under section 869(d)(2)(B) of this title (article 69(d)(2)(B)).

(d) DUTIES.—

(1) CASES APPEALED BY ACCUSED.—

(A) IN GENERAL.—In any case before the Court of Criminal Appeals under subsection (b), the Court may act only with respect to the findings and sentence as entered into the record under section 860c of this title (article 60c). The Court may affirm only such findings of guilty as the Court finds correct in law, and in fact in accordance with subparagraph (B).

(B) FACTUAL SUFFICIENCY REVIEW.—

(i) In an appeal of a finding of guilty under subsection (b), the Court may consider whether the finding is correct in fact upon request of the accused if the accused makes a specific showing of a deficiency in proof.

(ii) After an accused has made such a showing, the Court may weigh the evidence and determine controverted questions of fact subject to—

(I) appropriate deference to the fact that the trial court saw and heard the witnesses and other evidence; and

(II) appropriate deference to findings of fact entered into the record by the military judge.

(iii) If, as a result of the review conducted under clause (ii), the Court is clearly convinced that the finding of guilty was against the weight of the evidence, the Court may dismiss, set aside, or modify the finding, or affirm a lesser finding.

(2) ERROR OR EXCESSIVE DELAY.—In any case before the Court of Criminal Appeals under subsection (b), the Court may provide appropriate relief if the accused demonstrates error or excessive delay in the processing of the court-martial after the judgment was entered into the record under section 860c of this title (article 60c).

(e) CONSIDERATION OF SENTENCE.—

(1) IN GENERAL.—In considering a sentence on appeal, other than as provided in section 856(d) of this title (article 56(d)), the Court of Criminal Appeals may consider—

(A) whether the sentence violates the law;

(B) whether the sentence is inappropriately severe—

(i) if the sentence is for an offense for which the President has not established a sentencing parameter pursuant to section 539E(e) of the National Defense Authorization Act for Fiscal Year 2022; or

(ii) in the case of an offense for which the President has established a sentencing parameter pursuant to section 539E(e) of the National Defense Authorization Act for Fiscal Year 2022, if the sentence is above the upper range of such sentencing parameter;

(C) in the case of a sentence for an offense for which the President has established a sentencing parameter pursuant to section 539E(e) of the National Defense Authorization Act for Fiscal Year 2022, whether the sentence is a result of an incorrect application of the parameter;

(D) whether the sentence is plainly unreasonable; and

(E) in review of a sentence to death or to life in prison without eligibility for parole determined by the members in a capital case under section 853(c) of this title (article 53(c)), whether the sentence is otherwise appropriate, under rules prescribed by the President.

(2) RECORD ON APPEAL.—In an appeal under this subsection or section 856(d) of this title (article 56(d)), other than review under subsection (b)(2) of this section, the record on appeal shall consist of—

(A) any portion of the record in the case that is designated as pertinent by any party;

(B) the information submitted during the sentencing proceeding; and

(C) any information required by rule or order of the Court of Criminal Appeals.

(f) LIMITS OF AUTHORITY.—

(1) SET ASIDE OF FINDINGS —

(A) IN GENERAL—If the Court of Criminal Appeals sets aside the findings, the Court—

(i) may affirm any lesser included offense; and

(ii) may, except when prohibited by section 844 of this title (article 44), order a rehearing.

(B) DISMISSAL WHEN NO REHEARING ORDERED.—If the Court of Criminal Appeals sets aside the findings and does not order a rehearing, the Court shall order that the charges be dismissed.

(C) DISMISSAL WHEN REHEARING IMPRACTICABLE.—

(i) IN GENERAL.—Subject to clause (ii), if the Court of Criminal Appeals orders a rehearing on a charge and the convening authority finds a rehearing impracticable, the convening authority may dismiss the charge.

(ii) CASES REFERRED BY SPECIAL TRIAL COUNSEL.—If a case was referred to trial by a special trial counsel, a special trial counsel shall determine if a rehearing is impracticable and shall dismiss the charges if the special trial counsel so determines.

(2) SET ASIDE OF SENTENCE.—If the Court of Criminal Appeals sets aside the sentence, the Court may—

(A) modify the sentence to a lesser sentence; or

(B) order a rehearing.

(3) ADDITIONAL PROCEEDINGS.—If the Court of Criminal Appeals determines that additional proceedings are warranted, the Court may order a hearing as may be necessary to address a substantial issue, subject to such limitations as the Court may direct and under such regulations as the president may prescribe. If the Court of Appeals for the Armed Forces determines that additional proceedings are warranted, the Court of Criminal Appeals shall order a hearing or other proceeding in accordance with the direction of the court of Appeals for the Armed Forces.

(g) ACTION IN ACCORDANCE WITH DECISIONS OF COURTS.—The Judge Advocate General shall, unless there is to be further action by the President, the Secretary concerned, the Court of Appeals for the Armed Forces, or the Supreme Court, instruct the appropriate authority to take action in accordance with the decision of the Court of Criminal Appeals.

(h) RULES OF PROCEDURE.—The Judge Advocates General shall prescribe uniform rules of procedure for Courts of Criminal Appeals and shall meet periodically to formulate policies and procedure in regard to review of court-martial cases in the offices of the Judge Advocates General and by Courts of Criminal Appeals.

(i) PROHIBITION ON EVALUATION OF OTHER MEMBERS OF COURTS.—No member of a Court of Criminal Appeals shall be required, or on his own initiative be permitted, to prepare, approve, disapprove, review, or submit, with respect to any other member of the same or another Court of Criminal Appeals, an effectiveness, fitness, or efficiency report, or any other report or document used in whole or in part for the purpose of determining whether a member of the armed forces is qualified to be advanced in grade, or in determining the assignment or transfer of a member of the armed forces, or in determining whether a member of the armed forces should be retained on active duty.

(j) INELIGIBILITY OF MEMBERS OF COURTS TO REVIEW RECORDS OF CASES INVOLVING CERTAIN PRIOR MEMBER SERVICE.—No member of a Court of Criminal Appeals shall be eligible to review the record of any trial if such member served as investigating officer in the case or served as a member of the court-martial before which such trial was conducted, or served as military judge, trial or defense counsel, or reviewing officer of such trial.

§867. Art. 67. Review by the Court of Appeals for the Armed Forces

(a) The Court of Appeals for the Armed Forces shall review the record in—

(1) all cases in which the sentence, as affirmed by a Court of Criminal Appeals, extends to death;

(2) all cases reviewed by a Court of Criminal Appeals which the Judge Advocate General, after appropriate notification to the other Judge Advocates General and the Staff Judge Advocate to the Commandant of the Marine Corps, orders sent to the Court of Appeals for the Armed Forces for review; and

(3) all cases reviewed by a Court of Criminal Appeals in which, upon petition of the accused and on good cause shown, the Court of Appeals for the Armed Forces has granted a review.

(b) The accused may petition the Court of Appeals for the Armed Forces for review of a decision of a Court of Criminal Appeals within 60 days from the earlier of—

(1) the date on which the accused is notified of the decision of the Court of Criminal Appeals; or

(2) the date on which a copy of the decision of the Court of Criminal Appeals, after being served on appellate counsel of record for the accused (if any), is deposited in the United States mails for delivery by first-class certified mail to the accused at an address provided by the accused or, if no such address has been provided by the accused, at the latest address listed for the accused in his official service record.

The Court of Appeals for the Armed Forces shall act upon such a petition promptly in accordance with the rules of the court.

(c)(1) In any case reviewed by it, the Court of Appeals for the Armed Forces may act only with respect to—

(A) the findings and sentence set forth in the entry of judgment, as affirmed or set aside as incorrect in law by the Court of Criminal Appeals;

(B) a decision, judgment, or order by a military judge, as affirmed or set aside as incorrect in law by the Court of Criminal Appeals; or

(C) the findings set forth in the entry of judgment, as affirmed, dismissed, set aside, or modified by the Court of Criminal Appeals as incorrect in fact under section 866(d)(1)(B) of this title (article 66(d)(1)(B)).

(2) In a case which the Judge Advocate General orders sent to the Court of Appeals for the Armed Forces, that action need be taken only with respect to the issues raised by him.

(3) In a case reviewed upon petition of the accused, that action need be taken only with respect to issues specified in the grant of review.

(4) The Court of Appeals for the Armed Forces shall take action only with respect to matters of law.

(d) If the Court of Appeals for the Armed Forces sets aside the findings and sentence, it may, except where the setting aside is based on lack of sufficient evidence in the record to support the findings, order a rehearing. If it sets aside the findings and sentence and does not order a rehearing, it shall order that the charges be dismissed.

(e) After it has acted on a case, the Court of Appeals for the Armed Forces may direct the Judge Advocate General to return the record to the Court of Criminal Appeals for further review in accordance with the decision of the court. Otherwise, unless there is to be further action by the President or the Secretary concerned, the Judge Advocate General shall instruct the convening authority to take action in accordance with that decision. If the court has ordered a rehearing, but the convening authority finds a rehearing impracticable, he may dismiss the charges. Notwithstanding the preceding sentence, if a case was referred to trial by a special trial counsel, a special trial counsel shall determine if a rehearing is impracticable and shall dismiss the charges if the special trial counsel so determines.

§867a. Art. 67a. Review by the Supreme Court

(a) Decisions of the United States Court of Appeals for the Armed Forces are subject to review by the Supreme Court by writ of certiorari as provided in section 1259 of title 28. The Supreme Court may not review by a writ of certiorari under this section any action of the United States Court of Appeals for the Armed Forces in refusing to grant a petition for review.

(b) The accused may petition the Supreme Court for a writ of certiorari without prepayment of fees and costs or security therefor and without filing the affidavit required by section 1915(a) of title 28.

§868. Art. 68. Branch offices

The Secretary concerned may direct the Judge Advocate General to establish a branch office with any command. The branch office shall be under an Assistant Judge Advocate General who, with the consent of the Judge Advocate General, may establish a Court of Criminal Appeals with one or more panels. That Assistant Judge Advocate General and any Court of Criminal Appeals established by him may perform for that command under the general supervision of the Judge Advocate General, the respective duties which the Judge Advocate General and a Court of Criminal Appeals established by the Judge Advocate General would otherwise be required to perform as to all cases involving sentences not requiring approval by the President.

§869. Art. 69. Review by Judge Advocate General

(a) IN GENERAL.—Upon application by the accused or receipt of the record pursuant to section 864(c)(3) of this title (article 64(c)(3)) and subject to subsections (b), (c), and (d), the Judge Advocate General may—

(1) with respect to a summary court-martial, modify or set aside, in whole or in part, the findings and sentence; or

(2) with respect to a general or special court-martial, order such court-martial to be reviewed under section 866 of this title (article 66).

(b) TIMING.—

(1) To qualify for consideration, an application under subsection (a) must be submitted to the Judge Advocate General not later than—

(A) for a summary court-martial, one year after the date of completion of review under section 864 of this title (article 64); or

(B) for a general or special court-martial, one year after the end of the 90-day period beginning on the date the accused is provided notice of appellate rights under section 865(c) of this title (article 865(c)), unless the accused submitted a waiver or withdrawal of appellate review under section 861 of this title (article 61) before being provided notice of appellate rights, in which case the application must be submitted to the Judge Advocate General not later than one year after the entry of judgment under section 860c of this title (article 60c).

(2) The Judge Advocate General may, for good cause shown, extend the period for submission of an application, except that—

(A) in the case of an application for review of a summary court martial, the Judge Advocate may not consider an application submitted more than three years after the completion date referred to in paragraph (1)(A); and

(B) in case of an application for review of a general or special court-martial, the Judge Advocate may not consider an application submitted more than three years after the end of the applicable period under paragraph (1)(B).

(c) SCOPE.—

(1)(A) In a case reviewed under section 864 of this title (article 64), the Judge Advocate General may set aside the findings or sentence, in whole or in part, on the grounds of newly discovered evidence, fraud on the court, lack of jurisdiction over the accused or the offense, error prejudicial to the substantial rights of the accused, or the appropriateness of the sentence.

(B) In setting aside findings or sentence, the Judge Advocate General may order a rehearing, except that a rehearing may not be ordered in violation of section 844 of this title (article 44).

(C) If the Judge Advocate General sets aside findings and sentence and does not order a rehearing, the Judge Advocate General shall dismiss the charges.

(D)(i) Subject to clause (ii), if the Judge Advocate General sets aside findings and orders a rehearing and the convening authority determines that a rehearing would be impracticable, the convening authority shall dismiss the charges.

(ii) If a case was referred to trial by a special trial counsel, a special trial counsel shall determine if a rehearing is impracticable and shall dismiss the charges if the special trial counsel so determines.

(2) In a case reviewed under section 865(b) of this title (article 65(b)), review under this section is limited to the issue of whether the waiver or withdrawal of an appeal was invalid under the law. If the Judge Advocate General determines that the waiver or withdrawal of an appeal was invalid, the Judge Advocate General shall send the case to the Court of Criminal Appeals.

(d) COURT OF CRIMINAL APPEALS.—

(1) A Court of Criminal Appeals may review the action taken by the Judge Advocate General under subsection (c)(1) in a case submitted to the Court of Criminal Appeals by the accused in an application for review.

(2) The Court of Criminal Appeals may grant an application under paragraph (1) only if—

(A) the application demonstrates a substantial basis for concluding that the action on review under subsection (c) constituted prejudicial error; and

(B) the application is filed not later than the earlier of—

(i) 60 days after the date on which the accused is notified of the decision of the Judge Advocate General; or

(ii) 60 days after the date on which a copy of the decision of the Judge Advocate General is deposited in the United States mails for delivery by first-class certified mail to the accused at an address provided by the accused or, if no such address has been provided by the accused, at the latest address listed for the accused in his official service record.

(3) The submission of an application for review under this subsection does not constitute a proceeding before the Court of Criminal Appeals for purposes of section 870(c)(1) of this title (article 70(c)(1)).

(e) ACTION ONLY ON MATTERS OF LAW.—Notwithstanding section 866 of this title (article 66), in any case reviewed by a Court of Criminal Appeals under subsection (d), the Court may take action only with respect to matters of law.

§870. Art. 70. Appellate counsel

(a) The Judge Advocate General shall detail in his office one or more commissioned officers as appellate Government counsel, and one or more commissioned officers as appellate defense counsel, who are qualified under section 827(b)(1) of this title (article 27(b)(1)).

(b) Appellate Government counsel shall represent the United States before the Court of Criminal Appeals or the Court of Appeals for the Armed Forces when directed to do so by the Judge Advocate General. Appellate Government counsel may represent the United States before the Supreme Court in cases arising under this chapter when requested to do so by the Attorney General.

(c) Appellate defense counsel shall represent the accused before the Court of Criminal Appeals, the Court of Appeals for the Armed Forces, or the Supreme Court—

(1) when requested by the accused;

(2) when the United States is represented by counsel; or

(3) when the Judge Advocate General has sent the case to the Court of Appeals for the Armed Forces.

(d) The accused has the right to be represented before the Court of Criminal Appeals, the Court of Appeals for the Armed Forces, or the Supreme Court by civilian counsel if provided by him.

(e) Military appellate counsel shall also perform such other functions in connection with the review of court martial cases as the Judge Advocate General directs.

(f) To the greatest extent practicable, in any capital case, at least one defense counsel under subsection (c) shall, as determined by the Judge Advocate General, be learned in the law applicable to such cases. If necessary, this counsel may be a civilian and, if so, may be compensated in accordance with regulations prescribed by the Secretary of Defense.

§872. Art. 72. Vacation of suspension

(a) Before the vacation of the suspension of a special court-martial sentence which as approved includes a bad-conduct discharge, or of any general court-martial sentence, the officer having special court-martial jurisdiction over the probationer shall hold a hearing on the alleged violation of probation. The special court-martial convening authority may detail a judge advocate, who is certified under section 827(b) of this title (article 27(b)), to conduct the hearing. The probationer shall be represented at the hearing by counsel if the probationer so desires.

(b) The record of the hearing and the recommendation of the officer having special court-martial jurisdiction shall be sent for action to the officer exercising general court-martial jurisdiction over the probationer. If the officer exercising general court-martial jurisdiction vacates the suspension, any unexecuted part of the sentence, except a dismissal, shall be executed, subject to applicable restrictions in section 857 of this title (article 57)). The vacation of the suspension of a dismissal is not effective until approved by the Secretary concerned.

(c) The suspension of any other sentence may be vacated by any authority competent to convene, for the command in which the accused is serving or assigned, a court of the kind that imposed the sentence.

§873. Art. 73. Petition for a new trial

At any time within three years after the date of the entry of judgment under section 860c of this title (article 60c), the accused may petition the Judge Advocate General for a new trial on the grounds of newly discovered evidence or fraud on the court. If the accused's case is pending before a Court of Criminal Appeals or before the Court of Appeals for the Armed Forces, the Judge Advocate General shall refer the petition to the appropriate court for action. Otherwise the Judge Advocate General shall act upon the petition.

§874. Art. 74. Remission and suspension

(a) The Secretary concerned and, when designated by him, any Under Secretary, Assistant Secretary, Judge Advocate General, or commanding officer may remit or suspend any part or amount of the unexecuted part of any sentence, including all uncollected forfeitures other than a sentence approved by the President. However, in the case of a sentence of confinement for life without eligibility for parole that is adjudged for an offense committed after October 29, 2000, after the sentence is ordered executed, the authority of the Secretary concerned under the preceding sentence (1) may not be delegated, and (2) may be exercised only after the service of a period of confinement of not less than 20 years.

(b) The Secretary concerned may, for good cause, substitute an administrative form of discharge for a discharge or dismissal executed in accordance with the sentence of a court-martial.

§875. Art. 75. Restoration

(a) Under such regulations as the President may prescribe, all rights, privileges, and property affected by an executed part of a court-martial sentence which has been set aside or disapproved, except an executed dismissal or discharge, shall be restored unless a new trial or rehearing is ordered and such executed part is included in a sentence imposed upon the new trial or rehearing.

(b) If a previously executed sentence of dishonorable or bad-conduct discharge is not imposed on a new trial, the Secretary concerned shall substitute therefor a form of discharge authorized for administrative issuance unless the accused is to serve out the remainder of his enlistment.

(c) If a previously executed sentence of dismissal is not imposed on a new trial, the Secretary concerned shall substitute therefor a form of discharge authorized for administrative issue, and the commissioned officer dismissed by that sentence may be reappointed by the President alone to such commissioned grade and with such rank as in the opinion of the President that former officer would have attained had he not been dismissed. The reappointment of such a former officer shall be without regard to the existence of a vacancy and shall affect the promotion status of other officers only insofar as the President may direct. All time between the dismissal and the reappointment shall be considered as actual service for all purposes, including the right to pay and allowances.

(d) The President shall prescribe regulations, with such limitations as the President considers appropriate, governing eligibility for pay and allowances for the period after the date on which an executed part of a court-martial sentence is set aside.

§876. Art. 76. Finality of proceedings, findings, and sentences

The appellate review of records of trial provided by this chapter, the proceedings, findings, and sentences of courts-martial as approved, reviewed, or affirmed as required by this chapter, and all dismissals and discharges carried into execution under sentences by courts-martial following approval, review, or affirmation as required by this chapter, are final and conclusive. Orders publishing the proceedings of courts-martial and all action taken pursuant to those proceedings are binding upon all departments, courts, agencies, and officers of the United States, subject only to action upon a petition for a new trial as provided in section 873 of this title (article 73) and to action by the Secretary concerned as provided in section 874 of this title (article 74) and the authority of the President.

§876a. Art. 76a. Leave required to be taken pending review of certain court-martial convictions

Under regulations prescribed by the Secretary concerned, an accused who has been sentenced by a court-martial may be required to take leave pending completion of action under this subchapter if the sentence includes an unsuspended dismissal or an unsuspended dishonorable or bad-conduct discharge. The accused may be required to begin such leave on the date of the entry of judgment under section 860c of this title (article 60c) or at any time after such date, and such leave may be continued until the date on which action under this subchapter is completed or may be terminated at any earlier time.

§876b. Art. 76b. Lack of mental capacity or mental responsibility: commitment of accused for examination and treatment

(a) PERSONS INCOMPETENT TO STAND TRIAL.—

(1) In the case of a person determined under this chapter to be presently suffering from a mental disease or defect rendering the person mentally incompetent to the extent that the person is unable to understand the nature of the proceedings against that person or to conduct or cooperate intelligently in the defense of the case, the general court-martial convening authority for that person shall commit the person to the custody of the Attorney General.

(2) The Attorney General shall take action in accordance with section 4241(d) of title 18.

(3) If at the end of the period for hospitalization provided for in section 4241(d) of title 18, it is determined that the committed person's mental condition has not so improved as to permit the trial to proceed, action shall be taken in accordance with section 4246 of such title.

(4)(A) When the director of a facility in which a person is hospitalized pursuant to paragraph (2) determines that the person has recovered to such an extent that the person is able to understand the nature of the proceedings against the person and to conduct or cooperate intelligently in the defense of the case, the director shall promptly transmit a notification of that determination to the Attorney General and to the general court-martial convening authority for the person. The director shall send a copy of the notification to the person's counsel.

(B) Upon receipt of a notification, the general court-martial convening authority shall promptly take custody of the person unless the person covered by the notification is no longer subject to this chapter. If the person is no longer subject to this chapter, the Attorney General shall take any action within the authority of the Attorney General that the Attorney General considers appropriate regarding the person.

(C) The director of the facility may retain custody of the person for not more than 30 days after transmitting the notifications required by subparagraph (A).

(5) In the application of section 4246 of title 18 to a case under this subsection, references to the court that ordered the commitment of a person, and to the clerk of such court, shall be deemed to refer to the general court-martial convening authority for that person. However, if the person is no longer subject to this chapter at a time relevant to the application of such section to the person, the United States district court for the district where the person is hospitalized or otherwise may be found shall be considered as the court that ordered the commitment of the person.

(b) PERSONS FOUND NOT GUILTY BY REASON OF LACK OF MENTAL RESPONSIBILITY.—

(1) If a person is found by a court-martial not guilty only by reason of lack of mental responsibility, the person shall be committed to a suitable facility until the person is eligible for release in accordance with this section.

(2) The court-martial shall conduct a hearing on the mental condition in accordance with subsection (c) of section 4243 of title 18. Subsections (b) and (d) of that section shall apply with respect to the hearing.

(3) A report of the results of the hearing shall be made to the general court-martial convening authority for the person.

(4) If the court-martial fails to find by the standard specified in subsection (d) of section 4243 of title 18 that the person's release would not create a substantial risk of bodily injury to another person or serious damage of property of another due to a present mental disease or defect—

(A) the general court-martial convening authority may commit the person to the custody of the Attorney General; and

(B) the Attorney General shall take action in accordance with subsection (e) of section 4243 of title 18.

(5) Subsections (f), (g), and (h) of section 4243 of title 18 shall apply in the case of a person hospitalized pursuant to paragraph (4)(B), except that the United States district court for the district where the person is hospitalized shall be considered as the court that ordered the person's commitment.

(c) GENERAL PROVISIONS.—

(1) Except as otherwise provided in this subsection and subsection (d)(1), the provisions of section 4247 of title 18 apply in the administration of this section.

(2) In the application of section 4247(d) of title 18 to hearings conducted by a court-martial under this section or by (or by order of) a general court-martial convening authority under this section, the reference in that section to section 3006A of such title does not apply.

(d) APPLICABILITY.—

(1) The provisions of chapter 313 of title 18 referred to in this section apply according to the provisions of this section notwithstanding section 4247(j) of title 18.

(2) If the status of a person as described in section 802 of this title (article 2) terminates while the person is, pursuant to this section, in the custody of the Attorney General, hospitalized, or on conditional release under a prescribed regimen of medical, psychiatric, or psychological care or treatment, the provisions of this section establishing requirements and procedures regarding a person no longer subject to this chapter shall continue to apply to that person notwithstanding the change of status.

SUBCHAPTER X—PUNITIVE ARTICLES

Sec.	Art.	
877.	77.	Principals.
878.	78.	Accessory after the fact.
879.	79.	Conviction of offense charged, lesser included offenses, and attempts.
880.	80.	Attempts.
881.	81.	Conspiracy.
882.	82.	Soliciting commission of offenses.
883.	83.	Malingering.
884.	84.	Breach of medical quarantine.
885.	85.	Desertion.
886.	86.	Absence without leave.
887.	87.	Missing movement; jumping from vessel.
887a.	87a.	Resistance, flight, breach of arrest, and escape.
887b.	87b.	Offenses against correctional custody and restriction.
888.	88.	Contempt toward officials.
889.	89.	Disrespect toward superior commissioned officer; assault of superior commissioned officer.
890.	90.	Willfully disobeying superior commissioned officer.
891.	91.	Insubordinate conduct toward warrant officer, noncommissioned officer, or petty officer.
892.	92.	Failure to obey order or regulation.
893.	93.	Cruelty and maltreatment.
893a.	93a.	Prohibited activities with military recruit or trainee by person in position of special trust.
894.	94.	Mutiny or sedition.
895.	95.	Offenses by sentinel or lookout.
895a.	95a.	Disrespect toward sentinel or lookout.
896.	96.	Release of prisoner without authority; drinking with prisoner.
897.	97.	Unlawful detention.
898.	98.	Misconduct as prisoner.
899.	99.	Misbehavior before the enemy.
900.	100.	Subordinate compelling surrender.
901.	101.	Improper use of countersign.
902.	102.	Forcing a safeguard.
903.	103.	Spies.
903a.	103a.	Espionage.
903b.	103b.	Aiding the enemy.
904.	104.	Public records offenses.
904a.	104a.	Fraudulent enlistment, appointment, or separation.
904b.	104b.	Unlawful enlistment, appointment, or separation.
905.	105.	Forgery.
905a.	105a.	False or unauthorized pass offenses.
906.	106.	Impersonation of officer, noncommissioned or petty officer, or agent or official.
906a.	106a.	Wearing unauthorized insignia, decoration, badge, ribbon, device, or lapel button.
907.	107.	False official statements; false swearing.
907a.	107a.	Parole violation.
908.	108.	Military property of United States—Loss, damage, destruction, or wrongful disposition.
908a.	108a.	Captured or abandoned property.
909.	109.	Property other than military property of United States—Water, spoilage, or destruction.
909a.	109a.	Mail matter: wrongful taking, opening, etc.
910.	110.	Improper hazarding of vessel or aircraft.
911.	111.	Leaving scene of vehicle accident.
912.	112.	Drunkenness and other incapacitation offenses.
912a.	112a.	Wrongful use, possession, etc., of controlled substances.
913.	113.	Drunken or reckless operation of a vehicle, aircraft or vessel.
914.	114.	Endangerment offenses.
915.	115.	Communicating threats.
916.	116.	Riot or breach of peace.
917.	117.	Provoking speeches or gestures.
917a.	117a.	Wrongful broadcast or distribution of intimate visual images.
918.	118.	Murder.
919.	119.	Manslaughter.
919a.	119a	Death or injury of an unborn child.
919b.	119b	Child endangerment.
920.	120.	Rape and sexual assault generally.
920a.	120a	Mails: deposit of obscene matter.
920b.	120b.	Rape and sexual assault of a child.
920c.	120c.	Other sexual misconduct.
921.	121.	Larceny and wrongful appropriation.
921a.	121a.	Fraudulent use of credit cards, debit cards, and other access devices.
921b.	121b.	False pretenses to obtain services.
922.	122.	Robbery.
922a.	122a	Receiving stolen property.
923.	123.	Offenses concerning Government computers.
923a.	123a.	Making, drawing, or uttering check, draft, or order without sufficient funds.
924.	124.	Frauds against the United States.
924a.	124a.	Bribery.
924b.	124b.	Graft.
925.	125.	Kidnapping.
926.	126.	Arson; burning property with intent to defraud.
927.	127.	Extortion.
928.	128.	Assault.
928a.	128a.	Maiming.
928b.	128b.	Domestic violence.
929.	129.	Burglary; unlawful entry.
930.	130.	Stalking.
931.	131.	Perjury.
931a.	131a	Subornation of perjury.
931b.	131b.	Obstructing justice.
931c.	131c.	Misprision of serious offense.
931d.	131d	Wrongful refusal to testify.

931e.	131e.	Prevention of authorized seizure of property.
931f.	131f.	Noncompliance with procedural rules.
931g.	131g.	Wrongful interference with adverse administrative proceeding.
932.	132.	Retaliation.
933.	133.	Conduct unbecoming an officer.
934.	134.	General article.

§877. Art. 77. Principals

Any person punishable under this chapter who—

(1) commits an offense punishable by this chapter, or aids, abets, counsels, commands, or procures its commission; or

(2) causes an act to be done which if directly performed by him would be punishable by this chapter;

is a principal.

§878. Art. 78. Accessory after the fact

Any person subject to this chapter who, knowing that an offense punishable by this chapter has been committed, receives, comforts, or assists the offender in order to hinder or prevent his apprehension, trial, or punishment shall be punished as a court-martial may direct.

§879. Art. 79. Conviction of offense charged, lesser included offenses, and attempts

(a) IN GENERAL.—An accused may be found guilty of any of the following:

(1) The offense charged.

(2) A lesser included offense.

(3) An attempt to commit the offense charged.

(4) An attempt to commit a lesser included offense, if the attempt is an offense in its own right.

(b) LESSER INCLUDED OFFENSE DEFINED.—In this section (article), the term "lesser included offense" means—

(1) an offense that is necessarily included in the offense charged; and

(2) any lesser included offense so designated by regulation prescribed by the President.

(c) REGULATORY AUTHORITY.—Any designation of a lesser included offense in a regulation referred to in subsection (b) shall be reasonably included in the greater offense.

§880. Art. 80. Attempts

(a) An act, done with specific intent to commit an offense under this chapter, amounting to more than mere preparation and tending, even though failing, to effect its commission, is an attempt to commit that offense.

(b) Any person subject to this chapter who attempts to commit any offense punishable by this chapter shall be punished as a court-martial may direct, unless otherwise specifically prescribed.

(c) Any person subject to this chapter may be convicted of an attempt to commit an offense although it appears on the trial that the offense was consummated.

§881. Art. 81. Conspiracy

(a) Any person subject to this chapter who conspires with any other person to commit an offense under this chapter shall, if one or more of the conspirators does an act to effect the object of the conspiracy, be punished as a court-martial may direct.

(b) Any person subject to this chapter who conspires with any other person to commit an offense under the law of war, and who knowingly does an overt act to effect the object of the conspiracy, shall be punished, if death results to one or more of the victims, by death or such other punishment as a court-martial or military commission may direct, and, if death does not result to any of the victims, by such punishment, other than death, as a court-martial or military commission may direct.

§882. Art. 82. Soliciting commission of offenses

(a) SOLICITING COMMISSION OF OFFENSES GENERALLY.—Any person subject to this chapter who solicits or advises another to commit an offense under this chapter (other than an offense specified in subsection (b)) shall be punished as a court-martial may direct.

(b) SOLICITING DESERTION, MUTINY, SEDITION, OR MISBEHAVIOR BEFORE THE ENEMY.—Any person subject to this chapter who solicits or advises another to violate section 885 of this title (article 85), section 894 of this title (article 94), or section 899 of this title (article 99)—

(1) if the offense solicited or advised is attempted or is committed, shall be punished with the punishment provided for the commission of the offense; and

(2) if the offense solicited or advised is not attempted or committed, shall be punished as a court-martial may direct.

§883. Art. 83. Malingering

Any person subject to this chapter who, with the intent to avoid work, duty, or service—

(1) feigns illness, physical disablement, mental lapse, or mental derangement; or

(2) intentionally inflicts self-injury;

shall be punished as a court-martial may direct.

§884. Art. 84. Breach of medical quarantine

Any person subject to this chapter—

(1) who is ordered into medical quarantine by a person authorized to issue such order; and

(2) who, with knowledge of the quarantine and the limits of the quarantine, goes beyond those limits before being released from the quarantine by proper authority;

shall be punished as a court-martial may direct.

§885. Art. 85. Desertion

(a) Any member of the armed forces who—

(1) without authority goes or remains absent from his unit, organization, or place of duty with intent to remain away therefrom permanently;

(2) quits his unit, organization, or place of duty with intent to avoid hazardous duty or to shirk important service; or

(3) without being regularly separated from one of the armed forces enlists or accepts an appointment in the same or another one of the armed forces without fully disclosing the fact that he has not been regularly separated, or enters any foreign armed service except when authorized by the United States;

is guilty of desertion.

(b) Any commissioned officer of the armed forces who, after tender of his resignation and before notice of its acceptance, quits his post or proper duties without leave and with intent to remain away therefrom permanently is guilty of desertion.

(c) Any person found guilty of desertion or attempt to desert shall be punished, if the offense is committed in time of war, by death or such other punishment as a court-martial may direct, but if the desertion or attempt to desert occurs at any other time, by such punishment, other than death, as a court-martial may direct.

§886. Art. 86. Absence without leave

Any member of the armed forces who, without authority—

(1) fails to go to his appointed place of duty at the time prescribed;

(2) goes from that place; or

(3) absents himself or remains absent from his unit, organization, or place of duty at which he is required to be at the time prescribed;

shall be punished as a court-martial may direct.

§887. Art. 87. Missing movement; jumping from vessel

(a) MISSING MOVEMENT.—Any person subject to this chapter who, through neglect or design, misses the movement of a ship, aircraft, or unit with which the person is required in the course of duty to move shall be punished as a court-martial may direct.

(b) JUMPING FROM VESSEL INTO THE WATER.—Any person subject to this chapter who wrongfully and intentionally jumps into the water from a vessel in use by the armed forces shall be punished as a court-martial may direct.

§887a. Art. 87a. Resistance, flight, breach of arrest, and escape

Any person subject to this chapter who—

(1) resists apprehension;

(2) flees from apprehension;

(3) breaks arrest; or

(4) escapes from custody or confinement;

shall be punished as a court-martial may direct.

§887b. Art. 87b. Offenses against correctional custody and restriction

(a) ESCAPE FROM CORRECTIONAL CUSTODY.—Any person subject to this chapter—

(1) who is placed in correctional custody by a person authorized to do so;

(2) who, while in correctional custody, is under physical restraint; and

(3) who escapes from the physical restraint before being released from the physical restraint by proper authority;

shall be punished as a court-martial may direct.

(b) BREACH OF CORRECTIONAL CUSTODY.—Any person subject to this chapter—

(1) who is placed in correctional custody by a person authorized to do so;

(2) who, while in correctional custody, is under restraint other than physical restraint; and

(3) who goes beyond the limits of the restraint before being released from the correctional custody or relieved of the restraint by proper authority;

shall be punished as a court-martial may direct.

(c) BREACH OF RESTRICTION.—Any person subject to this chapter—

(1) who is ordered to be restricted to certain limits by a person authorized to do so; and

(2) who, with knowledge of the limits of the restriction, goes beyond those limits before being released by proper authority;

shall be punished as a court-martial may direct.

§888. Art. 88. Contempt toward officials

Any commissioned officer who uses contemptuous words against the President, the Vice President, Congress, the Secretary of Defense, the Secretary of a military department, the Secretary of Homeland Security, or the Governor or legislature of any State, Commonwealth, or possession in which he is on duty or present shall be punished as a court-martial may direct.

§889. Art. 89. Disrespect toward superior commissioned officer; assault of superior commissioned officer

(a) DISRESPECT.—Any person subject to this chapter who behaves with disrespect toward that person's superior commissioned officer shall be punished as a court-martial may direct.

(b) ASSAULT.—Any person subject to this chapter who strikes that person's superior commissioned officer or draws or lifts up any weapon or offers any violence against that officer while the officer is in the execution of the officer's office shall be punished—

(1) if the offense is committed in time of war, by death or such other punishment as a court-martial may direct; and

(2) if the offense is committed at any other time, by such punishment, other than death, as a court-martial may direct.

§890. Art. 90. Willfully disobeying superior commissioned officer

Any person subject to this chapter who willfully disobeys a lawful command of that person's superior commissioned officer shall be punished—

(1) if the offense is committed in time of war, by death or such other punishment as a court-martial may direct; and

(2) if the offense is committed at any other time, by such punishment, other than death, as a court-martial may direct.

§891. Art. 91. Insubordinate conduct toward warrant officer, noncommissioned officer, or petty officer

Any warrant officer or enlisted member who—

(1) strikes or assaults a warrant officer, noncommissioned officer, or petty officer, while that officer is in the execution of his office;

(2) willfully disobeys the lawful order of a warrant officer, noncommissioned officer, or petty officer; or

(3) treats with contempt or is disrespectful in language or deportment toward a warrant officer, noncommissioned officer, or petty officer, while that officer is in the execution of his office;

shall be punished as a court-martial may direct.

§892. Art. 92. Failure to obey order or regulation

Any person subject to this chapter who—

(1) violates or fails to obey any lawful general order or regulation;

(2) having knowledge of any other lawful order issued by a member of the armed forces, which it is his duty to obey, fails to obey the order; or

(3) is derelict in the performance of his duties;

shall be punished as a court-martial may direct.

§893. Art. 93. Cruelty and maltreatment

Any person subject to this chapter who is guilty of cruelty toward, or oppression or maltreatment of, any person subject to his orders shall be punished as a court-martial may direct.

§893a. Art. 93a. Prohibited activities with military recruit or trainee by person in position of special trust

(a) ABUSE OF TRAINING LEADERSHIP POSITION.—Any person subject to this chapter—

(1) who is an officer, a noncommissioned officer, or a petty officer;

(2) who is in a training leadership position with respect to a specially protected junior member of the armed forces; and

(3) who engages in prohibited sexual activity with such specially protected junior member of the armed forces;

shall be punished as a court-martial may direct.

(b) ABUSE OF POSITION AS MILITARY RECRUITER.—Any person subject to this chapter—

(1) who is a military recruiter and engages in prohibited sexual activity with an applicant for military service; or

(2) who is a military recruiter and engages in prohibited sexual activity with a specially protected junior member of the armed forces who is enlisted under a delayed entry program;

shall be punished as a court-martial may direct.

(c) CONSENT.—Consent is not a defense for any conduct at issue in a prosecution under this section (article).

(d) DEFINITIONS.—In this section (article):

(1) SPECIALLY PROTECTED JUNIOR MEMBER OF THE ARMED FORCES.—The term "specially protected junior member of the armed forces" means—

(A) a member of the armed forces who is assigned to, or is awaiting assignment to, basic training or other initial active duty for training, including a member who is enlisted under a delayed entry program;

(B) a member of the armed forces who is a cadet, a midshipman, an officer candidate, or a student in any other officer qualification program; and

(C) a member of the armed forces in any program that, by regulation prescribed by the Secretary concerned, is identified as a training program for initial career qualification.

(2) TRAINING LEADERSHIP POSITION.—The term "training leadership position" means, with respect to a specially protected junior member of the armed forces, any of the following:

(A) Any drill instructor position or other leadership position in a basic training program, an officer candidate school, a reserve officers' training corps unit, a training program for entry into the armed forces, or any program that, by regulation prescribed by the Secretary concerned, is identified as a training program for initial career qualification.

(B) Faculty and staff of the United States Military Academy, the United States Naval Academy, the United States Air Force Academy, and the United States Coast Guard Academy.

(3) APPLICANT FOR MILITARY SERVICE.—The term "applicant for military service" means a person who, under regulations prescribed by the Secretary concerned, is an applicant for original enlistment or appointment in the armed forces.

(4) MILITARY RECRUITER.—The term "military recruiter" means, a person who, under regulations prescribed by the Secretary concerned, has the primary duty to recruit persons for military service.

(5) PROHIBITED SEXUAL ACTIVITY.—The term "prohibited sexual activity" means, as specified in regulations prescribed by the Secretary concerned, inappropriate physical intimacy under circumstances described in such regulations.

§894. Art. 94. Mutiny or sedition

(a) Any person subject to this chapter who—

(1) with intent to usurp or override lawful military authority, refuses, in concert with any other person, to obey orders or otherwise do his duty or creates any violence or disturbance is guilty of mutiny;

(2) with intent to cause the overthrow or destruction of lawful civil authority, creates, in concert with any other person, revolt, violence, or other disturbance against that authority is guilty of sedition;

(3) fails to do his utmost to prevent and suppress a mutiny or sedition being committed in his presence, or fails to take all reasonable means to inform his superior commissioned officer or commanding officer of a mutiny or sedition which he knows or has reason to believe is taking place, is guilty of a failure to suppress or report a mutiny or sedition.

(b) A person who is found guilty of attempted mutiny, mutiny, sedition, or failure to suppress or report a mutiny or sedition shall be punished by death or such other punishment as a court-martial may direct.

§895. Art. 95. Offenses by sentinel or lookout

(a) DRUNK OR SLEEPING ON POST, OR LEAVING POST BEFORE BEING RELIEVED.—Any sentinel or lookout who is drunk on post, who sleeps on post, or who leaves post before being regularly relieved, shall be punished—

(1) if the offense is committed in time of war, by death or such other punishment as a court-martial may direct; and

(2) if the offense is committed other than in time of war, by such punishment, other than death, as a court-martial may direct.

(b) LOITERING OR WRONGFULLY SITTING ON POST.—Any sentinel or lookout who loiters or wrongfully sits down on post shall be punished as a court-martial may direct.

§895a. Art. 95a. Disrespect toward sentinel or lookout

(a) DISRESPECTFUL LANGUAGE TOWARD SENTINEL OR LOOKOUT.—Any person subject to this chapter who, knowing that another person is a sentinel or lookout, uses wrongful and disrespectful language that is directed toward and within the hearing of the sentinel or lookout, who is in the execution of duties as a sentinel or lookout, shall be punished as a court-martial may direct.

(b) DISRESPECTFUL BEHAVIOR TOWARD SENTINEL OR LOOKOUT.—Any person subject to this chapter who, knowing that another person is a sentinel or lookout, behaves in a wrongful and disrespectful manner that is directed toward and within the sight of the sentinel or lookout, who is in the execution of duties as a sentinel or lookout, shall be punished as a court-martial may direct.

§896. Art. 96. Release of prisoner without authority; drinking with prisoner

(a) RELEASE OF PRISONER WITHOUT AUTHORITY.—Any person subject to this chapter—

(1) who, without authority to do so, releases a prisoner; or

(2) who, through neglect or design, allows a prisoner to escape; shall be punished as a court-martial may direct, whether or not the prisoner was committed in strict compliance with the law.

(b) DRINKING WITH PRISONER.—Any person subject to this chapter who unlawfully drinks any alcoholic beverage with a prisoner shall be punished as a court-martial may direct.

§897. Art. 97. Unlawful detention

Any person subject to this chapter who, except as provided by law, apprehends, arrests, or confines any person shall be punished as a court-martial may direct.

§898. Art. 98. Misconduct as prisoner

Any person subject to this chapter who, while in the hands of the enemy in time of war—

(1) for the purpose of securing favorable treatment by his captors acts without proper authority in a manner contrary to law, custom, or regulation, to the detriment of others of whatever nationality held by the enemy as civilian or military prisoners; or

(2) while in a position of authority over such persons maltreats them without justifiable cause; shall be punished as a court-martial may direct.

§899. Art. 99. Misbehavior before the enemy

Any member of the armed forces who before or in the presence of the enemy—

(1) runs away;

(2) shamefully abandons, surrenders, or delivers up any command, unit, place, or military property which it is his duty to defend;

(3) through disobedience, neglect, or intentional misconduct endangers the safety of any such command, unit, place, or military property;

(4) casts away his arms or ammunition;

(5) is guilty of cowardly conduct;

(6) quits his place of duty to plunder or pillage;

(7) causes false alarms in any command, unit, or place under control of the armed forces;

(8) willfully fails to do his utmost to encounter, engage, capture, or destroy any enemy troops, combatants, vessels, aircraft, or any other thing, which it is his duty so to encounter, engage, capture, or destroy; or

(9) does not afford all practicable relief and assistance to any troops, combatants, vessels, or aircraft of the armed forces belonging to the United States or their allies when engaged in battle; shall be punished by death or such other punishment as a court-martial may direct.

§900. Art. 100. Subordinate compelling surrender

Any person subject to this chapter who compels or attempts to compel the commander of any place, vessel, aircraft, or other military property, or of any body of members of the armed forces, to give it up to an enemy or to abandon it, or who strikes the colors or flag to an enemy without proper authority, shall be punished by death or such other punishment as a court-martial may direct.

§901. Art. 101. Improper use of countersign

Any person subject to this chapter who in time of war discloses the parole or countersign to any person not entitled to receive it or who gives to another who is entitled to receive and use the parole or countersign a different parole or countersign from that which, to his knowledge, he was authorized and required to give, shall be punished by death or such other punishment as a court-martial may direct.

§902. Art. 102. Forcing a safeguard

Any person subject to this chapter who forces a safeguard shall suffer death or such other punishment as a court-martial may direct.

§903. Art. 103. Spies

Any person who in time of war is found lurking as a spy or acting as a spy in or about any place, vessel, or aircraft, within the control or jurisdiction of any of the armed forces, or in or about any shipyard, any manufacturing or industrial plant, or any other place or institution engaged in work in aid of the prosecution of the war by the United States, or elsewhere, shall be tried by a general court-martial or by a military commission and on conviction shall be punished by death or such other punishment as a court-martial or a military commission may direct. This section does not apply to a military commission established under chapter 47A of this title.

§903a. Art. 103a. Espionage

(a)(1) Any person subject to this chapter who, with intent or reason to believe that it is to be used to the injury of the United States or to the advantage of a foreign nation, communicates, delivers, or transmits, or attempts to communicate, deliver, or transmit, to any entity described in paragraph (2), either directly or indirectly, anything described in paragraph (3) shall be punished as a court-martial may direct, except that if the accused is found guilty of an offense that directly concerns (A) nuclear weaponry, military spacecraft or satellites, early warning systems, or other means of defense or retaliation against large scale attack, (B) war plans, (C) communications intelligence or cryptographic information, or (D) any other major weapons system or major element of defense strategy, the accused shall be punished by death or such other punishment as a court-martial may direct.

(2) An entity referred to in paragraph (1) is—

(A) a foreign government;

(B) a faction or party or military or naval force within a foreign country, whether recognized or unrecognized by the United States; or

(C) a representative, officer, agent, employee, subject, or citizen of such a government, faction, party, or force.

(3) A thing referred to in paragraph (1) is a document, writing, code book, signal book, sketch, photograph, photographic negative, blueprint, plan, map, model, note, instrument, appliance, or information relating to the national defense.

(b)(1) No person may be sentenced by court-martial to suffer death for an offense under this section (article) unless—

(A) the members of the court-martial unanimously find at least one of the aggravating factors set out in subsection (c); and

(B) the members unanimously determine that any extenuating or mitigating circumstances are substantially outweighed by any aggravating circumstances, including the aggravating factors set out in subsection (c).

(2) Findings under this subsection may be based on—

(A) evidence introduced on the issue of guilt or innocence;

(B) evidence introduced during the sentencing proceeding; or

(C) all such evidence.

(3) The accused shall be given broad latitude to present matters in extenuation and mitigation.

(c) A sentence of death may be adjudged by a court-martial for an offense under this section (article) only if the members unanimously find, beyond a reasonable doubt, one or more of the following aggravating factors:

(1) The accused has been convicted of another offense involving espionage or treason for which either a sentence of death or imprisonment for life was authorized by statute.

(2) In the commission of the offense, the accused knowingly created a grave risk of substantial damage to the national security.

(3) In the commission of the offense, the accused knowingly created a grave risk of death to another person.

(4) Any other factor that may be prescribed by the President by regulations under section 836 of this title (article 36).

§903b. Art. 103b. Aiding the enemy

Any person who—

(1) aids, or attempts to aid, the enemy with arms, ammunition, supplies, money, or other things; or

(2) without proper authority, knowingly harbors or protects or gives intelligence to, or communicates or corresponds with or holds any intercourse with the enemy, either directly or indirectly; shall suffer death or such other punishment as a court-martial or military commission may direct. This section does not apply to a military commission established under chapter 47A of this title.

§904. Art. 104. Public records offenses

Any person subject to this chapter who, willfully and unlawfully—

(1) alters, conceals, removes, mutilates, obliterates, or destroys a public record; or

(2) takes a public record with the intent to alter, conceal, remove, mutilate, obliterate, or destroy the public record;

shall be punished as a court-martial may direct.

§904a. Art. 104a. Fraudulent enlistment, appointment, or separation

Any person who—

(1) procures his own enlistment or appointment in the armed forces by knowingly false representation or deliberate concealment as to his qualifications for that enlistment or appointment and receives pay or allowances thereunder; or

(2) procures his own separation from the armed forces by knowingly false representation or deliberate concealment as to his eligibility for that separation;

shall be punished as a court-martial may direct.

§904b. Art. 104b. Unlawful enlistment, appointment, or separation

Any person subject to this chapter who effects an enlistment or appointment in or a separation from the armed forces of any person who is known to him to be ineligible for that enlistment, appointment, or separation because it is prohibited by law, regulation, or order shall be punished as a court-martial may direct.

§905. Art. 105. Forgery

Any person subject to this chapter who, with intent to defraud—

(1) falsely makes or alters any signature to, or any part of, any writing which would, if genuine, apparently impose a legal liability on another or change his legal right or liability to his prejudice; or

(2) utters, offers, issues, or transfers such a writing, known by him to be so made or altered;

is guilty of forgery and shall be punished as a court-martial may direct.

§905a. Art. 105a. False or unauthorized pass offenses

(a) WRONGFUL MAKING, ALTERING, ETC.—Any person subject to this chapter who, wrongfully and falsely, makes, alters, counterfeits, or tampers with a military or official pass, permit, discharge certificate, or identification card shall be punished as a court-martial may direct.

(b) WRONGFUL SALE, ETC.—Any person subject to this chapter who wrongfully sells, gives, lends, or disposes of a false or unauthorized military or official pass, permit, discharge certificate, or identification card, knowing that the pass, permit, discharge certificate, or identification card is false or unauthorized, shall be punished as a court-martial may direct.

(c) WRONGFUL USE OR POSSESSION.—Any person subject to this chapter who wrongfully uses or possesses a false or unauthorized military or official pass, permit, discharge certificate, or identification card, knowing that the pass, permit, discharge certificate, or identification card is false or unauthorized, shall be punished as a court-martial may direct.

§906. Art. 106. Impersonation of officer, noncommissioned or petty officer, or agent or official

(a) IN GENERAL.—Any person subject to this chapter who, wrongfully and willfully, impersonates—

(1) an officer, a noncommissioned officer, or a petty officer;

(2) an agent of superior authority of one of the armed forces; or

(3) an official of a government; shall be punished as a court-martial may direct.

(b) IMPERSONATION WITH INTENT TO DEFRAUD.—Any person subject to this chapter who, wrongfully, willfully, and with intent to defraud, impersonates any person referred to in paragraph (1), (2), or (3) of subsection (a) shall be punished as a court-martial may direct.

(c) IMPERSONATION OF GOVERNMENT OFFICIAL WITHOUT INTENT TO DEFRAUD.—Any person subject to this chapter who, wrongfully, willfully, and without intent to defraud, impersonates an official of a government by committing an act that exercises or asserts the authority of the office that the person claims to have shall be punished as a court-martial may direct.

§906a. Art. 106a. Wearing unauthorized insignia, decoration, badge, ribbon, device, or lapel button

Any person subject to this chapter—

(1) who is not authorized to wear an insignia, decoration, badge, ribbon, device, or lapel button; and

(2) who wrongfully wears such insignia, decoration, badge, ribbon, device, or lapel button upon the person's uniform or civilian clothing; shall be punished as a court-martial may direct.

§907. Art. 107. False official statements; false swearing

(a) FALSE OFFICIAL STATEMENTS.—Any person subject to this chapter who, with intent to deceive—

(1) signs any false record, return, regulation, order, or other official document, knowing it to be false; or

(2) makes any other false official statement knowing it to be false; shall be punished as a court-martial may direct.

(b) FALSE SWEARING.—Any person subject to this chapter—

(1) who takes an oath that—

(A) is administered in a matter in which such oath is required or authorized by law; and

(B) is administered by a person with authority to do so; and

(2) who, upon such oath, makes or subscribes to a statement; if the statement is false and at the time of taking the oath, the person does not believe the statement to be true, shall be punished as a court-martial may direct.

§907a. Art. 107a. Parole violation

Any person subject to this chapter—

(1) who, having been a prisoner as the result of a court-martial conviction or other criminal proceeding, is on parole with conditions; and

(2) who violates the conditions of parole; shall be punished as a court-martial may direct.

§908. Art. 108. Military property of United States—Loss, damage, destruction, or wrongful disposition

Any person subject to this chapter who, without proper authority—

(1) sells or otherwise disposes of;

(2) willfully or through neglect damages, destroys, or loses; or

(3) willfully or through neglect suffers to be lost, damaged, destroyed, sold, or wrongfully disposed of; any military property of the United States, shall be punished as a court-martial may direct.

§908a. Art. 108a. Captured or abandoned property

(a) All persons subject to this chapter shall secure all public property taken from the enemy for the service of the United States, and shall give notice and turn over to the proper authority without delay all captured or abandoned property in their possession, custody, or control.

(b) Any person subject to this chapter who—

(1) fails to carry out the duties prescribed in subsection (a);

(2) buys, sells, trades, or in any way deals in or disposes of captured or abandoned property, whereby he receives or expects any profit, benefit, or advantage to himself or another directly or indirectly connected with himself; or

(3) engages in looting or pillaging; shall be punished as a court-martial may direct.

§909. Art. 109. Property other than military property of United States—Waste, spoilage, or destruction

Any person subject to this chapter who willfully or recklessly wastes, spoils, or otherwise willfully and wrongfully destroys or damages any property other than military property of the United States shall be punished as a court-martial may direct.

§909a. Art. 109a. Mail matter: wrongful taking, opening, etc.

(a) TAKING.—Any person subject to this chapter who, with the intent to obstruct the correspondence of, or to pry into the business or secrets of, any person or organization, wrongfully takes mail matter before the mail matter is delivered to or received by the addressee shall be punished as a court-martial may direct.

(b) OPENING, SECRETING, DESTROYING, STEALING.—Any person subject to this chapter who wrongfully opens, secretes, destroys, or steals mail matter before the mail matter is delivered to or received by the addressee shall be punished as a court-martial may direct.

§910. Art. 110. Improper hazarding of vessel or aircraft

(a) WILLFUL AND WRONGFUL HAZARDING.—Any person subject to this chapter who, willfully and wrongfully, hazards or suffers to be hazarded any vessel or aircraft of the armed forces shall be punished by death or such other punishment as a court-martial may direct.

(b) NEGLIGENT HAZARDING.—Any person subject to this chapter who negligently hazards or suffers to be hazarded any vessel or aircraft of the armed forces shall be punished as a court-martial may direct.

§911. Art. 111. Leaving scene of vehicle accident

(a) DRIVER.—Any person subject to this chapter—

(1) who is the driver of a vehicle that is involved in an accident that results in personal injury or property damage; and

(2) who wrongfully leaves the scene of the accident—

(A) without providing assistance to an injured person; or

(B) without providing personal identification to others involved in the accident or to appropriate authorities;

shall be punished as a court-martial may direct.

(b) SENIOR PASSENGER.—Any person subject to this chapter—

(1) who is a passenger in a vehicle that is involved in an accident that results in personal injury or property damage;

(2) who is the superior commissioned or noncommissioned officer of the driver of the vehicle or is the commander of the vehicle; and

(3) who wrongfully and unlawfully orders, causes, or permits the driver to leave the scene of the accident—

(A) without providing assistance to an injured person; or

(B) without providing personal identification to others involved in the accident or to appropriate authorities; shall be punished as a court-martial may direct.

§912. Art. 112. Drunkenness and other incapacitation offenses

(a) DRUNK ON DUTY.—Any person subject to this chapter who is drunk on duty shall be punished as a court-martial may direct.

(b) INCAPACITATION FOR DUTY FROM DRUNKENNESS OR DRUG USE.—Any person subject to this chapter who, as a result of indulgence in any alcoholic beverage or any drug, is incapacitated for the proper performance of duty shall be punished as a court-martial may direct.

(c) DRUNK PRISONER.—Any person subject to this chapter who is a prisoner and, while in such status, is drunk shall be punished as a court-martial may direct.

§912a. Art. 112a. Wrongful use, possession, etc., of controlled substances

(a) Any person subject to this chapter who wrongfully uses, possesses, manufactures, distributes, imports into the customs territory of the United States, exports from the United States, or introduces into an installation, vessel, vehicle, or aircraft used by or under the control of the armed forces a substance described in subsection (b) shall be punished as a court-martial may direct.

(b) The substances referred to in subsection (a) are the following:

(1) Opium, heroin, cocaine, amphetamine, lysergic acid diethylamide, methamphetamine, phencyclidine, barbituric acid, and marijuana and any compound or derivative of any such substance.

(2) Any substance not specified in clause (1) that is listed on a schedule of controlled substances prescribed by the President for the purposes of this article.

(3) Any other substance not specified in clause (1) or contained on a list prescribed by the President under clause (2) that is listed in schedules I through V of section 202 of the Controlled Substances Act (21 U.S.C. 812).

§913. Art. 113. Drunken or reckless operation of a vehicle, aircraft, or vessel

(a) Any person subject to this chapter who—

(1) operates or physically controls any vehicle, aircraft, or vessel in a reckless or wanton manner or while impaired by a substance described in section 912a(b) of this title (article 112a(b)), or

(2) operates or is in actual physical control of any vehicle, aircraft, or vessel while drunk or when the alcohol concentration in the person's blood or breath is equal to or exceeds the applicable limit under subsection (b),

shall be punished as a court-martial may direct.

(b)(1) For purposes of subsection (a), the applicable limit on the alcohol concentration in a person's blood or breath is as follows:

(A) In the case of the operation or control of a vehicle, aircraft, or vessel in the United States, such limit is the lesser of—

(i) the blood alcohol content limit under the law of the State in which the conduct occurred, except as may be provided under paragraph (2) for conduct on a military installation that is in more than one State; or

(ii) the blood alcohol content limit specified in paragraph (3).

(B) In the case of the operation or control of a vehicle, aircraft, or vessel outside the United States, the applicable blood alcohol content limit is the blood alcohol content limit specified in paragraph (3) or such lower limit as the Secretary of Defense may by regulation prescribe.

(2) In the case of a military installation that is in more than one State, if those States have different blood alcohol content limits under their respective State laws, the Secretary may select one such blood alcohol content limit to apply uniformly on that installation.

(3) For purposes of paragraph (1), the blood alcohol content limit with respect to alcohol concentration in a person's blood is

0.08 grams of alcohol per 100 milliliters of blood and with respect to alcohol concentration in a person's breath is 0.08 grams of alcohol per 210 liters of breath, as shown by chemical analysis. The Secretary may by regulation prescribe limits that are lower than the limits specified in the preceding sentence, if such lower limits are based on scientific developments, as reflected in Federal law of general applicability.

(4) In this subsection:

(A) The term "blood alcohol content limit" means the amount of alcohol concentration in a person's blood or breath at which operation or control of a vehicle, aircraft, or vessel is prohibited.

(B) The term "United States" includes the District of Columbia, the Commonwealth of Puerto Rico, the Virgin Islands, Guam, and American Samoa and the term "State" includes each of those jurisdictions.

§914. Art. 114. Endangerment offenses

(a) RECKLESS ENDANGERMENT.—Any person subject to this chapter who engages in conduct that—

(1) is wrongful and reckless or is wanton; and

(2) is likely to produce death or grievous bodily harm to another person; shall be punished as a court-martial may direct.

(b) DUELING.—Any person subject to this chapter—

(1) who fights or promotes, or is concerned in or connives at fighting a duel; or

(2) who, having knowledge of a challenge sent or about to be sent, fails to report the facts promptly to the proper authority; shall be punished as a court-martial may direct.

(c) FIREARM DISCHARGE, ENDANGERING HUMAN LIFE.—Any person subject to this chapter who, willfully and wrongly, discharges a firearm, under circumstances such as to endanger human life shall be punished as a court-martial may direct.

(d) CARRYING CONCEALED WEAPON.—Any person subject to this chapter who unlawfully carries a dangerous weapon concealed on or about his person shall be punished as a court-martial may direct.

§915. Art. 115. Communicating threats

(a) COMMUNICATING THREATS GENERALLY.—Any person subject to this chapter who wrongfully communicates a threat to injure the person, property, or reputation of another shall be punished as a court-martial may direct.

(b) COMMUNICATING THREAT TO USE EXPLOSIVE, ETC.—Any person subject to this chapter who wrongfully communicates a threat to injure the person or property of another by use of (1) an explosive, (2) a weapon of mass destruction, (3) a biological or chemical agent, substance, or weapon, or (4) a hazardous material, shall be punished as a court-martial may direct.

(c) COMMUNICATING FALSE THREAT CONCERNING USE OF EXPLOSIVE, ETC.—Any person subject to this chapter who maliciously communicates a false threat concerning injury to the person or property of another by use of (1) an explosive, (2) a weapon of mass destruction, (3) a biological or chemical agent, substance, or weapon, or (4) a hazardous material, shall be punished as a court-martial may direct. As used in the preceding sentence, the term "false threat" means a threat that, at the time the threat is communicated, is known to be false by the person communicating the threat.

§916. Art. 116. Riot or breach of peace

Any person subject to this chapter who causes or participates in any riot or breach of the peace shall be punished as a court-martial may direct.

§917. Art. 117. Provoking speeches or gestures

Any person subject to this chapter who uses provoking or reproachful words or gestures towards any other person subject to this chapter shall be punished as a court-martial may direct.

§917. Art. 117a. Wrongful broadcast or distribution of intimate visual images

(a) PROHIBITION. Any person subject to this chapter—

(1) who knowingly and wrongfully broadcasts or distributes an intimate visual image of another person or a visual image of sexually explicit conduct involving a person who—

(A) is at least 18 years of age at the time the intimate visual image or visual image of sexually explicit conduct was created;

(B) is identifiable from the intimate visual image or visual image of sexually explicit conduct itself, or from information displayed in connection with the intimate visual image or visual image of sexually explicit conduct; and

(C) does not explicitly consent to the broadcast or distribution of the intimate visual image or visual image of sexually explicit conduct;

(2) who knows or reasonably should have known that the intimate visual image or visual image of sexually explicit conduct was made under circumstances in which the person depicted in the intimate visual image or visual image of sexually explicit conduct retained a reasonable expectation of privacy regarding any broadcast or distribution of the intimate visual image or visual image of sexually explicit conduct;

(3) who knows or reasonably should have known that the broadcast or distribution of the intimate visual image or visual image of sexually explicit conduct is likely—

(A) to cause harm, harassment, intimidation, emotional distress, or financial loss for the person depicted in the intimate visual image or visual image of sexually explicit conduct; or

(B) to harm substantially the depicted person with respect to that person's health, safety, business, calling, career, financial condition, reputation, or personal relationships; and

(4) whose conduct, under the circumstances, had a reasonably direct and palpable connection to a military mission or military environment, is guilty of wrongful distribution of intimate visual images or visual images of sexually explicit conduct and shall be punished as a court-martial may direct.

(b) DEFINITIONS. In this section:

(1) BROADCAST. The term 'broadcast' means to electronically transmit a visual image with the intent that it be viewed by a person or persons.

(2) DISTRIBUTE. The term 'distribute' means to deliver to the actual or constructive possession of another person, including transmission by mail or electronic means.

(3) INTIMATE VISUAL IMAGE. The term 'intimate visual image' means a visual image that depicts a private area of a person.

(4) PRIVATE AREA. The term 'private area' means the naked or underwear-clad genitalia, anus, buttocks, or female areola or nipple.

(5) REASONABLE EXPECTATION OF PRIVACY. The term 'reasonable expectation of privacy' means circumstances in which a reasonable person would believe that a private area of the person, or sexually explicit conduct involving the person, would not be visible to the public.

(6) SEXUALLY EXPLICIT CONDUCT. The term 'sexually explicit conduct' means actual or simulated genital-genital contact, oral-genital contact, anal-genital contact, or oral-anal contact, whether between persons of the same or opposite sex, bestiality, masturbation, or sadistic or masochistic abuse.

(7) VISUAL IMAGE. The term 'visual image' means the following:

(A) Any developed or undeveloped photograph, picture, film, or video.

(B) Any digital or computer image, picture, film, or video made by any means, including those transmitted by any means, including streaming media, even if not stored in a permanent format.

(C) Any digital or electronic data capable of conversion into a visual image.

§918. Art. 118. Murder

Any person subject to this chapter who, without justification or excuse, unlawfully kills a human being, when he—

(1) has a premeditated design to kill;

(2) intends to kill or inflict great bodily harm;

(3) is engaged in an act which is inherently dangerous to another and evinces a wanton disregard of human life; or

(4) is engaged in the perpetration or attempted perpetration of burglary, rape, rape of a child, sexual assault, sexual assault of a child, aggravated sexual contact, sexual abuse of a child, robbery, or aggravated arson; is guilty of murder, and shall suffer such punishment as a court-martial may direct, except that if found guilty under clause (1) or (4), he shall suffer death or imprisonment for life as a court-martial may direct.

§919. Art. 119. Manslaughter

(a) Any person subject to this chapter who, with an intent to kill or inflict great bodily harm, unlawfully kills a human being in the heat of sudden passion caused by adequate provocation is guilty of voluntary manslaughter and shall be punished as a court-martial may direct.

(b) Any person subject to this chapter who, without an intent to kill or inflict great bodily harm, unlawfully kills a human being—

(1) by culpable negligence; or

(2) while perpetrating or attempting to perpetrate an offense, other than those named in clause (4) of section 918 of this title (article 118), directly affecting the person; is guilty of involuntary manslaughter and shall be punished as a court-martial may direct.

§919a. Art. 119a. Death or injury of an unborn child

(a)(1) Any person subject to this chapter who engages in conduct that violates any of the provisions of law listed in subsection (b) and thereby causes the death of, or bodily injury (as defined in section 1365 of title 18) to, a child, who is in utero at the time the conduct takes place, is guilty of a separate offense under this section and shall, upon conviction, be punished by such punishment, other than death, as a court-martial may direct, which shall be consistent with the punishments prescribed by the President for that conduct had that injury or death occurred to the unborn child's mother.

(2) An offense under this section does not require proof that—

(i) the person engaging in the conduct had knowledge or should have had knowledge that the victim of the underlying offense was pregnant; or

(ii) the accused intended to cause the death of, or bodily injury to, the unborn child.

(3) If the person engaging in the conduct thereby intentionally kills or attempts to kill the unborn child, that person shall, instead of being punished under paragraph (1), be punished as provided under sections 880, 918, and 919(a) of this title (articles 80, 118, and 119(a)) for intentionally killing or attempting to kill a human being.

(4) Notwithstanding any other provision of law, the death penalty shall not be imposed for an offense under this section.

(b) The provisions referred to in subsection (a) are sections 918, 919(a), 919(b)(2), 920(a), 922, 926, 928, and 928a of this title (articles 118, 119(a), 119(b)(2), 120(a), 122, 126, 128, and 128a.

(c) Nothing in this section shall be construed to permit the prosecution—

(1) of any person for conduct relating to an abortion for which the consent of the pregnant woman, or a person authorized by law to act on her behalf, has been obtained or for which such consent is implied by law;

(2) of any person for any medical treatment of the pregnant woman or her unborn child; or

(3) of any woman with respect to her unborn child.

(d) In this section, the term "unborn child" means a child in utero, and the term "child in utero" or "child, who is in utero" means a member of the species homo sapiens, at any stage of development, who is carried in the womb.

§919b. Art. 119b. Child endangerment

Any person subject to this chapter—

(1) who has a duty for the care of a child under the age of 16 years; and

(2) who, through design or culpable negligence, endangers the child's mental or physical health, safety, or welfare; shall be punished as a court-martial may direct.

§920. Art. 120. Rape and sexual assault generally

(a) RAPE.—Any person subject to this chapter who commits a sexual act upon another person by—

(1) using unlawful force against that other person;

(2) using force causing or likely to cause death or grievous bodily harm to any person;

(3) threatening or placing that other person in fear that any person will be subjected to death, grievous bodily harm, or kidnapping;

(4) first rendering that other person unconscious; or

(5) administering to that other person by force or threat of force, or without the knowledge or consent of that person, a drug,

intoxicant, or other similar substance and thereby substantially impairing the ability of that other person to appraise or control conduct;

is guilty of rape and shall be punished as a court-martial may direct.

(b) SEXUAL ASSAULT.—Any person subject to this chapter who—

(1) commits a sexual act upon another person by—

(A) threatening or placing that other person in fear;

(B) making a fraudulent representation that the sexual act serves a professional purpose; or

(C) inducing a belief by any artifice, pretense, or concealment that the person is another person;

(2) commits a sexual act upon another person—

(A) without the consent of the other person; or

(B) when the person knows or reasonably should know that the other person is asleep, unconscious, or otherwise unaware that the sexual act is occurring; or

(3) commits a sexual act upon another person when the other person is incapable of consenting to the sexual act due to—

(A) impairment by any drug, intoxicant, or other similar substance, and that condition is known or reasonably should be known by the person; or

(B) a mental disease or defect, or physical disability, and that condition is known or reasonably should be known by the person;

is guilty of sexual assault and shall be punished as a court-martial may direct.

(c) AGGRAVATED SEXUAL CONTACT.—Any person subject to this chapter who commits or causes sexual contact upon or by another person, if to do so would violate subsection (a) (rape) had the sexual contact been a sexual act, is guilty of aggravated sexual contact and shall be punished as a court-martial may direct.

(d) ABUSIVE SEXUAL CONTACT.—Any person subject to this chapter who commits or causes sexual contact upon or by another person, if to do so would violate subsection (b) (sexual assault) had the sexual contact been a sexual act, is guilty of abusive sexual contact and shall be punished as a court-martial may direct.

(e) PROOF OF THREAT.—In a prosecution under this section, in proving that a person made a threat, it need not be proven that the person actually intended to carry out the threat or had the ability to carry out the threat.

(f) DEFENSES.—An accused may raise any applicable defenses available under this chapter or the Rules for Court-Martial. Marriage is not a defense for any conduct in issue in any prosecution under this section.

(g) DEFINITIONS.—In this section:

(1) SEXUAL ACT.—The term "sexual act" means—

(A) the penetration, however, slight, of the penis into the vulva or anus or mouth;

(B) contact between the mouth and the penis, vulva, scrotum, or anus; or

(C) the penetration, however slight, of the vulva or penis or anus of another by any part of the body or any object, with an intent to abuse, humiliate, harass, or degrade any person or to arouse or gratify the sexual desire of any person.

(2) Sexual contact.—The term "sexual contact" means touching, or causing another person to touch, either directly or through the clothing, the vulva, penis, scrotum, anus, groin, breast, inner thigh, or buttocks of any person, with an intent to abuse, humiliate, harass, or degrade any person or to arouse or gratify the sexual desire of any person. Touching may be accomplished by any part of the body or an object.

(3) GRIEVOUS BODILY HARM.—The term "grievous bodily harm" means serious bodily injury. It includes fractured or dislocated bones, deep cuts, torn members of the body, serious damage to internal organs, and other severe bodily injuries. It does not include minor injuries such as a black eye or a bloody nose.

(4) FORCE.—The term "force" means—

(A) the use of a weapon;

(B) the use of such physical strength or violence as is sufficient to overcome, restrain, or injure a person; or

(C) inflicting physical harm sufficient to coerce or compel submission by the victim.

(5) UNLAWFUL FORCE.—The term "unlawful force" means an act of force done without legal justification or excuse.

(6) THREATENING OR PLACING THAT OTHER PERSON IN FEAR.—The term "threatening or placing that other person in fear" means a communication or action that is of sufficient consequence to cause a reasonable fear that non-compliance will result in the victim or another person being subjected to the wrongful action contemplated by the communication or action.

(7) CONSENT.—

(A) The term "consent" means a freely given agreement to the conduct at issue by a competent person. An expression of lack of consent through words or conduct means there is no consent. Lack of verbal or physical resistance does not constitute consent. Submission resulting from the use of force, threat of force, or placing another person in fear also does not constitute consent. A current or previous dating or social or sexual relationship by itself or the manner of dress of the person involved with the accused in the conduct at issue does not constitute consent.

(B) A sleeping, unconscious, or incompetent person cannot consent. A person cannot consent to force causing or likely to cause death or grievous bodily harm or to being rendered unconscious. A person cannot consent while under threat or in fear or under the circumstances described in subparagraph (C) or (D) of subsection (b)(1).

(C) All the surrounding circumstances are to be considered in determining whether a person gave consent.

(8) Incapable of consenting.—The term "incapable of consenting" means the person is—

(A) incapable of appraising the nature of the conduct at issue; or

(B) physically incapable of declining participation in, or communicating unwillingness to engage in, the sexual act at issue.

§920a. Art. 120a. Mails: deposit of obscene matter

Any person subject to this chapter who, wrongfully and knowingly, deposits obscene matter for mailing and delivery shall be punished as a court-martial may direct.

§920b. Art. 120b. Rape and sexual assault of a child

(a) RAPE OF A CHILD.—Any person subject to this chapter who—

(1) commits a sexual act upon a child who has not attained the age of 12 years; or

(2) commits a sexual act upon a child who has attained the age of 12 years by—

(A) using force against any person;

(B) threatening or placing that child in fear;

(C) rendering that child unconscious; or

(D) administering to that child a drug, intoxicant, or other similar substance; is guilty of rape of a child and shall be punished as a court-martial may direct.

(b) SEXUAL ASSAULT OF A CHILD.—Any person subject to this chapter who commits a sexual act upon a child who has attained the age of 12 years is guilty of sexual assault of a child and shall be punished as a court-martial may direct.

(c) SEXUAL ABUSE OF A CHILD.—Any person subject to this chapter who commits a lewd act upon a child is guilty of sexual abuse of a child and shall be punished as a court-martial may direct.

(d) AGE OF CHILD.—

(1) UNDER 12 YEARS.—In a prosecution under this section, it need not be proven that the accused knew the age of the other person engaging in the sexual act or lewd act. It is not a defense that the accused reasonably believed that the child had attained the age of 12 years.

(2) UNDER 16 YEARS.—In a prosecution under this section, it need not be proven that the accused knew that the other person engaging in the sexual act or lewd act had not attained the age of 16 years, but it is a defense in a prosecution under subsection (b) (sexual assault of a child) or subsection (c) (sexual abuse of a child), which the accused must prove by a preponderance of the evidence, that the accused reasonably believed that the child had attained the age of 16 years, if the child had in fact attained at least the age of 12 years.

(e) PROOF OF THREAT.—In a prosecution under this section, in proving that a person made a threat, it need not be proven that the person actually intended to carry out the threat or had the ability to carry out the threat.

(f) MARRIAGE.—In a prosecution under subsection (b) (sexual assault of a child) or subsection (c) (sexual abuse of a child), it is a defense, which the accused must prove by a preponderance of the evidence, that the persons engaging in the sexual act or lewd act were at that time married to each other, except where the accused commits a sexual act upon the person when the accused knows or reasonably should know that the other person is asleep, unconscious, or otherwise unaware that the sexual act is occurring or when the other person is incapable of consenting to the sexual act due to impairment by any drug, intoxicant, or other similar substance, and that condition was known or reasonably should have been known by the accused.

(g) CONSENT.—Lack of consent is not an element and need not be proven in any prosecution under this section. A child not legally married to the person committing the sexual act, lewd act, or use of force cannot consent to any sexual act, lewd act, or use of force.

(h) DEFINITIONS.—In this section:

(1) SEXUAL ACT AND SEXUAL CONTACT.—The terms "sexual act" and "sexual contact" have the meanings given those terms in section 920(g) of this title (article 120(g)), except that the term "sexual act" also includes the intentional touching, not through the clothing, of the genitalia of another person who has not attained the age of 16 years with an intent to abuse, humiliate, harass, degrade, or arouse or gratify the sexual desire of any person.

(2) FORCE.—The term "force" means—

(A) the use of a weapon;

(B) the use of such physical strength or violence as is sufficient to overcome, restrain, or injure a child; or

(C) inflicting physical harm.

In the case of a parent-child or similar relationship, the use or abuse of parental or similar authority is sufficient to constitute the use of force.

(3) THREATENING OR PLACING THAT CHILD IN FEAR.—The term "threatening or placing that child in fear" means a communication or action that is of sufficient consequence to cause the child to fear that non-compliance will result in the child or another person being subjected to the action contemplated by the communication or action.

(4) CHILD.—The term "child" means any person who has not attained the age of 16 years.

(5) LEWD ACT.—The term "lewd act" means—

(A) any sexual contact with a child;

(B) intentionally exposing one's genitalia, anus, buttocks, or female areola or nipple to a child by any means, including via any communication technology, with an intent to abuse, humiliate, or degrade any person, or to arouse or gratify the sexual desire of any person;

(C) intentionally communicating indecent language to a child by any means, including via any communication technology, with an intent to abuse, humiliate, or degrade any person, or to arouse or gratify the sexual desire of any person; or

(D) any indecent conduct, intentionally done with or in the presence of a child, including via any communication technology, that amounts to a form of immorality relating to sexual impurity which is grossly vulgar, obscene, and repugnant to common propriety, and tends to excite sexual desire or deprave morals with respect to sexual relations.

§920c. Art. 120c. Other sexual misconduct

(a) INDECENT VIEWING, VISUAL RECORDING, OR BROADCASTING.—Any person subject to this chapter who, without legal justification or lawful authorization—

(1) knowingly and wrongfully views the private area of another person, without that other person's consent and under circumstances in which that other person has a reasonable expectation of privacy;

(2) knowingly photographs, videotapes, films, or records by any means the private area of another person, without that other person's consent and under circumstances in which that other person has a reasonable expectation of privacy; or

(3) knowingly broadcasts or distributes any such recording that the person knew or reasonably should have known was made under the circumstances proscribed in paragraphs (1) and (2);

is guilty of an offense under this section and shall be punished as a court-martial may direct.

(b) FORCIBLE PANDERING.—Any person subject to this chapter who compels another person to engage in an act of prostitution with any person is guilty of forcible pandering and shall be punished as a court-martial may direct.

(c) INDECENT EXPOSURE.—Any person subject to this chapter who intentionally exposes, in an indecent manner, the genitalia, anus, buttocks, or female areola or nipple is guilty of indecent exposure and shall by punished as a court-martial may direct.

(d) DEFINITIONS.—In this section:

(1) ACT OF PROSTITUTION.—The term "act of prostitution" means a sexual act or sexual contact (as defined in section 920(g) of this title (article 120(g))) on account of which anything of value is given to, or received by, any person.

(2) PRIVATE AREA.—The term "private area" means the naked or underwear-clad genitalia, anus, buttocks, or female areola or nipple.

(3) REASONABLE EXPECTATION OF PRIVACY.—The term "under circumstances in which that other person has a reasonable expectation of privacy" means—

(A) circumstances in which a reasonable person would believe that he or she could disrobe in privacy, without being concerned that an image of a private area of the person was being captured; or

(B) circumstances in which a reasonable person would believe that a private area of the person would not be visible to the public.

(4) BROADCAST.—The term "broadcast" means to electronically transmit a visual image with the intent that it be viewed by a person or persons.

(5) DISTRIBUTE.—The term "distribute" means delivering to the actual or constructive possession of another, including transmission by electronic means.

(6) INDECENT MANNER.—The term "indecent manner" means conduct that amounts to a form of immorality relating to sexual impurity which is grossly vulgar, obscene, and repugnant to common propriety, and tends to excite sexual desire or deprave morals with respect to sexual relations.

§921. Art. 121. Larceny and wrongful appropriation

(a) Any person subject to this chapter who wrongfully takes, obtains, or withholds, by any means, from the possession of the owner or of any other person any money, personal property, or article of value of any kind—

(1) with intent permanently to deprive or defraud another person of the use and benefit of property or to appropriate it to his own use or the use of any person other than the owner, steals that property and is guilty of larceny; or

(2) with intent temporarily to deprive or defraud another person of the use and benefit of property or to appropriate it to his own use or the use of any person other than the owner, is guilty of wrongful appropriation.

(b) Any person found guilty of larceny or wrongful appropriation shall be punished as a court-martial may direct.

§921a. Art. 121a. Fraudulent use of credit cards, debit cards, and other access devices

(a) IN GENERAL.—Any person subject to this chapter who, knowingly and with intent to defraud, uses—

(1) a stolen credit card, debit card, or other access device;

(2) a revoked, cancelled, or otherwise invalid credit card, debit card, or other access device; or

(3) a credit card, debit card, or other access device without the authorization of a person whose authorization is required for such use; to obtain money, property, services, or anything else of value shall be punished as a court-martial may direct.

(b) ACCESS DEVICE DEFINED.—In this section (article), the term "access device" has the meaning given that term in section 1029 of title 18.

§921b. Art. 121b. False pretenses to obtain services

Any person subject to this chapter who, with intent to defraud, knowingly uses false pretenses to obtain services shall be punished as a court-martial may direct.

§922. Art. 122. Robbery

Any person subject to this chapter who takes anything of value from the person or in the presence of another, against his will, by means of force or violence or fear of immediate or future injury to his person or property or to the person or property of a relative or member of his family or of anyone in his company at the time of the robbery, is guilty of robbery and shall be punished as a court-martial may direct.

§922a. Art. 122a. Receiving stolen property

Any person subject to this chapter who wrongfully receives, buys, or conceals stolen property, knowing the property to be stolen property, shall be punished as a court-martial may direct.

§923. Art. 123. Offenses concerning Government computers

(a) IN GENERAL.—Any person subject to this chapter who—

(1) knowingly accesses a Government computer, with an unauthorized purpose, and by doing so obtains classified information, with reason to believe such information could be used to the injury of the United States, or to the advantage of any foreign nation, and intentionally communicates, delivers, transmits, or causes to be communicated, delivered, or transmitted such information to any person not entitled to receive it;

(2) intentionally accesses a Government computer, with an unauthorized purpose, and thereby obtains classified or other protected information from any such Government computer; or

(3) knowingly causes the transmission of a program, information, code, or command, and as a result of such conduct, intentionally causes damage without authorization, to a Government computer; shall be punished as a court-martial may direct.

(b) DEFINITIONS.—In this section:

(1) The term "computer" has the meaning given that term in section 1030 of title 18.

(2) The term "Government computer" means a computer owned or operated by or on behalf of the United States Government.

(3) The term "damage" has the meaning given that term in section 1030 of title 18.

§923a. Art. 123a. Making, drawing, or uttering check, draft, or order without sufficient funds

Any person subject to this chapter who—

(1) for the procurement of any article or thing of value, with intent to defraud; or

(2) for the payment of any past due obligation, or for any other purpose, with intent to deceive; makes, draws, utters, or delivers any check, draft, or order for the payment of money upon any bank or other depository, knowing at the time that the maker or drawer has not or will not have sufficient funds in, or credit with, the bank or other depository for the payment of that check, draft, or order in full upon its presentment, shall be punished as a court-martial may direct. The making, drawing, uttering, or delivering by a maker or drawer of a check, draft, or order, payment of which is refused by the drawee because of insufficient funds of the maker or drawer in the drawee's possession or control, is prima facie evidence of his intent to defraud or deceive and of his knowledge of insufficient funds in, or credit with, that bank or other depository, unless the maker or drawer pays the holder the amount due within five days after receiving notice, orally or in writing, that the check, draft, or order was not paid on presentment. In this section, the word "credit" means an arrangement or understanding, express or implied, with the bank or other depository for the payment of that check, draft, or order.

§924. Art. 124. Frauds against the United States

Any person subject to this chapter—

(1) who, knowing it to be false or fraudulent—

(A) makes any claim against the United States or any officer thereof; or

(B) presents to any person in the civil or military service thereof, for approval or payment, any claim against the United States or any officer thereof;

(2) who, for the purpose of obtaining the approval, allowance, or payment of any claim against the United States or any officer thereof—

(A) makes or uses any writing or other paper knowing it to contain any false or fraudulent statements;

(B) makes any oath to any fact or to any writing or other paper knowing the oath to be false; or

(C) forges or counterfeits any signature upon any writing or other paper, or uses any such signature knowing it to be forged or counterfeited;

(3) who, having charge, possession, custody or control of any money, or other property of the United States, furnished or intended for the armed forces thereof, knowingly delivers to any person having authority to receive it, any amount thereof less than that for which he receives a certificate or receipt; or

(4) who, being authorized to make or deliver any paper certifying the receipt of any property of the United States furnished or intended for the armed forces thereof, makes or delivers to any person such writing without having full knowledge of the truth of the statements therein contained and with intent to defraud the United States; shall, upon conviction, be punished as a court-martial may direct.

§924a. Art. 124a. Bribery

(a) ASKING, ACCEPTING, OR RECEIVING THING OF VALUE.—Any person subject to this chapter—

(1) who occupies an official position or who has official duties; and

(2) who wrongfully asks, accepts, or receives a thing of value with the intent to have the person's decision or action influenced with respect to an official matter in which the United States is interested; shall be punished as a court-martial may direct.

(b) PROMISING, OFFERING, OR GIVING THING OF VALUE.—Any person subject to this chapter who wrongfully promises, offers, or gives a thing of value to another person, who occupies an official position or who has official duties, with the intent to influence the decision or action of the other person with respect to an official matter in which the United States is interested, shall be punished as a court-martial may direct.

§924b. Art. 124b. Graft

(a) ASKING, ACCEPTING, OR RECEIVING THING OF VALUE.—Any person subject to this chapter—

(1) who occupies an official position or who has official duties; and

(2) who wrongfully asks, accepts, or receives a thing of value as compensation for or in recognition of services rendered or to be rendered by the person with respect to an official matter in which the United States is interested; shall be punished as a court-martial may direct.

(b) PROMISING, OFFERING, OR GIVING THING OF VALUE.—Any person subject to this chapter who wrongfully promises, offers, or gives a thing of value to another person, who occupies an official position or who has official duties, as compensation for or in recognition of services rendered or to be rendered by the other person with respect to an official matter in which the United States is interested, shall be punished as a court-martial may direct.

§925. Art. 125. Kidnapping

Any person subject to this chapter who wrongfully—

(1) seizes, confines, inveigles, decoys, or carries away another person; and

(2) holds the other person against that person's will; shall be punished as a court-martial may direct.

§926. Art. 126. Arson; burning property with intent to defraud

(a) AGGRAVATED ARSON.—Any person subject to this chapter who, willfully and maliciously, burns or sets on fire an inhabited dwelling, or any other structure, movable or immovable, wherein, to the knowledge of that person, there is at the time a human being, is guilty of aggravated arson and shall be punished as a court-martial may direct.

(b) SIMPLE ARSON.—Any person subject to this chapter who, willfully and maliciously, burns or sets fire to the property of another is guilty of simple arson and shall be punished as a court-martial may direct.

(c) BURNING PROPERTY WITH INTENT TO DEFRAUD.—Any person subject to this chapter who, willfully, maliciously, and with intent to defraud, burns or sets fire to any property shall be punished as a court-martial may direct.

§927. Art. 127. Extortion

Any person subject to this chapter who communicates threats to another person with the intention thereby to obtain anything of value or any acquittance, advantage, or immunity is guilty of extortion and shall be punished as a court-martial may direct.

§928. Art. 128. Assault

(a) ASSAULT.—Any person subject to this chapter who, unlawfully and with force or violence—

(1) attempts to do bodily harm to another person;

(2) offers to do bodily harm to another person; or

(3) does bodily harm to another person; is guilty of assault and shall be punished as a court-martial may direct.

(b) AGGRAVATED ASSAULT.—Any person subject to this chapter—

(1) who, with the intent to do bodily harm, offers to do bodily harm with a dangerous weapon;

(2) who, in committing an assault, inflicts substantial bodily harm or grievous bodily harm on another person; or

(3) who commits an assault by strangulation or suffocation;

is guilty of aggravated assault and shall be punished as a court-martial may direct.

(c) ASSAULT WITH INTENT TO COMMIT SPECIFIED OFFENSES.—

(1) IN GENERAL.—Any person subject to this chapter who commits assault with intent to commit an offense specified in paragraph (2) shall be punished as a court-martial may direct.

(2) OFFENSES SPECIFIED.—The offenses referred to in paragraph (1) are murder, voluntary manslaughter, rape, sexual assault, rape of a child, sexual assault of a child, robbery, arson, burglary, and kidnapping.

§928a. Art. 128a. Maiming

Any person subject to this chapter who, with intent to injure, disfigure, or disable, inflicts upon the person of another an injury which—

(1) seriously disfigures his person by any mutilation thereof;

(2) destroys or disables any member or organ of his body; or

(3) seriously diminishes his physical vigor by the injury of any member or organ; is guilty of maiming and shall be punished as a court-martial may direct.

§928b. Art. 128b. Domestic Violence

Any person who—

(1) commits a violent offense against a spouse, an intimate partner, or an immediate family member of that person;

(2) with intent to threaten or intimidate a spouse, an intimate partner, or an immediate family member of that person—

(A) commits an offense under this chapter against any person; or

(B) commits an offense under this chapter against any property, including an animal;

(3) with intent to threaten or intimidate a spouse, an intimate partner, or an immediate family member of that person, violates a protection order;

(4) with intent to commit a violent offense against a spouse, an intimate partner, or an immediate family member of that person, violates a protection order; or

(5) assaults a spouse, an intimate partner, or an immediate family member of that person by strangling or suffocating

shall be punished as a court-martial may direct.

§929. Art. 129. Burglary; unlawful entry

(a) BURGLARY.—Any person subject to this chapter who, with intent to commit an offense under this chapter, breaks and enters the building or structure of another shall be punished as a court-martial may direct.

(b) UNLAWFUL ENTRY.—Any person subject to this chapter who unlawfully enters—

(1) the real property of another; or

(2) the personal property of another which amounts to a structure usually used for habitation or storage; shall be punished as a court-martial may direct.

930. Art. 130. Stalking

(a) IN GENERAL.—Any person subject to this chapter—

(1) who wrongfully engages in a course of conduct directed at a specific person that would cause a reasonable person to fear death or bodily harm, including sexual assault, to himself or herself, to a member of his or her immediate family, or to his or her intimate partner;

(2) who has knowledge, or should have knowledge, that the specific person will be placed in reasonable fear of death or bodily harm, including sexual assault, to himself or herself, to a member of his or her immediate family, or to his or her intimate partner; and

(3) whose conduct induces reasonable fear in the specific person of death or bodily harm, including sexual assault, to himself or herself, to a member of his or her immediate family, or to his or her intimate partner;

is guilty of stalking and shall be punished as a court-martial may direct.

(b) DEFINITIONS.—In this section:

(1) The term "conduct" means conduct of any kind, including use of surveillance, the mails, an interactive computer service, an electronic communication service, or an electronic communication system.

(2) The term "course of conduct" means—

(A) a repeated maintenance of visual or physical proximity to a specific person;

(B) a repeated conveyance of verbal threat, written threats, or threats implied by conduct, or a combination of such threats, directed at or toward a specific person; or

(C) a pattern of conduct composed of repeated acts evidencing a continuity of purpose.

(3) The term "repeated", with respect to conduct, means two or more occasions of such conduct.

(4) The term "immediate family", in the case of a specific person, means—

(A) that person's spouse, parent, brother or sister, child, or other person to whom he or she stands in loco parentis; or

(B) any other person living in his or her household and related to him or her by blood or marriage.

(5) The term "intimate partner", in the case of a specific person, means—

(A) a former spouse of the specific person, a person who shares a child in common with the specific person, or a person who cohabits with or has cohabited as a spouse with the specific person; or

(B) a person who has been in a social relationship of a romantic or intimate nature with the specific person, as determined by the length of the relationship, the type of relationship, and the frequency of interaction between the persons involved in the relationship.

§931. Art. 131. Perjury

Any person subject to this chapter who in a judicial proceeding or in a course of justice willfully and corruptly—

(1) upon a lawful oath or in any form allowed by law to be substituted for an oath, gives any false testimony material to the issue or matter of inquiry; or

(2) in any declaration, certificate, verification, or statement under penalty of perjury as permitted under section 1746 of title 28, subscribes any false statement material to the issue or matter of inquiry; is guilty of perjury and shall be punished as a court-martial may direct.

§931a. Art. 131a. Subornation of perjury

(a) IN GENERAL.—Any person subject to this chapter who induces and procures another person—

(1) to take an oath; and

(2) to falsely testify, depose, or state upon such oath; shall, if the conditions specified in subsection (b) are satisfied, be punished as a court-martial may direct.

(b) CONDITIONS.—The conditions referred to in subsection (a) are the following:

(1) The oath is administered with respect to a matter for which such oath is required or authorized by law.

(2) The oath is administered by a person having authority to do so.

(3) Upon the oath, the other person willfully makes or subscribes a statement.

(4) The statement is material.

(5) The statement is false.

(6) When the statement is made or subscribed, the person subject to this chapter and the other person do not believe that the statement is true.

§931b. Art. 131b. Obstructing justice

Any person subject to this chapter who engages in conduct in the case of a certain person against whom the accused had reason to believe there were or would be criminal or disciplinary proceedings pending, with intent to influence, impede, or otherwise obstruct the due administration of justice shall be punished as a court-martial may direct.

§931c. Art. 131c. Misprision of serious offense

(a) IN GENERAL.—Any person subject to this chapter—

(1) who knows that another person has committed a serious offense; and

(2) wrongfully conceals the commission of the offense and fails to make the commission of the offense known to civilian or military authorities as soon as possible; shall be punished as a court-martial may direct.

§931d. Art. 131d. Wrongful refusal to testify

Any person subject to this chapter who, in the presence of a court-martial, a board of officers, a military commission, a court of inquiry, preliminary hearing, or an officer taking a deposition, of or for the United States, wrongfully refuses to qualify as a witness or to answer a question after having been directed to do so by the person presiding shall be punished as a court-martial may direct.

§931e. Art. 131e. Prevention of authorized seizure of property

Any person subject to this chapter who, knowing that one or more persons authorized to make searches and seizures are seizing, are about to seize, or are endeavoring to seize property, destroys, removes, or otherwise disposes of the property with intent to prevent the seizure thereof shall be punished as a court-martial may direct.

§931f. Art. 131f. Noncompliance with procedural rules

Any person subject to this chapter who—

(1) is responsible for unnecessary delay in the disposition of any case of a person accused of an offense under this chapter; or

(2) knowingly and intentionally fails to enforce or comply with any provision of this chapter regulating the proceedings before, during, or after trial of an accused; shall be punished as a court-martial may direct.

§931g. Art. 131g. Wrongful interference with adverse administrative proceeding

Any person subject to this chapter who, having reason to believe that an adverse administrative proceeding is pending against any person subject to this chapter, wrongfully acts with the intent—

(1) to influence, impede, or obstruct the conduct of the proceeding; or

(2) otherwise to obstruct the due administration of justice; shall be punished as a court-martial may direct.

§932. Art. 132. Retaliation

(a) IN GENERAL.—Any person subject to this chapter who, with the intent to retaliate against any person for reporting or planning to report a criminal offense, or making or planning to make a protected communication, or with the intent to discourage any person from reporting a criminal offense or making or planning to make a protected communication—

(1) wrongfully takes or threatens to take an adverse personnel action against any person; or

(2) wrongfully withholds or threatens to withhold a favorable personnel action with respect to any person; shall be punished as a court-martial may direct.

(b) DEFINITIONS.—In this section:

(1) The term "protected communication" means the following:

(A) A lawful communication to a Member of Congress or an Inspector General.

(B) A communication to a covered individual or organization in which a member of the armed forces complains of, or discloses information that the member reasonably believes constitutes evidence of, any of the following:

(i) A violation of law or regulation, including a law or regulation prohibiting sexual harassment or unlawful discrimination.

(ii) Gross mismanagement, a gross waste of funds, an abuse of authority, or a substantial and specific danger to public health or safety.

(2) The term "Inspector General" has the meaning given that term in section 1034(j) of this title.

(3) The term "covered individual or organization" means any recipient of a communication specified in clauses (i) through (v) of section 1034(b)(1)(B) of this title.

(4) The term "unlawful discrimination" means discrimination on the basis of race, color, religion, sex, or national origin.

§933. Art. 133. Conduct unbecoming an officer

Any commissioned officer, cadet, or midshipman who is convicted of conduct unbecoming an officer shall be punished as a court-martial may direct.

§934. Art. 134. General article

Though not specifically mentioned in this chapter, all disorders and neglects to the prejudice of good order and discipline in the armed forces, all conduct of a nature to bring discredit upon the armed forces, and crimes and offenses not capital, of which persons subject to this chapter may be guilty, shall be taken cognizance of by a general, special, or summary court-martial, according to the nature and degree of the offense, and shall be punished at the discretion of that court. As used in the preceding sentence, the term "crimes and offenses not capital" includes any conduct engaged in outside the United States, as defined in section 5 of title 18, that would constitute a crime or offense not capital if the conduct had been engaged in within the special maritime and territorial jurisdiction of the United States, as defined in section 7 of title 18.

SUBCHAPTER XI. MISCELLANEOUS PROVISIONS

§935. Art. 135. Courts of inquiry

(a) Courts of inquiry to investigate any matter may be convened by any person authorized to convene a general court-martial or by any other person designated by the Secretary concerned for that purpose, whether or not the persons involved have requested such an inquiry.

(b) A court of inquiry consists of three or more commissioned officers. For each court of inquiry the convening authority shall also appoint counsel for the court.

(c)(1) Any person subject to this chapter whose conduct is subject to inquiry shall be designated as a party.

(2) Any person who is (A) subject to this chapter, (B) employed by the Department of Defense, or (C) with respect to the Coast Guard, employed by the department in which the Coast Guard is operating when it is not operating as a service in the Navy, and who has a direct interest in the subject of inquiry has the right to be designated as a party upon request to the court.

(3) Any person designated as a party shall be given due notice and has the right to be present, to be represented by counsel, to cross-examine witnesses, and to introduce evidence.

(d) Members of a court of inquiry may be challenged by a party, but only for cause stated to the court.

(e) The members, counsel, the reporter, and interpreters of courts of inquiry shall take an oath to faithfully perform their duties.

(f) Witnesses may be summoned to appear and testify and be examined before courts of inquiry, as provided for courts-martial.

(g) Courts of inquiry shall make findings of fact but may not express opinions or make recommendations unless required to do so by the convening authority.

(h) Each court of inquiry shall keep a record of its proceedings, which shall be authenticated by the signatures of the president and counsel for the court and forwarded to the convening authority. If the record cannot be authenticated by the president, it shall be signed by a member in lieu of the president. If the record cannot be authenticated by the counsel for the court, it shall be signed by a member in lieu of the counsel.

§936. Art. 136. Authority to administer oaths

(a) The following persons on active duty or performing inactive-duty training may administer oaths for the purposes of military administration, including military justice:

(1) All judge advocates.

(2) All summary courts-martial.

(3) All adjutants, assistant adjutants, acting adjutants, and personnel adjutants.

(4) All commanding officers of the Navy, Marine Corps, and Coast Guard.

(5) All staff judge advocates and legal officers, and acting or assistant staff judge advocates and legal officers.

(6) All other persons designated by regulations of the armed forces or by statute.

(b) The following persons on active duty or performing inactive-duty training may administer oaths necessary in the performance of their duties:

(1) The president, military judge, trial counsel, and assistant trial counsel for all general and special courts-martial.

(2) The president and the counsel for the court of any court of inquiry.

(3) All officers designated to take a deposition.

(4) All persons detailed to conduct an investigation.

(5) All recruiting officers.

(6) All other persons designated by regulations of the armed forces or by statute.

(c) Each judge and senior judge of the United States Court of Appeals for the Armed Forces shall have the powers relating to oaths, affirmations, and acknowledgements provided to justices and judges of the United States by section 459 of title 28.

§937. Art. 137. Articles to be explained

(a) ENLISTED MEMBERS.—

(1) The sections (articles) of this chapter specified in paragraph (3) shall be carefully explained to each enlisted member at the time of (or within fourteen days after)—

(A) the member's initial entrance on active duty; or

(B) the member's initial entrance into a duty status with a reserve component.

(2) Such sections (articles) shall be explained again—

(A) after the member has completed six months of active duty or, in the case of a member of a reserve component, after the member has completed basic or recruit training; and

(B) at the time when the member reenlists.

(3) This subsection applies with respect to sections 802, 803, 807–815, 825, 827, 831, 837, 838, 855, 877–934, and 937–939 of this title (articles 2, 3, 7–15, 25, 27, 31, 37, 38, 55, 77–134, and 137–139).

(b) OFFICERS.—

(1) The sections (articles) of this chapter specified in paragraph (2) shall be carefully explained to each officer at the time of (or within six months after)—

(A) the initial entrance of the officer on active duty as an officer; or

(B) the initial commissioning of the officer in a reserve component.

(2) This subsection applies with respect to the sections (articles) specified in subsection (a)(3) and such other sections (articles) as the Secretary concerned may prescribe by regulation.

(c) TRAINING FOR CERTAIN OFFICERS.—Under regulations prescribed by the Secretary concerned, officers with the authority to convene courts-martial or to impose non-judicial punishment shall receive periodic training regarding the purposes and administration of this chapter. Under regulations prescribed by the Secretary of Defense, officers assigned to duty in a combatant command, who have such authority, shall receive additional specialized training regarding the purposes and administration of this chapter with respect to joint commands and combatant commands.

(d) AVAILABILITY AND MAINTENANCE OF TEXT.—The text of this chapter and the text of the regulations prescribed by the President under this chapter shall be—

(1) made available to a member on active duty or to a member of a reserve component, upon request by the member, for the member's personal examination; and

(2) maintained by the Secretary of Defense in electronic formats that are updated periodically and made available on the Internet.

§938. Art. 138. Complaints of wrongs

Any member of the armed forces who believes himself wronged by his commanding officer, and who, upon due application to that commanding officer, is refused redress, may complain to any superior commissioned officer, who shall forward the complaint to the officer exercising general court-martial jurisdiction over the officer against whom it is made. The officer exercising general court-martial jurisdiction shall examine into the complaint and take proper measures for redressing the wrong complained of; and he shall, as soon as possible, send to the Secretary concerned a true statement of that complaint, with the proceedings had thereon.

§939. Art. 139. Redress of injuries to property

(a) Whenever complaint is made to any commanding officer that willful damage has been done to the property of any person or that his property has been wrongfully taken by members of the armed forces, he may, under such regulations as the Secretary concerned may prescribe, convene a board to investigate the complaint. The board shall consist of from one to three commissioned officers and, for the purpose of that investigation, it has power to summon witnesses and examine them upon oath, to receive depositions or other documentary evidence, and to assess the damages sustained against the responsible parties. The assessment of damages made by the board is subject to the approval of the commanding officer, and in the amount approved by him shall be charged against the pay of the offenders. The order of the commanding officer directing charges herein authorized is conclusive on any disbursing officer for the payment by him to the injured parties of the damages so assessed and approved.

(b) If the offenders cannot be ascertained, but the organization or detachment to which they belong is known, charges totaling the amount of damages assessed and approved may be made in such proportion as may be considered just upon the individual members thereof who are shown to have been present at the scene at the time the damages complained of were inflicted, as determined by the approved findings of the board.

§940. Art. 140. Delegation by the President

The President may delegate any authority vested in him under this chapter, and provide for the subdelegation of any such authority.

§940a. Art. 140a. Case management; data collection and accessibility

(a) IN GENERAL.—The Secretary of Defense, in consultation with the Secretary of Homeland Security, shall prescribe uniform standards and criteria for conduct of each of the following functions at all stages of the military justice system (including with respect to the Coast Guard), including pretrial, trial, post-trial, and appellate processes, using, insofar as practicable, the best practices of Federal and State courts:

(1) Collection and analysis of data concerning substantive offenses and procedural matters in a manner that facilitates case management and decision making within the military justice system, and that enhances the quality of periodic reviews under section 946 of this title (article 146).

(2) Case processing and management.

(3) Timely, efficient, and accurate production and distribution of records of trial within the military justice system.

(4) Facilitation of access to docket information, filings, and records, taking into consideration restrictions appropriate to judicial proceedings and military records.

(b) PROTECTION OF CERTAIN PERSONALLY IDENTIFIABLE INFORMATION.—Records of trial, docket information, filings, and other records made publicly accessible in accordance with the uniform standards and criteria for conduct established by the Secretary under subsection (a) shall restrict access to personally identifiable information of minors and victims of crime (including victims of sexual assault and domestic violence), as practicable to the extent such information is restricted in electronic filing systems of Federal and State courts.

(c) INAPPLICABILITY TO CERTAIN DOCKETS AND RECORDS.—Nothing in this section shall be construed to provide public access to docket information, filings, or records that are classified, subject to a judicial protective order, or ordered sealed.

(d) PRESERVATION OF COURT-MARTIAL RECORDS WITHOUT DISREGARD TO OUTCOME.—The standards and criteria prescribed by the Secretary of Defense under subsection (a) shall provide for the preservation of general and special court-martial records, without regard to the outcome of the proceeding concerned, for not fewer than 15 years.

SUBCHAPTER XII. UNITED STATES COURT OF APPEALS FOR THE ARMED FORCES

§941. Art. 141. Status

There is a court of record known as the United States Court of Appeals for the Armed Forces. The court is established under article I of the Constitution. The court is located for administrative purposes only in the Department of Defense.

§942. Art. 142. Judges

(a) NUMBER.—The United States Court of Appeals for the Armed Forces consists of five judges.

(b) APPOINTMENT; QUALIFICATION.—

(1) Each judge of the court shall be appointed from civilian life by the President, by and with the advice and consent of the Senate, for a specified term determined under paragraph (2). A judge may serve as a senior judge as provided in subsection (e).

(2)(A) The term of a judge shall expire as follows:

(i) In the case of a judge who is appointed after January 31 and before July 31 of any year, the term shall expire on July 31 of the year in which the fifteenth anniversary of the appointment occurs.

(ii) In the case of a judge who is appointed after July 31 of any year and before February 1 of the following year, the term shall expire fifteen years after such July 31.

(B) If at the time of the appointment of a judge the date that is otherwise applicable under subparagraph (A) for the expiration of the term of service of the judge is the same as the date for the expiration of the term of service of a judge already on the court, then the term of the judge being appointed shall expire on the first July 31 after such date on which no term of service of a judge already on the court will expire.

(3) No person may be appointed to be a judge of the court unless the person is a member of the bar of a Federal court or the highest court of a State.

(4) A person may not be appointed as a judge of the court within seven years after retirement from active duty as a commissioned officer of a regular component of an armed force.

(c) REMOVAL.—Judges of the court may be removed from office by the President, upon notice and hearing, for—

(1) neglect of duty;

(2) misconduct; or

(3) mental or physical disability. A judge may not be removed by the President for any other cause.

(d) PAY AND ALLOWANCES.—Each judge of the court is entitled to the same salary and travel allowances as are, and from time to time may be, provided for judges of the United States Courts of Appeals.

(e) SENIOR JUDGES.—(1)(A) A former judge of the court who is receiving retired pay or an annuity under section 945 of this title (article 145) or under subchapter III of chapter 83 or chapter 84 of title 5 shall be a senior judge. The chief judge of the court may call upon an individual who is a senior judge of the court under this subparagraph, with the consent of the senior judge, to perform judicial duties with the court—

(i) during a period a judge of the court is unable to perform his duties because of illness or other disability;

(ii) during a period in which a position of judge of the court is vacant; or

(iii) in any case in which a judge of the court recuses himself.

(B) If, at the time the term of a judge expires, no successor to that judge has been appointed, the chief judge of the court may call upon that judge (with that judge's consent) to continue to perform judicial duties with the court until the vacancy is filled. A judge who, upon the expiration of the judge's term, continues to perform judicial duties with the court without a break in service under this subparagraph shall be a senior judge while such service continues.

(2) A senior judge shall be paid for each day on which he performs judicial duties with the court an amount equal to the difference between—

(A) the daily equivalent of the annual rate of pay provided for a judge of the court; and

(B) the daily equivalent of the annuity of the judge under section 945 of this title (article 145), the applicable provisions of title 5, or any other retirement system for employees of the Federal Government under which the senior judge receives an annuity.

(3) A senior judge, while performing duties referred to in paragraph (1), shall be provided with such office space and staff assistance as the chief judge considers appropriate and shall be entitled to the per diem, travel allowances, and other allowances provided for judges of the court.

(4) A senior judge shall be considered to be an officer or employee of the United States with respect to his status as a senior judge, but only during periods the senior judge is performing duties referred to in paragraph (1). For the purposes of section 205 of title 18, a senior judge shall be considered to be a special government employee during such periods. Any provision of law that prohibits or limits the political or business activities of an employee of the United States shall apply to a senior judge only during such periods.

(5) The court shall prescribe rules for the use and conduct of senior judges of the court. The chief judge of the court shall transmit such rules, and any amendments to such rules, to the Committee on Armed Services of the Senate and the Committee on Armed Services of the House of Representatives not later than 15 days after the issuance of such rules or amendments, as the case may be.

(6) For purposes of subchapter III of chapter 83 of title 5 (relating to the Civil Service Retirement and Disability System) and chapter 84 of such title (relating to the Federal Employees' Retirement System) and for purposes of any other Federal Government retirement system for employees of the Federal Government—

(A) a period during which a senior judge performs duties referred to in paragraph (1) shall not be considered creditable service;

(B) no amount shall be withheld from the pay of a senior judge as a retirement contribution under section 8334, 8343, 8422, or 8432 of title 5 or under any other such retirement system for any period during which the senior judge performs duties referred to in paragraph (1);

(C) no contribution shall be made by the Federal Government to any retirement system with respect to a senior judge for any period during which the senior judge performs duties referred to in paragraph (1); and

(D) a senior judge shall not be considered to be a reemployed annuitant for any period during which the senior judge performs duties referred to in paragraph (1).

(f) SERVICE OF ARTICLE III JUDGES.—(1) The Chief Justice of the United States, upon the request of the chief judge of the court, may designate a judge of a United States court of appeals or of a United States district court to perform the duties of judge of the United States Court of Appeals for the Armed Forces—

(A) during a period a judge of the court is unable to perform his duties because of illness or other disability;

(B) in any case in which a judge of the court recuses himself; or

(C) during a period when there is a vacancy on the court and in the opinion of the chief judge of the court such a designation is necessary for the proper dispatch of the business of the court.

(2) The chief judge of the court may not request that a designation be made under paragraph (1) unless the chief judge has determined that no person is available to perform judicial duties with the court as a senior judge under subsection (e).

(3) A designation under paragraph (1) may be made only with the consent of the designated judge and the concurrence of the chief judge of the court of appeals or district court concerned.

(4) Per diem, travel allowances, and other allowances paid to the designated judge in connection with the performance of duties for the court shall be paid from funds available for the payment of per diem and such allowances for judges of the court.

(g) EFFECT OF VACANCY ON COURT.—A vacancy on the court does not impair the right of the remaining judges to exercise the powers of the court.

§943. Art. 143. Organization and employees

(a) CHIEF JUDGE.—

(1) The chief judge of the United States Court of Appeals for the Armed Forces shall be the judge of the court in regular active service who is senior in commission among the judges of the court who—

(A) have served for one or more years as judges of the court; and

(B) have not previously served as chief judge.

(2) In any case in which there is no judge of the court in regular active service who has served as a judge of the court for at least one year, the judge of the court in regular active service who is senior in commission and has not served previously as chief judge shall act as the chief judge.

(3) Except as provided in paragraph (4), a judge of the court shall serve as the chief judge under paragraph (1) for a term of five years. If no other judge is eligible under paragraph (1) to serve as chief judge upon the expiration of that term, the chief judge shall continue to serve as chief judge until another judge becomes eligible under that paragraph to serve as chief judge.

(4)(A) The term of a chief judge shall be terminated before the end of five years if—

(i) the chief judge leaves regular active service as a judge of the court; or

(ii) the chief judge notifies the other judges of the court in writing that such judge desires to be relieved of his duties as chief judge.

(B) The effective date of a termination of the term under subparagraph (A) shall be the date on which the chief judge leaves regular active service or the date of the notification under subparagraph (A)(ii), as the case may be.

(5) If a chief judge is temporarily unable to perform his duties as a chief judge, the duties shall be performed by the judge of the court in active service who is present, able and qualified to act, and is next in precedence.

(b) PRECEDENCE OF JUDGES.—The chief judge of the court shall have precedence and preside at any session that he attends. The other judges shall have precedence and preside according to the seniority of their original commissions. Judges whose commissions bear the same date shall have precedence according to seniority in age.

(c) STATUS OF CERTAIN POSITIONS.—

(1) Attorney positions of employment under the Court of Appeals for the Armed Forces are excepted from the competitive service. A position of employment under the court that is provided primarily for the service of one judge of the court, reports directly to the judge, and is a position of a confidential character is excepted from the competitive service. Appointments to positions referred to in the preceding sentences shall be made by the court, without the concurrence of any other officer or employee of the executive branch, in the same manner as appointments are made to other executive branch positions of a confidential or policy-determining character for which it is not practicable to examine or to hold a competitive examination. Such positions shall not be counted as positions of that character for purposes of any limitation on the number of positions of that character provided in law.

(2) In making appointments to the positions described in paragraph (1), preference shall be given, among equally qualified persons, to persons who are preference eligibles (as defined in section 2108(3) of title 5).

§944. Art. 144. Procedure

The United States Court of Appeals for the Armed Forces may prescribe its rules of procedure and may determine the number of judges required to constitute a quorum.

§945. Art. 145. Annuities for judges and survivors

(a) RETIREMENT ANNUITIES FOR JUDGES.—

(1) A person who has completed a term of service for which he was appointed as a judge of the United States Court of Appeals for the Armed Forces is eligible for an annuity under this section upon separation from civilian service in the Federal Government. A person who continues service with the court as a senior judge under section 942(e)(1)(B) of this title (article 142(e)(1)(B)) upon the expiration of the judge's term shall be considered to have been separated from civilian service in the Federal Government only upon the termination of that continuous service.

(2) A person who is eligible for an annuity under this section shall be paid that annuity if, at the time he becomes eligible to receive that annuity, he elects to receive that annuity in lieu of any other annuity for which he may be eligible at the time of such election (whether an immediate or a deferred annuity) under subchapter III of chapter 83 or subchapter II of chapter 84 of title 5 or any other retirement system for civilian employees of the Federal Government. Such an election may not be revoked.

(3)(A) The Secretary of Defense shall notify the Director of the Office of Personnel Management whenever an election under paragraph (2) is made affecting any right or interest under subchapter III of chapter 83 or subchapter II of chapter 84 of title 5 based on service as a judge of the United States Court of Appeals for the Armed Forces.

(B) Upon receiving any notification under subparagraph (A) in the case of a person making an election under paragraph (2), the Director shall determine the amount of the person's lump-sum credit under subchapter III of chapter 83 or subchapter II of chapter 84 of title 5, as applicable, and shall request the Secretary of the Treasury to transfer such amount from the Civil Service Retirement and Disability Fund to the Department of Defense Military Retirement Fund. The Secretary of the Treasury shall make any transfer so requested.

(C) In determining the amount of a lump-sum credit under section 8331(8) of title 5 for purposes of this paragraph—

(i) interest shall be computed using the rates under section 8334(e)(3) of such title; and

(ii) the completion of 5 years of civilian service (or longer) shall not be a basis for excluding interest.

(b) AMOUNT OF ANNUITY.—The annuity payable under this section to a person who makes an election under subsection (a)(2) is 80 percent of the rate of pay for a judge in active service on the United States Court of Appeals for the Armed Forces as of the date on which the person is separated from civilian service.

(c) RELATION TO THRIFT SAVINGS PLAN.—Nothing in this section affects any right of any person to participate in the thrift savings plan under section 8351 of title 5 or subchapter III of chapter 84 of such title.

(d) SURVIVOR ANNUITIES.—The Secretary of Defense shall prescribe by regulation a program to provide annuities for survivors and former spouses of persons receiving annuities under this section by reason of elections made by such persons under subsection (a)(2). That program shall, to the maximum extent practicable, provide benefits and establish terms and conditions that are similar to those provided under survivor and former spouse annuity programs under other retirement systems for civilian employees of the Federal Government. The program may include provisions for the reduction in the annuity paid the person as a condition for the survivor annuity. An election by a judge (including a senior judge) or former judge to receive an annuity under this section terminates any right or interest which any other individual may have to a survivor annuity under any other retirement system for civilian employees of the Federal Government based on the service of that judge or former judge as a civilian officer or employee of the Federal Government (except with respect to an election under subsection (f)(1)(B)).

(e) COST-OF-LIVING INCREASES.—The Secretary of Defense shall periodically increase annuities and survivor annuities paid under this section in order to take account of changes in the cost of living. The Secretary shall prescribe by regulation procedures for increases in annuities under this section. Such system shall, to the maximum extent appropriate, provide cost-of-living adjustments that are similar to those that are provided under other retirement systems for civilian employees of the Federal Government.

(f) ELECTION OF JUDICIAL RETIREMENT BENEFITS.—

(1) A person who is receiving an annuity under this section by reason of service as a judge of the court and who later is appointed as a justice or judge of the United States to hold office during good behavior and who retires from that office, or from regular active service in that office, shall be paid either (A) the annuity under this section, or (B) the annuity or salary to which he is entitled by reason of his service as such a justice or judge of the United States, as determined by an election by that person at the time of his retirement from the office, or from regular active service in the office, of justice or judge of the United States. Such an election may not be revoked.

(2) An election by a person to be paid an annuity or salary pursuant to paragraph (1)(B) terminates (A) any election previously made by such person to provide a survivor annuity pursuant to subsection (d), and (B) any right of any other individual to receive a survivor annuity pursuant to subsection (d) on the basis of the service of that person.

(g) SOURCE OF PAYMENT OF ANNUITIES.—Annuities and survivor annuities paid under this section shall be paid out of the Department of Defense Military Retirement Fund.

(h) ELIGIBILITY TO ELECT BETWEEN RETIREMENT SYSTEMS.—

(1) This subsection applies with respect to any person who—

(A) prior to being appointed as a judge of the United States Court of Appeals for the Armed Forces, performed civilian service of a type making such person subject to the Civil Service Retirement System; and

(B) would be eligible to make an election under section 301(a)(2) of the Federal Employees' Retirement System Act of 1986, by virtue of being appointed as such a judge, but for the fact that such person has not had a break in service of sufficient duration to be considered someone who is being reemployed by the Federal Government.

(2) Any person with respect to whom this subsection applies shall be eligible to make an election under section 301(a)(2) of the Federal Employees' Retirement System Act of 1986 to the same extent and in the same manner (including subject to the condition set forth in section 301(d) of such Act) as if such person's appointment constituted reemployment with the Federal Government.

§946. Art. 146. Military Justice Review Panel

(a) ESTABLISHMENT.—The Secretary of Defense shall establish a panel to conduct independent periodic reviews and assessments of the operation of this chapter. The panel shall be known as the "Military Justice Review Panel" (in this section referred to as the "Panel").

(b) MEMBERS.—

(1) NUMBER OF MEMBERS—The Panel shall be composed of thirteen members.

(2) APPOINTMENT OF CERTAIN MEMBERS—Each of the following shall appoint one member of the Panel:

(A) The Secretary of Defense (in consultation with the Secretary of the department in which the Coast Guard is operating when it is not operating as a service in the Navy).

(B) The Attorney General.

(C) The Judge Advocates General of the Army, Navy, Air Force, and Coast Guard, and the Staff Judge Advocate to the Commandant of the Marine Corps.

(3) APPOINTMENT OF REMAINING MEMBERS BY SECRETARY OF DEFENSE—The Secretary of Defense shall appoint the remaining members of the Panel, taking into consideration recommendations made by each of the following:

(A) The chairman and ranking minority member of the Committee on Armed Services of the Senate and the Committee on Armed Services of the House of Representatives.

(B) The Chief Justice of the United States.

(C) The Chief Judge of the United States Court of Appeals for the Armed Forces.

(c) QUALIFICATIONS OF MEMBERS.—The members of the Panel shall be appointed from among private United States citizens with expertise in criminal law, as well as appropriate and diverse experience in investigation, prosecution, defense, victim representation, or adjudication with respect to courts-martial, Federal civilian courts, or State courts.

(d) CHAIR.—The Secretary of Defense shall select the chair of the Panel from among the members.

(e) TERM; VACANCIES.—Each member shall be appointed for a term of eight years, and no member may serve more than one term. Any vacancy shall be filled in the same manner as the original appointment.

(f) REVIEWS AND REPORTS.—

(1) INITIAL REVIEW OF RECENT AMENDMENTS TO UCMJ.—During fiscal year 2021, the Panel shall conduct an initial review and assessment of the implementation of the amendments made to this chapter during the preceding five years. In conducting the initial review and assessment, the Panel may review such other aspects of the operation of this chapter as the Panel considers appropriate.

(2) SENTENCING DATA COLLECTION AND REPORT.—During fiscal year 2020, the Panel shall gather and analyze sentencing data collected from each of the armed forces from general and special courts-martial applying offense-based sentencing under section 856 of this title (article 56). The sentencing data shall include the number of accused who request member sentencing and the number who request sentencing by military judge alone, the offenses which the accused were convicted of, and the resulting sentence for each offense in each case. The Judge Advocates General and the Staff Judge Advocate to the Commandant of the Marine Corps shall provide the sentencing data in the format and for the duration established by the chair of the Panel. The analysis under this paragraph shall be included in the assessment required by paragraph (1).

(3) PERIODIC COMPREHENSIVE REVIEWS.—During fiscal year 2024 and every eight years thereafter, the Panel shall conduct a comprehensive review and assessment of the operation of this chapter.

(4) PERIODIC INTERIM REVIEWS.—During fiscal year 2028 and every eight years thereafter, the Panel shall conduct an interim review and assessment of such other aspects of the operation of this chapter as the Panel considers appropriate. In addition, at the request of the Secretary of Defense, the Panel may, at any time, review and assess other specific matters relating to the operation of this chapter.

(5) REPORTS.—With respect to each review and assessment under this subsection, the Panel shall submit a report to the Committees on Armed Services of the Senate and House of Representatives. Each report—

(A) shall set forth the results of the review and assessment concerned, including the findings and recommendations of the Panel; and

(B) shall be submitted not later than December 31 of the calendar year in which the review and assessment is concluded.

(g) HEARINGS.—The Panel may hold such hearings, sit and act at such times and places, take such testimony, and receive such evidence as the Panel considers appropriate to carry out its duties under this section.

(h) INFORMATION FROM FEDERAL AGENCIES.—Upon request of the chair of the Panel, a department or agency of the Federal Government shall provide information that the Panel considers necessary to carry out its duties under this section.

(i) ADMINISTRATIVE MATTERS.—

(1) MEMBERS TO SERVE WITHOUT PAY.—Members of the Panel shall serve without pay, but shall be allowed travel expenses, including per diem in lieu of subsistence, at rates authorized for employees of agencies under subchapter I of chapter 57 of title 5, while away from their homes or regular places of business in the performance of services for the Panel.

(2) STAFFING AND RESOURCES.—The Secretary of Defense shall provide staffing and resources to support the Panel.

(j) CHAPTER 10 OF TITLE 5.—Chapter 10 of title 5 shall not apply to the Panel.

§946a. Art. 146a. Annual reports

(a) COURT OF APPEALS FOR THE ARMED FORCES.—Not later than December 31 of each year, the Court of Appeals for the Armed Forces shall submit a report that, with respect to the previous fiscal year, provides information on the number and status of completed and pending cases before the Court, and such other matters as the Court considers appropriate regarding the operation of this chapter.

(b) SERVICE REPORTS.—Not later than December 31 of each year, the Judge Advocates General and the Staff Judge Advocate to the Commandant of the Marine Corps shall each submit a report, with respect to the preceding fiscal year, containing the following:

(1) Data on the number and status of pending cases.

(2) Information on the appellate review process, including—

(A) information on compliance with processing time goals;

(B) descriptions of the circumstances surrounding cases in which general or special court-martial convictions were

(i) reversed because of command influence or denial of the right to speedy review or

(ii) otherwise remitted because of loss of records of trial or other administrative deficiencies;

(C) an analysis of each case in which a provision of this chapter was held unconstitutional; and

(D) an analysis of each case in which a Court of Criminal Appeals made a final determination that a finding of a court-martial was clearly against the weight of the evidence, including an explanation of the standard of appellate review applied in such case.

(3)(A) An explanation of measures implemented by the armed force involved to ensure the ability of judge advocates—

(i) to participate competently as trial counsel and defense counsel in cases under this chapter;

(ii) to preside as military judges in cases under this chapter; and

(iii) to perform the duties of Special Victims' Counsel, when so designated under section 1044e of this title.

(B) The explanation under subparagraph (A) shall specifically identify the measures that focus on capital cases, national security cases, sexual assault cases, and proceedings of military commissions.

(4) The independent views of each Judge Advocate General and of the Staff Judge Advocate to the Commandant of the Marine Corps as to the sufficiency of resources available within the respective armed forces, including total workforce, funding, training, and officer and enlisted grade structure, to capably perform military justice functions.

(5) Such other matters regarding the operation of this chapter as may be appropriate.

(c) SUBMISSION.—Each report under this section shall be submitted—

(1) to the Committee on Armed Services of the Senate and the Committee on Armed Services of the House of Representatives; and

(2) to the Secretary of Defense, the Secretaries of the military departments, and the Secretary of the department in which the Coast Guard is operating when it is not operating as a service in the Navy.

APPENDIX 2.1
DISPOSITION GUIDANCE

This Appendix provides non-binding guidance issued by the Secretary of Defense, in consultation with the Secretary of Homeland Security, pursuant to Article 33 (Disposition Guidance) of the Uniform Code of Military Justice (UCMJ), 10 U.S.C. § 833.

SECTION 1: IN GENERAL

1.1. Policy.

a. This Appendix provides guidance regarding factors that convening authorities, commanders, special trial counsel, staff judge advocates, and other judge advocates should consider when exercising their duties with respect to the disposition of charges and specifications under the UCMJ, and to further promote the purposes of military law.[1]

b. This Appendix supplements the Manual for Courts-Martial. The guidance in this Appendix does not require a particular disposition decision or other action in any given case. Accordingly, the disposition factors set forth in this Appendix are cast in general terms, with a view to providing guidance rather than mandating results. The intent is to promote regularity without regimentation, encourage consistency without sacrificing necessary flexibility, and provide the flexibility to apply these factors in a manner that facilitates the fair and effective response to local conditions in the interest of justice and good order and discipline.

1.2. Purpose. This guidance is intended to:

a. Set forth factors for consideration by those assigned responsibility under the UCMJ for disposing of alleged violations of the UCMJ on how best to exercise their authority in a reasoned and structured manner, consistent with the principle of fair and evenhanded administration of the law;

b. Promote the fair and effective exercise of prosecutorial discretion and foster confidence on the part of the public and Service members that disposition decisions will be made rationally and objectively on the merits of each case;

c. Serve as a training tool for convening authorities, commanders, special trial counsel, staff judge advocates, and other judge advocates involved in the disposition process;

d. Contribute to the effective utilization of the Government's law enforcement and prosecutorial resources;

e. Enhance the relationship between military commanders; special trial counsel; staff judge advocates; other judge advocates involved in the disposition process; and law enforcement agencies, including military criminal investigative organizations (MCIOs), with respect to investigations and charging decisions; and

f. Guide the significant decision whether to prosecute a matter at court-martial recognizing the profound consequences for the accused and crime victims regardless of the outcome.

[1] "The purposes of military law are to promote justice, to deter misconduct, to facilitate appropriate accountability, to assist in maintaining good order and discipline in the armed forces, to promote efficiency and effectiveness in the military establishment, and thereby to strengthen the national security of the United States." Manual for Courts-Martial, United States, Pt. I, ¶ 3 (2024 ed.).

1.3. Scope. This Appendix is designed to promote the reasoned exercise of discretion with respect to the following:

a. Initiating and declining action under the UCMJ;

b. Selecting appropriate charges and specifications;

c. Special trial counsel's decisions to prefer or refer a charge or defer an alleged offense;

d. Selecting the appropriate type of court-martial or alternative mode of disposition, if any;

e. Preliminary hearing officers' disposition recommendations; and

f. Entering into a plea agreement.

1.4. Non-Litigability. This Appendix was developed solely as a matter of internal policy in accordance with Article 33. This Appendix is not intended to, does not, and may not be relied upon to create a right, benefit, or defense, substantive or procedural, enforceable at law or in equity by any person and may not be relied upon by any party or person in litigation with the United States.

SECTION 2: CONSIDERATIONS IN ALL CASES

2.1. Interests of Justice and Good Order and Discipline. The military justice system is a powerful tool that promotes justice and assists in maintaining good order and discipline while protecting the rights of Service members. In determining whether the interests of justice and good order and discipline are served by trial by court-martial or other disposition in a case, the factors listed below should be considered. The weight and priority given to each of these factors may vary depending on the facts and circumstances of the case.

a. Whether admissible evidence will probably be sufficient to obtain and sustain a finding of guilty in a trial by court-martial when viewed objectively by an unbiased factfinder;

b. The truth-seeking function of trial by court-martial;

c. The nature, seriousness, and circumstances of the alleged offense and the accused's culpability in connection with the alleged offense;

d. Input, if any, from law enforcement agencies involved in or having an interest in the specific case;

e. The accused's willingness to cooperate in the investigation or prosecution of others;

f. The accused's criminal history or history of misconduct, whether military or civilian, if any;

g. The probable sentence or other consequences to the accused of a finding of guilty;

h. The impact and appropriateness of alternative disposition options—including nonjudicial punishment or administrative action—with respect to the accused's potential for continued service and the responsibilities of the command with respect to justice and good order and discipline.

i. In cases involving an individual who is a victim of the alleged offense as defined by Article 6b(b), that individual's views as to disposition;

j. The extent of the harm caused to any victim of the alleged offense;

k. The availability and willingness of the victim of the alleged offense and other witnesses to testify;

l. The effect of the alleged offense on the morale, health, safety, welfare, and good order and discipline of the command;

m. The extent to which the conduct tends to bring discredit upon the armed forces;

n. Whether the alleged offense occurred during wartime, combat, or contingency operations; and

o. The mission-related responsibilities of the command.

2.2. Consultation with a Judge Advocate. Commanders and convening authorities shall at all times communicate directly with their assigned judge advocates in matters relating to the administration of military justice (*see* R.C.M. 105).

2.3. Referral.

a. Probable cause must exist for each charge and specification referred to a court-martial (*see* R.C.M. 601(d)(1)). In addition to the consideration required by R.C.M. 601(d)(2),[2] when making a referral decision, the referral authority should also consider the matters described in paragraph 2.1 of this appendix.

b. A special trial counsel should not refer, and a staff judge advocate or other judge advocate involved in the disposition process should not recommend that a convening authority refer, a charge to a court-martial unless the special trial counsel, staff judge advocate, or other judge advocate believes that the Service member's conduct constitutes an offense under the UCMJ and that the admissible evidence will probably

[2] "Referral authorities shall consider whether the admissible evidence will probably be sufficient to obtain and sustain a conviction." Rule for Courts-Martial 601(d)(2), Manual for Courts-Martial, United States (2024 ed.).

be sufficient to obtain and sustain a finding of guilty when viewed objectively by an unbiased factfinder.

c. A convening authority should not refer a charge to a court-martial unless the admissible evidence will probably be sufficient to obtain and sustain a finding of guilty when viewed objectively by an unbiased factfinder. In assessing whether there is sufficient admissible evidence, a convening authority should consider the advice of a staff judge advocate or other judge advocate authorized to provide pretrial advice.

2.4. Determining the Charges and Specifications to Refer. A referral authority should avoid referring multiple charges when they would:

a. Unnecessarily complicate the prosecution of the most serious readily provable alleged offense or offenses;

b. Unnecessarily exaggerate the nature and extent of the accused's alleged criminal conduct or add unnecessary confusion to the issues at court-martial;

c. Unnecessarily expose the accused to a harsher potential sentence or range of punishments than the circumstances of the case justify; or

d. Be disposed of more appropriately through an alternative disposition.

2.5. Determining the Appropriate Type of Court-Martial. In determining the appropriate type of court-martial, a convening authority should consider the advice of a staff judge advocate or other judge advocate authorized to provide pretrial advice. Additionally, a referral authority should consider:

a. The interests of justice and good order and discipline (*see* paragraph 2.1);

b. The authorized maximum and minimum punishments for the charged offenses;

c. Any unique circumstances in the case requiring immediate disposition of the charges;

d. Whether the type of court-martial would unnecessarily expose the accused to a harsher potential sentence or range of punishments than the circumstances of the case justify; and

e. Whether the potential of the accused for rehabilitation and continued service would be better addressed in a specific type of court-martial.

2.6. Alternatives to Referral. In determining whether to refer charges and specifications, a referral authority should consider whether an adequate alternative to referral exists. If an adequate alternative to referral exists, in addition to the considerations in paragraph 2.1, a referral authority should consider:

a. The effect of the alternative disposition on the interests of justice and good order and discipline;

b. The options available under the alternative disposition;

c. The views of the victim of the alleged offense, if any, concerning the alternative disposition of the case; and

d. The likelihood of an effective outcome.

2.7. Inappropriate Considerations. The disposition determination must not be influenced by:

a. The accused's race; ethnicity; religion; sex; gender (including gender identity); sexual orientation; national origin; or lawful political association, activities, or beliefs;

b. The personal feelings of anyone authorized to recommend, advise, or make a decision as to disposition of alleged offenses concerning the accused, the accused's associates, the victim of the alleged offense, or any witness;

c. The time and resources already expended in the investigation of the case;

d. The possible effect of the disposition determination on the commander's, convening authority's, or special trial counsel's military career or other professional or personal circumstances;

e. Political pressure to take or not to take specific actions in the case; or

f. Improper consideration of the race; ethnicity; religion; sex; gender (including gender identity); sexual orientation; national origin; or lawful political association, activities, or beliefs of the victim of an alleged offense.

SECTION 3: SPECIAL CONSIDERATIONS

3.1. Prosecution in Another Jurisdiction. When the accused is subject to effective prosecution in another jurisdiction, a convening authority should consider the advice of a staff judge advocate or other judge advocate authorized to provide pretrial advice. Additionally, a referral authority should consider the following additional factors when determining disposition:

a. The strength of the other jurisdiction's interest in prosecution;

b. The other jurisdiction's ability and willingness to prosecute the case effectively;

c. The probable sentence or other consequences if the accused were to be convicted in the other jurisdiction;

d. The views of the victim of the alleged offense, if any, as to the desirability of prosecution in the other jurisdiction;

e. Applicable policies derived from agreements with the Department of Justice and foreign governments regarding the exercise of military jurisdiction; and

f. The likelihood that the nature of the proceedings in the other jurisdiction will satisfy the interests of justice and good order and discipline in the case, including any burdens on the command with respect to the need for witnesses to be absent from their military duties, and the potential for swift or delayed disposition in the other jurisdiction.

3.2. Plea Agreements. In accordance with Article 53a, the referral authority may enter into an agreement with an accused concerning disposition of the charges and specifications and the sentence that may be imposed. A convening authority should consider the advice of a staff judge advocate or other judge advocate authorized to provide pretrial advice. Additionally, a referral authority should consider the following additional factors in determining whether it would be appropriate to enter into a plea agreement in a particular case:

a. The accused's willingness to cooperate in the investigation or prosecution of others;

b. The nature and seriousness of the charged offense or offenses;

c. The accused's remorse or contrition and willingness to assume responsibility for the accused's conduct;

d. Restitution, if any;

e. The accused's criminal history or history of misconduct, whether military or civilian;

f. The desirability of prompt and certain disposition of the case and of related cases;

g. The likelihood of obtaining a finding of guilty at court-martial;

h. The probable effect on victims of alleged offenses and witnesses;

i. The probable sentence or other consequences if the accused is convicted;

j. The public and military interest in having the case tried rather than disposed of by a plea agreement;

k. The time and expense associated with trial and appeal;

l. The views of the victim of an alleged offense with regard to prosecution, the terms of the anticipated agreement, and alternative disposition; and

m. The potential of the accused for rehabilitation and continued service.

3.3. Agreements Concerning Disposition of Charges and Specifications. With respect to plea agreements regarding the disposition of charges and specifications, the plea agreement should require the accused to plead guilty to charges and specifications that:

a. Appropriately reflect the nature and extent of the criminal conduct;

b. Are supported by an adequate factual basis;

c. Would support the imposition of an appropriate sentence under all the circumstances of the case;

d. Do not adversely affect the investigation or prosecution of others suspected of misconduct; and

e. Appropriately serve the interests of justice and good order and discipline.

3.4 Agreements Concerning Sentence Limitations. A plea agreement should ensure that any sentence limitation takes into consideration the sentencing guidance set forth in Article 56(c).

****

Analysis:

This appendix implements Article 33, UCMJ, as amended by Section 5204 of the Military Justice Act of 2016, Division E of the National Defense Authorization Act for Fiscal Year 2017, Pub. L. No. 114-328, 130 Stat. 2000 (2016), and section 12 of Executive Order 13825 of March 1, 2018. The disposition factors contained in this appendix are adapted primarily from three sources: the Principles of Federal Prosecution issued by the Department of Justice; the American Bar Association, Criminal Justice Standards for the Prosecution Function; and the National District Attorneys Association, National Prosecution Standards. Practitioners are encouraged to familiarize themselves with the disposition factors contained in this appendix as well as those related civilian prosecution function standards. The disposition factors have been adapted with a view toward the unique nature of the military justice system.

APPENDIX 3
DoD Instruction 5525.07

Department of Defense
INSTRUCTION

June 18, 2007
NUMBER 5525.07

GC, DoD/IG DoD

SUBJECT:

Implementation of the Memorandum of Understanding (MOU) Between the Departments of Justice (DoJ) and Defense Relating to the Investigation and Prosecution of Certain Crimes

References:

(a) DoD Directive 5525.7, "Implementation of the Memorandum of Understanding Between the Department of Justice and the Department of Defense Relating to the Investigation and Prosecution of Crimes," January 22, 1985 (hereby canceled)

(b) Acting Deputy Secretary of Defense Memorandum, "DoD Directives Review - Phase II," July 13, 2005

(c) DoD Directive 5145.1, "General Counsel of the Department of Defense," May 2, 2001

(d) DoD Directive 5106.01, "Inspector General of the Department of Defense," April 13, 2006

(e) through (h), see Enclosure 1

1. REISSUANCE AND PURPOSE

This Instruction:

1.1. Reissues Reference (a) as a DoD Instruction in accordance with the guidance in Reference (b) and the authority in References (c) and (d).

1.2. Updates policy, assigns responsibilities, and supplements the MOU between the Departments of Justice and Defense Relating to the Investigation and Prosecution of Certain Crimes (Reference (e)) at Enclosure 1, pursuant to References (c) and (d).

2. APPLICABILITY AND SCOPE

2.1 This Instruction applies to the Office of the Secretary of Defense, the Military Departments, the Chairman of the Joint Chiefs of Staff, the Combatant Commands, the Office of the Inspector General of the Department of Defense (IG DoD), the Defense Agencies, the DoD Field Activities, and all other organizational entities within the Department of Defense (hereafter referred to collectively as the "DoD Components").

2.2. The term "DoD criminal investigative organizations," as used herein, refers collectively to the United States Army Criminal Investigation Command, Naval Criminal Investigative Service, U.S. Air Force Office of Special Investigations, and Defense Criminal Investigative Service, Office of the IG DoD.

3. POLICY

It is DoD policy to maintain effective working relationships with the DoJ in the investigation and prosecution of crimes involving DoD programs, operations, or personnel.

4. PROCEDURES

With respect to inquiries for which the DoJ has assumed investigative responsibility based on Reference (e), the DoD criminal investigative organizations should seek to participate jointly with DoJ investigative agencies whenever the inquiries relate to DoD programs, operations, or personnel. This applies to cases referred to the Federal Bureau of Investigation under paragraph C.1.a. of Reference (e) as well as to those cases for which a DoJ investigative agency is assigned primary investigative responsibility by a DoJ prosecutor. The DoD Components shall comply with the terms of Reference (e) and DoD Supplemental Guidance in Enclosure 2.

5. RESPONSIBILITIES

5.1. The IG DoD, shall:

5.1.1. Establish procedures to implement the investigative policies set forth in this Instruction.

5.1.2. Monitor compliance by DoD criminal investigative organizations with the terms of Reference (c).

5.1.3. Provide specific guidance regarding investigative matters, as appropriate.

5.2. The General Counsel of the Department of Defense (GC, DoD), shall:

5.2.1. Establish procedures to implement the prosecutive policies as set forth in Reference (e) and consistent with the DoD Supplemental Guidance provided in Enclosure 2, the Uniform Code of Military Justice (Reference (f)) and the Manual for Courts-Martial (Reference (g)).

5.2.2. Monitor compliance by the DoD Components regarding the prosecutive aspects of Reference (e).

5.2.3. Provide specific guidance on the investigation and prosecution of those crimes addressed in Reference (e), as appropriate.

5.2.4. Modify the DoD Supplemental Guidance in Enclosure 2 with the concurrence of the IG DoD, after coordinating with the affected DoD Components.

5.3. The Secretaries of the Military Departments shall establish procedures to implement the policies set forth in this Instruction.

6. EFFECTIVE DATE

This Instruction is effective immediately upon signing by both of the following, whichever date is later.

Signed by Claude M. Kicklighter
Inspector General Department of Defense

Signed by Daniel J. Dell'Orto, Acting
General Counsel Department of Defense

Enclosures – 2

E1. References, continued

E2. DoD Supplemental Guidance to the MOU Between the Departments of Justice and Defense Relating to the Investigation and Prosecution of Certain Crimes

E1. ENCLOSURE 1

REFERENCES, continued

(e) Memorandum of Understanding between the Departments of Justice and Defense Relating to the Investigation and Prosecution of Certain Crimes, August 1981[1]

(f) Chapter 47 of title 10, United States Code, "Uniform Code of Military Justice (UCMJ)"

(g) Manual for Courts-Martial, United States, 2005 (R.C.M. 704)

(h) Title 18 of the United States Code

E2. ENCLOSURE 2

DoD SUPPLEMENTAL GUIDANCE TO THE MOU BETWEEN THE DEPARTMENTS OF JUSTICE AND DEFENSE RELATING TO THE INVESTIGATION AND PROSECUTION OF CERTAIN CRIMES

This enclosure contains the verbatim text of

[1] For copies of the signed Memorandum of Understanding, contact the Office of the Deputy General Counsel (Personnel and Health Policy), 1600 Defense Pentagon, Washington, D.C. 20301-1600

Reference (e). Matter that is identified as "DoD Supplemental Guidance" has been added by the Department of Defense. DoD Components shall comply with the MOU and the DoD Supplemental Guidance.

MEMORANDUM OF UNDERSTANDING BETWEEN THE DEPARTMENTS OF JUSTICE AND DEFENSE RELATING TO THE INVESTIGATION AND PROSECUTION OF CERTAIN CRIMES

A. PURPOSE, SCOPE AND AUTHORITY

This Memorandum of Understanding (MOU) establishes policy for the Department of Justice and the Department of Defense with regard to the investigation and prosecution of criminal matters over which the two Departments have jurisdiction. This memorandum is not intended to confer any rights, benefits, privileges or form of due process procedure upon individuals, associations, corporations, or other persons or entities.

This Memorandum applies to all components and personnel of the Department of Justice and the Department of Defense. The statutory bases for the Department of Defense and the Department of Justice investigation and prosecution responsibilities include, but are not limited to:

1. Department of Justice: Titles 18, 21 and 28 of the United States Code; and

2. Department of Defense: The Uniform Code of Military Justice, Title 10, United States Code, Sections 801-940; the Inspector General Act of 1978, Title 5 United States Code, Appendix 3; and Title 5 United States Code, Section 301.

B. POLICY

The Department of Justice has primary responsibility for enforcement of federal laws in the United States District Courts. The Department of Defense has responsibility for the integrity of its programs, operations and installations and for the discipline of the Armed Forces. Prompt administrative actions and completion of investigations within the two (2) year statute of limitations under the Uniform Code of Military Justice require the Department of Defense to assume an important role in federal criminal investigations. To encourage joint and coordinated investigative efforts, in appropriate cases where the Department of Justice assumes investigative responsibility for a matter relating to the Department of Defense, it should share information and conduct the inquiry jointly with the interested Department of Defense investigative agency.

It is neither feasible nor desirable to establish inflexible rules regarding the responsibilities of the Department of Defense and the Department of Justice as to each matter over which they may have concurrent interest. Informal arrangements and agreements within the spirit of this MOU are permissible with respect to specific crimes or investigations.

C. INVESTIGATIVE AND PROSECUTIVE JURISDICTION

1. *CRIMES ARISING FROM THE DEPARTMENT OF DEFENSE OPERATIONS*

a. *Corruption Involving the Department of Defense Personnel*

The Department of Defense investigative agencies will refer to the FBI on receipt all significant allegations of bribery and conflict of interest involving military or civilian personnel of the Department of Defense. In all corruption matters that are the subject of a referral to the FBI, the Department of Defense shall obtain the concurrence of the Department of Justice prosecutor or the FBI before initiating any independent investigation preliminary to any action under the Uniform Code of Military Justice. If the Department of Defense is not satisfied with the initial determination, the matter will be reviewed by the Criminal Division of the Department of Justice.

The FBI will notify the referring agency promptly

regarding whether they accept the referred matters for investigation. The FBI will attempt to make such decision in one (1) working day of receipt in such matters.

DoD Supplemental Guidance

A. Certain bribery and conflict of interest allegations (also referred to as "corruption" offenses in the MOU) are to be referred immediately to the FBI.

B. For the purposes of this section, bribery and conflict of interest allegations are those which would, if proven, violate sections 201, 203, 205, 208, 209, or 219 of title 18, United States Code (Reference (h)).

C. Under paragraph C.1.a., DoD criminal investigative organizations shall refer to the FBI those "significant" allegations of bribery and conflict of interest that implicate directly military or DoD civilian personnel, including allegations of bribery or conflict of interest that arise during the course of an ongoing investigation.

1. All bribery and conflict of interest allegations against present, retired, or former General or Flag officers and civilians in positions above the GS-15 and equivalent levels, the Senior Executive Service, and the Executive Level will be considered "significant" for purposes of referral to the FBI.

2. In cases not covered by subsection C.1., of this supplemental guidance, the determination of whether the matter is "significant" for purposes of referral to the FBI should be made in light of the following factors: sensitivity of the DoD program involved, amount of money in the alleged bribe, number of DoD personnel implicated, impact on the affected DoD program, and with respect to military personnel, whether the matter normally would be handled under Reference (f). Bribery and conflicts of interest allegations warranting consideration of Federal prosecution, which were not referred to the FBI based on the application of these guidelines and not otherwise disposed of under Reference (f), will be developed and brought to the attention of the Department of Justice through the "conference" mechanism described in paragraph C.1.b of Reference (e).

D. Bribery and conflict of interest allegations when military or DoD civilian personnel are not subjects of the investigations are not covered by the referral requirement of paragraph C.1.a. of Reference (e). Matters in which the suspects are solely DoD contractors and their subcontractors, such as commercial bribery between a DoD subcontractor and a DoD prime contractor, do not require referral upon receipt to the FBI. The "conference" procedure described in paragraph C.1.b. of Reference (e) shall be used in these types of cases.

E. Bribery and conflict of interest allegations that arise from events occurring outside the United States, its territories, and possessions, and requiring investigation outside the United States, its territories, and possessions need not be referred to the FBI.

F. The 1984 MOU references a two (2) year statute of limitations in effect for some Uniform Code of Military Justice offenses. Section 843 of Reference (f), governing statute of limitations has been amended several times since signing the MOU, applying generally a 5 year statute of limitation. It remains important that administrative actions and investigations be completed in a timely manner in order to meet the statute of limitations requirements for the respective offenses, while keeping in mind that the applicable statute of limitation of a particular offense is that which was in effect at the time the offense was committed.

b. *Frauds Against the Department of Defense and Theft and Embezzlement of Government Property*

The Department of Justice and the Department of Defense have investigative responsibility for frauds against the Department of Defense and theft and embezzlement of Government property from the Department of Defense. The Department of Defense will investigate frauds against the Department of Defense and theft of government property from the Department of Defense. Whenever a Department of Defense investigative agency identifies a matter which, if developed by investigation, would warrant federal prosecution, it will confer with the United

States Attorney or the Criminal Division, the Department of Justice, and the FBI field office. At the time of this initial conference, criminal investigative responsibility will be determined by the Department of Justice in consultation with the Department of Defense.

DoD Supplemental Guidance

A. Unlike paragraph C.1.a. of Reference (e), paragraph C.1.b. does not have an automatic referral requirement. Under paragraph C.1.b, DoD criminal investigative organizations shall confer with the appropriate Federal prosecutor and the FBI on matters which, if developed by investigation, would warrant Federal prosecution. This "conference" serves to define the respective roles of DoD criminal investigative organizations and the FBI on a case-by-case basis. Generally, when a conference is warranted, the DoD criminal investigative organization shall arrange to meet with the prosecutor and shall provide notice to the FBI that such meeting is being held. Separate conferences with both the prosecutor and the FBI normally are not necessary.

B. When investigations are brought to the attention of the Federal Procurement Fraud Unit (FPFU), such contact will satisfy the "conference" requirements of paragraph C.1.b. of Reference (e) as both the prosecutor and the FBI.

C. Mere receipt by DoD criminal investigative organizations of raw allegations of fraud or theft does not require conferences with the DoJ and the FBI. Sufficient evidence should be developed before the conference to allow the prosecutor to make an informed judgment as to the merits of a case dependent upon further investigation. However, DoD criminal investigative organizations should avoid delay in scheduling such conferences, particularly in complex fraud cases, because an early judgment by a prosecutor can be of assistance in focusing the investigation on those matters that most likely will result in criminal prosecution.

2. *CRIMES COMMITTED ON MILITARY INSTAL-LATIONS*

a. *Subject(s) can be Tried by Court-Martial or are Unknown*

Crimes (other than those covered by paragraph C.1.) committed on a military installation will be investigated by the Department of Defense investigative agency concerned and, when committed by a person subject to the Uniform Code of Military Justice, prosecuted by the Military Department concerned. The Department of Defense will provide immediate notice to the Department of Justice of significant cases in which an individual subject/victim is other than a military member or dependent thereof.

b. *One or More Subjects cannot be Tried by Court-Martial*

When a crime (other than those covered by paragraph C.1.) has occurred on a military installation and there is reasonable basis to believe that it has been committed by a person or persons, some or all of whom are not subject to the Uniform Code of Military Justice, the Department of Defense investigative agency will provide immediate notice of the matter to the appropriate Department of Justice investigative agency unless the Department of Justice has relieved the Department of Defense of the reporting requirement for that type of class of crime.

DoD Supplemental Guidance

A. Subsection C.2. of Reference (e) addresses crimes committed on a military installation other than those listed in paragraphs C.1.a. (bribery and conflict of interest) and C.1.b. (fraud, theft, and embezzlement against the Government).

B. Unlike paragraph C.1.a. of Reference (e), which requires "referral" to the FBI of certain cases, and paragraph C.1.b, which requires "conference" with respect to certain cases, subsection C.2. requires only that "notice" be given to DoJ of certain cases. Relief from the reporting requirement of subsectionnC.2. may be granted by the local U.S. attorney as to types or classes of cases.

C. For purposes of paragraph C.2.a. (when the

subjects can be tried by court-martial or are unknown), an allegation is "significant" for purposes of required notice to the DoJ only if the offense falls within the prosecutorial guidelines of the local U.S attorney. Notice should be given in other cases when the DoD Component believes that Federal prosecution is warranted or otherwise determines that the case may attract significant public attention.

3. *CRIMES COMMITTED OUTSIDE MILITARY INSTALLATIONS BY PERSONS WHO CAN BE TRIED BY COURT-MARTIAL*

a. *Offense is Normally Tried by Court-Martial*

Crimes (other than those covered by paragraph C.1.) committed outside a military installation by persons subject to the Uniform Code of Military Justice which, normally, are tried by court-martial will be investigated and prosecuted by the Department of Defense. The Department of Defense will provide immediate notice of significant cases to the appropriate Department of Justice investigative agency. The Department of Defense will provide immediate notice in all cases where one or more subjects is not under military jurisdiction unless the Department of Justice has relieved the Department of Defense of the reporting requirement for that type or class or crime.

DoD Supplemental Guidance

For purposes of this paragraph, an allegation is "significant" for purposes of required notice to the DoJ only if the offense falls within prosecutorial guidelines of the local U.S. attorney. Notice should be given in other cases when the DoD Component believes that Federal prosecution is warranted, or otherwise determines that the case may attract significant public attention.

b. *Crimes Related to Scheduled Military Activities*

Crimes related to scheduled Military activities outside of a military installation, such as organized maneuvers in which persons subject to the Uniform Code of Military Justice are suspects, shall be treated as if committed on a military installation for purposes of this Memorandum. The FBI or other Department of Justice investigative agency may assume jurisdiction with the concurrence of the United States Attorney or the Criminal Division, Department of Justice.

c. *Offense is not Normally Tried by Court-Martial*

When there are reasonable grounds to believe that a Federal crime (other than those covered by paragraph C.1.) normally not tried by court-martial, has been committed outside a military installation by a person subject to the Uniform Code of Military Justice, the Department of Defense investigative agency will immediately refer the case to the appropriate Department of Justice investigative agency unless the Department of Justice has relieved the Department of Defense of the reporting requirements for the type or class of crime.

D. REFERRALS AND INVESTIGATIVE ASSISTANCE

1. *REFERRALS*

Referrals, notices, reports, requests and the general transfer of information under this Memorandum normally should be between the FBI or other Department of Justice investigative agency and the appropriate Department of Defense investigative agency at the field level.

If a Department of Justice investigative agency does not accept a referred matter and the referring Department of Defense investigative agency then, or subsequently, believes that evidence exists supporting prosecution before civilian courts, the Department of Defense agency may present the case to the United States Attorney or the Criminal Division, Department of Justice, for review.

2. *INVESTIGATIVE ASSISTANCE*

In cases where a Department of Defense or Department of Justice investigative agency has primary responsibility and it requires limited assistance to pursue outstanding leads, the investigative agency requiring assistance will promptly advise the appropriate investigative agency in the other Department and, to the extent authorized by law and regulations, the requested assistance should be provided without assuming responsibility for the investigation.

F. PROSECUTION OF CASES

1. With the concurrence of the Department of Defense, the Department of Justice will designate such Department of Defense attorneys as it deems desirable to be Special Assistant United States Attorneys for use where the effective prosecution of cases may be facilitated by the Department of Defense attorneys.

2. The Department of Justice will institute civil actions expeditiously in United States District Courts whenever appropriate to recover monies lost as a result of crimes against the Department of Defense; the Department of Defense will provide appropriate assistance to facilitate such actions.

3, The Department of Justice prosecutors will solicit the views of the Department of Defense prior to initiating action against an individual subject to the Uniform Code of Military Justice.

4. The Department of Justice will solicit the views of the Department of Defense with regard to its Department of Defense-related cases and investigations in order to effectively coordinate the use of civil, criminal and administrative remedies.

DoD Supplemental Guidance

Prosecution of Cases and Grants of Immunity

A. The authority of court-martial convening authorities to refer cases to trial, approve pretrial agreements, and issue grants of immunity under Reference (f) extends only to trials by court-martial. In order to ensure that such actions do not preclude appropriate action by Federal civilian authorities in cases likely to be prosecuted in the U.S. district courts, court-martial convening authorities shall ensure that appropriate consultation as required by this enclosure has taken place before trial by court-martial, approval of a pretrial agreement, or issuance of a grant of immunity in cases when such consultation is required.

B. Only a general court-martial convening authority may grant immunity under Reference (f), and may do so only in accordance with Rule for Courts-Martial 704 of Reference (g).

1. Under Reference (f), there are two types of immunity in the military justice system:

a. A person may be granted transactional immunity from trial by court-martial for one or more offenses under Reference (f).

b. A person may be granted testimonial immunity, which is immunity from the use of testimony, statements, and any information directly or indirectly derived from such testimony or statements by that person in a later court-marital.

2. Before a grant of immunity under Reference (f), the general court-martial convening authority shall ensure that there has been appropriate consultation with the DoJ with respect to offenses in which consultation is required by this enclosure.

3. A proposed grant of immunity in a case involving espionage, subversion, aiding the enemy, sabotage, spying, or violation of rules or statutes concerning classified information or the foreign relations of the United States shall be forwarded to the GC, DoD for the purpose of consultation with the DoJ. The GC, DoD shall obtain the views of other appropriate elements of the Department of Defense in furtherance of such consultation.

C. The authority of court-martial convening authorities extends only to grants of immunity from action under Reference (f). Only the Attorney General or other authority designated under sections 6001-6005 of Reference (h) may authorize action to obtain a grant of immunity with respect to trials in the U.S. district courts.

F. MISCELLANEOUS MATTERS

1. *THE DEPARTMENT OF DEFENSE ADMINISTRATIVE ACTIONS*

Nothing in this Memorandum limits the Department of Defense investigations conducted in support of administrative actions to be taken by the Department of Defense. However, the Department of Defense investigative agencies will coordinate all such investigations with the appropriate Department of Justice prosecutive agency and obtain the concurrence of the Department of Justice prosecutor or the Department of Justice investigative agency prior to conducting any administrative investigation during the pendency of the criminal investigation or prosecution.

2. *SPECIAL UNIFORM CODE OF MILITARY JUSTICE FACTORS*

In situations where an individual subject to the Uniform Code of Military Justice is a suspect in any crime for which a Department of Justice investigative agency has assumed jurisdiction, if a Department of Defense investigative agency believes that the crime involves special factors relating to the administration and discipline of the Armed Forces that would justify its investigation, the Department of Defense investigative agency will advise the appropriate Department of Justice investigative agency or the Department of Justice prosecuting authorities of these factors. Investigation of such a crime may be undertaken by the appropriate Department of Defense investigative agency with the concurrence of the Department of Justice.

3. *ORGANIZED CRIME*

The Department of Defense investigative agencies will provide to the FBI all information collected during the normal course of agency operations pertaining to the element generally known as "organized crime" including both traditional (La Cosa Nostra) and nontraditional organizations whether or not the matter is considered prosecutable. The FBI should be notified of any investigation involving any element of organized crime and may assume jurisdiction of the same.

4. *DEPARTMENT OF JUSTICE NOTIFICATIONS TO DEPARTMENT OF DEFENSE INVESTIGATIVE AGENCIES*

a. The Department of Justice investigative agencies will promptly notify the appropriate Department of Defense investigative agency of the initiation of the Department of Defense related investigations which are predicated on other than a Department of Defense referral except in those rare instances where notification might endanger agents or adversely affect the investigation. The Department of Justice investigative agencies will also notify the Department of Defense of all allegations of the Department of Defense related crime where investigation is not initiated by the Department of Justice.

b. Upon request, the Department of Justice investigative agencies will provide timely status reports on all investigations relating to the Department of Defense unless the circumstances indicate such reporting would be inappropriate.

c. The Department of Justice investigative agencies will promptly furnish investigative results at the conclusion of an investigation and advise as to the nature of judicial action, if any, taken or contemplated.

d. If judicial or administrative action is being considered by the Department of Defense, the Department of Justice will, upon written request, provide existing detailed investigative data and documents (less any federal grand jury material, disclosure of which would be prohibited by Rule 6(e), Federal Rules of Criminal Procedure), as well as agent testimony for use in judicial or administrative proceedings, consistent with Department of Justice and other federal regulations. The ultimate use of the information shall be subject to the concurrence of the federal prosecutor during the pendency of any related investigation or prosecution.

5. *TECHNICAL ASSISTANCE*

a. The Department of Justice will provide to the Department of Defense all technical services normally available to federal investigative agencies.

b. The Department of Defense will provide assistance to the Department of Justice in matters not relating to the Department of Defense as permitted by law and implementing regulations.

6. *JOINT INVESTIGATIONS*

a. To the extent authorized by law, the Department of Justice investigative agencies and the Department of Defense investigative agencies may agree to enter into joint investigative endeavors, including undercover operations, in appropriate circumstances. However, all such investigations will be subject to Department of Justice guidelines.

b. The Department of Defense, in the conduct of any investigation that might lead to prosecution in Federal District Court, will conduct the investigation consistent with any Department of Justice guidelines. The Department of Justice shall provide copies of all relevant guidelines and their revisions.

DoD Supplemental Guidance

When DoD procedures concerning apprehension, search and seizure, interrogation, eyewitnesses, or identification differ from those of DoJ, DoD procedures will be used, unless the DoJ prosecutor has directed that DoJ procedures be used instead. DoD criminal investigators should bring to the attention of the DoJ prosecutor, as appropriate, situations when use of DoJ procedures might impede or preclude prosecution under Reference (f).

7. *APPREHENSION OF SUSPECTS*

To the extent authorized by law, the Department of Justice and the Department of Defense will each promptly deliver or make available to the other suspects, accused individuals and witnesses where authority to investigate the crimes involved is lodged in the other Department. This MOU neither expands nor limits the authority of either Department to perform apprehensions, searches, seizures, or custodial interrogations.

G. EXCEPTION

This Memorandum shall not affect the investigative authority now fixed by the 1979 "Agreement Governing the Conduct of the Defense Department Counterintelligence Activities in Conjunction with the Federal Bureau of Investigation" and the 1983 Memorandum of Understanding between the Department of Defense, the Department of Justice and the FBI concerning "Use of Federal Military Force in Domestic Terrorist Incidents."

APPENDIX 4
MEMORANDUM OF UNDERSTANDING BETWEEN THE DEPARTMENTS OF JUSTICE AND TRANSPORTATION (COAST GUARD) RELATING TO THE INVESTIGATIONS AND PROSECUTION OF CRIMES OVER WHICH THE TWO DEPARTMENTS HAVE CONCURRENT JURISDICTION

Whereas, certain crimes committed by Coast Guard personnel subject to the Uniform Code of Military Justice may be prosecuted by Coast Guard tribunals under the Code or by civilian authorities in the Federal Courts; and

Whereas, it is recognized that although the administration and discipline of the Coast Guard requires that certain types of crimes committed by its personnel be investigated by that service and prosecuted before Coast Guard military tribunals other types of crimes committed by such military personnel should be investigated by civil authorities and prosecuted before civil tribunals; and

Whereas, it is recognized that it is not feasible to impose inflexible rules to determine the respective responsibility of the civilian and Coast Guard military authorities as to each crime over which they may have concurrent jurisdiction and that informal arrangements and agreements may be necessary with respect to specific crimes or investigations; and

Whereas, agreement between the Department of Justice and the Department of Transportation (Coast Guard) as to the general areas in which they will investigate and prosecute crimes to which both civil and military jurisdiction attach will, nevertheless, tend to make the investigation and prosecution of crimes more expeditious and efficient and give appropriate effect to the policies of civil government and the requirements of the United States Coast Guard;

It is hereby agreed and understood between the Department of Justice and the Department of Transportation (Coast Guard) as follows:

1. *Crimes committed on military installations (including aircraft and vessels).* Except as hereinafter indicated, all crimes committed on a military installation by Coast Guard personnel subject to the Uniform Code of Military Justice shall be investigated and prosecuted by the Coast Guard if the Coast Guard makes a determination that there is a reasonable likelihood that only Coast Guard personnel subject to the Uniform Code of Military justice are involved in such crimes as principles or accessories, and except in extraordinary cases, that there is no victim other than persons who are subject to the Uniform Code of Military Justice or who are bona fide dependents or members of a household of military or civilian personnel residing on the installation. Unless such a determination is made, the Coast Guard shall promptly advise the Federal Bureau of Investigation of any crime committed on a military installation if such crime is within the investigative authority of the Federal Bureau of Investigation. The Federal Bureau of Investigation shall investigate any serious crime of which it has been so advised for the purpose of prosecution in the civil courts unless the Department of Justice determines that investigation and prosecution may be conducted more efficiently and expeditiously by the Coast Guard. Even if the determination provided for in the first sentence of this paragraph is made by the Coast Guard, it shall promptly advise the Federal Bureau of Investigation of any crime committed on a military installation in which there is a victim who is not subject to the Uniform Code of Military Justice or a bona fide dependent or member of the household of military or civilian personnel residing on the installation and that the Coast Guard is investigating the crime because it has been determined to be extraordinary. The Coast Guard shall promptly advise the Federal Bureau of Investigation whenever the crime, except in minor offenses, involves fraud against the government, misappropriation, robbery, or theft of government property of funds, or is of a similar nature. All such crimes shall be investigated by the Coast Guard unless it receives prompt advise that the Department of Justice has determined that the crime should be investigated by the Federal Bureau of Investigation and that the Federal Bureau of Investigation will undertake the investigation for the purpose of prosecution in the civil courts.

2. *Crimes committed outside of military installations.* Except as herein after indicated , all crimes committed outside of military installations, which fall within the investigative jurisdiction of the Federal Bureau of Investigation and in which there is involved as a suspect an individual subject to the Uniform Code of Military Justice, shall be investigated by the Federal Bureau of Investigation for the purpose of prosecution in civil courts, unless the Department of Justice determines that investigation and prosecution may be conducted more efficiently and expeditiously by other authorities. All such crimes which come first to the attention of Coast Guard authorities shall be referred promptly by them to the Federal Bureau of Investigation, unless relieved of this requirement by the Federal Bureau of Investigation as to particular types or classes of crime. However, whenever Coast Guard military personnel are engaged in scheduled military activities outside of military installations such as organized maneuvers or organized movement, the provisions of paragraph 1 above shall apply, unless persons not subject to the Uniform Code of Military Justice are involved as principals, accessories or victims. If, however, there is involved as a suspect or as an accused in any crime committed outside of a military installation and falling within the investigative authority of the Federal Bureau of Investigation, an individual who is subject to the Uniform Code of Military Justice and if the Coast Guard authorities

believe that the crime involves special factors relating to the administration and discipline of the Coast Guard which would justify investigation by them for the purpose of prosecution before a Coast Guard military tribunal, they shall promptly advise the Federal Bureau of Investigation of the crime and indicate their views on the matter. Investigation of such a crime may be undertaken by the Coast Guard military authorities if the Department of Justice agrees.

3. *Transfer of investigative authority.* An investigative body of the Coast Guard which has initiated an investigation pursuant to paragraphs 1 and 2 hereof, shall have exclusive investigative authority and may proceed therewith to prosecution. If, however, any Coast Guard investigative body comes to the view that effectuation of those paragraphs requires the transfer of investigative authority over a crime, investigation of which has already been initiated by that or by any other investigative body, it shall promptly advise the other interested investigative body of its views. By agreement between the Departments of Justice and Transportation (Coast Guard), investigative authority may then be transferred.

4. *Administrative action.* Exercise of exclusive investigative authority by the Federal Bureau of Investigation pursuant to this agreement shall not preclude Coast Guard military authorities from making inquiries for the purpose of administrative action related to the crime being investigated. The Federal Bureau of Investigation will make the results of its investigations available to Coast Guard military authorities for use in connection with such action. Whenever possible, decisions with respect to the application in particular cases of the provisions of this Memorandum of Understanding will be made at the local level, that is, between the Special Agent in Charge of the local office of the Federal Bureau of Investigation and the local Coast Guard military commander.

5. *Surrender of suspects.* To the extent of the legal authority conferred upon them, the Department of Justice and Coast Guard military authorities will each deliver to the other promptly suspects and accused individuals if authority to investigate the crimes in which such accused individuals and suspects are involved is lodged in the other by paragraphs 1 and 2 hereof. Nothing in this memorandum shall prevent the Coast Guard from prompt arrest and detention of any person subject to the Uniform Code of Military Justice whenever there is knowledge or reasonable basis to believe that such a person has committed an offense in violation of such code and detaining such person until he is delivered to the Federal Bureau of Investigation if such action is required pursuant to this memorandum.

APPROVED:

/s/ Alan S. Boyd
Alan S. Boyd
Secretary of Transportation
Date: 24 October 1967

/s/ Ramsey Clark
Ramsey Clark
Attorney General
Date: 9 October 1967

APPENDIX 5

The Department of Defense Forms Management Program provides the following blank forms for reference and use in military justice processing. This is a non-exhaustive list. The forms are available at https://www.esd.whs.mil/Directives/forms/.

Form Number	Form Name
DD Form 453	Subpoena to Testify and/or Produce or Permit Inspection of Items in a Court Martial
DD Form 453-1	Travel Order
DD Form 454	Warrant of Attachment
DD Form 455	Report of Proceedings to Vacate Suspension of a Court-Martial Sentence
DD Form 456	Interrogatories and Depositions
DD Form 457	Preliminary Hearing Officer's Report
DD Form 458	Charge Sheet
DD Form 490	Certified Record of Trial
DD Form 491	Summarized Record of Trial
DD Form 491-1	Summarized Record of Trial – Article 39(A) Session
DD Form 493	Extract of Military Records of Previous Convictions
DD Form 494	Court-Martial Data Sheet
DD Form 1722	Request for Trial Before Military Judge Alone
DD Form 2654	Involuntary Allotment Notice and Processing
DD Form 2329	Record of Trial by Summary Court-Martial
DD Form 2330	Waiver/Withdrawal of Appellate Rights in General and Special Courts-Martial Subject to Review by a Court of Military Review
DD Form 2331	Waiver/Withdrawal of Appellate Rights in General Courts-Martial Subject to Examination in the Office of the Judge Advocate General
DD Form 2698	Application for Transitional Compensation
DD Form 2701	Initial Information for Victims and Witnesses of Crime
DD Form 2702	Court-Martial Information for Victims and Witnesses of Crime
DD Form 2703	Post-Trial Information for Victims and Witnesses of Crime
DD Form 2704	Victim/Witness Certification and Election Concerning Prisoner Status
DD Form 2704-1	Victim Election of Post-Trial and Appellate Rights
DD Form 2705	Notification to Victim/Witness of Prisoner Status
DD Form 2706	Annual Report on Victim and Witness Assistance
DD Form 2707	Confinement Order
DD Form 2707-1	Department of Defense Report of Result of Trial
DD Form 2708	Receipt for Pretrial/Post-Trial Prisoner or Detained Person
DD Form 2717	Department of Defense Voluntary/Involuntary Appellate Leave Action
DD Form 2873	Military Protective Order
DD Form 3056	Search and Seizure Warrant Pursuant to 18 U.S.C. § 2703
DD Form 3057	Application for Search and Seizure Warrant Pursuant to 18 U.S.C. § 2703

Appendix 6 – RESERVED

THIS PAGE LEFT INTENTIONALLY BLANK.

Appendix 7 – RESERVED

THIS PAGE LEFT INTENTIONALLY BLANK.

APPENDIX 8
GUIDE FOR SUMMARY COURTS-MARTIAL

[General Note to SCM: It is not the purpose of this guide to answer all questions which may arise during a trial. When this guide, chapter 13 of the Rules for Courts-Martial, and other legal materials available fail to provide sufficient information concerning law or procedure, the summary court-martial should seek advice on these matters from a judge advocate. *See* R.C.M. 1301(b). If the accused has obtained, or wishes to obtain, defense counsel, *see* R.C.M. 1301(e). The SCM should examine the format for record of trial at appendix 9. It may be useful as a checklist during the proceedings to ensure proper preparation after trial. The SCM should become familiar with this guide before using it. Instructions for the SCM are contained in brackets, and should not be read aloud. Language in parentheses reflects optional or alternative language. The SCM should read the appropriate language aloud.]

Preliminary Proceeding

Identity of SCM

SCM: I am ____________. I have been detailed to conduct a summary court-martial (by Summary Court-Martial Convening Order (Number ______), Headquarters, _________ , dated [see convening order]).

Referral of charges to trial

Charges against you have been referred to me for trial by summary court-martial by ([*name and title of convening authority*]) on ([*date of referral*]) [see block IV on page 2 of charge sheet].

[Note 1. Hand copy of charge sheet to the accused.]

Providing the accused with charge sheet

I suggest that you keep this copy of the charge sheet and refer to it during the trial. The charges are signed by [see first name at top of page 2 of charge sheet], a person subject to the Uniform Code of Military Justice, as accuser, and are properly sworn to before a commissioned officer of the armed forces authorized to administer oaths.

(_________ ordered the charges to be preferred.) The charges allege, in general, violation of Article ______, in that you __________, (and Article ______, in that you _______). I am now going to tell you about certain rights you have in this trial. You should carefully consider each explanation because you will soon have to decide whether to object to trial by summary court-martial. Until I have completed my explanation, do not say anything except to answer the specific questions which I ask you. Do you understand that?

ACC: _______________.

Duties of SCM

SCM: As summary court-martial it is my duty to obtain and examine all the evidence concerning any offense(s) to which you plead not guilty, and to thoroughly and impartially inquire into both sides of the matter. I will call witnesses for the prosecution and question them, and I will help you in cross-examining those witnesses. I will help you obtain evidence and present the defense. This means that one of my duties is to help you present your side of the case. You may also represent yourself, and if you do, it is my duty to help you. You are presumed to be innocent until your guilt has been

		proved by legal and competent evidence beyond a reasonable doubt. If you are found guilty of an offense, it is also my duty to consider matters which might affect the sentence, and then to adjudge an appropriate sentence. Do you understand that?
	ACC:	______________.
Right to object to SCM	SCM:	You have the absolute right to object to trial by summary court-martial. If you object the appropriate authority will decide how to dispose of the case. The charges may be referred to a special or general court-martial, or they may be dismissed, or the offenses charged may be disposed of by (nonjudicial punishment [if not previously offered and refused] or) administrative measures. [*See* R.C.M. 306.] Do you understand that?
	ACC:	______________.
Right to inspect allied papers and personnel records.	SCM:	You may inspect the allied papers and personnel records [Hand those documents which are available to the accused for examination in your presence.] (You may also inspect [*identify personnel records or other documents which are not present*] which are located at __________. You may have time to examine these if you wish.)
Witnesses/other evidence for the government	SCM:	The following witnesses will probably appear and testify against you: __________________. The following documents and physical evidence will probably be introduced: ______________________.
Right to cross-examine		After these witnesses have testified in response to my questions, you may cross-examine them. If you prefer, I will do this for you after you inform me of the matters about which you want the witness to be questioned. Do you understand that?
	ACC:	______________.
Right to present evidence	SCM:	You also have the right to call witnesses and present other evidence. This evidence may concern any or all of the charges. (I have arranged to have the following witnesses for you present at the trial.) I will arrange for the attendance of other witnesses and the production of other evidence requested by you. I will help you in any way possible. Do you understand that?
	ACC:	______________.
Evidence to be considered	SCM:	In deciding this case, I will consider only evidence introduced during the trial. I will not consider any other information, including any statements you have made to me, which is not introduced in accordance with the Military Rules of Evidence during the court-martial. Do you understand that?

ACC: _______________.

Right to remain silent

SCM: You have the absolute right during this trial to choose not to testify and to say nothing at all about the offense(s) with which you are charged. If you do not testify, I will not hold it against you in any way. I will not consider it as an admission that you are guilty. If you remain silent, I am not permitted to question you about the offense(s).

Right to testify concerning the offense(s)

However, if you choose, you may be sworn and testify as a witness concerning the offense(s) charged against you. If you do that, I will consider your testimony just like the testimony of any other witness.

[Note 2. Use the following if there is only one specification.]

If one specification

If you decide to testify concerning the offense, you can be questioned by me about the whole subject of the offense. Do you understand that?

ACC: _______________.

[Note 3. Use the following if there is more than one specification.]

If more than one specification

SCM: If you decide to testify, you may limit your testimony to any particular offense charged against you and not testify concerning any other offense(s) charged against you. If you do this, I may question you about the whole subject of the offense about which you testify, but I may not question you about any offense(s) concerning which you do not testify. Do you understand that?

ACC: _______________.

Right to testify, remain silent or make an unsworn statement in extenuation and mitigation

SCM: In addition, if you are found guilty of an offense, you will have the right to testify under oath concerning matters regarding an appropriate sentence. You may, however, remain silent, and I will not hold your silence against you in any way. You may, if you wish, make an unsworn statement about such matters. This statement may be oral, in writing, or both. If you testify, I may cross-examine you. If you make an unsworn statement, however, I am not permitted to question you about it, but I may receive evidence to contradict anything contained in the statement. Do you understand that?

ACC: _______________.

Maximum punishment

SCM: If I find you guilty (of the offense) (of any of the offenses charged), the maximum sentence which I am authorized to impose is:

[Note 4. For an accused of a pay grade of E–4 or below, proceed as follows.]

E-4 and below

(l) reduction to lowest enlisted pay grade; and

(2) forfeiture of two-thirds of 1 month's pay; and

(3) confinement for l month.

[Note 5. For an accused of a pay grade above E–4, proceed as follows.]

E-5 and above

(1) reduction to the next inferior pay grade; and

(2) forfeiture of two-thirds of 1 month's pay; and

(3) restriction to specified limits for 2 months.

SCM: Do you understand the maximum punishment which this court-martial is authorized to adjudge?

ACC: _______________.

Plea options

SCM: You may plead not guilty or guilty to each offense with which you are charged. You have an absolute right to plead not guilty and to require that your guilt be proved beyond a reasonable doubt before you can be found guilty. You have the right to plead not guilty even if you believe you are guilty. Do you understand that?

ACC: _______________.

SCM If you believe you are guilty of an offense, you may, but are not required to, plead guilty to that offense. If you plead guilty to an offense, you are admitting that you committed that offense, and this court-martial could find you guilty of that offense without hearing any evidence, and could sentence you to the maximum penalty I explained to you before. Do you understand that?

ACC: _______________.

Lesser included offenses

SCM: [Examine the list of lesser included offenses under each punitive article alleged to have been violated. *See* Appendix 12A. If a lesser included offense may be at issue, give the following advice.] You may plead not guilty to Charge _______, Specification ______, as it now reads, but plead guilty to the lesser offense of __________, which is included in the offense charged. Of course, you are not required to do this. If you do, then I can find you guilty of this lesser offense without hearing evidence on it. Furthermore, I could still hear evidence on the greater offense for purposes of deciding whether you are guilty of it. Do you understand that?

ACC: _______________.

SCM: Do you need more time to consider whether to object to trial by summary court-martial or to prepare for trial?

ACC: _______________.

SCM: [If time is requested or otherwise appropriate.] We will convene the court-martial at ________. When we convene, I will ask you whether you object to trial by summary court-martial. If you do not object, I will then ask for your pleas to the charge(s) and specification(s), and for you to make any motions you may have.

Trial Proceedings

Convene

SCM: This summary court-martial is now in session.

Objection/consent to trial by SCM

SCM: Do you object to trial by summary court-martial?

ACC: _______________.

Entries on record of trial

[Note 6. If there is an objection, adjourn the court-martial and return the file to the convening authority. If the accused does not object, proceed as follows. The accused may be asked to initial the notation on the record of trial that the accused did or did not object to trial by summary court-martial. This is not required, however.]

Readings of the charges

SCM: Look at the charge sheet. Have you read the charge(s) and specification(s)?

ACC: _______________.

SCM: Do you want me to read them to you?

ACC: [If accused requests, read the charge(s) and specification(s).]

Arraignment

SCM: How do you plead? Before you answer that question, if you have any motion to dismiss (the) (any) charge or specification, or for other relief, you should make it now.

ACC: _______________.

Motions

[Note 7. If the accused makes a motion to dismiss or to grant other relief, or such a motion is raised by the summary court-martial, do not proceed with the trial until the motions have been decided. *See* R.C.M. 905–907, and R.C.M. 1304(b)(2)(C). After any motions have been disposed of and if termination of the trial has not resulted, have the accused enter pleas and proceed as indicated below.]

Pleas

ACC: I plead: _______________.

[Note 8. If the accused refuses to plead to any offense charged, enter pleas of not guilty. If the accused refuses to enter any plea, evidence must be presented to establish that the accused is the person named in the specification(s) and is subject to court-martial jurisdiction. *See* R.C.M. 202, 1301(c)]

[Note 9. If the accused pleads not guilty to all offenses charged, proceed to the section entitled "Procedures-Not Guilty Pleas."]

[Note 10. If the accused pleads guilty to one or more offenses, proceed as follows.]

Procedures-guilty pleas

SCM: I will now explain the meaning and effect of your pleas, and question you so that I can be sure you understand. Refer to the charge(s) and specification(s). I will not accept your pleas of guilty unless you understand their meaning and effect. You are legally and morally entitled to plead not guilty even though you believe you are guilty, and to require that your guilt be proved beyond a reasonable doubt. A plea of guilty is the strongest form of proof known to the law. On your pleas of guilty alone, without receiving any evidence, I can find you guilty of the offense(s) to which you have pleaded guilty. I will not accept your pleas unless you realize that by your pleas you admit every element of the offense(s) to which you have pleaded guilty, and that you are pleading guilty because you really are guilty. If you are not convinced that you are in fact guilty, you should not allow anything to influence you to plead guilty. Do you understand that?

ACC: ______________.

SCM: Do you have any questions?

ACC: ______________.

SCM: By your pleas of guilty you give up three very important rights. (You keep these rights with respect to any offense(s) to which you have pleaded not guilty.) The rights which you give up when you plead guilty are:

First, the right against self-incrimination. This means you give up the right to say nothing at all about (this) (these) offense(s) to which you have pleaded guilty. In a few minutes I will ask you questions about (this) (these) offense(s), and you will have to answer my questions for me to accept your pleas of guilty.

Second, the right to a trial of the facts by this court-martial. This means you give up the right to have me decide whether you are guilty based upon the evidence which would be presented.

Third, the right to be confronted by and to cross-examine any witnesses against you. This means you give up the right to have any witnesses against you appear, be sworn and testify, and to cross-examine them under oath.

Do you understand these rights?

ACC: ______________.

SCM: Do you understand that by pleading guilty you give up these rights?

ACC: ______________.

SCM On your pleas of guilty alone you could be sentenced to ________________.

[Note 11. Re-read the appropriate sentencing section at notes 4 or 5 above unless the summary court-martial is a rehearing or new or other trial, in which case see R.C.M. 810(d).]

SCM: Do you have any questions about the sentence which could be imposed as a result of your pleas of guilty?

ACC: ______________.

SCM: Has anyone made any threat or tried in any other way to force you to plead guilty?

ACC: ______________.

Pretrial agreement

SCM: Are you pleading guilty because of any promises or understandings between

you and the convening authority or anyone else?

ACC: ______________.

[Note 12. If the accused answers yes, the summary court-martial must inquire into the terms of such promises or understandings in accordance with R.C.M. 910.

[Note 13. If the accused has pleaded guilty to a lesser included offense, also ask the following question.]

Effect of guilty pleas to lesser included offenses

SCM: Do you understand that your plea of guilty to the lesser included offense of admits all the elements of the offense charged except the element(s) of , and that no proof is necessary to establish those elements admitted by your pleas?

ACC: ______________.

SCM: The following elements state what would have to be proved beyond a reasonable doubt before the court-martial could find you guilty if you had pleaded not guilty. As I read each of these elements to you, ask yourself whether each is true and whether you want to admit that each is true, and then be prepared to discuss each of these elements with me when I have finished. The elements of the offense(s) which your pleas of guilty admit are

[Note 14. Read the elements of the offense(s) from the appropriate punitive article in Part IV. This advice should be specific as to names, dates, places, amounts, and acts.]

Do you understand each of the elements of the offense(s)?

ACC: ______________.

SCM: Do you believe, and admit, that taken together these elements correctly describe what you did?

[Note 15. The summary court-martial should now question the accused about the circumstances of the offense(s) to which the accused has pleaded guilty. The accused will he placed under oath for this purpose. See oath below. The purpose of these questions is to develop the circumstances in the accused's own words, so that the summary court-martial may determine whether each element of the offense(s) is established.]

Oath to accused for guilty plea inquiry	SCM:	Do you (swear) (affirm) that the statements you are about to make shall be the truth, the whole truth, and nothing but the truth (so help you God)?
	ACC:	______________.
	SCM:	Do you have any questions about the meaning and effect of your pleas of guilty?
	ACC:	______________.
	SCM:	Do you believe that you understand the meaning and effect of your pleas of guilty?
Determination of providence of pleas of guilty		[Note 16. Pleas of guilty may not be accepted unless the summary court-martial finds that they are made voluntarily and with understanding of their meaning and effect, and that the accused has knowingly, intelligently, and consciously waived the rights against self-incrimination, to a trial of the facts by a court-martial, and to be confronted by the witnesses. Pleas of guilty may be improvident when the accused makes statements at any time during the trial which indicate that there may be a defense to the offense(s), or which are otherwise inconsistent with an admission of guilt. If the accused makes such statements and persists in them after questioning, then the summary court-martial must reject the accused's guilty pleas and enter pleas of not guilty for the accused. Turn to the section entitle "Procedures-Not Guilty Pleas" and continue as indicated. If (the) (any of the) accused's pleas of guilty are found provident, the summary court-martial should announce findings as follows.]
Acceptance of guilty pleas	SCM:	I find that the pleas of guilty are made voluntarily and with understanding of their meaning and effect. I further specifically find that you have knowingly, intelligently, and consciously waived your rights against self-incrimination, to a trial of the facts by a court-martial, and to be confronted by the witnesses against you. Accordingly, I find the pleas are provident, and I accept them. However, you may ask to take back your guilty pleas at any time before the sentence is announced. If you have a sound reason for your request, I will grant it. Do you understand that?
	ACC:	______________.
If any not guilty pleas remain		[Note 17. If no pleas of not guilty remain, go to note 26. If the accused has changed pleas of guilty to not guilty, if the summary court-martial has entered pleas of not guilty to any charge(s) and specification(s), or if the accused has pleaded not guilty to any of the offenses or pleaded guilty to a lesser included offense, proceed as follows.]
Witnesses for the accused	SCM:	If there are witnesses you would like to call to testify for you, give me the name, rank, and organization or address of each, and the reason you think they should be here, and I will arrange to have them present if their testimony would be material. Do you want to call witnesses?
	ACC:	______________.
		[Note 18. The summary court-martial should estimate the length of the case and arrange for the attendance of witnesses. The prosecution evidence should be presented before evidence for the defense.]
Calling witnesses	SCM:	I call as a witness ___________.

Witness oath

SCM: [To the witness, both standing] Raise your right hand.

Do you swear (or affirm) that the evidence you shall give in the case now in hearing shall be the truth, the whole truth, and nothing but the truth (, so help you God)? [Do not use the phrase, "so help you God," if the witness prefers to affirm.]

WIT: _________.

SCM: Be seated. State your full name, rank, organization, and armed force ([or if a civilian witness] full name, city and state of residence, and occupation).

WIT: _________.

[Note 19. The summary court-martial should question each witness concerning the alleged offense(s). After direct examination of each witness, the accused must be given an opportunity to cross-examine. If the accused declines to cross-examine the witness, the summary court-martial should ask any questions that it feels the accused should have asked. If cross-examination occurs, the summary court-martial may ask questions on redirect examination and the accused may ask further questions in recross examination.]

[Note 20. After each witness has testified, instruct the witness as follows.]

SCM: Do not discuss this case with anyone except the accused, counsel, or myself until after the trial is over. Should anyone else attempt to discuss this case with you, refuse to do so and report the attempt to me immediately. Do you understand that?

WIT: _________.

Recalling witnesses

[Note 21. Witnesses may be recalled if necessary. A witness who is recalled is still under oath and should be so reminded.]

[Note 22. After all witnesses against the accused have been called and any other evidence has been presented, the summary court-martial will announce the following.]

SCM: That completes the evidence against you. I will now consider the evidence in your favor.

Presentation of defense case

[Note 23. Witnesses for the accused should now be called to testify and other evidence should be presented. Before the defense case is terminated the summary court-martial should ask the accused if there are other matters the accused wants presented. If the accused has not testified, the summary court-martial should remind the accused of the right to testify or to remain silent.]

Closing argument

SCM: I have now heard all of the evidence. You may make an argument on this evidence before I decide whether you are guilty or not guilty.

Deliberations on findings

[Note 24. The court-martial should normally close for deliberations. If the summary court-martial decides to close, proceed as follows.]

SCM: The court-martial is closed so that I may review the evidence. Wait outside the courtroom until I recall you.

[Note 25. The summary court-martial should review the evidence and applicable law. It must acquit the accused unless it is convinced beyond a reasonable doubt by the evidence it has received in court in the presence of the accused that each element of the alleged offense(s) has been proved beyond a reasonable doubt. *See* R.C.M. 918. It may not consider any facts that were not admitted into evidence, such as a confession or admission of the accused that was excluded because it was taken in violation of Mil. R. Evid. 304. In accordance with R.C.M. 1304(b)(2)(F), the summary court-martial shall apply the principles of R.C.M. 918 in determining the findings.]

Announcing the findings

[Note 26. The summary court-martial should recall the accused, who will stand before the court-martial when findings are announced. All findings including any findings of guilty resulting from guilty pleas, should be announced at this time. The following forms should be used in announcing findings.]

Not guilty of all offenses

SCM: I find you of (the) (all) Charge(s) and Specification(s): Not Guilty.

Guilty of all offenses

I find you of (the) (all) Charge(s) and Specification(s): Guilty.

Guilty of some but not all offenses

I find you of (the) Specification (________) of (the) Charge (___): Not Guilty; of (the) Specification (______) of (the) Charge (___): Guilty; of (the) Charge (______): Guilty.

Guilty of lesser included offense or with exceptions and substitutions

I find you of (the Specification (________) of (the) Charge (___): Guilty, except the words ______ and; (substituting therefor, respectively, the words _______ and _______); of the excepted words: Not Guilty; (of the substituted words: Guilty;) of the Charge: (Guilty) (Not Guilty, but Guilty of a violation of Article ______, UCMJ, a lesser included offense).

Entry of findings

[Note 27. The summary court-martial shall note all findings on the record of trial.]

Procedure if total acquittal

[Note 28. If the accused has been found not guilty of all charges and specifications, adjourn the court-martial, excuse the accused, complete the record of trial, and return the charge sheet, personnel records, allied papers, and record of trial to the convening authority.]

Procedure if any findings of guilty

[Note 29. If the accused has been found guilty of any offense, proceed as follows.]

Presentence procedure

SCM: I will now receive information in order to decide on an appropriate sentence. Look at the information concerning you on the front page of the charge sheet. Is it correct?

[Note 30. If the accused alleges that any of the information is incorrect, the summary court-martial must determine whether it is correct and correct the charge sheet, if necessary.]

[Note 31. Evidence from the accused's personnel records, including evidence favorable to the accused, should now be received in accordance with R.C.M. 1001(b)(2). These records should be shown to the accused.]

SCM: Do you know any reason why I should not consider these?

ACC: _______________.

[Note 32. The summary court-martial shall resolve objections under R.C.M. 1002(b)(2) and the Military Rules of Evidence and then proceed as follows. *See also* R.C.M. 1001(b)(3), (4), and (5) concerning other evidence which may be introduced.]

Victim's Right to be heard on sentencing

[Note 33. A crime victim has the right to be reasonably heard at presentencing hearing. *See* R.C.M. 1001(c) and 1304(a)(4)(D). A "crime victim" is an individual who has suffered direct physical, emotional, or pecuniary harm as a result of the commission of an offense of which the accused was found guilty.]

SCM: Is there a crime victim in this case that wishes to submit a sworn or unsworn statement?

[Note 34. The crime victim may make a sworn statement, and be subject to cross-examination. The crime victim can elect to submit an unsworn statement, and may not be subjected to cross-examination. The content of statements may only include victim impact and matters in mitigation.]

Extenuation and mitigation

SCM: In addition to the information already admitted which is favorable to you, and which I will consider, you may call witnesses who are reasonably available, you may present evidence, and you may make a statement. This information may be to explain the circumstances of the offense(s), including any reasons for committing the offense(s), and to lessen the punishment for the offense(s) regardless of the circumstances. You may show particular acts of good conduct or bravery, and evidence of your reputation in the service for efficiency, fidelity, obedience, temperance, courage, or any other trait desirable in a good servicemember. You may call available witnesses or you may use letters, affidavits, certificates of military and civil officers, or other similar writings. If you introduce such matters, I may receive written evidence for the purpose of contradicting the matters you presented. If you want me to get some military records that you would otherwise be unable to obtain, give me a list of these documents. If you intend to introduce letters, affidavits, or other documents, but you do not have them, tell me so that I can help you get them. Do you understand that?

ACC: _______________.

Rights of accused to testify, remain silent, and make an unsworn statement

SCM: I informed you earlier of your right to testify under oath, to remain silent, and to make an unsworn statement about these matters.

SCM: Do you understand these rights?

ACC: _______________.

SCM: Do you wish to call witnesses or introduce anything in writing?

ACC: _______________.

Questions concerning pleas of guilty

[Note 35. If as a result of matters received on sentencing, including the accused's testimony or an unsworn statement, any matter is disclosed which is inconsistent with the pleas of guilty, the summary court-martial must immediately inform the accused and resolve the matter. *See* Note 16.]

Argument on sentence

SCM: You may make an argument on an appropriate sentence.

ACC: _______________.

Deliberations prior to announcing sentence

[Note 36. After receiving all matters relevant to sentencing, the summary court-martial should normally close for deliberations. If the summary court-martial decides to close, proceed as follows.]

Closing the court-martial	SCM:	This court-martial is closed for determination of the sentence. Wait outside the courtroom until I recall you.

[Note 37. *See* Appendix 11 concerning proper form of sentence. Once the summary court-martial has determined the sentence, it should reconvene the court-martial and announce the sentence as follows.]

Announcement of sentence	SCM:	Please rise. I sentence you to __________.

[Note 38. If the sentence includes confinement, advise the accused as follows.]

SCM: You have the right to request in writing that [name of convening authority] defer your sentence to confinement. Deferment is not a form of clemency and is not the same as suspension of a sentence. It merely postpones the running of a sentence to confinement.

[Note 39. Whether or not the sentence includes confinement, advise the accused as follows.]

SCM: You have the right to submit in writing a petition or statement to the convening authority. This statement may include any matters you feel the convening authority should consider, a request for clemency, or both. This statement must be submitted within 7 days, unless you request and convening authority approves an extension of up to 20 days. After the convening authority takes action, your case will be reviewed by a judge advocate for legal error. You may suggest, in writing, legal errors for the judge advocate to consider. If, after final action has been taken in your case, you believe that there has been a legal error, you may request review of your case by The Judge Advocate General of ____________. Do you understand these rights?

ACC: ______________.

Adjourning the court-martial	SCM:	This court-martial is adjourned.

Entry on charge sheet

[Note 40. Record the sentence in the record of trial, inform the convening authority of the findings, recommendations for suspension, if any, and any deferment request. If the sentence includes confinement, arrange for the delivery of the accused to the accused's commander, or someone designated by the commander, for appropriate action. Ensure that the commander is informed of the sentence. Complete the record of trial and forward to the convening authority.]

Appendix 9 – RESERVED

THIS PAGE LEFT INTENTIONALLY BLANK.

APPENDIX 10
FORMS FOR ACTIONS (CASES REFERRED BEFORE 1 JANUARY 2019)

The Forms in this appendix are guides for preparation of the convening authority's initial action for cases referred before 1 January 2019. Guidance is also provided for actions under MCM (2016), R.C.M. 1112(f). Appendix 11 contains Forms for later actions. The Forms are guidance only, and are not mandatory. They do not provide for all cases. It may be necessary to combine parts of different Forms to prepare an action appropriate to a specific case. Extreme care should be exercised in using these Forms and in preparing actions. See MCM (2016), R.C.M. 1107(f) concerning contents of the convening authority's action.

In addition to the matters contained in the Forms below, the action should show the headquarters and place, or the ship, of the convening authority taking the action, and the date of the action. The signature of the convening authority is followed by the grade and unit of the convening authority, and "commander" or "commanding" as appropriate.

Further, convening authorities must include in the record of trial a written explanation for (1) actions on findings to dismiss or change any charge or specification of qualifying offenses, and (2) actions to disapprove, commute, or suspend the adjudged sentence for an other than qualifying offense. Written explanations are not required in cases involving at least one pre-24 June 2014 offense, even for action concerning offenses that would otherwise require written explanation. The written explanation should not be written on the action itself.

When the sentence includes confinement, the place of confinement is designated in the action unless the Secretary concerned prescribes otherwise. If the place of confinement is designated in the action, service regulations should be consulted first. *See* MCM (2016) R.C.M. 1113(e)(2)(C).

In actions on a summary court-martial, when the action is written on the record of trial (*see* Appendix 9) the words "In the case of ______________" may be omitted.

The convening authority should state in the action or elsewhere in a document maintained in the record of trial that the convening authority considered the matters required by R.C.M. 1107 and whether the convening authority considered any discretionary matters under that Rule.

INITIAL ACTION ON COURT-MARTIAL SENTENCE—FINDINGS NOT AFFECTED

Forms 1–10 are appropriate when the adjudged sentence does not include death, dismissal, or a dishonorable or bad-conduct discharge. An adjudged sentence of confinement for more than six months may not be disapproved, commuted, or suspended absent (1) a pre-trial agreement providing for such action, (2) a trial counsel recommendation for clemency for substantial assistance by the accused in the investigation and/or prosecution of another case; or (3) conviction in the same case for at least one offense occurring prior to 24 June 2014.

Adjudged sentence approved and ordered executed without modification. See MCM (2016), R.C.M. 1107(f)(4).

1. In the case of _____________ the sentence is approved and will be executed. (_______ is designated as the place of confinement.)

Adjudged sentence modified. See MCM (2016), R.C.M. 1107(d)(1), (f)(4).

Adjudged sentence approved in part and ordered executed.

2. In the case of _____________ only so much of the sentence as provides for _____________ is approved and will be executed. (__________ is designated as the place of confinement.)

Adjudged sentence approved; part of confinement changed to forfeiture of pay.

3. In the case of _____________, so much of the sentence extending to _______ months of

confinement is changed to forfeiture of $ ____ pay per month for months. The sentence as changed is approved and will be executed. (____________ is designated as the place of confinement.)

Credit for illegal pretrial confinement. See R.C.M. MCM (2016), 305(k); 1107(f)(4)(F).

In the case of ____________, the sentence is approved and will be executed. The accused will be credited with ____ days of confinement against the sentence to confinement. (_________ is designated as the place of confinement.)

Suspension of sentence. See MCM (2016), R.C.M. 1107(f)(4)(B); 1108.

Adjudged sentence approved and suspended.

5. In the case of ____________, the sentence is approved. Execution of the sentence is suspended for _______ (months) (years) at which time, unless the suspension is sooner vacated, the sentence will be remitted without further action.

Adjudged sentence approved; part of sentence suspended.

6. In the case of ____________, the sentence is approved and will be executed but the execution of that part of the sentence extending to (confinement) (confinement in excess of months) (forfeiture of pay) (__) is suspended for (months) (years), at which time, unless the suspension is sooner vacated, the suspended part of the sentence will be remitted without further action. (______ is designated as the place of confinement.)

Deferment of confinement and termination of deferment. See MCM (2016), R.C.M. 1101(c); 1107(f)(4)(E).

Adjudged sentence approved; confinement deferred pending final review.

7. In the case of ____________, the sentence is approved and, except for that portion extending to confinement, will be executed. Service of the sentence to confinement (is) (was) deferred effective (date), and will not begin until (the conviction is final) (date) (______), unless sooner rescinded by competent authority.

Adjudged sentence approved; deferment of confinement terminated.

8. In the case of ____________, the sentence is approved and will be executed. The Service of the sentence to confinement was deferred on (date). (_________ is designated as the place of confinement.)

Adjudged sentence approved; deferment of confinement terminated previously.

9. In the case of ____________, the sentence is approved and will be executed. The service of the sentence to confinement was deferred on (date), and the deferment ended on (date). (_________ is designated as the place of confinement.)

Disapproval of sentence; rehearing on sentence only ordered. See MCM (2016), R.C.M. 1107(e), (f).

10. In the case of ____________, it appears that the following error was committed: (evidence of a previous conviction of the accused was erroneously admitted) (____________). This error was prejudicial as to the sentence. The sentence is disapproved. A rehearing is ordered before a (summary) (special) (general) court-martial to be designated.

When the adjudged sentence includes death, dismissal, or a dishonorable or a bad-conduct discharge, Forms 1-10 are generally appropriate, but several will require modification depending on the action to be taken. One reason for this is because Article 60 now limits the authority to modify an adjudged dismissal, dishonorable discharge, or bad-conduct discharge. Generally, an adjudged punitive discharge may not be disapproved, commuted, or suspended, absent (1) a pre-trial agreement providing for such action, (2) a trial counsel recommendation for clemency for substantial assistance by the accused in the investigation and/or prosecution of another case, or (3) conviction in the same case for at least one offense occurring prior to 24 June 2014. For certain sex offenses occurring on or after 24 June 2014, Article 56(b) imposes a mandatory dishonorable discharge or dismissal, even when at least one offense in the same case occurs prior to 24 June 2014. When acting, pursuant to a pre-trial agreement, on a punitive discharge required by Article 56(b), Article 56(b) limits such action to commutation of the dishonorable discharge to a bad conduct discharge. This action is not authorized for dismissals pursuant to Article 56(b).

A second reason that several of the Forms require modification is that death, dismissal, or a dishonorable or bad-conduct discharge may not be ordered executed in the initial action. Therefore, unless an adjudged punishment of death, dismissal, or a dishonorable or bad-conduct discharge is disapproved, changed to another punishment, or (except in the case of death) suspended, the initial action must specifically except such punishments from the order of execution. This is done by adding the words "except for the part of the sentence extending to (death) (dismissal) (dishonorable discharge) (bad-conduct discharge)," after the words "is approved and" and before the words "will be executed" in the action. (A death sentence cannot be suspended. *See* MCM (2016), R.C.M. 1108(b).)

Forms 11-14 provide examples of actions when the sentence includes death, dismissal, or a dishonorable or bad-conduct discharge.

Adjudged sentence approved and, except for death, dismissal, or discharge, ordered executed. See MCM (2016), R.C.M. 1107(f)(4).

11. In the case of ____________, the sentence is approved and, except for the part of the sentence extending to (death) (dismissal) (dishonorable discharge) (bad-conduct discharge), will be executed. (_______ is designated as the place of confinement.)

Adjudged sentence modified. See MCM (2016), R.C.M. 1107(d)(1), (f)(4). If the part of the sentence providing for death, dismissal, or a dishonorable or a bad-conduct discharge is disapproved, *see* Form 2 above.

12. In the case of ____________, only so much of the sentence as provides for (death) (dismissal) (a dishonorable discharge) (a bad-conduct discharge) (and __________ [specify each approved punishment]) is approved and, except for the part of the sentence extending to (death) (dismissal) (dishonorable discharge) (bad-conduct discharge), will be executed. (____________ is designated as the place of confinement.)

Adjudged sentence approved; discharge changed to confinement.

13. In the case of ____________, so much of the sentence extending to a (dishonorable discharge) (bad-conduct discharge) is changed to confinement for ______ months (thereby making the period of confinement _____ total months). The sentence as changed is approved and will be executed. (____________ is designated as the place of confinement.)

Suspension of sentence. See MCM (2016), R.C.M. 1107(f)(4)(B); 1108(d). If the portion of the sentence extending to dismissal or a dishonorable or a bad-conduct discharge is suspended, Form 5 or Form 6 may be used, as appropriate. If parts of the sentence other than an approved dismissal or discharge are suspended, the following form may be used:

Adjudged sentence approved; part of sentence, other than dismissal or dishonorable or bad-conduct discharge, suspended.

14. In the case of ____________, the sentence is approved and, except for that part of the sentence extending to (dismissal) (a dishonorable discharge) (a bad-conduct discharge), will be executed, but the execution of that part of the sentence adjudging (confinement) (confinement in excess of____________) (forfeiture of pay) (__________) is suspended for ________ (months) (years) at which time, unless the suspension is sooner vacated, the suspended part of the sentence will be

remitted without further action. (_____________ is designated as the place of confinement.)

INITIAL ACTION ON COURT-MARTIAL WHEN FINDINGS AFFECTED

Findings are addressed in the action only when any findings of guilty are disapproved, in whole or part. *See* MCM (2016), R.C.M. 1107(c), (f)(3). The action must also indicate what action is being taken on the sentence. Appropriate parts of the foregoing Forms for Action on the sentence may be substituted in the following examples as necessary. Under Article 60, convening authorities may only act to dismiss or change any charge or specification if such offenses are qualifying offenses, pre-24 June 2014 offenses, or heard in the same case as a pre-24 June 2014 offense. In cases of legal error when action on findings are not authorized, convening authorities may wish to consider deferring punishment until completion of review in accordance with R.C.M. 110 1(c)(6)(A).

Some findings of guilty disapproved; adjudged sentence approved.

15. In the case of _____________, the finding of guilty of Specification 2, Charge I is disapproved. Specification 2, Charge I is dismissed. The sentence is approved and (, except for that part of the sentence extending to ((dismissal) (a dishonorable discharge) (a bad-conduct discharge),) will be executed. (_____________ is designated as the place of confinement.)

Finding of guilty of lesser included offense approved; adjudged sentence modified.

16. In the case of _____________, the finding of guilty of Specification 1, Charge II is changed to a finding of guilty of (assault with a means likely to produce grievous bodily harm, to wit: a knife) (absence without authority from the (unit) (ship) (_____________) alleged from (date) to (date) in violation of Article 86) (_____________). Only so much of the sentence as provides for _____________ is approved and (,except for the part of the sentence extending to ((dismissal) (dishonorable discharge) (bad-conduct discharge)), will be executed. (_____________ is designated as the place of confinement.)

Some findings of guilty and sentence disapproved; combined rehearing ordered. See 1107(e). A rehearing may not be ordered if any sentence is approved. *See* MCM (2016) R.C.M. 1107(c); (e).

17. In the case of _____________, it appears that the following error was committed: (Exhibit 1, a laboratory report, was not properly authenticated and was admitted over the objection of the defense) (_____________). This error was prejudicial as to Specifications 1 and 2 of Charge II. The findings of guilty as to Specifications 1 and 2 of Charge II and the sentence are disapproved. A combined rehearing is ordered before a court-martial to be designated.

All findings of guilty and sentence disapproved; rehearing ordered. See MCM (2016), R.C.M. 1107(c).

18. In the case of _____________, it appears that the following error was committed: (evidence offered by the defense to establish duress was improperly excluded) (_____________). This error was prejudicial to the rights of the accused as to all findings of guilty. The findings of guilty and the sentence are disapproved. A rehearing is ordered before a court-martial to be designated.

All findings of guilty and sentence disapproved based on jurisdictional error; another trial ordered. See MCM (2016), R.C.M. 1107(e)(3). This Form may also be used when a specification fails to state an offense.

19. In the case of _____________, it appears that (the members were not detailed to the court-martial by the convening authority) (_____________). The proceedings, findings, and sentence are invalid. Another trial is ordered before a court-martial to be designated.

All findings of guilty and sentence disapproved; charges dismissed. See MCM (2016), R.C.M. 1107(c).

20 In the case of _____________, the findings of guilty and the sentence are disapproved. The charges

are dismissed.

ACTION ON A REHEARING

The action on a rehearing is the same as an action on an original court-martial in most respects. It differs first in that, as to any sentence approved following the rehearing, the accused must be credited with those parts of the sentence previously executed or otherwise served. Second, in certain cases the convening authority must provide for the restoration of certain rights, privileges, and property. *See* MCM (2016), R.C.M. 1107(f)(5)(A). Under Article 60, convening authorities may only act to dismiss or change any charge or specification if such offenses are qualifying offenses, pre-24 June 2014 offenses, or heard in the same case as a pre-24 June 2014 offense.

Action on rehearing; granting credit for previously executed or served punishment.

21. In the case of _____________, the sentence is approved and (, except for the portion of the sentence extending to ((dismissal) (dishonorable discharge) (bad-conduct discharge)), will be executed. The accused will be credited with any portion of the punishment served from (date) to (date) under the sentence adjudged at the former trial of this case.

Action on rehearing; restoration of rights.

22. In the case of _____________, the findings of guilty and the sentence are disapproved and the charges are dismissed. All rights, privileges, and property of which the accused has been deprived by virtue of the execution of the sentence adjudged at the former trial of this case on (date) will be restored.

23. In the case of _____________, the accused was found not guilty of all the charges and specifications which were tried at the former hearing. All rights, privileges, and property of which the accused has been deprived by virtue of the execution of the sentence adjudged at the former trial of this case on (date) will be restored.

WITHDRAWAL OF PREVIOUS ACTION

Form 24 is appropriate for withdrawal of an earlier action. *See* MCM (2016), R.C.M. 1107(f)(2) concerning modification of an earlier action. Form 24a is appropriate for withdrawal of previous action pursuant to instructions from reviewing authority pursuant to MCM (2016), R.C.M. 1107(f)(2) or (g).

24. In the case of _____________, the action taken by (me) (my predecessor in command) on (date) is withdrawn and the following substituted therefor:

24a. In the case of _____________, in accordance with instructions from (The Judge Advocate General) (the Court of Criminal Appeals) pursuant to Rule for Courts-Martial [1107(f)(2)] [1107(g)], the action taken by (me) (my predecessor in command) is withdrawn. The following is substituted therefor:

_____________________.

FORMS FOR ACTIONS APPROVING AND SUSPENDING PUNISHMENTS MENTIONED IN ARTICLE 58a AND RETAINING ACCUSED IN PRESENT OR INTERMEDIATE GRADE.

Under the authority of Article 58a, the Secretary concerned may, by regulation, limit or specifically preclude the reduction in grade which would otherwise be effected under that Article upon the approval of certain court-martial sentences by the convening authority. The Secretary concerned may provide in regulations that if the convening or higher authority taking action on the case suspends those elements of the sentence that are specified in Article 58a the accused may be retained in the grade held by the accused at the time of the sentence or in any intermediate grade. Forms 25-27 may be used by the convening or higher authority in effecting actions authorized by the Secretary concerned in regulations pursuant to the authority of Article 58a.

If the convening authority or higher authority, when taking action on a case in which the sentence includes a punitive discharge, confinement, or hard labor without confinement, elects to approve the sentence and to retain the enlisted member in the grade held by that member at the time of sentence or in any intermediate grade, that authority may do so if permitted by regulations of the Secretary concerned whether or not the sentence also includes a reduction to the lowest enlisted grade, by using one of the following Forms of Action. The first action, Form 25, is appropriate when the sentence does not specifically provide for reduction. The second and third actions, Forms 26 and 27, are appropriate when the sentence specifically provides for reduction to the grade of E-1. The action set forth in Form 26 is intended for a case in which the accused is to be probationally retained in the grade held by that accused at the time of sentence. The action set forth in Form 27 is for a case in which the accused is to serve probationally in an intermediate grade.

Note that the following limitations on post-trial authority may affect the applicability of the Forms 25-27. An adjudged sentence of confinement for more than six months may not be disapproved, commuted, or suspended absent (1) a pre-trial agreement providing for such action, (2) a trial counsel recommendation for clemency for substantial assistance by the accused in the investigation and/or prosecution of another case; or (3) conviction in the same case for at least one offense occurring prior to 23 June 2014. For certain sex offenses occurring on or after 24 June 2014, Article 56(b) imposes a mandatory dishonorable discharge or dismissal, even when at least one offense in the same case occurs prior to 23 June 2014. When acting, pursuant to a pre-trial agreement, on a punitive discharge required by Article 56(b), Article 56(b) limits such action to commutation of the dishonorable discharge to a bad conduct discharge. This action is not authorized for dismissals pursuant to Article 56(b).

Automatic reduction suspended; sentence does not specifically include reduction.

25. In the case of _____________, the sentence is approved and will be executed, but the execution of that part of the sentence extending to (a dishonorable discharge) (a bad-conduct discharge) (confinement) (hard labor without confinement) (and) is suspended for (months) (years) at which time, unless the suspension is sooner vacated, the suspended part of the sentence will be remitted without further action. The accused will (continue to) serve in the grade of ___ unless the suspension of (the dishonorable discharge) (the bad-conduct discharge) (confinement) (hard labor without confinement) is vacated, in which event the accused will be reduced to the grade of E-1 at that time.

Automatic reduction and adjudged reduction to E-l suspended; accused retained in grade previously held.

26. In the case of _____________, the sentence is approved and will be executed, but the execution of that part of the sentence extending to (a dishonorable discharge) (a bad-conduct discharge) (confinement) (hard labor without confinement) (_____________), and reduction to the grade of E-1, is suspended for ___ (months) (years), at which time, unless the suspension is sooner vacated, the suspended part of the sentence will be remitted without further action. The accused will continue to serve in the grade of___ unless the suspension of (the dishonorable discharge) (the bad-conduct discharge) (confinement) (hard labor without confinement), or reduction to the grade of E-1, is vacated, in which event the accused will be reduced to the grade of E-1 at that time

Automatic reduction and adjudged reduction to E-l suspended; accused retained in intermediate grade.

27. In the case of _____________, the sentence is approved and will be executed but the execution of that part of the sentence extending to (a dishonorable discharge) (a bad-conduct discharge) (confinement) (hard labor without confinement), and that part of the reduction which is in excess of reduction to the grade of_______ is suspended for _____ (months) (years) at which time, unless the suspension is sooner vacated, the suspended part of the sentence will be remitted without further action. The accused will serve in the grade of _____ unless the suspension of (the dishonorable discharge) (bad-conduct discharge) (confinement) (hard labor without confinement), or reduction to the grade of E-1, is vacated, in which event the accused will be reduced to the grade of E-1 at that time.

ACTION UNDER MCM (2016), R.C.M. 1112(f).

The Forms for Action for the officer taking action under R.C.M. 1112(f) are generally similar to the foregoing actions. The officer taking action under R.C.M. 1112(f) may order executed all parts of the approved sentence, including a dishonorable or bad-conduct discharge, except those parts which have been suspended without later vacation unless the record must be forwarded under R.C.M. 1112(g)(1). *See* MCM (2016), R.C.M. 1113(c)(1)(A). The following are additional Forms which may be appropriate:

Sentence approved when convening authority suspended all or part of it.

28. In the case of _____________, the sentence as approved and suspended by the convening authority is approved.

Sentence approved and, when confinement was deferred, ordered executed. See MCM (2016), R.C.M. 1101(c)(6).

29. In the case of _____________, the sentence is approved and the confinement will be executed. The service of the sentence to confinement was deferred on (date). (_____________ is designated as the place of confinement.)

Sentence includes unsuspended dishonorable or bad-conduct discharge; order of execution. See MCM (2016), R.C.M. 1113(c)(1) and (2).

30. In the case of _____________, the sentence is approved. The (dishonorable discharge) (bad-conduct discharge) will be executed.

Findings and sentence disapproved; restoration as to parts ordered executed by convening authority. See MCM (2016), R.C.M. 1208.

31. In the case of _____________, the findings of guilty and the sentence are disapproved. The charges are dismissed. (The accused will be released from the confinement adjudged by the sentence in this case and all) (All) rights, privileges, and property of which the accused has been deprived by virtue of the findings and sentence disapproved will be restored.

Findings and sentence disapproved; rehearing authorized. See MCM (2016), R.C.M. 1112(f).

32. In the case of _____________, it appears that the following error was committed: (Exhibit 1, a statement of the accused, was not shown to have been preceded by Article 31 warnings as required and was admitted over the objection of the defense) (_____________). This error was prejudicial to the rights of the accused as to the findings and the sentence. The case is returned to the convening authority who may order a rehearing or dismiss the charges.

Action taken is less favorable to the accused than that recommended by the judge advocate. See MCM (2016), R.C.M. 1112(f), (g).

33. In the case of _____________, the sentence is approved. As this action is less favorable to the accused than that recommended by the judge advocate, the record and this action shall be forwarded to the Judge Advocate General for review under Article 69(b).

Action when approved sentence includes dismissal. See MCM (2016), R.C.M. 1113(c)(2).

34. In the case of _____________, the sentence is approved. The record shall be forwarded to the [Secretary concerned].

APPENDIX 11
FORMS FOR COURT-MARTIAL ORDERS
(CASES REFERRED BEFORE 1 JANUARY 2019)

a. Forms for initial promulgating orders

[Note. The following is a form applicable in promulgating the results of trial and the action of the convening authority in all general and special court-martial cases. Omit the marginal side notes in drafting orders. *See* R.C.M. 1114(c) (MCM 2016)]

Heading

(General) (Special) (Headquarters) (USS)

Court-Martial Order No. ___________ ____________________

[Note. The date must be the same as the date of the convening authority's action, if any.]

(Grade) (Name) (SSN) (Armed Force)

(Unit)

Arraignment

was arraigned (at/on board) on the following offenses at a court-martial convened by (this command) (Commander, _______________).

Offenses

CHARGE I. ARTICLE 86. Plea: G. Finding: G.

Specification 1: Unauthorized absence from unit from 1 April 1984 to 31 May 1984. Plea: G. Finding: G.

[Note. Specifications may be reproduced verbatim or may be summarized. Specific factors, such as value, amount, and other circumstances which affect the maximum punishment should be indicated in a summarized specification. Other significant matters contained in the specification may be included. If the specification is copied verbatim, include any amendment made during trial. Similarly, information included in a summarized specification should reflect any amendment to that information made during the trial.]

Specification 2: Failure to repair on 18 March 1984. Plea: None entered. Finding: Dismissed on motion of defense for failure to state an offense.

[Note. If a finding is not entered to a specification because, for example, a motion to dismiss was granted, this should be noted where the finding would otherwise appear.]

CHARGE II. ARTICLE 91. Plea: NG. Finding: NG, but G of a violation of ARTICLE 92.

Specification: Disobedience of superior noncommissioned officer on 30 March 1984 by refusing to inspect sentinels on perimeter of bivouac site. Plea: NG. Finding: G, except for disobedience of superior noncommissioned officer, substituting failure to obey a lawful order to inspect sentinels on perimeter of bivouac site.

CHARGE III. ARTICLE 112a. Plea: G. Finding: G.

Specification 1: Wrongful possession of 150 grams of marijuana on 24 March 1984. Plea: G. Finding: G.

Specification 2: Wrongful use of marijuana while on duty as a sentinel on 24 March 1984. Plea: G. Finding G.

Specification 3: Wrongful possession of heroin with intent to distribute on 24 March 1984. Plea: NG. Finding: G.

CHARGE IV. ARTICLE 121. Plea: NG. Finding: G.

Specification: Larceny of property of a value of $150.00 on 27 March 1984. Plea: NG. Finding: G, except the word "steal," substituting "wrongfully appropriate."

Acquittal

If the accused was acquitted of all charges and specifications, the date of the acquittal should be shown: "The findings were announced on ______________."

SENTENCE

Sentence adjudged on ____________ _____________: Dishonorable discharge, forfeiture of all pay and allowances, confinement for 2 years, and reduction to the lowest enlisted grade.

Action of convening authority

ACTION

[Note. Summarize or enter verbatim the action of the convening authority. Whether or not the action is recited verbatim, the heading, date, and signature block of the convening authority need not be copied from the action if the same heading and date appear at the top of this order and if the name and rank of the convening authority are shown in the authentication.]

Authentication

[Note. *See* R.C.M. 1114(e) concerning authentication of the order.]

Joint or common trial

[Note. In case of a joint or common trial, separate trial orders should be issued for each accused. The description of the offenses on which each accused was arraigned may, but need not, indicate that there was a co-accused.]

b. *Forms for supplementary orders promulgating results of affirming action*

[Note. Court-martial orders publishing the final results of cases in which the President or the Secretary concerned has taken final action are promulgated by departmental orders. In other cases, the final action may be promulgated by an appropriate convening authority, or by an officer exercising general court-martial jurisdiction over the accused at the time of final action, or by the Secretary concerned. The following sample forms may be used where such a promulgating order is published in the field. These forms are guides. Extreme care should be exercised in using them. If a sentence as ordered into execution or suspended by the convening authority is affirmed without modifications and there has been no modification of the findings, no supplementary promulgating order is required.]

Heading

**See* above.

Sentence

-Affirmed

In the (general) (special) court-martial case of *(name, grade or rank, branch of service, and SSN of accused,)* the sentence to bad-conduct discharge, forfeiture of, and confinement for, as promulgated in (General) (Special) Court-Martial Order No. _________, (Headquarters) (Commandant ________, Naval Region) ________ dated , has been finally affirmed. Article 71(c) having been complied with, the bad-conduct discharge will be executed.

or

-Affirmed in part

In the (general) (special) court-martial case of *(name, grade or rank, branch of service, and SSN of accused,)* only so much of the sentence promulgated in (General) (Special) Court-Martial Order No. ____, (Headquarters) (Commandant, _____ Naval Region) _____, dated _____, as provides for _____, has been finally affirmed. Article 71(c) having been complied with, the bad-conduct discharge will be executed.

or

In the (general) (special) court-martial case of *(name, grade or rank, branch of service, and SSN of accused,)* the findings of guilty of Charge II and its specification have been set aside and only so much of the sentence promulgated in (General) (Special) Court-Martial Order No. _____, (Headquarters) (Commandant, _____, Naval Region) _____, dated _____, as provides for _____, has been finally affirmed. Article 71(c) having been complied with, the bad-conduct discharge will be executed.

or

Affirmed in part; prior order of execution set aside in part

In the (general) (special) court-martial case of *(name, grade or rank, branch of service, and SSN of accused,)* the proceedings of which are promulgated in (General) (Special) Court-Martial Order No. ____, (Headquarters) (Commandant, _____Naval Region) _____, dated _____, the findings of guilty of Charge I and its specification, and so much of the sentence as in excess of have been set aside and the sentence, as thus modified, has been finally affirmed. Article 71(c) having been complied with, all rights, privileges, and property of which the accused has been deprived by virtue of the findings of guilty and that portion of the sentence so set aside will be restored.

Finding and sentence set aside

In the (general)(special) court-martial case of *(name, grade or rank, branch of service, and SSN, of accused,)* the findings of guilty and the sentence promulgated by (General) (Special) Court-Martial Order No. _____, (Headquarters) (Commandant, _____Naval Region), _____, dated _____, were set aside on _____. (The charges are dismissed. All rights, privileges, and property of which the accused has been deprived by virtue of the findings of guilty and the sentence so set aside will be restored.) (A rehearing is ordered before another court-martial to be designated.)

Authentication

See R.C.M. 1114(e).

c. *Forms for orders remitting or suspending unexecuted portions of sentence*

Heading

See a above

Remissions; suspension
See R.C.M. 1108

The unexecuted portion of the sentence to _____, in the case of *(Name, grade or rank, branch of service and SSN of accused,)* promulgated in (General) (Special) Court-Martial Order No. _____, (this headquarters) (this ship) (Headquarters _____) (USS _____), _____, _____, is (remitted) (suspended for _____, months, at which time, unless the suspension is sooner vacated, the unexecuted portion of the sentence will be remitted without further action).

Authentication

See R.C.M. 1114(e).

d. *Forms for orders vacating suspension*

[Note. Orders promulgating the vacation of the suspension of a dismissal will be published by departmental orders of the Secretary concerned. Vacations of any other suspension of a general court-martial sentence, or of a special court-martial sentence that as approved and affirmed includes a bad-conduct discharge or confinement for one year, will be promulgated by the officer exercising general court-martial jurisdiction over the probationer (Article 72(b)). The vacation of suspension of any other sentence may be promulgated by an appropriate convening authority under Article 72(c). See R.C.M. 1109.]

Heading — *See a* above

Vacation of Suspension — So much of the order published in (General) (Special) (Summary) (Court-Martial Order No. _____) (the record of summary court-martial), (this headquarters) (this ship) (Headquarters _____) (USS _____), _____. _____, in the case of *(name, grade or rank, branch of service, and SSN)*, as suspends, effective _____, execution of the approved sentence to (a bad-conduct discharge) (confinement for (months) (years)) (forfeiture of _____), (and subsequently modified by (General) (Special) Court-Martial Order No. _____, (this headquarters) (this ship) (Headquarters _____) (USS _____), _____. _____, is vacated. (The unexecuted portion of the sentence to will be executed.) (_____is designated as the place of confinement.)

[Note. *See* R.C.M. 1113 concerning execution of the sentence.]

Authentication — *See* R.C.M. 1114(e).

e. *Forms for orders terminating deferment*

[Note: When any deferment previously granted is rescinded after the convening authority has taken action in the case, such rescission will be promulgated in a supplementary order. *See* R.C.M. 1101(c)(7)(C).]

Heading — *See a* above

Rescission of deferment — The deferment of that portion of the sentence that provides for confinement for (months) (years) published in (General) (Special) Court-Martial Order _____ (this headquarters) (this ship) (Headquarters _____) (USS _____), _____, in the case of *(name, grade or rank, branch of service, and SSN of accused)* (is rescinded) (was rescinded on _____.) The portion of the sentence to confinement will be executed. (_____ is designated as the place of confinement.)

Authentication — *See* R.C.M. 1114(e).

[Note. Deferment may be terminated by an appropriate authority once the conviction is final under Article 71(c) and R.C.M. 1208(a). *See* R.C.M. 1101(c)(7).]

Heading — *See a* above

In the (general) (special) court-martial case of *(name, grade or rank, branch of service, and SSN of accused,)* the sentence to confinement (and _____), as promulgated in (General) (Special) Court-Martial Order No. _____, (Headquarters) (Commandant, _____ Naval Region) _____, dated _____, has been finally affirmed. Service of confinement was deferred on _____. Article 71(c) having been complied with, the (bad-conduct discharge and the) sentence to confinement will be executed. (_____ is designated as the place of confinement.)

Authentication — *See* R.C.M. 1114(e).

APPENDIX 12
MAXIMUM PUNISHMENT CHART

This chart was compiled for convenience purposes only and is not the authority for specific punishments. See Part IV and R.C.M. 1003 for specific limits and additional information concerning maximum punishments.

Article	*Offense*	*Discharge*	*Confinement*	*Forfeitures*
77	Principals (*see* Part IV, Para. 1 and pertinent offenses)			
78	Accessory after the fact (*see* Part IV, Para. 2.d.)			
79	Conviction of offense charged, lesser included offenses, and attempts (*see* Part IV, Para. 3 and pertinent offenses)			
80	Attempts (*see* Part IV, Para. 4.d.)			
81	Conspiracy (*see* Part IV, Para. 5.d.)			
82	Soliciting commission of offenses			
	Solicitation of espionage	DD, BCD	Life[4]	Total
	Solicitation of desertion; mutiny or sedition; misbehavior before the enemy (*see* Part IV, Para 6.d.2.)			
	Solicitation of all other offenses (*see* Part IV, Para 6.d.3.)			
83	Malingering			
	Feigning illness, physical disablement, mental lapse, or mental derangement			
	In time of war, or in a hostile pay zone	DD, BCD	3 yrs.	Total
	Other	DD, BCD	1 yr.	Total
	Intentional self-inflicted injury			
	In time of war, or in a hostile fire pay zone	DD, BCD	10 yrs.	Total
	Other	DD, BCD	5 yrs.	Total
84	Breach of medical quarantine			
	Breach of medical quarantine involving a quarantinable communicable disease defined by 42 CFR 70.1	DD, BCD	1 yr.	Total
	Breach of medical quarantine	BCD	6 mos.	2/3 6 mos.
85	Desertion			
	In time of war	Death, DD, BCD	Life[4]	Total
	Intent to avoid hazardous duty or to shirk important services[1]	DD, BCD	5 yrs.[1]	Total
	Other cases			
	Terminated by apprehension	DD, BCD	3 yrs.[1]	Total
	Terminated otherwise	DD, BCD	2 yrs.[1]	Total
86	Absence without leave			
	Failing to go, going from appointed place of duty	None	1 mo.	2/3 1 mo.
	Absence from unit, organization, etc.			
	Not more than 3 days	None	1 mo.	2/3 1 mo.
	More than 3, not more than 30 days	None	6 mos.	2/3 6 mos.
	More than 30 days	DD, BCD	1 yr.	Total
	More than 30 days and terminated by apprehension	DD, BCD	18 mos.	Total
	Absence from guard or watch	None	3 mos.	2/3 3 mos.
	Absence from guard or watch with intent to abandon	BCD	6 mos.	Total
	Absence with intent to avoid maneuvers or field exercises	BCD	6 mos.	Total
87	Missing movement; jumping from vessel			
	Missing movement			
	Design	DD, BCD	2 yrs.	Total
	Neglect	BCD	1 yr.	Total
	Jumping from vessel into the water	BCD	6 mos.	Total
87a	Resistance, flight, breach of arrest, and escape			
	Resisting apprehension	BCD	1 yr.	Total
	Flight from apprehension	BCD	1 yr.	Total
	Breaking arrest	BCD	6 mos.	Total
	Escape from custody, pretrial confinement, or confinement pursuant to Article 15	DD, BCD	1 yr.	Total
	Escape from post-trial confinement	DD, BCD	5 yrs.	Total
87b	Offenses against correctional custody and restriction			
	Escape from correctional custody	DD, BCD	1 yr.	Total
	Breach of correctional custody	BCD	6 mos.	Total
	Breach of restriction	None	1 mo.	2/3 1 mo.
88	Contempt toward officials	Dismissal	1 yr.	Total

APPENDIX 12

This chart was compiled for convenience purposes only and is not the authority for specific punishments. See Part IV and R.C.M. 1003 for specific limits and additional information concerning maximum punishments.

Article	*Offense*	*Discharge*	*Confinement*	*Forfeitures*
89	Disrespect toward superior commissioned officer; assault of superior commissioned officer			
	Disrespect toward superior commissioned officer			
	In command	BCD	1 yr.	Total
	In rank	BCD	6 mos.	Total
	Striking, drawing or lifting up a weapon or offering any violence to superior commissioned officer in execution of office			
	In time or war	Death, DD, BCD	Life[4]	Total
	Other[1]	DD, BCD	10 yrs.[1]	Total
90	Willfully disobeying superior commissioned officer			
	In time of war	Death, DD, BCD	Life[4]	Total
	Other[1]	DD, BCD	5 yrs.[1]	Total
91	Insubordinate conduct toward warrant officer, noncommissioned officer, or petty officer			
	Striking or assaulting:			
	Warrant officer	DD, BCD	5 yrs.	Total
	Superior noncommissioned or petty officer	DD, BCD	3 yrs.	Total
	Other noncommissioned or petty officer	DD, BCD	1 yr.	Total
	Willfully disobeying:			
	Warrant officer	DD, BCD	2 yrs.	Total
	Noncommissioned or petty officer	BCD	1 yr.	Total
	Contempt or disrespect:			
	Warrant officer	BCD	9 mos.	Total
	Superior noncommissioned or petty officer	BCD	6 mos.	Total
	Other noncommissioned or petty officer	None	3 mos.	2/3 3 mos.
92	Failure to obey order or regulation			
	Violation of or failure to obey general order or regulation[2]	DD, BCD	2 yrs.	Total
	Violation of or failure to obey other lawful order[2]	BCD	6 mos.	Total
	Dereliction in performance of duties			
	Through neglect or culpable inefficiency	None	3 mos.	2/3 3 mos.
	Through neglect or culpable inefficiency resulting in death or grievous bodily harm	BCD	18 mos.	Total
	Willful	BCD	6 mos.	Total
	Willful dereliction of duty resulting in death or grievous bodily harm	DD, BCD	2 yrs.	Total
93	Cruelty and maltreatment	DD, BCD	3 yrs.	Total
93a	Prohibited activities with military recruit or trainee by person in position of special trust	DD, BCD	5 yrs.	Total
94	Mutiny or sedition	Death, DD, BCD	Life[4]	Total
95	Offenses by sentinel or lookout			
	Drunk or sleeping on post, or leaving post before being relieved			
	In time of war	Death, DD, BCD	Life[4]	Total
	While receiving special pay under 37 USC 310	DD, BCD	10 yrs.	Total
	In all other places	DD, BCD	1 yr.	Total
	Loitering or wrongfully sitting on post by a sentinel or lookout			
	In time of war or while receiving special pay under 37 USC 310	DD, BCD	2 yrs.	Total
	Other cases	BCD	6 mos.	Total
95a	Disrespect toward sentinel or lookout	None	3 mos.	2/3 3 mos.
96	Release of prisoner without authority; drinking with prisoner			
	Releasing a prisoner without authority	DD, BCD	2 yrs.	Total
	Allowing a prisoner to escape through neglect	BCD	2 yrs.	Total
	Allowing a prisoner to escape through design	DD, BCD	5 yrs.	Total
	Drinking with prisoner	None	1 yr.	2/3 1 yr.
97	Unlawful Detention	DD, BCD	3 yrs.	Total
98	Misconduct as prisoner	DD, BCD	Life[4]	Total
99	Misbehavior before the enemy	Death, DD, BCD	Life[4]	Total
100	Subordinate compelling surrender	Death, DD, BCD	Life[4]	Total
101	Improper use of countersign	Death, DD, BCD	Life[4]	Total
102	Forcing a safeguard	Death, DD, BCD	Life[4]	Total

MAXIMUM PUNISHMENT CHART

This chart was compiled for convenience purposes only and is not the authority for specific punishments. See Part IV and R.C.M. 1003 for specific limits and additional information concerning maximum punishments.

Article	*Offense*	*Discharge*	*Confinement*	*Forfeitures*
103	Spies	Death, DD, BCD	Life[4]	Total
103a	Espionage			
	Espionage as a capital offense	Death, DD, BCD	Life[4]	Total
	Espionage or attempted espionage	DD, BCD	Life[4]	Total
103b	Aiding the enemy	Death, DD, BCD	Life[4]	Total
104	Public records offenses	DD, BCD	3 yrs.	Total
104a	Fraudulent enlistment, appointment, or separation			
	Fraudulent enlistment or appointment	DD, BCD	2 yrs.	Total
	Fraudulent separation	DD, BCD	5 yrs.	Total
104b	Unlawful enlistment, appointment, or separation	DD, BCD	5 yrs.	Total
105	Forgery	DD, BCD	5 yrs.	Total
105a	False or unauthorized pass offenses			
	Possessing or using with intent to defend or deceive, or making, altering, counterfeiting, tampering with, or selling	DD, BCD	3 yrs.	Total
	All other cases	BCD	6 mos.	Total
106	Impersonation of officer, noncommissioned or petty officer, or agent or official			
	With intent to defraud	DD, BCD	3 yrs.	Total
	All other cases	BCD	6 mos.	Total
106a	Wearing unauthorized insignia, decoration, badge, ribbon, device, or lapel button			
	Wrongful wearing of the Medal of Honor; Distinguished Service Cross; Navy Cross; Air Force Cross; Silver Star; Purple Heart; or a valor device on any personal award	BDC	1 yr.	Total
	All other cases	BCD	6 mos.	Total
107	False official statements; false swearing			
	False official statement	DD, BCD	5 yrs.	Total
	False swearing	DD, BCD	3 yrs.	Total
107a	Parole violation	BCD	6 mos.	2/3 6 mos.
108	Military property; loss, damage, destruction, disposition			
	Selling or otherwise disposing			
	Of a value of $1,000 or less	BCD	1 yr.	Total
	Of a value of more than $1,000 or any firearm or explosive	DD, BCD	10 yrs.	Total
	Damaging, destroying, losing or suffering to be lost, damaged, destroyed, sold, or wrongfully disposed:			
	Through neglect, of a value or damage of			
	$1,000 or less	None	6 mos.	2/3 6 mos.
	More than $1,000	BCD	1 yr.	Total
	Willfully, of a value or damage of			
	$1,000 or less	BCD	1 yr.	Total
	More than $1,000, or of any firearm or explosive	DD, BCD	10 yrs.	Total
108a	Captured or abandoned property			
	Captured, abandoned property; failure to secure, etc.			
	Of a value of $1,000 or less	BCD	6 mos.	Total
	Of a value of more than $1,000 or any firearm or explosive	DD, BCD	5 yrs.	Total
	Looting or pillaging	DD, BCD	Life[4]	Total
109	Property other than military property of United States: Waste, spoilage, or destruction			
	Wasting or spoiling, non-military property – real property of a value of:			
	$1,000 or less	BCD	1 yr.	Total
	More than $1,000	DD, BCD	5 yrs.	Total
	Damaging any property other than military property of the United States of:			
	$1,000 or less	BCD	1 yr.	Total
	More than $1,000	DD, BCD	5 yrs.	Total
	Destroying any property other than military property of the United States valued at:			
	$1,000 or less	BCD	1 yr.	Total

APPENDIX 12

This chart was compiled for convenience purposes only and is not the authority for specific punishments. See Part IV and R.C.M. 1003 for specific limits and additional information concerning maximum punishments.

Article	*Offense*	*Discharge*	*Confinement*	*Forfeitures*
	More than $1,000	DD, BCD	5 yrs.	Total
109a	Mail matter: Wrongful taking, opening, etc.	DD, BCD	5 yrs.	Total
110	Improper hazarding of vessel or aircraft			
	Willfully and wrongfully	Death, DD, BCD	Life[4]	Total
	Negligently	DD, BCD	2 yrs.	Total
111	Leaving scene of vehicle accident	BCD	6 mos.	Total
112	Drunkenness and other incapacitation offenses			
	Drunk on duty	BCD	9 mos.	Total
	Incapacitation for duty from drunkenness or drug use	None	3 mos.	2/3 3 mos.
	Drunk prisoner	None	3 mos.	2/3 3 mos.
112a	Wrongful use, possession, etc., of controlled substances			
	Wrongful use, possession, manufacture, or introduction of controlled substance			
	Amphetamine, cocaine, heroin, lysergic acid diethylamide, marijuana (except possession of less than 30 grams or use of marijuana), methamphetamine, opium, phencyclidine, secobarbital, and Schedule I, II, III controlled substances	DD, BCD	5 yrs.	Total
	Marijuana (possession of less than 30 grams or use), phenobarbital, and Schedule IV and V controlled substances	DD, BCD	2 yrs.	Total
	Wrongful distribution, possession, manufacture, or introduction of controlled substance with intent to distribute, or wrongful importation or exportation of a controlled substance			
	Amphetamine, cocaine, heroin, lysergic and diethylamide, marijuana, methamphetamine, opium, phencyclidine, secobarbital, and schedule I, II, and III controlled substances	DD, BCD	15 yrs.	Total
	Phenobarbital and Schedule IV and V controlled substances	DD, BCD	10 yrs.	Total
113	Drunken or reckless operation of a vehicle, aircraft, or vessel			
	Resulting in personal injury	DD, BCD	18 mos.	Total
	No personal injury involved	BCD	6 mos.	Total
114	Endangerment offenses	DD, BCD	1 yr.	Total
115	Communicating threats			
	Threats and false threats generally	DD, BCD	3 yrs.	Total
	Threats and false threats concerning use of explosives, etc.	DD, BCD	10 yrs.	Total
116	Riot or breach of peace			
	Riot	DD, BCD	10 yrs.	Total
	Breach of the peace	None	6 mos.	2/3 6 mos.
117	Provoking speeches or gestures	None	6 mos.	2/3 6 mos.
117a	Wrongful broadcast or distribution of intimate visual images	DD, BCD	2 yrs.	Total
118	Murder			
	Article 118(1) or (4)	Death, mandatory minimum life with parole, DD, BCD	Life[4]	Total
	Article 118(2) or (3)	DD, BCD	Life[4]	Total
119	Manslaughter			
	Voluntary manslaughter	DD, BCD	15 yrs.	Total
	Involuntary manslaughter	DD, BCD	10 yrs.	Total
	Voluntary manslaughter of a child under 16 years of age	DD, BCD	20 yrs.	Total
	Involuntary manslaughter of a child under 16 years of age	DD, BCD	15 yrs.	Total
119a	Death or injury of an unborn child (*see* Part IV, para 58.d.)			
119a	Injuring or killing an unborn child	Such punishment, other than death, as a court-martial may direct, but such punishment shall be consistent with the punishment had the bodily injury or death occurred to the		

MAXIMUM PUNISHMENT CHART

This chart was compiled for convenience purposes only and is not the authority for specific punishments. See Part IV and R.C.M. 1003 for specific limits and additional information concerning maximum punishments.

Article	*Offense*	*Discharge*	*Confinement*	*Forfeitures*
		unborn child's mother.		
	Attempting to kill an unborn child	Such punishment, other than death, as a court-martial may direct, but such punishment shall be consistent with the punishment had the attempt been made to kill the unborn child's mother.		
	Intentionally killing an unborn child	Such punishment, other than death, as a court-martial may direct, but such punishment shall be consistent with the punishment had the death occurred to the unborn child's mother.		
119b	Child endangerment			
	Endangerment by design resulting in grievous bodily harm	DD, BCD	8 yrs.	Total
	Endangerment by design resulting in harm	DD, BCD	5 yrs.	Total
	Other cases by design	DD, BCD	4 yrs.	Total
	Endangerment by culpable negligence resulting in grievous bodily harm	DD, BCD	3 yrs.	Total
	Endangerment by culpable negligence resulting in harm	BCD	2 yrs.	Total
	Other cases by culpable negligence	BCD	1 yr.	Total
120	Rape and sexual assault generally			
	Rape	Mandatory DD[5]	Life[4]	Total
	Sexual assault	Mandatory DD[5]	30 yrs.	Total
	Aggravated sexual contact	DD, BCD	20 yrs.	Total
	Abusive sexual contact	DD, BCD	7 yrs.	Total
120a	Mails: deposit of obscene matter	DD, BCD	3 yrs.	Total
120b	Rape and sexual assault of a child			
	Rape of a child	Mandatory DD[5]	Life[4]	Total
	Sexual assault of a child	Mandatory DD[5]	30 yrs.	Total
	Sexual abuse of a child			
	Cases involving sexual contact	DD, BCD	20 yrs.	Total
	Other cases	DD, BCD	15 yrs.	Total
120c	Other sexual misconduct			
	Indecent viewing	DD, BCD	1 yr.	Total
	Indecent recording	DD, BCD	5 yrs.	Total
	Broadcasting or distributing of an indecent recording	DD, BCD	7 yrs.	Total
	Forcible pandering	DD, BCD	20 yrs.	Total
	Indecent exposure	DD, BCD	1 yr.	Total
	[Note: The Article 120, 120b, and 120c maximum punishments apply to offenses committed after 1 January 2019. *See* Appendices 17, 20, 21, and 20.]			
121	Larceny and wrongful appropriation			
	Larceny			
	Property of a value of $1,000 or less	BCD	1 yr.	Total
	Military property of a value of more than $1,000 or of any military motor vehicle, aircraft, vessel, firearm, or explosive.	DD, BCD	10 yrs.	Total

APPENDIX 12

This chart was compiled for convenience purposes only and is not the authority for specific punishments. See Part IV and R.C.M. 1003 for specific limits and additional information concerning maximum punishments.

Article	*Offense*	*Discharge*	*Confinement*	*Forfeitures*
	Property other than military property of a value of more than $1,000 or any motor vehicle, aircraft, vessel, firearm, or explosive not included in subparagraph d.(1)(b)	DD, BCD	5 yrs.	Total
	Wrongful appropriation			
	Of a value of $1,000 or less	None	3 mos.	2/3 3 mos.
	Of a value of more than $1,000	BCD	1 yr.	Total
	Of any motor vehicle, aircraft, vessel, firearm, explosive, or military property of a value of more than $1,000	DD, BCD	2 yrs.	Total
121a	Fraudulent use of credit cards, debit cards, and other access devices			
	Fraudulent use of a credit card, debit card, or other access device to obtain property of a value of $1,000 or less	BCD	10 yrs.	Total
	Fraudulent use during any 1-year period of a credit card, debit card, or other access device to obtain property the aggregate value of which is more than $1,000	DD, BCD	15 yrs.	Total
121b	False pretenses to obtain services			
	Of a value of $1,000 or less	BCD	1 yr.	Total
	Of a value of more than $1,000	DD, BCD	5 yrs.	Total
122	Robbery			
	When committed with a dangerous weapon	DD, BCD	15 yrs.	Total
	All other cases	DD, BCD	10 yrs.	Total
122a	Receiving stolen property			
	Receiving, buying, or concealing stolen property of a value of $1,000 or less	BCD	1 yr.	Total
	Receiving, buying, or concealing stolen property of a value of more than $1,000	DD, BCD	3 yrs.	Total
123	Offenses concerning Government computers			
	Unauthorized distribution of classified information obtained from a Government computer	DD, BCD	10 yrs.	Total
	Unauthorized access of a Government computer and obtaining classified or other protected information	DD, BCD	5 yrs.	Total
	Causing damage to a Government computer	DD, BCD	10 yrs.	Total
123a	Making, drawing, or uttering check, draft, or order without sufficient funds			
	For the procurement of any article or thing of value, with intent to defraud, in the face amount of:			
	$1,000 or less	BCD	6 mos.	Total
	More than $1,000	DD, BCD	5 yrs.	Total
	For the payment of any past due obligation, or for any other purpose, with intent to deceive	BCD	6 mos.	Total
124	Frauds against the United States			
	Article 124(1) and (2)	DD, BCD	5 yrs.	Total
	Article 124(3) and (4)			
	When amount is $1,000 or less	BCD	6 mos.	Total
	When amount is more than $1,000	DD, BCD	5 yrs.	Total
124a	Bribery	DD, BCD	5 yrs.	Total
124b	Graft	DD, BCD	3 yrs.	Total
125	Kidnapping	DD, BCD	Life[4]	Total
126	Arson; burning property with intent to defraud			
	Aggravated arson	DD, BCD	25 yrs.	Total
	Simple arson, where property value is:			
	$1,000 or less	DD, BCD	5 yrs.	Total
	More than $1,000	DD, BCD	10 yrs.	Total
	Burning with intent to defraud	DD, BCD	10 yrs.	Total
127	Extortion	DD, BCD	3 yrs.	Total
128	Assault			
	Simple assault			
	Generally	None	3 mos.	2/3 3 mos.
	When committed with a firearm/other dangerous weapon	DD, BCD	2 yrs.	Total
	When committed with a loaded firearm	DD, BCD	4 yrs.	Total

MAXIMUM PUNISHMENT CHART

This chart was compiled for convenience purposes only and is not the authority for specific punishments. See Part IV and R.C.M. 1003 for specific limits and additional information concerning maximum punishments.

Article	*Offense*	*Discharge*	*Confinement*	*Forfeitures*
	Battery			
	Assault consummated by a battery	BCD	6 mos.	Total
	Assault upon a commissioned officer of the armed forces of the United States or of a friendly foreign power, not in the execution of office	DD, BCD	3 yrs.	Total
	Assault upon a warrant officer, not in the execution of office	DD, BCD	18 mos.	Total
	Assault upon a noncommissioned or petty officer, not in the execution of office	BCD	6 mos.	Total
	Assault upon a sentinel or lookout in the execution of duty, or upon any person who, in the execution of office, is performing security police, military police, shore patrol, master at arms, or other military or civilian law enforcement duties	DD, BCD	3 yrs.	Total
	Assault consummated by a battery upon a child under 16 years, spouse, intimate partner, or an immediate family member	DD, BCD	2 yrs.	Total
	Aggravated assault			
	Aggravated assault with a dangerous weapon			
	When committed with a loaded firearm	DD, BCD	8 yrs.	Total
	When committed upon a child under the age of 16 years, spouse, intimate partner, or an immediate family member	DD, BCD	5 yrs.	Total
	Other cases	DD, BCD	3 yrs.	Total
	Aggravated assault in which substantial bodily harm in inflicted			
	When the injury is inflicted with a loaded firearm	DD, BCD	8 yrs.	Total
	When the injury is inflicted upon a child under the age of 16 years, spouse, intimate partner, or an immediate family member	DD, BCD	6 yrs.	Total
	Other cases	DD, BCD	3 yrs.	Total
	Aggravated assault in which grievous bodily harm is inflicted			
	When the injury is inflicted with a loaded firearm	DD, BCD	10 yrs.	Total
	When the injury is inflicted upon a child under the age of 16 years, spouse, intimate partner, or an immediate family member	DD, BCD	8 yrs.	Total
	Other cases	DD, BCD	5 yrs.	Total
	Assault with intent to commit specified offenses			
	Assault with the intent to commit murder, rape, or rape of a child	DD, BCD	20 yrs.	Total
	Assault with intent to commit voluntary manslaughter, robbery, arson, burglary, and kidnapping	DD, BCD	10 yrs.	Total
128a	Maiming	DD, BCD	20 yrs.	Total
128b	Domestic Violence			
	Commission of a violent offense against a spouse, an intimate partner, or an immediate family member.	DD, BCD	Underlying offense plus 3 yrs.	Total
	Commission of a violation of the UCMJ against any person with the intent to threaten or intimidate a spouse, an intimate partner, or an immediate family member of that person	DD, BCD	Underlying offense plus 3 yrs.	Total
	Commission of a violation of the UCMJ against any property, including an animal, with the intent to threaten or intimidate a spouse, intimate partner, or an immediate family member of that person	DD, BCD	Underlying offense plus 3 yrs.	Total
	Violation of a protective order with the intent to threaten or intimidate a spouse, an intimate partner, or an immediately family member of that person	DD, BCD	3 yrs.	Total
	Violation of a protective order with the intent to commit a violent offense against a spouse, an intimate partner, or an immediate family member of that person	DD, BCD	5 yrs.	Total
	Assaulting a spouse, an intimate partner, or an immediate family member of that person by strangulation or suffocation			
	Aggravated assault by strangulation or suffocation when committed upon a child under the age of 16 years.	DD, BCD	11 yrs.	Total
	Other cases	DD, BCD	8 yrs.	Total

APPENDIX 12

This chart was compiled for convenience purposes only and is not the authority for specific punishments. See Part IV and R.C.M. 1003 for specific limits and additional information concerning maximum punishments.

Article	*Offense*	*Discharge*	*Confinement*	*Forfeitures*
129	Burglary; unlawful entry			
	Burglary (with intent to commit an offense punishable under Article 118-120, 120b-121, 122, 125-128a, or 130)	DD, BCD	10 yrs.	Total
	Burglary (with intent to commit any other offense punishable under the UCMJ)	DD, BCD	5 yrs.	Total
	Unlawful entry	BCD	6 mos.	Total
130	Stalking	DD, BCD	3 yrs.	Total
131	Perjury	DD, BCD	5 yrs.	Total
131a	Subornation of perjury	DD, BCD	5 yrs.	Total
131b	Obstructing justice	DD, BCD	5 yrs.	Total
131c	Misprision of serious offense	DD, BCD	3 yrs.	Total
131d	Wrongful refusal to testify	DD, BCD	5 yrs.	Total
131e	Prevention of authorized seizure of property	DD, BCD	5 yrs.	Total
131f	Noncompliance with procedural rules			
	Unnecessary delay in disposing of case	BCD	6 mos.	Total
	Knowingly and intentionally failing to enforce or comply with provisions of the UCMJ	DD, BCD	5 yrs.	Total
131g	Wrongful interference with adverse administrative proceedings	DD, BCD	5 yrs.	Total
132	Retaliation	DD, BCD	3 yrs.	Total
133	Conduct unbecoming an officer	Dismissal	1 yr. or as prescribed	Total
134	Animal abuse			
	Abuse, neglect, or abandonment of an animal	BCD	1 yr.	Total
	Abuse, neglect, or abandonment of a public animal	BCD	2 yrs.	Total
	Sexual act with an animal or cases where the accused caused the serious injury or death of the animal	DD, BCD	5 yrs.	Total
	Bigamy	DD, BCD	2 yrs.	Total
	Check, worthless making and uttering – by dishonorably failing to maintain funds	BCD	6 mos.	Total
	Child pornography			
	Possessing, receiving, or viewing child pornography	DD, BCD	10 yrs.	Total
	Possessing child pornography with intent to distribute	DD, BCD	15 yrs.	Total
	Distributing child pornography	DD, BCD	20 yrs.	Total
	Producing child pornography	DD, BCD	30 yrs.	Total
	Debt, dishonorably failing to pay	BCD	6 mos.	Total
	Disloyal statements	DD, BCD	3 yrs.	Total
	Disorderly conduct, drunkenness			
	Disorderly conduct			
	Under such circumstances as to bring discredit upon the military Service	None	4 mos.	2/3 4 mos.
	Other cases	None	1 mo.	2/3 1 mo.
	Drunkenness			
	Aboard ship or under such circumstances as to bring discredit upon the military Service	None	3 mos.	2/3 3 mos.
	Other cases	None	1 mo.	2/3 1 mo.
	Drunk and disorderly			
	Aboard ship	BCD	6 mos.	Total
	Under such circumstances as to bring discredit upon the military Service	None	6 mos.	2/3 6 mos.
	Other cases	None	3 mos.	2/3 3 mos.
	Extramarital sexual conduct	DD, BCD	1 yr.	Total
	Firearm, discharging – through negligence	None	3 mos.	2/3 3 mos.
	Fraternization	Dismissal	2 yrs.	Total
	Gambling with subordinate	None	3 mos.	2/3 3 mos.
	Homicide, negligent	DD, BCD	3 yrs.	Total
	Indecent conduct	DD, BCD	5 yrs.	Total
	Indecent language			
	Communicated to any child under the age of 16 years	DD, BCD	2 yrs.	Total
	Other cases	BCD	6 mos.	Total

MAXIMUM PUNISHMENT CHART

This chart was compiled for convenience purposes only and is not the authority for specific punishments. See Part IV and R.C.M. 1003 for specific limits and additional information concerning maximum punishments.

Article	*Offense*	*Discharge*	*Confinement*	*Forfeitures*
	Pandering and prostitution			
	Prostitution and patronizing a prostitute	DD, BCD	1 yr.	Total
	Pandering	DD, BCD	5 yrs.	Total
	Self-injury without intent to avoid service			
	In time of war or in a hostile fire pay zone	DD, BCD	5 yrs.	Total
	Intentional self-inflicted injury	DD, BCD	2 yrs.	Total
134	Sexual Harassment	DD, BCD	2 yrs.	Total
134	Straggling	None	3 mos.	2/3 3 mos.

Notes:

1. Suspended in time of war

2. *See* paragraph 18d(1) & (2) Note, Part IV

3. When any offense under paragraph 50, Part IV, is committed: while the accused is on duty as a sentinel or lookout; on board a vessel or aircraft used by or under the control of the armed forces; in or at a missile launch facility used by or under the control of the armed forces; while receiving special pay under 37 U.S.C. sec. 310; in time of war; or in a confinement facility used by or under the control of the armed forces, the maximum period of confinement authorized for such offense shall be increase by 5 years.

4. With or without the eligibility for parole.

5. A dishonorable discharge may be reduced to a bad-conduct discharge by the convening authority in accordance with a plea agreement.

APPENDIX 12A

PRESIDENTIALLY-PRESCRIBED LESSER INCLUDED OFFENSES PURSUANT TO ARTICLE 79(b)(2), UNIFORM CODE OF MILITARY JUSTICE

This authoritative list provides actual notice of factually similar lesser included offenses designated by the President, pursuant to Article 79(b)(2), that are "reasonably included" in the greater offense. The military justice system has unique, but closely related, military offenses, which are not "necessarily included" lesser offenses under the "elements test." *See United States v. Teters*, 37 M.J. 370 (C.A.A.F. 1993); *see also United States v. Jones*, 68 M.J. 465 (C.A.A.F. 2009). This list is exhaustive as to those lesser included offenses (called "reasonably included offenses" in the chart below) that the President has designated pursuant to Article 79(b)(2). However, this list is not intended to address, and does not address, those offenses that are necessarily included in a charged offense and are therefore lesser included offenses pursuant to Article 79(b)(1).

Article	Offense (Part IV Citation)	Reasonably Included Offense (RIO) Article	RIO (Part IV Citation)
85 - Desertion	Para. 9.b.(1)-(3)	85 - Desertion	Para. 9.b.(4)
87a - Resistance, flight, breach of arrest, and escape	Par. 12.b.(5)	86 - Absent without leave	Para. 10.b.(3)
87b - Offenses against correctional custody and restriction	Para. 13.b.(1)	86 - Absent without leave	Para. 10.b.(3)
93a - Prohibited activities with military recruit or trainee by person in position of special trust	Para. 20.b.(1); 20.b.(2)	93 - Cruelty and maltreatment	Para. 19.b.
94 - Mutiny or sedition	Para. 21.b.(1)	94 - Mutiny or sedition	Para. 21.b.(6)
100 - Subordinate compelling surrender	Para. 28.b.(1)	100 - Subordinate compelling surrender	Para. 28.b.(2)
103a - Espionage	Para. 32.b.(1)	103a - Espionage	Para. 32.b.(2)
103b - Aiding the enemy	Para. 33.b.(1)	103b - Aiding the enemy	Para. 33.b.(2)
104b - Unlawful enlistment, appointment, or separation	Para. 36.b.	107 - False official statements; false swearing	Para. 41.b.(1)
118 - Murder	Para. 56.b.(1); 56.b.(2); 56.b.(3); 56.b.(4)	114 - Endangerment Offenses	Para. 52.b.(1)
119 - Manslaughter	Para. 57.b.(1)	114 - Endangerment Offenses	Para. 52.b.(1)

119a - Death or injury of an unborn child	Para. 58.b.(2); 58.b.(4)	119a - Death or injury of an unborn child	Para. 58.b.(3)
120 - Rape and Sexual Assault	Para. 60.b.(1)	128 - Assault with intent to commit specified offenses (rape)	Para. 77.b.(3)
120 - Rape and Sexual Assault	Para. 60.b.(2)	128 - Assault with intent to commit specified offenses (sexual assault)	Para. 77.b.(3)
120b - Rape of a child	Para. 62.b.(1)	128 - Assault with intent to commit specified offenses (rape of a child)	Para. 77.b.(3)
120b - Rape of a child	Para. 62.b.(2)	128 - Assault with intent to commit specified offenses (sexual assault of a child)	Para. 77.b.(3)
128 - Assault	Para. 77.b.(2); 77.b.(3); 77.b.(4); 77.b.(5)	128 - Assault	Para. 77.b.(1)
134 - Check, worthless making and uttering by dishonorably failing to maintain funds	Para. 94.b.	134 - Debt, dishonorably failing to pay	Para. 96.b.
134 - Child pornography	Para. 95.b.(1); 95.b.(2); 95.b.(3); 95.b.(4)	134 - Indecent conduct	Para. 104.b.
134 - Disloyal statements	Para. 97.b.	88 - Contempt toward officials	Para. 14.b.

Appendix 12B

Offense Category	Months
1	0–12
2	1–36
3	30–120
4	120–240
5	240–480
6	Confinement for life with eligibility for parole

Sentencing Parameter Table – Confinement Range Categories

Note: For all above categories, if the confinement portion of the maximum authorized punishment for the offense is less than the Offense Category's confinement maximum, the lesser confinement portion of the maximum authorized punishment shall control as the recommended maximum confinement time for that offense. At a special court-martial, for an offense that is a category 3 offense or greater, the jurisdictional maximum period of confinement (12 months) constitutes the parameters; however, the military judge may impose a period of confinement less than the jurisdictional maximum period of confinement upon finding specific facts that warrant such a sentence.

Appendix 12C – Offense Category Chart

Article	*Offense*	*Offense Category*
77	Principals	Dependent on underlying offense
78	Accessory after the fact	Dependent on underlying offense
79	Conviction of offense charged, lesser included offenses, and attempts	Dependent on underlying offense
80	Attempts	Dependent on underlying offense
81	Conspiracy	Dependent on underlying offense
82	Soliciting commission of offenses	
	Solicitation of espionage	Category 4
	Solicitation of desertion, mutiny or sedition, misbehavior before the enemy if committed or attempted	Dependent on underlying offense
	Solicitation of desertion in time of war if not committed or attempted	Criteria
	Solicitation of desertion if not committed or attempted	Category 1
	Solicitation of mutiny or sedition if not committed or attempted	Category 3
	Solicitation of misbehavior before enemy if not committed or attempted	Category 3
	Solicitation of other offense regardless of whether committed or attempted	Dependent on underlying offense
83	Malingering	
	Feigning illness, physical disablement, mental lapse, or mental derangement	
	In time of war or in a hostile fire pay zone	Criteria
	Other	Category 1
	Intentional self-inflicted injury	
	In time of war or in a hostile fire pay zone	Criteria
	Other	Category 2
84	Breach of medical quarantine	
	Breach of medical quarantine involving a quarantinable communicable disease defined by 42 CFR 70.1	Category 1
	Breach of medical quarantine	Category 1
85	Desertion	
	In time of war	Criteria
	Intent to avoid hazardous duty or to shirk important services	Category 2
	Other cases	
	Terminated by apprehension	Category 2
	Terminated otherwise	Category 1
86	Absence without leave	
	Failing to go, going from appointed place of duty	Category 1
	Absence from unit, organization, etc.	
	Not more than 3 days	Category 1
	More than 3, not more than 30 days	Category 1
	More than 30 days	Category 1
	More than 30 days and terminated by apprehension	Category 1
	Absence from guard or watch	Category 1
	Absence from guard or watch with intent to abandon	Category 1
	Absence with intent to avoid maneuvers or field exercises	Category 1
87	Missing movement; jumping from vessel	
	Missing movement	
	Design	Category 2
	Neglect	Category 1
	Jumping from vessel into the water	Category 1
87a	Resistance, flight, breach of arrest, and escape	
	Resisting apprehension	Category 1
	Flight from apprehension	Category 1
	Breaking arrest	Category 1
	Escape from custody, pretrial confinement, or confinement pursuant to Article 15	Category 1
	Escape from post trial confinement	Category 2
87b	Offenses against correctional custody and restriction	
	Escape from correctional custody	Category 1
	Breach of correctional custody	Category 1
	Breach of restriction	Category 1

Article	*Offense*	*Offense Category*
88	Contempt toward officials	Category 1
89	Disrespect toward superior commissioned officer; assault of superior commissioned officer	
	Disrespect toward superior commissioned officer	
	In command	Category 1
	In rank	Category 1
	Striking, drawing, or lifting up a weapon or offering any violence to superior commissioned officer in execution of office	
	In time or war	Criteria
	Other	Category 2
90	Willfully disobeying superior commissioned officer	
	In time of war	Criteria
	Other	Category 2
91	Insubordinate conduct toward warrant officer, noncommissioned officer, or petty officer	
	Striking or assaulting	
	Warrant officer	Category 2
	Superior noncommissioned or petty officer	Category 2
	Other noncommissioned or petty officer	Category 1
	Willfully disobeying	
	Warrant officer	Category 1
	Noncommissioned or petty officer	Category 1
	Contempt or disrespect	
	Warrant officer	Category 1
	Superior noncommissioned or petty officer	Category 1
	Other noncommissioned or petty officer	Category 1
92	Failure to obey order or regulation	
	Violation of or failure to obey general order or regulation	Category 1
	Violation of or failure to obey other lawful order	Category 1
	Dereliction in performance of duties	
	Through neglect or culpable inefficiency	Category 1
	Through neglect or culpable inefficiency resulting in death or grievous bodily harm	Category 2
	Willful	Category 1
	Willful dereliction of duty resulting in death or grievous bodily harm	Category 2
93	Cruelty and maltreatment	Category 1
93a	Prohibited activities with military recruit or trainee by person in position of special trust	Category 2
94	Mutiny or sedition	Criteria
95	Offenses by sentinel or lookout	
	Drunk or sleeping on post, or leaving post before being relieved	
	In time of war	Criteria
	While receiving special pay under 37 USC 310	Criteria
	In all other places	Category 1
	Loitering or wrongfully sitting on post by a sentinel or lookout	
	In time of war or while receiving special pay under 37 USC 310	Criteria
	Other cases	Category 1
95a	Disrespect toward sentinel or lookout	Category 1
96	Release of prisoner without authority; drinking with prisoner	
	Releasing a prisoner without authority	Category 2
	Allowing a prisoner to escape through neglect	Category 1
	Allowing a prisoner to escape through design	Category 2
	Drinking with prisoner	Category 1
97	Unlawful Detention	Category 2
98	Misconduct as prisoner	Criteria
99	Misbehavior before the enemy	Criteria
100	Subordinate compelling surrender	Criteria
101	Improper use of countersign	Criteria
102	Forcing a safeguard	Criteria
103	Spies	Category 5
103a	Espionage	
	Espionage as a capital offense	Category 5
	Espionage or attempted espionage	Category 5

Article	Offense	Offense Category
103b	Aiding the enemy	Criteria
104	Public records offenses	Category 2
104a	Fraudulent enlistment, appointment, or separation	
	Fraudulent enlistment or appointment	Category 2
	Fraudulent separation	Category 2
104b	Unlawful enlistment, appointment, or separation	Category 2
105	Forgery	Category 2
105a	False or unauthorized pass offenses	
	Possessing or using with intent to defend or deceive, or making, altering, counterfeiting, tampering with, or selling	Category 2
	All other cases	Category 1
106	Impersonation of officer, noncommissioned or petty officer, or agent or official	
	With intent to defraud	Category 2
	All other cases	Category 1
106a	Wearing unauthorized insignia, decoration, badge, ribbon, device, or lapel button	
	Wrongful wearing of the Medal of Honor; Distinguished Service Cross; Navy Cross; Air Force Cross; Silver Star; Purple Heart: or a valor device on any personal award	Category 1
	All other cases	Category 1
107	False official statements; false swearing	
	False official statement	Category 2
	False swearing	Category 1
107a	Parole violation	Category 1
108	Military property of United States—Loss, damage, destruction, or wrongful disposition	
	Selling or otherwise disposing	
	Of a value of $1,000 or less	Category 1
	Of a value of more than $1,000 or any firearm or explosive	Category 2
	Damaging, destroying, losing or suffering to be lost, damaged, destroyed, sold, or wrongfully disposed	
	Through neglect, of a value or damage of	
	Of a value of $1,000 or less	Category 1
	Of a value of more than $1,000	Category 1
	Willfully, of a value or damage of	
	$1,000 or less	Category 1
	More than $1,000 or of any firearm or explosive	Category 2
108a	Captured or abandoned property	
	Captured, abandoned property; failure to secure, etc.	
	Of a value of $1,000 or less	Category 1
	Of a value of more than $1,000 or any firearm or explosive	Category 2
	Looting or pillaging	Criteria
109	Property other than military property of United States— Waste, spoilage, or destruction	
	Wasting, spoiling, destroying, or damaging non-military property	
	Of a value of $1,000 or less	Category 1
	Of a value of more than $1,000	Category 2
109a	Mail matter: wrongful taking, opening, etc.	Category 2
110	Improper hazarding of vessel or aircraft	
	Willfully and wrongfully	Criteria
	Negligently	Category 2
111	Leaving scene of vehicle accident	Category 1
112	Drunkenness and other incapacitation offenses	
	Drunk on duty	Category 1
	Incapacitation for duty from drunkenness or drug use	Category 1
	Drunk prisoner	Category 1

Article	*Offense*	*Offense Category*
112a	Wrongful use, possession, etc., of controlled substances	
	Wrongful use, possession, manufacture, or introduction of controlled substance	
	Wrongful use or possession of amphetamine, cocaine, heroin, lysergic acid diethylamide, marijuana, methamphetamine, opium, phencyclidine, secobarbital, and Schedule I, II, and III controlled substances	Category 1
	Wrongful manufacture or introduction of amphetamine, cocaine, heroin, lysergic acid diethylamide, marijuana, methamphetamine, opium, phencyclidine, secobarbital, and Schedule I, II, and III controlled substances	Category 2
	Wrongful use, possession, manufacture, or introduction of phenobarbital and Schedule IV and V controlled substances	Category 1
	Wrongful distribution, possession, manufacture, or introduction of controlled substance with intent to distribute, or wrongful importation or exportation of a controlled substance	
	Amphetamine, cocaine, heroin, lysergic acid diethylamide, marijuana, methamphetamine, opium, phencyclidine, secobarbital, and Schedule I, II, and III controlled substances	Category 2
	Phenobarbital and schedule IV and V controlled substances	Category 2
113	Drunken or reckless operation of a vehicle, aircraft, or vessel	
	Resulting in personal injury	Category 2
	No personal injury involved	Category 1
114	Endangerment offenses	
	Carrying concealed weapon	Category 1
	Discharging firearm, willfully, under such circumstances as to endanger human life	Category 1
	Reckless endangerment	Category 1
	Dueling	Category 1
115	Communicating threats	
	Threats and false threats generally	Category 2
	Threats and false threats concerning use of explosives, etc.	Category 3
116	Riot or breach of peace	
	Riot	Category 3
	Breach of the peace	Category 1
117	Provoking speeches or gestures	Category 1
117a	Wrongful broadcast or distribution of intimate visual images	Category 2
118	Murder	
	Article 118(1) or (4)	Category 6
	Article 118(2) or (3)	Category 5
119	Manslaughter	
	Voluntary manslaughter	Category 4
	Involuntary manslaughter	Category 3
	Voluntary manslaughter of a child under 16 years of age	Category 4
	Involuntary manslaughter of a child under 16 years of age	Category 3
119a	Death or injury of an unborn child	
	Injuring or killing an unborn child	Dependent on underlying offense
	Attempting to kill an unborn child	Dependent on underlying offense
	Intentionally killing an unborn child	Dependent on underlying offense
119b	Child endangerment	
	Endangerment by design resulting in grievous bodily harm	Category 3
	Endangerment by design resulting in harm	Category 2
	Other cases by design	Category 2
	Endangerment by culpable negligence resulting in grievous bodily harm	Category 2
	Endangerment by culpable negligence resulting in harm	Category 2
	Other cases by culpable negligence	Category 1

Article	*Offense*	*Offense Category*
120	Rape and sexual assault generally	
	Rape	Category 4
	Sexual assault	Category 3
	Aggravated sexual contact	Category 3
	Abusive sexual contact	Category 2
120a	Mails: deposit of obscene matter	Category 2
120b	Rape and sexual assault of a child	
	Rape of a child	Category 5
	Sexual assault of a child	Category 4
	Sexual abuse of a child	
	Cases involving sexual contact	Category 3
	Other cases	Category 3
120c	Other sexual misconduct	
	Indecent viewing	Category 1
	Indecent recording	Category 2
	Broadcasting or distributing of an indecent recording	Category 2
	Forcible pandering	Category 3
	Indecent exposure	Category 1
121	Larceny and wrongful appropriation	
	Larceny	
	Property of a value of $1,000 or less	Category 1
	Military property of a value of more than $1,000 or of any military motor vehicle, aircraft, vessel, firearm, or explosive	Category 2
	Property other than military property of a value of more than $1,000 or any motor vehicle, aircraft, vessel, firearm, or explosive	Category 2
	Wrongful appropriation	
	Of a value of $1,000 or less	Category 1
	Of a value of more than $1,000	Category 1
	Of any motor vehicle, aircraft, vessel, firearm, explosive, or military property of a value of more than $1,000	Category 1
121a	Fraudulent use of credit cards, debit cards, and other access devices	
	Fraudulent use of a credit card, debit card, or other access device to obtain property of a value of $1,000 or less	Category 1
	Fraudulent use during any 1-year period of a credit card, debit card, or other access device to obtain property the aggregate value of which is more than $1,000	Category 2
121b	False pretenses to obtain services	
	Of a value of $1,000 or less	Category 1
	Of a value of more than $1,000	Category 2
122	Robbery	
	When committed with a dangerous weapon	Category 3
	All other cases	Category 3
122a	Receiving stolen property	
	Receiving, buying, or concealing stolen property of a value of $1,000 or less	Category 1
	Receiving, buying, or concealing stolen property of a value of more than $1,000	Category 2
123	Offenses concerning Government computers	
	Unauthorized distribution of classified information obtained from a Government computer	Category 3
	Unauthorized access of a Government computer and obtaining classified or other protected information	Category 2
	Causing damage to a Government computer	Category 3
123a	Making, drawing, or uttering check, draft, or order without sufficient funds	
	For the procurement of any article or thing of value, with intent to defraud, in the face amount of:	
	$1,000 or less	Category 1
	More than $1,000	Category 2
	For the payment of any past due obligation, or for any other purpose, with intent to deceive	Category 1

Article	*Offense*	*Offense Category*
124	Frauds against the United States	
	Article 124(1) and (2)	Category 2
	Article 124(3) and (4)	
	When amount is $1,000 or less	Category 1
	When amount is more than $1,000	Category 2
124a	Bribery	Category 2
124b	Graft	Category 2
125	Kidnapping	Category 3
126	Arson; burning property with intent to defraud	
	Aggravated arson	Category 3
	Simple arson, where property value is:	
	$1,000 or less	Category 1
	More than $1,000	Category 2
	Burning with intent to defraud	Category 2
127	Extortion	Category 2
128	Assault	
	Simple assault	
	Generally	Category 1
	When committed with an unloaded firearm	Category 2
	Battery	
	Assault consummated by a battery	Category 1
	Assault upon a commissioned officer of the armed forces of the United States or of a friendly foreign power, not in the execution of office ...	Category 2
	Assault upon a warrant officer, not in the execution of office	Category 2
	Assault upon a noncommissioned or petty officer, not in the execution of office	Category 1
	Assault upon a sentinel or lookout in the execution of duty, or upon any person who, in the execution of office, is performing security police, military police, shore patrol, master at arms, or other military or civilian law enforcement duties	Category 2
	Assault consummated by a battery upon a child under 16 years ...	Category 2
	Assault with intent to commit murder or rape	Category 3
	Assault with intent to commit voluntary manslaughter, robbery, arson, burglary, or kidnapping	Category 3
	Aggravated assault	
	Aggravated assault with a dangerous weapon	
	When committed with a loaded firearm	Category 3
	When committed upon a child under the age of 16 years	Category 3
	Other cases	Category 2
	Aggravated assault in which substantial bodily harm in inflicted	
	When the injury is inflicted with a loaded firearm	Category 3
	When the injury is inflicted upon a child under the age of 16 years	Category 3
	Other cases	Category 2
	Aggravated assault in which grievous bodily harm is inflicted	
	When the injury is inflicted with a loaded firearm	Category 3
	When the injury is inflicted upon a child under the age of 16 years	Category 3
	Other cases	Category 2
	Aggravated assault by strangulation or suffocation	
	When committed upon a child under the age of 16 years ..	Category 3
	Other cases	Category 2
128a	Maiming	Category 3
128b	Domestic Violence	
	Commission of violent offense against spouse, intimate partner, or immediate family member of that person	Dependent on underlying offense
	Commission of UCMJ violation against any person with intent to threaten or intimidate spouse, intimate partner, or immediate family member of that person	Dependent on underlying offense

Article	Offense	Offense Category
	Commission of UCMJ violation against any property, including animal, with intent to threaten or intimidate spouse, intimate partner, or immediate family member of that person	Dependent on underlying offense
	Violation of protection order with intent to threaten or intimidate spouse, intimate partner, or immediate family member of that person	Category 2
	Violation of protection order with intent to commit a violent offense against spouse, intimate partner, or immediate family member of that person	Category 2
	Assaulting spouse, intimate partner, or immediate family member of that person by strangulation or suffocation	
	Aggravated assault by strangulation or suffocation when committed upon a child under 16 years	Category 3
	Other cases	Category 2
129	Burglary; unlawful entry	
	Burglary (with intent to commit an offense punishable under Article 118–120, 120b–121, 122, 125–128a, or 130)	Category 3
	Burglary (with intent to commit any other offense punishable under the UCMJ)	Category 2
	Unlawful entry	Category 1
130	Stalking	Category 2
131	Perjury	Category 2
131a	Subornation of perjury	Category 2
131b	Obstructing justice	Category 2
131c	Misprision of serious offense	Category 2
131d	Wrongful refusal to testify	Category 2
131e	Prevention of authorized seizure of property	Category 1
131f	Noncompliance with procedural rules	
	Unnecessary delay in disposing of case	Category 1
	Knowingly and intentionally failing to enforce or comply with provisions of the UCMJ	Category 2
131g	Wrongful interference with adverse administrative proceeding	Category 2
132	Retaliation	Category 2
133	Conduct unbecoming an officer.	Criteria
134	General article	Criteria
	Animal abuse	
	Abuse, neglect, or abandonment of an animal	Category 1
	Abuse, neglect, or abandonment of a public animal	Category 1
	Sexual act with an animal or cases where the accused caused the serious injury or death of the animal	Category 2
	Bigamy	Category 1
	Check, worthless making and uttering – by dishonorably failing to maintain funds	Category 1
	Child pornography	
	Possessing, receiving, or viewing child pornography	Category 2
	Possessing child pornography with intent to distribute	Category 3
	Distributing child pornography	Category 3
	Producing child pornography	Category 4
	Debt, dishonorably failing to pay	Category 1
	Disloyal statements	Category 1
	Disorderly conduct, drunkenness	
	Disorderly conduct	
	Under such circumstances as to bring discredit upon the military Service	Category 1
	Other cases	Category 1
	Drunkenness	
	Aboard ship or under such circumstances as to bring discredit upon the military Service	Category 1
	Other cases	Category 1

Article	*Offense*	*Offense Category*
134	Drunk and disorderly	
	Aboard ship	Category 1
	Under such circumstances as to bring discredit upon the military Service	Category 1
	Other cases	Category 1
	Extramarital sexual conduct	Category 1
	Firearm, discharging – through negligence	Category 1
	Fraternization	Category 1
	Gambling with subordinate	Category 1
	Homicide, negligent	Category 2
	Indecent conduct	Category 2
	Indecent language	
	Communicated to any child under the age of 16 years	Category 2
	Other cases	Category 1
	Pandering and prostitution	
	Prostitution and patronizing a prostitute	Category 1
	Pandering	Category 2
	Self-injury without intent to avoid service	
	In time of war or in a hostile fire pay zone	Criteria
	Intentional self-inflicted injury	Category 1
	Sexual harassment	Category 2
	Straggling	Category 1

Appendix 12D - List of Sentencing Criteria Offenses

UCMJ Article	Title
82	Solicitation to desert (in time of war)
83	Malingering (in time of war or in hostile fire pay zone)
85	Desertion (in time of war)
89	Striking, drawing, or lifting up a weapon or offering any violence to superior commissioned officer in execution of office (in time of war)
90	Willfully disobeying a lawful order of superior commissioned officer (in time of war)
94	Mutiny or sedition
95	Offenses by sentinel or lookout (in time of war or while receiving special pay under 37 U.S.C. 310)
98	Misconduct as prisoner
99	Misbehavior before the enemy
100	Subordinate compelling surrender
101	Improper use of countersign
102	Forcing a safeguard
103b	Aiding the enemy
108a	Captured or abandoned property (looting or pillaging)
110	Improper hazarding of vessel or aircraft (willfully and wrongfully)
133	Conduct unbecoming an officer
134	General article
134	Self-injury without intent to avoid service (in time of war or in a hostile fire pay zone)

SENTENCING CRITERIA

The military judge shall consider the sentencing criteria established for the following offenses:

Article 82. Solicitation to desert *(in time of war).*

The age and experience of the accused;

Any mental impairment or deficiency of the accused;

Whether the offense disrupted or, in any way, impacted the operations of any organization;

Whether the offense caused damage to the national security of the United States, regardless of whether the accused intended such damage;

Whether the offense was committed in a way or under circumstances that unlawfully and substantially endangered the life of one or more persons; and

Whether the offense was committed in territory in which the United States or an ally of the United States was then an occupying power or in which the United States Armed Forces were then engaged in a contingency operation or active hostilities.

Article 83. Malingering *(in time of war or in hostile fire pay zone).*

The age and experience of the accused;

Any mental impairment or deficiency of the accused;

Whether the offense was committed before or in the presence of the enemy;

Whether the offense disrupted or, in any way, impacted the operations of any organization;

Whether the offense caused damage to the national security of the United States, regardless of whether the accused intended such damage;

Whether the offense was committed in a way or under circumstances that unlawfully and substantially endangered the life of one or more persons;

Whether the offense was committed to avoid the movement of a vessel or hazardous duty or shirk important service; and

Whether the offense was committed in territory in which the United States or an ally of the United States was then an occupying power or in which the United States Armed Forces were then engaged in a contingency operation or active hostilities.

Article 85. Desertion *(in time of war).*

The age and experience of the accused;

Any mental impairment or deficiency of the accused;

Whether the offense was committed before or in the presence of the enemy;

Whether the offense was committed while the accused was under charges, investigation, or adverse action;

Whether the offense caused damage to the national security of the United States, regardless of whether the accused intended such damage;

Whether the offense disrupted or, in any way, impacted the operations of any organization;

Whether the offense was committed to avoid the movement of a vessel or hazardous duty or shirk important service;

Whether the offense was committed in a way or under circumstances that unlawfully and substantially endangered the life of one or more persons; and

Whether the offense was committed in a way or under circumstances such that the location from which the accused absented himself or remained absent was a territory in which the United States or an ally of the United States was then an occupying power or in which the United States Armed Forces were then engaged in a contingency operation or active hostilities.

Article 89. Striking, drawing, or lifting up a weapon or offering any violence to superior commissioned officer in execution of office *(in time of war).*

The age and experience of the accused;

Any mental impairment or deficiency of the accused;

Whether the offense disrupted or, in any way, impacted the operations of any organization;

Whether the offense was committed to avoid the movement of a vessel or hazardous duty or shirk important service;

Whether the offense was committed before or in the presence of the enemy;

Whether the offense was committed before or in the presence of other members of the accused's or the superior commissioned officer's unit;

Whether the offense caused damage to the national security of the United States, regardless of whether the accused intended such damage;

The status of the superior commissioned officer and command relationship to the accused;

Whether the accused abused a position of trust or authority, or used specialized skill or training, in a manner that significantly facilitated the offense;

The amount of force or violence used or threatened by the accused and other participants in the offense;

The nature or extent of any injuries suffered by the victim;

Whether the offense was committed in a way that created, or under circumstances creating, a substantial risk of bodily harm or death to any person;

Whether the offense involved the conscious or reckless disregard of a risk of death or serious bodily harm to any person;

Whether the offense involved possession of a dangerous weapon; and

Whether the offense was committed in territory in which the United States or an ally of the United States was then an occupying power or in which the United States Armed Forces were then engaged in a contingency operation or active hostilities.

Article 90. Willfully disobeying a lawful order of superior commissioned officer *(in time of war).*

The age and experience of the accused;

Any mental impairment or deficiency of the accused;

Whether the offense disrupted or, in any way, impacted the operations of any organization;

Whether the offense was committed to avoid the movement of a vessel or hazardous duty or shirk important service;

Whether the offense was committed before or in the presence of the enemy;

Whether the offense was committed before or in the presence of other members of the accused's or the superior commissioned officer's unit;

Whether the offense caused damage to the national security of the United States, regardless of whether the accused intended such damage;

The status of the superior commissioned officer and command relationship to the accused;

Whether the accused abused a position of trust or authority, or used specialized skill or training, in a manner that significantly facilitated the offense;

Whether the offense was committed in a way that created, or under circumstances creating, a substantial risk of bodily harm or death to any person;

Whether the offense involved the conscious or reckless disregard of a risk of death or serious bodily harm to any person;

Whether the offense involved possession of a dangerous weapon; and

Whether the offense was committed in territory in which the United States or an ally of the United States was then an occupying power or in which the United States Armed Forces were then engaged in a contingency operation or active hostilities.

Article 94. Mutiny or sedition.

The age and experience of the accused;

Any mental impairment or deficiency of the accused;

The accused's relationship to the military or civil authority against which the accused committed the mutiny or sedition;

Whether the offense disrupted or, in any way, impacted the operations of any organization;

Whether the offense was committed to avoid the movement of a vessel or hazardous duty or shirk important service;

Whether the offense was committed before or in the presence of the enemy;

Whether the offense caused damage to the national security of the United States, regardless of whether the accused intended such damage;

Whether the accused was the actual perpetrator of the offense or was a principal whose participation in the offense was major;

Whether the accused was an organizer, leader, manager, or supervisor in the offense and the number of other participants in the offense;

Whether the accused was a minimal or minor participant in the offense;

Whether the accused abused a position of trust or authority, or used specialized skill or training, in a manner that significantly facilitated the offense;

The amount of force or violence used or threatened by the accused and other participants in the offense;

The nature or extent of any injuries suffered by any victims of the offense;

The nature or extent of any public or private property damage related to the offense;

Whether the offense was committed in a way or under circumstances that unlawfully and substantially endangered the life of one or more persons;

Whether the offense involved the conscious or reckless disregard of a risk of death or serious bodily harm to any person;

Whether the offense involved possession of a dangerous weapon;

Whether the offense involved the conscious or reckless disregard of a risk of serious damage to public or private property; and

Whether the offense was committed in territory in which the United States or an ally of the United States was then an occupying power or in which the United States Armed Forces were then engaged in a contingency operation or active hostilities.

Article 95. Offenses by sentinel or lookout ***(in time of war or while the accused was receiving special pay under 37 U.S.C 310).***

The age and experience of the accused;

Any mental impairment or deficiency of the accused;

Whether the offense disrupted or, in any way, impacted the operations of any organization;

Whether the offense was committed to avoid the movement of a vessel or hazardous duty or shirk important service;

Whether the offense was committed before or in the presence of the enemy;

Whether the offense caused damage to the national security of the United States, regardless of whether the accused intended such damage;

Whether the offense was committed in a way or under circumstances that unlawfully and substantially endangered the life of one or more persons; and

Whether the offense was committed in territory in which the United States or an ally of the United States was then an occupying power or in which the United States Armed Forces were then engaged in a contingency operation or active hostilities.

Article 98. Misconduct as prisoner.

The age and experience of the accused;

Any mental impairment or deficiency of the accused;

Whether the offense caused damage to the national security of the United States, regardless of whether the accused intended such damage;

Whether the accused was the actual perpetrator of the offense or was a principal whose participation in the offense was major;

Whether the accused was an organizer, leader, manager, or supervisor in the offense and the number of other participants in the offense;

Whether the accused was a minimal or minor participant in the offense;

Whether the accused abused a position of trust or authority, or used specialized skill or training, in a manner that significantly facilitated the offense;

The nature of any maltreatment inflicted on other prisoners;

The amount of force or violence used or threatened by the accused and other participants in the offense;

The nature or extent of any injuries suffered by any victims of the offense;

Whether the offense was committed in a way or under circumstances that unlawfully and substantially endangered the life of one or more persons;

Whether the offense involved the conscious or reckless disregard of a risk of death or serious bodily harm to any person;

Whether the offense involved possession of a dangerous weapon;

The nature of any benefits or improvements enjoyed by the accused as a result of his or her conduct; and

Whether the offense was committed in territory in which the United States or an ally of the United States was then an occupying power or in which the United States Armed Forces were then engaged in a contingency operation or active hostilities.

Article 99. Misbehavior before the enemy.

The age and experience of the accused;

Any mental impairment or deficiency of the accused;

Whether the offense disrupted or, in any way, impacted the operations of any organization.

Whether the offense caused damage to the national security of the United States, regardless of whether the accused intended such damage;

Whether the accused abused a position of trust or authority, or used specialized skill or training, in a manner that significantly facilitated the offense;

Whether the accused was the actual perpetrator of the offense or was a principal whose participation in the offense was major;

Whether the accused was an organizer, leader, manager, or supervisor in the offense and the number of other participants in the offense;

Whether the accused was a minimal or minor participant in the offense;

Whether the offense was committed in a way or under circumstances that unlawfully and substantially endangered the life of one or more persons;

Whether the offense involved the conscious or reckless disregard of a risk of death or serious bodily harm to any person;

Whether the offense involved possession of a dangerous weapon;

Whether the offense was committed in a way that created, or under circumstances creating, a substantial risk of bodily harm or death to any person; and

Whether the offense was committed in territory in which the United States or an ally of the United States was then an occupying power or in which the United States Armed Forces were then engaged in a contingency operation or active hostilities.

Article 100. Subordinate compelling surrender.

The age and experience of the accused;

Any mental impairment or deficiency of the accused;

The nature of the conflict or hostilities in which the accused's unit was engaged;

Whether the offense was committed in the immediate presence of the enemy;

Whether the offense caused damage to the national security of the United States, regardless of whether the accused intended such damage;

Whether the offense impacted the operations of any organization in addition to the unit of the accused;

Whether the offense was committed in a way or under circumstances that unlawfully and substantially endangered the life of one or more persons;

Whether the offense was committed in territory in which the United States or an ally of the United States was then an occupying power or in which the United States Armed Forces were then engaged in a contingency operation or active hostilities;

Whether the accused abused a position of trust or authority, or used specialized skill or training, in a manner that significantly facilitated the offense;

Whether the offense was committed for the purpose of receiving money or a thing of value;

Whether the accused was the actual perpetrator of the offense or was a principal whose participation in the offense was major;

Whether the accused was an organizer, leader, manager, or supervisor in the offense and the number of other participants in the offense; and

Whether the accused was a minimal or minor participant in the offense.

Article 101. Improper use of countersign.

The age and experience of the accused;

Any mental impairment or deficiency of the accused;

Whether the offense was committed before or in the presence of the enemy;

Whether the offense caused damage to the national security of the United States, regardless of whether the accused intended such damage;

Whether the offense was committed in a way or under circumstances that unlawfully and substantially endangered the life of one or more persons;

Whether the offense was committed in territory in which the United States or an ally of the United States was then an occupying power or in which the United States Armed Forces were then engaged in a contingency operation or active hostilities;

Whether the accused abused a position of trust or authority, or used specialized skill or training, in a manner that significantly facilitated the offense; and

Whether the offense was committed for the purpose of receiving money or a thing of value.

Article 102. Forcing a safeguard.

The age and experience of the accused;

Any mental impairment or deficiency of the accused;

That nature of the person or persons, place, or property intended to be protected by the safeguard;

Whether the offense was committed before or in the presence of the enemy;

Whether the offense caused damage to the national security of the United States, regardless of whether the accused intended such damage;

Whether the offense was committed in a way or under circumstances that unlawfully and substantially endangered the life of one or more persons;

Whether the offense was committed in territory in which the United States or an ally of the United States was then an occupying power or in which the United States Armed Forces were then engaged in a contingency operation or active hostilities;

Whether the accused abused a position of trust or authority, or used specialized skill or training, in a manner that significantly facilitated the offense;

Whether the offense was committed for the purpose of receiving money or a thing of value;

Whether any person or persons, place, or property intended to be protected by the safeguard was injured or damaged;

Whether the accused was the actual perpetrator of the offense or was a principal whose participation in the offense was major;

Whether the accused actually knew of the safeguard;

Whether the accused was an organizer, leader, manager, or supervisor in the offense and the number of other participants in the offense; and

Whether the accused was a minimal or minor participant in the offense.

Article 103b. Aiding the enemy

The age and experience of the accused;

Any mental impairment or deficiency of the accused;

Whether the accused abused a position of trust or authority, or used specialized skill or training, in a manner that significantly facilitated the offense;

Whether the offense disrupted or, in any way, impacted the operations of any organization;

Whether the accused intended to cause damage to national security;

Whether the offense caused damage to the national security of the United States, regardless of whether the accused intended such damage;

Whether the offense involved the conscious or reckless disregard of a risk of death or serious bodily harm to any person;

Whether the offense involved possession of a dangerous weapon;

Whether the offense was committed in a way or under circumstances that unlawfully and substantially endangered the life of one or more persons; and

Whether the offense was committed in territory in which the United States or an ally of the United States was then an occupying power or in which the United States Armed

Forces were then engaged in a contingency operation or active hostilities.

Article 108a. Captured or abandoned property *(looting or pillaging)*

The age and experience of the accused;

Any mental impairment or deficiency of the accused;

Whether the offense was committed before or in the presence of the enemy;

Whether the offense caused damage to the national security of the United States, regardless of whether the accused intended such damage;

Whether the offense was committed in territory in which the United States or an ally of the United States was then an occupying power or in which the United States Armed Forces were then engaged in a contingency operation or active hostilities;

Whether the accused was the actual perpetrator of the offense or was a principal whose participation in the offense was major;

Whether the accused was an organizer, leader, manager, or supervisor in the offense and the number of other participants in the offense;

Whether the accused was a minimal or minor participant in the offense;

Whether the accused abused a position of trust or authority, or used specialized skill or training, in a manner that significantly facilitated the offense;

Whether the offense involved the conscious or reckless disregard of a risk of death or serious bodily harm to any person;

Whether the offense involved possession of a dangerous weapon;

Whether the offense was committed in a way or under circumstances that unlawfully and substantially endangered the life of one or more persons;

Whether the offense involved the conscious or reckless disregard of a risk of serious damage to public or private property;

The amount of force or violence used or threatened by the accused and other participants in the offense;

The value and nature of the captured or abandoned property; and

The amount of restitution, if any, paid by the accused.

Article 110. Improper hazarding of vessel or aircraft ***(willfully and wrongfully).***

The age and experience of the accused;

Any mental impairment or deficiency of the accused;

The position, responsibility, and authority of the accused at the time of the offense;

Whether the offense caused damage to the vessel or aircraft and the amount and type of damage;

Whether the accused committed the offense with the intent to prevent the vessel's or aircraft's deployment, movement, or departure;

Whether the offense occurred in a time of active hostilities;

Whether the offense disrupted or, in any way, impacted the operations of any organization;

Whether the offense caused damage to the national security of the United States, regardless of whether the accused intended such damage;

Whether the offense involved the conscious or reckless disregard of a risk of death or serious bodily harm to any person;

Whether the accused abused a position of trust or authority, or used specialized skill or training, in a manner that significantly facilitated the offense;

Whether the accused was an organizer, leader, manager, or supervisor in the offense and the number of other participants in the offense; and

Whether the accused was the actual perpetrator of the offense or was a principal whose participation in the offense was major.

Article 133. Conduct unbecoming an officer.

The age and experience of the accused;

Any mental impairment or deficiency of the accused;

The sentencing parameter for the most analogous enumerated offense;

The grade of the accused;

Whether the offense occurred in a time of active hostilities;

Whether the offense disrupted or, in any way, impacted the operations of any organization;

Whether the offense caused damage to the national security of the United States, regardless of whether the accused intended such damage;

Whether the offense involved a severe lack of integrity and judgment;

Whether the offense involved the conscious or reckless disregard of a risk of death or serious bodily harm to any person; and

Whether the accused abused a position of trust or authority, or used specialized skill or training, in a manner that significantly facilitated the offense.

Article 134. General article.

(A) For offenses under Article 134's "disorders and neglects to the prejudice of good order and discipline" or "conduct of a nature to bring discredit upon the armed forces" clause that are not listed in Part IV of the Manual for Courts-Martial:

(1) For offenses for which the maximum punishment is calculated pursuant to

Rule for Courts-Martial 1003(c)(l)(B)(i), the sentencing parameter for the offense that provided the maximum punishment.

(2) For offenses for which the maximum punishment is calculated by reference to a provision of the United States Code pursuant to Rule for Courts-Martial 1003(c)(l)(B)(ii), the Federal Sentencing Guideline range for the offense that provided the maximum punishment.

(3) For offenses for which the maximum punishment is calculated by reference to a custom of the applicable service pursuant to Rule for Courts-Martial 1003(c)(l)(B)(ii), the sentencing parameter for the most analogous enumerated offense.

(B) For offenses under Article 134's "crimes and offenses not capital" clause, the Federal Sentencing Guideline range for the underlying offense.

Article 134. Self-injury without intent to avoid service in a time of war or in a hostile fire pay zone.

The age and experience of the accused;

Any mental impairment or deficiency of the accused;

Whether the offense was committed before or in the presence of the enemy;

Whether the offense disrupted or, in any way, impacted the operations of any organization;

Whether the offense caused damage to the national security of the United States, regardless of whether the accused intended such damage;

Whether the offense was committed in a way or under circumstances that unlawfully and substantially endangered the life of one or more persons; and

Whether the offense was committed in territory in which the United States or an ally of the United States was then an occupying power or in which the United States Armed Forces were then engaged in a contingency operation or active hostilities."

Appendix 13 – RESERVED

THIS PAGE LEFT INTENTIONALLY BLANK.

Appendix 14 – RESERVED

THIS PAGE LEFT INTENTIONALLY BLANK.

APPENDIX 15
ANALYSIS OF THE COMPOSITION OF THE MANUAL, THE PREAMBLE, AND THE RULES FOR COURTS-MARTIAL

Introduction

The Manual for Courts-Martial, United States (2024 edition) implements the military justice reforms enacted by the National Defense Authorization Act for Fiscal Year 2020, Pub. L. 116-92, 133 Stat. 1198 (2019); William M. (Mac) Thornberry National Defense Authorization Act for Fiscal Year 2021, Pub. L. 116-283, 134 Stat. 3388 (2020); National Defense Authorization Act for Fiscal Year 2022, Pub. L. No. 117-81, 135 Stat. 1541 (2021) and the James M. Inhofe National Defense Authorization Act for Fiscal Year 2023, Pub. L. No. 263, 136 Stat 2395 (2022). It also incorporates two Executive Orders, namely Executive Order No. 14062 (Jan. 26, 2022) and Executive Order No. 14103 (July 28, 2023).

History of the Manual for Courts-Martial. The President traditionally has exercised the power to make rules for the government of the military establishment, including rules governing courts-martial. *See* W. Winthrop, *Military Law and Precedents* 27–28 (2d ed. 1920 reprint). Such rules have been promulgated under the President's authority as commander-in-chief, *see* U.S. Const., Art. II, sec. 2, cl.1., and, at least since 1813, such power also has been provided for in statutes. *See* W. Winthrop, *supra*, at 26–27. Article 36 of the Uniform Code of Military Justice provides such authority. *See also* Articles 18 and 56. *See generally Hearings on H.R. 3804 Before the Military Personnel Subcomm. of the House Comm. on Armed Services*, 96th Cong., 1st Sess. 5–6, 14, 17–18, 20–21, 52, 106 (1979). In 1979, Article 36 was amended to clarify the broad scope of the President's rulemaking authority for courts-martial. Act of November 9, 1979, Pub. L. No. 96–107, Section 801(b), 93 Stat. 810,811. *See generally Hearings on H.R. 3804, supra.*

In the nineteenth century the President promulgated, from time to time, regulations for the Army. Those regulations were published in various forms, including "Manuals." W. Winthrop, *supra*, at 28. Such publications were not limited to court-martial procedures and related matters; however, they were more in the nature of compendiums of military law and regulations. The early manuals for courts-martial were informal guides and were not promulgated by the President. *See* MCM, 1895 at 1, 2; MCM, 1905 at 3; MCM, 1910 at 3; MCM, 1917 at III. *See also* MCM, 1921 at XIX.

The forerunner of the modern *Manual for Courts-Martial* was promulgated by the Secretary of War in 1895. *See* MCM, 1895 at 2. *See also* Hearings on H.R. 3805, *supra*, at 5. (Earlier Manuals were prepared by individual authors. *See e.g.*, A. Murray, *A Manual for Courts-Martial* (3d ed. 1893); H. Coppée, *Field Manual for Courts-Martial* (1863)). Subsequent Manuals through MCM, 1969 (Rev.) have had the same basic format, organization, and subject matter as MCM, 1895, although the contents have been modified and considerably expanded. *See, e.g.*, MCM, 1921 at XIX–XX. The format was been a paragraph format, numbered consecutively and divided into chapters. The subject matter included pretrial, trial, and post-trial procedure. In MCM, 1917, rules of evidence and explanatory materials on the punitive articles were included. *See* MCM, 1917 at XIV. The 1921 Manual for Courts-Martial was the first to be promulgated by the President. *See* MCM, 1921 at XXVI.

Background of this Manual. During the drafting of the Military Rules of Evidence (*see* Analysis, Part III, introduction, *infra*), the drafters identified several portions of MCM, 1969 (Rev.) in which they considered revisions appropriate. Consideration was given to amending MCM, 1969 (Rev.) in specific areas. However, the project to draft the Military Rules of Evidence had demonstrated the value of a more comprehensive examination of existing law. In addition, changing the format of the Manual for Courts-Martial was considered desirable. In this regard it should be noted that, as indicated above, the basic format and organization of the Manual for Courts-Martial had remained the same for over 80 years, although court-martial practice and procedure had changed substantially.

Upon completion of the Military Rules of Evidence in early 1980, the General Counsel, Department of Defense, with the concurrence of the Judge Advocates General, directed that the Manual for Courts-Martial be revised. There were four basic goals for the revision. First, the new Manual was to conform to federal practice to the extent possible, except where the Uniform Code of Military Justice requires otherwise or where specific military requirements render such conformity impracticable. *See* Article 36. Second, current court-martial practice and applicable judicial precedent was to be thoroughly examined and the Manual was to be brought up to date, by modifying such practice and precedent or conforming to it as appropriate. Third, the format of the Manual was to be modified to make it more useful to lawyers (both military and civilian) and nonlawyers. Specifically, a rule as opposed to paragraph format was to be used and prescriptive rules would be separated from nonbinding discussion. Fourth, the procedures in the new Manual had to be workable across the spectrum of circumstances in which courts-martial are conducted, including combat conditions.

These goals were intended to ensure that the Manual for Courts-Martial continues to fulfill its fundamental purpose as a comprehensive body of law governing the trial of courts-martial and as a guide for lawyers and nonlawyers in the operation and application of such law. It was recognized that no single source could resolve all issues or answer all questions in the criminal process. However, it was determined that the Manual for Courts-Martial should be sufficiently comprehensive, accessible, and understandable so it could be reliably used to dispose of matters in the military justice system properly, without the necessity to consult other sources, as much as reasonably possible.

The Joint Service Committee on Military Justice was tasked with the project. In the summer of 1980, the Navy and Army prepared an initial outline of the new Manual. Drafting was done by the Working Group of the Joint Service Committee on Military Justice.

The Working Group drafted the Manual in fourteen increments. Each increment was circulated by each service to various field offices for comment. Following such comment, each increment was reviewed in the respective offices of the Judge Advocates General, the Director, Judge Advocate Division, Headquarters, USMC, and the Chief Counsel, USCG, and in the Court of Military Appeals. Following such review, the Joint Service Committee met and took action on each increment. After all increments had been reviewed and approved, the Code Committee approved the draft.

Following approval by the Code Committee, the draft was made available for comment by the public. 48 Fed. Reg. 23688 (May 26, 1983). In September and October 1983, the comments were reviewed. The Working Group prepared numerous modifications in the draft based on comments from the public and from within the Department of Defense, and on judicial decisions and other developments since completion of the draft. In October 1983, the Joint Service Committee approved the draft for forwarding to the General Counsel, Department of Defense, for submission to the

President after coordination by the Office of Management and Budget.

On November 18, 1983, Congress passed the Military Justice Act of 1983. This act was signed into law by the President on December 6, 1983, Pub. L. No. 98–209, 97 Stat. 1393 (1983). The Working Group had previously drafted proposed modifications to the May 1983 draft which would be necessary to implement the act. These proposed modifications were approved by the Joint Service Committee in November 1983 and were made available to the public for comment in December 1983. 48 Fed. Reg. 54263 (December 1, 1983). These comments were reviewed and modifications made in the draft by the Working Group, and the Joint Service Committee approved these changes in January 1984. The draft of the complete Manual and the proposed executive order were forwarded to the General Counsel, Department of Defense in January 1984. These were reviewed and forwarded to the Office of Management and Budget in January 1984. They were reviewed in the Departments of Justice and Transportation. The Executive Order was finally prepared for submission to the President, and the President signed it on 13 April 1984.

A note on citation form. The drafters generally have followed *The Bluebook, A Uniform System of Citation* (21st ed. 2020), subject to the following.

This edition of the Manual for Courts-Martial is referred to generally as "this Manual." The Rules for Courts-Martial are cited, *e.g.*, as R.C.M. 101. The Military Rules of Evidence are cited, *e.g.*, as Mil. R. Evid. 101. Other provisions of this Manual are cited to the applicable part and paragraph, *e.g.*, MCM, Part V, paragraph 1a(1) (2024).

Previous editions of the Manual for Courts-Martial will be referred to as "MCM, (XXXX edition)."

The Uniform Code of Military Justice, 10 U.S.C. Sections 801–946a, is cited as follows: Each individual section is denominated in the statute as an "Article" and is cited to the corresponding Article. *E.g.*, 10 U.S.C. Section 801 is cited as "Article 1"; 10 U.S.C. Section 802 is cited as "Article 2"; 10 U.S.C. Section 940 is cited as "Article 140." The entire legislation, Articles 1 through 146a, is referred to as "the Code" or "the UCMJ" without citation to the United States Code.

When a change from MCM, 2016 is based on the Military Justice Act of 2016 or subsequent legislation, this will be noted in the analysis, with citation to the appropriate section of the act.

Composition of the Manual for Courts-Martial

Executive Order

The Manual for Courts-Martial consists of the Preamble; Rules for Courts-Martial; Military Rules of Evidence; the Punitive Articles; Nonjudicial Punishment Procedure; Appendix 12A, Presidentially-Prescribed Lesser Included Offenses pursuant to Article 79(b)(2), Uniform Code of Military Justice; Appendix 12B, Sentencing Parameter Table—Confinement Range Categories; Appendix 12C—Offense Category Chart; and Appendix 12D—List of Sentencing Criteria Offenses. Each rule states binding requirements except when the text of the rule expressly provides otherwise. Normally, failure to comply with a rule constitutes error. See Article 59 concerning the effect of errors.

a. *Supplementary Materials*

As a supplement to the Manual, the Department of Defense, in conjunction with the Department of Homeland Security, has published a Discussion (accompanying the Preamble, the Rules for Courts-Martial, the Military Rules of Evidence, and the Punitive Articles), this Analysis, and various Appendices.

(1) *The Discussion*

The Discussion is intended by the drafters to serve as a treatise. To the extent that the Discussion uses terms such as "must" or "will," it is solely for the purpose of alerting the user to important legal consequences that may result from binding requirements in the Executive Order, judicial decisions, or other sources of binding law. The Discussion itself, however, does not have the force of law, even though it may describe legal requirements derived from other sources. It is in the nature of treatise, and may be used as secondary authority. The inclusion of both the President's rules and the drafters' informal discussion in the basic text of the Manual provides flexibility not available in pre-1984 editions of the Manual, and should eliminate questions as to whether an item is a requirement or only guidance. *See e.g., United States v. Baker*, 14 M.J. 361, 373 (C.M.A. 1973). In this Manual, if matter is included in a rule or paragraph, it is intended that the matter be binding, unless it is clearly expressed as precatory. A rule is binding even if the source of the requirement is a judicial decision or a statute not directly applicable to courts-martial. If the President had adopted a rule based on a judicial decision or a statute, subsequent repeal of the statute or reversal of the judicial decision does not repeal the rule. On the other hand, if the President did not choose to "codify" a principle or requirement derived from a judicial decision or other source of law but the drafters considered it sufficiently significant that the Manual's users should be aware of it, such matter is addressed in the Discussion. The Discussion is revised from time to time as warranted by changes in applicable law.

(2) *The Analysis*

The Analysis sets forth the nonbinding views of the drafters as to the basis for each rule or paragraph, as well as the intent of the drafters, particularly with respect to the purpose of substantial changes in present law. The Analysis is intended to be a guide in interpretation. Users are reminded, however, that primary reliance should be placed on the plain words of the rules. In addition, it is important to remember that the Analysis solely represents the views of staff personnel who worked on the project, and does not necessarily reflect the views of the President in approving it, or of the officials who formally recommended approval to the President.

The Analysis frequently refers to judicial decisions and statutes from the civilian sector that are not applicable directly to courts-martial. Subsequent modification of such sources of law may provide useful guidance in interpreting rules, and the drafters do not intend that citation of a source in this Analysis should preclude reference to subsequent developments for purposes of interpretation. At the same time, the user is reminded that the amendment of the Manual is the province of the President. Developments in the civilian sector that affect the underlying rationale for a rule do not affect the validity of the rule except to the extent otherwise required as a matter of statutory or constitutional law. The same is true with respect to rules derived from the decisions of military tribunals. Once incorporated into the Executive Order, such matters have an independent source of authority and are not dependent upon continued support from the judiciary. Conversely, to the extent that judicial precedent is set forth only in the Discussion or is otherwise omitted from the Rules or the Discussion, the continuing validity of the precedent will depend on the force of its rationale, the doctrine of *stare decisis*, and similar jurisprudential considerations. Nothing in this Introduction should be interpreted to suggest that the placement of matter in the Discussion (or the Analysis), rather than the rule, is to be taken as disapproval of the precedent or as an invitation for a court to take a different approach; rather, the difficult drafting problem of choosing between a codification and common law approach to the law frequently resulted in noncodification of decisions which had the unanimous support of the drafters. To the extent that future changes are made in the Rules or Discussion, corresponding materials will be included in the Analysis.

(3) The Appendices

Except for Appendix 2.1 and Appendices 12A-D, the Appendices are approved by the General Counsel of the Department of Defense and provide supplementary, non-binding materials to assist Manual users. While Appendix 2 offers a reproduction of the Uniform Code of Military Justice for user convenience, it is advisable to consult with the official and most up-to-date version of the law published by the Office of Law Revision Counsel at https://uscode.house.gov. When referencing excerpts of law or legal authority contained within the appendices, it is advisable to cross-reference the cited law or authority. For details on the issuing authority and scope of Appendix 2.1 and Appendices 12A-D, please refer to the respective sections.

PART I. PREAMBLE

Introduction.

The preamble is based on paragraphs 1 and 2 of MCM, 1969 (Rev.).

1. Sources of military jurisdiction

This subsection is based on paragraph 1 of MCM, 1969 (Rev.). The provisions of the Constitution which are sources of jurisdiction of military courts or tribunals include: Art I, sec. 8, cl. 1, 9–16, 18; Art. II, sec. 2; Art. IV, sec. 4; and the Fifth Amendment. As to sources in international law, see *e.g., Ex Parte Quirin*, 317 U.S. 1 (1942); Geneva Convention Relative to the Treatment of Prisoners of War, Aug. 12, 1949, arts. 82–84, 6 U.S.T. 3316, 3382, T.I.A.S. No. 3365, 75 U.N.T.S. 287.

2. Exercise of military jurisdiction

Subsection (a) is based on the first paragraph of paragraph 2 of MCM, 1969 (Rev.).

For additional materials on martial law, see W. Winthrop, *Military Law and Precedent* 817–30 (2d ed. 1920 reprint); *Ex parte Milligan,* 71 U.S. (4 Wall.) 2 (1866). *See also* paragraph 3, sec. 1 of MCM, 1910 (concerning the exercise of martial law over military affiliated persons).

For additional materials on military government, *see* W. Winthrop, *supra* at 798–817; *Madsen v. Kinsella*, 343 U.S. 341(1952); *Mechanics' and Traders' Bank v. Union Bank*, 89 U.S. (22 Wall.) 276 (1875).

For additional materials on the exercise of military jurisdiction under the law of war, *see* W. Winthrop, *supra* at 831–46; *Trials of War Criminals Before the Nuremberg Tribunals* (U.S. Gov't Printing Off., 1950–51); *Trials of the Major War Criminals Before the International Military Tribunal* (International Military Tribunal, Nuremberg 1947); *In re Yamashita*, 327 U.S. 1 (1946); *Ex parte Quirin, supra; Ex parte Milligan, supra*; Articles 18 and 21. Subsection (b) is based on the second paragraph of paragraph 2 of MCM, 1969 (Rev.). *See also* Article 21; DA PAM 27–174, *supra* at paragraph 1–5 *a*; W. Winthrop, *supra at* 802–05, 835–36. As to provost courts, *see also Hearings on H.R. 2498 Before a Subcomm. of the House Comm. on Armed Services*, 81st Cong., 1st Sess. 975, 1061 (1949). As to trial of prisoners of war, see *Article* 2(a)(9) and Article 102, 1949 Geneva Convention Relative to the Treatment of Prisoners of War, *supra.*

3. Purpose of military law

See generally Chappell v. Wallace, 462 U.S. 296 (1983); *Parker v. Levy*, 417 U.S. 733 (1974); S. Rep. No. 53, 98th Cong., 1st Sess. 2–3 (1983). For a discussion of the nature and purpose of military law, see R. Everett, *Military Justice in the Armed Forces of the United States* (1956); J. Bishop, *Justice Under Fire* (1974); Hodson, *Military Justice: Abolish or Change?*, 22 Kan. L. Rev. 31 (1975), *reprinted in* Mil. L. Rev. Bicent. Issue 579 (1976); Hansen, *Judicial Functions for the Commander*, 41 Mil.L.Rev. 1 (1968); *Hearings on H.R. 2498 Before a Subcomm. of the House Comm. on Armed Services*, 81st Cong., 1st Sess. 606, 778–86 (1949); H. Moyer, *Justice and the Military* 5–23 (1972).

2023 Amendment: Paragraph 3 was revised to note that the purposes of military law include deterring misconduct and facilitating appropriate accountability.

4. The Evolving Military Justice System

2023 Amendment: A new paragraph 4 was added to discuss the evolution of the military justice system, including the reforms enacted by the National Defense Authorization Act for Fiscal Year 2022, Pub. L. No. 117-81, 135 Stat. 1546 (2021) [hereinafter FY2022 NDAA].

5. Structure and application of the Manual for Courts-Martial

Self-explanatory. *See also* the *Introduction* of the *Analysis*.

2023 Amendment: Paragraph 4 was renumbered as paragraph 5. Citations to the Department of Defense issuance governing the Joint Service Committee on Military Justice were updated.

PART II. RULES FOR COURTS-MARTIAL

CHAPTER I. GENERAL PROVISIONS

Rule 101 Scope, title

This rule is taken from Rule 101 of the MCM (2016 edition) without amendment.

Rule 102 Purpose and construction

This rule is taken from Rule 102 of the MCM (2016 edition) without amendment.

Rule 103 Definitions and rule of construction

This rule is taken from Rule 103 of the MCM (2016 edition) with the following amendments:

2018 Amendment: R.C.M. 103(1), (2), and (3) are renumbered as R.C.M. 103(2), (3), and (4); R.C.M. 103(16) through (18) are renumbered as R.C.M. 103(17) through (19); R.C.M. 103(19) through (21) are renumbered R.C.M. 103(21) through (23). The definition of "UCMJ" is moved from R.C.M. 103(4) to R.C.M. 103(20).

R.C.M. 103(1) is amended and clarifies the reference to "appellate military judge" means a judge of a Court of Criminal Appeals.

R.C.M. 103(8)(D) is amended and implements Article 16, as amended by Section 5161 of the Military Justice Act of 2016, Division E of the National Defense Authorization Act for Fiscal Year 2017, Pub. L. No. 114-328, 130 Stat. 2000 (2016), as further amended by Section 1081(c)(1)(C) of the National Defense Authorization Act for Fiscal Year 2018, Pub. Law. No. 115-91, 131 Stat. 1283 (2017), which authorizes a convening authority to refer charges to a special court-martial consisting of a military judge alone under such limitations as the President may prescribe by regulation.

R.C.M. 103(11) is amended and updates a description of the federal law definition of "explosive."

R.C.M. 103(15) is amended and implements Article 1, as amended by Section 5101 of the Military Justice Act of 2016, Division E of the National Defense Authorization Act for Fiscal Year 2017, Pub. L. No. 114-328, 130 Stat. 2000 (2016), as further amended by Sections 1081(a)(21) and 1081(c)(1)(A) of the National Defense Authorization Act for Fiscal Year 2018, Pub. Law. No. 115-91, 131 Stat. 1283 (2017), which amends the definition of "military judge."

R.C.M. 103(16) is amended and implements Articles 19, 26a, and 30a, as amended by Sections 5163, 5185, and 5202 of the Military Justice Act of 2016, Division E of the National Defense Authorization Act for Fiscal Year 2017, Pub. L. No. 114-328, 130 Stat. 2000 (2016), which authorizes the use of military magistrates; Article 30a was amended by Section 531(b) of the National Defense Authorization Act for Fiscal Year 2018, Pub. Law. No. 115-91, 131 Stat. 1283 (2017).

R.C.M. 103(17) is amended and clarifies the definition of "party" to include acting on behalf of a party in pre-referral and post-referral proceedings under these rules.

R.C.M. 103(22) is amended and aligns the definitions of "writings" and "recordings" with Mil. R. Evid. 1001.

The Discussion accompanying R.C.M. 103(23) is amended and reflects current statutory provisions.

2023 Amendments: R.C.M. 103(10), (12), and (23) are amended to provide definitions regarding special trial counsel authorities. *See* Subtitle D, FY2022 NDAA. Other definitions are renumbered as appropriate without further amendment.

R.C.M. 103(12) defines the phrase "exercise authority over," which is statutory language in Article 24a. The definition clarifies how a special trial counsel can exercise authority over an offense to the exclusion of a commander. The definition ensures that a special trial counsel and a convening authority each know when they are responsible for disposing of an offense.

R.C.M. 103(23) defines the term "referral authority." This term is used throughout the R.C.M.s to discuss roles and responsibilities of the special trial counsel or the convening authority, as applicable."

Rule 104 Command influence

This rule is taken from R.CM. 104 of the MCM (2016 edition), with the following amendments:

2018 Amendment: The Discussion accompanying R.C.M. 104(b)(2)(B) is amended to reflect the reorganization of the punitive articles in the Military Justice Act of 2016. *See* Articles 79-134, as amended by Sections 5401-5452 of the Military Justice Act of 2016, Division E of the National Defense Authorization Act for Fiscal Year 2017, Pub. L. No. 114-328, 130 Stat. 2000 (2016), as further amended by Section 1081(c) of the National Defense Authorization Act for Fiscal Year 2018, Pub. L. No. 115-91, 131 Stat. 1283 (2017).

2023 Amendments: The title of the rule is amended to reflect the change to Article 37. *See* National Defense Authorization Act for Fiscal Year 2020, Pub. L. No. 116-92, 133 Stat. 1359 (2019). The text of the rule is amended to implement changes to Article 37 as well as to clarify the role and responsibilities of special trial counsel.

R.C.M. 104(a)(2)(B)(ix) is added to include "taking action on the findings or sentence," and all subsequent paragraphs are redesignated.

Rule 105 Direct communication: convening authorities and staff judge advocates; among staff judge advocates

This rule is taken from Rule 105 of the MCM (2016 edition) with the following amendments:

2023 Amendments: R.C.M. 105(c) is new and clarifies the ability to communicate with special trial counsel.

R.C.M. 105(d) is new and clarifies that all communications must be free from unlawful or unauthorized influence or coercion per Article 37, UCMJ.

Rule 106 Delivery of military offenders to civilian authorities

This rule is taken from Rule 106 of the MCM (2016 edition) with the following amendment: the Discussion accompanying R.C.M. 106 is amended to correct a cross-reference.

Rule 107 Dismissed officer's right to request trial by court-martial

This rule is taken from Rule 107 of the MCM (2016 edition) without substantive amendment.

Rule 108 Rule of court

This rule is taken from Rule 108 of the MCM (2016 edition) without amendment.

Rule 109 Professional supervision of military judges and counsel

This rule is taken from Rule 109 of the MCM (2016 edition) with the following amendment:

2018 Amendment: The title of R.C.M. 109 and its accompanying Discussions are amended and reflect Articles 6a and 26a, as added by Sections 5104 and 5185 of the Military Justice Act of 2016, Division E of the National Defense Authorization Act for Fiscal Year 2017, Pub. L. No. 114-328, 130 Stat. 2000 (2016), which adds military magistrates to those judicial personnel included in procedures relating to the investigation and disposition of matters pertaining to the fitness of military judges, and authorizes the Judge Advocate General to certify the qualifications of military magistrates, respectively.

CHAPTER II. JURISDICTION

Rule 201 Jurisdiction in general

This rule is taken from Rule 201 of the MCM (2016 edition) with the following amendments:

2018 Amendment: The Discussion accompanying R.C.M. 201(b)(5) is amended and deletes a reference to R.C.M. 810(d).

R.C.M. 201(c), which addressed contempt, is deleted. See R.C.M. 809 for procedures and standards for contempt proceedings and the exercise of contempt authority by judicial officers under Article 98.

R.C.M. 201(f)(1)(A)(i), R.C.M. 201(f)(1)(D), and the Discussion accompanying R.C.M. 201(g) are amended to reflect the reorganization of the punitive articles in the Military Justice Act of 2016. *See* Articles 79-134, as amended by Sections 5401-5452 of the Military Justice Act of 2016, Division E of the National Defense Authorization Act for Fiscal Year 2017, Pub. L. No. 114-328, 130 Stat. 2000 (2016), as further amended by Section 1081(c) of the National Defense Authorization Act for Fiscal Year 2018, Pub. Law. No. 115-91, 131 Stat. 1283 (2017).

R.C.M. 201(f)(1)(D) and (f)(2)(D) are amended and eliminate redundancies and reflect the dates of applicability set forth in Section 1705(c) of the National Defense Authorization Act for Fiscal Year 2014, Pub. L. No. 113-66, 127 Stat. 672, 960 (2013).

The Discussion accompanying R.C.M. 201(f)(2)(D) is amended to update a citation.

R.C.M. 201(f)(2)(B)(ii) is amended and implements Articles 16 and 19, as amended by Sections 5161 and 5163 of the Military Justice Act of 2016, Division E of the National Defense Authorization Act for Fiscal Year 2017, Pub. L. No. 114-328, 130 Stat. 2000 (2016), as further amended by Section 1081(c)(1)(C) of the National Defense Authorization Act for Fiscal Year 2018, Pub. Law. No. 115-91, 131 Stat. 1283 (2017), which eliminate special courts-martial without a military judge and authorize a convening authority to refer charges to a special court-martial consisting of a military judge alone under such limitations as the President may prescribe by regulation.

R.C.M. 201(f)(2)(E) and the accompanying Discussion are new and reflect Article 16, as amended by Section 5161 of the Military Justice Act of 2016, Division E of the National Defense Authorization Act for Fiscal Year 2017, Pub. L. No. 114-328, 130 Stat. 2000 (2016), as further amended by Section 1081(c)(1)(C) of the National Defense Authorization Act for Fiscal Year 2018, Pub. Law. No. 115-91, 131 Stat. 1283 (2017), which authorizes a convening authority to refer charges to a special court-martial consisting of a military judge alone under such limitations as the President may prescribe by regulation.

2023 Amendments: R.C.M. 201(e) is amended to clarify the procedure for reciprocal jurisdiction among the services.

The Discussion accompanying R.C.M. 201(b)(3) is amended to reflect that a referral to a general court-martial or special court-martial, when done at the direction of a special trial counsel for covered offenses, does not make the convening authority an accuser for purposes of R.C.M. 307. *See* FY2022 NDAA.

The Discussion accompanying R.C.M. 201(d)(3) is amended to reflect the document title of the memorandum of understanding (MOU) between the Department of Justice (DOJ) and Department of Defense at Appendix 3 and to note a similar MOU between the DOJ and the Department of Transportation for the U.S. Coast Guard at Appendix 4.

R.C.M. 201(f)(2)(C) is amended to account for referral of capital offenses by special trial counsel to special court-martial.

Rule 202 Persons subject to jurisdiction of courts-martial

This rule is taken from Rule 202 of the MCM (2016 edition) with the following amendments:

2018 Amendment: Paragraph (1) of the Discussion accompanying R.C.M. 202(a) and the Discussion accompanying R.C.M. 202(c) are amended to reflect the reorganization of the punitive articles in the Military Justice Act of 2016. *See* Articles 79-134, as amended by Sections 5401-5452 of the Military Justice Act of 2016, Division E of the National Defense Authorization Act for Fiscal Year 2017, Pub. L. No. 114-328, 130 Stat. 2000 (2016), as further amended by Section 1081(c) of the National Defense Authorization Act for Fiscal Year 2018, Pub. Law. No. 115-91, 131 Stat. 1283 (2017).

Paragraph (5) of the Discussion accompanying R.C.M. 202(a) is amended and reflects Article 2(a)(3), as amended by Section 5102 of the Military Justice Act of 2016, Division E of the National Defense Authorization Act for Fiscal Year 2017, Pub. L. No. 114-328, 130 Stat. 2000 (2016), which revises UCMJ jurisdiction over reservists to cover periods incident to inactive-duty training.

Rule 203 Jurisdiction over the offense

This rule is taken from Rule 203 of the MCM (2016 edition) with the following amendment:

2018 Amendment: The Discussion accompanying R.C.M. 203 is amended and adds a reference to R.C.M. 201(f) with respect to the punishment limitations applicable to specific types of courts-martial.

Rule 204 Jurisdiction over certain reserve component personnel

This rule is taken from Rule 204 of the MCM (2016 edition) with the following amendment:

2018 Amendment: R.C.M. 204(d) is amended and implements Article 2(a)(3), as amended by Section 5102 of the Military Justice Act of 2016, Division E of the National Defense Authorization Act for Fiscal Year 2017, Pub. L. No. 114-328, 130 Stat. 2000 (2016), which revises UCMJ jurisdiction over reservists to cover periods incident to inactive-duty training.

CHAPTER III. INITIATION OF CHARGES; APPREHENSION; PRETRIAL RESTRAINT; RELATED MATTERS

Rule 301 Report of offense

This rule is taken from Rule 301 of the MCM (2016 edition) with the following amendment:

2023 Amendment: Subparagraph (c) is added to ensure special trial counsel are made aware of all allegations of covered offenses. A special trial counsel must exercise authority over a covered offense and has exclusive authority to determine whether a reported offense is a covered offense.

Rule 302 Apprehension

This rule is taken from Rule 302 of the MCM (2016 edition) with the following amendments:

2018 Amendment: The Discussion accompanying R.C.M. 302(a)(1) is amended and updates cross-references.

R.C.M. 302(e)(2)(A) is amended and updates cross-references to the Military Rules of Evidence.

R.C.M. 302(e)(2)(B) is amended and reflects exigent circumstances under which an apprehension may be made in a private dwelling.

2023 Amendments: The Discussion accompanying R.C.M. 302(b)(3) is amended to replace "passion" with "possession."

The Discussion accompanying R.C.M. 302(c) is amended to remove the proposition that "reasonable grounds" is equivalent to "probable cause."

Rule 303 Preliminary inquiry into reported offenses

This rule is taken from Rule 303 of the MCM (2016 edition) with the following amendment:

2018 Amendment: The Discussion accompanying R.C.M. 303 is amended and reflects Section 1742 of the National Defense Authorization Act for Fiscal Year 2014, Pub. L. No. 113-66, 127 Stat. 980 (2013), which mandated that commanders refer reports of sex-related offenses involving members of the armed forces in their chain of command to the appropriate military criminal investigative organization.

Rule 303A Determination by special trial counsel to exercise authority

2023 Amendment: This rule is new and describes the initial determinations special trial counsel shall make prior to exercising authority over an offense.

Rule 304 Pretrial restraint

This rule is taken from Rule 304 of the MCM (2016 edition) with the following amendments:

2018 Amendment: The Discussion accompanying R.C.M. 304(a)(4) is amended and reflects the reorganization of the punitive articles in the Military Justice Act of 2016. *See* Articles 79-134, as amended by Sections 5401-5452 of the Military Justice Act of 2016, Division E of the National Defense Authorization Act for Fiscal Year 2017, Pub. L. No. 114-328, 130 Stat. 2000 (2016), as further amended by Section 1081(c) of the National Defense Authorization Act for Fiscal Year 2018, Pub. Law. No. 115-91, 131 Stat. 1283 (2017).

2023 Amendment: R.C.M. 304(f) is added and ensures timely notice is given to special trial counsel when an accused suspected of a covered offense is placed under pretrial restraint. All other paragraphs are redesignated, without further amendment, to accommodate the addition of the new R.C.M. 304(f).

Rule 305 Pretrial confinement

This rule is taken from Rule 305 of the MCM (2016 edition) with the following amendments:

2018 Amendment: R.C.M. 305 is amended throughout the rule and replaces the term "prisoner" with the term "confinee."

The Discussion accompanying R.C.M. 305(a) is amended and reflects Article 12, as amended by Section 5122 of the Military Justice Act of 2016, Division E of the National Defense Authorization Act for Fiscal Year 2017, Pub. L. No. 114-328, 130 Stat. 2000 (2016), with respect to confinement of members of the armed forces in immediate association with enemy prisoners and other specified individuals.

R.C.M. 305(k) is amended and updates cross-references applicable to administrative credit against the sentenced adjudged for confinement served as a result of noncompliance with R.C.M. 305(f), (h), (i), or (j).

R.C.M. 305(m)(1) and (2) are amended and update cross-references.

The Discussion accompanying R.C.M. 305(m) is amended and clarifies that operational exceptions permitted to the requirements of certain provisions of R.C.M. 305 do not constitute exceptions to the requirements of Article 31(b).

The Discussion accompanying R.C.M. 305(n) is amended and clarifies the meaning of the term "victim of an alleged offense" as it pertains to this rule.

2023 Amendments: R.C.M. 305(f) is added to ensure timely notice is given to special trial counsel when an accused suspected of a covered offense is placed in pretrial confinement. All other paragraphs are redesignated, without further amendment, to accommodate the addition of the new R.C.M. 305(f).

R.C.M. 305(j), now R.C.M. 305(k), is amended to provide procedures for pre-referral review of a pretrial confinement determination.

Rule 306 Initial disposition for offenses over which special trial counsel does not exercise authority

This rule is taken from Rule 306 of the MCM (2016 edition) with the following amendments:

2018 Amendment: The Discussion accompanying R.C.M. 306(a) is amended and reflects that the Initial Disposition Authority for certain sex-related offenses is a commander in the grade of O-6 or above possessing at least special court-martial convening authority.

The Discussion accompanying R.C.M. 306(b) is amended and refers to the non-binding disposition guidance required by Article 33, as amended by Section 5204 of the Military Justice Act of 2016, Division E of the National Defense Authorization Act for Fiscal Year 2017, Pub. L. No. 114-328, 130 Stat. 2000 (2016). *See* Appendix 2.1.

The Discussion accompanying R.C.M. 306(c)(2) is relocated and accompanies R.C.M. 306(c)(1).

R.C.M. 306(e)(1) is amended and reflects the reorganization of the punitive articles in the Military Justice Act of 2016. *See* Articles 79-134, as amended by Sections 5401-5452 of the Military Justice Act of 2016, Division E of the National Defense Authorization Act for Fiscal Year 2017, Pub. L. No. 114-328, 130 Stat. 2000 (2016), as further amended by Section 1081(c) of the National Defense Authorization Act for Fiscal Year 2018, Pub. Law. No. 115-91, 131 Stat. 1283 (2017).

R.C.M. 306(e)(3) is amended and clarifies that, under such regulations as the Secretary may prescribe, if no charges are preferred for an alleged sex-related offense, if the commander learns of any decision by civilian authorities to prosecute or not prosecute the offense in civilian court, the commander shall ensure the victim is notified.

2023 Amendment: R.C.M. 306 is amended to articulate command authority to make an initial disposition determination on reported offenses when a special trial counsel is not exercising authority or has deferred.

Rule 306A Initial disposition for offenses over which special trial counsel exercises authority

2023 Amendment: This rule is new and describes the manner in which a special trial counsel disposes of offenses over which the special trial counsel has exercised authority. Under R.C.M. 307(a), any person subject to the UCMJ may prefer charges. If someone other than a special trial counsel prefers a charge for a covered offense, a special trial counsel must exercise authority over that offense upon learning of the preferral of the charge. Special trial counsel have exclusive authority to dispose of preferred charges for covered offenses, and any other offenses over which a special trial counsel has exercised authority, regardless of who preferred the charges.

Rule 307 Preferral of charges

This rule is taken from Rule 307 of the MCM (2016 edition) with the following amendments:

2018 Amendment: R.C.M. 307(b) is amended and implements Article 30, as amended by Section 5201 of the Military Justice Act of 2016, Division E of the National Defense Authorization Act for Fiscal Year 2017, Pub. L. No. 114-328, 130 Stat. 2000 (2016).

The Discussion accompanying R.C.M. 307(c)(3) is amended and reflects the reorganization of the punitive articles in the Military Justice Act of 2016 and the addition of Appendix 12A with respect to lesser included offenses. *See* Articles 79-134, as amended by Sections 5401-5452 of the Military Justice Act of 2016, Division E of the National Defense Authorization Act for Fiscal Year 2017, Pub. L. No. 114-328, 130 Stat. 2000 (2016), as further amended by Section 1081(c) of the National Defense Authorization Act for Fiscal Year 2018, Pub. Law. No. 115-91, 131 Stat. 1283 (2017).

R.C.M. 307(c)(4) is amended and deletes the last sentence.

The Discussion accompanying R.C.M. 307(c)(4) is amended to address the differences between multiplicity and unreasonable multiplication of charges, and to alert practitioners that use of the phrase "multiplicity in sentencing," is confusing and should be avoided. *See United States v. Campbell*, 71 M.J. 19 (C.A.A.F. 2012).

2023 Amendment: R.C.M. 307(b)(3) is added to clarify that preferral of charges by remote means is authorized.

Rule 308 Notification to accused of charges and required disclosures

This rule is taken from Rule 308 of the MCM (2016 edition) with the following amendments:

2023 Amendment: R.C.M. 308(c) and (d) incorporate language regarding disclosures that was previously located in R.C.M. 404A(a)(1), (b), (c), and (d) in the MCM (2019 edition). Additionally, R.C.M. 308(c) specifically identifies the items accompanying the charges that are required for initial disclosure, and R.C.M. 308(d)(2) clarifies work product not subject to disclosure.

Rule 309 Pre-referral judicial proceedings

2018 Amendment: R.C.M. 309 is new and implements Article 30a, as added by Section 5202 of the Military Justice Act of 2016, Division E of the National Defense Authorization Act for Fiscal Year 2017, Pub. L. No. 114-328, 130 Stat. 2000 (2016), as amended by Section 531(b) of the National Defense Authorization Act for Fiscal Year 2018, Pub. L. No. 155-91, 131 Stat. 1283 (2017), which establishes the matters that may be addressed by a military judge or military magistrate in a pre-referral proceeding.

2023 Amendment: R.C.M. 309(a) is amended to limit the authority of the military judge in the pre-referral context.

R.C.M. 309(b)(4)-(10) are added to include matters that may be adjudicated at a pre-referral hearing under Article 30a. Of note, R.C.M. 309(b)(3)(10) is added to allow a party to ask a military judge to consider whether to order a pre-referral deposition.

R.C.M. 309(e) is amended to ensure the record from any pre-referral hearing in a case involving a special trial counsel is forwarded to the special trial counsel.

CHAPTER IV. FORWARDING AND DISPOSITION OF CHARGES

Rule 401 Forwarding and disposition of charges in general

This rule is taken from Rule 401 of the MCM (2016 edition) with the following amendments:

2018 Amendment: The Discussions accompanying R.C.M. 401(b) and (c) are amended and refer to the non-binding disposition guidance required by Article 33, as amended by Section 5204 of the Military Justice Act of 2016, Division E of the National Defense Authorization Act for Fiscal Year 2017, Pub. L. No. 114-328, 130 Stat. 2000 (2016). *See* Appendix 2.1.

2023 Amendment: R.C.M. 401 and the Discussions are amended to articulate command authority over the forwarding and disposition of charges when a special trial counsel has not exercised authority or has deferred.

Rule 401A. Disposition of charges over which a special trial counsel exercises authority and has not deferred

2023 Amendment: R.C.M. 401A and the Discussions are new and describe the process special trial counsel must employ to dispose of preferred charges.

Rule 402 Action by commander not authorized to convene courts-martial

This rule is taken from Rule 402 of the MCM (2016 edition) with the following amendments:

2023 Amendment: R.C.M. 402 is amended to clarify the role of special trial counsel.

Rule 403 Action by commander exercising summary court-martial jurisdiction

This rule is taken from Rule 403 of the MCM (2016 edition) with the following amendments:

2018 Amendment: The Discussions accompanying R.C.M. 403 are amended and update cross-references. R.C.M. 403(b)(4) is amended and implements Article 18, as amended by Section 1705(b) of the National Defense Authorization Act for Fiscal Year 2014, Pub. L. No. 113-66, 127 Stat. 672 (2013), as further amended by Section 5162 of the Military Justice Act of 2016, Division E of the National Defense Authorization Act for Fiscal Year 2017, Pub. L. No. 114-328, 130 Stat. 2000 (2016), which limits jurisdiction for certain sex-related offenses to general courts-martial.

2023 Amendment: R.C.M. 403 is amended to clarify the role of special trial counsel.

Rule 404 Action by Commander exercising special court-martial jurisdiction

This rule is taken from Rule 404 of the MCM (2016 edition) with the following amendments:

2018 Amendment: R.C.M. 404(4) and the accompanying Discussion are amended and reflect Article 18, as amended by Section 1705(b) of the National Defense Authorization Act for Fiscal Year 2014, Pub. L. No. 113-66, 127 Stat. 672 (2013), as further amended by Section 5162 of the Military Justice Act of 2016, Division E of the National Defense Authorization Act for Fiscal Year 2017, Pub. L. No. 114-328, 130 Stat. 2000 (2016), which limits jurisdiction for certain sex-related offenses to general courts-martial.

2023 Amendment: R.C.M. 404 is amended to clarify the role of special trial counsel.

Rule 404A Initial Disclosures [Removed]

This rule is taken from Rule 404A of the MCM (2016 edition) with the following amendments:

2018 Amendments: The rule is renamed "Initial disclosures."

R.C.M. 404A(a) is amended and establishes the Government's disclosure requirements at preferral of charges and at the direction of a preliminary hearing.

The Discussion accompanying R.C.M. 404A(c) is amended and updates a cross-reference.

The Discussion accompanying R.C.M. 404A(d) is amended and updates a reference.

2023 Amendment: R.C.M. 404A is removed. The substance of the rule is incorporated into R.C.M. 308 and R.C.M. 405.

Rule 405 Preliminary hearing

This rule is taken from Rule 405 of the MCM (2016 edition) with the following amendments:

2018 Amendment: R.C.M. 405 and the accompanying Discussions are amended and reflect Articles 6b, 30a, 32, 33, 46, and 47, as amended or added by Sections 5105, 5202, 5203, 5204, and 5229 of the Military Justice Act of 2016, Division E of the National Defense Authorization Act for Fiscal Year 2017, Pub. L. No. 114-328, 130 Stat. 2000 (2016). Article 6b is further amended by Sections 531(a), 1081(a)(22), and 1081(c)(1)(B) of the National Defense Authorization Act for Fiscal Year 2018, Pub. L. No. 155-91, 131 Stat. 1283 (2017). Article 30a is amended by Section 531(b) of the National Defense Authorization Act for Fiscal Year 2018, Pub. L. No. 155-91, 131 Stat. 1283 (2017).

The Discussions following R.C.M. 405(i)(2)(D), R.C.M. 405(j)(8), and R.C.M. 405(k)(3) are new and reflect that the terms of a sealing order may authorize listed persons or entities to examine or receive disclosure of sealed materials outside of the procedures set forth in R.C.M. 1113(b).

2023 Amendments by Annex 1 of Executive Order No. 14103 (July 28, 2023):

R.C.M. 405(f), now R.C.M. 405(g), is amended to clarify the rights of the accused at a preliminary hearing.

R.C.M. 405(h)(3)(B)(iii), now R.C.M. 405(i)(3)(B)(iii), is amended to clarify the use of an investigative subpoena for evidence not under the control of the Government during a preliminary hearing.

R.C.M. 405(i)(2)(A), now R.C.M. 405(j)(2)(A), is amended to change "any alleged victim's sexual predisposition" to "the alleged victim's sexual predisposition." Additionally, subparagraph (i) is amended to replace "Mil. R. Evid. 412(b)(1)(A) or (B)" with "Mil. R. Evid. 412(b)(1) or (2)," and subparagraph (ii) is amended to remove "relevant" from the determination.

R.C.M. 405(j)(3), now R.C.M. 405(k)(3), is amended to clarify that preliminary hearings should remain open to the public whenever possible, whether conducted in person or via remote means. R.C.M. 405(j)(4), now R.C.M. 405(k)(4), is amended to clarify the requirements for an accused to appear via remote means at a preliminary hearing.

2023 Amendments by Annex 2 of Executive Order No. 14103 (July 28, 2023):

R.C.M. 405(c) is amended to clarify special trial counsel's role in determining whether a preliminary hearing is required.

R.C.M. 405(d) is added to incorporate disclosures previously contained in R.C.M. 404A. Other paragraphs are renumbered to accommodate this addition.

R.C.M. 405(d), now R.C.M. 405(e), is amended to add that for preliminary hearings, special trial counsel shall detail counsel for the Government consistent with regulations prescribed by the Secretary concerned.

R.C.M. 405(e), now R.C.M. 405(f), is amended to require the preliminary hearing officer to provide notice to the convening authority and submit a copy of the preliminary hearing report to a special trial counsel if an uncharged covered offense is adduced during the preliminary hearing.

R.C.M. 405(k)(4) is amended to clarify that remote presence of the accused for a preliminary hearing is authorized.

Rule 406 Pretrial advice and special trial counsel determinations

This rule is taken from Rule 406 of the MCM (2016 edition) with the following amendments:

2018 Amendments: R.C.M. 406(a) and (b) and the accompanying Discussions are amended and reflect Article 34, as amended by Section 5205 of the Military Justice Act of 2016, Division E of the National Defense Authorization Act for Fiscal Year 2017, Pub. L. No. 114-328, 130 Stat. 2000 (2016), which requires a convening authority to consult a judge advocate on relevant legal issues before referring charge(s) and specification(s) to a special court-martial and also prohibits a convening authority from referring charge(s) and specification(s) to a general court-martial unless a staff judge advocate provides written advice stating that the specification alleges an offense under the UCMJ, there is probable cause to believe that the accused committed the offense charged, and a court-martial would have jurisdiction over the accused and the offense. Prior to referring charge(s) and specification(s) to a general court-martial, the staff judge advocate is also required to provide a recommendation as to the disposition that should be made of the charges and specifications by the convening authority in the interest of justice and discipline. *See also* R.C.M. 601(d).

The Discussion accompanying R.C.M. 406(a) is amended and refers to the non-binding disposition guidance required by Article 33, as amended by Section 5204 of the Military Justice Act of 2016, Division E of the National Defense Authorization Act for Fiscal Year 2017, Pub. L. No. 114-328, 130 Stat. 2000 (2016). *See* Appendix 2.1.

2023 Amendment by Annex 1 of Executive Order No. 14103 (July 28, 2023): R.C.M. 406(c) is added to address distribution of written advice from the staff judge advocate if charges are referred to a general court-martial.

2023 Amendments by Annex 2 of Executive Order No. 14103 (July 28, 2023): R.C.M. 406(a)(2) is amended to incorporate R.C.M. 406A.

R.C.M. 406(c) is amended to account for the written determination made by special trial counsel if charges are referred to a general or special court-martial.

Rule 406A Pretrial advice before referral to special court-martial [REMOVED]

2018 Amendments: R.C.M. 406A is new and implements Article 34(b), as amended by Section 5202 of the Military Justice Act of 2016, Division E of the National Defense Authorization Act for Fiscal Year 2017, Pub. L. No. 114-328, 130 Stat. 2000 (2016), which requires a convening authority to consult a judge advocate on relevant legal issues before referring charge(s) and specification(s) to a special court-martial.

The Discussion accompanying R.C.M. 406A(a) is amended and refers to guidance concerning disposition of charges and specifications required by Article 33, as amended by Section 5204 of the Military Justice Act of 2016, Division E of the National Defense Authorization Act for Fiscal Year 2017, Pub. L. No. 114-328, 130 Stat. 2000 (2016). *See* Appendix 2.1.

2023 Amendment: R.C.M. 406A is removed. The substance of the rule is incorporated into R.C.M. 406.

Rule 407 Action by commander exercising general court-martial jurisdiction

This rule is taken from Rule 407 of the MCM (2016 edition) with the following amendments:

2018 Amendments: R.C.M. 407(a)(4) and the accompanying Discussion are amended and reflect Article 18, as amended by Section 1705(b) of the National Defense Authorization Act for Fiscal Year 2014, Pub. L. No. 113-66, 127 Stat. 672 (2013), as further amended by Section 5162 of the Military Justice Act of 2016, Division E of the National Defense Authorization Act for Fiscal Year 2017, Pub. L. No. 114-328, 130 Stat. 2000 (2016), which limits jurisdiction over certain sex-related offenses to general courts-martial.

The Discussion accompanying R.C.M. 407(a)(6) is amended and refers to Sections 1744(b)-(d) of the National Defense Authorization Act for Fiscal Year 2014, Pub. L. No. 113-66, 127 Stat. 980 (2013), as amended by the Section 541 of the Carl Levin and Howard P. "Buck" McKeon National Defense Authorization Act for Fiscal Year 2015, Pub. L. 113-291, 128 Stat. 3371 (2014), which require higher level review with respect to certain decisions involving allegations of sex-related offenses.

2023 Amendment: R.C.M. 407 is amended to clarify the role of special trial counsel.

CHAPTER V. COURT-MARTIAL COMPOSITION AND PERSONNEL; CONVENING COURTS-MARTIAL

Rule 501 Composition and personnel of courts-marital

This rule is taken from Rule 501 of the MCM (2016 edition) with the following amendments:

2018 Amendment: R.C.M. 501(a) and the accompanying Discussion are amended and reflect Articles 16, 25a, and 29, as amended by Sections 5161, 5183, and 5187 of the Military Justice Act of 2016, Division E of the National Defense Authorization Act for Fiscal Year 2017, Pub. L. No. 114-328, 130 Stat. 2000 (2016), as further amended by Section 1081(c)(1)(C) of the National Defense Authorization Act for Fiscal Year 2018, Pub. Law. No. 115-91, 131 Stat. 1283 (2017), which require a set number of members for capital and non-capital general courts-martial and special courts-martial, eliminate special courts-martial without a military judge, establish a special court-martial consisting of a military judge alone with certain limitations on offenses and punishments, and authorize the convening authority to detail alternate members to general and special courts-martial.

The Discussion accompanying R.C.M. 501(c) in the MCM (2016 edition), which addressed court reporters, is deleted.

Rule 502 Qualifications and duties of personnel of court-martial

This rule is taken from Rule 502 of the MCM (2016 edition) with the following amendments:

2018 Amendment: R.C.M. 502(a)(1) is amended and implements Article 25, as amended by Section 5182 of the Military Justice Act of 2016, Division E of the National Defense Authorization Act for Fiscal Year 2017, Pub. L. No. 114-328, 130 Stat. 2000 (2016), which permits a convening authority to detail enlisted members to general and special courts-martial without requiring a request for such members from an enlisted accused.

R.C.M. 502(a)(2) and the accompanying Discussion are amended and reflect Articles 29 and 53, as amended by Sections 5187 and 5236 of the Military Justice Act of 2016, Division E of the National Defense Authorization Act for Fiscal Year 2017, Pub. L. No. 114-328, 130 Stat. 2000 (2016), as further amended by Section 1081(c)(1)(G) of the National Defense Authorization Act for Fiscal Year 2018, Pub. Law. No. 115-91, 131 Stat. 1283 (2017), which authorizes the convening authority to detail alternate members to general and special courts-martial and addresses sentencing for capital offenses.

R.C.M. 502(c) and the accompanying Discussion are amended and reflect Articles 26 and 26a, as amended and added, respectively, by Sections 5184 and 5185 of the Military Justice Act of 2016, Division E of the National Defense Authorization Act for Fiscal Year 2017, Pub. L. No. 114-328, 130 Stat. 2000 (2016), which establish qualifications and minimum tour lengths for trial judges and authorizes the Secretary concerned to establish a military magistrate program.

R.C.M. 502(d)(1) and (2) and the accompanying Discussion are amended and reflect Article 27, as amended by Section 5186 of the Military Justice Act of 2016, Division E of the National Defense Authorization Act for Fiscal Year 2017, Pub. L. No. 114-328, 130 Stat. 2000 (2016), with respect to the qualifications of trial counsel, assistant trial counsel, defense counsel, assistant and associate defense counsel, individual military counsel, civilian defense counsel, and counsel learned in the law applicable to capital cases.

R.C.M. 502(d)(3) and the accompanying Discussion are amended and address disqualification of appellate military judges and counsel for witnesses and victims.

The Discussion accompanying R.C.M. 502(d)(4) is amended and updates cross-references, reflects trial counsel's duties with regard to victims' rights, and reflects the elimination of special courts-martial without a military judge. *See* Articles 6b and 16, as amended by Sections 5105 and 5161 of the Military Justice Act of 2016, Division E of the National Defense Authorization Act for Fiscal Year 2017, Pub. L. No. 114-328, 130 Stat. 2000 (2016). Article 6b is further amended by Sections 531(a), 1081(a)(22), and 1081(c)(1)(B) of the National Defense Authorization Act for Fiscal Year 2018, Pub. Law. No. 115-91, 131 Stat. 1283 (2017). Article 16 is further amended by Section 1081(c)(1)(C) of the National Defense Authorization Act for Fiscal Year 2018, Pub. Law. No. 115-91, 131 Stat. 1283 (2017).

The Discussion accompanying R.C.M. 502(d)(5) is amended and clarifies defense counsel's duties in light of substantial changes to post trial and appellate practice in the Military Justice Act of 2016.

2023 Amendments: R.C.M. 502(a)(2)(A) is amended to account for changes in the sentencing procedures in Articles 53 and 56, UCMJ, providing for judge-alone sentencing in all special and non-capital general court-martial cases, enacted by Section 539E of FY2022 NDAA.

R.C.M. 502(d)(1)(C) is new and describes the qualifications of special trial counsel and requires a special trial counsel be detailed to all cases referred by special trial counsel.

R.C.M. 502(d)(3)(A) is amended to clarify that a special trial is not disqualified as an accuser by making a determination to prefer or refer a charge.

The Discussion accompanying R.C.M. 502(d)(4) is amended to clarify that the convening authority is responsible for addressing irregularities in the convening orders and allied papers in all cases. For cases over which a special trial counsel has exercised authority and has not deferred, the special trial counsel is responsible for addressing any irregularity in a charge. For cases in which the convening authority has referred the charges, the convening authority is responsible for addressing any irregularity in a charge.

Rule 503 Detailing members, military judge, and counsel, and designating military magistrates

This rule is taken from Rule 503 of the MCM (2016 edition) with the following amendments:

2018 Amendment: R.C.M. 503(a)(1) and (2) and the accompanying Discussions are amended and reflect Articles 25, 25a, and 29, as amended by Sections 5182, 5183, and 5187 of the Military Justice Act of 2016, Division E of the National Defense Authorization Act for Fiscal Year 2017, Pub. L. No. 114-328, 130 Stat. 2000 (2016), regarding detailing of members, excusal of members, and impanelment of alternate members.

R.C.M. 503(a)(4) is new and implements Article 16, as amended by Section 5161 of the Military Justice Act of 2016, Division E of the National Defense Authorization Act for Fiscal Year 2017, Pub. L. No. 114-328, 130 Stat. 2000 (2016), as further amended by Section 1081(c)(1)(C) of the National Defense Authorization Act for Fiscal Year 2018, Pub. Law. No. 115-91, 131 Stat. 1283 (2017), which permits a convening authority to refer charge(s) and specification(s) to a special court-martial consisting of a military judge alone under such limitations as the President may prescribe by regulation.

R.C.M. 503(b)(4) is new and implements Articles 19 and 30a, as amended by Sections 5163 and 5202 of the Military Justice Act of 2016, Division E of the National Defense Authorization Act for Fiscal Year 2017, Pub. L. No. 114-328, 130 Stat. 2000 (2016), and Article 30a is further amended by Section 531(b) of the National Defense Authorization Act for Fiscal Year 2018, Pub. L. No. 155-91, 131 Stat. 1283 (2017), which authorizes military judges to detail military magistrates, if authorized under regulations of the Secretary concerned, to preside over certain pre-referral proceedings and special courts-martial consisting of a military judge alone in specified circumstances.

R.C.M. 503(c)(1) is amended and implements Article 27, as amended by Section 5186 of the Military Justice Act of 2016, Division E of the National Defense Authorization Act for Fiscal Year 2017, Pub. L. No. 114-328, 130 Stat. 2000 (2016), with respect to counsel learned in the law applicable to capital cases.

2023 Amendments: R.C.M. 503(a)(1) is amended to reference Article 25, UCMJ, and to require the convening authority to provide a list of detailed members to the military judge to randomize in accordance with R.C.M. 911.

The Discussion accompanying R.C.M. 503(a)(1) is amended to require the convening authority to detail a sufficient number of qualified persons. In order to determine a sufficient number of qualified persons to detail to a court-martial, the convening authority, as advised by the staff judge advocate, should consider the following non-exclusive list of factors to ensure an adequate number of members remains after challenges: operational necessity; forum of the court-martial; availability of Article 25, UCMJ, qualified servicemembers to the convening authority; anticipated awareness of, and knowledge regarding, the parties or facts of the case; and the capability to detail additional members to the convening order.

The Discussion accompanying R.C.M. 503(a)(2) is amended to remove the reference to member sentencing.

Rule 504 Convening courts-martial

This rule is taken from Rule 504 of the MCM (2016 edition) with the following amendments:

2018 Amendment: R.C.M. 504(d) is amended and aligns with the 2018 amendments to R.C.M. 503(a).

2023 Amendment: R.C.M. 504(c)(1) is amended to clarify that a commanding officer shall not be considered an accuser solely due to the role of the commanding officer in convening a special or general court-martial to which charges and specifications were referred by a special trial counsel.

Rule 505 Changes of members, military judge, and counsel

This rule is taken from Rule 505 of the MCM (2016 edition) with the following amendments:

2018 Amendment: R.C.M. 505(a) is amended and aligns with the 2018 Amendments to R.C.M. 503(b)(4) regarding military magistrates.

R.C.M. 505(b) is amended and aligns with the 2018 Amendments to R.C.M. 1202 regarding the certification of the record of trial.

R.C.M. 505(c)(2) is amended and aligns with the 2018 Amendments to R.C.M. 501 and 912A regarding fixed panel sizes in general and special courts-martial and the procedure for excusing excess members at impanelment. The Discussion accompanying R.C.M.505(c)(2) is new.

R.C.M. 505(e) is amended and describes the circumstances in which the military magistrate can be changed before and after assembly of the court-martial. The Discussion accompanying R.C.M. 505(e) is new.

R.C.M. 505(f) is amended and describes the circumstances in which good cause would exist to change the military magistrate.

2023 Amendment: R.C.M. 505(c) is amended to specify that the convening authority must follow the procedures in R.C.M 503(a) when detailing additional members to a court-martial.

Rule 506 Accused's rights to counsel

This rule is taken from Rule 506 of the MCM (2016 edition) with the following amendment:

2018 Amendment: R.C.M. 506(a) and the accompanying Discussion are amended and align with the 2018 Amendments to R.C.M. 502(d)(2)(C) regarding the detailing of defense counsel in capital cases.

CHAPTER VI. REFERRAL, SERVICE, AMENDMENT, AND WITHDRAWAL OF CHARGES

Rule 601 Referral

This rule is taken from Rule 601 of the MCM (2016 edition), as amended by Exec. Order No. 13825, 83 Fed. Reg. 9889 (March 1, 2018), with the following amendments:

2018 Amendment: R.C.M. 601(a) is amended and clarifies that referral is the order of a convening authority that charges and specifications against an accused will be tried by a specified court-martial.

R.C.M. 601(d) is amended and implements Article 34(b), as amended by Section 5205 of the Military Justice Act of 2016, Division E of the National Defense Authorization Act for Fiscal Year 2017, Pub. L. No. 114-328, 130 Stat. 2000 (2016), which requires a convening authority to consult a judge advocate on relevant legal issues before referring charge(s) and specification(s) to a special court-martial and also prohibits a convening authority from referring charge(s) and specification(s) to a general court-martial unless a staff judge advocate provides written advice stating that the specification alleges an offense under the UCMJ, there is probable cause to believe that the accused committed the offense charged, and a court-martial would have jurisdiction over the accused and the offense. Prior to referring charge(s) and specification(s) to a general court-martial, the staff judge advocate is also required to provide a recommendation to the convening authority as to the disposition that should be made of the charges and specifications by the convening authority in the interest of justice and discipline. *See also* R.C.M. 406.

The Discussion accompanying R.C.M. 601(d)(1) is amended and references Appendix 2.1 (Non-binding disposition guidance), and reflects Article 33, as amended by Section 5204 of the Military Justice Act of 2016, Division E of the National Defense Authorization Act for Fiscal Year 2017, Pub. L. No. 114-328, 130 Stat. 2000 (2016).

The Discussion accompanying R.C.M. 601(d)(2) is new and reflects the opportunity of the accused to waive the preliminary hearing and the rules regarding waiver or forfeiture for failure to object to a defect under R.C.M. 601.

The Discussion accompanying R.C.M. 601(d)(3) is new and references limitations on referral of charges and specifications to special courts-martial.

R.C.M. 601(e)(1) is amended and implements Article 16, as amended by Section 5161 of the Military Justice Act of 2016, Division E of the National Defense Authorization Act for Fiscal Year 2017, Pub. L. No. 114-328, 130 Stat. 2000 (2016), as further amended by Section 1081(c)(1)(C) of the National Defense Authorization Act for Fiscal Year 2018, Pub. L. No. 115-91, 131 Stat. 1283 (2017), concerning referring charges and specifications in a capital case or in a special court-martial consisting of a military judge alone under Article 16(c)(2)(A).

2023 Amendment: R.C.M. 601(a) is amended to allow for referral by special trial counsel.

The Discussion accompanying R.C.M. 601(a) deletes the reference to elements of referral of charges because it is not applicable to cases referred by a special trial counsel.

R.C.M. 601(b) is amended to allow for referral by special trial counsel.

R.C.M. 601(c) is amended to clarify that a special trial counsel is not disqualified from referring a charge as a result of having preferred the charge or having directed that the charge be preferred.

R.C.M. 601(d)(1) is amended to describe the process for referral of charges by special trial counsel.

R.C.M. 601(d)(2) is new and requires referral authorities to consider whether admissible evidence will probably be sufficient to obtain and sustain a conviction. This provision is consistent with the Principles of Federal Prosecution, Section 9-27.220 (updated January 2023) and Appendix 2.1 of the MCM. This provision does not alter the probable cause standard for referral. It does not expand the disclosure and discovery requirements of R.C.M. 308 and 701.

R.C.M. 601(e) is amended to allow for referral by special trial counsel.

The Discussion accompanying R.C.M 601(e) clarifies that a special trial counsel is not authorized to refer a charge to a special court-martial consisting of a military judge alone under Article 16(c)(2)(A).

The Discussion accompanying R.C.M. 601(e)(2) is amended to remove the language encouraging the convening authority to refer all known charges to a single court-martial, as this guidance may interfere with special trial counsel's exclusive authority.

R.C.M. 601(g)(2) is added, and the Discussion to R.C.M. 601(g) is amended, to allow for a convening authority to transfer charges to a parallel convening authority within the limitations prescribed by the Secretary concerned to avoid interfering with special trial counsel's exclusive authority.

Rule 602 Service of charges

This rule is taken from Rule 602 of the MCM (2016 edition) with the following amendment:

2018 Amendment: R.C.M. 602 is amended and implements Article 35, as amended by Section 5206 of the Military Justice Act of 2016, Division E of the National Defense Authorization Act for Fiscal Year 2017, Pub. L. No. 114-328, 130 Stat. 2000 (2016) regarding the time periods applicable to service of charges and commencement of trial, and sets forth the consequences for defense failure to object to proceeding during the applicable period

Rule 603 Changes to charges and specifications

This rule is taken from Rule 603 of the MCM (2016 edition) with the following amendments:

2018 Amendment: R.C.M. 603 and the accompanying Discussions are revised and clarify the definition of major and minor changes that may be made to charges and specifications that have been referred to trial by court-martial, and the timing requirements for making such changes to the charges and specifications.

2023 Amendment: R.C.M. 603(a) is amended to clarify the role of special trial counsel.

Rule 604 Withdrawal of charges

This rule is taken from Rule 604 of the MCM (2016 edition) with the following amendment:

2023 Amendment: R.C.M. 604(a) and its Discussion are amended to clarify the role of special trial counsel.

CHAPTER VII. PRETRIAL MATTERS

Rule 701 Discovery

This rule is taken from Rule 701 of the MCM (2016 edition) as amended by Exec. Order No. 13825, 83 Fed. Reg. 9889 (March 1, 2018), with the following amendments.

2018 Amendment: The amendments to R.C.M. 701 clarify discovery practice in the military justice system. The amendments enhance efficiency and ensure the prompt disposition of offenses, while at the same time ensuring fairness to the accused and the equal opportunity of both the prosecution and defense to obtain witnesses and evidence guaranteed by Article 46.

R.C.M. 701(a) is amended and aligns with the 2018 Amendments to the disclosure provisions of R.C.M. 404A.

The Discussion accompanying R.C.M. 701(a) is new and addresses the purposes of discovery in the military justice system.

R.C.M. 701(a)(2)(A)(i) and (a)(2)(B)(i) are amended and specify the scope of trial counsel discovery obligations. The provisions broaden the scope of discovery, requiring disclosure of items that are "relevant" rather than "material" to defense preparation of a case, and adding a requirement to disclose items the government anticipates using in rebuttal.

R.C.M. 701(a)(3) and (5), and R.C.M 701(b)(1)(A) and (C)(i) are amended and require the trial counsel and defense counsel to provide contact information, rather than addresses, of witnesses.

R.C.M. 701(a)(6)(D) is added and clarifies that trial counsel must disclose to defense counsel information adverse to the credibility of prosecution witnesses or evidence. *See Strickler v. Greene*, 527 U.S. 263, 280 (1999) (duty to disclose evidence favorable to the defense applies even in the absence of a request by the defense and encompasses impeachment evidence as well as exculpatory evidence).

The Discussion accompanying R.C.M. 701(a)(6) is amended and reflects that trial counsel may disclose information earlier than required by R.C.M. 701 or in addition to that required by the rule; that trial counsel have a continuing duty to disclose information favorable to the defense and should exercise due diligence and good faith in learning about such evidence; and should not avoid pursuit of information that may be harmful to the prosecution's case; and to update cross-references.

R.C.M. 701(b)(2) and the accompanying Discussion are amended and require that the defense provide notice of certain defenses in writing.

R.C.M. 701(b)(3) is amended and permits the trial counsel to copy or photograph the items listed for disclosure by the defense.

The Discussion accompanying R.C.M. 701(b)(5) is amended and updates cross-references.

The Discussion accompanying R.C.M. 701(d) is new and reflects that trial counsel should advise authorities involved in the case of their duty to identify, preserve, and disclose to trial counsel the information required to be disclosed under R.C.M. 701.

R.C.M. 701(e)(1) is amended and conforms to Article 6b, as amended by Section 5105 of the Military Justice Act of 2016, Division E of the National Defense Authorization Act for Fiscal Year 2017, Pub. L. No. 114-328, 130 Stat. 2000 (2016), as further amended by Sections 531(a), 1081(a)(22), and 1081(c)(1)(B) of the National Defense Authorization Act for Fiscal Year 2018, Pub. L. No. 115-91, 131 Stat. 1283 (2017).

R.C.M. 701(g)(2) is amended and clarifies the applicability of Part III of the Manual for Courts-Martial to the examination of materials by the military judge *in camera*. R.C.M. 701(g)(2) is further amended and clarifies the responsibilities of the military judge with respect to sealing materials and attaching materials examined to the record of trial.

The Discussion accompanying R.C.M. 701(g)(2) is new and addresses considerations relevant to the military judge's authority to regulate discovery in order to achieve the purposes of the Rule and reflects that the terms of a sealing order may authorize listed persons or entities to examine or receive disclosure of sealed materials outside the procedures set forth in R.C.M. 1113(b).

2023 Amendment: R.C.M. 701(a)(1) is amended to clarify which papers accompanying the charges must be provided to the defense as soon as practicable after service of charges.

Rule 702 Depositions

2018 Amendment: This rule is taken from Rule 702 of the MCM (2016 edition) with substantial amendments, clarifies the circumstances in which depositions may be ordered and their uses at trial, and reflects Article 49, as amended by Section 5231

of the Military Justice Act of 2016, Division E of the National Defense Authorization Act for Fiscal Year 2017, Pub. L. No. 114-328, 130 Stat. 2000 (2016), and the consequence for failure to object prior to or during a deposition, or to written interrogatories.

2023 Amendment: R.C.M. 702(b) is amended to clarify who can order a deposition.

Rule 703 Production of witnesses and evidence

2018 Amendment: This rule is taken from Rule 703 of the MCM (2016 edition) with substantial amendments and clarifies the procedures for requesting the production of witnesses and evidence at trial. The amendments are as follows:

R.C.M. 703(d) is amended and clarifies the distinction between expert witnesses and expert consultants. *See, e.g., United States v. Warner*, 62 M.J. 114 (C.A.A.F. 2005): *United States v. Turner*, 28 M.J. 487 (C.M.A. 1989); *United States v. Langston*, 32 M.J. 894 (A.F.C.M.R. 1991).

R.C.M. 703(g)(3)(C) and (D) and the Discussion accompanying R.C.M. 703(g)(3)(C) are new and reflect Article 46, as amended by Section 5228 of the Military Justice Act of 2016, Division E of the National Defense Authorization Act for Fiscal Year 2017, Pub. L. No. 114-328, 130 Stat. 2000 (2016), which authorizes the issuance of a pre-referral investigative subpoena under specified circumstances.

R.C.M. 703(g)(3)(C)(i) and (ii) and the accompanying Discussions are new. R.C.M. 703(g)(3)(C)(i) describes requirements for investigative subpoenas; R.C.M. 703(g)(3)(C)(ii) establishes a category of investigative subpoenas with respect to personal or confidential information of a victim consistent with the Fed. R. Crim. P. 17. This category of investigative subpoenas has special notice requirements, with appropriate exceptions for exceptional circumstances. The Discussion accompanying R.C.M. 703(g)(3)(C)(ii) also clarifies the meaning of the term "victim" for purposes of this provision.

R.C.M. 703(g)(3)(G) and (H) and the Discussion accompanying R.C.M. 703(g)(3)(H)(i) are amended and reflect Articles 30a and 46, as added and amended, respectively, by Sections 5202 and 5228 of the Military Justice Act of 2016, Division E of the National Defense Authorization Act for Fiscal Year 2017, Pub. L. No. 114-328, 130 Stat. 2000 (2016), which authorizes a military judge to review requests for relief from subpoenas prior to referral. Article 30a was amended by Section 531(b) of the National Defense Authorization Act for Fiscal Year 2018, Pub. L. No. 115-91, 131 Stat. 1283 (2017).

R.C.M. 703(g)(4) is new and reflects that a request for subpoena may be accompanied by a request that the custodian of the evidence take all necessary step to preserve records and other evidence until such time as the items may be produced or inspected. *Cf. United States v. Stellato*, 74 M.J. 473 (C.A.A.F. 2015).

2023 Amendments by Annex 1 of Executive Order No. 14103 (July 28, 2023):

R.C.M 703(d) is amended to require the Services to promulgate regulations for government and defense funding of expert witnesses and consultants.

R.C.M. 703(g)(3)(G), now R.C.M. 703(g)(3)(I), is amended to allow a named victim in a specification to request relief.

2023 Amendments by Annex 2 of Executive Order No. 14103 (July 28, 2023): R.C.M. 703(d)(2) is amended to change "shall" to "may" which recognizes the defense may continue to request funding of expert witnesses and consultants by the Government.

RCM 703(d)(2) is amended to add the "appointment" of an expert in addition to the "employment" or "funding" of an expert to account for the appointment of employees of the government.

R.C.M. 703(d)(2)(A) is amended to expand the types of defense requests that may be raised before the military judge (previously the defense could only raise a "denied defense request" before the military judge).

R.C.M. 703(d)(3) is added to require notice by both parties for expert witnesses.

R.C.M. 703(g)(3)(D) is added to allow the defense to request a subpoena, after referral, for witnesses *ex parte* from the military judge and require the military judge to issue such a subpoena if the witness's testimony is determined to be relevant and necessary.

R.C.M. 703(g)(3)(E) is amended to account for the addition of R.C.M. 703(g)(3)(D).

R.C.M. 703(g)(3)(F) is added to account for the addition of R.C.M. 703(g)(3)(D) by requiring notice to all parties for any subpoena issued for a witness post-referral, unless the military judge issues a protective order.

All other paragraphs are shifted to accommodate the additions in R.C.M. 703(g)(3) without further amendment.

Rule 703A Warrant or order for wire or electronic communication

2018 Amendment: R.C.M. 703A is new and implements Article 46, as amended by Section 5228 of the Military Justice Act of 2016, Division E of the National Defense Authorization Act for Fiscal Year 2017, Pub. L. No. 114-328, 130 Stat. 2000 (2016), which provides authority for a military judge to issue a warrant or order for the disclosure of the contents of electronic communications by a provider of an electronic communication service or a remote computing service. *See also* 18 U.S.C. §§ 2703 and 2711, as amended by Section 5228 of the Military Justice Act of 2016, Division E of the National Defense Authorization Act for Fiscal Year 2017, Pub. L. No. 114-328, 130 Stat. 2000 (2016).

Rule 704 Immunity

This rule is taken from Rule 704 of the MCM (2016 edition) as amended by Exec. Order No. 13825, 83 Fed. Reg. 9889 (March 1, 2018), with the following amendments:

2018 Amendment: The Discussion accompanying R.C.M. 704(d) is amended and updates cross-references and reflects the reorganization of the punitive articles in the Military Justice Act of 2016. See Articles 79-134, as amended by Sections 5401-5452 of the Military Justice Act of 2016, Division E of the National Defense Authorization Act for Fiscal Year 2017, Pub. L. No. 114-328, 130 Stat. 2000 (2016), as further amended by Section 1081(c) of the National Defense Authorization Act for Fiscal Year 2018, Pub. L. No. 115-91, 131 Stat. 1283 (2017).

2023 Amendments: R.C.M. 704(c) and its Discussion are amended to allow a special trial counsel designated by the Secretary concerned (or that individual's designee) to grant immunity for offenses over which a special trial counsel has exercised authority and not deferred.

R.C.M. 704(d)(1) is amended to allow the special trial counsel designated by the Secretary concerned (or that individual's designee) to grant immunity.

R.C.M. 704(d)(2) is amended to move language from the Discussion into the rule and clarify that the convening authority, not the special trial counsel designated by the Secretary concerned, shall order a person subject to the UCMJ who receives a grant of immunity to answer questions pursuant to that grant of immunity.

R.C.M. 704(e) is amended to allow the special trial counsel designated by the Secretary concerned to grant immunity."

Rule 705 Plea agreements

This rule is taken from Rule 705 of the MCM (2016 edition) with the following amendments:

2018 Amendment: R.C.M. 705 and the accompanying Discussions are substantially amended and reflect Article 53a, as added by Section 5237 of the Military Justice Act of 2016, Division E of the National Defense Authorization Act for Fiscal Year 2017, Pub. L. No. 114-328, 130 Stat. 2000 (2016), as amended by Sections 531(d) and 1081(c)(1)(H) of the National Defense Authorization Act for Fiscal Year 2018, Pub. Law. No. 115-91, 131 Stat. 1283 (2017), and Articles 33, 56 and 60, as amended by Sections 5204, 5301 and 5321 of the Military Justice Act of 2016, Division E of the National Defense Authorization Act for Fiscal Year 2017, Pub. L. No. 114-328, 130 Stat. 2000 (2016). Article 56 was further amended by Section 531(e) of the National Defense Authorization Act for Fiscal Year 2018, Pub. Law. No. 115-91, 131 Stat. 1283 (2017).

The Discussion following R.C.M. 705(d)(1)(C) is new and reflects the role of the military judge and the members in adjudging a sentence as part of a plea agreement.

R.C.M. 705(e) of the MCM (2016 edition) is renumbered as R.C.M. 705(f) and is amended and allows a military judge to notify a court-martial of the existence of a plea agreement upon either the request of an accused or to prevent a manifest injustice.

2023 Amendment by Annex 1 of Executive Order No. 14103 (July 28, 2023): R.C.M. 705(d)(1) is amended to allow the Secretary concerned to prescribe limitations pursuant to R.C.M. 705(a), and R.C.M. 705(d)(1)(D) is added to clarify that a plea agreement may include a specified sentence or portion of a sentence that shall be imposed by the court-martial.

2023 Amendment by Annex 2 of Executive Order No. 14103 (July 28, 2023): R.C.M. 705(a) and its Discussion are amended to account for plea agreements in cases over which a special trial counsel has exercised authority and not deferred. Under Article 53a, UCMJ, such plea agreements may only be entered into between a special trial counsel and the accused. Such plea agreements shall be subject to the same limitations and conditions applicable to other plea agreements under Article 53a, UCMJ. However, upon acceptance by the military judge of a general or special court-martial, a plea agreement shall bind the parties (including the convening authority and special trial counsel in the case of a plea agreement entered into under Article 53a(a)(3)) and the court-martial. R.C.M 705(a) requires plea agreements to be subject to limitations as prescribed by the Secretary concerned in order to provide clarity regarding the binding authority of a plea agreement.

R.C.M. 705(b) and its Discussion are amended to account for plea agreements in cases over which a special trial counsel has exercised authority and not deferred. R.C.M. 705(b)(3) is added to allow a promise by either the convening authority or a special trial counsel to take other action within their authority to be included in the plea agreement.

R.C.M. 705(c) is amended to account for plea agreements in cases over which a special trial counsel has exercised authority and not deferred.

R.C.M. 705(e) and its Discussion are amended to account for plea agreements in cases over which a special trial counsel has exercised authority and not deferred.

Rule 706 Inquiry into the mental capacity or mental responsibility of the accused

This rule is taken from Rule 706 of the MCM (2016 edition) with the following amendments:

2023 Amendments by Annex 1 of Executive Order No. 14103 (July 28, 2023): R.C.M. 706(b)(1) is amended to add authority for a military judge or magistrate to order an inquiry into the mental capacity or mental responsibility of an accused before referral, in accordance with R.C.M. 309.

R.C.M. 706(c)(3)(A) is amended to clarify that the only counsel entitled to the board's ultimate conclusions are government and defense counsel.

2023 Amendment by Annex 2 of Executive Order No. 14103 (July 28, 2023): R.C.M. 706(b) is amended to allow any applicable convening authority to order an inquiry into the mental capacity or mental responsibility of an accused. An "applicable convening authority" means a convening authority with authority over the accused.

Rule 707 Speedy trial

This rule is taken from Rule 707 of the MCM (2016 edition) with the following amendments:

2018 Amendment: R.C.M. 707(b)(3)(A) is amended and clarifies the effect of dismissal of charges or mistrial on the 120-day time period in which to bring a case to trial. The rule addresses both the circumstance where the accused, on the date of dismissal or mistrial, is under pretrial restraint and the circumstance where the accused, on the date of dismissal or retrial, is not under pretrial restraint. *See United States v. Anderson*, 50 M.J. 447 (C.A.A.F. 1997).

R.C.M. 707(e) is amended and clarifies the consequences of a plea of guilty on speedy trial issues as to the offense to which a plea of guilty is entered.

R.C.M. 707(f) is new and mandates that the trial of an accused held in pretrial restraint under R.C.M. 304(a)(3)-(4) be given priority, consistent with the Speedy Trial Act, *see* 18 U.S.C. § 3164 and Article 10, as amended by Section 5121 of the Military Justice Act of 2016, Division E of the National Defense Authorization Act for Fiscal Year 2017, Pub. L. No. 114-328, 130 Stat. 2000 (2016).

2023 Amendments by Annex 1 of Executive Order No. 14103 (July 28, 2023): R.C.M. 707(c)(1) is amended to remove the language authorizing the Secretary concerned to prescribe regulations allowing for a military judge to resolve requests for pretrial delay.

R.C.M. 707(e) is amended to clarify that the accused is waiving, not forfeiting, speedy trial issues by pleading guilty.

2023 Amendment by Annex 2 of Executive Order No. 14103 (July 28, 2023): R.C.M. 707(b)(3)(D) is amended to clarify when the 120-day time period for a rehearing begins for charges and specifications referred by special trial counsel.

R.C.M. 707(c)(1) and its Discussion are amended to require notification to the defense regarding pretrial delay requests. The rule is further amended by removing language from the Discussion and adding it to the rule to authorize the convening authority to delegate approval of pretrial delay requests to the preliminary hearing officer.

The Discussion accompanying R.C.M. 707(e) is removed.

CHAPTER VIII. TRIAL PROCEDURE GENERALLY

Rule 801 Military judge's responsibility; other matters

This rule is taken from Rule 801 of the MCM (2016 edition) with the following amendments:

2018 Amendments: The Discussion accompanying R.C.M. 801(a) is amended and reflects the elimination of special courts-martial without a military judge. *See* Article 16, as amended by Section 5161 of the Military Justice Act of 2016, Division E of the National Defense Authorization Act for Fiscal Year 2017, Pub. L. No. 114-328, 130 Stat. 2000 (2016), as further amended by Section 1081(c)(1)(C) of the National Defense Authorization Act for Fiscal Year 2018, Pub. Law. No. 115-91, 131 Stat. 1283 (2017).

The Discussion accompanying R.C.M. 801(a)(3) is amended and updates a cross-reference.

R.C.M. 801(a)(6) and the Discussion accompanying R.C.M. 801(a)(6)(E) are amended and reflect Article 6b, as amended by Section 5105 of the Military Justice Act of 2016, Division E of the National Defense Authorization Act for Fiscal Year 2017, Pub. L. No. 114-328, 130 Stat. 2000 (2016), as further amended by Sections 531(a), 1081(a)(22), and 1081(c)(1)(B) of the National Defense Authorization Act for Fiscal Year 2018, Pub. Law. No. 115-91, 131 Stat. 1283 (2017). The Discussion accompanying R.C.M 801(a)(6)(E) also clarifies the meaning of the term "victim of an offense under the UCMJ" as it pertains to this rule.

R.C.M. 801(e) and (f) are amended and reflect the elimination of special courts-martial without a military judge. *See* Article 16, as amended by Section 5161 of the Military Justice Act of 2016, Division E of the National Defense Authorization Act for Fiscal Year 2017, Pub. L. No. 114-328, 130 Stat. 2000 (2016), as further amended by Section 1081(c)(1)(C) of the National Defense Authorization Act for Fiscal Year 2018, Pub. Law. No. 115-91, 131 Stat. 1283 (2017).

The Discussion accompanying R.C.M. 801(e)(4) is amended and updates cross-references, and reflects the elimination of special courts-martial without a military judge. *See* Article 16, as amended by Section 5161 of the Military Justice Act of 2016, Division E of the National Defense Authorization Act for Fiscal Year 2017, Pub. L. No. 114-328, 130 Stat. 2000 (2016), as further amended by Section 1081(c)(1)(C) of the National Defense Authorization Act for Fiscal Year 2018, Pub. Law. No. 115-91, 131 Stat. 1283 (2017).

The Discussion accompanying R.C.M. 801(e)(5) is amended and reflects the elimination of special courts-martial without a military judge. *See* Article 16, as amended by Section 5161 of the Military Justice Act of 2016, Division E of the National Defense Authorization Act for Fiscal Year 2017, Pub. L. No. 114-328, 130 Stat. 2000 (2016), as further amended by Section 1081(c)(1)(C) of the National Defense Authorization Act for Fiscal Year 2018, Pub. Law. No. 115-91, 131 Stat. 1283 (2017).

Rule 802 Conferences

This rule is taken from Rule 802 of the MCM (2016 edition) with the following amendments.

2018 Amendment: R.C.M. 802(a) is amended and reflects Article 30a, as added by Section 5202 of the Military Justice Act of 2016, Division E of the National Defense Authorization Act for Fiscal Year 2017, Pub. L. No. 114-328, 130 Stat. 2000 (2016), as amended by Section 531(b) of the National Defense Authorization Act for Fiscal Year 2018, Pub. L. No. 155-91, 131 Stat. 1283 (2017), which provides the authority for military judges to preside over specified proceedings prior to referral.

Subsection (f) is amended and reflects the elimination of special courts-martial without a military judge. *See* Article 16, as amended by Section 5161 of the Military Justice Act of 2016, Division E of the National Defense Authorization Act for Fiscal Year 2017, Pub. L. No. 114-328, 130 Stat. 2000 (2016), as further amended by Section 1081(c)(1)(C) of the National Defense Authorization Act of 2018, Pub. Law. No. 115-91, 131 Stat. 1283 (2017).

Rule 803 Court-martial sessions with members under Article 39(a)

This rule is taken from Rule 803 of the MCM (2016 edition) with the following amendments:

2018 Amendment: R.C.M. 803 is amended and reflects the requirement for an entry of judgment in special and general courts-martial. *See* Article 60c, as added by Section 5324 of the Military Justice Act of 2016, Division E of the National Defense Authorization Act for Fiscal Year 2017, Pub. L. No. 114-328, 130 Stat. 2000 (2016). The last line of R.C.M. 803 is deleted and reflects the elimination of special courts-martial without a military judge. *See* Articles 16, 25, and 53, as amended by Sections 5161, 5182, and 5236, respectively, of the Military Justice Act of 2016, Division E of the National Defense Authorization Act for Fiscal Year 2017, Pub. L. No. 114-328, 130 Stat. 2000 (2016), as further amended by Sections 1081(c)(1)(C) and 1081(c)(1)(G) of the National Defense Authorization Act for Fiscal Year 2018, Pub. Law. No. 115-91, 131 Stat. 1283 (2017).

The Discussion accompanying R.C.M. 803 is amended and reflects changes to court-martial forums, the establishment of military judge alone sentencing as the default rule, and the elimination of special courts-martial without a military judge. *See* Articles 16, 25, and 53, as amended by Sections 5161, 5182, and 5236, respectively, of the Military Justice Act of 2016, Division E of the National Defense Authorization Act for Fiscal Year 2017, Pub. L. No. 114-328, 130 Stat. 2000 (2016), as further amended by Sections 1081(c)(1)(C) and 1081(c)(1)(G) of the National Defense Authorization Act for Fiscal Year 2018, Pub. Law. No. 115-91, 131 Stat. 1283 (2017).

Rule 804 Presence of the accused at trial proceedings

This rule is taken from Rule 804 of the MCM (2016 edition) with the following amendments:

2018 Amendments: The Discussion accompanying R.C.M. 804(a) is new and reflects the accused's entitlement to travel allowances for official travel to attend military justice proceedings.

R.C.M. 804(b) is amended and reflects the requirements of Article 39(b) with respect to remote proceedings and the physical presence of defense counsel with the accused, and prohibits the use of remote sessions for presentencing proceedings.

2023 Amendments by Annex 1 of Executive Order No. 14103 (July 28, 2023): R.C.M. 804(b) is amended to allow the use of remote sessions for presentencing proceedings under certain specified circumstances.

2023 Amendment by Annex 2 of Executive Order No. 14103 (July 28, 2023): R.C.M. 804 is rewritten to consolidate the rules pertaining to presence at court-martial proceedings generally.

R.C.M. 804(a) contains the provisions regarding the presence of the accused at court-martial proceedings previously addressed in R.C.M. 804. R.C.M. 804(a)(3) addresses the use of audiovisual technology to accomplish the presence of the accused in specific circumstances and allows the military judge to order presence by remote means for Article 39(a) sessions. R.C.M. 804(a)(3)(B) limits the accused's presence by remote means to guilty pleas and presentencing procedures unless: exceptional circumstances exist, the defense counsel is co-located with the accused, and the accused consents.

The Discussion accompanying R.C.M. 804(a) is deleted to remove an incorrect reference to the Joint Travel Regulations.

The Discussion accompanying R.C.M. 804(a)(2) (formerly R.C.M. 804(c)) is amended to remove the language not requiring the accused to consent to presence by remote means, consistent with amendments to R.C.M. 804.

The Discussion in R.C.M. 804(c)(1) (formerly R.C.M. 805(b)) is amended to remove the reference to member sentencing.

R.C.M. 804(d) (formerly R.C.M. 805(c)) is amended to account for special trial counsel presence in cases where a special trial counsel is detailed. A special trial counsel may determine his or her presence is not required, so long as another trial counsel, who is qualified according to R.C.M. 502(d), is present. The rule is also amended by explicitly providing the option in Article 39(a) sessions for counsel to satisfy the presence requirement through the use of audiovisual technology pursuant to R.C.M. 804(a)(3).

R.C.M. 804(e) is new and permits the remote presence of the victim and victims' counsel in limited circumstances.

Rule 805 [Reserved]

This rule is taken from Rule 805 of the MCM (2016 edition) with the following amendments:

2018 Amendment: R.C.M. 805(a) is amended and reflects the elimination of special courts-martial without a military judge. *See* Article 16, as amended by Section 5121 of the Military Justice Act of 2016, Division E of the National Defense Authorization Act for Fiscal Year 2017, Pub. L. No. 114-328, 130 Stat. 2000 (2016), as further amended by Section 1081(c)(1)(C) of the National Defense Authorization Act for Fiscal Year 2018, Pub. Law. No. 115-91, 131 Stat. 1283 (2017).

R.C.M. 805(b) and the accompanying Discussion are amended and reflect Articles 16 and 25, as amended by Sections 5161 and 5182 of the Military Justice Act of 2016, Division E of the National Defense Authorization Act for Fiscal Year 2017, Pub. L. No. 114-328, 130 Stat. 2000 (2016), as further amended by Section 1081(c)(1)(C) of the National Defense Authorization Act for Fiscal Year 2018, Pub. Law. No. 115-91, 131 Stat. 1283 (2017), which requires the use of fixed panel sizes, permits the accused the ability to request specified officer or enlisted composition, and permits the accused to elect sentencing by members, except where the court-martial is composed of a military judge alone.

R.C.M. 805(c) is amended and reflects the requirements of Article 39(b), with respect to remote proceedings and the physical presence of defense counsel with the accused, and prohibits the use of remote means to conduct presentencing proceedings.

The Discussion accompanying R.C.M. 805(c) is amended and updates cross-references.

R.C.M. 805(d) is amended and reflects Article 29(f), as amended by Section 5187 of the Military Justice Act of 2016, Division E of the National Defense Authorization Act for Fiscal Year 2017, Pub. L. No. 114-328, 130 Stat. 2000 (2016), which provides the option of playing an audio recording of the trial to newly detailed panel members and judges.

2023 Amendment: R.C.M. 805 is incorporated into an updated R.C.M. 804. R.C.M. 805 is now "Reserved" for future use.

Rule 806 Public trial

This rule is taken from Rule 806 of the MCM (2016 edition) with the following amendments:

2018 Amendment: R.C.M. 806(b)(1) is amended and deletes a provision addressing exclusion of spectators, which is now addressed in R.C.M. 806(b)(2).

R.C.M. 806(b)(2) is amended and addresses exclusion of spectators.

R.C.M. 806(b)(3) is amended and addresses the right of the victim not to be excluded. The Discussion accompanying R.C.M. 806(b)(3) is amended and addresses additional matters pertaining to victims, and clarifies the meaning of the term "victim of an alleged offense" as it pertains to this rule.

R.C.M. 806(b)(4) and (6) are deleted and the subject matter of those provisions is now addressed in a new R.C.M. 806(b)(3) and the accompanying Discussion.

R.C.M. 806(b)(5) is redesignated as R.C.M. 806(b)(4), and the accompanying Discussion is amended and updates cross-references.

R.C.M. 806(d) is amended and reflects the elimination of special courts-martial without a military judge. *See* Article 16, as amended by Section 5121 of the Military Justice Act of 2016, Division E of the National Defense Authorization Act for Fiscal Year 2017, Pub. L. No. 114-328, 130 Stat. 2000 (2016), as further amended by Section 1081(c)(1)(C) of the National Defense Authorization Act for Fiscal Year 2018, Pub. Law. No. 115-91, 131 Stat. 1283 (2017).

Rule 807 Oaths

This rule is taken from Rule 807 of the MCM (2016 edition) without substantive amendment.

Rules 808 Record of trial

This rule is taken from Rule 808 of the MCM (2016 edition) with the following amendments:

2018 Amendment: R.C.M. 808 is amended and updates a cross-reference.

The Discussion accompanying R.C.M. 808 is deleted in its entirety and the subject matter is covered by the 2018 Amendments to R.C.M. 1112.

Rule 809 Contempt proceedings

This rule is taken from Rule 809 of the MCM (2016 edition) with the following amendments:

2018 Amendment: R.C.M. 809(a) and (b) and the Discussion accompanying R.C.M. 809(a) are amended and reflect Article 48(a), as amended by Section 5230 of the Military Justice Act of 2016, Division E of the National Defense Authorization Act for Fiscal Year 2017, Pub. L. No. 114-328, 130 Stat. 2000 (2016), which uses the term "judicial officer." The use of the term reflects that judges are not detailed to courts of inquiry, and that judges serving on the Court of Appeals for the Armed Forces and the Courts of Criminal Appeals are not "detailed" to those courts in the sense that military judges are "detailed" to courts-martial.

The Discussion following R.C.M. 809(a) is further amended and reflects that, since 2011, the contempt power includes "indirect" contempts in addition to "direct" contempts. *See* Article 48, as amended by Section 542 of the Ike Skelton National Defense Authorization Act for Fiscal Year 2011, Pub. L. No. 111-383, 124 Stat. 4218 (2011), as further amended by Section 5230 of the Military Justice Act of 2016, Division E of the National Defense Authorization Act for Fiscal Year 2017, Pub. L. No. 114-328, 130 Stat. 2000 (2016), as further amended by Section 1081(c)(1)(F) of the National Defense Authorization Act for Fiscal Year 2018, Pub. Law. No. 115-91, 131 Stat. 1283 (2017).

R.C.M. 809(d) is amended and reflects Article 48, as amended by Section 5230 of the Military Justice Act of 2016, Division E of the National Defense Authorization Act for Fiscal Year 2017, Pub. L. No. 114-328, 130 Stat. 2000 (2016), as further amended by Section 1081(c)(1)(F) of the National Defense Authorization Act for Fiscal Year 2018, Pub. Law. No. 115-91, 131 Stat. 1283 (2017), which provides for appellate review of contempt punishments when imposed by military judges and military magistrates.

R.C.M. 809(e) is amended and addresses when execution of a sentence of contempt begins to run or becomes effective and the permissible maximum punishments that may be imposed for contempt *See* Article 48, as amended by Section 542 of the Ike Skelton National Defense Authorization Act for Fiscal Year 2011, Pub. L. No. 111-383, 124 Stat. 4218 (2011), as further amended by Section 5230 of the Military Justice Act of 2016, Division E of the National Defense Authorization Act for Fiscal Year 2017, Pub. L. No. 114-328, 130 Stat. 2000 (2016), as further amended by Section 1081(c)(1)(F) of the National Defense Authorization Act for Fiscal Year 2018, Pub. Law. No. 115-91, 131 Stat. 1283 (2017).

R.C.M. 809(f) is amended and reflects that judicial officers may exercise contempt authority and requires that a person held in contempt be informed of the procedures for review of a finding of contempt. *See* Article 48, as amended by Section 5230 of the Military Justice Act of 2016, Division E of the National Defense Authorization Act for Fiscal Year 2017, Pub. L. No. 114-328, 130 Stat. 2000 (2016), as further amended by Section 1081(c)(1)(F) of the National Defense Authorization Act for Fiscal Year 2018, Pub. Law. No. 115-91, 131 Stat. 1283 (2017).

Rule 810 Procedures for rehearing's, new trials, other trials, and remands

This rule is taken from Rule 810 of the MCM (2016 edition) with the following amendments:

2018 Amendment: R.C.M. 810(a)-(d) and the accompanying Discussions are amended and reflect Article 63, as added by Section 5327 of the Military Justice Act of 2016, Division E of the National Defense Authorization Act for Fiscal Year 2017, Pub. L. No. 114-328, 130 Stat. 2000 (2016), as amended by Section 531(i) of the National Defense Authorization Act for Fiscal Year 2018, Pub. Law. No. 115-91, 131 Stat. 1283 (2017), which addressed the limitations on sentences at rehearing's.

R.C.M. 810(f) is new and reflects Article 66(f)(3), as amended by Section 5330 of the Military Justice Act of 2016, Division E of the National Defense Authorization Act for Fiscal Year 2017, Pub. L. No. 114-328, 130 Stat. 2000 (2016), as further amended by Sections 531(j) and 1081(c)(1)(K) of the National Defense Authorization Act for Fiscal Year 2018, Pub. Law. No. 115-91, 131 Stat. 1283 (2017), and reflects, but does not expand, current practice regarding *DuBay* hearings. *See United States v. DuBay*, 37 C.M.R. 411 (C.M.A. 1967).

2023 Amendment: R.C.M. 810 is amended to account for rehearings in cases over which a special trial counsel has exercised authority. Specifically, R.C.M. 810(f) adds a requirement to notify special trial counsel because, in cases which were referred by a special trial counsel, special trial counsel exercise exclusive authority to determine whether an ordered rehearing is impracticable.

811 Stipulations

This rule is taken from Rule 811 of the MCM (2016 edition) without substantive amendment.

Rule 812 Joint and common trials

This rule is taken from Rule 812 of the MCM (2016 edition) with the following amendment:

2018 Amendment: The Discussion accompanying R.C.M. 812 is amended and addresses the differences between a joint and a common trial. *See* Major Robert S. Stubbs II, USMC, *Joint and Common Trials*, 1956 JAG Journal 16 (September-October).

Rule 813 Announcing personnel of the courts-martial and the accused

This rule is taken from Rule 813 of the MCM (2016 edition) with the following amendment:

2018 Amendment: R.C.M. 813(a)(3) is amended and reflects the elimination of special courts-martial without a military judge. *See* Article 16, as amended by Section 5161 of the Military Justice Act of 2016, Division E of the National Defense Authorization Act for Fiscal Year 2017, Pub. L. No. 114-328, 130 Stat. 2000 (2016), as further amended by Section 1081(c)(1)(C) of the National Defense Authorization Act for Fiscal Year 2018, Pub. Law. No. 115-91, 131 Stat. 1283 (2017).

2023 Amendment: R.C.M. 813 is amended to omit from announcement during the opening session of the court-martial, the name, rank, or position of the convening authority, with the exception of the Secretary concerned, the Secretary of Defense, or the President.

APPENDIX 15

CHAPTER IX. TRIAL PROCEDURE THROUGH FINDINGS

Rule 901 Opening session

This rule is taken from Rule 901 of the MCM (2016 edition) with the following amendments:

2018 Amendment: The Discussion following R.C.M. 901(a) is amended and provides a cross-reference reflecting applicable waiting periods between service of charges and commencement of trial by special and general courts-martial. *See* Article 35, as amended by Section 5206 of the Military Justice Act of 2016, Division E of the National Defense Authorization Act for Fiscal Year 2017, Pub. L. No. 114-328, 130 Stat. 2000 (2016).

R.C.M. 901(d)(2) and the Discussion accompanying R.C.M. 901(d)(3) are amended and reflect Article 27, as amended by Section 5186 of the Military Justice Act of 2016, Division E of the National Defense Authorization Act for Fiscal Year 2017, Pub. L. No. 114-328, 130 Stat. 2000 (2016) which requires, to the greatest extent practicable, that at least one defense counsel in a capital case be learned in the law applicable to capital cases.

R.C.M. 901(e) is amended and provides for the conduct of designated procedures without the members present, and to reflect the elimination of special courts-martial without a military judge. *See* Article 16, as amended by Section 5161 of the Military Justice Act of 2016, Division E of the National Defense Authorization Act for Fiscal Year 2017, Pub. L. No. 114-328, 130 Stat. 2000 (2016), as further amended by Section 1081(c)(1)(C) of the National Defense Authorization Act for Fiscal Year 2018, Pub. Law. No. 115-91, 131 Stat. 1283 (2017).

Rule 902 Disqualification of military judge

This rule is taken from Rule 902 of the MCM (2016 edition) with the following amendments:

2018 Amendment: R.C.M. 902(c)(1) is amended and reflects Article 30a, as added by Section 5202 of the Military Justice Act of 2016, Division E of the National Defense Authorization Act for Fiscal Year 2017, Pub. L. No. 114-328, 130 Stat. 2000 (2016), as amended by Section 531(b) of the National Defense Authorization Act for Fiscal Year 2018, Pub. L. No. 155-91, 131 Stat. 1283 (2017), which provides limited pre-referral authority to the military judge.

R.C.M. 902(c)(3) is deleted and reflects the elimination of special courts-martial without a military judge. *See* Article 16, as amended by Section 5161 of the Military Justice Act of 2016, Division E of the National Defense Authorization Act for Fiscal Year 2017, Pub. L. No. 114-328, 130 Stat. 2000 (2016), as further amended by Section 1081(c)(1)(C) of the National Defense Authorization Act for Fiscal Year 2018, Pub. Law. No. 115-91, 131 Stat. 1283 (2017).

2023 Amendment: R.C.M. 902(b)(3) is amended to clarify that a military judge is disqualified if the military judge has previously referred any charges as the special trial counsel in that case.

Rule 902A Application of sentencing rules [Removed]

2018 Amendment: R.C.M. 902A is new and implements Section 5542 of the National Defense Authorization Act for Fiscal Year 2017, Pub. L. No. 114-328, 130 Stat. 2000 (2016), which establishes effective dates for the amendments made by the Military Justice Act of 2016 and authorizes the President to prescribe regulations regarding applicable sentencing rules. R.C.M. 902A applies in cases where charges were referred to trial by court-martial after the effective date designated by the President for offenses allegedly committed both before and on or after the effective date. (Note, see text of Section 531(o), NDAA 2018).

2023 Amendment: R.C.M. 902A is removed. The substance of the rule is incorporated into the new R.C.M. 925.

Rule 903 Accused's elections on composition of court-martial

This rule is taken from Rule 903 of the MCM (2016 edition) with the following amendments:

2018 Amendment: R.C.M. 903 and its accompanying Discussion are amended and reflect Article 25, as amended by Section 5182 of the Military Justice Act of 2016, Division E of the National Defense Authorization Act for Fiscal Year 2017, Pub. L. No. 114-328, 130 Stat. 2000 (2016), which permits an accused to elect trial by military judge alone or by members, and, if the accused is enlisted, trial by a panel with at least one-third enlisted members or by an all-officer panel, and the elimination of special courts-martial without a military judge. *See* Article 16, as amended by Section 5161 of the Military Justice Act of 2016, Division E of the National Defense Authorization Act for Fiscal Year 2017, Pub. L. No. 114-328, 130 Stat. 2000 (2016), as further amended by Section 1081(c)(1)(C) of the National Defense Authorization Act for Fiscal Year 2018, Pub. Law. No. 115-91, 131 Stat. 1283 (2017).

Rule 904 Arraignment

This rule is taken from Rule 904 of the MCM (2016 edition) with the following amendment:

2018 Amendment: The Discussion accompanying R.C.M. 904 is amended and reflects the elimination of special courts-martial without a military judge. *See* Article 16, as amended by Section 5161 of the Military Justice Act of 2016, Division E of the National Defense Authorization Act for Fiscal Year 2017, Pub. L. No. 114-328, 130 Stat. 2000 (2016), as further amended by Section 1081(c)(1)(C) of the National Defense Authorization Act for Fiscal Year 2018, Pub. Law. No. 115-91, 131 Stat. 1283 (2017).

Rule 905 Motions generally

This rule is taken from Rule 905 of the MCM (2016 edition) with the following amendments:

2018 Amendment: The Discussion accompanying R.C.M. 905(b)(3) and (4) and R.C.M. 905(d) is amended and cross-references are updated.

R.C.M. 905(e) is amended and clarifies the applicability throughout the Manual of the concepts of waiver and forfeiture.

R.C.M. 905(f) and the Discussion accompanying R.C.M. 905(d) are amended to reflect the requirement for an entry of judgment in special and general courts-martial and the elimination of authentication of the record of trial. *See* Article 60c, as added by Section 5324 of the Military Justice Act of 2016, Division E of the National Defense Authorization Act for Fiscal Year 2017, Pub. L. No. 114-328, 130 Stat. 2000 (2016).

R.C.M. 905(h) is amended and authorizes the military judge to exercise his or her discretion to determine whether an Article 39(a) session is necessary for the resolution of a motion.

2023 Amendment: R.C.M. 905(e)(2) is amended to require a motion for failure of a charge to allege an offense to be raised before adjournment.

The Discussion to R.C.M. 905(g) is amended to account for special trial counsel.

Rule 906 Motions for appropriate relief

This rule is taken from Rule 906 of the MCM (2016 edition) with the following amendments.

2018 Amendment: R.C.M. 906(b)(4) is amended and clarifies the provisions governing amendment of charges after referral.

The Discussion accompanying R.C.M. 905(b)(5) is amended and updates a cross-reference and reflects the addition of Appendix 12A with respect to lesser included offenses. *See* Article 79, as amended by Section 5402 of the Military Justice Act of 2016, Division E of the National Defense Authorization Act for Fiscal Year 2017, Pub. L. No. 114-328, 130 Stat. 2000 (2016).

The Discussion accompanying R.C.M. 906(b)(7) is amended and updates a cross-reference.

R.C.M. 906(b)(10) is amended and addresses the standards applicable to severance of charges in capital and non-capital cases.

R.C.M. 906(b)(12) and the accompanying Discussion are amended and clarify the remedies available to address findings of unreasonable multiplication of charges in light of the requirement for segmented sentencing by military judges. *See* Article 56, as amended by Section 5301 of the Military Justice Act of 2016, Division E of the National Defense Authorization Act for Fiscal Year 2017, Pub. L. No. 114-328, 130 Stat. 2000 (2016), as further amended by Section 531(e) of the National Defense Authorization Act for Fiscal Year 2018, Pub. Law. No. 115-91, 131 Stat. 1283 (2017).

2023 Amendment: R.C.M. 906(b)(3) is amended to account for written determinations made by special trial counsel.

The Discussion accompanying R.C.M. 906(b)(10) is amended to delete the statement that all known charges should ordinarily be tried at a single court-martial.

R.C.M. 906(b)(12) is amended to delete references to member sentencing and move language from the Discussion to the rule stating that the ruling ordinarily should be deferred until after findings are entered.

Rule 907 Motions to dismiss

This rule is taken from Rule 907 of the MCM (2016 edition) with the following amendments: *2018 Amendment*: R.C.M. 907(b)(2)(C) and the accompanying Discussion are amended and reflect Article 44, as amended by Section 5226 of the Military Justice Act of 2016, Division E of the National Defense Authorization Act for Fiscal Year 2017, Pub. L. No. 114-328, 130 Stat. 2000 (2016), regarding the point when jeopardy attaches in a court-martial.

R.C.M. 907(b)(2)(D)(iii) is deleted and R.C.M. 907(b)(2)(D)(iv) is redesignated as R.C.M. 907(b)(2)(D)(iii).

Rule 908 Appeal by the United States

This rule is taken from Rule 908 of the MCM (2016 edition) with the following amendments:

2018 Amendment: R.C.M. 908(a) is amended and implements Article 62, as amended by Section 5326 of the Military Justice Act of 2016, Division E of the National Defense Authorization Act for Fiscal Year 2017, Pub. L. No. 114-328, 130 Stat. 2000 (2016), as further amended by Section 531(h) of the National Defense Authorization Act for Fiscal Year 2018, Pub. Law. No. 115-91, 131 Stat. 1283 (2017), which authorizes a Government appeal when a military judge sets aside a panel's guilty verdict. The Discussion accompanying R.C.M. 908(a) is new.

R.C.M. 908(b)(5) is amended and implements Article 54, as amended by Section 5238 of the Military Justice Act of 2016, Division E of the National Defense Authorization Act for Fiscal Year 2017, Pub. L. No. 114-328, 130 Stat. 2000 (2016), which requires the certification of the record of trial.

The Discussion accompanying R.C.M. 908(b)(7) is new and reflects changes to the jurisdiction of the Courts of Criminal Appeals. See Article 66(b), as amended by Section 5330 of the Military Justice Act of 2016, Division E of the National Defense Authorization Act for Fiscal Year 2017, Pub. L. No. 114-328, 130 Stat. 2000 (2016), as further amended by Sections 531(j) and 1081(c)(1)(K) of the National Defense Authorization Act for Fiscal Year 2018, Pub. Law. No. 115-91, 131 Stat. 1283 (2017), which provides that the Courts of Criminal Appeals maintain jurisdiction to review a case under Article 66(b) regardless of the sentence imposed when the government has filed an appeal under Article 62 or Article 56.

The Discussion accompanying R.C.M. 908(c) is new and reflects that the Government may appeal a sentence under certain circumstances and utilizing certain procedures. *See* Article 56, as amended by Section 5301 of the Military Justice Act of 2016, Division E of the National Defense Authorization Act for Fiscal Year 2017, Pub. L. No. 114-328, 130 Stat. 2000 (2016), as further amended by Section 531(e) of the National Defense Authorization Act for Fiscal Year 2018, Pub. Law. No. 115-91, 131 Stat. 1283 (2017).

R.C.M. 908(d) of the MCM (2016 edition) is deleted and reflects the elimination of special courts-martial without a military judge. *See* Article 16, as amended by Section 5163 of the Military Justice Act of 2016, Division E of the National Defense Authorization Act for Fiscal Year 2017, Pub. L. No. 114-328, 130 Stat. 2000 (2016), as further amended by Section 1081(c)(1)(C) of the National Defense Authorization Act for Fiscal Year 2018, Pub. Law. No. 115-91, 131 Stat. 1283 (2017).

2023 Amendment: R.C.M. 908(b)(6) is amended to move the requirement that The Judge Advocate General decides whether to file the appeal with the Court of Criminal Appeals to R.C.M. 908(b)(7).

R.C.M. 908(b)(7) is amended to clarify who is responsible for determining whether to file an appeal on behalf of the United States.

The Discussion accompanying R.C.M. 908(c) is amended to recognize that a special trial counsel may ask the Judge Advocate General to certify a case to the Court of Appeals for the Armed Forces.

Rule 909 Capacity of the accused to stand trial by court-martial

This rule is taken from Rule 909 of MCM (2016 edition) with the following amendments:

2023 Amendment by Annex 1 of Executive Order No. 14103 (July 28, 2023): R.C.M. 909(c)(2), now R.C.M. 909(c)(3), is added to permit the government or the accused to request that the military judge conduct a hearing to determine the mental capacity of the accused any time prior to referral.

2023 Amendment by Annex 2 of Executive Order No. 14103 (July 28, 2023):

R.C.M. 909(c)(2) is added to clarify that the convening authority, not the special trial counsel, takes action on the results of an inquiry under R.C.M. 706.

R.C.M. 909(g) is amended to account for cases in which a special trial counsel has exercised authority and not deferred.

Rule 910 Pleas

This rule is taken from Rule 910 of the MCM (2016 edition) with the following amendments:

2018 Amendment: R.C.M. 910(a)(1) is amended and implements Article 45, as amended by Section 5227 of the Military Justice Act of 2016, Division E of the National Defense Authorization Act for Fiscal Year 2017, Pub. L. No. 114-328, 130 Stat. 2000 (2016), which permits a military judge to accept a guilty plea in a capital case except where death is the mandatory punishment. Although the 2016 Amendments eliminated the sentence of death as a mandatory punishment for any offense, the prohibition against accepting a guilty plea in a capital case where death is the mandatory punishment is retained.

The Discussion accompanying R.C.M. 910(a)(1) is amended and reflects the addition of Appendix 12A with respect to lesser included offenses and reflects that no offenses carry a mandatory penalty of death. *See* Article 79, as amended by Section 5402 of the Military Justice Act of 2016, Division E of the National Defense Authorization Act for Fiscal Year 2017, Pub. L. No. 114-328, 130 Stat. 2000 (2016).

R.C.M. 910(c)(1) and the accompanying Discussion are amended and reflect changes to plea agreements and the sentencing proceeding in courts-martial. *See* Article 53a, as added by Section 5237 of the Military Justice Act of 2016, Division E of the National Defense Authorization Act for Fiscal Year 2017, Pub. L. No. 114-328, 130 Stat. 2000 (2016), as amended by Sections 531(d) and 1081(c)(1)(H) of the National Defense Authorization Act for Fiscal Year 2018, Pub. Law. No. 115-91, 131 Stat. 1283 (2017); and Article 56, as amended by Section 5301 of the Military Justice Act of 2016, Division E of the National Defense Authorization Act for Fiscal Year 2017, Pub. L. No. 114-328, 130 Stat. 2000 (2016), as further amended by Section 531(e) of the National Defense Authorization Act for Fiscal Year 2018, Pub. Law. No. 115-91, 131 Stat. 1283 (2017).

R.C.M. 910(c)(6) and the accompanying Discussion are new and reflect forum options for sentencing under the Military Justice Act of 2016. *See* Articles 53 and 56, as amended by Sections 5236 and 5301 of the Military Justice Act of 2016, Division E of the National Defense Authorization Act for Fiscal Year 2017, Pub. L. No. 114-328, 130 Stat. 2000 (2016). Article 56 was further amended by Section 531(e) of the National Defense Authorization Act for Fiscal Year 2018, Pub. Law. No. 115-91, 131 Stat. 1283 (2017).

R.C.M. 910(f) and the accompanying Discussions are amended and reflect changes to plea agreement practice in the military as a result of the Military Justice Act of 2016. *See* Article 53a, as added by Section 5237 of the Military Justice Act of 2016, Division E of the National Defense Authorization Act for Fiscal Year 2017, Pub. L. No. 114-328, 130 Stat. 2000 (2016), as amended by Sections 531(d) and 1081(c)(1)(H) of the National Defense Authorization Act for Fiscal Year 2018, Pub. Law. No. 115-91, 131 Stat. 1283 (2017).

R.C.M. 910(g) is amended and implements Articles 45 and 19, as amended by Sections 5227 and 5163 of the Military Justice Act of 2016, Division E of the National Defense Authorization Act for Fiscal Year 2017, Pub. L. No. 114-328, 130 Stat. 2000 (2016), which removed the requirement for the Services to maintain separate rules authorizing entry of a finding of guilty without a vote when a guilty plea has been accepted and eliminated special courts-martial without a military judge.

R.C.M. 910(h) is amended by deleting paragraph (3) and reflects the manner in which the military judge addresses the plea agreement under R.C.M. 910(f).

R.C.M. 910(i) is deleted. The requirement for a certified record of guilty plea proceedings is governed by R.C.M. 1112, 1114 and 1305.

R.C.M. 910(j) is redesignated as 910(i) and reflects the application of plain-error review to errors concerning guilty pleas raised for the first time on appeal. *See* Article 45, as amended by Section 5227 of the Military Justice Act of 2016, Division E of the National Defense Authorization Act for Fiscal Year 2017, Pub. L. No. 114-328, 130 Stat. 2000 (2016).

2023 Amendments: R.C.M. 910(f)(8) is added to establish the criteria a military judge shall use to reject a plea agreement.

R.C.M. 910(a) and its Discussion are amended to remove references to guilty pleas in cases in which death is the mandatory punishment. There no longer are any offenses for which a death sentence is mandatory.

The Discussions accompanying R.C.M. 910(f)(5) and (g) are amended to delete references to member sentencing.

R.C.M. 910(j) is amended to add that an accused waives any objections for non-jurisdictional defects in a plea of guilty.

The Discussion accompanying R.C.M. 910(j) is amended to change "forfeiture" to "waiver" and remove the "harmless error" standard.

Rule 911 Randomization and assembly of the court-martial panel

This rule is taken from Rule 911 of the MCM (2016 edition) with the following amendments:

2018 Amendment: The Discussion accompanying R.C.M. 911 is amended and authorizes the convening authority to refer charges to a special court-martial consisting of a military judge alone under such limitations as the President may prescribe by regulation, and updates a cross-reference. *See* Articles 16 and 19, as amended by Sections 5161 and 5163 of the Military Justice Act of 2016, Division E of the National Defense Authorization Act for Fiscal Year 2017, Pub. L. No. 114-328, 130 Stat. 2000 (2016).

2023 Amendments: R.C.M. 911 is amended to require randomization of court-martial members prior to assembly. Additionally, the amended rule describes the role of the military judge in the randomization process, to include determining how many members must be present at the initial session, how to temporarily excuse members, and how to cause members to be sworn before announcing the assembly of the court-martial.

R.C.M. 911(g) is amended to account for the randomization process in R.C.M. 911 and clarifies that each party is entitled to a peremptory challenge when additional members not previously subject to peremptory challenge are present and sworn.

The Discussion accompanying R.C.M. 911 is amended to delete reference to the order in which members are sworn at a court-martial.

Rule 912 Challenge of selection of members; examination and challenges of members

This rule is taken from Rule 912 of the MCM (2016 edition) with the following amendments:

2018 Amendment: R.C.M. 912(a)(1) is amended and reflects the authority of the convening authority to detail alternate members. *See* Article 29, as amended by Section 5187 the Military Justice Act of 2016, Division E of the National Defense Authorization Act for Fiscal Year 2017, Pub. L. No. 114-328, 130 Stat. 2000 (2016).

The Discussion accompanying R.C.M. 912(a)(1) is amended and updates a cross-reference.

R.C.M. 912(b)(3) is amended and clarifies that failure to make a timely motion challenging the selection of the members shall forfeit, but not waive, the improper selection, except in specified circumstances where the failure to make a timely motion neither forfeits nor waives the improper selection.

R.C.M. 912(f)(4) is amended and implements Article 25, as amended by Section 5182 of the Military Justice Act of 2016, Division E of the National Defense Authorization Act for Fiscal Year 2017, Pub. L. No. 114-328, 130 Stat. 2000 (2016), which eliminates the prohibition against detailing enlisted members from the same unit.

The Discussion accompanying R.C.M. 912(f)(4) is amended and updates a cross-reference.

R.C.M. 912(f)(5) is new and addresses the assignment of random numbers to members following challenges for cause for the purpose of impaneling members and alternate members as set forth in R.C.M. 912A.

The Discussion accompanying R.C.M. 912(g)(2) is amended and reflects the requirement for a specified number of members in special and general courts-martial. *See* Article 16, as amended by Section 5161 of the Military Justice Act of 2016, Division E of the National Defense Authorization Act for Fiscal Year 2017, Pub. L. No. 114-328, 130 Stat. 2000 (2016), as further amended by Section 1081(c)(1)(C) of the National Defense Authorization Act for Fiscal Year 2018, Pub. Law. No. 115-91, 131 Stat. 1283 (2017).

R.C.M. 912(h) of the MCM (2016 edition) is deleted and R.C.M. 912(i) is redesignated as R.C.M. 912(h). This reflects the elimination of special courts-martial without a military judge. *See* Article 16, as amended by Section 5161 of the Military Justice Act of 2016, Division E of the National Defense Authorization Act for Fiscal Year 2017, Pub. L. No. 114-328, 130 Stat. 2000 (2016), as further amended by Section 1081(c)(1)(C) of the National Defense Authorization Act for Fiscal Year 2018, Pub. Law. No. 115-91, 131 Stat. 1283 (2017).

2023 Amendments: R.C.M. 912 is amended to account for the randomized selection of detailed members to serve on a court-martial panel as required by R.C.M. 911. R.C.M. 912(f)(5) is deleted because R.C.M. 911 requires assignment of random numbers to detailed members prior to examination and challenges.

R.C.M. 912(g) is amended to describe the updated process for challenging a member peremptorily. *See* Article 41(c) and *United States v. Carter*, 25 M.J. 471 (C.M.A. 1988).

Rule 912A Impaneling members and alternate members

2018 Amendment: R.C.M. 912A is new and implements Articles 16, 25, and 29, as amended by Sections 5161, 5182, and 5187 of the Military Justice Act of 2016, Division E of the National Defense Authorization Act for Fiscal Year 2017, Pub. L. No. 114-328, 130 Stat. 2000 (2016), regarding the process for impaneling members after challenges for cause and peremptory challenges, and the process for impaneling alternate members if authorized by the convening authority. Article 16 was further amended by Section 1081(c)(1)(C) of the National Defense Authorization Act for Fiscal Year 2018, Pub. Law. No. 115-91, 131 Stat. 1283 (2017).

2023 Amendment: R.C.M. 912A(a) is amended to account for the randomization process in R.C.M. 911. Additionally, R.C.M. 912A(a)(4) is amended to prevent notifying alternate members that they are alternate members until the start of deliberations.

R.C.M. 912A(c) and (d) are amended to describe how the military judge orders additional detailed members to be present at the court-martial when the number of members is insufficient.

R.C.M. 912A(d)(3)(C) is added to allow the convening authority to instruct the military judge to prioritize impaneling a specific number of alternate enlisted members before impaneling alternate officer members.

Rule 912B Excusal and replacement of members after impanelment

2018 Amendment: R.C.M. 912B is new and implements Article 29, as amended by Section 5187 of the Military Justice Act of 2016, Division E of the National Defense Authorization Act for Fiscal Year 2017, Pub. L. No. 114-328, 130 Stat. 2000 (2016), which prescribes the process by which impaneled members may be excused and replaced by alternate members or additionally detailed members.

Rule 913 Presentation of the case on the merits

This rule is taken from Rule 913 of the MCM (2016 edition) with the following amendments:

2018 Amendment: The Discussion to R.C.M. 913(c)(2) is amended and updates a cross-reference.

The Discussion to R.C.M. 913(c)(3) is amended and deletes the first sentence, which reflected that views and inspections should be permitted only in extraordinary circumstances.

Rule 914 Production of statements of witnesses

This rule is taken from Rule 914 of MCM (2016 edition) with the following amendments:

2023 Amendments: R.C.M. 914(e) is amended to address situations in which there is a failure to produce a statement in good faith.

R.C.M. 914(e) is amended to change "trial counsel" to "Government."

Rule 914A Use of remote live testimony of a child

This rule is taken from Rule 914A of the MCM (2016 edition) without amendment.

Rule 914B Use of remote testimony

This rule is taken from Rule 914B of MCM (2016 edition) without amendment.

Rule 915 Mistrial

This rule is taken from Rule 915 of the MCM (2016 edition) with the following amendment:

2018 Amendment: The Discussion accompanying R.C.M. 915(b) is deleted and reflects the elimination of special courts-martial without a military judge. *See* Article 16, as amended by Section 5161 of the Military Justice Act of 2016, Division E of the National Defense Authorization Act for Fiscal Year 2017, Pub. L. No. 114-328, 130 Stat. 2000 (2016), as further amended by Section 1081(c)(1)(C) of the National Defense Authorization Act for Fiscal Year 2018, Pub. Law. No. 115-91, 131 Stat. 1283 (2017).

Rule 916 Defense

This rule is taken from Rule 916 of MCM (2016 edition) with the following amendments:

2018 Amendment: The Discussion accompanying R.C.M. 916(e)(2)(B) is amended to align with Article 128, as amended by Section 5441 of the Military Justice Act of 2016, Division E of the National Defense Authorization Act for Fiscal Year 2017, Pub. L. No. 114-328, 130 Stat. 2000 (2016), as further amended by 1081(c)(1)(P) of the National Defense Authorization Act for Fiscal Year 2018, Pub. Law. No. 115-91, 131 Stat. 1283 (2017).

R.C.M. 916(e)(3) and (5) and the Discussion accompanying R.C.M. 916(j) and R.C.M. 916(l)(2) are amended and reflect the reorganization of the punitive articles in the Military Justice Act of 2016. *See* Articles 79-134, as amended by Sections 5401-5452 of the Military Justice Act of 2016, Division E of the National Defense Authorization Act for Fiscal Year 2017, Pub. L. No. 114-328, 130 Stat. 2000 (2016), as further amended by Section 1081(c) of the National Defense Authorization Act for Fiscal Year 2018, Pub. Law. No. 115-91, 131 Stat. 1283 (2017).

The Discussion accompanying R.C.M. 916(k)(1) is amended and updates a cross-reference.

R.C.M. 916(k)(3)(B) and the accompanying discussion are amended and reflect the elimination of special courts-martial without a military judge. *See* Article 16, as amended by Section 5161 of the Military Justice Act of 2016, Division E of the National Defense Authorization Act for Fiscal Year 2017, Pub. L. No. 114-328, 130 Stat. 2000 (2016), as further amended by Section 1081(c)(1)(C) of the National Defense Authorization Act for Fiscal Year 2018, Pub. Law. No. 115-91, 131 Stat. 1283 (2017).

2022 Amendment: R.C.M. 916(e)(3) and (e)(5) are amended to include Article 128b, UCMJ.

2023 Amendment: R.C.M. 916(e)(2) is amended to change "assault with a dangerous weapon or means likely to produce death or grievous bodily harm" to "aggravated assault."

Rule 917 Motion for finding of not guilty

This rule is taken from Rule 917 of the MCM (2016 edition) with the following amendments:

2018 Amendment: R.C.M. 917(a) is amended and allows a military judge to rule on a motion under R.C.M. 917 after a panel returns findings, similar to the practice in U.S. District Court. *See* Fed. R. Crim. P. 29; *United States v. Wilson*, 420 U.S. 332 (1975).

The Discussion accompanying R.C.M. 917(a) is new and refers to R.C.M. 908(a) concerning the ability of the Government to file an interlocutory appeal when the military judge sets aside a panel's finding of guilty. *See* Article 62, as amended by Section 5326 of the Military Justice Act of 2016, Division E of the National Defense Authorization Act for Fiscal Year 2017, Pub. L. No. 114-328, 130 Stat. 2000 (2016), as further amended by Section 531(h) of the National Defense Authorization Act for Fiscal Year 2018, Pub. Law. No. 115-91, 131 Stat. 1283 (2017).

The Discussion accompanying R.C.M. 917(c) is amended and reflects the elimination of special courts-martial without a military judge. *See* Article 16, as amended by Section 5161 of the Military Justice Act of 2016, Division E of the National Defense Authorization Act for Fiscal Year 2017, Pub. L. No. 114-328, 130 Stat. 2000 (2016), as further amended by Section 1081(c)(1)(C) of the National Defense Authorization Act for Fiscal Year 2018, Pub. Law. No. 115-91, 131 Stat. 1283 (2017).

R.C.M. 917(f) is amended and permits the military judge to reconsider a denial of a motion for a finding of not guilty at any time before entry of judgment. *See* Article 60c, as added by Section 5324 of the Military Justice Act of 2016, Division E of the National Defense Authorization Act for Fiscal Year 2017, Pub. L. No. 114-328, 130 Stat. 2000 (2016).

Rule 918 Finding

This rule is taken from Rule 918 of the MCM (2016 edition) with the following amendments:

2018 Amendment: The Discussion accompanying R.C.M. 918(a)(1) is amended and clarifies when the fact finder may consider a lesser included offense if the evidence fails to prove the offense charged. *See* Article 79, as amended by Section 5402 of the Military Justice Act of 2016, Division E of the National Defense Authorization Act for Fiscal Year 2017, Pub. L. No. 114-328, 130 Stat. 2000 (2016).

The Discussion accompanying R.C.M. 918(a)(2) is amended and reflects the reorganization of the punitive articles in the Military Justice Act of 2016. *See* Articles 79-134, as amended by Sections 5401-5452 of the Military Justice Act of 2016, Division E of the National Defense Authorization Act for Fiscal Year 2017, Pub. L. No. 114-328, 130 Stat. 2000 (2016), as further amended by Section 1081(c) of the National Defense Authorization Act for Fiscal Year 2018, Pub. Law. No. 115-91, 131 Stat. 1283 (2017).

R.C.M. 918(b) is amended and requires the entry of special findings prior to the entry of judgment. *See* Article 60c, as added by Section 5324 of the Military Justice Act of 2016, Division E of the National Defense Authorization Act for Fiscal Year 2017, Pub. L. No. 114-328, 130 Stat. 2000 (2016).

2023 Amendment: R.C.M. 918(a)(1)(B) is amended to remove "named" before "lesser included offenses."

Rule 919 Argument by counsel on findings

This rule is taken from Rule 919 of the MCM (2016 edition) with the following amendment:

2018 Amendment: R.C.M. 919(c) is amended and addresses the consequences of a failure to object to error in argument.

Rule 920 Instructions on findings

This rule is taken from Rule 920 of the MCM (2016 edition) with the following amendments:

2018 Amendment: The Discussion accompanying R.C.M. 920(e) is amended and reflects the two statutory grounds by which to designate an offense as lesser included: those offenses that are "necessarily included" in the greater offense, and those offenses designated in regulations prescribed by the President that are "reasonably included" in the greater offense. *See* Article 79, as amended by Section 5402 of the Military Justice Act of 2016, Division E of the National Defense Authorization Act for Fiscal Year 2017, Pub. L. No. 114-328, 130 Stat. 2000 (2016).

R.C.M. 920(f) is amended and addresses the consequences of a failure to object to an instruction or the omission of an instruction.

2023 Amendment: R.C.M. 920(g) is added to prohibit instructions on a lesser included offense when both parties agree to its waiver.

Rule 921 Deliberations and voting on findings

This rule is taken from Rule 921 of the MCM (2016 edition) with the following amendment:

2018 Amendment: R.C.M. 921(c) and the accompanying Discussion are amended and reflect Article 52, as amended by Section 5235 of the Military Justice Act of 2016, Division E of the National Defense Authorization Act for Fiscal Year 2017, Pub. L. No. 114-328, 130 Stat. 2000 (2016), concerning voting on findings in a non-capital case.

Rule 922 Announcement of findings

This rule is taken from Rule 922 of the MCM (2016 edition) with the following amendments:

2018 Amendment: R.C.M. 922(a) is amended and conforms to Article 53, as amended by Section 5236 of the Military Justice Act of 2016, Division E of the National Defense Authorization Act for Fiscal Year 2017, Pub. L. No. 114-328, 130 Stat. 2000 (2016), as further amended by Section 1081(c)(1)(G) of the National Defense Authorization Act for Fiscal Year 2018, Pub. Law. No. 115-91, 131 Stat. 1283 (2017).

R.C.M. 922(b) and the accompanying Discussion are amended and conform to changes regarding the acceptance of guilty pleas by the military judge and the announcement of findings by the members.

2023 Amendment: The Discussion accompanying R.C.M. 922(a) is removed.

Rule 923 Impeachment of findings

This rule is taken from Rule 923 of MCM (2016 edition) without substantive amendment.

Rule 924 Reconsideration of findings

This rule is taken from Rule 924 of the MCM (2016 edition) with the following amendments:

2018 Amendment: R.C.M. 924(b) is amended and implements Article 52, as amended by Section 5235 of the Military Justice Act of 2016, Division E of the National Defense Authorization Act for Fiscal Year 2017, Pub. L. No. 114-328, 130 Stat. 2000 (2016), which reflects the changes in voting requirements. The subsection is also amended and reflects the elimination of any provisions imposing a mandatory death penalty.

R.C.M. 924(c) is amended and reflects the requirement for an entry of judgment and the elimination of authentication of the record of trial. *See* Article 60c, as added by Section 5324 of the Military Justice Act of 2016, Division E of the National Defense Authorization Act for Fiscal Year 2017, Pub. L. No. 114-328, 130 Stat. 2000 (2016).

2023 Amendment: R.C.M. 924(c)(2) is amended to replace "in the case of a complete acquittal" with "where there are no findings of guilty."

Rule 925 Application of sentencing rules

2023 Amendment: This rule is new and identifies which sentencing rules apply at a court-martial in order to carry out the amendments of Articles 53 and 56, UCMJ, as enacted by Section 539E of FY2022 NDAA. R.C.M. 925 determines the applicable sentencing rules based on the date of an offense for which the accused has been found guilty. If the accused is convicted of any offense committed on or before December 27, 2023, the court-martial shall follow the sentencing rules in effect at the time of the offense. R.C.M. 902A(d), regarding the accused's irrevocable election made prior to arraignment, is no longer applicable. If the accused is convicted only of non-capital offenses occurring after December 27, 2023, then the court-martial shall follow R.C.M. 925(c)(2), and the military judge shall sentence the accused.

CHAPTER X. SENTENCING

Rule 1001 Presentencing procedure

This rule is taken from Rule 1001 of the MCM (2016 edition) with the following amendments:

2018 Amendment: R.C.M. 1001 is amended and implements Articles 25, 53 and 56, as amended by Sections 5182, 5236, and 5301 of the Military Justice Act of 2016, Division E of the National Defense Authorization Act for Fiscal Year 2017, Pub. L. No. 114-328, 130 Stat. 2000 (2016). Article 56 was further amended by Section 531(e) of the National Defense Authorization Act for Fiscal Year 2018, Pub. Law. No. 115-91, 131 Stat. 1283 (2017). R.C.M. 1001(b)(1), (b)(2), and (h) set forth the consequences for failure to object to matters presented by the prosecution or argument on sentence.

The Discussion following R.C.M. 1001(b)(3)(C) is amended and reflects the new requirement for the entry of judgment in R.C.M. 1111.

R.C.M. 1001(c) is new and incorporates R.C.M. 1001A of the MCM (2016 edition).

2023 Amendments: R.C.M. 1001(a)(1) is amended to remove the reference to the accused's sentencing election to reflect the amendments of Articles 53 and 56, as enacted by Section 539E of FY2022 NDAA.

R.C.M. 1001(b)(2) and R.C.M. 1001(b)(3)(B) are amended to relocate a provision designating the point at which a summary court-martial conviction is admissible evidence of character of prior service of the accused during a sentencing proceeding.

R.C.M. 1001(b)(4) is amended to include additional aggravating factors, such as pregnancy and gender identity.

R.C.M. 1001(c)(1) is amended to permit a crime victim to make a request for a specific sentence in a non-capital case in sentencing proceedings conducted by a military judge in accordance with Section 539E of FY2022 NDAA.

R.C.M. 1001(c)(2)(B) is amended to strike the word "directly" in subparagraph (c)(2)(B) to allow victims to discuss the impacts of crimes upon others, such as family members.

R.C.M. 1001(c)(2)(D)(i) is amended and a Discussion section is added to reflect that, in capital courts-martial, the "right to be reasonably heard" may not include a recommendation of a specific sentence. *See Booth v. Maryland*, 482 U.S. 496 (1987); *Bosse v. Oklahoma*, 580 U.S. 1 (2016) (per curium).

R.C.M. 1001(c)(2)(D)(ii) is amended to add the right of a crime victim to be heard on any objection to an unsworn statement.

R.C.M. 1001(c)(3) is amended to permit a crime victim to recommend a specific sentence. However, note that R.C.M. 1001(c)(2)(D)(i) is amended to prohibit a crime victim's statement in a capital case from including a recommendation of a specific sentence.

R.C.M. 1001(c)(5) is amended to allow a crime victim's unsworn statement to be made by the crime victim, counsel representing the crime victim, or both. It is also amended to remove the procedure for reviewing a victim's proffer of an unsworn statement in sentencing proceedings conducted by military judges in accordance with Section 539E of FY2022 NDAA. The purpose of the amendment is to streamline the process, allowing victims to express crime impacts and allowing defense counsel to object or rebut as necessary.

R.C.M. 1001(f)(1) is amended to clarify that during presentencing proceedings, a dispute as to the production of a witness at Government expense is a matter within the discretion of the military judge.

R.C.M. 1001(h) is amended to specify that the trial counsel's argument may not speak for the convening authority or any other higher authority. That revision prohibits a trial counsel's sentencing argument from purporting to speak on behalf of a special trial counsel's leadership.

Rule 1002 Sentencing determination

This rule is taken from Rule 1002 of the MCM (2016 edition) with the following amendments:

2018 Amendment: This rule and its accompanying Discussions amend R.C.M. 1002 of the MCM (2016 edition) in its entirety and implement Articles 25, 53, 53a, and 56, as amended by Sections 5182, 5236, 5237, and 5301 of the Military Justice Act of 2016, Division E of the National Defense Authorization Act for Fiscal Year 2017, Pub. L. No. 114-328, 130 Stat. 2000 (2016), which provides an accused the option to elect sentencing by members in lieu of sentencing by military judge in a general or special court-martial with a military judge and members; reflects that sentences adjudged by a military judge shall provide for segmented sentences of confinement and fines; and sets forth statutory guidance for determining an appropriate sentence. Article 53a was further amended by Sections 531(d) and 1081(c)(1)(H) of the National Defense Authorization Act for Fiscal Year 2018, Pub. L. No. 115-91, 131 Stat. 1283 (2017).

Article 56 was further amended by Section 531(e) of the National Defense Authorization Act for Fiscal Year 2018, Pub. L. No. 115-91, 131 Stat. 1283 (2017).

2023 Amendments: R.C.M. 1002(a)(1) and its accompanying Discussion are amended to clarify that plea agreements for sentences less than the mandatory minimum are prohibited, unless otherwise authorized. "Unless otherwise authorized" provides for the possibility that future amendments to the UCMJ may specifically authorize plea agreements for sentences less than the mandatory minimum for violations of Article 118(1) and (4), UCMJ.

R.C.M. 1002(a)(2) is added to incorporate sentencing parameters and criteria. R.C.M. 1002(a)(2), now R.C.M. 1002(a)(3), is amended to clarify when a military judge may reject a plea agreement, in accordance with the Section 539E of FY2022 NDAA.

R.C.M. 1002(b)-(d) are amended and combined into subsection (b), deleting all references to sentencing forum selection and sentencing by members in noncapital cases.

R.C.M. 1002(e) is incorporated into an updated R.C.M. 1004.

The remaining sections are renumbered accordingly.

Rule 1003 Punishments

This rule is taken from Rule 1003 of the MCM (2016 edition) with the following amendments:

2018 Amendment: R.C.M. 1003(b)(2) is amended by adding the last sentence, which is consistent with *United States v. Warner*, 25 M.J. 64 (C.M.A. 1987).

R.C.M. 1003(c)(1)(C) is amended and removes discussion of the available remedies for Multiplicity and Unreasonable Multiplication of Charges. Such remedies are addressed in R.C.M. 906(b)(12).

The discussion immediately following R.C.M. 1003(c)(1)(C) is replaced with language directing practitioners to R.C.M. 906(b)(12).

2023 Amendments: R.C.M. 1003(b) is amended to clarify when forfeitures greater than two-thirds' pay may be imposed.

R.C.M. 1003(b)(5) is amended to clarify that the maximum duration of restriction that may be adjudged is two months. In calculating the maximum authorized sentence for an accused sentenced to both confinement and restriction in the same case, each month of confinement is equal to two months of restriction. For example, an accused may be sentenced to two months of restriction and also no more than five months of confinement for violating Article 91 for contempt or disrespect towards a superior noncommissioned or petty officer, which has a maximum confinement of six months.

R.C.M. 1003(c)(1) is amended to reflect the military sentencing parameter provisions of Section 539E(c) of FY2022 NDAA.

R.C.M. 1003(c)(2)(A)(ii) is deleted and the remaining subsections are renumbered. Under the amended rule, a commissioned or warrant officer or a cadet or midshipman can be sentenced to confinement by a special or general court-martial.

Rule 1004 Capital cases

This rule is taken from Rule 1004 of the MCM (2016 edition) with the following amendments:

2018 Amendment: R.C.M. 1004(a)(2) is amended and implements Articles 45 and 52, as amended by Sections 5227 and 5235 of the Military Justice Act of 2016, Division E of the National Defense Authorization Act for Fiscal Year 2017, Pub. L. No. 114-328, 130 Stat. 2000 (2016).

R.C.M. 1004(b)(4) is amended and clarifies that the members must find unanimously that at least one of the aggravating factors under subsection (c) existed beyond a reasonable doubt before death may be adjudged.

R.C.M. 1004(b)(6) is amended and requires that the military judge instruct the members of the charges and specifications for which they shall determine a sentence, because the accused has the option to choose sentencing by members, rather than the military judge, for those charges and specifications for which death may not be adjudged, in accordance with R.C.M. 1002(b)(2).

A Discussion is added after R.C.M. 1004(b)(6) and addresses an accused's right to elect sentencing by members in lieu of sentencing by military judge. *See* Articles 25 and 53 as amended by Sections 5182 and 5236 of the Military Justice Act of 2016, Division E of the National Defense Authorization Act for Fiscal Year 2017, Pub. L. No. 114-328, 130 Stat. 2000 (2016).

R.C.M. 1004(b)(7) is amended and reflects the requirement that members must unanimously concur in a finding of the existence of at least one aggravating factor and unanimously find that the extenuating and mitigating circumstances are substantially outweighed by any aggravating circumstances before a sentence of death may be considered.

R.C.M. 1004(c)(3) is amended and deletes the reference to Article 120.

R.C.M. 1004(c)(4) is amended and deletes the reference to Article 120 and reflects the reorganization of the punitive articles. *See* Articles 79-134, as amended by Sections 5401-5452 of the Military Justice Act of 2016, Division E of the National Defense Authorization Act for Fiscal Year 2017, Pub. L. No. 114-328, 130 Stat. 2000 (2016), as further amended by Section 1081(c) of the National Defense Authorization Act for Fiscal Year 2018, Pub. Law. No. 115-91, 131 Stat. 1283 (2017).

R.C.M. 1004(c)(6) is amended and deletes the reference to Article 120.

R.C.M. 1004(c)(7)(B) is amended and adds the phrase "a separate murder, or" and deletes the reference to forcible sodomy and reflects the reorganization of the punitive articles. *See* Articles 79-134, as amended by Sections 5401-5452 of the Military Justice Act of 2016, Division E of the National Defense Authorization Act for Fiscal Year 2017, Pub. L. No. 114-328, 130 Stat. 2000 (2016), as further amended by Section 1081(c) of the National Defense Authorization Act for Fiscal Year 2018, Pub. Law. No. 115-91, 131 Stat. 1283 (2017).

R.C.M. 1004(c)(8) is amended and deletes the reference to forcible sodomy and reflects the reorganization of the punitive articles. *See* Articles 79-134, as amended by Sections 5401-5452 of the Military Justice Act of 2016, Division E of the National Defense Authorization Act for Fiscal Year 2017, Pub. L. No. 114-328, 130 Stat. 2000 (2016), as further amended by Section 1081(c) of the National Defense Authorization Act for Fiscal Year 2018, Pub. Law. No. 115-91, 131 Stat. 1283 (2017).

R.C.M. 1004(c)(9) is deleted.

R.C.M. 1004(c)(11) is amended and reflects the reorganization of the punitive articles. *See* Articles 79-134, as amended by Sections 5401-5452 of the Military Justice Act of 2016, Division E of the National Defense Authorization Act for Fiscal Year 2017, Pub. L. No. 114-328, 130 Stat. 2000 (2016), as further amended by Section 1081(c) of the National Defense Authorization Act for Fiscal Year 2018, Pub. Law. No. 115-91, 131 Stat. 1283 (2017).

R.C.M. 1004(d) is deleted and subsection "(e)" is redesignated as subsection "(d)" and reflects the reorganization of the punitive articles and the removal of the mandatory death penalty for spying. *See* Section 5414 of the Military Justice Act of 2016, Division E of the National Defense Authorization Act for Fiscal Year 2017, Pub. L. No. 114-328, 130 Stat. 2000 (2016)(eliminating mandatory death penalty for spying). *See* Articles 79-134, as amended by Sections 5401-5452 of the Military Justice Act of 2016, Division E of the National Defense Authorization Act for Fiscal Year 2017, Pub. L. No. 114-328, 130 Stat. 2000 (2016), as further amended by Section 1081(c) of the National Defense Authorization Act for Fiscal Year 2018, Pub. Law. No. 115-91, 131 Stat. 1283 (2017).

2023 Amendment: R.C.M. 1004 is amended to consolidate the rules pertaining to sentencing in capital cases (R.C.M. 1004-1006, 1008, and 1009). Additionally, it accounts for the authority of special trial counsel in the referral process and amends the procedure for member voting in capital cases.

R.C.M. 1004(f)(4) is amended to replace the phrase "shall constitute waiver of the objection" with "forfeits the objection," aligning it with established definitions of waiver and forfeiture.

Rule 1005 Reconsideration of sentence in noncapital cases

This rule is taken from Rule 1005 of the MCM (2016 edition) with the following amendments:

2018 Amendment: The Discussion after R.C.M. 1005(e)(1) is amended and includes instructions to the members regarding the available range of permissible punishments when a plea agreement contains sentencing limitations.

The discussion after R.C.M. 1005(e)(5) is amended and reflects the terms of Article 56(c), as amended by Section 5301 of the Military Justice Act of 2016, Division E of the National Defense Authorization Act for Fiscal Year 2017, Pub. L. No. 114-328, 130 Stat. 2000 (2016), as further amended by Section 531(e) of the National Defense Authorization Act for Fiscal Year 2018, Pub. Law. No. 115-91, 131 Stat. 1283 (2017).

R.C.M. 1005(e)(6) is new and implements Article 56(c), as amended by Section 5301 of the Military Justice Act of 2016, Division E of the National Defense Authorization Act for Fiscal Year 2017, Pub. L. No. 114-328, 130 Stat. 2000 (2016), as further amended by Section 531(e) of the National Defense Authorization Act for Fiscal Year 2018, Pub. Law. No. 115-91, 131 Stat. 1283 (2017).

R.C.M. 1005(e)(7) is new and allows a military judge to provide additional instructions as may be required.

R.C.M. 1005(f) is amended and changes "waiver" to "forfeiture" when a party fails to object to an instruction or to omission of an instruction before the members close to deliberate on the sentence.

2023 Amendment: R.C.M. 1005 is a re-written version of R.C.M. 1009. It explains the process for reconsideration in noncapital cases and accounts for the authorities of special trial counsel in the reconsideration process.

Rule 1006 Deliberations and voting on sentence

This rule is taken from Rule 1006 of the MCM (2016 edition) with the following amendments:

2018 Amendment: R.C.M. 1006(a) is amended and implements Articles 25 and 53 as amended by Sections 5182 and 5236 of the Military Justice Act of 2016, Division E of the National Defense Authorization Act for Fiscal Year 2017, Pub. L. No. 114-328, 130 Stat. 2000 (2016).

R.C.M. 1006(d)(4)(B) of the MCM (2016 edition) is deleted and R.C.M. 1006(d)(4)(C) is redesignated as (d)(4)(B). This provision and its accompanying Discussion are amended and implement Article 52 as amended by Section 5235 of the Military Justice Act of 2016, Division E of the National Defense Authorization Act for Fiscal Year 2017, Pub. L. No. 114-328, 130 Stat. 2000 (2016).

R.C.M. 1006(d)(6) is new and implements Art 53a, as added by Section 5237 of the Military Justice Act of 2016, Division E of the National Defense Authorization Act for Fiscal Year 2017, Pub. L. No. 114-328, 130 Stat. 2000 (2016), amended by Sections 531(d) and 1081(c)(1)(H) of the National Defense Authorization Act for Fiscal Year 2018, Pub. Law. No. 115-91, 131 Stat. 1283 (2017).

R.C.M. 1006(e) is amended and implements Articles 52, 53, and 56 as amended by Sections 5235, 5236, and 5301 of the Military Justice Act of 2016, Division E of the National Defense Authorization Act for Fiscal Year 2017, Pub. L. No. 114-328, 130 Stat. 2000 (2016). Article 56 was further amended by Section 531(e) of the National Defense Authorization Act for Fiscal Year 2018, Pub. Law. No. 115-91, 131 Stat. 1283 (2017).

Rule 1007 Announcement of sentence

This rule is taken from Rule 1007 of the MCM (2016 edition) with the following amendments:

2018 Amendment: R.C.M. 1007(a) and its accompanying Discussion are amended and implement Article 53 as amended by Section 5236 of the Military Justice Act of 2016, Division E of the National Defense Authorization Act for Fiscal Year 2017, Pub. L. No. 114-328, 130 Stat. 2000 (2016), as further amended by Section 1081(c)(1)(G) of the National Defense Authorization Act for Fiscal Year 2018, Pub. Law. No. 115-91, 131 Stat. 1283 (2017).

R.C.M. 1007(b) and its accompanying Discussion are amended and conform with changes made to R.C.M. 1002. This rule reflects the accused's right to elect member sentencing in lieu of military judge sentencing for non-capital offenses and the requirement for the military judge to announce the sentence promptly after it has been determined.

Rule 1008 Impeachment of sentence

This rule is taken from Rule 1008 of the MCM (2016 edition) without substantive amendment.

Rule 1009 [Reserved]

This rule is taken from Rule 1009 of the MCM (2016 edition) with the following amendments:

2018 Amendments: R.C.M. 1009 and its accompanying Discussion are amended and implement Articles 52 and 53, as amended by Sections 5235 and 5236 of the Military Justice Act of 2016, Division E of the National Defense Authorization Act for Fiscal Year 2017, Pub. L. No. 114-328, 130 Stat. 2000 (2016), regarding reconsideration of the sentence, including in a capital sentencing proceeding.

R.C.M. 1009(b)(3) is new and reflects the addition of Article 53a, as added by Section 5237 of the Military Justice Act of 2016, Division E of the National Defense Authorization Act for Fiscal Year 2017, Pub. L. No. 114-328, 130 Stat. 2000 (2016), as amended by Section 531(d) and 1081(c)(1)(H) of the National Defense Authorization Act for Fiscal Year 2018, Pub. L. No. 115-91, 131 Stat. 1283 (2017).

2023 Amendment: R.C.M. 1009 is incorporated into an updated R.C.M. 1004. R.C.M. 1009 is now "Reserved" for future use. Portions of the rule that pertained to capital cases were moved to R.C.M. 1004. Provisions no longer applicable in light of changes to sentencing procedures enacted by Section 539E of FY2022 NDAA were deleted.

Rule 1010 Notice concerning post-trial and appellate rights

This rule is taken from Rule 1010 of the MCM (2016 edition) with the following amendments:

2018 Amendment: R.C.M. 1010 is amended and implements Articles 60a, 60b, 61, 64-67, and 69, as amended by Sections 5322, 5323, 5325, 5328, 5329, 5330, 5331, and 5333 of the Military Justice Act of 2016, Division E of the National Defense Authorization Act for Fiscal Year 2017, Pub. L. No. 114-328, 130 Stat. 2000 (2016), regarding appellate procedure.

The Discussion following R.C.M. 1010(d) is amended and corrects a cross-reference.

Rule 1011 Adjournment

This rule is taken from Rule 1011 of the MCM (2016 edition) without substantive amendment. The Discussion accompanying R.C.M. 1011 is amended and corrects a cross-reference.

CHAPTER XI. POST-TRIAL PROCEDURE

Rule 1101 Statement of trial results

2018 Amendment: R.C.M. 1101 ("Report of result of trial; post-trial restraint; deferment of confinement, forfeitures and reduction in grade; waiver of Article 58b forfeitures") of the MCM (2016 edition) is deleted.

R.C.M. 1101 ("Statement of trial results") and its accompanying Discussion are new. R.C.M. 1101 implements Article 60, as amended by Section 5321 of the Military Justice Act of 2016, Division E of the National Defense Authorization Act for Fiscal Year 2017, Pub. L. No. 114-328, 130 Stat. 2000 (2016), regarding the requirement that the military judge of a general or special court-martial enter into the record of trial a document entitled "Statement of Trial Results.

2023 Amendment by Annex 1 of Executive Order No. 14103 (July 28, 2023): R.C.M. 1101(e) is new and describes how the Statement of Trial Results may be modified.

Rule 1102 Execution and effective date of sentences

2018 Amendment: R.C.M. 1102 ("Post-trial Sessions") of the MCM (2016 edition) is deleted.

R.C.M. 1102 ("Execution and effective date of sentences") and its accompanying Discussion are new. R.C.M. 1102 implements Articles 57 and 60-60c, as amended by Sections 5302, 5321, 5322, 5323 and 5324 of the Military Justice Act of 2016, Division E of the National Defense Authorization Act for Fiscal Year 2017, Pub. L. No. 114-328, 130 Stat. 2000 (2016), regarding the execution and effective date of sentences.

2023 Amendment: R.C.M. 1102(b)(1) is amended and R.C.M. 1102(b)(6) is added to clarify language for enlisted reductions in grade.

Rule 1102A [REMOVED]

2018 Amendment: R.C.M. 1102A ("Post-trial hearing for person found not guilty only by reason of lack of mental responsibility") of the MCM (2016 edition) is deleted and its provisions are incorporated into R.C.M. 1105 without substantial amendment.

Rule 1103 Deferment of confinement, forfeitures, and reduction in grade; waiver of Article 58b forfeitures

2018 Amendment: R.C.M. 1103 ("Preparation of record of trial") of the MCM (2016 edition) as amended by Exec. Order No. 13825, 83 Fed. Reg. 9889 (March 1, 2018), is deleted.

R.C.M. 1103 ("Deferment of confinement, forfeitures, and reduction in grade; waiver of Article 58b forfeitures") and its accompanying Discussion are new. R.C.M. 1103 implements Article 57(b), as amended by Section 5302 of the Military Justice Act of 2016, Division E of the National Defense Authorization Act for Fiscal Year 2017, Pub. L. No. 114-328, 130 Stat. 2000 (2016).

R.C.M. 1103 also incorporates portions of R.C.M. 1101 and 1107 of the MCM (2016 edition), regarding deferment of confinement, forfeitures, and reduction in grade, as well as waiver of Article 58b forfeitures.

2023 Amendment: R.C.M. 1103(a)(1) is amended to add a notice requirement to special trial counsel in cases over which special trial counsel has exercised authority when there is a request by an accused for deferment of confinement, forfeitures, and reduction in grade and when the convening authority makes a decision on the request.

Rule 1103A [REMOVED]

2018 Amendment: R.C.M. 1103A ("Sealed exhibits and proceedings") of the MCM (2016 edition) as amended by Exec. Order No. 13825, 83 Fed. Reg. 9889 (March 1, 2018), and its accompanying Discussion are deleted and its provisions are incorporated into R.C.M. 1113.

Rule 1104 Post-trial motions and proceedings

2018 Amendment: R.C.M. 1104 ("Records of trial: Authentication; service; loss; correction; forwarding") of the MCM (2016 edition) and its accompanying Discussion are deleted.

R.C.M. 1104 ("Post-trial motions and proceedings") and its accompanying Discussion are new. R.C.M. 1004 implements the provisions of Articles 60-60c, as amended by Sections 5321, 5322, 5323, and 5324 of the Military Justice Act of 2016, Division E of the National Defense Authorization Act for Fiscal Year 2017, Pub. L. No. 114-328, 130 Stat. 2000 (2016), and authorizes the filing of post-trial motions before entry of judgment.

R.C.M. 1104 also incorporates portions of R.C.M. 1102 of the MCM (2016 edition).

2023 Amendment: R.C.M. 1104(e) is amended to require notice to victims of certain post-trial motions and hearings.

Rule 1105 Post-trial hearing for person found not guilty only by reason of lack of mental responsibility

2018 Amendment: RCM 1105 ("Matters submitted by the accused") of the MCM (2016 edition) and its accompanying Discussion are deleted.

R.C.M. 1105 ("Post-trial hearing for person found not guilty only by reason of lack of mental responsibility") is new and incorporates R.C.M. 1102A of the MCM (2016 edition) regarding a post-trial hearing for a person found not guilty only by reason of lack of mental responsibility without substantive amendments.

Rule 1105A [REMOVED]

2018 Amendment: R.C.M. 1105A ("Matters submitted by a crime victim") of the MCM (2016 edition) and its accompanying Discussion are deleted and its provisions are substantially incorporated into R.C.M. 1106A.

Rule 1106 Matters submitted by accused

2018 Amendment: R.C.M. 1106 ("Recommendation of the staff judge advocate or legal officer") of the MCM (2016 edition) and its accompanying Discussion are deleted.

R.C.M. 1106 ("Matters submitted by the accused") and its accompanying Discussion are new and incorporate portions of R.C.M. 1105 of the MCM (2016 edition) addressing the post-trial submission of matters to the convening authority by the accused.

Rule 1106A Matters submitted by crime victim

2018 Amendment: R.C.M. 1106A and its accompanying Discussion are new and incorporate portions of R.C.M. 1105A of the MCM (2016 edition) addressing the post-trial submission of matters by the crime victim to the convening authority.

Rule 1107 Suspension of execution of sentence; remission

2018 Amendment: R.C.M. 1107 ("Action by convening authority") of the MCM (2016 edition) and its accompanying Discussion are deleted.

R.C.M. 1107 ("Suspension of execution of sentence; remission") is new and implements Articles 60-60c, as amended by Sections 5321, 5322, 5323, and 5324 of the Military Justice Act of 2016, Division E of the National Defense Authorization Act for Fiscal Year 2017, Pub. L. No. 114-328, 130 Stat. 2000 (2016), regarding suspension of a sentence and the remission of a sentence in limited circumstances.

The rule incorporates portions of R.C.M. 1108 of the MCM (2016 edition).

2023 Amendment: R.C.M. 1107(b)(2) is amended to clarify that only the convening authority may suspend the unexecuted portions of the sentence.

Rule 1108 Vacation of suspension of sentence

2018 Amendment: R.C.M. 1108 ("Suspension of execution of sentence; remission") of the MCM (2016 edition) and its accompanying Discussion are deleted.

R.C.M. 1108 ("Vacation of suspension of sentence") and its accompanying Discussion are new. R.C.M. 1108 implements Articles 60-60c and 72 as amended by Sections 5321, 5322, 5323, 5324, and 5335 of the Military Justice Act of 2016, Division E of the National Defense Authorization Act for Fiscal Year 2017, Pub. L. No. 114-328, 130 Stat. 2000 (2016), regarding procedures for the vacation of a suspension of a sentence.

R.C.M. 1108 incorporates portions of R.C.M. 1109 of the MCM (2016 edition).

Rule 1109 Reduction of sentence, general and special courts-martial

2018 Amendment: R.C.M. 1109 ("Vacation of suspension of sentence") of the MCM (2016 edition), as amended by Exec. Order No. 13825, 83 Fed. Reg. 9889 (March 1, 2018), and it's accompanying Discussion, are deleted.

R.C.M. 1109 ("Reduction of Sentence, general and special courts-martial") and its accompanying Discussion are new. R.C.M. 1109 implements Articles 60-60c, as amended by Sections 5321, 5322, 5323, and 5324 of the Military Justice Act of 2016, Division E of the National Defense Authorization Act for Fiscal Year 2017, Pub. L. No. 114-328, 130 Stat. 2000 (2016), regarding the reduction of a sentence in specified general or special court-martials.

R.C.M. 1109 incorporates portions of R.C.M. 1107 of the MCM (2016 edition).

2023 Amendment: R.C.M. 1109(e) is amended to clarify that only the convening authority may act on reducing the sentence of the accused for substantial assistance. R.C.M. 1109(g)(2) is amended to expand the written requirement to explain when any part of a sentence is reduced, commuted, or suspended.

Rule 1110 Action by convening authority in certain general and special court-martial

2018 Amendment: R.C.M. 1110 ("Waiver or withdrawal of appellate review") of the MCM (2016 edition) and its accompanying Discussion are deleted.

R.C.M. 1110 ("Action by convening authority in certain general and special courts-martial") and its accompanying Discussion are new. R.C.M. 1110 implements Articles 60-60c, as amended by Sections 5321, 5322, 5323, and 5324 of the Military Justice Act of 2016, Division E of the National Defense Authorization Act for Fiscal Year 2017, Pub. L. No. 114-328, 130 Stat. 2000 (2016), regarding the action that the convening authority may take in certain general and special courts-martial.

R.C.M. 1110 incorporates portions of R.C.M. 1107 of the MCM (2016 edition).

Rule 1111 Entry of judgment

2018 Amendment: R.C.M. 1111 ("Disposition of the record of trial after action") of the MCM (2016 edition) and its accompanying Discussion are deleted.

R.C.M. 1111 ("Entry of judgment") and its accompanying Discussion are new. R.C.M. 1111 implements Articles 60c and 63, as added by Sections 5324 and 5327 of the Military Justice Act of 2016, Division E of the National Defense Authorization Act for Fiscal Year 2017, Pub. L. No. 114-328, 130 Stat. 2000 (2016). Article 63 was amended by Section 531(i) of the National Defense Authorization Act for Fiscal Year 2018, Pub. L. No. 115-91, 131Stat. 1283 (2017).

The entry of judgment replaces the action by the convening authority as the means by which the trial proceedings terminate and the appellate process begins. The judgment replaces the promulgating order as the document that reflects the outcome of the court-martial.

2023 Amendment: R.C.M. 1109(e) is amended to clarify the process for a military judge to modify a judgment.

Rule 1112 Certification of record of trial; general and special courts-martial

2018 Amendment: R.C.M. 1112 ("Review by a judge advocate") of the MCM (2016 edition) and its accompanying Discussion are deleted.

R.C.M. 1112 ("Certification of record of trial; general and special courts-martial") and its accompanying Discussion are new. R.C.M. 1112 implements Articles 54 and 60-60c, as amended by Sections 5238, 5321, 5322, 5323, and 5324 of the Military Justice Act of 2016, Division E of the National Defense Authorization Act for Fiscal Year 2017, Pub. L. No. 114-328, 130 Stat. 2000 (2016), providing for the certification and contents of records of trial in general and special courts-martial.

R.C.M. 1112 incorporates portions of R.C.M. 1103 of the MCM (2016 edition).

The Discussion following R.C.M. 1112(e)(3)(B)(iii) reflects that the terms of a sealing order may authorize listed persons or entities to examine or receive disclosure of sealed materials outside of the procedures set forth in R.C.M. 1113(b).

2023 Amendment by Annex 1 of Executive Order No. 14103 (July 28, 2023): R.C.M. 1112(b)(5) is amended to require the election for application of sentencing rules in effect on or after January 1, 2019, to be included in the record of trial.

2023 Amendment by Annex 3 of Executive Order No. 14103 (July 28, 2023): The former provisions of R.C.M. 1112(b)(5) are deleted because the accused's sentencing election will no longer be applicable under the sentencing reform measures enacted by Section 539E(c) of FY2022 NDAA. Subsequent subparagraphs are redesignated.

Rule 1113 Sealed exhibits, proceedings, and other materials

2018 Amendment: R.C.M. 1113 ("Execution of sentences") of the MCM (2016 edition) and its accompanying Discussion are deleted.

R.C.M. 1113 ("Sealed exhibits and proceedings") and its accompanying Discussion are new and incorporate R.C.M. 1103A of the MCM (2016 edition) as amended by Exec. Order No. 13825, 83 Fed. Reg. 9889 (March 1, 2018). R.C.M. 1113(b) conforms to changes in R.C.M. 1112(c) regarding certification of records of trial.

The Discussion following R.C.M. 1113(b) is new and reflects

that the terms of a sealing order may authorize listed persons or entities to examine or receive disclosure of sealed materials outside of the procedures set forth in R.C.M. 1113(b).

2023 Amendment by Annex 1 of Executive Order No. 14103 (July 28, 2023): R.C.M. 1113(b)(3)(C) is amended to add the Judge Advocates General to those empowered to authorize the disclosure of sealed materials. The authority of the Judge Advocates General applies in cases eligible for review under R.C.M. 1203 or 1204

2023 Amendment by Annex 2 of Executive Order No. 14103 (July 28, 2023): R.C.M. 1113(b)(1) is amended to authorize special trial counsel to examine and disclose sealed materials for the purposes of making a determination on referral.

Rule 1114 Transcription of proceedings

2018 Amendment: R.C.M. 1114 ("Promulgating orders") of MCM (2016 edition) and its accompanying Discussion are deleted.

R.C.M. 1114 ("Transcription of proceedings") and its accompanying Discussion are new. R.C.M. 1114 implements Article 54(c), as amended by Section 5238 of the Military Justice Act of 2016, Division E of the National Defense Authorization Act for Fiscal Year 2017, Pub. L. No. 114-328, 130 Stat. 2000 (2016), regarding the contents of a record of trial.

Rule 1115 Waiver or withdrawal of appellate review

R.C.M. 1115 ("Waiver or withdrawal of appellate review") and its accompanying Discussion are new and are taken from Rule 1110 of the MCM (2016 edition) with the following amendments:

2018 Amendment: R.C.M. 1115 and its accompanying Discussion are new. R.C.M. 1115 implements Article 61, as amended by Section 5325 of the Military Justice Act of 2016, Division E of the National Defense Authorization Act for Fiscal Year 2017, Pub. L. No. 114-328, 130 Stat. 2000 (2016), regarding waiver or withdrawal of appellate review.

2023 Amendment: R.C.M. 1115(a) is amended to reflect the expansion of appeal-as-of-right to the Courts of Criminal Appeals enacted by Section 544 of the James M. Inhofe NDAA for FY 2023, Pub. L. No. 117-263, 136 Stat. 2395, 2582 (2022) [hereinafter FY2023 NDAA].

Rule 1116 Transmittal of records of trial for general and special courts-martial

2018 Amendment: R.C.M. 1116 ("Transmittal of records of trial for general and special courts-martial") and its accompanying Discussion are new. R.C.M. 1116 implements Articles 65 and 66, as amended by Sections 5329 and 5330 of the Military Justice Act of 2016, Division E of the National Defense Authorization Act for Fiscal Year 2017, Pub. L. No. 114-328, 130 Stat. 2000 (2016), regarding the transmittal of records of trial in general and special courts-martial to the Judge Advocate General and the Courts of Criminal Appeals. Article 66 was further amended by Sections 531(j) and 1081(c)(1)(K) of the National Defense Authorization Act for Fiscal Year 2018, Pub. Law. No. 115-91, 131 Stat. 1283 (2017).

2023 Amendment: R.C.M. 1116(c) is amended to reflect the expansion of appeal-as-of-right to the Courts of Criminal Appeals enacted by Section 544 of FY2023 NDAA.

Rule 1117 Appeal of sentence by the United States

2018 Amendment. R.C.M. 1117 ("Appeal of sentence by the United States") and its accompanying Discussion are new. R.C.M. 1117 implements Article 56(d), as added by Section 5301 of the Military Justice Act of 2016, Division E of the National Defense Authorization Act for Fiscal Year 2017, Pub. L. No. 114-328, 130 Stat. 2000 (2016), as amended by Section 531(e) of the National Defense Authorization Act for Fiscal Year 2018, Pub. Law. No. 115-91, 131 Stat. 1283 (2017).

2023 Amendments: R.C.M. 1117(a) is amended to permit the Government to appeal a sentence to the Court of Criminal Appeals on the grounds that the sentence is a result of an incorrect application of a sentencing parameter or criterion, as authorized by Article 56(d), UCMJ.

R.C.M. 1117(c)(3) is amended to require that the statement of reasons in support of an appeal under R.C.M. 1117(a)(2) identify the parameters or criteria at issue and the facts supporting how the parameters or criteria were applied incorrectly. The subsequent paragraphs are redesignated.

R.C.M. 1117(e), which provided a standard for what is "plainly unreasonable," is removed, thereby enabling the application of those words according to their plain language as provided in Article 66(e). Likewise, R.C.M. 1117(c)(3) is redesignated as R.C.M. 1117(c)(4) and the following words are deleted: "because no reasonable sentencing authority would adjudge such a sentence in view of the record before the sentencing authority at the time the sentence was announced under R.C.M. 1007.

CHAPTER XII. APPEALS AND REVIEW

Rule 1201 Review by the Judge Advocate General

This rule is taken from Rule 1201 of the MCM (2016 edition) with the following amendments:

2018 Amendment: R.C.M. 1201 and its accompanying Discussion are amended. R.C.M. 1201 implements Articles 65, 66, and 69, as amended by Sections 5329, 5330, and 5333 of the Military Justice Act of 2016, Division E of the National Defense Authorization Act for Fiscal Year 2017, Pub. L. No. 114-328, 130 Stat. 2000 (2016), regarding the post-trial review of certain records of trial by the Judge Advocate General. Article 66 was further amended by Sections 531(j) of and 1081(c)(1)(K) of the National Defense Authorization Act for Fiscal Year 2018, Pub. Law. No. 115-91, 131 Stat. 1283 (2017).

2023 Amendments: R.C.M. 1201(f)(4) is amended to account for special trial counsel.

R.C.M. 1201(h) is amended to reflect the limitations of Article 69 appeals in general and special court-martial cases as enacted by Section 544(c) of FY2023 NDAA.

Rule 1202 Appellate counsel

This rule is taken from Rule 1202 of the MCM (2016 edition) with the following amendments:

2018 Amendment: R.C.M. 1202(b)(2)(A) is amended and implements Article 65, as amended by Section 5329 of the Military Justice Act of 2016, Division E of the National Defense Authorization Act for Fiscal Year 2017, Pub. L. No. 114-328, 130

Stat. 2000 (2016), as further amended by Section 1081(c)(1)(J) of the National Defense Authorization Act for Fiscal Year 2018, Pub. Law. No. 115-91, 131 Stat. 1283 (2017), addressing the requirement to detail appellate defense counsel to review cases eligible for direct appeal.

R.C.M. 1202(c) and its accompanying Discussion are new. R.C.M. 1202(c) implements Article 70, as amended by Section 5334 of the Military Justice Act of 2016, Division E of the National Defense Authorization Act for Fiscal Year 2017, Pub. L. No. 114-328, 130 Stat. 2000 (2016), addressing the requirements regarding counsel learned in the law applicable to capital cases.

2023 Amendments: Rule 1202(a)(2)(A) is amended to account for expanded appellate rights pursuant to Section 544 of FY2023 NDAA.

Rule 1202(c) is amended to account for the application of regulations of the Department of Homeland Security that would govern the compensation of appellate defense counsel for cases arising in the Coast Guard. Also, the word "death" is substituted for "the death penalty"; this change is stylistic in nature and not substantive.

Rule 1203 Review by a Court of Criminal Appeals

This rule is taken from Rule 1203 of the MCM (2016 edition) with the following amendments:

2018 Amendment: R.C.M. 1203 and its accompanying Discussion are amended and implements Articles 65, 66, and 69, as amended by Sections 5329, 5330, and 5333 of the Military Justice Act of 2016, Division E of the National Defense Authorization Act for Fiscal Year 2017, Pub. L. No. 114-328, 130 Stat. 2000 (2016), regarding review by a Court of Criminal Appeals and minimum tour lengths for appellate military judges. Article 66 was further amended by Sections 531(j) of and 1081(c)(1)(K) of the National Defense Authorization Act for Fiscal Year 2018, Pub. Law. No. 115-91, 131 Stat. 1283 (2017).

2023 Amendment: R.C.M. 1203(e)(2) is added to address when a finding is set aside. The convening authority or special trial counsel, as applicable, shall determine if a rehearing is impracticable and, if so, determine whether to dismiss a charge. All subsequent sections are redesignated.

R.C.M. 1203(e)(2), now R.C.M. 1203(e)(3), is amended to authorize special trial counsel to determine if a rehearing is impracticable when a sentence is set aside. If special trial counsel determines a rehearing is impracticable as to sentencing, special trial counsel may dismiss the applicable charges. Alternatively, if special trial counsel makes a determination to not dismiss the applicable charges, the convening authority shall order a sentence of no punishment be imposed.

Rule 1204 Review by the Court of Appeals for the Armed Forces

This rule is taken from Rule 1204 of the MCM (2016 edition) with the following amendments:

2018 Amendment: R.C.M. 1204(a)(2) is amended and implements Article 67, as amended by Section 5331 of the Military Justice Act of 2016, Division E of the National Defense Authorization Act for Fiscal Year 2017, Pub. L. No. 114-328, 130 Stat. 2000 (2016), which requires that the Judge Advocate General provide appropriate notification to all other Judge Advocates General and the Staff Judge Advocate to the Commandant of the Marine Corps before certifying a case to the Court of Appeals for the Armed Forces.

2023 Amendment: R.C.M. 1204 is amended to account for special trial counsel determining if a rehearing is impracticable.

Rule 1205 Review by the Supreme Court

This rule is taken from Rule 1205 of the MCM (2016 edition) with the following amendments.

2018 Amendment: R.C.M. 1205(a) is amended and changes the reference to "Article 67(h)" and replaces it with "Article 67a." Technical corrections are made to references to Article 67(a)(1), (2), and (3).

Rule 1206 Powers and responsibilities of the Secretary

This rule is taken from Rule 1206 of the MCM (2016 edition) with the following amendments:

2018 Amendment: The Discussion to R.C.M. 1206(a) is amended and changes the reference to "Article 71(b)" and replaces it with "Article 57(a)(4)."

Rule 1207 Sentences requiring approval by the President

This rule is taken from Rule 1207 of the MCM (2016 edition) with the following amendments:

2018 Amendment: The Discussion to R.C.M. 1207 is amended and changes the reference to "Article 71(a)" and replaces it with "Article 57(a)(3)."

Rule 1208 Restoration

This rule is taken from Rule 1208 of the MCM (2016 edition) with the following amendments:

2018 Amendment: R.C.M. 1208(b) is amended and implements Article 75, as amended by Section 5337 of the Military Justice Act of 2016, Division E of the National Defense Authorization Act for Fiscal Year 2017, Pub. L. No. 114-328, 130 Stat. 2000 (2016). R.C.M. 1208 now requires that in certain cases where an executed part of a court-martial sentence is set aside pending a rehearing, new trial, or other trial, that those punishments shall not be enforced from the effective date of the order setting aside that punishment.

R.C.M. 1208(a), 1208(b) and the Discussion to R.C.M. 1208(b) are amended and insert a reference to entry of a new judgment in the case.

2023 Amendment by Annex 1 of Executive Order No. 14103 (July 28, 2023): R.C.M. 1208(c) is added to clarify the effective date of the new sentence after a previous sentence has been set aside or disapproved.

Rule 1209 Finality of courts-martial

This rule is taken from Rule 1209 of the MCM (2016 edition) with the following amendments:

2018 Amendment: R.C.M. 1209 and its Discussion are amended and implement Articles 64, 65, and 69, as amended by Sections 5328, 5329, and 5333 of the Military Justice Act of 2016, Division E of the National Defense Authorization Act for Fiscal Year 2017, Pub. L. No. 114-328, 130 Stat. 2000 (2016), regarding the finality of courts-martial.

Rule 1210 New trial

This rule is taken from Rule 1210 of the MCM (2016 edition) with the following amendments:

2018 Amendment: R.C.M. 1210 is amended and implements Article 73, as amended by Section 5336 of the Military Justice Act of 2016, Division E of the National Defense Authorization Act for Fiscal Year 2017, Pub. L. No. 114-328, 130 Stat. 2000 (2016), which increases the time in which an accused must file a petition for a new trial from two years to three years after entry of judgment. R.C.M. 1210 is amended and includes references to the entry of judgment in accordance with the addition of Article 60c, as reflected in Section 5324 of the Military Justice Act of 2016, Division E of the National Defense Authorization Act for Fiscal Year 2017, Pub. L. No. 114-328, 130 Stat. 2000 (2016).

The Discussion accompanying R.C.M. 1210(f)(3) is amended and corrects a cross-reference.

2023 Amendment: R.C.M. 1210(h) is amended to change "convening authority" to "appropriate authority" to account for special trial counsel.

CHAPTER XIII. SUMMARY COURTS-MARTIAL

Rule 1301 Summary courts-martial

This rule is taken from Rule 1301 of the MCM (2016 edition) with the following amendments:

2018 Amendment: R.C.M. 1301(b) is amended and implements Article 20, as amended by Section 5164 of the Military Justice Act of 2016, Division E of the National Defense Authorization Act for Fiscal Year 2017, Pub. L. No. 114-328, 130 Stat. 2000 (2016), which clarifies that a summary court-martial is not a criminal forum and a finding of guilt does not constitute a criminal conviction. This change does not deprive an accused at a summary court-martial of the protections previously applicable at a summary court-martial, to include the right to confront witnesses.

R.C.M. 1301(c) and the Discussion to R.C.M. 1301(c) are amended and align with the prohibition against trying certain offenses at a summary court-martial and the elimination of the discrete offense of forcible sodomy in accordance with Sections 5162 and 5439 of the Military Justice Act of 2016, Division E of the National Defense Authorization Act for Fiscal Year 2017, Pub. L. No. 114-328, 130 Stat. 2000 (2016).

Rule 1302 Convening a summary court-martial

This rule is taken from Rule 1302 of the MCM (2016 edition) without substantive amendment.

Rule 1303 Right to object to trial by summary court-martial

This rule is taken from Rule 1303 of the MCM (2016 edition) without substantive amendment.

Rule 1304 Trial procedure

This rule is taken from Rule 1304 of the MCM (2016 edition) with the following amendments:

2018 Amendment: R.C.M. 1304(a)(4) and the accompanying Discussion are new and address the rights of a victim at summary courts-martial in accordance with Article 6b as amended by Section 5105 of the Military Justice Act of 2016, Division E of the National Defense Authorization Act for Fiscal Year 2017, Pub. L. No. 114-328, 130 Stat. 2000 (2016), as further amended by Sections 531(a), 1081(a)(22) and 1081(c)(1)(B) of the National Defense Authorization Act for Fiscal Year 2017, Pub. L. No. 115-91, 131 Stat. 1283 (2017). The Discussion accompanying R.C.M. 1304(a)(4)(E) clarifies the meaning of the term "victim" as it pertains to this provision. R.C.M. 1304(b)(2)(F)(ii) is amended and directs the summary court-martial to use the procedures in R.C.M. 1001 and 1002 and the principles in the remainder of Chapter X in determining a sentence, with some exceptions.

2023 Amendment by Annex 1 of Executive Order No. 14103 (July 28, 2023): R.C.M. 1304(b)(2)(F) is amended to correct a scrivener's error.

Rule 1305 Record of trial

This rule is taken from Rule 1305 of the MCM (2016 edition) with the following amendments:

2018 Amendment: R.C.M. 1305(c) and (d) and the Discussion accompanying R.C.M. 1305(c), (d), and (e) are amended and reflect Article 54, as amended by Section 5238 of the Military Justice Act of 2016, Division E of the National Defense Authorization Act for Fiscal Year 2017, Pub. L. No. 114-328, 130 Stat. 2000 (2016), which requires a certified record of trial in a summary court-martial.

R.C.M. 1305(d) is amended to include a cross-reference to procedures for classified information in the record of trial, and conforms with changes to Article 54 to provide procedures for the correction of a record of trial in a summary court-martial.

Rule 1306 Post-trial procedure, summary court-martial

2018 Amendment: This rule is taken from Rule 1306 of the MCM (2016 edition) with the following amendments:

R.C.M. 1306 and its accompanying Discussion are amended and consolidate the post-trial process for summary courts-martial into one rule and removes most of the prior cross references to the post-trial process prescribed for general and special courts-martial. The rule is further amended to reflect the changes to post-trial and appellate procedures in summary courts-martial required by the changes to Articles 60b, 64, and 69 as amended by Sections 5323, 5328, and 5333 of the Military Justice Act of 2016, Division E of the National Defense Authorization Act for Fiscal Year 2017, Pub. L. No. 114-328, 130 Stat. 2000 (2016).

2023 Amendment: R.C.M. 1306 is amended to clarify the convening authority may approve the sentence as adjudged.

Rule 1307 Review of summary courts-martial by a judge advocate

2018 Amendment: R.C.M. 1307 and its accompanying Discussion are new. R.C.M. 1307 implements Articles 64 and 69, as amended by Sections 5328 and 5333 of the Military Justice Act of 2016, Division E of the National Defense Authorization Act for Fiscal Year 2017, Pub. L. No. 114-328, 130 Stat. 2000 (2016), which provides for review of the record of trial of a summary court-martial by a judge advocate and permits an accused to apply for appellate review for correction of legal error.

APPENDIX 16
ANALYSIS OF THE MILITARY RULES OF EVIDENCE

SECTION I
General Provisions

Rule 101 Scope

This rule is taken from Rule 101 of the MCM (2016 edition) with the following amendments:

2018 Amendment: Mil. R. Evid. 101(c)(1) is amended and reflects the elimination of special courts-martial without a military judge and to include within the definition of military judge a military magistrate who has been designated to preside at a special court-martial or pre-referral proceedings under Article 30a. *See* Articles 16 and 30a, as amended and added, respectively, by Sections 5161 and 5202 of the Military Justice Act of 2016, Division E of the National Defense Authorization Act for Fiscal Year 2017, Pub. L. No. 114-328, 130 Stat. 2000 (2016), as further amended and amended, respectively, by Sections 1081(c)(1) and 531(b), respectively, of the National Defense Authorization Act for Fiscal Year 2018, Pub. L. No. 155-91, 131 Stat. 1283 (2017).

Mil. R. Evid. 101(c)(2) is amended and aligns military rules regarding electronically stored information with Federal civilian practice and the broader definitions of "writing" contained in R.C.M. 103 and Mil. R. Evid. 1001. The new language is based on Fed. R. Evid. 101(b)(6).

Rule 102 Purpose

This rule is taken from Rule 102 of the MCM (2016 edition) without amendment.

Rule 103 Rulings on evidence

This rule is taken from Rule 103 of the MCM (2016 edition) without amendment.

Rule 104 Preliminary questions

This rule is taken from Rule 104 of the MCM (2016 edition) with the following amendment:

2018 Amendment: Mil. R. Evid. 104(c) is amended and reflects the elimination of special courts-martial without a military judge. *See* Article 16, as amended by Section 5161 of the Military Justice Act of 2016, Division E of the National Defense Authorization Act for Fiscal Year 2017, Pub. L. No. 114-328, 130 Stat. 2000 (2016), as amended by Section 1081(c)(1)(C) of the National Defense Authorization Act for Fiscal Year 2018, Pub. Law. No. 115-91, 131 Stat. 1283 (2017).

Rule 105 Limiting evidence that is not admissible against other parties or for other purposes

This rule is taken from Rule 105 of the MCM (2016 edition) without amendment.

Rule 106 Remainder of or related writings or recorded statements

This rule is taken from Rule 106 of the MCM (2016 edition) without amendment.

SECTION II

Judicial Notice

Rule 201 Judicial notice of adjudicative facts

This rule is taken from Rule 201 of the MCM (2016 edition) without amendment.

Rule 202 Judicial notice of law

This rule is taken from Rule 202 of the MCM (2016 edition) without amendment.

SECTION III

Exclusionary Rules And Related Matters Concerning Self-Incrimination, Search And Seizure, And Eyewitness Identification

Rule 301 Privilege concerning compulsory self-incrimination

This rule is taken from Rule 301 of the MCM (2016 edition) without amendment.

Rule 302 Privilege concerning mental examination of an accused

This rule is taken from Rule 302 of the MCM (2016 edition) without amendment.

Rule 303 Degrading questions

This rule is taken from Rule 303 of the MCM (2016 edition) without amendment.

Rule 304 Confessions and admissions

This rule is taken from Rule 304 of the MCM (2016 edition) with the following amendment:

2018 Amendment: Mil. R. Evid. 304(f)(7) is amended and reflects the elimination of special courts-martial without a military judge. *See* Article 16, as amended by Section 5161 of the Military Justice Act of 2016, Division E of the National Defense Authorization Act for Fiscal Year 2017, Pub. L. No. 114-328, 130

Stat. 2000 (2016), as amended by Section 1081(c)(1)(C) of the National Defense Authorization Act for Fiscal Year 2018, Pub. Law. No. 115-91, 131 Stat. 1283 (2017).

Rule 305 Warnings about rights

This rule is taken from Rule 305 of the MCM (2016 edition) without amendment.

Rule 306 Statements by one of several accused

This rule is taken from Rule 306 of the MCM (2016 edition) without amendment.

Rule 311 Evidence obtained from unlawful searches and seizures

This rule is taken from Rule 311 of the MCM (2016 edition), as amended by Exec. Order No. 13825, 83 Fed. Reg. 9889 (March 1, 2018), with the following amendments.

2023 Amendments:

Mil. R. Evid. 311(c)(3) is amended to expand the good faith exception. *See United States v. Perkins*, 78 M.J. 381 (C.A.A.F. 2019).

Mil. R. Evid. 311(d)(4)(B) is amended to include references to omitting a material fact knowingly and intentionally or with reckless disregard for the truth. *See United States v. Garcia*, 80 M.J. 379 (C.A.A.F. 2020).

Rule 312 Body views and intrusions

This rule is taken from Rule 312 of the MCM (2016 edition) without amendment. The Discussion following Mil. R. Evid. 312(f) has been updated.

Rule 313 Inspections and inventories in the Armed Forces

This rule is taken from Rule 313 of the MCM (2016 edition) without amendment.

Rule 314 Searches and requiring probable cause

This rule is taken from Rule 314 of the MCM (2016 edition) without amendment.

Rule 315 Probable cause searches

This rule is taken from Rule 315 of the MCM (2016 edition) with the deletion of the Discussion following Mil. R. Evid. 315(a) and the following additional amendments:

2023 Amendments:

Mil. R. Evid. 315(b)(2) is amended to add a reference to search warrants under R.C.M. 703A.

Mil. R. Evid. 315(b)(3) is amended to clarify that only a military judge may issue a warrant for wire or electronic communications.

Mil. R. Evid. 315(d)(3) is amended to add a "Other competent search authority" to the list of those who may authorize a search.

Rule 316 Seizures

This rule is taken from Rule 316 of the MCM (2016 edition) without amendment.

Rule 317 Interception of wire and oral communications

This rule is taken from Rule 317 of the MCM (2016 edition) without amendment.

Rule 321 Eyewitness identification

This rule is taken from Rule 321 of the MCM (2016 edition) without amendment.

SECTION IV

Relevancy And Its Limits

Rule 401 Test for relevant evidence

This rule is taken from Rule 401 of the MCM (2016 edition) without amendment.

Rule 402 General admissibility of relevant evidence

This rule is taken from Rule 402 of the MCM (2016 edition) without amendment.

Rule 403 Excluding relevant evidence for prejudice, confusion, waste of time, or other reasons

This rule is taken from Rule 403 of the MCM (2016 edition) without amendment.

Rule 404 Character evidence, crimes or other acts

This rule is taken from Rule 404 of the MCM (2016 edition) with the following amendments:

2018 Amendment: Mil. R. Evid. 404(a)(2)(A) is amended and reflects the reorganization of the punitive articles in the Military Justice Act of 2016. *See* Articles 79-134, as amended by Sections 5401-5452 of the Military Justice Act of 2016, Division E of the National Defense Authorization Act for Fiscal Year 2017, Pub. L. No. 114-328, 130 Stat. 2000 (2016), as amended by Section 1081(c) of the National Defense Authorization Act for Fiscal Year 2018, Pub. Law. No. 115-91, 131 Stat. 1283 (2017).

2023 Amendment:

Mil. R. Evid. 404(b)(3) is amended to align with the Federal Rules of Evidence.

Rule 405 Methods of proving character

This rule is taken from Rule 405 of the MCM (2016 edition) without amendment.

Rule 406 Habit; routine practice

This rule is taken from Rule 406 of the MCM (2016 edition) without amendment.

Rule 407 Subsequent remedial measures

This rule is taken from Rule 407 of the MCM (2016 edition) without amendment.

Rules 408 Compromise offers and negotiations

This rule is taken from Rule 408 of the MCM (2016 edition) without amendment.

Rule 409 Offers to pay medical and similar expenses

This rule is taken from Rule 409 of the MCM (2016 edition) without amendment.

Rule 410 Pleas, plea discussions, and related statements

This rule is taken from Rule 410 of the MCM (2016 edition) without amendment.

Rule 411 Liability insurance

This rule is taken from Rule 411 of the MCM (2016 edition) without amendment.

Rule 412 Sex offense cases: The victim's sexual behavior or predisposition

This rule is taken from Rule 412 of the MCM (2016 edition) with the following amendments:

2018 Amendment: Mil. R. Evid. 412(b) is amended and more closely aligns with Federal Rule of Evidence 412. The amendment also addresses the Court of Appeals for the Armed Forces' opinion in *United States v. Gaddis*, 70 M.J. 248 (C.A.A.F. 2011) with regard to evidence the admission of which is required by the United States Constitution.

In *United States v. Banker*, 60 M.J. 215, 223 (C.A.A.F. 2004), the Court of Appeals for the Armed Forces indicated that when assessing whether evidence satisfies Military Rule of Evidence 412's requirement that its probative value outweighs the danger of unfair prejudice, one factor to be considered is the "prejudice to the victim's legitimate privacy interests." In 2007, the President codified that standard in Military Rule of Evidence 412, adding to the rule that evidence is admissible under the rule if "the probative value of such evidence outweighs the danger of unfair prejudice to the alleged victim's privacy." Exec. Order No. 13,447, Annex, § 2(a) (Sept. 28, 2007). The Court of Appeals for the Armed Forces subsequently cautioned that the revised Military Rule of Evidence 412 "has the potential to lead military judges to exclude constitutionally required evidence merely because its probative value does not outweigh the danger of prejudice to the alleged victim's privacy, which would violate the Constitution." *Gaddis*, 70 M.J. at 254. A rule that invites constitutional error, with its attendant risk of appellate reversal and even unjust convictions, is not in the interest of the accused, the government, or the alleged victim. Additionally, the current rule is in tension with Article 36(a) of the Uniform Code of Military Justice, 10 U.S.C. § 836(a), which generally requires that the evidentiary rules prescribed by the President be, "as far as he considers practicable" consistent with "the rules of evidence generally recognized in the trial of criminal cases in the United States district courts." The portion of Military Rule of Evidence 412 added in 2007 is inconsistent with the portion of Federal Rule of Evidence 412 that applies in criminal cases; however, *Banker* prescribed an additional test of admissibility that made it impracticable to follow Federal Rule of Evidence 412 in full. *Gaddis*' repudiation of *Banker*, *see* 70 M.J. at 256, however, eliminated that concern with regard to the test for admissibility of constitutionally required evidence. Thus, it is no longer impracticable for courts-martial to follow the same admissibility test for constitutionally required evidence as in Federal Rule of Evidence 412. Accordingly, to comply with Article 36(a), Military Rule of Evidence 412, as it pertains to constitutionally required evidence, is revised to comport with the portion of Federal Rule of Evidence 412 that applies in criminal cases The balancing test for the admission of evidence that is not required by the Constitution remains unchanged.

Mil. R. Evid. 412(c)(2) is amended and updates a cross-reference to R.C.M. 1103A, which is deleted and redesignated as R.C.M. 1113.

Rule 413 Similar crimes in sexual offense cases

This rule is taken from Rule 413 of the MCM (2016 edition) without amendment.

Rule 414 Similar crimes in child-molestation cases

This rule is taken from Rule 414 of the MCM (2016 edition) without amendment.

SECTION V

Privileges

Rule 501 Privilege in general

This rule is taken from Rule 501 of the MCM (2016 edition) without amendment.

Rule 502 Lawyer-client privilege

This rule is taken from Rule 502 of the MCM (2016 edition) without amendment.

Rule 503 Communications to clergy

This rule is taken from Rule 503 of the MCM (2016 edition) with the following amendment:

2023 Amendment:

Mil. R. Evid. 503 is amended to use gender-neutral language.

Rule 504 Marital privilege

This rule is taken from Rule 504 of the MCM (2016 edition) without amendment.

Rule 505 Classified information

This rule is taken from Rule 505 of the MCM (2016 edition) with the following amendments:

2018 Amendment: Mil. R. Evid. 505, as amended by Exec. Order No. 13825, 83 Fed. Reg. 9889 (March 1, 2018), further amends Mil. R. Evid. 505(j)(3), 505(k)(1)(B), and 505(l) updates cross-references to R.C.M. 701(g)(2) and R.C.M. 1103A (which is deleted and redesignated as R.C.M. 1113), and updates cross-references to R.C.M. 1103(h) and 1104(b)(1)(D), which are deleted and redesignated as R.C.M. 1112(e)(3).

2023 Amendment:

Mil. R. Evid. 505(f)(4) is amended to account for special trial counsel.

Rule 506 Government information

This rule is taken from Rule 506 of the MCM (2016 edition) with the following amendments:

2018 Amendment: Mil. R. Evid. 506, as amended by Exec. Order No. 13825, 83 Fed. Reg. 9889 (March 1, 2018), further amends Mil. R. Evid. 506(b) and broadens the scope of the rule to cover classified information. The government may now claim a privilege with respect to classified information under either Mil. R. Evid. 505 or Mil. R. Evid. 506, or both.

The Discussion accompanying Mil. R. Evid. 506(b) is new.

Mil. R. Evid. 506(j)(3), 506(l)(2), and 506(m) are amended and update cross-references to R.C.M. 1103A, which is deleted and redesignated as R.C.M. 1113.

2023 Amendment:

Mil. R. Evid. 506(f)(4) is amended to account for special trial counsel.

Rule 507 Identity of informants

This rule is taken from Rule 507 of the MCM (2016 edition) with the following amendment:

2023 Amendment:

Mil. R. Evid. 507(e)(3) is amended to account for special trial counsel."

Rule 508 Political vote

This rule is taken from Rule 508 of the MCM (2016 edition) without amendment.

Rule 509 Deliberations of courts and juries

This rule is taken from Rule 509 of the MCM (2016 edition) without amendment.

Rule 510 Waiver of privilege by voluntary disclosure

This rule is taken from Rule 510 of the MCM (2016 edition) without amendment.

Rule 511 Privileged matter disclosed under compulsion or without opportunity to claim privilege

This rule is taken from Rule 511 of the MCM (2016 edition) without amendment.

Rule 512 Comment upon or inference from claim of privilege; instruction

This rule is taken from Rule 512 of the MCM (2016 edition) with the following amendment:

2018 Amendment: Mil. R. Evid. 512(b) is amended and reflects the elimination of special courts-martial without a military judge. *See* Article 16, as amended by Section 5161 of the Military Justice Act of 2016, Division E of the National Defense Authorization Act for Fiscal Year 2017, Pub. L. No. 114-328, 130 Stat. 2000 (2016), as further amended by Section 1081(c)(1)(C) of the National Defense Authorization Act for Fiscal Year 2018, Pub. Law. No. 115-91, 131 Stat. 1283 (2017).

Rule 513 Psychotherapist—patient privilege

This rule is taken from Rule 513 of the MCM (2016 edition) with the following amendments:

2018 Amendment: Mil. R. Evid. 513, as amended by Exec. Order No. 13825, 83 Fed. Reg. 9889 (March 1, 2018), amends Mil. R. Evid. 513(c) and provides that a patient may authorize trial counsel or any counsel representing the patient to claim the privilege on his or her behalf.

Mil. R. Evid. 513(e)(3)(A) is amended and clarifies the required findings of a military judge prior to conducting an in-camera review of protected records or communications to determine whether the records or communications must be produced or admitted into evidence.

Mil. R. Evid. 513(e)(6) is amended and updates cross-references to R.C.M. 701(g)(2) and R.C.M. 1103A (which is deleted and redesignated as R.C.M. 1113).

Rule 514 Victim advocate—victim privilege

This rule is taken from Rule 514 of the MCM (2016 edition) with the following amendments:

2018 Amendment: Mil. R. Evid. 514, as amended by Exec. Order No. 13825, 83 Fed. Reg. 9889 (March 1, 2018), amends Mil. R. Evid. 514(b)(2) and clarifies the definition of a "victim advocate" in this rule as a person, other than a prosecutor, trial counsel, any victim's counsel, law enforcement officer, or military criminal investigator in the case.

Mil. R. Evid. 514(e)(3)(A) is amended and clarifies the required findings of a military judge prior to conducting an in-camera review of protected records or communications to determine whether the records or communications must be produced or admitted into evidence.

Mil. R. Evid. 514(e)(6) is amended and updates cross-references to R.C.M. 701(g)(2) and R.C.M. 1103A (which is deleted and redesignated as R.C.M. 1113).

SECTION VI

Witnesses

Rule 601 Competency to testify in general

This rule is taken from Rule 601 of the MCM (2016 edition) without amendment.

Rule 602 Need for personal knowledge

This rule is taken from Rule 602 of the MCM (2016 edition) without amendment.

Rule 603 Oath or affirmation to testify truthfully

This rule is taken from Rule 603 of the MCM (2016 edition) without amendment.

Rule 604 Interpreter

This rule is taken from Rule 604 of the MCM (2016 edition) without amendment.

Rule 605 Military Judge's competency as a witness

This rule is taken from Rule 605 of the MCM (2016 edition) without amendment.

Rule 606 Member's competency as a witness

This rule is taken from Rule 606 of the MCM (2016 edition) with the following amendment:

2018 Amendment: Mil. R. Evid. 606(a) is amended and reflects the elimination of special courts-martial without a military judge. *See* Article 16, as amended by Section 5161 of the Military Justice Act of 2016, Division E of the National Defense Authorization Act for Fiscal Year 2017, Pub. L. No. 114-328, 130 Stat. 2000 (2016), as further amended by Section 1081(c)(1)(C) of the National Defense Authorization Act for Fiscal Year 2018, Pub. Law. No. 115-91, 131 Stat. 1283 (2017).

Rule 607 Who may impeach a witness

This rule is taken from Rule 607 of the MCM (2016 edition) without amendment.

Rule 608 A witness' character for truthfulness or untruthfulness

This rule is taken from Rule 608 of the MCM (2016 edition) without amendment.

Rule 609 Impeachment by evidence of a criminal conviction or finding of guilty by summary court-marital

This rule is taken from Rule 609 of the MCM (2016 edition) with the following amendment:

2018 Amendment: Mil. R. Evid. 609 is amended throughout and reflects changes to Article 20, UCMJ, implementing the Supreme Court's ruling in *Middendorf v. Henry*, 425 U.S. 25 (1976) (summary court-martial is not a "criminal prosecution" within the meaning of the Sixth Amendment). *See* Article 20, as amended by Section 5164 of the Military Justice Act of 2016, Division E of the National Defense Authorization Act for Fiscal Year 2017, Pub. L. No. 114-328, 130 Stat. 2000 (2016).

Rule 610 Religious beliefs or opinions

This rule is taken from Rule 610 of the MCM (2016 edition) without amendment.

Rule 611 Mode and order of examining witnesses and presenting evidence

This rule is taken from Rule 611 of the MCM (2016 edition) with the following amendment:

2023 Amendment:

Mil. R. Evid. 611(d)(2) is amended to clarify the definition of domestic violence.

Rule 612 Writing used to refresh a witness' memory

This rule is taken from Rule 612 of the MCM (2016 edition) without amendment.

Rule 613 Witness' prior statement

This rule is taken from Rule 613 of the MCM (2016 edition) without amendment.

Rule 614 Court-martials calling or examining a witness

This rule is taken from Rule 614 of the MCM (2016 edition) without amendment.

Rule 615 Excluding witnesses

This rule is taken from Rule 615 of the MCM (2016 edition) without amendment.

SECTION VII

Opinions And Expert Testimony

Rule 701 Opinion testimony by lay witnesses

This rule is taken from Rule 701 of the MCM (2016 edition) without amendment.

Rule 702 Testimony by expert witnesses

This rule is taken from Rule 702 of the MCM (2016 edition) without amendment.

Rule 703 Bases of an expert's opinion testimony

This rule is taken from Rule 703 of the MCM (2016 edition) without amendment.

Rule 704 Opinion on an ultimate issue

This rule is taken from Rule 704 of the MCM (2016 edition) without amendment.

Rule 705 Disclosing the facts or data underlying an expert's opinion

This rule is taken from Rule 705 of the MCM (2016 edition) without amendment.

Rule 706 Court-appointed expert witnesses

This rule is taken from Rule 706 of the MCM (2016 edition) without amendment.

Rule 707 Polygraph examinations

This rule is taken from Rule 707 of the MCM (2016 edition) without amendment.

SECTION VIII

Hearsay

Rule 801 Definitions that apply to this section; exclusions from hearsay

This rule is taken from Rule 801 of the MCM (2016 edition) without amendment.

Rule 802 The rule against hearsay

This rule is taken from Rule 802 of the MCM (2016 edition) without amendment.

Rule 803 Exceptions to the rule against hearsay – regardless of whether the declarant is available as a witness

This rule is taken from Rule 803 of the MCM (2016 edition) with the following amendments:

2023 Amendments:

Mil. R. Evid. 803(16) is amended to change the definition of an ancient document to one that was prepared before January 1, 1998.

Mil. R. Evid. 803(22) is amended to correct a scrivener's error.

Rule 804 Exceptions to the rule against hearsay – when the declarant is unavailable as a witness

This rule is taken from Rule 804 of the MCM (2016 edition) with the following amendment:

2018 Amendment: Mil. R. Evid. 804(a)(6) is amended and reflects amendments to Article 49 and deletes the cross-reference to Article 49(d)(2). *See* Article 49, as amended by Section 532, Carl Levin and Howard P. "Buck" McKeon National Defense Authorization Act for Fiscal Year 2015, Pub. L. No. 113-291, 128 Stat. 3292 (2014).

Rule 805 Hearsay within hearsay

This rule is taken from Rule 805 of the MCM (2016 edition) without amendment.

Rule 806 Attacking and supporting the declarant's credibility

This rule is taken from Rule 806 of the MCM (2016 edition) without amendment.

Rule 807 Residual exception

This rule is taken from Rule 807 of the MCM (2016 edition) with the following amendment:

2023 Amendment:

Mil. R. Evid. 807 is amended to align with the Federal Rules of Evidence.

SECTION IX

Authentication And Identification

Rule 901 Authenticating or identifying evidence

This rule is taken from Rule 901 of the MCM (2016 edition) without amendment.

Rule 902 Evidence that is self-authenticating

This rule is taken from Rule 902 of the MCM (2016 edition) with the following amendments:

2023 Amendments:

Mil. R. Evid. 902(12) is added and reserved.

Mil. R. Evid. 902(13) is added and allows "Certified Records Generated by an Electronic Process or System" to be self-authenticating.

Mil. R. Evid. 902(14) is added and allows "Certified Data Copied from an Electronic Device Storage Medium, or File" to be self-authenticating.

Rule 903 Subscribing witness' testimony

This rule is taken from Rule 903 of the MCM (2016 edition) without amendment.

SECTION X

Contents Of Writings, Recordings, And Photographs

Rule 1001 Definitions that apply to this section

This rule is taken from Rule 1001 of the MCM (2016 edition) without amendment.

Rule 1002 Requirement of the original

This rule is taken from Rule 1002 of the MCM (2016 edition) without amendment.

Rue 1003 Admissibility of duplicates

This rule is taken from Rule 1003 of the MCM (2016 edition) without amendment.

Rule 1004 Admissibility of other evidence of content

This rule is taken from Rule 1004 of the MCM (2016 edition) without amendment.

Ruel 1005 Copies of public records to prove content

This rule is taken from Rule 1005 of the MCM (2016 edition) without amendment.

Rule 1006 Summaries to prove content

This rule is taken from Rule 1006 of the MCM (2016 edition) without amendment.

Rule 1007 Testimony or statement of a party to prove content

This rule is taken from Rule 1007 of the MCM (2016 edition) without amendment.

Rule 1008 Functions of the military judge and the members

This rule is taken from Rule 1008 of the MCM (2016 edition) without amendment.

SECTION XI

Miscellaneous Rules

Rules 1101 Applicability of these rules

This rule is taken from Rule 1101 of the MCM (2016 edition) with the following amendments:

2018 Amendment: Mil. R. Evid. 1101(a) is amended and reflects that the Military Rules of Evidence also apply to pre-referral proceedings under Article 30a. *See* Article 30a, as added by Section 5202 of the Military Justice Act of 2016, Division E of the National Defense Authorization Act for Fiscal Year 2017, Pub. L. No. 114-328, 130 Stat. 2000 (2016), as amended by Section 531(b) of the National Defense Authorization Act for Fiscal Year 2018, Pub. L. No. 155-91, 131 Stat. 1283 (2017).

Rule 1102 Amendments

This rule is taken from Rule 1102 of the MCM (2016 edition) without amendment.

Rule 1103 Title

This rule is taken from Rule 1103 of the MCM (2016 edition) without amendment.

APPENDIX 17
ANALYSIS OF PUNITIVE ARTICLES

1. Article 77 (10 U.S.C. 877)—Principals

This paragraph is taken, without change, from paragraph 1 (Article 77—Principals) of the MCM (2016 edition).

2. Article 78 (10 U.S.C. 878)—Accessory after the fact

This paragraph is taken from paragraph 2 (Article 78—Accessory after the fact) of the MCM (2016 edition), with the following amendments:

2018 Amendment: c. *Explanation*. (2) *Failure to report offense*. This subparagraph is amended and reflects that the offense of misprision of a serious offense has been relocated from Article 134 to Article 131c as part of the Military Justice Act of 2016's realignment of the punitive articles. The substance of the offense remains the same. *See* Article 131c, as added by Section 5446 of the Military Justice Act of 2016, Division E of the National Defense Authorization Act for Fiscal Year 2017, Pub. L. No. 114-328, 130 Stat. 2000 (2016).

Subparagraph d. *Lesser included offenses* from the MCM (2016 edition) has been deleted. Subparagraphs e. *Maximum punishment* and f. *Sample specification* from the MCM (2016 edition) have been redesignated as subparagraphs d. and e. respectively. For lesser included offenses, see Appendix 12A.

3. Article 79 (10 U.S.C 879)—Conviction of offense charged, lesser included offenses, and attempts

This paragraph is taken from paragraph 3 (Article 79—Conviction of lesser included offenses) of the MCM (2016 edition) with the following amendments:

2018 Amendment: a. *Text of statute*. Article 79 is amended and provides two statutory grounds for identifying "lesser included offenses." Under the first, the lesser offense must be "necessarily included" in the greater offense. *See, e.g.*, the elements test articulated in *United States v. Jones*, 68 M.J. 465, 470 (C.A.A.F. 2010); *United States v. Alston*, 69 M.J. 214, 216 (C.A.A.F. 2010). Under the second, the offense must be expressly designated by the President as a lesser included offense. The President's authority extends only to an offense "reasonably included" in the greater offense. The President has done so in Appendix 12A. *See* Article 79 as amended by Section 5402 of the Military Justice Act of 2016, Division E of the National Defense Authorization Act for Fiscal Year 2017, Pub. L. No. 114-328, 130 Stat. 2000 (2016).

b. *Explanation*.

Subparagraph b.2. sets forth an explanation of "necessarily included offenses." Subparagraph b.3. explains the President's express authority under Article 79 to designate certain closely related offenses to be "reasonably included" lesser offenses of greater ones, including offenses that do not strictly meet the "necessarily included" elements test. Whether "necessarily included" or "reasonably included," a lesser included offense must be raised by the evidence at trial. That is, while all presidentially designated lesser included offenses (*see* Appendix 12A) qualify as lesser included offenses, a party is not entitled to an instruction on a lesser included offense if the evidence at trial does not reasonably raise it. *See United States v. Bean*, 62 M.J. 264, 265 (C.A.A.F. 2005).

2023 Amendment: Subparagraph b. *Explanation* (4) *Sua sponte duty* is amended to align with R.C.M. 920(g) allowing the parties to waive instructions on a lesser included offense.

4. Article 80 (10 U.S.C. 880)—Attempts

This paragraph is taken from paragraph 4 (Article 80—Attempts), of the MCM (2016 edition) with the following amendments:

2018 Amendment: c. *Explanation*. (6) *Attempts not under Article 80*. This subparagraph is amended and reflects that the offenses of Article 104—Aiding the enemy and Article 106a—Espionage are renumbered Articles 103b and 103a respectively, under Section 5401 of the Military Justice Act of 2016, Division E of the National Defense Authorization Act for Fiscal Year 2017, Pub. L. No. 114-328, 130 Stat. 2000 (2016).

Subparagraph d. *Lesser included offenses* from the MCM (2016 edition) has been deleted. Subparagraphs e. *Maximum punishment* and f. *Sample specification* from the MCM (2016 edition) have been redesignated as subparagraphs d. and e. respectively. For lesser included offenses, see Appendix 12A.

d. *Maximum punishment*.

This subparagraph is amended and reflects that the offense of forcible sodomy under Article 125 is now addressed under Article 120. *See* Section 5430 of the Military Justice Act of 2016, Division E of the National Defense Authorization Act for Fiscal Year 2017, Pub. L. No. 114-328, 130 Stat. 2000 (2016), as further amended by Section 1081(c)(1)(O) of the National Defense Authorization Act for Fiscal Year 2018, Pub. Law. No. 115-91, 131 Stat. 1283 (2017).

5. Article 81 (10 U.S.C. 881)—Conspiracy

This paragraph is taken from paragraph 5 (Article 81—Conspiracy) of the MCM (2016 edition) with the following amendment:

2018 Amendment: Subparagraph d. *Lesser included offenses* from the MCM (2016 edition) has been deleted. Subparagraphs e. *Maximum punishment* and f. *Sample specification* from the MCM (2016 edition) have been redesignated as subparagraphs d. and e. respectively. For lesser included offenses, see Appendix 12A.

6. Article 82 (10 U.S.C. 882)—Soliciting commission of offenses

This paragraph is taken from paragraphs 6 (Article 82—Solicitation) and 105 (Article 134—Soliciting another to commit an offense) of the MCM (2016 edition) with the following amendments:

2018 Amendment: a. *Text of Statute*. Article 82 is revised and incorporates the solicitation of any offense under the UCMJ in one consolidated statute. Specifically, the former Article 134—Soliciting another to commit an offense, MCM (2016 edition), is relocated to Article 82 pursuant to Section 5403 of the Military Justice Act of 2016, Division E of the National Defense Authorization Act for Fiscal Year 2017, Pub. L. No. 114-328, 130 Stat. 2000 (2016), as further amended by Section 1081(c)(1)(M) of the National Defense Authorization Act for Fiscal Year 2018, Pub. Law. No. 115-91, 131 Stat. 1283 (2017). Soliciting another to commit a criminal offense is a well-recognized concept in criminal law that does not rely upon the "terminal element" of Article 134 as the basis for its criminality.

Accordingly, the newly consolidated Article 82 does not require proof of the Article 134 "terminal element."

Subparagraph d. *Lesser included offenses* from the MCM (2016 edition) has been deleted. Subparagraphs e. *Maximum punishment* and f. *Sample specification* from the MCM (2016 edition) have been redesignated as subparagraphs d. and e. respectively. For lesser included offenses, see Appendix 12A.

d. *Maximum Punishment.* The maximum authorized confinement for solicitation to commit desertion, mutiny or sedition, or misbehavior before the enemy where the offense is not committed or attempted is changed to confinement for 15 years or the maximum confinement for the underlying offense, whichever is lesser. The maximum authorized punishment for solicitation to commit unspecified offenses is changed to a dishonorable discharge, forfeiture of all pay and allowances, and confinement for 10 years, or the maximum punishment for the underlying offense, whichever is lesser.

2023 Amendment. Paragraph 6.d. is amended to clarify the maximum punishment for solicitation offenses.

7. Article 83 (10 U.S.C. 883)—Malingering

This paragraph is taken from paragraph 40 (Article 115—Malingering) of the MCM (2016 edition) with the following amendments:

This offense is relocated to its current position, without substantive change, pursuant to Section 5404 of the Military Justice Act of 2016, Division E of the National Defense Authorization Act for Fiscal Year 2017, Pub. L. No. 114-328, 130 Stat. 2000 (2016).

2018 Amendment: Subparagraph d. *Lesser included offenses* from the MCM (2016 edition) has been deleted. Subparagraphs e. *Maximum punishment* and f. *Sample specification* from the MCM (2016 edition) have been redesignated as subparagraphs d. and e. respectively. For lesser included offenses, see Appendix 12A.

8. Article 84 (10 U.S.C. 884)—Breach of medical quarantine

The Article 134 offense of Quarantine: medical, breaking is relocated from paragraph 100 of the MCM (2016 edition) to Article 84 pursuant to Section 5405 of the Military Justice Act of 2016, Division E of the National Defense Authorization Act for Fiscal Year 2017, Pub. L. No. 114-328, 130 Stat. 2000 (2016). Proof of the Article 134 "terminal element" is no longer required.

2018 Amendment: c. *Explanation.* Formal medical quarantines are addressed in DoDI 6200.03, Public Health Emergency Management within the Department of Defense, March 5, 2010 (Change 2, effective October 2, 2013). This instruction provides an example of a commander's power to institute medical quarantines as an incidence of command, but the commander's power generally to institute a medical quarantine is not limited to the situations discussed in DoDI 6200.03. Quarantines may include, but are not limited to, orders to remain within a restricted area and to submit to diagnostic or medical treatment. *See id.* at Enclosure 3, ¶2(c)–(e), (h), 4a(7)(a)–(i).

Subparagraph d. *Lesser included offenses* from the MCM (2016 edition) has been deleted. Subparagraphs e. *Maximum punishment* and f. *Sample specification* from the MCM (2016 edition) have been redesignated as subparagraphs d. and e. respectively. For lesser included offenses, see Appendix 12A.

d. *Maximum Punishment.* A new maximum punishment category is added and aligns this offense with federal law (*see* 42 U.S.C. § 271) by enhancing maximum punishments for breaking of medical quarantines declared in reference to a "quarantinable communicable disease." Under 42 U.S.C. § 271, a "quarantinable communicable disease" extends to those diseases defined by the President by Executive Order. The President has done so in Executive Order 13295 (April 4, 2003, as amended July 3, 2014), now promulgated in 42 C.F.R. §70.1.

9. Article 85 (10 U.S.C. 885)—Desertion

This paragraph is taken, without substantive change, from paragraph 9 (Article 85—Desertion) of the MCM (2016 edition).

2018 Amendment: Subparagraph d. *Lesser included offenses* from the MCM (2016 edition) has been deleted. Subparagraphs e. *Maximum punishment* and f. *Sample specification* from the MCM (2016 edition) have been redesignated as subparagraphs d. and e. respectively. For lesser included offenses, see Appendix 12A.

10. Article 86 (10 U.S.C. 886)—Absence without leave

This paragraph is taken, without substantive change, from paragraph 10 (Article 86—Absence without leave) of the MCM (2016 edition).

2018 Amendment: Subparagraph d. *Lesser included offenses* from the MCM (2016 edition) has been deleted. Subparagraphs e. *Maximum punishment* and f. *Sample specification* from the MCM (2016 edition) have been redesignated as subparagraphs d. and e. respectively. For lesser included offenses, see Appendix 12A.

11. Article 87 (10 U.S.C. 887)—Missing movement; jumping from vessel

This paragraph is taken from paragraphs 11 (Article 87—Missing movement) and 91 (Article 134—Jumping from vessel into the water) of the MCM (2016 edition) with the following amendments:

2018 Amendment: a. *Text of Statute.* The Article 134 offense of jumping from a vessel into the water is relocated to Article 87 pursuant to Section 5406 of the Military Justice Act of 2016, Division E of the National Defense Authorization Act for Fiscal Year 2017, Pub. L. No. 114-328, 130 Stat. 2000 (2016). The substance of both offenses remains the same with the exception of the removal of the terminal element from the former Article 134 offense.

Subparagraph b. *Elements.* The two elements "that the accused missed the movement" and "through design or neglect" from paragraph 11.b.(3) and (4) of the MCM (2016 edition) are combined into a single sentence "that the accused missed the movement through design or neglect."

A new Discussion is added following paragraph 11.c.(2)

Subparagraph d. *Lesser included offenses* from the MCM (2016 edition) has been deleted. Subparagraphs e. *Maximum punishment* and f. *Sample specification* from the MCM (2016 edition) have been redesignated as subparagraphs d. and e. respectively. For lesser included offenses, see Appendix 12A.

12. Article 87a (10 U.S.C. 887a)—Resistance, flight, breach of arrest, and escape

This paragraph is taken from paragraph 19 (Article 95—Resistance, flight, breach, of arrest, and escape) of the MCM (2016 edition). This offense is relocated to its current position, without substantive change, pursuant to Section 5401 of the Military Justice Act of 2016, Division E of the National Defense Authorization Act for Fiscal Year 2017, Pub. L. No. 114-328, 130 Stat. 2000 (2016).

2018 Amendment: Subparagraph d. *Lesser included offenses* from the MCM (2016 edition) has been deleted. Subparagraphs e. *Maximum punishment* and f. *Sample specification* from the MCM (2016 edition) have been redesignated as subparagraphs d. and e. respectively. For lesser included offenses, see Appendix 12A.

13. Article 87b (10 U.S.C. 887b)—Offenses against correctional custody and restriction

This paragraph is taken from paragraph 70 (Article 134—Correctional custody—offenses against) and paragraph 102 (Article 134—Restriction, breaking) of the MCM (2016 edition). These offenses are consolidated and relocated to Article 87b pursuant to Section 5407 of the Military Justice Act of 2016, Division E of the National Defense Authorization Act for Fiscal Year 2017, Pub. L. No. 114-328, 130 Stat. 2000 (2016). Proof of the Article 134 "terminal element" is no longer required.

2018 Amendment: Subparagraph d. *Lesser included offenses* from the MCM (2016 edition) has been deleted. Subparagraphs e. *Maximum punishment* and f. *Sample specification* from the MCM (2016 edition) have been redesignated as subparagraphs d. and e. respectively. For lesser included offenses, see Appendix 12A.

14. Article 88 (10 U.S.C. 888)—Contempt toward officials

This paragraph is taken, without substantive change, from paragraph 12 (Article 88—Contempt toward officials) of the MCM (2016 edition).

2018 Amendment: Subparagraph d. *Lesser included offenses* from the MCM (2016 edition) has been deleted. Subparagraphs e. *Maximum punishment* and f. *Sample specification* from the MCM (2016 edition) have been redesignated as subparagraphs d. and e. respectively. For lesser included offenses, see Appendix 12A.

15. Article 89 (10 U.S.C. 889)—Disrespect toward superior commissioned officer; assault of superior commissioned officer

This paragraph is taken from paragraphs 13 (Article 89—Disrespect toward superior commissioned officer) and 14 (Article 90—Assaulting or willfully disobeying superior commissioned officer) of the MCM (2016 edition) with the following amendments:

2018 Amendment: a. *Text of Statute*. Article 89 is amended and incorporates the offense of willfully assaulting a superior commissioned officer, which is relocated from Article 90 MCM (2016 edition) pursuant to Section 5408 of the Military Justice Act of 2016, Division E of the National Defense Authorization Act for Fiscal Year 2017, Pub. L. No. 114-328, 130 Stat. 2000 (2016).

c. *Explanation*.

(1) *Superior commissioned officer*. The definition of superior commissioned officer is changed from MCM (2016 edition), Part IV, subparagraph 13.c.(1). The definition of "superior commissioned officer," as revised, removes the separate Service distinction.

Subparagraph d. *Lesser included offenses* from the MCM (2016 edition) has been deleted. Subparagraphs e. *Maximum punishment* and f. *Sample specification* from the MCM (2016 edition) have been redesignated as subparagraphs d. and e. respectively. For lesser included offenses, see Appendix 12A.

d. Maximum punishment. The maximum punishment is adjusted and differentiates situations where the disrespect is directed at a superior commissioned officer in command from situations where a commissioned officer is superior in rank.

16. Article 90 (10 U.S.C. 890)—Willfully disobeying superior commissioned officer

This paragraph is taken from paragraph 14 (Article 90—Assaulting or willfully disobeying superior commissioned officer) of the MCM (2016 edition) with the following amendments:

2018 Amendment: a. *Text of Statute*. Article 90 is amended by relocating the offense of "striking or assaulting superior commissioned officer" to Article 89 pursuant to Sections 5408 and 5409 of the Military Justice Act of 2016, Division E of the National Defense Authorization Act for Fiscal Year 2017, Pub. L. No. 114-328, 130 Stat. 2000 (2016).

c. *Explanation* (1) *Superior commissioned officer*. The definition of superior commissioned officer is changed from MCM (2016 edition), Part IV, subparagraph 13.c.(1). The definition of "superior commissioned officer," as revised, removes the separate Service distinction. Subparagraph 16.c.(2)(a)(iii), as revised, explains the basis for the authority of the issuing officer.

Subparagraph d. *Lesser included offenses* from the MCM (2016 edition) has been deleted. Subparagraphs e. *Maximum punishment* and f. *Sample specification* from the MCM (2016 edition) have been redesignated as subparagraphs d. and e. respectively. For lesser included offenses, see Appendix 12A.

17. Article 91 (10 U.S.C. 891)—Insubordinate conduct toward warrant officer, noncommissioned officer, or petty officer

This paragraph is taken from paragraph 15 (Article 91—Insubordinate conduct toward warrant officer, noncommissioned officer, or petty officer) of the MCM (2016 edition) without substantive change.

2018 Amendment: Subparagraph d. *Lesser included offenses* from the MCM (2016 edition) has been deleted. Subparagraphs e. *Maximum punishment* and f. *Sample specification* from the MCM (2016 edition) have been redesignated as subparagraphs d. and e. respectively. For lesser included offenses, see Appendix 12A.

18. Article 92 (10 U.S.C. 892)—Failure to obey order or regulation

This paragraph is taken from paragraph 16, (Article 92—Failure to obey order or regulation) of the MCM (2016 edition) without substantive change.

2018 Amendment: Subparagraph d. *Lesser included offenses* from the MCM (2016 edition) has been deleted. Subparagraphs e. *Maximum punishment* and f. *Sample specification* from the MCM (2016 edition) have been redesignated as subparagraphs d. and e. respectively. For lesser included offenses, see Appendix 12A.

19. Article 93 (10 U.S.C. 893)—Cruelty and maltreatment

This paragraph is taken from paragraph 17 (Article 93—Cruelty and maltreatment) of the MCM (2016 edition) with the following amendments:

2018 Amendment: Subparagraph d. *Lesser included offenses* from the MCM (2016 edition) has been deleted. Subparagraphs e. *Maximum punishment* and f. *Sample specification* from the MCM (2016 edition) have been redesignated as subparagraphs d. and e. respectively. For lesser included offenses, see Appendix 12A.

d. Maximum punishment. The maximum authorized confinement for a violation of Article 93 is increased from two years to three years

2023 Amendment: Subparagraph c. *Explanation* (2) *Nature of the Act* is amended to clarify the definition of sexual harassment for purposes of Article 93.

20. Article 93a (10 U.S.C. 893a)—Prohibited activities with military recruit or trainee by person in position of special trust

2018 Amendment: This article is a new enumerated provision and implements Article 93a, as added by Section 5410 of the Military Justice Act of 2016, Division E of the National Defense Authorization Act for Fiscal Year 2017, Pub. L. No. 114-328, 130 Stat. 2000 (2016), and criminalizes acts of "prohibited sexual activity" specified in regulations by the Secretary concerned, between those in positions of special trust and junior military members in initial active duty training, officer qualification programs, other training programs for initial career qualification, in a delayed entry program, or applicants for military service.

2023 Amendment: Subparagraph b. *Elements* is amended to change the knowledge requirement to "knew" from "knew, or reasonably should have known" for both offenses under Article 93a. For subparagraph b(2), elements (c) and (d) are combined into one paragraph. Subparagraph c. *Explanation* is amended to add an explanation of "Prohibited activity" and update the definition of "Knowledge." Subparagraph e. *Sample specifications* is amended to reflect the amendments in Subparagraph b.

21. Article 94 (10 U.S.C. 894)—Mutiny or sedition

This paragraph is taken from paragraph 18 (Article 94—Mutiny and sedition) of the MCM (2016 edition) without substantive change.

2018 Amendment: Subparagraph c.(4)(b) is amended and clarifies the definition of "superior commissioned officer."

Subparagraph d. *Lesser included offenses* from the MCM (2016 edition) has been deleted. Subparagraphs e. *Maximum punishment* and f. *Sample specification* from the MCM (2016 edition) have been redesignated as subparagraphs d. and e. respectively. For lesser included offenses, see Appendix 12A.

22. Article 95 (10 U.S.C. 895)—Offenses by sentinel or lookout

This paragraph is taken from paragraph 38 (Article 113—Misbehavior of sentinel or lookout) and the portions of paragraph 104 (Article 134—Sentinel or lookout: offenses against or by) relating to the offense of "Loitering or wrongfully sitting on post by a sentinel or lookout" of the MCM (2016 edition) with the following amendments: This offense is relocated from subparagraph 104.b.(2) of Article 134 of the MCM (2016 edition) pursuant to Section 5411 of the Military Justice Act of 2016, Division E of the National Defense Authorization Act for Fiscal Year 2017, Pub. L. No. 114-328, 130 Stat. 2000 (2016). Proof of the "terminal element" of Article 134 is no longer required.

2018 Amendment: Subparagraph d. *Lesser included offenses* from the MCM (2016 edition) has been deleted. Subparagraphs e. *Maximum punishment* and f. *Sample specification* from the MCM (2016 edition) have been redesignated as subparagraphs d. and e. respectively. For lesser included offenses, see Appendix 12A.

23. Article 95a (10 U.S.C. 895a)—Disrespect toward sentinel or lookout

This paragraph is taken from the portions of paragraph 104 (Article 134—Sentinel or lookout: offenses against or by) of the MCM (2016 edition) relating to the offense of "Disrespect to a sentinel or lookout." This offense is relocated to its current position pursuant to Section 5412 of the Military Justice Act of 2016, Division E of the National Defense Authorization Act for Fiscal Year 2017, Pub. L. No. 114-328, 130 Stat. 2000 (2016) with the following amendments: Proof of the Article 134 "terminal element" is no longer required.

2018 Amendment: Subparagraph d. *Lesser included offenses* from the MCM (2016 edition) has been deleted. Subparagraphs e. *Maximum punishment* and f. *Sample specification* from the MCM (2016 edition) have been redesignated as subparagraphs d. and e. respectively. For lesser included offenses, see Appendix 12A.

24. Article 96 (10 U.S.C. 896)—Release of prisoner without authority; drinking with prisoner

This paragraph is taken from paragraphs 20 (Article 96—Releasing prisoner without authority) and 74 (Article 134—Drinking liquor with prisoner) of the MCM (2016 edition) with the following amendments: These offenses were relocated and consolidated pursuant to Section 5413 of the Military Justice Act of 2016, Division E of the National Defense Authorization Act for Fiscal Year 2017, Pub. L. No. 114-328, 130 Stat. 2000 (2016). The term "suffers" was stricken and replaced with "allows" and reflects modern usage of terminology; and in the case of the "drinking with prisoner" offense, the scope of the offense was extended to apply to any person who unlawfully drinks an alcoholic beverage with a prisoner. Proof of the "terminal element" of Article 134 is no longer required.

2018 Amendment: c. *Explanation* (5) *Drinking with prisoner*. This explanation clarifies that drinking with a prisoner is unlawful unless competent authority has granted the accused specific permission to consume alcohol with a prisoner.

Subparagraph d. *Lesser included offenses* from the MCM (2016 edition) has been deleted. Subparagraphs e. *Maximum punishment* and f. *Sample specification* from the MCM (2016 edition) have been redesignated as subparagraphs d. and e. respectively. For lesser included offenses, see Appendix 12A.

d. *Maximum punishment.* The maximum authorized confinement for allowing a prisoner to escape through neglect is increased from one to two years; the maximum authorized confinement for allowing a prisoner to escape through design is increased from two to five years. The maximum authorized confinement and period of forfeitures of two-thirds pay per month for drinking with a prisoner is increased from three months to one year.

25. Article 97 (10 U.S.C. 897)—Unlawful detention

This paragraph is taken, without substantive change, from paragraph 21 (Article 97—Unlawful detention) of the MCM (2016 edition) with the following amendments:

2018 Amendment: Subparagraph d. *Lesser included offenses* from the MCM (2016 edition) has been deleted. Subparagraphs e. *Maximum punishment* and f. *Sample specification* from the MCM (2016 edition) have been redesignated as subparagraphs d. and e. respectively. For lesser included offenses, see Appendix 12A.

26. Article 98 (10 U.S.C. 898)—Misconduct as prisoner

This paragraph is taken from paragraph 29 (Article 105—Misconduct as a prisoner) of the MCM (2016 edition) with the following amendments: This offense is relocated to its current position, pursuant to Section 5401 of the Military Justice Act of 2016, Division E of the National Defense Authorization Act for Fiscal Year 2017, Pub. L. No. 114-328, 130 Stat. 2000 (2016).

2018 Amendment: Subparagraph d. *Lesser included offenses* from the MCM (2016 edition) has been deleted. Subparagraphs e. *Maximum punishment* and f. *Sample specification* from the MCM (2016 edition) have been redesignated as subparagraphs d. and e. respectively. For lesser included offenses, see Appendix 12A.

27. Article 99 (10 U.S.C. 899)—Misbehavior before the enemy

This paragraph is taken, without substantive change, from paragraph 23 (Article 99—Misbehavior before the enemy) of the MCM (2016 edition) with the following amendments:

2018 Amendment: Subparagraph d. *Lesser included offenses* from the MCM (2016 edition) has been deleted. Subparagraphs e. *Maximum punishment* and f. *Sample specification* from the MCM (2016 edition) have been redesignated as subparagraphs d. and e. respectively. For lesser included offenses, see Appendix 12A.

28. Article 100 (10 U.S.C. 900)—Subordinate compelling surrender

This paragraph is taken from paragraph 24 (Article 100—Subordinate compelling surrender) of the MCM (2016 edition) with the following amendments:

2018 Amendment: Subparagraph d. *Lesser included offenses* from the MCM (2016 edition) has been deleted. Subparagraphs e. *Maximum punishment* and f. *Sample specification* from the MCM (2016 edition) have been redesignated as subparagraphs d. and e. respectively. For lesser included offenses, see Appendix 12A.

29. Article 101 (10 U.S.C. 901)—Improper use of countersign

This paragraph is taken from paragraph 25 (Article 101—Improper use of a countersign) of the MCM (2016 edition) with the following amendments:

2018 Amendment: Subparagraph d. *Lesser included offenses* from the MCM (2016 edition) has been deleted. Subparagraphs e. *Maximum punishment* and f. *Sample specification* from the MCM (2016 edition) have been redesignated as subparagraphs d. and e. respectively. For lesser included offenses, see Appendix 12A.

30. Article 102 (10 U.S.C. 902)—Forcing a safeguard

This paragraph is taken from paragraph 26 (Article 102—Forcing a safeguard) of the MCM (2016 edition) with the following amendments:

2018 Amendment: Subparagraph d. *Lesser included offenses* from the MCM (2016 edition) has been deleted. Subparagraphs e. *Maximum punishment* and f. *Sample specification* from the MCM (2016 edition) have been redesignated as subparagraphs d. and e. respectively. For lesser included offenses, see Appendix 12A.

31. Article 103 (10 U.S.C. 903)—Spies

This paragraph is taken from paragraph 30 (Article 106—Spies) of the MCM (2016 edition) with the following amendments: This offense is relocated to its current position pursuant to Section 5401 of the Military Justice Act of 2016, Division E of the National Defense Authorization Act for Fiscal Year 2017, Pub. L. No. 114-328, 130 Stat. 2000 (2016) and is amended to remove the mandatory death penalty.

2018 Amendment: Subparagraph d. *Lesser included offenses* from the MCM (2016 edition) has been deleted. Subparagraphs e. *Maximum punishment* and f. *Sample specification* from the MCM (2016 edition) have been redesignated as subparagraphs d. and e. respectively. For lesser included offenses, see Appendix 12A.

d. *Maximum punishment.* As amended, death is the maximum authorized punishment for the offense, rather than a mandatory punishment.

32. Article 103a (10 U.S.C. 903a)—Espionage

This paragraph is taken from paragraph 30a (Article 106a—Espionage) of the MCM (2016 edition) with the following amendments: This offense is relocated to its current position pursuant to Section 5401 Military Justice Act of 2016, Division E of the National Defense Authorization Act for Fiscal Year 2017, Pub. L. No. 114-328, 130 Stat. 2000 (2016).

2018 Amendment: Subparagraph d. *Lesser included offenses* from the MCM (2016 edition) has been deleted. Subparagraphs e. *Maximum punishment* and f. *Sample specification* from the MCM (2016 edition) have been redesignated as subparagraphs d. and e. respectively. For lesser included offenses, see Appendix 12A.

33. Article 103b (10 U.S.C. 903b)—Aiding the enemy

This paragraph is taken from paragraph 28 (Article 104—Aiding the enemy) of the MCM (2016 edition) with the following amendments: This offense is relocated to its current position pursuant to Section 5401 Military Justice Act of 2016, Division E of the National Defense Authorization Act for Fiscal Year 2017, Pub. L. No. 114-328, 130 Stat. 2000 (2016).

2018 Amendment: Subparagraph d. *Lesser included offenses* from the MCM (2016 edition) has been deleted. Subparagraphs e. *Maximum punishment* and f. *Sample specification* from the MCM (2016 edition) have been redesignated as subparagraphs d. and e. respectively. For lesser included offenses, see Appendix 12A.

34. Article 104 (10 U.S.C. 904)—Public records offenses

This paragraph is taken from paragraph 99 (Article 134—Public record: altering, concealing, removing, mutilating, obliterating, or destroying) of the MCM (2016 edition) and is relocated to Article 104 pursuant to Section 5415 of the Military Justice Act of 2016, Division E of the National Defense Authorization Act for Fiscal Year 2017, Pub. L. No. 114-328, 130 Stat. 2000 (2016) with the following amendments: Proof of the Article 134 "terminal element" is no longer required.

2018 Amendment: Subparagraph d. *Lesser included offenses* from the MCM (2016 edition) has been deleted. Subparagraphs e. *Maximum punishment* and f. *Sample specification* from the MCM (2016 edition) have been redesignated as subparagraphs d. and e. respectively. For lesser included offenses, see Appendix 12A.

35. Article 104a (10 U.S.C. 904a)—Fraudulent enlistment, appointment, or separation

This paragraph is taken from paragraph 7 (Article 83—Fraudulent enlistment, appointment, or separation) of the MCM (2016 edition) with the following amendments: This offense is relocated to and is relocated to Article 104a pursuant to Section 5452 of the Military Justice Act of 2016, Division E of the National Defense Authorization Act for Fiscal Year 2017, Pub. L. No. 114-328, 130 Stat. 2000 (2016).

2018 Amendment: Subparagraph d. *Lesser included offenses* from the MCM (2016 edition) has been deleted. Subparagraphs e. *Maximum punishment* and f. *Sample specification* from the MCM (2016 edition) have been redesignated as subparagraphs d. and e. respectively. For lesser included offenses, see Appendix 12A.

36. Article 104b (10 U.S.C. 904b)—Unlawful enlistment, appointment, or separation

This paragraph is taken from paragraph 8 (Article 84—Effecting unlawful enlistment, appointment, or separation) of the MCM (2016 edition) with the following amendments: This offense is relocated to Article 104b pursuant to Section 5452of the Military Justice Act of 2016, Division E of the National Defense Authorization Act for Fiscal Year 2017, Pub. L. No. 114-328, 130 Stat. 2000 (2016).

2018 Amendment: Subparagraph d. *Lesser included offenses* from the MCM (2016 edition) has been deleted. Subparagraphs e. *Maximum punishment* and f. *Sample specification* from the MCM (2016 edition) have been redesignated as subparagraphs d. and e. respectively. For lesser included offenses, see Appendix 12A.

37. Article 105 (10 U.S.C. 905)—Forgery

This paragraph is taken from paragraph 48 (Article 123—Forgery) of the MCM (2016 edition) with the following amendments: This offense is relocated to Article 105 pursuant to Section 5401 of the Military Justice Act of 2016, Division E of the National Defense Authorization Act for Fiscal Year 2017, Pub. L. No. 114-328, 130 Stat. 2000 (2016).

2018 Amendment: Subparagraph d. *Lesser included offenses* from the MCM (2016 edition) has been deleted. Subparagraphs e. *Maximum punishment* and f. *Sample specification* from the MCM (2016 edition) have been redesignated as subparagraphs d. and e. respectively. For lesser included offenses, see Appendix 12A.

38. Article 105a (10 U.S.C. 905a)—False or unauthorized pass offenses

This paragraph is taken from paragraph 77 (Article 134—False pretenses, obtaining services under) of the MCM (2016 edition) pursuant to Section 5416 of the Military Justice Act of 2016, Division E of the National Defense Authorization Act for Fiscal Year 2017, Pub. L. No. 114-328, 130 Stat. 2000 (2016) with the following amendments: Proof of the Article 134 "terminal element" is no longer required.

2018 Amendment: Subparagraph d. *Lesser included offenses* from the MCM (2016 edition) has been deleted. Subparagraphs e. *Maximum punishment* and f. *Sample specification* from the MCM (2016 edition) have been redesignated as subparagraphs d. and e. respectively. For lesser included offenses, see Appendix 12A.

39. Article 106 (10 U.S.C. 906)—Impersonation of officer, noncommissioned or petty officer, or agent or official

This paragraph is taken from paragraph 86 (Article 134—Impersonating a commissioned, warrant, noncommissioned, or petty officer, or an agent or official) of the MCM (2016 edition) with the following amendments: This offense is relocated to Article 106 pursuant to Section 5417 of the Military Justice Act of 2016, Division E of the National Defense Authorization Act for Fiscal Year 2017, Pub. L. No. 114-328, 130 Stat. 2000 (2016). Proof of the Article 134 "terminal element" is no longer required.

2018 Amendment: a. *Text of statute*. The phrase "commissioned, warrant officer" is replaced with "officer." This change aligns this offense with the definition of "officer" under 10 U.S.C. § 101(b)(1) which defines "officer" to mean a commissioned or warrant officer.

c. *Explanation* (2) *Officer*. This provision is added to the MCM and explains that the definition of "officer" for purposes of this statute is derived from the existing definition of that term in 10 U.S.C. § 101(b)(1).

Subparagraph d. *Lesser included offenses* from the MCM (2016 edition) has been deleted. Subparagraphs e. *Maximum punishment* and f. *Sample specification* from the MCM (2016 edition) have been redesignated as subparagraphs d. and e. respectively. For lesser included offenses, see Appendix 12A.

40. Article 106a (10 U.S.C. 906a)—Wearing unauthorized insignia, decoration, badge, ribbon, device, or lapel button

This paragraph is taken from paragraph 113 (Article 134—Wearing unauthorized insignia, decoration, badge, ribbon, device, or lapel button) of the MCM (2016 edition) with the following amendments: This offense is relocated to Article 106a pursuant to Section 5418 of the Military Justice Act of 2016, Division E of the National Defense Authorization Act for Fiscal Year 2017, Pub. L. No. 114-328, 130 Stat. 2000 (2016). Proof of the Article 134 "terminal element" is no longer required.

2018 Amendment: c. *Explanation* (1) *In general*. The MCM (2016 edition) did not provide an explanation for this provision. An explanation is added and clarifies the gravamen of this offense, the scope of unauthorized wear, and knowledge.

d. *Maximum punishment*. The maximum authorized confinement is increased from six months to a year for violations of the article involving specified medals and awards.

Subparagraph d. *Lesser included offenses* from the MCM (2016 edition) has been deleted. Subparagraphs e. *Maximum punishment* and f. *Sample specification* from the MCM (2016 edition) have been redesignated as subparagraphs d. and e. respectively. For lesser included offenses, see Appendix 12A.

41. Article 107 (10 U.S.C. 907)—False official statements; false swearing

This paragraph is taken from paragraphs 31 (Article 107—False official statement) and 79 (Article 134—False swearing) of the MCM (2016 edition) with the following amendments: The offense of false swearing is relocated from Article 134, MCM (2016 edition), to Article 107 pursuant to Section 5419 of the Military Justice Act of 2016, Division E of the National Defense Authorization Act for Fiscal Year 2017, Pub. L. No. 114-328, 130 Stat. 2000 (2016). Proof of the Article 134 "terminal element" of Article 134 is no longer required.

2018 Amendment: c. *Explanation*. (1)(b) *Official statements*. This explanation is revised and clarifies whether a statement relates to the official duties of the speaker or hearer. *See United States v. Spicer*, 71 M.J. 470 (C.A.A.F. 2013). *See also United States v. Passut*, 73 M.J. 27 (C.A.A.F. 2014), and *United States v. Capel*, 71 M.J. 485 (C.A.A.F. 2013).

Subparagraph d. *Lesser included offenses* from the MCM (2016 edition) has been deleted. Subparagraphs e. *Maximum punishment* and f. *Sample specification* from the MCM (2016 edition) have been redesignated as subparagraphs d. and e. respectively. For lesser included offenses, see Appendix 12A.

42. Article 107a (10 U.S.C. 907a)—Parole violation

This paragraph is taken from paragraph 97a (Article 134—Parole, violation of) of the MCM (2016 edition) with the following amendments: The offense is relocated from Article 134, MCM (2016 edition), to Article 107a pursuant to Section 5420 of the Military Justice Act of 2016, Division E of the National Defense Authorization Act for Fiscal Year 2017, Pub. L. No. 114-328, 130 Stat. 2000 (2016). Proof of the Article 134 "terminal element" of Article 134 is no longer required.

Subparagraph d. *Lesser included offenses* from the MCM (2016 edition) has been deleted. Subparagraphs e. *Maximum punishment* and f. *Sample specification* from the MCM (2016 edition) have been redesignated as subparagraphs d. and e. respectively. For lesser included offenses, see Appendix 12A.

43. Article 108 (10 U.S.C. 908)—Military property of United States—Loss, damage, destruction, or wrongful disposition

This paragraph is taken from paragraph 32 (Article 108—Military property of United States Loss, damage, destruction, or wrongful disposition) of the MCM (2016 edition) with the following amendments:

2018 Amendment: c. *Explanation*. Subparagraph c.(4) *Firearms and Explosives* clarifies that the term "explosive" specifically includes ammunition.

Subparagraph d. *Lesser included offenses* from the MCM (2016 edition) has been deleted. Subparagraphs e. *Maximum punishment* and f. *Sample specification* from the MCM (2016 edition) have been redesignated as subparagraphs d. and e. respectively. For lesser included offenses, see Appendix 12A.

d. *Maximum punishment*. The threshold amount for purposes of the maximum punishment in relation to the qualifying value of property concerned is amended to $1,000 and aligns with the division between felony and misdemeanor penalties for property offenses in federal civilian law for equivalent misconduct. *See* 18 U.S.C. § 1361.

44. Article 108a (10 U.S.C. 908a)—Captured or abandoned property

This paragraph is taken from paragraph 27 (Article 103—Captured or abandoned property) of the MCM (2016 edition) and is relocated to Article 108a pursuant to Section 5401 of the Military Justice Act of 2016, Division E of the National Defense Authorization Act for Fiscal Year 2017, Pub. L. No. 114-328, 130 Stat. 2000 (2016) with the following amendments:

2018 Amendment: c. *Explanation*. Subparagraph c.(6) *Firearms and explosives* is added and aligns it with an identical provision in paragraph 43.

Subparagraph d. *Lesser included offenses* from the MCM (2016 edition) has been deleted. Subparagraphs e. *Maximum punishment* and f. *Sample specification* from the MCM (2016 edition) have been redesignated as subparagraphs d. and e. respectively. For lesser included offenses, see Appendix 12A.

d. *Maximum Punishment*. The threshold amount for purposes of the maximum punishment in relation to the qualifying value of the property concerned is amended to $1,000 and aligns with the division between felony and misdemeanor penalties for property offenses in civilian jurisdictions. Maximum punishments focus on the amount of damage inflicted and the value of the property destroyed.

45. Article 109 (10 U.S.C. 909)—Property other than military property of United States—Waste, spoilage, or destruction

This paragraph is taken from paragraph 33 (Article 109—Property other than military property of the United States—waste, spoilage, or destruction) of the MCM (2016 edition) with the following amendments:

2018 Amendments: b. *Elements.* The maximum punishment categories are reorganized into three separate categories reflecting the type of property involved and the type of action being taken against the property.

Subparagraph d. *Lesser included offenses* from the MCM (2016 edition) has been deleted. Subparagraphs e. *Maximum punishment* and f. *Sample specification* from the MCM (2016 edition) have been redesignated as subparagraphs d. and e. respectively. For lesser included offenses, see Appendix 12A.

d. *Maximum Punishment.* The threshold amount for purposes of the maximum punishment in relation to the qualifying value of the property concerned is amended to $1,000 and aligns with the division between felony and misdemeanor penalties for property offenses in civilian jurisdictions. Maximum punishments focus on the amount of damage inflicted and the value of the property destroyed. The maximum punishments are also further divided based on the nature of the property and the extent of the damage.

46. Article 109a (10 U.S.C. 909a)—Mail matter: wrongful taking, opening, etc.

This paragraph is taken from paragraph 93 (Article 134—Mail: taking, opening, secreting, destroying, or stealing) of the MCM (2016 edition) with the following amendments: The offense is relocated from Article 134, MCM (2016 edition), to Article 109a pursuant to Section 5421 of the Military Justice Act of 2016, Division E of the National Defense Authorization Act for Fiscal Year 2017, Pub. L. No. 114-328, 130 Stat. 2000 (2016). Proof of the Article 134 "terminal element" of Article 134 is no longer required.

Subparagraph d. *Lesser included offenses* from the MCM (2016 edition) has been deleted. Subparagraphs e. *Maximum punishment* and f. *Sample specification* from the MCM (2016 edition) have been redesignated as subparagraphs d. and e. respectively. For lesser included offenses, see Appendix 12A.

47. Article 110 (10 U.S.C. 910)—Improper hazarding of vessel or aircraft

This paragraph is taken from paragraph 34 (Article 110—Improper hazarding of a vessel) of the MCM (2016 edition) with the following amendments:

2018 Amendment: a. *Text of statute.* This offense is amended and includes improper hazarding of an aircraft, and accordingly is retitled "Improper hazarding of vessel or aircraft."

Subparagraph d. *Lesser included offenses* from the MCM (2016 edition) has been deleted. Subparagraphs e. *Maximum punishment* and f. *Sample specification* from the MCM (2016 edition) have been redesignated as subparagraphs d. and e. respectively. For lesser included offenses, see Appendix 12A.

48. Article 111 (10 U.S.C. 911)—Leaving scene of vehicle accident

This paragraph is taken from paragraph 82 (Article 134—Fleeing scene of accident) of the MCM (2016 edition) with the following amendments: The offense is relocated from Article 134, MCM (2016 edition), to Article 111 pursuant to Section 5423 of the Military Justice Act of 2016, Division E of the National Defense Authorization Act for Fiscal Year 2017, Pub. L. No. 114-328, 130 Stat. 2000 (2016). Proof of the Article 134 "terminal element" of Article 134 is no longer required.

2018 Amendment: Subparagraph d. *Lesser included offenses* from the MCM (2016 edition) has been deleted. Subparagraphs e. *Maximum punishment* and f. *Sample specification* from the MCM (2016 edition) have been redesignated as subparagraphs d. and e. respectively. For lesser included offenses, see Appendix 12A.

49. Article 112 (10 U.S.C. 912)—Drunkenness and other incapacitation offenses

This paragraph is taken from paragraphs 36 (Article 112—Drunk on duty), 75 (Article 134—Drunk Prisoner) and 76 (Article 134—Drunkenness—incapacitation for performance of duties through prior wrongful indulgence in intoxicating liquor or any drug) of the MCM (2016 edition) with the following amendments: The offense is now Article 112 pursuant to Section 5424 of the Military Justice Act of 2016, Division E of the National Defense Authorization Act for Fiscal Year 2017, Pub. L. No. 114-328, 130 Stat. 2000 (2016). Proof of the Article 134 "terminal element" of Article 134 is no longer required.

2018 Amendment: a. *Text of statute.* The new text reflects the migration of paragraphs 75 and 76 from Article 134 offenses in the MCM (2016 edition) to Article 112; proof of the terminal element of Article 134 is no longer required. This migration places the similar offenses of drunk on duty, drunk prisoner, and incapacitation for duty under the same UCMJ article.

(2) *Incapacitation for duty from drunkenness or drug use.* Under paragraph 76 of the MCM (2016 edition) wrongful indulgence in alcohol or drugs was required. The word wrongful has been removed from the incapacitation for duty from drunkenness or drug use offense; the act of being incapacitated for duty is itself wrongful in the military context. However, this offense retains the affirmative defense formerly utilized in the paragraph 76 of the MCM (2016 edition) namely: that at the time of the offense the accused neither knew, nor reasonably should have known, that he or she was assigned to, or susceptible to recall for, military duties. *See* subparagraph 49.c.(2)(b). Likewise, the defenses of accident (*see* R.C.M. 916(f)) and mistake of fact (*see* R.C.M. 916 (j)) continue to apply to instances where the accused accidentally or mistakenly consumed drugs or alcohol, not knowing them to be such at the time of ingestion.

c. *Explanation.* (1) *Drunk on Duty.* (a) *Drunk.* This definition is taken from subparagraph 35.c.(6), MCM (2016 edition).

(2) *Incapacitation for duty from drunkenness or drug use.* (a) *Incapacitated.* The cross-reference to the explanation of drunk is changed to reflect the relocation of that definition from subparagraph 35.c.(6), MCM (2016 edition) to subparagraph 49.c.(1)(a).

(3) *Drunk prisoner.* (a) *Prisoner.* The cross-reference to the explanation of prisoner is changed and reflects the Military Justice Act of 2016's relocation of the former Article 134—Drinking liquor with prisoner offense paragraph 74 of the MCM (2016 edition) to Article 96.

(b) *Drunk. See* subparagraph 51.c.(6). The definition of drunk is changed and reflects the lower blood alcohol content limits set forth in Article 113 pursuant to Section 5425, Military Justice Act of 2016, Division E of the Nationall Defense Authorization Act for Fiscal Year 2017, Pub. L. No. 114-328, 130 Stat. 2000 (2016) and the relocation of that definition from subparagraph 35.c.(6), MCM (2016 edition), to subparagraph 49.c.(1)(a).

Subparagraph d. *Lesser included offenses* from the MCM (2016 edition) has been deleted. Subparagraphs e. *Maximum punishment* and f. *Sample specification* from the MCM (2016 edition) have been redesignated as subparagraphs d. and e. respectively. For lesser included offenses, see Appendix 12A.

50. Article 112a (10 U.S.C. 912a)—Wrongful use, possession, etc., of controlled substances

This paragraph is taken from paragraph 37 (Article 112a—Wrongful use, possession, etc., of controlled substances) of the MCM (2016 edition) with the following amendments:

2018 Amendment: Subparagraph d. *Lesser included offenses* from the MCM (2016 edition) has been deleted. Subparagraphs e. *Maximum punishment* and f. *Sample specification* from the MCM (2016 edition) have been redesignated as subparagraphs d. and e. respectively. For lesser included offenses, see Appendix 12A.

51. Article 113 (10 U.S.C. 913)—Drunken or reckless operation of a vehicle, aircraft, or vessel

This paragraph is taken from paragraph 35 (Article 111—Drunken or reckless operation of a vehicle, aircraft, or vessel) of the MCM (2016 edition). This offense is relocated to its current position pursuant to Section 5452 of the Military Justice Act of 2016, Division E of the National Defense Authorization Act for Fiscal Year 2017, Pub. L. No. 114-328, 130 Stat. 2000 (2016) with the following amendments:

2018 Amendment: a. *Text of statute*. The substance of the offense remains the same, except for a lower blood alcohol content limit with respect to alcohol concentration in a person's blood pursuant to Section 5425 of the NDAA for FY17. The Secretary may by regulation prescribe limits that are lower if such lower limits are based on scientific developments, as reflected in federal civilian law of general applicability.

Subparagraph d. *Lesser included offenses* from the MCM (2016 edition) has been deleted. Subparagraphs e. *Maximum punishment* and f. *Sample specification* from the MCM (2016 edition) have been redesignated as subparagraphs d. and e. respectively. For lesser included offenses, see Appendix 12A.

2023 Amendment: Paragraph 51.d. was amended to correct a scrivener's error.

52. Article 114 (10 U.S.C. 914)—Endangerment Offenses

This paragraph is taken from paragraphs 39 (Article 114—Dueling), 81 (Article 134—Firearm, discharging—willfully, under such circumstances as to endanger human life), 100a (Article 134—Reckless endangerment), and 112 (Article 134—Weapon: concealed, carrying) of the MCM (2016 edition) with the following amendments: These offenses are relocated and consolidated into the newly titled Article 114—Endangerment offenses pursuant to Section 5426 of the Military Justice Act of 2016, Division E of the National Defense Authorization Act for Fiscal Year 2017, Pub. L. No. 114-328, 130 Stat. 2000 (2016). Proof of the Article 134 "terminal element" is no longer required.

2018 Amendment: Subparagraph d. *Lesser included offenses* from the MCM (2016 edition) has been deleted. Subparagraphs e. *Maximum punishment* and f. *Sample specification* from the MCM (2016 edition) have been redesignated as subparagraphs d. and e. respectively. For lesser included offenses, see Appendix 12A.

d. *Maximum punishment*. By prescribing one maximum punishment for all of these offenses, the 2018 Amendments authorize the imposition of a dishonorable discharge for reckless endangerment and for carrying a concealed weapon. Previously, a bad-conduct discharge but not a dishonorable discharge was a portion of the maximum authorized punishment for those offenses.

53. Article 115 (10 U.S.C. 915)—Communicating threats

This paragraph is taken from paragraphs 109 (Article 134—Threat or hoax designed or intended to cause panic or public fear) and 110 (Article 134—Threat, communicating) of the MCM (2016 edition) with the following amendments: These offenses are consolidated and relocated to their current position pursuant to Section 5427 of the Military Justice Act of 2016, Division E of the National Defense Authorization Act for Fiscal Year 2017, Pub. L. No. 114-328, 130 Stat. 2000 (2016). Proof of the Article 134 "terminal element" is no longer required. The explanations for threat and wrongful are amended and are consistent with *Elonis v. United States*, 135 S.Ct. 2001 (2015), and *United States v. Rapert*, 75 M.J. 164 (C.A.A.F. 2016).

2018 Amendment: Subparagraph d. *Lesser included offenses* from the MCM (2016 edition) has been deleted. Subparagraphs e. *Maximum punishment* and f. *Sample specification* from the MCM (2016 edition) have been redesignated as subparagraphs d. and e. respectively. For lesser included offenses, see Appendix 12A.

54. Article 116 (10 U.S.C. 916)—Riot or breach of peace

This paragraph is taken from paragraph 41 (Article 116—Riot or breach of peace) of the MCM (2016 edition) and is relocated to Article 116 pursuant to Section 5452 of the Military Justice Act of 2016, Division E of the National Defense Authorization Act for Fiscal Year 2017, Pub. L. No. 114-328, 130 Stat. 2000 (2016) with the following amendments:

2018 Amendment: Subparagraph d. *Lesser included offenses* from the MCM (2016 edition) has been deleted. Subparagraphs e. *Maximum punishment* and f. *Sample specification* from the MCM (2016 edition) have been redesignated as subparagraphs d. and e. respectively. For lesser included offenses, see Appendix 12A.

55. Article 117 (10 U.S.C. 917)—Provoking speeches or gestures

This paragraph is taken from paragraph 42 (Article 117—Provoking speeches or gestures) of the MCM (2016 edition) with the following amendments:

2018 Amendment: Subparagraph d. *Lesser included offenses* from the MCM (2016 edition) has been deleted. Subparagraphs e. *Maximum punishment* and f. *Sample specification* from the MCM (2016 edition) have been redesignated as subparagraphs d. and e. respectively. For lesser included offenses, see Appendix 12A.

2023 Amendment: Amended to remove a note that is no longer applicable due to the promulgation of paragraph 55a by Executive Order 14062.

55a. Article 117a (10 U.S.C. 917a)—Wrongful broadcast or distribution of intimate visual images

2022 Amendment: This is a new enumerated offense pursuant to Section 533 of the National Defense Authorization Act for Fiscal Year 2018, Pub. L. No. 115-91, 131 Stat. 1283 (2017), which criminalizes the wrongful broadcast or distribution of intimate visual images.

56. Article 118 (10 U.S.C. 918)—Murder

This paragraph is taken from paragraph 43 (Article 118—Murder) of the MCM (2016 edition) with the following amendments:

2018 Amendment: c. *Explanation* (5)(b) *Separate offenses*. This subparagraph is amended and conforms to the amendments to Articles 120 and 125 from Sections 5430 and 5439 of the Military Justice Act of 2016, Division E of the National Defense Authorization Act for Fiscal Year 2017, Pub. L. No. 114-328, 130 Stat. 2000 (2016). The specific listing of offenses that may be charged separately also is amended to reflect the list of felony-murder offenses contained at Article 118(4).

2018 Amendment: Subparagraph d. *Lesser included offenses* from the MCM (2016 edition) has been deleted. Subparagraphs e. *Maximum punishment* and f. *Sample specification* from the MCM (2016 edition) have been redesignated as subparagraphs d. and e. respectively. For lesser included offenses, see Appendix 12A.

57. Article 119 (10 U.S.C. 919)—Manslaughter

This paragraph is taken from paragraph 44 (Article 119—Manslaughter) of the MCM (2016 edition) with the following amendments:

2018 Amendment: b. *Elements* (2)(d) clarifies the relationship between involuntary manslaughter and murder perpetrated during the commission of certain offenses and conforms to the amendments to Articles 118 and 120 from Sections 5428 and 5430 of the Military Justice Act of 2016, Division E of the National Defense Authorization Act for Fiscal Year 2017, Pub. L. No. 114-328, 130 Stat. 2000 (2016). Forcible sexual misconduct previously addressed under Article 125 (MCM 2016) is now addressed in Articles 120 and 134 (Animal abuse).

Subparagraph d. *Lesser included offenses* from the MCM (2016 edition) has been deleted. Subparagraphs e. *Maximum punishment* and f. *Sample specification* from the MCM (2016 edition) have been redesignated as subparagraphs d. and e. respectively. For lesser included offenses, see Appendix 12A.

58. Article 119a (10 U.S.C. 919a)—Death or injury of an unborn child

This paragraph is taken from paragraph 44a (Article 119a—Death or injury of an unborn child) of the MCM 2016, as amended by Section 1031(c)(1)(N) of the National Defense Authorization Act for Fiscal Year 2018, Pub. Law. No. 115-91, 131 Stat. 1283 (2017), with the following amendments:

2018 Amendment: a. *Text of statute*. The phrase "authorized by state or federal law to perform abortions" was removed from this subparagraph's recital of the text of Article 119a because that phrase does not appear in the statute. *See* Pub. L. No. 1018-212, § 3; 118 Stat. 568 (April 1, 2004).

Subparagraph d. *Lesser included offenses* from the MCM (2016 edition) has been deleted. Subparagraphs e. *Maximum punishment* and f. *Sample specification* from the MCM (2016 edition) have been redesignated as subparagraphs d. and e. respectively. For lesser included offenses, see Appendix 12A.

59. Article 119b (10 U.S.C. 919b)—Child endangerment

This paragraph is taken from paragraph 68a (Article 134—Child endangerment) of the MCM (2016 edition) and is relocated to Article 116 pursuant to Section 5429 of of the Military Justice Act of 2016, Division E of the National Defense Authorization Act for Fiscal Year 2017, Pub. L. No. 114-328, 130 Stat. 2000 (2016). Proof of the Article 134 "terminal element" is no longer required.

2018 Amendment: c. *Explanation*. (2) The phrase "even though such harm would not necessarily be the natural and probable consequences of such acts. In this regard," was removed from this subparagraph.

Subparagraph d. *Lesser included offenses* from the MCM (2016 edition) has been deleted. Subparagraphs e. *Maximum punishment.* and f. *Sample specification.* from the MCM (2016 edition) have been redesignated as subparagraphs d. and e. respectively. For lesser included offenses, see Appendix 12A.

60. Article 120 (10 U.S.C. 920)—Rape and sexual assault generally

This paragraph is taken from paragraph 45 (Article 120—Rape and sexual assault generally) of MCM (2016 edition) with the following amendments that implement Article 120, as amended by Section 5430 of the Military Justice Act of 2016, Division E of the National Defense Authorization Act for Fiscal Year 2017, Pub. L. No. 114-328, 130 Stat. 2000 (2016), as further amended by Section 1081(c)(1)(O) of the National Defense Authorization Act for Fiscal Year 2018, Pub. Law. No. 115-91, 131 Stat. 1283 (2017).*2018 Amendment:* a. *Text of statute.* The definition of sexual act is amended.

b. *Elements.* The elements are consolidated to eliminate redundancy in repeating the specific intent necessary to accomplish a sexual act and sexual contact because the definitions of sexual act and sexual contact already contain within them the mens rea element of specific intent.

c. *Explanation.* (4) Consent as an element was removed from the explanation. Section 5430 of the Military Justice Act of 2016, Division E of the National Defense Authorization Act for Fiscal Year 2017, Pub. L. No. 114-328, 130 Stat. 2000 (2016) amended Article 120 to include lack of consent as an element in Article 120(b)(2), Sexual Assault.

(5) Scope of threatening or placing that other person in fear emphasizes that threatening or placing that other person in fear explicitly includes, but is not limited to, abuse of military rank, position, or power, in order to engage in a sexual act or contact with a victim. *See United States v. Simpson*, 58 M.J. 368, 377 (C.A.A.F. 2003) (listing seven factors "demonstrating the relationship between the offenses at issue and Appellant's superior rank and position" in a case involving "constructive force" under the pre-2007 version of Article 120).

Subparagraph d. *Lesser included offenses* from the MCM (2016 edition) has been deleted. Subparagraphs e. *Maximum punishment.* and f. *Sample specification.* from the MCM (2016 edition) have been redesignated as subparagraphs d. and e. respectively. For lesser included offenses, see Appendix 12A.

e. *Sample specifications*. The sample specifications are consolidated to include the various acts constituting: (a) rape; (b) sexual assault; (c) aggravated sexual contact; and (d) abusive sexual contact, by consolidating the descriptions of a sexual act or sexual contact within each overarching specification.

2023 Amendment: Subparagraph e. *Sample specifications* is amended to add "[(directly) (through the clothing)]" for all offenses under "Aggravated sexual contact" and "Abusive sexual contact."

61. Article 120a (10 U.S.C. 920a)—Mails: deposit of obscene matter

This paragraph is taken from paragraph 94 (Article 134—Mails: depositing or causing to be deposited obscene matters in) of the MCM (2016 edition) and is relocated to Article 120a pursuant to Section 5431of the Military Justice Act of 2016, Division E of the National Defense Authorization Act for Fiscal Year 2017, Pub. L. No. 114-328, 130 Stat. 2000 (2016) with the following amendments. Proof of the Article 134 "terminal element" is no longer required. See *Miller v. United States*, 413 U.S. 15 (1973), for a discussion of the definition of obscenity.

2018 Amendment: Subparagraph d. *Lesser included offenses* from the MCM (2016 edition) has been deleted. Subparagraphs e. *Maximum punishment* and f. *Sample specification* from the MCM (2016 edition) have been redesignated as subparagraphs d. and e. respectively. For lesser included offenses, see Appendix 12A.

62. Article 120b (10 U.S.C. 920b)—Rape and sexual assault of a child

This paragraph is taken from paragraph 47 (Article 120b—Rape and sexual assault of a child) of the MCM (2016 edition) with the following amendments:

2018 Amendment: a. *Text of statute*. The definition of sexual act conforms to Article 120(g) as amended by Section 5430 of the Military Justice Act of 2016, Division E of the National Defense Authorization Act for Fiscal Year 2017, Pub. L. No. 114-328, 130 Stat. 2000 (2016). Consistent with federal civilian law, sexual acts with children under Article 120b include the intentional touching of the genitalia of a child under the age of 16 (committed by a person over the age of 16), when accomplished with either the intent to abuse, humiliate, harass, or degrade the victim, or to arouse or gratify the sexual desire of any person.

b. *Elements*. The elements are consolidated and eliminate redundancy in repeating the specific intent necessary to accomplish a sexual act and sexual contact. The definitions of sexual act and sexual contact already contain the mens rea element of specific intent.

Subparagraph d. *Lesser included offenses* from the MCM (2016 edition) has been deleted. Subparagraphs e. *Maximum punishment* and f. *Sample specification* from the MCM (2016 edition) have been redesignated as subparagraphs d. and e. respectively. For lesser included offenses, see Appendix 12A.

e. *Sample specifications*. The sample specifications are consolidated and include the various acts constituting rape of a child and sexual assault of a child, by consolidating the descriptions of a sexual act or sexual contact within each overarching specification.

63. Article 120c (10 U.S.C. 920c)—Other sexual misconduct

This paragraph is taken from paragraph 45c (Article 120c—Other sexual misconduct) of the MCM (2016 edition) with the following amendments:

2018 Amendment: Subparagraph d. *Lesser included offenses* from the MCM (2016 edition) has been deleted. Subparagraphs e. *Maximum punishment* and f. *Sample specification* from the MCM (2016 edition) have been redesignated as subparagraphs d. and e. respectively. For lesser included offenses, see Appendix 12A.

d. *Maximum punishment*. The maximum punishment for forcible pandering is increased and aligns with federal civilian law. *See* 18 U.S.C. § 2422.

2023 Amendment: Subparagraph b. *Elements* is amended to add "without legal justification or lawful authorization" for the offenses of "Indecent viewing," "Indecent recording," "Broadcast of an indecent recording," and "Distribution of an indecent recording." Subparagraph e. *Sample specifications* is amended to reflect the amendments in Subparagraph b.

64. Article 121 (10 U.S.C. 921)—Larceny and wrongful appropriation

This paragraph is amended and reflects the addition of Article 121a to the UCMJ by Section 5432 of the Military Justice Act of 2016, Division E of the National Defense Authorization Act for Fiscal Year 2017, Pub. L. No. 114-328, 130 Stat. 2000 (2016). Other than the deletion of portions of the explanation dealing with matters now covered by Article 121a, this section is taken from paragraph 46 of the MCM (2016 edition).

2018 Amendment: Subparagraph d. *Lesser included offenses* from the MCM (2016 edition) has been deleted. Subparagraphs e. *Maximum punishment* and f. *Sample specification* from the MCM (2016 edition) have been redesignated as subparagraphs d. and e. respectively. For lesser included offenses, see Appendix 12A.

d. *Maximum punishment*. The maximum punishments for Wrongful appropriation of property of a value more than $1000 is increased and aligns with corresponding federal civilian practice under 18 U.S.C. § 661 (Theft within special maritime and territorial jurisdiction) and § 641 (Theft of public money, property, or records). The threshold amount for purposes of the maximum punishment in relation to the qualifying value of the property concerned is amended to $1,000 and aligns with the division between felony and misdemeanor penalties for property offenses in federal civilian law. The difference in the maximum authorized confinement for larceny of military versus non-military property in the lower-value category is eliminated.

2023 Amendment: Paragraph 64.d.(1)(c) is amended to correct a scrivener's error.

65. Article 121a (10 U.S.C. 921a)—Fraudulent use of credit cards, debit cards, and other access devices

This offense is new and addresses misconduct previously charged as an obtaining-type larceny offense under paragraph 46 (Article 121–Larceny) the MCM (2016 edition), and is similar to 18 U.S.C. § 1029. This offense is created pursuant to pursuant to Section 5432 of the Military Justice Act of 2016, Division E of the National Defense Authorization Act for Fiscal Year 2017, Pub. L. No. 114-328, 130 Stat. 2000 (2016). The offense focuses on the intent of the accused and technology used. This punitive article applies to situations where an accused has no authorization to use the access device from a person whose authorization is required, as well as situations where an accused exceeds the authorization of a person whose authorization is required for such use. *See United States v. Simpson*, 77 M.J. 279 (C.A.A.F. 2018) and cases cited therein.

66. Article 121b (10 U.S.C. 921b)—False pretenses to obtain services

This paragraph is taken from paragraph 78 (Article 134—False pretenses: obtaining services under) of the MCM (2016 edition) pursuant to Section 5433 of the Military Justice Act of 2016, Division E of the National Defense Authorization Act for Fiscal Year 2017, Pub. L. No. 114-328, 130 Stat. 2000 (2016) with the following amendments. Proof of the Article 134 "terminal element" is no longer required.

2018 Amendment: Subparagraph d. *Lesser included offenses* from the MCM (2016 edition) has been deleted. Subparagraphs e. *Maximum punishment* and f. *Sample specification* from the MCM (2016 edition) have been redesignated as subparagraphs d. and e. respectively. For lesser included offenses, see Appendix 12A.

d. *Maximum punishment*. The maximum punishment for the lower-value category is increased, and aligns with federal civilian practice under 18 U.S.C. § 661 (Theft within special maritime and territorial jurisdiction). The threshold amount for purposes of the maximum punishment in relation to the qualifying value of the property concerned is amended to $1,000 and aligns with the division between felony and misdemeanor penalties for property offenses in federal civilian law.

67. Article 122 (10 U.S.C. 922)—Robbery

This paragraph is taken from paragraph 47 (Article 122—Robbery) of the MCM (2016 edition) with the following amendments: This offense is relocated to its current position Section 5434 of the Military Justice Act of 2016, Division E of the National Defense Authorization Act for Fiscal Year 2017, Pub. L. No. 114-328, 130 Stat. 2000 (2016).

2018 Amendment: a. *Statutory Text*. Consistent with equivalent misconduct under federal civilian law (see 18 U.S.C. § 2111), the element of "with the intent to deprive permanently" is removed from the offense of Article 122—Robbery. The gravamen of the offense is the forcible taking of a victim's property in the presence of a victim.

Subparagraph d. *Lesser included offenses* from the MCM (2016 edition) has been deleted. Subparagraphs e. *Maximum punishment* and f. *Sample specification* from the MCM (2016 edition) have been redesignated as subparagraphs d. and e. respectively. For lesser included offenses, see Appendix 12A.

d. *Maximum Punishment*. The maximum punishment categories of robbery are aligned with federal civilian law to authorize a maximum punishment of 15 years confinement for any robbery committed with a "dangerous weapon," not limited to firearms.

68. Article 122a (10 U.S.C. 922a)—Receiving stolen property

This paragraph is taken from paragraph 106 (Article 134—Stolen property: knowingly receiving, buying, or concealing) of the MCM (2016 edition) with the following amendments. This offense is relocated from Article 134 to Article 122a pursuant to Section 5435 of the Military Justice Act of 2016, Division E of the National Defense Authorization Act for Fiscal Year 2017, Pub. L. No. 114-328, 130 Stat. 2000 (2016). Proof of the Article 134 "terminal element" is no longer required.

2018 Amendment: Subparagraph d. *Lesser included offenses* from the MCM (2016 edition) has been deleted. Subparagraphs e. *Maximum punishment* and f. *Sample specification* from the MCM (2016 edition) have been redesignated as subparagraphs d. and e. respectively. For lesser included offenses, see Appendix 12A.

d. *Maximum punishment*. The maximum punishments are increased, and align with corresponding federal civilian practice under 18 U.S.C. § 662 (Receiving stolen property within special maritime and territorial jurisdiction). The threshold amount for purposes of the maximum punishment in relation to the qualifying value of the property concerned is amended to $1,000 and aligns with the division between felony and misdemeanor penalties for property offenses in federal civilian law.

69. Article 123 (10 U.S.C. 923)—Offenses concerning Government computers

This offense is new pursuant to Section 5436 of the Military Justice Act of 2016, Division E of the National Defense Authorization Act for Fiscal Year 2017, Pub. L. No. 114-328, 130 Stat. 2000 (2016). The offense is similar to 18 U.S.C. § 1030, but does not supersede or preempt the assimilation of 18 U.S.C. § 1030 or other Title 18 offenses under Article 134, clause 3. Also, this offense does not supersede or preempt Department of Defense and Service regulations applicable to offenses concerning Government computers, applied via Article 92. This offense is directed at certain types of criminal conduct concerning Government computers. For other types of criminal conduct concerning computers, including private computers, persons subject to this chapter may also be subject to 18 U.S.C. § 1030, and other criminal statutes, via clause 3 of Article 134, as well as orders and regulations via Article 92. *See* Report of the Military Justice Review Group Part I: UCMJ Recommendations (December 22, 2015). For explanation of Controlled Unclassified Information, see DoDM 5200.01-V4 (February 24, 2012).

2023 Amendment: Subparagraph c. *Explanation* (1) *Access* is amended to include "computer system or computer network.

70. Article 123a (10 U.S.C. 923a)—Making, drawing, or uttering check, draft, or order without sufficient funds

This paragraph is taken from paragraph 49 (Article 123a—Making, drawing, or uttering check, draft, or order without sufficient funds) of the MCM (2016 edition) with the following amendments:

2018 Amendment: Subparagraph d. *Lesser included offenses* from the MCM (2016 edition) has been deleted. Subparagraphs e. *Maximum punishment* and f. *Sample specification* from the MCM (2016 edition) have been redesignated as subparagraphs d. and e. respectively. For lesser included offenses, see Appendix 12A.

d. *Maximum punishment*. The threshold amount for purposes of the maximum punishment in relation to the qualifying value of the property concerned is amended to $1,000 and aligns with the division between felony and misdemeanor penalties for property offenses in federal civilian law.

71. Article 124 (10 U.S.C. 924)—Frauds against the United States

This paragraph is taken from paragraph 58 (Article 132—Frauds against the United States) of the MCM (2016 edition) with the following amendments. This offense is relocated to Article 124 pursuant to Section 5401 of the Military Justice Act of 2016, Division E of the National Defense Authorization Act for Fiscal Year 2017, Pub. L. No. 114-328, 130 Stat. 2000 (2016).

2018 Amendment: Subparagraph d. *Lesser included offenses* from the MCM (2016 edition) has been deleted. Subparagraphs e. *Maximum punishment* and f. *Sample specification* from the MCM (2016 edition) have been redesignated as subparagraphs d. and e. respectively. For lesser included offenses, see Appendix 12A.

d. *Maximum punishment*. The threshold amount for purposes of the maximum punishment in relation to the qualifying value of the property concerned is amended to $1,000 and aligns with the division between felony and misdemeanor penalties for property offenses in federal civilian law.

72. Article 124a (10 U.S.C. 924a)—Bribery

This paragraph is taken from portions of paragraph 66 (Article 134—Bribery and graft) of the MCM (2016 edition), related to the offense of bribery pursuant to Section 5437 of the Military Justice Act of 2016, Division E of the National Defense Authorization Act for Fiscal Year 2017, Pub. L. No. 114-328, 130 Stat. 2000 (2016) with the following amendments. Proof of the Article 134 "terminal element" is no longer required.

2018 Amendment: Subparagraph d. *Lesser included offenses* from the MCM (2016 edition) has been deleted. Subparagraphs e. *Maximum punishment* and f. *Sample specification* from the MCM (2016 edition) have been redesignated as subparagraphs d. and e. respectively. For lesser included offenses, see Appendix 12A.

73. Article 124b (10 U.S.C. 924b)—Graft

This paragraph is taken from portions of paragraph 66 (Article 134—Bribery and graft) of the MCM (2016 edition), related to the offense of graft; pursuant to Section 5437 of the Military Justice Act of 2016, Division E of the National Defense Authorization Act for Fiscal Year 2017, Pub. L. No. 114-328, 130 Stat. 2000 (2016) with the following amendments. Proof of the Article 134 "terminal element" is no longer required.

2018 Amendment: Subparagraph d. *Lesser included offenses* from the MCM (2016 edition) has been deleted. Subparagraphs e. *Maximum punishment* and f. *Sample specification* from the MCM (2016 edition) have been redesignated as subparagraphs d. and e. respectively. For lesser included offenses, see Appendix 12A.

74. Article 125 (10 U.S.C. 925)—Kidnapping

This paragraph is taken from paragraph 92 (Article 134—Kidnapping) of the MCM (2016 edition) pursuant to Section 5439 of the Military Justice Act of 2016, Division E of the National Defense Authorization Act for Fiscal Year 2017, Pub. L. No. 114-328, 130 Stat. 2000 (2016) with the following amendments. Proof of the Article 134 "terminal element" is no longer required.

2018 Amendment: Subparagraph c.(5) has deleted the sentence from the MCM (2016 edition) that discussed kidnapping in the context of a parent or legal guardian.

Subparagraph d. *Lesser included offenses* from the MCM (2016 edition) has been deleted. Subparagraphs e. *Maximum punishment* and f. *Sample specification* from the MCM (2016 edition) have been redesignated as subparagraphs d. and e. respectively. For lesser included offenses, see Appendix 12A.

75. Article 126 (10 U.S.C. 926)—Arson; burning property with intent to defraud

This paragraph is taken from paragraphs 52 (Article 126—Arson) and 67 (Article 134—Burning with intent to defraud) of the MCM (2016 edition) pursuant to Section 5440 of the Military Justice Act of 2016, Division E of the National Defense Authorization Act for Fiscal Year 2017, Pub. L. No. 114-328, 130 Stat. 2000 (2016) with the following amendments. Proof of the Article 134 "terminal element" is not required.

2018 Amendment: Article 126 is amended and incorporates burning with intent to defraud in conjunction with the Military Justice Act of 2016's reorganization of the punitive articles. The offense of burning with intent to defraud remains substantively the same, except proof of the Article 134 terminal element is no longer required.

b.(1). The elements of aggravated arson were amended and proof that the property belonged to a certain person and was of a certain value is not required. *See United States v. Desha*, 23 M.J. 66 (C.A.A.F. 1986) (affirming an aggravated arson conviction holding that Congress eliminated the common-law requirement that the property burned be "of another").

b.(2). The element of simple arson that required that the dwelling or structure be of a certain value was removed. An enhanced punishment is available for property of a value of more than $1,000.

c.(2)(a). The definition of "inhabited dwelling" aligns with *United States v. Duke*, 16 C.M.A. 460 (C.M.A. 1966).

Subparagraph d. *Lesser included offenses* from the MCM (2016 edition) has been deleted. Subparagraphs e. *Maximum punishment* and f. *Sample specification* from the MCM (2016 edition) have been redesignated as subparagraphs d. and e. respectively. For lesser included offenses, see Appendix 12A.

d. *Maximum punishment*. The maximum authorized confinement for both aggravated arson and simple arson are increased.

76. Article 127 (10 U.S.C. 927)—Extortion

This paragraph is taken from paragraph 53 (Article 127—Extortion) of the MCM (2016 edition) with the following amendments:

2018 Amendment: Subparagraph d. *Lesser included offenses* from the MCM (2016 edition) has been deleted. Subparagraphs e. *Maximum punishment* and f. *Sample specification* from the MCM (2016 edition) have been redesignated as subparagraphs d. and e. respectively. For lesser included offenses, see Appendix 12A.

77. Article 128 (10 U.S.C. 928)—Assault

This paragraph is taken from paragraphs 54 (Article 128—Assault) and 64 (Article 134—Assault—with intent to commit murder, voluntary manslaughter, rape, robbery, sodomy, arson, burglary, or housebreaking) of the MCM (2016 edition) pursuant to Section 5441 of the Military Justice Act of 2016, Division E of the National Defense Authorization Act for Fiscal Year 2017, Pub. L.

No. 114-328, 130 Stat. 2000 (2016), as further amended by Section 1081(c)(1)(P) of the National Defense Authorization Act for Fiscal Year 2018, Pub. L. No. 115-91, 131 Stat. 1283 (2017). with the following amendments:

2018 Amendment: a. *Text of statute*. (b) *Aggravated Assault*. Two amendments to this statute align it more closely with federal civilian practice under 18 U.S.C. § 113. First, the phrase "or other means or force likely to result in death or grievous bodily harm" has been removed from the statutory definition of "aggravated assault," and replaced with the phrase "dangerous weapon." This eliminates the likelihood of harm analysis previously necessary under the MCM (2016 edition) for this offense, and allows the offense to focus solely on the intent of the accused. In turn, the phrase "dangerous weapon" focuses on the capability of any object to inflict death or grievous bodily harm. *See* c. *Explanation* (5)(a)(iii). Second, the intent necessary to complete an aggravated assault is modified to no longer require the specific intent to commit substantial or grievous bodily harm. This change aligns the specific intent requirement to federal civilian law under 18 U.S.C. § 113. Pursuant to Section 533 of the John S. McCain National Defense Authorization Act for Fiscal Year 2019, Pub. L. No. 115-232, 132 Stat. 1636 (2018), subparagraph a. Text of the statute is amended to add element (b)(3).

(c) *Assault with intent to commit specified offenses*. The offense of assault with intent to commit specified offenses is taken from paragraph 64 (Article 134—Assault—with intent to commit murder, voluntary manslaughter, rape, robbery, forcible sodomy, arson, burglary, or housebreaking) of the MCM (2016 edition) in conjunction with the Military Justice Act of 2016's reorganization of the punitive articles. *See* Appendix 23, subparagraph 64.c. *Explanation* of the MCM (2016 edition). The scope of the offense remains substantively the same with two exceptions: (1) the offense now lists rape of a child, sexual assault, sexual assault of a child, and kidnapping, as specified offenses; and (2) proof of the terminal element of Article 134 is no longer required.

c. *Explanation*.(1) *Substantial bodily harm*. The definition of substantial bodily harm aligns with 18 U.S.C. § 113(b)(1). It provides a middle tier of harm between bodily harm and grievous bodily harm. The definition of grievous bodily harm aligns with the definition of serious bodily injury under 18 U.S.C. § 113(b)(2), which is the highest tier of bodily injury.

(5)(a)(iii) *Dangerous weapon*. The definition of dangerous weapon focuses attention on the nature of the weapon involved and the accused's intent to commit any bodily harm. To qualify as a dangerous weapon, it is sufficient that "an instrument [is] capable of inflicting death or serious bodily injury." *United States v. Sturgis*, 48 F.3d 784, 787 (4th Cir. 1995). *See also United States v. Bey*, 667 F.2d 7, 11 (5th Cir. 1982) (citation and internal quotation omitted) ("[w]hat constitutes a dangerous weapon depends not on the nature of the object itself but on its capacity, given the manner of its use, to endanger life or inflict great bodily harm.")

(5)(b)(i). Assault resulting in substantial or grievous bodily harm requires only a finding of general intent. *See United States v. Davis*, 237 F.3d 942, 944 (8th Cir. 2001).

Subparagraph d. *Lesser included offenses* from the MCM (2016 edition) has been deleted. Subparagraphs e. *Maximum punishment* and f. *Sample specification* from the MCM (2016 edition) have been redesignated as subparagraphs d. and e. respectively. For lesser included offenses, see Appendix 12A.

d. *Maximum punishment*. Two new maximum punishment categories were added: (1) infliction of substantial bodily harm and (2) assaulting a spouse, intimate partner, or an immediate family member.

2022 Amendment: Subparagraph b. *Elements* is amended to remove references to "a spouse, intimate partner, or an immediate family member of the accused" for all applicable elements; those scenarios are now covered by Article 128b. Subsequent parallel amendments are made to subparagraphs c-e. *Subparagraph b.* Elements is amended to add the offense of "Aggravated Assault by strangulation or suffocation." Subsequent parallel amendments are added to subparagraphs c-e.

2023 Amendment: The descriptor for subparagraph d. *Maximum punishment* (1)(b) is amended to read, "When committed with an unloaded firearm or other dangerous weapon." Subparagraph d.(1)(b) is further amended to change the maximum confinement from three years to two years. Subparagraph d.(1)(c) is added. The maximum punishment under subparagraph d.(5)(b) is amended to align with the offense under subparagraph c.(6)(d)."

78. Article 128a (10 U.S.C. 928a)—Maiming

This paragraph is taken from paragraph 50 (Article 124—Maiming) of the MCM (2016 edition) with the following amendments. This offense is relocated to its current position pursuant to Section 5401 of the Military Justice Act of 2016, Division E of the National Defense Authorization Act for Fiscal Year 2017, Pub. L. No. 114-328, 130 Stat. 2000 (2016).

2018 Amendment: Subparagraph d. *Lesser included offenses* from the MCM (2016 edition) has been deleted. Subparagraphs e. *Maximum punishment* and f. *Sample specification* from the MCM (2016 edition) have been redesignated as subparagraphs d. and e. respectively. For lesser included offenses, see Appendix 12A.

78a. Article 128b (10 U.S.C. 928b)—Domestic Violence

2022 Amendment: This is a new punitive article enacted by Section 532 of the John S. McCain National Defense Authorization Act for Fiscal Year 2019, Pub. L. No. 115-232, 132 Stat. 1636 (2018), which criminalizes domestic violence.

79. Article 129 (10 U.S.C. 929)—Burglary; unlawful entry

This paragraph is taken from paragraphs 55 (Article 129—Burglary), 56 (Article 130—Housebreaking), and 111 (Article 134—Unlawful entry) of the MCM (2016 edition) and is consolidated pursuant to Section 5442 of the Military Justice Act of 2016, Division E of the National Defense Authorization Act for Fiscal Year 2017, Pub. L. No. 114-328, 130 Stat. 2000 (2016) with the following amendments:

2018 Amendment: a. *Text of statute*. The common law elements of nighttime and dwelling house are eliminated as elements of the offense of burglary.

b. *Elements*. The list of offenses that qualify for enhanced maximum punishment is amended to reflect the Military Justice Act of 2016's reorganization of the punitive articles.

c. *Explanation*. The definition of "Building, structure" is taken, without change, from paragraph 56 of the MCM (2016 edition).

Subparagraph d. *Lesser included offenses* from the MCM (2016 edition) has been deleted. Subparagraphs e. *Maximum punishment* and f. *Sample specification* from the MCM (2016 edition) have been redesignated as subparagraphs d. and e. respectively. For lesser included offenses, see Appendix 12A.

f. *Sample specifications*. The sample specifications are modeled after those contained under paragraphs 55, 56, and 111 of the MCM (2016 edition).

80. Article 130 (10 U.S.C. 930)—Stalking

This offense is taken from paragraph 45a (Article 120a Stalking) of the MCM (2016 edition) and is modified pursuant to Section 5443 of the Military Justice Act of 2016, Division E of the National Defense Authorization Act for Fiscal Year 2017, Pub. L. No. 114-328, 130 Stat. 2000 (2016) with the following amendments:

2018 Amendment: a. *Text of statute*. This statute is amended and extends the conduct covered to include cyberstalking and threats to intimate partners. This aligns the offense with similar misconduct under 18 U.S.C. § 2261A.

c. *Explanation*. The definition of bodily harm is based on subparagraph 77.c.(1)(a).

Subparagraph d. *Lesser included offenses* from the MCM (2016 edition) has been deleted. Subparagraphs e. *Maximum punishment* and f. *Sample specification* from the MCM (2016 edition) have been redesignated as subparagraphs d. and e. respectively. For lesser included offenses, see Appendix 12A.

81. Article 131 (10 U.S.C. 931)—Perjury

This paragraph is taken from paragraph 57 (Article 131—Perjury) of the MCM (2016 edition) with the following amendments:

2018 Amendment: Subparagraph d. *Lesser included offenses* from the MCM (2016 edition) has been deleted. Subparagraphs e. *Maximum punishment* and f. *Sample specification* from the MCM (2016 edition) have been redesignated as subparagraphs d. and e. respectively. For lesser included offenses, see Appendix 12A.

82. Article 131a (10 U.S.C. 931a)—Subornation of perjury

This paragraph is taken from paragraph 98 (Article 134—Perjury: subornation of) of the MCM (2016 edition) with the following amendments. The offense is relocated to Article 131a pursuant to Section 5444 of the Military Justice Act of 2016, Division E of the National Defense Authorization Act for Fiscal Year 2017, Pub. L. No. 114-328, 130 Stat. 2000 (2016). Proof of the Article 134 "terminal element" is no longer required.

2018 Amendment: Subparagraph d. *Lesser included offenses* from the MCM (2016 edition) has been deleted. Subparagraphs e. *Maximum punishment* and f. *Sample specification* from the MCM (2016 edition) have been redesignated as subparagraphs d. and e. respectively. For lesser included offenses, see Appendix 12A.

83. Article 131b (10 U.S.C. 931b)—Obstructing justice

This paragraph is taken from paragraph 96 (Article 134—Obstructing justice) of the MCM (2016 edition) with the following amendments. The offense is relocated to Article 131b pursuant to Section 5445 of the Military Justice Act of 2016, Division E of the National Defense Authorization Act for Fiscal Year 2017, Pub. L. No. 114-328, 130 Stat. 2000 (2016). Proof of the Article 134 "terminal element" is no longer required.

2018 Amendment: Subparagraph c. *Explanation* has been updated and reflects Article 20, as amended by Section 5164 of the Military Justice Act of 2016, Division E of the National Defense Authorization Act for Fiscal Year 2017, Pub. L. No. 114-328, 130 Stat. 2000 (2016), which clarifies that a summary court-martial is not a criminal forum. The *Explanation* also reflects the reorganization of Article 98, Noncompliance with procedural rules, from paragraph 22 of MCM (2016 edition) to paragraph 87 (Article 131f), pursuant to Section 5201 of the Military Justice Act of 2016, Division E of the National Defense Authorization Act for Fiscal Year 2017, Pub. L. No. 114-328, 130 Stat. 2000 (2016).

Subparagraph d. *Lesser included offenses* from the MCM (2016 edition) has been deleted. Subparagraphs e. *Maximum punishment* and f. *Sample specification* from the MCM (2016 edition) have been redesignated as subparagraphs d. and e. respectively. For lesser included offenses, see Appendix 12A.

84. Article 131c (10 U.S.C. 931c)—Misprision of serious offense

This paragraph is taken from paragraph 95 (Article 134—Misprision of a serious offense) of the MCM (2016 edition) with the following amendments. The offense is relocated to Article 131c pursuant to Section 5446 of the Military Justice Act of 2016, Division E of the National Defense Authorization Act for Fiscal Year 2017, Pub. L. No. 114-328, 130 Stat. 2000 (2016). Proof of the Article 134 "terminal element" is no longer required.

2018 Amendment: Subparagraph d. *Lesser included offenses* from the MCM (2016 edition) has been deleted. Subparagraphs e. *Maximum punishment* and f. *Sample specification* from the MCM (2016 edition) have been redesignated as subparagraphs d. and e. respectively. For lesser included offenses, see Appendix 12A.

85. Article 131d (10 U.S.C. 931d)—Wrongful refusal to testify

This paragraph is taken from paragraph 108 (Article 134—Testify: wrongful refusal) of the MCM (2016 edition) with the following amendments. The offense is relocated to Article 131d pursuant to Section 5447 of the Military Justice Act of 2016, Division E of the National Defense Authorization Act for Fiscal Year 2017, Pub. L. No. 114-328, 130 Stat. 2000 (2016). Proof of the Article 134 "terminal element" is no longer required.

2018 Amendment: Subparagraph d. *Lesser included offenses* from the MCM (2016 edition) has been deleted. Subparagraphs e. *Maximum punishment* and f. *Sample specification* from the MCM (2016 edition) have been redesignated as subparagraphs d. and e. respectively. For lesser included offenses, see Appendix 12A.

86. Article 131e (10 U.S.C. 931e)—Prevention of authorized seizure of property

This paragraph is taken from paragraph 103 (Article 134—Seizure: destruction, removal, or disposal of property to prevent) of the MCM (2016 edition) with the following amendments. The offense is relocated to Article 131e pursuant to Section 5448 of the Military Justice Act of 2016, Division E of the National Defense Authorization Act for Fiscal Year 2017, Pub. L. No. 114-328, 130

Stat. 2000 (2016). Proof of the Article 134 "terminal element" is no longer required.

2018 Amendment: Subparagraph d. *Lesser included offenses* from the MCM (2016 edition) has been deleted. Subparagraphs e. *Maximum punishment* and f. *Sample specification* from the MCM (2016 edition) have been redesignated as subparagraphs d. and e. respectively. For lesser included offenses, see Appendix 12A.

d. *Maximum punishment*. The authorized punishment for the offense is modified and aligns with federal civilian law for similar misconduct. *See* 18 U.S.C. § 2232.

87. Article 131f (10 U.S.C. 931f)—Noncompliance with procedural rules

This paragraph is taken from paragraph 22 (Article 98—Noncompliance with procedural rules) of the MCM (2016 edition) with the following amendments. This offense is relocated to its current position, pursuant to Section 5401 of the Military Justice Act of 2016, Division E of the National Defense Authorization Act for Fiscal Year 2017, Pub. L. No. 114-328, 130 Stat. 2000 (2016).

2018 Amendment: Subparagraph d. *Lesser included offenses* from the MCM (2016 edition) has been deleted. Subparagraphs e. *Maximum punishment* and f. *Sample specification* from the MCM (2016 edition) have been redesignated as subparagraphs d. and e. respectively. For lesser included offenses, see Appendix 12A.

88. Article 131g (10 U.S.C. 931g)—Wrongful interference with adverse administrative

This paragraph is taken from paragraph 96a (Article 134—Wrongful interference with an adverse administrative proceeding) of the MCM (2016 edition) with the following amendments. The offense is relocated to Article 131g pursuant to Section 5449 of the Military Justice Act of 2016, Division E of the National Defense Authorization Act for Fiscal Year 2017, Pub. L. No. 114-328, 130 Stat. 2000 (2016). Proof of the Article 134 "terminal element" is no longer required.

2018 Amendment: Subparagraph d. *Lesser included offenses* from the MCM (2016 edition) has been deleted. Subparagraphs e. *Maximum punishment* and f. *Sample specification* from the MCM (2016 edition) have been redesignated as subparagraphs d. and e. respectively. For lesser included offenses, see Appendix 12A.

89. Article 132 (10 U.S.C. 932) —Retaliation

This is a new enumerated offense pursuant to Section 5450 of the Military Justice Act of 2016, Division E of the National Defense Authorization Act for Fiscal Year 2017, Pub. L. No. 114-328, 130 Stat. 2000 (2016), as further amended by Section 1081(c)(1)(Q) of the National Defense Authorization Act for Fiscal Year 2018, Pub. Law. No. 115-91, 131 Stat. 1283 (2017), which supplements and does not preempt Service regulations that address other types or categories of prohibited retaliatory actions. *See also* 10 U.S.C. § 1034, 18 U.S.C. § 1513. Service regulations may specify additional types of retaliatory conduct punishable at court-martial under Article 92 or Article 134.

2023 Amendment: Subparagraph c. *Explanation* (2)(b) is added to expand the definition of "Personnel action" to include actions affect civilian employees.

90. Article 133 (10 U.S.C. 933)—Conduct unbecoming an officer

This paragraph is taken from paragraph 59 (Article 133—Conduct unbecoming an officer and a gentleman) of the MCM (2016 edition) with the following amendments:

2018 Amendment: c. *Explanation* (1) *Gentleman*. This subparagraph is amended to emphasize that the term "gentleman" connotes failings in an officer's personal character, regardless of gender.

Subparagraph d. *Lesser included offenses* from the MCM (2016 edition) has been deleted. Subparagraphs e. *Maximum punishment* and f. *Sample specification* from the MCM (2016 edition) have been redesignated as subparagraphs d. and e. respectively. For lesser included offenses, see Appendix 12A.

2023 Amendment: Pursuant to Section 532 of the National Defense Authorization Act for Fiscal Year 2022, Pub. L. No 117-81, 135 Stat. 1546 (2021), the name of this article and the text of the statute are amended to remove "and a gentleman." Subparagraph b. *Elements* (2) is amended to remove "and a gentleman." Subparagraph c. *Explanations* is re-written in their entirety to clarify the meaning of "officership" and to update the explanation of the nature of the offense.

91. Article 134 (10 U.S.C. 934)—General article

This paragraph is taken from paragraph 60 (Article 134—General Article) of the MCM (2016 edition), and reflects two significant changes to designated Article 134 offenses within the MCM (2016 edition), namely, (1) the "relocation" of 36 of the 53 Article 134 offenses listed in MCM (2016 edition) to the enumerated punitive articles (Articles 80-132); and (2) the statutory amendment to Article 134 to provide extraterritorial jurisdiction for noncapital federal crimes committed outside of the United States which otherwise require commission of the offense "within the special maritime and territorial jurisdiction of the United States."

2018 Amendment: a. *Statutory text*. Article 134 is amended and specifically provides that under clause 3, extraterritorial jurisdiction exists over non-capital federal crimes committed outside the United States which include as an element that the crime occur "within the special maritime or territorial jurisdiction of the United States." Clause 3 aligns the prosecutorial scope of noncapital federal offenses under Article 134 with the prosecutorial scope of 18 U.S.C. § 3261 (applicable to civilian misconduct). This extraterritorial jurisdiction does not extend to 18 U.S.C. § 13—Federal Assimilative Crimes Act—which requires the commission of the offense concerned upon an enclave of federal exclusive or concurrent jurisdiction.

b. *Elements*. The terminal element for each Article 134 offense is revised as follows: "That, under the circumstances, the conduct of the accused was either: (i) to the prejudice of good order and discipline in the armed forces; (ii) was of a nature to bring discredit upon the armed forces; or (iii) to the prejudice of good order and discipline in the armed forces and of a nature to bring discredit upon the armed forces." See RCM 307(c)(3) regarding the form for alleging this terminal element.

c. *Explanation*. Subparagraph c.(4) is amended and clarifies the categories of federal crimes and offenses which may be prosecuted under clause (3), Article 134.

(6) *Drafting specifications for Article 134 offenses*. The third paragraph in the Discussion following subparagraph c.(6)(a) is consistent with *United States v. Miles*, 71 M.J. 671 (N.M. Ct. Crim.

App. 2012) and R. Peter Masterton, "A View From the Bench: Prohibition on Disjunctive Charging Using 'Or'", *A View From the Bench: Prohibition on Disjunctive Charging Using 'Or,'* ARMY LAW., May 2012.

92. Article 134—(Animal abuse)

This paragraph is taken from paragraph 61 (Article 134—Animal Abuse) of the MCM (2016 edition) with the following amendments:

2018 Amendment: Subparagraph d. *Lesser included offenses* from the MCM (2016 edition) has been deleted. Subparagraphs e. *Maximum punishment* and f. *Sample specification* from the MCM (2016 edition) have been redesignated as subparagraphs d. and e. respectively. For lesser included offenses, see Appendix 12A.

93. Article 134—(Bigamy)

This paragraph is taken from paragraph 65 (Article 134—Bigamy) of the MCM (2016 edition) with the following amendments:

2018 Amendment: Subparagraph d. *Lesser included offenses* from the MCM (2016 edition) has been deleted. Subparagraphs e. *Maximum punishment* and f. *Sample specification* from the MCM (2016 edition) have been redesignated as subparagraphs d. and e. respectively. For lesser included offenses, see Appendix 12A.

94. Article 134—(Check, worthless making and uttering—by dishonorably failing to maintain funds)

This paragraph is taken from paragraph 68 (Article 134—Check, worthless, making and uttering—by dishonorably failing to maintain funds) of the MCM (2016 edition) with the following amendments:

2018 Amendment: Subparagraph d. *Lesser included offenses* from the MCM (2016 edition) has been deleted. Subparagraphs e. *Maximum punishment* and f. *Sample specification* from the MCM (2016 edition) have been redesignated as subparagraphs d. and e. respectively. For lesser included offenses, see Appendix 12A.

95. Article 134—(Child pornography)

This paragraph is taken from paragraph 68b (Article 134—Child pornography) of the MCM (2016 edition) with the following amendments:

2018 Amendment: c. *Explanation* (1) *In general*. The scope of child pornography under Article 134 is broader than the scope of child pornography criminalized under 18 U.S.C. § 2252A. *Cf. Ashcroft v. Free Speech Coalition*, 535 U.S. 234 (2002). Article 134 includes visual depictions of what appear to be minors engaged in sexually explicit conduct within the definition of child pornography. *See United States v. Blouin*, 74 M.J. 247 (C.A.A.F. 2015); *United States v. Forney*, 67 M.J. 271, 275 (C.A.A.F. 2009); *United States v. Brisbane*, 63 M.J. 106, 116 (C.A.A.F. 2006); *United States v. Roderick*, 62 M.J. 425, 429 (C.A.A.F. 2006); *United States v. Reeves*, 62 M.J. 88, 96 (C.A.A.F. 2005); *United States v. Mason*, 60 M.J. 15, 19 (C.A.A.F. 2004); *United States v. O'Connor*, 58 M.J. 450 (C.A.A.F. 2003).

(2) *Federal "Child pornography" and "Obscenity" offenses* and (3) *State "child pornography" and "obscenity" offenses* are new and emphasize that Article 134—(Child pornography) is not intended to preempt applicable federal and state child pornography and obscenity statutes. (2) and (3) also discuss the circumstances under which these federal and state child pornography and obscenity statutes may be charged under Article 134, clauses 2 and 3.

(10) *Sexually explicit conduct*. The amendments do not change the usefulness of the "*Dost* factors" in determining whether a particular image qualifies as a "lascivious exhibition", for purposes of this offense. *United States v. Dost*, 636 F.Supp. 828, 832 (S.D. Ca. 1986), *aff'd sub nom United States v. Wiegand*, 812 F.2d 1239 (9th Cir. 1987). The *Dost* factors are also commonly employed by federal civilian and military courts in interpreting "lascivious exhibition" for purposes of 18 U.S.C. § 2252A. *See United States v. Roderick*, 62 M.J. 425, 430 (C.A.A.F. 2006).

Subparagraph d. *Lesser included offenses* from the MCM (2016 edition) has been deleted. Subparagraphs e. *Maximum punishment* and f. *Sample specification* from the MCM (2016 edition) have been redesignated as subparagraphs d. and e. respectively. For lesser included offenses, see Appendix 12A.

96. Article 134—(Debt, dishonorably failing to pay)

This paragraph is taken from paragraph 71 (Article 134—Debt: dishonorable failing to pay) of the MCM (2016 edition) with the following amendments:

2018 Amendment: Subparagraph d. *Lesser included offenses* from the MCM (2016 edition) has been deleted. Subparagraphs e. *Maximum punishment* and f. *Sample specification* from the MCM (2016 edition) have been redesignated as subparagraphs d. and e. respectively. For lesser included offenses, see Appendix 12A.

97. Article 134—(Disloyal statements)

This paragraph is taken from paragraph 72 (Article 134—Disloyal statements) of the MCM (2016 edition) with the following amendments:

2018 Amendment: Subparagraph d. *Lesser included offenses* from the MCM (2016 edition) has been deleted. Subparagraphs e. *Maximum punishment* and f. *Sample specification* from the MCM (2016 edition) have been redesignated as subparagraphs d. and e. respectively. For lesser included offenses, see Appendix 12A.

98. Article 134—(Disorderly conduct, drunkenness)

This paragraph is taken from paragraph 73 (Article 134—Disorderly conduct, drunkenness) of the MCM (2016 edition) with the following amendments:

2018 Amendment: Subparagraph d. *Lesser included offenses* from the MCM (2016 edition) has been deleted. Subparagraphs e. *Maximum punishment* and f. *Sample specification* from the MCM (2016 edition) have been redesignated as subparagraphs d. and e. respectively. For lesser included offenses, see Appendix 12A.

99. Article 134—(Extramarital sexual conduct)

This paragraph is drawn from paragraph 62 (Article 134 Adultery) of the MCM (2016 edition) with the following amendments:

2018 Amendment: This offense does not preempt any additional lawful regulations prescribed by a proper authority to proscribe additional forms of improper extramarital conduct by military personnel. Violations of such regulations, directives, or orders may be punishable under Article 92. *See* paragraph 18.

b. *Elements*. The definition of extramarital conduct is consistent with the definition of sexually explicit conduct under 18 U.S.C. § 2256(2)(A)(i) and is gender neutral.

c. *Explanation*. (1) *Nature of the offense* was deleted and replaced with *Conduct prejudicial to good order and discipline or of a nature to bring discredit upon the armed forces*. Subparagraph c.(1)(h) from the MCM (2016 edition) regarding legal separations is now an affirmative defense. Subparagraph c.(1)(h) now lists pending legal dissolution as a factor in assessing whether the conduct at issue meets a terminal element.

(4) *Legal separation*. This is a new affirmative defense. In order for the affirmative defense to apply, both parties to the conduct must either be legally separated or unmarried. That is, it is not an affirmative defense if the accused is legally separated but the co-actor is still married. By the same token, it is an affirmative defense if the accused is legally separated and the co-actor is unmarried.

Subparagraph d. *Lesser included offenses* from the MCM (2016 edition) has been deleted. Subparagraphs e. *Maximum punishment* and f. *Sample specification* from the MCM (2016 edition) have been redesignated as subparagraphs d. and e. respectively. For lesser included offenses, see Appendix 12A.

100. Article 134—(Firearm, discharging—through negligence)

This paragraph is taken from paragraph 80 (Article 134—Firearm, discharging through negligence) of the MCM (2016 edition) with the following amendments:

2018 Amendment: Subparagraph d. *Lesser included offenses* from the MCM (2016 edition) has been deleted. Subparagraphs e. *Maximum punishment* and f. *Sample specification* from the MCM (2016 edition) have been redesignated as subparagraphs d. and e. respectively. For lesser included offenses, see Appendix 12A.

101. Article 134—(Fraternization)

This paragraph is taken from paragraph 83 (Article 134—Fraternization) of the MCM (2016 edition) with the following amendments:

2018 Amendment: Subparagraph d. *Lesser included offenses* from the MCM (2016 edition) has been deleted. Subparagraphs e. *Maximum punishment* and f. *Sample specification* from the MCM (2016 edition) have been redesignated as subparagraphs d. and e. respectively. For lesser included offenses, see Appendix 12A.

102. Article 134—(Gambling with subordinate)

This paragraph is taken from paragraph 84 (Article 134—Gambling with subordinate) of the MCM (2016 edition) with the following amendments:

2018 Amendment: Subparagraph d. *Lesser included offenses* from the MCM (2016 edition) has been deleted. Subparagraphs e. *Maximum punishment* and f. *Sample specification* from the MCM (2016 edition) have been redesignated as subparagraphs d. and e. respectively. For lesser included offenses, see Appendix 12A.

103. Article 134—(Homicide, negligent)

This paragraph is taken from paragraph 85 (Article 134—Homicide, negligent) of the MCM (2016 edition) with the following amendments:

2018 Amendment: Subparagraph d. *Lesser included offenses* from the MCM (2016 edition) has been deleted. Subparagraphs e. *Maximum punishment* and f. *Sample specification* from the MCM (2016 edition) have been redesignated as subparagraphs d. and e. respectively. For lesser included offenses, see Appendix 12A.

104. Article 134—(Indecent conduct)

This paragraph is taken from paragraph 90 (Article 134—Indecent conduct) of the MCM (2016 edition) with the following amendments:

2018 Amendment: Subparagraph d. *Lesser included offenses* from the MCM (2016 edition) has been deleted. Subparagraphs e. *Maximum punishment* and f. *Sample specification* from the MCM (2016 edition) have been redesignated as subparagraphs d. and e. respectively. For lesser included offenses, see Appendix 12A.

105. Article 134—(Indecent language)

This paragraph is taken from paragraph 89 (Article 134—Indecent language) of the MCM (2016 edition) with the following amendments:

2018 Amendment: Subparagraph d. *Lesser included offenses* from the MCM (2016 edition) has been deleted. Subparagraphs e. *Maximum punishment* and f. *Sample specification* from the MCM (2016 edition) have been redesignated as subparagraphs d. and e. respectively. For lesser included offenses, see Appendix 12A.

106. Article 134—(Pandering and prostitution)

This paragraph is based on paragraph 97 (Article 134—Pandering and prostitution) of the MCM (2016 edition) with the following amendments:

2018 Amendment: (c)(1) *Sexual act*. The definition of "sexual act" conforms to Article 120(g) as amended by Section 5430 of the Military Justice Act of 2016, Division E of the National Defense Authorization Act for Fiscal Year 2017, Pub. L. No. 114-328, 130 Stat. 2000 (2016).

Subparagraph d. *Lesser included offenses* from the MCM (2016 edition) has been deleted. Subparagraphs e. *Maximum punishment* and f. *Sample specification* from the MCM (2016 edition) have been redesignated as subparagraphs d. and e. respectively. For lesser included offenses, see Appendix 12A.

107. Article 134—(Self-injury without intent to avoid service)

This paragraph is taken from paragraph 103a (Article 134—Self-injury without intent to avoid service) of the MCM (2016 edition).

2018 Amendment: Subparagraph d. *Lesser included offenses* from the MCM (2016 edition) has been deleted. Subparagraphs e. *Maximum punishment.* and f. *Sample specification.* from the MCM (2016 edition) have been redesignated as subparagraphs d. and e. respectively. For lesser included offenses, see Appendix 12A.

107a. Article 134—(Sexual Harassment)

2023 Amendment: This is a new enumerated offense establishing sexual harassment as a stand-alone offense under Article 134, UCMJ. *See* National Defense Authorization Act for Fiscal Year 2022, Pub. L. No. 117-81, § 539D, 135 Stat. 1546 (2021).

108. Article 134—(Straggling)

This paragraph is taken from paragraph 107 (Article 134—Straggling) of the MCM (2016 edition).

2018 Amendment: Subparagraph d. *Lesser included offenses* from the MCM (2016 edition) has been deleted. Subparagraphs e. *Maximum punishment.* and f. *Sample specification.* from the MCM (2016 edition) have been redesignated as subparagraphs d. and e. respectively. For lesser included offenses, see Appendix 12A.

109. Article 134—(Visual depiction, nonconsensual distribution or broadcast)

This paragraph is taken from paragraph 114 (Article 134—(Visual depiction, nonconsensual distribution or broadcast) of the MCM (2016 edition), as amended by Exec. Order No. 13825, 83 Fed. Reg. 9889 (March 1, 2018) without substantive amendment.

2018 Amendment: Subparagraph d. *Lesser included offenses* from the MCM (2016 edition) has been deleted. Subparagraphs e. *Maximum punishment.* and f. *Sample specification.* from the MCM (2016 edition) have been redesignated as subparagraphs d. and e. respectively. For lesser included offenses, see Appendix 12A.

APPENDIX 18
ANALYSIS OF NONJUDICIAL PUNISHMENT PROCEDURE

1. General

c. *Purpose*. This paragraph is based on the legislative history of Article 15, both as initially enacted and as modified in 1962. *See generally* H.R.Rep. No. 491, 81st Cong., 1st Sess. 14–15 (1949); S.Rep. No. 1911, 87th Cong., 2d Sess. (1962).

d. *Policy*. Subparagraph (1) is based on paragraph 129*a* of MCM, 1969 (Rev.). Subparagraph (2) is based on the last sentence of paragraph 129*a* of MCM, 1969 (Rev.) and on service regulations. *See, e.g.*, AR 27–10, para. 3–4 *b* (1 Sep. 1982); JAGMAN sec. 0101. *Cf.* Article 37. Subparagraph (3) is based on the second paragraph 129b *of* MCM, 1969 (Rev.).

e. *Minor offenses*. This paragraph is derived from paragraph 128*b* of MCM, 1969 (Rev.), service regulations concerning "minor offenses" (*see, e.g.*, AR 27–10, para. 3–3*d* (1 Sep. 1982); AFR 111–9, para. 3*a*(3) (31 Aug. 1979)); *United States v. Fretwell,* 11 U.S.C.M.A. 377, 29 C.M.R. 193 (1960). The intent of the paragraph is to provide the commander with enough latitude to appropriately resolve a disciplinary problem. Thus, in some instances, the commander may decide that nonjudicial punishment may be appropriate for an offense that could result in a dishonorable discharge or confinement for more than 1 year if tried by general court-martial, e.g., failure to obey an order or regulation. On the other hand, the commander could refer a case to a court-martial that would ordinarily be considered at nonjudicial punishment, e.g., a short unauthorized absence, for a servicemember with a long history of short unauthorized absences, which nonjudicial punishment has not been successful in correcting.

2018 Amendment: Paragraph 1.e. is amended and addresses the definition of minor offense.

f. Limitations *on nonjudicial punishment.*

(1) *Double punishment prohibited.* This subparagraph is taken from the first paragraph of paragraph 128*d* of MCM, 1969 (Rev.). Note that what is prohibited is the service of punishment twice. Where nonjudicial punishment is set aside, this does not necessarily prevent reimposition of punishment and service of punishment not previously served.

(2) *Increase in punishment prohibited.* This paragraph is taken from the second paragraph of paragraph 128*d* of MCM, 1969 (Rev.).

(3) *Multiple punishment prohibited.* This paragraph is based on the guidance for court-martial offenses, found in paragraph 30g and 33*h* of MCM, 1969 (Rev.).

(4) *Statute of limitations.*

2018 Amendment: Paragraph 1.f.(4) is amended and clarifies that a member may waive the statute of limitations applicable to nonjudicial punishment. This is consistent with court-martial practice. *See United States v. Moore*, 32 M.J. 170 (CMA 1991).

2023 Amendment: Paragraph 1.f.(4) is amended to update the citation to Article 43, UCMJ.

(5) *Civilian courts.* This paragraph is derived from service regulations (*see, e.g.*, AR 27–10, chap. 4 (1 Sep. 1982)) and is intended to preclude the possibility of a servicemember being punished by separate jurisdictions for the same offense, except in unusual cases.

g. *Relationship of nonjudicial punishment to administrative corrective measures.* This paragraph is derived from paragraph 128*c of* MCM, 1969 (Rev.) and service regulations.

h. *Burden of proof.*

2023 Amendment: This paragraph is amended to establish "preponderance of the evidence" as the burden of proof for imposition and appellate adjudication of nonjudicial punishment.

i. Effect *of errors.* This paragraph is taken from paragraph 130 of MCM, 1969 (Rev.).

j. *Applicable standards.*

2023 Amendment: This paragraph was deleted from subparagraph (h) and is now added to a new subparagraph (j). This subsection clarifies that nonjudicial punishment proceedings conducted in a combatant or joint command are to be conducted in accordance with the implementing regulations and procedures of the service of which the accused is a member. l. *2018 Amendments*: Paragraph 1.e. is amended and addresses the definition of minor offense. Paragraph 1.f.(4) is amended and clarifies that a member may waive the statute of limitations applicable to nonjudicial punishment. This is consistent with court-martial practice. *See United States v. Moore*, 32 M.J. 170 (CMA 1991).

2. Who may impose nonjudicial punishment

This paragraph is taken from paragraph 128*a* of MCM, 1969 (Rev.) and service regulations. *See, e.g.*, AR 27–10, para. 3–7 (1 Sep. 1982); JAGMAN sec. 0101; AFR 111–9, para. 3 (31 Aug. 1979). Additional guidance in this area is left to Secretarial regulation, in accordance with the provisions of Article 15(a).

2005 Amendment: Subsection (2) was amended to clarify the authority of the commander of a joint command to impose nonjudicial punishment upon service members of the joint command.

3. Right to demand trial

This paragraph is taken from Article 15(a) and paragraph 132 of MCM, 1969 (Rev.).

2018 Amendment: Paragraph 3 is amended and addresses nonjudicial punishment of a person attached to or embarked in a vessel.

4. Procedure

This paragraph is based on paragraph 133 of MCM, 1969 (Rev.) and service regulations. It provides a uniform basic procedure for nonjudicial punishment for all the services. Consistent with the purposes of nonjudicial punishment (*see* S.Rep. No. 1911, 87th Cong. 2d Sess. 4 (1962)) it provides due process protections and is intended to meet the concerns expressed in the Memorandum of Secretary of Defense Laird, 11 January 1973. *See also United States v. Mack*, 9 M.J. 300, 320–21 (C.M.A. 1980). The Report of the Task Force on the Administration of Military Justice in the Armed Forces, 1972, and GAO Report to the Secretary of Defense, *Better Administration of Military Article 15 Punishments for Minor Offenses is Needed*, September 2, 1980, were also considered.

Note that there is no right to consult with counsel before deciding whether to demand trial by court-martial. Unless other- wise prescribed by the Secretary concerned, the decision whether to permit a member to consult with counsel is left to the commander. In *United States v. Mack, supra,* records of punishments where such opportunity was not afforded (except when the member was attached to or embarked in a vessel) were held inadmissible in courts-martial.

1986 Amendment: Subparagraph (c)(2) was amended to state clearly that a servicemember has no absolute right to refuse to appear personally before the person administering the nonjudicial punishment proceeding. In addition, Part V was amended throughout to use the term "nonjudicial punishment authority" in circumstances where the proceeding could be administered by a commander, officer in charge, or a principal assistant to a general court-martial convening authority or general or flag officer.

5. Punishments

This paragraph is taken from paragraph 131 of MCM, 1969 (Rev.). Subparagraph b(2)(b)4 is also based on S.Rep. 1911, 87th Cong., 1st Sess. 7 (1962). Subparagraph c(4) is also based on *id.* at 6–7 and *Hearings Before a Subcomm. of the House Comm. on Armed Services*, 87th Cong., 1st Sess. 33 (1962). Detention of pay was deleted as a punishment because under current centralized pay systems, detention of pay is cumbersome, ineffective, and seldom used. The concept of apportionment, authorized in Article 15(b) and set forth in paragraph 131*d* of MCM, 1969 (Rev.), was eliminated as unnecessary and confusing. Accordingly, the Table of Equivalent Punishments is no longer necessary. Subparagraph d, in concert with the elimination of the apportionment concept, will ease the commanders burden of determining an appropriate punishment and make the implementation of that punishment more efficient and understandable.

1987 Amendment: Subparagraph e was redesignated as subparagraph g and new subparagraphs e and f were added to implement the amendments to Articles 2 and 3, UCMJ, contained in the "Military Justice Amendments of 1986," tit. VIII, § 804, National Defense Authorization Act for fiscal year 1987, Pub. L. No. 99–661, 100 Stat. 3905 (1986).

1990 Amendment: Subsection (c)(8) was amended to incorporate the statutory expansion of jurisdiction over reserve component personnel provided in the Military Justice Amendments of 1990, tit. XIII, § 1303, National Defense Authorization Act of Fiscal Year 1990, Pub. L. 101–189, 103 Stat. 1352 (1989).

2007 Amendment: Paragraph 5.c.(8) was amended because Hardship Duty Pay (HDP) superseded Foreign Duty Pay (FDP) on 3 February 1999. HDP is payable to members entitled to basic pay. The Secretary of Defense has established that HDP will be paid to members (a) for performing specific missions, or (b) when assigned to designated areas.

2018 Amendment: Subparagraphs 5.b.(2)(A)(i) and 5.b.(2)(B)(i) are amended and reflect the elimination of confinement on bread and water or diminished rations as an authorized nonjudicial punishment in Section 5141 of the Military Justice Act of 2016, Division E of the National Defense Authorization Act for Fiscal Year 2017, Pub. L. No. 114-328, 130 Stat. 2000 (2016).

2018 Amendment: Subparagraph 5.c.(1) is amended and reflects the elimination of confinement on bread and water or diminished rations as an authorized nonjudicial punishment in Section 5141 of the Military Justice Act of 2016, Division E of the National Defense Authorization Act for Fiscal Year 2017, Pub. L. No. 114-328, 130 Stat. 2000 (2016).

2018 Amendment: Subparagraph 5.d.(1) is amended and reflects the elimination of confinement on bread and water or diminished rations as an authorized nonjudicial punishment in Section 5141 of the Military Justice Act of 2016, Division E of the National Defense Authorization Act for Fiscal Year 2017, Pub. L. No. 114-328, 130 Stat. 2000 (2016).

2018 Amendment: Paragraphs 5.b.(2)(A)(i), 5.b.(2)(B)(i), 5.c.(5), and 5.d.(2) are amended and address the authorized punishments.

6. Suspension, mitigation, remission, and setting aside

This paragraph is taken from Article 15, paragraph 134 of MCM 1969 (Rev.), and service regulations. *See e.g.*, AR 27–10, paras. 3–23 through 3–28 (1 Sep. 1982); JAGMAN sec. 0101; AFR 111–9, para 7 (31 Aug 1979). Subparagraph a dealing with suspension was expanded to: require a violation of the code during the period of suspension as a basis for vacation action, and to explain that vacation action is not in itself nonjudicial punishment and does not preclude the imposition of nonjudicial punishment for the offenses upon which the vacation action was based. Subparagraph a(4) provides a procedure for vacation of suspended nonjudicial punishment. This procedure parallels the procedure found sufficient to make admissible in courts-martial records of vacation of suspended nonjudicial punishment. *United States v. Covington*, 10 M.J. 64 (C.M.A. 1980).

1990 Amendment: A new subsection a(4) was added to permit punishment imposed under Article 15 to be suspended based on conditions in addition to violations of the UCMJ. This affords the same flexibility given to authorities who suspend punishment adjudged at court-martial under R.C.M. 1108(c). Experience has demonstrated the necessity and utility of such flexibility in the nonjudicial punishment context.

2018 Amendment: Subparagraph 6.d is amended and reflects the elimination of confinement on bread and water or diminished rations as an authorized nonjudicial punishment in Section 5141 of the Military Justice Act of 2016, Division E of the National Defense Authorization Act for Fiscal Year 2017, Pub. L. No. 114-328, 130 Stat. 2000 (2016).

2018 Amendment: Paragraphs 6.b.(2) and b.(3) are amended and address mitigation and remission of authorized punishments.

7. Appeals

This paragraph is taken from paragraph 135 of MCM, 1969 (Rev.) and service regulations dealing with appeals. *See* AR 27–10, paras. 3–29 through 3–35 (1 Sep. 1982); JAGMAN 0101; AFR 111–9, para. 8 (31 Aug. 1981). Subparagraph (d) requires an appeal to be filed within 5 days or the right to appeal will be waived, absent unusual circumstances. This is a reduction from the 15 days provided for in paragraph 135 and is intended to expedite the appeal process. Subparagraph f(2) is intended to promote sound practice, that is, the superior authority should consider many factors when reviewing an appeal, and not be limited to matters submitted by the appellant or the officer imposing the punishment. Subparagraph f(3) provides for "additional proceedings" should a punishment be set aside due to a procedural error. This is consistent with court-martial practice and intended to ensure that procedural errors do not prevent appropriate disposition of a disciplinary matter.

8. Records of nonjudicial punishment

This paragraph is taken from Article 15(g) and paragraph 133c of MCM, 1969 (Rev).

APPENDIX 19
HISTORICAL EXECUTIVE ORDERS

Each Executive Order is available online at the Joint Service Committee's website at the following address: http://jsc.defense.gov.

EXECUTIVE ORDER 12473
49 Fed Reg. 17152 (Apr. 23, 1984)
President Ronald W. Reagan (Apr. 13, 1984)

EXECUTIVE ORDER 12484
49 Fed. Reg. 28825 (July 17, 1984)
President Ronald W. Reagan (July 13, 1984)

EXECUTIVE ORDER 12550
51 Fed. Reg. 6497 (Feb. 25, 1986)
President Ronald W. Reagan (Feb. 19, 1986)

EXECUTIVE ORDER 12586
52 Fed. Reg. 7103 (Mar. 9, 1987)
President Ronald W. Reagan (Mar. 3, 1987)

EXECUTIVE ORDER 12708
55 Fed. Reg. 11353 (Mar. 27, 1990)
President George H.W. Bush (Mar. 23, 1990)

EXECUTIVE ORDER 12767
56 Fed. Reg. 30284 (July 1, 1991)
President George H.W. Bush (June 27, 1991)

EXECUTIVE ORDER 12888
58 Fed. Reg. 69153 (Dec. 29, 1993)
President William J. Clinton (Dec. 23, 1993)

EXECUTIVE ORDER 12936
59 Fed. Reg. 59075 (Nov. 15 1994)
President William J. Clinton (Nov. 10, 1994)

EXECUTIVE ORDER 12960
60 Fed. Reg. 26647 (May 17, 1995)
President William J. Clinton (May 12, 1995)

EXECUTIVE ORDER 13086
63 Fed. Reg. 30065 (June 2, 1998)
President William J. Clinton (May 27, 1998)

EXECUTIVE ORDER 13140
64 Fed. Reg. 55115 (Oct. 12, 1999)
President William J. Clinton (Oct. 6, 1999)

EXECUTIVE ORDER 13262
67 Fed. Reg. 18773 (Apr. 17, 2002)
President George W. Bush (Apr. 11, 2002)

EXECUTIVE ORDER 13365
69 Fed. Reg. 71333 (Dec. 8, 2004)
President George W. Bush (Dec. 3, 2004)

EXECUTIVE ORDER 13387
70 Fed. Reg. 60697 (Oct. 18, 2005)
President George W. Bush (Oct. 14, 2005)

EXECUTIVE ORDER 13430
72 Fed. Reg. 20213 (Apr. 23, 2007)
President George W. Bush (Apr. 18, 2007)

EXECUTIVE ORDER 13447
72 Fed. Reg. 56179 (Oct. 2, 2007)
President George W. Bush (Sep. 28, 2007)

EXECUTIVE ORDER 13468
73 Fed. Reg. 43827 (July 28, 2008)
President George W. Bush (July 24, 2008)

EXECUTIVE ORDER 13552
75 Fed. Reg. 54263 (Sep. 3, 2010)
President Barack H. Obama (Aug 31, 2010)

APPENDIX 19

EXECUTIVE ORDER 13593
76 Fed. Reg. 78451 (Dec. 16, 2011)
President Barack H. Obama (Dec. 13, 2011)

EXECUTIVE ORDER 13643
78 Fed. Reg. 29559 (May 21, 2013)
President Barack H. Obama (May 15, 2013)

EXECUTIVE ORDER 13669
79 Fed. Reg. 34999 (June 18, 2014)
President Barack H. Obama (June 13, 2014)

EXECUTIVE ORDER 13696
80 Fed. Reg. 35781 (June 22, 2015)
President Barack H. Obama (June 17, 2015)

EXECUTIVE ORDER 13730
81 Fed. Reg. 33331 (May 26, 2016)
President Barack H. Obama (May 20, 2016)

EXECUTIVE ORDER 13740
81 Fed. Reg. 65175 (Sep. 22, 2016)
President Barack H. Obama (Sep. 16, 2016)

EXECUTIVE ORDER 13825
83 Fed. Reg. 9889 (Mar. 8, 2018)
President Donald J. Trump (Mar. 1, 2018)

EXECUTIVE ORDER 14062
87 Fed. Reg. 4763 (Jan. 31, 2022)
President Joseph R. Biden (Jan. 26, 2022)

EXECUTIVE ORDER 14103
88 Fed. Reg. 50535 (Aug. 2, 2023)
President Joseph R. Biden (Jul. 28, 2023)

APPENDIX 20
PUNITIVE ARTICLES APPLICABLE TO SEXUAL OFFENSES COMMITTED PRIOR TO 1 OCTOBER 2007

The punitive articles contained in this appendix were replaced or superseded by changes to Article 120, Uniform Code of Military Justice, contained in the National Defense Authorization Act for Fiscal Year 2006. Article 120 was amended again by the National Defense Authorization Act for Fiscal Year 2012. Each version of Article 120 is located in a different part of this Manual. For offenses committed prior to 1 October 2007, the relevant sexual offense provisions and analysis are contained in this appendix and listed below. For offenses committed during the period 1 October 2007 through 27 June 2012, the relevant sexual offense provisions and analysis are contained in Appendix 28. For offenses committed on or after 28 June 2012, the relevant sexual offense provisions are contained in Part IV of this Manual (Articles 120, 120b, and 120c).

45. Article 120—Rape and carnal knowledge

a. *Text.*

(a) Any person subject to this chapter who commits an act of sexual intercourse by force and without consent, is guilty of rape and shall be punished by death or such other punishment as a court-martial may direct.

(b) Any person subject to this chapter who, under circumstances not amounting to rape, commits an act of sexual intercourse with a person—

(1) who is not his or her spouse; and

(2) who has not attained the age of sixteen years, is guilty of carnal knowledge and shall be punished as a court-martial may direct.

(c) Penetration, however slight, is sufficient to complete either of these offenses.

(d)(1) In a prosecution under subsection (b), it is an affirmative defense that—

(A) the person with whom the accused committed the act of sexual intercourse had at the time of the alleged offense attained the age of twelve years; and

(B) the accused reasonably believed that the person had at the time of the alleged offense attained the age of 16 years.

(2) The accused has the burden of proving a defense under subparagraph (d)(1) by a preponderance of the evidence.

b. *Elements.*

(1) *Rape.*

(a) That the accused committed an act of sexual intercourse; and

(b) That the act of sexual intercourse was done by force and without consent.

(2) *Carnal knowledge.*

(a) That the accused committed an act of sexual intercourse with a certain person;

(b) That the person was not the accused's spouse; and

(c)(1) That at the time of the sexual intercourse the person was under the age of 12; or

(2) That at the time of the sexual intercourse the person had attained the age of 12 but was under the age of 16.

c. *Explanation.*

(1) *Rape.*

(a) *Nature of offense.* Rape is sexual intercourse by a person, executed by force and without consent of the victim. It may be committed on a victim of any age. Any penetration, however slight, is sufficient to complete the offense.

(b) *Force and lack of consent.* Force and lack of consent are necessary to the offense. Thus, if the victim consents to the act, it is not rape. The lack of consent required, however, is more than mere lack of acquiescence. If a victim in possession of his or her mental faculties fails to make lack of consent reasonably manifest by taking such measures of resistance as are called for by the circumstances, the inference may be drawn that the victim did consent. Consent, however, may not be inferred if resistance would have been futile, where resistance is overcome by threats of death or great bodily harm, or where the victim is unable to resist because of the lack of mental or physical faculties. In such a case there is no consent and the force involved in penetration will suffice. All the surrounding circumstances are to be considered in determining whether a victim gave consent, or whether he or she failed or ceased to resist only because of a reasonable fear of death or grievous bodily harm. If there is actual consent, although obtained by fraud, the act is not rape, but if to the accused's knowledge the victim is of unsound mind or unconscious to an extent rendering him or her incapable of giving consent, the act is rape. Likewise, the acquiescence of a child of such tender years that he or she is incapable of understanding the nature of the act is not consent.

(c) *Character of victim. See* Mil. R. Evid. 412 concerning rules of evidence relating to an alleged rape victim's character.

(2) *Carnal knowledge.* "Carnal knowledge" is sexual intercourse under circumstances not amounting to rape, with a person who is not the accused's spouse and who has not attained the age of 16 years. Any penetration, however slight, is sufficient to complete the offense. It is a defense, however, which the accused must prove by a preponderance of the evidence, that at the time of the act of sexual intercourse, the person with whom the accused committed the act of sexual intercourse was at least 12 years of age, and that the accused reasonably believed that this same person was at least 16 years of age.

d. *Lesser included offenses.*

(1) *Rape.*

(a) Article 128—assault; assault consummated by a battery

(b) Article 134—assault with intent to commit rape

(c) Article 134—indecent assault

(d) Article 80—attempts

(e) Article 120(b)—carnal knowledge

(2) *Carnal knowledge.*

(a) Article 134—indecent acts or liberties with a person under 16

(b) Article 80—attempts

e. *Maximum punishment.*

(1) *Rape.* Death or such other punishment as a court-martial may direct.

(2) *Carnal knowledge with a child who, at the time of the offense, has attained the age of 12 years.* Dishonorable discharge, forfeiture of all pay and allowances, and confinement for 20 years.

(3) *Carnal knowledge with a child under the age of 12 years at the time of the offense.* Dishonorable discharge, forfeiture of all pay and allowances, and confinement for life without eligibility for parole.

f. *Sample specifications.*

(1) *Rape.* In that (personal jurisdiction data), did, (at/on board — location) (subject - matter jurisdiction data, if required), on or about __________, rape, __________ (a person under the age of 12) (a person who had attained the age of 12 but was under the age of 16).

(2) *Carnal knowledge.* In that (personal jurisdiction data), did, (at/on board — location) (subject - matter jurisdiction data, if required), on or about __________, commit the offense of carnal knowledge with __________, (a person under the age of 12) (a person who attained the age of 12 but was under the age of 16).

63. Article 134—(Assault—indecent)

a. *Text. See* paragraph 60.

b. *Elements.*

(1) That the accused assaulted a certain person not the spouse of the accused in a certain manner;

(2) That the acts were done with the intent to gratify the lust or sexual desires of the accused; and

(3) That, under the circumstances, the conduct of the accused was to the prejudice of good order and discipline in the armed forces or was of a nature to bring discredit upon the armed forces.

c. *Explanation.* See paragraph 54c for a discussion of assault. Specific intent is an element of this offense. For a definition of 'indecent', *see* paragraph 90*c*.

d. *Lesser included offenses.*

(1) Article 128—assault consummated by a battery; assault

(2) Article 134—indecent acts

(3) Article 80—attempts

e. *Maximum punishment.* Dishonorable discharge, forfeiture of all pay and allowances, and confinement for 5 years.

f. *Sample specification.* In that (personal jurisdiction data), did (at/on board—location), (subject-matter jurisdiction data, if required), on or about __________, commit an indecent assault upon a person not his/her wife/husband by __________, with intent to gratify his/her (lust) (sexual desires).

87. Article 134—(Indecent acts or liberties with a child)

a. *Text. See* paragraph 60.

b. *Elements.*

(1) *Physical contact.*

(a) That the accused committed a certain act upon or with the body of a certain person;

(b) That the person was under 16 years of age and not the spouse of the accused;

(c) That the act of the accused was indecent;

(d) That the accused committed the act with intent to arouse, appeal to, or gratify the lust, pas- sions, or sexual desires of the accused, the victim, or both; and

(e) That, under the circumstances, the conduct of the accused was to the prejudice of good order and discipline in the armed forces or was of a nature to bring discredit upon the armed forces.

(2) *No physical contact.*

(a) That the accused committed a certain act;

(b) That the act amounted to the taking of indecent liberties with a certain person;

(c) That the accused committed the act in the presence of this person;

(d) That this person was under 16 years of age and not the spouse of the accused;

(e) That the accused committed the act with the intent to arouse, appeal to, or gratify the lust, passions, or sexual desires of the accused, the victim, or both; and

(f) That, under the circumstances, the conduct of the accused was to the prejudice of good order and discipline in the armed forces or was of a nature to bring discredit upon the armed forces.

c. *Explanation.*

(1) *Consent.* Lack of consent by the child to the act or conduct is not essential to this offense; consent is not a defense.

(2) *Indecent liberties.* When a person is charged with taking indecent liberties, the liberties must be taken in the physical presence of the child, but physical contact is not required. Thus, one who with the requisite intent exposes one's private parts to a child under 16 years of age may be found guilty of this offense. An indecent liberty may consist of communication of indecent language as long as the communication is made in the physical presence of the child.

(3)*Indecent. See* paragraph 89c and 90c.

d. *Lesser included offense.*

(1) Article 134—indecent acts with another

(2) Article 128—assault; assault consummated by a battery

(3) Article 80—attempts

e. *Maximum punishment.* Dishonorable discharge, forfeiture of all pay and allowances, and confinement for 7 years.

f. *Sample specification.* In that (personal jurisdiction data), did, (at/on board — location) (subject - matter jurisdiction data, if required), on or about __________, (take (indecent) liberties with) (commit an indecent act (upon) (with) the body of) __________, a (female) (male) under 16 years of age, not the (wife) (husband) of the said __________, by (fondling (her) (him) and placing his/her hands upon (her) (his) leg and private parts) (   ), with intent to (arouse) (appeal to) (gratify) the (lust) (passion) (sexual desires) of the said (   ).

88. Article 134—(Indecent exposure)

a. *Text. See paragraph* 60.

b. *Elements.*

(1) That the accused exposed a certain part of the accused's body to public view in an indecent manner;

(2) That the exposure was willful and wrongful; and

(3) That, under the circumstances, the accused's conduct was to the prejudice of good order and discipline in the armed forces or was of a nature to bring discredit upon the armed forces.

c. *Explanation.* "Willful" means an intentional exposure to public view. Negligent indecent exposure is not punishable as a violation of the code. See paragraph 90c concerning "indecent."

d. *Lesser included offense.* Article 80—attempts

e. *Maximum punishment.* Bad - conduct discharge, forfeiture of all pay and allowances, and confinement for 6 months.

f. *Sample specification.* In that (personal jurisdiction data), did (at/on board—location) (subject-matter jurisdiction data, if required), on or about __________ while (at a barracks window) ( ) willfully and wrongfully expose in an indecent manner to public view his or her __________.

90. Article 134—(Indecent acts with another)

a. *Text. See paragraph* 60.

b. *Elements.*

(1) That the accused committed a certain wrongful act with a certain person;

(2) That the act was indecent; and

(3) That, under the circumstances, the conduct of the accused was to the prejudice of good order and discipline in the armed forces or was of a nature to bring discredit upon the armed forces.

c. *Explanation.* "Indecent" signifies that form of immorality relating to sexual impurity which is not only grossly vulgar, obscene, and repugnant to common propriety, but tends to excite lust and deprave the morals with respect to sexual relations.

d. *Lesser included offense.* Article 80—attempts

e. *Maximum punishment.* Dishonorable discharge, forfeiture of all pay and allowances, and confinement for 5 years.

f. *Sample specification.* In that (personal jurisdiction data), did (at/on board—location) (subject-matter jurisdiction data, if required), on or about __________, wrongfully commit an indecent act with by __________.

Appendix 20 Analysis Follows:

The analysis was inserted into this appendix to accompany the version of Article 120, and other punitive sexual offense articles, applicable to offenses committed before 1 October 2007. For offenses committed during the period 1 October 2007 through 27 June 20 12, analysis related to Article 120 is contained in Appendix 21. For offenses committed between 28 June 2012, and 31 December 2018 analysis related to Article 120, 120b, and 120c is contained in Appendix 22.]

45. Article 120—Rape and carnal knowledge

b. *Elements. 2004 Amendment:* Paragraph 45(b)(2) was amended to add two distinct elements of age based upon the 1994 amendment to paragraph 45(e). See also concurrent change to R.C.M. 307(c)(3) and accompanying analysis.

c. *Explanation.* This paragraph is based on para- graph 199 of MCM, 1969 (Rev). The third paragraph of paragraph 199 (a) was deleted as unnecessary. The third paragraph of paragraph 199(b) was deleted based on the preemption doctrine. *See United States v. Wright*, 5 M.J. 106 (C.M.A. 1978); *United States v. Norris*, 2 U.S.C.M.A. 236, 8 C.M.R. 36 (1953). *Cf. Williams v. United States*, 327 U.S. 711 (1946) (scope of preemption doctrine). The Military Rules of Evidence deleted the requirement for corroboration of the victim's testimony in rape and similar cases under former paragraph 153 *a* of MCM, 1969. *See* Analysis, Mil. R. Evid. 412.

d. *Lesser included offenses.* Carnal knowledge was deleted as a lesser included offense of rape in view of the separate elements in each offense. Both should be separately pleaded in a proper case. *See generally United States v. Smith*, 7 M.J. 842 (A.C.M.R. 1979).

1993 Amendment. The amendment to para 45*d*(1) represents an administrative change to conform the Manual with case authority. Carnal knowledge is a lesser included offense of rape where the pleading alleges that the victim has not attained the age of 16 years. *See United States v. Baker*, 28 M.J. 900 (A.C.M.R. 1989); *United States v. Stratton*, 12 M.J. 998 (A.F.C.M.R. 1982), pet. *denied*, 15 M.J. 107 (C.M.A. 1983); *United States v. Smith*, 7 M.J. 842 (A.C.M.R. 1979).

e. *Maximum punishment.*

1994 Amendment. Subparagraph *e* was amended by creating two distinct categories of carnal knowledge for sentencing purposes -- one involving children who had attained the age of 12 years at the time of the offense, now designated as subparagraph e(2), and the other for those who were younger than 12 years. The latter is now designated as subparagraph e(3). The punishment for the older children was increased from 15 to 20 years confinement. The maximum confinement for carnal knowledge of a child under 12 years was increased to life. The purpose for these changes is to bring the punishments more in line with those for sodomy of a child under paragraph 51e of this part and with the Sexual Abuse Act of 1986, 18 U.S.C. §§ 2241–2245. The alignment of the maximum punishments for carnal knowledge with those of sodomy is aimed at paralleling the concept of gender–

neutrality incorporated into the Sexual Abuse Act.

1995 Amendment. The offense of rape was made gender neutral and the spousal exception was removed under Article 120(a). National Defense Authorization Act for Fiscal Year 1993, Pub. L. No. 10 2–484, 106 Stat. 2315, 2506 (1992).

Rape may "be punished by death" only if constitutionally permissible. In Coker *v. Georgia*, 433 U.S. 584 (1977), the Court held that the death penalty is "grossly disproportionate and excessive punishment for the rape of an adult woman," and is "therefore forbidden by the Eighth Amendment as cruel and unusual punishment." *Id.* at 592 (plurality opinion). *Coker*, however, leaves open the question of whether it is permissible to impose the death penalty for the rape of a minor by an adult. *See Coker*, 433 U.S. at 595. *See Leatherwood v. State*, 548 So.2d 389 (Miss. 1989) (death sentence for rape of minor by an adult is not cruel and unusual punishment prohibited by the Eighth Amendment). *But see Buford v. State*, 403 So.2d 943 (Fla. 1981) (sentence of death is grossly disproportionate for sexual assault of a minor by an adult and consequently is forbidden by Eighth Amendment as cruel and unusual punishment).

1998 Amendment: In enacting section 1113 of the National Defense Authorization Act for Fiscal Year 1996, Pub. L. No. 104-106, 110 Stat. 186, 462 (1996), Congress amended Article 120, UCMJ, to make the offense gender neutral and create a mistake of fact as to age defense to a prosecution for carnal knowledge. The accused must prove by a preponderance of the evidence that the person with whom he or she had sexual intercourse was at least 12 years of age, and that the accused reasonably believed that this person was at least 16 years of age.

f. *Sample Specification. 2004 Amendment:* Paragraph 45(f)(2) was amended to aid practitioners in charging the two distinct categories of carnal knowledge created in 1994. For the same reason paragraph 45(f)(1) was amended to allow for contingencies of proof because carnal knowledge is a lesser-included offense of rape if properly pleaded. *See also* concurrent change to R.C.M.307(c)(3) and accompanying analysis.

63. Article 134—(Assault—indecent)

c. *Explanation.* This paragraph is based on paragraph 213*f*(2) of MCM, 1969 (Rev.). *See United States v. Caillouette*, 12 U.S.C.M.A. 149, 30 C.M.R. 149 (1961) regarding specific intent. *See also United States v. Headspeth*, 2 U.S.C.M.A. 635, 10 C.M.R. 133 (1953).

Gender-neutral language has been used in this paragraph, as well as throughout this Manual. This will eliminate any question about the intended scope of certain offenses, such as indecent assault such as may have been raised by the use of the masculine pronoun in MCM, 1969 (Rev.). It is, however, consistent with the construction given to the former Manual. *See, e.g., United States v. Respess*, 7 M.J. 566 (A.C.M.R. 1979). *See generally* 1 U.S.C. § 1 ("unless the context indicates otherwise … words importing the masculine gender include the feminine as well ….").

d. *Lesser included offenses. See United States v. Thacker*, 16 U.S.C.M.A. 408, 37 C.M.R. 28 (1966); *United States v. Jackson*, 31 C.M.R. 738 (A.F.B.R. 1962).

2007 Amendment: This paragraph has been replaced in its entirety by paragraph 45. *See* Article 120 (e) Aggravated Sexual Contact, (h) Abusive Sexual Contact, and (m) Wrongful Sexual Contact.

87. Article 134—(Indecent acts or liberties with a child)

c. *Explanation.* This paragraph is based on paragraph 213*f*(3) of MCM, 1969 (Rev.). *See also United States v. Knowles*, 15 U.S.C.M.A. 404, 35 C.M.R. 376 (1965); United *States v. Brown*, 3 U.S.C.M.A. 454, 13 C.M.R. 454, 13 C.M.R. 10 (1953); *United States v. Riffe*, 25 C.M.R. 650 (A.B.R. 1957), pet. *denied*, 9 U.S.C.M.A. 813, 25 C.M.R. 486 (1958). "Lewd" and "lascivious" were deleted because they are synonymous with indecent. *See id. See also paragraph* 90c.

2007 Amendment. This paragraph has been replaced in its entirety by paragraph 45. *See* Article 120 (g) Aggravated Sexual Contact with a Child, (i) Abusive Sexual Contact with a Child, and (j) Indecent Liberty with Child.

88. Article 134—(Indecent exposure)

c. *Explanation.* This paragraph and is based on *United States v. Manos*, 8 U.S.C.M.A. 734, 25 C.M.R. 238 (1958). *See also United States v. Caune*, 22 U.S.C.M.A. 200, 46 C.M.R. 200 (1973); *United States v. Conrad*, 15 U.S.C.M.A. 439, 35 C.M.R. 411 (1965).

e. *Maximum punishment.* The maximum punishment has been increased to include a bad-conduct discharge. Indecent exposure in some circumstances (e.g., in front of children, but without the intent to incite lust or gratify sexual desires necessary for indecent acts or liberties) is sufficiently serious to authorize a punitive discharge.

2007 Amendment: This paragraph has been replaced in its entirety by paragraph 45. *See* Article 120(n) Indecent Exposure.

90. Article 134—(Indecent acts with another)

c. Explanation. This and is based on *United States v. Holland*, 12 U.S.C.M.A. 444, 31 C.M.R. 30 (1961); *United States v. Gaskin*, 12 U.S.C.M.A. 419, 31 C.M.R. 5 (1962); United *States v. Sanchez*, 11 U.S.C.M.A. 216, 29 C.M.R. 32 (1960); *United States v. Johnson*, 4 M.J. 770 (A.C.M.R. 1978). “Lewd” and “lascivious” have been deleted as they are synonymous with “indecent.” *See id.*

APPENDIX 21
PUNITIVE ARTICLES APPLICABLE TO SEXUAL OFFENSES COMMITTED DURING THE PERIOD 1 OCTOBER 2007 THROUGH 27 JUNE 2012

The punitive articles contained in this appendix were replaced or superseded by Articles 120, 120b, and 120c, Uniform Code of Military Justice, as amended or established by the National Defense Authorization Act for Fiscal Year 2012. Article 120 was previously amended by the National Defense Authorization Act for Fiscal Year 2006. Each version of Article 120 is located in a different part of this Manual. For offenses committed prior to 1 October 2007, the relevant sexual offense provisions are contained in Appendix 20. For offenses committed during the period 1 October 2007 through 27 June 2012, the relevant sexual offense provisions are contained in this appendix and listed below. For offenses committed between 28 June 2012 and 31 December 2018, the relevant sexual offense provisions are contained in Appendix 22.

45. Article 120—Rape, sexual assault, and other sexual misconduct

a. *Text of statute.*

(a) *Rape.* **Any person subject to this chapter who causes another person of any age to engage in a sexual act by—**

(1) **using force against that other person;**

(2) **causing grievous bodily harm to any person;**

(3) **threatening or placing that other person in fear that any person will be subjected to death, grievous bodily harm, or kidnapping;**

(4) **rendering another person unconscious; or**

(5) **administering to another person by force or threat of force, or without the knowledge or permission of that person, a drug, intoxicant, or other similar substance and thereby substantially impairs the ability of that other person to appraise or control conduct; is guilty of rape and shall be punished as a court-martial may direct.**

(b) *Rape of a child.* **Any person subject to this chapter who—**

(1) **engages in a sexual act with a child who has not attained the age of 12 years; or**

(2) **engages in a sexual act under the circumstances described in subsection (a) with a child who has attained the age of 12 years; is guilty of rape of a child and shall be punished as a court-martial may direct.**

(c) *Aggravated sexual assault.* **Any person subject to this chapter who—**

(1) **causes another person of any age to engage in a sexual act by—**

(A) **threatening or placing that other person in fear (other than by threatening or placing that other person in fear that any person will be subjected to death, grievous bodily harm, or kidnapping); or**

(B) **causing bodily harm; or**

(2) **engages in a sexual act with another person of any age if that other person is substantially incapacitated or substantially incapable of—**

(A) **appraising the nature of the sexual act;**

(B) **declining participation in the sexual act; or**

(C) **communicating unwillingness to engage in the sexual act; is guilty of aggravated sexual assault and shall be punished as a court-martial may direct.**

(d) *Aggravated sexual assault of a child.* **Any person subject to this chapter who engages in a sexual act with a child who has attained the age of 12 years is guilty of aggravated sexual assault of a child and shall be punished as a court-martial may direct.**

(e) *Aggravated sexual contact.* **Any person subject to this chapter who engages in or causes sexual contact with or by another person, if to do so would violate subsection (a) (rape) had the sexual contact been a sexual act, is guilty of aggravated sexual contact and shall be punished as a court-martial may direct.**

(f) *Aggravated sexual abuse of a child.* **Any person subject to this chapter who engages in a lewd act with a child is guilty of aggravated sexual abuse of a child and shall be punished as a court-martial may direct**

(g) *Aggravated sexual contact with a child.* **Any person subject to this chapter who engages in or causes sexual contact with or by another person, if to do so would violate subsection (b) (rape of a**

child) had the sexual contact been a sexual act, is guilty of aggravated sexual contact with a child and shall be punished as a cour-martial may direct.

(h) *Abusive sexual contact.* **Any person subject to this chapter who engages in or causes sexual contact with or by another person, if to do so would violate subsection (c) (aggravated sexual assault) had the sexual contact been a sexual act, is guilty of abusive sexual contact and shall be punished as a court-martial may direct.**

(i) *Abusive sexual contact with a child.* **Any person subject to this chapter who engages in or causes sexual contact with or by another person, if to do so would violate subsection (d) (aggravated sexual assault of a child) had the sexual contact been a sexual act, is guilty of abusive sexual contact with a child and shall be punished as a court-martial may direct.**

(j) *Indecent liberty with a child.* **Any person subject to this chapter who engages in indecent liberty in the physical presence of a child—**

(1) **with the intent to arouse, appeal to, or gratify the sexual desire of any person; or**

(2) **with the intent to abuse, humiliate, or degrade any person; is guilty of indecent liberty with a child and shall be punished as a court-martial may direct.**

(k) *Indecent act.* **Any person subject to this chapter who engages in indecent conduct is guilty of an indecent act and shall be punished as a court-martial may direct.**

(l) *Forcible pandering.* **Any person subject to this chapter who compels another person to engage in an act of prostitution with another person to be directed to said person is guilty of forcible pandering and shall be punished as a court-martial may direct.**

(m) *Wrongful sexual contact.* **Any person subject to this chapter who, without legal justification or lawful authorization, engages in sexual contact with another person without that other person's permission is guilty of wrongful sexual contact and shall be punished as a court-martial may direct.**

(n) *Indecent exposure.* **Any person subject to this chapter who intentionally exposes, in an indecent manner, in any place where the conduct involved may reasonably be expected to be viewed by people other than members of the actor's family or household, the genitalia, anus, buttocks, or female areola or nipple is guilty of indecent exposure and shall be punished as a court-martial may direct.**

(o) *Age of child.*

(1) *Twelve years.* **In a prosecution under subsection (b) (rape of a child), subsection (g) (aggravated sexual contact with a child), or subsection (j) (indecent liberty with a child), it need not be proven that the accused knew that the other per-on engaging in the sexual act, contact, or liberty had not attained the age of 12 years. It is not an affirmative defense that the accused reasonably believed that the child had attained the age of 12 years.**

(2) *Sixteen years.* **In a prosecution under subsection (d) (aggravated sexual assault of a child), subsection (f) (aggravated sexual abuse of a child), subsection (i) (abusive sexual contact with a child), or subsection (j) (indecent liberty with a child), it need not be proven that the accused knew that the other person engaging in the sexual act, contact, or liberty had not attained the age of 16 years. Unlike in paragraph (1), however, it is an affirmative defense that the accused reasonably believed that the child had attained the age of 16 years.**

(p) *Proof of threat.* **In a prosecution under this section, in proving that the accused made a threat, it need not be proven that the accused actually intended to carry out the threat.**

(q) *Marriage.*

(1) *In general.* **In a prosecution under paragraph (2) of subsection (c) (aggravated sexual assault), or under subsection (d) (aggravated sexual assault of a child), subsection (f) (aggravated sexual abuse of a child), subsection (i) (abusive sexual contact with a child), subsection (j) (indecent liberty with a child), subsection (m) (wrongful sexual contact), or subsection (n) (indecent exposure), it is an affirmative defense that the accused and the other person when they engaged in the sexual act, sexual contact, or sexual conduct were married to each other.**

(2) *Definition* **For purposes of this**

subsection, a marriage is a relationship, recognized by the laws of a competent State or foreign jurisdiction, between the accused and the other person as spouses. A marriage exists until it is dissolved in accordance with the laws of a competent State or foreign jurisdiction.

(3) *Exception.* Paragraph (1) shall not apply if the accused's intent at the time of the sexual conduct is to abuse, humiliate, or degrade any person.

(r) *Consent and mistake of fact as to consent.* Lack of permission is an element of the offense in subsection (m) (wrongful sexual contact). Consent and mistake of fact as to consent are not an issue, or an affirmative defense, in a prosecution under any other subsection, except they are an affirmative defense for the sexual conduct in issue in a prosecution under subsection (a) (rape), subsection (c) (aggravated sexual assault), subsection (e) (aggravated sexual contact), and subsection (h) (abusive sexual contact).

(s) *Other affirmative defenses not precluded.* The enumeration in this section of some affirmative defenses shall not be construed as excluding the existence of others.

(t) *Definitions.* In this section:

(1) *Sexual act.* The term "sexual act" means—

(A) contact between the penis and the vulva, and for purposes of this subparagraph contact involving the penis occurs upon penetration, however slight; or

(B) the penetration, however slight, of the genital opening of another by a hand or finger or by any object, with an intent to abuse, humiliate, harass, or degrade any person or to arouse or gratify the sexual desire of any person.

(2) *Sexual contact.* The term "sexual contact" means the intentional touching, either directly or through the clothing, of the genitalia, anus, groin, breast, inner thigh, or buttocks of another person, or intentionally causing another person to touch, either directly or through the clothing, the genitalia, anus, groin, breast, inner thigh, or buttocks of any person, with an intent to abuse, humiliate, or degrade any person or to arouse or gratify the sexual desire of any person.

(3) *Grievous bodily harm.* The term "grievous bodily harm" means serious bodily injury. It includes fractured or dislocated bones, deep cuts, torn members of the body, serious damage to internal organs, and other severe bodily injuries. It does not include minor injuries such as a black eye or a bloody nose. It is the same level of injury as in section 928 (article 128) of this chapter, and a lesser degree of injury than in section 2246(4) of title 18.

(4) *Dangerous weapon or object.* The term "dangerous weapon or object" means—

(A) any firearm, loaded or not, and whether operable or not;

(B) any other weapon, device, instrument, material, or substance, whether animate or inanimate, that in the manner it is used, or is intended to be used, is known to be capable of producing death or grievous bodily harm; or

(C) any object fashioned or utilized in such a manner as to lead the victim under the circumstances to reasonably believe it to be capable of producing death or grievous bodily harm.

(5) *Force.* The term "force" means action to compel submission of another or to overcome or prevent another's resistance by—

(A) the use or display of a dangerous weapon or object;

(B) the suggestion of possession of a dangerous weapon or object that is used in a manner to cause another to believe it is a dangerous weapon or object; or

(C) physical violence, strength, power, or restraint applied to another person, sufficient that the other person could not avoid or escape the sexual conduct.

(6) *Threatening or placing that other person in fear.* The term "threatening or placing that other person in fear" under paragraph (3) of subsection (a) (rape), or under subsection (e) (aggravated sexual contact), means a communication or action that is of sufficient consequence to cause a reasonable fear that non-compliance will result in

the victim or another person being subjected to death, grievous bodily harm, or kidnapping.

(7) *Threatening or placing that other person in fear.*

(A) *In general.* **The term "threatening or placing that other person in fear" under paragraph (1)(A) of subsection (c) (aggravated sexual assault), or under subsection (h) (abusive sexual contact), means a communication or action that is of sufficient consequence to cause a reasonable fear that non-compliance will result in the victim or another being subjected to a lesser degree of harm than death, grievous bodily harm, or kidnapping.**

(B) *Inclusions.* **Such lesser degree of harm includes—**

(i) **physical injury to another person or to another person's property; or**

(ii) **a threat—**

(I) to accuse any person of a crime;

(II) to expose a secret or publicize an asserted fact, whether true or false, tending to subject some person to hatred, contempt, or ridicule; or

(III) through the use or abuse of military position, rank, or authority, to affect or threaten to affect, either positively or negatively, the military career of some person.

(8) *Bodily harm.* **The term "bodily harm" means any offensive touching of another, however slight.**

(9) *Child.* **The term "child" means any person who has not attained the age of 16 years.**

(10) *Lewd act.* **The term "lewd act" means—**

(A) **the intentional touching, not through the clothing, of the genitalia of another person, with an intent to abuse, humiliate, or degrade any person, or to arouse or gratify the sexual desire of any person; or**

(B) **intentionally causing another person to touch, not through the clothing, the genitalia of any person with an intent to abuse, humiliate or degrade any person, or to arouse or gratify the sexual desire of any person.**

(11) *Indecent liberty.* **The term "indecent liberty" means indecent conduct, but physical contact is not required. It includes one who with the requisite intent exposes one's genitalia, anus, buttocks, or female areola or nipple to a child. An indecent liberty may consist of communication of indecent language as long as the communication is made in the physical presence of the child. If words designed to excite sexual desire are spoken to a child, or a child is exposed to or involved in sexual conduct, it is an indecent liberty; the child's consent is not relevant.**

(12) *Indecent conduct.* **The term "indecent conduct" means that form of immorality relating to sexual impurity that is grossly vulgar, obscene, and repugnant to common propriety, and tends to excite sexual desire or deprave morals with respect to sexual relations. Indecent conduct includes observing, or making a videotape, photograph, motion picture, print, negative, slide, or other mechanically, electronically, or chemically reproduced visual material, without another per- son's consent, and contrary to that other person's reasonable expectation of privacy, of—**

(A) **that other person's genitalia, anus, or buttocks, or (if that other person is female) that person's areola or nipple; or**

(B) **that other person while that other person is engaged in a sexual act, sodomy (under section 925 (article 125) of this chapter), or sexual contact.**

(13) *Act of prostitution.* **The term "act of prostitution" means a sexual act, sexual contact, or lewd act for the purpose of receiving money or other compensation.**

(14) *Consent.* **The term "consent" means words or overt acts indicating a freely given agreement to the sexual conduct at issue by a competent person. An expression of lack of consent through words or conduct means there is no consent. Lack of verbal or physical resistance or submission resulting from the accused's use of force, threat of force, or placing another person in fear does not constitute consent. A current or previous dating relationship by itself or the manner of dress of the person involved with the accused in the sexual conduct at issue shall not constitute consent. A person cannot consent to**

sexual activity if—

(A) **under 16 years of age; or**

(B) **substantially incapable of—**

(i) **appraising the nature of the sexual conduct at issue due to—**

(I) mental impairment or unconsciousness resulting from consumption of alcohol, drugs, a similar substance, or otherwise; or

(II) mental disease or defect that renders the person unable to understand the nature of the sexual conduct at issue;

(ii) **physically declining participation in the sexual conduct at issue; or**

(iii) **physically communicating unwillingness to engage in the sexual conduct at issue.**

(15) *Mistake of fact as to consent.* **The term "mistake of fact as to consent" means the accused held, as a result of ignorance or mistake, an incorrect belief that the other person engaging in the sexual conduct consented. The ignorance or mistake must have existed in the mind of the accused and must have been reasonable under all the circumstances. To be reasonable, the ignorance or mistake must have been based on information, or lack of it, that would indicate to a reasonable person that the other person consented. Additionally, the ignorance or mistake cannot be based on the negligent failure to discover the true facts. Negligence is the absence of due care. Due care is what a reasonably careful person would do under the same or similar circumstances. The accused's state of intoxication, if any, at the time of the offense is not relevant to mistake of fact. A mistaken belief that the other person consented must be that which a reasonably careful, ordinary, prudent, sober adult would have had under the circumstances at the time of the offense.**

(16) *Affirmative defense.* **The term "affirmative defense" means any special defense that, although not denying that the accused committed the objective acts constituting the offense charged, denies, wholly, or partially, criminal responsibility for those acts. The accused has the burden of proving the affirmative defense by a preponderance of evidence. After the defense meets this burden, the prosecution shall have the burden of proving beyond a reasonable doubt that the affirmative defense did not exist.**

b. *Elements.*

(1) *Rape.*

(a) *Rape by using force.*

(i) That the accused caused another person, who is of any age, to engage in a sexual act by using force against that other person.

(b) *Rape by causing grievous bodily harm.*

(i) That the accused caused another person, who is of any age, to engage in a sexual act by causing grievous bodily harm to any person.

(c) *Rape by using threats or placing in fear.*

(i)That the accused caused another person, who is of any age, to engage in a sexual act by threatening or placing that other person in fear that any person will be subjected to death, grievous bodily harm, or kidnapping.

(d) *Rape by rendering another unconscious.*

(i) That the accused caused another person, who is of any age, to engage in a sexual act by rendering that other person unconscious.

(e) *Rape by administration of drug, intoxicant, or other similar substance.*

(i) That the accused caused another person, who is of any age, to engage in a sexual act by administering to that other person a drug, intoxicant, or other similar substance;

(ii) That the accused administered the drug, intoxicant or other similar substance by force or threat of force or without the knowledge or permission of that other person; and

(iii) That, as a result, that other person's ability to appraise or control conduct was substantially impaired.

(2) *Rape of a child.*

(a) *Rape of a child who has not attained the age of 12 years.*

(i) That the accused engaged in a sexual act with a child; and

(ii) That at the time of the sexual act the child had not attained the age of twelve years.

(b) *Rape of a child who has attained the age of 12 years but has not attained the age of 16 years by using force.*

(i) That the accused engaged in a sexual act with a child;

(ii) That at the time of the sexual act the child had attained the age of 12 years but had not attained the age of 16 years; and

(iii) That the accused did so by using force against that child.

(c) *Rape of a child who has attained the age of 12 years but has not attained the age of 16 years by causing grievous bodily harm.*

(i) That the accused engaged in a sexual act with a child;

(ii) That at the time of the sexual act the child had attained the age of 12 years but had not attained the age of 16 years; and

(iii) That the accused did so by causing grievous bodily harm to any person.

(d) *Rape of a child who has attained the age of 12 years but has not attained the age of 16 years by using threats or placing in fear.*

(i) That the accused engaged in a sexual act with a child;

(ii)That at the time of the sexual act the child had attained the age of 12 years but had not attained the age of 16 years; and

(iii) That the accused did so by threatening or placing that child in fear that any person will be subjected to death, grievous bodily harm, or kidnapping.

(e) *Rape of a child who has attained the age of 12 years but has not attained the age of 16 years by rendering that child unconscious.*

(i) That the accused engaged in a sexual act with a child;

(ii) That at the time of the sexual act the child had attained the age of 12 years but had not attained the age of 16 years; and

(iii) That the accused did so by rendering that child unconscious.

(f) *Rape of a child who has attained the age of 12 years but has not attained the age of 16 years by administration of drug, intoxicant, or other similar substance.*

(i) That the accused engaged in a sexual act with a child;

(ii) That at the time of the sexual act the child had attained the age of 12 years but had not attained the age of 16 years; and

(iii)(a) That the accused did so by administering to that child a drug, intoxicant, or other similar substance;

(b) That the accused administered the drug, intoxicant, or other similar substance by force or threat of force or without the knowledge or permission of that child; and

(c) That, as a result, that child's ability to appraise or control conduct was substantially impaired.

(3) *Aggravated sexual assault.*

(a) *Aggravated sexual assault by using threats or placing in fear.*

(i) That the accused caused another person, who is of any age, to engage in a sexual act; and

(ii) That the accused did so by threatening or placing that other person in fear that any person would be subjected to bodily harm or other harm (other than by threatening or placing that other person in fear that any person would be subjected to death, grievous bodily harm, or kidnapping).

(b) *Aggravated sexual assault by causing bodily harm.*

(i)That the accused caused another person, who is of any age, to engage in a sexual act; and

(ii) That the accused did so by causing bodily harm to another person.

(c) *Aggravated sexual assault upon a person substantially incapacitated or substantially incapable of appraising the act, declining participation, or communicating unwillingness.*

(i) That the accused engaged in a sexual act with another person, who is of any age; and

(Note: add one of the following elements)

(ii) That the other person was substantially incapacitated;

(iii) That the other person was substantially incapable of appraising the nature of the sexual act;

(iv) That the other person was substantially incapable of declining participation in the sexual act; or

(v) That the other person was substantially incapable of communicating unwillingness to engage in the sexual act.

(4) *Aggravated sexual assault of a child who has attained the age of 12 years but has not attained the age of 16 years.*

(a) That the accused engaged in a sexual act with a child; and

(b) That at the time of the sexual act the child had attained the age of 12 years but had not attained the age of 16 years.

(5) *Aggravated sexual contact.*

(a) *Aggravated sexual contact by using force.*

(i)(a) That the accused engaged in sexual contact with another person; or

(b) That the accused caused sexual contact with or by another person; and

(ii) That the accused did so by using force against that other person.

(b) *Aggravated sexual contact by causing grievous bodily harm.*

(i)(a) That the accused engaged in sexual contact with another person; or

(b) That the accused caused sexual contact with or by another person; and

(ii) That the accused did so by causing grievous bodily harm to any person.

(c) *Aggravated sexual contact by using threats or placing in fear.*

(i)(a) That the accused engaged in sexual contact with another person; or

(b) That the accused caused sexual contact with or by another person; and

(ii) That the accused did so by threatening or placing that other person in fear that any person will be subjected to death, grievous bodily harm, or kidnapping.

(d) *Aggravated sexual contact by rendering another unconscious.*

(i)(a) That the accused engaged in sexual contact with another person; or

(b) That the accused caused sexual contact with or by another person; and

(ii) That the accused did so by rendering that other person unconscious.

(e) *Aggravated sexual contact by administration of drug, intoxicant, or other similar substance.*

(i)(a) That the accused engaged in sexual contact with another person; or

(b) That the accused caused sexual contact with or by another person; and

(ii)(a) That the accused did so by administering to that other person a drug, intoxicant, or other similar substance;

(b) That the accused administered the drug, intoxicant, or other similar substance by force or threat of force or without the knowledge or permission of that other person; and

(c) That, as a result, that other person's ability to appraise or control conduct was substantially impaired.

(6) *Aggravated sexual abuse of a child.*

(a) That the accused engaged in a lewd act; and

(b) That the act was committed with a child who has not attained the age of 16 years.

(7) *Aggravated Sexual Contact with a Child.*

(a) *Aggravated sexual contact with a child who has not attained the age of 12 years.*

(i)(a) That the accused engaged in sexual contact with a child; or

(b) That the accused caused sexual contact with or by a child or by another person with a child; and

(ii) That at the time of the sexual contact the child had not attained the age of twelve years.

(b) *Aggravated sexual contact with a child who has attained the age of 12 years but has not attained the age of 16 years by using force.*

(i)(a) That the accused engaged in sexual contact with a child; or

(b) That the accused caused sexual contact

with or by a child or by another person with a child; and

(ii) That at the time of the sexual contact the child had attained the age of 12 years but had not attained the age of 16 years; and

(iii) That the accused did so by using force against that child.

(c) *Aggravated sexual contact with a child who has attained the age of 12 years but has not attained the age of 16 years by causing grievous bodily harm.*

(i)(a) That the accused engaged in sexual contact with a child; or

(b) That the accused caused sexual contact with or by a child or by another person with a child; and

(ii) That at the time of the sexual contact the child had attained the age of 12 years but had not attained the age of 16 years; and

(iii) That the accused did so by causing grievous bodily harm to any person.

(d) *Aggravated sexual contact with a child who has attained the age of 12 years but has not attained the age of 16 years by using threats or placing in fear.*

(i)(a) That the accused engaged in sexual contact with a child; or

(b) That the accused caused sexual contact with or by a child or by another person with a child; and

(ii) That at the time of the sexual contact the child had attained the age of 12 years but had not attained the age of 16 years; and

(iii) That the accused did so by threatening or placing that child or that other person in fear that any person will be subjected to death, grievous bodily harm, or kidnapping.

(e) *Aggravated sexual contact with a child who has attained the age of 12 years but has not attained the age of 16 years by rendering another or that child unconscious.*

(i)(a) That the accused engaged in sexual contact with a child; or

(b) That the accused caused sexual contact with or by a child or by another person with a child; and

(ii) That at the time of the sexual contact the child had attained the age of 12 years but had not attained the age of 16 years; and

(iii) That the accused did so by rendering that child or that other person unconscious.

(f) *Aggravated sexual contact with a child who has attained the age of 12 years but has not attained the age of 16 years by administration of drug, intoxicant, or other similar substance.*

(i)(a) That the accused engaged in sexual contact with a child; or

(b)That the accused caused sexual contact with or by a child or by another person with a child; and

(ii) That at the time of the sexual contact the child had attained the age of 12 years but had not attained the age of 16 years; and

(iii)(a) That the accused did so by administering to that child or that other person a drug, intoxicant, or other similar substance;

(b) That the accused administered the drug, intoxicant, or other similar substance by force or threat of force or without the knowledge or permission of that child or that other person; and

(c) That, as a result, that child's or that other person's ability to appraise or control conduct was substantially impaired.

(8) *Abusive sexual contact.*

(a) *Abusive sexual contact by using threats or placing in fear.*

(i)(a) That the accused engaged in sexual contact with another person; or

(b) That the accused caused sexual contact with or by another person; and

(ii) That the accused did so by threatening or placing that other person in fear that any person would be subjected to bodily harm or other harm (other than by threatening or placing that other person in fear that any person would be subjected to death, grievous bodily harm, or kidnapping).

(b) *Abusive sexual contact by causing bodily harm.*

(i)(a) That the accused engaged in sexual contact with another person; or

(b) That the accused caused sexual contact with or by another person; and

(ii) That the accused did so by causing bodily

harm to another person.

(c) *Abusive sexual contact upon a person substantially incapacitated or substantially incapable of appraising the act, declining participation, or communicating unwillingness.*

(i)(a) That the accused engaged in sexual contact with another person; or

(b) That the accused caused sexual contact with or by another person; and

(Note: add one of the following elements)

(ii) That the other person was substantially incapacitated;

(iii) That the other person was substantially incapable of appraising the nature of the sexual contact;

(iv) That the other person was substantially incapable of declining participation in the sexual contact; or

(v) That the other person was substantially incapable of communicating unwillingness to engage in the sexual contact.

(9) *Abusive sexual contact with a child.*

(i)(a) That the accused engaged in sexual contact with a child; or

(b) That the accused caused sexual contact with or by a child or by another person with a child; and

(ii) That at the time of the sexual contact the child had attained the age of 12 years but had not attained the age of 16 years.

(10) *Indecent liberty with a child.*

(a) That the accused committed a certain act or communication;

(b) That the act or communication was indecent;

(c) That the accused committed the act or communication in the physical presence of a certain child;

(d) That the child was under 16 years of age; and

(e) That the accused committed the act or communication with the intent to:

(i) arouse, appeal to, or gratify the sexual desires of any person; or

(ii) abuse, humiliate, or degrade any person.

(11) *Indecent act.*

(a) That the accused engaged in certain conduct; and

(b) That the conduct was indecent conduct.

(12) *Forcible pandering.*

(a) That the accused compelled a certain person to engage in an act of prostitution; and

(b) That the accused directed another person to said person, who then engaged in an act of prostitution.

(13) *Wrongful sexual contact.*

(a) That the accused had sexual contact with another person;

(b) That the accused did so without that other person's permission; and

(c) That the accused had no legal justification or lawful authorization for that sexual contact.

(14) *Indecent exposure.*

(a) That the accused exposed his or her genitalia, anus, buttocks, or female areola or nipple;

(b) That the accused's exposure was in an indecent manner;

(c) That the exposure occurred in a place where the conduct involved could reasonably be expected to be viewed by people other than the accused's family or household; and

(d) That the exposure was intentional.

c. *Explanation.*

(1) *Definitions.* The terms are defined in Paragraph 45a.(t), supra.

(2) *Character of victim.* See Mil. R. Evid. 412 concerning rules of evidence relating to the character of the victim of an alleged sexual offense.

(3) *Indecent.* In conduct cases, "indecent" generally signifies that form of immorality relating to sexual impurity that is not only grossly vulgar, obscene, and repugnant to common propriety, but also tends to excite lust and deprave the morals with respect to sexual relations. Language is indecent if it tends reasonably to corrupt morals or incite libidinous thoughts. The language must violate community standards.

d. *Lesser included offenses.* The following lesser included offenses are based on internal cross-references provided in the statutory text of Article 120. See subsection (e) for a further listing of possible lesser included offenses.

(1) *Rape.*

(a) Article 120—Aggravated sexual contact

(b) Article 134—Assault with intent to commit rape

(c) Article 128—Aggravated assault; Assault; Assault consummated by a battery

(d) Article 80—Attempts

(2) *Rape of a child.*

(a) Article 120—Aggravated sexual contact with a child; Indecent act

(b) Article 134—Assault with intent to commit rape

(c) Article 128—Aggravated assault; Assault; Assault consummated by a battery; Assault consummated by a battery upon a child under 16

(d) Article 80—Attempts

(3) *Aggravated sexual assault.*

(a) Article 120—Abusive sexual contact

(b) Article 128—Aggravated assault; Assault; Assault consummated by a battery

(c) Article 80—Attempts

(4) *Aggravated sexual assault of a child.*

(a) Article 120—Abusive sexual contact with a child; Indecent act

(b) Article 128—Aggravated assault; Assault; Assault consummated by a battery; Assault consummated by a battery upon a child under 16

(c) Article 80—Attempts

(5) *Aggravated sexual contact.*

(a) Article 128—Aggravated assault; Assault; Assault consummated by a battery

(b) Article 80—Attempts

(6) *Aggravated sexual abuse of a child.*

(a) Article 120—Indecent act

(b) Article 128—Assault; Assault consummated by a battery; Assault consummated by a battery upon a child under 16

(c) Article 80—Attempts

(7) *Aggravated sexual contact with a child.*

(a) Article 120—Indecent act

(b) Article 128—Assault; Assault consummated by a battery; Assault consummated by a battery upon a child under 16

(c) Article 80—Attempts

(8) *Abusive sexual contact.*

(a) Article 128—Assault; Assault consummated by a battery

(b) Article 80—Attempts

(9) *Abusive sexual contact with a child.*

(a) Article 120—Indecent act

(b) Article 128—Assault; Assault consummated by a battery; Assault consummated by a battery upon a child under 16

(c) Article 80—Attempts

(10) *Indecent liberty with a child.*

(a) Article 120—Indecent act

(b) Article 80—Attempts

(11) *Indecent act.* Article 80—Attempts

(12) *Forcible pandering.* Article 80—Attempts

(13) *Wrongful sexual contact* Article 80—Attempts

(14) *Indecent exposure.* Article 80—Attempts

e. *Additional lesser included offenses.* Depending on the factual circumstances in each case, to include the type of act and level of force involved, the following offenses may be considered lesser included in addition to those offenses listed in subsection d. (See subsection (d) for a listing of the offenses that are specifically cross-referenced within the statutory text of Article 120.) The elements of the proposed lesser included offense should be compared with the elements of the greater offense to determine if the elements of the lesser offense are derivative of the greater offense and vice versa. See Appendix 23 for further explanation of lesser included offenses.

(1)(a) *Rape by using force.* Article 120—Indecent act; Wrongful sexual contact

(1)(b) *Rape by causing grievous bodily harm.* Article 120—Aggravated sexual assault by causing bodily harm; Abusive sexual contact by causing bodily harm;

Indecent act; Wrongful sexual contact

(1)(c) *Rape by using threats or placing in fear.* Article 120—Aggravated sexual assault by using threats or placing in fear; Abusive sexual contact by using threats or placing in fear; Indecent act; Wrongful sexual contact

(1)(d) *Rape by rendering another unconscious.* Article 120—Aggravated sexual assault upon a person substantially incapacitated; Abusive sexual contact upon a person substantially incapacitated; Indecent act; Wrongful sexual contact

(1)(e) *Rape by administration of drug, intoxicant, or other similar substance.* Article 120—Aggravated sexual assault upon a person substantially incapacitated; Abusive sexual contact upon a person substantially incapacitated; Indecent act; Wrongful sexual contact

(2)(a) - (f) *Rape of a child who has not attained 12 years; Rape of a child who has attained the age of 12 years but has not attained the age of 16 years.* Article 120—Aggravated sexual assault of a child; Aggravated sexual abuse of a child; Abusive sexual contact with a child; Indecent liberty with a child; Wrongful sexual contact

(3) *Aggravated sexual assault.* Article 120—Wrongful sexual contact; indecent act

(4) *Aggravated sexual assault of a child.* Article 120—Aggravated sexual abuse of a child; Indecent liberty with a child; Wrongful sexual contact

(5)(a) *Aggravated sexual contact by force.* Article 120—Indecent act; Wrongful sexual contact

(5)(b) *Aggravated sexual contact by causing grievous bodily harm.* Article 120—Abusive sexual contact by causing bodily harm; Indecent act; Wrongful sexual contact

(5)(c) *Aggravated sexual contact by using threats or placing in fear.* Article 120—Abusive sexual contact by using threats or placing in fear; Indecent act; Wrongful sexual contact

(5)(d) *Aggravated sexual contact by rendering another unconscious.* Article 120—Abusive sexual contact upon a person substantially incapacitated; Indecent act; Wrongful sexual contact

(5)(e) *Aggravated sexual contact by administration of drug, intoxicant, or other similar substance.* Article 120—Abusive sexual contact upon a person substantially incapacitated; Indecent act; Wrongful sexual contact

(6) *Aggravated sexual abuse of a child.* Article 120—Aggravated sexual contact with a child; Aggravated sexual abuse of a child; Indecent liberty with a child; Wrongful sexual contact

(7) *Aggravated sexual contact with a child.* Article 120—Abusive sexual contact with a child; Indecent liberty with a child; Wrongful sexual contact

(8) *Abusive sexual contact.* Article 120—Wrong- ful sexual contact; Indecent act

(9) *Abusive sexual contact with a child.* Article 120—Indecent liberty with a child; Wrongful sexual contact

(10) *Indecent liberty with a child.* Article 120—Wrongful sexual contact

f. *Maximum punishment.*

(1) *Rape and rape of a child.* Death or such other punishment as a court martial may direct.

(2) *Aggravated sexual assault.* Dishonorable discharge, forfeiture of all pay and allowances, and confinement for 30 years.

(3) *Aggravated sexual assault of a child who has attained the age of 12 years but has not attained the age of 16 years, aggravated sexual abuse of a child, aggravated sexual contact, and aggravated sexual contact with a child.* Dishonorable discharge, forfeiture of all pay and allowances, and confinement for 20 years.

(4) *Abusive sexual contact with a child and indecent liberty with a child.* Dishonorable discharge, forfeiture of all pay and allowances, and confinement for 15 years.

(5) *Abusive sexual contact.* Dishonorable discharge, forfeiture of all pay and allowances, and confinement for 7 years.

(6) *Indecent act or forcible pandering.* Dishonorable discharge, forfeiture of all pay and allowances, and confinement for 5 years.

(7) *Wrongful sexual contact or indecent exposure.* Dishonorable discharge, forfeiture of all pay and allowances, and confinement for 1 year.

g. *Sample specifications*

(1) *Rape*

(a) *Rape by using force.*

(i) *Rape by use or display of dangerous weapon or object.* In that __________ (personal jurisdiction data), did (at/on board-location) (subject-matter jurisdiction data, if required), on or about __________20 _____, cause __________ to engage in a sexual act, to wit: __________, by (using a dangerous weapon or object, to wit: __________ against (him)(her)) (displaying a dangerous weapon or object, to wit: __________ to (him)(her)).

(ii) *Rape by suggestion of possession of dangerous weapon or object.* In that __________ (personal jurisdiction data), did (at/on board-location) (subject-matter jurisdiction data, if required), on or about __________20 _____, cause __________ to engage in a sexual act, to wit: __________, by the suggestion of possession of a dangerous weapon or an object that was used in a manner to cause (him) (her) to believe it was a dangerous weapon or object.

(iii) *Rape by using physical violence, strength, power, or restraint to any person.* In that __________ (personal jurisdiction data), did (at/on board-location) (subject-matter jurisdiction data, if required), on or about __________20 _____, cause __________ to engage in a sexual act, to wit: __________, by using (physical violence)(strength)(power)(restraint applied to __________), sufficient that (he)(she) could not avoid or escape the sexual conduct.

(b) *Rape by causing grievous bodily harm.* In that __________ (personal jurisdiction data), did (at/on board-location) (subject-matter jurisdiction data, if required), on or about __________20 _____, cause __________ to engage in a sexual act, to wit: __________, by causing grievous bodily harm upon (him)(her)(__________), to wit: a (broken leg)(deep cut)(fractured skull)(__________).

(c) *Rape by using threats or placing in fear.* In that __________ (personal jurisdiction data), did (at/on board-location) (subject-matter jurisdiction data, if required), on or about __________20 _____, cause __________ to engage in a sexual act, to wit: __________, by [threatening][placing (him)(her) in fear] that (he)(she)(__________) will be subjected to (death)(grievous bodily harm)(kidnapping) by __________.

(d) *Rape by rendering another unconscious.* In that __________ (personal jurisdiction data), did (at/on board-location) (subject-matter jurisdiction data, if required), on or about __________20 _____, cause __________ to engage in sexual act, to wit: __________, by rendering (him)(her) unconscious.

(e) *Rape by administration of drug, intoxicant, or other similar substance.* In that __________ (personal jurisdiction data), did (at/on board-location) (subject-matter jurisdiction data, if required), on or about __________20 _____, cause __________ to engage in a sexual act, to wit: __________, by administering to (him)(her) a drug, intoxicant, or other similar substance, (by force)(by threat of force)(without (his)(her) knowledge or permission), and thereby substantially impaired (his)(her) ability to [(appraise)(control)][(his)(her)] conduct.

(2) *Rape of a child.*

(a) *Rape of a child who has not attained the age of 12 years.* In that __________ (personal jurisdiction data), did (at/on board-location) (subject-matter jurisdiction data, if required), on or about __________20 _____, engage in a sexual act, to wit: __________ with __________, a child who had not attained the age of 12

(b) *Rape of a child who has attained the age of 12 years but has not attained the age of 16 years by using force.*

(i) *Rape of a child who has attained the age of 12 years but has not attained the age of 16 years by use or display of dangerous weapon or object.* In that __________ (personal jurisdiction data), did (at/on board-location) (subject-matter jurisdiction data, if required), on or about __________20 _____, engage in a sexual act, to wit: __________, with __________, a child who had attained the age of 12 years, but had not attained the age of 16 years, by (using a dangerous weapon or object, to wit: __________ against (him)(her))(displaying a dangerous weapon or object, to wit: __________ to (him)(her)).

(ii) *Rape of a child who has attained the age of 12 years but has not attained the age of 16 years by suggestion of possession of dangerous weapon or object.* In that __________ (personal jurisdiction data), did (at/on board-location) (subject-matter jurisdiction data, if required), on or about __________20 _____, engage in a sexual act, to wit: __________, with __________, a child who had attained the age of 12 years, but had not attained the age of 16 years, by suggestion of possession of a dangerous weapon or an object that was used in a manner to cause (him)(her) to believe it was a dangerous weapon or object.

(iii) *Rape of a child who has attained the age of 12 years but has not attained the age of 16 years by using physical violence, strength, power, or restraint to any person.* In that __________ (personal jurisdiction data), did (at/on board-location) (subject-matter jurisdiction data, if required), on or about __________20 _____, engage in a sexual act, to wit: __________ with __________, a child who had not attained the age of 12 years, but had not attained the age of 16 years, by using (physical violence)(strength)(power)(restraint applied to __________) sufficient that (he)(she) could not avoid or escape the sexual conduct.

(c) *Rape of a child who has attained the age of 12 years but has not attained the age of 16 years by causing grievous bodily harm.* In that __________ (personal jurisdiction data), did (at/on board-location) (subject-matter jurisdiction data, if required), on or about __________20 _____, engage in a sexual act, to wit: __________, with __________, a child who had attained the age of 12 years, but had not attained the age of 16 years, by causing grievous bodily harm upon (him)(her)(__________), to wit: a (broken leg)(deep cut)(fractured skull)(__________).

(d) *Rape of a child who has attained the age of 12 years but has not attained the age of 16 years by using threats or placing in fear.* In that __________ (personal jurisdiction data), did (at/on board-location) (subject-matter jurisdiction data, if required), on or about __________20 _____, engage in a sexual act, to wit: __________, with __________, a child who had attained the age of 12 years, but had not attained the age of 16 years, by [threatening][placing (him)(her) in fear] that (he)(she)(__________) would be subjected to (death)(grievous bodily harm)(kidnapping) by __________.

(e) *Rape of a child who has attained the age of 12 years but has not attained the age of 16 years by rendering that child unconscious.* In that __________ (personal jurisdiction data), did (at/on board-location) (subject-matter jurisdiction data, if required), on or about __________20 _____, engage in a sexual act, to wit: __________, with __________, a child who had attained the age of 12 years, but had not attained the age of 16 years, by rendering (him)(her) unconscious.

(f) *Rape of a child who has attained the age of 12 years but has not attained the age of 16 years by administration of drug, intoxicant, or other similar substance.* In that __________ (personal jurisdiction data), did (at/on board-location) (subject-matter jurisdiction data, if required), on or about __________20 _____, engage in a sexual act, to wit: __________, with __________, a child who had attained the age of 12 years, but had not attained the age of 16 years, by administering to (him)(her) a drug, intoxicant, or other similar substance (by force)(by threat of force)(without (his)(her) knowledge or permission), and thereby substantially impaired (his)(her) ability to [(appraise)(control)][(his)(her)] conduct.

(3) *Aggravated sexual assault.*

(a) *Aggravated sexual assault by using threats or placing in fear.* In that __________ (personal jurisdiction data), did (at/on board-location)(subject-matter jurisdiction data, if required), on or about __________ 20_____, cause __________ to engage in a sexual act, to wit: __________ by [threatening][placing(him)(her) in fear of][(physical injury to __________)(injury to __________'s property)(accusation of crime)(exposition of secret)(abuse of military position)(__________)].

(b) *Aggravated sexual assault by causing bodily harm.* In that __________(personal jurisdiction data), did (at/on board-location)(subject-matter jurisdiction data, if required), on or about __________ 20_____, cause __________ to engage in a sexual act, to wit: __________by causing bodily harm upon (him)(her)(__________), to wit: __________.

(c) *Aggravated sexual assault upon a person substantially incapacitated or substantially incapable of appraising the act, declining participation, or communicating unwillingness.* In that __________ (personal jurisdiction data), did (at/on board-location)(subject-matter jurisdiction data, if required), on or about __________ 20_____, engage in a sexual act, to wit: __________ with __________, who was (substantially incapacitated) [substantially incapable of (appraising the nature of the sexual act)(declining participation in the sexual act)(communicating unwillingness to engage in the sexual act)].

(4) *Aggravated sexual assault of a child who has attained the age of 12 years but has not attained the age of 16 years.* In that __________ (personal jurisdiction data), did (at/on board-location)(subject-matter jurisdiction data, if required), on or about __________ 20_____, engage in a sexual act, to wit: __________ with __________, who had attained the age of 12 years, but had not attained the age of 16 years.

(5) *Aggravated sexual contact.*

(a) *Aggravated sexual contact by using force.*

(i) *Aggravated sexual contact by use or display of dangerous weapon or object.* In that __________(personal jurisdiction data), did (at/on board location)(subject-matter jurisdiction data, if required), on or about __________ 20_____, [(engage in sexual contact, to wit: __________ with __________)(cause __________ to engage in sexual contact, to wit: __________, with__________)(cause sexual contact with or by __________, to wit: __________)] by (using a dangerous weapon or object, to wit: __________ against (him)(her))(displaying a dangerous weapon or object, to wit: __________ to (him)(her))

(ii) *Aggravated sexual contact by suggestion of possession of dangerous weapon or object.* In that __________(personal jurisdiction data), did (at/on board-location)(subject-matter jurisdiction data, if required), on or about __________ 20_____, [(engage in sexual contact, to wit: __________ with __________)(cause __________ to engage in sexual contact, to wit: __________, with __________)(cause sexual contact with or by __________, to wit: __________)] by the suggestion of possession of a dangerous weapon or an object that was used in a manner to cause (him)(her)(__________) to believe it was a dangerous weapon or object.

(iii) *Aggravated sexual contact by using physical violence, strength, power, or restraint to any person.* In that __________ (personal jurisdiction data), did (at/on board-location)(subject-matter jurisdiction data, if required), on or about __________ 20_____, [(engage in sexual contact, to wit: __________with __________)(cause __________ to engage in sexual contact, to wit: __________, with __________)(cause sexual contact with or by __________, to wit: __________)] by using (physical violence) (strength) (power) (restraint applied to __________), sufficient that (he)(she)(__________) could not avoid or escape the sexual conduct.

(b) *Aggravated sexual contact by causing grievous bodily harm.* In that __________ (personal jurisdiction data), did (at/on board-location)(subject-matter jurisdiction data, if required), on or about __________ 20_____, [(engage in sexual contact, to wit: __________with __________)(cause __________ to engage in sexual contact, to wit: __________, with __________)(cause sexual contact with or by __________, to wit: __________)] by causing grievous bodily harm upon (him)(her)(__________), to wit: a (broken leg)(deep cut)(fractured skull)(__________).

(c) *Aggravated sexual contact by using threats or placing in fear.* In that __________ (personal jurisdiction data), did (at/on board-location)(subject-matter jurisdiction data, if required), on or about __________ 20_____, [(engage in sexual contact, to wit: __________with __________)(cause __________ to engage in sexual contact, to wit: __________, with __________)(cause sexual contact with or by __________, to wit: __________)] by [threatening (him)(her)(__________)][(placing (him)(her)(__________) in fear] that (he)(she)(__________) will be subjected to (death)(grievous bodily harm)(kidnapping) by __________.

(d) *Aggravated sexual contact by rendering another unconscious.* In that __________ (personal jurisdiction data), did (at/on board-location)(subject-matter jurisdiction data, if required), on or about __________ 20_____, [(engage in sexual contact, to wit: __________with __________)(cause __________ to engage in sexual contact, to wit: __________, with __________)(cause sexual contact with or by __________, to wit: __________)] by rendering (him)(her)(__________) unconscious.

(e) *Aggravated sexual contact by administration of drug, intoxicant, or other similar substance.* In that __________ (personal jurisdiction data), did (at/on board-location)(subject-matter jurisdiction data, if required), on or about __________ 20_____, [(engage in sexual contact, to wit: __________with __________)(cause __________ to engage in sexual contact, to wit: __________, with __________)(cause sexual contact with or by __________, to wit: __________)] by administering to (him)(her)(__________) a drug, intoxicant, or other similar substance, (by force)(by threat of force)(without (his)(her)(__________) knowledge or permission), and thereby substantially impaired (his)(her)(__________) ability to [(appraise)(control)][(his)(her)] conduct.

(6) *Aggravated sexual abuse of a child.* In that __________ (personal jurisdiction data), did (at/on board-location)(subject-matter jurisdiction data, if required), on or about __________ 20_____, engage in lewd act, to wit: __________ with __________, a child who had not attained the age of 16 years.

(7) *Aggravated sexual contact with a child.*

(a) *Aggravated sexual contact with a child who has not attained the –age of 12 years.* In that __________ (personal jurisdiction data), did (at/on board-location)(subject-matter jurisdiction data, if required), on or about __________ 20_____,[(engage in sexual contact, to wit: __________with __________, a child who had not attained the age of 12 years)(cause __________ to engage in sexual contact, to wit: __________, with __________, a child who has not attained the age of 12 years)(cause sexual contact with or by __________, to wit: __________, a child who has not attained the age of 12 years)]

(b) *Aggravated sexual contact with a child who has attained the age of 12 years but has not attained the age of 16 years by using force.*

(i) *Aggravated sexual contact with a child who has attained the age of 12 years but has not attained the age of 16 years by use or display of dangerous weapon or object.* In that __________ (personal jurisdiction data), did (at/on board-location)(subject-matter jurisdiction data, if required), on or about __________ 20_____,[(engage in sexual contact, to wit: __________with __________, a child who had attained the age of 12 years, but had not attained the age of 16 years)(cause __________ to engage in sexual contact, to wit: __________, with __________, a child who had attained the age of 12 years, but had not attained the age of 16 years)(cause sexual contact with or by __________, to wit: __________, a child who had attained the age of 12 years, but had not attained the age of 16 years)] by (using a dangerous weapon or object, to wit: __________ against (him)(her)(__________))(displaying a dangerous weapon or object, to wit: __________ to (him)(her)(__________)).

(ii) *Aggravated sexual contact with a child who has attained the age of 12 years but has not attained the age of 16 years by suggestion of possession of dangerous weapon or object.* In that __________ (personal jurisdiction data), did (at/on board-location)(subject-matter jurisdiction data, if required), on or about __________ 20_____,[(engage in sexual contact, to wit: __________with __________, a child who had attained the age of 12 years, but had not attained the age of 16 years)(cause __________ to engage in sexual contact, to wit: __________, with __________, a child who had attained the age of 12 years, but had not attained the age of 16 years)(cause sexual contact with or by __________, to wit: __________, a child who had attained the age of 12 years, but had not attained the age of 16 years)] by the suggestion of possession of a dangerous weapon or an object that was used in a manner to cause (him)(her)(__________) to believe it was a dangerous weapon or object.

(iii) *Aggravated sexual contact with a child who has attained the age of 12 years but has not attained the age of 16 years by using physical violence, strength, power, or restraint to any person.* In that __________ (personal jurisdiction data), did (at/on board-location)(subject-matter jurisdiction data, if required), on or about __________ 20_____,[(engage in sexual contact, to wit: __________with __________, a child who had attained the age of 12 years, but had not attained the age of 16 years)(cause __________ to engage in sexual contact, to wit: __________, with __________, a child who had attained the age of 12 years, but had not attained the age of 16 years)(cause sexual contact with or by __________, to wit: __________, a child who had attained the age of 12 years, but had not attained the age of 16 years)] by using (physical violence)(strength)(power)(restraint applied to __________) sufficient that (he)(she)(__________) could not avoid or escape the sexual conduct.

(c) *Aggravated sexual contact with a child who has attained the age of 12 years but has not attained the age of 16 years by causing grievous bodily harm* In that __________ (personal jurisdiction data), did (at/on board-location)(subject-matter jurisdiction data, if required), on or about __________ 20_____,[(engage in sexual contact, to wit: __________with __________, a child who had attained the age of 12 years, but had not attained the age of 16 years)(cause __________ to engage in sexual contact, to wit: __________, with __________, a child who had attained the age of 12 years, but had not attained the age of 16 years)(cause sexual contact with or by __________, to wit: __________, a child who had attained the age of 12 years, but had not attained the age of 16 years)] by causing grievous bodily harm upon (him)(her)(__________), to wit: a (broken leg)(deep cut)(fractured skull)(__________).

(d) *Aggravated sexual contact with a child who has attained the age of 12 years but has not attained the age of 16 years by using threats or placing in fear* In that __________ (personal jurisdiction data), did (at/on board-location)(subject-matter jurisdiction data, if required), on or about __________ 20_____,[(engage in sexual contact, to wit: __________with __________, a child who had attained the age of 12 years, but had not attained the age of 16 years)(cause __________ to engage in sexual contact, to wit: __________, with __________, a child who had attained the age of 12 years, but had not attained the age of 16 years)(cause sexual contact with or by __________, to wit: __________, a child who had attained the age of 12 years, but had not attained the age of 16 years)] by [threatening][placing (him)(her)(__________) in fear] that (he)(she)(__________) will be subjected to (death)(grievous bodily harm)(kidnapping) by __________.

(e) *Aggravated sexual contact with a child who has attained the age of 12 years but has not attained the age of 16 years by rendering that child or another unconscious* In that __________ (personal jurisdiction data), did (at/on board-location)(subject-matter jurisdiction data, if required), on or about __________ 20_____,[(engage in sexual contact, to wit: __________with __________, a child who had attained the age of 12 years, but had not attained the age of 16 years)(cause __________ to engage in sexual contact, to wit: __________, with __________, a child who had attained the age of 12 years, but had not attained the age of 16 years)(cause sexual contact with or by __________, to wit: __________, a child who had attained the age of 12 years, but had not attained the age of 16 years)] by rendering (him)(her)(__________) unconscious.

(f) *Aggravated sexual contact with a child who has attained the age of 12 years but has not attained the age of 16 years by administration of drug, intoxicant, or other similar substance* In that __________ (personal jurisdiction data), did (at/on board-location)(subject-matter jurisdiction data, if required), on or about __________ 20_____,[(engage in sexual contact, to wit: __________with __________, a child who had attained the age of 12 years, but had not attained the age of 16 years)(cause __________ to engage in sexual contact, to wit: __________, with __________, a child who had attained the age of 12 years, but had not attained the age of 16 years)(cause sexual contact with or by __________, to wit: __________, a child who had attained the age of 12 years, but had not attained the age of 16 years)] by administering to (him)(her)(__________) knowledge or permission), and thereby substantially impaired (his)(her)(__________) ability to [(appraise)(control)][(his)(her)] conduct.

(8) *Abusive sexual contact.*

(a) *Abusive sexual contact by using threats or placing in fear.* . In that __________ (personal jurisdiction data), did (at/on board-location)(subject-matter jurisdiction data, if required), on or about __________ 20_____, [engage in sexual contact, to wit: __________ with __________)(cause __________ to engage in sexual contact, to wit: __________, with __________)(cause sexual contact with or by __________, to wit: __________)] by [(threatening)(placing (him)(her)(__________) in fear of)][physical injury to __________)(injury to __________'s property)(accusation of crime)(exposition of secret)(abuse of military position)(__________)].

(b) *Abusive sexual contact by causing bodily harm.* In that __________ (personal jurisdiction data), did (at/on board-location)(subject-matter jurisdiction data, if required), on or about __________ 20_____, [engage in sexual contact, to wit: __________ with

__________)(cause __________ to engage in sexual contact, to wit: __________, with __________)(cause sexual contact with or by __________, to wit: __________)] by causing bodily harm upon (him)(her)(__________), to wit: (__________).

(c) *Abusive sexual contact by engaging in a sexual act with a person substantially incapacitated or substantially incapable of appraising the act, declining participation, or substantially incapable of communicating unwillingness.* In that __________ (personal jurisdiction data), did (at/on board-location)(subject-matter jurisdiction data, if required), on or about __________ 20_____, [engage in sexual contact, to wit: __________ with __________)(cause __________ to engage in sexual contact, to wit: __________, with __________)(cause sexual contact with or by __________, to wit: __________)] while (he)(she)(__________) was [substantially incapacitated][substantially incapable of (appraising the nature of the sexual contact)(declining participation in the sexual contact)(communicating unwillingness to engage in the sexual contact)].

(9) *Abusive sexual contact with a child.* In that __________ (personal jurisdiction data), did (at/on board-location)(subject-matter jurisdiction data, if required), on or about __________ 20_____,[(engage in sexual contact, to wit: __________with __________, a child who had attained the age of 12 years, but had not attained the age of 16 years)(cause __________ to engage in sexual contact, to wit: __________, with __________, a child who had attained the age of 12 years, but had not attained the age of 16 years)(cause sexual contact with or by __________, a child who had attained the age of 12 years, but had not attained the age of 16 years, to wit: __________)]

(10) *Indecent liberties with a child.* In that __________ (personal jurisdiction data), did (at/on board-location)(subject-matter jurisdiction data, if required), on or about __________ 20_____, (take indecent liberties)(engage in indecent conduct) in the physical presence of __________, a (female)(male) under 16 years, by (communicating the words: to wit: __________)(exposing one's private parts, to wit: __________)(__________), with the intent to [(arouse)(appeal to)(gratify) the (sexual desire) of the __________ (or __________)][(abuse)(humiliate)(degrade) __________].

(11) *Indecent act.* In that __________ (personal jurisdiction data), did (at/on board-location)(subject-matter jurisdiction data, if required), on or about __________ 20_____, wrongfully commit indecent conduct, to wit __________.

(12) *Forcible pandering.* In that __________ (personal jurisdiction data), did (at/on board-location)(subject-matter jurisdiction data, if required), on or about __________ 20_____, compel __________ to engage in [(a sexual act)(sexual contact)(lewd act), to wit: __________] for the purpose of receiving money or other compensation with __________ (a) person(s) to be directed to (him)(her) by the said __________.

(13) *Wrongful sexual contact.* In that __________ (personal jurisdiction data), did (at/on board-location)(subject-matter jurisdiction data, if required), on or about __________ 20_____, engage in sexual contact with __________, to wit: __________, and such sexual contact was without legal justification or lawful authorization and without the permission of __________.

(14) *Indecent exposure.* In that __________ (personal jurisdiction data), did (at/on board-location)(subject-matter jurisdiction data, if required), on or about __________ 20_____, intentionally (expose in an indecent manner (his)(her)(__________)(__________) while (at the barracks window)(in a public place)(__________)."

Appendix 21 Analysis Follows:

[Note:The analysis was inserted into this appendix to accompany the version of Article 120 applicable to offenses committed during the period 1 October 2007 through 27 June 2012. For offenses committed prior to 1 October 2007, analysis related to Article 120 and other punitive articles applicable to sexual offenses is contained in Appendix 20. For offenses committed between 28 June 2012 and 31 December 2018, analysis related to Article 120, 120b, and 120c is contained in Appendix 22.]

45. Article 120—Rape, sexual assault, and other sexual misconduct

2007 Amendment: Changes to this paragraph are contained in Div. A. Title V. Subtitle E, Section 552(a)(1) of the National Defense Authorization Act for Fiscal Year 2006, P.L. 109-163, 119 Stat. 3257 (6 January 2006), which supersedes the previous paragraph 45, Rape and Carnal Knowledge, in its entirety and replaces paragraph 45 with Rape, sexual assault and other sexual misconduct. In accordance with Section 552(c) of that Act, the amendment to the Article applies only with respect to offenses committed on or after 1 October 2007.

Nothing in these amendments invalidates any nonjudicial punishment proceeding, restraint, investigation, referral of charges, trial in which arraignment occurred, or other action begun prior to 1 October 2007. Any such nonjudical punishment proceeding, restraint, investigation, referral of charges, trial in which arraignment occurred, or other action may proceed in the same manner and with the same effect as if these amendments had not been prescribed.

This new Article 120 consolidates several sexual misconduct offenses and is generally based on the Sexual Abuse Act of 1986, 18 U.S.C. Sections 2241-2245. The following is a list of offenses that have been replaced by this new paragraph 45:

(1) Paragraph 63, 134 Assault - Indecent, has been replaced in its entirety by three new offenses under paragraph 45. *See* subsections (e) Aggravated Sexual Contact, (h) Abusive Sexual Contact, and (m) Wrongful Sexual Contact.

(2) Paragraph 87, 134 Indecent Acts or Liberties with a Child, has been replaced in its entirety by three new offenses under paragraph 45. *See* subsections (g) Aggravated Sexual Contact with a Child, (i) Abusive Sexual Contact with a Child, and (j) Indecent Liberty with a Child.

(3) Paragraph 88, Article 134 Indecent Exposure, has been replaced in its entirety by a new offense under paragraph 45. *See* subsection (n) Indecent Exposure.

(4) Paragraph 90, Article 134 Indecent Acts with Another, has been replaced in its entirety by a new offense under paragraph 45. *See* subsection (k) Indecent Act.

(5) Paragraph 97, Article 134 Pandering and Prostitution, has been amended. The act of compelling another person to engage in an act of prostitution with another person will no longer be an offense under paragraph 97 and has been replaced by a new offense under paragraph 45. *See* subsection (l), Forcible Pandering.

c. *Explanation.* Subparagraph (3), definition of "indecent," is taken from paragraphs 89.c and 90.c of the Manual (2005 ed.) and is intended to consolidate the definitions of "indecent," as used in the former offenses under Article 134 of "Indecent acts or liberties with a child," "Indecent exposure," and "Indecent acts with another," formerly at paragraphs 87, 88, and 90 of the 2005 Manual, and "Indecent language," at paragraph 89. The application of this sin- gle definition of "indecent" to the offenses of "Indecent liberty with a child," "Indecent act," and "Indecent exposure" under Article 120 is consistent with the construction given to the former Article 134 offenses in the 2005 Manual that were consolidated into Article 120. *See e.g. United States v. Negron*, 60 M.J. 136 (C.A.A.F. 2004).

d. *Additional Lesser Included Offenses.* The test to determine whether an offense is factually the same as another offense, and therefore lesser-included to that offense, is the "elements" test. *United States v. Foster*, 40 M.J. 140, 142 (C.M.A. 1994). Under this test, the court considers "whether each provision requires proof of a fact which the other does not." *Blockburger*, 284 U.S. 299 at 304 (1932). Rather than adopting a literal application of the elements test, the Court stated that resolution of lesser-included claims "can only be resolved by lining up elements realistically and determining whether each element of the supposed 'lesser' offense is rationally derivative of one or more elements of the other offense - and vice versa." *Foster*, 40 M.J. at 146. Whether an offense is a lesser-included offense is a matter of law that the Court will consider de novo. *United States v. Palagar*, 56 M.J. 294, 296 (C.A.A.F. 2002).

e. *Maximum punishment. See 1995 Amendment* regarding maximum punishment of death.

APPENDIX 22
PUNITIVE ARTICLES APPLICABLE TO SEXUAL OFFENSES COMMITTED BETWEEN 28 JUNE 2012 AND 31 DECEMBER 2018

[Note: This statute applies to offenses committed between 28 June 2012 and 31 December 2018. Previous versions of Article 120 are located as follows: for offenses committed on or before 30 September 2007, *see* Appendix 20; for offenses committed during the period 1 October 2007 through 27 June 2012, *see* Appendix 21.]

45. Article 120—Rape and sexual assault generally

a. *Text of statute.*

(a) *Rape.* Any person subject to this chapter who commits a sexual act upon another person by—

(1) using unlawful force against that other person;

(2) using force causing or likely to cause death or grievous bodily harm to any person;

(3) threatening or placing that other person in fear that any person will be subjected to death, grievous bodily harm, or kidnapping;

(4) first rendering that other person unconscious; or

(5) administering to that other person by force or threat of force, or without the knowledge or consent of that person, a drug, intoxicant, or other similar substance and thereby substantially impairing the ability of that other person to appraise or control conduct; is guilty of rape and shall be punished as a court- martial may direct.

(b) *Sexual Assault.* Any person subject to this chapter who—

(1) commits a sexual act upon another person by—

(A) threatening or placing that other person in fear;

(B) causing bodily harm to that other person;

(C) making a fraudulent representation that the sexual act serves a professional purpose; or

(D) inducing a belief by any artifice, pretense, or concealment that the person is another person;

(2) commits a sexual act upon another person when the person knows or reasonably should know that the other person is asleep, unconscious, or otherwise unaware that the sexual act is occurring; or

(3) commits a sexual act upon another person when the other person is incapable of consenting to the sexual act due to—

(A) impairment by any drug, intoxicant, or other similar substance, and that condition is known or reasonably should be known by the person; or

(B) a mental disease or defect, or physical disability, and that condition is known or reasonably should be known by the person; is guilty of sexual assault and shall be punished as a court-martial may direct.

(c) *Aggravated Sexual Contact.* Any person subject to this chapter who commits or causes sexual contact upon or by another person, if to do so would violate subsection (a) (rape) had the sexual contact been a sexual act, is guilty of aggravated sexual contact and shall be punished as a court-martial may direct.

(d) *Abusive Sexual Contact.* Any person subject to this chapter who commits or causes sexual contact upon or by another person, if to do so would violate subsection (b) (sexual assault) had the sexual contact been a sexual act, is guilty of abusive sexual contact and shall be punished as a court-martial may direct.

(e) *Proof of Threat.* In a prosecution under this section, in proving that a person made a threat, it need not be proven that the person actually intended to carry out the threat or had the ability to carry out the threat.

(f) *Defenses.* An accused may raise any applicable defenses available under this chapter or the Rules for Court-Martial. Marriage is not a defense for any conduct in issue in any prosecution under this section.

(g) *Definitions.* In this section:

(1) *Sexual act.* The term 'sexual act' means—

(A) contact between the penis and the vulva or anus or mouth, and for purposes of this subparagraph contact involving the penis occurs

upon penetration, however slight; or

(B) the penetration, however slight, of the vulva or anus or mouth of another by any part of the body or by any object, with an intent to abuse, humiliate, harass, or degrade any person or to arouse or gratify the sexual desire of any person.

(2) *Sexual contact.* The term 'sexual contact' means—

(A) touching, or causing another person to touch, either directly or through the clothing, the genitalia, anus, groin, breast, inner thigh, or buttocks of any person, with an intent to abuse, humiliate, or degrade any person; or

(B) any touching, or causing another person to touch, either directly or through the clothing, any body part of any person, if done with an intent to arouse or gratify the sexual desire of any person.

Touching may be accomplished by any part of the body.

(3) *Bodily harm.* The term 'bodily harm' means any offensive touching of another, how- ever slight, including any nonconsensual sexual act or nonconsensual sexual contact.

(4) *Grievous bodily harm.* The term 'grievous bodily harm' means serious bodily injury. It includes fractured or dislocated bones, deep cuts, torn members of the body, serious damage to internal organs, and other severe bodily injuries. It does not include minor injuries such as a black eye or a bloody nose.

(5) *Force.* The term 'force' means—

(A) the use of a weapon;

(B) the use of such physical strength or violence as is sufficient to overcome, restrain, or injure a person; or

(C) inflicting physical harm sufficient to coerce or compel submission by the victim.

(6) *Unlawful Force.* The term 'unlawful force' means an act of force done without legal justification or excuse.

(7) *Threatening or placing that other person in fear.* The term 'threatening or placing that other person in fear' means a communication or action that is of sufficient consequence to cause a reasonable fear that non-compliance will result in the victim or another person being subjected to the wrongful action contemplated by the communication or action.

(8) *Consent.*

(A) The term 'consent' means a freely given agreement to the conduct at issue by a competent person. An expression of lack of consent through words or conduct means there is no consent. Lack of verbal or physical resistance or submission resulting from the use of force, threat of force, or placing another person in fear does not constitute consent. A current or previous dating or social or sexual relationship by itself or the manner of dress of the person involved with the accused in the conduct at issue shall not constitute consent.

(B) A sleeping, unconscious, or incompetent person cannot consent. A person cannot consent to force causing or likely to cause death or grievous bodily harm or to being rendered un- conscious. A person cannot consent while under threat or fear or under the circumstances de- scribed in subparagraph (C) or (D) of subsection (b)(1).

(C) Lack of consent may be inferred based on the circumstances of the offense. All the surrounding circumstances are to be considered in determining whether a person gave consent, or whether a person did not resist or ceased to resist only because of another person's actions.

b. *Elements.*

(1) *Rape involving contact between penis and vulva or anus or mouth.*

(a) By unlawful force

(i) That the accused committed a sexual act upon another person by causing penetration, how- ever slight, of the vulva or anus or mouth by the penis; and

(ii) That the accused did so with unlawful force.

(b) *By force causing or likely to cause death or grievous bodily harm*

(i)That the accused committed a sexual act upon another person by causing penetration, however slight, of the vulva or anus or mouth by the penis; and

(ii) That the accused did so by using force causing or likely to cause death or grievous bodily harm to any person.

(c) *By threatening or placing that other person in fear that any person would be subjected to death, grievous bodily harm, or kidnapping*

(i) That the accused committed a sexual act upon another person by causing penetration, however slight, of the vulva or anus or mouth by the penis; and

(ii) That the accused did so by threatening or placing that other person in fear that any person would be subjected to death, grievous bodily harm, or kidnapping.

(d) *By first rendering that other person unconscious*

(i) That the accused committed a sexual act upon another person by causing penetration, however slight, of the vulva or anus or mouth by the penis; and

(ii) That the accused did so by first rendering that other person unconscious.

(e) *By administering a drug, intoxicant, or other similar substance*

(i) That the accused committed a sexual act upon another person by causing penetration, however slight, of the vulva or anus or mouth by the penis; and

(ii) That the accused did so by administering to that other person by force or threat of force, or without the knowledge or permission of that person, a drug, intoxicant, or other similar substance and thereby substantially impairing the ability of that other person to appraise or control conduct.

(2) *Rape involving penetration of the vulva or anus or mouth by any part of the body or any object.*

(a) *By force*

(i) That the accused committed a sexual act upon another person by causing penetration, however slight, of the vulva or anus or mouth of another person by any part of the body or by any object;

(ii) That the accused did so with unlawful force; and

(iii) That the accused did so with an intent to abuse, humiliate, harass, or degrade any person or to arouse or gratify the sexual desire of any person.

(b) *By force causing or likely to cause death or grievous bodily harm*

(i) That the accused committed a sexual act upon another person by causing penetration, however slight, of the vulva or anus or mouth of another person by any part of the body or by any object;

(ii) That the accused did so by using force causing or likely to cause death or grievous bodily harm to any person; and

(iii) That the accused did so with an intent to abuse, humiliate, harass, or degrade any person or to arouse or gratify the sexual desire of any person.

(c) *By threatening or placing that other person in fear that any person would be subjected to death, grievous bodily harm, or kidnapping*

(i) That the accused committed a sexual act upon another person by causing penetration, however slight, of the vulva or anus or mouth of another person by any part of the body or by any object;

(ii) That the accused did so by threatening or placing that other person in fear that any person would be subjected to death, grievous bodily harm, or kidnapping; and

(iii) That the accused did so with an intent to abuse, humiliate, harass, or degrade any person or to arouse or gratify the sexual desire of any person.

(d) *By first rendering that other person unconscious*

(i) That the accused committed a sexual act upon another person by causing penetration, however slight, of the vulva or anus or mouth of another person by any part of the body or by any object;

(ii) That the accused did so by first rendering that other person unconscious; and

(iii) That the accused did so with an intent to abuse, humiliate, harass, or degrade any person or to arouse or gratify the sexual desire of any person.

(e) *By administering a drug, intoxicant, or other similar substance*

(i) That the accused committed a sexual act upon another person by causing penetration, however slight, of the vulva or anus or mouth of another person by any part of the body or by any object;

(ii) That the accused did so by administering to that other person by force or threat of force, or without the knowledge or permission of that person, a drug, intoxicant, or other similar substance and thereby substantially impairing the ability of that other person to appraise or control conduct; and

(iii) That the accused did so with an intent to abuse, humiliate, harass, or degrade any person or to arouse or gratify the sexual desire of any person.

(3) *Sexual assault involving contact between penis and vulva or anus or mouth.*

(a) *By threatening or placing that other person in fear*

(i) That the accused committed a sexual act upon another person by causing penetration, however slight, of the vulva or anus or mouth by the penis; and

(ii) That the accused did so by threatening or placing that other person in fear.

(b) *By causing bodily harm*

(i) That the accused committed a sexual act upon another person by causing penetration, however slight, of the vulva or anus or mouth by the penis; and

(ii) That the accused did so by causing bodily harm to that other person.

(c) *By fraudulent representation*

(i) That the accused committed a sexual act upon another person by causing penetration, however slight, of the vulva or anus or mouth by the penis; and

(ii) That the accused did so by making a fraudulent representation that the sexual act served a professional purpose.

(d) *By false pretense*

(i) That the accused committed a sexual act upon another person by causing penetration, however slight, of the vulva or anus or mouth by the penis; and

(ii) That the accused did so by inducing a belief by any artifice, pretense, or concealment that the accused is another person.

(e) *Of a person who is asleep, unconscious, or otherwise unaware the act is occurring*

(i) That the accused committed a sexual act upon another person by causing penetration, however slight, of the vulva or anus or mouth by the penis;

(ii) That the other person was asleep, unconscious, or otherwise unaware that the sexual act was occurring; and

(iii) That the accused knew or reasonably should have known that the other person was asleep, unconscious, or otherwise unaware that the sexual act was occurring.

(f) *When the other person is incapable of consenting*

(i) That the accused committed a sexual act upon another person by causing penetration, however slight, of the vulva or anus or mouth by the penis;

(ii) That the other person was incapable of consenting to the sexual act due to:

(A) Impairment by any drug, intoxicant or other similar substance; or

(B) A mental disease or defect, or physical disability; and

(iii) That the accused knew or reasonably should have known of the impairment, mental disease or defect, or physical disability of the other person.

(4) *Sexual assault involving penetration of the vulva or anus or mouth by any part of the body or any object.*

(a) By threatening or placing that other person in fear

(i) That the accused committed a sexual act upon another person by causing penetration, however slight, of the vulva or anus or mouth by any part of the body or by any object;

(ii) That the accused did so by threatening or placing that other person in fear; and

(iii) That the accused did so with an intent to abuse, humiliate, harass, or degrade any person or to arouse or gratify the sexual desire of any person.

(b) *By causing bodily harm*

(i) That the accused committed a sexual act upon another person by causing penetration, however slight, of the vulva or anus or mouth by any part of the body or by any object;

(ii) That the accused did so by causing bodily harm to that other person; and

(iii) That the accused did so with an intent to abuse, humiliate, harass, or degrade any person or to arouse or gratify the sexual desire of any person.

(c) *By fraudulent representation*

(i) That the accused committed a sexual act upon another person by causing penetration, however slight, of the vulva or anus or mouth by any part of the body or by any object;

(ii) That the accused did so by making a fraudulent representation that the sexual act served a professional purpose when it served no professional purpose; and

(iii) That the accused did so with an intent to abuse, humiliate, harass, or degrade any person or to arouse or gratify the sexual desire of any person.

(d) *By false pretense*

(i) That the accused committed a sexual act upon another person by causing penetration, however slight, of the vulva or anus or mouth by any part of the body or by any object;

(ii) That the accused did so by inducing a belief by any artifice, pretense, or concealment that the accused is another person; and

(iii) That the accused did so with an intent to abuse, humiliate, harass, or degrade any person or to arouse or gratify the sexual desire of any person.

(e) *Of a person who is asleep, unconscious, or otherwise unaware the act is occurring*

(i) That the accused committed a sexual act upon another person by causing penetration, however slight, of the vulva or anus or mouth by any part of the body or by any object;

(ii) That the other person was asleep, unconscious, or otherwise unaware that the sexual act was occurring;

(iii) That the accused knew or reasonably should have known that the other person was asleep, unconscious, or otherwise unaware that the sexual act was occurring.

(iv) That the accused did so with an intent to abuse, humiliate, harass, or degrade any person or to arouse or gratify the sexual desire of any person.

(f) *When the other person is incapable of consenting*

(i) That the accused committed a sexual act upon another person by causing penetration, however slight, of the vulva or anus or mouth by any part of the body or by any object;

(ii) That the other person was incapable of consenting to the sexual act due to:

(A) Impairment by any drug, intoxicant or other similar substance; or

(B) A mental disease or defect, or physical disability;

(iii) That the accused knew or reasonably should have known of the impairment, mental disease or defect, or physical disability of the other person; and

(iv) That the accused did so with intent to abuse, humiliate, harass, or degrade any person or to arouse or gratify the sexual desire of any person.

(5) *Aggravated sexual contact involving the touching of the genitalia, anus, groin, breast, inner thigh, or buttocks of any person.*

(a) *By force*

(i) That the accused committed sexual contact upon another person by touching, or causing another person to touch, either directly or through the clothing, the genitalia, anus, groin, breast, inner thigh, or buttocks of any person;

(ii) That the accused did so with unlawful force; and

(iii) That the accused did so with an intent to abuse, humiliate, harass, or degrade any person or to arouse or gratify the sexual desire of any person.

(b) *By force causing or likely to cause death or grievous bodily harm*

(i) That the accused committed sexual contact upon another person by touching, or causing another person to touch, either directly or through the clothing, the genitalia, anus, groin, breast, inner thigh, or buttocks of any person;

(ii) That the accused did so by using force causing or likely to cause death or grievous bodily harm to any person; and

(iii) That the accused did so with an intent to abuse, humiliate, harass, or degrade any person or to arouse or gratify the sexual desire of any person.

(c) *By threatening or placing that other person in fear that any person would be subjected to death, grievous bodily harm, or kidnapping*

(i) That the accused committed sexual contact upon another person by touching, or causing another person to touch, either directly or through the clothing, the genitalia, anus, groin, breast, inner thigh, or buttocks of any person;

(ii) That the accused did so by threatening or placing that other person in fear that any person would be subjected to death, grievous bodily harm, or kidnapping; and

(iii) That the accused did so with an intent to abuse, humiliate, harass, or degrade any person or to arouse or gratify the sexual desire of any person.

(d) *By first rendering that other person*

unconscious

(i) That the accused committed sexual contact upon another person by touching, or causing another person to touch, either directly or through the clothing, the genitalia, anus, groin, breast, inner thigh, or buttocks of any person;

(ii) That the accused did so by first rendering that other person unconscious; and

(iii) That the accused did so with intent to abuse, humiliate, harass, or degrade any person or to arouse or gratify the sexual desire of any person.

(e) *By administering a drug, intoxicant, or other similar substance*

(i) That the accused committed sexual contact upon another person by touching, or causing another person to touch, either directly or through the clothing, the genitalia, anus, groin, breast, inner thigh, or buttocks of any person;

(ii) That the accused did so by administering to that other person by force or threat of force, or without the knowledge or permission of that person, a drug, intoxicant, or other similar substance and thereby substantially impairing the ability of that other person to appraise or control conduct; and

(iii) That the accused did so with intent to abuse, humiliate, harass, or degrade any person or to arouse or gratify the sexual desire of any person.

(6) *Aggravated sexual contact involving the touching of any body part of any person.*

(a) By force

(i) That the accused committed sexual contact upon another person by touching, or causing another person to touch, any body part of any person;

(ii) That the accused did so with unlawful force; and

(iii) That the accused did so with intent to arouse or gratify the sexual desire of any person.

(b) *By force causing or likely to cause death or grievous bodily harm*

(i) That the accused committed sexual contact upon another person by touching, or causing another person to touch, any body part of any person;

(ii) That the accused did so by using force causing or likely to cause death or grievous bodily harm to any person; and

(iii) That the accused did so with intent to arouse or gratify the sexual desire of any person.

(c) *By threatening or placing that other person in fear that any person would be subjected to death, grievous bodily harm, or kidnapping*

(i) That the accused committed sexual contact upon another person by touching, or causing another person to touch, any body part of any person;

(ii) That the accused did so by threatening or placing that other person in fear that any person would be subjected to death, grievous bodily harm, or kidnapping; and

(iii) That the accused did so with intent to arouse or gratify the sexual desire of any person.

(d) By first rendering that other person unconscious

(i) That the accused committed sexual contact upon another person by touching, or causing another person to touch, any body part of any person;

(ii) That the accused did so by first rendering that other person unconscious; and

(iii) That the accused did so with intent to arouse or gratify the sexual desire of any person.

(e) *By administering a drug, intoxicant, or other similar substance*

(i) That the accused committed sexual contact upon another person by touching, or causing another person to touch, any body part of any person;

(ii) That the accused did so by administering to that other person by force or threat of force, or without the knowledge or permission of that person, a drug, intoxicant, or other similar substance and thereby substantially impairing the ability of that other person to appraise or control conduct; and

(iii) That the accused did so with intent to arouse or gratify the sexual desire of any person.

(7) *Abusive sexual contact involving the touching of the genitalia, anus, groin, breast, inner thigh, or buttocks of any person.*

(a) *By threatening or placing that other person in fear*

(i) That the accused committed sexual contact upon another person by touching, or causing another person to touch, either directly or through the clothing, the genitalia, anus, groin, breast, inner thigh, or buttocks of any person;

(ii) That the accused did so by threatening or placing that other person in fear; and

(iii) That the accused did so with intent to abuse, humiliate, harass, or degrade any person or to arouse or gratify the sexual desire of any person.

(b) *By causing bodily harm*

(i) That the accused committed sexual contact upon another person by touching, or causing another person to touch, either directly or through the clothing, the genitalia, anus, groin, breast, inner thigh, or buttocks of any person;

(ii) That the accused did so by causing bodily harm to that other person; and

(iii) That the accused did so with intent to abuse, humiliate, harass, or degrade any person or to arouse or gratify the sexual desire of any person.

(c) *By fraudulent representation*

(i) That the accused committed sexual contact upon another person by touching, or causing another person to touch, either directly or through the clothing, the genitalia, anus, groin, breast, inner thigh, or buttocks of any person;

(ii) That the accused did so by making a fraudulent representation that the sexual act served a professional purpose; and

(iii) That the accused did so with intent to abuse, humiliate, harass, or degrade any person or to arouse or gratify the sexual desire of any person.

(d) *By false pretense*

(i) That the accused committed sexual contact upon another person by touching, or causing another person to touch, either directly or through the clothing, the genitalia, anus, groin, breast, inner thigh, or buttocks of any person;

(ii) That the accused did so by inducing a belief by any artifice, pretense, or concealment that the accused is another person; and

(iii) That the accused did so with intent to abuse, humiliate, harass, or degrade any person or to arouse or gratify the sexual desire of any person.

(e) *Of a person who is asleep, unconscious, or otherwise unaware the act is occurring*

(i) That the accused committed sexual contact upon another person by touching, or causing another person to touch, either directly or through the clothing, the genitalia, anus, groin, breast, inner thigh, or buttocks of any person;

(ii) That the other person was asleep, unconscious, or otherwise unaware that the sexual act was occurring;

(iii) That the accused knew or reasonably should have known that the other person was asleep, unconscious, or otherwise unaware that the sexual act was occurring; and

(iv) That the accused did so with intent to abuse, humiliate, harass, or degrade any person or to arouse or gratify the sexual desire of any person.

(f) *When the other person is incapable of consenting*

(i) That the accused committed sexual contact upon another person by touching, or causing another person to touch, either directly or through the clothing, the genitalia, anus, groin, breast, inner thigh, or buttocks of any person;

(ii) That the other person was incapable of consenting to the sexual act due to:

(A) Impairment by any drug, intoxicant or other similar substance; or

(B) A mental disease or defect, or physical disability;

(iii) That the accused knew or reasonably should have known of the impairment, mental disease or defect, or physical disability of the other person; and

(iv) That the accused did so with intent to abuse, humiliate, harass, or degrade any person or to arouse or gratify the sexual desire of any person.

(8) *Abusive sexual contact involving the touching of any body part of any person.*

(a) By threatening or placing that other person in fear

(i) That the accused committed sexual contact upon another person by touching, or causing another person to touch, any body part of any person;

(ii) That the accused did so by threatening or placing that other person in fear; and

(iii) That the accused did so with intent to arouse or gratify the sexual desire of any person.

(b) *By causing bodily harm*

(i) That the accused committed sexual contact upon another person by touching, or causing another person to touch, any body part of any person;

(ii) That the accused did so by causing bodily harm to that other person; and

(iii) That the accused did so with intent to arouse or gratify the sexual desire of any person.

(c) *By fraudulent representation*

(i) That the accused committed sexual contact upon another person by touching, or causing another person to touch, any body part of any person;

(ii) That the accused did so by making a fraudulent representation that the sexual act served a professional purpose when it served no professional purpose; and

(iii) That the accused did so with intent to arouse or gratify the sexual desire of any person.

(d) *By false pretense*

(i) That the accused committed sexual contact upon another person by touching, or causing another person to touch, any body part of any person;

(ii) That the accused did so by inducing a

belief by any artifice, pretense, or concealment that the accused is another person; and

(iii) That the accused did so with intent to arouse or gratify the sexual desire of any person.

(e) *Of a person who is asleep, unconscious, or otherwise unaware the act is occurring*

(i) That the accused committed sexual contact upon another person by touching, or causing another person to touch, any body part of any person;

(ii) That the other person was asleep, unconscious, or otherwise unaware that the sexual act was occurring;

(iii) That the accused knew or reasonably should have known that the other person was asleep, unconscious, or otherwise unaware that the sexual act was occurring; and

(iv) That the accused did so with intent to arouse or gratify the sexual desire of any person.

(f) *When the other person is incapable of consenting*

(i) That the accused committed sexual contact upon another person by touching, or causing another person to touch, any body part of any person;

(ii) That the other person was incapable of consenting to the sexual act due to:

(A) Impairment by any drug, intoxicant, or other similar substance; or

(B) A mental disease or defect, or physical disability;

(iii) That the accused knew or reasonably should have known of the impairment, mental disease or defect, or physical disability of the other person; and

(iv) That the accused did so with intent to arouse or gratify the sexual desire of any person.

c. *Explanation.*

(1) In general. Sexual offenses have been separated into three statutes: adults (120), children (120b), and other offenses (120c).

(2) Definitions. The terms are defined in Paragraph 45.a.(g).

(3) Victim character and privilege. See Mil. R Evid. 412 concerning rules of evidence relating to the character of the victim of an alleged sexual offense. See Mil. R. Evid. 514 concerning rules of evidence relating to privileged communications between the victim and victim advocate.

(4) Consent as an element. Lack of consent is not an element of any offense under this paragraph unless expressly stated. Consent may be relevant for other purposes.

d. *Lesser included offenses.* See paragraph 3 of this part and Appendix 12A.

e. *Maximum punishments.*

(1) *Rape.* Forfeiture of all pay and allowances, and confinement for life without eligibility for parole. Mandatory minimum – Dismissal or dishonorable discharge.

(2) *Sexual assault.* Forfeiture of all pay and allowances and confinement for 30 years. Mandatory minimum – Dismissal or dishonorable discharge.

(3) *Aggravated sexual contact.* Dishonorable discharge, forfeiture of all pay and allowances, and confinement for 20 years.

(4) *Abusive sexual contact.* Dishonorable discharge, forfeiture of all pay and allowances, and confinement for 7 years.

f. *Sample specifications.*

(1) *Rape involving contact between penis and vulva or anus or mouth.*

(a) *By force.* In that (personal jurisdiction data), did (at/on board location), on or about___________, commit a sexual act upon by causing penetration of ___________'s (vulva) (anus) (mouth) with ___________'s penis, by using unlawful force.

(b) *By force causing or likely to cause death or grievous bodily harm.* In that (personal jurisdiction data), did (at/on board location), on or about 20 , commit a sexual act upon ___________ by causing penetration of ___________'s (vulva) (anus) (mouth) with ___________'s penis, by using force likely to cause death or grievous bodily harm to ___________, to wit: ___________.

(c) *By threatening or placing that other person in fear that any person would be subjected to death, grievous bodily harm, or kidnapping.* In that (personal jurisdiction data), did (at/on board location), on or about ____. 20__ , commit a sexual act upon ___________ by causing penetration of ___________'s (vulva) (anus) (mouth) with ___________'s penis, by (threatening ___________) (placing ___________ in fear) that would be subjected to (death) (grievous bodily harm) (kidnapping).

(d) *By first rendering that other person unconscious.* In that (personal jurisdiction data), did (at/on board location), on or about ____. 20__ , commit a sexual act upon by ___________ causing penetration of ___________'s (vulva) (anus) (mouth) with ___________'s penis, by first rendering ___________ unconscious by ___________.

(e) *By administering a drug, intoxicant, or other*

similar substance. In that (personal jurisdiction data), did (at/on board location), on or about ____. 20__, commit a sexual act upon by causing penetration of __________'s (vulva) (anus) (mouth) with __________'s penis, by administering to __________ (by force) (by threat of force) (without the knowledge or permission of __________) a (drug) (intoxicant) (list other similar substance), to wit: __________, thereby substantially impairing the ability of __________ to appraise or control his/her conduct.

(2) *Rape involving penetration of genital opening by any part of the body or any object.*

(a) *By force.* In that (personal jurisdiction data), did (at/on board location), on or about _____, 20__, commit a sexual act upon _________, by penetrating the (vulva) (anus) (mouth) of _________ with (list body part or object) by using unlawful force, with an intent to (abuse) (humiliate) (harass) (degrade) (arouse/gratify the sexual desire of) _________.

(b) By force causing or likely to cause death or grievous bodily injury. In that (personal jurisdiction data), did (at/on board location), on or about _____, 20__, commit a sexual act upon _________, by penetrating the (vulva) (anus) (mouth) of _________ with (list body part or object) by using force likely to cause death or grievous bodily harm to, to wit: _________, with an intent to (abuse) (humiliate) (harass) (degrade) (arouse/gratify the sexual desire of).

(c) *By threatening or placing that other person in fear that any person would be subjected to death, grievous bodily harm, or kidnapping.* In that (personal jurisdiction data), did (at/on board location), on or about____. 20__, commit a sexual act upon _________, by penetrating the (vulva) (anus) (mouth) of _________ with (list body part or object) by (threatening) (placing _________ in fear) that _________ would be subjected to (death) (grievous bodily harm) (kidnapping), with an intent to (abuse) (humiliate) (harass) (degrade) (arouse/gratify the sexual desire of) _________.

(d) *By first rendering that other person unconscious.* In that (personal jurisdiction data), did (at/on board location), on or about _____, 20__, commit a sexual act upon ________, by penetrating the (vulva) (anus) (mouth) of _________ with (list body part or object) by first rendering_________ unconscious, with an intent to (abuse) (humiliate) (harass) (degrade) (arouse/gratify the sexual desire of) _________.

(e) *By administering a drug, intoxicant, or other similar substance.* In that (personal jurisdiction data), did (at/on board location), on or about____. 20__, commit a sexual act upon _________, by penetrating the (vulva) (anus) (mouth) of _________ with (list body part or object) by administering to _________ (by force) (by threat of force) (without the knowledge or permission of _________) a (drug) (intoxicant) (list other similar substance), to wit: _________, thereby substantially impairing the ability of _________ to appraise or control his/her conduct, with an intent to (abuse) (humiliate) (harass) (degrade) (arouse/gratify the sexual desire of) _________.

(3) *Sexual assault involving contact between penis and vulva or anus or mouth.*

(a) *By threatening or placing that other person in fear.* In that (personal jurisdiction data), did (at/on board location), on or about _____, 20_____, commit a sexual act upon _________, by causing penetration of _________'s (vulva) (anus) (mouth) with _________'s penis, by (threatening _________) (placing _________ in fear).

(b) *By causing bodily harm.* In that (personal jurisdiction data), did (at/on board location), on or about____. 20__, commit a sexual act upon _________, by causing penetration of _________'s (vulva) (anus) (mouth) with _________'s penis by causing bodily harm to _________, to wit: _________.

(c) *By fraudulent representation.* In that (personal jurisdiction data), did (at/on board location), on or about____. 20__, commit a sexual act upon _________, by causing penetration of _________'s (vulva) (anus) (mouth) with _________'s penis by making a fraudulent representation that the sexual act served a professional purpose, to wit: _________.

(d) *By false pretense.* In that (personal jurisdiction data), did (at/on board location), on or about _____, 20__, commit a sexual act upon _________, by causing penetration of _________'s (vulva) (anus) (mouth) with _________'s penis by inducing a belief by (artifice) (pretense) (concealment) that the said accused was another person.

(e) *Of a person who is asleep, unconscious, or otherwise unaware the act is occurring.* In that (personal jurisdiction data), did (at/on board location), on or about _____, 20__, commit a sexual act upon

_________, by causing penetration of _________'s (vulva) (anus) (mouth) with _________'s penis when he/she knew or reasonably should have known that _________ was (asleep) (unconscious) (unaware the sexual act was occurring due to_________).

(f) *When the other person is incapable of consenting.* In that (personal jurisdiction data), did (at/on board location), on or about _____, 20__, commit a sexual act upon _________, by causing penetration of _________'s (vulva) (anus) (mouth) with _________'s penis, when_________ was incapable of consenting to the sexual act because he/she [was impaired by (a drug, to wit: _________) (an intoxicant, to wit: _________) ( )] [had a (mental disease, to wit: _________) (mental defect, to wit: _________) (physical disability, to wit: _________)], a condition that was known or reasonably should have been known by the said accused.

(4) *Sexual assault involving penetration of vulva or anus or mouth by any part of the body or any object.*

(a) *By threatening or placing that other person in fear.* In that (personal jurisdiction data), did (at/on board location), on or about _____, 20____, commit a sexual act upon _________, by penetrating the (vulva) (anus) (mouth) of _________ with (list body part or object), by (threatening _________) (placing _________ in fear), with an intent to (abuse) (humiliate) (harass) (degrade) (arouse) (gratify the sexual desire of) _________.

(b) *By causing bodily harm.* In that (personal jurisdiction data), did (at/on board location), on or about _____, 20__, commit a sexual act upon _________, by penetrating the (vulva) (anus) (mouth) of _________ with (list body part or object), by causing bodily harm to _________, to wit: _________ with an intent to (abuse) (humiliate) (harass) (degrade) (arouse) (gratify the sexual desire of) _________.

(c) *By fraudulent representation.* In that (personal jurisdiction data), did (at/on board location), on or about _____, 20__, commit a sexual act upon _________, by penetrating the (vulva) (anus) (mouth) of _________ with (list body part or object), by making a fraudulent representation that the sexual act served a professional purpose, to wit: _________, with an intent to (abuse) (humiliate) (harass) (degrade) (arouse) (gratify the sexual desire of) _________.

(d) By false pretense. In that (personal jurisdiction data), did (at/on board location), on or about _____, 20__, commit a sexual act upon _________, by penetrating the (vulva) (anus) (mouth) of _________ with (list body part or object), by inducing a belief by (artifice) (pretense) (concealment) that the said accused was another person, with an intent to (abuse) (humiliate) (harass) (degrade) (arouse) (gratify the sexual desire of) _________.

(e) *Of a person who is asleep, unconscious, or otherwise unaware the act is occurring.* In that (personal jurisdiction data), did (at/on board location), on or about _____, 20__, commit a sexual act upon _________, by penetrating the (vulva) (anus) (mouth) of _________ with (list body part or object), when he/she knew or reasonably should have known that _________ was (asleep) (unconscious) (unaware the sexual act was occurring due to), with an intent to (abuse) (humiliate) (harass) (degrade) (arouse) (gratify the sexual desire of) _________.

(f) *When the other person is incapable of consenting.* In that (personal jurisdiction data), did (at/ on board location), on or about _____, 20__, commit a sexual act upon _________, by penetrating the (vulva) (anus) (mouth) of with (list body part or object), when _________ was incapable of consenting to the sexual act because he/she [was impaired by (a drug, to wit: _________) (an intoxicant, to wit: _________) ( )] [had a (mental disease, to wit: _________) (mental defect, to wit: _________) (physical disability, to wit: _________)], a condition that was known or reasonably should have been known by the said accused, with an intent to (abuse) (humiliate) (harass) (degrade) (arouse) (gratify the sexual desire of) _________.

(5) *Aggravated sexual contact involving the touching of the genitalia, anus, groin, breast, inner thigh, or buttocks of any person.*

(a) *By force.* In that (personal jurisdiction data), did (at/on board location), on or about _____, 20__, [(touch) (cause to touch)] [(directly) (through the clothing)] the (genitalia) (anus) (groin) (breast) (inner thigh) (buttocks) of _________, by using unlawful force, with an intent to (abuse) (humiliate) (degrade) (arouse) (gratify the sexual desire of) _________.

(b) *By force causing or likely to cause death or grievous bodily harm.* In that (personal jurisdiction data), did (at/on board location), on or about _____, 20__, [(touch) (cause _________ to touch)] [(directly) (through the clothing)] the (genitalia) (anus) (groin) (breast) (inner thigh) (buttocks) of _________, by using force likely to cause death or grievous bodily harm to ________, to wit: ________, with an intent to (abuse) (humiliate) (degrade) (arouse) (gratify the sexual desire of) ________.

(c) *By threatening or placing that other person in fear that any person would be subjected to death, grievous bodily harm, or kidnapping.* In that (personal jurisdiction data), did (at/on board location), on or about _____, 20__, [(touch) (cause ________ to touch)] [(directly) (through the clothing)] the (genitalia) (anus) (groin) (breast) (inner thigh) (buttocks) of ________, by (threatening ________) (placing ______ in fear) that ________ would be subjected to (death) (grievous bodily harm) (kidnapping), with an intent to (abuse) (humiliate) (degrade) (arouse) (gratify the sexual desire of) ________.

(d) *By first rendering that other person unconscious.* In that (personal jurisdiction data), did (at/on board location), on or about ____. 20__, [(touch) (cause ________ to touch)] [(directly) (through the clothing)] the (genitalia) (anus) (groin) (breast) (inner thigh) (buttocks) of ________, by rendering ________ unconscious by ________, with an intent to (abuse) (humiliate) (degrade) (arouse) (gratify the sexual desire of) .

(e) *By administering a drug, intoxicant, or other similar substance.* In that (personal jurisdiction data), did (at/on board location), on or about____. 20__, [(touch) (cause ________ to touch)] [(directly) (through the clothing)] the (genitalia) (anus) (groin) (breast) (inner thigh) (buttocks) of ________, by administering to ________ (by force) (by threat of force) (without the knowledge or permission of____) a (drug) (intoxicant) (___) thereby substantially impairing the ability of ________ to appraise or control his/her conduct, with an intent to (abuse) (humiliate) (degrade) (arouse) (gratify the sexual desire of) ________.

(6) *Aggravated sexual contact involving the touching of any body part of any person.*

(a) *By force.* In that (personal jurisdiction data), did (at/on board location), on or about____. 20__, [(touch) (cause ________ to touch)] [(directly) (through the clothing)] (name of body part) of ________, by using unlawful force, with an intent to (arouse) (gratify the sexual desire of) ________.

(b) *By force causing or likely to cause death or grievous bodily harm.* In that (personal jurisdiction data), did (at/on board location), on or about____. 20__, [(touch) (cause ________ to touch)] [(directly) (through the clothing)] (name of body part) of ________, by using force likely to cause death or grievous bodily harm to ________, to wit: ________, with an intent to (arouse) (gratify the sexual desire of) ________.

(c) *By threatening or placing that other person in fear that any person would be subjected to death, grievous bodily harm, or kidnapping.* In that (personal jurisdiction data), did (at/on board location), on or about____. 20__, [(touch) (cause to touch)] [(directly) (through the clothing)] (name of body part) of ________, by (threatening ________) (placing ________ in fear) that ________ would be subjected to (death) (grievous bodily harm) (kidnapping), with an intent to (arouse) (gratify the sexual desire of) ________.

(d) By first rendering that other person unconscious. In that (personal jurisdiction data), did (at/on board location), on or about____. 20__, [(touch) (cause ________to touch)] [(directly) (through the clothing)] (name of body part) of _______, by rendering ________ unconscious by ________, with an intent to (arouse) (gratify the sexual desire of) ________.

(e) By administering a drug, intoxicant, or other similar substance. In that (personal jurisdiction data), did (at/on board location), on or about____. 20__, [(touch) (cause ________ to touch)] [(directly) (through the clothing)] (name of body part) of ________, by administering to ________ (by force) (by threat of force) (without the knowledge or permission of ________) a (drug) (intoxicant) (____) and thereby substantially impairing the ability of ________ to appraise or control his/her conduct, with an intent to (arouse) (gratify the sexual desire of) ________.

(7) *Abusive sexual contact involving the touching of the genitalia, anus, groin, breast, inner thigh, or buttocks of any person.*

(a) *By threatening or placing that other person in fear.* In that (personal jurisdiction data), did (at/on board location), on or about____. 20__, [(touch) (cause another person to touch)] [(directly) (through the clothing)] the (genitalia) (anus) (groin) (breast) (inner thigh) (buttocks) of ________ by (threatening ________) (placing ________ in fear), with an intent to (abuse) (humiliate) (degrade) (arouse) (gratify the sexual desire of) ________.

(b) *By causing bodily harm.* In that (personal jurisdiction data), did (at/on board location), on or about____. 20__, [(touch) (cause another person to touch)] [(directly) (through the clothing)] the (genitalia) (anus) (groin) (breast) (inner thigh) (buttocks) of _________ by causing bodily harm to _________, to wit: _________, with an intent to (abuse) (humiliate) (degrade) (arouse) (gratify the sexual desire of) _________.

(c) *By fraudulent representation.* In that (personal jurisdiction data), did (at/on board location), on or about____. 20__, [(touch) (cause another person to touch)] [(directly) (through the clothing)] the (genitalia) (anus) (groin) (breast) (inner thigh) (buttocks) of _________ by making a fraudulent representation that the sexual contact served a professional purpose, to wit: _________, with an intent to (abuse) (humiliate) (degrade) (arouse) (gratify the sexual desire of) _________.

(d) *By false pretense.* In that (personal jurisdiction data), did (at/on board location), on or about ____. 20__, [(touch) (cause another person to touch)] [(directly) (through the clothing)] the (genitalia) (anus) (groin) (breast) (inner thigh) (buttocks) of _________ by inducing a belief by (artifice) (pretense) (concealment) that the said accused was another person, with an intent to (abuse) (humiliate) (degrade) (arouse) (gratify the sexual desire of) _________.

(e) *Of a person who is asleep, unconscious, or otherwise unaware the act is occurring.* In that (personal jurisdiction data), did (at/on board location), on or about____. 20__, [(touch) (cause another person to touch)] [(directly) (through the clothing)] the (genitalia) (anus) (groin) (breast) (inner thigh) (buttocks) of _________ when he/she knew or reasonably should have known that _________ was (asleep) (unconscious) (unaware the sexual contact was occur- ring due to _________), with an intent to (abuse) (humiliate) (degrade) (arouse) (gratify the sexual desire of) _________.

(f) *When that person is incapable of consenting.* In that (personal jurisdiction data), did (at/on board location), on or about____. 20__, [(touch) (cause another person to touch)] [(directly) (through the clothing)] the (genitalia) (anus) (groin) (breast) (inner thigh) (buttocks) of _________ when _________ was incapable of consenting to the sexual contact because he/she [was impaired by (a drug, to wit: _________) (an intoxicant, to wit: _________) ( )] [had a (mental disease, to wit: _________) (mental defect, to wit: _________) (physical disability, to wit: _________)] and this condition was known or reasonably should have been known by _________, with an intent to (abuse) (humiliate) (degrade) (arouse) (gratify the sexual desire of) _________.

(8) Abusive sexual contact involving the touching of any body part of any person.

(a) *By threatening or placing that other person in fear.* In that (personal jurisdiction data), did (at/on board location), on or about____. 20__, [(touch) (cause another person to touch)] [(directly) (through the clothing)] the (name of body part) of _________ by (threatening _________) (placing in _________ fear), with an intent to (arouse) (gratify the sexual desire of) _________.

(b) *By causing bodily harm.* In that (personal jurisdiction data), did (at/on board location), on or about____. 20__, [(touch) (cause another person to touch)] [(directly) (through the clothing)] the (name of body part) of _________by causing bodily harm to _________, to wit: _________, with an intent to (arouse) (gratify the sexual desire of) _________.

(c) *By fraudulent representation.* In that (personal jurisdiction data), did (at/on board location), on or about____. 20__, [(touch) (cause another person to touch)] [(directly) (through the clothing)] the (name of body part) of _________by making a fraudulent representation that the sexual contact served a professional purpose, to wit: _________, with an intent to (arouse) (gratify the sexual desire of) _________.

(d) *By false pretense.* In that (personal jurisdiction data), did (at/on board location), on or about____. 20__, [(touch) (cause another person to touch)] [(directly) (through the clothing)] the (name of body part) of _________ by inducing a belief by (artifice) (pretense) (concealment) that the said accused was another person, with an intent to (arouse) (gratify the sexual desire of) _________.

(e) *Of a person who is asleep, unconscious, or otherwise unaware the act is occurring.* In that (personal jurisdiction data), did (at/on board location), on or about____. 20__, [(touch) (cause another person to touch)] [(directly) (through the clothing)] the (name of body part) of _________when he/she knew or reasonably should have known that _________ was (asleep) (unconscious) (unaware the sexual contact was occurring due to _________), with an intent to (arouse) (gratify the sexual desire of) _________.

(f) *When that person is incapable of consenting.* In that (personal jurisdiction data), did (at/on board location), on or about____. 20__, [(touch) (cause another person to touch)] [(directly) (through the clothing)] the (name of body part) of _________ when _________ was incapable of consenting to the sexual contact because he/she [was impaired by (a drug, to wit: _________) (an intoxicant, to wit: _________) ( )] [had a (mental disease, to wit: _________) (mental defect, to wit: _________) (physical disability, to wit: _________)], a condition that was known or reasonably should have been known by _________, with an intent to (arouse) (gratify the sexual desire of) _________.

45a. Article 120a—Stalking

a. *Text of statute.*

(a) Any person subject to this section:

(1) who wrongfully engages in a course of conduct directed at a specific person that would cause a reasonable person to fear death or bodily harm, including sexual assault, to himself or herself or a member of his or her immediate family;

(2) who has knowledge, or should have knowledge, that the specific person will be placed in reasonable fear of death or bodily harm, including sexual assault, to himself or herself or a member of his or her immediate family; and

(3) whose acts induce reasonable fear in the specific person of death or bodily harm, including sexual assault, to himself or herself or to a member of his or her immediate family;

is guilty of stalking and shall be punished as a court-martial may direct.

(b) In this section:

(1) The term "course of conduct" means:

(A) a repeated maintenance of visual or physical proximity to a specific person; or

(B) a repeated conveyance of verbal threat, written threats, or threats implied by con- duct, or a combination of such threats, directed at or towards a specific person.

(2)The term "repeated," with respect to conduct, means two or more occasions of such conduct.

(3)The term "immediate family," in the case of a specific person, means a spouse, parent, child, or sibling of the person, or any other family member, relative, or intimate partner of the person who regularly resides in the household of the person or who within the six months preceding the commencement of the course of conduct regularly resided in the household of the person.

b. *Elements.*

(1) That the accused wrongfully engaged in a course of conduct directed at a specific person that would cause a reasonable person to fear death or bodily harm to himself or herself or a member of his or her immediate family;

(2) That the accused had knowledge, or should have had knowledge, that the specific person would be placed in reasonable fear of death or bodily harm to himself or herself or a member of his or her immediate family; and

(3) That the accused's acts induced reasonable fear in the specific person of death or bodily harm to himself or herself or to a member of his or her immediate family.

c. *Explanation.* See Paragraph 54c(1)(a) for an explanation of "bodily harm".

d. Lesser included offenses. See paragraph 3 of this part and Appendix 12A.

e. *Maximum punishment.* Dishonorable discharge, forfeiture of all pay and allowances, and confinement for 3 years.

f. Sample Specification.

In that _________ (personal jurisdiction data), who (knew)(should have known) that _________ would be placed in reasonable fear of (death)(bodily harm) to (himself) (herself) (_________, a member of his or her immediate family) did (at/on board—location), (subject-matter jurisdiction data, if required), (on or about____. 20__)(from about to about 20), wrongfully engage in a course of conduct directed at _________, to wit: _________ thereby inducing in _________, a reasonable fear of (death)(bodily harm) to (himself)(herself) (, a member of his or her immediate family).

45b. Article 120b—Rape and sexual assault of a child

[Note: This statute applies to offenses committed between 28 June 2012 and 31 December 2018. Article 120b is a new statute designed to address only child sexual offenses. Previous versions of child sexual offenses are located as follows: for offenses committed on or before 30 September 2007, see Appendix 20; for offenses committed during the period 1 October 2007 through 27 June 2012, see Appendix 21.]

a. *Text of Statute*

(a) *Rape of a Child.* Any person subject to this

chapter who—

(1) commits a sexual act upon a child who has not attained the age of 12 years; or

(2) commits a sexual act upon a child who has attained the age of 12 years by—

(A) using force against any person;

(B) threatening or placing that child in fear;

(C) rendering that child unconscious; or

(D) administering to that child a drug, in toxicant, or other similar substance; is guilty of rape of a child and shall be punished as a court-martial may direct.

(b) *Sexual Assault of a Child.* Any person subject to this chapter who commits a sexual act upon a child who has attained the age of 12 years is guilty of sexual assault of a child and shall be punished as a court-martial may direct.

(c) *Sexual Abuse of a Child.* Any person subject to this chapter who commits a lewd act upon a child is guilty of sexual abuse of a child and shall be punished as a court-martial may direct.

(d) Age of Child.

(1) *Under 12 years.* In a prosecution under this section, it need not be proven that the accused knew the age of the other person engaging in the sexual act or lewd act. It is not a defense that the accused reasonably believed that the child had attained the age of 12 years.

(2) *Under 16 years.* In a prosecution under this section, it need not be proven that the accused knew that the other person engaging in the sexual act or lewd act had not attained the age of 16 years, but it is a defense in a prosecution under subsection (b) (sexual assault of a child) or subsection (c) (sexual abuse of a child), which the accused must prove by a preponderance of the evidence, that the accused reasonably believed that the child had attained the age of 16 years, if the child had in fact attained at least the age of 12 years.

(e) *Proof of Threat.* In a prosecution under this section, in proving that a person made a threat, it need not be proven that the person actually intended to carry out the threat or had the ability to carry out the threat.

(f) *Marriage.* In a prosecution under subsection (b (sexual assault of a child) or subsection (c) (sexual abuse of a child), it is a defense, which the accused must prove by a preponderance of the evidence, that the persons engaging in the sexual act or lewd act were at that time married to each other, except where the accused commits a sexual act upon the person when the accused knows or reasonably should know that the other person is asleep, unconscious, or otherwise unaware that the sexual act is occurring or when the other person is incapable of consenting to the sexual act due to impairment by any drug, intoxicant, or other similar substance, and that condition was known or reasonably should have been known by the accused.

(g) *Consent.* Lack of consent is not an element and need not be proven in any prosecution under this section. A child not legally married to the person committing the sexual act, lewd act, or use of force cannot consent to any sexual act, lewd act, or use of force.

(h) *Definitions.* In this section:

(1) *Sexual act and sexual contact.* The terms 'sexual act' and 'sexual contact' have the meanings given those terms in section 920(g) of this title (article 120(g)).

(2) *Force.* The term 'force' means—

(A) the use of a weapon;

(B) the use of such physical strength or violence as is sufficient to overcome, restrain, or injure a child; or

(C) inflicting physical harm. In the case of a parent-child or similar relation- ship, the use or abuse of parental or similar authority is sufficient to constitute the use of force.

(3) *Threatening or placing that child in fear.* The term 'threatening or placing that child in fear' means a communication or action that is of sufficient consequence to cause the child to fear that non-compliance will result in the child or another person being subjected to the action contemplated by the communication or action.

(4) *Child.* The term 'child' means any person who has not attained the age of 16 years.

(5) *Lewd act.* The term 'lewd act' means—

(A) any sexual contact with a child;

(B) intentionally exposing one's genitalia, anus, buttocks, or female areola or nipple to a child by any means, including via any communication technology, with an intent to abuse, humiliate, or degrade any person, or to arouse or gratify the sexual desire of any person;

(C) intentionally communicating indecent language to a child by any means, including via any communication technology, with an intent to abuse, humiliate, or degrade any person, or to

arouse or gratify the sexual desire of any person; or

(D) any indecent conduct, intentionally done with or in the presence of a child, including via any communication technology, that amounts to a form of immorality relating to sexual impurity which is grossly vulgar, obscene, and repugnant to common propriety, and tends to excite sexual desire or deprave morals with respect to sexual relations.

b. *Elements.*

(1) *Rape of a child involving contact between penis and vulva or anus or mouth.*

(a) *Rape of a child who has not attained the age of 12.*

(i) That the accused committed a sexual act upon a child causing penetration, however slight, by the penis of the vulva or anus or mouth; and

(ii) That at the time of the sexual act the child had not attained the age of 12 years.

(b) *Rape by force of a child who has attained the age of 12.*

(i) That the accused committed a sexual act upon a child causing penetration, however slight, by the penis of the vulva or anus or mouth; and

(ii) That at the time of the sexual act the child had attained the age of 12 years but had not attained the age of 16 years, and

(iii) That the accused did so by using force against that child or any other person.

(c) *Rape by threatening or placing in fear a child who has attained the age of 12.*

(i) That the accused committed a sexual act upon a child causing penetration, however slight, by the penis of the vulva or anus or mouth;

(ii) That at the time of the sexual act the child had attained the age of 12 years but had not attained the age of 16 years; and

(iii) That the accused did so by threatening the child or another person or placing that child in fear.

(d) *Rape by rendering unconscious a child who has attained the age of 12.*

(i) That the accused committed a sexual act upon a child causing penetration, however slight, by the penis of the vulva or anus or mouth;

(ii) That at the time of the sexual act the child had attained the age of 12 years but had not attained the age of 16 years; and

(iii) That the accused did so by rendering that child unconscious.

(e) *Rape by administering a drug, intoxicant, or other similar substance to a child who has attained the age of 12.*

(i) That the accused committed a sexual act upon a child causing penetration, however slight, by the penis of the vulva or anus or mouth;

(ii) That at the time of the sexual act the child had attained the age of 12 years but had not attained the age of 16 years; and

(iii) That the accused did so by administering to that child a drug, intoxicant, or other similar substance.

(2) *Rape of a child involving penetration of vulva or anus or mouth by any part of the body or any object.*

(a) *Rape of a child who has not attained the age of 12.*

(i) That the accused committed a sexual act upon a child by causing penetration, however slight, of the vulva or anus or mouth of the child by any part of the body or by any object;

(ii) That at the time of the sexual act the child had not attained the age of 12 years; and

(iii) That the accused did so with an intent to abuse, humiliate, harass, or degrade any person or to arouse or gratify the sexual desire of any person.

(b) *Rape by force of a child who has attained the age of 12.*

(i) That the accused committed a sexual act upon a child by causing penetration, however slight, of the vulva, anus, or mouth of the child by any part of the body or by any object;

(ii) That at the time of the sexual act the child had attained the age of 12 years but had not attained the age of 16 years;

(iii) That the accused did so by using force against that child or any other person; and

(iv) That the accused did so with an intent to abuse, humiliate, harass, or degrade any person or to arouse or gratify the sexual desire of any person.

(c) *Rape by threatening or placing in fear a child who has attained the age of 12.*

(i) That the accused committed a sexual act upon a child by causing penetration, however slight, of the vulva or anus or mouth of the child by any part of the body or by any object;

(ii) That at the time of the sexual act the child had attained the age of 12 years but had not attained the age of 16 years;

(iii) That the accused did so by threatening the

child or another person or placing that child in fear; and

(iv) That the accused did so with an intent to abuse, humiliate, harass, or degrade any person or to arouse or gratify the sexual desire of any person.

(d) *Rape by rendering unconscious a child who has attained the age of 12.*

(i) That the accused committed a sexual act upon a child by causing penetration, however slight, of the vulva or anus or mouth of the child by any part of the body or by any object;

(ii) That at the time of the sexual act the child had attained the age of 12 years but had not attained the age of 16 years;

(iii) That the accused did so by rendering that child unconscious; and

(iv) That the accused did so with an intent to abuse, humiliate, harass, or degrade any person or to arouse or gratify the sexual desire of any person.

(e) *Rape by administering a drug, intoxicant, or other similar substance to a child who has attained the age of 12.*

(i) That the accused committed a sexual act upon a child by causing penetration, however slight, of the vulva or anus or mouth of the child by any part of the body or by any object;

(ii) That at the time of the sexual act the child had attained the age of 12 years but had not attained the age of 16 years;

(iii) That the accused did so by administering to that child a drug, intoxicant, or other similar substance; and

(iv) That the accused did so with an intent to abuse, humiliate, harass, or degrade any person or to arouse or gratify the sexual desire of any person.

(3) *Sexual assault of a child.*

(a) *Sexual assault of a child who has attained the age of 12 involving contact between penis and vulva or anus or mouth.*

(i) That the accused committed a sexual act upon a child causing contact between penis and vulva or anus or mouth; and

(ii) That at the time of the sexual act the child had attained the age of 12 years but had not attained the age of 16 years.

(b) *Sexual assault of a child who has attained the age of 12 involving penetration of vulva or anus or mouth by any part of the body or any object.*

(i) That the accused committed a sexual act upon a child by causing penetration, however slight, of the vulva or anus or mouth of the child by any part of the body or by any object;

(ii) That at the time of the sexual act the child had attained the age of 12 years but had not attained the age of 16 years; and

(iii) That the accused did so with an intent to abuse, humiliate, harass, or degrade any person or to arouse or gratify the sexual desire of any person.

(4) *Sexual abuse of a child.*

(a) *Sexual abuse of a child by sexual contact involving the touching of the genitalia, anus, groin, breast, inner thigh, or buttocks of any person.*

(i) That the accused committed sexual contact upon a child by touching, or causing another person to touch, either directly or through the clothing, the genitalia, anus, groin, breast, inner thigh, or buttocks of any person; and

(ii) That the accused did so with intent to abuse, humiliate, harass, or degrade any person or to arouse or gratify the sexual desire of any person.

(b) *Sexual abuse of a child by sexual contact involving the touching of any body part.*

(i) That the accused committed sexual contact upon a child by touching, or causing another person to touch, either directly or through the clothing, any body part of any person; and

(ii) That the accused did so with intent to arouse or gratify the sexual desire of any person.

(c) *Sexual abuse of a child by indecent exposure.*

(i) That the accused intentionally exposed his or her genitalia, anus, buttocks, or female areola or nipple to a child by any means; and

(ii) That the accused did so with an intent to abuse, humiliate or degrade any person, or to arouse or gratify the sexual desire of any person.

(d) *Sexual abuse of a child by indecent communication.*

(i) That the accused intentionally communicated indecent language to a child by any means; and

(ii) That the accused did so with an intent to abuse, humiliate or degrade any person, or to arouse or gratify the sexual desire of any person.

(e) *Sexual abuse of a child by indecent conduct.*

(i) That the accused engaged in indecent conduct, intentionally done with or in the presence of a child; and

(ii) That the indecent conduct amounted to a form of immorality relating to sexual impurity which is grossly vulgar, obscene, and repugnant to common propriety, and tends to excite sexual desire or deprave morals with respect to sexual relations.

c. *Explanation.*

(1) *In general.* Sexual offenses have been separated into three statutes: adults (120), children (120b), and other offenses (120c).

(2) *Definitions.* Terms not defined in this paragraph are defined in paragraph 45b.a.(h), supra.

d. *Lesser included offenses.* See paragraph 3 of this part and Appendix 12A.

e. *Maximum punishment.*

(1) Rape of a child. Forfeiture of all pay and allowances, and confinement for life without eligibility for parole. Mandatory minimum – Dismissal or dishonorable discharge.

(2) Sexual assault of a child. Forfeiture of all pay and allowances, and confinement for 30 years. Mandatory minimum – Dismissal or dishonorable discharge.

(3) Sexual abuse of a child.

(a) *Cases involving sexual contact.* Dishonorable discharge, forfeiture of all pay and allowances, and confinement for 20 years.

(b) *Other cases.* Dishonorable discharge, forfeiture of all pay and allowances, and confinement for 15 years.

f. *Sample specifications.*

(1) Rape of a child involving contact between penis and vulva or anus or mouth.

(a) *Rape of a child who has not attained the age of 12.* In that (personal jurisdiction data), did (at/on board location), on or about____. 20__, commit a sexual act upon ___________, a child who had not attained the age of 12 years, by causing penetration of ___________'s (vulva) (anus) (mouth) with ___________'s penis.

(b) *Rape by force of a child who has attained the age of 12 years.* In that (personal jurisdiction data), did (at/on board location), on or about____. 20__, commit a sexual act upon ___________, a child who had attained the age of 12 years but had not attained the age of 16 years, by causing penetration of ___________'s (vulva) (anus) (mouth) with ___________'s penis, by using force against ___________, to wit: ___________.

(c) *Rape by threatening or placing in fear a child who has attained the age of 12 years.* In that (personal jurisdiction data), did (at/on board location), on or about____. 20__, commit a sexual act upon ___________, a child who had attained the age of 12 years but had not attained the age of 16 years, by causing penetration of_________'s (vulva) (anus) (mouth) with ___________'s penis by (threatening ___________) (placing ___________in fear).

(d) *Rape by rendering unconscious of a child who has attained the age of 12 years.* In that (personal jurisdiction data), did (at/on board location), on or about____. 20__, commit a sexual act upon ___________, a child who had attained the age of 12 years but had not attained the age of 16 years, by causing penetration of ___________'s (vulva) (anus) (mouth) with ___________'s penis by rendering ___________ unconscious by ___________.

(e) *Rape by administering a drug, intoxicant, or other similar substance to a child who has attained the age of 12 years.* In that (personal jurisdiction data), did (at/on board location), on or about____. 20__, commit a sexual act upon ___________, a child who had attained the age of 12 years but had not attained the age of 16 years, by causing penetration of ___________'s (vulva) (anus) (mouth) with ___________'s penis by administering to a (drug) (intoxicant) ( ), to wit: ___________.

(2) *Rape of a child involving penetration of the vulva or anus or mouth by any part of the body or any object.*

(a) *Rape of a child who has not attained the age of 12.* In that (personal jurisdiction data), did (at/on board location), on or about____. 20__, commit a sexual act upon ___________, a child who had not attained the age of 12 years, by penetrating the (vulva) (anus) (mouth) of ___________ with (list body part or object), with an intent to (abuse) (humiliate) (harass) (degrade) (arouse) (gratify the sexual desire of) ___________.

(b) *Rape by force of a child who has attained the age of 12 years.* In that (personal jurisdiction data), did (at/on board location), on or about____. 20__, commit a sexual act upon ___________, a child who had attained the age of 12 years but had not attained the age of 16 years, by penetrating the (vulva) (anus) (mouth) of ___________ with (list body part or object), by using force against ___________, with an intent to (abuse) (humiliate) (harass) (degrade) (arouse) (gratify the sexual desire of) ___________.

(c) *Rape by threatening or placing in fear a child who has attained the age of 12 years.* In that (personal jurisdiction data), did (at/on board location), on or about ____. 20__, commit a sexual act upon ___________, a child who had attained the age of 12 years but had not attained the age of 16 years, by penetrating the (vulva) (anus) (mouth) of

___________ with (list body part or object), by (threatening ___________) (placing ___________ in fear), with an intent to (abuse) (humiliate) (harass) (degrade) (arouse) (gratify the sexual desire of) ___________.

(d) *Rape by rendering unconscious of a child who has attained the age of 12 years.* In that (personal jurisdiction data), did (at/on board location), on or about____. 20__, commit a sexual act upon ___________, a child who had attained the age of 12 years but had not attained the age of 16 years, by penetrating the (vulva) (anus) (mouth) of ___________ with (list body part or object), by rendering ___________ unconscious, with an intent to (abuse) (humiliate) (harass) (degrade) (arouse) (gratify the sexual desire of) ___________.

(e) *Rape by administering a drug, intoxicant, or other similar substance to a child who has attained the age of 12 years.* In that (personal jurisdiction data), did (at/on board location), on or about____. 20__, commit a sexual act upon ___________, a child who had attained the age of 12 years but had not attained the age of 16 years, by penetrating the (vulva) (anus) (mouth) of ___________ with (list body part or object), by administering to ___________ a (drug) (intoxicant) ( ), to wit: ___________, with an intent to (abuse) (humiliate) (harass) (degrade) (arouse) (gratify the sexual desire of) ___________.

(3) *Sexual assault of a child.*

(a) *Sexual assault of a child who has attained the age of 12 years involving contact between penis and vulva or anus or mouth.* In that (personal juris- diction data), did (at/on board location), on or about____. 20__, commit a sexual act upon ___________, a child who had attained the age of 12 years but had not attained the age of 16 years, by causing penetration of ___________'s (vulva) (anus) (mouth) with ___________'s penis.

(b) *Sexual assault of a child who has attained the age of 12 years involving penetration of vulva or anus or mouth by any part of the body or any object.* In that (personal jurisdiction data), did (at/on board location), on or about____. 20__, commit a sexual act upon ___________, a child who had attained the age of 12 years but had not attained the age of 16 years, by penetrating the (vulva) (anus) (mouth) of ___________with (list body part or object), with an intent to (abuse) (humiliate) (harass) (degrade) (arouse) (gratify the sexual desire of) ___________.

(4) *Sexual abuse of a child.*

(a) *Sexual abuse of a child involving sexual contact involving the touching of the genitalia, anus, groin, breast, inner thigh, or buttocks of any person.* In that (personal jurisdiction data), did (at/on board location), on or about____. 20__, commit a lewd act upon ___________, a child who had not attained the age of 16 years, by intentionally [(touching) (causing ___________to touch)] [(directly) (through the clothing)] the (genitalia) (anus) (groin) (breast) (inner thigh) (buttocks) of ___________, with an intent to (abuse) (humiliate) (degrade) ___________.

(b) *Sexual abuse of a child involving sexual contact involving the touching of any body part of any person.* In that (personal jurisdiction data), did (at/on board location), on or about____. 20__, commit a lewd act upon ___________, a child who had not attained the age of 16 years, by intentionally exposing [his (genitalia) (anus) (buttocks)] [her (genitalia) (anus) (buttocks) (areola) (nipple)] to ___________, with an intent to (abuse) (humiliate) (harass) (degrade) (arouse) (gratify the sexual desire of) ___________.

(c) *Sexual abuse of a child involving indecent exposure.* In that (personal jurisdiction data), did (at/on board location), on or about____. 20__, commit a lewd act upon ___________, a child who had not attained the age of 16 years, by intentionally [(touching)(causing _________ to touch)] [(directly) (through the clothing)] (name of body part) of ___________, with an intent to (arouse) (gratify the sexual desire of) ___________.

(d) *Sexual abuse of a child involving indecent communication.* In that (personal jurisdiction data), did (at/on board location), on or about____. 20__, commit a lewd act upon ___________, a child who had not attained the age of 16 years, by intentionally communicating to ___________ indecent language to wit: ___________, with an intent to (abuse) (humiliate) (harass) (degrade) (arouse) (gratify the sexual desire of) ___________.

(e) *Sexual abuse of a child involving indecent conduct.* In that (personal jurisdiction data), did (at/ on board location), on or about____. 20__, commit a lewd act upon ___________, a child who had not attained the age of 16 years, by engaging in indecent conduct, to wit: ___________, intentionally done (with) (in the presence of) ___________, which conduct amounted to a form of immorality relating to sexual impurity which is grossly vulgar, obscene, and repugnant to common propriety, and tends to excite sexual desire or deprave morals with respect to sexual relations.

45c. Article 120c—Other sexual misconduct

[Note: This statute applies to offenses committed between 28 June 2012 and 31 December 2018. Article 120c is a new statute designed to address miscellaneous sexual misconduct. Previous versions of these offenses are located as follows: for offenses committed on or before 30 September 2007, see Appendix 20; for offenses committed during the period 1 October 2007 through 27 June 2012, see Appendix 21.]

a. *Text of Statute*

(a) *Indecent Viewing,* Visual Recording, or Broadcasting. Any person subject to this chapter who, without legal justification or lawful authorization—

(1) knowingly and wrongfully views the private area of another person, without that other person's consent and under circumstances in which that other person has a reasonable expectation of privacy;

(2) knowingly photographs, videotapes, films, or records by any means the private area of another person, without that other person's consent and under circumstances in which that other person has a reasonable expectation of privacy; or

(3) knowingly broadcasts or distributes any such recording that the person knew or reasonably should have known was made under the circumstances proscribed in paragraphs (1) and (2); is guilty of an offense under this section and shall be punished as a court-martial may direct.

(b) *Forcible Pandering.* Any person subject to this chapter who compels another person to engage in an act of prostitution with any person is guilty of forcible pandering and shall be punished as a court-martial may direct.

(c) *Indecent Exposure.* Any person subject to this chapter who intentionally exposes, in an indecent manner, the genitalia, anus, buttocks, or female areola or nipple is guilty of indecent exposure and shall by punished as a court-martial may direct.

(d) *Definitions.* In this section:

(1) *Act of prostitution.* The term 'act of prostitution' means a sexual act or sexual contact (as defined in section 920(g) of this title (article 120(g))) on account of which anything of value is given to, or received by, any person.

(2) *Private area.* The term 'private area' means the naked or underwear-clad genitalia, anus, buttocks, or female areola or nipple.

(3) *Reasonable expectation of privacy.* The term 'under circumstances in which that other person has a reasonable expectation of privacy' means—

(A) circumstances in which a reasonable person would believe that he or she could disrobe in privacy, without being concerned that an image of a private area of the person was being captured; or

(B) circumstances in which a reasonable person would believe that a private area of the person would not be visible to the public.

(4) *Broadcast.* The term 'broadcast' means to electronically transmit a visual image with the intent that it be viewed by a person or persons.

(5) *Distribute.* The term 'distribute' means delivering to the actual or constructive possession of another, including transmission by electronic means.

(6) *Indecent manner.* The term 'indecent manner' means conduct that amounts to a form of immorality relating to sexual impurity which is grossly vulgar, obscene, and repugnant to common propriety, and tends to excite sexual desire or deprave morals with respect to sexual relations.

b. *Elements.*

(1) *Indecent viewing.*

(a) That the accused knowingly and wrongfully viewed the private area of another person;

(b) That said viewing was without the other person's consent; and

(c) That said viewing took place under circumstances in which the other person had a reasonable expectation of privacy.

(2) *Indecent recording.*

(a) That the accused knowingly recorded (photographed, videotaped, filmed, or recorded by any means) the private area of another person;

(b) That said recording was without the other person's consent; and

(c) That said recording was made under circumstances in which the other person had a reasonable expectation of privacy.

(3) *Broadcasting of an indecent recording.*

(a) That the accused knowingly broadcast a certain recording of another person's private area;

(b) That said recording was made or broadcast

without the other person's consent;

(c) That the accused knew or reasonably should have known that the recording was made or broadcast without the other person's consent;

(d) That said recording was made under circumstances in which the other person had a reasonable expectation of privacy; and

(e) That the accused knew or reasonably should have known that said recording was made under circumstances in which the other person had a reasonable expectation of privacy.

(4) *Distribution of an indecent visual recording.*

(a) That the accused knowingly distributed a certain recording of another person's private area;

(b) That said recording was made or distributed without the other person's consent;

(c) That the accused knew or reasonably should have known that said recording was made or distributed without the other person's consent;

(d) That said recording was made under circumstances in which the other person had a reasonable expectation of privacy; and

(e) That the accused knew or reasonably should have known that said recording was made under circumstances in which the other person had a reasonable expectation of privacy.

(5) *Forcible pandering.* That the accused compelled another person to engage in an act of prostitution with any person.

(6) *Indecent exposure.*

(a) That the accused exposed his or her genitalia, anus, buttocks, or female areola or nipple;

(b) That the exposure was in an indecent manner; and

(c) That the exposure was intentional.

c. *Explanation.*

(1) *In general.* Sexual offenses have been separated into three statutes: adults (120), children (120b), and other offenses (120c).

(2) *Definitions.*

(a) Recording. A "recording" is a still or moving visual image captured or recorded by any means.

(b) Other terms are defined in paragraph 45c.a.(d), supra.

d. *Lesser included offenses. See paragraph 3 of this part and Appendix 12A.*

e. *Maximum punishment.*

(1) *Indecent viewing.* Dishonorable discharge, forfeiture of all pay and allowances, and confinement for 1 year.

(2) *Indecent visual recording.* Dishonorable discharge, forfeiture of all pay and allowances, and confinement for 5 years.

(3) *Broadcasting or distribution of an indecent visual recording.* Dishonorable discharge, forfeiture of all pay and allowances, and confinement for 7 years.

(4) *Forcible pandering.* Dishonorable discharge, forfeiture of all pay and allowances, and confinement for 12 years.

(5) *Indecent exposure.* Dishonorable discharge, forfeiture of all pay and allowances, and confinement for 1 year.

f. *Sample specifications.*

(1) *Indecent viewing, visual recording, or broadcasting.*

(a) *Indecent viewing.* In that (personal jurisdiction data), did (at/on board location), on or about____. 20__, knowingly and wrongfully view the private area of ___________, without (his) (her) consent and under circumstances in which (he) (she) had a reasonable expectation of privacy.

(b) *Indecent visual recording.* In that (personal jurisdiction data), did (at/on board location), on or about____. 20__, knowingly (photograph) (videotape) (film) (make a recording of) the private area of ___________, without (his) (her) consent and under circumstances in which (he) (she) had a reasonable expectation of privacy.

(c) *Broadcasting or distributing an indecent visual recording.* In that (personal jurisdiction data), did (at/on board location), on or about____. 20__, knowingly (broadcast) (distribute) a recording of the private area of ___________, when the said accused knew or reasonably should have known that the said recording was (made) (and/or) (distributed/ broadcast) without the consent of ___________ and under circumstances in which (he) (she) had a reasonable expectation of privacy.

(2) *Forcible pandering.* In that (personal jurisdiction data), did (at/on board location), on or about____. 20__, wrongfully compel ___________ to engage in (a sexual act) (sexual contact) with ___________, to wit: ___________, for the purpose of receiving (money) (other compensation) (___________).

(3) *Indecent exposure.* In that (personal jurisdiction data), did (at/on board location), on or about____. 20__, intentionally expose [his (genitalia) (anus) (buttocks)] [her (genitalia) (anus) (buttocks) (areola) (nipple)] in an indecent manner, to wit: ___________.

97. Article 134—(Pandering and prostitution)

a. *Text of statute. See* paragraph 60.

b. *Elements.*

(1) Prostitution.

(a) That the accused engaged in a sexual act with another person not the accused's spouse;

(b) That the accused did so for the purpose of receiving money or other compensation;

(c) That this act was wrongful; and

(d) That, under the circumstances, the conduct of the accused was to the prejudice of good order and discipline in the armed forces or was of a nature to bring discredit upon the armed forces.

(2) *Patronizing a prostitute.*

(a) That the accused engaged in a sexual act with another person not the accused's spouse;

(b) That the accused compelled, induced, enticed, or procured such person to engage in a sexual act in exchange for money or other compensation; and

(c) That this act was wrongful; and

(d) That, under the circumstances, the conduct of the accused was to the prejudice of good order and discipline in the armed forces or was of a nature to bring discredit upon the armed forces.

(3) *Pandering by inducing, enticing, or procuring act of prostitution.*

(a) That the accused induced, enticed, or procured a certain person to engage in a sexual act for hire and reward with a person to be directed to said person by the accused;

(b) That this inducing, enticing, or procuring was wrongful;

(c) That, under the circumstances, the conduct of the accused was to the prejudice of good order and discipline in the armed forces or was of a nature to bring discredit upon the armed forces.

(4) *Pandering by arranging or receiving consideration for arranging for a sexual act.*

(a) That the accused arranged for, or received valuable consideration for arranging for, a certain person to engage in a sexual act with another person;

(b) That the arranging (and receipt of consideration) was wrongful; and

(c) That, under the circumstances, the conduct of the accused was to the prejudice of good order and discipline in the armed forces or was of a nature to bring discredit upon the armed forces.

c. *Explanation.*

(1) Prostitution may be committed by males or females.

(2) Sexual act. See paragraph 45.a.(g)(1).

d. *Lesser included offenses.* See paragraph 3 of this part and Appendix 12A.

e. *Maximum punishment.*

(1) Prostitution and patronizing a prostitute. Dishonorable discharge, forfeiture of all pay and allowances, and confinement for 1 year.

(2) Pandering. Dishonorable discharge, forfeiture of all pay and allowances, and confinement for 5 years.

f. Sample specifications.

(1) *Prostitution.*

In that _________ (personal jurisdiction data), did, (at/on board-location) (subject-matter jurisdiction data, if required), on or about____. 20__, wrongfully engage in (a sexual act) (sexual acts) with , a person not his/her spouse, for the purpose of receiving (money) (   ), and that said conduct was (to the prejudice of good order and discipline in the armed forces) (of a nature to bring discredit upon the armed forces) (to the prejudice of good order and discipline in the armed forces and was of a nature to bring discredit upon the armed forces).

(2) *Patronizing a prostitute.*

In that _________ (personal jurisdiction data), did, (at/on board location) (subject-matter jurisdiction data, if required), on or about____. 20__, wrongfully (compel) (induce) (entice) (procure) _________, a person not his/her spouse, to engage in (a sexual act) (sexual acts) with the accused in exchange for (money) (_________), and that said conduct was (to the prejudice of good order and discipline in the armed forces) (of a nature to bring discredit upon the armed forces) (to the prejudice of good order and discipline in the armed forces and was of a nature to bring discredit upon the armed forces).

(3) *Inducing, enticing, or procuring act of prostitution.*

In that _________ (personal jurisdiction data), did (at/on board-location) (subject-matter jurisdiction data, if required), on or about____. 20__, wrongfully (induce)(entice)(procure) _________ to engage in (a sexual act) (sexual acts for hire and reward) with persons to be directed to him/her by the said _________, and that said conduct was (to the prejudice of good order and discipline in the armed forces) (of a nature to bring discredit upon the armed forces) (to the prejudice of good order and discipline in the armed forces and was of a nature to bring discredit upon the armed forces).

(4) *Arranging, or receiving consideration for arranging for sexual intercourse or sodomy.*

In that _________ (personal jurisdiction data), did, (at/on board-location) (subject-matter jurisdiction data, if required), on or about____. 20__, wrongfully (arrange for) (receive valuable consideration, to wit: _________ on account of arranging for) _________ to engage in (an act) (acts) of (sexual intercourse) (sodomy) with _________, and that said conduct was (to the prejudice of good order and discipline in the armed forces) (of a nature to bring discredit upon the armed forces) (to the prejudice of good order and discipline in the armed forces and was of a nature to bring discredit upon the armed forces).

MCM INDEX

INDEX

INDEX

www.ingramcontent.com/pod-product-compliance
Lightning Source LLC
LaVergne TN
LVHW081959200926
848481LV00010B/2769
* 9 7 8 1 5 9 8 0 4 9 8 3 1 *